Twentieth-Century Literary Criticism

Volume 8

Twentieth-Century Literary Criticism

**Excerpts from Criticism of the
Works of Novelists, Poets, Playwrights,
Short Story Writers, and Other Creative Writers
Who Lived between 1900 and 1960,
from the First Published Critical Appraisals
to Current Evaluations**

**Sharon K. Hall
Editor**

**Thomas Ligotti
James E. Person, Jr.
Associate Editors**

**Gale Research Company
Book Tower
Detroit, Michigan 48226**

STAFF

Sharon K. Hall, *Editor*

Thomas Ligotti, James E. Person, Jr., *Associate Editors*

Mark W. Scott, *Senior Assistant Editor*

Earlene M. Alber, Jane Dobija, Kathleen Gensley, Sandra Giraud, Denise B. Grove, Marie Lazzari,
Denise Wiloch, *Assistant Editors*

Phyllis Carmel Mendelson, Dennis Poupard, *Contributing Editors*

Carolyn Bancroft, *Production Supervisor*
Lizbeth A. Purdy, *Production Coordinator*
Frank James Borovsky, Laura L. Britton, Paula J. DiSante, Serita Lanette Lockard, Brenda
Marshall, Marie M. Mazur, Gloria Anne Williams, *Editorial Assistants*

Robert J. Elster, Jr., *Research Coordinator*
Ann Marie Dadah, Jeannine Schiffman Davidson, Robert J. Hill, James A. MacEachern, Carol
Angela Thomas, *Research Assistants*

Linda M. Pugliese, *Manuscript Coordinator*
Donna D. Craft, *Assistant Manuscript Coordinator*
Colleen M. Crane, Maureen A. Puhl, Rosetta Irene Simms, *Manuscript Assistants*

L. Elizabeth Hardin, *Permissions Supervisor*
Filomena Sgambati, *Permissions Coordinator*
Janice M. Mach, *Assistant Permissions Coordinator*
Patricia A. Seefelt, *Photo Permissions*
Anna Pertner, Mary P. McGrane, Susan D. Nobles, *Permissions Assistants*
Elizabeth Babini, Margaret Chamberlain, Virgie T. Leavens, Joan B. Weber, *Permissions Clerks*

Library of Congress Catalog Card Number 76-46132

ISBN 0-8103-0219-5
ISSN 0276-8178

CONTENTS

5

PREFACE

It is impossible to overvalue the importance of literature in the intellectual, emotional, and spiritual evolution of humanity. Literature is that which both lifts us out of everyday life and helps us to better understand it. Through the fictive life of an Emma Bovary, a Lambert Strether, a Leopold Bloom, our perceptions of the human condition are enlarged, and we are enriched.

Literary criticism is a collective term for several kinds of critical writing: criticism may be normative, descriptive, textual, interpretive, appreciative, generic. It takes many forms: the traditional essay, the aphorism, the book or play review, even the parodic poem. Perhaps the single unifying feature of literary criticism lies in its purpose: to help us to better understand what we read.

The Scope of the Book

The usefulness of Gale's *Contemporary Literary Criticism (CLC)*, which excerpts criticism on current writing, suggested an equivalent need among literature students and teachers interested in authors of the period 1900 to 1960. The great poets, novelists, short story writers, and playwrights of this period are by far the most popular writers for study in high school and college literature courses. Moreover, since contemporary critics continue to analyze the work of this period—both in its own right and in relation to today's tastes and standards—a vast amount of relevant critical material confronts the student.

Thus, *Twentieth-Century Literary Criticism (TCLC)* presents significant passages from published criticism on authors who died between 1900 and 1960. Because of the difference in time span under consideration *(CLC* considers authors living from 1960 to the present), there is no duplication between *CLC* and *TCLC*.

Each volume of *TCLC* is carefully designed to present a list of authors who represent a variety of genres and nationalities. The length of an author's section is intended to be representative of the amount of critical attention he or she has received in the English language. Articles and books that have not been translated into English are excluded. An attempt has been made to identify and include excerpts from the seminal essays on each author's work. Additionally, as space permits, especially insightful essays of a more limited scope are included. Thus *TCLC* is designed to serve as an introduction for the student of twentieth-century literature to the authors of that period and to the most significant commentators on these authors.

Each *TCLC* author section represents the scope of critical response to that author's work: some early criticism is presented to indicate initial reactions, later criticism is selected to represent any rise or fall in an author's reputation, and current retrospective analyses provide students with a modern view. Since a *TCLC* author section is intended to be a definitive overview, the editors include between 30 and 35 authors in each 600-page volume (compared to approximately 75 authors in a *CLC* volume of similar size) in order to devote more attention to each author. An author may appear more than once because of the great quantity of critical material available, or because of the resurgence of criticism generated by events such as an author's centennial or anniversary celebration, the republication of an author's works, or publication of a newly translated work or volume of letters.

The Organization of the Book

An author section consists of the following elements: author heading, biocritical introduction, principal works, excerpts of criticism (each followed by a citation), and, beginning with Volume 3, an annotated bibliography of additional reading.

- The *author heading* consists of the author's full name, followed by birth and death dates. The unbracketed portion of the name denotes the form under which the author most commonly wrote. If an author wrote consistently under a pseudonym, the pseudonym will be listed in the author heading and the real name given in parentheses on the first line of the biocritical introduction. Also located at the beginning of the biocritical introduction are any name variations under which an author wrote, including transliterated forms for authors whose languages use nonroman alphabets. Uncertainty as to a birth or death date is indicated by a question mark.

- The *biocritical introduction* contains biographical and other background information about an author that will elucidate his or her creative output. Parenthetical material following several of the biocritical introductions includes references to biographical and critical reference series published by the Gale Research Company. These include *Dictionary of Literary Biography* and past volumes of *TCLC*.

- The *list of principal works* is chronological by date of first book publication and identifies genres. In the case of foreign authors where there are both foreign language publications and English translations, the title and date of the first English-language edition are given in brackets. Unless otherwise indicated, dramas are dated by first performance, not first publication.

- *Criticism* is arranged chronologically in each author section to provide a perspective on any changes in critical evaluation over the years. In the text of each author entry, titles by the author are printed in boldface type. This allows the reader to ascertain without difficulty the works discussed. For purposes of easier identification, the critic's name and the publication date of the essay are given at the beginning of each piece of criticism. Unsigned criticism is preceded by the title of the journal in which it appeared. For an anonymous essay later attributed to a critic, the critic's name appears in brackets in the heading and in the citation.

- A complete *bibliographical citation* designed to facilitate location of the original essay or book by the interested reader accompanies each piece of criticism. An asterisk (*) at the end of a citation indicates the essay is on more than one author.

- The *annotated bibliography* appearing at the end of each author section suggests further reading on the author. In some cases it includes essays for which the editors could not obtain reprint rights. An asterisk (*) at the end of a citation indicates the essay is on more than one author.

Each volume of *TCLC* includes a cumulative index to critics. Under each critic's name is listed the author(s) on which the critic has written and the volume and page where the criticism may be found. *TCLC* also includes a cumulative index to authors with the volume numbers in which the author appears in boldface after his or her name. A cumulative nationality index is another useful feature in *TCLC*. Author names are arranged alphabetically under their respective nationalities and followed by the volume number(s) in which they appear.

Acknowledgments

No work of this scope can be accomplished without the cooperation of many people. The editors especially wish to thank the copyright holders of the excerpts included in this volume, the permission managers of many book and magazine publishing companies for assisting us in locating copyright holders, and the staffs of the Detroit Public Library, University of Detroit Library, University of Michigan Library, and Wayne State University Library for making their resources available to us. We are also grateful to Michael F. Wiedl III for his assistance with copyright research and to Norma J. Merry for her editorial assistance.

Suggestions Are Welcome

Several features have been added to *TCLC* since its original publication in response to various suggestions:

- Since Volume 2—An *Appendix* which lists the sources from which material in the volume is reprinted.

- Since Volume 3—An *Annotated Bibliography* for additional reading.

- Since Volume 4—*Portraits* of the authors.

- Since Volume 6—A *Nationality Index* for easy access to authors by nationality.

If readers wish to suggest authors they would like to have covered in future volumes, or if they have other suggestions, they are cordially invited to write the editor.

AUTHORS TO APPEAR
IN FUTURE VOLUMES

Ady, Endre 1877-1919
Agate, James 1877-1947
Agustini, Delmira 1886-1914
Aldrich, Thomas Bailey
    1836-1907
Annensy, Innokenty
    Fyodorovich 1856-1909
Arlen, Michael 1895-1956
Barea, Arturo 1897-1957
Barry, Philip 1896-1946
Bass, Eduard 1888-1946
Benét, William Rose 1886-1950
Benson, E(dward) F(rederic)
    1867-1940
Benson, Stella 1892-1933
Beresford, J(ohn) D(avys)
    1873-1947
Besant, Annie(Wood) 1847-1933
Bethell, Mary Ursula 1874-1945
Binyon, Laurence 1869-1943
Blackmore, R(ichard) D(odd-
    ridge) 1825-1900
Blasco Ibanez, Vicente
    1867-1928
Bojer, Johan 1872-1959
Borowski, Tadeusz 1924-1951
Bosman, Herman Charles
    1905-1951
Bottomley, Gordon 1874-1948
Bourget, Paul 1852-1935
Bourne, George 1863-1927
Brandes, Georg (Morris Cohen)
    1842-1927
Broch, Herman 1886-1951
Bromfield, Louis 1896-1956
Bryusov, Valery (Yakovlevich)
    1873-1924
Byrne, Donn (Brian Oswald
    Donn-Byre) 1889-1928
Caine, Hall 1853-1931
Campana, Dina 1885-1932
Campbell, (William) Wilfred
    1861-1918
Cannan, Gilbert 1884-1955
Churchill, Winston 1871-1947
Corelli, Marie 1855-1924
Corvo, Baron (Frederick William
    Rolfe) 1860-1913
Crane, Stephen 1871-1900
Crawford, F. Marion 1854-1909
Croce, Benedetto 1866-1952
Davidson, John 1857-1909
Day, Clarence 1874-1935
Dazai, Osamu 1909-1948
Delafield, E.M. (Edme Elizabeth
    Monica de la Pasture)
    1890-1943
DeMorgan, William 1839-1917
Doblin, Alfred 1878-1957
Douglas, Lloyd C(assel)
    1877-1951
Douglas, (George) Norman
    1868-1952
Dreiser, Theodore 1871-1945
Drinkwater, John 1882-1937

Duun, Olav 1876-1939
Fadeyev,Alexandr 1901-1956
Feydeau, Georges 1862-1921
Field, Michael (Katherine Harris
    Bradley 1846-1914 and Edith
    Emma Cooper 1862-1913)
Field, Rachel 1894-1924)
Fisher, Rudolph 1897-1934
Flecker, James Elroy 1884-1915
France, Anatole (Anatole
    Thibault) 1844-1924
Freeman, John 1880-1929
Freeman, Mary E. (Wilkins)
    1852-1930
Gilman, Charlotte (Anna Perkins
    Stetson) 1860-1935
Gippius Or Hippius, Zinaida
    (Nikolayevna) 1869-1945
Glyn, Elinor 1864-1943
Gogarty, Oliver St. John
    1878-1957
Golding, Louis 1895-1958
Gosse, Edmund 1849-1928
Gould, Gerald 1885-1936
Grahame, Kenneth 1859-1932
Gray, John 1866-1934
Grieg, Nordahl 1902-1943
Guiraldes, Ricardo 1886-1927
Gumilyov, Nikolay 1886-1921
Gwynne, Stephen Lucius
    1864-1950
Haggard, H(enry) Rider
    1856-1925
Hale, Edward Everett 1822-1909
Hall, (Marguerite) Radclyffe
    1886-1943
Harris, Frank 1856-1931
Hearn, Lafcadio 1850-1904
Hergesheimer,Joseph 1880-1954
Hernandez, Miguel 1910-1942
Herrick, Robert 1868-1938
Hewlett, Maurice 1861-1923
Heym, Georg 1887-1912
Heyward, DuBose 1885-1940
Hichens, Robert 1864-1950
Hilton, James 1900-1954
Hofmannsthal, Hugo Von
    1874-1926
Holtby, Winifred 1898-1935
Hope, Anthony 1863-1933
Hudson, Stephen 1868-1944
Hudson, W(illiam) H(enry)
    1841-1922
Ivanov, Vyacheslav Ivanovich
    1866-1949
Jacobs, W(illiam) W(ymark)
    1863-1943
James, Will 1892-1942
Jerome, Jerome K(lapka)
    1859-1927
Jones, Henry Arthur 1851-1929
Kaiser, Georg 1878-1947
Kuttner, Henry 1915-1958
Kuzmin, Mikhail Alexseyevich
    1875-1936

Lang, Andrew 1844-1912
Larbaud, Valery 1881-1957
Lawson, Henry 1867-1922
Leverson, Ada 1862-1933
Lewisohn, Ludwig 1883-1955
Lindsay, (Nicholas) Vachel
    1879-1931
London, Jack 1876-1916
Lonsdale, Frederick 1881-1954
Loti, Pierre 1850-1923
Lowndes, Marie Belloc
    1868-1947
Lucas, E(dward) V(errall)
    1868-1938
Lynd, Robert 1879-1949
MacArthur, Charles
    1895-1956
MacDonald, George
    1824-1905
Machado de Assis, Joaquim
    Maria 1839-1950
Mann, Heinrich 1871-1950
Manning, Frederic
    1887-1935
Marinetti, Filippo Tommaso
    1876-1944
Marriott, Charles 1869-1957
Martin du Gard, Roger
    1881-1958
Mencken, H(enry) L(ouis)
    1880-1956
Meredith, George 1828-1909
Mistral, Frédéric 1830-1914
Mitchell, Margaret
    1900-1949
Monro, Harold 1879-1932
Moore, Thomas Sturge
    1870-1944
Morgan, Charles 1894-1958
Morley, Christopher
    1890-1957
Murray, (George) Gilbert
    1866-1957
Nervo, Amado 1870-1919
Nietzsche, Friedrich
    1844-1900
Norris, Frank 1870-1902
Olbracht, Ivan (Kemil
    Zeman) 1882-1952
Ortega y Gasset, Jose
    1883-1955
Péguy, Charles 1873-1914
Pinero, Arthur Wing
    1855-1934
Pontoppidan, Henrik
    1857-1943
Porter, Eleanor H(odgman)
    1868-1920
Porter, Gene(va) Stratton
    1886-1924
Powys, T(heodore) F(rancis)
    1875-1953
Quiller-Couch, Arthur
    1863-1944
Rappoport, Solomon
    1863-1944

Reed, John (Silas)
    1887-1920
Reid, Forrest 1876-1947
Riley, James Whitcomb
    1849-1916
Rinehart, Mary Roberts
    1876-1958
Roberts, Elizabeth Madox
    1886-1941
Rolland, Romain 1866-1944
Rölvaag, O(le) E(dvart)
    1876-1931
Rosenberg, Isaac 1870-1918
Rourke, Constance 1885-1941
Roussel, Raymond 1877-1933
Runyon, (Alfred) Damon
    1884-1946
Sabatini, Rafael 1875-1950
Santayana, George 1863-1952
Schreiner, Olive (Emilie
    Albertina) 1855-1920
Seeger, Alan 1888-1916
Service, Robert 1874-1958
Seton, Ernest Thompson
    1860-1946
Slater, Francis Carey
    1875-1958
Slesinger, Tess 1905-1945
Sologub, Fyodor 1863-1927
Squire, J(ohn) C(ollings)
    1884-1958
Steiner, Rudolph 1861-1925
Stockton, Frank R.
    1834-1902
Sudermann, Hermann
    1857-1938
Symons, Arthur 1865-1945
Tabb, John Bannister
    1845-1909
Tarkington, Booth
    1869-1946
Teilhard de Chardin, Pierre
    1881-1955
Tey, Josephine (Elizabeth
    Mackintosh) 1897-1952
Thomas, (Philip) Edward
    1878-1917
Toller, Ernst 1893-1939
Turner, W(alter) J(ames)
    R(edfern) 1889-1946
Vachell, Horace Annesley
    1861-1955
Valera y Alcala Galiano,
    Juan 1824-1905
Van Dine, S.S. (William H.
    Wright) 1888-1939
Van Doren, Carol
    1885-1950
Vazov, Ivan 1850-1921
Vian, Boris 1878-1959
Wallace, Edgar 1874-1932
Wallace, Lewis 1827-1905
Washington, Booker
    T(aliaferro) 1856-1915
Webb, Mary 1881-1927

Authors to Appear in Future Volumes

Webster, Jean 1876-1916
Welch, Denton 1917-1948

Wells, Carolyn 1869-1942
Wister, Owen 1860-1938

Wren, P(ercival)
  C(hristopher) 1885-1941

Wylie, Francis Brett
  1844-1954

Readers are cordially invited to suggest additional authors to the editors.

Guillaume Apollinaire

1880-1918

(Born Wilhelm Apollinaris de Kostrowitzki; also Kostrowitski, and Kostrowitzky) French poet, dramatist, critic, short story writer, and novelist.

A quintessential modernist, Apollinaire is one of the most important poets of the early twentieth century. His career, despite its brevity, spanned such nineteenth-century literary movements as symbolism and such twentieth-century movements as futurism and cubism. During various periods his work shows affinities with each of these movements. Apollinaire was, however, more than an artist formed by trends and traditions, for he himself helped to shape the modernist schools that followed him.

There is a significant relationship between Apollinaire's life and his work. According to most sources, he was born in Rome, the illegitimate son of a Polish mother, and spent much of his youth traveling around Europe before finally settling in Paris. With such a background he developed a cosmopolitan outlook and became fascinated with a variety of studies. His interest in art, for example, led to his becoming a significant critic and early promoter of the cubists. He mixed with a bohemian group of artists which included Picasso and Marcel Duchamp, and he became himself an offbeat model of the definitive bohemian. Apollinaire had always lived somewhere on the fringe of a stable society, and at one point he was unjustly imprisoned in connection with the theft of the *Mona Lisa*. This experience was expressed through a series of poems written during his incarceration, one example of the autobiographical element in his writing. Another example of the relationship between Apollinaire's art and life is the wartime poetry chronicling his duty at the front during World War I. A head wound sent him back to Paris, where he died on Armistice Day of influenza.

Apollinaire's earliest publication, *L'enchanteur pourrissant* and *L'hérésiarque et cie,* are collections of short stories which exhibit a major trait of all his subsequent works: the unrestricted use of imagination. Fantastic characters and situations are used freely throughout these stories. Like the symbolist writers before him, Apollinaire repudiated the realistic approach to writing and the limits it imposed. But rather than following symbolism's self-imposed exile from everyday reality, Apollinaire's works display a whole-hearted attempt to confront and transform wordly experience in all its aspects, from the advancements of technology to the tragedies of war. As Anna Balakian has observed, Apollinaire's ambition was "to change the world through language." Among the author's other works of fiction, the novel *Le poète assassiné (The Poet Assasinated)* introduces the poet as a creator of new worlds, a role that Apollinaire himself took on in his major works, the poetry collections *Alcools* and *Calligrammes (Calligrams).*

Both *Alcools* and *Calligrams* are notable for their stylistic experimentation and the novelty of their themes. Apollinaire based many of his poems on subjects not often treated in serious poetry before him, particularly subjects from contemporary life. He also treated traditional poetic themes, such as the poet's experience of war or romance, in ways that ex-

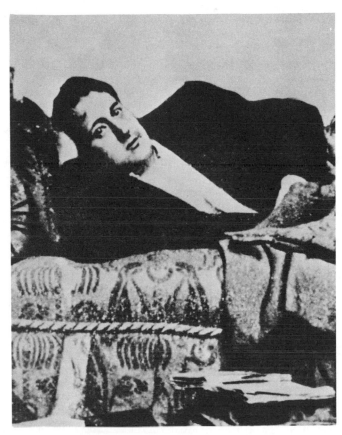

pressed an astonishing willingness to contemplate the severest emotions from new points of view. However, Apollinaire's unique and liberating sense of humor serves more to clarify rather than diminish the poignancy of his often tragic themes. He frequently achieves this effect through the stylistic innovations which a number of critics view as his most significant contribution to modern poetry. Apollinaire's first major collection of poetry, *Alcools,* was in many ways traditional in style until, at the last moment, he instructed the printer to leave all punctuation out of the manuscript. The stylistic result is apparent throughout the works of poets writing after Apollinaire. In addition to its technical importance, *Alcools* contains what critics regard as Apollinaire's most successful individual poems, such as "Zone" and "La chanson du mal-aimé" ("Song of the Ill-Beloved"), which transcribe the full range and complexity of their author's vision.

When Apollinaire returned to Paris after his service in the First World War, he saw the staging of his drama *Les mamelles de Tirésias (The Breasts of Tiresias).* After considering other designations for the play, he finally subtitled it a *drame surrealiste.* This epithet was later adopted by the surrealists to describe their delirium-like approach to art and experience. Throughout Apollinaire's works, from his concrete poems written in the shape of various objects to pornographic extravaganzas like *Les onze mille verges (The Debauched Hospodar)*, there exist numerous examples of those artistic traits which lead the surrealists and other literary experimentalists to claim him as one of their predecessors. Undoubtedly the most outstanding quality of Apollinaire was his constant vitality and his willingness to take risks. It is perhaps this spirit that makes Apollinaire's name synonymous with literary innovation.

(See also *TCLC*, Vol. 3.)

PRINCIPAL WORKS

L'enchanteur pourrissant (short stories) 1909
L'hérésiarque et cie (short stories) 1910
    [*The Heresiarch and Co.*, 1965; also published as *The Wandering Jew, and Other Stories*, 1967]
Le bestiaire; ou, Cortège d'Orphée (poetry) 1911
Alcools (poetry) 1913
    [*Alcools*, 1964]
Méditations esthétiques: Les peintres cubistes (criticism) 1913
    [*The Cubist Painters: Aesthetic Meditations, 1913*]
Le poète assassiné (novel) 1916
    [*The Poet Assassinated*, 1923]
Vitam impedere amori (poetry) 1917
Calligrammes (poetry) 1918
    [*Calligrams*, 1970]
L'esprit nouveau et les poètes (essay) 1918
Les mamelles de Tirésias (drama) 1918
    [*The Breasts of Tiresias* published in journal *Odyssey*, 1961]
La femme assise (novel) 1920
Il y a (poetry) 1925
Les onze mille verges (novel) 1948
    [*The Debauched Hospodar*, 1953]
Couleur de temps (drama) 1949

S. A. RHODES (essay date 1938)

[Apollinaire] wanted his *Calligrammes* to speak to the eye as well as to the mind and the senses. He carved some of them, accordingly, in the shape objects assume and suggest in the universe. But behind this external semblance lies concealed an inner image of the poetic reality they emulate and contain. The reader must unveil every poem for himself. His heart-shaped poem *Coeur* resembles a candle-flame burning upside down; his *Œillet* exhales the perfume of a carnation, and is fashioned like a flower; his *Jet d'Eau* imitates the graceful cascade of a fountain. Its syllables echo the melancholy swash of falling waters. (p. 303)

Some of his *Calligrammes* seem to be composed with disconnected images. The imagination must leap from one to the other, perform somersaults that contradict the laws of logic and academic gravity. Others are told in a tone of confidence, seeming to have sprung without premeditation from a conversation, a promenade in the countryside, a ride along the boulevards. He aimed to bridge the distance that divides poetry and daily living. He did not seek to put into figurative speech the formless aspects of things he conceived, however. He knew the limitations of his typographical innovations. "They are an idealization of free-verse," he declared, and a typographical

precision at a time when typography is ending its career brilliantly, at the dawn of other means of expression through the phonograph and cinématograph." He believed, nevertheless, that they afforded a new sensibility a means of expressing itself anew. Croniamantal, the hero of his novel *Le Poète assassiné*, writes his last poem in regular verse as

> Luth
> Zut!

and immediately after he composes his last irregular poem also, so as to break with all verse. He wished to do away with all rhetoric and formalism in art. He did not apologize for his seeming verbal eccentricities, or for their shortcomings. "It is the first book of its kind," he observed regarding *Calligrammes*. "Others will follow on the road to perfection." To the very end of his life he held firmly to this faith. "If I end my experiments," he confided to André Billy, "it will be because I shall have become weary of being treated as a scatterbrain, for innovations seem absurd to those who are satisfied to languish in a rut." (pp. 303-04)

Of the two novels Apollinaire wrote, the better known, *Le Poète assassiné*, is a social travesty of Rabelaisian quality and intensity, more Quixotic, and closer to the heart of the poet than any of his other prose writings. This tale of the mock-heroic massacre of the poets is especially interesting on account of the light it throws on the inner inquietude and pessimism of the poet. "Real glory," bellows Horace Tograth, the antagonist of the poet in the novel, "has forsaken poetry for science, philosophy, acrobatics, philanthropy, sociology, etc. There is no more room for poets in modern society. The prizes awarded to them belong to the workers, the acrobats, the philanthropists, the sociologists, etc. Let them disappear. Lycurgus banished them from the Republic; let them be banished from the earth." Thus begins, in the story, the massacre of the innocents, until all are killed, including its hero Croniamantal, save the prince of poets who, being held in protective imprisonment, escapes death, and is present, later, at the unveiling of a statue to the memory of the martyred Croniamantal.

The other full novel of Apollinaire, *La Femme assise*, presents picturesque side-pictures of the Montparnasse of the post-war era. Aside from that, it reveals the poet's proneness for romanesque situations. It is a patchwork of whimsical and bizarre yarns which are darned together with difficulty. The tales collected in *l'Hérésiargue et Cie*, and in the volume that contains *Le poète assassiné*, are of a higher calibre. They are truculent narratives of heretics and lunatics, of knavery and mystery. Here the exotic and prosaic, the ironic and melodramatic mingle together to form a strange panorama of society on the verge of a chimerical reality. They recreate the spirit and atmosphere of Villiers de l'Isle-Adam's *Contes cruels*, and are worthy of being classed beside them. (pp. 305-06)

Apollinaire associates his sentimental journey with the variegated spectacle of life in the adolescent years of the century. His poetry becomes in turn a multicolored reflection of that multifarious reality. His intellectual and emotional nimbleness and alertness commingle to set off the fireworks of his creative imagination. He sees everything, senses everything, experiences everything. In consequence, his inspiration is multiple, ever new and refreshing. He fuses and confuses the lines of demarcation artificially erected between social and poetical territories. His field lies in the *terra incognita* of art, where he sows the seeds of his earthly captivity, and where he harvests strange flowers that may seem to the alien in spirit like hybrids between lovely orchids and some forbidding cacti. He remains a passionate poet, mindful of the machanism of daily activities, and yet courageously faithful to his poetic pilgrimage. For there is enough routine in life to mould or distort the human heart. His poetry is the expression of a vibrating mode of life, a restatement of its ultimate and potent values. It represents a genuine attempt to create a form of simultaneous lyricism—globular, integral, mystical. It is an illustration of that "re-organization of lyricism," he wished to engineer, that "inner restraint" he advocated, that "surrealism" which he finally introduced into the poetic vocabulary, in contrast to the "sur-naturalism" embraced by the previous generation of poets.

The ways of the poet within this "inner restraint" are not always smooth or easy to tread upon. His poems are often like fabulous, beautiful conches. The creatures that were lodged in them once upon a time have escaped, some with cries of pain, others humming unearthly strains. Something of their melodies has continued to vibrate within their spiral chambers. The wind-ing, inner ways of Apollinaire's poems, the vowels and con-sonants that wall them, have likewise retained for ever the echo of the music he has sung into them. Placed against our mind's ears, they resound with a harmony of exquisite timbre, though they may seem, indeed, bizarre to the external eye.

Apollinaire composes a music in the necromantic laboratory of his sensibility disturbing alike to the glossaries of men and to their tranquillity. His imagination sails upon a sea of restless quests, and his words, like sea-foam, swell upon a sea of restless quests, and his words, like sea-foam, swell over its waves, rhythmically, unfathomably escaping towards unseen shores. (pp. 306-08)

He felt he was the mouthpiece of his age. He invented new sounds, new voices, drawn from body and heart, from earth and sky. He mixed the elements of this alchemy with cunning witchery. And he brought out of his inner fire a magic gold that was held to be counterfeit in the outworn exchange of versifiers. But underneath his strangely alluring alloy glitters a metal that would find currency in Parnassus. (p. 308)

S. A. Rhodes, "Guillaume Apollinaire," in The French Review (copyright 1938 by the American Association of Teachers of French), Vol. XI, No. 4, February, 1938, pp. 303-19.

DAVID I. GROSSVOGEL   (essay date 1958)

Guillaume Apollinaire appended a foreword to a previously written play of his own, **Les Mamelles de Tirésias**. . . . Though couched amidst irrelevant remarks about Malthusianism, this preface attempted more than merely to raise some cheerful nonsense to the level of a pamphlet: it was in effect Apolli-naire's *ars dramatica*.

The preface begins as a protest—and at first, the very protest seems anodine. Apollinaire wants to lift the theater out of the rut into which it has fallen because of vulgar naturalism. Ref-erence is made to the successors of Victor Hugo and to the vacuity of subsequent "local color," the inevitable pendant of that skillful deception—naturalism—which Apollinaire wishes to supersede. In this phase of its development, the author's theory is too negatively circumscribed to afford much promise. Indeed, Jeanine Moulin (*Guillaume Apollinaire: Textes inédits* . . .) reminds the modern reader that this *drame surréaliste* which today enjoys a cognomen that has gathered literary fame, was to have been labeled simply *surnaturaliste;* Pierre Albert-

Birot, Apollinaire's publisher, suggested the more ambiguous term *surréaliste* whose implied extensions proved so felicitous.

But the suggestive word benefits even the theorist, and in calling for a return to "nature," though stipulating that this never be through servile imitation, Apollinaire finds his de-scription adumbrating an esthetics: "When man wished to im-itate walking, he fashioned the wheel that in no way resembles a leg. He thus achieved surrealism without knowing it." The theorist is now ready to turn from controversy to the devel-opment of his own concepts. He finds that a more viable drama will strive to concern itself with its own particular esthetics rather than with the usual surface imitations of life. . . . [Apol-linaire] is discovered demanding of the theater essentially what Antonin Artaud (*Le Théâtre et son double* . . .) was to for-mulate: "The theater will be able to become itself again—that is to say, a means of providing true illusion—only by giving the spectator genuine dream precipitates."

Since the drama will be an essential and collective experience rather than a game made posible because of coincidentally valid facets (repeatedly, in preface and prologue, Apollinaire warns against *trompe-l'oeil* shallowness), the audience will be drawn into the dramatic rite. He mentions as a hoped-for means of achieving this integration a double theater in the round, one that will bound the spectators from without as well, through an external, circular stage.

This theater, not about life but generating instead a life truly its own, will reject the strictures of any one genre. Such is anyway the author's cast: "It is impossible for me to decide whether or not this drama is serious. [. . .] I preferred to allow a free flow to that *fantaisie* which is my way of interpreting nature, *fantaisie*, which, according to the days, evidences vary-ing degrees of melancholy, satire or lyricism." The word *fan-taisie* is a felicitous one—the conscious author assumes the mantle which he and his public know to be his and suggests through the word those qualities of imaginativeness, conceptual freedom, spontaneity, and surprise found in his poetic opus. . . . That Apollinaire's artistic climate indeed required that *fantaisie* alluded to, is confirmed by the withering of subsequent drama which was not granted such a climate. In **Couleur du temps,** "Drama in Three Acts and in Verse" . . . there remains little more than the author's war-inspired and maudlin sentiment.

Couleur du temps sends the prophetic poet Nyctor, a scientist, and a magnate in a plane-born quest for Peace. Protracted stopovers on a battlefield to rescue the mother of a dead soldier, and on a desert island to snatch away a repentant criminal, fail to prevent the discovery of Peace—a beautiful woman encased in a polar ice-block, "this peace so white and beautiful / So still and, in a word, so dead," over whom the four men fight and die. Many of the symbols are familiar: their neoteric had been the poet Apollinaire's for many years; the visionary Nyc-tor is the chanter of **La Chanson du mal-aimé** and **"La Jolie Rousse";** the plane has already appeared in **"Zone,"** etc. But those unredeemed symbols now remain solemnly pedestrian. Nyctor is earthbound through partisan concerns; the plane, whose modernism no longer stuns nor uplifts, has become merely an unwieldy conveyance; the island from which "le solitaire" is removed, although it is hopefully anticipated as harboring "Serpents and also poetical monsters / Which we shall invent in order to please you" is a flat and moralizing landscape alongside that of "Onirocritique." Mavise, *la fi-ancée*, a momentary echo of the already saddened poet in **"La Jolie Rousse,"** protests: "Though drunken with a will to fight / They would compel me to accept / The ignominious and sad peace / That blankets this deserted isle,'' but she is rapidly sacrificed as merely a woman to Nyctor and remains in the end a useless and passive commentator.

Apollinaire claims to have written all but the prologue and the last scene of *Les Mamelles de Tirésias* in 1903. The life and color which it evinces by comparison with *Couleur du temps* place it at any rate before the tragic spring of 1916. The title suggests the pertness and the ambiguity of the play: Thérèse's breasts fly out as toy balloons that she might shed her womanhood and become a ''man''—Tirésias. Her husband, the moralizing force in this play concerned with repopulation, then takes over the duties of child-bearing, a task he prolifically accomplishes only to have a more subdued Thérèse return to him as the curtain falls.

[Pascal Pia (*Apollinaire par lui-même*)] notes that in chapter IV of Apollinaire's *Le Poète assassiné* . . . , the embryo of a similar plot had been sketched. . . . (pp. 30-3)

The same novel, in which a Lacouff first appears (he does so later in *Les Mamelles*), also contains a number of other burlesque outlines whose purpose is to ridicule the then prevalent forms of drama. In these outlines, the author is merely spoofing, albeit with verve reminiscent of Jarry. . . . However, in transferring such a satirical outline to the full dimensions of the stage, Apollinaire has had to shift his sights. What had been a simply destructive protest will now attempt to be construction as well: the protest gives way to the exemplar. Whereas the spurious plot outline merely pretends to be a play in order to mock real plays, the real play now created by Apollinaire will seek substance, in conformity with the ideals of the preface—from within itself rather than through parody. It might not be amiss to note here that Apollinaire's third and last dramatic attempt extant, *Casanova* . . . , which is called *comédie parodique,* fails, betraying in its very title the substance of those ideals. *Casanova* was to have been the libretto for a comic opera, an episode drawn from the Italian adventurer's life, and as such, the pastiche of an Italianate genre which Apollinaire might have remembered from the pre-war days when he had written *Le Théâtre italien.* . . . Perhaps the subdued author of *Vitam Impendere Amori* . . . was consciously seeking elsewhere an effervescence no longer in him. Whether or not such speculation be valid, the contrived and glossy fun of *Casanova* remains bookish and static even in its sallies: the promise of the stage has not been fulfilled.

In *Les Mamelles de Tirésias,* Apollinaire has chosen laughter from the start, the indecision of his preface notwithstanding. Pascal Pia, who believes that *Les Mamelles* was written in 1916, bases a part of his evidence on a tone which he finds reminiscent of the first poems of *Calligrammes.* Availing himself of a fun-seeking device at least as old as Aucassin's visit to Torelore, Apollinaire has retained, as in his comic sketch, the inversion of sexual functions. In line with this facetious mood, the play favors puns, elementary figures of intellectual laughter, which it occasionally strings out at length. . . . (pp. 34-5)

Apollinaire acknowledges in his preface that he would have no objections to formulate were even the comic elements to gain the upper hand. . . . He takes note of accusations according to which he has availed himself of means used in revues and defends himself against these accusations, but only casually, as he has no fundamental objection to them either.

However, whether Apollinaire's comic ambivalence be genuine or simply retrospective, his humor eventually acquires other dimensions; the play is quite obviously not simply a

revue. The puns, while still at the intellectual level, partake of multiple extensions: in II, iv, for example, the *scène*-Seine play on words indicates universality as well as dramatic essence and condensation. In so doing, it echoes the fundamental equivoque of the entire play which is laid in Zanzibar (frequently identified with Paris by participants), a city that derives its name from a homonymous dice game whose attribute is the megaphone shaped like a huge dice box and used by various actors at intervals throughout the play. The pun upon which the physical locus of the play is established has moved, like that of its hero, beyond mere intellectual oscillations—it truly partakes of two inherencies.

Such devices, if they merely seek to extend the fun-making into new dimensions, and properly scenic ones, are innocuous enough. However, Apollinaire's preface speaks of ''sufficient newness to shock and rouse to indignation.'' The word ''striking'' is used to designate the new esthetics that aim at a spectator ''struck.'' Shock is indeed a mechanism of laughter— just as newness is concomitant with artistic transmutation. But neither requires outrage to the beholder. Artistic newness is a re-creation in which the spectator participates, and the shock that leads to mirth is sufficiently mild to be overcome through laughter. Thus the implications of Apollinaire's troubled awareness are not that the experiment might fail, making its author merely another writer of farces, but rather that the farce might prove unable to disguise the perpetration of new modes. At this level the mirth shields a revolutionary, someone who wishes to upset, whose voice, when it sought no protective mask, had pleaded in **''La Jolie Rousse''**: ''Pity on us forever struggling at the brink / Of the unbounded and of what is yet to come.''

This is the voice that had elevated all things surprising, the new and the unknown, to the level of an esthetics and whose literary testament, *L'Esprit nouveau,* was read by Apollinaire in 1917: ''The new spirit is also to be found in the astounding. The astounding is that which is most alive and most fresh in that spirit.'' Few of Apollinaire's commentators have failed to note his motto ''I astonish''—one spoken evidently in full cognizance of its etymon.

The theater is quite properly a place of wonderment and, therefore, developing a genuinely theatrical esthetics might indeed have been for Apollinaire not only a congenial but a fruitful issue. Thérèse's breasts flying out to the audience (and later, as the curtain comes down, being tossed out as plentiful rubber balls to that audience) gave evidence of the author's concerns. Whereas Jarry's initial shock had suddenly severed stage and audience, this action allows Apollinaire a mechanism of surprise while at the same time it facilitates psychological communication across the footlights (all this quite apart from the cumulative effect of the sexual note which must certainly have been hoped for by the author of *Ombre de mon amour*). The audience thus intimately participant was the one for whom the theater in the round had been planned. (pp. 36-8)

Avowedly, the play is a cubist experiment, one that came to life under the sponsorship of the cubist publication *Sic.* . . . [Marcel Adéma] recalls how a certain number of cubist painters disavowed Apollinaire after the performance, accusing him of having ridiculed them. This particular protest is curious in view of the close contact Apollinaire had enjoyed with so many of the group and its sympathizers, like Picasso, Braque, Chirico, Picabia, and the many articles he had written for *Les Soirées de Paris* on behalf of the new school. These articles, gathered in 1913 and published as *Les Peintres cubistes* (originally titled

Méditations esthétiques) contain some of the first and more perceptive definitions of cubism attempted hitherto.

Apollinaire first defines the new movement's program—methods and aims:

> Wishing to attain dimensions of the ideal, no longer limiting themselves to humanity, the young painters offer us works that are more cerebral than sensual.
>
> What makes cubism different from the old style of painting is the fact that it is not an imitative art but a conceptual art striving to achieve creation.

He sees four tendencies of this new art, or better, two paths of what he calls the *art pur* and two others of a trend that fails to merit that denomination. Among the genuine art forms are scientific cubism and orphic cubism. Scientific cubism strives to create new artistic entities with elements derived not from the "reality" of vision but from the reality of a true knowledge. Orphic cubism substitutes, for the essentially factual components of scientific cubism, components entirely created by the artist though endowed by him with vital "reality." To further delineate these two art forms, their anti-forms are also described. Corresponding to a debasement of scientific cubism is physical cubism built with elements merely understood by the eye, while orphic cubism gives way, at an inferior level, to instinctive cubism, which is the compound of shapes created by an artist lacking either fundamental artistic perception or belief. (p. 38)

How close the positive aspects of this program are to the dramatic ideals set forth in the preface of *Les Mamelles* need hardly be emphasized. Picasso is naturally cited as an exponent of both scientific and orphic cubism and the reference to Picasso in Apollinaire's play as the author of "a canvas that moves" calls to mind the fact that, in turning to the stage, Apollinaire had tried to create a play "that moves." Properly speaking, *Les Mamelles de Tirésias* is an attempted cubist drama, one that will, in conformity with the cubist esthetics, reject imitation for creation and hope to achieve thereby an artistic truth derived from the medium itself. (pp. 38-40)

This attempt to give an additional dimension to the reality of the canvas, one already evident in Cézanne, undoubtedly accounts for the meaning of "a canvas that moves." And in this way, the puns alluded to (*scène*-Seine, Zanzibar, etc.) attempt first an intellectual and then an artistic oscillation between the idea and the stage reality. However, in reference to the visual demands of the stage, these intellectual or semi-intellectual transmutations give way to wholly physical ones. Thus it is that Thérèse undergoes sexual changes on stage; that her husband creates a baby reporter by mixing in his crib scraps of things associated with the journalistic trade. . . . As ambiguous as the ambivalent hero whose oscillations are visible on stage, are those further modulations emphasized by the very voice of the stage—most frequently by the "people" of Zanzibar, actually a sound-effects man (an obvious reminiscence of Jarry's stage theory) whose presence within the action creates and cancels a number of the sounds which that action requires. (pp. 40-1)

Thus, the new drama was orphic, according to Apollinaire's definition, when its cubism established areas of ambiguous intellectual inferences, and scientific when the stage relied on visual, mechanical tricks to implement its dramatic simultaneities.

The supreme achievement of this ambiguous art was to have extended its area of ambivalence to include the audience in its fluctuation. The supertheater in the round was to have been in reality a single cubist unit—the play engulfing stage and audience alike—of which the spectatress previously mentioned remains a vestigial witness. It is ironic that this climactic aim should have been in fact the undoing of the entire experiment. The failure of Apollinaire's cubist drama, whose esthetics were so closely patterned on the successful experiments of the cubist painters, was a failure to account for the basic differences between the dramatic and other art forms. Indications of this potential failure are deducible fairly early from the poet's excessive cult of surprise. (p. 41)

[Apollinaire's] experiment was fated, in common with all experiments, to elicit first the laughter of the uninitiated before being able to induce response. Such awkward laughter, born of uneasiness rather than of assimilative triumph, must be imputed to Apollinaire himself if his sincerity (confirmed by his cubist ethics and the dramatic esthetics of Jarry which *Les Mamelles* so frequently illustrates) is to be credited. The intimate experience which the theater in the round would have anticipated, demanded first human presence and second, total dedication. . . . Healthy laughter, already frustrated by the absence of realistic surfaces, becomes spiritless or hostile through such accumulative alienation.

In fact, the mechanical aspect of its performers slowly mires the action of these two acts whose dynamism seldom appears to stem from true spontaneity: the experimenter repeatedly betrays the comic author and the latter finds himself betrayed in turn. Harbingers of laughter must offer an initial threat to the intimate familiarity of spectator and actor: the figures of Apollinaire elicit at best mild admiration.

In *Les Mamelles,* the quest for laughter not infrequently dominates the experiment and the play loses form. It is no longer easy to understand readily why the husband speaks with a distinctly Belgian accent off stage and loses it after he has appeared. . . . It is hard thereafter to tell whether the original performance had the gendarme and the journalist played by women for any particular purpose or merely because of nonchalance towards the over-all validity of the performance. One inclines to the latter belief after having failed to find any essential reason for their existence and noting the episodic form of the play as it moves fitfully to its ineffectual conclusion.

One will likewise impugn the entire cubist experiment when its devices are viewed as stage actions rather than illustrative material for that experiment. *Casanova,* an undramatic stage materialization of an aspect of the author's earlier romanticism (albeit presented as a pastiche) and *Couleur du temps,* the ponderous restatement of a number of conceits, point to the primary failure of *Les Mamelles:* the failure of a drama to draw substance from its own soil. The failure is the more noticeable in that, as a truly perceptive theorist, Apollinaire had understood this dramatic necessity. The form of *Les Mamelles de Tirésias* as it now exists would appear to be the instance of an initial betrayal of the dramatist by the experimenter and thereafter betrayal of the experimenter by the uneasy dramatist seeking to disguise the experimenter's excesses.

Upon such grounds, the dramatic experiment could not fructify: the experimental is awkwardly obvious, surprise frustrates the communion, mechanical artifacts inhibit the human. Even the farce is seldom funny, for unlike Jarry, whom Apollinaire admired for his genuine truculence, the author himself seems to have remained outside the circle of his synthetic creation. And so the cubist drama remains an odd assemblage of disjointed parts out of whose hermaphroditism the dream world was to have soared. (pp. 44-6)

David I. Grossvogel, "Les enfants terribles: Jarry, Apollinaire, Cocteau," in his The Self-Conscious Stage in Modern French Drama *(copyright © 1958 Columbia University Press; reprinted by permission of the publisher), Columbia University Press, 1958 (and reprinted as* 20th Century French Drama *by Gordian Press, 1967), pp. 19-67.*

L. C. BREUNIG (essay date 1964)

Mr. [C. A.] Hackett admits that in the work of Apollinaire "there are individual verses, refrains and short lyrics which have more than a period interest," but he concludes that the best work is "that which reflects the work of other and greater poets, such as Villon, Rimbaud and Verlaine."

Such an evaluation is based, it seems to us, upon an oversimplification. . . . (p. 67)

Certainly the poetry of Apollinaire is more complex. It contains elements, it must contain elements, which account for its continued appeal a half-century later. Without attempting . . . to discuss them all we would like to examine a single but a very essential element, or rather a tone in this poetry which would seem to have considerable resonance in the nineteen sixties. The contemporaries of Apollinaire, those of the "banquet years," were not particularly sensitive to it, but thanks to Surrealism we are able to hear it more clearly. It is the laughter of Apollinaire.

In 1940 Breton published his *Anthologie de l'humour noir,* a collection which in addition to such masters of "black humor" as Swift, Lichtenberg and De Quincey includes the Surrealists Vaché, Rigaud, Dali, Prévert and, among the few writers of the immediately preceding generation, Apollinaire. In his presentation Breton recalls the sound of Apollinaire's laugh as he himself had actually heard it before the poet's death in 1918. "It made the same noise as a first burst of hailstones on a window pane." The implication is that this laugh had nothing contagious about it; it caused no merriment but rather a shudder. Was it not a sudden outburst of the more inhuman, unfeeling, destructive side of the poet's nature?

The excerpts from Apollinaire in Breton's Anthology, most of them in prose, are not among his more significant work, and what Breton fails to stress is that one can hear these "hailstones" not only in many of the weird tales of *L'Hérésiarque et Cie* or the more sinister episodes of *Le Poète assassiné* and *La Femme assise* but also in the pages of lyric poetry upon which Apollinaire's reputation stands, in *Alcools* and *Calligrammes.*

What is the nature of this laughter? For ears which are attuned to it today it has a remarkable resemblance with that which is heard less perhaps in the novel or the poetry of the last few years than in the theatre of the avant-garde. Indeed Breton, if he so desired, could publish a new edition of his Anthology for the present decade to include, in all fairness, more of the Surrealists of his own generation such as Artaud and Vitrac (whom he had "excommunicated") and in addition excerpts from Ionesco, Beckett, Genet, Tardieu, Arrabal, Obaldia, Vian

and others. He could give, for example, the scene from Vitrac's *Les Mystères de l'amour* in which the author, having failed to commit suicide, comes on stage still bleeding and laughing uproariously; the passage from the beginning of Ionesco's *Les Chaises* where the pathetic old man and his wife shake with laughter as he repeats the same inane story ("Alors on arri. . . .") that they have heard every evening for the last sixty-five years. . . . This is not comedy in the traditional sense. The author does not wish to elicit laughter but rather, as Ionesco specifically indicates at the end of *Jacques ou la soumission,* "to provoke in the audience a painful sentiment of malaise. . . ." (pp. 67-8)

[Our aim] is merely to invite the reader to look again at the lyric poetry of Apollinaire with today's very somber laughter still echoing in his ears.

We discover first that we do not need to rely on Breton's testimony alone, for Apollinaire describes his own laugh. . . .

> You make fun of yourself and like the fire of hell your laughter crackles / The sparks of your laughter gild the depths of your life / It's a painting hung in a somber museum / And sometimes you go to have a close look at it.

Breton's image has changed here into that of little crackling flames, but the troubling effect is the same. The poet is speaking to himself. Heautontimoroumenos-like he is both the one laughing and the one laughed at. And as he steps up closer to himself he realizes that beneath the gentle, tender sentimental self lies the infernal, destructive force which was to chill Breton.

In some poems Apollinaire transfers this laugh to another character, usually a woman, and portrays himself as the victim. In such cases he becomes the traditional "mal-aimé," Guillaume who suffers from the perverse capriciousness of Mareye, Annie, Marie, Lou and Madeleine and who in his more grief-stricken moments sees himself as Orpheus being torn to pieces by the Maenads. This theme is of course as old as poetry itself, but the distinctiveness, the modernity, if you will, of Apollinaire lies in the very intensity of the harsh, sadistic laugh which reveals a monstrous degree of insensitivity. At times it becomes an atrocious grimace, mechanical, fixed, like a whinny, and creating between the two beings a wide, mysterious void which alienates them beyond all hope. The haunting sound of this laughter echoes throughout the work. (p. 69)

An awareness of this sound helps us to reread certain poems with a deeper sense of their meaning. The very possibility that Salome (**"Salomé"**) is not broken-hearted over the death of John the Baptist, that her feverish burst of frivolity is perhaps authentic makes the death of her victim even more horrible. (p. 70)

The sound is even more disquieting, however, when it emerges from the poet himself. In **"Poème lu au mariage d'André Salmon"** Apollinaire recalls the birth within him of his black humor. . . . Here Apollinaire takes the place of the Maenads. The dying Orpheus seems to symbolize all the sorrow, and of course the self-pity within the poets themselves, sentiments which they suddenly demolish with a guffaw that bursts forth like breaking glass. (pp. 70-1)

One of the most powerful examples of these explosive outbursts comes in the middle of **"La Chanson du mal-aimé."** The Zaporogian Cossacks, who have just received the order to surrender to the Sultan of Constantinople, compose with a burst of mirthless laughter their foul-mouthed reply. For them the laugh is an act of defiance, but for the poet-lover it is a purge for his grief and his mortification at finding himself the victim of a passionate and impossible attachment. And indirectly through a kind of "poetic logic" the impassive young English girl who inspired the poem is splattered by the most ungallant ribaldry which follows.

Once we realize that Apollinaire chose consciously or unconsciously to laugh infernally, to stand alongside the Maenads, to become himself the destructive force we can appreciate more fully some of the incongruous juxtapositions which so puzzled his contemporaries. In an essay on Picasso he once wrote that "surprise laughs savagely in the pure light" of the artist's paintings. The technique of surprise, which he made so much of without ever defining it adequately, takes on more meaning if we associate it with the explosive quality of his own "savage" laughter. Many of the devices of surprise such as the juxtaposition of the tender and the grotesque, of gravity and triviality or, as in the example we have just seen, the sudden intrusion of obscenities into a sentimental mood seem to stem from the poet's decision to let "the fire of his laughter crackle." (p. 71)

This black humor is nowhere more apparent than in the war poetry. . . . Apollinaire, like Jarry, turns the tragic inside out and by making death a subject for laugher conveys more freshly all its horror. Face to face with it he can affect the most insensitive cheerfulness, a kind of amused detachment, or a puckish smile. In **"Merveilles de la guerre"** the bursting shells in the darkness remind him of a huge banquet. . . . Who would have said that one could be so casual, so jaunty when one is in the trenches, ready to be blown up at any moment?

In **"Chant d'honneur"** the poet recalls the sight of four dead soldiers still standing upright in the trench. . . . Four Towers of Pisa! What are we to make of this delightful simile which derives from such detached, almost callous, indifference? This is not irony in the usual sense; Apollinaire in fact was rarely ironical. Nor can one accuse him of cynicism. Only a few lines later he will address his comrades in the most moving terms. . . . It seems rather that as a lyric poet speaking in the first person Apollinaire plays the role of both author and characters in his own "theatre of the absurd." He can make the most abrupt leaps from the anguished, heavy-hearted self within him who feels as deeply as the writers of today the tragedy of man's condition, to himself as *persona,* detached, inhuman, an "image d'Epinal" soldier, "Guy au galop," a stranger as mysterious and alarming as the stylized, Guignol characters we see in the theatre today. The laughter of Apollinaire in such cases is also on stage. And like the mask-maker of Marcel Marceau, holding the two masks of Tragedy and Comedy and putting now one, now the other on his face in rapid-fire succession, the lines of Apollinaire with their sudden shifts often convey a single sentiment, neither tragic nor comic and yet containing both, the sentiment of the absurd.

The power of the Theatre of the Absurd comes from the fact that beneath the vaudeville gags, the word-play and the farcical nonsense the audience senses the author's earnestness, his deep concern before what he feels to be the "non-sense" of the world itself. It is unlikely that Apollinaire had any clearly formulated notion of the absurd, and his own moods were undoubtedly more personal and less representative of any collective anxiety in the world of his day. Nevertheless, in its fusion of laughter and despair, whatever its causes, his poetry produces a malaise that we are perhaps more sensitive to than

his contemporaries. The playwrights of today tend to hide their own anguish beneath the laughter of their characters whereas Apollinaire as a poet was more inclined to alternate the two elements within a single poem. Although the method may be different the emotional effect is nonetheless much the same.

And it is largely Surrealism that we have to thank for this affiliation. By revealing those mysterious and irrational recesses of the mind from which the "hailstones" of laughter emerge, Surrealism has attuned us to the poetic impact of a new kind of theatre and at the same time has disclosed a new tone in the poet whose signature, in black ink, was "Tout terriblement Guillaume Apollinaire." (pp. 72-3)

> *L. C. Breunig, "The Laughter of Apollinaire," in* Yale French Studies *(copyright © Yale French Studies 1964), No. 31, 1964, pp. 66-73.*

ARMINEL MARROW   (essay date 1968)

The definition of basic terms is our first concern. A *pun* might be said to be a *perceived identity in the shape of words,* remembering that words are the raw material of the poet.

Image, metaphor & analogy might be collectively described as *perceived identity or similarity in the shape of objects*—that is, in the subject-matter on which the poet works.

A picture-poem is different again, for it seeks to express and explore the sensed, "secret" identity of word and object. . . .

[All three] attempt to find "short cuts to reality"—the deep, brilliant illumination that surpasses the words it uses. This rôle of illumination, long a function of image, has not always been accepted as part of pun, nor, for that matter, of picture-poem. But Apollinaire did come to take this function seriously.

To begin with a fairly simple, rather humorous calligramme, let us look at *Aussi bien que les cigales.* Apollinaire is in a mood of jocular exhortation, persistent as the cicada. (pp. 295-96)

Since the picture of the insect is made up of words about it, it would be true to say that the cicada *is its own meaning.* This meaning, to the poet, has four main elements: [joy, initiation, violence and courage, and song]. . . . (p. 296)

[Thus] the cicada *embodies,* for Apollinaire, the same values as the soldier and the poet: it is associated with the virtues of courage and of aspiration.

Coeur, couronne et miroir is a group of three apparently unrelated picture-poems, offering other aspects of the calligramme technique.

Coeur gives a picture version of a metaphor found elsewhere in Apollinaire's poetry: that is, the heart as an upside-down flame. A comical metaphor? Yes, but how accurate nonetheless!

What seems to be almost nonsensical in verbal terms is simple and self-evident in the picture. It is possible to rationalize it, of course, and come up with a verbal explanation like this: "ma flamme" is an antique way of saying love (read heart); the poet rejuvenates the image by qualifying it—ma flamme *renversée*. This implies the reverses of fortune suffered by his still incandescent heart. But these implications and subtleties are to be drawn from the words, not the picture. The picture dispels ambiguities: it *is* both flame and heart. It is a picture-pun.

Line is simple; words are subtle. But the basis of the words *is* the line, and their complexities are inspired by the line itself. In this little poem, puzzle and solution, complexity and simplicity, combine in gently humorous balance.

Couronne, like the cicada, is an emblem poem. It is on a variation of the same theme, too: the poet as hero. The crown, symbol of kingship, is the property of the poet, king of men; and the modern poet is, in a sense, the heir of the dying race of kings, for he is intrepid hero, visionary, and seeker of truth.

The drawing is again simple, crown meaning king or greatness. And again it is through the words that ambiguity arises: but this time it is grammatical. If read "Les rois qui meurent tour à tour", there is a sadness and sense of inevitable decay, not uncharacteristic of the nostalgic side of Apollinaire. But if read ". . . tour à tour renaissent au coeur des poètes", the emphasis is triumphant. And is it not true that the crown emblem does imply both life and death? continuity in impermanence?

The pivot phrase is "tour à tour"; and appropriately it is also the pivotal central line of the drawing.

Miroir is one of Apollinaire's best calligrammes. Simple, yet mysterious, shape and word illuminating each other, it achieves a rare harmony and sophistication.

In the oval mirror is Guillaume Apollinaire. The mirror is his poetry. It is not an ordinary mirror, but "ce miroir"—a mirror made of words.

In his poetry the poet lives more truly than in real life, for the life of the imagination, which excludes contingencies, is a life of *essence*. Angel, or spirit, is the essence of life, as the metaphysical and alchemistical philosophers decided long ago. The reflection in an ordinary mirror, because it does not contain this essence, is a false copy, embodying only the inessential traits, the contingencies.

Hence, the stark signature, Guillaume Apollinaire, *is* Guillaume Apollinaire in a way that a mirror-image never can be. It is his *created self*—created by and in poetry, shaped by imagination.

There is perhaps also an implication that the "ultimate reality" is not this created self within the magic circle of words, nor yet the living self which creates, but lies in the relationship between essence and existence.

Yet, with all this subtlety and seriousness of implication, with its hints of sorcery and name-taboo symbolism, there is the hint of a whimsical smile: for the way the poet is "contained" in the mirror is really almost comic. And perhaps that trace of a smile is Apollinaire's most authentic signature. (pp. 296-98)

Puns exploit the likenesses in words: this coincidence in word-shape can be interpreted as implying a special relationship between the different objects indicated.

Images exploit likenesses in objects, likenesses which may be either physical or spiritual.

Calligrammes are more difficult to fit into this pattern, but could, I think, be defined as exercises in full coincidence, whereas puns and images are concerned with partial coincidence. What is it, for example, that the word "crown" and the object-crown have in common? A number of associations: an emotional shape if you like.

Within the range of the calligrammes we have examined, it is possible to distinguish different degrees of "coincidence". Some picture-poems are distinctly emblematic in character, for example. In these, the drawing shows the visible entity; the words describe the non-visible attributes of the thing. The shape and the words are distinct, separate: two quite different ways of perceiving. This is the case in *Aussi bien que les cigales*, and in *Couronne.*

Others are picture-puns: *Coeur* being the simplest of these. Like the word-pun, which relies on coincidence of word-shape representing quite different objects, this is based upon a coincidence of object-shape representing two quite different things, two distinct words. As the pun creates a special and significant relationship between its disparate objects, so too does the dual-direction calligramme. (pp. 299-300)

To Apollinaire, fascinated by signs and symbols, coincidence was not mere chance, but the mark of a secret, subtle relationship. Each thing has its deeper meanings, its silent ties with experiences and attitudes. Any particular object is not only itself, but embodies other objects, like it in shape. This is not the ambiguity of Symbolism, the system of correspondences which implies a dualistic concept of the universe, but rather the ambiguity of Surrealism, metamorphosis within a monistic universe.

It is perhaps this, most important of all, if not always successfully expressed, that Apollinaire seems to be trying to suggest in these picture-poems. It is the puns of form itself, and the ambiguities of shapes. It is the emotional morphology which arises directly from the physical shape of objects. (pp. 300-01)

Arminel Marrow, "Form and Meaning in Apollinaire's Picture-Poems," in Australian Journal of French Studies, *Vol. V, No. 3, September-December, 1968, pp. 295-302.*

LAURENCE M. PORTER　　(essay date 1970)

"Zone" presents on a small scale the retrospective view *Alcools* provides on a large one. The title *Alcools,* like the one it replaced (*Eau-de-vie*), suggests a life whose supreme value is to drink from the fount of "sensations fortes," both those experienced in the present and those remembered from the past. . . . But having surveyed memories ranging from his childhood to the present, the poet of "Zone" finds that his life-style of intoxication has provided some moments of joy, but has led to no lasting achievement. . . . [The] poet finds himself in an emotional "Zone." "Zone" . . . serves as a metaphor for the painful state of transition between an old self and a new one as yet undiscovered. A dwellingplace for outcasts, located between country and city, childhood and maturity, innocence and experience, this purgatorial region expresses the puberty of the soul.

Throughout **"Zone,"** flashes of joy and humor alternate with deep despair to express a mercurial personality. . . . The poet avidly grasps for sources of joy, and finds them all unstable. His quests for an ecstasy that is at first intellectual, then emotional, and finally physical, constitute a series of defensive strategies intended to obliterate the pain of self-confrontation, which nevertheless draws inexorably nearer to the poet. The frequent changes from "tu" to "je" and back again in the poet's self-address communicate his effort at objective self-examination, which repeatedly breaks down before the onslaughts of self-pity. (pp. 286-87)

Paradoxically, Apollinaire—like Baudelaire, Rimbaud, and Mallarmé—attains an artistic triumph by rendering eloquently into poetry the intense experience of failure. Apollinaire recognized this success when he had completed his poem. His removal of all punctuation from the proofs of *Alcools* communicates a sense of liberation: without punctuation, the poems' flow of words can simulate the movement of a stream of consciousness proceeding by free association, and untrammeled by logical or formal boundaries. With renewed self-confidence, Apollinaire also revised **"Zone"** so as to attenuate its expression of disgust at life, and to convey the experience of religious ecstasy. . . . [In] the history of the composition of the poem, the superadded vision represents a victory for the imagination, which recaptures its pristine vigor and reintegrates religious experience with the modern world. **"Zone"** proves therapeutic. By creating it, Apollinaire escapes the tyranny of his past sensibility and finds the equilibrium of self-acceptance expressed by the innovative freedom of his later work. (p. 295)

> Laurence M. Porter, *"The Fragmented Self of Apollinaire's 'Zone'," in* L'Esprit Créateur *(copyright © 1970 by L'Esprit Créateur), Vol. X, No. 4, Winter, 1970, pp. 285-95.*

ANNA BALAKIAN   (essay date 1970)

Since the end of the nineteenth century a rift had taken place between science and art which was growing wider and wider. . . .

This conflict is vividly demonstrated by Apollinaire in his *Le Poète Assassiné*. . . . Much of this Rabelaisian novelette is autobiographical. We trace the fantastically confused origin and international upbringing of the poet-hero, Croniamental, which parallels closely the apocryphal data about Apollinaire's own early years. (p. 81)

Croniamental comes face to face with the archenemy of poets, not the smug unimaginative bourgeois, but the champion of the scientists, Horace Tograth, who demands the killing of all poets because they have been overrated and are contributing nothing valuable to present civilization. . . .

Croniamental protests furiously against this persecution of the artists, and pays with his life. Yet Apollinaire leaves an undertone of criticism directed not exclusively against the philistine debaser of the poet, but also against the artist in general who has partially merited the attack. He indicates that the fault for this apparent impotence of poets is partly the public's, that public which demands boredom and unhappiness as the subject matter of literature. . . . (p. 82)

Although in *Le Poète Assassiné* the conflict between science and art ends in tragedy and defeat for the artist, Apollinaire rejected in his own life and writings the secondary role attributed to the artist in the world of new values. He sought a conciliation between the work of the scientist and of the modern artist. He called himself and those like him "pilgrims of perdition" because they were risking what intellectual security they had as artists to explore the uncertain and the unproven. . . .

The need for inventiveness to preserve the prestige of the twentieth-century artist in competition with the twentieth-century technologist was first illustrated through Apollinaire's negative reaction to the existing imitative and autobiographical novel much in vogue then in France. As principal reviewer on the staff of *La Phalange* for a number of years, early in his career, he found ample opportunity to criticize the unoriginality of the novel form. Even when commending what he considered an exceptional one such as *Tzimin-Choc* by Louis-Bréon he makes of it an opportunity to chide the average contemporary novelist for his superficial realism, for his recourse to the easy autobiographical material. And yet he somehow hopes that a change of direction is at hand. . . . (p. 83)

While literature had been neglecting imagination, science had learned to make maximum use of it. (p. 84)

Why not a parallel between the creativeness of applied science and that of the arts? In his preface to **Les Mamelles de Tirésias** he fabricated the word "surreal" to designate the human ability to create the unnatural, and he pointed out that man's first surrealistic act was the creation of the wheel, which imitates the physical function of motion but creates a form entirely independent of forms known to exist in nature. The wheel becomes for him a product of purely creative work on the part of man, a manifestation of unconscious surrealism. . . . The same independence from natural objects, which the technologist had achieved by his inventions, and through which he revolutionized the physical appearance of the world, should be sought by the artist in his own medium. To Apollinaire the acquisition of that freedom was to be the fundamental attainment of the modern mind. (pp. 84-5)

Since the scientist had become not a destroyer of fantasy but a producer of marvels, his inventiveness should prove a challenge and an incentive to the artist. . . .

Art's pitfalls in recent times had been its imitative approach to nature. . . . (p. 85)

The symbolists had had a similar notion about the "interiority" of art but they had feared the object, feared the *concrete,* which they had mistaken for the *natural.* To point out the difference Apollinaire made up the word "surreal" as opposed to "symbolist." True to this distinction the culmination of the symbolist attitude was to be abstract art and not surrealism.

Although Apollinaire showed a certain affinity at first with Marinetti and other futurists, he soon noticed something superficial in the way the futurists extolled science. . . .

Apollinaire's relations with the cubist painters were of a much more fundamental nature. He found in the cubists the truest competitors of the imaginative technologists. As the perfect illustration of his own theories he defined cubism in **Les Peintres Cubistes** . . . as "an art of conception which tends to rise to the level of creation." (p. 86)

He discovered in the works of the cubists the fourth dimension of reality, which he deemed not only a proof of creativeness but of divinity. . . . Through his observations of the cubists' activities he was able to make a crucial distinction between the new and the old mental formation of the artist: the traditional artist is a sieve of human experiences and, stimulated by the muse, he is a facile interpreter of life; while the new artist, like the scientist, plods from effort to effort in the process of construction, unaided by divine inspiration, but possessing himself the grains of divinity.

Apollinaire's friendship with Picasso, Braque, Picabia, and the Douanier Rousseau made him a better apologist for the new art than the painters themselves could have been, thus setting a precedent for closer association between the arts of painting and writing, a relationship which was to prove so significant and influential in the development of dadaism and surrealism. (p. 87)

Apollinaire's importance lies not so much in being the originator of an attitude as in having stated it more provocatively and held to it more persistently than his contemporaries. His ideas on art did not remain in the realm of theories but were illustrated consciously in the major portion of his poetic work.

Apollinaire was not a suggestive artist in the manner of the symbolists. Like the magician that he wished to emulate, the poet tried to infuse his work with unexpected sparks: visions, concretely resplendent and limitless, meant to surprise and mystify the reader in the way that a rabbit is pulled out of a sleeve. . . .

His earliest poetical work, *L'Enchanteur Pourissant (The Rotting Enchanter)* . . . , depicts the imprisonment of the enchanter by those who exploit his power but also prophesies the magician's eventual resurrection. (p. 88)

He is then dead only in the eyes of the world, and he will come back to earth when humanity is again ready to reclaim him. Apollinaire sees this time as close and bases his whole optimism on the fact that man's inventive spirit has again become ignited with the advent of the new century. (p. 89)

The symbol of the immortal Merlin dead to mortal man is an obsessive image for Apollinaire and the basis for his poetic vision which he tries to shape through the fusion of the finite with the infinite, what he calls "reasonable irreality." In *L'Enchanteur Pourrissant* all the apocalyptic events that Apollinaire describes in the ambience of the enchanter are marked by a language that tries to waive the contradictions of physical reality which it expresses.

L'Enchanteur Pourrissant ends with a piece of writing called "Onirocritique," which is a natural appendix to his work. It represents Apollinaire's earliest example of inventive writing: in an apocalyptic vision of the universe he combines creatures and disintegrates them into a hundred feet, eyes, in an ever-changing panorama; sounds are transformed into beings, silence into movement, trees consume stars; and each reader is left with his own interpretation of the imagery. Apollinaire was to adhere all his life to this faith in the poet, which he had expressed in this early piece of writing. Later in "Les Collines" he was indeed to announce that the resurrection of the old enchanter was at hand, and that he was about to arise again from his man-imposed grave. (pp. 89-90)

The two basic anthologies *Alcools* and *Calligrammes,* in which he collected his poetic writings, contain two types of poems, both inspirational to the future surrealists, although in different ways: the poem-manifesto and the poem-illustration, the first giving comfort, the second being more relevant to the techniques of surrealist writing. . . .

[In *Alcools*], his first collection of verse, we find instances of the same mixture of perspectives and sensations. Just as the technologist formed a new world of realities with existing matter, Apollinaire believed that words could make and unmake a universe. He attempted to use his "five senses and a few more" to string side by side images often logically disconnected, demanding of the reader leaps and bounds of the imagination to keep pace with his self-characterized "oblong" vision. His dislocations of temporal and spatial perspective defy ordinary reality but are of this earth in their tactility, colors, and scents. "Cortège" presents one of the most incoherent yet challenging visions in the theme of the inverted flight of a bird and its effects on the relativity of land, sky, and light. . . . (p. 90)

On the other hand a poem such as **"Poème au Mariage d'André Salmon"** offers nothing new in terms of illustration of a new aesthetics; it could even be considered redundant in its repetitions and in the direct form of its communication of Apollinaire's joyful celebration of his friend's consummation of love. But it is an inventory of work in progress as far as his poetic destiny is concerned. It is in this poem that Apollinaire uses the expression "pilgrims of perdition" to characterize what he and his friend had attempted to do: to catch the eye of a dying Orpheus, to seize the divine fire, to learn also to laugh, and to ignite words with new meanings, i.e., to change the world through language,—an objective that the surrealists were to make distinctly their major concern. (p. 91)

[*Calligrammes*] is a more striking example of his inventive approach to writing. The theme in this collection of poetry is the newness of the world: new fires, new forms, new colors impatient to be given reality. The wand which has brought about the return of the "age of magic" is said to be the war. . . . In a poem called **"War"** he bids his readers not to cry over the horrors of war but instead to realize that, while before we only knew the surface of earth and sea, now we could reach deeper below and higher into space. (p. 92)

In *Calligrammes* Apollinaire used juxtaposition and discarded symmetry and order much more than in his previous works. These poems are circumstantial in the sense that their point of departure is a factual event or concrete detail of the color of the times. But the submarine cables, the planes fighting overhead, the bombs, the flares, the telephone or the phonograph, each serves as an impetus to new imagery surpassing its circumstantial nature and announcing to Apollinaire the need to alert and sharpen the senses.

When Apollinaire was criticized for the obscurity of the symbols in his play, *Les Mamelles de Tirésias,* he defended himself by stating that true symbolism, like the Sibylline Oracles, lends itself to many meanings, "to numerous interpretations that sometimes contradict each other." *Calligrammes* fearlessly illustrates this theory, thereby setting a new relationship between the artist and his audience: if the writer or painter is no longer to be a mere interpreter of life but a creator, then his erstwhile role of interpreter will be transferred to the reader or spectator, who loses his passive task of absorbing and feeling the message of the artist and assumes the more creative role of relating the sensations of the artist to his own experiences and his own faculties of imagination and association. Thus in their flexibility, the visions of the artist are set to a perpetual motion of interpretations, which may in themselves be a form of creative activity. This same technique, called by the uninitiated the obscurity of modern art forms, was to become the *sine qua non* of the works of the dadaist and surrealist disciples of Apollinaire.

Here again we have manifesto poems, particularly in **"Les Collines"** and in the last of the series, **"La Jolie Rousse."** Both poems written in very direct and clear discourse have in their linguistic structure none of the sibylline character, but oracular they are and their augury is of joy and wisdom as Apollinaire foresees a future where "machines may begin to think" where the "depths of conscience will be explored" and "other worlds will be discovered." (pp. 92-3)

In **"La Jolie Rousse"** he seems to talk to those who are resisting the change prophesied in **"Les Collines."** He identifies with the renovators in the struggle between Order and Adventure, which as he sees it the war had brought to a head. . . . Apollinaire believed that ''The domain of the imagination is reality,'' a concept that was to be accepted by the surrealists as the focal point of all their efforts to intensify life and enrich vision. (pp. 93-4)

Perhaps, in the long run, the greatest mark left by Apollinaire on the current of ideas will be the break he dared to make with the *mal-du-siècle* attitude which had played the poetic strings of melancholy in the nineteenth century, and had then continued uninterrupted through an undetermined state called ''inquiétude'' or uneasiness over the modern world's ills shared by the leading writers before and after World War I. . . . Apollinaire is one of the very first to have felt that dejected, introspective brooding could not be a characteristic of the modern mind. ''This pessimism more than a century old, ancient enough for such a boring thing,'' should, he said in *Les Mamelles de Tirésias*, be now replaced. The fat, jovial, buoyant cosmopolite had had his share of disappointments in life, but he always maintained his hope in the future with its challenges and surprises. In the words of his friend Philippe Soupault, who recalled Apollinaire's character after his death, he was ''the being most happy to be alive'' and although sometimes sad, languorous and melancholy, yet never one who despaired. (pp. 94-5)

It seems incontestable that Apollinaire changed the key of the poet from the minor one of the symbolists to a more vigorous and more exalting harmony. If he is right in believing in the energy of creativeness of the modern mind and in thus establishing a *mystique* of the *here and now*, he is indeed a herald of a new age of enchantment and will loom more and more prodigious in the history of ideas as well as of literature. (p. 99)

> Anna Balakian, ''Apollinaire and L'esprit nouveau,'' in her Surrealism: The Road to the Absolute (copyright © 1959, 1970 by Anna Balakian; reprinted by permission of the author), revised edition, Dutton, 1970, pp. 80-99.

NORMA RINSLER (essay date 1971)

Apollinaire's war poems have generally met with unfavourable criticism. They may have suffered from their proximity, in *Calligrammes,* to 'experimental' poems whose seriousness is often doubted. . . . [Critics reasoned that] Apollinaire is 'playing with words', and therefore playing with life; yet it appears, here and elsewhere, that Apollinaire is really being criticized not for what he said, but for what he did not say.

[Louis] Aragon recalls that since Apollinaire did not celebrate the war in the manner of 'Maeterlinck, Paul Fort ou Paul Claudel', the younger poets admired his images, accepting 'certains mots' as expressions of 'l'ironie et l'émotion indirecte'. . . . In 1935, Aragon's anxiety to confess his own sins led him to misrepresent Apollinaire. His original estimate of those 'certains mots' was a true one. By 1935, he had decided that Apollinaire ought to have challenged the patriotic poets with explicit protest; and he accused him of irresponsibility. Others have followed suit; but what, in this context, does 'irresponsibility' mean? Aragon commends Henri Barbusse's novel *Le Feu* as a true picture of the war. . . . [But] the unrelieved gloom of *Le Feu*, however admirable its intentions, is as false, in its own way, as the visions of the patriotic poets. . . . (p. 169)

Apollinaire, who was not French, saw the war as his chance to create a permanent link with his adopted country: to be prepared to die for France was a way of belonging. Between his first rejection by the Army and his eventual enlistment,

Apollinaire saw civilian society as a 'paradis artificiel': real life was at the Front. There was a widespread feeling that the war was the necessary purification before a new order could begin. Apollinaire rejected his former self-centred life . . . [and in *Ode*] he heralds a new union of human lives, no longer a cautious coexistence, but a genuine interpenetration. This he calls *amour,* which means nothing less than total fusion, a battle in which both sides must win and both lose, in which each attacks and each surrenders. At this stage, like his English contemporaries, he was more concerned with the effects of the war on peacetime attitudes than with the nature of the war itself, about which he knew nothing as yet. . . . Rupert Brooke (*Peace*) likewise rejected the 'little emptiness of love' he had known before. Apollinaire had not the same revulsion from sexual contact, and his love more easily progressed from *amour* in a narrow context to *Amour* in a universal one, with no real change in its nature; but he welcomed the change in scope, and one finds in his poems, as in Brooke's, the feeling that there was a new truth just within reach. . . . (pp. 170-71)

The prospect of action filled him, as it did others, with intense excitement, and with a sense of being bound more closely to his fellow-soldiers than he had ever been to a woman. (p. 172)

In view of this rejection of women, the eroticism of many of Apollinaire's war poems may seem paradoxical. But eroticism is an abstraction, which can thrive on hatred or indifference as well as on love. In an unnatural world like the Western Front, the mind seeks above all to keep its balance. Poets like Edmund Blunden and Robert Graves saved their reason through imagination of rural England: they withdrew from their surroundings to a calm, unpeopled landscape of the mind. Apollinaire found his salvation in an impersonal eroticism. For a while his imagination continued to picture Lou, until one day he wrote to a girl named Madeleine whom he had met in a train. She replied, and the passion transferred itself to her, fully-formed and obsessive. It was certainly not love, but neither was it merely lust. She represented a normal world, safe, quiet, clean and orderly, 'une femme, une chambre', and he kept himself hopeful and aware by using her remembered (or imagined) beauty to stimulate his senses. . . . Apollinaire had always used eroticism as an element of what he calls 'surprise'. In fact, the celebrated image of the *canons-priapes* was not inspired by his experiences at the Front: Michel Décaudin points out that it appears in the manuscript of *Le Poète assassiné* which dates from early 1914, and in another of even earlier date. But in war, erotic imagery was no longer a device to affect the reader. Apollinaire was not writing for the general public. He was using eroticism to protect himself from the *abrutissement* to which many less robust spirits succumbed. (pp. 173-74)

Nevertheless, the poems in which Apollinaire fuses love, death, war and the natural world have a disturbing quality unlike that of poems in which other poets contemplate these things. Firstly, Apollinaire rarely contemplates; he lives and describes each moment with intense involvement, refusing himself, and the reader, the comfortable distance of contemplation. Secondly, he effects a genuine fusion of a most unusual kind. . . . Apollinaire does not place love and war in opposition: they are one and the same. He tries in this way to incorporate the accidents of war into something more continuous. His use of erotic imagery (though admittedly it appears too conscious in the less successful poems) is an attempt to assert the primacy of continuing life over death, and of love over hate. It has nothing to do with the conventional linking of virility and aggression. There is joy in virility, at least in the early poems, but there is no aggression in the service of hate. . . . [Knowing] that only genuine feelings survived in the trenches, he could think of war as love—'O Guerre / Multiplication de l'amour' (*Oracles . . .*)—just as he thought of love as war. What he achieved in both cases was a rare fusion of love and aggression, making the one serve the other.

What began as a vision later became deliberate self-intoxication. . . . The turning-point comes late in 1915, with Apollinaire's commission and transfer to the infantry. The change in his situation was radical, yet his critics generally base their arguments solely on examples from the early poems. (pp. 174-76)

The early optimism about a better future was gone. The only way to avoid fear was not to think of the future at all. This necessarily meant that all sense of purpose vanished, leaving only a sense of pride in doing well what had to be done, and of intensified kinship with those who were bound by the same necessity. . . . [In *Exercice*] Apollinaire shows how this attitude detaches a man from life, so that the presence of death becomes less alien. His infantrymen, like Wyndham Lewis's, hardly notice the shells; like monks they have trained themselves to the patient rhythm of an ascetic life which expects nothing of this world, and thus is not afraid of leaving it. . . . (p. 177)

Concentration on the present moment magnifies all the details of a man's surroundings. He will generally try to make them fill the range of his vision, excluding that other world which would make plain their horror or strangeness. The result is a fragmentation of consciousness: all details are equally significant, and there is no attempt to place them in a meaningful pattern: it is precisely their meaning which the soldier is trying to ignore. Apollinaire succeeds in recreating this state of mind by simple juxtaposition; a number of observed, remembered and imagined details are placed side by side, introduced flatly by 'Il y a . . .', so that all are separate and equal. . . . The technique is most effective in *Qu'est-ce qui se passe.* . . . The poet, on guard, is an unmoving, watchful eye. His physical vision observes the landscape, while his imagination ranges to places and things he cannot see, swelling the movement of the verse and spilling over into the next line in a sudden brilliant vision of spring blossom. As his fancy reaches its most distant point, his physical eye brings him back to the soldiers nearby, and his ear perceives the distant guns; the movement of the verse slows and stops as he recalls the friends he has lost. The lack of comment enhances the mysterious fusion of all these elements into a state of mind which the reader shares. Time is an eternal present, and the only relations are spatial ones. Fact and fancy, emotion and perception, are made equivalent, so that we cannot seize on any one element and value it in relation to the others. . . .

Fragmentation makes it possible for isolated details of the landscape to be appreciated aesthetically, without regard to their moral significance. Apollinaire is not unique in this respect. . . . The human mind protects itself by using its powers of dissociation. The artillery in the Great War saw the action from a sufficient distance to allow them such detachment; the infantry had to create a mental distance, if suffering and death were not to become unbearably real to them. (pp. 178-79)

Insensibility is a defence against both fear and guilt: and guilt took complex forms, especially among the officers, who felt responsibile for their men, yet remote from them, and less exposed to danger. Apollinaire was saved from the worst of

this by his gift (confirmed by everyone who met him) of identifying himself with his companions. He was able to feel with his men, instead of feeling for them. . . . It made him incapable of sustained insensibility, which is a defence by exclusion. His more characteristic solution was one of inclusion: he links himself through love with civilians and soldiers, animals and machines, life and death. . . . This bond made it impossible to ignore the horrors around him; but he does not isolate the horrors, and thus achieves a balanced vision of the world, in which the dreadful and the beautiful live side by side, and in which, as in life, they are sometimes one and the same. This wholeness gives his war poems a peculiar strength. True tragedy, as distinct from pathos, depends on the sense of a moral order. That sense is present in Apollinaire's war poems, not as a theoretical notion, but as a wholeness apprehended directly in contact with men and things. He creates a harmony of life and death which gives both greater significance.

The presence of death is given perspective by his use of verse forms normally associated with a quite different mood, as in *Exercice* with its folk-song rhythm. Sometimes a snatch of real folk-song relates his shattered world to a continuing tradition. . . . (pp. 180-81)

[Apollinaire made] a final comment on the war, in a verse-play, *Couleur de Temps,* which was in rehearsal when he died in 1918. One character in his play, burdened with the guilt of an ancient betrayal, sees death in battle as an absolution. . . . The poet is sadly aware that the human race has a vested interest in war, which offers a violent but effective solution to many otherwise insoluble problems. The other characters in his play are prepared to die for the various absolutes in which they believe, for beauty, or knowledge, or peace. They are all ironically given the same absolute: death; for the one thing they do not understand is 'amour', which is life.

There seems little justification for accusing Apollinaire of having tried to beautify war. He achieved in the end a remarkably coherent vision of an experience that entirely defeated many poets. Perhaps his ability to find a way of talking about an unprecedented situation was due precisely to the fact that he had no preconceived ideas about what war poetry ought to be. With his characteristic *disponibilité,* he allowed the experience as he lived it to determine the words on the page. It is difficult to agree with Breton that Apollinaire merely demonstrates the 'insuffisance' of poetry when faced with 'real life'. Not only does he restore a certain dignity to 'art', but he also reasserts the dignity of life. . . . In *Calligrammes* there is none of the deliciously melting melancholy of *Alcools,* none of the pathos and the graceful self-pity; the voice is sharper, more robust, the pity is turned towards others. These poems go beyond pathos and posturing to a feeling of tragedy which is muted but real. If *Calligrammes* is less consistently successful than *Alcools,* it nevertheless represents a victory. . . . (pp. 184-85)

Norma Rinsler, "The War Poems of Apollinaire," in French Studies, *Vol. XXV, No. 2, April, 1971, pp. 169-86.*

ALBERT BERMEL (essay date 1974)

The Breasts of Tiresias is the most famous unknown play of the century. Apollinaire inadvertently secured it an entry in the index of every textbook on the modern theater when he subtitled it "a surrealist drama," and made his own name a stepping-stone in the history of the French avant-garde set down somewhere between Jarry and Ionesco. But the play itself is seldom discussed and even more seldom performed, a curious fate for a work that predates almost every dramatic innovation of recent years, from non-psychological characters and the reversal of sex roles to satire on our upstart civilization and on traditional forms of theater.

To start with, the hero is a woman. Her name is Thérèse. She walks onstage wearing a long blue dress and a blue face. The print on the dress—monkeys and painted fruit—could be a comment on the play's tropical, pre-Tanzanian setting, the island of Zanzibar. The blue face could denote several things— anemia, a low temperature, the cosmetic smeared on by some Arab women to proclaim their modesty (Zanzibar was once the center of a flourishing slave trade conducted by Arab merchants), or even woad, for Thérèse would like to become, without further delay, a sort of neo-Boadicean warrior. . . . Between sneezes, cackles, a fit of hysterics, the noise of broken dishes, and her imitation of the sound of a train, Thérèse recites a list of further resolutions. She intends to become a parliamentary deputy, a lawyer, a senator, a cabinet minister, and president of the state, among other ambitions, which, in 1917 when the play was first staged, could not be seriously entertained in France, Zanzibar, or anywhere else by a woman.

However, Thérèse is not going to remain a woman. She opens her blouse. Her breasts fly out. One is red, the other blue to match her face. They float upward like balloons but are attached to her by strings. She pulls the strings to make them dance. Then she explodes them with a lighter. And to take her transsexual conversion a step further she sprouts an instant beard and mustache. So perhaps her blue face denotes her rebirth— blue for a boy.

Her unnamed Husband, a baker, is heard offstage asking for lard. "Listen to him," says Thérèse, "he only thinks of love." The Husband appears. He mistakes the mustached and bearded Thérèse for a man who has killed his wife and put on her clothes. *They fight,* says a stage direction, and *she overpowers him.* She then tells him she is walking out on him and taking with her a chamber pot, a basin, and a urinal, which he understands to be, respectively, a piano, a violin, and a butter dish. Whereupon she hurls herself on him and *takes off his trousers, undresses herself, hands him her skirt, ties him up, puts on the trousers, cuts her hair, and puts on a top hat.* Now she has completed the transition. . . . Too far? Or not far enough? The joke has hardly begun, for the Husband follows her lead. When a woman steps out of her feminine role and insists on making war, not babies, it is up to the man. In less than a day the Husband becomes the mother of 40,050 children which he fabricates out of ink, paper, and glue. He does this for the sake of his nation and its survival; he undertakes a personal program of repopulation; he is willing to go through pain and self-denial. But lo—he prospers. . . . During twelve strenuous hours (this play has a unity of time!) while the Husband becomes famous for his mass-rearing of remunerative children, Thérèse becomes famous as the general of the Zanzibar army and a deputy in its legislature. That same evening she returns from her labors disguised as a Fortuneteller whose skull is lit from within by electricity. She praises the Husband and informs him that he will be "a millionaire ten times over": she literally tells *fortunes.* Then she rips off the disguise: she is the original Thérèse, only a Thérèse on top of her luck, a Thérèse who has seen the light and has a skullful of electricity to prove it. Success has gone to her heart. She has brought home the chamber pot, the basin, and the urinal, as well as a new conviction that "we've got to love or I'll die." This belief

reconciles her with the Husband, who was asking at the start for nothing but lard—lovemaking. She now flirts with the spectators by throwing balls and balloons at them. (pp. 172-74)

But keeping one's eye on this particular play is not easy. A pioneering drama, it contains sixteen scenes which assail us with varied and skittish wonders. Two men named Presto and Lacouf put in brief appearances. If Thérèse and the Husband are interchangeable opposites, Presto and Lacouf are undifferentiated. A director might elect to have them performed by contrasting buffo actors—fat and thin, tall and short, timid and aggressive—but Apollinaire gives no hints. From the dialogue we gather that Lacouf has won at a game of cards; Presto has lost. Are they gamblers? Is one lucky and the other reckless? The play does not say. It presents them engaging in a short argument over whether they are in Zanzibar or Paris. The argument ends when they produce cardboard revolvers, fire at one another, are both killed, and both come back to life. During the action they will shoot one another dead three times and three times doggedly revive. What are Presto the loser and Lacouf the winner all about?

Well, Zanzibar is not only the location of the play. It is the name of a French game of chance, the card game Presto and Lacouf have been playing. Lacouf, who maintains that they are in Paris, is a winner and cannot be wrong. This particular Zanzibar *is* Paris; they are playing a Parisian scene in a game of chance. Since a performance in a playhouse is also a game of chance, Apollinaire's nonsense begins to look less nonsensical.

The four roles—one can hardly call them "characters"—of Thérèse-Tiresias, the Husband, Presto, and Lacouf are even less defined than the "types" are in a nineteenth-century farce like [Eugène] Labiche's *Pots of Money (La Cagnotte).* By less defined I mean not only less realized but also less restricted. Whatever they do is plausible; and they are capable of anything. There is no story in the past to govern their future. But in the drama, as in life, a vacuum is abhorrent. Something must take the place of personality. That something is animated objects. In *Pots of Money* objects are nearly as necessary to the action as the characters are. In *The Breasts of Tiresias* objects have become human. The most conspicuous one is a Newsstand, which remains on display throughout and is interpreted by an actress. The Newsstand sings, dances, and even has a few ruminative lines to speak. (pp. 174-75)

[Apollinaire's] play also comes equipped with a prologue, spoken by a character called the Director; a written preface; and verses (bouquets, really) addressed to the actors in the first production. Like the dedicatory letter to [Bernand Shaw's] *Man and Superman* . . . these additional elements help us to understand what the playwright is getting at by elaborating on his attitude toward his work. Apollinaire seems to be constructing a theoretical plinth out of women's liberation and the failure of the French population to multiply. The preface says, "We don't make children any more in France because we don't make love often enough," a poisoned barb when aimed at Frenchmen. But repopulation and equality of the sexes are not the only social issues raised by the play. A third is the destructiveness of war, which Apollinaire connects to the other two. (p. 175)

The Breasts of Tiresias had its first production during the First World War. Apollinaire himself had been invalided out of the army after a head wound and a trepanning operation. (He was to die two days before the Armistice in 1918.) A character called the Director, who appears only in the Prologue and not in the action, is an army officer just home from the front, like the author. After having lived through the heavy bombardments in the trenches which "put out the stars" and "even murdered the constellations," he hopes the audience

> Will be inclined to profit
> From all the lessons that the play contains
> And so that the earth will be starred with the
>   glances of infants
> Even more numerous than the twinkling stars
> Hear O Frenchmen the lesson of war
> And make children you that made few before. . . .

The play can therefore be construed as a dramatization of these three issues of the time, as of our time. It can also be construed as a warming. France's population will dwindle if French-women keep pressing for equal (or better-than-equal) rights, instead of renouncing them as Thérèse does when she returns to the Husband and says, "We [France] must love or I [France] will die." The same will happen if France keeps going to war.

Apollinaire says with admirable understatement that *The Breasts of Tiresias* is composed in a "less somber style" than that of the drawing-room problem play, which had dominated the French stage for three-quarters of a century. It demonstrates how topical material can be presented in the theater with farcical effects and imaginative mockery, but without ever losing sight of the main themes. These boil down to the lapel slogan: Make love, not war.

But how much notice are we supposed to take of the farcical, mocking tone? Does it compromise the themes? In his preface Apollinaire writes, "I cannot possibly decide if this drama is serious or not. Its aim is to interest and entertain. That is the aim of every dramatic work." We can readily see why he feels doubtful about whether his play is or is not serious. It has a thesis, that the fertile shall inherit the earth. It is an antiwar play that corresponds in some particulars to the *Lysistrata*. And yet, trying to persuade people to stop making war and start making children, however virtuous an endeavor for a play-wright, seems unlikely to bring results when he fools about with the issues in so many ways. Apollinaire was an art critic of long standing and, like Shaw, the most discerning critic of his time in his chosen field. As with Shaw, we can look past the theoretical issues and at the measures the play proposes. "It is up to the authorities to act," says the preface, "to facilitate marriages, to encourage fruitful love above all else; the other important questions such as that of child labor will then be easily resolved for the good and honor of the country." . . . This is blatant irony. The authorities are "to encourage fruitful love," and "the other important questions" will be "easily resolved." Apollinaire is making social proposals and laughing up his sleeve at his own proposals, acting as the critic of his own work.

In the preface and subtitle to this play Apollinaire coined the word "surrealist." The prologue goes on to tell us that sur-realism can "bring forth life itself in all its truth," as against ordinary realism, which photographs "the so-called slice of life." (pp. 176-77)

Apollinaire has joined in the twentieth-century quest for a the-ater that is inherently theatrical. Not until playwrights under-stand the theater's limitations can they surmount them and explore what he calls the "infinite possibilities" by the "rea-sonable use of the improbable." In the play he shows that the limitations have not as yet been approached (in 1917), and that

destruction must precede the rebuilding. The technique he em-ploys for this destruction and rebuilding is the miracle—sudden mutation.

He gives us many examples of the miracle in the theater. Thérèse turns into Tiresias, her breasts into disposable bal-loons, her husband into a mother, Zanzibar into Paris, the Newsstand into a character with moving arms and a talent for dance, song, and speech. (p. 177)

Apollinaire tears down conventions of the realistic theater such as boundaries between the sexes, boundaries between life and death, between species and numbers. The unity of place, which he adopts, is a joke if the audience can be in three places at once—Paris, Zanzibar, and the playhouse. . . . The author wants these convention-smashing miracles to look casual, like the game of chance called Zanzibar, but he does not intend to relinquish control at any moment; he remains the play's deity. "His universe," explains the prologue, "is his stage / Within it he is the creating god." (p. 178)

[Tiresias] presents an ideal, an evolutionary step past humanity and in the direction of the superhuman. He combines earthly *knowing* culled over an exceptionally long lifetime with unearthly *seeing* which includes the arts of foresight and the black arts of sorcery. He is the spiritual father needed by a community because of his three roles: as a priest he interprets the will of the gods; as an elder and revered statesman-citizen he has earned a temporal authority that may challenge the will of kings like Oedipus, Pentheus, or Creon; as a man-plus-woman he provides unarguably experienced counsel. Such a fatherly ideal has persisted through history, and not only in Western cul-tures. . . .

In Apollinaire's hands Tiresias, that memory from antiquity, undergoes drastic revision. If Tiresias was successively man, woman, man, Thérèse is successively woman, man, woman. If Tiresias was old, Thérèse is young. If Tiresias was from Thebes, one of the cradles of European civilization, Thérèse is from Zanzibar, an island outpost of Africa—but a Zanzibar with Parisian flavoring. If Tiresias was an impartial observer and seer, Thérèse is a doer, a mainspring of the action. (p. 180)

The reasons for these mutations of the venerable prophet seem to me to lie in Apollinaire's subversiveness, his resolve to undercut the dignity of the myth, to belittle the lofty ideal. As a fictitious figure, a literary concept, Tiresias is all very well. As a human being he would be insufferable, politically and morally neutral, so confident of his foresight, so complacent about his superior function and other people's miseries that he would never stick his neck out. He is a preacher who has no stake in the life around him, only a faith in the inexorability of fate. He has belonged to both sexes; now he transcends sex, which is like saying that he transcends living. In the new characterization, Apollinaire substitutes jocosity for prophecy, as when Thérèse returns as the Fortuneteller whose head is lit up. By the end of the play Apollinaire has elbowed the old prig off his pedestal. (pp. 180-81)

Apollinaire's Thérèse is not a version of Tiresias but a retort to him. Giving up her masculine ambitions constitutes a pos-itive gesture, not a sexist surrender to woman's oppressed role as mere wife. She is making the conventional dramatic choice between love and duty and saying that duty is worthless without love. But even then the play is laughing at itself. When Thérèse tosses balloons and balls into the auditorium what she is doing in effigy is offering the lookers-on a free supply of toy sexual equipment. (p. 181)

Albert Bermel, "Apollinaire's Male Heroine," in Twentieth Century Literature *(copyright 1974, Hofstra University Press), Vol. 20, No. 3, July, 1974, pp. 172-82.*

MICHAEL PERKINS　(essay date 1976)

[Two] different approaches to erotic writing, one soft, evocative, and within a conventional literary tradition, the other harsh, explicit and obsessive, represent between their extremes the kind of erotic novel that was being published in Europe between the late nineteenth century and 1925.

[In this period there is, besides Pierre Louÿs, only one] author of erotic novels whose work must be mentioned: the poet Guillaume Apollinaire. Apollinaire's status as a major figure in French poetry is secure. Although he died in 1918 of injuries suffered earlier in the First World War, it was he who first used the word *surrealist* (a literary method by which the automatic, uncensored responses of the unconscious are employed to create a dream world and transform ordinary reality) and his influence on later writers has been considerable. Yet this poet of delicate lyrics and *avant-garde* formulations had another career: he wrote two erotic novels, one so brutal it is pseudo-Sadean, *The Debauched Hospodar;* the other, *Memoirs of a Young Rakehell,* bucolic and almost certainly autobiographical. In addition, he was something of a scholar in erotic literature. He wrote prefaces to erotic books, assisted in their publication, and compiled bibliographies in the genre, a French Pisanus Fraxi.

The sadism of *The Debauched Hospodar* is casually excessive, so quick and gruesomely comic it is a parody of Sadean fiction rather than a sadistic novel. Mony Vibescu is a Roumanian "Hospodar" (equivalent to the title of subprefect in France) who becomes bored with the pleasures of Bucharest and decides that he must have a woman of Paris. He goes to say goodbye to a friend and finds him with two pretty girls. An orgy follows, in which Mony is buggered at pistol point by his friend. The pace is frenzied from the start, increasing in tempo as Mony arrives in Paris and immediately becomes involved with two women who urge him to beat them with a coachman's whip. As an indication of the degree of sadism in the novel, this flagellation scene comes to seem mild when compared with the range of debauchery Apollinaire employs: murders, necrophilia, cannibalism, impalements, the rape of a child by her father, even a black mass. Apollinaire deliberately set out to violate every moral convention, in order perhaps to demonstrate—by exaggeration to the point of mania—that nothing is out of bounds in literature. Ufortunately, although this demonstration succeeds as a *tour de force,* the novel suffers from a lack of characterization and a haphazard plot.

Memoirs of a Young Rakehell, the brief narrative of a boy's sexual awakening, is as different from *The Debauched Hospodar* as black is from white. As the boy learns about sex from spying on his sister and timidly attempting to seduce the family maid, an atmosphere of highly charged adolescent sexuality is slowly developed. Although obscenities are used freely, there is something sweetly innocent about the novelist's use of fanciful imagery in describing sexual acts. (pp. 43-4)

Memoirs of a Young Rakehell is as conventional an erotic novel as *The Debauched Hospodar* is unconventional; like Louÿs, Apollinaire was capable of both extremes. . . .

[Louÿs's] *Mother's Three Daughters* and *The Debauched Hospodar* fit into one category, and [Louÿs's] *Aphrodite* and *Memoirs of a Young Rakehell* into another. The first is assaultive, in that books like *The Debauched Hospodar* attempt to overwhelm the reader's sense by a shock treatment that is apt to horrify or repulse; this is the Dionysian impulse to destruction which found its literary expression in Sade. The second is seductive. Novels like *Aphrodite,* and *Memoirs of a Young Rakehell* to a lesser extent, attempt through a softer, more sensuous approach to seduce the reader into not only accepting the author's depiction of sexuality as an accurate reflection of the reader's own sexuality, but to entertain and stimulate as well. These two lines of erotic writing, the assaultive and the seductive, can be followed throughout the history of modern erotic literature. Between them, they enclose a majority of work in the genre, although there is a third mode, the philosophical, exemplified by the work of Georges Bataille.

Apollinaire's career as an erotic writer is the link between Sade in the eighteenth century, and the group of writers attracted to erotic literature in the late nineteen-twenties. (p. 45)

Apollinaire reaffirmed the validity of the assaultive approach in *The Debauched Hospodar,* freeing erotic novelists from the euphemistic conventions of Victorian erotica. . . . (p. 66)

Michael Perkins, "The Innocence of Evil," in his The Secret Record: Modern Erotic Literature *(copyright © 1976 by Michael Perkins; abridged by permission of William Morrow & Company, Inc.), Morrow, 1976, pp. 40-66.**

WILLARD BOHN　(essay date 1977)

In July 1914, Guillaume Apollinaire, who was at that time the leader of the Parisian avant-garde, composed an important pantomime in collaboration with three other artists: *A quelle heure un train partira-t-il pour Paris? (What Times Does A Train Leave For Paris?).* . . . Modeled on a 1913 poem by Apollinaire, **"The Musician of Saint Merry,"** the pantomime featured a scenario by Apollinaire, "music by Alberto Savinio, sets and staging by Francis Picabia and Marius de Zayas" according to the title page. Unfortunately, no contributions by the latter three individuals have been discovered—if indeed these ever existed. . . . In 1917, concurrent with the production of *The Breasts of Tiresias,* Apollinaire apparently attempted to revive his original project as a ballet, but his death in 1918 effectively relegated this project to oblivion. While the 1914 scenario is ostensibly Apollinaire's independent creation, it is readily apparent that his fellow collaborators contributed various ideas that helped to determine the eventual shape of the pantomime. Analysis of influential currents and cross-currents reveals, as we will see, that Apollinaire was indebted to the Italian Futurists as well.

The plot of *What Times Does A Train Leave For Paris?* is deceptively simple. On the whole it follows that of the original poem quite closely, except for the final scene which was invented specifically for the pantomime. With the exception of this scene, the major innovations are limited to stage effects and costumes. (p. 73)

The sources of the mysterious protagonist of *What Time Does A Train Leave For Paris?,* as well as his multiple meanings, are debatable to say the least. **"The Musician of Saint Merry"** gives us two brief descriptions: he is "A man with no eyes no nose and no ears," and "The young man was dark with a strawberry tint to his cheeks." The scenario for the pantomime also calls him a "faceless musician." Given the total absence of any physiognomy, except for a mouth, this character is readily imaginable as a human body surmounted by a smooth, spherical head. The plot and characterization seem to indicate two major sources for this figure: folklore and anatomy. In the first instance, Apollinaire's debt to the famous fable of the Pied Piper of Hamlin is obvious. Nevertheless, although his central character and basic plot structure come from the fable, Apollinaire seems merely to have taken the story for his starting point—amused by the idea of changing a rat-catcher into a woman-catcher. The second source seems more important. As several critics have shown, Apollinaire's original poem derives much of its inspiration from the ancient Greek legends surrounding Orpheus, Pan, and Dionysos. It is doubtful, however, if any of these figures can be said to constitute a *source,* properly speaking. The same is true of Beelzebub and Thanatos, with whom the faceless man has also been identified. To the best of my knowledge, no one has indicated what certainly must be the principal source of this character: the male sexual organ. The actual staging of the poem and the protagonist's costume, as described by Savinio, would have left little doubt in the minds of the audience as to the real identity of the faceless man.

In support of a phallic interpretation it should be noted that the pantomime contains a multitude of sexual symbols, many of which are given monumental status. Masculine symbols—including the flute, the luminous column, the Eiffel Tower, and the Tall Factory Chimney—are deliberately juxtaposed with feminine counterparts: the fountain, an open door, some broken windows, the vacant house, the Arc de Triomphe, and Notre Dame cathedral. Their prominence and number indicate the importance Apollinaire attached to them. This is particularly true of the monuments, whose presence looms over the entire pantomime and which give the impression of being eternal witnesses of mankind. Omnipresent sphinx-like guardians representing the basic principles of life, they reflect a belief in a dualistic universe governed by sexual forces. In this context the most meaningful framework within which to consider these symbols is that of fertility ritual—ceremonial actions which are intended to assure the fecundity of the earth or of a particular woman or group of women. For one thing, the pantomime contains an overt reference to African rites. Among the subjects chosen to represent the variety of life, Apollinaire specifically includes "The Dionysian religious life of equatorial Africa" ("La vie religieuse et panique de l'Afrique équatoriale," Scene 4). For another, the adjective "panique," which actually evokes the lascivious behavior of the god Pan, serves to link African myth and ritual to the ancient Greek legends of death and rebirth. Like their African counterparts, the Greek beliefs found expression in numerous fertility ceremonies. Not only is one such rite specifically evoked in the pantomime—the annual procession of the phallus in honor of Dionysos—its structure was super-imposed on that of the Pied Piper fable to determine the pantomime's basic form. To be sure, not all fertility rites involve some form of phallic worship, but many do. In this particular instance the women who follow the musician in a hypnotic state clearly represent worshippers fallen in ecstasy before the sacred phallus.

"Primitive" religion employs a great deal of sexual symbolism in general but usually in a passive manner—for example in its mythology. In most fertility rites, however, the symbolism suddenly becomes *active,* i.e., capable of influencing material events. In a sense the distinction between symbol and object symbolized vanishes, for it is assumed that the interaction of symbols—manipulated artificially—will produce a parallel interaction of the corresponding objects in nature. This is the basic assumption of all imitative magic, an assumption that also underlies the sexual symbolism in *What Time.* While Apollinaire doubtless did not believe in the magical efficacy of his symbols, it is important to note that he uses them as if he actually did. In effect ritual assumed a generative function in the origin of the pantomime to such an extent that the distinction between the two modes of expression tends to disappear. The erotic mixing of male and female symbols is perhaps more understandable if we translate the principle of imitative magic into psychological terms: wishful thinking. . . . Thus *What Time Does A Train Leave For Paris?* is as much as anything a product of the poet's own libido. On one level at least, it represents a dramatization of the sexual tensions, of the psychological preoccupations of Apollinaire. After all, it is he who is the protagonist of his own story, the mysterious musician "playing the tune that I am singing and that I invented" (**"The Musician of Saint Merry"**). He frankly admits, at the beginning of both the poem and the pantomime, that what we are about to see is his internal life, where fantasy is king: "I sing all the possibilities of myself beyond this world and the stars." We are thus confronted with a grandiose sexual fantasy on the part of Apollinaire in which a personification of his own sexual member plays the starring role, an example of phallic narcissism translated into artistic terms.

The pantomime functions on several other levels as well, two of which are not immediately accessible to the audience. We know, for instance, that in May 1913 Apollinaire conducted a guided tour of the Saint Merry quarter of Paris for a group interested in local history and architecture. One suspects that *What Time* is partly a fantasized version of this tour, which may have included a number of attractive women. In any case, the identification of the protagonist with Apollinaire becomes even more certain. Similarly, residents of Paris would immediately recognize the quarter as one in which prostitution has been rampant for centuries. *What Time* must also be seen therefore as a reenactment of the drama of daily life in this neighborhood, portraying the numerous streetwalkers in pursuit of their customers and livelihood—appropriately symbolized by a phallus. It should be noted, however, that a more general point of view is equally valid. For on still another level this multi-faceted work constitutes a universal drama, the drama of the Eternal Feminine fascinated by, and in pursuit of, the Eternal Masculine. On this same level the sexual symbols in the background can be seen to be part of a cosmic *weltanschauung* in which masculine and feminine principles confront—*interpenetrate*—each other in a universal dance of life. As the month of courtship and fertility par excellence, May proves to be an apt choice for the numerous dramas contained in Apollinaire's pantomime. *What Time* thus proves to be a psycho-sexual complex functioning simultaneously on a multitude of different levels. Its implications range from the particular to the general, from the personal to the universal. (pp. 76-9)

As far as technical innovations are concerned, it would seem that Apollinaire was influenced considerably by the Italian Futurists, most of whom he knew personally. One finds, for example, in his *Futurist Anti-tradition* (June 29, 1913) the seeds of numerous ideas in the pantomime, ranging from "Dance labor or pure choreography" to "universal Mimicry and the Art of lights." While this manifesto was conceived as a summary of the various avant-garde tendencies of the day, it also summarizes all the proclamations the Futurists had issued up to that point. Thus Apollinaire's advocacy of a "captivated life or phonocinematography" is mostly his own idea, but the recommendation of a "Total music and Art of noises" is taken directly from Luigi Russolo's manifesto, *The Art of Noises* (March 11, 1913) in which the latter foresees a new kind of music based on six different types of noises. It is worth noting that both these ideas are realized to some extent in *What Time,* where various noises are synchronized with the projections. Thus, for example, the moving pictures projected by the Eiffel Tower in Scene 2 are accompanied by the following: "city sounds, automobile horns, bells, klaxons, the crackling of wireless telegraphy." (pp. 79-80)

What Times Does A Train Leave For Paris? also presents many dadaistic aspects, suggesting that it may possibly reflect Picabia's influence. One thinks of the poet who salutes with an automatic (mechanical) gesture, of the absurd conclusion, of the choice of a title having no connection with the story, of the automatic sovereign (Napoleon III) and his nose-blowing followers, of the faceless protagonist and the bizarre women who pursue him. In addition, the perverse humor characterizing much of the pantomime resembles the sort of *humour noir* which was to become a Picabia trademark. (pp. 80-1)

In the last analysis, while Apollinaire borrowed from various sources, *What Times Does A Train Leave For Paris?* is very much his own work. A dramatic synthesis of his experience and aesthetic theories, it leads directly to the revolutionary play *The Breasts of Tiresias. . . .* Like the pantomime, this play—the first to bear the subtitle "drame surréaliste"—is stamped with its author's personality throughout. In addition, *The Breasts of Tiresias* reveals numerous traces of *What Time,* which in effect constitute dramatic remembrances of the 1914 avant-garde experiments. Some of the traces are not particularly apparent; others are easier to identify. . . . [An] identical pattern is discernible in Apollinaire's use of megaphones to amplify the voice, a device much in evidence in *The Breasts of Tiresias* which features a megaphone in the shape of a dice-box. The prologue to the play leads one to believe that this constitutes a remembrance of Apollinaire's service in the artillery, where megaphones were used to give orders over the noise of the cannons (cf. the poem "**Cotton in Your Ears**"). However, it is now evident that this stage device was borrowed from *What Time* where it has an identical function. As in the case of the placards and characters such as Presto and Lacouf, the original source of the megaphone was the music hall and the circus—considered by the Futurists to be the epitome of modern theater. (pp. 82-3)

As for *The Breasts of Tiresias,* if the lesser borrowings from the pantomime concern the use of certain props, the more readily identifiable borrowings have to do with specific costumes. For example, one of the most important characters in the play is modeled on Apollinaire's red and blue women. As unlikely as it may seem at first, this person is none other than the neophyte feminist Thérèse, who deserts her husband and becomes Tiresias. This identification is unmistakable, for she is described in considerable detail at the beginning of the play. There Apollinaire expressly informs us that in addition to wearing a long blue dress adorned with monkeys and painted fruits, she possesses a face to match—namely a "*visage bleu.*" (p. 84)

The foregoing study has, I hope, made clear what a remarkable work we have in *What Times Does A Train Leave For Paris?* The fact that this avant-garde creation dates from 1914 makes it especially interesting. For it is evident that it prefigures—that indeed it predicts—the appearance of the Dada movement

a full two years before the term "Dada" was coined. This actually is not terribly surprising in view of the fact that all four collaborators were to become involved in this movement to different degrees, were indeed to help determine the form it would take. Picabia, of course, was destined to play a role in its development whose importance would be equaled only by that of Tristan Tzara. It is apparent in any case that Apollinaire's influence on Dada was much greater than anyone has realized. Given the identities of the four collaborators, one feels justified in claiming for *What Time* the role and title of "The First Dada Play." With respect to Apollinaire's own artistic development, we have see that what he called *surréalisme* in 1917 existed already in 1914. Baptized initially as "surnaturalisme," it was essentially an anti-realistic method of apprehending and re-formulating reality. Nowhere is the process better illustrated than in *What Time.* This is an exciting work, both visually and conceptually, exemplifying Apollinaire's preoccupation with newness, modernity, simultaneity, spontaneity, juxtaposition, and surprise. There is, moreover, a sort of *tension* in the pantomime between the real and the unreal, between the natural and the unnatural, that keeps the reader and spectator continually off balance. It is exactly this kind of complex interplay between real and imaginary frames of reference that we find later in *The Breasts of Tiresias.*

In view of the fact that it was Apollinaire who first invented the term "surrealism," one would probably be justified in also bestowing upon *What Time* the title of "The First Surrealist Play." More significantly, the existence of this pantomime has important implications for the history of modern drama as well as for Apollinaire's dramatic work in general. Critics have occasionally claimed, for example, that *The Breasts of Tiresias* was merely a clever imitation of Jean Cocteau's *Parade,* performed one month earlier. The discovery of *What Time* effectively refutes this argument by showing that Apollinaire was writing similar plays a good three years before. It is evident that the later play owes almost nothing to Cocteau's work—as Apollinaire protested on several occasions—and that it derives instead from his dramatic experiments in 1914. The significance of Apollinaire's contributions to the modern French theater increases accordingly. While the importance of the pantomime for the history of modern drama and for Apollinaire's own development is undeniably great, it is a work which also deserves our admiration in its own right. Its history has been rather paradoxical. Originally a poem, then a pantomime, later a ballet, it was quite influential even though it was never performed or published. Apparently left unfinished, its production rendered impossible first by the outbreak of World War I, then by the death of Apollinaire, it testifies nevertheless to the creative vigor of its author and to the artistic fertility of the years immediately preceding the war. (pp. 85-6)

Willard Bohn, "A New Play by Apollinaire," in Comparative Drama *(© copyright 1977, by the Editors of* Comparative Drama*), Vol. II, No. 1, Spring, 1977, pp. 73-87.*

ROSS FELD (essay date 1981)

[*Calligrammes* was Apollinaire's] last major corpus of poems. At its overture, less devoted Apollinairians have been known to seize the moment and slip out the side exits. Some of the more committed who stay in their seats wouldn't mind a little editing, and it's the rare faithful who are entirely satisfied with these last works. The honeyed tenor of *Alcools'* love laments is only intermittently on stage; whapping war noises so drown him out that he quickly learns to incorporate them. . . . (p. 25)

Unless one accepts that Apollinaire's First World War was a spectacle of effortfulness rather than a midden of effect, it is hard to make sense of these poems at all. He was more likely to admire the living breathing Senegalese soldier sharing his trench than remark upon the one possibly dead only ten minutes later. The range of his pre-war, mid-war, and post-war labors equably encompassed wasn't-it-wacky enlistment memoirs; painstakingly composed "shaped" poems; simple, often riggish love notes to Madeleine Pagès or to Louise de Coligny-Chatillon; poems that take head-on note of carnage (*"Le Palais du Tonnerre," "Merveille de la Guerre"*) while refusing to denude it of nobility by calling it waste; and long, touching millenarian odes to the coming age of paradise (*"Les Collines," "La Jolie Rousse"*) despite a head wound and a lurking death. A far cry from Wilfred Owen, for sure.

Less than a quarter of *Calligrammes* consists of actual "calligrams"—the graphically designed shaped-poems—yet the impression they make is disproportionate. As the book and the war progressed (because, for the most part, Apollinaire wrote and even self-published these poems while actually at the front), there are fewer and fewer. The first major one to appear, *"Lettre-Océan"* . . . is the richest, most firmly and formally self-assured. Rendered like fat-cracklings out of the occasion of a sea voyage to Mexico made by Apollinaire's brother Albert, the calligram distributes a "simultanist" collage of different typefaces, stamps, place names, slivers of speech and gossip, onomatopoeia, and smutty throwaways into a visual pattern that chiefly apes radio waves and Mayan calendars. Yet despite all the mini-relaxations of its postcard-y parts, the whole displays . . . a remarkable "sobriety": Da but not yet Dada, a firecracker gone off inside a tightly-lidded box. Apollinaire's inherent orderliness plays some part in this, also the tonguetip-between-teeth sedulousness of labor one can imagine such a poem requiring; as with most conscious experiments in literature, a slight but inescapable just-so fustiness lies over the surface of the composition, defending its newness while also discouraging its re-reading.

With the exception of *"Lettre-Océan"* and a 1915 calligram, *"Aussi Bien que les Cigales,"* whose reiteration of one basic phrase is reminiscent of Gertrude Stein, few of the other calligrams are so theoretically adventurous. (pp. 26-7)

Depending, then, on how seriously you take Apollinaire as a poet (and you can love him but still not take him too seriously; for many he's the boy-man, the teddy bear of French literary history); and depending on what you believe his intentions were, you can take these "beautiful writings" as anything from game to poetic breakthrough. As game, a poet's brilliant rebuses sent back to amuse his mistresses, they are very charming. The care that went into them (remembering that Apollinaire is juggling typefaces and paste-ups while resting against a gunnery emplacement) testifies to a faith in invention and sensibility literally unshakable, undislodged by even the worst concussive yap. As documentary souvenirs, mimetically expressing the discontinuities of war, they are at least as effective, coming as they do from behind the lines of Apollinaire's take on life. . . . And as an arm of the Cubist remaking of reality, speeding up meaning by slowing down recognition, the calligrams surely reach out most hopefully. In *Les Peintres cubistes,* Apollinaire had already described truth as mere communication, "plastic writing" always at the right temperature for perfect elasticity. Yet the calligram, taken down from the-

ory's shelf, is a clunky, näive, nearly pious thing when set next to even the most mediocre Cubist canvas. . . . [Exegesis] itself is an iron rod thrown into a shaped-poem's combine, bringing it to an immediate halt. It is one of the well-acknowledged foxinesses of language to suggest the purely spatial—only to then presently disappear from and transcend it. One definition of literary style, in fact, could be the speed with which this transcendence is quickened or slowed. If I want to still the choirs of meaning that hover over the plainest sentence or line and thus be able to use it visually, I've got to first make that sentence or line inhospitably numb: shatter or fuse it against its imminent straightening into independent meaning. Contemporary concrete poetry, child of the calligrams, has been illustrating this process of synesthesia-made-anesthesia with some clarity. Hypnosis or else costiveness; the ruined, repeated, or solo-word poem being generally more cozy swaddled in the grey blankets of neurology than sporting the gayer interpretive colors of literary ambiguity, accident, mistake.

It hadn't ever got that far with Apollinaire, however. Big wishes aside, his calligram stayed essentially a primitive pun. And as happens with a pun, it's best left made only once. Gesture is always a key to Apollinaire—and since gesture arises from role, the key is at work in the late non-calligram war poems as well. Apollinaire the unhappy lover—the passive *mal-aimé*—is a more comforting figure than Apollinaire the soldier, but the *mal-aimé* had already showed signs of change by 1914. Apollinaire had done some growing-up. *"Le Musicien de Saint-Merry"* . . . is figured around a Chiricesque mannequin who, with a magic flute, is able to gather in all the women of Paris and lead them into permanent oblivion. Vengeance is mine, saith the Poet—one of the perquisites—but the practical lessons of a strenuous amorous life had finally, too, resulted in a stronger man. (pp. 27-9)

Much as we'd like to think otherwise, Apollinaire was not, therefore, lost on the battlefield, wondering helplessly to what bootless pass his life had come that he should suddenly wind up here. What remained in him of the *mal-aimé* could take refuge from rejection in the sole company of other men. The inveterate armchair traveller, forever leaping his poetic imagination over distances to the Rhine, the coast of Texas, Vancouver, the Antilles, Mexico, New York, found the front agreeably foreign: close yet far, like a Kierkegaardian repetition. The sophisticate was treated to fascinating and awesome theater. . . . (p. 29)

Because many of the earliest war poems are calligrams, like [*"Visée,"*] . . . we can for a time excuse them as the stenography of a stunned observer. Uncrabbed, uncrimpled, untricky, the non-shaped poems will (our pacifism hopes) be able to ultimately renounce the slaughter. But in a poem like *"La Nuit d'Avril 1915,"* a fire-fight at night: *La fôret merveilleuse où je vis donne un bal / La mitrailleuse joue un air à triplescroches;* The marvelous forest where I live is giving a ball / The machine gun plays a tune in three-fourths time. In *"Le Palais du Tonnerre"* (**Thunder's Palace**), the trenches are described with novelistic scrupulosity (and acceptance). In *"Désir,"* the German lines Apollinaire finds himself firing into blindly evoke a yet more macrocosmic victory . . . in which mix the personae of Genghis Khan, Baedeker, and Don Juan—a thousand Leporellos around the last in a "Night that is violet and violent and dark and momentarily full of gold / Night of men only." In a poem such as this, or one like *"A l'Italie,"* Apollinaire exhibits no higher ethical pusillanimity: he wants his army to win, to beat the Boche, to kill them. When there's horror, it seems to him mostly a product of deceleration.

"Merveille de la Guerre" is perhaps the best summing-up. Flares are dancing ladies, a daily apotheosis "of all my Berenices whose hair has turned to / comets' tails." The light overhead is "as lovely as if life itself issued from those who are dying." (pp. 30-1)

So it isn't a callous barbarian here. With women, or in exotic places of the imagination, or on the planes of cubism and admixtures of simultanism, the many-in-one—riding a parabolic curve—is where to find the true Apollinarian *I*. Roger Shattuck has helpfully isolated it: "He increasingly sought himself *outside* himself. It is as if his *I* were the exterior world from which, once he had radiated himself into it, he could look back wistfully and indulgently upon his old self as a pathetic object." A sleeve turned inside out. And in a recent essay focusing on Dowell, that most eelish narrator of Ford's *The Good Soldier*, Denis Donoghue points out something that applies, I think, as well and snugly to Apollinaire: "The gestures by which he answers contingency make him immune to it. No wonder he survives its attack."

While immunity through gesture could not guarantee Apollinaire safe corporeal passage through war (even his helmet was unable to do that), it did allow the potentials of his art through. And potential—ardor, reach—was for Apollinaire the very crux. (The octopus, three-hearted and ink-throwing, was a favorite autobiographical image, see *"Océan de Terre"*. . . .) It wasn't in Apollinaire's power to too-abruptly categorize war—or anything—as abomination. That would have stunted the image-seeding faculty, would have packed shut the "starry head"— precious rarity in a situation where one was lucky to keep any head at all. If the non-calligram poems of Apollinaire's war never once wholly succeed, at least they still fail from on high. Gliding down off a perch of dogged spiritual innocence that isn't quite—*"Bouche ouverte sur un harmonium / C'était une voix faite d'yeux"; Mouth open above a harmonium / It was a voice composed of eyes (*"Souvenirs"*)—they are arguably more *possible*, i.e., erotic, than any French poems since those of the troubadors. If Apollinaire could love (and suffer) this, he could love anything. (p. 32)

Ross Feld, "Headless, with Flares," in Parnassus. Poetry in Review (copyright © Poetry in Review Foundation), Vol. 9, No. 1, Spring-Summer, 1981, pp. 17-32.

ADDITIONAL BIBLIOGRAPHY

Bohn, Willard. "Apollinaire and de Chirico: The Making of the Mannequins.' *Comparative Literature* XXVII, No. 2 (Spring 1975): 153-65.*
  Development of the mannequin in art, especially as used in Apollinaire's 1913 poem "Le Musicien de Saint-Merry."

Breunig, LeRoy C. "The Chronology of Apollinaire's *Alcools*." *PMLA* LXVII, No. 7 (December 1952): 907-23.
  Regroups the poems of *Alcools* in their original order of composition, using biographical, stylistic, and thematic clues in establishing chronology. This essay is an interesting piece of scholarly detection which in addition to dating the poems also defines five distinct creative periods subsumed in the larger eras of Apollinaire's work.

Carmody, Francis J. *The Evolution of Apollinaire's Poetics, 1901-1914*. Berkeley: University of California Press, 1963, 130 p.

Technical philological analysis of Apollinaire's work.

Davies, Margaret. *Apollinaire*. London: Oliver & Boyd, 1964, 312 p.
  Study that tightly integrates critical and biographical material on Apollinaire.

Dutton, K. R. "Apollinaire and Communication." *Australian Journal of French Studies* V, No. 3 (September-December 1968): 303-28.
  Discussion of Apollinaire's poetic innovations, including their relationship to new forms in communication.

George, Emery E. "Calligrams in Apollinaire and in Trakl: A Psycho-stylistic Study." *Language and Style* 1, No. 1 (Winter 1968): 131-93.*
  Technical linguistic study of the ways Apollinaire and Georg Trakl, among others, form words into shapes to create and reinforce poetic meaning.

Greet, Anne Hyde. "Wordplay in Apollinaire's *Calligrammes*." *L'esprit créateur* X, No. 4 (Winter 1970): 296-307.
  Discusses puns, word associations, and other verbal devices in Apollinaire's war poems.

Lawler, James R. "Music and Poetry in Apollinaire." *French Studies* X, No. 4 (October 1956): 339-46.
  Draws parallels between Apollinaire's poetry and musical rhythms and structures. This essay contains an interesting section that analyzes as music a recording Apollinaire made of some of his poems.

Lawler, James R. "Rimbaud and Apollinaire." *French Studies* XIX, No. 3 (July 1965): 266-77.*
  Scholarly documentation of Apollinaire's knowledge of Rimbaud, presenting evidence for Rimbaud's influence on the later poet's work. The essay admits to being a brief exploratory investigation, though it does offer much useful substantiation toward its thesis.

Mackworth, Cecily. *Guillaume Apollinaire and the Cubist Life*. New York: Horizon Press, 1964, 244 p.
  Literary biography of Apollinaire focusing on his social and professional relationships with leading figures in the Cubist movement. The author's work is not treated critically in this study.

Melchiori, Giorgio. "Eliot and Apollinaire." *Notes and Queries* n.s. 11, No. 10 (October 1964): 385-86.*
  The influence of *Les mamelles de Tirésias* on T. S. Eliot.

St. Onge, Ronald Rene. "The Accursed Families of Apollinaire." *Kentucky Romance Quarterly* XXII, No. 1 (Winter 1975): 3-14.
  Discusses Apollinaire's negative depictions of family relationships in his work, and looks at the author's own hectic upbringing as a partial prototype for these "accursed families."

Shattuck, Roger. "Guillaume Apollinaire, 1880-1918." In his *The Banquet Years: The Arts in France, 1885-1918*, pp. 195-248. New York: Harcourt, Brace and Co., 1955.
  Anecdotal essay discussing Apollinaire's position in the artistic society of his time.

Steegmuller, Francis. *Apollinaire: Poet among Painters*. New York: Farrar, Straus and Co., 1963, 305 p.
  Biography of Apollinaire that traces many autobiographical references in the author's work.

Sullivan, Dennis G. "On Time and Poetry: A Reading of Apollinaire." *Modern Language Notes* 88, No. 4 (May 1973): 811-37.
  Highly philosophical approach to Apollinaire's poetic theory as it is articulated in his critical writing and implied in his poems.

Urdang, Constance. "The Hills of Guillaume Apollinaire." *Western Review* 22, No. 2 (Winter 1958): 117-23.
  Argues for the thematic unity of Apollinaire's "Les collines," contending that this unified structure distinguishes it from the disjointed poetry of surrealism.

Maurice Baring

1874-1945

English novelist, dramatist, parodist, autobiographer, essayist, journalist, biographer, poet, and critic.

During the early twentieth century, Baring was considered an unofficial partner with G. K. Chesterton and Hilaire Belloc in an Anglican-Catholic literary triumvirate, but he is little read today. During his long career, Baring wrote in many genres: of these, his novels, particularly *C, Cat's Cradle*, and *Daphne Adeane*, are his best known works. With a lucid style, slow pace, and subtle humor, Baring's novels illuminate European upper-class life, and appeal to a select readership.

Baring was born into one of the wealthiest families in England, and he received the education, culture, and opportunities for travel which laid the groundwork for his career. As a young man, he traveled to Germany and Italy to study languages, a lifelong interest; he eventually became fluent in seven languages besides English. Groomed for diplomatic work, Baring served Great Britain for three years in several European cities. Shortly after resigning from politics in 1901, he published his first important works: two collections of verse and short dramas, *The Black Prince* and *Gaston de foix*. For the next decade Baring wrote plays which were noted for their dryness and realism. He turned to journalism in 1904, covering the Russo-Japanese War for the London *Morning Post*. Writing from Manchuria and later from Moscow, Baring introduced his readers to Chekhov's drama and to the works of other Russian authors. He later wrote several acclaimed books on Russia and its literature, evidencing superb skill as a translator and scholar. Baring's reading of Chekhov and Turgenev led him to develop what Vernon Lee described as his "dry bony style, which looks like no style at all."

Baring began writing novels soon after World War I, beginning with *Passing By*, published in 1921. A common theme in such works as *Cat's Cradle, Robert Peckham*, and *C* is the conflict between passion and duty, treated from a Catholic eschatological view. Ironically, the fiction written after Baring's 1909 conversion is free of the overt religiosity that had offended some readers of his earlier dramas. He was "a moralist saved from moralizing by his sensitivity," according to Robert Speaight. Other books, popular with readers of Baring's day, are his autobiography, *The Puppet Show of Memory*, and the parodies, including *Dead Letters, Lost Diaries*, and *Lost Lectures*, which display the breadth of his reading. His scholarly books on Russian literature are still valued.

Critics often remark on the contrast between Baring's life and his fiction; the lively gentleman who would, on occasion, set his hair afire for the startled amusement of others, wrote with a deliberately flat style, often in a melancholy tone. As a result, reviewers often express greater admiration for the man than for his work, finding his novels tediously mannered and plodding. Other critics detect a purpose in Baring's technique, perceiving the style and tone as tools used to evoke subtly a brooding identification with the struggling protagonists and with the author's Christian humanist philosophy. "What I most admire about Baring's work," remarked François Mauriac, "is the sense he gives you of the penetration of grace."

Historical Pictures Service, Chicago

Baring's writings mark him as a representative of the long-vanished Edwardian upper class. Although critic Anne Fremantle has judged him to have attained the stature of Mauriac and Georges Bernanos, he is nearly forgotten today.

PRINCIPAL WORKS

Pastels and Other Rhymes (poetry) 1891
The Black Prince (drama and poetry) 1902
Gaston de foix (dramas) 1903
A Year in Russia (journalism) 1907
The Grey Stocking (drama) 1908
*Dead Letters (fictional letters) 1910
*Diminutive Dramas (dramas) 1910
Landmarks in Russian Literature (criticism) 1910
*Lost Diaries (fictional journals) 1913
In Memoriam: Auberon Herbert (poetry) 1917
Passing By (novel) 1921
Overlooked (novel) 1922
The Puppet Show of Memory (autobiography) 1922
A Triangle (novel) 1923
C (novel) 1924
Cat's Cradle (novel) 1925
Daphne Adeane (novel) 1926
French Literature (criticism) 1927

*These works were published as *Unreliable History* in 1919.

BERNARD SHAW　(essay date 1908)

I thought [*The Grey Stocking*] quite successful, both as an experiment and in the ordinary way of the stage. I have only two cavils to make. I think the scene in the last act, where the Johnny in the brown suit told Miss Braithwaite that he knew that she was in love with the other man, was questionable, partly because it was abominably indelicate of the brown bounder to force a confidence on the woman like that (she would never have forgiven him for it), and partly because you had already worked this stunt for all it was worth, and concerning the same man, the Russian, with another couple. The second cavil is at the first act. On consideration, however, I withdraw it, and approve of the first act. It was heroic to impose all that twaddle on the audience, and to insist on their being patient with it and reflecting on it and even aesthetically enjoying it merely as twaddle, in stupendous contrast with silent omnipresent reality; but the old Adam in me rebelled against such a waste of opportunities for so many good old stage laughs. (p. 148)

I do not see why the dickens you should not go regularly into the trade of playwriting. I thought that some of the scenes in *The Grey Stocking* showed a very rare sort of dramatic tact— a power of letting go a thing at the right moment instead of wallowing in it and getting hopelessly messed up with it, as most of our good, thick, average professionals do. The real difficulty of course is that you draw Society as it really is, and not as our good public conceives it. Also they take the bogus criticisms quite seriously. Not even ——'s clowning prevented them from taking that judgment of current literature, which she fires off before leaving, otherwise than with Tennysonian seriousness. (p. 149)

> *Bernard Shaw, in his letter to Maurice Baring on June 1, 1908 (reprinted by permission of The Society of Authors on behalf of the Bernard Shaw Estate), in* Maurice Baring *by Ethel Smyth, William Heinemann Ltd, 1938, pp. 148-49.*

MAX BEERBOHM　(essay date 1908)

It is evident the playwright who deals in heroes, villains, buffoons, queer people who are either doing or suffering either tremendous or funny things, has a very valuable advantage over the playwright who deals merely in humdrum you and me. The dramatist has his material as spring-board. The adramatist must be very much an athlete.

Is Mr. Maurice Baring such an one? His play, **"The Grey Stocking,"** . . . gives me the impression that he is very athletic by nature, but that he has not "trained" quite hard enough. His next play I shall probably enjoy more than I enjoyed this one (and that is saying much), not only because he is doubtless

training hard for it at this moment, but also because I shall know just what to expect. I had not expected adramaturgy. I was on the look-out for things happening; and the fact that nothing happened rather bothered me. . . . Mr. Baring ought to have given his play a more explicit title—"The Potterers," or something like that. For they are all of them potterers, these creatures of Mr. Baring's fancy. Mentally they are alert enough. They talk about all the fashionable topics, and talk well. Not that the play is "a conversation" à la G.B.S. After a while there are signs that the persons of the play are to be more than talkers at large, and that we are to see them under stress of particular emotion—see their souls at work. Lady Sybil Alston is married to a very religious man. A bore is always a rather dangerous person in a play: he is so apt to bore the audience. Mr. Baring is to be congratulated on having created a bore who really amuses us. Lady Sybil, not sharing our amusement, contracts a sentiment for an attractive foreigner who is staying in her house. . . . However, she has a regular lover. With him she goes motoring. The other people in the house are rather uneasy when night falls and the couple has not returned. The couple does return, however, a little later. So *that* is all right. Also, it is all right about Lady Sybil and the foreigner. He does not care for her enough to elope with her. Nor does she care for him enough to elope with him; she prefers to remain with the tedious husband. Well, all this is very true to average life. But in a play where nothing comes of anything, and where no one is an outwardly exciting person, we must be made to know the characters very intimately: else we are in danger of inanition. Mr. Baring gives us deliciously clever sketches of his characters; but he does not give us the full, deep portraits that are needed. (pp. 514-16)

> *Max Beerbohm, "An Adramatist" (originally published in* The Saturday Review, *London, Vol. 105, No. 2745, June 6, 1908), in his* Around Theatres *(reprinted by permission of Mrs. Eva Reichmann), revised edition, Rupert Hart-Davis, 1953, pp. 512-16.*

ARNOLD BENNETT　(essay date 1910)

I have read with very great interest Mr. Maurice Baring's new volume about Russia, **"Landmarks in Russian Literature."** . . . It deals with Gogol, Tourgenieff, Dostoievsky, Tolstoy, and Tchehkoff. It is unpretentious. It is not "literary." I wish it had been more literary. Mr. Baring seems to have a greater love for literature than an understanding knowledge of it. He writes like a whole-hearted amateur, guided by common-sense and enthusiasm, but not by the delicate perceptions of an artist. He often says things, or says things in a manner, which will assuredly annoy the artist. Thus his curt, conventional remarks about Zola might have been composed for a leading article in the *Morning Post,* instead of for a volume of literary criticism. Nevertheless, I cannot be cross with him. In some ways his book is illuminating. I mean that it has illuminated my darkness. His chapters on Russian characteristics and on realism in Russian literature are genuinely valuable. . . . Only a man who knows Russia very well, and who has a genuine affection for the Russian character, could have written these chapters. And I am ready to admit that they are more useful than many miles of appreciation in the delicate balancing manner of say an Arthur Symons. (pp. 208-09)

> *Arnold Bennett, "Tourgenieff and Dostoievsky" (originally published as "Books and Persons: An Occasional Causerie," in* The New Age, *Vol. VI, No. 22, March 31, 1910), in his* Books and Persons:

Being Comments on a Past Epoch, 1908-1911 *(copyright, 1917, by George H. Doran Company; copyright renewed © 1945 by Marie Marguerite Bennett), Doran, 1917, pp. 208-13.**

kind permission of J. C. Squire's son, Mr. Raglan Squire), Hodder & Stoughton, Limited, 1921 (and reprinted by Books for Libraries Press, 1971; distributed by Arno Press, Inc., pp. 93-9).

SOLOMON EAGLE [J.C. Squire]   (essay date 1919)

It is not a new thing to write letters from or dialogues between dead or legendary people. Englishmen, Frenchmen, and ancients have done it; possibly Czecho-Slovaks, but I do not know. . . . In our own day I do not know anybody who has done the thing better than Mr. Maurice Baring.

Before the war Mr. Baring published three volumes of short, light compositions which in various fashions put words into the mouths of the dead. These were: *Lost Diaries, Dead Letters* and *Diminutive Dramas*. Those who possess them cherish them as men of taste always cherish good books which are not so well known as they ought to be. . . . The third, the book of small dramas, some of which are frequently played in America, was, taken all through, the most uniformly amusing of the three. (pp. 93-4)

Mr. Baring's little plays are all much of a length, and the majority are comic representations, in prose, of historical or legendary characters in action. . . . A few are something other or something more. Some are contemporary and their characters invented. And two are parodies. Of these one is as good a burlesque of Maeterlinck (not a difficult butt) as has ever been written, and in the other Mr. Baring succeeds beautifully in the harder task of writing an Elizabethan play. The subject is the death of Alexander the Great; the manner is the manner not (except here and there) of Shakespeare but of his lesser and more ranting contemporaries. There is a touch of the Marlowe of *Tamerlane*. Alexander's long and eloquent speeches have too much of the old magic to amuse; the parody is most entertaining where the originals are most palpably weak and bombastic. (p. 95)

Two of the best for acting purposes are minute modern comedies. *The Drawback* is a conversation between a pair of lovers in the park, in which a most horrible revelation is made in a tantalisingly mysterious way. *The Greek Vase* is a bitter little scene between an artist and a dealer. *Don Juan's Failure*—Don Juan, drawn precisely as he must have been, comes up against an English ingénue—would also go well. Of the others I fancy for amateur actors *Catherine Parr, The Rehearsal, After Euripides, Electra, Calpurnia's Dinner Party*, and *King Alfred's Neat Herd*. (p. 96)

Catherine Parr is mild farce: a dialogue between Henry VIII and his last wife as to a watery egg the monarch has been given for breakfast. . . . This effort, I think, does not come into the category of dramas in which an attempt has seriously been made to re-create historical characters and scenes. But I think that the scene showing a rehearsal of *Macbeth*, and the part played therein by the modest, amiable, able and adaptable author is almost certainly accurate, and could be studied to advantage by all Shakespeare's biographers. (pp. 97-8)

I wish that with his gift for comic writing Mr. Baring would attempt something on the same lines as these dramas but a little longer. (p. 99)

Solomon Eagle [*pseudonym of J. C. Squire*], "'Diminutive Dramas'" (originally published in New Statesman, *Vol. XIII, No. 323, June 14, 1919), in his* Books in General *(copyright 1921; reprinted by*

REBECCA WEST   (essay date 1922)

Mr. Baring is often an artist and very memorably a poet. But in this quasi-novel [*Overlooked*] he is neither; he admits a larger circle than usual into the secret (for it will still be concealed from those of grosser mould) that he has a delightful personality. It is the story of a drama between two people, and how it appeared to their contemporaries. . . . She was a woman formed for love who had had a disappointing engagement in her youth, and since then had wilted in a destiny that if it was not actually ugly, was at least plain. When she meets the man who is a Russian, and who is all that Mr. Baring loves to tell us that Russians are, it means a happiness hardly to be believed in for both of them. . . . Now, these people were well-bred and reticent, and they play out their drama in the setting, specially compulsive of reserved behaviour, of a French spa. Mr. Baring's game is to show just how much the onlookers could make of the game. The narrator of the story sees nearly everything, though he is a blind man, because he is sensitive, sympathetic, and a gentleman. Mr. James Rudd, the novelist, who tries to make a novel of it, misses everything, because he is shallow and common and unresponsive to deep tides. Out of his descriptions of these two people one gets a lot of Mr. Baring's peculiar and delightful quality. . . . One finds, however, that this book bears traces of the disadvantages that private personality labours under as compared with artistic personality. No one makes a work of art without having some ideal of art which entails selection and rejection, and the artistic personality is consequently used to pruning itself. The private personality is used to extending and receiving social tolerance; and it is therefore rather apt to be without certain necessary austerities. In *Overlooked* Mr. Baring makes one catch one's breath by letting Mr. Rudd say depreciatingly of the Russian that "he had not got further than Miss Austen and he was taken in by Chesterton." The implication staggers one, and of all modern authors the one that the spirit of Miss Austen would be mostly likely to dislike would be the flushed author of *Lepanto;* and to couple these two incompatibles as the likely preferences of a cultured man is an extreme courtesy to a contemporary that ought to take place in the home, but not in that serious thing, a printed book. One feels the social atmosphere again when Mr. Baring inserts into his book a short story by James Rudd, which has the stupendous specific gravity of that heaviest of all known substances, an unsuccessful parody. One feels as one might at a party when Uncle (who will delude himself that he can talk American) tells his longest story about the Express Company tourists in Venice, but one remembers at the time that Uncle is a great dear. That, indeed, must be one's attitude to *Overlooked*. As a novel it hardly exists; as a sample of Mr. Baring it is, of course, auriferous. (p. 690)

Rebecca West, "Notes on Novels: 'Overlooked'," in New Statesman (© 1922 The Statesman Publishing Co. Ltd.), Vol. XIX, No. 494, September 30, 1922, pp. 690, 692.

MAURICE BARING   (essay date 1925)

[My *Cat's Cradle*] is a true story. The main facts, strange facts, improbable facts, are all true; even the frame, the setting, is near the truth, although I invented it. You can find the story in the old files of a newspaper; but, in turning the true story into fiction, I had to attenuate the facts, to foreshorten, to lessen, to diminish, to tone down; because what is true in life is not necessarily true in art—the old tag about *le vrai et le vraisemblable*—and to give to fiction the appearance of reality, to make the reader swallow it, you must needs temper the powder of fact with the jam of (relative) probability. The reader could not have swallowed the crude improbable facts of this tale neat and undiluted from the glass of fiction—he would have said they were impossible; so I have toned down the truth, and in a way spoilt the story and made another.

The story has a moral.

You will perceive what that moral is should you read it, but, in case you don't read the book, I will tell you what that moral is presently. Before I do that I want to digress for a moment. You will remember that years ago, when we were young, merry, and very, very wise, people used to talk a good deal about "Art for Art's sake," and maintain that a work of art with a moral was a contradiction in terms. Strangely enough, they used to regard as their masters men who not only practised, but even preached the direct opposite: Baudelaire, for instance.

Strangely enough, too, sometimes the fruit of their theories was poor as a work of art, but powerful as a sermon: instances will leap readily to your mind. But it always seemed to me that if life has a moral (which it seems never to be without), and if art be the reflection of life, art must have a moral too. (pp. v-vi)

To go on to the moral of this book.

It has been expressed by Cervantes in Spanish. Here are his words. I read them long before I ever thought of writing the book, and, I may say, to satisfy the lions, that I wrote the book first and deduced the moral afterwards.

"Solo se vence la pasion amorosa con huilla, y que nadie se ha poner á brazos con tan poderoso enemigo, porque es menester fuerzas divinas para vencer las suyas humanas." ("Love is too strong to be overcome by anything except flight, no mortal creature ought to be so presumptuous as to stand the encounter, since there is need of something more than human, and indeed a heavenly force, to confront and vanquish that human passion.")

It has also been admirably expressed, partly in English and partly in French, in a poem by yourself, composed at my table, and in my presence:

> "The Love of God which leads to realms above
> Is *contre-carréd* by the god of Love."

"*Contre-carréd*": yes. That is to say, met, counteracted, assailed, undermined, thwarted, checked at every turn, but not necessarily *defeated*, not necessarily *check-mated*, by the god of Love . . . in this case . . . but, if you want to know how this applies to my story, you must read it. . . . (pp. viii-ix)

> *Maurice Baring, "Dedication to Hillary Belloc," in his* Cat's Cradle *(reprinted by permission of the Estate of the late Maurice Baring), William Heinemann Ltd, 1925, pp. v-xii.*

V. S. PRITCHETT   (essay date 1930)

Mr. Baring's unfailing good taste is both a virtue and a chilling limitation. His art has the pallor and melancholy diffidence of those people who are too well-bred and too passive to experience any drama but the dramas of conscience, any tragedy but that which arises out of the conflict of good manners and timid rightness with crude, unmannerly life. These tragedies, or, rather, these resignations, he polishes until they gleam with a haunting and impeccable *tristesse*. **Robert Peckham** is of this order. It is a historical story selected with perfect unobtrusiveness from religious confusions of the reigns of Henry the Eighth and Mary, and is concerned with Robert Peckham's inability to accept the Reformation, and his failure to stand out frankly against his father, the King's adviser, who held that loyalty to the King did not imply disloyalty to Rome. Robert Peckham's hesitations harden to a negative austerity with the years, and finally send him in old age to lonely exile in Rome. . . . The veins of Mr. Baring's marble creatures have no blood. The cold stone of conscience holds them irrevocably apart. Yet Mr. Baring persuades one to feel an inexpressible sadness, the sadness that haunts the everlasting exile and distance of figures on an urn. The story is flawlessly constructed. (p. 1067)

> *V. S. Pritchett, "The English Heart," in* The Spectator *(© 1930 by The Spectator; reprinted by permission of The Spectator), Vol. 144, No. 5322, June 28, 1930, pp. 1064-067.**

ALLARDYCE NICOLL   (essay date 1934)

From the critic of acting . . . we demand a strange combination of qualities. First, he must have enthusiasm, for out of enthusiasm is all great criticism born. Combined with that, however, must go a rational and intellectual power of evaluation and judgment. The ability to recognize the true relationship between the art of the actor and the dramatic rôle he interprets is a third quality, and still another is the possessing a power of observation abnormally acute, a keen swiftness of vision, an almost superhuman skill in grasping shadowy and evanescent material. (pp. 628-29)

[Although Mr. Baring's **Sarah Bernhardt**] lacks the complete combination of critical talents, those qualities which he does bring to the treatment of his subject are . . . fundamentally valuable. His manner is restrained; . . . [he offers an] essentially sober and unadorned record. Of his own limitations Mr. Baring is well aware. "To write the life of Sarah Bernhardt," he says, "it would require another Sarah Bernhardt: that is to say, someone who could do in biography what she could do in acting." In that sentence lies the whole truth: to write adequately on Edmund Kean was needed the genius of a [William] Hazlitt; on Ellen Terry, the genius of a Shaw. Hazlitts and Shaws are not common and, recognizing this, Mr. Baring has done well to restrict himself in scope. By doing so, he has succeeded in producing a book which may heartily be welcomed—a record of the impressions made on his mind by Bernhardt's performances, a record valuable for its thoroughness and its firmness even although it be wanting in the richer music of Hazlitt's style. (p. 630)

> *Allardyce Nicoll, "The Art of Bernhardt," in* The Yale Review *(© 1934 by Yale University; reprinted by permission of the editors), Vol. XXIII, No. 3, March, 1934, pp. 628-30.**

WILLIAM LYON PHELPS   (essay date 1935)

[Maurice Baring] is one of the most brilliant of contemporary men of letters; original, learned, wise, witty, humorous, tender, sympathetic, whose published works show an extraordinary versatility. He is a novelist, critic, poet, dramatist, historian, and his autobiography, **"The Puppet Show of Memory,"** is one of the most charming books of the twentieth century. . . .

And I do not know where one can find anywhere a more beautiful case of loyalty to a school than in what Mr. Baring says in **"Lost Lectures"** about Eton. . . .

Mr. Baring says that every moment of his years at Eton he would like to live over again; that he is certain it is the best school that ever existed; that in every athletic contest he wants Eton to win. He says this with a jolly laugh, but it is refreshing, like all antiseptic laughter.

There is a quality in everything this man writes; it is difficult to describe this. But remembering that he is as modest as he is distinguished, that he combines humor with reverence, a passionate loyalty with outrageous mirth, we may come near to understanding him.

William Lyon Phelps, "Maurice Baring," in Commonweal (copyright © 1935 Commonweal Publishing Co., Inc.; reprinted by permission of Commonweal Publishing Co., Inc.), Vol. XXII, No. 18, August 30, 1935, p. 423.

HILAIRE BELLOC (essay date 1935)

I have finished **Darby and Joan.** It is *very good.* . . .

Its quality is the sequence of human life. This you attempt, this you have attained. There is in it the exact balance of motive and the frustration which gives reality to any mood of human life purporting to be real. It is, I assure you, a great achievement. . . . On the top of that you write with deliberate restraint, a quality which people are always praising, because they think it national, but which is less *practised* here [in England] than anywhere. (p. 253)

On all this side matter, the book is perfect. For the purpose of the method it has exactly the material required, exceeding neither in the number of the relations nor in the irrelevancy of minor experiences. This last is the worst pitfall menacing those who work after this manner. It is hardly ever avoided, and as far as I can note after a very careful reading, there is no line in **Friday's Business** where the temptation has caught you. The chief danger lay in the small talk of the diplomatic circle; but I do not think there was half a line too much.

Now as to manner: and that is the more difficult point when you are doing this in the English language. The reason the French have been led to the method is that *la langue Française ignore l'homonyme.* Armed with this weapon of incalculable value, the Frenchman can write "I saw a pig", and it means exactly that. But in English pretty well every word, or at any rate every general word, has a vague edge to it. On that depend the English effects which a French translation cannot give; but on the other hand, it makes the full value of extreme economy a dreadfully difficult thing to attain. It is attained when the reader is in the writer's own mood; it is missed in proportion as the reader's mind is apart from that mood.

It is on this account that I have always said of your books written in this manner that they must be read consecutively, at once and as a whole. Thus the writer's mood is caught, preserved, enhanced.

You have deliberately chosen a handicap in **Friday's Business** of having a very strong emotion near the outset of the book.

It was a great advantage to **Cat's Cradle** that there is ascent in moments of emotion from the beginning to the end, the penultimate stab being the love scene and the ultimate and sharpest stab the memory of the child at the mother's death and her speaking its name. However, having deliberately chosen this other sequence in **Friday's Business,** you have got away with it all right; only, inevitably, you burden yourself for this reason:— that the growing into the writer's mood by the reader is made less gradual and therefore less easy. I do not discover the penultimate stab before the last, the death; but perhaps I shall discover it on a second reading.

In the use of the arrangement of words there is nothing to be criticised and that, in this method, is the most difficult virtue to sustain. It is of course a talent peculiarly your own; I should have no idea how to do it and I do not know anyone else who could do it for more than a page or two. I could not keep it up beyond three sentences. The penalty exacted by the time in which we live for a gift of that kind is having to wait for its recognition; but you may be confident that it is startlingly present; and to me, as one reader at least, more striking than the economy of matter or the accord with life, though both are very marked throughout. (pp. 253-54)

Hilaire Belloc, in his letter to Maurice Baring on December 7, 1935, in his Letters from Hilaire Belloc, edited by Robert Speaight (copyright © 1958 by Hilary Belloc; reprinted by permission of A D Peters & Co Ltd), Hollis & Carter, 1958, pp. 253-54.

JOSEPH J. REILLY (essay date 1939)

The writings of Belloc and of the late Gilbert Chesterton have overshadowed those of Maurice Baring, the third member of that extraordinary fellowship. Everybody knows that *Lepanto* is one of the most gorgeous poems in the language and that *Marie Antoinette* ranks among the memorable biographies of our time, but few are aware that Baring is equally many-sided and that his beauty of style, deep human sympathies, and psychological penetration help to make him one of the most important of contemporary British novelists. He has been many things, diplomat, journalist, soldier, critic, and poet, and won distinction in every role. In 1909 he became a Catholic, "the only action of my life," he wrote, "which I am quite certain I have never regretted." It is necessary to know this in order to understand his outlook on life as it is revealed in his novels.

Baring selects his characters, settings, and incidents from the life he knows best. Most of his people have means and culture, they recruit the diplomatic service and the civil professions, and they are equally at home at great country houses, embassy dinners, and continental watering places. His men are decent, intelligent, unspiritual, and, all told, undistinguished. His chief concern is with women and he draws them with delicacy, sureness of touch, and extraordinary insight. (p. 11)

In all but one of Baring's most important novels it is a woman who plays the leading part. Why? Because in Baring's view women are more interesting. Why that? Because morally they are more self-sufficient, their emotions are subtler, deeper, and more enduring, and finally because they have a certain spirituality at the core and a greater capacity for self-dedication and sacrifice. If they do not inspire men to great achievements they are capable of banishing emptiness from their lives and bringing harmony to their souls; should they fail, the fault is less with them than with their stars or with the instability or blindness of the men.

Baring pictures them as lovely and gracious with a light in their eyes when young, a thinly veiled sadness when mature, and always a distinction elusive but unmistakable. (p. 12)

It is the social not the business side of life to which we are introduced; not offices or shops or surging crowds, but concerts, exhibitions, dinner parties, varied by week-ends at shooting lodges in Scotland or holidays in Cornwall or along the upper Thames or on the Continent. . . . [Beneath] the well-bred restraint of Baring's people burn the fires of those passions which are in all the children of men; the same temptations, the same divided loyalties, the same ills of mind and spirit are their equal heritage. If Baring's interests center in the Colonel's Lady rather than in Judy O'Grady, he knows that every hunger of heart, every impulse which Judy experiences is shared by her more highly placed sister-under-the-skin. (pp. 12-13)

In the typical Baring novel a young girl marries at eighteen or twenty. She is fresh, unspoiled, and docile. If she has had an early love affair, it is usually with a romantic young man who cares deeply but whose lack of money or prospects provides older heads with a reason for interfering and preaching with ultimate success the superior wisdom of marrying the man of their choice. (Baring treats these youthful affairs with understanding and reverence and he provides for their culminating episode a setting whose loveliness recalls the fourteenth chapter of *Richard Feverel*.) In any case she has had little experience with life, and when a man of means and position, usually her senior by ten or twelve years, is attracted by her youth and beauty, her elders manage matters with "sense" and the marriage occurs with "everybody" present. There is a honeymoon in the country, a return to London, the opening of the town house—and then the real story is ready to unfold.

The society which the bride glimpsed before but becomes a part of now is composed of people with whom restraint and good breeding are essential and the ultimate condemnation is to behave badly. It is a sophisticated society like Henry James's and Galsworthy's, half pagan and inwardly restive, which lives by its own code, prizing a pledged word more than continence and demanding that its members, in deference to the outer decencies, affect to believe that their spouses, however notorious their "affairs," are above suspicion. To find consolation for a husband's or a wife's infidelity is general and, according to the code, so natural that the opposite course arouses comment.

The typical Baring heroine does not yield herself to the semi-paganism in which this society is steeped, for within her is an unconscious and saving grace. Besides, she finds satisfaction in a fine home, a husband universally deemed desirable, and the novelty of a situation never experienced before. Soon, sometimes tragically soon, she comes to realize that what counts most is none of these things but her relations with her husband. That realization reacts in different ways but it leads in every case to one discovery, the discovery that love complete, reciprocal, absorbing, love as the grand passion beside which all else in life shrinks to nothingness is wanting. It is this passion, a noble and transcendent thing, which Baring's heroines crave and to which they are capable of sacrificing every lesser good. It is this passion, let me repeat, which fails to find fulfilment in their marriage. Therein lie the seeds of tragedy. Fanny Choyce, loving her husband dearly, finds him giving her everything but the one thing necessary; and Mrs. Housman *(Passing By)* give everything only to meet with neglect and infidelity. Where love or jealousy is awakened Baring's women and most of his men are extraordinarily perceptive. They do not need anything

so gross as an affirmation or a denial, an unearthed letter or a warning from a meddler. As with Henry James's women the intonation of a voice, a moment's silence, a look meaningless to all the world else, tells everything.

Thus what follows belongs in each case to the hidden drama of life; on the surface little happens, but in the relations of husband and wife certain imperceptible but subtle changes occur sensed by each in turn but overtly unacknowledged. The rift steadily widens until at last the woman is oppressed by a sense of the emptiness of life or of her personal isolation and moral loneliness. Wealth, social success, even children, serve less to mitigate this feeling than to accentuate the absence of the one essential thing. Then one day a man comes into her life, subtly different from all the others, who gradually fills its emptiness and re-establishes her sense of participation in life and the joy of it. And so at last the high moment comes, love awakens love, the grand passion is born, and the woman's heart (the ultimate center, let me repeat, of Baring's interest) comes into its own. (pp. 13-15)

In this hour of rapture all the operations of life seem suspended; it is as if the lovers were beyond the reach of man and fate.

But our days are not lived thus. (p. 15)

[Apprehension] dogs the lovers' steps; the man's mind, the woman's conscience, find no rest; something will happen, *must* happen; they feel (the woman more acutely) that they are living beneath a suspended sword or are drifting downstream to a whirlpool. Then one day—a matter of months, a matter of years—the sword falls: the forces of Fate (or Destiny, if you prefer, or Providence), temporarily halted, resume their imperious march; the evasion of the inevitable comes to an end, and, for the woman, "Duty and inclination," in Stevenson's fine phrase, "come nobly to the grapple." Sometimes, as with Madame D'Alberg, Hyacinth Wake *(Daphne Adeane)*, and Mrs. Housman *(Passing By)*, we are not permitted to see that duel but merely to surmise its intensity from the character of the woman and the aftermath; sometimes, as with Princess Blanche and more especially Fanny Choyce, we are given the struggle in full view and then Baring's treatment is admirable for its firmness and delicacy. (p. 16)

It would be a mistake to suppose that all Baring's novels follow an identical pattern. The pattern varies in many details and in accordance with the character of the woman who plays the chief part. (p. 17)

[The] first blunder of Baring's women is not a deliberate piece of wrong-doing: it is a mistake in judgment, in entering upon a marriage in deference to the wishes of a parent or without understanding (how can a girl of eighteen or twenty understand?) the innumerable compromises and delicate adjustments involved in the most fundamental and hazardous of life's relationships and the unpredictable reactions which make or mar it. Having taken that first step she cannot turn back or free herself from the new obligations in which she has become enmeshed. It is when she tries that she finds herself inviting the counterstroke of Fate (or Providence); it is when she persists that its weight falls. Is this realism? Of the most essential kind. Do we find it upsetting? Tragically so. Can we change it? No, says Baring, and Thomas Hardy would agree with him. Why not? Because life is like that, full of imperfect understanding and innocent hopes defeated and moral waste so vast and seemingly so purposeless. Whence comes all this tragedy inexplicable because counter to the instincts of human justice? From the malicious Overlord, says Hardy, ("President of the Immortals,'' he calls him in *Tess),* who toys with his creatures as a cat with a mouse, and, suddenly wearying of the sport, destroys them with a blow. Baring disagrees. Our individual tragedies, he says in his most moving novel, *The Coat Without Seam,* are like the patches and stains on the wrong side of a perfectly woven garment. The disfigurements come from our faulty vision, our awkward fingers; the perfection of its seamless beauty from One whose eyes can see all things, even men's secret thoughts, and whose hands can shape all things, even their broken hearts, to a nobler destiny than they dare to dream. It is this faith which Baring won by the step he has ''never regretted,'' and which Hardy desired in vain. How shall we face life and live it through? With stoicism, says Hardy, in which there is no hope. With resignation, says Baring, which alone brings healing and peace.

Baring's ideal woman is Daphne Adeane, a Catholic, ''a will of steel in a frail body,'' whose name is given to a novel in which she never appears, since like Tom Outland in Willa Cather's *Professor's House,* she had died before the story opens. But, again like Outland, she is a living influence throughout and is the most effective of the characters because morally the strongest, spiritually the most valiant. (pp. 19-20)

Baring is never directly didactic. His Catholics, even his priests, explain the teachings of their faith only when asked, and confess that life poses to them as to non-believers questions which evade all logic but that of faith. Baring is too good an artist and too honest an observer to imply that people who inherit or accept Catholicism escape devastating temptations or always defeat them. Much is given them, but the final effort, the will to victory, as with Hyacinth Wake, only they themselves can supply. . . .

Of Baring's novels *Cat's Cradle* is the most ambitious, *The Coat Without Seam* the most deeply felt, *The Lonely Lady of Dulwich* the most deftly done, *Friday's Business* the most satiric, *A Triangle* the subtlest, *Daphne Adeane* all told the finest. Long after one is finished with Baring's novels scenes from them cling to the memory: the pleasure party on the Thames in *Robert Peckham* with the song of the revellers and the serenity of a summer afternoon stilling for a little hour and for the last time the tumult in Robert's heart; the final chapter of *Friday's Business,* marked by Hardy's irony of circumstance and Maupassant's detachment. . . . (p. 20)

Baring's literary relationships are numerous. Like Browning he believes in love at first sight, not because it is a vulgar passion easily aroused but because it is the mutual recognition of the kinship of two souls, which comes with the swiftness of light and the suddenness of a revelation. . . . Again like Browning he is acutely aware of that hidden place where the motive-forces of every man dwell, a place of mystery and unsoundable depths. Unlike Browning he has never sought to penetrate its final and darker secrets—he has for instance written nothing comparable to ''My Last Duchess'' or ''Any Wife to Any Husband''—but he points the way for the imaginative reader with a subtlety so extraordinary that it often goes unnoticed. The device by which Browning in *The Ring and the Book* exposed to full view the limitations of human insight (by presenting the opinions of ''one half Rome, the other half Rome, and the Tertium Quid'') Baring has successfully adopted in narrower compass when treating Blanche's departure from her husband's home and Daphne Adeane's secret, and throughout two shorter novels, *A Triangle* and *Overlooked.*

Baring's concern with men and women of the leisure class and his interest in the psychological effects of action rather than in

action itself, recall Henry James. But Henry James got to the point where he placed art above life . . . as if people existed to be studied under the microscope and to be meticulously reported on, after tortuous explorations of their souls and minds. . . . With Baring art is a means not an end; it exists to present life; the sense of time with him as with Tolstoi is never lost. Indeed it is a part of Baring's purpose to keep us aware of its onward march as of the footsteps of an unseen monitor who whispers that the night cometh when no man shall work—or play or marry or give in marriage.

As a contemporary portrayer of English society prior to the World War Baring challenges comparison with Galsworthy. Each presents men and women of some culture but scant faith, a society which took its pleasures furtively before 1914 and flauntingly thereafter. Both men are keen, sensitive, deeply sympathetic; each is a romantic, honestly facing reality and striving to picture it faithfully. Baring is a cosmopolitan who has seen life on many fronts and is free from Galsworthy's insularity. Baring is more objective in treatment and creates sympathy for his characters without betraying his personal partiality. Thus one cannot be sure what he thinks of Rose Mary Clifford *(Cat's Cradle),* a woman hard at the core, but Galsworthy' liking for the self-righteous Irene *(Forsythe Saga)*—one of the most unloveable women in modern fiction—is transparent.

A chief source of Baring's power is his rich and inexhaustible sentiment; Galsworthy's primary weakness is his sentimentalism (sentiment over-ripe and touched with decay) which permits him to believe that ''love'' (meaning physical passion) is its own justification, that ''Spring in the blood'' excuses a flirtation with fatal consequences, and that an embezzler who commits suicide deserves our sympathy if he prepares for the deed like an Epicurean and consummates it like a Stoic. . . . [Galsworthy] says as an Epicurean ''You have the right to be happy,'' and admonishes as a Stoic, ''Do not lose your form.''

If on rare occasions Baring's men strive and cry or fail to keep their form, his women never do. Except for Mrs. Bucknell in *C* (Baring's Becky Sharp) they know the difference between love and its counterfeit, they have a moral sense, and sooner or later they learn the wisdom of renunciation whose ways alone are peace. In all Baring's novels there is a sense of the pathos of life, the tears of things. Why then are they not depressing? Because they present reality without bitterness and with infinite compassion and unfailing beauty. (pp. 21-3)

Joseph J. Reilly, ''The Novels of Maurice Baring'' (originally published in The Catholic World, *Vol. CL, No. 896, November, 1939), in his* Of Books and Men *(copyright © 1942, 1970 by Joseph J. Reilly; reprinted by permission of Julian Messner, a Simon & Schuster division of Gulf & Western Corporation), Julian Messner, Inc., 1942, pp. 11-23.*

RICHARD CHURCH   (essay date 1948)

Of all modern British authors, Maurice Baring is the most difficult to write about. This is due, I think, to the incompatibility between his personality and his character. . . . [His biographer, Dame Ethel Smyth, found him] a person of rare charm, with a playful humour and a wayward attitude towards the conventions of life. The testimony of his two great friends, Hilaire Belloc and G. K. Chesterton, bears out the truth of this portrait. I would add that Baring's own book, *The Puppet Show of Memory* amplifies the portrait. It is one of his most beautiful books. (pp. 72-3)

But this side of the man, with his aristocratic eccentricities, his practical jokes, his indifference to the conventions and to the correct moves in career-making, does not appear in his writing. On the contrary, as soon as we come to the world of his art, we come to a bare, desolate land, whose beauties emerge only gradually, after we have become acclimatized. Both in verse and prose he wrote with a deliberate flatness, a drooping rhythm, as though a great weariness and desolation of spirit possessed him. The general aspect of his work is one of sadness, a deep sadness that is less active than pessimism, but more penetrating. It comes upon the soul of the reader, producing a sense of loneliness, of being face to face with oneself and finding the company inadequate. It penetrates even further, and ends—or rather it does not end, for there is no end to this influence—by forcing the reader to a contact with Baring's own refuge from this desolation. His refuge was the Roman Catholic Church. The story of his conversion is laconic and terse, but it is devastating in its effect. (See *The Puppet Show of Memory*.)

But even with this sustenance, age-old, and with all the incidence of European culture which meant so much to the author, he could not escape from the Catullus-like despair which was part of his temperament. Below his social high spirits, deeper than his devout faith, moved this restless imagination. Its most tragic expression is found in the two great novels *C* and *The Coat without Seam,* and probably in *Cat's Cradle*. Behind his work lies the wide culture into which he was born. Behind that culture lies the desperate spirit looking in vain for certainty. The search has given his work a strange power, an almost hypnotic force that belies the laconic literary style which is its vehicle. (pp. 73-4)

> *Richard Church, "Maurice Baring: 1874-1945," in his* British Authors: A Twentieth-Century Gallery with 53 Portraits *(reprinted by permission of the Estate of Richard Church and Laurence Pollinger Limited), revised edition, Longmans Green and Co., 1948, pp. 72-4.*

RONALD A. KNOX (essay date 1948)

[There are] certain rare intellects which aspire to a sublime ignorance in vain. They cannot choose but learn. Maurice's nature was one which constantly absorbed, as it constantly exuded, something which (for want of a less abused word) you can only label "culture". . . . [The] classics he read in form must have got under his skin, I suppose, without his noticing it. For, whether it was the mind of a scholar or no, his mind was soaked in the classics. (p. 109)

I have often wondered, but never asked, whether *"C"* was consciously the story of Catullus re-written, as *Darby and Joan* was Mary Queen of Scots re-written (one of its reviewers said the thing could not have happened in real life). A psychologist would pounce on the similarity between the names Catullus and Caryll, the names Lesbia and Leila, as proof of unconscious association. But, then, it would have been very like Maurice to do it on purpose by way of scoring off the psychologist.

Be that as it may, those early books of his which were afterwards bound together under the title *Unreliable History* are heavily overweighted on the classical side. More than half of the *Diminutive Dramas*, more than a third of the *Lost Letters,* and a quarter of the *Lost Diaries,* have a classical setting. Nor

do I think he was ever better inspired than when he thus played on the eternal themes in Greek or Latin dress. **"Ariadne in Naxos"**, for instance, and **"From the Mycenae papers"**, give you his minute observation of the opposite sex almost better than his novels do. The utter simplicity of the décor suited his genius. And I never remember discovering, or having pointed out to me, a single lapse of scholarship in the whole of the three volumes.

But perhaps the most striking proof of his love for antiquity came at the very end of his literary carrer. . . . *Have You Anything to Declare?* is to some people the most cherished of his books. And one extraordinary thing about it is that roughly a third of the material in it dates back before Dante. Of course, he may have chosen too many of those earlier extracts, not guessing how long the book would be. Yet it is surely remarkable that a man so widely read in English literature, and in the literature of five other great modern languages, should have made such a generous allowance for the Latin and Greek to which his Eton form-masters would have pronounced him impervious. The truth is, I think, that he took an exceptional delight in *translation;* in the delicate shades of difference which manifest themselves when the same idea is perfectly expressed first in one language and then in another. . . . If it be scholarship to take an almost gluttonous delight in the deft manipulation by which an idea, or set of ideas, is taken out of one language and put into another, to that extent he was a scholar.

Yet more I think he was, in the literary sense of the word, a humanist. He went largely, no doubt, to the Romantics for his inspiration. But there was a restraint about everything he wrote which is utterly classical. (pp. 110-12)

> *Ronald A. Knox, "On the Effect of the Classics on Maurice Baring's Mind," in* Maurice Baring: A Postscript with Some Letters and Verse *by Laura Lovat (copyright 1948 by Sheed & Ward, Inc.; reprinted with permission from Andrews and McMeel, Inc.), Sheed and Ward, Inc., 1948, pp. 107-12.*

G. K. CHESTERTON (essay date 1950)

Mr. Maurice Baring, the chief Puppet-Master of the *Puppet-Show of Memory,* has included in a recent reprint [of *Diminutive Dramas*], I am glad to see, an item that I have loved long since and lost awhile, in the form of a scene from the old Drury Lane sort of Harlequinade, recast in the manner of the mystical plays of Maeterlinck, [*The Blue Harlequin*]. . . . It is a queer thing to note the extent to which the world has become silent about Maeterlinck; though it may be the more impressive to the remaining followers of so eloquent an admirer of silence. Whatever be the cause, it certainly was not that his work was devoid of a very individual imaginative quality. . . . But the matter only arises here in relation to this little literary jest about the Pantomime, which I always felt to be one of Mr. Baring's most charming fancies. Of course [*The Blue Harlequin*] is a very good burlesque of Maeterlinck; it is also in a sense a very good burlesque of the Pantomime; and the latter is the more delicate achievement. Every healthy person wishes to make fun of a serious thing; but it is generally almost impossible to make fun of a funny thing. But in this case the notion of fun or burlesque must not be confused in either case with any idea of hostility, or even of satire. Parody does not consist merely of contrast; at its best it rather consists of a superficial contrast covering a substantial congruity. The bitter sort of burlesque may exist, and have a right to exist; but it is doubtful whether in this particular form the bitterest is the best. The one sort of parodist will naturally parody the sort of style he dislikes. But the other sort of parodist will always prefer to parody the style he likes. (pp. 53-4)

> G. K. Chesterton, "The Pantomime," in his The Common Man (reprinted by permission of the Estate of the late G. K. Chesterton), Sheed and Ward, Inc., 1950, pp. 53-9.

DAVID LODGE (essay date 1960)

The novels of Maurice Baring, which in his own lifetime enjoyed a small but discriminating readership, seem now to have passed into total eclipse. At first glance this does not seem surprising. The superficial impression given by his work is that of a Marxist parody of decadent capitalist literature. It cannot be denied that Baring created a 'world', but the question presents itself: is this world, or Baring's treatment of it, significant? His world is narrow and exclusive, inhabited only by the aristocracy and landed gentry; those not belonging to these classes exist merely to open the front door and bring in the tea. (p. 262)

This in itself, of course, is not enough to condemn Baring. The 'worlds' of several great novelists—Henry James and Proust for example—are just as narrow and exclusive. But the novels of Maurice Baring are less immediately recognizable as literature than the novels of James or Proust. The level, polished surfaces of Baring's novels seem to elude the critic's grasp; his style is spare and functional; there is nothing of Proust's rich sensuous appeal, no 'thrills of recognition'; there is nothing of James' artful syntax, suggestive imagery, architectonic skill. There is little variation of tempo, little humour. Baring excluded so much from his novels that we doubt, for a moment, whether he included anything at all. But on closer examination we perceive that he is, after all, a novelist worthy of serious critical attention: a novelist of artistic and philosophical integrity, working carefully within the limits of his experience and ability, master of a style which, if somewhat dry and unexciting, is perfectly suited to his needs, and possessed of a personal vision which reveals in the narrow and exclusive society he studies patterns of universal significance. (pp. 262-63)

Baring began writing novels at a fairly late stage of his career, and drew mainly on his experience of the late Victorian and Edwardian periods. His work is thus marked by an attitude of retrospection, in which his complex emotional response to his own social *milieu*—nostalgia, pity, admiration, melancholy and a qualified pessimism—is ordered and defined.

Equally important is the gap between his adoption of the Catholic faith and the commencement of his work as a novelist, which allowed him satisfactorily to absorb Catholicism into his philosophy of life. Before his reception into the Catholic Church, Baring's mind had been formed by his deep love for and considerable knowledge of classical literature. The peculiar, haunting quality of Baring's vision of life, as revealed in his novels, is its fusion of the pagan and the Christian: the amelioration of the pagan conception of tragedy—stoical acceptance of the workings of Nemesis—by the Christian mystery of forgiveness.

This fusion of pagan and Christian pervades all Baring's work, but it is perhaps most explicit in *Daphne Adeane*. . . . The heroine, Fanny, is faced with an agonizing dilemma: while her husband, Michael, whom she has ceased to love, is at war,

she falls in love with another man, Francis Greene. Her husband is reported missing, and, after several years, is presumed dead. Fanny and Francis are planning to marry, when a message arrives stating that Michael has reappeared after suffering from loss of memory. Fanny is faced with the alternatives of asking for a divorce or resuming married life with a man whom she no longer loves. In her distraction she seeks the advice of a priest, Fr Rendall, though she is herself not a Catholic or a Christian. Inevitably, he advises her to give up Francis. She says she cannot, because, as a 'pagan', she cannot accept his premises. (p. 263)

A little later in their conversation Fr Rendall says:

> 'You say you are a pagan. What is, in your opinion, the fundamental idea of Paganism? What is the essence of Greek tragedy?'
>
> 'Sacrifice,' said Fanny, without hesitation.
>
> 'There,' said Fr Rendall; 'now believe me that in every act of sacrifice we make there is a *balm*, and in every act of self that we make there is an after-taste of fire, smoke, dust and ash.'

Fanny ultimately accepts Fr Rendall's advice, and begins life again with Michael. Baring manipulates the connotations of 'pagan' and 'sacrifice' in a way which, if he were writing a study in comparative religion, would be suspect. But the imaginative artist may legitimately employ such methods to define his interpretation of life.

The idea developed in the passage just quoted is of crucial importance to the understanding of Baring's work. In most of the novels, as in *Daphne Adeane,* it is expressed in terms of a conflict between human and divine love. (pp. 263-64)

Baring's integrity as a novelist would not allow him to suggest that divine love is always triumphant. One of his best novels, *C. . . . ,* was aptly described by a contemporary reviewer as 'a study in the temperament of failure'. It is concerned with the hero's experience of 'pain, unmixed pain, infinite bitterness, and a tragic realization of the pity and waste of things'— the result of his infatuation with a corrupt and worthless woman, Leila Bucknell. In *C.,* as so often in Henry James' novels, evil is manifested by betrayal in human relationships. The scene in which C. observes Leila dining with another man in a Parisian café has the same force as that in *The Ambassadors,* where Strether sees Chad and Mme de Vionnet on the river. Baring carefully prepares the scene in order to wring from it the fullest irony. Leila and C. have just concluded an idyllic holiday together in France, at the end of which C. is at last convinced that she has pledged her love exclusively to him. On his departure for England she bids him a tearful and tender farewell. C. is unexpectedly delayed in Paris, and is invited by a friend to make up a party of four. That evening, dining in an open-air cafe, he sees Leila in high spirits, dining with a man who, his friends assure him, is notorious as her latest lover. To complete the irony, it is to this man that Beatrice is unhappily married—Beatrice, whom C. had loved in his youth, until his mother selfishly prevented their intended marriage. (p. 264)

C. is Baring's most exhaustive and pessimistic study of human passion. Although Leila's shallowness, vulgarity and corruption is patent, even to C. himself, and although Beatrice, after the death of her husband, offers C. a second chance of peace and pure love, and the recovery of his lost innocence, he cannot cut himself free from his infatuation. In Baring's vision, love, even the most soiled and selfish love, has a fatal and inexorable power against which there is only one resource: *'la grace surnaturelle, révélation d'un autre amour'*. C. lacked this resource—hence his failure. But Blanche, the heroine of *Cat's Cradle* . . . , discovers it just when her life seems, like C.'s, to have been desolated by her own selfish and undisciplined passions.

Cat's Cradle seems to me to be at once the finest and the most typical of Baring's books. In this novel the characteristic features of his vision of life—the attitude of detached yet concerned retrospection, the fusion of pagan and Christian schemes of retribution and forgiveness, and the conflict between human and divine love—are combined in a skilfully executed work of impressive proportions. (p. 265)

Most of Baring's characters make early in life a fatal mistake which pursues them like a Nemesis all through their lives. Blanche is no exception. At an early age she falls in love with Sidney Hope, a young soldier without prospects. She accepts the well-intentioned but misguided advice of her father, breaks off her engagement to Sidney, and marries an Anglo-Italian prince, Guido Roccapalumba, whom she does not love. (pp. 265-66)

It does not take Blanche long to realize that she has married a jealous neurotic. Yet she cannot escape from him, because divorce is taboo in her social circle, and, more importantly, because she becomes a Catholic. A few years after her marriage, Blanche is tormented by the spectacle of Sidney Hope's unexpected inheritance of a rich estate, and she perceives the pattern of Nemesis that is to dominate her life. . . . (p. 266)

Guido arranges a separation, and Blanche occupies herself with the upbringing of her niece and ward, the cold and jealous Rose Mary. Guido dies, and Blanche, still beautiful despite her years, looks hopefully towards [Bernard Lacey, a scion of the old English Catholic gentry]. He visits her and says he is thinking of getting married; she is overjoyed until she realizes that he is referring to Rose Mary. Nevertheless she deliberately misunderstands him, and compromises him into proposing to her. Rose Mary understands the situation, and hates Blanche for her duplicity. From his God's-eye vantage-point Baring notes that Rose Mary does not even give Blanche credit for her moment of genuine misunderstanding: he delights in these fine distinctions. Of course Blanche is no happier than before, as Bernard falls more deeply in love with Rose Mary. . . . A malicious woman gives Blanche irrefutable evidence that Bernard is in love with Rose Mary—a revelation that is no less crushing because of Blanche's existing suspicions. The moral history of Blanche reaches its climax [as] she understands and accepts the pattern of retribution running through her life. . . . (pp. 266-67)

The scheme of crime and punishment expounded here is pagan in that retribution is seen to follow *in this life;* but Christian in that the adjustment of punishment to crime is ordered with strict justice, and not at the whim of a blind and malicious 'President of the Immortals'. (I use the terms 'pagan' and 'Christian', of course, in the sense in which Baring understood them.) The efficacy of the Christian scheme becomes explicit a little further on, when Blanche at last escapes from her Nemesis by an interior act of sacrifice:

> She prayed to be saved from herself for what remained of her life, not to do more harm, not to cause further unhappiness. . . . And it was then the wound caused by the whole situation

seemed to pierce her soul, and, as it pierced it, healed it. . . .

> Blanche felt at that moment that she would for the rest of her life be able to sacrifice herself. She made the supreme act of self-sacrifice; she knew now that from henceforth she would never grudge Bernard his love for another; she would be able to live without help, without friends, without love. . . . And from the act of inner self-sacrifice and renunciation she made, came balm; just as hitherto, from every act of self-indulgence she had ever made, had come a sense of scorching ashes.

This conception of sacrifice and renunciation closely resembles the solution offered to Fanny by Fr Rendall in *Daphne Adeane,* even to verbal echoes—'balm' and 'ashes'.

There is no 'objective correlative' to this metamorphosis in Blanche's character: she dies shortly afterwards, to outside observers a lonely and disappointed woman. But to have provided an objective correlative in the form of some dramatic change of heart in Bernard or Rose Mary would have compromised Baring's honest and generally pessimistic judgement of human nature. If the supreme act of self-sacrifice, and death, have released Blanche from the whirligig of human passion, the other characters are still trapped on it. Bernard marries Rose Mary after Walter's death, and it seems that this pair at least have achieved happiness. But in the last pages of the novel the shadow of the war encroaches on their marriage, and with it the slighter but more sinister shadow of a woman. Two people are chattering at a party:

> 'Is Bernard here tonight? I haven't seen him.'
>
> 'He's at a table right over there, having supper with his back to us.'
>
> 'I can't see who that is with him.'
>
> 'It's Mrs Bucknell.'
>
> 'Leila?'
>
> 'Yes.'
>
> 'Is she just as pretty as ever?'
>
> 'Just.'
>
> 'She has never been a friend of Bernard's, has she?'
>
> 'No, not yet, that I know of.'

This superficially unremarkable passage is an excellent example of Baring's unobtrusive skill as a novelist. The dialogue is effortlessly natural, yet packed with significant undertones and ironies, conveying a judgement on the speakers themselves (and by implication on the social group they represent), as well as suggesting the commencement of another selfish and sterile intrigue. To appreciate the full force of the loaded phrase 'not yet', we must, of course, have read *C.*

Both *C.* and *Cat's Cradle* belong to the genre of the 'life novel'. Both possess the most palpable characteristic of this form— length: each novel runs to more than seven hundred pages. In this respect they stand apart from the rest of Baring's novels. But the great length of *C.* and *Cat's Cradle* can be justified. Length, as Charles du Bos has said with reference to Baring's work, is a *'nécessité primordiale du roman, qui se propose de nous mettre en possession d'un monde'*. The evocation of a 'world' in historical perspective—aristocratic Europe from 1870 to 1914, is particularly important in *Cat's Cradle*. Nearly all Baring's novels are distinguished by a sense of period, by a mood of retrospection, but seldom is this effect obtained with such an elaboration of detail as in *Cat's Cradle*. (pp. 267-69)

Another significant departure in *C.* and *Cat's Cradle* from Baring's previous practice was the abandonment of experiments with the 'point of view' for a more traditional narrative method. *C.* is presented as a fictionalized memoir based on private papers; though it is written mainly from *C.*'s point of view, Baring frequently assumes omniscience in order to give extension to the web in which his hero becomes trapped. In *Cat's Cradle,* though the narrative is mainly concerned with the life of Blanche, the God's-eye view is all-pervasive, tracing the ironic and disastrous pattern of events from above.

On the whole Baring seems happier with the more traditional method. Although the use of the point of view in *Passing By* is entirely successful, it degenerates into an academic exercise in the two novels that follow, *Overlooked* and *A Triangle;* while all the novels that follow *Daphne Adeane* are marred by a deliberate arbitrariness and artificiality of design. If one hesitates to endorse André Maurois' description of Baring as *'un grand romancier'*, it is because only four of his books are free from serious shortcomings of this kind: *Passing By, C., Cat's Cradle* and *Daphne Adeane.* And even these novels are impaired by an excessive reticence about certain areas of experience. Baring's principal theme was the rivalry of human and divine love; he insisted that only supernatural grace could fortify the soul against the assaults of human passion. One feels that this conflict—which Baring presented with such order and logic— would have been more intense and dramatic if the human passion had been more immediately recognizable as a product of man's sensual nature.

When these reservations have been made, however, it seems to me that Baring remains a writer who deserves and rewards serious consideration. The fact that his work lies outside the most interesting trends and developments in English fiction of the twentieth century perhaps explains why he has been more fully appreciated in France than in his own country. But the value of Baring's novels lies in their content rather than their form, in the patterns he perceived and revealed in the chaotic flux of experience. The significance of his achievement in this respect has not always been acknowledged. (pp. 269-70)

> David Lodge, ''Maurice Baring, Novelist: A Reappraisal,'' in The Dublin Review, *Vol. 234, No. 485, Autumn, 1960, pp. 262-70.*

PAUL HORGAN (essay date 1969)

[Let us look] closely at the literary work of [Baring], who was so observant of the universally human under the particular and transient style of his time.

He was a votary of a vocation all but vanished—that is, a writer accomplished and expressive in all literary forms, from poetry to drama, journalism to the novel, the critical essay to the learned literary spoof. With so much to cover, we have little opportunity to do justice to all these, and I shall give most of my attention to his pastiches and his novels, in which, I think, his most expressive work is to be found. But a word or two

along the rest of the line will be useful in developing a view of his quality.

In 1904 he gave up what began as a career in diplomacy . . . and went as a reporter for the *Morning Post* to cover the Russo-Japanese War. . . . [His] first dispatch came from Moscow and it introduced the art of Anton Chekhov to the general English world, for he saw a performance of *Uncle Vanya* at the Arts Theatre and immediately knew he had come into communion with a new literary vision. His review of the performance is the first chapter in his collected volume of reports and impressions called *With the Russians in Manchuria.* The pieces in general skilfully demonstrate his idea of his task: 'The essence of journalism,' he said, 'is sensation captured on the wing.'

In 1914 he came to war again, this time as a volunteer officer attached to the headquarters of the Royal Flying Corps. . . . (pp. 10-11)

After the war he published a book called *R.F.C. H.Q.,* an excellent record of early air warfare. (p. 11)

Here we can leave the soldier resting in honour upon his arms and return to the man of letters.

The theatre deeply engaged him, both as observer and as playwright. (p. 12)

It was inevitable that he should write plays—ambitious, full-length pieces, meant to be acted. He wrote also many short and witty parodies and pastiches in dramatic form, but these were clearly meant only for the page and the eye. The earliest of his serious plays belong to a *genre* which, once respectable, now raises qualms, for they were poetic dramas, written in blank verse, full of studied archaisms, operatic situations, lost gallantries, over-significant incantations, and the rest.

He had somewhat better fortune with drawing-room comedies set in his own period and written in the almost telegraphic dialogue which he used in his fiction. Several of these plays had productions in respectable art theatres, but none succeeded, and what is probably his best play, *His Majesty's Embassy,* has never been produced at all—professionally, anyhow.

Max Beerbohm reviewed Baring's play *The Grey Stocking* in the *Saturday Review* on 6 June 1908 [see excerpt above]. . . . He ended his review with the statement that 'Mr Baring gives us deliciously clever sketches of his characters; but he does not give us the full, deep portraits that are needed'.

Actually, in present reading, the play seems to present only one adequately drawn character, Miss Farrer, a novelist with a cult for saying flatly what she thinks, which on principle is the opposite of what everybody else thinks. She puts us in mind of Dame Ethel Smyth, as she weaves in and out of the main idea of the play without actually contributing to it. This is a limp exercise in unhappy marriage, with hopeless and muted love outside it, in a symmetry which seems contrived and undramatic, offering not one but two such situations. We are sure that Baring is referring to people he knows and can talk about; but to animate them on the stage is quite another matter. And yet, 'Some of the scenes in *The Grey Stocking*', wrote Bernard Shaw to Maurice Baring, 'show a very rare sort of dramatic talent' [see excerpt above]. . . . (pp. 12-13)

Another play, *The Green Elephant,* offers an entirely different tone and energy. It is designed after French farce—rapid entrances and exits, wildly involved plot, confusions, lies, intrigues of love and crime concerning jewels stolen at a weekend party in a country house—all laid on with a bare-faced air of plausibility which is naïvely theatrical. The play's action has rather the air of children acting—'being' and 'declaring'—things patently unbelievable, and believed only through a conspiracy of politeness. If his earlier play was formless, this one is over-plotted and too rigidly formalized. Again, only one character, Lady Warburton, seems to contain the breath of life.

In *A Double Game* it is atmosphere which seems to consume the author's available vitality at the expense of other values. It is a play of the revolutionary movement of 1907 in Russia. While it has some dramatic tension, and certainly suggests Baring's love of the Russians and knowledge of their style, the 'Russianism' of it seems synthetic, and the end is a finale in the manner of Chekhov, with a pistol-shot and suicide offstage. Again, the individual characters merely seem to have lines to speak, without the inner energies of life which would make them into genuine creations. (pp. 13-14)

In *His Majesty's Embassy* Baring used materials he knew well, combining the schoolboy antics of junior diplomatic clerks with a hopeless love-affair at ambassadorial level. The play conjures up, out of insistent trivia of the daily diplomatic round, but with the tyrannical and reckless power of all secrets, the central love story, an affair between the British ambassador to Rome and the wife of a sophisiticated member of the Italian Diplomatic Corps. The story is made of heartbreak and helplessness, and convention protects itself, and the train-guard blows his whistle, and on goes the current, sweeping into separate channels the lives that long to come together, however disastrous the brink of the falls waiting ahead. Of this play *The Times* of London said that it was a 'fragment of English life as alive as it is unique'; and we have a hint that in any but a commercially controlled theatre Baring might eventually have achieved recognition as a playwright; for, again, Shaw wrote to Ethel Smyth that 'It was really a calamity that the theatre was incapable of him'. . . . But if he failed in the theatres of the West End of London, Baring left evidence in his published plays of how delicately he could lay back the layers of convention to reveal the passions that society both generated and concealed. (pp. 14-15)

[Baring] wrote poetry from his boyhood onward. At Eton in 1891 he engaged a printer to produce a small volume called *Pastels and Other Rhymes,* containing verses seriously intended, which inevitably, in the tone of a responsive schoolboy, echoed the current styles of Wilde, Morris, and the pre-Raphaelite vision. A booklet of prose, *Damozel Blanche and Other Faery Tales,* printed for him in the same year, was also consciously literary, as its title suggests.

His poetry had only a few themes—the same ones which informed his novels. These were nostalgia, death, love recognized but unrealizable, honour, God's mysterious way and power. Over much of the verse lingers an air of weekendish polite accomplishment, conventional and pallidly felicitous. But the best of it holds true emotion, contained in formal rhymes, stanzas, and metres, yet with an effect of inner freedom which is particularly his own—possibly the metaphor for his life as well as for his art.

His best poetry is to be found in a handful of sonnets; in several long elegies for friends lost in war (written in a flowing form of ode with irregular lines and deliberately simple rhymes which summon up feeling through the effects of simple literate speech); and in a small group of translations of Russian lyrics which survive as English poetry while scholars praise them as suc-

cessful equivalents of Russian originals. Poetry was not Baring's major achievement—and yet his love of the act of poetry, his ingenuousness which was so intuitive as to lie far beyond sophistication, and his vulnerability to true feeling, all entitle him to inclusion among the lesser spirits who have so loved the English language and voice that their proper element can be said to be that of poetry, however small their contribution to the great stream of English verse may be. Valuable as he is as a poet in his best poems, it is in his best novels that his poetic gift most truly rests plain; for what his poems celebrate under strick metrical governance finds its most convincing presence as it hovers insubstantially behind the lines of his prose. He was one of those artists in literature whose quality comes into view not at once but only after a long time and many pages in its presence. The brief lyric and even the funerary panegyric of several pages do not allow this emergence its full opportunity.

His versatility expressed his many responses to be external terms of life, each demanding its characteristic style or medium. Delight in literature required him to compose essays and criticism, impressions and prose sketches, which he gathered in various volumes. His most notable work in literary study is his small book, *An Outline of Russian Literature,* written for the Home University Library Series. Along with the thin volume by Lytton Strachey on French literature, done for the same series, Baring's book on the Russians is a model of its kind. (pp. 15-16)

The last categories of his abundant production—he published almost fifty books—whose air and substance I shall try to suggest are two: the first, his literary jokes; the second, his major novels.

When I say literary jokes I do not mean to suggest offhand japes or mockeries. On the contrary, Baring's literary jokes are to be taken with respect for all the ingenuity, the extended and expert knowledge, and the special sense of fun, out of which they are made. . . . Literature could have its meaning for him as a playful as well as a serious *genre,* and he kept alive into maturity the schoolboy's genius for historical travesty, sublimely wrongheaded construction, and inventive misunderstanding. Much British humour is built upon these foundations; and Baring refined the use of them in a delicious set of nonsense inventions published first in three separate volumes as *Diminutive Dramas, Dead Letters,* and *Lost Diaries,* which he later collected in one volume under the title *Unreliable History.*

Typically in these pieces . . . he took a famous historical or literary situation or set of characters and treated them in the accents of the modern and social condition. The colloquial is imposed on the classical, the suburban upon the historically august, the irreverent upon the sacrosanct; and the results, informed with all the range and penetration of Baring's knowledge, are hilarious to the degree in which the reader shares Baring's culture and its allusions. (p. 17)

There is no point in being pedantic about all this aspect of Baring's multifarious talent, but it is of interest to note that his inspired triflings with solemn matters for the most part had the added interest of good scholarship. (p. 20)

After Maurice Baring's first appearance in print in 1891, thirty years elapsed before he published his first novel, *Passing By.* . . . In the meantime he had worked in all the other forms of writing available to a man of letters, including the prose sketch and the short story. . . . (pp. 20-1)

The Glass Mender is a book of fourteen fairy tales which echoed his youthful study period of living in with a German professor's family at Hildesheim—but made non-Germanic and light to the point of triviality. Almost all of them begin with the words 'Once upon a time' and in their deliberately naïve presentation of little lyric loves in an atmosphere of sadness and perishable beauty they recall the rare and the precious after the manner of the *Yellow Book*. Another book of short inventions in the style of fairy tales was *Orpheus in Mayfair*. These are slender pieces, for the most part artificially symbolic, rather than rewarding for their inherent narrative value or charm of expression. One is a parody of history in the manner of Hilaire Belloc, but here it is only the terrible facts behind the burlesqued subject—the torture and death of Edward II at Berkeley Castle—which lend any meaning to it; and it is also a rare, possibly the only, example of a lapse of taste or sensibility in Baring's work, for the tragedy of Edward does not invite spoofing. He was more generally successful in the book which he called *Half a Minute's Silence and Other Stories,* though many of the stories were reprinted from *Orpheus in Mayfair.* (p. 21)

His novels were generally built around the chronicle of a complete life. His typical ones carry the central character from infancy to death, and in doing so traverse both outer and inner worlds. *C,* a novel of some three hundred thousand words, takes Caryl Bramsley (the title is the initial of his first name, the nickname by which he was always known) through his discoveries in the act of maturing, enlightenment through literature, music and art, and love, sorrow, passion and futility, faith and death. All through this novel, as in many of his others, is woven the pathos of the absolutely certain, young, inexperienced people who are at the mercy of the absolutely forgetful, experienced elders. The strongest themes are those of love and of that inner need for a purpose or at least a grasp in life which answers more than simple material requirements. It is the total architecture of a life that interests him rather than its high-keyed details or moments. He is a novelist with a long view and an enclosing faith. (p. 26)

The lesser novels plays variations on such themes, and several of them suggest in their very titles—*Passing By, Overlooked, The Lonely Lady of Dulwich, Comfortless Memory*—the ingrained melancholy, the sense of detached loss, the hurt regard of life, which linger between the lines of all of Baring's fiction. . . .

If all his novels are love stories, they are all unhappy ones. All his lovers are star-crossed, and this arises, we feel, less out of a story-teller's dramatic necessity than out of an unshakable view of life. Love is the worst thing that can happen, and at the same time it is the only thing worth wanting. (p. 27)

And yet love in Maurice Baring's novels is more often a fatal accident than a blessing. In his anthology, *Have You Anything To Declare?* he quotes a passage from *Don Quixote* which could stand as an epigraph for many of his stories: 'Love is too strong to be overcome by anything except flight, nor ought mortal creature to be so presumptuous as to stand the encounter, since there is need of something more than human, and indeed heavenly, powers to vanquish human passion.' (pp. 27-8)

Behind all the chivalric chastity of the bachelors in his stories who say 'I shall never marry', there is, through sheer weight of their number, a hint that they cherished their self-denial. If they must settle for a memory of love, a love denied by fateful circumstance, even of a love only imagined, it is clear that to the best of their knowledge his people projected an utterly lofty

ideal of life. The novel *Daphne Adeane* is built round the theme of a dead lady so lovely and so much beloved that she remains greatly influential as a memory in many lives. Her power in memory is so great that it seems to be stated with the effect of a principle. The novel is a biography of a *ghost* of love, and of how the echo, its repeated manifestations in later lives, goes on, without change in essence or design for ever and ever. Embodied in others, love itself lives on memory. If it comes too near, all there is to do—Baring quoted the Cervantes passage several times in his works—is to flee it, for otherwise there was no denial possible.

Why to flee? Because for the most of human life, love is a misfortune. (p. 37)

It is Baring's triumph that, in a literary world generally oriented to scepticism, he is able to make religion a matter of reality and importance in his writing. It is for his characters and in the fabric of his world a reality in respect to social condition, a reality in culture, and a reality in what is most significant of all, private conviction. His manners as a Catholic apologist are better than those of other English literary men of his persuasion. He is never bantering or patronizing, like Chesterton, or rude, impatient and contemptuous like Evelyn Waugh, or glumly rebellious, like Graham Greene. He is always delicately respectful of explanations of life that differ from his own; and in fact he is scrupulous to echo the sceptical world's case against the Catholic Church. (p. 41)

The theme of the social difficulties attending Catholicism in upper-class life runs through many of his novels, determining private lives, and wreaking earthly unhappiness in the name of an unearthly happiness certain to come in eternity. But not until his last two novels did he dramatize with full zeal the passionate power of the Catholic cause as a course leading not to private misery and public inconvenience, but straight to martyrdom, executed on the public stage of history. *Robert Peckham* and *In My End Is My Beginning* are historical novels set in Tudor times. The central issue is that which divided England between the old religion and the reformed. Robert Peckham must remain true to Rome, and in the other novel Mary Queen of Scots—for it is her tragic history which is played out there—knows that she goes to her death for her Faith as much as for any other political reason. Here the theological argument is entwined with large issues in history—the arch of events, passions, and varying orthodoxies (political and theological) of the time, and it takes its place as proper to the material and holds us fascinated.

One of the strengths of *Robert Peckham* is that Robert and the others interest us for their own human sake, and as we go with their story we go with the ethical argument which lies at the root of their relationships. Baring makes, as always, a more than intelligent and fair case for the Reformer opposition. The novel follows his familiar diagonals of personal involvement, criss-crossings of love, suppressed, with all but hopeless inner commitments. Honour, retribution, a life-tissue of mistakes, God's law, appear again. In his style for the two novels, he has recourse to only a few repeated archaisms to suggest the period. (pp. 43-4)

[In] his long novel about Mary of Scotland, he gives us an experiment in form—to have four young women of the queen's bedchamber tell her story, covering much the same ground, with the first three coming to a halt just short of the queen's execution; then letting the fourth tell the same story and bring it all the way to its terrible end. The difficulty here is that there is small evidence of any difference in character or style between the four, and whatever variations there are in the narrative, these seldom seem significant. The effect of the book is that of a love song to Mary of Scotland, in four long prose stanzas, and perhaps it is fair to see the whole composition as a late and lavish gesture of that chivalry with which earlier novels celebrated ladies unattainable in life, as this one made love to one unattainable in history. Both in **Robert Peckham** and **In My End Is My Beginning** there are rhapsodic passages about the Queen—everyone had but to see her only once to be ready to die of love for her. Again Baring attempted to animate the historical novel with fresh ideas of form. It does not here succeed, and, though it is a wholly serious work, its 'scholarly' method makes us sight for his much earlier triumphs in 'unreliable history' with their brief, hilarious impersonations of historical persons in their period trappings.

These were among Maurice Baring's last novels. . . . His other, lesser, novels—**Passing By, A Triangle, Darby and Joan, Comfortless Memory, Friday's Business, Tinker's Leave**—give us his familiar virtues and fleeting echoes of an appealing self but without the pressing energy of his fullest use of his material. (p. 45)

In a summary of his career in 1945 *The Times* of London was able to say, 'Time may perhaps confirm the judgement of those who see in him one of the subtlest, profoundest, and most original of recent English writers.' (p. 47)

> *Paul Horgan, "Introduction" (1969), in his* Maurice Baring Restored *(reprinted by permission of Farrar, Straus and Giroux, Inc.; all rights reserved), Farrar, Straus and Giroux, 1970, pp. 1-52.*

EDMUND WILSON   (essay date 1971)

It is possible to read a good deal of Maurice Baring—his poetry, his plays, and many of his novels—and find him thin and insipid. I have had the experience, and I know very well how discouraging this writer can be if one comes to him in the setting of his generation—of Wells and Bennett, of Shaw, Chesterton, and Belloc. . . . He, like them, did a great deal of journalism, yet he belonged to a different world, and it is difficult for the reader not to think of him as an aristocratic amateur. One has to adjust oneself to his constituting a very peculiar case before one is able to see how accomplished and able he was, and to know how to separate the Baring who was interesting from the Baring who may seem a phantom. (p. 77)

I agree in general with Paul Horgan about the relative importance of Baring's works [see excerpt above]. The four departments I would recommend are (I) his eight books about Russia, of which only the two small volumes on Russian literature . . . are still in print. Maurice Baring was perhaps the only Englishman who really knew the country well and who was also an excellent writer. *The Mainsprings of Russia* and *The Russian People* are probably the best surveys of the history of Russia, the best analyses of Russian society that had at that time been published in English. They may seem today a little old-fashioned—the author speaks often of "the Russian soul"—but anyone who is interested in Soviet Russia would find it worthwhile to read them, for written before the collapse of old Russia, they show how this had been led up to and how similar, after all, conditions under the czar were to conditions under the present government. . . . [In his *Landmarks in Russian Literature* and *An Outline of Russian Literature,* as well as in his *Oxford Book of Russian Verse*] . . . , he performed for the

English a service similar to that which that other Russophile from the diplomatic service, the Vicomte Melchior de Vogüé, had done in his pioneering book *Le Roman Russe* in 1886. . . . [Baring] has written the most accurate appreciations of Pushkin that I have ever seen in English.

My second recommendation of the Baring that is worth reading is his long novel called simply *C.* I have read a number of Baring's novels. They all display his intimate knowledge of the international social world, the wide range of his cultural interests, and his dry, end-of-the-century wit. . . . All these books carry one along and hold one's interest to the usually pathetic end. But I have found that I cannot remember most of them only a few days after I have read them. The characters are pale, seem mere names, sometimes hard to distinguish from one another. They are, in fact, so little differentiated that one can rarely recognize the same characters when they turn up in different books. The chronicle of their social life becomes so monotonous and tiresome that one sometimes wonders what effect their creator is aiming at. We are invariably told who all the guests at all the dinners were and who sat next to whom, and a chapter is likely to end, "Then he turned to Lady —— on his left." When Baring wants, as he frequently does, to break off relations between his people, he can always have them shifted to another embassy or make them go somewhere else for their health. Is this due to an obsession on Baring's part with the kind of life he describes? The imputation of being too fond of this life seems to have been the only criticism to which he was at all sensitive—as in his reactions to a letter from Vernon Lee, quoted by Ethel Smyth, and in reproaches to Pushkin for his waste of energy in an addiction to worldly frivolities. We wonder, in reading *Cat's Cradle,* whether the author may not be trying to underline the dreariness of the social life that muffles the tragedy of the heroine. One sympathizes with Vernon Lee when she tells him that she does not find this novel "anything like as good as *C.,*" and continues, "Even the English part seems to me inordinately full of trifling detail without realisation of the chief figures. (The men are all interchangeable.) But—but—but—you have somehow, and perhaps by this very thinness of texture, contrived to give an extraordinary essence of passion; rather like what music gives. . . . Of course I *dislike* your people, personally. I dislike their mixture of footling uselessness and devouring passion (they have *time* for it, as they never do anything but go to parties) and I dislike their (and your) Catholic other-worldliness: I abominate such making light of life and its . . . well! *uniqueness.*" . . . Maurice Baring's principal themes are the Catholic religion and love. Yet we never understand the inevitability of the conversion of the principal characters, or of Maurice Baring himself, and we never can movingly imagine the passionate relations of his lovers, which are invariably buried at such depths of discretion. In *Cat's Cradle,* we wonder why Bernard, who has been so much in love with Blanche, does not pounce on her as soon as he sees her again. But in Baring's novels nobody pounces, any more than the characters are allowed to be seen at moments of religious revelation; nor would the ladies allow themselves to be pounced upon any more than the lovers would be capable of pouncing. Though, at the moment that I am writing, sex is being made so baldly explicit that it ceases to be attractive, we cannot but feel that Baring's novels need at least a touch of Lady Chatterley. They are, however, usually doomed to be long-protracted tales of frustration. The heroine marries the wrong man or is a Catholic and has scruples against getting a divorce, or the hero, as in *The Coat Without Seam,* is unable to bring himself to take advantage of the opportunities offered him. This undoubtedly was one of the causes—as in the case of Henry James, whose lovers are always renouncing—of the lack of popularity of these novels in relation to Galsworthy's or Wells's. And they do not even seem much to have impinged on the consciousness of the literary world, of his brother and sister writers. (pp. 78-83)

Yet *C.* is by far, it seems to me, the best novel of Baring's of those I have read. It contains his two most memorable characters: Leila Bucknell, the irresistible siren and invincibly successful bitch, who manages to be financed by a succession of lovers without losing her position in smart society; and Lady Hengrave, the hero's mother, who represents everything most correct, most self-confident, and most discouraging in the solid upper-class world. Though C. himself, in love with and betrayed by Leila, and tactfully thwarted by his mother, is the invariable Baring hero, delicately responsive to music and poetry, who comes to a sad end, both these ladies are treated with a good deal of humor and are really fine comic creations. (p. 83)

The third department of Baring's writing that I want to commend to the reader is the sequence of burlesques and parodies that he published between 1910 and 1913: *Dead Letters, Diminutive Dramas,* and *Lost Diaries*—later reprinted in one volume as *Unreliable History.* One of the favorite devices here is to make the famous figures of the literature or history of whatever country or period talk and behave like the English characters of Baring's contemporary novels. Thus Catullus's Lesbia, writing from Baiae to a girl friend in Athens, and Charmian, writing of a dinner in Rome, are made to sound exactly like Leila Bucknell, and Lady Macbeth, writing to Lady Macduff, to invite her to stay at the castle and, if possible, bring her little boy, maintains the dignified, friendly tone of Lady Hengrave reasoning with C. to dissuade him from marrying a Catholic (p. 84)

The fourth section of Baring's work that cannot be disregarded is that of his literary criticism, with which must be considered his anthologies. These latter are of a peculiarly personal kind. They include his two volumes of *Algae,* which he subtitled **"Anthologies of Phrases,"** and his late substantial book, *Have You Anything to Declare?,* a compilation of favorite passages from a lifetime of multilingual reading. The *Algae* consist of very short bits of verse and prose from the literatures of eight languages. By isolating these lines and phrases thus and giving each one a page, he lends them a special distinction—as Eliot does the passages he borrows or quotes—of which one may not have been aware if one has met them in rapid reading. Maurice Baring's own poetry is not very impressive. His early lyrics are like old-fashioned undergraduate verse—too many sighs and roses, lilies and asphodels, too much unevocative reference to gold and silver and the sun and the moon and the stars—and his later long elegies on the death of friends and of a nephew, which have sometimes been much applauded, seem to me uninterestingly conventional. Yet in his sonnets one occasionally finds lines which might perhaps satisfy the taste that compiled these fastidious anthologies. . . . (pp. 86-7)

Baring's two collections of essays, *Lost Lectures* and *Punch and Judy,* have, no doubt because their tone seems rather casual, been undeservedly neglected. He is particularly good on French literature. . . . One may not be able to agree with him that La Fontaine is the greatest French poet, but if you want to understand what the French admire in their poetry, you cannot do better than read Baring on Racine of his review of *The Oxford Book of French Verse. Have You Anything to Declare?,* which he calls a "notebook with commentaries," also

shows Baring at his best as a critic. . . . I have read in this book many times. It would, I should think, be worth studying—though not perhaps in a college course—by anyone with literary ambitions. Baring was a fine connoisseur of writing and an excellent guide to style. (pp. 87-8)

[The best of Baring's books,] although infused with a sense of comedy, never carry practical joking and compulsively violent behavior as far as Baring did in his life. . . . He called himself a troll, and I believe that his impulses to do something unconventional at variance with his deadpan appearance were protests against the world of Lady Hengrave and the routines of the country house and of the diplomatic service, in the latter of which he once frightened into collapse one of the women who worked in the office by sending her, compressed in a dispatch box, one of those snakes that pop out. He seems to be protesting thus against his own dignified presence, as he is in his parodies of solemn speeches and official justifications. . . . But this *esprit de contradiction* is usually very quiet and itself appears quite well bred. It is only when one catches its flavor that Maurice Baring becomes entertaining, and only if one responds to what Vernon Lee calls the musical charm of his writing that one can become mildly addicted to Baring. . . . But one remembers him not as the block-like books that fill up the shelves of one's library or as the solid dreams those books project but as the varied conversation, at times almost opalescent, of a very pleasant companion, whom it is always refreshing to listen to, even if one may not always remember exactly what it was he said. (pp. 90-1)

Edmund Wilson, "How Not to Be Bored by Maurice Baring" (originally published in The New Yorker, *Vol. XLVII, No. 31, September 18, 1971), in his* The Devils and Canon Barham: Ten Essays on Poets, Novelists and Monsters *(reprinted by permission of Farrar, Straus and Giroux, Inc.; copyright © 1971, 1973 by Elena Wilson, Executrix of the Estate of Edmund Wilson), Farrar, Straus and Giroux, 1973, pp. 77-91.*

ADDITIONAL BIBLIOGRAPHY

Belloc, Hilaire. *Letters from Hilaire Belloc.* Edited by Robert Speaight. London: Hollis & Carter, 1958, 313 p.
　　Contains a letter to Baring, dated 22 December 1927, finding *French Literature* an "extraordinary" work.

Fremantle, Anne. "'. . . Since Maurice Died'." *Commonweal* XLII, No. 18 (15 February 1946): 446-49.
　　An excellent biographical and critical essay.

Hanighen, Frank C. "The Art of Maurice Baring." *The Bookman,* New York LXXV, No. 4 (August 1932): 321-26.
　　A general critical outline of Baring's theories and technique.

Las Vergnas, Raymond. "Maurice Baring." In his *Chesterton, Belloc, Baring,* translated by C. C. Martindale, S. J., pp. 88-133. New York: Sheed & Ward, 1938.
　　A cogent biocritical essay.

Lovat, Laura. *Maurice Baring: A Postscript.* New York: Sheed & Ward, 1948, 116 p.
　　Contains a glowing memoir by Lady Lovat about Baring, a selection of Baring's verse and letters, a letter on Baring from Princess Marthe Bibesco to Lady Lovat, and Ronald Knox's essay "On the Effect of the Classics on Maurice Baring's Mind," excerpted above.

Marsh, Edward. ''Maurice Baring.'' In his *A Number of People: A Book of Reminiscences,* pp. 65-94. New York, London: Harper & Brothers Publishers, 1939.
  Recounts numerous meetings and conversations with Baring.

Smyth, Ethel. *Maurice Baring.* London: William Heinemann, 1938, 348 p.
  An adoring biography, written by one of Baring's long-time friends. The book reprints several letters from Vernon Lee to Baring; one of which states, ''Your plays at present are like a Handel opera. Three or four divine airs in pages of dull recitative.'' Letters by other notable contemporaries are also included.

Pío Baroja (y Nessi)

1872-1956

Spanish novelist, poet, short story writer, and essayist.

Baroja is the dominant novelist of modern Spanish literature. While critics sometimes place him among the "generation of '98" writers, he himself disclaimed this inclusion. Baroja's sense of individuality also informs his style and approach to his subjects: isolated and cynical. A conflict between vital and antivital aspects of existence appears as a major theme in his work. Paramount to Baroja's vision is the judgment that human nobility is an illusion.

Baroja was born in San Sebastian in the Basque provinces. He studied medicine in Madrid and for a short time was a practicing physician. It was in Madrid that he became familiar with the lowlife degradation so often depicted in his novels, most notably the trilogy *La lucha por la vida*. Throughout his literary career Baroja attracted both accolades and condemnations, even threat of exile, because of the frank and outspoken nature of his works. Baroja was a self-revealing author, and many of his numerous essay collections, including *Juventud, egolatría (Youth and Egolatry)*, are autobiographical in fact, while novels such as *El árbol de la ciencia (The Tree of Knowledge)* are autobiographical in spirit.

Fiction was Baroja's favored genre and his output was extensive. Most of his novels were published in trilogies; those written before 1912 are the most important and convey the life Baroja lived and observed. Baroja's first novel, *La casa de Aizgorri (The House of the Aizgorri)*, is grouped in the trilogy *Tierra Vasco* and is among a series of works that survey Basque culture as it succumbs to vice and industrialization. Also included in *Tierra Vasco* is the novel *Zalacaín el adventurero*, a narrative reviving the picaresque style of Golden Age Spain. Among the novels in his next trilogy, *La vida fantastica, Camino de perfección* features as a protagonist the kind of wandering neurasthenic outcast who is a typically Barojan character type: an idealist who discovers there are no enduring ideals. In *Aurora roja (Red Dawn)*, from the widely acclaimed trilogy *La lucha por la vida*, Baroja again exposes the hopelessness of idealism and the moral impotence of intellectuals. From the trilogy *El pasado*, the novels *Los últimos románticos* and *Las tragedias grotescas* are concerned with Spanish culture in Paris of the 1860s. The trilogy *La raza* consists of *La dama errante*, with its anarchistic interests; *La ciudad de laniebla*, about the Spanish colony in London; and the semiautobiographical *The Tree of Knowledge*. In the works of the trilogy *Las ciudades*, Baroja emphasizes the failings of contemporary society. Representative is the novel *El mayorazgo de Labraz (The Lord of Labraz)*, which serves as a good example of Baroja's frequently displayed power to depict a decayed town and its inhabitants. The most significant work Baroja wrote after 1912 is the multivolume *Las memorias de un hombre de acción*. Aubrey F.G. Bell has stated that the episodes of this opus are "etched with a vividness so intense that they warrant us in placing Don Pio Baroja among the great writers of the Twentieth Century."

Baroja wrote spontaneously and seldom revised his work. Critics often point out that his novels are episodic and loosely

structured. For some this looseness is a positive quality indicating an imaginative and vital temperament, while others find it merely reveals a lack of discipline and a disdain for artistry. Another major critical concern deals with Baroja's characterization. While the influence of the "generation of '98" was to encourage penetration of the "soul" of the individual, Baroja, searching for this soul in Spain, usually found only a sick will, disenchantment, animal hunger, and suffering. These qualities characterize the crowd of outcasts which occur throughout his work. A striking feature of Baroja's work is his contempt for various social institutions, including the family, the Catholic church and the Spanish aristocracy. Baroja made no secret of even his most iconoclastic opinions and throughout his long life he expressed them freely. It is usually this quality of honest spontaneity that earns the highest praise from readers and critics of Baroja's work.

PRINCIPAL WORKS

La casa de Aizgorri (novel) 1900
  [*The House of the Aizgorri*, 1958]
Vidas sombrías (short stories) 1900
Aventures, inventos y mixtificaciones de Silvestre Paradox
  (novel) 1901

Camino de perfección   (novel)   1902
El mayorazgo de Labraz   (novel)   1903
   [*The Lord of Labraz*, 1926]
Aurora roja   (novel)   1904
   [*Red Dawn*, 1924]
La busca   (novel)   1904
   [*The Quest*, 1922]
Mala hierba   (novel)   1904
   [*Weeds*, 1923]
El tablado de Arlequín   (essays)   1904
La feria de los discretos   (novel)   1905
   [*The City of the Discreet*, 1917]
Paradox, rey   (novel)   1906
   [*Paradox, King*, 1931]
Los últimos románticos   (novel)   1906
Las tragedias grotescas   (novel)   1907
La dama errante   (novel)   1908
La ciudad de la niebla   (novel)   1909
Zalacaín el aventurero   (novel)   1909
César o nada   (novel)   1910
   [*Caesar or Nothing*, 1919]
El árbol de la ciencia   (novel)   1911
   [*The Tree of Knowledge*, 1928]
Las inquietudes de Shanti Andía   (novel)   1911
   [*The Restlessness of Shanti Andía* published in *The
      Restlessness of Shanti Andía, and Other Writings*, 1959]
El mundo es ansí   (novel)   1912
Las memorias de un hombre de acción. 22 vols.   (novels)
   1913-35
Juventud, egolatría   (essays)   1917
   [*Youth and Egolatry*, 1920]
Nuevo tablado de Arlequín   (essays)   1917
La sensualidad pervetida   (novel)   1920
La leyenda de Juan de Alzate   (novel)   1922
El laberinto de las sirenas   (novel)   1923
El gran torbellino del mundo   (novel)   1926
Las veleidadas de la fortuna   (novel)   1926
Los amores tardíos   (novel)   1927
Los pilotos de altura   (novel)   1929
La estrella del capitan Chimista   (novel)   1930
Canciones del suburbio   (poetry)   1944
Memorias. 6 vols.   (autobiography)   1944-49
Obras completas. 8 vols.   (novels, short stories, poetry,
   and essays)   1946-51

FEDERICO de ONIS   (essay date 1919)

From the first the literary personality of Pio Baroja has afforded a sharp note of originality which sets him off, not only from all who came before him but from his contemporaries and his successors. At the close of the nineteenth century, when he began to write, the realistic novel in its last phase was still dominant, that type of novel which in twenty-five years had produced in Spain such figures as [Benito Pérez] Galdos, [Juan] Valera, and [José Maria de] Pereda first, and later Paudo Bazan, Palacio Valdea, and Leopolde Aias. . . .

Pío Baroja, Azorin, [Ramon Maria de] Valle-Inclan are the exponents of the diverse forms that the novel has assumed in Spain in the twentieth century.

There is a sharp line of demarkation between the two moments, between the two generations that lived side by side, yet between whom there lies the distance of two epochs. In style and expression, in emotions and vision the second generation represents a profound and violent reaction against the first. The reaction which took place at the end of the century in all the world against the naturalistic novel and the renascence of every subjective tendency, spiritualistic, mystic, and romantic, produced a particularly deep reverberation in Spain, where it was intensified by the national hyperaesthesia brought on by the tragic situation of those years. This group of writers is often called in Spain "the generation of 98," thus uniting this brilliant literary and artistic flowering to the date of the last colonial disaster.

A longing to penetrate into the depths of the soul of the individual and of the nation and to achieve the most honest and sincere form of expression was the only common bond between these men. In all the rest their passionate desire for originality and self-expression started them off in the most opposed directions. . . . Pio Baroja is sincere and ingenuous to the point of cynicism, as spontaneous and natural as though there had never been literature before him. . . .

[His] novels are always a personal expression of the author; the world seen through eyes that are at once childlike and skeptical, sad and humorous. This lyric quality of Baroja is in no way incompatible with his seeing the reality, with his catching the fleeting soul of passing objects, the peculiar tint of the place and the occasion; but always enveloped in and colored by his personality, which views the world through ingenuous yet weary eyes. And throughout his work there runs a philosophy which would be pessimistic were it not for its saving humor.

It can be easily seen from the foregoing that there is a striking similarity between the work of Baroja and that of the Russians. There is in this fact a coincidence, not an influence. Spain and Russia, despite the great differences that exist between them, offer striking similarities. And the individuality which is the dominant note of Baroja's work has not been learned in any school. It has ever been a marked feature of the Spanish character.

Baroja has demonstrated throughout his work a profound sympathy with those beings that show an exaggerated or abnormal development of personality, incapable of associating themselves with others, vagabonds like the adventurers and rogues of old, who wander through life without ever finding quiet or repose; types which Spanish life has always afforded in extraordinary variety and abundance. And the reader of Baroja sees through these erratic, illogical beings an illogical world, a world in which things happen and pass as incessantly as in life itself.

It is therefore idle to seek in his novels a harmonious structure, orderly, rounded and complete. For the spirit of Baroja is as errant as that of his characters; he loves digressing; he delights in details. And in this very fact lies his originality and charm. Some have called these qualities defects, as they have his careless, natural, but vigorous and spontaneous style, when it is precisely these apparent defects that constitute his never-to-be-forgotten enchantment. . . .

["**Caesar or Nothing**"] is perhaps not the best of Baroja's novels, but it is the one which assembles more of the traits and characteristics of the author. There are two parts quite distinct from each other, the first of which takes place in Italy and which has the varied, discursive, almost cinematographic, character which has already been pointed out in Baroja's works; through it there passes a dizzying procession of landscapes, cities, personages, all caught, so to speak, on the wing, in their momentary, fleeting attitude, which have been noted with admirable exactitude, and commented on with a fresh and occasionally cruel humor. The second and, in my opinion, more powerful part occurs in Spain and gives a vivid impression of one of the paralyzed cities, into the crannies of whose soul Baroja has penetrated with acuteness. The leading character, he who would be Caesar or nothing, is one of those types so frequent in Baroja, a mixture of weakness and strength, a man with a sick will. . . .

Any one who wishes to know the soul of Spain of today, or at least one phase of it, the saddest and most pessimistic, perhaps, but not therefore less real, should read carefully the novels of Baroja, which are, at the same time, one of Spain's finest contributions to modern literature.

> Federico de Onís, "Pío Baroja and the Contemporary Spanish Novel," in The New York Times Book Review (© 1919 by The New York Times Company; reprinted by permission), May 4, 1919, p. 257.

JOHN DOS PASSOS (essay date 1922)

The moon shines coldly out of an intense blue sky where a few stars glisten faint as mica. Shadow fills half the street, etching a silhouette of roofs and chimneypots and cornices on the cobblestones, leaving the rest very white with moonlight. The façades of the houses, with their blank windows, might be carved out of ice. In the dark of a doorway a woman sits hunched under a brown shawl. Her head nods, but still she jerks a tune that sways and dances through the silent street out of the accordion on her lap. A little saucer for pennies is on the step beside her. In the next doorway two guttersnipes are huddled together asleep. The moonlight points out with mocking interest their skinny dirt-crusted feet and legs stretched out over the icy pavement, and the filthy rags that barely cover their bodies. Two men stumble out of a wineshop arm in arm, poor men in corduroy, who walk along unsteadily in their worn canvas shoes, making grandiloquent gestures of pity, tearing down the cold hard façades with drunken generous phrases, buoyed up by the warmth of the wine in their veins.

That is Baroja's world: dismal, ironic, the streets of towns where industrial life sits heavy on the neck of a race as little adapted to it as any in Europe. No one has ever described better the shaggy badlands and cabbage-patches round the edges of a city, where the debris of civilization piles up ramshackle suburbs in which starve and scheme all manner of human detritus. . . . Outside of Russia there has never been a novelist so taken up with all that society and respectability reject.

Not that the interest in outcasts is anything new in Spanish literature. Spain is the home of that type of novel which the pigeonhole-makers have named picaresque. These loafers and wanderers of Baroja's, like his artists and grotesque dreamers and fanatics, all are the descendants of the people in the *Quijote* and the *Novelas Ejemplares,* of the rogues and bandits of the Lazarillo de Tormes, who through *Gil Blas* invaded France and England, where they rollicked through the novel until Mrs. Grundy and George Eliot packed them off to the reform school. But the rogues of the seventeenth century were jolly rogues. They always had their tongues in their cheeks, and success rewarded their ingenious audacities. The moulds of society had

not hardened as they have now; there was less pressure of hungry generations. Or, more probably, pity had not come in to undermine the foundations. (pp. 84-7)

Baroja's outcasts are no longer jolly knaves who will murder a man for a nickel and go on their road singing "Over the hills and far away"; they are men who have not had the willpower to continue in the fight for bread, they are men whose nerve has failed, who live furtively on the outskirts, snatching a little joy here and there, drugging their hunger with gorgeous mirages.

One often thinks of Gorki in reading Baroja, mainly because of the contrast. Instead of the tumultuous spring freshet of a new race that drones behind every page of the Russian, there is the cold despair of an old race, of a race that lived long under a formula of life to which it has sacrificed much, only to discover in the end that the formula does not hold. (p. 88)

[Baroja] says in one of his books that the only part a man of the middle classes can play in the reorganization of society is destructive. He has not undergone the discipline, which can only come from common slavery in the industrial machine, necessary for a builder. His slavery has been an isolated slavery which has unfitted him forever from becoming truly part of a community. He can use the vast power of knowledge which training has given him only in one way. His great mission is to put the acid test to existing institutions, and to strip the veils off them. I don't want to imply that Baroja writes with his social conscience. He is too much of a novelist for that, too deeply interested in people as such. But it is certain that a profound sense of the evil of existing institutions lies behind every page he has written, and that occasionally, only occasionally, he allows himself to hope that something better may come out of the turmoil of our age of transition.

Only a man who had felt all this very deeply could be so sensitive to the new spirit—if the word were not threadbare one would call it religious—which is shaking the foundations of the world's social pyramid, perhaps only another example of the failure of nerve, perhaps the triumphant expression of a new will among mankind. (pp. 93-4)

Baroja's most important work lies in the four series of novels of the Spanish life he lived, in Madrid, in the provincial towns where he practiced medicine, and in the Basque country where he had been brought up. The foundation of these was laid by *El Arbol de la Ciencia* ("The Tree of Knowledge"), a novel half autobiographical describing the life and death of a doctor, giving a picture of existence in Madrid and then in two Spanish provincial towns. Its tremendously vivid painting of inertia and the deadening under its weight of intellectual effort made a very profound impression in Spain. Two novels about the anarchist movement followed it, *La Dama Errante,* which describes the state of mind of forward-looking Spaniards at the time of the famous anarchist attempt on the lives of the king and queen the day of their marriage, and *La Ciudad de la Niebla,* about the Spanish colony in London. Then came the series called *La Busca* ("The Search"), which to me is Baroja's best work, and one of the most interesting things published in Europe in the last decade. It deals with the lowest and most miserable life in Madrid and is written with a cold acidity which Maupassant would have envied and is permeated by a human vividness that I do not think Maupassant could have achieved. All three novels, *La Busca, Mala Hierba,* and *Aurora Roja,* deal with the drifting of a typical uneducated Spanish boy, son of a maid of all work in a boarding house, through different strata of Madrid life. They give a sense of unadorned reality very rare in any literature, and besides their power as novels are immensely interesting as sheer natural history. The type of the *golfo* is a literary discovery comparable with that of Sancho Panza by Cervántes.

Nothing that Baroja has written since is quite on the same level. The series *El Pasado* ("The Past") gives interesting pictures of provincial life. *Las Inquietudes de Shanti Andia* ("The Anxieties of Shanti Andia"), a story of Basque seamen which contains a charming picture of a childhood in a seaside village in Guipuzcoa, delightful as it is to read, is too muddled in romantic claptrap to add much to his fame. *El Mundo es Así* ("The World is Like That") expresses, rather lamely it seems to me, the meditations of a disenchanted revolutionist. The latest series, *Memorias de un Hombre de Acción,* a series of yarns about the revolutionary period in Spain at the beginning of the nineteenth century, though entertaining, is more an attempt to escape into a jolly romantic past the realities of the morose present than anything else. *César o Nada,* translated into English under the title of "**Aut Caesar aut Nullus**" is also less acid and less effective than his earlier novels. That is probably why it was chosen for translation into English. We know how anxious our publishers are to furnish food easily digestible by weak American stomachs.

It is silly to judge any Spanish novelist from the point of view of form. Improvisation is the very soul of Spanish writing. In thinking back over books of Baroja's one has read, one remembers more descriptions of places and people than anything else. In the end it is rather natural history than dramatic creation. But a natural history that gives you the pictures etched with vitriol of Spanish life in the end of the nineteenth and the beginning of the twentieth century which you get in these novels of Baroja's is very near the highest sort of creation. If we could inject some of the virus of his intense sense of reality into American writers it would be worth giving up all these stale conquests of form we inherited from Poe and O. Henry. The following, . . . from the preface of *La Dama Errante,* is Baroja's own statement of his aims. And certainly he has realized them.

"Probably a book like *La Dama Errante* is not of the sort that lives very long; it is not a painting with aspirations towards the museum but an impressionist canvas; perhaps as a work it has too much asperity, is too hard, not serene enough.

"This ephemeral character of my work does not displease me. We are men of the day, people in love with the passing moment, with all that is fugitive and transitory and the lasting quality of our work preoccupies us little, so little that it can hardly be said to preoccupy us at all." (pp. 96-100)

> *John Dos Passos, "A Novelist of Revolution," in his* Rosinante to the Road Again *(copyright 1922 by George H. Doran Company; copyright renewed © 1949 by John Dos Passos; reprinted by permission of the Literary Estate of John Dos Passos), Doran, 1922, pp. 80-100.*

SALVADOR de MADARIAGA (essay date 1923)

[With] the same singlemindedness, the same courage, and the same uncompromising fierceness with which Loyola fought for Christ in the sixteenth century, Pio Baroja, born in the nineteenth century, battles for Truth. (p. 112)

[For] Baroja, refinement is on a higher plane than nature, difficult to attain, still more to keep. And thus the carelessness and primitiveness of his style appear at first as the easiest path for a nature poorly gifted with the sense of refinement. This racial characteristic takes in Baroja a certain boorish aspect which is peculiar to his own individual nature. Baroja is a solitary man, and, like most solitary men, he tends to divide the world into two parts: himself, and the rest. Hence an exaggerated, if perhaps unconscious, sense of the importance of his ways and a tendency to strike the world by saying unusually hard things in an unusually hard way. (p. 114)

Were there none but negative features in his style no one would read him. Yet Baroja is widely read and daily gains ground. This, in so far as style is concerned, is due to the fact that in renouncing most of the attractive methods of the literary art, he has gained a freer scope for the intensity and power of his vision. The result is a writing which for directness and simplicity has no rival in Spain. Baroja merely states. . . . There is no doubt in all this, a scruple for truthfulness. . . . [Baroja] came to write his novels in a disconnected succession of short episodes, having no particular rhythm or shape, beginning just anyhow and ending just any way, having no other relations than those between the characters which run through them, and no other unity than a vague continuity in time and the mood of the whole novel which they build up ultimately by their cumulative effect. (pp. 115-17)

Realism is generally the healthy reaction of a community against its own tendency to hide away its more unpleasant aspects. It is therefore but natural that eagerness for truth in a novelist should manifest itself in the emphasizing of the sordid side of reality. The picaresque novels and Baroja have this feature in common. Baroja seems to prefer for his subjects the evils which seethe in an atmosphere of destitution. No other Spanish author has dwelt more frequently and insistently on the peculiar aspect which human nature takes under the grey twilight ever hovering over the borders of hunger. Hunger and poverty were also familiar subjects with the picaresque authors, but how differently treated! For, though picaresque in many of his subjects, Baroja can hardly be described as such if the mood be considered in which he approaches them. The picaresque authors were wholly indifferent to the ethical aspects of the life they depicted. . . . Baroja, on the other hand, is deeply concerned with the ethical monstrosity of the horrors which he illustrates. Nor is his concern due to any hard and fast theory of conduct. On ethics his ideas seem to be as fluid, nay, as confused, as in all other realms of human thought. What troubles him is not sin but suffering. It is the sight of humanity dishonoured by disease, divided by crime and brute authority, left to her weakness, tricked by nature, exposed to the animal shame of hunger. (pp. 117-18)

[Baroja is] a repressed sentimentalist, who refuses to show his feeling, partly from pride, partly from timidity, partly from a self-conscious fear of the ridicule attached to sentiment in a country in which fire is more prized than water. But though not expressed nor even admitted, feeling is there as it were in an undercurrent, or rather in a parallel current. (p. 119)

There is in Baroja's latent protest against the sufferings of children and animals a touch of irritation at the irrationality of a world in which such things can happen. It is a mere heightening of his general attitude to all evil, due partly to a sentimental cause—his special solicitude for the victims—partly also to a logical cause—that, in the case of defenceless and innocent victims, the monstrosity and uncalled-for character of evil is most repellent. . . . This earnestness of his outlook, and the uncompromising way in which he keeps to his level and refuses to waste time on minor matters, constitute the positive element of his art. We go to Baroja knowing that his novels deal with acts and motives that matter. We go to him knowing that, right or wrong, he is sincere, and that no tradition, no prejudice, no social respect will prevail upon his sense of truth.

And yet, having read him with more respect than real pleasure, we come to the conclusion that there is something unsatisfactory about his work. Our first objection may be summed up in one word: disorder. . . . [The] mere examination of his style brings us to the conclusion that it is the expression of a mind which has little natural clearness and little also of that acquired clearness which is at bottom what we understand by 'culture'. (pp. 119-21)

Baroja is far from being an ignorant man. Not only does he possess the professional knowledge of a doctor of medicine, but he has read widely, scientific as well as philosophic and literary books, both old and new. Yet, despite all this reading, he can hardly be described as a cultured man. There is something in his nature which seems to be as rebellious to culture as it is to refinement. It is probably that same incapacity for following up first inspirations, impressions, thoughts, and weaving them into a complex unity. (pp. 121-22)

There is a pride in him which leads him to minimize or ridicule, or both, whatever force he feels he does not possess. And in his curious antagonism towards France we may perhaps find the root of his refractoriness to culture. France is one of the favourite objects of his scorn. . . . In France, by the action of centuries of refinement, the world is naturally seen in an intellectual order which gives a majesty and a harmony to what otherwise would be a chaos as formless, if as lively, as one of Baroja's novels. This capacity for intellectual vision has been denied Baroja, and the lack of it is apparent not only in the loose texture of his style and in his utter lack of all sense of composition, but also in a certain feeling of helplessness which is never absent from the intellect that has not found its bearings as from the heart that has not found its faith. (pp. 122-23)

His hatred for priests and all kinds of religion can only be compared superficially with that shallow rationalism which the indiscriminate spread of so-called education tends to foster in Spain as elsewhere. . . . Now, this irritation itself belongs to the religious, not to the 'cultural' or scientific order, which of itself is dispassionate and calm. Hence an amusing discord within Baroja's attitude towards religion and its ministers. For while he dismisses the one and the other as vestiges of error and superstition, he does so in a manner which strangely resembles that which it means to disown. But of these contradictions between manner and substance, between thought and the vital texture of thought, the Basque race in general and Baroja in particular, present abundant examples.

Deprived of a religious explanation of the world, Baroja turns to science. . . . This idea of reason as the guiding light of the world of men is expanded by Baroja to embrace all nature, and results in a picture in which every stone, tree, animal, star, man, voices his own point of view. Yet here, in his scientific mood, no less than in his creative capacity, Baroja fails to unite, to make a whole out of his cacophony of separate voices. As a thinker no less than as an artist he remains in the first stage of perception, a recorder of disconnected facts. (pp. 123-25)

[This] results from that all-important deficiency in Baroja's character as an artist: his utter lack of lyrical power. . . . Baroja [reveals] an underworld of anti-poetical feeling similar to his feelings against religion and against France—three revelations respectively of his lack of poetry, of religion, and of refinement. . . . He is genuinely sensitive, not merely aesthetically, but humanly and ethically so. He is, indeed, far more sensitive as a man than as an artist. Yet, he is loveless. His sensitiveness is purely receptive and never results in an outgoing flow of feeling. It adds to his burden of pain—a pain in which the physical and the mental elements predominate over the emotional; but it never brings him any pleasure. His reaction to nature's sights and doings, particularly to those of human nature, is we feel, a kind of shrinking, as of a nerve that is being irritated by an experimenter; never of that expanding quality which is the privilege of great, all-embracing hearts. He carries into his views of love that unfortunate absorption by the physical which is the hallmark of his medical studies and tends to degrade all affection to the level of disease or of vice. His attitude towards women is free and masterful enough when he deals with the lowest types of feminine degradation. But when he attempts to rise higher in the spiritual scale he is awkward, distant, and scornful, with an undercurrent of repressed irritation always ready to burst out into the open. True to his physiological interpretation of man-and-woman love, he seems to incline towards [a] type of masculine, headstrong woman. . . . It is this absence of all sense of love, whether human or divine, which dries up the springs of poetry in Baroja. Feeling is there and moves darkly in the recesses of his being. But he will not let go. He is a grown-up man, an Arch-European, believing in reason and no sentiment. And as he thinks more of what he is than of what he would fain feel if only he dared, poetry in him is stillborn. (pp. 125-26)

Salvador de Madariaga, "Pio Baroja," in his The Genius of Spain and Other Essays on Spanish Contemporary Literature *(reprinted by permission of Oxford University Press), Oxford University Press, Oxford, 1923, pp. 111-27.*

G. D. EATON (essay date 1925)

[*Red Dawn*] is good, to me, for several reasons, not the least of which is that it exposes the vapidity of intellectuals when they attempt to thresh out their ideas and theories before each other. Baroja, with his conceptions—superior as they are—has doubtless suffered confusion, like the characters in his book, when his anarchical views have come into conflict with views of persons of similar kidney.

The book exposes, too, the futility of the idealist who would save mankind, the heartbreak which surely must beset this sort of man, and the advantage which schemers inevitably take of his deep kindliness.

The propaganda in the work is merely that of urging persons to be restless, whether as anarchists, socialists, nihilists, or what not. No specific end has Baroja in sight—only an aim. He believes in nothing as absolute and, save for his militancy, is a brother to the late Anatole France. Baroja's exposition of the various theories of various groups shows the infinite and hopeless conflicts of such theories. His one approach to a fairly conclusive truth comes from the mouth of a character, on the attaining of liberty: "First by money. Then by thinking."

The narrative is utterly without coherence until the last hundred pages. The scene shifts amazingly and without apparent reason. (p. 443)

Too often, I have felt, in the presence of foreigners, that they occupied another branch of the philogenetic tree, that they were tangibly different from my American friends and neighbors (although I know better). What a feeling of strangeness comes over me when I see, for instance, a group of swarthy Spaniards, large-headed and black-eyed! They seem another species. In Baroja's books, as in stories by Maupassant, as in Balzac's "César Birotteau," I forget the strangeness. "El Madrileño" becomes John Smith and the foreign flavor is gone. Yes, the flavor is gone, but the common delectable salt of all humanity remains. (pp. 443-44)

> *G. D. Eaton, "A Propagandist Novel," in* The Saturday Review of Literature *(copyright © 1925 by Saturday Review; all rights reserved; reprinted by permission), Vol. 1, No. 24, January 10, 1925, pp. 443-44.*

JOHN T. REID (essay date 1937)

There are many difficulties involved in the investigation of the social ideas of Pío Baroja; principal among them is one inherent in any attempt to trace the opinions of a writer who is primarily a novelist—the task of determining to what extent the author expresses himself through his characters. . . . In his novels are scores of strange individuals who flicker momentarily on the scene, sketched only in coarse outline, and then slip rapidly away. Others are more fully portrayed and seem to express in their spiritual struggles and meditations the author's own efforts to see a confused world clearly. Generally speaking, these are the characters which one must follow in order to arrange a compendium of Baroja's social thought. When their experiences and reactions are checked against those which Baroja has elsewhere avowed as his own, we see that certain of his protagonists are more or less faithful mouthpieces of their creator; especially is this true of Andrés Hurtado (*El árbol de la ciencia*), Luis Murguía (*La sensualidad pervertida*), Fermín (*Los visionarios*), Larrañaga (*Las agonías de nuestro tiempo:* trilogy), and, to a lesser extent, César (*César o nada*).

A second obstacle in the path of presenting an integrated outline of Baroja's social ideology is that of the real and apparent inconsistencies which often occur in his opinions. (pp. 60-1)

[There is an affinity between Baroja] and one of his favorite authors, Friedrich Nietzsche. It is probable that many of the contradictions in Baroja result from a desire to imitate the critical method of the German philosopher. . . . [It] seems evident that his inveterate habit of opposing the commonplace, regardless of consistency, is borrowed to some extent from his German predecessor. (p. 62)

Pío Baroja, although he disclaims connection with the so-called Generation of 1898, is no exception to the predominantly destructive spirit current among the end-of-the-century critics. Almost unanimously his commentators have agreed that one of the unchanging factors of his work, if not the main factor, is his rebellious custom of tearing down. (p. 64)

Baroja is not always consistent in an unreserved faith in the role of science in the future of the human race. He realizes that the naïve reliance on the boundless virtue of the scientific method alone is too simplified an approach to the solution of human problems. There is apparently a conflict in his mind between the claims of the intellectual way of science and truth and the vital way of illusion and opportunism, which is most graphically set forth in *El árbol de la ciencia*. This novel is

almost a spiritual autobiography, as Baroja himself points out. (p. 68)

In spite of his vacillations of confidence in the value and application of the scientific method, Baroja's net attitude is one of respect and faith, especially when the method of science and that of religion conflict: "This is the characteristic thing about the Basque novelist: to oppose religion and science, and to value science far above any religion or attitude of religious mysticism." (p. 71)

In such pronouncements about modern mechanical progress, he identifies himself with a current prevalent in modern thought, liberal and otherwise. (p. 75)

In spite of his violent rejection of liberalism as it has been embodied in Spanish political thought, Baroja nevertheless claims to be a true liberal in his fashion: "I have been and am a liberal and an undisciplined individualist." He carefully separates what he considers the wheat from the chaff in his concept of liberalism. I have already stressed his preference for its destructive side. In so far as liberalism attacks the social system of the past in Spain and fights organized religious prejudices, Baroja favors it. As long as liberalism is the aggressive critic of the status quo, he stands with it; but as soon as it becomes established in power and attempts to realize its constructive aims, such as parliamentary democracy, Baroja parts company with it in disgust. (p. 79)

Liberty is almost a keynote in the writings of Baroja. Primarily it is not a liberty of legal formulas, but a personal independence, a fierce, anarchistic desire to be free from constraint, to do as he pleases, untrammeled by any human institution: "The only blessing that man has is liberty; the more the better." (p. 80)

[Baroja also believes there] should be a government of the intelligent, those who are conscious of the needs and conditions of their country, over the nonintelligent: "In this way we would have an absolutism of the intelligent over the nonintelligent, of those spirits which have reached a high stage of development over those who are lazy or asleep." (p. 83)

How can Baroja reconcile a dictatorial ideal with his expressed love of liberty? He realizes this conflict when he says: "From a human point of view the perfect society would be one which would defend the interests of the country as a whole and yet, at the same time, make room for individual interests; one that would give the individual the advantages of work in common and the most absolute liberty; one which would multiply the individual's chances for work and give him personal independence. This would be a good and a just system."

The details of achieving an equilibrium of this sort, so eagerly sought by modern Liberals, are lacking, unfortunately, in the work of Pío Baroja. (p. 85)

By democracy Baroja means, not a spirit of genuine helpful love for all humanity, but the political system which tends to give the reins of government to the masses, resulting in the "absolutism of numbers." (p. 86)

Like all good individualists, Baroja also fears the tendency of socialism to make of the state a dominating and oppressive machine. (p. 95)

Setting aside the question of the faults and virtues of socialism, Baroja has said on more than one occasion that some form of collective organization on socialistic lines is the inevitable outline of the future state: ". . . I imagine that the future will be socialist; but, in spite of this, I feel a profound dislike for socialist doctrines.'' (pp. 97-8)

Becoming still more practical, he states that communism cannot be feasible in Spain now, because Spain is surrounded by capitalist countries which would immediately pounce on a communist Spain and crush it. With all these factors in mind, Baroja concludes that communism "in a country such as Spain would be absolute misery."

His judgment of communism is of peculiar importance in relation to his liberalism, since there is a tendency among some commentators to feel that the greatest conflict at present in social thought is one between the two systems. . . . (p. 102)

[Radicalism] in Spain has frequently assumed the characteristic form of anarchism rather than socialism. As a careful observer of the Spanish scene Baroja has shown that both the theory and the practical results of anarchism have a powerful fascination for him. Nearly all of his books contain references to it, and several are concerned directly with a kind of anatomy of anarchism. In one of the latter, *Aurora roja,* he provides in fictional form a conscientious and detailed study of the movement and its representatives. It will clarify this discussion if I summarize his classification of the anarchists as he has known them in Spain.

First he describes the rebellious individual, the philosophical anarchist, who, by either nature or intellectual conviction, is irked by authority. He cares little about concrete economic problems, and his protest is entirely personal and egoistic. The second type is the humanitarian anarchist, represented by one of the main figures of the novel, Juan, an artist. His anarchism arises from a sincere sympathy for the misery and suffering of the poor and oppressed; it is directed by sentiment, emotion, and a religious faith in the goodness of man if loosed from the shackles of authority, rather than by the intellect. It results in a passionate hatred of any and all authority; he dreads socialistic as well as capitalistic regulation and repression. He will go to any lengths of terrorism and destruction to further his dream of an altruistic, completely free society. The third type is the opposite extreme, the anarchist with parliamentary inclinations, who is really more of a Republican than an anarchist; he wants to formalize the anarchist meetings and talk politics. The last type belongs to the lunatic fringe; he is the insanely destructive anarchist whose aim is annihilation, without any fixed ideal to motivate him.

The program of individual terror and violence, represented in the last kind of anarchist described, is the tenet of anarchism most obviously repugnant to the average citizen. There is no doubt of Baroja's censure of this procedure. In *Aurora roja* he gives a terrible and vivid picture of one of the numerous anarchist bomb outrages in a Barcelona theater. Manuel, the novel's principal character, as he sees the dead and the dying writhing in blood and agony, exclaims that the perpetrators are fully as base and despicable as the cruelest exploiters. Propaganda by violence, according to Pepe Morales, is nothing more than a crime. Acceptance of such principles could justify the violence of the worst bandit or despot. (pp. 102-03)

[But the] chief reproach which Baroja casts at anarchism in Spain is based on different grounds. Even more than those of socialism or communism, the doctrines of anarchism are a religious dogma: "Really the only revolutionary philosophy today among the masses is the anarchist; but the anarchist philosophy is instinctive, dependent on the sentiments, and it

assumes the character of a religious dogma, which is absurd and childish.'' (pp. 103-04)

However, his objections to the anarchist mode of thought do not constitute a blanket condemnation. There are two factors in their ideology which command sympathy from him: the sincere, self-denying love of humanity which he says is characteristic of some anarchists; and their function as implacable critics of existing institutions. (p. 106)

With these somewhat eclectic judgments about anarchism before us, it is not easy to dismiss Baroja bluntly as an anarchist without qualification, as some critics have done, or to state categorically what his net attitude is toward the anarchist doctrines. (pp. 108-09)

While Baroja rejects democracy, republicanism, socialism, communism, and anarchism in their present crystallized forms as acceptable solutions for the social future, he is not indifferent to the poverty and misery which in principle are the *raison d'être* of these movements for change. . . . In his trilogy *La lucha por la vida,* Baroja draws a detailed and naturalistic picture of the suffering and hopelessness in the tenement districts of Madrid. Sick, drunken men, quarreling women, prostitutes, filthy beggars, all pass in sordid procession; as a contrast we see elegant dandies who laugh and joke with the prostitutes, indifferent to the sordid poverty everywhere.

In *La ciudad de la niebla* the author gives a pathetic description of the downtrodden social outcasts in London, the capital of one of the countries which has supposedly advanced most. . . .

In the pages of one of his more recent novels, *Los visionarios,* there are numerous references to the deplorable conditions of the Andalusian agricultural workers. . . . (p. 111)

While he is occasionally pessimistic about the underlying spirit of slavery among the poor, he generally places the blame for their miserable condition squarely on the social injustice of our civilization. (p. 112)

One of his favorite targets is the Spanish aristocracy. Although no advocate of democracy, as we have seen, Baroja feels that the aristocrats and pseudo aristocrats contribute nothing to Spanish society and are useless and undesirable, a race of incapable degenerates and alcoholics, lacking in culture, intelligence, and, worst of all, in directive social intelligence. (pp. 112-13)

A social hierarchy is necessary, but it should be a rational one, not made up of corrupt *nouveaux riches.* Culture, which Baroja deifies, is aristocratic; the cat, which he also admires, is an aristocratic animal; but it is the aristocracy of talent and intelligence to which he refers. (p. 113)

Thus far the discussion of Baroja's ideology has been chiefly concerned with his attitude toward the general outline of liberalism and the political theories related to it. What does he say about the more specific problems which have been integrally connected with liberal programs? (p. 114)

A concern for the social freedom of women is often regarded as a tenet of neo-liberalism. . . . In Spain the emancipation of women from conventional limitations is complicated by the particularly strong tradition which determines the sphere of woman's activities and by the intense devotion of Spanish women to the Catholic Church. (p. 117)

What must be done, thinks Baroja, is to educate women to collaborate in the problems of society outside the home: "Neither man nor woman should impose their respective points of view on life. Any society which attempts to eliminate the influence of women is an anomalous one. In Spanish society woman is kept in the home; she is not allowed to exercise the influence of her intelligence or her heart, and the result is that she dominates through her baser instincts.

"And this is what must be avoided. In order to avoid it, it is necessary to *secularize* woman, take her out of the cloister of the home, where she conspires against human progress, make of her a collaborator instead of an enemy."

He realizes that this would be no easy task. Spanish women are hedged about with so many agelong traditions that persistent, tireless effort will be necessary to change things. Further, emancipation will not destroy the home, as many claim; rather will it strengthen its solidarity with bonds of sympathy and understanding. The home and the family, as they have existed, are in Baroja's view by no means perfect institutions: "The family, like all human institutions, has been a fountainhead of repression, injustice, and sorrow." In particular, Baroja has objected to the so-called "double standard." He fails to see why marital infidelity should be considered a minor sin for a husband and a crime for a wife. Although mutual tolerance and pardon can be the way out of many marital conflicts for the chosen few, divorce should be possible as a logical and sensible procedure. Birth control, which has encountered strong opposition in Catholic Spain, appears also to Baroja to be an aid to marital felicity. (pp. 118-19)

In spite of the desire that Baroja has shown to change the status of women in Spain, he has been very frank in his criticism of certain trends which the feminist movement has taken. He complains that whereas many women have thrown off their old modesty and are living in a freer moral manner, instead of thereby deepening their intellectual and artistic life they are reducing themselves to nothing more than personified sexual desire. (p. 120)

[Baroja's] agnostic attitude naturally makes him an enemy of the Church as a repository of absolute truth. . . .

Following a nineteenth-century tradition, exemplified in Herbert Spencer and Thomas Huxley, Baroja states that science has undermined the foundations of religion. Even in rural Spain, where Catholicism is so strong, he contends that half the believers would desert the Church if scientific theories were popularized among them. Science is clear, confident, constructive; religion is mysterious and obscure. (p. 127)

Fear and reverence for God are emotions which Baroja professes never to have felt, and, echoing Nietzsche, he considers the fear of the Christian for his God a sign of slavery. He also follows the German philosopher in his detestation of the doctrine of original sin. Such a dogma cannot be in harmony with scientific thinking, which envisages an evolution of man from an anthropoid to his present status, rather than a retrogression from a primitive state of purity to one of inherent evil.

In regard to many aspects of the ritual of the Catholic Church Baroja displays not only disapproval but also considerable irreverence. (pp. 127-28)

[A] phase of religion which provokes his ire is its morality, both theoretical and practical. . . . Vice is really ridiculous to a clear-minded person, and had the Church not put an aura about it everyone would simply scoff at it. . . .

Especially in the realm of sex Baroja insists that the Christian idea of sin has led to prostitution and all its horrors. Eroticism

and exaggerated sexual appetites he believes should be considered not as moral sins but rather as abnormalities to be treated scientifically. (p. 129)

Whatever his judgment of the doctrines and representatives of the Church may be, a more important point in relation to Baroja's liberalism must, of course, be his view of the position of the Catholic Church relative to the social problems of Spain. Like the typical Spanish anticlerical, he habitually links the Church, the Army, and the wealthy bourgeois State together as the hateful triumvirate, the target of the nineteenth-century radical tradition. (p. 136)

The respect for tradition which is fostered by Catholicism, Baroja says, often stands in the way of progress through scientific evaluation of the bases of our society; not all that is traditional is bad, but the Church's accent on traditionalism excludes the possibility of intelligent selection of the good from the bad. He adds that the power of the Church in Spain is one of the main causes for the decadent state of the country; its baneful influence is most clearly seen in the rural villages. The peasants live in misery and poverty partly because they support starched Church dignitaries in Spain and in Rome. While the poor die of hunger, the ceremonies of the Church continue in heedless splendor. In the Basque provinces, the Carlists and the Jesuits have wrought havoc with the people: "In the rural villages they have driven out the natural kindness of the peasants, they have dried up their imagination and filled them with bad ideas." . . . Above all, Baroja says, the Catholic tradition has stultified thought in Spain and failed to encourage wide and independent reading. (pp. 137-38)

> *John T. Reid, in his* Modern Spain and Liberalism: A Study in Literary Contrasts *(reprinted with the permission of the publishers, Stanford University Press; copyright 1937 by the Board of Trustees of the Leland Stanford Junior University; copyright renewed 1965), Stanford University Press, 1937, 236 p.**

ANTHONY KERRIGAN   (essay date 1959)

Despite his nearly one hundred novels, there are some grounds for believing that Pío Baroja was not a novelist at all. He began publishing in the first years of this century, and the two books that appeared that year were *Vidas sombrías* (a collection of short stories), and *The House of the Aizgorri* (a "Novel in Seven Acts"—a novel in dialogue form, or play). His last books were the seven volumes of *Memoirs,* and in writing them he availed himself of whole sections taken from his works of fiction, for his novels were of the same stuff as the chronicle of his own history—his lived life or "novel of himself," as Ortega would have called it.

Late in his career, Baroja also issued a first book of verse, *Canciones del suburbio* ("Songs of the Suburb"), a book which Azorín calls a condensation of his originality, and which Cela considers an index of the man and his style and the single best book by which to know him.

Between the first and last books were the dozens of novels. But were they, after all, of any more homogeneous an order than the final *Memoirs* or the first novel in dialogue? Baroja's novels characteristically lack all novelistic development, or argument, or plot. (pp. 17-18)

In Baroja, the trajectory of a voyage, or a choreographic wandering—transposed from the Spanish picaresque narrative along with the traditional running social criticism—is likely to be the only impelling force. Characters appear and many never reappear. There are stories within the story which dwarf the original narrative. Apart from the predisposition of the Generation of '98 to subordinate the totality of the plot to the peculiarity of the individual, there is in Baroja a willfulness in the characters that makes them act with an omnipotent near-blindness. Only in certain of the Basque stories does Baroja achieve the insight expressed by Antonio Machado, the poet of the generation:

> The eye you see
> is not an eye because you see it
> but an eye because it sees you.

The reciprocity between the characters present in Unamuno in the form of mutual anguish or concern is absent in Baroja. And yet the differences between Baroja and the other writers of '98 are matched by more important similarities.

Baroja's man of action—or often man of activity, for his ceaseless action may be only conversational or at best conspiratorial (in the words of Ortega, "Thinking can be action, while the movement and tussle in sports, for instance, are no part of action")—is the fictional counterpart of Ortega's man becoming what he is by his enforced acting in the world. In Baroja the struggle of the hero to be, to impose himself on chaos, is the equivalent of the moral need to act in Ortega. Fullfilment in action against or in one's circumstance, the conscious transformation of reality, is the climactic point in Ortega's thought and in Baroja's novels. The stag clearing its way through the woods as it (almost aesthetically) flees, the hound extending itself as it pursues, the hunter spiritually "beside himself" in the electrically enlivened landscape: this is the moment of decisive being, or "vital reason" in Ortega's philosophy, and it is toward this paradigm that Baroja strives, though he constantly and wryly lets us see that his heroes are never quite up to their own ideal of action. And if, as similarly occurs in Sterne's *Tristram Shandy*, despite endless coming and going the hero is never fully born or never born to any purpose, there is nevertheless a verisimilitude of action which serves as well as life to test the circumstance of would-be heroes.

In the sense of an elaboration, there is no "style" in Baroja, his style being an attempt to bypass rhetoric in order to reach the things described. And Baroja is as sure-footed as a goat in choosing his ground and his stepping stones.

It is with the element of style which is selectivity that Baroja is most sensitive and most decisive. His dramatic end he achieves by understatement. What he chooses to say is a résumé of the unsaid, and his characters are sketched with the rapidity of a sharp-eyed master draftsman. His visual approach is that of an artist filling his sketchbook. The Madrid books are triumphs of a black and white technique; the Basque books have pages of subtle water color and occasionally the larger composition of a colorist working in oils.

The poetry of his prose is quickened by his pantheistic feeling for nature; there is a Celtic peopling of the forests and watercourses, a druidical awe before trees and rocks. In *Shanti Andia* the Basque coast is alive with titanic struggle and microcosmic forces, and natural description tends toward verse: "The brackish seaweed forms into skeins like long leashes, and bladderwrack and jellyfish shimmer in the sand." Luis Navascués puts into English a line from *Camino de perfección* which typifies Baroja's naturalism: "What a beautiful poem the bishop's body in a peaceful field!"

His first book, the collection of short pieces, many of which were written while he was a village doctor at Cestona and some of which were published in Salmerón's republican paper, was, like James Joyce's *Dubliners,* both a gallery of frustrated figures and a prelude that stated a number of themes in the compositions to follow. Like *Dubliners,* which was written (though not published) in the same years, the stories were typically without plot, and they were written in the same atmosphere of melancholy stultification. Baroja's Madrid loafer "expects nothing from anyone," and "probably has few friends, perhaps none—a sign of intelligence." The heroes of **"The Bakers"** bicker and quarrel at the funeral of one of their number. The sky in **"The Charcoal Maker"** is like a "gray winding sheet waving in the wind," and the charcoal maker himself, high in the Basque mountains, throws stones blindly down into the valley when he hears that he is to be drafted. And **"The Master of the Cage,"** who is God, is deafened by caged mankind. The author records pointless deaths and even more senseless lives with a late-Romantic pessimism and disenchantment. In the Basque stories . . . , Baroja adumbrated the writing that would deal with nature and men in the land of his birth. (pp. 18-20)

> Anthony Kerrigan, *"The World of Pío Baroja,"* in The Restlessness of Shanti Andia and Other Writings *by Pío Baroja (copyright © by the University of Michigan 1959), University of Michigan Press, 1959, pp. 3-30.*

SHERMAN H. EOFF　(essay date 1961)

[There are] two major aspects of [Baroja's] philosophical outlook, the one indicating a forced acceptance of an unhappy lot and the other expressing an undying aspiration. . . .

He was a writer of modest ambitions and modest claims, content to express his sharp criticism and his whimsical musings in simple, unpretentious tales. He utilized a great variety of vantage points from which to observe the human race but in no single work did he plunge deeply into a chosen subject. It has seemed proper, therefore, . . . [to discuss] two novels which, taken together, may be considered a fairly accurate account of Baroja's essential outlook: *El árbol de la ciencia,* which is predominantly reflective, and *Zalacaín el aventurero,* which is predominantly fanciful. With widely differing emphasis the novels illustrate respectively two fundamental aspects of Baroja the novelist: the gloomy philosopher and the dreamer. (p. 166)

In [*El árbol de la ciencia*] the problem of personal orientation in life overwhelms the central character, whose quest for a satisfying philosophy is fraught with disillusionment. The story of Andrés Hurtado is in a sense an account of social maladjustment. In a sense, too, the novel is autobiographical, for it reflects the author's own unhappy experience as medical student and practicing physician for the period of a few youthful years. (p. 167)

In his efforts to solve his problem from a rational approach, Andrés begins with Kant's reasoning on the question of reality. Holding long discussions with his doctor uncle, Iturrioz, which make the novel seem at times like an essay rather than a narrative development, he arrives at a logical, if uncomfortable, concept of the individual's destiny. He accepts Kant's conclusion that we cannot know what lies beyond phenomena and that knowable reality exists only in the individual mind. But he cannot agree with Kant's insistence upon the necessity for directing one's life as though the presence of a benevolent God or Law were provable. Instead, he declares that "After Kant, the world is blind." . . . Life is uninteresting because it holds no ''future'' for the individual, who exists only as a momentary flash of intelligence, an incidental excrescence of matter, and then disappears into nothingness. The fundamental conflict in Andrés is between a materialistic concept of the universe and a desire to believe in the importance of individuality as a dignified and undying reality. If the subjective values necessary to the second concept cannot be honored, life is indeed boring.

The big question for Andrés to answer, then, is what to do with his life, believing as he is compelled to believe that he has little significance in the universe when considered as an individual. There are, in the opinion of Iturrioz, only two possible solutions for a man who would maintain his peace of mind: either an abstention from life, and an indifferent contemplation of everything, or limited action within a small area. The second of these two solutions is a semiactive, or semipassive, stand which allows the individual to indulge his idealistic impulses, thus partially countering his boredom, without falling victim to the folly of opposing the general rule of a materialistic universe. Andrés, whose reading of Schopenhauer has inclined him decidedly toward inactivity, chooses a course of limited action, making a modest affirmation of individuality by carrying out the practice of medicine. (pp. 167-69)

After a period of tentative, unenthusiastic participation, Andrés makes one major effort to plunge decisively and optimistically into the stream of life—to engage himself, as one would say about a Sartrian protagonist. He does so by marrying Lulú. . . . Andrés' wife dies at the birth of a son, and he, once more overwhelmed by the ruthlessness of life, commits suicide. He has reached for the illusion of happiness and succumbs before the vision of a muddy life stream conjured up under the shadows of the tree of knowledge. (p. 170)

The dreamworld aspect, which comes to view in *El árbol de la ciencia* with just enough countercharge to endow the tragedy of individuality with dignity if not with stalwart heroism, assumes a dominant position in *Zalacaín el aventurero*. Somber philosophical thought in this novel is to be detected largely by inference, but if we keep in mind the author's strong philosophical bent, as seen in *El árbol de la ciencia* and many other stories, its presence can be felt hovering over the whole like an invisible cloud. The somberness is couched in a decided lyricism that converts the story into a soft recollection and suggests above all else a philosophical concept of time. Like other writers of his day, Baroja is oppressed by thoughts of a natural process grinding its way through endlessly recurring cycles toward no apparent end or purpose. In addition to this nineteenth-century biological orientation, he also reflects a prominent trend in which naturalistic emphasis shifts from physiology and psychology to more abstract subjects. (p. 172)

Within a short period following the publication of his *Evolution créatrice* in 1907, [Henri] Bergson was widely known and discussed; and since he was a very influential philosopher in the early part of the century, especially in his antirationalistic bent, it is only natural that we think of him when dealing with a novel of that epoch that raises the question of human experience viewed as duration. *Zalacaín el aventurero* by Pío Baroja is just such a novel, and although one would be mistaken to confine it within a close relationship to Bergsonian or any other philosophical thought, it can be profitably appraised in the light of Bergson's *Matière et mémoire*. The relationship is to be found in the observation of two aspects of time: one, exhibiting a multiplicity of moments or occurrences as perceived in the world of ordinary experience; the other, underscoring memory or spirit, the immaterial world which is re-

moved from perception and action in the direction of dream. In Baroja's novel the first aspect impresses itself in the narration of a rapid succession of loosely connected happenings which constitute the bulk of the novel's action and the second aspect looms suddenly and dramatically in the conclusion. (p. 175)

The author's casual summation of personal experiences that apparently lead only to an empty beyond prompts us to ask whether or not the hero's restless activity can be regarded as anything but a futile substitute for hope of participating in an endless present. The word ''action'' is very prominent in criticism of Baroja and in his own vocabulary, but the meaning of the word as illustrated in his novels can almost be limited to mere ''movement.'' If, as Andrés argues in *El árbol de la ciencia* . . . , truth is attainable only within small, arbitrary limits, one is easily persuaded to accept the immediate circumstance as true and enjoyable even though certain to be quickly erased. On the other hand, if one tries to relate the circumstance to a universal truth, one becomes lost in unreality and may be inclined to regard grandiose ideas, such as individual immortality, as hardly worth the effort of sustained thought. One may therefore decide to confine one's attention to small day-to-day experiences, free of the responsibility of relating them to a meaningful whole, content to discover what lies around the corner, and sometimes plainly seeking escape from boredom. So it is that the incidents in Zalacaín's life follow their own whimsical way, rising briefly in their separateness and being always replaced by other incidents equally transient and equally unnecessary to the creation of a sense of completion. The author's technique produces an effect of sharp contrast between disconnected particulars of the immediate world and a formless beyond that is always erasing them.

Action, then, as Baroja interprets it, is primarily the restless movement of one who longs for an unknowable something and yet scarcely ventures more than the satisfaction of curiosity with respect to things close at hand. Zalacaín, with all his restlessness, is really a bystander who watches his earthly destiny transpire in a rapid succession of casually related happenings, and then faces suddenly an immensity that fuses all fleeting events in one vast stream of memory. As though playing a dual role, he is the illusory reality of successive moments and the vague constituent of an endless duration. It is in this connection that Bergson's *Matière et mémoire* comes to mind. (pp. 180-81)

Now, Zalacaín's history can quite justifiably and pleasurably be viewed as materializing on a plane of action, that is, movement, and then fading into the realm of pure memory on the plane of dream. Linkage between the two planes in the form of a recollection partially perceptual and partially dreamlike is indicated by a nostalgic tone in reference to concrete places, by the youth's dreams of freedom and heroic deeds, and by the delicate evocation of heroic personality from the past—the allusion, for example, to Ulysses when Zalacaín is detained in the home of Linda and, again, at the time of Zalacaín's death, the reference to the horn of Roland. The dreamlike quality overwhelms all else in the conclusion; but before this we witness—on the plane of action—the steady rhythm of time marking off the passage of life as perceived and rationalized by intellect. The incidents, large and small, sprinkled along the hero's path and held together by little more than chronological relatedness, are like the ticking of a clock marking off minutes of a life span. Chance happenings and passing acquaintances—listening to songs and stories around a kitchen fireside, planting a flag on the wall of an enemy city and being acclaimed a hero for the daring, wandering along the streets of an ancient city in company with a foreign newspaper correspondent—take their place alongside love, marriage, and death and contribute with equal magnitude to the impression of a moving chain of independent objects forcefully speaking for the extended world of matter. These are the blocks of time that conform to the natural inclination of intellect to specify a deterministic necessity of mechanical succession. In Zalacaín's life they constitute a kaleidoscopic panorama of things, from which the individual remains detached, knowing that his reality cannot be identified with them. Yet the freedom from mechanism which Bergson offers can hardly be enjoyed if it must merge with a vast sea of unconsciousness; and since Baroja does not willingly bow down to the Great Unconscious, he chooses to emphasize the dream aspect of Bergson's thesis. This alteration is only slightly more heartening, because the spirit world in which personal continuity is assured is scarcely more than an abstraction bearing the name of memory and holding appeal to a person's fancy but hardly satisfying the rationalistic part of his intelligence. (pp. 181-82)

The suggestion of Bergson's conception of time and memory seems very strong in *Zalacaín el aventurero,* but there is no need to interpret the novel exclusively in the light of Bergson's viewpoint. The ideas that found their way into Baroja's writings come from many sources. Especially to be remembered are two lines of thought known to be influential on Baroja's thinking in general: the Nietzschean call to positive action and the stronger, more hypnotic Schopenhauerian inducement toward anesthesia. Pertinent to our present discussion are some of Nietzsche's ardent assertions expressing the wish to raise the individual to glorious heights and to have man transcend himself. (p. 183)

Nietzsche's superman is to a very large degree a protest against the all-powerful, solutive "Will to Live" of Schopenhauer, which is an unindividuated "striving forward in boundless space, without rest and without end." Now, Zalacaín is an "arrow of longing for the other shore who seeketh to create beyond himself." He, too, is a protest against the Schopenhauerian Will that recognizes no individual will; but there is a marked difference in the tone of protest. Nietzsche tries to liberate himself from the thought of "willing to become non-willing," calling it "a fabulous song of madness," and declaring rebelliously that "Something higher than reconciliation must the Will will which is the Will to Power." Baroja, on the other hand, is not possessed of Nietzsche's fiery determination to have the self lift itself by its own bootstraps. He merely wishes that it could be done, and in a melancholy, nostalgic mood drifts into a dreamworld where time flows endlessly. The quiet passivity of Schopenhauer thus asserts its dominance over Nietzsche. (p. 184)

Reading the unpretentious *Zalacaín el aventurero,* one is left with a haunting remembrance, as of a youth standing on the banks of the stream of time, yearning to venture from its unindividuated flow whence he came, resigned to the necessity for eventual fusion again, and yet hopeful that some moment of his temporality may have established its permanency. The story, therefore, is not altogether a dream. The author is protesting against death, but is so possessed of the idea of individuality as to wish its immortal nature into reality and thus, perhaps, to prove it. (p. 185)

Sherman H. Eoff, "The Persuasion to Passivity," in his The Modern Spanish Novel: Comparative Essays Examining the Philosophical Impact of Science on

Fiction *(reprinted by permission of New York University Press; copyright © 1961 by New York University), New York University Press, 1961, pp. 148-85.* *

D. L. SHAW (essay date 1963)

Baroja asserts that his novels arose spontaneously out of an inner framework of personal experience, supported by observation of life; that their main concern is with content; and that their content is largely *reportaje* of contemporary life seen above all in terms of 'human units' (*i.e.* characters) whose joys, sorrows and opinions constitute the element of substantial importance. What this means in practice is that we can define the typical Barojan novel as a biographical account of an ideologically conceived central character. (p. 151)

The chief characteristic is the domination of the narrative by a single personage, the novel being constructed as far as possible within the limits of his character and temperament. . . . Thus a single chain of incidents, without sub-plot, parallelism or complex internal structure, usually solicits the reader's attention. The events follow one another in the order in which they strike the hero; his range of vision is the book's stage. Where any change of situation occurs off that stage, it is usually reported to the reader in a brief summary at the moment when it first affects the hero. . . . Four consequences follow. One is a natural reaction away from the novelesque. There is a narrow limit to the number of untoward and extraordinary incidents which can be made to enter the field of direct experience of a single character without straining the reader's credulity, unless, of course, that character is a Zalacaín or an Aviraneta. . . . But the real problem of monolinear narrative, growing by accretion in this way, is tempo. . . . The travelogue-technique employed in many novels is inseparable from this preference for unhurried rhythm, lending as it does an appearance of movement not borne out by the actual progress forward of the narrative. Thirdly there is the question of the other characters. These come to depend entirely on the hero. Once out of the range of his attention their hold on life is broken. . . . The notoriously poor love-interest in Baroja's novels is partially due to his unwillingness to start them off with both a hero and a heroine, dividing the reader's interest between the two. Instead the heroines are introduced or brought to the fore only as the hero's development permits. . . . A final consequence arising from the dominance of the novels by the central character concerns their general shape and balance, which again come to depend exclusively on the hero's psychological evolution. . . . Since it is the ideological conception of the central character which in turn determines his evolution, we may now pass to the second element in our definition [of the typical Barojan novel].

The strong ideological factor in Baroja's novels has two principal effects on their technique. The first and most obvious is the tendency to manipulate the narrative, that is, to select and adjust the incidents so as to make them fit the theme. (pp. 152-53)

The second effect of Baroja's ideological preoccupations is revealed by the fact that the outstanding characteristic of his heroes is not their activeness, as critics will keep insisting, but their articulacy: they are not so much people as attitudes to life. . . . Oral self-revelation and discussion are among the chief activities of the central characters. Interlocutors, therefore, play an important part in the narrative. While Baroja occasionally finds them something to *do,* more commonly he makes no pretence that they are there for any other reason than to talk to the hero. (p. 154)

These, then, are some of the major characteristics we expect to find in a Barojan novel. It is hoped that the following analysis of two specific novels will both confirm and amplify what has already been said. The two novels selected, *César o nada* and *El gran torbellino del mundo,* offer a reasonable field for comparative study. Sixteen years separate their dates of publication; the former is the outstanding example of the Vitalist phase of Baroja's production, the latter, with its general stocktaking of attitudes and ideas, is a fundamental novel of his second manner. In both, the general lay-out and divisions of the narrative are characteristically interesting. Azorín and Baroja, not content with breaking down the rounded periods of nineteenth-century style into shorter and more suggestive phrases, applied the same technique to the chapter. Ceasing to be a carefully constructed unity, it became simply a unit. This fragmentation is carried to the extreme by Baroja, whose drastically shortened chapters are in turn often broken down into sections hardly more than a paragraph long under cross headings. His arguments in favour of this system in the prologue to *Páginas escogidas* . . . are unconvincing, but the fact remains that the chapter, reduced to its components and strung out as it were horizontally, instead of being built into a pattern, is the basic structural element. (pp. 154-55)

[*César o nada* and *El gran torbellino del mundo*] illustrate the pattern described earlier. A brief tabularization of their similarities produces the following recapitulation:

(a) Both novels were quite rapidly written: *César o nada* in not more than a year, *El gran torbellino del mundo* in less. This is not exceptional for Baroja, who rarely spent more than a year on any one novel. Some, *e.g. Los caudillos de 1830, La senda dolorosa* and *Los pilotos de altura,* were written in three months or less, while *Paradox rey* was written in a fortnight.

(b) Both novels are blanketed by the hero and patterned by his development. There is no other independent character and no sub-plot.

(c) In both novels the most important single element is dialogue, which is adapted to a wide variety of functions.

(d) The lay-out of the novels illustrates the progressive fragmentation of the narrative characteristic in Baroja.

(e) The background of both novels, together with many of the characters and events, reflects Baroja's reliance on *cosas y tipos vistos.*

(f) Both novels are deliberately made to end unhappily, more in accordance with Baroja's ideology than from internal necessity.

One question remains: is it possible to discern an evolution in Baroja's narrative technique? Evidently it is, within narrow limits. The true evolution is, of course, between the respective attitudes of César and Larrañaga, but this is accompanied by a slight variation of manner. What is primarily evident is Baroja's increasing inability to keep his stories moving. The later ideology has very limited fictional possibilities: abstention is a theme which lends itself to few variations and, having given of its best early in *La sensualidad pervertida,* soon shows signs of exhaustion. Once the vitalistic prop is lost the protagonists of the later biographical novels progressively cease to be what they must be when everything depends exclusively on them,

that is, *casos psicológicos de interés.* Lacking tense novelesque situations, the novels tend to become humdrum in spite of the scene's being shifted about, or the inclusion of observed details and characters, or the narrative's being cut up into as many bits as possible. It is interesting to note that the abandonment of serious narrative elements altogether and their replacement by satirical travelogue-reportage, as in *Los visionarios,* bring a conspicuous improvement. It is probable that with age Baroja's unconscious control over the narrative and the range of his powers of anticipation shortened. Although the tendency away from plot is visible from the earliest novels, those written before 1912 on the whole retain strong and unifying centres of interest. Later works tend more and more to exhibit the characteristics of piecemeal writing instead of the kind of unconscious architecture which presumably led Galdós to praise the technique of *La lucha por la vida.* Posterity will probably be unkind to them. (pp. 158-59)

D. L. Shaw, "Two Novels of Baroja: An Illustration of His Technique," in Bulletin of Hispanic Studies *(© copyright 1963 Liverpool University Press), Vol. XL, 1963, pp. 151-59.*

LEO L. BARROW　(essay date 1971)

[The] negative factor plays an important role in the contemporary novels of Spain. . . . (pp. 7-8)

Baroja assuredly is one of that group of writers who, as the first step in his creative process, said "no" to the world around him. (p. 8)

The negative qualities in Baroja's novels are by no means a natural consequence of the particular time, place, and setting chosen for it. All the towns which serve as a background for Baroja's novels seem to be alike in that they are all gloomy, lonely, isolated, and barren, towns on which Baroja's antivital atmosphere has been superimposed. Baroja has not rejected any device that might make them seem more morbid and depressing. The same can be said of his novels as a whole. He always seems to bring in additions to reinforce the atmosphere, even though these are entirely unrelated to the main body of the novel. The literary quotes and the many tales of famous hangings and assassinations provide excellent examples.

The conclusion emerging from this adding of unrelated material to strengthen the total atmospherical impression is that the consistent dark and depression serve a vital artistic purpose in Baroja's novels. It is not simply an atmosphere which any sensitive person might feel upon exposure to the multifarious aspects of Spain and the universe reflected in Baroja's novels. Neither is it, necessarily, the atmosphere which Baroja senses when he encounters the same aspects in real life. It is rather the atmosphere which Baroja feels he must create and intensify to establish his novelistic world. Evidently he considers blacking-out of large areas of the novelistic world a most important and completely necessary step in its creation, "Destruir es crear."

Once it becomes clear that the atmosphere which floods Baroja's novels with darkness has a purely creative raisón d'être, insight is gained into the nature and essence of this creation. The darkened atmosphere evidently does not form a part of the essential creation; it serves only as background. Although it forms the bulk of the novelistic world, it fails to cause the most intense impact on the emotional and esthetic sensibilities of the reader. It is not the vital atmosphere of the novel, but rather the antivital part of it. There is a sharp division between the two atmospheres.

This division gives firm indications of some of the things which are to be part of Baroja's essential creation. By elimination it becomes obvious that this essence will contain nothing of the ideological—all ideologies are relegated to the antivital. The same can be applied to the decadent and the lifeless, the solitary, and the dismal rainy side of the weather.

This elimination suggests that the essential in his novels will bear no tag. It will of necessity be nameless and without affiliation. Part of this essence will be composed of human solidarity, human solidarity achieved without ideologies. This peculiar human solidarity will generally be achieved through the mutual seeking of those things, like food and shelter, which support life. The bright clear day and morning sunshine will play an important part in this essential creation and will be intimately connected to it. Most of those things that basically contribute to human life will form part of this creation—the warmth of a fire; the pleasure of food when one is hungry; the pure physical love of a healthy woman unadulterated by religious, social or mystic concepts; procreation of children; and sheer physical activity.

All these matters seem to be carefully set aside from the antivital. Within Baroja's novelistic orb, they are tangible realities that stand in bright and sharp relief against the dark, unreal, and indeterminate background. (pp. 93-4)

Baroja seems quite aware of the fact that men need vital illusions in large or small quantities, in order to survive. (p. 104)

The variations of this fiction, so propitious for Baroja's novelistic art, seem to be endless. Few, perhaps none, of the characters are exempt from dependence on it. Some of the characters are guided by literature, which shapes their lives. . . . Subliterature, in the form of superstitions, tall tales, proverbs, etc., forms an important section of this vital illusion. Baroja's characters reject huge proportions of this vital illusion, but they always seem left with a vestige, a small particle of fiction to which they cling. (p. 105)

Given Baroja's method of revelation of his characters in which he consistently strives to rid his protagonist of all that might be superficial in the way of illusions or material surroundings, it is easy to understand how his characters never quite achieve greatness. (p. 118)

The answer to the question of greatness is not a direct one, nor is it easy to formulate. Baroja, however, tends to defend these poor creatures whom he has gone to considerable trouble and ingenuity to reveal by saying that they are real, sincere, and most human. This very lack of greatness, this lack of any great occidentally recognized virtue, is probably their most human attribute. (p. 119)

Baroja, then, uses a single technique in revealing almost all of his major characters. The characters do not grow through the process of gradual accruement. They are not the sum total of many ideas and things. They tend to shrink and become smaller and smaller. They are taken away from family and friends and stripped of material possessions and basic ideas and beliefs. They are revealed and not developed. (p. 120)

From the consistency and thoroughness with which this method of character revelation is carried out, one must conclude that the end product, the revealed protagonist, is most important to Baroja. However, this revealed character does not impress one, at first, as a vehicle capable of tremendous emotional and intellectual appeal. At the end of the novel, Baroja's protagonist is best defined as *poca cosa,* as a man who is not much, hardly anything, a very little thing.

As the reader encounters more and more of Baroja's protagonists, his sensibilities become more finely attuned to the little bit of humanity revealed in each novel. This increased sensibility helps him to perceive more instantaneously and more tangibly the physical minutiae of sensation which surround him. Almost without exception Baroja's insignificant protagonists have a hypersensitivity and appreciativeness of the most vital, physical sensations: sunshine, warmth, color, movement, air, etc. These were the last things to be taken away from Don Luis in *El cantor vagabundo.* ''There was nothing left for him: only the light of the sun and the breeze and the color of the sea, but this no longer gave him any illusion, but rather tired him.'' . . . Besides this refinement of the reader's sensitivity to selected minutiae of physical sensations, strong emotional and intellectual undertones begin to emanate from the little derelict bits of humanity. These ''little'' men come to represent a quasi affirmation of man's littleness and insignificance or a quasi denial of his greatness. In them is an ever-increasing suggestion that this is all man is, that there is nothing more—that man is, after all, in unadorned essence, *poca cosa.* The poignant suggestion is reiterated at the end of almost every novel. (pp. 120-21)

Running parallel to the idea ''This is all there is to man,'' is the suggestion that, if there is something more, man's sensibility must be too awkward and too obscured to perceive it. One of the strongest hindrances to finding anything more in this little man, in this little thing, is the obfuscation caused by traditional vital illusions, many of which presuppose a completely false and antiquated means for measuring man. (p. 121)

When man's vital illusions become universalized and standardized they become clumsy tools for the understanding and measuring of man. It is only when individual man, with little assistance or guidance, welds into a highly personal illusion a personal handful of ideas and things which surround him that this fiction becomes revealing. Even then, it tends to reveal an essential need of the individual rather than an essential part of his being. Thus Baroja takes great pains with many or most of his novels to show the difference between the suggestive and illuminating potential of a personal vital fiction and the dark and antivital sameness of those fabricated by time and what he might call many generations of *farsantes.* The basic difference seems to be that the traditional vital illusions, the official dogma of things and ideas, come from outside the individual, not forming an integral part of his being, while the personal ones come from within, expressing—or suggesting, at least—one of his vital needs.

Thus Baroja's stripped and misplaced men stand alone in their human littleness at the end of the novel. They seem to represent, not the result and final conclusion of the investigation into the essential nature of humanity, but rather its beginning. They seem to mark the first step, point out its fundamental direction. This direction, which so carefully reveals these little men, seems to be a living negation of the efficaciousness of all the literary and intellectual apparatus intended to plumb the depths of their being and reveal their most essential humanity.

When fully cognizant of the method and purpose of Baroja's character revelation, it is easy to see the necessity for extreme care in creating an antivital atmosphere. Baroja seems to feel that this is the only atmosphere in which he can hope to get a glimpse of undistorted humanity. Man, in an atmosphere charged and turbulent with emotions, ideas, truths, philosophies (Baroja would say) may be greater, more powerful, perhaps even a superman, but he will be deformed, false. This is the atmosphere which creates *mixtificadores* and *farsantes,* as Baroja calls them.

This protagonist, then, is the beginning of Baroja's positive answer to a sad, negative, chaotic world. (pp. 121-22)

There can be little doubt that Baroja shows a predilection for certain types and a great disdain for others. (p. 126)

Baroja's minor characters are interesting and seem the product of an inventive genius because they have undergone the same process of revelation outside of the novel as his protagonists did within it. Life has stripped them of much of the exterior and revealed their true human essence. Baroja has been criticized for not developing more fully the novelistic potentiality of these individuals. He seems to limit himself to finding them, introducing them into novels, and then letting them disappear. . . . (p. 134)

The strange vagabonds and mystics who flit through the pages are the poetic essence of what Baroja wanted to find. They are what his eyes have been seeking, what he expected and hoped for. The creation, then, has taken place in Baroja's own mind before he discovers these outcasts and vagabonds who serve only to authenticate his rather poetic image of them. Baroja does not look for complex characters; consequently he does not find them. Instead he finds a rather poetic simplicity that stands isolated in the world. (p. 137)

Baroja's characters must fit into a greatly reduced and deflated novelistic orb. Much of the material that would amplify and enrich their lives has been removed or negated.

Given the profusion of the secondary characters and the reduced simplicity of their human essence, Baroja is confronted with the problem of revealing them with a minimum of words and devices. He is faced with the necessity of transplanting the character he sees or feels, neatly and precisely into his novelistic world. He has to reveal him with a minimum of words and a simple technique. Baroja is not interested in the standard classifications. He would like to disregard them completely, destroy them, and start anew. (p. 138)

Baroja's minor characters, so different one from another, are united by their consistent negation of almost all systematic value systems, philosophical truths, and social mores. For them, life's highest value may well be a plot of ground in the cemetery for the cultivation of cabbage. Their only philosophical truth may well be a self-deception, the illusion that they can paint when they cannot. Their social relations may be reduced to the company of their favorite dog. These little creatures, shunned and pushed aside by a hard and sometimes hostile world, stand as living negations of man's greatness. (p. 142)

The three facets of Baroja's creativity point toward a negation of the importance of all other members of the human race except self, a negation of most traditional virtues, and a negation of the form and subject of traditional poetry.

No one can doubt the importance of *yoísmo* in the works of Don Pío Baroja. Critics who have commented on his works have ranked this tendency to project himself into his novels as one of the most important facets of his artistic technique. (p. 162)

Baroja, in fact, seems to write mostly for himself. . . .

One of Baroja's principal justifications of this *yoísmo* is that today he thinks we seek the man behind the work and not the work itself. . . .

Nearly every prologue written by Baroja is a means of calling the reader's attention to himself. The prologue is one method of placing himself in the center of the novelistic orb to be created. Unlike many authors who step aside after this personal introduction, Baroja maintains this spotlighted position and seems to remain omnipresent throughout the novel.

By now, the reader has become aware of another aspect of Baroja's *yoísmo*. When Baroja speaks of the novel in general, he is almost exclusively concerned with his own novels. (p. 164)

The unequivocal stamp of originality that each character bears should caution against lumping them into one mold and saying categorically that they are all Baroja. (p. 166)

Baroja, who is ever present in his own novels as an entity of fiction as well as the author of that fiction, enriches his own novelistic reality by attributing certain qualities to his fictional characters. (p. 167)

In a sense, this sensitive comprehension of the generally by-passed and forgotten multitudes who appear and disappear in his novels without scheme or pattern can be considered as a further, perhaps more subtle and poetic projection of his own ego. Baroja leads us to consider this possibility while discussing the real interests which a criminal holds for us, and thus for himself. (p. 168)

Baroja's extreme sensibility comes from an almost complete ego-identification with these characters who are cut adrift from the norms of life. This ego-identification tends to be momentary. One is reminded of Baroja's statement that one cannot add to a character, one cannot dwell upon the complexities of his life, if these complexities of life do not exist. This seems to be another way of saying that one's ego-identification with a certain character cannot be sustained. It seems to be a rather poetical flickering of humanity that for a moment reaches a full comprehension of the character through the realization that a very fine line of circumstance separates the observer and his mode of life from that of the observed. (pp. 168-69)

Baroja appears to be striving for just this type of momentary identification or fusion of human sympathies. In the severely reduced and darkened ambient of his novels he sees, momentarily sympathizes with, and with great sensibility reflects, the humanity of these characters. Thus when the critics speak of the acutely human qualities of Baroja's characters, part of this human feeling comes from Baroja's own reaction to them. Author and character, for a moment only, are humanely fused into one, within the novelistic orb. The characters themselves are not only limited by the fact that they have been chosen because they were already limited, and by the fact that they are more observed than invented, but they are also limited by Baroja's own wealth of human sympathy, by his store of sentimentalism which gradually exhausts itself. (p. 170)

Baroja's consistent attempts in his novelistic world to strike out and destroy that which does not appeal to his reserve of sentiment or to his human sensibilities are balanced by his poetical effusion before all which sincerely does affect him. Ramón Sender sees Baroja's poetic effusion in the presence of all that strikes his peculiar sensibilites as his greatest virtue. Few critics have failed to find this lyrical vein in his novels.

Baroja has several names for this lyrical quality. At times he refers to it as his sentimentalism; other times he speaks of it as a tendency toward romanticism. On other occasions he refers to it as sensibility. It seems quite obvious that these terms point up Baroja's desire to capture what he considers the fragmentary poetic essence of his novelistic world. (p. 171)

The important thing is that in the midst of a reduced and deflated novelistic world Baroja became enthused over something, and this enthusiasm was manifested in spontaneous lyrical outbursts.

Interestingly enough the objects which elicit Baroja's lyrical response, like the characters fill his novels, are all quite liberated. They have been cast aside and forgotten by the progressive march of society. The old merry-go-round no longer exists at the time Baroja sings its virtues. The same can be said for the ceroplastic art and other objects. Most of them are described as old because they have been by-passed by time. . . . (p. 172)

Baroja's *yoísmo* forces him, or at least allows him, to occupy an inordinate amount of space and importance in his novelistic world, thereby denying this space and importance to his characters. His own character and personality are constantly being projected into his novels, overshadowing and belittling the characters found within, reducing them to a kind of human insignificance. Baroja, considered a great novelist, created only one, if not great, at least complex character, Don Pío Baroja. Undoubtedly, one of the keys to this creation is the systematic negation of the qualities of greatness and complexity in the little human entities that people the nooks and corners of his novels.

Baroja's egotism and his momentary ego-identification with only a limited range of people and objects represent almost total negation of virtue for virtue's sake. For Baroja, virtue operates only when there is ego-involvement or when the individual's sensibility allows him to conceive the possibility of ego-involvement. According to Baroja, one can feel pity for a beggar only if he recognizes the possibility of one day having to beg himself. In any case the ego-identification must be short-lived because the self quickly returns to its own ego-centered moment, to the joy of plenty. Baroja might well say that charity is fine, but who wants to spend three chapters with a beggar. The beggar receives one or two paragraphs before the ego-identification dissolves.

In a sense Baroja's poetic moments are the result of the strong projection of his *yoísmo* and the limitation of his ego-identification. Knowing full well that he could choose and cultivate whatever *yo* or group of *yoes* that he wished, he chose and cultivated the one best suited to the ephemeral identification with special subjects and objects, those which had undergone a process of negation in real life. Thus Baroja's poetic vision may well have been the result of a deliberate limitation. Rejecting the traditional forms and subjects of poetry, he attuned his sensibility to the forms and subjects poetry has rejected or ignored. The negation lies in both the perceiver and the form and subject perceived. His vision may merit the term "lyrical" since it is uniquely Barojian. After all, doesn't negation enter into every lyrical poet's vision of reality? Doesn't he tend to reject even the possibility of any other vision and project only his own? (pp. 179-80)

Baroja is closely related to the novelists and other writers of his own century, so many of whom created sad, negative worlds. The novelistic worlds of Joyce, Proust, Moravia, Pietro Spina, Camus, Greene, and Faulkner are essentially sad and negative. Baroja's own generation, the Generation of 98, is outstanding in the creation of sad and negative worlds. Some of the best novelistic and literary talents of this century have dedicated themselves to the creation of dark, antivital nihilistic worlds.

Baroja's answer to this nihilistic world links him closely to the writers of this century. R.W.B. Lewis's observation that the answer James Joyce and Proust give—that the artistic experience is to be the only positive value—seems adequate and just. His affirmation that the other writers treated in his study give a human answer is also justified. Both the answers are partial and limited, and they are stated artistically and never overtly and dogmatically. . . .

Baroja's answer to the dark and antivital world he created is also a partial one and is expressed artistically and not overtly or as a dogma. It is also a human answer, an answer concerned with that which is most basic and essential to humanity. This positive answer to a negative world is reduced and limited to those things which are available to the senses, to the surroundings that are most essential to the animal or biological existence of man. (p. 192)

> *Leo L. Barrow, in his* Negation in Baroja: A Key to His Novelistic Creativity *(reprinted by permission of The University of Arizona Press, Tucson; copyright © 1971 The Arizona Board of Regents), University of Arizona Press, 1971, 238 p.*

BEATRICE P. PATT   (essay date 1971)

Baroja's first collection of short stories was published in 1900 under the general title of *Vidas sombrías (Somber Lives)*. (p. 78)

As the title suggests, *Somber Lives* is a melancholy book, full of delicate feeling poetically expressed. The concerns of the Generation of 1898 for everyday life, for the enduring traditions of the humble people, in short, for "infrahistory," is particularly apparent in this collection. The vein of tenderness in Baroja, which diminished with the passage of time and with the concomitant acquisition of many opinions, is at its freshest and most poignant in this youthful work.

La casa de Aizgorri (The House of Aizgorri), published in the same year as *Somber Lives*, stands somewhat apart from the mainstream of the author's production in both form and content. At first conceived as a play, it is in effect a novel in dialogue form. (pp. 80-1)

It is the derivative nature of the work that both sets it apart from the bulk of Baroja's production and links it with some of the pieces in *Somber Lives*. The idea of the hereditary taint owes much to Ibsen and [the author of *Degeneration*, Max] Nordau and the sharp line of demarcation between the symbols of good and evil recall the stylized, rhetorical dramas of the nineteenth century. Everything is clear in *The House of Aizgorri*, there are no ambiguities, there is no greyness. (p. 81)

Similar in ethical intent is *El mayorazgo de Labraz (The Lord of Labraz)*, published three years later. *The Lord of Labraz* is a somber novel, medieval in atmosphere, and romantic in spirit. Baroja had gone to Labraz, a decrepit and moribund *pueblo terrible* because its lugubrious atmosphere was in keeping with his anguished spirit, deeply saddened by "the destruction of [my] romantic illusions." Availing himself of an old and respectable fictional device, Baroja states that his novel is merely a transcription of a fantasy imagined by the Englishman Mister Samuel Bothwell Crawford. Mister Bothwell, as he is usually designated in the novel, therefore plays the dual role of playwright and actor, mirroring the double role often played by Baroja. When Bothwell begins to express the author's opinions, the reader is introduced into a hall of mirrors. (pp. 81-2)

It is evident that Baroja's view of mankind made it relatively easy for him to depict collective evil and vice, but what he fails to do in this novel is to portray evil successfully in an individualized fashion. . . . The evil that the author sees is a characteristic of the generic *homo sapiens,* for nowhere are there concrete, full-scale villains, capable of overflowing a page and filling a book. (p. 83)

The romantic nature of *The Lord of Labraz* places the work at the head of a long line of rather melodramatic novels of fantasy produced by Baroja over his long life-span. In works of this type the critical note becomes attenuated over the years while the melodrama is noticeably accentuated. . . .

Between *The House of Aizgorri* and *The Lord of Labraz,* neither of which is distinguished for its originality, Baroja wrote *Aventuras, inventos y mixtificaciones de Silvestre Paradox (Adventures, Inventions and Hoaxes of Silvestre Paradox),* the first novel that can be labelled, *a posteriori,* genuinely Barojian. In the *Adventures* . . . , published in 1901, Baroja finds his authentic style, and the texture and tone are as unmistakably his in this early work as they are in [*El árbol de la ciencia (The Tree of Knowledge)*] or [*La sensualidad pervertida (Sublimated Sensuality)*]. (p. 84)

With the publication of [*Camino de perfeccion (The Way to Perfection)*] in 1902, Baroja emerges as a serious novelist-critic, joining Azorín as spokesman for the Generation of 1898. The vitriolic tone is an augury of the sharply critical novels and essays yet to come, and the central themes reflect the readings and synthesize the preoccupations of his cogenerationists. (p. 88)

The style of the novel is alternately lyrical and strident; while the landscapes of Spain, sometimes radiant, sometimes grim, are painted with the delicate brush of the impressionist, the institutions of Spain are probed with a merciless scalpel. With its harsh social criticism and its portrayal of a fundamentally flawed protagonist, *The Way to Perfection* takes its place next to Azorín's *La Voluntad* as one of the earliest authentic literary manifestations of the temper of the Generation of 1898, but does not fully indicate the path that Baroja was later to follow with such consistency in his major works. The progression from the representation of a partial alter ego, as exemplified by Silvestre Paradox and Dr. Labarta in 1901, is irregular and full of gaps; the free utilization by the author of Nordau and Nietzsche in the delineation of Ossorio's personality indicates strongly that the latter is not a link in the progression.

La lucha por la vida (The Struggle for Life) is the trilogy published in 1904 which earned for its author the Orteguian designation *el Homero de la canalla* (''the Homer of the rabble''). In [*La busca (The Quest)* and *Mala hierba (Weeds)*], the first two novels of the series, the writer becomes the photographer and poet of the slums of Madrid; thieves and prostitutes, murderers and Don Juans, confidence men and degenerates, the hungry and the needy, crowd the pages of a work dedicated to the exploration of all the manifestations of abject misery that an urban center can produce. The wind and the cold, the rain and the snow are chronicled with the precision of a meteorological report, and the teeming sublife of Madrid at night and by day is observed and catalogued with the zeal of a scientist. Baroja has called both novels a copy from nature,

with antecedents in the Spanish picaresque novel, in Dickens, the Russians, and in French serial literature of the *bas fonds* (lower depths). (pp. 93-4)

The whole of *The Struggle for Life* is in fact an illustration of Goethe's statement that reality has more genius than invention. Baroja paints observed details and creates multitudes of rapid vignettes; the total number of figures in the three novels is enormous and the variety of episodes and subplots makes a detailed summary extremely lengthy. If the vision of *The Struggle for Life* is Goyesque, the execution is by Breughel. (p. 96)

Baroja's view throughout the work is compassionate and humane, yet at the same time puritanical in its insistence on morality, work, and steadfastness. For all its crude realism, the note of sentimentality is not absent. . . . Baroja is not yet ready to follow his own thinking to its logical conclusion but seeks, however artificially, to mitigate the consequences of his apparent nihilism. . . .

One year after the publication of *The Struggle for Life,* the puritanical collector of specimens from the lower depths again takes up the cudgels in defense of morality and decency. In [*La feria de los discretos (The School for Rogues)*] what has been implicit all along is now explicit: paradise is reserved for the pure in heart. (pp. 96-7)

The mystery surrounding the hero's origin as well as the proliferation of subplots and episodes involving gambling, kidnapping, and robbery, *inter alia,* make the association with serialized novels inevitable and give the reader the uneasy feeling that he has inadvertently stumbled into a theatre specializing in plays of the Romantic era. (p. 98)

Paradox Rey, (Paradox, King), which followed the *Adventures* . . . after a period of five years, is a sequel only in the sense that Silvestre Paradox and Don Avelino again figure prominently in the plot. *Paradox, King,* like *The House of Aizgorri,* is a dialogued novel, a form Baroja used infrequently but with considerable skill. (pp. 98-9)

Baroja classifies *Paradox, King* as half-fantasy, half-satirical poem and it is in this work, particularly, that his formidable comic talents are most apparent. The arthritic, the author informs his readers, is timid and melancholy, ill-tempered and hypochondriacal, but ''. . . comedy often emerges in the midst of ill temper.'' The misanthropy in *Paradox, King* is obviously of the jovial type described by Escobedo in *The School for Rogues.* The opportunity to feel *robinsoniano* (like Robinson Crusoe) fills Baroja with youthful cheer and vitality, and it is this vigor that gives to the work its bright ebullience.

Los últimos románticos (The Last Romantics) and *Las tragedias grotescas (Grotesque Tragedies),* published in 1906 and 1907 respectively, reveal in a more convincing manner than *The School for Rogues* the author's consuming interest in nineteenth-century history. . . . In accordance with his belief that only relatively recent history can be recreated with any sense of reality and vividness, Baroja sets both novels in Paris in the last years of the Second Empire. The materialism, vanity, and corruption as well as the revolutionary fervor of the era are conveyed through the descriptions of the amatory escapades and the political involvements of a group of French aristocrats, Spanish émigrés, and miscellaneous adventurers and idealists. (pp. 100-01)

Some of the non-historical aspects of the two novels again reveal Baroja's love for romantic fiction: a letter, a picture, blackmail, discoveries of hidden identities, the claiming of a fortune, still mar the author's plots. The valuable aspects of the work lie in the sensitive descriptions of the old and picturesque Paris and in the evocations of the Spanish émigrés living in that city in the 1860's. (pp. 101-02)

The recent past rather than the nineteenth century supplies the material for [*Ladama errante (The Wandering Lady)* and *La ciudad de la niebla (The City of Fog)*], published in 1908 and 1909 subsequent to a visit to London. . . .

[*The Wandering Lady*] is in many respects a travel book of the variety cultivated first by Azorín and Unamuno and later by Ortega and Cela, the plot merely serving as a pretext for the evocation of landscape and incident. (p. 103)

The City of Fog is the London novel for which *The Wandering Lady* was the preparation. . . .

The discurisve tone that is usually associated with the Barojian novel is more in evidence in these two novels than in the previous works. (p. 104)

The Paris novels and *The City of Fog,* in particular, are of greater interest for their atmosphere than for their ideological content, and the poet is far more persuasive than the social critic. The Madrid, Paris, and London novels are antivalentines, loving evocations of the abject and dismal as well as of the romantic and the picturesque; the authentic valentine can be addressed only to the Basque countryside and to its heroes. . . . [*Zalacaín el aventurero (Zalacaín the Adventurer)*] found great favor both in Spain and abroad, and was considered by Baroja to be one of his best novels. The popularity of *Zalacaín* may have done much to bring the name of the author to the public, but its merit lies less in its intrinsic excellence than in its interest as a rehearsal for the Aviraneta series. (p. 105)

Zalacaín is the most objective of Baroja's early novels and it is his only extended work that is truly redolent of youth. Basque songs are interpolated into the text, and Baroja's almost Cervantine custom of including independent narratives sometimes yields surprisingly happy results. (p. 106)

Baroja decided to compose a work with a modern setting, but with reminiscences of the Borgia type; [*César o nada (Caesar or Nothing)*], which was published in 1910 after having appeared serially in *El Radical,* was the result. Aside from its function as a surrogate historical novel, *Caesar or Nothing* is also the reflection of the author's first serious brush with politics, for it was in 1909 that Baroja ran unsuccessfully for municipal councilman. . . . (p. 107)

Baroja's ambiguous portrayal of Moncada has given rise to contradictory interpretations. Gonzalo Sobejano considers Moncada *el hombre de acción que más cerca está de la Voluntad nietzscheana* . . . ("the man of action who comes closest to the Nietzschean Will . . .") while Sherman Eoff considers *Caesar or Nothing* to go counter to Nietzsche's aggressive egoism, for César ". . . attempts self-glorification in a Machiavellian way and is made to know . . . the futility of his ego." Moncada's dual nature . . . accommodates either interpretation.

The *Adventures, The Way to Perfection,* and *Caesar or Nothing* can be regarded as Baroja's modern reworking of the medieval debate between water and wine, between carnality and self-denial. The elements of the modern debate have been transformed and the new struggle is acted out between affirmation and negation, between vitality and passivity, between life-giv-

ing and life-destroying tendencies. To the so-far uncommitted author, neither side appears to win and the contest ends in a draw. . . .

[*Las inquietudes de Shanti Andía (The Restlessness of Shanti Andía)*] made its appearance one year after the publication of *Caesar or Nothing,* and on the surface at least, it is difficult to conceive of two more widely differing novels. (p. 110)

Baroja could have said with Faust *zwei Seelen wohnen, ach! in meiner Brust* ("two souls are housed, alas, in my breast"). One of Baroja's tendencies is dynamic and restless, craving constant movement; the innumerable adventures in *Zalacaín* and *The Restlessness of Shanti Andía* and the veritable shower of episodes in *The Struggle for Life* fulfill this need. The other tendency, contemplative and philosophical, lies just below the surface, a variety of figured bass. All is vanity, the author whispers, all effort and life itself are futile. In *The Restlessness of Shanti Andía* the novelist seeks once again to mitigate the consequences of his lucid pessimism. . . . The conflict between affirmation and negation remains unresolved.

The closing lines of the novel, "But there was something of the precursor in him." although far from explicit, have the effect of mitigating the tragedy of Hurtado's death. The latter can be considered a precursor to the extent that he prefigures the new man who will be capable of both contemplation and action, who will be able to sustain his vitality and exercise his will despite his knowledge, despite his awareness of the precarious nature of existence. In a reminiscence of Zarathustra, Baroja implies that what is not fulfilled in the present will be fulfilled in the future: the new man will affirm life in the face of death. He will be, in short, the existentialist hero. (p. 116)

The Tree of Knowledge is Baroja's most authentic novel because it is his least contrived; invention is subordinated to reality with respect to atmosphere, incident, and character. Nothing was ever to be more vivid to the author than the years of his youth, and the inclusion in the novel of many real characters recollected from his student days is indicative of Baroja's reluctance, not to say refusal, to sever the link with his earlier self. (p. 117)

The purely autobiographical character of many aspects of the novel accounts for its dense atmosphere of emotion recollected and incident relived, but it is the principal character who gives *The Tree of Knowledge* its never-to-be-repeated vitality. Andrés Hurtado is perhaps Baroja's only fully realized fictional protagonist; he lives, he suffers, and he changes, responding to his environment with the sensitivity of a finely-tuned instrument. Paradoxically, it is his role as Baroja's mirror that gives him his authenticity and freedom. As the author unwinds the film of his earlier life, Andrés is on each successive frame, appearing to have no prior identity, but observed in the process of becoming. It is this becoming that gives to Hurtado his particular flesh-and-blood quality, a quality noticeably absent from most of the novelist's main characters. Hurtado has what Ortega called a *quehacer vital* (a vital task), and the content of his life is the attempted fulfillment of this *quehacer.* The fact that the task itself is more of a beginning than an end does not diminish its value; the search for an acceptable method of confronting the world is the proper occupation of the philosopher. Where Hurtado failed, others would succeed. (p. 120)

The episodes included in [*El mundo es ansí (The Way of the World)*] belong to a somewhat older Baroja, the man in his thirties who was less affected by what he saw and what he did. . . .

If this particular novel does not appear to have fully engaged either Baroja's mind or sentiments, a further cause may be sought in his involvement with the figure of Aviraneta. It was in 1911 that the novelist became interested in the somewhat shadowy figure of this distant relative and began to do some research with a view to devoting a chapter to him. This short piece ultimately expanded into the twenty-two volumes that make up the Aviraneta series [*Las memorias de un hombre de acción (Memoirs of a Man of Action)*]. (p. 125)

The ubiquitous Aviraneta, by virtue of a long life that stretched from the War of Independence to within a year of the establishment of the First Republic, and by virtue of his blood relationship to Baroja, was admirably suited to the author's needs. . . .

Baroja's novels in the Aviraneta series constitute "imaginary reportage" rather than completely accurate history, hence the freedom of the novelist to invent and reinvent. Baroja's insistence on the rôle of the imagination should not, however, lead the reader to false conclusions. He consulted whatever historical documents were available to him as is evident from his accounts in the prologue to *Aviraneta, o la vida de un conspirador (Aviraneta, or the Life of a Conspirator)* and in the *Memoirs.* (p. 126)

In Aviraneta there is more restlessness than striving, less will to power than indiscriminate political dabbling. Aviraneta, like his presumed opposite José Larrañaga, goes out with more of a whimper than a bang. Maravall has called Baroja a novelist of the *élan vital,* but this élan belongs to virtually every aspect of the *Memoirs of a Man of Action* with the exception of Aviraneta. The interference of the author's temperament and, to a lesser degree, his experiences, makes of the archadventurer a figure smaller than life. (p. 128)

Aviraneta weaves in and out of the novels in his long series, sometimes all but forgotten in the mass of details on battles, conspiracies, Freemasonry, and royal scandals. Secondary plots abound, and hundreds of characters sail briefly into the reader's field of vision, soon to disappear without a trace. At the end of the last volume, *Desde el principio hasta el fin (From the Beginning to the End),* Baroja takes leave of Aviraneta as his fellow countryman and "coreligionist in liberalism, individualism, and in a somewhat unfortunate life." The violence that underlies the series proceeds from the events themselves and the collision of opposing forces, with Aviraneta's voice often drowned by the clashing cymbals and thunderous drum rolls of this heroic symphony. (p. 134)

Between 1917, by which time six volumes of the Aviraneta series had appeared, and 1919, when three more had been written, Baroja published several collections of essays: *Juventud, egolatría (Youth, Egolatry)* and *Nuevo tablado de Arlequín (New Harlequinade),* . . . *Las horas solitarias (Solitary Hours)* . . . , and *Momentum catastrophicum (Time of Crisis)* and *La caverna del humorismo (The Grotto of Humor).* . . . The shift from the personal narrative to the form of the essay is, in reality, scarcely perceptible. Baroja's fictions often resemble essays and vice versa. . . . (pp. 134-35)

The Tree of Knowledge and *Sublimated Sensuality* together provide Baroja's intellectual and sentimental biography up to 1920. That Baroja had finally reached a *modus vivendi* with himself is evident in the shift from Hurtado's anguished rejection of life to Murguía's half-willing acceptance. He lacks, to use Machado's phrase, "physiological joy," but his self-characterization as "a rotted fruit on the tree of life" is too highly

colored. Murguía is not a brilliant social success, surely, yet he is less a failure than he would like to believe. There is a disparity between Murguía's behavior, which is not particularly striking for its outlandishness, and his theorizing about himself. He is not quite the misfit he declares he is. In comparison with Andrés Hurtado, he is almost a social butterfly, and Hurtado did not become a semi-hermit until the latter part of his life. Baroja surrounds Murguía with his now-familiar philosophical ideas, but this protagonist is not easily drowned in literature. The faun, the satyr, still peers out from the side of the vase. (p. 143)

[*El laberintade las sirenas (The Labyrinth of the Sirens)*] is a purely visual book, a work of the imagination rather than of the intellect. The sea, the weather, the changing light are painted with the delicacy of the artist's brush, and the author's facility for detailed description is given the freest possible rein. Baroja's artistic sensibility, often submerged under a wealth of ideological digressions in so many of the other works, here holds sway, and is perhaps the only *raison d'être* of the novel. *The Labyrinth of the Sirens* apparently did not displease Baroja entirely, for in **"Ciudades de Italia" ("Cities of Italy")** he diffidently suggests that some aspects of the novel may not be "entirely bad." It seems ungrateful to disagree with so modest a judgment. (pp. 144-45)

The nostalgia for a world where adventure replaces ratiocination and where unreality can be lavishly embroidered with rich detail holds Baroja in its iron grasp even during the years of the Spanish Civil War and the ensuing World War, as evidenced by a collection of four stories written between 1928 and 1941 and published under the general title of *Los impostores joviales (The Jovial Imposters).* (p. 146)

[*El cura de Monleón (The Curate of Monleón)*] is both the story of the priest Javier Olarán and an historical survey of Christianity. . . . The loss of faith or the struggle to believe achieves the dimensions of tragedy in the hands of Unamuno, but when Baroja takes up the theme he is floundering in uncharted waters. The failure to give solidity to . . . Javier is the measure of Baroja's radical incapacity to so much as imagine the agonies that doubt and incredulity inflict on the truly religious; the dark night of the soul is as alien to the author as a sustained period of exhilarating exuberance. (pp. 152-53)

[*Intermedios (Intermezzi)*] provides excellent illustrations of the short sketch that was Baroja's specialty; bohemians, eccentrics, imposters, anarchists, and mystics pass in rapid succession, some receiving the benefit of only a short but vivid paragraph. Reminiscences, anecdotes, observations on literary topics, even playlets, round out the exceedingly heterogeneous collection. (p. 157)

[The *Vitrina pintoresca (Picturesque Showcase)*] touches on a variety of topics including hangmen, beggars, Jesuits, Freemasons, and Jews; an essay on the rivers of Spain is followed by a "travellers' bestiary" as the concrete and the abstract, the past and the present, history and folklore occupy the author's restless attention. One essay, entitled **"Epigrafía callejera" ("Street Signs"),** represents Baroja at his humorous best, while the pieces on carnivals, fairs, and the old streets of Madrid once again reveal Baroja's love for the outlandish and the mysterious.

The essay **"Nuestra juventud" ("Our Youth")** is a self-interview which casts an interesting light on the nature of the author's true tastes. . . .

Juan Uribe Echevarría uses the apt designation of *microensay-ismo* (''microessayism'') to describe the special nature of the Barojian essay. This ''microessay,'' with its opportunities for the quick rendition of impressions or the synthetic imparting of information, is Baroja's most authentic genre. What is chaos in a novel is diversity in the essay, and the movement and change that are so often unmotivated in the works of fiction are fully justified in collections that do not pretend to unity or harmony. (p. 158)

[*Susana (Susana)*], exemplifies what must finally be called the impermeability of the author, the radical inability to reflect the outer world without at the same time casting his own shadow. The badly articulated plot of *Susana* purportedly concerns the ill-fated love of Miguel Salazar for the Susana of the title, and the details need not detain the serious reader. (pp. 158-59)

[It] might be more accurate to consider *Susana* less of a joke than the visible and concrete evidence of failing powers and flagging resources. (p. 159)

The complete works of Baroja are a chronicle of the author's times, the concrete evidence of a talent that is primarily re-portorial. That the sum is greater than the parts is beyond question, although the difficulty of reading the collected works is not to be underestimated. The sensation of *déjà vu* is at times overpowering, for the totality of Baroja's production is an outstanding example of literary overkill.

Camilo José Cela, one of Spain's most prominent contemporary literary figures, has affirmed that Baroja opened the doors to *una España novelesca,* revealing the infinite possibilities of the novelistic art: . . . *de Baroja sale toda la novela española a él posterior* (''the entire Spanish novel after Baroja stems from him''). (p. 171)

Beatrice P. Patt, in her Pío Baroja *(copyright ©1971 by Twayne Publishers, Inc.; reprinted with the permission of Twayne Publishers, a Division of G. K. Hall & Co., Boston), Twayne, 1971, 208 p.*

CURTIS MILLNER (essay date 1975)

A large portion of the criticism of Pío Baroja's novels says or implies that these novels are not structured in an internally consistent and artistically economical way. These critics say or imply that a typical Baroja novel characteristically does not concentrate on a single, sharply-focused topic and then proceed to develop that topic with an economy of artistic means. My own experience in reading, studying, and teaching Baroja's novels has been that this is not true. I find that the typical Baroja novel is both structurally consistent and artistically economical. I would like to demonstrate that this is true by specifying the structural consistency and the artistic economy of *El árbol de la ciencia,* which is one of Baroja's most representative novels. (p. 99)

Professor Robert W. Hatton [gives] this admirable summary of the plot: ''Andrés Hurtado, the protagonist, is a young, sensitive medical student in Spain searching for a meaning in life. At odds with the world around him, he experiences withdrawal symptoms, plunging into a philosophical consideration of man and his existence. Unable to reconcile his own moral and spiritual code of conduct with that of what he views as a degenerate society, Andrés commits suicide.'' This plot summary implies that the manifest interests of the novelist converge on a single, well-defined topic: the process by which the protagonist comes to discover who he is and what the outside

world is in relation to him. Until we examine the text, we do not know if, in fact, Baroja develops this topic in a way which is consistent and economical; but the sharpness and the single mindedness with which the topic is focused certainly afford the writer an excellent opportunity for making a tightly-knit book if he should choose to do so. (pp. 99-100)

[The] book does indeed have a single topic: the process by which Andrés Hurtado becomes aware of himself, his world, and of the relationship between himself and his world, and his reaction to that awareness. The question now is whether Baroja develops this topic consistently and economically, without digressing into other activities.

The titles of the 7 sections of the novel would suggest that he does precisely that. Each of the section titles implies that the section deals either with Andrés Hurtado's life experiences or his reaction to those experiences. . . . Many of the section titles call our attention to the process of learning by experience: the first section is called ''La vida de un estudiante en Madrid,'' and the last three sections are called ''La experiencia en el pueblo,'' ''La experiencia en Madrid,'' and ''La experiencia del hijo.'' The second section, ''Las carnarias,'' clearly fits into this same category of learning from life experience. The remaining section titles quite obviously refer to the reactions to which Hurtado's experiences give rise: ''Tristezas y dolores'' (3rd section), and ''Inquisiciones'' (4th section).

What attracts one's attention in the chapter titles is the overwhelming preponderance of the substantive: people, places, things, and conditions are named in the chapter titles and thereby objectified. The implication of both the section and the chapter titles is that Andrés Hurtado's life process is based on a system in which the passing phenomenalizations of the outer world are objectified into abstractions. These objectified phenomena are then regarded by Hurtado as examples of general categories into which one can conveniently fit all aspects of human life. This process begins and ends in intellectualization. The way in which all of this is structured by Baroja is what is interesting to me: Hurtado's world, through some kind of happy fortuity, seems to present Andrés with exactly the kinds of experiences that he needs in order to arrive at certain generalizations about himself, his world, and how they relate to each other. This fortuitousness is of course not fortuitous at all, but rather a direct response to the technical need to keep all of the material in the book sharply focused on the single topic of Hurtado's growing awareness of himself and of his world. The exterior structure of the novel merely implies the possibility of this peculiarly convenient juxtapositioning of the protagonist and his world. We must examine the interior structure of the book itself to see if this is in fact the procedure that Baroja uses.

In short, the nature of the exterior structure of the book implies that its interior structure is both consistent and economical. It seems likely that the material inside the novel will be sharply focused on a single preoccupation which will then be consistently and economically developed without digression. Let us examine the interior structure of the novel to see if this is the case.

The consistency of the material inside *El árbol de la ciencia* is based on two fixed factors which are in constant conflict with each other: Andrés Hurtado's sustained search for meaning in the world on the one hand, and the world's continuing refusal to afford him that meaning on the other. The plot traces the ups and downs and the ultimate resolution of that struggle. This conflict is achieved technically by causing Andrés to have certain experiences to which he reacts either emotionally or, more often, intellectually. If the novel is to have the proper structural consistency and economy, all of the episodes of the plot should serve the sole purpose of elucidating the nature and/or the results of Hurtado's conflicts with his world. Any episode, any of Hurtado's experiences or encounters which do not serve this purpose, would be artistic flaws in the book. I have found no such non-functional episodes in *El árbol de la ciencia*. Andrés Hurtado's experiences are carefully chosen for him by Baroja. The lack of non-functional or discursive episodes is not accidental. In this novel, Baroja is not, as many critics have implied, merely picturing, to no particular purpose, the chaotic, unstructured world "out there." Instead, he is carefully tracing (actually, creating) the fluctuations and ultimate resolution of the precisely defined and doggedly executed project of his protagonist for interpenetrating with that world. No real life in the real world could be lived in such a perfect one-to-one relationship in which every single life experience is viable raw material for the project of interpenetration with the world. In that sense and to that extent, *El árbol de la ciencia* is not a realistic novel. (pp. 101-03)

By demonstrating the structural consistency and artistic economy of *El árbol de la ciencia,* which is Baroja's most representative novel, I mean to imply that many of his novels have those same characteristics. The failure of many critics to recognize such characteristics in Baroja's novels springs from the identification that the critics make between the diffuse real life of the novelist and the highly-structured novelized life of his sometimes autobiographical protagonist. Baroja drew upon the personal experiences of his own life in order to invent the life of his protagonist, but this process was based on selection and ordering and not duplication. Baroja's demonstrated intention was not to reproduce faithfully his own life but rather to communicate a point of view about human life in general held by the novelist at the moment of writing his novel. (pp. 104-05)

> *Curtis Millner, "Structural Consistency and Artistic Economy in 'El arbol de la ciencia',"* in Revista de Estudios Hispánicos *(reprinted by permission of The University of Alabama Press), Vol. IX, No. 1, January, 1975, pp. 99-105.*

ADDITIONAL BIBLIOGRAPHY

Anderson, James Anthony. "Conrad and Baroja: Two Spiritual Exiles." *Kwartalnik Neofilologiczny* XX, No. 4 (1973): 363-71.*
Compares themes and techniques in the works of Joseph Conrad and Baroja.

Baroja, Pío. "Myself: A Spanish Novelist Turns His Hand to Aphorisms." *The Living Age* 337, No. 4346 (15 September 1929): 114-18.
Thoughts of Baroja on such topics as "Sensibility," "Anarchy," and "Aspirations of Change."

Bell, Aubrey F. G. "The Novel." In his *Contemporary Spanish Literature*, pp. 39-150. New York: Alfred A. Knopf, 1925.
Survey of Baroja's fiction.

Bloom, Leonard. "Pío Baroja and the Basque Language." *Romance Notes* XI, No. 3 (Spring 1970): 557-68.
Discourse on *euskera*, the language of the Basque country.

Borenstein, Walter. "Baroja's Uncomplimentary Stereotype of the Latin American." *Symposium* XI, No. 1 (Spring 1957): 46-60.
Reveals Baroja's condemnatory attitude toward Latin Americans.

Borenstein, Walter. "The Failure of Nerve: The Impact of Pío Baroja's Spain on John Dos Passos." In *Nine Essays in Modern Literature,* edited by Donald E. Stanford, pp. 63-87. Baton Rouge: Louisiana State University Press, 1965.*
Influence of Baroja and the Spanish experience on John Dos Passos.

Boyd, Ernest. "Pío Baroja." In his *Studies from Ten Literatures,* pp. 72-86. 1925. Reprint. Port Washington, N.Y.: Kennikat Press, 1968.
Survey of Baroja's works.

Bruyne, Jacques de. "Aspects of Pío Baroja's Anticlericalism." *Neophilologus* LX, No. 1 (January 1976): 56-74.
Investigation of anticlericalism in Baroja, its modes of expression, and its etiology.

Ciplijauskaité, Biruté. "The 'Noventayochistas' and the Carlist Wars." *Hispanic Review* 44, No. 3 (Summer 1976): 265-79.*
Compares the historical novels of Baroja, Valle-Inclán, and Unamuno.

Drake, William A. "Pío Baroja." In his *Contemporary European Writers,* pp. 114-23. New York: The John Day Co., 1928.
Overview of Baroja's works.

Fox, E. Inman. "Baroja and Schopenhauer." *Revue de littérature comparée* XXXVII, No. 3 (July-September 1963): 350-59.*
Influence of Schopenhauer on Baroja.

Hatton, Robert W. "Reviews: *El arbol de la ciencia.*" *Hispania* 54, No. 2 (May 1971): 414.
Reviews an edition of *El arbol de la ciencia* that has been adapted for college Spanish classes.

Litvak, Lily. *A Dream of Arcadia: Anti-Industrialism in Spanish Literature 1895-1905.* Austin: University of Texas Press, 1975, 278 p.*
Details Baroja's disdain for the squalor resulting from modern industrialism.

Lovett, Gabriel H. "Two Views of Guerrilla Warfare: Galdós' 'Juan Martín el Empecinado' and Baroja's 'El Escuadron del Brigante'." *Revista de Estudios Hispanicos* VI, No. 3 (October 1972): 335-44.*
Explains how Pérez Galdós and Baroja deal with the guerrilla aspect of Spain's War of Independence against Napoleon.

Mencken, H. L. Introduction to *Youth and Egolatry,* by Pío Baroja, pp. 11-20. New York: A. Knopf, 1920.
Discusses Baroja's position in contemporary Spain.

Olstad, Charles. "Symbolic Structure in Baroja's *Camino de perfeccion.*" *Kentucky Romance Quarterly* XXIII, No. 4 (1976): 451-65.
Parallels the hero-quest myth with the efforts of Ossorio, the protagonist of Baroja's *Camino de perfeccion.*

Sender, Ramón. "Posthumous Baroja." *New Mexico Quarterly* XXX, No. 1 (Spring 1960): 6-10.
Brief biographical characterization of Baroja.

Shaw, D. L. "A Reply to 'Deshumanización'—Baroja on the Art of the Novel." *Hispanic Review* XXV, No. 2 (April 1957): 105-11.*
Discusses the artistic views of José Ortega y Gasset and Baroja.

Starkie, Walter. "Some Novelists of Modern Spain." *The Nineteenth Century and After* 48, No. 583 (September 1925): 452-61.*
Examines Baroja's stylistic tendencies, and those of other Spanish writers.

Templin, E. H. "Pío Baroja: Three Pivotal Concepts." *Hispanic Review* 12, No. 4 (October 1944): 306-29.
Discusses character psychology in Baroja's novels.

"People." *Time* LXVIII, No. 18 (29 October 1956): 47.*
Account of Ernest Hemingway's visit to the dying Baroja. Hemingway declared to the Spanish author: "I deplore the fact that you have not yet received a Nobel Prize, especially when it was given to so many who deserved it less, like me, who am only an adventurer."

Maxim Gorky

1868-1936

(Also transliterated as Maksim; also Gorki, Gorkii, and Gor'ky; pseudonym of Aleksei Maksimovich Peshkov; also transliterated as Alexey, Alexei, and Aleksey; also Maximovich and Mikhaylovich; also Pyeshkov) Russian novelist, dramatist, short story writer, essayist, autobiographer, diarist, and poet.

Gorky is recognized as one of the earliest and foremost exponents of socialist realism in literature. His brutal, yet romantic, portraits of Russian life and his sympathetic depictions of the working class had an inspirational effect on the oppressed people of his native land. From 1910 until his death, Gorky was considered Russia's greatest living writer; today he is acclaimed in the Soviet Union as the voice of the proletariat and the model for all future writers. Gorky the tramp, the rebel, is as much a legend as the strong, individual characters presented in his stories. His hero was a new type in the history of Russian literature—a figure drawn from the masses of a growing industrialized society; his most famous novel, *Mat' (Mother)*, was the first in that country to portray the factory worker as a force destined to break down the existing order.

Gorky was orphaned at the age of ten and raised by his maternal grandparents. He was often treated harshly by his grandfather, and it was from his grandmother that Gorky received what little kindness he experienced as a child. During his thirteenth year, Gorky ran away from Nizhniy Novgorod, the city of his birth (now called Gorky) and lived a precarious existence as a tramp and vagrant, wandering from one job to another. Frequently beaten by his employers, nearly always hungry and ill-clothed, Gorky came to know the seamy side of Russian life as few writers before him. At the age of nineteen, he attempted suicide by shooting himself in the chest. The event became a turning point in Gorky's life; his outlook changed from one of despair to one of hope. Within a few years he began publishing stories in the provincial press. Written under the pseudonym Maxim Gorky (Maxim the Bitter), these stories stressed the strength and individualism of the Russian peasant. When they were collected and published in *Ocherki i rasskazy*, Gorky gained recognition throughout Russia. His second volume of stories, *Rasskazy*, along with the production of his controversial play *Na dne (The Lower Depths)*, assured his success and brought him acclaim in western Europe and the United States. Gorky's fame in the West coincided with increasing suspicion from the Russian authorities, who considered the author a source of the country's growing political unrest. In 1901 he was briefly jailed for publishing the revolutionary poem "Pesnya o burevestnike" ("Song of the Stormy Petrel") in a Marxist review. Three years later, he established the Znanie publishing firm to provide a forum for socially conscious writers. The friendship and advice of Nikolai Lenin strengthened Gorky's growing political radicalism. He was very active during the revolution of 1905, and after its failure he was forced to flee abroad. He was allowed to return home in 1913, and again he resumed his revolutionary activities. After the 1917 Revolution, Gorky did his best to help a number of authors and scientists during these years of political chaos. He left Russia one last time and settled on the island

of Capri for health reasons. In 1928 he returned to a national celebration of his literary, cultural, and moral contributions to the socialist cause, which took place on his sixtieth birthday. His death several years later, allegedly by poisoning, is still enveloped in mystery.

Gorky's work can be divided into three distinct groups. The first comprises his short stories, which many critics consider superior to his novels. In a highly romantic manner, these stories portray the subjugation of Russian peasants and down-and-outers. Many of these tales, such as "Makar Chudra" and "Chelkash," are based on actual peasant legends and allegories. In them Gorky championed the wisdom and self-reliance of his vagabonds over the brutality of the decaying bourgeoisie. One of the most accomplished of these stories is "Dvádtssat' shest' i odná" ("Twenty-Six Men and a Girl"), a tale in which Gorky described the sweatshop conditions in a provincial bakery. The second group consists of Gorky's autobiographical works, notably the trilogy *Detstvo (My Childhood)*, *V liudiakh (In the World)*, and *Moe universitety (My Universities)*, and his reminiscences of Tolstoy, *Vospominaniya o Lve Nikolaieviche Tolstom' (Reminiscences of Leo Nicolayevitch Tolstoi)*. The trilogy is considered one of the finest autobiographies in the Russian language. The work reveals Gorky as an acute observer of detail with a particular talent for describing people. The third group, by far the largest, consists of a number of novels and plays which are not as artistically successful as his short stories and autobiography. Gorky's first novel, *Foma Gordeyev (Foma Gordeiev)*, illustrates his characteristic admiration for the hard-working, honest individual. He contrasts the rising capitalist Ignat Gordeyev with his feeble, intellectual son Foma, a "seeker after the meaning of life," as are many of Gorky's other characters. The novel was the first of many in which the author portrayed the rise of Russian capitalism. Of all Gorky's novels, *Mother* is perhaps the least artistic, though it is interesting from a historical perspective as his only long work devoted to the Bolshevik movement. Among the twelve plays Gorky wrote between 1901 and 1913, only one, *The Lower Depths*, deals with the "dregs of society." Though the play has most of the structural faults of his other plays, primarily one-dimensional characters and a didactic tone, it is still regarded as one of the greatest proletarian dramas of the twentieth century. Gorky's other plays, including *Meshchane (The Smug Citizens)*, *Varvary (The Barbarians)*, and *Yegor Bulychyov i drugiye (Yegor Bulichov and Others)*, focus either on the intelligentsia or on the struggle between capitalist and socialist forces in pre-Soviet Russia.

Despite his success and importance as a socialist writer, most modern critics agree that Gorky deserves little of the idolatrous attention which has been lavished upon him. They argue that his work suffers from an overly dramatic quality, a coarse, careless style, and an externally imposed structure which results in fiction motivated by ideology rather than artistry. Many critics suggest that his failure to develop his characters and his tendency to lapse into irrelevant discussions about the meaning of life greatly damages the seriousness of his subjects. However, it is in his short stories and, especially, in his autobiography that Gorky fully realized his artistic powers. In these works he managed to curb his ideology and focus on those talents for which he has been consistently lauded: realistic description and the ability to portray the brutality of his environment. It is for these that Gorky has been called by Stefan Zweig, one of "the few genuine marvels of our present world."

While critical regard for his work fluctuates, Gorky himself has passed into history not only as a remarkable personality, but also as the precursor of socialist realism and, therefore, an important stimulus in twentieth-century Russian literature. With Vladimir Mayakovsky and Aleksandr Blok, he was one of the few Russian writers who played an equally important part in his country both before and after the Bolshevik Revolution. Although Gorky was an intellectual, and thus distanced from the common people who overthrew the Czarists and Mensheviks, he used his influence and talent after October 1917 to prevent the revolution from consuming itself in a savage blood-frenzy. As Janko Lavrin has noted, "It was here that his personality and his work served as a bridge between the creative values of the old intelligentsia culture and the culture of the risen masses, anxious to build up a new world."

PRINCIPAL WORKS

Ocherki i rasskazy. 3 vols. (short stories) 1898-99
Foma Gordeyev (novel) 1900
  [*Foma Gordeiev*, 1901]
Rasskazy. 9 vols. (short stories) 1900-10
Orlóff and His Wife (short stories) 1901
Meshchane (drama) 1902
  [*The Smug Citizens*, 1906; also published as *The Petty Bourgeois*, 1972]

Na dne (drama) 1902
  [*The Lower Depths*, 1912]
Dachniki (drama) 1904
  [*Summer Folk*, 1905]
Creatures that Once Were Men (short stories) 1905
Varvary (drama) 1906
  [*The Barbarians* published in *Seven Plays of Maxim Gorky*, 1945]
Mat' (novel) 1907
  [*Mother*, 1907]
Ispoved (novel) 1908
  [*A Confession*, 1910]
Chelkash, and Other Stories (short stories) 1915
V liudiakh (autobiography) 1916
  *[*In the World*, 1917; also published as *My Apprenticeship*, 1952]
Vospominaniya o Lve Nikolaieviche Tolstom' (memoirs) 1919
  [*Reminiscences of Leo Nicolayevitch Tolstoi*, 1920]
Moi universitety (autobiography) 1923
  *[*My University Days*, 1923; also published as *My Universities*, 1952]
Zametki iz dnevnika. Vospominaniya (diary) 1924
  [*Fragments from My Diary*, 1924]
Delo Artamonovykh (novel) 1925
  [*The Artamonov Business*, 1948]
Zhizn' Klima Samgina. 4 vols. (novel) 1927-36
  [Published in four volumes: *Bystander*, 1930; *The Magnet*, 1931; *Other Fires*, 1933; *The Specter*, 1938]
Detstvo (autobiography) 1928
  *[*My Childhood*, 1915]
Dvádtsat' shest' i odná (short stories) 1928
  [*Twenty-Six Men and a Girl*, 1902]
Sobranie sochinenii. 4 vols. (short stories, novels, dramas, essays, and poems) 1928-30
Yegor Bulychyov i drugiye (drama) 1932
  [*Yegor Bulichov and Others* published in *The Last Plays of Maxim Gorki*, 1937]
Zhizn' Matveya Kozhemyakina (novel) 1933
The Last Plays of Maxim Gorky (dramas) 1937
Seven Plays of Maxim Gorky (dramas) 1945
Orphan Paul (novel) 1946
Reminiscences (autobiography) 1946

*These works were published as *Autobiography of Maxim Gorky* in 1949.

ANTON TCHEKHOV (essay date 1898)

You ask what my opinion is about your stories. My opinion? Yours is an unmistakable talent, and a real, great talent. For instance, in your story **"In the Steppe"** it is expressed with extraordinary power, and I was even seized with envy that it was not I who wrote it. You are an artist, a wise man; you feel superbly, you are plastic; that is, when you describe a thing you see it and touch it with your hands. That is real art. There you have my opinion, and I am very glad to be able to express it to you. I repeat, I am very glad, and if we came to know each other and talk for an hour or two you would be convinced how highly I value you, and what hopes I build on your talent.

Shall I speak now of defects? But that is not so easy. To speak of the defects of a talent is like speaking of the defects of a great tree growing in the orchard; the chief consideration is not the tree itself, but the taste of the man who is looking at the tree. Is not that so?

I shall begin by saying that, in my opinion, you do not use sufficient restraint. You are like a spectator in the theatre who expresses his rapture so unreservedly that he prevents both himself and others from listening. Particularly is this lack of restraint felt in the descriptions of Nature with which you interrupt your dialogues; when one reads those descriptions one wishes they were more compact, shorter, put, say, into two or three lines. The frequent mention of tenderness, whispering, velvetiness, and so on, gives to these descriptions a certain character of rhetoric and monotony—and they chill the reader, almost tire him. Lack of restraint is felt also in the descriptions of women (**"Malva,"** **"On the Rafts"**) and in the love scenes. It is not vigour, nor breadth of touch, but plain unreserve. Then there is a frequent use of words unsuitable in stories of your type. "Accompaniment," "disc," "harmony"—such words mar. You talk often about waves. In your descriptions of educated people there is a feeling of strain, and, as it were, wariness; that is not because you have not sufficiently observed educated people; you know them, but you do not know precisely from what side to approach them. (pp. 261-62)

> *Anton Tchekhov, in his letter to Maxim Gorki on December 3, 1898, in* The Life and Letters of Anton Tchekhov, *edited and translated by S. S. Koteliansky and Philip Tomlinson (reprinted with permission of Macmillan Publishing Co., Inc., acting as agent for Crowell Collier & Macmillan, Ltd., formerly part of Cassell Ltd.), George H. Doran Company, 1925, Cassell & Co., 1925, pp. 261-62.*

ANTON TCHEKHOV   (essay date 1899)

Apparently you haven't quite understood me. I did not write to you of the crudeness but of the unfitness of foreign, not genuinely Russian, or rarely used words. With other writers such words as, for instance, "fatalistically" pass unnoticed, but your things are musical, harmonious, so that any crude little touch screams at the top of its voice. Of course, this is a matter of taste, and perhaps this is a sign of excessive irritability in me, or of the conservatism of a man who long ago adopted definite habits. In descriptions I can put up with "collegiate councillor" and "captain of the second rank," but "flirt" and "champion" (when they are used in descriptions) arouse my disgust.

Are you a self-taught man? In your stories you are a complete artist, and a cultured one in the truest sense. Least of all is crudeness charactertistic of you; are are wise, and your feelings are subtle and elegant. Your best things are **"In the Steppe"** and **"On the Rafts"**—did I write to you about that? These are superb things, models; one sees in them an artist who has passed through a very good school. I do not think I am mistaken. The only defect is lack of restraint, lack of grace. When a man spends the fewest number of movements on a certain definite action, that is grace. In your expenditure there is felt excess.

The descriptions of nature are artistic; you are a real landscape painter. But the frequent personification (anthropomorphism)—the sea breathes, the sky gazes, the steppe caresses, Nature whispers, speaks, mourns, and so on—such personifications make the descriptions somewhat monotonous, at times sugary, at times vague. Colour and expressiveness in descriptions of Nature are attained only by simplicity, by such simple phrases as "the sun set," "it became dark," "it began to rain," and so on—and that simplicity is inherent in you to a high degree, rare to anyone among the novelists. . . . (pp. 262-63)

> *Anton Tchekhov, in his letter to Maxim Gorki on January 3, 1899, in* The Life and Letters of Anton Tchekhov, *edited and translated by S. S. Koteliansky and Philip Tomlinson (reprinted with permission of Macmillan Publishing Co., Inc., acting as agent for Crowell Collier & Macmillan, Ltd., formerly part of Cassell Ltd.), George H. Doran Company, 1925, Cassell & Co., 1925, pp. 262-63.*

GEORGE CLIFTON EDWARDS   (essay date 1902)

Probably what attracted many readers to **"Foma Gordyeff,"** the first long novel by Maxim Gorky, was the announcement spread far and wide that here was the successor of Tolstoy, and at first one who had come to the book with the expectation of finding this true feels a keen disappointment. Stylistically there is not the slightest resemblance. Gorky chooses his words because they seem apt from a rhetorical standpoint and his scenes for their dramatic significance; Tolstoy seems to choose his because with his personages it is not possible to choose others. There are many places where in the work of the younger man you stop and say, "How clever! brilliant! cutting!" and then you go back to see just how the thought is running. The artlessness of Tolstoy's style is paralleled by that of his plot. The lives and struggles of his chief characters are of such concern to him that there is given them a pulsing vitality that it is possible to find in the work of no other novelist. In reading **"Foma Gordyeff"** you wonder if there could have been such a man, but there is no wonder in the case of "Anna Karenina," only pity and sympathy for her fate-dogged life.

There is a resemblance, however, closer than any external one could be, in feeling. Both of these men write from a sympathy with the down-trodden almost too deep for words, and they both write with that lack of silly optimism which those who do not think immediately denounce as pessimism. If pessimism means a weak surrender to evils too great for living, they are not pessimists; but if it means the open-eyed recognition of the fact that the condition of the world is just about as bad as it possibly could be at this day and time, then both are pessimists. But the word "pessimism" is not a deadly epithet even when applied to men whose strength is small, much less when applied to these two strong men. The one thing most deadening to all religion now is a calm and self-satisfied indifference that thinks that all is well because all of its narrow circle seems to be well; a pharisaical attitude of mind to which the blankest negation is to be preferred if only it can jolt into some sort of dissatisfaction. This is a service for tragedy and not for time destroyers. And to say that Gorky's work is of this type is at the outset to give it high praise.

"Foma Gordyeff" is a tragedy just as clearly as "Hamlet" is a tragedy. In both cases there is a soul-perplexed and weak struggling with problems too great to present solution, and in both cases the death that comes is a God-given relief. Foma's father and his mother are both out of the ordinary, made so perhaps to explain how there could be struck from the vicious selfishness of the Russian merchant class fire enough to show forth a soul. For this merchant class is brutal; brutal too not in the cold, thin style of American money getters, but with all the full-bloodedness and mass that we know as Russian for good or evil. The wealthy Russian merchant is only Tolstoy's most powerful and grasping peasant come to town and accommodated to the advanced ways of getting much for little. In his former weaker state the peasant saw men who were higher in the world than he seeking first money, houses, and land, and he sought them. By his own vigor he got them; and then he stops to think. His old aim of life (getting wealth) existing no longer as an aim, he has before him two things—to go on securing wealth which he sees he does not need, or to sit in idleness. The former, the American method, wears out the seeker and he has no life; and the other unlooses a volcano of passions, in the outbreak of which there is not the least consideration for a glozing etiquette. Now Ignat Gordyeff, Foma's father, belonged to the latter class, spending his time in alternate spasms of money-getting and of debauchery. This Ignat, who has never *lived,* who has never been out of the grasp of the two animal instincts of acquiring wealth and of raging with lust, has the responsibility of setting a son out in the world. . . . There is nothing in life more keenly pathetic or more common than the attempt that Ignat makes to talk seriously to Foma on the latter's return from his first business trip and his first debauch; the vanity of this father's trying to tell his son how to live when he himself never knew! There is the earnest desire of the father to say something at this crisis, the feeling that there has been done a wrong, the haste to have the unpleasant thing uttered, and the vain sinking back into commonplaces that must come when one man tries to restrain his brother from an evil that he does not see is an evil in his case also.

When Ignat dies, the son does not fall into sottishness because he has in him the disturbing element of a conscience. What made his father see, in crises, that there was an evil, is with Foma always, for his life is but one long crisis. He sees that the life that is lived around him is not life but death; but what resource is there against it? The thread of consistency that runs through his life is the feeling, now vague, now expressed, of the mystery of life: "I understand nothing, my dear fellow," he says at one time; "I simply wish to live." This is the reason for his succumbing to the physical charm of the peasant women on his first trip, the blind effort to see into the mystery of life; this, the reason for debauch after debauch, for discussion after discussion, for the final outbreak at the Pharisee's dinner—the outbreak that made it possible for his fox of an uncle to cage him as insane.

Evidently this book is not one to be chosen if one seek mere amusement or an intellectual anaesthetic in the face of stern life. It is a tragedy, and, unlike the tragedy that we generally think of when this word is used, one that comes home to the heart of every man who looks at life with a mind and a conscience. By society to-day, with its widely printed and often spoken word of Christ, and its every organization based on any principle save that of Christ, Gorky is tortured, and so he wrote the book. If any man is trying to think out these things, **"Foma Gordyeff"** will stimulate and enlighten him. It will give him no definite directions—no book can—but it will show him how the same life with which he is struggling strikes a man of genius and purpose. Gorky himself is struggling blindly with the world, but with great strength. He forces on his readers the reality of life, gives his best thoughts in reference to it, and then demands: "And what think you?" (pp. 234-37)

George Clifton Edwards, "Maxim Gorky," in The Sewanee Review *(reprinted by permission of the editor and The University of the South), Vol. X, No. 2, April, 1902, pp. 234-37.*

E. J. DILLON   (essay date 1902)

The deftness and grace with which Gorky personifies nature and blends elemental forces with human beings in a harmonious picture, intermingling sound with colour and fragrance with form, is unrivalled in Russian literature. His men and women, nay the readers themselves, become as the lotus-eaters whose souls are delighted with visions of glory and bliss. For the Over-tramp is a clever impressionist. Like the representatives of the latest school of pictorial art he paints what seems, rather than what is, utilising the fact that upon the cultured men of this nervous age—their perception of the real having become highly sensitised—impressions react more quickly and are more faithfully mirrored than in the minds of their fathers. Instead therefore of taking an impression by itself, and letting it unfold and grow gradually from germ to flower, he at once throws it into space, scattering its elements broadcast among the objects that lie around, aware that all the light-rays they reflect will again converge in the inner eye of the beholder. A complex soul-state is thus made to shimmer in many facets, and the reader glancing simultaneously at these receives the impress of a picture which is one and indivisible. . . . Light and shadow, sea and sky, rain and wind, the gloom and squalor of a hovel, the grey breadth of the cheerless steppe, play on the souls of the susceptible reader as on a chorded instrument, accompanying the words and actions of the *dramatis personæ,* and creating a tone of sentiment congruous with the tale. Maxim Gorky, relying largely upon this curious fact, often preludes his psychological dramas with soul-subduing or stirring accords of this music of nature, and while the heartstrings of the reader are still vibrating in sympathetic response the human figures thus heralded enter upon the stage. Again after an exciting episode in the story, the lulling breath of faint winds sighing over the Bessarabian wolds soothes the fierce fever and brings with it a presentiment of coming calm. Or it is the howling of the storm, which stirs not the sea only but our very soul to its depths, attuning it to a mood responsive to the wild enthusiasms or savage despair of its hero.

Take, for example, the frame of the richly coloured picture he has painted of the graceful, free, and shameless Malva, a Phryne of the slums. . . . (pp. 313-15)

[Here, Gorky] blends his tints with harmonious effect, and sounds, scents, colours, flow in upon our souls in soothing or stimulating streams, calling forth impressions, inducing moods which can be uttered only in the divine language of Beethoven or Chopin. The consummate art with which he thus draws upon nature, working her sombre hues into the cold greys of his melancholy men and women, is calculated to thrill the hearts of his sensitive countrymen. And yet he is attracted much less by the beautiful in nature than by the sublime. He makes the boundless, monotonous steppe and the restless waste of waters the background of most of his mournful pictures, and they spread themselves out before the gaze of the beholder in forms and colours and combinations which the inartistic eye had never before suspected. (pp. 316-17)

It is in the just perception of this mystic closeness of touch between men and nature that Gorky has outdone all his predecessors. The subtle action and reaction of such disparate objects acquire under his treatment a soft consciousness which only poetic pantheism can bestow. Animals, trees, the water, the mould, darkness and light, are fused by his fiery fancy into one universal soul, the will-o'-the-wisp of intellect being quenched for ever. (p. 318)

[His] outcasts can dispense with regulated human intercourse as they can do without a bed or a roof. They stand aloof each one by himself, in a certain sense entire men, bad or diseased, if you will, but at least true to their nature. It is their destiny—so they feel—to bring forth thorns, and they make no endeavour to palm them off as figs or grapes, like many of the wiser in their generation, who know better than they do; and that is an item to their credit.

Gorky is a consummate master of the short sketch, the *genre:* a waste of water or a wilderness of grey land as background and two or three human figures as *dramatis personæ,* and the picture is complete. His force lies in showing—unconsciously it may be—that however begrimed, the human soul can never wholly shed the fragrance of the paradise from which it has been expelled: selfishness, baseness, cruelty, murder itself may blacken and disfigure it, but beneath the ugly crust of crime the spirit of the Godhead is still alive though imprisoned, and may even be conjured up by those who utter the magic word, whether or not they know its virtue. It was a real *tour de force* thus to throw the glamour of poetry on the loathsomeness of latter-day lepers. To paint the idylls of squalid beggars and hardened criminals from whom almost every trace of the human spirit has seemingly vanished, and to allow them to gather a certain quality of nobility from the background of the vast steppe, the boundless ocean, was an undertaking worthy of a poet; and had he thus broken through our brutal classification of men, and widened the range of human sympathy by purely artistic methods, the praise lavished upon his achievement would have been well deserved. But instead of approaching Art in the humble spirit of self-surrender, and helping others to a pleasurable apprehension of life by presenting it as it appeared—not indeed to the will which feels attracted or repelled, but to the passionless æsthetic sense—Gorky deliberately strove to touch his readers' sensibilities on behalf not only of his wayward men and women, but also of their subversive principles.

Of this deadly sin against Art we have seen the disastrous effects in his shorter sketches, many of which a wise selection would have excluded from his collected writings; but it offends us still more in his ambitious flights, his attempts at novel writing, lacking, as he does, that architectural conception which sees and realises unity in plurality, harmony in discord. In **"Foma Gordyeeff,"** for example, he has merely set side by side a number of figures, some of them palpitating with life, after the naïve manner of those early Italian masters who juxtaposed several scenes on one and the same canvas, with no coordination of parts, no growth of design, no organic completeness, but each independent of the others, like Russian tramps in real life. (pp. 319-21)

Evidently Maxim Gorky is gifted with a marvellous power of seeing life, especially those morbid phases of it with which he himself came mostly in contact, and of reproducing his sense of those in a series of realistic pictures which burn themselves on the reader's mind, throwing him into the swiftly changing moods of the actors of the drama. For Gorky's character penetrates his production, his own heart and soul animate his creations, his thoughts and feelings are theirs, nor is he wont to keep the smallest portion of himself in reserve, as it were, for any sudden emergency. He cannot wholly detach himself from his work, his æsthetic intuition, the inner mirror, which he holds up to nature and to men is but imperfectly shielded from the sullying breath of the individual will. Impassioned and impetuous, he is incapable of leaving a certain space between himself and the types which he calls into being. Hence he, too, like them, is buffeted and torn by wild storms of emotion, for his entire being is on the surface of the wind-lashed water, instead of partly reposing, like a mighty iceberg, in the calm depths below. It is impossible not to feel when reading the life-story of Ignat, the father of Foma Gordyeeff, and still more that of Ilya Loonyeff [in **"A Trio"**], which occasionally turns the microscope upon the nauseous workings of gross temptations, that if he should ever find the secret—and he seems to be moving up close to it of late—of eliminating that baneful subjective element, wholly alien from art, which so often intrudes upon and mars his best work, Russia may indeed find in him the legitimate successor to the illustrious author of "Anna Karenyina." (pp. 348-49)

> *E. J. Dillon, in his* Maxim Gorky: His Life and Writings, *Isbister and Company Limited, 1902, 390 p.*

MAX BEERBOHM (essay date 1903)

I am all for relaxing the girths of modern drama. The modern technique is much too tight, in my opinion. . . . [Any sign] of a movement towards looser form is always sped very heartily by me. But looseness of form is one thing, formlessness is another. Such devices as prologues, and epilogues, and scenes of mere conversation, are all quite defensible, quite commendable. But the line must be drawn somewhere, and drawn a long way before we come down to **"The Lower Depths"** of Gorki. There must be some kind of artistic unity—unity either of story or of idea. There must be a story, though it need not be stuck to like grim death; or there must be, with similar reservation, an idea. Gorki has neither asset. At any rate he does nothing with either asset. Enough that he gives us, honestly and fearlessly, "a slice of life"? Enough, certainly, if he did anything of the kind. But he doesn't. **"The Lower Depths"** is no "slice." It is chunks, hunks, shreds and gobbets, clawed off anyhow, chucked at us anyhow. "No thank you" is the only possible reception for such work. We are not at all squeamish. But we demand of the playwright who deals with ugly things, just as we demand of the playwright who deals with pretty things, something more than the sight of his subject-matter. . . . Æsthetic pain or pleasure depends not at all on the artist's material: it does depend, entirely, on the artist. A convenient proof of this law may be made through comparison of **"The Lower Depths"** with another foreign play, "The Good Hope," which the Stage Society produced in its past season. [Herman] Heijermans, its author, had taken a not less ghastly theme than Gorki's. Fisher-folk doomed to starve or to sacrifice their lives for the enrichment of an unscrupulous shipowner are not less ghastly a theme than are drink-sodden wastrels in a "night refuge." But Heijermans had an idea, and this idea he expressed, very beautifully, through a coherent story. He evoked, through art, a sense of pity and awe; and so he sent us away happy, despite our very real indignation that in real life such things should be. I would willingly subscribe something to any "fund for the amelioration of the condition of Dutch fishermen." But, also, I cherish the memory of a delightful afternoon. On the other hand, no "fund for the amelioration of the condition of wastrels in Moscow" would extract from me a brass farthing. I am not interested in them. I may become so, in the future. I shall become so, if some Russian artist arise and handle well the theme which Gorki has botched. If ever I meet Gorki, who is said to be an impressive person in real life, or if ever I read one of his books, which are said to be impressive, I shall be awakened doubtless, to a quick sympathy with Russian wastrels. But Gorki on the stage is merely a bore, and a disgusting bore. I dare say the characters in **"The Lower Depths"** are closely observed from life. But so are the figures in the lower depths of Madame Tussaud's quaint establishment. I defy you to leave the Chamber of Horrors a wiser and a better man, or a man conscious of an æsthetic impression. Where there is no meaning, no unity, nothing but bald and unseemly horror, you must needs be merely disgusted and anxious to change the subject. It is just possible, as I have hinted, that Gorki may have meant to express some sort of an idea. Let us credit him with having meant to express a very noble idea. But that idea is not enubilable from the muzzy maunderings of the wastrels. They maunder muzzily on, these wastrels, just as they would in real life; but no ray is cast from without on their darkness. There is an old man, who appears suddenly, and in whom we dimly descry a "raisonneur." But he disappears, not less suddenly, leaving behind him no lesson except a vague sentimental optimism. This lack of any underlying idea would not matter if there were any narrative unity. An artist has the right to tell a story without any criticism of its meaning. The story itself produces that artistic unity which, if there is no story, can be produced only by an underlying idea. But Gorki as story-teller is not less far to seek than Gorki as thinker. Two or three clumsy little bits of a story are wedged in here and there. But they have nothing to do with the play. (pp. 302-04)

Gorki's work is to dramaturgy as snap-shot photographs are to the art of painting; and a proscenium (literally a gold frame) deserves something better than the misuse of being made to nullify such value as such work may have. (p. 305)

> *Max Beerbohm, "The Lower Depths" (originally published in* The Saturday Review, *London, Vol. 96, No. 2510, December 5, 1903), in his* Around Theatres *(reprinted by permission of Mrs. Eva Reichmann), revised edition, Rupert Hart-Davis, 1953, pp. 302-05.**

JAMES HUNEKER   (essay date 1905)

After witnessing a performance of Maxim Gorky's *Nachtasyl—The Night Refuge* is a fair equivalent in English—one realizes, not without a shudder, that there are depths within depths, abysms beneath abysms, still unexplored by the dramatic adventurer. The late Emile Zola posed all his lifetime as the father of naturalism in literature; but he might have gone to school to learn the alphabet of his art at the knees of the young man from Nijni Novgorod, Maxim Gorky. That anarchist of letters has taught us lessons of the bitterest import, Gorky the Bitter One. (p. 269)

For years I have searched for the last word in dramatic naturalism, and in Gorky's *Nachtasyl* I found it. . . . Gorky, himself a lycanthrope, pessimist, despiser of his fellow-men, has assembled in this almost indescribable and unspeakable mélange—for it is not a play—a set of men and women whose very lives smell to heaven; the setting recalls one of his stories, *Men with Pasts*. (It is in *Orloff and his Wife*.)

An utter absence of theatricalism and a naïveté in dramatic feeling proclaim Gorky a man of genius and also one quite ignorant of the fundamental rules of the theatre. His four acts might be compressed into two, or, better still, into one. Only the fatigue and gloom engendered would interfere with this scheme, for there is far too much talk, far too little movement.

Gorky, like many uneducated men of power, loves to moralize, to discuss life and its meanings. He is at times veritably sophomoric in this respect. Long speeches are put into the mouths of his characters, who forthwith spout the most dreary commonplaces about destiny, luck, birth, and death.

The strength of the play lies in its presentation of character. Characterization, with a slender thread of narrative, no effective "curtains," comprises the material of this vivid experiment. Nevertheless, it burns the memory because of its shocking candour and pity-breeding truths. (pp. 272-73)

Gorky, like Gogol, loves to picture some poor wretch with a dominant passion, and then to place him in surroundings that will move the machinery of his being. And with all his hatred of life, of men, pity oozes from his pages, sometimes contemptuous, sometimes passionate, pity. *The Night Refuge* is a cellar with a kitchen, a few holes in the wall for sleeping purposes. Its counterpart exists in every great city. Thieves, prostitutes, men and women, the very dregs of life, pass their battered days and nights in these foul caves. (p. 273)

How to weave a play from such unpromising material must have puzzled Gorky. Evidently he did not try, preferring the easier way of letting his people tell their own stories and reducing technical construction to a mere dropping of the curtain from time to time. In fact, there is far more dramatic intrigue in Tolstoy's *Powers of Darkness*, of which this piece is really a pendant. Gorky does not fear the naked truth as do many literary artists who have social position and reputations to maintain. (p. 276)

The amateur of sensations, exquisite, morbid, or brutal, must feel after *Nachtasyl* that the bottomless pit has been almost plumbed. What further exploitation of woe, of crime, of humanity stripped of its adventitious social trappings, can be made? And this question is put by every generation without in the least stopping the fresh shaking up of the dramatic kaleidoscope. The Gorky play, even if it disgusts at times, at least arouses pity and terror, and thus, according to the classical formula, purges the minds of its spectators. Compared to the drama of lubricity manufactured in Paris and annually exported to America, this little study of a group of outcast men and women is a powerful moral lesson. That it is a play I do not assert, nor could it be put on the boards in America without a storm of critical and public censure. Americans go to the theatre to be amused and not to have their nerves assaulted. . . . The ugly cancers of the social system should never be exposed, especially by a candid hand! In art, to tell truths of this kind does not alone shame the devil, but outrages the community. No wonder Emperor William does not grace such performances by his presence. No wonder Gorky is a suspect in Russia. He tells the truth, which in the twentieth century is more dangerous than hammering dynamite! (pp. 283-84)

> *James Huneker, "Maxim Gorky's 'Nachtasyl'," in his* Iconoclasts, a Book of Dramatists: Ibsen, Strindberg, Becque, Hauptmann, Sudermann, Hervieu, Gorky, Duse and D'Annunzio, Maeterlinck and Bernard Shaw *(copyright © 1905 Charles Scribner's Sons), Charles Scribner's Sons, 1905, pp. 269-85.*

WILLION LYON PHELPS   (essay date 1911)

As an artist, [Gorki] will not bear a moment's comparison with Andreev; but some of his short stories and his play, *The Night Asylum,* have the genuine Russian note of reality, and a rude strength much too great for its owner's control. He has never written a successful long novel, and his plays have no coherence; but, after all, the man has the real thing—vitality. (p. 215)

[Gorki's full-length novels] have all the incoherence and slipshod workmanship of Dostoevski, without the latter's glow of brotherly love. His first real novel, *Foma Gordeev,* an epic of the Volga, has many beautiful descriptive passages, really lyric and idyllic in tone, mingled with an incredible amount of drivel. The character who plays the title-rôle is a typical Russian windbag, irresolute and incapable, like so many Russian heroes; but whether drunk or sober, he is destitute of charm. He is both dreary and dirty. The opening chapters are written with great spirit, and the reader is full of happy expectation. One goes farther and fares worse. After the first hundred pages, the book is a prolonged anti-climax, desperately dull. Altogether the best passage in the story is the description of the river in spring, impressive not merely for its beauty and accuracy of language, but because the Volga is interpreted as a symbol of the spirit of the Russian people, with vast but unawakened possibilities. (pp. 221-22)

The novel *Varenka Olessova* is a tedious book of no importance. The hero is, of course, the eternal Russian type, a man of good education and no backbone; he lacks resolution, energy, will power, and will never accomplish anything. . . . Contrasted with him is the girl Varenka, a simple child of nature, who prefers silly romances to Russian novels, and whose virgin naïveté is a constant puzzle to the conceited ass who does not know whether he is in love with her or not. Indeed, he asks himself if he is capable of love for any one. The only interesting pages in this stupid story are concerned with a discussion on reading, between Varenka and the young man, where her denunciation of Russian fiction is, of course, meant to proclaim its true superiority. In response to the question whether she reads Russian authors, the girl answers with conviction: ''Oh, yes! But I don't like them! . . . In Russian books, one cannot understand at all why the men continue to live. What's the use of writing books if the author has nothing remarkable to say?''

The long novel *Mother* is a good picture of life among the working-people in a Russian factory, that is, life as seen through Gorki's eyes; all cheerfulness and laughter are, of course, absent, and we have presented a dull monotone of misery. The factory itself is the villain of the story, and resembles some grotesque wild beast, that daily devours the blood, bone, and marrow of the throng of victims that enter its black jaws. The men, women, and children are represented as utterly brutalised by toil; in their rare moments of leisure, they fight and beat each other unmercifully, and even the little children get dead drunk. Socialist and revolutionary propaganda are secretly circulated among these stupefied folk, and much of the narrative is taken up with the difficulties of accomplishing this distribution; for the whole book itself is nothing but a revolutionary tract. The characters, including the pitiful Mother herself, are not vividly drawn, they are not alive, and one forgets them speedily; as for plot, there is none, and the book closes with the brutal murder of the old woman. It is a tedious, inartistic novel, with none of the relief that would exist in actual life. Turgenev's poorest novel, *Virgin Soil,* which also gives us a picture of a factory, is immensely superior from every point of view.

But if *Mother* is a dull book, *The Spy* is impossible. It is full of meaningless and unutterably dreary jargon; its characters are sodden with alcohol and bestial lusts. One abominable woman's fat body spreads out on an arm-chair ''like sour dough.'' And indeed, this novel bears about the same relation to a finished work of art that sour dough bears to a good loaf of bread. The characters are poorly conceived, and the story is totally without movement. Not only is it very badly written, it lacks even good material. The wretched boy, whose idiotic states of mind are described one after the other, and whose eventual suicide is clear from the start, is a disgusting whelp, without any human interest. One longs for his death with murderous intensity, and when, on the last page, he throws himself under the train, the reader experiences a calm and sweet relief.

Much of Gorki's work is like Swift's poetry, powerful not because of its cerebration or spiritual force, but powerful only from the physical point of view, from its capacity to disgust. It appeals to the nose and the stomach rather than to the mind and the heart. (pp. 223-26)

A distinguished American novelist has said that in Gorki ''seems the body without the soul of Russian fiction, and sodden with despair. The soul of Russian fiction is the great thing.'' This is, indeed, the main difference between his work and that of the giant Dostoevski. In the latter's darkest scenes the spiritual flame is never extinct.

Gorki lacks either the patient industry or else the knowledge necessary to make a good novel. He is seen at his best in short stories, for his power comes in flashes. In *Twenty-six Men and a Girl,* the hideous tale that gave him his reputation in America, one is conscious of the streak of genius that he undoubtedly possesses. The helpless, impotent rage felt by the wretched men as they witness the debauching of a girl's body and the damnation of her soul, is clearly echoed in the reader's mind. Gorki's notes are always the most thrilling when played below the range of the conventional instrument of style. This is not low life, it is sub-life.

He is, after all, a student of sensational effect; and the short story is peculiarly adapted to his natural talent. He cannot develop characters, he cannot manage a large group, or handle a progressive series of events. But in a lurid picture of the pit, in a flash-light photograph of an underground den, in a sudden vision of a heap of garbage with unspeakable creatures crawling over it, he is impressive. (pp. 227-28)

Gorki, in spite of his zeal for the revolutionary cause, has no remedy for the disease he calls Life. He is eaten up with rage at the world in general, and tries to make us all share his disgust with it. But he teaches us nothing; he has little to say that we can transmute into anything valuable. This is perhaps the reason why the world has temporarily, at any rate, lost interest in him. He was a new sensation, he shocked us, and gave us strange thrills, after the manner of new and unexpected sensations. Gorki came up on the literary horizon like an evil storm, darkening the sky, casting an awful shadow across the world's mirth and laughter, and making us shudder in the cold and gloom.

Gorki completely satisfied that strange but almost universal desire of well-fed and comfortable people to go slumming. (pp. 228-29)

But we soon had enough of it, and our experienced and professional guide failed to perceive the fact. He showed us more of the same thing, and then some more. Such sights and sounds—authentic visions and echoes of hell—merely repeated, began to lose their uncanny fascination. The man who excited us became a bore. For the worst thing about Gorki is his dull monotony, and vice is even more monotonous than virtue, perhaps because it is more common. Open the pages of almost any of his tales, it is always the same thing, the same criminals, the same horrors, the same broken ejaculations and brutish rage. Gorki has shown no capacity for development, no power of variety and complexity. His passion for mere effect has reacted unfavourably on himself. (pp. 229-30)

He is certainly not a great teacher, but he has the power to ask awkward questions so characteristic of Andreev, Artsybashev, and indeed of all Russian novelists. We cannot answer him with a shrug of the shoulders or a sceptical smile. He shakes the foundations of our fancied security by boldly questioning what we had come to regard as axioms. . . . Russian novelists are a thorn in the side of complacent optimism.

And yet surely, if life is not so good as it conceivably might be, it is not so darkly bitter as the Bitter One would have us believe. In a short article that he wrote about one of the playgrounds of America, he betrayed his own incurable jaundice. In the New York *Independent* for 8 August 1907, Gorki published a brilliant impressionistic sketch of Coney Island, and called it *Boredom.* Gorki at Coney Island is like Dante at a country fair. (pp. 230-31)

Gorki speaks poetically in his article of the "fantastic city all of fire" that one sees at night. But as he mingles with the throng, disgust fills his lonely heart. (pp. 231-32)

"In the glittering gossamer of its fantastic buildings, tens of thousands of grey people, like patches on the ragged clothes of a beggar, creep along with weary faces and colourless eyes. . . .

"But the precaution has been taken to blind the people, and they drink in the vile poison with silent rapture. The poison contaminates their souls. Boredom whirls about in an idle dance, expiring in the agony of its inanition. . . ." . . .

This sketch is valuable not merely because of the impression of a distinguished foreign writer of one of the sights of America, but because it raises in our minds an obstinate doubt of his capacity to tell the truth about life in general. Suppose a person who had never seen Coney Island should read Gorki's vivid description of it, would he really know anything about Coney Island? Of course not. The crowds at Coney Island are as different from Gorki's description of them as anything could well be. Now then, we who know the dregs of Russian life only through Gorki's pictures, can we be certain that his representations are accurate? Are they reliable history of fact, or are they the revelations of a heart that knoweth its own bitterness? (p. 233)

William Lyon Phelps, "Gorki," in his Essays on Russian Novelists *(reprinted with permission of Macmillan Publishing Co., Inc.; copyright 1911 by Macmillan Publishing Co., Inc.; renewed 1939 by William Lyon Phelps), Macmillan, 1911, pp. 215-33.*

D. S. MIRSKY (essay date 1926)

The greatest name in the realistic revival is Maxim Gorky's. Next to Tolstoy he is to-day the only Russian author of the modern period who has a really world-wide reputation and one which is not, like Chekhov's, confined to the *intelligentsias* of the various countries of the world. Gorky's career has been truly wonderful; risen from the lowest depths of the provincial proletariate, he was not thirty when he became the most popular writer and the most discussed man in Russia. After a period of dazzling celebrity during which he was currently placed by the side of Tolstoy, and unquestionably above Chekhov, his fame suffered an eclipse, and he was almost forgotten by the Russian educated classes. But his fame survived abroad and among the lower classes at home, and after 1917 his universal reputation and his connexion with the new rulers of Russia made him the obvious champion of Russian literature. However, this new position was due to his personal rather than to his literary merits, and though in the general opinion of competent people Gorky's last books (beginning with *Childhood* . . .) are superior to his early stories, his literary popularity is to-day quite out of proportion to what it was a quarter of a century ago. And those works by which he is most likely to survive as a classic will never have known the joy and wonder of immediate success. (pp. 106-07)

In all Gorky's early work his Realism is strongly modified by Romanticism, and it was this Romanticism that made for his success in Russia, although it was his Realism that carried it over the frontier. To the Russian reader the novelty of his early stories consisted in their bracing and dare-devil youthfulness; to the foreign public it was the ruthless crudeness with which he described his nether world. Hence the enormous difference between Russian and foreign appreciations of the early Gorky— it comes from a difference of background. Russians saw him against the gloom and depression of Chekhov and the other novelists of the eighties; foreigners, against a screen of conventional and reticent Realism of Victorian times. His very first stories are purely romantic. Such are his first published story, *Makar Chudra, The Old Woman Izergil* . . . and his early poetry. . . . (p. 112)

This Romanticism is very theatrical and tawdry, but it was genuinely infectious and did more to endear Gorky to the Chekhov-fed Russian reader than all the rest of his work. It crystallized in a philosophy which is expressed most crudely and simply in the very early parable of *The Siskin Who Lied and the Truth-loving Woodpecker,* and which may be formulated as a preference of a lie that elevates the soul to a depressing and ignoble truth.

By 1895 Gorky abandons the conventional stock-in-trade of his early gipsy and robber stories and develops a manner which combines realistic form and romantic inspiration. His first story, published in the "big" press, *Chelkash* . . . , is also one of the best. His subject is the contrast between the gay, cynical, and careless smuggler Chelkash and the lad he employs to help him in his dangerous business, a typical peasant, timid and greedy. The story is well constructed, and though the romantic glamour round Chelkash is anything but "realistic," his figure is drawn with convincing vividness. Other stories of the same kind are *Malva* . . . , who is a female Chelkash, and *My Fellow-Traveller* . . . , which from the point of view of character-drawing is perhaps the best of the lot; that primitive immoralist, the Georgian Prince Sharko, with whom the narrator makes on foot the long journey from Odessa to Tiflis, is a truly wonderful creation, which deserves to stand by the side of the best of his recent character sketches. There is not an ounce of idealization in Sharko, though it is quite obvious that the author's "artistic sympathy" is entirely on his side. One of the features of the early Gorky which won him most admirers was his way of "describing nature." A typical instance of this manner is the beginning of *Malva,* with the famous opening paragraph consisting of the two words, *"More smeyalos"* (The sea was laughing). But it must be confessed that the brightness of these descriptions has greatly faded and fails to-day to take us by storm. About 1897 Realism begins to outweigh Romanticism, and in *Ex-People (Byvshii lyudi* . . . ; in the English version,

Creatures That Once Were Men, an arbitrary mistranslation)
Realism is dominant, and the heroic gestures of Captain Ku-
valda fail to relieve the drab gloom of the setting. In this story
and in all other stories of these years, a feature appears which
was to be the undoing of Gorky: an immoderate love for "philosophical" conversations. As long as he kept free from it, he
gave proof of a great power of construction, a power which is
rare in Russian writers, and which gives some of his early
stories a solidness and cohesion almost comparable to Chekhov's. But he had not Chekhov's sense of artistic economy,
and though in such stories as *Her Lover* (in Russian, *Boles . . .*)
and *To Kill Time* (untranslated) the skeleton is firm and strong,
the actual texture of the story has not that inevitableness which
is the hall-mark of Chekhov. Besides (and in this respect Chekhov was not better), Gorky's Russia is "neutral," the words
are mere signs and have no individual life. If it were not for
certain catchwords, they might have been a translation from
any language. The only one of Gorky's early stories which
makes one forget all his shortcomings (except the mediocrity
of his style) is that which may be considered as closing the
period, *Twenty-six Men and a Girl.* . . . The story is cruelly
realistic. But it is traversed by such a powerful current of
poetry, by such a convincing faith in beauty and freedom and
in the essential nobility of man, and at the same time it is told
with such precision and necessity, that it can hardly be refused
the name of a masterpiece. It places Gorky, the young Gorky,
among the true classics of our literature. But *Twenty-six Men
and a Girl* is alone in its supreme beauty—and it is the last of
Gorky's early good work: for fourteen years he was to be a
wanderer in tedious and fruitless mazes. (pp. 112-14)

[Gorky's autobiographical works] have, up to the present, formed
the contents of five volumes: the three volumes of the autobiographical series [*Childhood, Among Strangers,* and *My Universities*] . . . , a volume of *Recollections* (of Tolstoy, Korolenko, Chekhov, Andreev, etc.); and *Notes from a Diary.* . . .
In these works Gorky has abandoned the form of fiction and
all (apparent) literary invention; he has also hidden himself
and given up taking any part in his characters' "quest for
truth." He is a realist, a great realist finally freed from all the
scales of romance, tendency, or dogma. He has finally become
an objective writer. This makes his autobiographical series one
of the strangest autobiographies ever written. It is about everyone except himself. His person is only the pretext round which
to gather a wonderful gallery of portraits. Gorky's most salient
feature in these books is his wonderful visual convincingness.
The man seems to be all eyes, and the reader sees, as if they
were painted, the wonderfully live and vivid figures of the
characters. We can never forget such figures as those of the
old Kashirins, his grandfather and grandmother; or of the good
Bishop Chrysanthus; or of that strange heathen and barbaric
orgy of the inhabitants of the little station (*My Universities*).
The series invariably produces an impression of hopeless gloom
and pessimism on the foreign, and even on the older Russian,
reader, but we who have been trained to a less conventional
and reticent realism than George Eliot's, fail to share that
feeling. Gorky is not a pessimist, and if he is, his pessimism
has nothing to do with his representation of Russian life, but
rather with the chaotic state of his philosophical views, which
he has never succeeded in making serve his optimism, in spite
of all his efforts in that direction. As it is, Gorky's autobiographical series represents the world as ugly but not unrelieved—the redeeming points, which may and must save humanity, are enlightenment, beauty, and sympathy. The other
two books reveal Gorky as an even greater writer than does
this autobiography. The English-speaking public has appreci-

ated the wonderful *Recollections of Tolstoy* (which appeared in
the *London Mercury* soon after their first publication), and in
speaking of Tolstoy I have mentioned them as the most worth-
while pages ever written about that great man. And this in
spite of the fact Gorky is most certainly nothing like Tolstoy's
intellectual equal. It is his eyes that see through, rather than
his mind that understands. The wonderful thing is that he saw
and noted down things other people were incapable of seeing,
or, if they saw, powerless to record. Gorky's image of Tolstoy
is rather destructive than constructive: it sacrifices the unity of
legend to the complexity of life. It deals a death-blow to the
hagiographical image of "St. Leo." Equally remarkable are
his *Recollections of Andreev,* which contain one of his best
chapters—the one which describes the heavy and joyless drunkenness of the younger writer. *Notes from a Diary* is a book
of characters. Nowhere more than here does Gorky reveal his
artist's love for his country, which is after all to him the best
country in the world in spite of all his Internationalism, of all
his scientific dreams, and of all the dirty things he has seen in
her. "Russia is a wonderful country, where even fools are
original," is the burden of the book. It is a collection of portraits, striking characters, and of glimpses of strange minds.
Originality is the keynote. Some of the characters are those of
very eminent men: two fragments are devoted to Alexander
Blok. Memorable Portraits are drawn of the well-known Old-
Believer millionaire Bugrov, who himself used to cultivate
Gorky as an original; and of Anna Schmidt, the mystical correspondent of Vladimir Soloviev. Other interesting chapters
are those on the morbid attraction exercised on human beings
by fires; and the uncanny things people sometimes do when
they are alone and don't expect to be overlooked. With the
exception of *Recollections of Tolstoy,* this last book is perhaps
the best Gorky ever wrote. Other stories have appeared in
periodicals signed by him which partly continue the manner
of *Notes from a Diary,* partly seem to indicate a return to more
conventional and constructed forms of fiction. This seems dangerous, but Gorky has so often deceived us by his developments
that this time our misgivings may again be deceived.

Gorky's last books have met with universal and immediate
appreciation. And yet he has not become a living literary influence. His books are read as freshly discovered classics, not
as novelties. In spite of his great personal part in the literature
of to-day (innumerable young writers look up to him as their
sponsor in the literary world), his work is profoundly unlike
all the work of the younger generation; first of all, for his
complete lack of interest in style, and, secondly, for his very
unmodern interest in human psychology. The retrospective
character of all his recent work seems to emphasize the impression that it belongs to a world that is no more ours. (pp. 118-
20)

> D. S. Mirsky, "Gorky," in his Contemporary Rus-
> sian Literature: 1881-1925 (copyright 1926 by Alfred
> A. Knopf, Inc.; reprinted by permission of the pub-
> lisher), Knopf, 1926, G. Routledge & Sons, 1926,
> pp. 106-20.

STEFAN ZWEIG (essay date 1929)

The effect of Gorki's first works was indescribably portentous,
like an upheaval, an alarm, a wrench, a breaking. Every one
felt that a different Russia from that of the past had here spoken
for the first time, that this voice came from the gigantic anguished breast of a whole people. Dostoevsky, Tolstoy, and
Turgenev, to be sure, had long before in noble visions given

some inkling of the Russian soul in its breadth and power. But here suddenly the same thing was presented differently, more vividly—not the soul merely, but the whole naked man, the pitilessly clear, authentic Russian reality. In those others Russian destiny floated in a spiritual element, in the stormy spheres of conscience—this wide-spread suffering, tension to the breaking point, the tragic knowledge of the course of world history. In Gorki, however, the Russian man arises not in the spirit but in flesh and blood, the shadowy nameless one takes definite form, becomes compelling reality. Gorki, in contrast to Tolstoy and Dostoevsky and [Ivan] Goncharov, has no comprehensive symbolical figures of world literature like, say, the four Karamazovs, like Oblomov, like Levin and Karatejev. It is no diminution of his greatness that Gorki has never sought to form a single symbol of the inward nature of the Russian soul, but has instead placed before us, so that we can seize and touch them, ten thousand living figures of individual men and women with penetration and detail, with incredible veracity and verisimilitude. Born of the people, he has in himself made visible a whole people. From all stages of misery, from all stations in life he has invoked figures—each one of unsurpassed fidelity to life—dozens, hundreds, thousands, an army of the poor and diseased. Instead of a comprehensive vision this glorious eye gives back to the living again in a thousand individual forms each man who met him in life. Therefore, for me, this remembering eye of Gorki belongs to the few genuine marvels of our present world, and I do not know what in the artcraft of our time can be even approximately compared in naturalness and exactitude to his art of observation. No shadow of the mystic dims this eye, there is no distorting flaw in this wonderful crystalline lens which neither enlarges nor diminishes, which never sees things obliquely or distorted, never falsely perceives them too bright or too dark. This eye sees only truly and clearly, but in unsurpassed truth and unexcelled clarity. What has once passed before this candid and just eye, this clearest and truest instrument of our newer art, remains undistorted, for this eye of Maxim Gorki forgets nothing—it gives purest and justest reality. (pp. 497-98)

[Maxim Gorky] did not, like Dostoevsky and Tolstoy, see the coming revolution as the product of a few over-excited and anarchistic intellectuals, as the realization of exactly thought out theories, but in him and in him alone will future history be able to read in chapter and verse that this uprising and revolt in Russia was organically an affair of the people. He has shown how in the masses, in millions of individual details, the tension grew to the unbearable. In his masterpiece, **"The Mother,"** one sees exactly how from the humblest men, from peasants, workers, from the uncultured and illiterate, the will concentrates in countless nameless sacrifices, and becomes tense before it bursts furiously forth in monstrous storm. No single man, but always the multitude, always the mass appears in his works as the holder of power; for because he himself was framed from a multitude, from the fullness of people, from the breadth of fate, this man perceives all that happens as universal experience. (p. 499)

Whoever knows Gorki's work knows the Russian people of today and in him the need and renunciation of all the oppressed; he knows with comprehending soul its rarest, most passionate emotion even as its wretched day by day existence. We can shudderingly experience in Gorki's books as in no others all the sorrows and trials of the transition period. And since we have learnt to feel with the Russian people in its most tragic hours, so now we can share the pride of Russia and experience its joy as our own, the proud joy of a people who have created

out of their own blood such a blameless and true artist. We recognize in him two who are one—Maxim Gorki, the people-made poet, and the Russian people become poet through him. (p. 501)

Stefan Zweig, "Maxim Gorki," in The Virginia Quarterly Review *(copyright, 1929, copyright renewed © 1956, by* The Virginia Quarterly Review, *The University of Virginia), Vol. 5, No. 4 (October, 1929), pp. 492-501.*

GLEB STRUVE   (essay date 1935)

[*Artamonov's Business*] was the first real novel Gorky wrote after . . . *Matvey Kozhemyakin*. It showed that he was by no means a spent force. It was better than any of his middle-period work and reminded one of the best passages of *Foma Gordeev*. There was in it even more firmness, concentration and solidity—which many of Gorky's novels lacked—in addition to his usual gift of keen observation. It is a story of a self-made bourgeois family in its three generations. All the characters: the old Artamonov, the founder of the family's prosperity, a strong, self-willed man; his sons and grandsons in whom there are already signs of imminent decay; their wives and other episodic figures are portrayed very vividly. As usual with Gorky the story combines great vigour and vitality with a keen vision of the gloomy, sombre side of life, not only in its outward manifestations, but also in the inner workings of human nature. In spite of the lifelikeness and variety of its characters, of whom Gorky shows not only their darker sides, there hangs about the whole story that atmosphere of gloom which is so characteristic of Gorky's view of old Russia, and one of the features of his Realism. It is felt also in his *Life of Klim Samgin,* a vast epic of forty years of Russian life, where the main attention is centred on the revolutionary *milieu* and its activity. This long-drawn novel lacks, however, the power and concentration of its predecessor.

Gorky's attitude to the Russia of the past is summed up well in the following words of Klim Samgin: "Everything is possible. Everything is possible in this mad country where men are desperately inventing themselves, and where all life is a bad invention."

In some of his recent stories Gorky has been trying to shift the focus of his Realism, to replace its usual "minus" sign by the "plus" sign in speaking of the Soviet realities. (pp. 7-8)

Gleb Struve, "Pre-Revolutionary Writers after 1924," in his Soviet Russian Literature *(Routledge & Kegan Paul Ltd.), Routledge & Kegan Paul, 1935, pp. 1-22.**

LEON TROTSKY   (essay date 1936)

Gorky died when there was nothing more for him to say. This makes quite bearable the decease of a great writer who has left a deep mark on the development of the Russian intelligentsia and the Russian working class during the last forty years.

Gorky started his literary career as a tramp poet. This was his best period as an artist. From the lower depths, Gorky carried to the Russian intelligentsia the spirit of daring, the romantic bravery of people who had nothing to lose. The Russian intelligentsia was preparing to break the chains of czarism. It needed daring. It passed on its spirit to the masses.

In the events of the revolution, however, there was no place for a real live tramp, excepting as a participant in robbery and pogroms. By December 1905 the Russian proletariat and the radical intelligentsia that was bearing Gorky on its shoulders met—in opposition. Gorky did the honest thing. It was, in its way, a heroic effort. He turned his face to the proletariat. The important product of this about-face was *Mother*. A wider vista opened to the writer, and he now dug deeper. But neither literary schooling nor political training could replace the splendid spontaneity of his first creative period. A tendency to cool reasoning made its appearance in the ambitious tramp. The artist began to resort to didacticism. During the years of reaction, Gorky shared himself out almost evenly between the working class, which had then abandoned the open political arena, and his old enemy-friend, the Russian intelligentsia, who had now taken unto themselves a new enthusiasm—religion. Together with the late [Anatoli] Lunacharsky, Gorky paid his tribute to the vogue of mysticism. As a monument to his spiritual capitulation, we have his weak novel *Confession*. (pp. 217-18)

The last period of his life was undoubtedly the period of his decline. But even this decline was a natural part of his life's orbit. His tendency to didacticism received now its great opportunity. He became the tireless teacher of young writers, even schoolboys. He did not always teach the right thing but he did it with sincere insistence and open generosity that more than made up for his too inclusive friendship with the bureaucracy. (p. 219)

The Soviet press is now piling over the writer's still warm form mountains of unrestrained praise. They call him no less than a "genius." They describe him as the "greatest genius." Gorky would have most likely frowned at this kind of praise. But the press serving bureaucratic mediocrity has its criteria. If Stalin, [Lazar] Kaganovich and [Anastas] Mikoyan have been raised to the rank of genius in their lifetime, one naturally cannot refuse Gorky the epithet upon his death. Gorky will enter the history of Russian literature as an unquestionably clear and convincing example of great literary talent, not touched, however, by the breath of genius. (p. 220)

> *Leon Trotsky, "Maxim Gorky," in his* Leon Trotsky On Literature and Art, *edited by Paul N. Siegel (copyright © 1970 by Pathfinder Press, Inc.), Pathfinder Press, 1970, pp. 217-20.*

ALDOUS HUXLEY (essay date 1939)

From the translation of Gorki's writings, what are the inferences that we are able to draw concerning the nature of his art? The most significant fact that seems to emerge is that Gorki was a writer who relied for the production of his effects at least as much upon verbal texture as upon composition. There have been great writers who cared as little for verbal texture as such painters as David and the Lenains cared for the texture of their pigment. There have been others for whom, as for Chardin or Rembrandt, surface quality has seemed as significant, as profoundly expressive, as structural form. Gorki belongs to the second category. (This is why, no doubt, his work is so hard to translate, why so few translations are satisfactory.) Some of his most fundamental ideas seem to be expressed by means of variations in the surface texture of his writing. For example, the idea that, beneath all the squalor and misery and cruelty of human life, and in spite of these things, there exists an underlying reality that would reveal itself, if only men would

take the trouble to uncover it, as beautiful and good—this idea is expressed almost entirely by means of variations in the verbal texture of the writing. It is not stated; it is implied by the arrangement of the words and phrases in which other matters are expressed. The device which Gorki most frequently employs for the rendering of this idea is a modulation, sudden and without transition, from the most brutal colloquialism into language of lyrical intensity and elevation. Such modulations are, of course, almost impossibly difficult to render in another language. But even from the most badly literal of translations we can see what it is that Gorki is after, we can infer the expressive subtlety of the original.

Gorki is not content to imply the existence of beauty latent in squalor, of an underlying goodness substantial to the evils and stupidities of common life. He is also concerned, in his works of fiction, to describe virtuous characters. **"The Hermit,"** for example, contains a subtly executed portrait of a good man, and one can find many other portraits of the same kind scattered through his writings.

Gorki's virtuous characters are interesting not only in themselves, but also because they illustrate very clearly the difficulties which imaginative writers have always had in portraying the good. Many writers have not even attempted the task. Thus, with the exception of the Duke in *Measure for Measure*, not one of Shakespeare's characters is an actively good person. (Incidentally, the Duke is not a person, but a symbol.) Of those who have attempted the task, practically all have chosen to portray good people who were, in some way or other, seriously defective. In this respect, Gorki's hermit is typical of his class. He is good—but on the verge of being dotty; good—but wholly uneducated; good—but childish to the point of having, in the innocence of his heart, deviated into incest; good—but utterly unaware of the larger problems of social life, accepting the existing social order unthinkingly, as a fish accepts the water in which it swims. We find some or all of these characteristics in the overwhelming majority of the virtuous characters in imaginative literature. (pp. vii-ix)

> *Aldous Huxley, in his foreword to* A Book of Short Stories *by Maxim Gorky, edited by Avrahm Yarmolinsky and Moura Budberg (copyright 1939 by Holt, Rinehart and Winston; copyright © 1967 by Avrahm Yarmolinsky and Baroness Moura Budberg; reprinted by permission of Holt, Rinehart and Winston, Publishers), Holt, Rinehart and Winston, 1939, pp. vii-x.*

JANKO LAVRIN (essay date 1945)

Gorky's creative urge came from his impulse to overcome his feeling of social inferiority, and the drabness of the life he saw around. He started to write as a self-assertive romantic, full of defiance. Instead of submitting to 'Chekhovian' resignation, he sounded a warlike clarion, in which there vibrated strength, self-reliance, and a youthful will to live fully and dangerously. Untrammelled by any taboos, traditions, and conventions, he chose characters most likely to express the same attitude towards life: tramps and roamers whose only home was the endless expanse of the steppes, and their favourite melody—the song of the winds, of the sea. The old gipsy Izegril, Tchelkash, the breezy Malva, or Varenka Olysova are some of them. To those he added the social outcasts of the towns, the 'people who once were humans'. In both cases he protested either against the drabness of life, or the injustice of our present system. Hence the scorn, the naïvely 'Nietzschean' insistence on the pride of the social underdog, in so many stories of his earlier period.

His flouting of all the bourgeois 'good and evil' was not devoid of nihilism. But even when his arguments were not convincing, his temperamental language appealed to those intellectuals who were tired of the moody impressionists. For there was vigour even in Gorky's rhetoric. In addition, he insisted on a change of life; on new aims and ideals, which could not fail to influence the younger generation. In [a] letter to Chekov, Gorky wrote these words which might well be applied to his own writings: 'Truly, at this moment one feels the need of heroics: there is a common desire for stimulating, brilliant things, for life, better, more beautiful. It is absolutely necessary for present-day literature to begin embellishing life a bit, and as soon as it begins to do so, life will take on colour; I mean men will begin to live a quickened, a brighter life.'

It was his romantic propensity to 'embellish life a bit' that was responsible both for his criticism of the life he saw around; and for the revolutionary character of his work. As the 'stormy petrel' of the revolution, he naturally adopted an appropriate manner. His style of that period was saturated, often rhetorical, full of colour, and at times irritatingly didactic. (pp. 139-40)

It was precisely [the] working men, 'tattered, drenched with sweat', that were eventually singled out by Gorky as the only hope for the future. In the smug Philistines he saw nothing but decay. He despised them and their bourgeois civilization with every fibre of his soul. His outraged sense of justice and his human pride rebelled against the capitalist order of life. It was partly through such an attitude that the former romantic Gorky arrived at the straightforward and rugged realism which links him up with one of the basic traditions of Russian literature as a whole. Equally strong is his emphasis on the quest for higher values; on the innate yearning for beauty and decency among the lowest: among those stepsons of life, who have no chance to gratify such an urge. Gorky's *Twenty-six Men and One Girl* is one of the finest stories of this kind.

Unfortunately, the seeker and reformer was too strong even in Gorky the artist to be able to abstain from reasoning and preaching. He often turned his characters into heralds of his own messages and ideas. Hence the impression as though a number of them were only acting their appointed parts. And what is more, those reasonings, discussions, and admonitions are often carried on in a bookish language. This duality intrudes too much into Gorky's plays and longer prose-works, especially those he wrote after 1905. It is disturbing in his first novel, *Foma Gordeyev* . . . , which presents an agitatedly drawn picture of the provincial trading bourgeoisie—with the 'superfluous' Foma, rebelling against his own class, in the centre. Like his less compact novel, *The Three of Them (Troe),* it has for its background a busy Volga town towards the end of the century. His *Mother* . . . , on the other hand, is crammed with socialistic outbursts and with protest. Full of defects, it preserves all the same its value as an epic of the Russian working-class life and struggle. The brewing revolutionary forces are strongly felt also in such long novels of manners as *The Chronicle of the Town Okurov* . . . and *Klim Samgin.* Yet Gorky's socialist propaganda is only another proof of his craving for justice which comes out in most of his works. (pp. 142-43)

It was from 1902 (after having joined the social-democrat party) that Gorky became didactic almost from a sense of duty. He also kept on writing articles and pamphlets—some of them rather high-pitched. There were doubts as to his further creative power, when he suddenly gave a new proof of it in *A Confession* and in several other works. His descriptions of the commercial bourgeoisie are particularly successful. And if his novel, *The Life of Klim Samgin,* with its background of the chaotic revolutionary Russia is much too long and diluted, he becomes highly condensed in his last and truly fine novel, *The Artamonov Business* . . . : a tale about three generations of commercial prosperity, founded on a crime, and destroyed by the recent revolution. But even as its best, Gorky's style looks much too improvised, if not careless. The structure of his works, too, is often mechanical, motivated rather by his ideological than his artistic urge. This is why he is prone to simplify not only ideas, but also psychology. In his lack of shades he mistakes, now and then, brutality for strength, and his love of glaring colours forms the greatest contrast to Chekhov's art. On the other hand, his observations are acute and shrewd. A proof of this are his studies of Tolstoy, Chekhov, and [Vladimir] Korolenko. His impression of Tolstoy in particular give an interesting clue to that great and puzzling figure.

Gorky can be regarded as a symbol of the transition period between the old and the new Russia. A restless intellectual nomad looking for an anchorage, he became a romantic of the revolution and incidentally a precursor of what is called at present 'socialist realism'. When the revolution broke out, he did his best to humanize it, to prevent it from degenerating into mere revolution for its own sake. It was here that his personality and his work served as a bridge between the creative values of the old intelligentsia culture and the culture of the risen masses, anxious to build up a new world. (pp. 143-44)

> *Janko Lavrin, "Maxim Gorky," in his* An Introduction to the Russian Novel *(reprinted by permission of the author), third edition, Methuen & Co. Ltd., 1945, pp. 136-44.*

GEORG LUKÁCS   (essay date 1950)

In Gorki's life-work as in that of many other great modern narrators—one need think only of Rousseau, Goethe or Tolstoy—the autobiographical element plays a very important part. Those great narrators who summed up the essential traits of their epoch in mighty works of literature, had themselves experienced in their own lives the emergence and maturing of the problems of the age. This process of digesting the historical content of an epoch is itself most characteristic for the epoch. (p. 221)

Gorki's own autobiographical writings, [*My Childhood, My Apprenticeship,* and *My Universities*], follow the tradition of the old classical autobiographies. One might even say that their distinctive characteristic, their *leitmotiv,* is precisely their extraordinary objectivity. This objectivity does not mean that the tone of the narration is impartial. The *tone* of Goethe's autobiographical writings is far more objective than Gorki's. The objectivity consists rather in the content of his autobiography, in the attitude to life expressed in it; it contains very little subjective, personal material.

Gorki shows us his development indirectly, through the circumstances, events, and personal contacts which have influenced it. Only at certain critical points does he sum up his subjective experience of the world as raising his personality to a higher level. But even this is not always a directly subjective summary; the reader is often made to see for himself Gorki's own evolution under the influence of objectively depicted events. (pp. 221-22)

This objectivity is the most subjective, most personal trait of Gorki's autobiography, for it is here that his profound ties with the life of the working masses, which is the basis of his implacable, militant humanism, finds expression. In the first pages of [*My Childhood*] he already reveals these ties very plainly. He says that the story of his childhood appears to him like a "sombre fairy-tale" which he must nevertheless truthfully tell, despite all the horrors it contains. (p. 222)

Only a passionate acceptance of the world such as it is, with all its inexhaustible multiplicity and incessant change, only a passionate desire to learn from the world; only love of reality, even though there are many abominations in it against which one has to struggle and which one hates—a love which is not hopeless because in the same reality one can see a road leading to human goodness—faith in life, and in its movement, through human endeavour towards something better, in spite of all the stupidity and evil manifested every day—only passionate receptivity, provides a foundation for a practical activity of the right kind.

This is optimism without illusions and Gorki possessed it. (p. 224)

Real types can be created only by writers who have an opportunity to make many well-founded comparisons between individuals, comparisons which are based on rich practical experience and which are such as to reveal the social and personal causes of affinities between individuals. The richer the life of the writer, the greater will be the depth from which he can bring up such affinities; the wider the compass embracing the unity of the personal and social elements in the type presented, the more genuine and the more interesting will the character be.

Gorki's autobiography shows us how a rich and eventful life developed in the young Gorki this faculty of creating types by comparing superficially quite different types. In this education of a great writer literature itself, of course, played a very important part. The young Gorki, still in his formation period, already saw that the great vocation of classical literature lay in teaching men to see and express themselves. From the outset Gorki always linked literature with life in his reading. As he read Balzac's *Eugenie Grandet,* he was not only delighted with the magnificent simplicity of the presentation—he immediately compared the old moneylender Grandet with his own grandfather. (pp. 225-26)

Gorki's autobiography shows us how a great poet of our time was born, how a child developed into a mirror of the world. Gorki's objective style emphasizes this character of the book. It shows Maxim Gorki as an important participant in the human comedy of pre-revolutionary Russia and it shows us life as the true teacher of every great poet. Gorki introduces us to this great teacher who formed him and shows us how it was done, how he, Gorki, was taught by life itself to be a man, a fighter and a poet. (p. 226)

> Georg Lukács, ''The Human Comedy of Pre-Revolutionary Russia'' (1950), in his Studies in European Realism: A Sociological Survey of the Writings of Balzac, Stendhal, Zola, Tolstoy, Gorki and Others, *translated by Edith Bone (copyright © The Merlin Press; reprinted by permission), Merlin Press, 1972, pp. 206-41.*

HELEN MUCHNIC (essay date 1951)

[On the face of it, O'Neill's *The Iceman Cometh* and Gorky's *The Lower Depths*] are very much alike, not only in setting,

plot, and structure, but in aesthetic conception; for they seem to be, and yet are not, ''slices of life.'' They are, more accurately, parables of life; and the social outcasts who people Harry Hope's ''cheap ginmill of the five-cent whiskey, last-resort variety'' and the ''cellar, resembling a cave,'' owned by Kostilev, are not, despite the naturalism of their portraiture, pictures of real men, but symbolic figures in a parable on man's fate. As such they are exceptionally well chosen; the ''dregs'' of society, as the mark of extreme failure, are distress signals which urge inquiry into the nature of human disaster and the responsibility for it. Both plays are plays of dialogue rather than action, and what is done in them, reversing the usual method of drama, is an illustration of what is said. In each, a group of individuals, loosely bound together by a familiarity which breeds tolerant indifference and boredom and with enough in common to represent mankind by and large, is confronted by a solitary outsider who considers himself, and is considered by the group, to be superior—to this extent, at least, that he is in a position to preach and to exhort them to a new way of life. In both plays this solitary individual is the repository of a ''truth'' unknown to the others, and in both, after a brief show of impressive authority, he leaves the scene of his activities in the same, or somewhat worse, condition than he had found it. Is the joke, then, on him? Are the tables turned? Is the prophet false, or at any rate, inadequate? And are the benighted souls whom he had tried to save in possession of a reality which his supposedly superior wisdom has not touched? Who, then, is better, and who is right? Who is to be blamed for the melancholy outcome of events, the prophet or those who refuse to become his disciples? The plays strike deep, deeper than their spoken arguments concerning the nature of truth and the value of illusion. Implicit in them are comparisons between theories of life and actual living, between idealism and reality: demands exacted by the mind and those made by the body, hope imposed by the spirit and the limits to hope set by the circumscribed potentialities of man; questions about the nature and the power of the will; and a search for an ethics that might be accepted as both just and possible in a human situation that is seen to be desperate. But here, with the kind of questions posed and the way they are examined, the similarities end. The answers given are amazingly different, and as one studies them one becomes aware that even the questions are not so similar as at first supposed.

Each play is constructed around a central character, and its meaning hinges on the interpretation of this man and of what he preaches, for he comes with a well-defined faith to correct his fellows; it is to him that they are constrained to respond individually and as a group, it is on him that thoughts and emotions converge. He is, in short, a test of moral principles, and the spectator must decide to what degree he should respect and trust him. In their natures, the two characters are entirely different. Gorky's Luke is a wanderer who, not from any newly found faith but from an accumulated store of sanctified dogma, hands out good advice wherever he happens to be to whoever will listen to him. He clucks sympathetically over men's complaints, tells little moral tales by way of illustrating his precepts, and, when the wretches he has been ''saving'' are drawn into a perilous situation and he himself is in danger of being caught and questioned by the authorities, slips out unperceived; for, with all his show of self-effacing, greathearted sympathy, he is not unmindful of his own safety—and he happens to be traveling without a passport. (pp. 99-101)

When *The Lower Depths* was first performed in 1902, Luke was presented as a saintly character, and the play was interpreted as a lesson in brotherly love. That had not been Gorky's intention, as he himself explained in interviews at the time and in an article of 1933 in which—having described four types of "consolers," the sincere (an extremely rare variety), the professional, the vain, and finally "the most dangerous, clever, well-informed, and eloquent" of them all, the coldhearted men who cared about nothing so much as their own peace and comfort and consoled only because they could not be bothered with complaints—he declared that Luke belonged in the last division. "In our days," he added, "the consoler can be presented on the stage only as a negative and comic figure."

Gorky had intended Satin to be the real hero, but muffed the effect by leaving him off stage in some of the crucial moments of the play. Satin is in every respect at opposite poles from Luke, whom he appraises with his native acumen and honest incivility. "Pulp for the toothless" he calls him, but admits that in theory, at least, the wanderer has the right idea about man: namely, that man is large and free and must not be hampered. Satin, who sneers when he is sober and is eloquent when drunk, who is not apart from but very much of the group, on the spot when he is needed, sensible, and, above all, realistic in his understanding of what his fellow men can and cannot do, has an undemonstrative, genuine sympathy which is infinitely more valuable than Luke's facile, softhearted, self-protecting kindliness. . . . From Satin's standpoint Luke's pampering consolations, when they are not positively harmful—as in the case of the Actor, for whose suicide Satin holds the old man responsible—are insulting to man. (pp. 101-02)

The "pipe dream" is the obvious leitmotif of *The Iceman Cometh,* as it is also that of *The Lower Depths,* the real theme of which, according to a splendid analysis by the Soviet Critic Iury Iuzovsky, is the question "What is Truth?" The characters of Gorky's play, this writer points out, are divided into well-marked groups with respect to the kind of truth they believe in: those, like the Actor, Pepel, Natasha, and Nastya, for whom illusion is truth; those, on the contrary, who believe only in the "truth of facts," like Bubnov, Kleshch, and the Baron, all of whom delight in pricking, variously, the bubble of man's hope—Bubnov with quiet satisfaction, Kleshch with bitterness, the Baron with a kind of sensual delight, "sneering out of envy," as Luke says of him; and, lastly, Luke and Satin who belong to neither category. . . . (pp. 102-03)

Nevertheless, whether they believe anything or not, the inhabitants of *The Lower Depths* retain, as individuals, a sense of their humanity and they suffer because of it; Circe has not deprived them of consciousness, and, even though they do not do very much, they retain the possibility of action. (p. 103)

The real difference between the characters in the two plays . . . is not that of social relationships but of the kind of illusion they cherish and the nature of the "truth" they are invited to adopt. If both plays can be said to deal with illusion and reality, these terms have different meanings for their authors. "Truth" or "reality" for Gorky is not a metaphysical but a humanist concept; it involves not so much a recognition of that which is or may be, immutably, as of that which may or may not be done at a given moment. Freedom of will is here based simply on a practical view of possibilities. O'Neill's position is more sophisticated and complex; for him there is no distinction between useful and useless illusions, and no naïve presentation of men as fully expressed by their beliefs. From an objective point of view, the "pipe dreams" here are all useless, but all are tragically inescapable and necessary to those who hold them. . . . The men of *The Lower Depths* are vaguely aware

of some great solution to existence which they have not yet discovered, and the play exhorts them to seek a way that will lead them to discover it; those of *The Iceman Cometh* have no thought of anything beyond their individual well-being, which by now has been reduced to the form of drunken senselessness, and the play turns out to be a study of the impossibility of getting at the truth, indeed, a warning of the danger of going after it. (p. 104)

What is at issue in Gorky's play is the relative usefulness—and *usefulness* is here the same as ultimate good—of two ideals: one, the Christian ideal of tender, pitying humility and inactive faith, the other, the materialist doctrine of forceful, self-reliant, practical action. In O'Neill's play the issue is the nature rather than the practicability of ideals. Social activity is the sphere of Gorky's thought, self-knowledge of O'Neill's. Though both are concerned with happiness, in *The Lower Depths* happiness is looked on as derivative, dependent on an intellectual grasp of values: let a man become conscious of his dignity and capacity, let him adopt an ideal which is possible for man, and he will realize it as an individual. . . . The reason Luke fails is that he is neither serious nor honest in his relations with men; but Hickey fails because, in his desire to rouse Circe's victims to their original status as human beings with insight into themselves, he has attempted the impossible, for most of them cannot be roused, and those who can will kill themselves once they have understood what they are. Gorky's "message" is seriously meant as a program of conduct; O'Neill's is a poetic statement of disaster, presented only for the contemplation of those who care to look below the surface of human activity. (p. 105)

The essential difference in the two [plays] is perhaps best embodied in the real heroes . . . : Satin, ruthless in his appraisal of individual failings but with a native respect for humanity and an ardent faith in its grandeur, and Larry, whose cynical philosophy is coupled with an instinctive sympathy of which he is ashamed, and whose sense of justice is based on a hopeless understanding of human beings. With these characters, it seems to me, their authors are identified: Gorky with the man of action, closely involved in the fate of his fellows, but more clear-eyed, farseeing, and confident than they, and able, therefore, to inspire them by a persuasive vision of their strength; O'Neill with the Grandstand Foolosopher, whose function it is to look unsquintingly on man's depravity and, when called upon, to discharge the unwelcome task not of judging men but of letting them pass judgment on themselves. The high point of Satin's act is a stirring speech on man, of Larry's, his waiting by the window to hear the sound of Parritt throwing himself from the fire escape (for Larry's finest deed is to free a man of guilt by driving him to suicide)—just as the purpose of Gorky's life was to stir men to action, and the function of O'Neill's has been to make them aware of the full meaning of the evil that is in them. (p. 108)

Helen Muchnic, "Circe's Swine: Plays by Gorky and O'Neill," (© copyright 1951 by University of Oregon; reprinted by permission of Comparative Literature), *in* Comparative Literature, *Vol. III, No. 2, Spring, 1951 (and reprinted in* O'Neill: A Collection of Critical Essays, *edited by John Gassner, Prentice-Hall, Inc., 1964, pp. 99-109).**

MARC SLONIM (essay date 1953)

When young Gorky passed from [the] romantic gypsies, Promethean Dankos, and heroic falcons [of his early tales] to more ordinary folk, he endowed his new heroes and heroines—tramps and prostitutes—with the same pride, strength, and love of freedom he had celebrated in his first legends. Chelkash (in the story of the same name), a wharf rat and a drunkard, despises the weakness and the bourgeois dreams of the peasant lad Gavrila, with whom he has temporarily joined forces; he has utter contempt for money and squanders it right and left whenever he manages to get any; he is ready to commit crime and robbery, since he accepts the laws of the human jungle: the merciless struggle for existence and the survival of the fittest. Malva, a Carmen of the Black Sea, maintains freedom in all her love affairs and always acts as an independent, strong-willed creature. In general, the strong men and women who maintain their individuality are Gorky's favorite heroes and heroines. He respects strength of character wherever he finds it—and this explains the note of admiration with which in his later works he portrayed not only rebels and revolutionaries but also those extremely predatory representatives of capitalism of whom he could hardly approve according to his political convictions. Silan Petrov, the boss in **'On the Rafts,'** one of Gorky's early stories, an old slave driver who is tireless in work and in love-making, is the prototype of Ilya Artamonov in the novel *The Artamonov Business* and is akin to old Bulychev in the play *Egor Bulychev and Others.* Vitality, pulsing life, the manifestation of primitive impulses—both moral and physical—appealed to Gorky, and in his first period he was the poet of what has come to be known as rugged individualism.

This was one of the reasons for the immediate success of his romantic and somewhat Nietzschean stories. Their impressionistic style was hardly a novelty in the late 'nineties, when various deviations from classical realism were prevalent. Their spirit, however, was something unexpected and novel, and it delighted readers who had become tired of the drab and bleak literary palette. The newcomer's picturesque brigands, romantic tramps, and legendary gypsies—all these magnificent specimens of manhood who vociferously proclaimed 'Life is narrow but my heart is wide'—created a startling eruption amid the depressing atmosphere of the period. (p. 133)

Unlike the Populists, who did pastels of the patience and saintliness of the traditional peasantry, Gorky portrayed the denizens of the slums, of the ports and lodging houses, as turbulent, violent, and seething with conscious and instinctive protest against the inhuman conditions in which they were compelled to exist. Yet poverty, crime, and despair could not kill the sparks of love and creativeness within them.

Still, it was not solely this affirmation of common humanity that made Gorky so popular. When Gorky was highly praised for having shown these qualities in his heroes, Tolstoy shrugged his shoulders and made a caustic remark: 'I knew long before Gorky that tramps have souls.' Much more significant was the refusal of his hoboes to be passive or to become resigned to their fate. They were wrathful, forceful human beings, ready to challenge the very order of things that turned them into thieves, drunkards, and derelicts. They symbolized the revolt of the downtrodden individual against the political and social machine that continued to exploit and crush them. This was the true message readers received from Gorky's stories and it found a response amid the general mood of the turn of the century, with its awakening of the masses and the increasing political activities of educated society.

The romantic tendency and the spirit of protest in Gorky's short stories between 1894 and 1898 ran parallel to the trend of critical realism: he concentrated more and more on the depic-

tion of poverty, ignorance, and the sufferings of the lower classes. The directness and even the brutality of these pictures led some critics to speak of Gorky's naturalism. If this term is applied as it was in connection with Zola, it becomes quite obvious that Gorky never aimed at the documentary objectivity of the French school: his tales always have warm lyrical overtones that are definitely lacking in the novels of the French master. Gorky painted the dregs of humanity with the passion and compassion of a romantic and a revolutionary. Certain defects of these works are due precisely to their emotional overflow: the pity, indignation, or anger of the author is all too vocal, and he uses almost melodramatic devices to score direct hits on the sympathy of his readers. Two *leit-motifs* are predominant in Gorky's work: realistic and crude representation of misery and violence, and a dream of humaneness and beauty that emphasizes the dreariness of reality, yet also builds up a sense of revolt. (pp. 134-35)

Although often marred by sentimentality [Gorky's] tales fitted into that great category of works about the 'wronged and the humiliated' which played such a prominent part in Russian letters. They revealed the same concern for the underdog, the same love for the 'little man' which has been so often considered the most characteristic trait of nineteenth-century Russian novelists. Their difference lay in that besides compassion and humanitarian sentimentalism Gorky displayed in his sketches other significant features. His realism was harsh, crude, pitiless; easy tears and sentimental situations did not hide the feelings of hatred and rebellion, which were completely lacking in Gogol, and were sublimated into preachments of Christian slave-morality in Dostoevsky. Although in many instances—particularly in his morbid interest in human suffering—Gorky has been linked to the latter, he is as far from the spirit of Christian quietism as was another writer who had influenced him—Saltykov-Shchedrin.

For Gorky evil is not a metaphysical problem as it is for the author of *The Brothers Karamazov,* or a result of the discrepancy between the truth of religion and the wrongs of civilization, as it is for Tolstoy: it is mainly a question of the ways of life, of its faulty organization, of material conditions and social wrongs. Man's sufferings are, for Gorky, caused by political despotism, class division, and social injustice. There is nothing vague about his criticism: like his predecessors of the 'forties and the 'sixties he is strongly attached to the earth. He was often reproached for his lack of depth, for his avoidance of the fundamental issues of human nature. But Gorky believed that the so-called metaphysical or philosophical approach to life which disregards the particular for imaginary generalities is hypocritical and obnoxious. A truthful and fearless observer, he scarcely saw anything beyond the concreteness of life as it is actually lived. Almost from the beginning of his literary career he evinced this tendency toward realism. He concentrated on the sordid details, primarily those of a physical nature: hunger, drunkenness, pain, filth, the lack of all physical essentials. With the exception of Dostoevsky, there is no other Russian writer of the nineteenth century who dealt as much as Gorky did with physical violence and murder. Whatever the psychological explanation may be in terms of Gorky's personality, it would be next to impossible to detect any grin of sadistic pleasure in his gruesome descriptions of wives mangled by their husbands, of vagabonds beaten up by police. . . . He had become aware of physical violence as a main feature of Russian life, and its exposé remained one of his principal objectives; he denounced it not only as an Asiatic heritage, a survival of the Tartar yoke, but also as a result of ignorance and oppression: the cruelty of the common people was bred by their misery and was a release as well as a compensation for their slavery. (pp. 135-36)

Most of the sketches and tales he wrote between 1892 and 1895 are weak and imitative, yet even in these attempts of the young writer, as well as in his more successful and occasionally brilliant stories of later years (1895-8 are the best of this period), there is a core of constant elements. The themes of violence, brutality, and despair appear even in *Paul the Unfortunate* (*Orphan Paul* in the English version), his first novel, which he refused—quite wisely—to include in his collected works, but the revision of which he began toward the end of his life. (p. 136)

In Gorky's early writings [the] theme of man's inhumanity to man runs parallel to two other powerful themes: humanity amid beastliness and man's yearning for liberation. The bakers in **'Twenty-six Men and a Girl,'** one of Gorky's best stories, lead the joyless existence of slaves, but they idealize Tania, a girl who personifies for them beauty and love. But when she fails to live up to this exalted idealization and succumbs to a soldier, they compensate for their frustration by vile oaths and atrocious behavior against their fallen idol. All of Gorky's unhappy heroes are forever seeking true love and freedom. (p. 137)

Gorky's artistry during the first period (1882-1902) was uneven. The tales that made him famous then have lost most of their charm for the reader of today. They are certainly colorful, dramatic, and vigorous, and already show that power of characterization which later was Gorky's principal asset as a writer. Their defects, however, are also patent: their primitive construction, a sentimentality so naïve as to border on bad taste, picturesque language, and lusty details lapsing into rhetoric and bathos. And the author is over-exuberant and high-pitched, using too many words of indignation and wrath or of tenderness and sympathy. He is, in general, inclined toward exaggeration and employs only blacks and whites. His philosophy is too obvious and his desire to put over a message and to convince the reader makes him obtrusive and didactic. The dramatic element is the dynamic force within his plots, yet he lacks the sense of structure. This is particularly evident in his first novels, such as *Three of Them*—an almost formless sequence of incidents, of isolated scenes and repulsive details; despite the intensity and rich texture of the narrative, it never acquires an organic unity.

The same may be said of *Foma Gordeyev* . . . , a novel that marked an important milestone in Gorky's literary development. It represents the Masters of Life, the rising capitalist class—a subject that fascinated Gorky and to which he was to return in later works. (p. 139)

The story of [Foma's] downfall is unfolded in a series of scenes, and although the main characters are masterfully drawn, with that abundance of vivid details so typical of Gorky's style, the novel leaves the impression that the author lacks control of his material—that he is, in fact, somewhat overwhelmed by it.

The looseness of construction is compensated for, however, by forceful descriptions of provincial life, and particularly by the 'national flavor' of the Volga merchants. This makes Gorky akin to the Regionalists and the Writers of the Soil. In general, Gorky's whole manner—his broad canvasses, colorful bold strokes, folkloristic reminiscences, popular expressions, and heroes who have not severed their ties with ancient customs and traditions—puts him close to . . . the Populists. What made him different from writers with Slavophile overtones, however,

was his decidedly Western and socialist orientation. He wanted to change the life he portrayed in his tales and novels, and he was convinced he had to contribute to that end not only by his writings but by direct activity as well. (pp. 139-40)

The period after the *Lower Depths* (from 1902 on) . . . culminated in *Mother,* the novel in which Gorky attempted to portray the revolutionary, the New Hero of his time. He had already outlined this type in some of his plays. . . . As material for *Mother,* Gorky utilized the strike and the political demonstrations that actually had taken place in 1902 in the industrial town of Sormovo, and the workman Peter Zalomov and his mother served as prototypes for the hero and his mother. . . . The aesthetic drawbacks of this work are obvious. Some of the minor characters are well drawn, but Paul and his comrades, as well as Nilovna herself, are done as smudged romantic stencils. The whole canvas utilizes but two colors: unrelieved black for officers, policemen, and other representatives of the ruling classes, and a poetic pastel pink for their opponents. The revolutionaries are so idealized that they become as sweet and unreal as angels in children's picture books. They all talk a great deal, as if they were reciting propaganda leaflets, and even Nilovna makes a speech after her arrest—a scene of brutality and martyrdom bringing the novel to a close. The rhetorical eloquence throughout makes the book's message too shrill and often distorts the contours of characters. From the first pages the reader can easily guess what is coming next, and the story follows an obvious pattern, with no surprises. The characters, except for Nilovna, are static and uniform, and the manner of description is two-dimensional and never conveys any feeling of depth. But the most exasperating thing about *Mother* is that while Russian revolutionaries have very often been men and women of extraordinary moral rectitude who lived and died like saints, when Gorky tried to portray them that way, the result was flat and false. The similarity of his heroes to actual persons has nothing to do with their artistic reality: they do not ring true and are not aesthetically convincing. (pp. 140-41)

The new period in Gorky's literary development, immediately following the publication of *Mother,* produced his most mature works. Between the thwarted Revolution of 1905 and the triumphant Revolution of 1917 he maintained all the good qualities of his early work and succeeded in overcoming many of his defects. While the intelligentsia fell prey to morbid disillusionment and escapism, Gorky continued to profess his faith in the inner goodness of man and kept his socialistic convictions, which were for him a logical corollary of his humaneness and his hatred of the iniquities and inequalities of Russian life. *Confession* and *Summer* . . . were strongly optimistic. Matthew, the hero of *Confession,* is a God-seeker, one of those Russian peasants who wandered through the country in search of true faith; he finally comes to the conclusion that humanity is God and that people, as a collective force, may truly work miracles. Egor Trofimov, the leading character in *Summer,* who was at one time a military clerk, propagandizes revolution among the peasants with a thoroughly Gorkian feeling of the saintliness of the cause, and the book ends on a symbolic, almost religious, note.

While *Confession* reflected the interest Russian intellectuals displayed after 1905 in religious problems, *Summer* was more in the traditional socialistic vein; both novels, however, were not without Populist overtones. They also had a strong folkloristic flavor—as a matter of fact, in his Italian exile Gorky spent a great deal of time studying folklore. Both novels are supposedly stories told by men whose style maintains all the inflections and peculiarities of popular idiom. Stylization, rhythmic divisions of sentences, inversions, and Biblical images prevail in *Confession* and make it highly lyrical and a trifle artificial. *Summer* is written in a simpler vein, although its hero also uses idiomatic expressions and occasionally talks like a village preacher. These two transitional works bear the stigmata of sentimentalism and of splashed primary colors, but they do reveal Gorky's intensified concern with his craftsmanship. In the years to come he retained his new manner of using folkloristic devices and poetic language, but with more discernment and a greater sense of proportion. In general, he became more sensitive to formal problems and consciously bridled his natural inclinations toward a profusion of language and a plethora of detail. He turned deliberately to realistic descriptions of Old Russia, and his later novels, drawn from his personal experience, remain his highest achievements. (pp. 142-43)

> Marc Slonim, ''Gorky,'' in his Modern Russian Literature: From Chekhov to the Present *(copyright © 1953 by Oxford University Press, Inc.; renewed 1981 by Tatiana Slonim; reprinted by permission of the publisher),* Oxford University Press, New York, 1953, pp. 125-52.

ALFRED KAZIN (essay date 1955)

In the course of his long revolutionary career, marked by so much painful self-education, literary success, and a stubborn dedication to basic human values stronger than his formal political beliefs, Maxim Gorky wrote several reminiscences of Russian writers that are peculiarly valuable. The finest of these are the notes on Tolstoy, which are surely among the most beautiful things ever written by one human being on the character of another. There is a memoir of Chekhov that is almost as fine, less notable only because the subject is less complex, and acrid memories of two friends from the ''decadent'' generation—the novelist Leonid Andreyev and the poet Alexander Blok. Gorky on Tolstoy, on Chekhov, and then on the melancholy and eccentric Andreyev and Blok, is like moving from the high blaze of summer in the Crimea, where Gorky knew Tolstoy in the latter's last years, to the dull winter of the Russian mind that followed the aborted revolution of 1905. Putting together Gorky's portraits of four master friends [in *Reminiscences*], we have his basic conception of Russia, of the writer in Russia, and of his quarrel with himself.

The portrait of Tolstoy is a masterpiece, set down in scattered notes that Gorky himself evidently did not mind losing at one time, so much had he revealed of himself in grappling with the fascinating mystery that was Tolstoy. Great in its insight into the ''old magician,'' whom Gorky adored and feared, it reveals more than he realized the liberating effect of Tolstoy's genius. (pp. 28-9)

Tolstoy was so strong that he bent the experience of life into a grotesque new shape to locate its ultimate meaning. But his real quest was the meaning of his formidable sincerity.

That there was such a quest, especially in Tolstoy's old age, was never lost on anyone near him. What is best in Gorky's portrait is that he makes us feel this continually in Tolstoy, and always in terms of his own respect for him—a respect that transcended resentment and went out in love and awe to the great writer seeking the meaning of his human strangeness. We have an appealing record of this in Gorky's description of

Tolstoy sitting alone at the edge of the sea, as if he had gone away into himself—as before his death he did flee from everyone, to die alone in the little railroad station at Astapovo. . . . (pp. 31-2)

Yet even after this, one feels in Gorky's notes the positive estrangement from Tolstoy. There was that in the older man which the younger could not recognize and which he feared; there was that which he feared because he could recognize it. Gorky was afraid of the whole moralistic and Gandhiesque side of Tolstoy's teaching because it rested on an indiscriminate religious affirmation to which he was susceptible. He liked to stress the beauty of positivism and secularism because he was afraid of losing his own hard-won faith in the revolution, and thus his principle of survival for himself and the Russian people. Tolstoy aroused in him those intense longings to burst the narrow bounds of revolutionary materialism which he knew could be exploited by the reactionary forces in Russian thought and earn him disfavor with the left. We know from the history of the Russian revolutionary movement that Gorky's religious promptings, in the confused period after 1905 when so many intellectuals sought to admit an idealistic principle into their thought, provoked contempt in Lenin. At the same time Gorky had a special need to believe in ''westernization,'' which he saw as the only counter to Russian despair and apathy. ''Culture,'' with its special resonance to a Russian intellectual outraged by the deprivations of his people, became his great belief. He insisted on it all the more because literature had raised him from the living death of the old Russia. Hence the sharpness with which he drew himself away from Tolstoy, as if to say: He can afford a metaphysics; I cannot. But hence, too, the shrewdness with which he exposed in Tolstoy the defects of the ''would-be saint.'' By this move he was trying to destroy simultaneously that which was genuine in him but false in Tolstoy.

When we turn to the descriptions of Chekhov, Andreyev and Blok we can see how avidly Gorky seized on those elements—particularly in Chekhov—which were overtly against the regime. He made a fellow-insurgent out of Chekhov, which the latter certainly was in his own way. But that way was so much subtler than Gorky's own, and so full of questionings and promptings on human nature in itself, that it is amusing to see how determinedly Gorky brought Chekhov's art down to his own level. His Chekhov is the tubercular doctor, rotting away in his small village, and dying of Russian life in the nineteenth century, *tout simple*. It is a very moving portrait, it is unquestionably a very true and keen portrait. But Gorky's Chekhov is too rationalist by far, too limited and thus too easily assimilable into the familiar canons of Russian criticism—a criticism always inseparable from the need to make of the writer a political demiurge.

Perhaps Gorky abbreviated Chekhov's personality so as to admit nothing which could cause him uneasiness. Tolstoy was too massively complex to bear elimination of a single trait; it was indeed just that preponderance of astonishing single traits that made him interesting. . . . It is obvious that Gorky could not bear to think of Chekhov as having a single fault. He does not attempt real criticism of Chekhov's work; in that he is one with his Western admirers. It was enough for Gorky that in this little man, whom Tolstoy also loved more than anyone else, there had been revealed so much ease in speaking the truth, and so deep a fund of personal nobility. Chekhov was the beautiful friend, the Spinoza in the Russian drama—Tolstoy, on the other hand, was the oracle speaking out of the dangerous Russian God-hunger; Andreyev and Blok were the gloomy contemporaries of Gorky's own literary world, too much like him in their inner restlessness to be admired. (pp. 33-5)

Alfred Kazin, "Maxim Gorky and Master Friends" (copyright 1946, 1974 by Alfred Kazin; reprinted by permission of Harcourt Brace Jovanovich, Inc.), in his The Inmost Leaf: A Selection of Essays, *Harcourt Brace Jovanovich, 1955, pp. 28-35.**

RONALD WILKS (essay date 1966)

My Childhood is amongst [Gorky's] finest works, and is one of the most moving descriptions of boyhood ever written. (p. 5)

The pages of *Childhood* are filled with a vast array of living people, all drawn with remarkable powers of observation: the pathetic apprentice, Tsiganok; the eccentric lodger who experiments with copper filings and acid; the cemetery watchman with his philosophizing on death and corruption, and his hair-raising stories; and the loathsome, oily army officer who becomes Gorky's stepfather.

And all these are seen perceptively through a child's eyes. Remarkably, Gorky can recall the actual sensations and reactions to the external world he experienced *as a child*. One of the first passages in the book which clearly demonstrates Gorky's wonderful evocation of the sensations of a child is the funeral scene, when his father is being buried one rainy afternoon. His thoughts are not about his father (who has just died from cholera) but about some frogs knocked down into the grave by clods of earth as the pit is being filled in. He is terrified for their sakes: he is too young to realize the real tragedy. This is surely how a child *would* think, and it is this psychological truth that underlies the whole book. Taste, touch, smell—all these sensations are described in such vivid detail that we seem to be experiencing them ourselves. And, more important than these bodily sensations, Gorky portrays the terror and fear that a child can feel when alone, lying delirious in an attic bedroom, or before some cruel beating.

What is amazing in this book is the compassion and understanding Gorky shows to mankind at its lowest. We are left, not with an impression of bitterness and cynicism, but with the assurance that the author, much though he suffered as a boy, still retains strong hopes that men will grow out of their evil ways in the end. (pp. 10-11)

Childhood has its faults. The descriptive passages, especially about nature, tend to be rhetorical and cliché-ridden and Gorky never forgets his moral message—the dignity and rights of the working man and the downtrodden—which at times develops into tiresome preaching. But these are minor blemishes on a book which, for all the cruelty and horror it describes, leaves the reader with a feeling that, after all, there is some hope for humanity. . . . With its psychological insight and depth of characterization, Gorky's *Childhood* is one of the great masterpieces of its kind. It is a living autobiography of the spirit, a confession in a sense, through which Gorky comes to terms with a squalid, cruel and depraved world, where justice has no place, and where men lust after money, and will spare nothing to get it. Reading it we enter into Russian life as it really was at the turn of the century, and this is an unforgettable experience. (pp. 11-12)

Ronald Wilks, in his introduction to My Childhood *by Maxim Gorky, translated by Ronald Wilks (copyright ©Ronald Wilks, 1966; reprinted by permission of Penguin Books Ltd.),* Penguin Books, 1966, pp. 5-12.

IRWIN WEIL (essay date 1966)

Within the socialist revolutionary movement [Gorky's novels] engendered great enthusiasm, and among the general run of Russian and European readers (as well as among some Americans and Asians) they seemed an entirely justified and necessary indictment of reactionary tsarist Russia. The very sociological influence of his novels was both a cause and a consequence of Gorky's incomplete success in bringing them under full esthetic control, for he was bitterly, deeply angry at the "merzosti" (one of his favorite words: "abominations") all around him in Russia. So anxious was he to eradicate them, to deal the blow that might help liberate his people, that he often fell into exaggerations or overstatements that unbalanced his writing. It was difficult for him to establish a form that would make of his polemics living situations, no matter how well he was able to catch the immediate moment. His writing, as a result, tends to vary between strongly perceived particular moments and tendentious, often overbearing generalizations.

Gorky's problems are perhaps nowhere more clearly presented than in his first novel, *Foma Gordeev*. ("Foma" is the Russian equivalent to "Thomas"; Gordeev, the last name, signifies "one of the proud.") While it is difficult to prove the Biblical connotation of this particular "Thomas," Gorky does in later novels specifically emphasize the concept of the "doubting Thomas," and there is a great deal of Biblical imagery in all his novels. The title character, Foma Gordeev, is the son of Ignat Gordeev, a wealthy, self-made Nizhny-Novgorod merchant who wants his son to carry on his thriving steamship business on the Volga River. Ignat, and after his death, Yakov Maiakin, Foma's uncle, try to persuade the young man to become one of the merchants, but from an early age Foma will not make his peace with the injustices and social inequalities that stem from the organization of the business whose profits he is to enjoy. He tries desperately to find a better way of life for himself; he is very heroic and very impulsive. His well-intended acts, however, are at best short-lived and at worst self-destructive; in the end, he succeeds only in debauching himself. The final result is a smashing victory for the older merchants and a complete rout·for Foma: the merchants force him into a role something like that of the traditional "village idiot." There are points at which the reader becomes quite impatient with the title character: Gorky sometimes permits Foma to be monumentally obtuse. But the protagonist is endowed with great sincerity and a minimum of sanctimoniousness. Since Foma acknowledges his personal weaknesses, the reader, after some hesitation, is prepared to identify with the tragedy in the novel. (pp. 44-6)

Many Soviet critics deny the existence of any problem of "fathers and sons" in the novel because, as they correctly point out, the reader finds sons on both sides of the ideological dividing line: Foma on one side, Taras on the other. But the fact that not all sons choose the revolutionary path does not prove the absence of the theme. Indeed, Turgenev's famous novel also had sons on both sides: Bazarov resisted and eventually perished while his friend, Arkady Kirsanov, accommodated and survived. The way Gorky's novel is constructed, the younger generation is faced by the fathers with a Draconian choice: either join us or be destroyed by us! In the beginning of the book, all the characters, including Yakov Maiakin, Taras's father, take it for granted that Taras has been exiled to Siberia as a revolutionary. Almost automatically, they come to the conclusion that anyone with Taras's energy and independence, who has gone out to Siberia for unknown reasons, must be a revolutionary, in conflict with the values of his father's generation. When Yakov Maiakin, who is one of the shrewdest characters in the novel, discovers his mistake, no one has to explain to him what a strong ally his son will be: the fact that the son has chosen the path of the father is evidence enough that the fathers have the situation so well in hand that for the sons there is simply no other choice. The theme of "fathers and sons" does not necessarily mean that every son will be pitted against every father. It does mean that every conscious young man of action will have his choices of action influenced by the position of the father.

Foma's fate must be the opposite of Taras's, for neither the circumstances of his society nor his own psychological make-up allows him the opportunity to carry through a successful revolt. His fate is quite different from that of later Gorky protagonists, who become successful revolutionaries by adopting the effective habits of the previous generation. Indeed, some of the later novels become almost Russian restatements of the ancient Greek familial legends in which family destruction becomes, in effect, the prerequisite to justice and social order. These later solutions, however, are still far removed from Foma's world; he can only struggle valiantly for a while against overwhelming forces. (pp. 48-9)

Foma Gordeev is not only the victim of unscrupulous merchants who seize his inheritance; he is also a victim of his own inability to handle his attraction toward other people, an attraction toward women, which he would be willing to admit, and a more complicated feeling toward the merchants and their society, which he would be unable to analyze, much less to admit. It would take a much stronger and more intelligent person than Foma—or else a very different society—to resolve these problems, and his perceptions, into a coherent whole. The confused situation in which Foma finds himself parallels, in important and moving ways, the situation of his creator. Gorky was drawn to elements in all of the worlds he presented, both as material for his literary imagination and as contributions toward a solution of the political and social problems that concerned him. But he took hold of them as disconnected fragments, impressive as such, but still the raw materials for a novel (or for a political program) rather than the completely finished literary product. (p. 52)

[During] his unhappy trip to the United States, Gorky had cut through the thematic contradictions and confusions of his previous works: he had found his Marxist revolutionary faith and resolved to express it directly and unambiguously. The result of his literary labors, completed on an upstate New York farm, turned out to be *Mother*—that paragon of Socialist Realism and *bête noire* of most of Gorky's non-Communist critics. The action of the novel describes the acquisition of revolutionary faith and the consequent revolutionary action of a young working man, Pavel Vlasov, culminating in his trial and imprisonment. Pavel's mother, Pelageia Nilovna Vlasova, who has watched and grown to sympathize with the revolutionary cause, continues his work until in the final episode, the tsarist police arrest her. The plot is simple and predictable: the revolutionaries carry on their activities as secretly as possible since they know that sooner or later they will be arrested when they make an open move, such as a demonstration on May Day. The revolutionary characters are uncomplicated and almost un-

marred by personal weaknesses of any kind; the one exception is Vesovshchikov, one of the group who expresses his hatred for the enemy rather crudely. His aberration is explained, however, in terms of his unenlightened surroundings rather than by any attempt to examine the inner world of this less than sympathetic character.

To criticize this work for its crudely simplified plot and characters, however, is to miss the *raison d'être* of the novel itself. Its social and political influence on the workers was enormous, and it moved them precisely in the direction that Gorky wished to move them. A whole Marxist generation found inspiration and encouragement in Gorky's whole-hearted and vigorous espousal of revolutionary doctrine. The expression of faith, uncomplicated by psychological complexities, does not necessarily make a bad work of art. The ancient and popular Russian tales, which depicted the lives of the great Christian saints—tales which were beloved by Gorky and later recommended by him as models of good writing—are examples of literature in which an unambiguous expression of faith does not militate against an esthetic effectiveness. And *Mother* if nothing is not a depiction of the lives of revolutionary saints and martyrs who thought that they themselves had very little chance of seeing success in their own lifetime but who nevertheless worked for the sake of future Russian generations.

What spoils the esthetic effectiveness of *Mother,* for those who do not see the simple expression of the revolutionary credo as a virtue that overrides all other possible considerations of the novel, is its language. Unfortunately, Gorky had not found a linguistic vehicle that was able to bear the ideological weight of the book. Its rhetoric is often embarrassingly simplistic for a writer of Gorky's previous accomplishments. . . . Just as often, Gorky makes the characters talk in the manner of rough street characters. But this style, used earlier by the author with such effectiveness, seems almost entirely out of place in *Mother;* the author is describing people without flaws, not "creatures who once were men," and street language simply does not sit well in the mouths of saints. The linguistic result is singularly lacking in harmonic sound or rhythm, especially to a reader who is familiar with Gorky's enormous linguistic and stylistic achievements in his earlier works. For tales about saints, the writer must find a special language, with its own rules, different from other languages of literary creation. The mixture of theological style and folklore in the lives of the Christian saints achieved just this special effect and, with it, their power to move the reader. Gorky, unfortunately for his own novel and for so many novels later to be influenced by *Mother,* was unable to find such a special style.

But *Mother* is not interesting solely or exclusively because of its historic and sociological influence on the revolutionary movement. In spite of its stylistic weaknesses, it is highly interesting esthetically from the point of view of Gorky's development as a prose writer. The book opens with a reprise of Gorky's early tramp character: Mikhail Vlasov, father of the revolutionary Pavel and an old worker at the factory that forms the center of the workers' settlement (a kind of urban area typical for pre-revolutionary Russia—the workers living in a concentrated area around the factory). He is completely brutalized by his hard and monotonous life at the factory and drinks excessively; when he is drunk, he wants to fight the whole world—which wisely fears him and avoids him then. After six pages, the author decrees death for his worker tramp; he does not allow the son to follow in the father's footsteps: Pavel tries vodka and ill-temper against his mother, but neither suits his temperament. In this novel, the protagonist does not have any trouble entering into the world of his mother, who is both considerate and kind. Gorky is determined not to let the nihilism of his former tramp characters dominate **Mother,** and the mood shifts violently after Mikhail's death and Pavel's coming to manhood. But Gorky pays a price for this exclusion: in eschewing almost completely the ethos and the world view of his tramps, he also loses their vitality, which played such an important part in his early writing. That Gorky had not yet found the basis for a new kind of literary vitality, based on the life of the right-thinking and right-acting individual, rather than on the life of the rebel, is clear in the characterization of Pavel and his friends, who move through the first half of the novel correctly, righteously—and lifelessly.

More interesting in this book are the feminine characters. Just like Foma Gordeev, Pavel Vlasov has his Pelageia and his Sasha; this time Sasha is the girl friend and Pelageia is the mother and title character of the novel. Unlike Foma, Pavel has succeeded in disciplining himself; consequently, he does not often give in to his feelings for Sasha, who is quite the opposite of the destructive Sasha of *Foma Gordeev.* The revolutionary and his girl friend consciously stay away from each other in order to avoid possible impediments to their struggle for the cause. It is interesting to note that again Gorky sees something essentially negative in the normal love relation. Granted, Pavel and Sasha are young people in the special circumstances created by the revolutionary moment, but a different sort of imagination could surely have found the way to describe them as both good revolutionaries and good lovers.

Instead, the title of Gorky's unambiguously revolutionary novel re-emphasizes the maternal as the basic standard for real human affection. Pelageia is a simple woman with all the virtues normally assigned to a good Christian. Gorky makes quite a point of her religious faith and takes great care that the young men in the atheist revolutionary circle around her son do not mock it; they even grant that her version of Christ is not completely contradictory to their own ideals. Furthermore, there is much Biblical imagery centering around Mother's ministrations to the revolutionaries. A good deal is made of her washing the feet of the unwashed, of a certain cup not passing her lips but her draining it if needs be. Indeed, at the very end of the novel, in its first edition, she comes close to saying, about the policemen who are arresting her, ''Forgive them, Father, for they know not what they do.''

Moreover, descriptions of sounds and places in the second half of the book become alive and vibrant when things are seen through Mother's eyes. These sections, together with the first seven pages, form the one important exception to the flatness of the author's language throughout the rest of the book. An example of this is Gorky's description of Mother's first experience with music played in separate harmonic parts. Her reactions are simple and touching; this is just the way a simple and noble nature would react after hearing complex music for the first time. There are several times when descriptions in the book take on a non-realistic quality, points at which conscious distortion becomes prominent; almost all of these moments are connected with Mother's personal perception. (pp. 53-7)

It is interesting that [the Symbolist] technique should appear in Gorky's most revolutionary novel at the moments when he is describing those scenes most intimately touched by the feelings and fears of Mother for her son: right after his arrest and at the beginning of the trial which will lead to his exile. When expressing what he undoubtedly considered to be the most

pathetic and moving scenes in the novel, in order to arouse sympathy for the persecuted revolutionaries he almost unconsciously resorted to the techniques of his Symbolist opponents, who intensely disliked his single-minded concentration on politics in literature. Even when he was being most unambiguously political in his work, Gorky was constantly groping for a different mode and style of expression. In this novel, just as in his others, the theme of revolution was uppermost; yet the themes of maternal love and of the necessity of the son to find his own path against the resistance of the older generation break through at the crucial points in the novel and seem to be responsible for Gorky's success in producing the emotion he wishes in the reader. It is hardly surprising that he did not stick to the revolutionary framework of **Mother** in his subsequent novels but instead branched out with some of the esthetic notions seen only in embryo in that novel. (pp. 58-9)

Irwin Weil, in his Gorky: His Literary Development and Influence on Soviet Intellectual Life *(copyright © 1966 by Random House, Inc.; reprinted by permission of the author), Random House, 1966, 238 p.*

F. M. BORRAS   (essay date 1967)

[Gorky's first attempt at a novel, **Paul the Wretched**], is the story of the life of an orphan, Pavel Gibly, from his birth to his imprisonment for the murder of the prostitute Natalya Krivtsova with whom he is in love. (p. 95)

This early work establishes the pattern for almost all of Gorky's subsequent attempts to write a novel. This pattern is the story of a man's life from his birth either to his death or to the occurrence of a catastrophe which brings about the destruction of his inner life. There is an obvious resemblance between the pattern of such works and that of Gorky's own autobiography, with the striking difference that Alexei Peshkov survives the trials and vicissitudes of his youth and early manhood and emerges triumphantly as Maxim Gorky the eminent writer. . . .

[Gorky's second novel, **Foma Gordeev**], follows the general pattern of the earlier novel, tracing the story of the hero's life from birth to an emotional crisis in early manhood which destroys his inner world. In each case this crisis is the culminating point of the hero's conflict with his surroundings which begins in youth and gains in intensity until it erupts, in Gibly's case, in the murder of his mistress, and in Gordeev's in an impassioned speech of moral condemnation of his fellow-merchants. (p. 96)

[In his short stories '**On a Raft**' and '**A Fit of the Blues**'] Gorky depicts the merchants Silan Petrov and Tikhon Pavlovich within the limits of a single incident which reveals how they think and act in a specific set of circumstances. In Ignat Gordeev, Foma's father, he draws a finished portrait of the type of boisterous, dynamic businessman of whom Petrov and Pavlovich were preliminary sketches. Ignat is the most sympathetic character in the whole of Gorky's early work, a true son of the writer's native region, the middle Volga, vital, creative, generous, and resolute. Gorky invests his hero with all the affection and admiration which he felt for men like him in real life, men whose commercial achievement delighted and flattered his regional compatriots. (p. 97)

Foma Gordeev is a failure as a novel because in it Gorky reduced a theme of great national significance—the conflict of historical forces in a large provincial town on the eve of a great revolution—to the story of one young hooligan's feud with his elders. Although within the confines of a short story Gorky at his best could develop a dramatic situation with great skill, within the longer framework of a novel he could not manage the interrelationships of a group of characters or conduct the unfolding of a series of events. Perhaps the best critical comment upon the artistic defects of *Foma Gordeev* was Gorky's own, made in a letter to the publisher, S. P. Doravatovsky, while he was still writing it: 'Much in it is superfluous and I do not know what to do with the essential and indispensable.' (pp. 103-04)

Gorky's next novel after *Foma Gordeev* was *The Three of Them*. . . . The hero of *The Three of Them*, Ilya Lunyev, is a boy who grows up among the filth and brutality of an urban slum, conceives a dream of middle-class respectability as the peak of human happiness, and achieves his dream through successful commercial activity, only to perceive that the social sphere to which he had so fervently aspired is morally corrupt. (pp. 104-05)

The 'three' of the title of this novel are Lunyev and his two boyhood friends, Yakov Filimonov and Pavel Grachev, the sons respectively of a publican and a blacksmith. The childhood and youth of these two boys is one long tale of suffering and misfortune, and at the end of the novel Filimonov is dying of consumption and Grachev is ill with venereal disease. Calamity after calamity overtakes them while Lunyev is growing ever more prosperous. The bitter contrast between Lunyev's well-being and the wretchedness of his old friends causes him great anguish and intensifies the discontent which he already feels with his material success through his growing disillusionment with middle-class morality. His spiritual drama, which is the theme of the novel, is made up of the inner conflict which arises in him through the interaction of these two factors. (pp. 105-06)

The resemblance of the plot of this novel to that of *Crime and Punishment* attracted the attention of the critics from the time of its publication. . . . Lunyev and Raskolnikov are similar in that they both commit murder for reasons unconnected with theft and steal during the carrying out of the murder, as it were to rationalize it. Both thereafter feel keener remorse for the theft than for the murder. With Lunyev the money becomes an object of irony because it enables him to achieve the *bourgeois* happiness he wants but comes to despise. This irony increases the agony of his inner crisis and makes him stamp and spit on Poluetakov's grave. Although not an irreligious man (he feels the falsity of his commercial ambitions most intensely in church) he is little troubled by the fact of being a murderer. . . . Lunyev, unlike Raskolnikov, remains convinced to the end that his reason for murdering another human being was a good one, but finds himself in an insoluble dilemma because the workings of his social (not his Christian) conscience make him incapable of enjoying the fruits of his crime, whereas his fellow-merchants live happily on the proceeds of every kind of crime, including murder. (pp. 106-07)

[The] message of Gorky's early stories was directed against the generally bewildered and passive mood of the Russian intelligentsia during the 'eighties, even though by the time he began his career that mood was passing. After 1905 he again planned to use his talent to combat the new predominant mood of political depression, which was more intense than that of twenty years before because it followed a period of almost manic elation. Thus he wrote of his purpose in writing *Mother*— 'to sustain the failing spirit of opposition to the dark and threatening forces in life'.

In pursuit of his goal Gorky presents a group of Social Democrat revolutionaries engaged in stimulating peasants and workers to revolt during the years immediately preceding 1905; their confidence in the rightness of their cause and its ultimate triumph, their mutual devotion, their indifference to personal interests contrast sharply with the pessimism, militant individualism, and sensual self-indulgence which Gorky saw as the basic vices of Russian society when the novel was written. (p. 109)

Gorky's attempt in *Mother* to reconcile in the figure of Pelageya Nilovna his socialist convictions with the religious aspirations he acquired in childhood from his grandmother and never completely lost was a reflection of the religious preoccupations widespread among the Russian intelligentsia after the failure of the revolution of 1905. Many Russian thinkers at this time, convinced of the impossibility of realizing the kingdom of God on earth, turned their attention to the seemingly more tractable problem of assuring their personal immortality in heaven. Gorky, however, from his Italian exile, kept his eyes firmly fixed upon the evils of this world, as exemplified in Russian reality, and sought in religious thinking stimulus to revive and sustain the revolutionary cause at home. . . . Rejecting traditional concepts of God which seemed to him either to sanction repression or to encourage resignation, he began to look for a new faith which would further the cause of the Russian revolution while still exalting Christian notions of freedom and justice. This new quest, which involved a search for suitable men and women to put the faith into practice, replaced after 1905 his earlier attempts to find a strong, individualistic hero. He has left an artistic record of his spiritual seeking during these years in the short novel *Confession*. . . . (pp. 112-13)

Confession is the account of the disillusionment of Matvei, an orphan boy, with traditional Christianity and his subsequent wandering through Russia in search of a new image of God. In describing this boy's physical vagabondage in quest of a spiritual ideal, Gorky is externalizing his own inner seeking. (p. 113)

In each of Gorky's novels so far examined, except *Mother*, the author has based his narrative upon the life story of a single young man. In each case this man's spiritual seeking, which constitutes the theme of the novel, is conditioned by his childhood experiences. . . . In each of these novels the hero's life story is followed up to his middle twenties, that is, approximately to the age at which Gorky closes his own autobiography. Each one of them is short. In *The Life of Matvei Kozhemyakin* . . . Gorky writes a very long novel in which he recounts the life of his hero from birth to his death at the age of about fifty-five. As in earlier works, he begins by relating the formation of a boy's outlook and personality under the influence of his surroundings; Matvei Kozhemyakin grows up in the small provincial town of Okurov, the son of Saveli Kozhemyakin, a self-made merchant in the style of Ignat Gordeev. In this novel, however, it is not Gorky's purpose to describe the inner conflicts of a merchant's son who does not wish to follow a commercial career. His attention is focused rather upon the town of Okurov, the manners and customs of which are the decisive influence upon the formation of his hero's personality. (pp. 115-16)

This novel is the story of a struggle between the forces of light, represented by Mansurova and Vasilev, and the forces of darkness, embodied in the life of Okurov, for the possession of a man's soul. The final result of this struggle is the total defeat of the forces of light—not only do Mansurova and Vasilev fail to change Kozhemyakin, but Mansurova's short sojourn in

Okurov adversely affects her sense of revolutionary purpose. . . . The defeat of Gorky's radical thinkers in this novel by the medieval atmosphere of Russian provincial life (the Russian people's Asiatic inheritance, insisted the writer) is as complete as the rout of his rebellious hobos by the nineteenth-century forces of law and order in his early stories. Like Dostoevsky, Gorky seeks God but shows the Devil as the stronger. (p. 117)

Like *Foma Gordeev* and *The Life of Matvei Kozhemyakin* [*The Artomonov Business*] depicts, against the mid-century background of ever-quickening commercial activity, the meteoric rise of a business founded by an ex-serf in a stagnant Russian provincial town. Whereas, however, the first of these novels is concerned with the inner life of the central character and the second with the intimate connexion between life in the town and the development of the hero's personality, the basic theme of the later novel, as the title makes clear, is the fate of the business itself. . . . Although the fate of the business (and with it that of Russian capitalism in general) is the basic theme of the novel, Gorky, always predominantly concerned with people, is more interested in the influence which its management exerts upon each member of the family than in the political and economic processes which result in its destruction. Because of the interweaving of the historical theme with personal destinies and the distribution of the narrative interest among three generations instead of its concentration upon one person, Gorky in this work could more justly claim to have written a true novel than in either of the other two. (p. 118)

The theme of *The Artomonov Business* is based upon the ideas Gorky had expressed many years earlier in the articles **'The Destruction of Personality'** and **'Notes on the petty bourgeois mentality',** and in the novel *Confession.* Gorky wishes us to compare, to their detriment, each succeeding member of the family with [the ex-serf] Ilya and to show how each generation, moving further away from the people, diminishes correspondingly in spiritual stature. This progressive estrangement is expressed in the deterioration of relations between the family and their workers. Ilya behaves very simply with them, attends their weddings and christenings, and they regard him as a peasant like themselves only more favoured by fortune. Pyotr is sullen and tyrannical with them because they represent the business cares which have spoilt his life. Alexei, half-nobleman, calls them rogues and ne'er-do-wells and scolds them. Yakov despises the workers, but he is terrified by the ever-growing proletarian movement. Miron understands that they are not concerned merely with obtaining reforms and attempts to win their co-operation by establishing for them libraries and sporting clubs, 'feeding wolves with carrots', as he puts it. Young Ilya, the Marxist, regards them, of course, in a different light from his relatives; in him, the best member of the third generation, old Ilya's oneness with the Russian people is restored, but whereas the commercial path chosen by the latter begins the alienation of the family from their own social class, his grandson's political activity reunites them, at least until the revolution. Gorky presents the short heyday of Russian capitalism as an aberration in the history of the nation.

Gorky wrote his last novel, *The Life of Klim Samgin,* during the years 1925 to 1936. His purpose in this work was to draw an epic picture of the ideological conflicts among the Russian intelligentsia from the mid eighteen-seventies to the revolution of 1917, and to fit into this picture a condemnatory portrait of his central character, Klim Samgin, a liberal intellectual. This was a most promising subject for a major novel, and Gorky's

work, if successful, would have been a significant contribution to world literature; unfortunately it is an abject failure. (pp. 125-26)

Gorky's long novel was foredoomed to failure when he decided to place at its centre such a footling nonentity as Samgin; the length of the work springs not from the significance of its subject but from the fact that the author enjoys venting his hatred on his puppet hero through four considerable volumes. The reader quickly tires of this protracted persecution. In a book of this length one would have expected Gorky to exploit his exceptional gifts of characterization and to compensate to some degree for the insignificance of his central character with a striking gallery of minor figures. Even in this realm, however, he fails utterly. As so often happened with him when he was dealing with members of the intelligentsia, he presents the great body of Samgin's innumerable acquaintances not as people but as vehicles for the expression of political, religious, and aesthetic opinions current during the decades covered by the action of the novel. In striving to impart ideological significance to all their personal relationships he destroys their reality as human beings. (p. 128)

> *F. M. Borras, in his* Maxim Gorky the Writer: An Interpretation *(© Oxford University Press 1967; reprinted by permission of Oxford University Press), Oxford University Press, Oxford, 1967, 195 p.*

BORIS BYALIK   (essay date 1968)

Gorky's manuscripts show the tremendous amount of work he put into *The Life of Klim Samgin:* almost the whole of his life as an artist was a prelude to the writing of the novel, and he continued his quest even after he began to write it. In the early version, the historical background of his story was still of relatively small importance, and the composition was entirely subordinate to the "history of a hollow soul." Gorky subsequently filled out the historical background, now and again subordinating the composition to it, and saying in many more of his letters that the whole was a "historical chronicle." Eventually he evolved the main principle behind the architectonics of the novel placing in juxtaposition "the history of a hollow soul"—the story of the "disintegration of the personality" of Klim Samgin and his like—and the logic of history, a chronicle of 40 years of life in Russia. (p. 148)

The Life of Klim Samgin is not just a summing up; it is a fresh, comprehensive and cogent picture of the historical tendencies which produced men like Samgin. He is a type on a par with the greatest in world literature. In fact, the name of this character has become a common noun for it is now used to designate a typical phenomenon of bourgeois reality of the imperialist epoch, an epoch of wars and revolutions smashing the old world and the pillars of its ideology. "Samginism" is the bankruptcy of individualism as a weapon of self-defence of the bourgeoisie and bourgeois intellectuals. It signifies the inefficacy of the philistine "spiritual make-up." (pp. 148-49)

In order to show the real class content of Samginism, Gorky surrounded Samgin with hundreds of characters who are in constant touch with him. Some put in only a fleeting appearance and depart after delivering themselves of one or two pithy statements. Others are seen again and again, each time in a different aspect, corresponding to the changing historical scene. Then there are Samgin's more or less constant companions. This numerous and varied host is the vehicle of diverse principles, beliefs and ideas—political, philosophical, aesthetic and so on. These ideas and their exponents help to shape Samgin's mind, either by subordinating him, or by repelling him and thus inducing him to defend himself. (p. 149)

The numerous characters of the novel may be variously grouped, depending on how they interact with Klim Samgin. Some of them are his doubles, revealing this or that of his traits and helping to show his true essence. There are the *agent provocateur* Nikonova, a woman with whom Samgin finds himself most at ease, and the informer Mitrofanov, whose "sober" views of life Samgin appreciates.

The characteristic thing is that he is apt to find his mental kin among those who have made a profession out of treachery.

A few other characters may be classified as Samgin's doubles only with substantial reservations. Their temperaments and fortunes are in no sense like Samgin's, but they happen to have tripped up on the same thing—the individualistic approach to life.

A special place belongs to the capitalists portrayed in the novel. They are the masters of the life in which Samgin hopes to find a quiet niche for himself, they are the fathers of the ideas that constitute the chief diet of his brain. Some of them give full and open vent to bourgeois principles, and while they are a motley crowd, they are in a way epitomized by Varavka, one of the "pioneers" of capitalist progress in Russia. Some of them have a tendency to "break out" of their proper *milieu*, like the highly complex Lyutov, who commits suicide, and the merchant woman Marina Zotova, who has a very prominent part to play in Samgin's life. Hers is a curious role, for she stands somewhere midway between Varavka (Samgin calls her "a petticoat Varavka") and Lyutov (the "redundant man" of the bourgeoisie whom Samgin thinks she somehow resembles). She matches the former in the frenzy of her money-grubbing, and the latter in the keenness of her perception that "this little old world of ours is going to pieces."

Apart from the numerous characters emphasizing Samgin's various traits or shedding light on the sources of his ideas and moods, there is an important gallery of characters whose presence spells the doom of Samginism and the whole of the old world. But let me say at this point that on the whole the characters in the novel should not be viewed only in connection with Samgin, an approach that would have been adequate had it been nothing but an exposé of Samginism, which it definitely is not. (pp. 149-50)

The Life of Klim Samgin is both a social and psychological novel showing the formation of Samgin's character, and a chronicle recording a number of historical facts and personalities. But both definitions fall short, because the novel and the chronicle are parts of a larger whole which could well be called an epopee.

The historical chronicle in *The Life of Klim Samgin* is merely the foundation on which is erected a broader, more generalized and truly epic portrayal of the destinies of the various classes in the people's revolution which unfolds under the leadership of the Communist Party. Samgin is repeatedly made to witness popular demonstrations and to admit that on each successive occasion the people are stronger, more united and more determined. (pp. 150-51)

What makes *The Life of Klim Samgin* so complex and original is the fact that it shows reality almost as Samgin sees it. Almost, but not quite, because it was not Gorky's task to show life through Samgin's dark glasses, but to discard and break them.

As in old Russian fairy-tales, where the hero is resurrected by first being sprinkled with the "water of death" and then with the "water of life," so in the novel, the reader is first plunged into the dull deadening bog of philistine thinking, and then led out into the bright world of progressive ideas, with reliable protection against the influence of Samginism. (p. 151)

[In a letter to Romain Rolland] Gorky said he linked up Samgin with literary characters like Stendhal's Julien Sorel, Goethe's Werther, [Alfred de] Musset's "son of the age," and [Paul] Bourget's "disciple." Hints of this link-up are given in the novel itself, as in the description of Marina Zotova's library, with its many novels about the "young man of the 19th century."

What then was behind the idea of comparing Samgin and these young men? It was that their attitude to life, once historically warranted, had lost its rationale in the new conditions. In making his comparison between the "redundant people" and Samgin, Gorky was in fact saying: anyone who took the attitude of the "young man of the 19th century" in this new epoch, the epoch of proletarian revolutions and great socialist transformations, would inevitably develop into a Samgin. Thus, Gorky's concept of the "history of a young man" as reflected in his novel, *The Life of Klim Samgin,* was of momentous importance, for it was shot through with his desire to safeguard readers, notably young people, from the venom of individualism, and to show man's great responsibility and great joy of living in the epoch when the people shape their own life.

The novel makes quite clear the tremendous possibilities which the art of socialist realism opens up for the artist. Gorky's novel also helps to see the connections running between this art and the best artistic traditions of the past, as well as its innovating character, which enables it to portray reality in its revolutionary development, as the triumphant shaping of history by the masses.

Two main themes run right through the whole of Gorky's writing: the resurrection of the human soul, and the disintegration of the personality. The former is most strikingly embodied in Gorky's *Mother,* and the latter in *The Life of Klim Samgin,* which shows the terrible emptiness in store for anyone who sets his ego against the people and tries to use it as a hideout in face of the inexorable march of history. (pp. 151-52)

Gorky's great epopee is not one of those books which provide recreation. Not at all. It is one of those works which demand of the reader an effort of all his intellectual powers, which augment with the reading of each page of this outstanding book. The reader is shown a whole new world, depicted with an incomparable knowledge of life and unsurpassed skill, as hundreds of human lives are unfolded in a complex and instructive panorama, and as the writer's sage and fearless thought illumines the past with the light of the future. (p. 152)

Boris Byalik, "A Great Epopee," in Soviet Literature *(© Soviet Literature, 1968), No. 3, 1968, pp. 147-52.*

ALLAN LEWIS (essay date 1971)

A detailed examination of [Gorky's *Yegor Bulitchev*] is essential in considering present-day trends in the theatre. It deserves to be better known in the Western world. *The Lower Depths* is too close to the influence of Chekhov; *Bulitchev* is the product of Gorky's maturity. It is assured, whereas the earlier play was still groping. *The Lower Depths* is a cry of rebellion, an inchoate, directionless struggle to free man, which in *Yegor Bulitchev* has crystallized into an awareness of responsibility. In this sense, Gorky has written a socialist play, perhaps the best that has come out of the Soviet theatre.

Yegor Bulitchev is in fact three plays, a trilogy composed on a grand scale, a document of history and people. The first play is called *Yegor Bulitchev and Others* and depicts the rotting away of the merchant class just before the Revolution of 1917; in the second, *Dostigaev and Others,* Yegor's business partner resists the changes of the Revolution; the final play, *Somov and Others,* is the story of socialist construction. *Yegor Bulitchev* is unquestionably the best of the three. (p. 120)

Like all of Gorky's work, the play is about people whose actions are conditioned by the social forces of which they themselves are an active element. Yet here, in addition, is a fuller canvas of society in collapse, with its abundance of dead mores, ignorance, and surviving folklore. The action is made up of the meaningful experiences of the day, yet towering above all is not a worker, a revolutionary hero typical of most Soviet plays, but a capitalist. Gorky had done the same before in his first novel, *Foma Gordeyev.* . . . [Yegor] is surrounded by a savage environment; he himself is brutal, yet he has an insatiable faith that, rotten as the world is, new avenues will be opened up by man into which the love of life can pour itself more creatively.

Gorky's heroes are of protest and unrest: either tramps, cold, hungry, but free, who have no superiors to command them; or strong, positive, lonesome men like Yegor. Strange heroes indeed for a collective society, but Gorky had one foot in each world, and his impressionable years had been spent under the czarist regime. From his youthful world he retained a belligerent humanitarianism and a respect for knowledge. In Yegor, these are transformed into the elements of modern tragedy—man struggling with hostile forces, sensing alternatives, willing to yield yet unable to do so, forced to fight to the end, succumbing only to death.

The tragic overtones make a sympathetic protagonist of Yegor. He is rude and insulting to his wife; he once had an affair with his wife's sister, the abbess; he has long carried on an affair with Glasha; he had married for money; his illegitimate daughter lives in the household; yet we admire Yegor and dislike his wife, for she is hypocritical, self-righteous, ignorant and weak, whereas he is direct, honest, lusty, bursting with life even in death. He has mastered the world of the merchant and found it wanting. He probes for new values, and is all too human—with too little and too late. He refuses to succumb to deception, religious chicanery, superstition, not because he is aloof and beyond them, but because he is part of them, has lived with them, and has risen by his own strength to reject them. (pp. 122-23)

Despite Gorky's expressed intentions, *Yegor Bulitchev* has little to do with the [Marxist theory of literature]. It is a play in the traditional realistic style. (pp. 126-27)

        Allan Lewis, "The Theatre of Socialist Realism— Maxim Gorky: 'Yegor Bulitchev'," *in his* The Contemporary Theatre: The Significant Playwrights of Our Time *(1971 by Allan Lewis; used by permission of Crown Publishers, Inc.), revised edition, Crown, 1971, pp. 111-27.*

JEFFREY BARTKOVICH (essay date 1973)

The predisposition for some people to view Gorky as a true humanitarian, a defender of the dregs of society, a moral protestor against the ugly side of reality, and as an artist whose characters depicted the loathsome and filthy, whose major themes exhibited the urge of degraded human beings to find in the world of existence some ray of sunlight and hope, and whose didacticism stressed the feeling that even the hearts of "ex-humans" retain sparks of true humanitarianism that may flare up if given the chance, may have been projecting their own idealistic thoughts upon a basically nihilistic writer. We can legitimize this view in respect to **"Twenty-six Men and a Girl,"** which takes its origins in the perception of Tanya as an embodiment of Truth, Beauty, and Goodness, the frame of reference in regard to the men's realization of Tanya's exposure, and the relationship of Tanya the Woman and Tanya the Idol.

The truly great commentator on women, Tolstoy, may have been hinting at the answer when he argued with Gorky that

> in a healthy girl chastity is not natural. 'If a girl who has turned fifteen is healthy, she desires to be touched and embraced. Her mind is still afraid of the unknown and of what she does not understand; that is what they call chastity and purity. But her flesh is already aware that the incomprehensible is right, lawful, and in spite of the mind, it demands fulfillment of the law.' . . . Then he began to speak about the girl in *Twenty-six and One,* using a stream of indecent words with a simplicity which seemed cynical. . . .

If this insight into the moral nature of women is correct, then Tanya the Woman forced men to accept a reality of life that they had been avoiding by their expectations and projections of Tanya as an Idol. Tanya did not deteriorate morally, she only responded in a more direct manner to the innate need to satisfy Tolstoy's "law" that was already existent in her nature.

Prior to her experience with the ex-soldier, Tanya's chastity manifested itself in her innocent acceptance of her role as Tanya the Idol as she daily descended to her subjects to receive their ritual sacrifices. This weak sanctity was elevated to moral virtue by the imaginative deceptions of the men and was established in the conventions and social expectations that Tanya willingly performed for her subjects. When the ex-soldier presented an opportunity for a more fulfilling display of the carnal passion, Tanya's proclivity to evil resigned her to the situation; and this released her from the restrictive proprieties that the men had imposed, and so produced a more mature and natural woman. This greater self-realization, self-expression, and self-acceptance allowed Tanya to withstand the "torrent of profanity and shameless taunts" of her distraught, disillusioned subjects. Unfortunately, however, she does not equate their contemptuous jealousy with the deprivation of their only illusion in a desolate, grim life.

Just as Tanya consummated herself as a woman and as a human, the ex-soldier's exploit forced a confrontation between the twenty-six men and the reality that they had been trying to evade. Previous to this occurrence, the twenty-six men were unwilling to tolerate the facts that they were "half-dead," that their senses were blunted by the "crushing burden of toil," that it was painful and hard for them as human beings to exist in a sterile immobile environment, and that the "hard labour was turning them into dumb oxen." To escape the bitterness and inhumanity of their condition, they sought ideal meanings and truths as things should be in Tanya, or at least a pretense that something better did exist; and to avoid the overwhelming harshness and crusing aspects of actuality, they fantasized an idyllic woman who would elevate them into a realm of subjective reality that had absolutely no foundations in objective reality. Perhaps in order for them to live, they needed the consolation of their own inner world of illusions; and if this non-existent state was destroyed, they would collapse. This is just what happened for the instant they recognized and admitted that their old ideals were but temporary joys and unfounded, they died a non-physical death for it "was more than they could endure." Once locked in their own idealism, they had been freed only to discover that goodness and truth did not dwell there, and their reality was nothing more than a painful existence. Their despair was both individual and cosmic. For the twenty-six men Tanya the Idol had been shattered, and their view of Tanya the Woman was beautiful but disgusting. As for the world, it had only to accept the ugly cruelty of its own situation.

It was significant that a female was chosen as the vessel of male idealism, for she became the source and the retribution of disillusionment. Yet, the foil of the seduced, whom the twenty-six idealists envisioned as the sanctuary of innocence and purity and the possessor of universal meaning and purpose, was the seducer himself. The ex-soldier became the means to dramatize the replacement of the vital ideal code of existence. How the thematic relationship between the twenty-six men and one girl comes clear. Just as the men tried to escape an understanding of their own condition in terms of their own humanity, so did they seek to explain their condition in a fantasized, idealized relation to an imaginative Idol. Likewise, just as they tried to avoid the real force working in the universe, so did they reject concupiscence as a force within Tanya and replaced it with Goodness. Finally, just as they tried to *create* meaning and purpose in their lives, so did they endow and stake their non-existent meaning and purpose with Tanya. But, with the destruction of the Dream came the realization that there is no purpose, nor any meaning. If the men found meaning, they had created it out of their own need; and that need would continue to exert influence even after the object endowed with the possible gratification was withdrawn. The twenty-six men discovered when their romanticism was shattered that in reality there was no ultimate cause for man's hope, for wasn't Tanya's defloration what each man secretly dreamed of obtaining? The ideals they believed in were human fabrications on how it all was. They "were left standing in the middle of the yard amid the mud, under the rain and a grey sky that had no sun in it. . . ." and in a universe that had no purposeful meaning. What was left but to shuffle "back to their damp stony dungeon" called life with a need that was their ultimate reality? (pp. 287-88)

> *Jeffrey Bartkovich, "Maxim Gorky's 'Twenty-Six Men and a Girl': The Destruction of an Illusion," in* Studies in Short Fiction *(copyright 1973 by Newberry College), Vol. X, No. 3, Summer, 1973, pp. 287-88.*

RUFUS W. MATHEWSON, JR.   (essay date 1975)

Mother contains two formulas often found in later Soviet fiction: the conversion of the innocent, the ignorant, or the misled to a richer life of participation in the forward movement of society; and the more important pattern of emblematic political heroism in the face of terrible obstacles. The first theme is embodied in the figure of the mother, whose life is transformed by affiliation with the revolutionary movement, and the second in the grim figure of her son, Pavel. Actually the two themes are interwoven, with Pavel acting as the principal agent in restoring his mother to a life of dignity and purpose. This relationship also illustrates the kind of inspiriting effect the image of Pavel is intended to have on the sympathetic reader.

Pavel's inspirational value derives from the moral qualities he displays and the kind of purposeful activity in which he displays them. When courage, endurance, strength of will are exercised in certain kinds of tactically "correct" political behavior, during the May Day parade, for example, it is always a calculated effect he aims for. His later defiance of the Tsarist court reflects a public, not a private, emotion in the sense that it is not a personal defense, but an occasion to instruct the masses in the workings of the hateful system. Pavel acts on this, and on all other occasions, out of two supplementary kinds of knowledge that make up class consciousness: the abstract generalizations about society learned from his precious books, plus the documentation of working-class misery which is daily before his eyes. Thus equipped with emotion and knowledge, Pavel goes forth to permanent battle with the status quo.

This, at least, is the way we are asked to read the novel. It may be read quite differently, however. The novel's conflict is posed between moral absolutes and the writer's attitude toward the conflict is not that of an observer but of a partisan who is, himself, engaged in the bitter class warfare. In this rigid opposition there is no opportunity for the emblematic good man to move in the area between good and evil, or to be involved with, tempted by, or overcome from within by evil. He may reproach himself for lacking the endurance he needs to carry out the tasks history has set for him. He may search his soul to find the courage he needs. He may examine the reasons which brought him to his exposed position. But he will not question the position itself. Evil is tangible and external, and all man's resources are needed to combat it. Since, according to the formula in *Mother,* the good man is the most distant from evil, he cannot yield to it without forfeiting his position in the novel's moral hierarchy. Pavel's revolutionary colleague, the Ukrainian, Andrei Nakhodka, asks a question which is vital for the revolutionary and suggests at the same time a fruitful approach for the writer to the tensions of revolutionary activity. After he has confessed to the murder of a police spy, he asks, in effect, what crimes he will commit in the name of the revolution, what violations of his private moral code are permissible (or bearable) for the dedicated man. But Nakhodka is too weak, too susceptible. He is a good-hearted follower, but not the leader Pavel is. In Pavel's eyes such questions have a certain validity, but they do not really concern *him,* and can always be resolved in the terms of his political-moral absolutes.

But the ease with which he does resolve them seriously challenges his adequacy as a literary portrait. He is, among other things, a fanatical moralizer and prophet. It may be argued that these qualities have been forced on him by the stringencies of his situation, or that they are inevitable costs of his kind of life. In any case they are there—we know because Gorky, perhaps unwittingly, shows them to us—to be accounted for, overcome, or read into any final assessment of his human worth. At the very least they are barriers to awareness, if not to action. By failing to record his hero's limitations fully Gorky has provided grounds for seriously questioning his human and literary judgment in this matter. (pp. 167-69)

When Nakhodka, whose humane awareness is in inverse proportion to his political effectiveness, reproaches [Pavel] for his harshness, and for acting the hero in front of his helpless mother,

Gorky the writer has brought to light a legitimate conflict of values. Pavel's pomposity, rigidity, and fixity of purpose, with their suggestions of sublimation and megalomania, are predictable consequences of his personality and of his way of life, as given. But Gorky the propagandist betrays his persuasive insight, a few moments later, by extracting a quick apology from Pavel. For the rest of the novel the insight is forgotten. Gorky's uncritical approval of Pavel is unmistakable as the latter grows into the most effective political leader in the area. Finally, when Pavel rises to speak at his trial, "A party man, I recognize only the court of my party and will not speak here in my defense," he has become in his own eyes the selfless incarnation of the public cause, without doubts, hesitations, or concern for personal loss, and Gorky, having surrendered his control over the character, can only agree.

The matter of tension between private and public life appears constantly, but it is resolved with one exception in favor of the latter. Sacrifice and suffering are often mentioned but seldom shown, and never explored to any depth. (pp. 169-70)

Only once does raw human experience force its way through the web of political rationalization. Nakhodka's anguish at his casual blow which turned out to be an act of murder bespeaks real inner conflict. He knows the conventional terms in which the crime can be justified, and he recites them with an air of conviction. . . . (p. 170)

The crime which is justifiable in public terms is nevertheless unacceptable to Nakhodka's moral sensibility. It is the most terrible and destructive act of self-renunciation the revolutionary can be asked to carry out, even though he believes, as he does it, that it is in the name of the time when "free men will walk on the earth" and "life will be one great service to man." . . .

Despite the congealed rhetoric, this is intelligible moral utterance, exposing grounds for the deepest division between the individual and his cause, including permanent banishment from the Utopia to come. One need not agree with his definition of the dilemma to see in this the germ of genuine tragic conflict, the real drama of the revolution's honorable casualties. Gorky does not develop it further. Pavel, who, with his mother, remains in the center of the stage, understands and sympathizes: "Andrei won't forgive himself soon," he says, "if he'll forgive himself at all." But he reduces it again to the comforting blacks and whites of the political morality which Andrei has for a moment seen through. . . . (p. 171)

The hardheaded visionaries of *Mother* . . . have their minds fixed firmly on the emergent future. They are struggling to forward a trend which, they are convinced, is both inevitable and infinitely preferable to the unbearable present. Gorky makes no attempt to hide his own partisanship in this contest. Completely identified with his protagonists, he is as committed as they are to the overthrow of life as it is, in the name of a compelling vision of life as it should be. But the question again arises: how can the conflict between future and present be dramatized within the confines of the realistic novel? Apart from the many "utopian" speculations in the novel, the desirability of the future can be suggested only indirectly, through the intensity of the characters' dedication to it. Otherwise the affirmative case must be set forth in declamatory assertions by the hero or his lieutenants. In spite of the endless, florid talk about the better world their personal struggle brings closer, what these men are fighting against is always more vividly realized than what they are fighting for. Their anger is thus

better motivated than their invincible optimism. In a novel of repeated tactical defeats this assurance is communicated only by defiant speeches.

The source of their optimism is a political truth founded upon abstractions. That the historical force championed by Pavel and his comrades is somehow benign is an assumption outside the novel which may or may not be accepted by the reader. Gorky's abandonment of a more traditional novelist's vantage for overt political commitment, therefore, prejudices any claims the novel may have to universal interest. The novel of open political partisanship can be acceptable only to like-minded readers. The only possibility of reaching a more indifferent audience rests in the acceptability or credibility of the human material—above all, of the hero—in the novel. And we have seen, I think, that the partisan blight has effectively neutralized his (or their) appeal.

The general difficulties we have indicated—involvement with the future, motivation by doctrine, and this writer's close identification with his heroes and with their cause—have one marked effect on the texture of the novel: it is shaped, down to the smallest technical details, by the spirit of political evangelism. It is not only that the climax of the novel is declamatory (Pavel's speech before the court), or that all the characters' actions and utterances are shaped by political considerations. The dialogue often resembles a verbal exchange of newspaper editorials, written in the turgid rhetoric which also disfigures Gorky's pamphleteering. The expository passages, the dramatic passages, the physical descriptions of the characters and of nature are likewise permeated with evangelism. As the mother goes down under the strangling fingers of the police spy at the novel's end she shouts a slogan, "You will not drown the truth in seas of blood." When Pavel has overcome her doubts about the essential justice of Nakhodka's act of homicide, "The mother arose agitated, full of a desire to fuse her heart into the heart of her son, into one burning, flaming torch." Class virtue manifests itself in the bodies, postures, faces, above all in the eyes of the characters. The eyes of the class enemy are muddy, bleared, or shifty, but, in the midst of his courtroom speech, "Pavel smiled, and the generous fire of his blue eyes blazed forth more brilliantly." At times Gorky comes very close to self-parody: "You'd better put on something; it's cold," one character remarks; and the other answers, "There's a fire inside of me." This is not simply bad writing but a striking example of the fusion of form and content. At the heart of the matter is Gorky's total partisanship. Under its influence all literary and human truth—even the truth of the physical universe—becomes subordinated to a single dogmatic view of political truth. (pp. 172-74)

Gorky knew that his approach to literature implied important departures from classical realism. In his letter to Chekhov about the need for "the heroic," Gorky exposed some of the thinking that underlay this demand:

> So there you go, doing away with realism. And I am extremely glad. So be it! And to hell with it! . . . Everyone wants things that are exciting and brilliant so that it won't be like life, you see, but superior to life, better, more beautiful. Present-day literature must definitely begin to color life and as soon as it does this, life itself will acquire color. That is to say, people will live faster, more brilliantly.

The "realism" that must give way to the "heroic" was neutral, he felt, hopeless, and rooted in the present, in life as it is; the "heroic" that was to replace it was not escapist, but functional, in that it was to quicken and change men's lives and set them in motion toward an unspecified vision of life as it should be. On the single occasion when this general feeling was translated into political myth-making, he invested the "color" and the promise in Pavel and the other Bolsheviks. This lapse has been seized upon and made the theoretical basis of "socialist romanticism," the ingredient of socialist realism which directs the writer not to a general heightening of experience as Gorky originally intended, but to the celebration of the emergent future exactly as it is defined in the Party program and in the five-year plans. This is the obligatory step beyond the present, beyond reality, beyond realism, and beyond the empirical truth that the figure of the Soviet hero must express. Pavel Vlasov is valued as an *ideological* portrait, made up of hope, doctrine, and tendency as much as he is of flesh and blood. Thus the grounds for doubting his human validity are built into the very basis of the theory he stands on. (pp. 175-76)

> *Rufus W. Mathewson, Jr., "Lenin and Gorky: The Turning Point," in his* The Positive Hero in Russian Literature *(reprinted with the permission of the publishers, Stanford University Press; © 1958, 1975 by the Board of Trustees of the Leland Stanford Junior University), second edition, Stanford University Press, 1975, pp. 156-76.**

GEORGETTE DONCHIN   (essay date 1976)

[Gorky's] first completed play, *Smug Citizens* . . . , gave him considerable trouble. He disliked it: 'It's bad. It is shrill, vain, and empty,' he wrote both to Andreyev and to Chekhov. His basic dramatic principles are already evident here. The play owes a great deal to Chekhov. The drama and the conflict between his characters take place in the everyday flow of life; the plot is weak and there is no real central protagonist. But the Chekhovian 'sub-text' and fine psychological characterisation are sorely missing. Chekhov immediately diagnosed the weaknesses: 'You force new, original people to sing new songs from a score that looks second-hand; you have four acts, the characters deliver moral lectures, the long drawn-out passages cause dismay . . .' Gorky differs from Chekhov, and this is characteristic of him as dramatist, in sharply differentiating his characters according to their ideology; their personal relationships only emphasise their ideological clashes. Thus the domestic two-generations conflict in *Smug Citizens,* vaguely reminiscent of [Aleksandr] Ostrovsky's plays, is projected onto a social canvas, and the play acquires a political dimension especially topical in pre-1905 Russia. *Smug Citizens* contained a new character, the worker Nil, hailed as the first proletarian type in the Russian theatre. Though rude and callous, he is an attempt at a positive character who, like Gorky himself, hates the small bourgeoisie and their philistinism. Gorky explained to Stanislavsky that Nil was 'a man calmly confident in his strength and in his right to change life', the shortcomings of which aroused in his soul 'only one feeling—a passionate desire to do away with them'. In the play, however, the calm confidence of Nil is not as apparent as his violent hatred. He is too loud and too ruthless in his denunciation, and unrelieved by doubts or weaknesses. Chekhov rightly considered *Smug Citizens* an immature work, but he pointed out that Gorky's merit was to have been the first writer in Russia and in the world to speak with contempt about philistinism at the very time when society was ready to protest.

Lower Depths proved a better play. More complex, it had a certain 'philosophical' interest, was permeated by a feeling of compassion for humanity—more effective than the crude hatred of *Smug Citizens*—and, above all, had a striking background, so much more colourful than the drabness in the preceding work. Once again, in form it looked back to Chekhov: in its plotless structure (though the loose scenes have more nodal points of dramatic interest than in Gorky's first play), in its absence of one central hero and its concentration on a collective group (here made socially and symbolically significant by the confines of the doss-house) and, above all, in its polyphonic dialogue (parallel speeches directed at no one in particular and punctured by expressive songs), though without the finesse of Chekhov's suggestion of the inner current of individual drama. Unlike the Chekhovian delicately understated and psychologically motivated characters, Gorky's thieves, murderers and prostitutes are sharply delineated and romantically exaggerated especially in their tedious speeches on the meaning of life and truth. They are individualised not so much by their individual drama as by their response to the kind of truth they believe in. Luka's arrival has activated for a while the stagnation of his dethroned social outcasts. His departure leads to both an optimistic assertion of human dignity and an act of despair, leaving enough room for varying interpretations of his role. The play's unprecedented success at the time no doubt was due to a combination of Gorky, Stanislavsky, and its contemporaneous relevance. Its initial impact on Western audiences can be easily explained, but by now the novelty of the naturalistic setting, of the sociopolitical undertones, and of the reflections on Man, Freedom, illusion and reality should have paled, yet the play is still periodically revived in the West. One of the great theatrical prototypes, *Lower Depths* remains a challenge to both producers and actors.

After 1902, Gorky wrote a series of plays attacking the new intelligentsia. *Summer Folk* . . . seems to take up where Chekhov's *Cherry Orchard* leaves off. It is a sprawling picture of the inheritors of the cherry orchard who, instead of creating a better world, have settled for the complacency and futility of their predecessors' lives. 'We do nothing except talk an awful lot,' says one character, while another ends a long diatribe on the intelligentsia's alienation from the masses with self-castigation: 'We have created our alienation ourselves . . . we deserve our torments.' *Summer Folk* is one of Gorky's most static plays, theatrically if not always thematically heavily indebted to Chekhov. Its characters are hardly ever more than two-dimensional. But Gorky was not interested: 'Summer Folk is not art,' he wrote in a revealing letter to Andreyev, 'but is a well-aimed shaft and I am glad, like a devil who has tempted the righteous to get shamefully drunk.' The topicality of the play excited the audiences of the day.

This kind of topicality proved to be the main redeeming feature of Gorky's subsequent plays which lacked the human interest of *Lower Depths*. [*Children of the Sun, The Barbarians* and *The Eccentrics*] . . . were all directed against the intellectuals, while *The Enemies* . . . portrayed a clash between factory owners and workers. There were also several plays on provincial merchants which were hardly ever staged. Gorky stopped writing for the theatre in 1917, but returned to it in the thirties to create his finest dramatic work, *Egor Bulychov and Others*. . . . (pp. 87-9)

The three acts of the play, which Gorky called 'scenes', depict the last days in the life of Egor Bulychov, a rich provincial merchant who knows he is dying of cancer and yet has still tremendous inner strength and zest for life. The time is the eve of the 1917 Revolution. Terrified of death, surrounded by scheming relatives who are waiting to divide the inheritance, incapable of believing in God, Bulychov refuses to submit. (p. 89)

The end of Bulychov's world is near in more than one sense. Events from the outside world filter through to him and he responds to them through the prism of his personal problem. He is aware of the corruption of the class that is toppling just as he is aware of the corruption of his family. He feels a stranger in their midst and realises that for thirty years he has been living 'in the wrong street'. The 'right street' seems to belong to the people—the class into which he was born but which he had deserted to make money, and which was not promoting the Revolution. And the people also include the only human beings for whom this warm, full-blooded man cares—his god-son, his illegitimate daughter, and his old servant and mistress.

As Bulychov is dying, he can hear the singing of marching Bolsheviks; it seems to him that they are singing his requiem.

At last Gorky the dramatist achieved what had eluded him all his life: a brilliant psychological drama with sociopolitical undertones and symbolic generalisation, closely knit together by the tragic figure of the protagonist, and illuminated by irony and humour. The political background is motivated and controlled by the psychological portraiture, and the dialogue is at once terse and suggestive. Never before has Gorky so well avoided overstatement and ideological abstraction. Despite the obvious connection of Egor Bulychov with Tolstoy's Ivan Ilyich, the play contains the whole of Gorky—his strong merchant type, his colourful rogues, the 'free' people who follow their instincts, the revolting philistines, the theme of truth and illusion—but this time handled with a sureness of touch and a restraint which reveal a truly great artist. (p. 90)

Gorky the playwright merits more attention than he has been given. As all his work, his plays are uneven. But in the final count, his contribution to drama is probably more noteworthy than his contribution to the Russian novel. (p. 91)

> *Georgette Donchin, "Gorky," in* Russian Literary Attitudes from Pushkin to Solzhenitsyn *by Richard Freeborn, Georgette Donchin, and N. J. Anning; edited by Richard Freeborn (© The Macmillan Press Limited 1976; by permission of Barnes & Noble Books, a Division of Littlefield, Adams & Co., Inc.; in Canada by Macmillan, London and Basingstoke), Barnes & Noble, 1976, Macmillan, 1976, pp. 79-98.*

EDITH OLIVER (essay date 1980)

[Maxim Gorky's **"Barbarians"**] opens in a public garden outside a provincial Russian town. The townsfolk assemble in twos and threes and engage in seemingly desultory conversation (desultory Russian conversation, that is. FIRST MAN: What I have is a mind that is restless. SECOND MAN: What you have is a personality that is unattractive), and the audience, one eye on the program, slowly sorts out the characters, attaching names and professions and relatives to them at exactly the right speed of dwindling confusion. The time is the early nineteen-hundreds, and the people are waiting for a pair of engineers who will bring the railroad to the town. The appearance of the engineers, near the end of the first act, launches the action, and by the time the play is over (and their job is finished) it is evident that nothing will ever be the same for anybody. The engineers are Tsyganov, a worldly, tired man, susceptible to pretty women, and Cherkoon, probably in his thirties, sexy, vindictive, and loutish, shrugging off his adoring

wife whenever he is on the make for another woman. A thick-skinned pair indeed, who at first would seem to be the barbarians of the title but, one soon realizes, are no coarser or more callous than most of the townspeople whose lives they reduce to rubble. The play is described as a comedy, and so it is, despite the cracks of breaking hearts, the sobs and gasps of humiliation, and the obligatory post-Chekhov pistol shot at the end. It's a comedy of obliviousness, stupidity, and insensitivity, in which much of the bad behavior verges on the farcical.

The script is as filled with incident as Gorky's **"Summerfolk."** . . . [Considering **"Barbarians"** I was struck] by the thought that Gorky is far more indulgent toward his audience than he is toward his characters; there are twenty-three of these, and few escape his scorn or contempt. It must be said at once that **"Barbarians"** is not nearly as good a play as **"Summerfolk;"** it is all right, but no better than that. Plot and any number of subplots aside, **"Barbarians"** is a multiple portrait of a town and its people, and most of the pleasure it affords is in performance. (pp. 99-100)

> *Edith Oliver, "The Theatre: 'Barbarians'," in* The New Yorker *(© 1980 by The New Yorker Magazine, Inc.), Vol. LVI, No. 10, April 28, 1980, pp. 99-100.*

ADDITIONAL BIBLIOGRAPHY

Borras, F. M. *Maxim Gorky and Lev Tolstoy.* Leeds, England: Leeds University Press, 1968, 19 p.
> Reprint of lecture delivered on the one hundredth anniversary of Gorky's birth, discussing his life and relationship with Tolstoy.

Bunin, Ivan. "Gorki." In his *Memories and Portraits*, pp. 71-81. Garden City, N.Y.: Doubleday & Co., 1951.
> Reminiscence in which Bunin reconstructs his acquaintance with Gorky.

Byalik, Boris. "Lenin and Gorky: Notes on Their Correspondence." *Soviet Literature*, No. 3: 110-17.*
> Notes on the correspondence between Lenin and Gorky. Byalik presents a number of the letters of Gorky and Lenin in an attempt to define their unique relationship.

Davies, Ruth. "Gorky: The End of the Beginning." In her *The Great Books of Russia*, pp. 364-92. Norman: University of Oklahoma Press, 1968.
> Biocritical discussion. Davies traces Gorky's development as the "first major Russian writer" who wrote specifically for and about the proletariat.

Gourfinkel, Nina. *Gorky.* Westport, Conn.: Greenwood Press, 1975, 192 p.
> A detailed biocritical account of Gorky's life and work. Gourfinkel supplements her study with extracts from his writings.

Hare, Richard. *Maxim Gorky: Romantic Realist and Conservative Revolutionary.* Westport, Conn.: Greenwood Press, 1978, 156 p.
> Biocritical study. Hare presents an illuminating account of Gorky's life and work, including numerous personal reminiscences of some of Gorky's contemporaries and letters Gorky wrote while living in the United States.

Holtzman, Filia. *The Young Maxim Gorky: 1868-1902.* New York: Columbia University Press, 1948, 256 p.
> Biography treating only Gorky's early years. Holtzman approaches Gorky as the symbol of "a new epoch in Russian literature."

Kaun, Alexander. *Maxim Gorky and His Russia.* New York: The Benjamin Blom Publishers, 1931, 620 p.

One of the first surveys of Gorky's life, written while he was still alive. Kaun asserts: "No author has known pre-Soviet Russia so well, and has described it with such poignant truthfulness, as Maxim Gorky."

Kostka, Edmund. "Maksim Gorky: Russian Writer with a Western Bent." *Rivista di letterature moderne e comparate* 23 (March 1970): 5-20.
Discussion of the influence of European thought and literature on Gorky's work.

Lamm, Martin. "Maxim Gorki." In his *Modern Drama*, translated by Karin Elliott, pp. 216-21. Oxford: Basil Blackwell, 1952.
Examination of Gorky's drama, with particular attention given to *The Lower Depths*. Lamm concludes that Gorky "never again fulfilled the expectations" which *The Lower Depths* had aroused.

Levin, Dan. *Stormy Petrel: The Life and Work of Maxim Gorky*. New York: Appleton-Century, 1965, 332 p.
Biocritical study. Levin comments on Gorky's work only in relation to his life.

Muchnic, Helen. "Maxim Gorky." In her *From Gorky to Pasternak: Six Writers in Soviet Russia*, pp. 29-103. New York: Random House, 1961.
General assessment of Gorky's work. Muchnic concludes that Gorky's "zeal for men prevented him from making the most of his unquestionable gift" as an artist.

Nilsson, Nils Åke. "Strindberg, Gorky and Blok." *Scando-Slavica* 4 (1958): 23-42.*
Discussion of the possible influence Strindberg exerted over Gorky's work.

Olgin, Moissaye J. *Maxim Gorky: Writer and Revolutionist*. New York: International Publishers, 1933, 64 p.
Biocritical study. Olgin offers commentary on Gorky's work, but focuses mainly on his revolutionary activities.

Persky, Serge. "Maxim Gorky." In his *Contemporary Russian Novelists*, translated by Frederick Eisemann, pp. 142-98. Boston: John W. Luce and Co., 1913.
General assessment of Gorky's work. Persky calls Gorky "the most original and, after Tolstoy, the most talented of modern Russian writers."

Pertsov, Victor. "The Pioneers: Notes on the Creative Method of Gorky and Mayakovsky." *Soviet Literature*, No. 11 (1968): 136-41.*
Examination of both Gorky's and Mayakovsky's aesthetic principles. Despite the dissimilarities in their respective styles, argues Pertsov, these authors share the same ideological and aesthetic attitudes towards reality.

Roskin, Alexander. *From the Banks of the Volga: The Life of Maxim Gorky*. Translated by D. L. Fromberg. New York: Philosophical Library, 1946, 126 p.
A noncritical account of Gorky's life through the 1917 revolution and the first years of the Soviet regime.

Wolfe, Bertram D. *The Bridge and the Abyss: The Troubled Friendship of Maxim Gorky and V. I. Lenin*. New York: Frederick A. Praeger, 1967, 180 p.*
Biocritical study. Wolfe attempts to shed new light on Gorky's character and work by examining "the peculiar ambivalence of his troubled and frequently stormy friendship with Lenin."

Yarmolinsky, Avrahm. "Maxim Gorky: Soviet Laureate." In his *The Russian Literary Imagination*, pp. 111-29. New York: Funk & Wagnalls, 1969.
Survey of Gorky's major work. Yarmolinsky concludes that Gorky was "an uneven writer, with some serious faults," and that "the best of him belongs to the past."

Zamyatin, Yevgeny. "Maxim Gorky." In his *A Soviet Heretic: Essays by Yevgeny Zamyatin*, edited and translated by Mirra Ginsberg, pp. 246-58. Chicago, London: The University of Chicago Press, 1970.
Personal reminiscences. Zamyatin constructs a portrait of Gorky's life as he knew it.

William Ernest Henley

1849-1903

English poet, editor, critic, essayist, and dramatist.

As editor of the *National Observer* and the *New Review,* Henley was an invigorating force in English literature, publishing and defending the early works of such writers as H. G. Wells, Thomas Hardy, and Bernard Shaw. As a poet he was a pioneer in the use of free verse, though he also wrote many poems that combine realistic social observation and description with traditional forms, such as the sonnet, the rondeau, and the rondel. His most famous poem, "Invictus," from *Poems,* demonstrates Henley's *braggadocio* style and optimistic spirit, two qualities apparent in much of his work. Henley was an important figure in the counter decadent movement of the 1890s and the leader of an imperialistic group of young writers, including Rudyard Kipling, Charles Whibley, and Robert Louis Stevenson, who stressed action, virility, and inner strength over alienation, effeminacy, and despair—characteristics they attributed to the decadents.

Henley was born in Gloucester, England, the son of lower-class parents. As a child he contracted a tubercular disease that affected his bone structure and necessitated the amputation of one foot. When it seemed evident that the other would be lost, Henley traveled to Edinburgh and sought the care of the surgeon Joseph Lister. Lister's painful treatment proved successful, and while recovering Henley began writing the impressionistic work "In Hospital," which established his poetic reputation. It was also during this period that he began his friendship with Stevenson, a close relationship that resulted in the writing and production of four plays before their bitter parting in 1888. (A few years earlier, Stevenson had portrayed Henley's alternately kind and brutal personality in the character of *Treasure Island*'s Long John Silver.) After leaving the infirmary, Henley earned his living mainly as an editor and literary critic, first with the *National Observer* and then with the *New Review* until his resignation in 1897. During this time he wrote his most vigorous and perceptive essays, in particular those on Robert Burns, Henry Fielding, William Hazlitt, and Tobias Smollett. Though he continued to write poetry throughout his life, Henley's later verse was never as accomplished or popular as his hospital poems.

Much of Henley's initial appeal was extraliterary, focusing on his courage and optimism in the face of extreme pain and poverty. *London Types* and the "In Hospital" poems in *A Book of Verses* are generally regarded as Henley's most vigorous poetic works. In his hospital verses, he describes an intense personal experience in language that is both realistic and impressionistic. His presentation of the hospital is graphically descriptive—almost journalistic—while his portrayal of the narrator's sensations are highly subjective. In his other memorable works, notably *London Types* and "London Voluntaries" in *The Song of the Sword and Other Verses* Henley displays a refined talent for portraiture and for visualizing his environment. Indeed, some critics, such as Alfred Noyes, have suggested that Henley was a significant poet not because of his realism or his experimentation in free verse, but rather because of his unique ability to paint settings and construct por-

traits. Since his death, Henley's poetry has been consistently criticized for its lack of imagery, for its nationalistic zeal, and for its didacticism. Often his stark observations do not fit the forms of his verse, and his early "bric-a-brac" poetry—rondeaus, villanelles, and ballads—holds little interest for the modern reader, despite its ornate charm.

Henley failed as a dramatist, and his collaboration with Stevenson produced four plays which are more interesting for what they attempt than for what they accomplish. Henley and Stevenson wanted to return melodrama to the English stage, and each of the plays, especially *Admiral Guinea* and *Macaire,* abound in adventure and sensationalism. Perhaps the most successful is *Macaire,* if only because the dialogue is witty, the characters somewhat well drawn, and the action aptly sustained.

Despite the quality of much of his creative work, Henley had little influence as a poet and almost none as a dramatist. It was as a critic and editor that Henley exercised the greatest influence on his age. His critical judgements were in large part founded on his own common sense and a high moral standard. *Views and Reviews* contains some of the most stimulating literary assessments in the whole of Victorian journalism. Many of Henley's essays are as fresh and informative today as they were at the time of their first publication. As an editor he helped raise the standards of nineteenth-century journalism and he established some of the most important writers of the twentieth century.

Henley's work characterizes an important period in English literature. At a time when aestheticism was at its peak, he was the most vocal and influential of the antidecadents. "Henley's verse echoed an important cultural force," according to Joseph M. Flora, "it touches part of the Victorian soul." For his verse and his prose, but particularly for his strident personality which ruled them both, Henley is remembered, in one critic's words, as the "Viking Chief of letters."

PRINCIPAL WORKS

Deacon Brodie: The Double Life [with Robert Louis Stevenson] (drama) 1882
A Book of Verses (poetry) 1888
Beau Austin [with Robert Louis Stevenson] (drama) 1890
Views and Reviews: Essays in Appreciation, Vol. 1 (criticism) 1890
The Song of the Sword, and Other Verses (poetry) 1892
Admiral Guinea [with Robert Louis Stevenson] (drama) 1897
London Types (poetry) 1898
Poems (poetry) 1898
Hawthorn and Lavender (poetry) 1899
For England's Sake (poetry) 1900
Macaire [with Robert Louis Stevenson] (drama) 1900
Views and Reviews: Essays in Appreciation, Vol. 2 (criticism) 1902
A Song of Speed (poetry) 1903
The Works of W. E. Henley. 7 vols. (poetry, essays, dramas, and criticism) 1908

OSCAR WILDE (essay date 1888)

"If I were king," says Mr. Henley in one of his most modest rondeaus,

> Art should aspire, yet ugliness be dear;
> Beauty, the shaft, should speed with wit for feather;
> And love, sweet love, should never fall to sere,
>   If I were king.

And these lines contain, if not the best criticism of his own work, certainly a very complete statement of his aim and motive as a poet. His little **"Book of Verse"** . . . reveals to us an artist who is seeking to find new methods of expression, and who has not merely a delicate sense of beauty and a brilliant fantastic wit, but a real passion also for what is horrible, ugly, or grotesque. No doubt everything that is worthy of existence is worthy also of art—at least, one would like to think so— but while echo or mirror can repeat for us a beautiful thing, to artistically render a thing that is ugly requires the most exquisite alchemy of form, the most subtle magic of transformation. To me there is more of the cry of Marsyas than of the singing of Apollo in the earlier poems of Mr. Henley's volume, the **"Rhymes and Rhythms in Hospital,"** as he calls them. But it is impossible to deny their power. Some of them are like bright, vivid pastels; others like charcoal drawings, with dull blacks and murky whites; others like etchings with deeply-bitten lines, and abrupt contrasts, and clever colour-sugges-

tions. In fact, they are like anything and everything, except perfected poems—that they certainly are not. They are still in the twilight. They are preludes, experiments, inspired jottings in a note-book, and should be heralded by a design of "Genius making Sketches." Rhyme gives architecture as well as melody to verse; it gives that delightful sense of limitation which in all the arts is so pleasurable, and is, indeed, one of the secrets of perfection; it will whisper, as a French critic has said, "things unexpected and charming, things with strange and remote relations to each other," and bind them together in indissoluble bonds of beauty; and in his constant rejection of rhyme Mr. Henley seems to me to have abdicated half his power. He is a *roi en exil* who has thrown away some of the strings of his lute, a poet who has forgotten the fairest part of his kingdom. (pp. 90-1)

Théophile Gautier once said that Flaubert's style was meant to be read, and his own style to be looked at. Mr. Henley's unrhymed rhythms form very dainty designs, from a typographical point of view. From the point of view of literature, they are a series of vivid concentrated impressions with a keen grip of fact, a terrible actuality, and an almost masterly power of picturesque presentation. But the poetic form—what of that? (pp. 92-3)

[The] most attractive thing in [**"Book of Verse"**] is no single poem that is in it, but the strong humane personality that stands behind both flawless and faulty work alike, and looks out through many masks, some of them beautiful, and some grotesque, and not a few mis-shapen. In the case of most of our modern poets, when we have analyzed them down to an adjective we can go no further, or we care to go no further, but with this book it is different. Through these reeds and pipes blows the very breath of life. It seems as if one could put one's hand upon the singer's heart and count its pulsations. There is something wholesome, virile, and sane about the man's soul. Anybody can be reasonable, but to be sane is not common; and sane poets are as rare as blue lilies, though they may not be quite so delightful.

> Let the great winds their worst and wildest blow,
> Or the gold weather round us mellow slow;
> We have fulfilled ourselves, and we can dare,
> And we can conquer, though we may not share
> In the rich quiet of the afterglow,
>   What is to come,

is the concluding stanza of the last rondeau—indeed, of the last poem in the collection, and the high serene temper displayed in these lines serves at once as keynote and keystone to the book. The very lightness and slightness of so much of the work, its careless moods and casual fancies, seems to suggest a nature that is not primarily interested in art—a nature, like Sordello's, passionately enamoured of life, and to which lyre and lute are things of less importance. From this mere joy of living, this frank delight in experience for its own sake, this lofty indifference, and momentary unregretted ardours, come all the faults and all the beauties of the volume. But there is this difference between them—the faults are deliberate and the result of much study, the beauties have the air of fascinating impromptus. Mr. Henley's healthy, if sometimes misapplied, confidence in the myriad suggestions of life gives them his charm. He is made to sing along the highways, not to sit down and write. If he took himself more seriously his work would become trivial. (pp. 95-6)

Oscar Wilde, "A Note on Some Modern Poets," in Woman's World, *Vol. II, No. 14, December, 1888 (and reprinted as ''Poems by Henley and Sharp,'' in his* The Artist As Critic: Critical Writings of Oscar Wilde, *edited by Richard Ellmann, W. H. Allen, 1970, pp. 90-100).**

ARTHUR SYMONS (essay date 1892)

In 1887 a volume of *Ballades and Rondeaus* appeared in the Canterbury Series under the editorship of Mr. Gleeson White. It was a collection of all the tolerable work in French forms that could be found in English and American literature, and its consequence (for our salvation) was such an indigestion of ingenuity that scarce a ballade, scarce a rondeau, has seen the light since its publication. As a curiosity the book had its interest; containing, as it did, some of the splendid work of Mr. Swinburne, the exquisite work of Mr. Dobson, it could not but have its value; but, after all, the main interest and value of the book lay in some five-and-thirty pieces signed W. E. Henley. . . . Written in the artificial forms of the ballade, the rondeau, the villanelle, they stood out from a mass of work, mainly artificial in substance as in form, by the freshness of their inspiration, the joyous individuality of their note. One felt that here was a new voice, and a voice with capacities for a better kind of singing. It was in answer to a demand which would take no denying—and how rarely does the British public ever make such demand!—that *A Book of Verses* appeared in the following year. It was a complete success—welcomed by the critics, talked about in the drawing-rooms, even bought for ready-money. In 1890 a volume of *Views and Reviews* was received with much curiosity, as a challenge that at all events had to be considered. Last year the play of *Beau Austin* (the work of Mr. Henley and Mr. Stevenson) was the literary sensation of the dramatic year, and, though not exactly a success on the boards, must be admitted to have presented to us the finest piece of comedy in action since *The School for Scandal.* And now *The Song of the Sword* comes, another challenge, and . . . in some sort a manifesto.

There is something revolutionary about all Mr. Henley's work; but it is in his poetry that the stirrings of a new element have worked to most effectual issues. This new volume of poems, by its very existence, is a vigorous challenge, a notable manifesto, on behalf of a somewhat new art—the art of modernity in poetry. Based on the same principles as *A Book of Verses,* it develops those principles yet further, and, in the "**London Voluntaries**" particularly, and in such poems as the second, twenty-second, and twenty-fourth of the "**Rhymes and Rhythms**," succeeds to a remarkable degree in working out a really modern art of verse. (pp. 182-83)

The style of the "**Hospital Sonnets**" is founded on the style of [Mr. George Meredith's] *Modern Love;* both from the rhymed and unrhymed poems in irregular metres, it is evident that Mr. Henley has learnt something from the odes of [Mr. Coventry Patmore's] *Unknown Eros;* there are touches of Walt Whitman, some of the notes of Heine; there is, too, something of the exquisitely disarticulated style of Verlaine. But with all this assimilation of influences that are in the air, Mr. Henley has developed for himself a style that becomes in the highest degree personal, and one realises behind it a most vigorous, distinct, and interesting personality. Alike as a human document, and as an artistic experiment, the "rhymes and rhythms" named "**In Hospital**" have a peculiar value. Dated from the Old Edinburgh Infirmary, 1873-75, they tell the story of life in hospital, from the first glimpse of the "tragic meanness" of stairs and corridors, through the horrors of the operation, by way of

visitors, doctors, and patients, to the dizzy rapture of the discharge, the freedom of wind, sunshine, and the beautiful world. . . . Here is a poetry made out of personal sensations, poetry which is half physiological, poetry which is pathology—and yet essentially poetry. . . . Mr. Henley has set himself to the task of rendering the more difficult poetry of the disagreeable. And in these wonderful poems—the sonnets and the "rhythms," as he calls his unrhymed verse—he has etched a series of impressions which are like nothing else that I know in poetry. What a triumph of remembered and recorded sensation is . . . , for instance, "**The Operation.**" . . . (pp. 185-86)

"**In Hospital**" gives us one side of Mr. Henley's talent, and it throws a vivid light on the conditions under which so much brave work has been done. For Mr. Henley, of all the poets of the day, is the most strenuously certain that life is worth living, the most eagerly defiant of fate, the most heroically content with death. There is, indeed, something of the spirit of Walt Whitman in his passion for living, his acceptance of the hour when man,

> Tired of experience, turns
> To the friendly and comforting breast
> Of the old nurse, Death.

His special "note," in the earlier work particularly, is a manly Bohemianism, a refreshingly reckless joy in the happy accidents of existence. Always insistently modern, with such fine use of "hansoms," of "fifth-floor windows," of bathers that "bob," of "washermaids" in the midst of "a shower of suds," he has set some of the most human of emotions to a music that is itself curiously modern. . . . (p. 187)

The most terrible poem in the new volume—a poem which may be compared and contrasted at once with Mr. Rudyard Kipling's "Tomlinson"—tells the tale of "deeds undone that hunger for their due," the rejection of death and the grave, and the frightful triumph of the worm:

> And writhing, fain
> And like a lover, he his fill shall take,
> Where no triumphant memory lives to make
> His obscene victory vain.

"**The Song of the Sword**," the splendidly eloquent "voice of the sword from the heart of the sword," is a hymn to the ecstasy of conflict, the quickening forces that advance the world. . . .

He is ashamed of none of the natural human instincts, and writes of women like a man, without effeminacy and without offence, content to be at one with the beneficent seasons, the will of nature. And has he not written, once and for all, the song of the soul of man in the shadow of the unknown? Such a song [as "**Invictus**"] is the equivalent of a great deed. (p. 189)

I find myself returning to the "**London Voluntaries**" as perhaps the most individual, the most characteristically modern, and the most entirely successful of Mr. Henley's work in verse. Here the subject is the finest of modern subjects, the pageant of London. Intensely personal in the feeling that transfuses the picture, it is with a brush of passionate impressionism that he paints for us the London of midsummer nights, London at "the golden end" of October afternoons, London cowering in winter under the Wind-Fiend "out of the poisonous east," London in all the ecstasy of spring. The style is freer, the choice of words, the direction of rhythms, more sure, the language more select and effectual in eloquence, than elsewhere. There is no eccentricity in rhythm, no experimentalising, nothing tentative. There is something classical—a note of *Lycidas*—in these most modern of poems, almost as if modernity had become classical. The outcome of many experiments, they have passed beyond that stage into the stage of existence.

Revolutionary always, Mr. Henley has had a wholesome but perilous discontent with the conventions of language and of verse. He is an artist who is also a critic, and the book of *Views and Reviews,* striking on its own account, has its value also in illustration of his artistic principles, preferences, and innovations. That book—"less a book," the author tells us, "than a mosaic of scraps and shreds recovered from the shot rubbish of some fourteen years of journalism"—shows us an active and varied intelligence, precipitately concerned with things in general, very emphatic in likes and dislikes, never quite dispassionately, always acutely, honestly, eagerly. His characteristics of feeling and expression, and not any reasoned or prejudiced partiality, make him the champion or the foe of every writer with whom he concerns himself. Brilliant, original, pictorial, his style tires by its pungency, dazzles by its glitter. Every word must be emphatic, every stroke must score heavily, every sentence must be an epigram or a picture or a challenge. With a preference, he tells us, for the "unobtrusive graces," for "tranquil writing," for "eloquence without adjectives," he is consistent in his negation of all these ideals of the urbane style. And, with this, immense cleverness, an acuteness that pierces and delights to pierce, an invention of phrases that is often of the essence of criticism, an extensive knowledge, extensive sympathies. His vocabulary is unusually large, and it is used, too recklessly indeed, but in a surprisingly novel, personal way. Turning to the poems, we find that the artist in verse is far more careful than the craftsman in prose, and that here he has curbed himself to a restraint in the debauch of coloured and sounding words, still sufficiently coloured and sounding for an equally novel and personal effect. What Mr. Henley has brought into the language of poetry is a certain freshness, a daring straightforwardness and pungency of epithet, very refreshing in contrast with the traditional limpness and timidity of the respectable verse of the day. One feels indeed at times that the touch is a little rough, the voice a trifle loud, the new word just a little unnecessary. But with these unaccustomed words and tones Mr. Henley does certainly succeed in flashing the picture, the impression upon us, in realising the intangible, in saying new things in a new and fascinating manner. (pp. 190-91)

["**London Voluntaries,**"] surely, is Mr. Henley's perfectly satisfactory work, his entirely characteristic rendering of modern subject-matter in appropriate form. A new subject, an individual treatment, a form which retains all that is helpful in tradition, while admitting all that is valuable in experiment: that, I think, is modernity becoming classical. (p. 192)

> Arthur Symons, "*Mr. Henley's Poetry*," *in* The Fortnightly Review *(reprinted by permission of Contemporary Review Company Limited), n.s. Vol. LII, August 1, 1892, pp. 182-92.*

BERNARD SHAW   (essay date 1895)

I see that Mr William Henley has just published in the *New Review* the version of [*Macaire*] which he made in collaboration with the late R. L. Stevenson. I read the work myself for the first time before the revival of the old version at the Lyceum Theatre; and it has always struck me as a part illustration of

the divorce of the stage from literature that we should have had, on the one hand, a famous writer of fiction collaborating with a born master of verse to rescue a famous old harlequinade from obsolescence, and, on the other, a revival of this harlequinade by our leading actor managing our leading theatre; yet that there was no thought of combining the two opportunities, the revival at the theatre proceeding contentedly with the old cheap and common dialogue, written originally with the idea that the play was a serious blood-and-thunder melodrama, whilst the new version circulated quietly in private as a booklet, and finally appears as a magazine contribution. It is a pity that Mr Henley could not very well print the old version in his *Review* side by side with the new, in order to shew, not only that the old is quite unreadable, and the new so wittily and whimsically turned that every phrase tickles, but that even the stage technique of the new is hugely superior to that of the old. Instead of two elaborate scenes, causing a long interval which a harlequinade will not bear, and entailing extra labor and expense, there is one scene all through, enabling the curtain to be dropped for a moment to point the situations and express conventionally the change from morning to bedtime, and from bedtime to murder-time, without perceptibly breaking the continuity of the extravaganza. The incongruous relics of the original folly of the author are swept away, and the whole brought into the vein of the fantastic variation by which Lemaître rescued the theme from obscurity. The effective situations are preserved and improved; Macaire retains all his old business except the creaking snuff-box, in exchange for which he acquires an epigrammatic philosophy expressed in lines which a distinguished actor need not be ashamed to speak; the ridiculous long-lost wife disappears; the gendarme and the innkeeper become amusing; the murder has the true touch of nightmare: in short, the two "literary men" have beaten the bungling stage "author" at his own craft in every point; outwritten him, outwitted him, outstaged him, and erased him from all future possibility in the eyes of every person of ordinary culture and intelligence who makes the comparison. And yet I have a grim conviction that actors will feel a mysterious "suitability to the stage" in the old version which is missing in the new. . . . The conception of theatrical art as the exploitation of popular superstition and ignorance, as the thrilling of poor bumpkins with ghosts and blood, exciting them with blows and stabs, duping them with tawdry affectations of rank and rhetoric, thriving parasitically on their moral diseases instead of purging their souls and refining their senses: this is the tradition that the theatre finds it so hard to get away from. (pp. 140-42)

[*Macaire,*] looked at in this light, immediately betrays innumerable deficiencies. The authors have brought a policeman on the stage without any sense of the audience's fear of a policeman and dreadful joy in seeing someone else arrested; they have introduced a nobleman without allowing his rank to strike at our servility or his gold at our envy; they have, with the insensibility of men who have never been hungry, brought wine and choice dishes on the stage without knowing their value when flourished properly in the faces of needy men; they have passed unconsciously over the "love" interest, forgetting that half the popular use of the boards is as a pedestal on which to set a well-painted, well-dressed woman in a strong light, to please the man who is tired of the mother of sorrows and drudgery at home; and they have put murder on the stage without calculating on the fact that murder is only a forbidden joy to people who know no other reasons than the gallows and the sixth commandment for not killing those whom they hate or whose property they covet. When the manager says of a play, "It is not suited to the stage," and the critic who has been long enough at his profession to pick up the managerial point of view follows with his *"Ce n'est pas du théâtre"*: that is fundamentally what they both mean, though superficially the matter may have a very different air. And it is because Stevenson and Mr Henley substituted for the low cunning and the cynical experience which makes effective melodramas out of such calculations, the higher qualities of wit, imagination, romance, and humor, applied with a literary workmanship which is at once curiously skilful and carelessly happy, that even the Lyceum Theatre dared not rise to their level.

Now that the collaboration of the authors of *Macaire* is broken up by the death of Stevenson, . . . one wonders whether Mr Henley will carry on the business alone. The charm of the pair was their combination of artistic faculty with a pleasant boyishness of imagination. Stevenson, always the older of the twain, shewed signs of growing up, and could even, when kept to the point by the collaboration of his stepson, produce stories that were not obviously the penny numbers of our boyhood rewritten by a fine hand. But Mr Henley defies the ravages of time. That amusing mixture of pedantry and hero-worship which marks the schoolboy's cult of athletics survives unabated and unenlightened in Mr Henley's cult of literature. He delights in puerile novels about prize-fighters like [my own] *Cashel Byron's Profession;* he has imagination without sense; he not only adores his literary and artistic heroes, but is violently jealous for their sakes of the reputations of all the others; his attitudes are reverently traditional; experience means to him the works of fiction he has read; at every turn of his pen he shews that cardinal quality of youth, its incapacity for apprehending life at first hand as distinguished from appreciating its presentations and formulations in art and social or scientific theory. And yet he has the romantic imagination and the fine gift of poetic speech which only need some concrete subject-matter—for really plays cannot, like poems or even articles, be made out of purely abstract indignation, scorn, defiance, and so on—to provide *Macaire, Admiral Guinea,* and the rest with more than worthy successors. (pp. 142-44)

Bernard Shaw, "Two Plays: 'Macaire'" (originally published in The Saturday Review, *London, Vol. 79, No. 2067, June 8, 1895), in his* Our Theatres in the Nineties, *Vol. I (reprinted by permission of The Society of Authors on behalf of the Bernard Shaw Estate), Constable and Company Limited, 1932, pp. 140-48.**

MAX BEERBOHM (essay date 1901)

What, precisely, was Mr. Henley's share in the plays done jointly by Robert Louis Stevenson and himself? (p. 146)

To evaluate, from a work produced by A and B, the share of B, your best way is to proceed by elimination. Analyse the work into its component parts—its matter, method, style, and so forth. Then set aside all that in it might be due to A, as A is known to you through the work done by him single-handed. The residue, presumably, must have been done by B. This presumption becomes a certainty if, referring to any work done by B singlehanded, you find that any of it coincides with that part of the joint work which does not seem to have been done by A. You may now, of course, find in the joint work things that could have been done either by A or by B. Some of the things that were A-like may, in the light of B's other work, seem to be equally B-like. For them you must give half-credit to both men. You may, on the other hand, find things that you

can attribute neither to A nor to B. For these, also, you will divide the credit. They are the result of fusion.

Apply this method to the two plays . . . **"Macaire"** and **"Beau Austin."** Take **"Macaire"** first. "A Melodramatic Farce" it is called, though it is rather a farce suddenly transformed, at last, into a melodrama. Stevenson, single-handed, was prolific of both these forms in his books. As examples of his farce we have the immortal "New Arabian Nights"; of his melodrama, "The Pavilion on the Links," "Dr. Jekyll and Mr. Hyde" and the greater part of every romance that he wrote. Therefore there is no reason why he should not have alone conceived the plot of **"Macaire."** There is (I forestall, unscientifically, the proper working of the process) very good reason to suppose that Mr. Henley did not conceive the plots of the plays written with Stevenson, inasmuch as he has never by himself shown any tendency to story-telling. As critic, as lyric and descriptive poet, he has been active. In fiction he has done nothing. Even if he had, the plot of **"Macaire"** (as also the plots of **"Deacon Brodie"** and **"Admiral Guinea"**) would obviously be Stevenson's. No one that has read "A Penny Plain and *2d.* Coloured"—and who with any love for the art of writing has not read that perfect essay many times?—could for one moment doubt the source of these plots. Out of Stevenson, by Skelt: that is their one possible pedigree. (p. 147)

[Now,] let us sum up the residue from what Stevenson might have done in it. Lo! There is no residue at all. Stevenson might have done the whole thing out of his own head. Appearances lead one to believe that he conceived the plot, drew the two important characters, wrote the dialogue. There is, on the other hand, nothing to stamp him surely as drawer of the subsidiary characters or as technical constructor. Thus the present inference from the evidence is that Mr. Henley may have constructed the play and drawn all the characters but Macaire and Bertrand. To test this inference, turn to Mr. Henley's record. He, as I have said, is a critic and a lyric and descriptive poet. Those qualities through which, in the arts of criticism and poetry, he has won his high reputation do not, certainly, obtrude themselves from **"Macaire."** Much in the play is characteristic of Stevenson, of Mr. Henley nothing. That Mr. Henley may have drawn the subordinate characters is, nevertheless, possible. As I said, any one could have drawn them. Also, being, like Stevenson, an amateur in dramaturgy, he may have been responsible for the construction. Such is the conclusion one draws as to Mr. Henley's share in the play. It is a conclusion not satisfactory to our general admiration of Mr. Henley. However, it is but an interim-conclusion. Mr. Henley, as I shall show, must have done more than what we can give him credit for at first sight.

With **"Beau Austin"** the case is much the same as with **"Macaire."** True, this play is a comedy, and comedy was not a form in which Stevenson dealt. At the same time, he, as being a creator in fiction, seems likelier than Mr. Henley to have conceived the plot of it. Moreover, the character of the Beau himself, round which everything revolves, is as thoroughly Stevensonian as the character of Macaire. It is, indeed, the character of Prince Florizel of Bohemia, realised on a comedic plane. Florizel as foreign potentate in modern London was farcical, but Florizel as dandy on the Pantiles becomes perfectly possible and comedic. That magnificence, that "stately and agreeable demeanour," that infinite span of condescension, become matter for smiles, for tears even, though before they could evoke only one's roars of ecstatic joy. Yes! surely, the Beau is Stevenson's. The paternity of Dorothy Musgrave is dubious. She is a shadow, and Stevenson, as we know, never could draw a woman. But then, the chances are that Mr. Henley, likewise, never could draw a woman. So let the credit for Dorothy Musgrave be divided between the two. Also the credit for the Aunt, the valet, and the other characters, who, though there is no reason to attribute them to Mr. Henley, do not remind one of any characters in Stevenson's books. The construction of the play—not inconsistent like the construction of **"Macaire"** but timid and frail—may be due to either of the authors. But the writing—again the writing seems authentically, exclusively, Stevenson's. "I am the rejected suitor of this young gentleman's sister, of Miss Musgrave. . . . See in how laughable a manner fate repaid me! The waiting-maid derided: the mistress denied, and now comes this very ardent champion who insults me." The voice is the voice of Florizel, in all its clear and mellifluous cadences, and there are none of those bristles that might betray to us the prose of Mr. Henley. Mr. Henley's prose-style is admirable, but it is essentially a bristling style. It sprouts, it pricks. It sprouts in uniformly brief sentences, pricks with uniformly sharp "points." It never waves and caresses, as did Stevenson's. The dialogue in **"Beau Austin"** waves and caresses in the truly Stevensonian mode. I am convinced that Mr. Henley did not write it. So far, then, the inference we have come to is that in **"Beau Austin"** Mr. Henley may have drawn Dorothy and the other minor characters, may have done the construction, and may, improbably, have conceived the main idea of the story, and that Stevenson did the rest. Again the conclusion leaves something to be desired by us admirers of Mr. Henley. Let me try to supply that something.

There must be some fallacy in the evidence from which we deduce that Mr. Henley played so small a part in the collaboration. If he had not played a part greater than it appears, the collaboration would have been a farcical affair, and Mr. Henley never would have allowed his name to be tacked on to plays with which he had had practically nothing to do. Can we reconcile the difference between what seems and what must have been? "Dexterously, good madonna." Mr. Henley, brought into contact with Stevenson was so affected by the fascinating personality of his companion that he lost his own identity, and became Stevenson, thought like Stevenson, felt like Stevenson, imagined like Stevenson, wrote—no, I cannot believe that any of the script was his. Stevenson wrote the plays, and Mr. Henley, to balance the collaboration, invented them. In the other collaborated works of Stevenson we do not wonder at our difficulty in determining what he did not do. Reading "The Dynamiter," we remember that the cleverness of all wives is soon assimilated to the cleverness of their husbands. Reading "The Wreckers," we easily extend this rule to clever stepsons. But that a material so definite, so tough, so trenchant as the mind of Mr. Henley should ever have been transformed by any one, is certainly, as the journalists say, "matter for no small surprise." It implies an elasticity of which we never should have suspected Mr. Henley, and for which we admire him all the more. And it is unique testimony to the glamour of "R.L.S." (pp. 149-51)

> *Max Beerbohm, "A Puzzle in Literary Drama" (originally published in* The Saturday Review, *London, Vol. 91, No. 2376, May 11, 1901), in his* Around Theatres *(reprinted by permission of Mrs. Eva Reichmann), revised edition, Rupert Hart-Davis, 1953, pp. 146-51.*

G. K. CHESTERTON (essay date 1908)

[The] modern literary method, that of exaggerating one's own peculiarities as if one were playing in a farce, gave the world a number of arresting and exciting personalities. Its great defect however was this: that it tended to give many men quite false personalities. I mean that even great men sometimes took so totally wrong a view of themselves that much of their work was wasted. They preferred their own masks to their own faces. They painted themselves so fiercely for the footlights that they concealed their own original good looks. It is only these men who had real reputations to spoil and spoilt them who are of any interest in literary history. (pp. 158-59)

One of these curious cases is that of W. E. Henley. He was a man who really suffered from the histrionic habit. He was a man of large heart who deliberately narrowed his heart. He was a man of large brain who deliberately narrowed his brain. He was a man thoroughly by nature a poet who forced himself, against all his own emotional trend, to be a boisterous and topical balladmonger. The critics of the future will have to take a great deal of trouble to extricate the real Henley from under the heavy accretions of the fictitious or dramatic Henley. But they will take the trouble; for they will be digging up gold.

No critic will ever be accused of misrepresenting Henley; the only man who misrepresented Henley was Henley himself. If we read those poems in which Henley was striking a deep note, as distinct from those in which he was thumping a tin kettle, we shall not find it at all difficult without having ever known him, to say what kind of man he was. He was a sad, sensitive and tender-hearted pessimist, who endured pain that came from nowhere, and enjoyed pleasure that came from nowhere, with the exquisite appreciation of some timid child in Maeterlinck's plays. He was not so much a Stoic as a tragic Epicurean. But he had this truly sublime quality in the highest type of Epicurean; that he enjoyed a pleasure so much that it reconciled him even to pain. He certainly believed (in his soul) that the rule of the universe was bad. But his glory was that he was ready to accept the rule for the sake of the exceptions. He enjoyed a red rose so poignantly and perfectly that he was ready to go through thorns for it, even though it was only an accident of the tree and not its crown. His poetry rose to its noblest height when he spoke of the strange joy of having snatched some good from an evil world. This led him to dwell much upon the past; and to him memory was a kind of intoxication. Neither he nor anyone else ever wrote anything much better or more real in its own way than those lines about things already secured. (pp. 159-60)

[As] I have said it is not very difficult to understand him. He was what every poet must be who shares the unbelief of his age; a man melancholy though not without happiness; a man reconciled to a second best. (p. 160)

Unfortunately in his life-time, and especially in his later years, Henley hid himself behind the mask of what he thought he ought to stand for. Somebody told him, or he somehow got into his head that he was the representative of rude energy and militant empire. His talents were entirely in the other direction. So far from specializing in strength he describes in his most penetrating poems a condition of beautiful weakness. So far from being by nature a prophet of the British Empire he had not the temperament to be a prophet of his own town or street. He did not believe in them enough; he did not believe much in anything. There were some things (it is true) which he definitely disbelieved in; he certainly had a sincere hatred for democracy and for Christian morals. But positive belief involves a certain simple fixity of the intellect which was not at all a part of his personality. He did not really believe even in the stone of the street or the stars in the sky. But he had this strange quality of a great imagination about him; that he could enjoy things even without believing in them.

This quite false conception of himself as a Raw Head and Bloody Bones produced a crop of poems which are not in Henley's good manner or even in his bad manner; they are not in Henley's manner at all. It would be untrue to say that Henley was ever a hypocrite; but some of his poems are hypocritical. **"The Song of the Sword"** is, I am afraid, hypocritical. It is all about the Lord and the Sword; two things that Henley knew nothing whatever about. Of the sword he had no grasp or experience, and in the Lord he didn't believe. The heavy Old Testament manner of the whole thing was utterly alien to his true nature which was sensitive and modern, exquisitely attuned to pleasure and to pain. He was not a solemn youth like David; he was an Epicurean invalid. A man more unmilitary cannot be conceived; if he had ever held a sword in his hand, he would have been filled either with pain at having to inflict wounds or with pleasure in inflicting them. Both these emotions are feminine and unsoldierly. And the most painful evidence of all of his unfitness for such topics can be found in this; that when he was attempting to be specially masculine he always came near to that most unmasculine of all ideas—cruelty.

But it is not with the false Henley, but the true Henley that the world will deal. He caused his own exquisite voice to be drowned in the clamour of his own quite fictitious reputation as a sort of a political ruffian. He drowned his own voice with his own drum. But anyone who cares today to take up one of his books of poems will suddenly find himself in an atmosphere utterly unexpected and very calm. He will break into a sudden stillness. He will read a few quiet poems about grey streets and silver sunsets. He will find that the poet has a peculiar power of describing the voiceless and neglected corners of a great city; the little grass-grown squares, the little streets that lead nowhere. The poet feels the lost parts of London as more lost than the lost parts of the wilderness; and he loves them more. He has an almost eerie power of realizing certain aimless emotions of an empty afternoon. All will seem full of a kind of quiet irrelevance; and yet the very foundations of the reader's heart will be moved. The sadness will only seem an expression of the sacred value of things; and as he walks home at evening after reading such a book, every paving-stone and lamp-post will be pathetic because it is precious. Nay, the world will seem brittle because it is precious; as if it might be broken, by accident. (pp. 160-62)

> *G. K. Chesterton, "W. E. Henley: Poet" (originally published in* The Bibliophile, *Vol. I, No. 1, March, 1908), in his* A Handful of Authors: Essay on Books and Writers, *edited by Dorothy Collins (reprinted by permission of Miss D. E. Collins), Sheed and Ward, Inc., 1953, pp. 157-62.*

W. B. YEATS   (essay date 1921)

Some quarter of an hour's walk from Bedford Park, out on the high road to Richmond, lived W. E. Henley, and I, like many others, began under him my education. . . . I disagreed with him about everything, but I admired him beyond words. With the exception of some early poems founded upon old French models I disliked his poetry, mainly because he wrote in *vers libre*, which I associated with . . . Bastien-Lepage's clownish peasant staring with vacant eyes at her great boots; and filled it with unimpassioned description of a hospital ward where his leg had been amputated. . . . Furthermore, Pre-Raphaelitism affected him as some people are affected by a cat in the room,

and though he professed himself at our first meeting without political interests or convictions, he soon grew into a violent Unionist and Imperialist. I used to say when I spoke of his poems, 'He is like a great actor with a bad part; yet who would look at Hamlet in the grave scene if Salvini played the grave-digger?' and I might so have explained much that he said and did. I meant that he was like a great actor of passion . . . and an actor of passion will display some one quality of soul, personified again and again, just as a great poetical painter, Titian, Botticelli, Rossetti, may depend for his greatness upon a type of beauty which presently we call by his name. . . . Half his opinions were the contrivance of a sub-consciousness that sought always to bring life to the dramatic crisis and expression to that point of artifice where the true self could find its tongue. Without opponents there had been no drama, and in his youth Ruskinism and Pre-Raphaelitism, for he was of my father's generation, were the only possible opponents. How could one resent his prejudice when, that he himself might play a worthy part, he must find beyond the common rout, whom he derided and flouted daily, opponents he could imagine moulded like himself? . . . He dreamed of a tyranny, but it was that of Cosimo de' Medici. (pp. 124-26)

> *W. B. Yeats, "The Trembling of the Veil: Four Years, 1887-1891" (originally published in* The London Mercury, *Vol. IV, No. 20, June, 1921), in his Autobiographies (reprinted with permission of Macmillan Publishing Co., Inc.; in Canada by M. B. Yeats, Anne Yeats; copyright 1916, 1935 by Macmillan Publishing Co., Inc., renewed 1944, 1963 by Bertha Georgie Yeats), Macmillan & Co Ltd, 1955, pp. 111-96.**

JOHN DRINKWATER   (essay date 1922)

Speaking of Byron, Henley says that he 'was not interested in words and phrases, but in the greater truths of destiny and emotion. His empire is over the imagination and the passions.' As a critical judgment this is far less shrewd than was common with Henley, but it is suggestive in relation to his own work as a poet. Henley was a remarkable figure in the literary world of his day, moving in no scholarly seclusion, but coming out into the open field of journalism, and bearing himself always with spirit and dignity. The best of his work is a durable contribution to the finest kind of popular criticism, vivid, far from unlearned, in close touch with the ordinary and confused affairs of life. On any given subject he might have to yield at points to the specialist, but few men have covered so wide a range with so warm an understanding and with a mind so well versed in the evidence of the case. It is as a critic that he will be remembered, and it is of his critical work that there is most to be said. But he produced a good deal of creative work, and, in common with most writers who work in both kinds, he no doubt hoped that it was in this that he came to his best achievement. So that, although on the whole it seems likely that this side of his expression will be the first to fade, it cannot be passed by without consideration.

'He was not interested in words and phrases, but in the greater truths of destiny and emotion.' This, in the last analysis, is true of Henley as a poet. He would have accepted the judgment with pride; and that he would have done so is indicative of his real weakness. When he adds that Byron's empire was over the imagination and the passions, he says more than justly can be put in for himself. Henley's poetic world was not that of passion and imagination, but that of clear-sighted morality, which was sometimes transfigured by indignation. It was in this world that he moved as a master in a great deal of his critical work. But it was a world that was, as it always must be, incomplete as an environment for rich poetic creation. In passing, it may be remarked that it merely is not true to say of Byron that in his great poetic moods, of which for all his failures he had as many as most poets, he was not interested in words and phrases. Byron knew, as in practice Henley did not, that, while it is passion and imagination that must condition the poetic faculty, the only possible consummation of that faculty comes through the most exact and disciplined ordering of words and phrases.

Henley brought to his poetry many beautiful qualities. He had real courage, he had a great-hearted tenderness, he hated Pecksniffs and impure Puritans; he was, in short, a very chivalrous man, with rare intellectual gifts. But he did not perceive that merely to be these things, while it might do anything else for you, could not make you into a poet. Every now and again this fine moral impetus in his being would move with such force as to achieve something which remains memorable and beyond the reach of any but poets of the most indisputable magic. Such pieces as **'Matri Delectissimae'** and **'On the Way to Kew,'** and the well-known **'Out of the night that covers me,'** and **'Or ever the knightly years were gone,'** are good things for any man to have written. . . . But Henley very rarely came to this excellence in his verse. The great body of it suffers from the fatal defect of having been subjected to no emotional selection, a defect which Henley very thoroughly understood when considering the work of other men. The sequence of Hospital sketches, for example, is no more than brilliant journalism. Brilliant journalism in its place is all very well; and, when a man aiming at it accomplishes it, all credit is due to him, but you cannot pass it off as poetry. These poems, one feels all the time as one reads them, are as much an accident as the occasion of Henley's being in the hospital at all. It is no case of carefully selected emotion being projected through an occasion that shall give it final form, as it seems to the poet; it is, rather, a vivid observation catching up this, that, and the other fragment of casual event and setting it down, not with imaginative but merely graphic power. (pp. 101-03)

On the whole, the volume of **Poems,** running to nearly three hundred pages, is the one of the five forming the admirable collected edition now published that is least likely to serve Henley's memory. He was a skilled writer always and handled many verse forms with ease, but only very rarely in any of them does he come to that last continence which is style. It is interesting to note that he often writes in a manner which is to-day supposed to be very revolutionary, but he seems to have done it without theories, merely because it was easy. (p. 103)

Before passing to the important Henley, the critic, a word must be said of the four plays that he wrote in collaboration with Stevenson. In these there are passages of patent merit. The Stevenson of 'Treasure Island' could not fail in the course of a long work to find moments of enchantment, flushed with the true broadside manner, and coloured of the best. And, given the situation right and the characters really agog, Henley had a gift of dramatic dialogue—if it was Henley's, as I suspect—that could firmly hold the stage for five minutes at a stretch. But these things do not make drama; and, as dramas, these four plays are the merest exercises, and very poor ones at that. It is incredible that two writers of such outstanding ability could at times become so jejune. It is all very well for men of genius to have larks, but even in their larks there must be some con-

science, and if there is any conscience in these plays I do not discover it. **'Admiral Guinea'** has scenes of the true Stevensonian glamour, but it has nothing else of the smallest dramatic truth. **'Robert Macaire'** is a very elaborate joke, which certainly does not come off in reading any more than I can believe it to come off on the stage. **'Beau Austin,'** although it has perhaps the best three minutes to be found in any of the plays, is no more than Sheridan-Goldsmith pastiche. And **'Deacon Brodie'** succeeds only in making villainy appear more imbecile than virtue. It is in this play, too, that we have the most hilarious examples of the abuse of soliloquy. Henley in his article on 'Othello' speaks of soliloquy as 'an expedient in dramatic art abominable to the play-going mind.' In that essay he is inclined to accept the device because of Shakespeare's use of it, not seeing that in its proper function it may be a magnificent element in great dramatic form. But that a critic who could raise the question at all should put his name to a play in which over and over again one of the characters speaks like this:

> 'Now for one of the Deacon's headaches! Rogues all, rogues all! *(Goes to clothes-press, and proceeds to change his coat.)* On with the new coat and into the new life! Down with the Deacon and up with the robber! . . . Only the stars to see me! *(Addressing the bed.)* Lie there, Deacon! sleep and be well to-morrow. As for me, I'm a man once more till morning. *(Gets out of the window.)*'

leaves one, as they say in the ring, guessing. They just won't do, and that is all there is to be said of the plays. (pp. 104-05)

Henley, the critic, is another matter altogether. It may sometimes be charged against him that he was superficial, and, in a way, justly. But it was a superficiality which Henley himself would have been at no pains to disown, since what is meant is not that he did not feel profoundly, but that his interests were chiefly along the highways of critical thought and creative effort, and that he was not much concerned with the remoter things of speculation nor with the rarer and more elusive kind of personality. The result is that a few readers will find Henley's pronouncement altogether shallow and ill-considered, in the case of a writer such as Landor, for example. (p. 106)

The outstanding quality of all Henley's work . . . is a moral courage of a particular strain which we to-day, taught by a generation of writers who in this at least have learnt wisdom, may find less unusual than it was, say in 1896, when [his] Burns essay was first published. Twenty-five years ago it was not difficult for a man to speak his mind about life; but, if he spoke with courage and independence, he was apt to find acceptance only among a small body of artists and thinkers. Thirty years had passed, it is true, since Swinburne sent the larger public into convulsions by 'Poems and Ballads'; but even after that lapse of time such a book would have been greeted with a considerable, if not an equal, storm of protest. To-day, however much it might flutter a few hearts, 'Poems and Ballads' would at least leave the moral sense of the public unshocked. And that this is so is largely due to writers, of whom Henley was by no means the least, who came out into the open and challenged, not a coterie but what is known as public opinion, with the declaration that nearly all moral judgments are immoral and that what really matters is not points of view but life. (p. 107)

It is [a] Christlike spirit that informs such essays as [those] of Henley on Fielding and Burns. Here was a critic who not only had his fine sense of literary excellence, but brought a real ethical standard to his appraising of it, a standard that recognised first and last that self-righteousness and morality cannot live together. The result is that in the study of Burns, for example, we have the whole of the man quite fearlessly set down—unstable, betrayed by circumstance into all sorts of follies and even worse, often enough spiritually thriftless, descending at times to the level of a mean antagonist, and, with it all, magnificent. Henley sees these defects in his hero, and is no more afraid of them than Burns himself was at pains to conceal them. He passes no moral judgment on them, since moral judgment is not his business. He merely perceives them, vividly, as part of a character, moving in its other scale to a courage, a generosity, and a passionate charity such as have never been excelled in any human heart. And this complete Burns is, for Henley, life, something to contemplate with all one's understanding and humility, something so much more marvellous in itself than it can be in the testing by preconceived standards. (p. 108)

[The] human quality in Henley's work would, it need hardly be said, not suffice in itself to make him the critic he is. It is, rather, that, when this nature in him is stirred, his critical faculty becomes alert also, and he discovers an authoritative sense of literary values. When, as in the case of Landor, the emotion of his subject escapes him, the expression of that emotion naturally enough seems to him to be in itself something inadequate. And all that can be said about it, as in every case of aesthetic appreciation, is that, so far as Henley's mind was concerned, the expression *was* inadequate. Landor remains, and Henley proves his worth elsewhere, and little harm is done. In the **'Fielding'** and **'Burns,'** on the other hand (one returns to these essays since, on the whole, they stand as the best of Henley's achievement), his personal sympathy with the life of his subject finds the nicest modulation in the analysis that he makes of the form in which that life found expression. And these papers are full not only of human understanding but of critical wisdom. We have not only warm-hearted persuasion, but a very rare insight into the processes of literary art. (p. 110)

On the whole, Henley stands for a quite definite thing in modern English letters. He was not a great imaginative writer; and, though he had a good style, it was not a notably distinguished one, such as, shall we say, that of Mr Edmund Gosse. Nor, on the other hand, was he a great and original moralist, moving in lonely ways of speculation. But he did perhaps as much as any writer of his time to enlighten the ever-vexed problem of the relation of morality to art. (p. 111)

[Henley] was a good man, and he loved goodness. He was under no illusions as to what goodness really was, and, as was shown by his acrimonious treatment of some of Stevenson's white-washers, he neither hoped nor wanted to find paragons of virtue among men. He was perfectly aware, too, that in this world of expediency the values of vice and virtue are continually falsified; so that he knew, for example, that in the sum Burns was a much better man than any of his detractors. But, when all is said, the fact remains that Henley did immensely cherish the ordinary decent things of charity and tolerance and fortitude and devotion. And, while he was the last man in the world to tell his fellows that they ought to foster these things, he was eager in his praises whenever he found them. Had he been a great creative artist, his world would have been alive with this best kind of virtue, and it would have been his to survive the common charge of sentimentalising life. As he was not a great creative artist, this instinct in him found its fullest

expression in criticism; and it does so in such a way as perhaps might persuade even the most intellectual critic that, in an artist, to be moral is not necessarily to be damned. (p. 112)

John Drinkwater, "William Ernest Henley," in The Quarterly Review, *Vol. 237, No. 470, January, 1922, pp. 101-12.*

ALFRED NOYES   (essay date 1924)

[The] peculiar gift of Henley, the gift that singles him out as a great writer, a major poet, not only from his contemporaries, but also from all his peers in the past, is his gift of portraiture. He is the Raeburn of English literature—our first, our only, and unapproachable portrait-painter in English verse. Others have excelled in other kinds; but this belongs to him alone. Not in the great masterpieces of our sonnet-literature, not in Rossetti, not in Wordsworth, not in Milton, not in Shakespeare even, shall we find that peculiar gift which is displayed over and over again in the work of Henley. Greater gifts we shall undoubtedly find; but not this particular gift. And he learned to use it in the long days when he was prisoned in that cold, clean hospital ward, half workhouse, half jail. (p. 84)

He hangs the naked corridors of the hospital with masterpieces of portraiture: the Scrubber of the Ward; . . . the Staff Nurses, old style and new; the Rescued Suicide, with his "unrazored features" ghastly brown against his pillow, and "throat so strangely bandaged."

Henley knew them all, talked with them all; and, like the great masters of his art on canvas, he painted their souls as well as their faces. He was quite conscious, too, of his aims in the matter, and not a little ambitious. . . . (pp. 85-6)

It is true that many of his lyrics are commonplace "echoes" (as he himself calls some of them), ballads and roundels that have been done far better by a hundred hands. There are, too, irregular odes, anthems, and voluntaries that contain much of the pomp and circumstance of words, but very little of the inner light that transfigures the similar work of Francis Thompson. His work in all these kinds has been praised and blamed indiscriminately; and this is a real injustice, for in his true gift he stood alone. A worse injustice has been done to him by those of his friends who realize the inadequacy of much that has been praised by the undiscriminating and would declare, like the *Dictionary of National Biography*, that "his verse was the occasional recreation of a life mainly occupied with editing and the criticism of literature and art," or that his value to posterity lies in the fact that he endured suffering with courage. (pp. 87-8)

The values of literature are not to be determined by impossible estimates of the comparative suffering in life of those who produced it. . . . All we are concerned with in art and literature is this one question, *Is the work good or bad?* If it be bad, then no desire or regret will make it valuable to the world. (p. 88)

Henley was a great artist. That is why the attention of the critic can safely be concentrated upon his work; for it is through his work that the great-hearted man still speaks to us. And, indeed, if there were one thing he tried to convey to us more than another, it was the everlasting joy that he found in life. (pp. 88-9)

Moreover, it is not in the words and phrases where he flings his crutch that he displays his greatest strength. The kind of violence which he occasionally shows in his verse is more symptomatic of his physical affliction than of his mental power. Strength in art and literature is nearly always accompanied by the rarest delicacy of workmanship. . . . This, as Henley himself knew, was the secret of Tennyson's delicate artistry and his power to put into a few lucid lines of *In Memoriam* the whole vast story of geology. Henley's own greatest work, his portraiture, is entirely free from the weakness of violence, for it was the outcome of his passion for life with all its humors. (pp. 89-90)

Plain-spoken as Henley always was, he knew not only his own aims but his own limitations. "I have no invention," he said, and he would probably have failed in his plays hopelessly had it not been for the collaboration of Stevenson. From first to last his real gift was that of portraiture, where invention was less necessary than insight into the hearts, minds, and souls of his sitters. (pp. 90-1)

Much of his patriotic verse was mere Prussianism. It is significant that even in his patriotic poetry Henley was at his best when he first personified England and then drew her portrait. (p. 91)

And after all, the distinguishing feature of his most famous poem, *Invictus,* is the fact that it is a portrait of the artist, painted by himself. No one who reads it aright will need to be assured that the greatness of this man is to be found in his poetical work, the best that he had to give us. . . . (p. 92)

> *Alfred Noyes, "The Poetry of W. E. Henley," in his* Some Aspects of Modern Poetry *(copyright, 1924, by Frederick A. Stokes Company; copyright renewed © 1952 by Alfred Noyes; reprinted by permission of the Literary Estate of Alfred Noyes), Stokes, 1924, pp. 81-92.**

JEROME HAMILTON BUCKLEY   (essay date 1945)

[From his 1875 essay on André Marie de Chénier] till the essay on *Othello* a few months before his death, Henley clung faithfully to his own critical standards. . . . Throughout his criticism his method was synthetic rather than analytical; he measured a literary work always in its relation to a literary context and never as an isolated aesthetic event. He was capable of capturing in a few brilliant generalizations the quality of a book or the spirit of an age; but he had neither the patience nor the power to trace to its origins a particular seminal idea or to describe in detail the processes by which a given poem had evolved. Avowedly "no metaphysician," he had no interest in logical deduction from abstract philosophic truth; with an invalid's faith in basic physical sensation, he reasoned empirically towards a coherent universe. By nature he was utterly unable to appreciate a literature of introspection; and all too readily he repudiated the artist wrapt in a contemplation of intangibles as one who sought to evade the realities of his world and his time. Without doubt his failure to achieve full sympathy with creative minds alien to his own placed his criticism under severe limitation. But from this failure alone arose his true significance as a critical force. He came at the close of a troubled era sick from its own doubt, weary of its febrile intellection. Yet once he had learned by painful experience his individual grammar of assent, he could in no way comprehend the Victorian denial, the omnipresent romantic *malaise dans une civilisation.* By an activist ethic he was prepared to accept the diversity of human nature as intrinsically good. Poetry, he said correcting Arnold, was nothing more than an "expression

of life." And in life, which meant the free exercise of an unconquerable soul, there was no place for a paralyzing despair.

In its most naïve form, activism led Henley to an admiration of lusty extrovert action as a prime source of literary material. . . . Dumas, Scott, Tolstoi, and the early English prose-masters before them, were all to a degree concerned with heroic values; and it was inevitable that the activist should applaud their effort.

Henley's "masculine protest," however, expressed itself critically not alone in his enjoyment of robustious elemental action; it had deeper and less direct implications. It brought him into immediate and lasting conflict not merely with the aesthetic "decadence," but also with the ideals and inhibitions of the same society against which the "decadents" themselves were reacting. Throughout his essays and reviews Henley repeatedly assailed Victorianism with all the "vigor" at his command. Against his father's generation and his own, he leveled charges sweeping enough to indict himself. The Victorian age was, he contended, "noisy and affected," with "an element of swagger in all its words and ways" and "a distressing and immoral turn for publicity." (pp. 162-64)

Decent, pharisaical, self-conscious, sentimental, the Victorians, taken by and large, were, as Henley saw them, both intellectually and emotionally dishonest. . . . Despite his own deliberate mannerism, his "swagger," his overstatement, Henley himself was fundamentally sincere in his revolt against a hollow convention. He was, of course, not alone in his rebellion. But, while the "decadents" sought escape from Victorianism in an unnatural perversion of its standards, Henley and his followers attacked an artificial restraint, explicitly in the interests of a sounder "moral health." The artist, they believed, had the right and duty to "select" his materials; but the artist who gingerly avoided certain subjects under taboo was guilty of unforgivable compromise with reality. Reticence, when it meant fear to discuss without equivocation the vital issues of modern life, was in nowise to be condoned. Sentiment, when it implied the glossing of an ugly truth, was not only unethical but also inartistic. From first to last the *National Observer* insisted upon a complete and disillusioned acceptance of the full experience. And from first to last in his own criticism Henley decried every evidence of hypocrisy, evasion, and obscurantism. His dissatisfaction with Victorian social morality induced him to praise and to publish the forbidden chapter of Hardy's *Tess.* And his righteous indignation at what seemed wilful distortion of fact prompted his notorious attack on the official biography of "Lewis" Stevenson. (pp. 164-65)

The aesthetes from the Swinburne of *Poems and Ballads* to the Wilde of *Salomé* turned in their reaction to Victorian art towards the literature of France. Henley himself had learned much concerning the discipline of metre from the fifteenth century formalists and from the Parnassians of the Second Empire. He had studied and imitated the technique of French romantic drama. He had introduced to an English public the work of the pre-impressionist French painters. And—what is more relevant to a discussion of his literary criticism—he had read deeply in Sainte-Beuve and Taine and had examined the first principles of contemporary French "realism." It was to be expected then that he should draw from the disillusioned Frenchmen support for his campaign against "middle-Victorian" sentimentalism. Nevertheless, on due consideration of the Flaubertian "realist's" claim to an honest portrayal of reality, he rejected the theory of art as incompatible with an activist's philosophy of life. For the ''realist'' proved hardly less inhibited than the sentimentalist and certainly more distrustful of high passion; while he laid a rightful emphasis on the clutch of circumstance, he failed to consider the individual's resistance to his fell destiny; there was no place in his factualism for ''the expression of human feeling in the coil of a tragic situation.'' (pp. 166-67)

''The way of realism,'' the path of honest acceptance and universal sympathy—herein lay for the activist the one possible approach to a sound philosophy of life. Yet the interests of ''Life,'' of the continuous process of growth and decay, were scarcely identical with the interests of ''Art,'' of completed patterns which allowed no continuum beyond themselves. From the outset, therefore, Henley found himself as critic of literature faced with the conflict between art and reality. At times he might make pretense of denying the conflict altogether, by relegating art to an entirely subordinate position; ''Byron and Burns,'' he once wrote, ''courted Life like a mistress, and made no more account of Art than many make of their wives, but were satisfied with companionship, and a pleasant house, and the presence of a goodly and fruitful issue.'' But his own work was sufficient proof that he could seldom follow Byron and Burns in taking art so for granted. Throughout his highly polished verse and prose he remained forever the deliberate craftsman, the self-conscious stylist. (p. 172)

[In his] criticism Henley approached a moral standard comparable to Ruskin's ideal of Purity. And in general Henley stood closer to the ''middle-Victorian'' aesthetician than he would ever have admitted. Like Ruskin, he believed that art was essentially a means of communication, that there existed between artist and spectator a bond of sympathy whereby an emotion might be passed from the creative to the receptive mind. The greatest and the most moral artist was he who saw deepest into the wholeness of things. And the greatest art was consequently that which showed the truest correspondence with reality and gave the best evidence of the creator's power of interpretation. (p. 174)

Despite his gusto of manner, his penchant for sweeping generalization, his habit of quoting and misquoting from memory, Henley himself displayed throughout his criticism an almost incredible erudition. Having read and assimilated the masterpieces of five languages, English, French, German, Italian, and Spanish, he brought to his essays and reviews an admirable capacity for comparative estimates. He made himself thoroughly familiar with the best that earlier critics had thought and said, and so prepared himself intelligently to refute any opinions that ran counter to his own conviction. Since he felt that biographical data might illuminate the character and intention of the author, he saturated himself in memoirs, diaries, and commonplace books; as a result, his monograph on Smollett revealed a firsthand knowledge of eighteenth century literary quarrels; and his survey of **''Byron's World,''** though written entirely without notes, betrayed a truly encyclopaedic command of Regency gossip. His shorter literary *aperçus* brilliantly measured each author against the other artists in his genre; a single paragraph ''placed'' Longfellow among the great sea poets; and a page served to touch off Balzac's unique contribution to European letters. His longer critical essays made deeper incursions into the backgrounds out of which the writer under scrutiny had emerged; the memorable Burns edition implied a detailed knowledge of countless minor dialect poets; and the sketch of Henry Fielding's career rested, in part at least, upon an examination of the record-books of the Old

Bailey sessions. But in all his studies, short or long, erudite or simply intuitive, Henley's first purpose was the discernment of the individuality stamped by the artist upon the matter of his creation.

The description of a master quality presented as many problems as its detection. Though well able to express his judgments in direct expository prose, Henley preferred a more dramatic critical method. In his terse *Views and Reviews* he strove to reduce his literary estimates to single impressions such as might be passed on to the reader in a handful of shining epigrams. . . . Yet it is a defect of Henley's own essays that much of the vivid impressionism seems too personal, too arbitrary, to have a firm objective basis. Invariably stimulating, his epigrams seldom appear other than brilliant impromptus; they indicate little of the careful consideration and genuine literary insight that went into their manufacture.

But the epigrammatic technique by no means accounts for the whole of Henley's critical method. The impressionism is counterbalanced by what might be called ''expressionism''; and this of its nature implies a deliberately impersonal approach to the art-object. By expressionism, Henley attempted to identify himself completely with the author's mind and thereby to re-create the author's world. ''In Herrick,'' he wrote, ''the air is fragrant with new-mown hay; there is a morning light upon all things; long shadows streak the grass, and on the eglantine swinging in the hedge the dew lies white and brilliant.'' . . . In such passages the poet and the critic were at one; the literature that struck a responsive chord in his mind became to Henley a present reality and so the actual stuff of inspiration. Through expressionism he achieved his strongest effects; so fully realized were his empathic judgments that there seemed nothing of subjective caprice in them.

In point of technique, Henley's literary criticism was not unlike that of Walter Pater, whose appreciations most fully had exploited the expressionistic method. Both critics approached a work of art with the bias of the individualist. Each evolved for his own use a highly personal style; Pater's prose moved by exquisite delays through long lingering periods; Henley's bristled with paradox and oxymoron, with sharp epigram and explosive epithet. And each sought for the distinctive trait, the master quality, of the author he would judge. But Pater's individualism was the philosophy of the aesthete who asked of art a refuge from the social conflict; whereas Henley's was the credo of the activist who felt a physical and moral duty strenuously to exercise his own soul in ''the brave gymnasium'' of time. The one doctrine was destined, even in spite of its teacher, to inspire the literature of ''decadence.'' The other served as a basis for Edwardian realism. (pp. 177-79)

[It was] Henley's place to guide Chesterton and Bennett and the younger generation as a whole away from Gallic pessimism, towards a more robust acceptance of reality; it [was] his function to reassert the fundamental heroic human values at a time when the sanctions behind them seemed rapidly to be crumbling. That these values were of prime significance as the basis of aesthetic expression, the Edwardian achievement in character-portrayal stands as sufficient proof. The fact that the neo-Georgian artist has repudiated them and so has sacrificed claim to a depiction of the whole truth, this is evidence only of their permanent validity. (p. 180)

Jerome Hamilton Buckley, in his William Ernest Henley: A Study in the ''Counter-Decadence'' of the 'Nineties *(copyright © 1945 by Princeton University Press; reprinted by permission of Princeton Univer-*

sity Press), Princeton University Press, 1945, 234 p.

JOHN GOULD FLETCHER   (essay date 1946)

[Henley's] poems—or rather, the best of them—are interesting examples of a type of *vers libre* which owes its inspiration almost solely to Heine, and especially to Heine's finest, the North Sea poems. . . . [There] is no doubt, that in his best poems, the Hospital sequence, the **London Voluntaries,** the **"Song of Speed"** written at the close of his life, Henley repeated, in large measure, the mingled sentimentality and irony that exist in Heine, who remained largely an unacknowledged master as far as he was concerned. That Heine is usually the better poet of the two cannot be doubted. There is a wordiness, a vague feeling for rhetorical flourishes, in the Englishman, that the exiled German Jew was able to avoid. And in middle-life, Henley himself turned away from this profitable and but little-trodden path, to develop into a skilled fashioner of what he himself called the "Bric-a-brac" school of verse:—the endless ballades, rondeaus, villanelles of the Austin Dobson, Andrew Lang type—against which Gerard Manley Hopkins protested at the time in his letters to Robert Bridges. He did this, because he instinctively put style above substance; the way of saying things above the thing said. In this, he was not only mistaken, but perverse; for the style, to amplify the French saying, is only the man in so far as the man, with all his faults and virtues, is able to fecundate and to fully employ the style. Perhaps Henley, with his limited strength, but bull-like drive of will, was never fully able to dominate and employ his own style completely to further his own purposes. . . . [His] self-conscious worship of style made of him rather more of a mere pattern-fashioner than a creator.

What remains? . . . I do not think it is too much to say that Henley's great monument, apart from his slang dictionary (which he did not live to complete) was that series of **"Tudor Translations"** which was completed with aid from his most faithful disciple, Charles Whibley. The happy possessor of one of these sets of thirty-two volumes has, at hand, one of the great monuments of a great age: and in setting up this monument, rather than in quarreling with the Philistines of the mid-Victorian period, or in writing the over-anthologized **"Invictus,"** Henley himself carved out a niche that abides in English literature. (pp. 719-20)

> *John Gould Fletcher, "Who Was Henley?" in* The Sewanee Review *(reprinted by permission of the editor;* © *1946, copyright renewed* © *1974, by The University of the South), Vol. LIV, No. 4, October-December, 1946, pp. 716-20.*

VIVIAN de SOLA PINTO   (essay date 1955)

[Henley] was an important pioneer of the new realism in English poetry. . . . The series of lyrics and sonnets first published as **Hospital Outlines** in the Cornhill Magazine . . . and included in his collected poems, under the title **In Hospital,** is one of the starting points of the English poetry of the modern crisis. It is highly significant that the subject of these poems is a hospital, the symbol both of the sickness of the modern world and its preoccupation with science. . . . (pp. 27-8)

These poems are, perhaps, the first resolute attempt in English to use ugliness, meanness and pain as subjects of poetry. Browning, indeed, had experimented in the use of ugliness,

but in his work it was always picturesque or grotesque and combined with some sort of moralizing explicit or implied. Henley's hospital poems are, perhaps, the first in which an English poet finds completely satisfactory images in the kind of ugliness peculiar to the modern world. . . . (p. 28)

Henley's unrhymed metres are descended from those of Heine, by whose work he was profoundly influenced; nevertheless they are different from Heine's and the best of them, in spite of dates, belong to the twentieth rather than to the nineteenth century. In a few poems he created irregular rhythms which are really expressive of the uprooted and divided modern consciousness. . . . (pp. 28-9)

One of the great needs of English poetry after the great Victorians was a new kind of verse free from the intolerable staleness of hackneyed rhymes and the smoothness of traditional rhythms. To create a "free" verse which would express by its movement the restlessness and spiritual disintegration of the modern world and yet would have a satisfying pattern, was a task which presented problems of immense difficulty, and Henley must be credited with the distinction of making the first resolute and intelligent attempt to solve them. His humorous realism, too, in such poems as **London Types** helped considerably in breaking down the pompous and orotund traditions of Victorian literary verse.

Henley's fine, courageous vision of external realities was not, unfortunately, matched by a corresponding intellectual and emotional maturity. The poverty of his inner life is revealed by the triviality of many of his ballades and rondeaux, and still more by the blustering imperialism of his political poems and the senseless swagger of his well-known and much anthologized **Invictus.** His patriotic poems suffered from exactly the same kind of hollowness as Blunt's anti-patriotic poems. . . . (p. 29)

> *Vivian de Sola Pinto, "The Two Voyages," in his* Crisis in English Poetry: 1880-1940, *second edition, Hutchinson's University Library, 1955, pp. 13-35.**

JOHN GROSS   (essay date 1969)

The *National Observer* played a considerable part in promoting the legends of late Victorian imperialism. It published, among other things, [Kipling's] *Barrack Room Ballads;* and during the years when he was editing it Henley himself emerged as a Bard of Empire. Although he had long been a romantic jingo, no one could have guessed it from his first collection of poems, **A Book of Verses** . . . , which consisted partly of ballades and other rondeliering trinkets ('A dainty thing's the villanelle'), partly of powerfully realistic *vers libre* sketches of hospital life. In 1892, however, he published **The Song of the Sword,** with its famous lyric **Pro Rege Nostro** ('What have I done for you, England, my England?') and its preposterous title-poem. . . . Henley's massacres all took place on paper: they were the daydreams of a frustrated cripple rather than positive calls to action. In his less feverish moods he wrote very different kinds of verse—brooding impressionistic townscapes, mostly. But the climate of the times encouraged him in his drum-and-trumpet posturings, and so did the set of journalists around him. He perpetrated some particularly fearsome doggerel at the time of the Boer War.

The favourable reception of **Views and Reviews** . . . enhanced his standing as a literary oracle. He described this collection as 'a mosaic of scraps and shreds recovered from the shot rubbish of some fourteen years of journalism', although it was in fact much more lovingly put together than this would suggest: there were sections instead of paragraphs, each with its indented rubric and its ornamental tailpiece. It is hard to see now why his criticism should ever have created much of a stir. He was widely read, and he could turn a jaunty epigram or fondle an exotic adjective in the Stevenson manner. But his opinions are nothing more than opinions, and most of his enthusiasms come across as robustious rather than robust. An exception might perhaps be made in favour of his comparative outspokenness about sex. It is something to find a Victorian critic who is capable, for example, of describing Mr B in *Pamela* as 'a kind of Walking Phallus'. And while he may not hit quite the right note in his essay on Burns when he calls him a 'lewd peasant of genius', his account of the poet is certainly preferable to the standard nineteenth-century bowdlerization. (D. H. Lawrence praises it in one of his letters.) Then, in addition to his criticism, and more usefully, Henley was an energetic anthologist, editor, and organizer of editorial projects. His outstanding achievement here was the splendid series of 'Tudor Translations', each with an introductory essay by a leading scholar of the day. Saintsbury was allotted Florio's *Montaigne*, for instance, W. P. Ker *Froissart*, Walter Raleigh *Castiglione*.

However, it was neither as a writer nor as an editor that Henley impressed his contemporaries most, but as a personality: the zestful warrior, the 'Viking Chief of letters'. (pp. 151-52)

> *John Gross, ''The Bookmen,'' in his* The Rise and Fall of the Man of Letters: A Study of the Idiosyncratic and the Humane in Modern Literature *(© 1969 by John Gross; reprinted by permission of Weidenfeld (Publishers) Limited), Macmillan, 1969, Weidenfeld & Nicholson, 1969, pp. 131-66.**

JOSEPH M. FLORA (essay date 1970)

In Hospital, a presentation in verse of a long hospital stay, is a sequence in which the reader can discern change, development, growth in the protagonist—mainly as the reader views the objective world of hospital life. As in Hemingway's fiction, inner realities emerge through careful presentation of the ''true.'' (Indeed, Hemingway portrayed his own hospital experience in several stories in essentially the ''In Hospital'' manner.) Form, as well as detail, makes the presentation realistic, a faithful representation of the hospital world; and form contributes greatly to the reader's experiencing the protagonist's psychological state. The sequence should be read as a whole: poem comments on poem as form comments on form. In *In Hospital* Henley developed a sonnet sequence into a more comprehensive experience than the sonnet by itself would permit.

How tonally unified *In Hospital* is can be seen in the fact that Henley did not include in it the ''embarrassing'' poem ''Invictus.'' That poem had, in fact, been written during Henley's long stay in the Edinburgh hospital. It was a part of his hospital experience, but he rightly judged it inappropriate for the sequence which depended on revealing the protagonist's emotions by underplaying them. Henley later printed the poem under *Echoes*, many poems beyond *In Hospital,* in the *Collected Works*. Surely, *In Hospital* has nothing of the tone nor any such statements of philosophy [of ''Invictus'']. . . . (p. 28)

Recently, John Ciardi has dismissed this poem, as ''perhaps the most widely known bad poem in English.'' For Ciardi, it is nothing but Henley's ''chest-thumping heroics.'' Henley wrote ''Invictus'' when he most had need of defiance, and, if he had not been defiant in refusing to follow the advice of medical authorities, he would have lost a second leg to the surgeon's knife. Defiance is muted in *In Hospital,* however much Henley might thump it in ''Invictus.'' The now very public ''Invictus'' (actually, Henley did not even give it a title, but settled for dedication to R. T. Hamilton Bruce) started as a very personal poem—and it suggests a direction in which all of his verse and life might have gone if he had not had something in himself like the Balzac motto prefacing *In Hospital* to warn him against too great egocentricity. (p. 29)

[When] Stevenson and Henley joined forces to write their first play, it is not surprising that Stevenson had a rough draft of a true Edinburgh story that had long before caught his interest. Nor is it surprising that each of the plays of the collaborators is set in the past—one far removed from the Victorian scene that both Henley and Stevenson frequently criticized: the eighteenth century. *Deacon Brodie* takes place about 1780; *Admiral Guinea,* about 1760; *Beau Austin* and *Macaire,* in 1820. (p. 36)

Deacon Brodie has a subtitle that is significant in light of Stevenson's later work: *The Double Life.* Although Stevenson's reputation is today far from what it was, *Dr. Jekyll and Mr. Hyde* is not likely soon to fade into obscurity; and two more adult romances, *Kidnapped* and *The Master of Ballantrae,* will continue to be read. In all three of these works, Stevenson makes important use of the double-life motif. William Brodie is Stevenson's first portrait of ''the beloved scoundrel,'' a concept which appealed to Henley as well as to Stevenson. (Indeed, Henley increasingly was Stevenson's beloved scoundrel. Stevenson's modeling Long John Silver on Henley was almost prophetic.) Reacting against Victorian pressures to keep personality in check, the scoundrel asserted that he would be ''master of his fate'' and ''captain of his soul.''

The real turning point for Deacon Brodie is, however, the loss of mastery over his own fate: Humphrey Moore usurps his position in the gang, and Brodie must take orders. (pp. 37-8)

Concomitant with the Deacon's active life is the play's most overt theme: criticism of hypocrisy. Aware of the duality in his own nature, Brodie implies that it must be so with all men. In the course of the play's action, he discovers some confirmation for this notion. His respectable, well-meaning uncle, William Lawson, the ''Procurator-Fiscal,'' buys illegal liquor, and Brodie later accuses him of this wrong. But in reality he joyously seizes his discovery as a sanction for his own duplicity. . . If Brodie's uncle bears some guilt, however, his father, his sister Mary, and her fiancé represent something very different dramatically and thereby make Brodie's deeds highly reprehensible. (p. 38)

The best moments in *Deacon Brodie* are those that involve the lowlife characters. On this score the melodrama in its use of lowlife characters, particularly in their language, has a claim to distinction. Stevenson returned frequently to lowlife characters in his fiction, and what he learned about them from Henley is not minimal. Henley himself had a lifelong interest in slang—his ballad **''Villon's Straight Tip to All Cross Coves''** is a remarkable tour de force attesting his proficiency. In the play, Humphrey Moore and George Smith speak in memorable accents. The role of Jean Watt, the Deacon's mistress, is decidedly a more lively one than that of Mary Brodie—Henley had more pleasure in treating sinners than saints. Read or played as pure melodrama (as its creators intended), *Deacon Brodie* has some very good moments. (p. 39)

[*Beau Austin*] is the quick-paced story of the celebrated Georgian beau, George Frederick Austin, and the events that made him a married man, even though one of his many admirers had concluded that "the very greatness of success condemns him to remain unmarried". . . . (p. 40)

Although the Sardou-like concentration of *Deacon Brodie* is not carried into *Beau Austin*, the latter play moves with marked rapidity—for which the musical inductions give the cue. The action of the play covers the space of ten hours, and the pace of the production must be accordingly brisk. The fast final scene is completely appropriate to the play's pace and theme. Dorothy falls into the arms of her hero exclaiming, "My hero! Take me! What you will." The Beau replies, "'My dear creature, remember you are in public.' *(Raising her)* 'Your Royal Highness, may I present you Mrs. George Frederick Austin?'" . . . And the curtain falls. Thus, without getting into the battle over the double standard that Arthur Wing Pinero's *The Second Mrs. Tanqueray* . . . would help keep popular in London, Henley and Stevenson—in Georgian rather than Victorian spirit—save the fallen woman's reputation and bring the Georgian dandy to contrition and magnanimity. Like an eighteenth-century Steele, they present us not with duel, but with near duels, and with spirited dialogue rather than the high sophistication of a Congreve. Not duplicity, but the essence of the gentleman is the source of admiration. But, denied Congreve's more penetrating glances at human nature, we are likewise denied memorable characterizations. Dorothy Musgrave can never compete with Congreve's Millimant—nor, of course, Beau Austin with his Mirabel. "Those Georgian days" of the play are as if never, never days. (p. 42)

[The] year they wrote *Beau Austin*, Henley and Stevenson also completed *Admiral Guinea*. Although this play has some lively scenes, *Admiral Guinea* is much inferior to *Beau Austin;* indeed, it is the most disappointing of the Henley-Stevenson plays. *Admiral Guinea* is a melodrama of sin and repentance, of appearance and reality, and of young lovers whose desired marriage is opposed by the girl's father. There are important differences, to be sure; but, basically, Henley and Stevenson are dealing with the same plot motifs they had used in *Deacon Brodie*. The potential for a serious study of evil is present, but the collaborators were more concerned with dramatic effects than with an examination of any "heart of darkness." (p. 43)

Macaire is the most even and the most consistently pleasing of the Henley-Stevenson collaboration. Whereas *Admiral Guinea* is mainly successful when the rogue Pew is present, *Macaire* has a rogue as its central figure and hence is focused on the kind of character that Henley and Stevenson were best at imagining. The play, written at the request of Mr. Beerbohm Tree (according to Edmund Gosse), is an adaptation of an old French melodrama—*L'Auberge des Adrets* by Benjamin Antier, Jean-Armand Saint-Amand, and Paulyanthe (Amand Lacoste). . . . (p. 50)

Speed has been the mark of the earlier plays of the collaboration, but it is especially important in *Macaire* where the spirit of the play is the "light fantastic." Indeed, the play is quite literally filled with music and dance. The dramatists envisioned that the time between the acts would be brief and the piece played "where it is merely comic in a vein of patter." . . . When we add to the lively stage business the simple but sharply distinguished background characters and the talk between Macaire and Bertrand, we easily have the Henley-Stevenson play that could still make a pleasant evening in the theater.

Macaire does best what both Henley and Stevenson could do with distinction—talk. A prime characteristic of the beloved scoundrel in all four of these plays—and also in Stevenson's fiction—is his ability to be a man of words as well as of action—which is, of course, what both of these victims of ill-health aspired to be. (pp. 50-1)

The plays themselves are interesting for what they try to do, for their gusto (sustained in the case of *Beau Austin* and *Macaire*), for the dialogue of lowlife. Undoubtedly, their authors wanted a neo-Romanticism on the English stage, but they produced no neo-Romantic play of absolute significance—as shortly thereafter Edmond Rostand did in France with *Cyrano de Bergerac*. . . . It is, moreover, ironical that Henley, having written poetry of the strongest realism and with some subtle psychological emphases, would turn so decidedly toward the romantic and melodramatic when he came to write drama. (pp. 53-4)

The poems gathered as **"Echoes"** reveal the poet at different moods in his life extending from the Margate year, 1872, the earliest year from which Henley preserved his poems, through 1888, that transition year in Henley's career when the Stevenson friendship ended, [his daughter] Margaret was born, and his mother died. These events—as well as his young love for Anna and the struggle over his leg—are all echoed in this grouping. And in it Henley placed the famous **"Invictus."** (p. 123)

Although *"Matri Dilectissimae"* is in free verse, almost all of the other echoes are short lyrics in very regular stanzas—ranging from the charm of **"The nightingale has a lyre of gold"** to the indifferent *Poem XI*. . . . (p. 124)

[In] **"Echoes"** Henley treats more vitally the theme of the rondel **"The ways of Death are soothing and serene."** The rhythm of the rondeau, its movement of a perfect cycle, its simple diction, all correspond with the perfect pattern Henley praised in **"What is to come."** There form *was* his main metaphor. The rondel form, however, worked against the theme Henley wanted to express. Allegorized Death cannot be so summarily, so liltingly dismissed. (p. 125)

The most moving statement of Henley's approach to Death is the free verse **"A late lark twitters."** The poem should be compared with the one Tennyson ordered placed as the final poem in all editions of his work, his "Crossing the Bar," which, incidentally, it predates. For the mid-Victorian there was the hope, but no certainty, that he would see his Pilot "face to face." For the late-Victorian—the activist who insisted that the only test of life was its creative living—there is not any longing for the Christian heaven. In the poem Henley slowly creates a picture of a late lark singing against the quiet of a sunset over "an old, gray city." With night comes the great gift of sleep. As many another nineteenth-century poet personalizes after creating a picture in nature, so Henley personalizes. But he is not moralizing; he voices an assured request, which is for him rather than for some reader in need of a moral. . . . Like many other Victorians, Henley is aware of duty, tasks, and wages. And, also like many of the Victorians, Henley found in responsibility the hope of a death that would be soothing and serene. His poem, however, leaves us with an image and rhythm which means shared experience, shared "prayer." (pp. 125-26)

The theme of [*Hawthorn and Lavender*] is caught in the lines from Shakespeare's Sonnet LXV which Henley had picked as an epigraph for Volume II of the definitive edition of his work:

''O, how shall summer's honey breath hold out / Against the wrackful siege of battering days?'' The white and pink blossoms and brightly colored fruit of hawthorn symbolize ''summer's honey breath''; and the pale purple flower, the lavender, symbolizes ''the wrackful siege of battering days.''

Although Henley's own pain and desire for easeful death come through clearly enough in the poems, the poems of hawthorn are more numerous and give the volume its most dominant colors. As in the earlier Henley poems, the theme here is not hawthorn and lavender as two separate things; rather hawthorn-and-lavender is ever Henley's theme. Death is still but Life in act, as Henley had described it in *''Matri Dilectissimae.''* (pp. 131-32)

Though many of the individual poems might seem merely competent, Henley is sometimes more than that; and, as a whole, *Hawthorn and Lavender* renders the feeling of Henley's love for Anna and his abiding confidence as death nears. In his more personal poems Henley escaped the confused syntax and the bizarre diction and reliance on a spasmodic punctuation that weaken many of his late ''free-verse'' poems. The poems that are directly personal convince us of a personality who has suffered but has also been deepened by life's battles. (p. 134)

Although Henley never accepted any creed, his poetry is certainly a record of a man who has become more fundamentally religious, a man of a religious conviction that saw no need of creed or ritual. His deepening religious sense finds its most vital expression in *Hawthorn and Lavender.* Yeats, who recognized the strain, tells a story of Henley's interest in the supernatural. Henley had seen a vision of his dead daughter and wanted to get to her. Yeats was touched by Henley's appeal and need. Although Henley apparently never pursued the magic that Yeats's friends had too lightly mocked, there is a calm throughout these late poems. (pp. 134-35)

In *London Voluntaries* Henley utilized more grandly the music metaphor that he had struck in the opening poem to *Hawthorn and Lavender.* In five poems—voluntaries—the poet plays in five different tempos; but, as in **''Praeludium''** of *Hawthorn and Lavender,* the song is visual. (p. 136)

If in these descriptive voluntaries Henley runs the risk of too great excitement and too extensive cataloguing, his experiments in picture and music have their appeal. Henley's Romantic faith is expressed only as it celebrates the several moods of the London scenes. Henley's voluntaries do not, of course, engage us in the way that Eliot's picture of urban life does. Henley's poems are far too diffuse. We need only to surrender to their Romantic vision—whereas Eliot requires great concentration; his scenes are dramatic rather than descriptive, and we earn our synthesis. But Henley's easier poem stands in a symbolic way to its age as Eliot's *The Waste Land* does to his. That such a vision was still possible in a late nineteenth-century poem is in itself remarkable. Amidst all the late nineteenth-century posing and celebration of the artistic over the natural, Henley made a spirited attempt to exult in the two as one. (p. 137)

Henley's enthusiasm for the work of Rudyard Kipling had inspired him to [write a] fairly long poem of high exuberance. That poem—*The Song of the Sword*—Henley dedicated to Kipling; it is now likely to be read not for its own sake but as a manifestation of jingoism. The sword's song is a blatantly militant exposition and exhortation. The sword declares its birth ''a proof'' of God's will, not *the* proof, but nevertheless an important one as it sifts nations. . . . Expressions like ''Ho!

then'' and numerous commands add to the sense of religious militancy. When Henley sent the poem to Frank Harris at the *Fortnightly Review,* an assistant wrote Henley regrets and thanks for a song which had sent Harris' thoughts ''back to Beowulf.'' Henley doubtless deserved more courteous treatment, but it is difficult to consider the effort more than a tour de force.

Shortly before his death in 1903, Henley wrote an even longer song, *A Song of Speed.* . . . The poem is dedicated to Alfred Harmsworth, who had given Henley a ride in his new Mercédes. Henley found the motoring experience exhilarating, and he made the automobile the major symbol of the poem; the Mercédes is ''one of God's messages,'' a message of progress, of advancement, indeed of miracle. It is doubtful that the poem is better than *The Song of the Sword;* the poem depends more on cataloguing, on seriatim. . . . As verse, the appeal of [*A Song of Speed*] is also slight. Henley himself must have felt the limits of such work, for in a letter to Whibley he later called the work ''an effusion.'' *A Song of Speed* is mainly of biographical interest. (pp. 138-39)

[Henley's] poetry records a spirit aware of the pain of life, but a spirit that would not allow pain to be the whole of it. Like *In Hospital,* the whole of Henley's poetry summarizes a spirit that would not—even in an age given to inner broodings—surrender to despair. (p. 141)

> *Joseph M. Flora, in his* William Ernest Henley *(copyright © 1970 by Twayne Publishers, Inc.; reprinted with the permission of Twayne Publishers, a Division of G. K. Hall & Co., Boston), Twayne, 1970, 171 p.*

NORMAN T. GATES   (essay date 1979)

[When Ezra Pound] came to form his revolutionary group of new poets, he nominated H. D., Richard Aldington, and himself as the original Imagists. These three contributed to *Des Imagistes* . . . , the first Imagist anthology, of which Wallace Martin says ''that it was largely responsible for the birth of what we consider 'modern poetry.''' . . . . [In 1933,] Aldington, referring to his own pre-1912 poetry, said:

> At length I grew disgusted with copying and (influenced by Greek Choruses and, strangely enough, Henley) began to write what I called ''rhythms,'' i.e., unrhymed pieces with no formal metrical scheme where the rhythm was created by a kind of inner chant.

Still later, looking back on earlier years, Aldington would say, ''What did the imagists achieve between 1912 and 1917? . . . They made free verse popular—it had already been used by Blake, Whitman, and Henley and by many of the French Symbolists.''

The text of Henley's poetry that Hulme, Aldington and their contemporaries would most likely have read would have been *Poems.* (p. 147)

In his **''Advertisement''** dated 4th September 1897, Henley introduces *Poems* and particularly mentions ''those unrhyming rhythms in which I had tried to quintessentialize, as (I believe) one scarce can do in rhyme, my impressions of the Old Edinburgh Infirmary.'' The poems to which Henley refers were about the period 1873-1875 when he was under Lister's care in Edinburgh; they comprise the first section of *Poems* and are entitled **''In Hospital.''**

There are twenty-nine poems grouped under the **"In Hospital"** caption, and, despite what Henley says, not all are "unrhyming rhythms." Twelve of them are, in fact, sonnets with regular rhyme schemes and metrical patterns. Another group are unrhymed but are structured metrically; only a minority of the poems in this section can properly be called free verse. Even among these, many of the lines can be scanned. (pp. 147-48)

Although Henley mentions only the "unrhymed rhythms" of **"In Hospital,"** there are many other examples of free verse in *Poems* which would have caught the eyes of the "new poets." Both ["**The Song of the Sword**" and "**Arabian Nights' Entertainments**"] . . . , which are given individual sections of the book, are written in free verse. **"The Song of the Sword,"** dedicated significantly to Rudyard Kipling, is as difficult to defend as some of Kipling's own jingoistic poetry which Henley published in the *Scots Observer* in that year. **"Arabian Nights' Entertainments,"** which recaptures a boy's enchantment by these magic stories, is a much better poem.

The twenty-three poems of the **"Bric-A-Brac"** section are all formally structured in rhyme and meter. As Professor Buckley says "perfection of form and vapidity of substance are the rule" here. Almost all of the poetry in the **"Echoes"** section of *Poems* is rhymed: of its forty-seven poems only five are written in true free verse, but one of these, [**"I.M.: Margaritae Soroi,"**] is a particularly fine example. Dr. Buckley suggests that "its only structural analogy in nineteenth century poetry is . . . to be found in the descriptive passages of Heine's *Nordsee*." (pp. 148-49)

Arthur Symons described the next section of *Poems,* **"London Voluntaries,"** when it first appeared in *The Song of the Sword and Other Verses* in 1892, as "the most individual, the most characteristically modern, and the most entirely successful of Mr. Henley's work in verse" [see excerpt above]. It is, however, written in irregular rhyme, and, therefore, in the strict sense of modern free verse, not pertinent to this inquiry, although the loosening of metrical form would certainly have interested the poets of the new century.

The final section of *Poems,* **"Rhymes and Rhythms,"** contains, as its title promises, more free verse than any other division of the book. Of its twenty-seven poems, almost half, including the **"Prologue"** and **"Epilogue"** are written in free verse. The opening stanzas of **"A Desolate Shore"** exemplify Henley's later free verse (and his unique personification of nature's usually romantic pairing—Moon and Sea). . . . (pp. 149-50)

Judging on the evidence of this inventory . . . of free verse in Henley's *Poems*—the book Hulme, Aldington and the other "new poets" would most likely have read—it would seem that . . . [they] were right to include Henley with Blake, Whitman, and the French Symbolists as one of the stepping stones used by modern poets to reach back to the poetic form of the Greek Choruses. (p. 150)

> *Norman T. Gates, "Henley and Free Verse in Modern Poetry," in* Four Decades of Poetry: 1890-1930 *(© Four Decades), Vol. II, No. 3, January, 1979, pp. 145-52.*

ADDITIONAL BIBLIOGRAPHY

Cohen, Edward H. *The Henley-Stevenson Quarrel.* Gainesville: The University Presses of Florida, 1974, 92 p.*

Examines the dissolution of the Henley-Stevenson friendship with the hope of shedding new light on the experiences behind the writers' literary creations.

Cohen, Edward H. "Uncollected Early Poems by William Ernest Henley." *Bulletin of the New York Public Library* (Spring 1976): 297-314.

Discussion of eight previously unpublished early poems by Henley. Cohen suggests that these poems, which appeared between 1869 and 1870 in the journal *Period,* provide evidence that Henley was originally influenced by Swinburne before he became active in the "counterdecadent" movement.

Connell, John. *W. E. Henley.* London: Constable Publishers, 1949, 385 p.

Biography based on the correspondence between Henley and Charles Whibley. Connell constructs an account of Henley's life by examining six volumes of letters to his close friend Whibley.

Cornford, L. Cope. *William Ernest Henley.* London: Constable and Co.; Boston, New York: Houghton Mifflin Co., 1913, 109 p.

Biocritical study by fellow-member of the "Henley regatta."

Elwin, Malcolm. "Andrew Lang and Other Critics." In his *Old Gods Falling,* pp. 182-217. New York: The Macmillan Co., 1939.*

Biography tracing Henley's years as an editor and literary critic.

Greene, Graham. "The Ugly Act." In his *The Lost Childhood and Other Essays,* pp. 129-31. London: Eyre & Spottiswoode, 1951.

A review of John Connell's *W. E. Henley,* focusing on Henley's quarrels with Stevenson and Wilde.

Gregory, Horace. "William Ernest Henley's Career." In his *Spirit of Time and Place,* pp. 113-21. New York: W. W. Norton & Co., 1973.

Biocritical discussion. Gregory examines Henley's relationship with and influence on other prominent writers of his time, such as Yeats and Shaw.

James, Henry. "Letter to Edmund Gosse." In his *The Letters of Henry James, Vol. I,* pp. 385-87, edited by Percy Lubbock. New York: Charles Scribner's Sons, 1920.

Contains a letter to Edmund Gosse, dated 20 November 1901, in which James comments on Henley's withering review of Graham Balfour's *Life of Robert Louis Stevenson.* James sees the critical article as the natural "overflow of Henley's gall."

Lucas, E. V. "W. E. Henley." In his *The Colvins and Their Friends,* pp. 106-33. London: Methuen & Co., 1928.

Correspondence between Henley and Sidney Colvin during the years 1879 to 1881.

Schaefer, William D. "Henley and 'The Hound of Heaven'." *Victorian Poetry* V, No. 3 (1967): 171-81.

Examination of Francis Thompson's possible influence on Henley. Schaefer suggests that Thompson's poem "The Hound of Heaven" was a source of inspiration and a model for Henley's *London Voluntaries.*

Shanks, Edward. "W. E. Henley." In his *First Essays on Literature,* pp. 245-50. 1923. Reprint. Freeport, N.Y.: Books for Libraries Press, 1968.

Critical survey. Shanks argues that Henley lacked the qualities to be even a marginal poet, but that he will be remembered as "a stimulating personality, and, above all, a stimulating editor."

Symons, Arthur. "The Revival of Henley." *The London Quarterly Review,* No. 273 (January 1922): 16-22.

A negative appraisal of Henley's career, written in a far different tone from Symons's early review of *The Song of the Sword* [see excerpt above]. Symons builds his essay around the key phrase: "He had no genius; he was not a great writer."

Thompson, Francis. "William Ernest Henley." In his *A Renegade Poet and Other Essays,* pp. 175-90. Boston: The Ball Publishing Co., 1910.

A critical essay gushing with praise for Henley's criticism and poetry.

Weygandt, Cornelius. ''The Beginnings of the New Order: Henley, Stevenson, and Davidson.'' In his *The Time of Yeats: English Poetry of To-day against an American Background,* pp. 30-66. 1937. Reprint. New York: Russell & Russell, 1969.*
  Lukewarm praise of Henley's work. Weygandt finds Henley to be a poet who was but sporadically touched by genius.

Williamson, Kennedy. *W. E. Henley: A Memoir.* London: Harold Shaylor, 1930, 296 p.
  Biography based on Williamson's reminiscences of Henley's life.

Paul (Johann Ludwig von) Heyse
1830-1914

German novella writer, translator, novelist, poet, dramatist, autobiographer, and critic.

Heyse is an acknowledged master of the novella. His most famous works, *Das Mädchen von Treppi (The Maiden of Treppi)* and *L'arrabiata*, are securely among the best German novellas ever written, though his proposal for structuring the novella—the controversial *Falkentheorie*—has prompted considerable critical debate. In contrast to contemporaries Gottfried Keller and Theodore Storm, who explored the individual's role within society, Heyse focused upon the individual's response to personal dilemmas. His work emphasizes the priority of individual conscience over the dictates of conventional ethics, a position stated most strongly in *The Maiden of Treppi* and in his finest novel, *Kinder der Welt (Children of the World)*. This stance led many of his contemporaries to label him a purveyor of immoral material.

Heyse, whose father and grandfather had been noted philologists, grew up in a scholarly, upper-middle-class home in Berlin. Travel and study in Italy inspired Heyse with love of that country and its language. He returned to Germany, studied philology, and received a doctorate in Romance languages. His earliest poetry, characterized by smooth craftsmanship and delicate language, was noticed by poet Emanuel Geibel, who brought Heyse to the attention of King Maximilian II of Bavaria. In 1854 the king invited Heyse to Munich, offering him a position as court poet. Heyse accepted the king's offer and quickly became a key figure in the *Münchner Dichterkreis*, the Munich poets' circle which met under royal patronage. The group included Geibel, Martin Greif, and Friedrich von Bodenstedt, and was devoted to a narrowly conceived formal beauty. In 1855 Heyse's professional career began with the critical success of the novella *L'arrabiata*. For the next thirty years he was recognized as one of the most important German writers of his day. In 1868 Geibel fell from royal favor and was dismissed from court. Heyse resigned his position as court poet in protest, but continued to work and live in Munich. His conservative aesthetic increasingly clashed with the growth of naturalism, which he felt dwelt unrealistically on the baser aspects of life. While the naturalists expanded the realms acceptable for artistic presentation Heyse stood fast, attacking the new movement through his naturalist parody, *Merlin*. During Heyse's last years, his reputation waned. Nevertheless, he was ennobled in 1910, the same year he received the Nobel prize in literature, becoming the first German so honored.

Critics have variously labeled Heyse a romantic, a realist, and a romantic realist. Despite such disagreement, they commend the charm and color of his early poetry and his facility with language, but do not attribute to it any lasting value. They praise Heyse's excellent translations from the Italian more than they do his own works. His *Falkentheorie*, though, has elicited much commentary. Heyse proposed that certain novellas should "present a significant human fate, an emotional, intellectual, or moral conflict that should reveal to the reader by means of an unusual happening a new aspect of human nature." Some critics view this as a confining prescription,

Courtesy of Prints and Photographs Division, Library of Congres

dictating a specified form for the writing of every novella. Recent criticism contends that Heyse's remarks express his personal preference, offering a formal device he found useful, but not binding, in composing novellas.

Throughout his career, Heyse stressed simplicity and clarity in form and content. He rejected the precepts of literary naturalism, upholding the concept of beauty in art and the nobility of human nature. His belief in individual freedom and self-determination remained constant in a time of changing aesthetic values. Of Heyse's sixty dramas, six novels, and over one hundred novellas and translations, only *L'arrabiata* and *The Maiden of Treppi* are frequently read. It is for these two works and for his outstanding translations that he is recognized today.

PRINCIPAL WORKS

Jungbrunnen (short story) 1849
L'arrabiata (novella) 1855; published in *Novellen*
   [*La rabbiata* published in *Four Phases of Love*, 1857; also
     published as *L'arrabiata*, 1867]
Novellen (novellas) 1855
   [*Four Phases of Love*, 1857; also published as *Love Tales*,
     1862]

Das Mädchen von Treppi   (novella)   1858; published in
   Neve Novellen
   [*The Maiden of Treppi,* 1874]
Neue Novellen   (novellas)   1858
Andrea Delfin   (novella)   1859
   [*Andrea Delfin,* 1864]
Hadrian   (drama)   1865
Hans Lange   (drama)   1866
   [*Hans Lange,* 1885]
Novellen und Terzinen   (novellas)   1867
Gesammelte Werke. 38 vols.   (poetry, novels, novellas, and
   dramas)   1871-1914
Kinder der Welt. 2 vols.   (novel)   1873
   [*Children of the World,* 1882]
Im Paradiese   (novel)   1875
   [*In Paradise,* 1878]
Zwei Gefangene   (novella)   1875
   [*Two Prisoners,* 1893]
Vetter Gabriel   (novella)   1886
*Italienische Dichter seit der Mitte der Achtzehn
   Jahrhunderts.* 5 vols.   (poetry and criticism)   1889-
   1905
Merlin. 3 vols.   (novel)   1892
Maria von Magdala   (drama)   1899
   [*Mary of Magdala,* 1900]
Jungenderrinnerungen und Bekenntnisse   (autobiography)
   1900
Die Hexe von Corso und andere novellen   (novellas)   1969

THE WESTMINSTER AND FOREIGN QUARTERLY REVIEW
(essay date 1858)

[Of Paul Heyse's] tales it is pleasant to be able to say that they are mostly genuine works, delightful to read, and infinitely superior to most of the fictions with which we are acquainted, not only in literary workmanship, and in artistic conception, but in dramatic power. In each volume there are four short tales. We prefer the "**Novellen**" to the "**Neue Novellen**" on the whole; but as the former have been translated into English by Mr. George Kingsley, under the somewhat unattractive title of "**Four Phases of Love**," we shall merely refer to them, urging the reader by all means to get sight of them, in English or in the original, for the sake of the exquisite story *La Rabbiata,* a perfect gem of a few pages, and the piquant little anecdote *Marion,* which ought to have been developed into a longer story. The "**Neue Novellen**" open with a story called *Das Mädchen von Treppi,* which is not only our favorite. . . . [but also] a good illustration of the author's powers. (pp. 502-03)

Unequal the tales are, but none of them are the product of the circulating library. Heyse writes a story because he has some psychological problem which demands artistic expression. . . . A keen and subtle insight into the working of passion, and a very charming style, distinguish his stories. What an Italian colour there is in [*Das Mädchen von Treppi!*] How the direct, simple, passionate nature of Fenice is exhibited in unforced, spontaneous touches! How *real* is this imaginative picture! Still more remarkable in this respect is *La Rabbiata.* In the *Blinden* and the *Kreisrichter* there is a want of steady psychological truth; in each there is a good idea, and some interesting pages, but we feel that the author has not mastered the secrets of his

characters, and that a deeper experience of life would have given another turn to these stories. (p. 515)

"Realism in Art: Recent German Fiction," in The Westminster and Foreign Quarterly Review *n.s. Vol. XIV, No. III, October 1, 1858, pp. 488-518.**

GEORG BRANDES   (essay date 1875)

With Heyse the "novelle" is not a picture of the times, or a *genre* painting; something always *does* happen with him, and it is always something unexpected. The plot, as a rule, is so arranged that at a certain point an unforseen change takes place; a surprise which, when the reader looks back, always proves to have had a firm and carefully prepared foundation in what went before. At this point the action sharpens; here the threads unite to form a knot from which they are spun around in an opposite direction. The enjoyment of the reader is based upon the art with which the purpose of the action is gradually more and more veiled and hidden from view, until suddenly the covering falls. His surprise is caused by the skill with which Heyse apparently strays farther and farther away from the goal which rose beyond the starting-point, until he finally discovers that he has been led through a winding path and finds himself exactly above the point where the story began. (pp. 84-5)

In the demand he makes on the "novelle," he has especially characterized the task he has imposed on himself and faithfully fulfilled. He prefers eccentric to typical everyday instances. As a rule, we are quite as sure of finding "the falcon" in his prose narratives, as a certain judge was of finding a woman at the bottom of every crime. In "**L'Arrabbiata**," the biting of a hand is "the falcon"; in the "**Bild der Mutter**" (**The Mother's Portrait**) it is the elopement; in "**Vetter [Cousin] Gabriel**," it is the letter copied from the "lover's letter-writer." If the reader will himself search for the aforesaid wild bird, he will gain an insight into the poet's method of composition. It is not always so easily captured as in the cases just cited. With a power of investigation, a nimble grace, which is rare in a man who is not of Roman race, Heyse has understood how to tie the knots of events and disentangle them again, to present and solve the psychologic problem which he has *isolated* in the "novelle." He has the faculty of singling out exceptional, unusual cases from the general state of culture, and the condition of the society of which he is a member, and presenting them purely and sharply in the form of a "novelle," without permitting the action to play into the unreal and fabulous, as is the wont of romantic novelists, and without ever allowing it to run into a merely epigrammatic point. His "novellen" are neither brief romances nor long anecdotes. They have at the same time fulness and strictly-defined form. And circumscribed as this form may be, it has yet proved itself sufficiently flexible to be able to embrace within its limits the most diverse materials. The "novellen" of Heyse play on many strings; most abundantly on the tender and the *spirituelle,* but also on the comic (as in the amusing tale, "**Die Wittwe von Pisa**"— **The Widow of Pisa**), the fantastic (as in the Hoffman-like "**Cleopatra**"); indeed, in a single instance, the awful (in the painful nocturne, "**Der Kinder Sünde der Väter Fluch**"—**The Sins of the Children the Curse of the Fathers**). The "novelle" as it is treated by Heyse borders on the provinces of Alfred de Musset, [Prosper Mérimée, Ernst Theodor Wilhelm Hoffman and Ludwig Tieck]; but has, however, its own special domain, as well as its very individual profile.

Meanwhile, ready as I am to recognize the significance of this sharp profile as the individual characteristic of the Heyse "novelle,'' and its significance for the novel in general as a work of art, it is equally hard for me to allow this to pass as the decisive norm for the estimation of individual stories. (pp. 86-7)

By the stress [Heyse] lays on what the novel within the novel is, he seems to oppose alike the overestimation of style, and of ideal purport. But of all his ''novellen'' in verse **''Der Salamander''** (The Salamander) appears to me to stand the highest; of his prose works **''Derletzte Centaur''** (The Last Centaur) is one of my favorites. The first of these seems to me to bear off the palm on account of the diction; the last, on account of the idea.

There is no need of taking pains to seek for a ''falcon'' in **''Salamander'';** there is no plot in it, the characters have no development worth mentioning, and yet every reader of any susceptibility will experience such lively enjoyment under the influence of the magic of these terzettos, that it will seem to him as if this poem, in addition to its own merits, possessed also all those which it lacks. Of the epic repose, of the objective style, which is Heyse's precise ideal in the domain of the ''novelle,'' not much will here be found. This epic repose is perhaps less adapted on the whole to the restless spirit of our time. The realization on this ideal of Heyse's has, properly speaking, only perfectly succeeded in the few prose ''novellen,'' which do not touch upon the civilization of modern society, as in those genial pasticcios of the olden time: **''Die Stickerin von Traviso''** and **''Geoffroy und Garcinde,''** where the noble, simple style of the old Italian or provençal form of narrative is idealized, or when the materials are taken from the life of the people in Italy or Tyrol; for the people in those lands are themselves a simple piece of the Middle Ages cast in *a form.* Such a story as that little jewel **''L'Arrabiata,''** which was the foundation of Heyse's fame, actually attains its rights through its plain, rigid setting; adorned with the decorations of style, or with psychologically polished facets, it would lose its entire beauty, if not become impossible. In the same way **''Die Stickerin von Treviso,''** which probably, next to the work just named, has reaped the greatest harvest of applause, in its touching simplicity and grandeur, is so thoroughly one with its chronicle form, that it cannot be conceived of without this. But in instances where scenes from purely modern civilization are described, the style cannot be too individual and nervous. Heyse himself cannot avoid making his aim in this respect proportionate to his materials; how feverish is the recital in the pretty invalid story in letters **''Unheilbar!''** (Incurable.) However, it is apparently with the utmost reluctance, and without the free exercise of his will, that he permits himself to be carried away into such a passionately surging and trembling style as in **''Salamander.''** This creation is pure style, its beauty depends wholly and entirely on the captivating charm of its metric diction, and yet throughout not a word will be found that is not to the purpose. The entire work teems with active life, every change in style is deeply felt and transparent; the struggling soul of the writer lies like an open book before the reader. The situations are insignificant and commonplace; no Bengal illumination, not even a final tableau. But these remarkable, incredibly beautiful, unnaturally easy, nervously passionate terzettos, which question and answer, jest, sing and lament, invest the theatrical, the enamored yet thoroughly composed blasé coquette, the heroine, and the passion she inspires, with such a charm that no exciting story, with crisis and pole, could be more captivating. Toward the close of the poem the glorious terzettos, which throughout have been transformed into quite a new species of metre, ring out in a manner as

surprising as it is genial and bold, in the chords of a triple ritornelle, invested with all the freshness of nature. Such a poem as this will maintain its place in spite of all theories.

Upon the whole, however, it seems to me that Heyse has formed an incorrect conception of the significance of poetic style. Theoretically, he fears its independent development, and cannot tolerate any works which are ''mere diction and style.'' Nevertheless, in such poems as **''Das Feenkind''** (The Fairy Child), and still more in such poems as **''Frauenemancipation''** (Female Emancipation), he has himself furnished productions of this kind. The first of these poems is refined and graceful, but the raillery in it is of too ample length—we do not care to eat an undue amount of whipped cream; the other, whose tendency, however, is the best, suffers from a loquacity without any salt. But a distinctly marked style is by no means the same thing as the formal virtuosoship of diction. That an artist of language like Heyse, the translator of Guisti, of the troubadours, of Italian and Spanish folk-songs, must possess this in the fullest degree, is understood as a matter of course. And yet the truly artistic style is not that formal grace which spreads uniformly over everything. Style, in the highest sense of the word, is fulfilment, a form completed from every point of view. Where the coloring of language, the phraseology, diction, and personal accent, still possess a certain abstract homogeneousness, where the author has failed to mirror the character at every essential point in all the outer forms, the drapery of language, of however light a texture it may consist, will hang stiff and dead about the personality of the speaker. The perfect modern style, on the contrary, envelops it as the flowing robe envelops the form of the Grecian orator, serving to relieve the attitude of the body and every movement. The diction of the mere virtuoso, even when ''brilliant,'' may be traditional and trivial; genuine style is never so. With the mode of narration of Heyse's ''novellen,'' I have not much fault to find; his dramatic diction, on the contrary, does not please me so well.

There are no doubt many who think that if Heyse's historic dramas have not gained the recognition accorded his ''novellen,'' it is because they are invested with too little action, and too much style. If the word style, however, be understood as I have here defined it, it should certainly rather be asserted that the iambic form used was worn threadbare, and that these works have not style enough. The diction in **''Elizabeth Charlotte,''** for example, neither sufficiently bears the coloring of the period in which the scenes are laid, nor of the persons who speak. Only compare it with the dry posthumous memoirs of the princess. The poet who, with his fabulous facility for orienting himself in every poetic form, can produce a drama as easily as he can tell a story, has taken his task almost too easily. The little tragedy **''Maria Moroni,''** a drama which may be ranked next to his ''novellen,'' through its plan as well as through its characterization, might worthily stand side by side with the Italian dramas of Alfred de Musset, of which it reminds us, were not its language-coloring by far too dull and cold. The dialogues of Musset not only sparkle with wit, but glow with ardor and with life. In his dramas Heyse is not personally present with his whole soul at every point. And yet this ''at every point'' is the style.

Inasmuch, therefore, as I have placed the highest estimate on **''Salamander,''** of all the versified ''novellen,'' on account of its excellence of diction, so for the sake of its idea I would give a high place to the prose narrative, **''Der letzte Centaur''** (The Last Centaur), although the latter is, at the same time, farthest removed from the requirements of the definition. It does not treat of an occurrence or a conflict in a defined sphere of life, nor of any especial psychologic instance, but of life itself; it permits the entire modern life to be mirrored at once within a narrow frame. A shot at the central point is so refreshing; why deny it? The peripheric character of some others of Heyse's works is to blame for their not being of greater interest. After reading through a long series of "novellen" one cannot help longing for an art form which is capable of embracing the more significant, universally current ideas and problems in poetic form.

Heyse's dramas are in the highest degree heterogeneous: civil tragedies, mythological, historic, patriotic plays of the most dissimilar artistic nature. His talent is so pliant that he feels at liberty to enter upon any theme. A strong impulse for the historical, Heyse has never had; his historical dramas have all sprung from a patriotic sentiment, and are effective chiefly through this sentiment. The one of his groups of dramas for which the poet is most noted is that which deals with antique subjects. At a time when modern political action was everywhere demanded of the higher drama, this employment of old Grecian and Roman materials was lamented over and derided in Germany, with an utter lack of comprehension. People asked what in all the world there was in such a subject as the rape of the Sabine women, or Meleager, or Hadrian, that could possibly interest the poet or any one else. To those who read critically it is very evident what must have attracted Heyse to these themes. They incorporate for him his favorite ideas concerning woman's love and woman's destiny, and his own being is mirrored in them. Any one who will compare the warm-blooded drama "**Meleager**" with Swinburne's "**Atalanta in Kalydon**," which handles the same material, will find occasion for many interestng observations, concerning the peculiarity of the two poets. "**Hadrian**" has perhaps perplexed the critic the most. What could attract the poet to a relation so wholly foreign to us as that between Hadrian and Antinous, one, too, that is so decidedly a reminder of the shady side of antique life, seems almost incomprehensible. I, for my part, rank "**Hadrian**" highest of all of Heyse's dramas. (pp. 88-93)

In this drama, by way of exception, all that is scenic is of the highest effect. The actual reason why Heyse, with all his great ability for the stage, still failed to meet with decided success in his dramas, is unquestionably because he does not possess the German pathos proper, that of Schiller. Not until the pathos is broken, not until it has become half pathological, is he able to treat it with entire originality. Genuine dramatic pathos from the depths of the heart, with him easily becomes inartistically national, patriotic, and somewhat commonplace. This is the reason why the representation of manly action proper is not his province. To however high a degree he may have command in his poetry over the passive qualities of manhood, such as dignity, earnestness, repose, dauntless courage, he nevertheless, like Goethe, wholly lacks the active momentum. A vigorous, effective plan of action that follows a defined goal is as little the essential part of his dramas as of his novels and romances. If there now and then appear an energetic action, it is occasioned by despair; the individual is forced into a dilemma in which the only apparent means of escape may be gained through the utmost daring alone. . . . Although from the reason already cited the genuine dramatic nerve and sinew are almost always lacking in Heyse's works, the hindrances which are placed in the way of the poet's decided success on the stage are not of such importance that he may not overcome them with time and celebrate a scenic triumph. (pp. 93-4)

["**Kinder der welt**"] is a dignified and nobel protest against those who would fetter freedom of thought and instruction in our day. It has to back it all polemics against dogmas. All its main personages, with a clear consciousness of their position, are made to live in that atmosphere of freer ideas, which is the vital air of modern times. It is one of those works which possess the intensity of a long-repressed, late-matured personal experience, and therefore has a vitality to which no awkwardness of form, no lack of form, can be prejudicial. The book, as a first attempt, is wanting in many of the elements of the genuine romance; the hero, as might have been expected, lacks much in resolution, in active manly vigor; it does not concentrate itself in a single, absolutely dominating interest; the all-engulfing erotic element does not permit the idea to stand forth clear and central, as it was conceived by the poet. . . . [The] entire little band of heroes of the book content themselves with the defensive, and when Edwin has finally completed his epoch-making work, the romance ends. Closely associated with this lack is the undue softness of feeling in those parts which treat of Balder. The absence of that strict observance of proportion and limits which distinguish Heyse's "novellen," is plainly felt in this romance. But how would it be possible that great merits in a work of such extent should not be purchased with some lacks. Not only have the ideal female characters here the same points of excellence as in the "novellen"; but the poet has also enlarged his sphere in a high degree; even the least ideal figures, Christiane, Mohr, Marquard, are incomparable. And what a flood of genuine humanity streams through this romance! What a fund of true, versatile culture it contains! It is not only a courageous book, it is also an edifying one. (pp. 95-6)

Freedom of thought was the fundamental idea of the "**Kinder der Welt**"; freedom of moral action is the fundamental idea of the romance "**Im Paradiese**," yet not in such a way that this work must be considered an attempt at justification; for if the freedom of thought Heyse advocates may be designated as absolute, the freedom of moral action is only relative. Moreover, "**Im Paradiese**" is a work of quite a different character than the first romance. Even the fact that the scenes of the early romance are laid in keen, critical Berlin, the second one in merry, pleasure-loving Munich, indicates the difference. While the "**Kinder der Welt**" may be called a philosophic romance, "**Im Paradiese**" is a sort of *roman comique* [comic novel], light, graceful, and full of a raillery blended with earnestness. Its greatest value is in being the psychology of an entire city of importance, and the portrait of the social and art circles of this city. All Munich is embraced in this book, and as a matter of course, the artist life of this city of artists occupies the main place. The conversations and reflections on art have not the useless and abstract character in the pages of this book that they assume in the ordinary art-romance; we feel that it is no theorist but a connoisseur who speaks, and a genuine studio atmosphere is diffused throughout all portions of the book. (pp. 97-8)

So far as the entanglements and composition of the plot are concerned, "**Im Paradiese**" denotes an undoubted progress. The interest is sustained throughout, and what is more, it continually increases; a commendation that cannot be bestowed on "**Kinder der Welt.**" Now and then, however, the means used to forward the plot are applied in rather an unskilful manner. . . . Yet in German romances not the plot, but the delineation of character is the main thing, and in almost all its subordinate figures this book reveals a new side of Heyse's talent. Such forms as Angelica, Rosenbusch, Kohl, Schnetz, have sportive, manifold life that formerly had been almost entirely excluded from Heyse's style. In a word, Heyse's mind has gained humor, the humor of mature manhood, one might almost say, of forty years of age; but a delicate sagacious, quiet humor which renders complete the gift of the poet and invests its coloring with the true blending.

We have run through the circle of ideas and forms in which this poetic soul has found its expression. We have seen how Heyse, at last, in the romance accommodated himself to the thought agitating modern times, and to which the "novellen" form was not able to give adequate space. Moreover, I pointed out one "novelle" which was not less distinguished by its fundamental thought than **"Der Salamander"** was by its style.

Each time that Heyse has attempted to gain a modern interest for ancient myths, he has been fortunate. The charming little youthful poem, **"Die Furie" (The Fury)**, is among the best that he has written. In a little drama, **"Perseus"** (not included in his collected works), he has given a new interpretation of the Medusa myth; he has felt pity for poor, beautiful Medusa, to whom was allotted the cruel fate of turning every one into stone, and he informs us that the envy of the goddesses who were jealous of her love for Perseus is alone to blame for this. Her head falls by the hand of her own lover, while she, in order not to harm him through her pernicious gaze, buries her face in the sand. Heyse has transformed the ancient myth into an original and sorrowful Märchen [fairytale]. The story of the **"Centaur"** is bright, and full of profound thought. . . . It is done with consummate art, and yet in the most natural way in the world. He first, so to speak, brings together two circles, then a third circle, and in the latter he conjures up the Centaur. The first circle is the world of the living, the second the world of the dead, the third easily and naturally comprises the world of the supernatural. The story begins, contrary to Heyse's custom, in a purely autobiographical way, therefore, with the strongest possible elements of reality. (pp. 98-9)

All the qualities which make a poetic work an enjoyment to the reader are combined in this "Märchen"; an exalted humor, which casts a gentle glow over all the details, the tenderest semi-tone and the finest clare-obscure, that permits the action of the piece to glide gently from the light of day into a dream of a circle of the dead, and then again allows the twilight of the shadow-world to be illumined by a sunbeam from old Hellas. Add to this a profound thought, which is entirely original to its poet. For this sportive tale is in reality a hymn to freedom in art as well as in life, and to freedom as Heyse has conceived it. In his eyes freedom does not consist in a struggle for freedom (as, for instance, in the case of the Norwegian author Henrik Ibsen), but it is the protest of nature against dogmas in the religious sphere, of nature against conventionality in the social and moral sphere. Through nature to freedom! that is his path and that his watchword. (pp. 102-03)

> *Georg Brandes, "Paul Heyse" (1875), in his* Eminent Authors of the Nineteenth Century, *translated by Rasmus B. Anderson, T. Y. Crowell & Co., 1886 (and reprinted in his* Creative Spirits of the Nineteenth Century, *translated by Rasmus B. Anderson, Thomas Y. Crowell Company, 1923, pp. 54-105).*

THE SPECTATOR   (essay date 1882)

Paul Heyse has won for himself a good name in German literature as the most elegant of living novelette-writers, one who tells in limpid and graceful prose, stories that have an imme-diate and agreeable aesthetic effect. And these stories are thoroughly characteristic of their writer. For Heyse loves to skim the surface of life, he is afraid of its deeper emotions, and even when a serious note is touched in his writings, it is rarely elicited by a nobler feeling than that of sensuous passion. It was therefore a great surprise when, just nine years ago, he suddenly came before the world, not only with a long novel in six closely-printed books, but with a novel that claimed to be a philosophical romance, written with a deep and moral purpose. Much discussed and criticised at first, it achieved finally little more than a *succès d'estime* [critical success], and we much question the wisdom of presenting the book to an English public. From the preface prefixed by the anonymous translator, we perceive that he or she (we incline to the latter supposition) treats the work as though it were a contribution of real value to the weary question whether morals rest upon a simply ethical or a theological basis. In real fact, the book is nothing of the kind; as a party manifesto, it is absolutely worthless. Heyse is too limited a thinker for his conclusions to have the slightest weight. He is nothing but a dilettante in psychology and philosophy, as in art. Thus he imagines the keynote of *Children of the World* to lie in the Schopenhauer philosophy, yet we doubt if the grim Sybarite of the Swan would recognise his own features as mirrored in the character of Toinette Marchand. The real truth is, that it is as a novel, and as a novel only, that *Children of the World* can be judged, and by that standard alone it can stand or fall. As a novel, it lacks homogeneity; the story is disjointed and involved, and in some of the most essential features so hopelessly obscure, that, for example, one incident may be interpreted in different ways, according to the reader's liking. For ourselves, after two careful perusals of the work, in the original and the translation, we are still uncertain whether a catastrophe took place in reality, or only in the imagination of the hysterical and overwrought female to whom it may, or may not, have happened. For actuality, a commodity in which Heyse does not deal, is more than commonly absent from a book which more than commonly required it.

It is not easy to tell the nominal story of *Children of the World,* for it contains several stories that run side by side. The main proposition is supposed to be the contrast between the so-called children of the world, i.e., the freethinkers, in contradistinction to the orthodox believers, self-styled children of God. But this proposition breaks down at once, and reveals Heyse as hopelessly unfair and one-sided. Or perhaps he is only ignorant, but if so, he should not have written about that of which he does not know. Not only religious professors, but humanity and good-sense are outraged in making a lying, fawning hypocrite the representative of the religious faction. No one, except perhaps a rabid atheist, can be so biassed as to imagine that this is a becoming representative of a creed which yet numbers among its adherents pure-minded and noble, even if narrow thinkers. Nor has the pious rascal even the merit of novelty to recommend him: he is a well-worn figure among the stock-in-trade of novel-writers; and yet on him rests all the onus of defending from scorn the religious believers, for the two other figures, also styled Children of God, play so secondary a part, and are so faintly depicted, that it is not possible to determine whether their professions rest upon sincere conviction or habit; and whether their gentleness and kindliness of feeling springs not rather from native goodness than from reasoned belief. What is a a latitudinarian? it has been rightly asked, but one whose views have breadth? yet in a book professedly written to spread latitudinarianism the writer at the outset stamps himself as lacking in the habit of mind essential to this dogma. A book like this can certainly not effect its purpose; it will convert the orthodox as little to tolerance as a tract impresses the man who refuses to think as a slave. As a polemic in behalf of toleration, the book is especially superfluous for England, where the State does not meddle with private convictions, and where religion is still something more living than an artificial dam raised by astute and unbelieving statesmen out of the decaying ruins of a shaken faith, a code of crystallised and lifeless dogmas, only kept in their place by aid of gendarmes. Such a religion must of necessity be false and empty, and can only survive so long as the patriarchal dream continues to exist that it is the duty of the State to watch over the theoretical opinions of its members, forgetting that deeds alone belong to its jurisdiction. It is perhaps therefore no wonder that Heyse can see nothing in religion beyond a *fable convenue* [accepted story].

In his freethinkers Heyse has given us more variety than in his believers. We are presented with a professor of philosophy, who reconciles the doctrines of Schopenhauer and Spinoza—in a fashion of Heyse's—an idealist, a kind-hearted but offensively sensuous materialist, a hedonist, an atheist, and a social democrat of the impracticable type to which these men too commonly belong in Germany, unhappily for the cause of liberty. The women are an ugly, middle-aged, hysterical pianoforte teacher; a young girl of Jewish blood by her mother's side, of Christian by her father's, "who finds it impossible to believe what she cannot comprehend;" and a mysterious character, Toinette, who starts up from no one knows where, and who, though the most interesting character in the book, has no more actuality than Goethe's Mignon. It is difficult to imagine how any one born into this terrestrial globe could be so ignorant, so irresponsible, as Toni is represented. . . . Her ultimate beloved, Edwin, the philosopher, has during her maidenhood tried in vain to cure her of her pessimism, and playing the part of an inverted Mephistopheles, endeavoured to make her love life. In this process he has hopelessly lost his heart, or far more correctly, he has become the victim of a morbid sensual passion, which Heyse seems unable to distinguish from love. Rejected by this fascinating syren to whom all men fall victims, Edwin consoles himself by contracting marriage with his pupil Lea. . . . The love-making of this pair is unutterably, though unintenionally, comic. Edwin begins by telling Lea the whole story of his infatuation for Toinette. "I was involved," he says, "in a passion which, like a demoniacal glamour, made me a stranger to myself," and adds that he is "a scarcely healed fugitive escaped out of a hard fight." He then proceeds to explain to her in the calmest, most metaphysical manner, what he feels for her (Lea), couching his language in scholastic terms borrowed from Spinoza, "as far as whom," he said smiling, "we had not come in our readings.". . . Why Edwin is held so irresistibly by all the women with whom he comes in contact, is far from clear. Indeed, in a book full of shadows, his figure is the most shadowy, a mere puppet, a lay figure, upon which the heroines pile their affections. We cannot see that any of the characters have flesh and blood, they are not even types of the personages they would represent. They are little else but marionnettes, pulled now with a transcendental string, now with a communistic, a musical, a philistine, and so forth. Few novels better exemplify the fatal tendency of German novelists to write of life as it is imagined, but not lived. In Heyse's short tales, where he only treats of an episode in a life, his incapacity to draw a complete character matters less. But in a novel, and especially one laid on such ambitious foundations, all-round characters are imperative. But Heyse can take hold of one point only in his figures, and this he fiercely illuminates with his magic lantern, with the fatal result

of leaving all the rest in preternatural darkness, and thus detracting from the possibility of feeling these people to be real. Every one of the characters in *Children of the World* is a fragment of a virtue or a characteristic which Heyse designed to illustrate. Even the most happy figure in the book, the cripple Balder, Edwin's brother, lacks substance. He is cousin-german to Dickens's Tiny Tim, but he has not his English rival's vitality. There is a want of real atmosphere about both characters and situations, both are too abstract, too over-refined. A writer who is not concrete must at least lead us into higher, more ideal regions of thought. Yet it is just here that Heyse fails, and notably in *Children of the World*. While treating of life in a dreamy, poetical manner, his people often act anything but poetically. There is a tone pervading his books that offends by its careless indifference to all morality. For virtue, there is little to choose between his believers or his freethinkers. As a book with a purpose, *Children of the World* is pointless; as a novel, inartistic; as a piece of reasoning, crude and jejune.

And yet, like all Heyse's works, this novel can be read, though we doubt, if stripped of its original grace of language, it will much commend itself to English readers. Still, there is undoubtedly a certain charm about Heyse's mode of writing that casts a spell over us while we read, forcing us to ignore his glaring improbabilities. The English translator has done his or her task in adequate, workmanlike style, and has clearly expended much pains on a most difficult, we had almost said hopeless, task; for Heyse's speech is a very apt illustration how the language of every country is an evidence in record of its characters and manners. Such situations, modes of thought and feeling as Heyse has depicted in *Children of the World* are imaginable in Germany and in the German tongue, but they lose a large part of their not too solid reality in their divorce from their native speech, gaining instead an uncomfortable semblance of absurdity and childishness. (pp. 1583-84)

"Books: 'Children of the World'," in The Spectator (© 1882 by The Spectator), Vol. 55, No. 2841, December 9, 1882, pp. 1583-84.

THE ATLANTIC MONTHLY (essay date 1893)

The appearance of Herr Paul Heyse's *Merlin,* in the sixtieth year of the author's age, recalls the fact that this is the age Goethe had reached when he wrote *Die Wahlverwandtschaften;* and just as Goethe went back, in the latter novel, to the idea that had given origin to *Werther,* so, by a further singular coincidence, does *Merlin* revive the moral that underlies *Kinder der Welt.* In Goethe's case, what is depicted is the conflict that arises when the passions of the individual run counter to the conventions of society. In Herr Paul Heyse's two romances, *Kinder der Welt* and *Merlin,* the Faustus creed is preached, that men may work out their own salvation without the conventional props of either society or religion. The hero of *Kinder der Welt,* who is wanting in all concern for social laws and regard for orthodoxy, is represented as being none the less happy and successful, inasmuch as he progresses steadily along the pathway of art. His duplicate, George, in *Merlin,* fails so to progress because he commits a fault, gives himself up to inactivity and remorse,—to remorse, which is retrospection, the very reverse of progress,—and ends, in consequence, most miserably.

The substance of the philosophy of the early romance is maintained intact, but *Merlin* adds to its pagan, masculine creed a provisional clause,—the clause, namely, that man may work out his own salvation, provided only he works. From the moral standpoint, this clause is, therefore, the new element which the book offers. And the fact that the spirit of the provision is qualifying reminds one again of Goethe and *Die Wahlver-wandtschaften;* for what is the moral resignation of the baron, in Goethe's later novel, but a modification of the mortal despair of Werther, the hero of the poet's younger days? Indeed, authors seldom lose altogether the insights of their youth, but, as we see, they broaden them. In old age the outer eye is farsighted. The inner eye, on the contrary, sees distant extremes in youth,—sees perfect success or Werther-like despairs. Betimes the spiritual eye takes note of averages and exceptions. And just as society makes laws first, then equity, so do poets first write books, then publish addenda; *Merlin* being such an addendum,—an addendum made by the author, in the decline of life, to the foregoing works of his early manhood. (pp. 410-11)

That the author should have been able to write it, as he declares he did, in the six weeks of the summer of 1891 is a fact that can be explained only by learning that the main contents of the romance are the ripened fruit of previous years of reflection: the writing was a gathering in rather than a sowing of ideas; a harvest, not a new creation. All the chief incidents of the plot were ready drawn twenty years ago or more, those of the earlier chapters being founded upon events in his own life. (p. 414)

Merlin, in short, was for many years the author's mental diary; and unless his present intention not to write his memoirs be given up, the literary student will hardly come into possession of a better guide through certain circumstances of Herr Heyse's literary life than this romance affords. It fills a place among his books corresponding to that which *The Mill on the Floss* fills among the writings of George Eliot; there are more personal reminiscences, or rather more analogies of personal reminiscences, in *Merlin*'s pages than have been confided to any other book. The complete author is here, even in such details as his methods and habits of work. . . . The personages of his tales, too, like those of his hero's, are creations of imagination; never does he model them (at least consciously) after his acquaintances in actual life. Just as George closes the window of his chamber that he may not see the peasant's wife as she sneaks at evening into the woods with her paramour, so does Heyse exclude from his poetic vision the gross figures of Labor and vile Lust. The factory in *Merlin* is kept characteristically in the background of the tale, whereas an open-air sermon of the factory doctor's is allowed to rise by force of innate grandeur into memorable prominence. George Falkner's scorn of fashion in literature, finally, and the front that he starts out to maintain against it, answer, in this symbolical and disguised biography, to the author's own literary attitude. (pp. 414-15)

The style in *Merlin* is broad throughout, and is the same for narrations, descriptive paragraphs, and conversations. A closer likeness to Goethe's *Wilhelm Meister* and *Elective Affinities,* in this particular, has not been produced of late years. Like these books, moreover, *Merlin* abounds with matter superfluous, with Confessions of a Beautiful Soul, in the form of poems, aphorisms, and fragments of tragedies: it is, in short, a genuine poet's vade mecum [manual], or precisely that which nearly every notable German romance of the elder novelists has been for three generations past. (p. 415)

> *"Paul Heyse," in* The Atlantic Monthly *(copyright © 1893, by The Atlantic Monthly Company, Boston, Mass.), Vol. 71, No. 425, March, 1893, pp. 410-15.*

WILLIAM WINTER (essay date 1903)

It is suggested to the readers and spectators of the drama of "Mary of Magdala" that it aims to depict a fanciful state of facts and circumstances, such as might have existed anterior to the establishment of Christianity, at a time when Jesus of Nazareth—around whom, although he is not introduced, the action circulates—was viewed exclusively as a man, and had not yet, in the eyes of any considerable number of persons, been invested with a sacred character. The picture of his personality that has been made in these imaginary scenes might seem sacrilegious, if this point of view were ignored. The allusions to him, under the various designations of Preacher, Prophet, Nazarene, etc., by Caiaphas, the High Priest of Jerusalem, by Flavius, the young Roman soldier, and by Judas,—here presented as a Hebrew patriot,—are such as might naturally be made, by different orders of men, with reference to a being human like themselves, and not, to their minds, in any sense divine; and, accordingly, these allusions should not be misconstrued as intending to disparage a Christian ideal. The defection of Judas from his leader is ascribed to loss of faith in that leader's ability and purpose forcibly to free the Jews from bondage to Rome, while his subsequent betrayal of that leader is attributed to frenzied rage,—Judas and Mary of Magdala having been lovers, and Mary, in her contrition and in her practical regneration, having broken that alliance, repudiated him, and given her heart to Heaven. The tendency of the drama, in the English form, as here printed, while telling a romantic story of action and depicting aspects of Hebrew life in ancient Jerusalem, is to diffuse an influence of charity and to suggest the celestial victory of a human soul, triumphant over sin and sorrow, through belief in Divine goodness. The German original . . . is human and compassionate in spirit; but it is neither poetical nor spiritual, and, in some particulars, it lacks refinement. Its exposition of the heroine's shame is somewhat needlessly specific and ample; its portrayal of Flavius, the young Roman lover, is carnal and coarse; and it makes the motive of Judas not only the fanatical resentment of a disappointed patriot, but the sensual jealousy of a discarded paramour. In its original form it would have proved offensive; in fact, it could not have been presented. The present adaptation, which was first written in prose and then rewritten in verse, presents the component parts of the original; but, in its treatment of them, it follows a free course, making essential modifications, alike in the structure, the character, and the tone, and resulting in a paraphrase. Upon a first reading of the German drama it seemed impracticable for the English stage; but a later study of it prompted the thought that, since the subject represented by the Magdalen has, whether for good or evil, become a stock theme in theatrical composition and almost continually recurrent on the stage, a salutary influence might, perhaps, be diffused by utilizing this fabric in a modified form; showing this representative type of degraded womanhood as a repentant sinner, and indicating—without either a specious embellishment of vicious life or a sentimental appeal to maudlin sympathy—the only refuge, comfort, and hope that the penitent can ever find. (pp. 5-6)

> *William Winter, in his preface to* Mary of Magdala: An Historical and Romantic Drama in Five Acts *by Paul Heyse, translated by William Winter, The Macmillan Company, 1903, pp. 5-7.*

LAWRENCE A. McLOUTH (essay date 1910)

Paul Heyse's literary works are divided into lyrics, tales in verse, short stories in prose, novels, dramas and some translations. His verse is finished, brilliant, full of color and harmony, but it never reaches the lyric heights of such great singers as Goethe, Heine, or Eichendorff. But none can deny its beauty. (pp. x-xi)

[Of Heyse's novels, *Kinder der Welt, Im Paradiese, Roman der Stiftsdame, Merlin, Über Allen Gipfeln,* and *Die Geburt der Venus,*] the first is the best. Perhaps, as Richard M. Meyer says, the short story writer has stood in the way of the novelist: that is, the quickly moving narrative, accustomed to stop when the climax is reached fails to interest the reader so keenly in the descending action. But in spite of all adverse criticism, deserved and undeserved, Heyse's novels are among the best that Germany has produced. . . .

He wrote some fifteen "novels in verse," as he calls them, the first, *Margherita Spoletina,* appearing in 1849, while Heyse was still a student in his teens, the last, *Das Feenkind,* belonging to the year 1868. The most ambitious and the longest is *Thekla, Ein Gedicht in neun Gesängen.* The character of these little epics is very uneven but all of them show unusual mastery of language and metrical form. As to content, some of them have no very strong moral foundation. Perhaps *Die Brüder* . . . though short, is the best. *Urica* . . . is a pessimistic tale of love between black and white. (p. xi)

Of his quite numerous dramas *Die Sabinerinnen* . . . won the prize offered by Maximilian II, but was never a great success; his *Hadrian* . . . stands in the same category as Goethe's *Tasso* and *Iphigenie* but at a very respectful distance, having beauty of form but very little action; his most popular play is *Hans Lange* . . . , while his *Colberg* . . . makes a hit on patriotic occasions; his *Wahrheit?* . . . is poor enough. The fact is, Heyse is a story teller, not a dramatist. (pp. xi-xii)

But it is in the short story, *die Novelle,* in contradistinction to the novel, *der Roman,* that Paul Heyse stands preeminent. Beginning with *Marion* . . . , and the beautiful *L'Arrabbiata.* . . , which latter made him famous at twenty-three, continuing with *Das Mädchen von Treppi* . . . and *Anfang und Ende* . . . , scarcely a year has passed without at least one or two successful stories from his facile pen, till now the number runs above one hundred. But he has never surpassed *L'Arrabbiata,* in which he at once struck the key-note of a successful story: supreme interest, a situation not a development, rapid action, beautiful, transparent language, only a few characters but all so well drawn that they fairly live and breathe before our eyes. Harmony and beauty are the characteristics—little of the rugged, angular strength of [Heinrich von] Kleist's *Michael Kohlhaas.* Heyse himself demanded of the *Novelle "eine starke Silhouette"* (a strong outline), and he put his theory into practice. Among so many stories it is no wonder that keen-eyed critics—whose works, by the way, will be no longer thought of, when *L'Arrabbiata* is still read and loved—have discovered, [with Richard M. Meyer,] that Heyse's greatest fault is that "The poet forgets that the external appearance should be only the key and symbol of the whole personality: he shows us actions, behind which we seek in vain warm life, psychology, connection in the higher sense." . . . But in spite of a few inferior stories, in spite of one or two faults to be discovered perhaps in several of them, still a score of them are admitted to be models of their kind, and Paul Heyse has contributed more than his fair share to the literature of the Nineteenth Century. (pp. xii-xiii)

> *Lawrence A. McLouth, "Biographical Sketch," in* Anfang und Ende *by Paul Heyse, edited by Lawrence A. McLouth (copyright © 1910 by Henry Holt and Company), Henry Holt and Company, 1910, pp. v-xiii.*

WILLIAM LYON PHELPS   (essay date 1914)

When I was a very young man, I came across an old paper-cover translation of Heyse's long novel, *The Children of the World.* I read it with such delight that I remember my first waking thoughts every day were full of happy anticipation. I lived with that group of characters, and whenever I open the book now, I find their charm as potent as ever. (p. 314)

On the twenty-first of January 1912, a glorious winter day, I went to see [Heyse], and literally sat at his feet. He was over eighty years old. . . . (p. 317)

I told him of my youthful enthusiasm for *The Children of the World.* He said with the utmost sincerity: "I never read any of my own works. I have forgotten practically everything in the book you admire. But I do remember that it does not express my real attitude towards life, only a certain viewpoint. Everyone who reads that story ought also to read my *Merlin,* as it supplies exactly the proper antidote. . . . I think the outlook for German literature in the next generation exceedingly bright. The air is full of signs of promise. For me—*ach, ich bin alter Herr!"* [ah, I am an old Man!] He said this with indescribable charm. (pp. 317-18)

> *William Lyon Phelps, "Conversations with Paul Heyse" (originally published in* The Yale Review, *n.s. Vol. III, No. 4, July, 1914), in his* Essays on Books *(reprinted with permission of Macmillan Publishing Co., Inc.; copyright 1914 by Macmillan Publishing Co., Inc.; renewed 1942 by William Lyon Phelps), Macmillan, 1914 (and reprinted by Macmillan, 1922), pp. 314-19.*

MAXIMILIAN J. RUDWIN   (essay date 1916)

In Heyse's **"Mary of Magdala"** and [Maurice] Maeterlinck's "Mary Magdalene" an indirect characterization of Christ is attempted by picturing his spirit and his influence over the central figure of the play. In the former play Christ keeps himself resolutely behind the stage, and in the latter he is seen only once for an instant just before the final curtain, walking past the window on the way to Caiaphas. (p. 281)

Though Maeterlinck's play is more poetic, Heyse's is more dramatic. Heyse's Mary of Magdala, who was married as a child to an old man, wins our sympathy in her revolt against her life and the laws of her religion, while Maeterlinck's Mary Magdalene, with sensuality as sole motive of her conduct, repels us. An especial feature of Heyse's dramatic version is Mary's association with Judas. This relationship formed before Judas met Jesus helps to make Judas humanly intelligible. Though full of resentment over Mary Magdalene's humiliation in Simon's house and her change of heart towards him, which he rightly attributes to Christ's influence, his betrayal of Jesus is primarily actuated by noble motives. This Judean zealot sees a great danger for the future of his country in the Galilean's teachings of non-resistance. "Love thine enemies and bless them that hate thee," is in the eyes of the patriot nothing short of treason. He considers it his duty to save Israel from the shame of seeing one of its sons, who was once called a saint, kiss the dust of the feet of the imperator. Judas has no use for a Messiahship of peace and meekness rather than of force, and he may also have a secret hope that when Jesus is seized he will resort to the power of the sword and redeem Israel from its oppressors. This humanization of the character of Judas alone will insure Heyse's play a place in the world's literature. (pp. 281-82)

Maximilian J. Rudwin, "Modern Passion Plays," in The Open Court *(reprinted by permission of The Open Court Publishing Company, La Salle, Illinois; copyright by The Open Court Publishing Company, 1916), Vol. XXX, No. 5, May, 1916, pp. 278-300.**

E. K. BENNETT (essay date 1934)

Compared with [Gottfried Keller and Theodor Storm], Paul Heyse, who was their friend as well as their contemporary, is the aesthete of the Novelle as well as its mass-producer. (p. 206)

The subject matter of [Heyse's] Novellen varies very much: there are Italienische Novellen, Meraner Novellen, Troubadour Novellen, Dorfnovelen and a majority dealing with the society of his days. The prevailing types, however, are those dealing with Italy or the Mediterranean generally, which is tantamount to saying, for Heyse, dealing with the 'land of beauty'; and the Novellen which treat psychological problems in modern society. Heyse was amongst other things a student of romance culture and literature in a dilettante fashion, and his Troubadour Novellen are monuments of his learning rather than of poetical imagination.

Aesthete and mass-producer—the two apparently contradictory terms and ideas—elucidate Heyse's position as a writer of Novellen and suggest at once the weakness and unsatisfactory nature of that position. . . . [He] is very little read nowadays. [Emil] Ermatinger writes of him: 'His Novellen are lacking in ideas and ultimately all dead, for the basic concepts of conventional morality, which are intended to give them life, are not ideas at all'. This severe judgment must be accepted with this reservation, that the critic is speaking here of Ideendichtung [idea, thought poetry] as such. Though Heyse's writings cannot claim to be Ideendichtung they contain many positive qualities which entitle them to respect and even admiration. Nevertheless the fact remains that they present a far more superficial view of life than the works of Keller, Storm or [Otto] Ludwig. . . . (pp. 206-07)

Paul Heyse was a man of independent means, greatly favoured by nature and circumstance, able to devote himself entirely to the cultivation of literature; and though he certainly was profoundly aware of his responsibilities to his art, so much so indeed that it may be said that the whole mass of his literary production—Novellen, dramas and lyrics—was an offering made by a devout votary on the altar of Beauty, yet, in respect of life he was, compared with Keller, Storm and [Eduard] Mörike, irresponsible. That is to say, he was not rooted in certain social forms of life in the same way as the others were, but was able to float arbitrarily on its surface. (pp. 207-08)

But Heyse came to be during his life-time the specialist and authority on the Novelle; and though the present generation may find less solid value in his works than in those of his greater contemporaries, yet he did some service to the genre as such in his insistence upon the observation of the form, and in his investigation of all possibilities of the genre. He enunciated the most popularly accepted theory of the Novelle—in his 'Falken-theorie'; he made a very admirable and useful collection of representative German Novellen which he published together with Hermann Kurz from 1871 onwards—a second collection with Ludwig Laistner was published between 1884

and 1888. To this collection—*Deutscher Novellenschatz*—he prefixed an essay on the Novelle, and each individual Novelle he supplied with a short critical introduction. His critical writings on the subject as well as his actual practice are concerned with the working out of the essential form of the Novelle; and in his *Fugenderin-nerungen und Bekenntnisse* he gives interesting accounts of his artistic procedure. In the chapter 'Aus der Werkstatt'' one can read with what conscientious care he approaches a subject, amplifies it, remodels it, motivates or suppresses until the subject is made to yield its maximum of effectiveness. One can see that hardly Otto Ludwig himself has considered the technique more carefully or brought it to a higher point of perfection as far as its effectiveness is concerned. . . . Yet with Heyse . . . it is purely an external matter, and the word 'effectiveness' stands with him in contrast to the word 'profundity'; his meticulous and praiseworthy skill in using his subject matter to the best possible advantage can achieve almost anything except inform that subject matter with an idea-significance which by his very nature he is unable to give it.

As it is significant for Storm that his characteristic form is the Erinnerungsnovelle [achievement story], so it is significant for Heyse that his characteristic form is what may be called the 'Bekanntschaftsnovelle' ['acquaintance story']—the term is something in the nature of unfavourable criticism. Hans Bracher in his work on the *Rahmenerzählung und Verwandtes bei Keller, Meyer, Storm* gives the following schema for Heyse's methods: 'He meets someone at the *table d'hôte*, in an hotel, on a journey who attracts his attention by some peculiarity. Heyse observes him silently and finds something enigmatical about him, makes his acquaintance, whereupon the person in question relates the story of his or her life'. And he sums up the method in the phrase: 'An hotel is the ideal place for the technique of the Bekanntschaftsnovelle. Heyse can't manage without it'. Heyse's attitude to the stories he tells is clearly much more irresponsible than that of Storm or Keller, much more arbitrarily individual. . . . In the framework stories of Storm and Keller, the connection between story-teller and the lives of the people whose stories are told is much more intimate and ethically responsible. With Heyse the connection is substantially mere curiosity. With all the skill which Heyse unfolds in the story itself, there is a lack of ethical motive for the telling of the story and the reader is frequently surprised to find that the principal character reveals the most secret affairs of his or her life to a person utterly unknown, whom he or she happens to meet in an hotel.

Heyse's first published Novelle, *L'Arrabbiata* . . . , has for its setting the Bay of Sorrento, and one may say that this type of natural beauty remains characteristic not only for his landscape but for his ideal of beauty altogether. *L'Arrabbiata* was for years cited as the most perfect specimen of the Novelle in European literature—an exaggerated estimate of it, certainly, though as far as the technique is concerned it reveals all the excellence and the essential qualities which Heyse in his later theoretical writings demands: it is a single incident isolated from the background, and having the strong-marked silhouette which impresses it upon the memory. (pp. 208-11)

It is in effect a very charming little idyll, without any very great depth or significance to it, such as there is consisting in the drawing of the fierce, untamed Lauretta, whose heart determines both in repulsion and surrender her course of action. And this type of woman reappears again and again in Heyse's stories—indeed his Novellen are nearly all about women.

Heyse has written several volumes of *Italienische Novellen*, and in all of them Italy is conceived of under the aspect of the 'land of art and beauty'—with Heyse it is always the oleograph Italy. There he is at home. The landscape contains shining sea, cypresses, marble villas, olive trees, dark-eyed maidens, the complete romantic *mise en scène*. Among Heyse's Novellen dealing with Italian subjects the following may be mentioned as being particularly good: [*Das Mädchen von Treppi, Die Stickerin von Treviso,* and *Nerina*]. . . , which deals with the sufferings of the Italian poet Leopardi. It will be observed that in all four Novellen the title refers to a heroine, who is the centre of interest.

But these Italian Novellen represent only one type; there are a great number, indeed the majority, which deal with the society of Heyse's own time. In these, as indeed in the Italian Novellen, the interest is nearly always in the psychology of some given person, and a great parade is made of the psychological problem as such. As examples of this type two of the better-known works, [*Zwei Gefangene* and *Himmlische und irdische Liebe*] . . . may be cited. It will astonish modern readers to know that in his own day Heyse was regarded as an extremely immoral writer, who upheld in his Novellen a code of morality which was subversive of the accepted one. (pp. 211-12)

Quite apart from the technical element of effectiveness which in itself secures a certain amount of popularity, it is clear that Heyse was popular in his day because he was in the bad sense 'modern'—up-to-date. He brought the latest daring attacks and rebellions against the accepted conventions of society. But in his attitude there was nothing profoundly ethical: he was not a moralist, like Nietzsche, shaking at the ethical foundations of his generation; he was merely a frondeur tilting at the social conventions of his generation. (p. 213)

Heyse's Novellen make on the whole pleasant reading. In addition to those already mentioned, the following would seem to reveal his art at its best: *Andrea Delfin* . . . , a moving story of Venice in the eighteenth century but with the ending *manqué; Der verlorene Sohn* . . . , a valiant attempt to achieve a really tragic situation; *Geoffroy und Garcinde* . . . , a Troubadour Novelle; *Der letzte Centaur* . . . , a characteristic presentation in fantastic and ironic form of the conflict between modern civilization and ancient naturalness. It is significant that most of the Novellen that can be read with pleasure today are those which deal with more exotic subject matter than the social conditions of Heyse's own time. Heyse tells often a good story and is technically free from faults. His form, like his style, like his tone, is polished, easy, 'weltmännisch' [urbane]. He writes an excellent German prose, but that, like everything about him, is lacking in those characteristic qualities which distinguish the greatest writers.

If it be asked what Heyse contributed to the development of the German Novelle, it must be admitted that his contribution in so far as it brings something new is rather to be deplored than welcomed. His positive merit lies in his reminder of the form, regarded as technique: the value of a careful examination and working out of the possibilities of the genre Novelle as such with a view to obtaining the maximum of effectiveness. But with regard to the content he sets the Novelle off upon a false track in laying the stress upon supposed individual psychological problems, which have ceased to be problems today. In all his numerous Novellen he contributes hardly anything which is really original and fruitful. (pp. 213-14)

E. K. Bennett, "The Psychological Novelle," in his A History of the German Novelle: From Goethe to Thomas Mann, *Cambridge at the University Press, 1934, pp. 206-30.*

HENRY SAFFORD KING   (essay date 1936)

[The] nineteenth century was convulsed by ideas handed down from the eighteenth, and Heyse and his contemporaries treated these ideas—sometimes with identical themes—in their stories. One of the ideas handed down from the French Revolution was "equality." A corollary of "equality" is the self-determination of woman. . . .

Heyse was apparently throughout his literary career a feminist. He never tires, in his stories, of showing the tension that arises from the meeting of two strong personalities, the seeming hostility that grows out of the interplay of these personalities; the instinctive urge of one to assert a superiority that will cause a submergence of the other; and the final resolution of the problem in the recognition of the rights of each. Heyse was never interested in the professional and political application of the "rights of women." Not jobs and votes for women, but the understanding of women and their elevation to a position of intelligent self-determination was his burning interest. He rings the changes on the theme of individual self-determination—for men as well as for women—and this theme is so prominent that it almost gives the lie to Spiero's statement that his Novellen were far removed from all *Tendenzpoesie* [trend poetry]. The *Tendenz* is unmistakable, but so skillfully woven into the body of the Novellen that it has escaped the eyes of the historians. Heyse was not merely the erotic writer which the historians agree that he was, but an out-and-out feminist; and if his problems have ceased to be problems today, it is only in the sense that they are no longer the subject of heated public controversy. Modern chivalry accepts Heyse's views, at least in public; but in private life, as long as men are physically superior to women, there will continue to be some who will lord it over women until the chivalry and insight of the few become the rule of the many. *Heyse's problems, instead of being outdated, are up to the minute in modernity.* (p. 96)

Heyse was a feminist, and his great urge was to show the validity of the idea of the self-determination of woman. In many Novellen he rings the changes of this theme: *L'Arrabbiata, Das Mädchen von Treppi, Marion, Im Grafenschloss, Vetter Gabriel, Die Reise nach dem Glück, Zwei Gefangene, Ein Ring, Das Glück von Rothenburg*—to mention a few at random. Nor did his view of self-determination imply the subordination of the man to the woman, as *Unvergessbare Worte, Er soll dein Herr sein* and *Das Glück von Rothenburg* clearly show. The key to his view of self-determination is found in the words *respect for human personality,* including respect for one's self. In Heyse's works the woman is elevated to a position of intelligence, where she seeks—and is often able—to know her own heart and mind and resist the temptation to throw herself away in the fatally wrong direction. In a clever poem entitled **"Frauenemanzipation"** Heyse exhorts women to think—not to play with thinking in a dilettante fashion: to develop a personality with a valid ideology, so that when the evil days come, as come they will, the woman can retire to the isle within, and be at peace. In the last two lines he slyly admits he may not wear just the cloth of a father confessor, but he protests that he is their friend just the same and—"time will tell!"

Heyse's Novellen do not have the stark realism, the tang of the soil, the almost homespun fiber of Keller's. Instead there is a fineness of texture that is consonant with his cultured personality. Into this texture are wrought many values of indubitable worth through the witchery of an inventive poetic imagination unequalled in German literature. (pp. 100-01)

> *Henry Safford King, "In Defense of Paul Heyse, Feminist," in* The German Quarterly *(copyright © 1936 by the American Association of Teachers of German), Vol. IX, No. 3, May, 1936, pp. 91-101.*

WALTER SILZ (essay date 1954)

Heyse wrote over one hundred Novellen, few of which are read today. He also edited, with Hermann Kurz, a collection of Novellen. In the Introduction to the first edition of this *Deutscher Novellenschatz*, and again thirty years later in his *Jugenderinnerungen und Bekenntnisse,* Heyse summed up his views, which culminate in the celebrated "Falkentheorie." The Novelle, he says, deals with significant human fate or conflict, revealing to us by means of an unusual happening a new aspect of human nature. It presents a specific case, sharply outlined within a restricted framework, just as the chemist must isolate the interaction of certain elements in his experiment to illustrate some law of Nature. The novel has a wider horizon and more manifold problems; it embraces various concentric "Lebenskreise" [life cycles]. The Novelle restricts itself to one circle and one conflict . . . , and it can suggest only in "abbreviation" the relation of its persons to the general life. . . . It has a definite individual character or "profile:" . . . , and it can be summarized in a few lines, as are the tales in Boccaccio's *Decamerone*. . . . From the story of the falcon in this work (the 9th story of the 5th day) Heyse derives his desideratum of the "Falke," that is, the specific thing that differentiates a particular Novelle from a thousand others.

Heyse's theory had considerable vogue for a time, but of late years it has been much criticised. Heyse discerned correctly the tendency of the Novelle toward delimitation and isolation and its concentration on one central conflict. It is true also that the story can usually be summed up in brief and striking, often paradoxical, formulation. But any great work of literature is likely to have a markedly individual "silhouette" which renders it unmistakable among its kind, and in making a sort of requirement of the "falcon" Heyse has stressed a feature of external form rather than internal organization. (pp. 4-5)

> *Walter Silz, "The Nature of the Novelle and of Poetic Realism," in his* Realism and Reality: Studies in the German Novelle of Poetic Realism *(copyright 1954 by The University of North Carolina Press), University of North Carolina Press, 1954, pp. 1-16.*

DONALD LoCICERO (essay date 1967)

From Heyse's initial statement about the *Novelle* it is evident that he does not view it as a literary form which is rigidly bound by unchanging formalistic requirements, but rather as an organically developing form. . . . Heyse . . . sees the *Novelle* as a form which no longer merely deals with a single, remarkable event, but one which should deal with the most important *social* or *socio-ethical* (sittlich) problems of the day. The only other requisite he sets for the genre is individuality of execution. . . . (p. 435)

Heyse repeatedly stresses the importance of the Russian writer, Turgenev, in the area of the *Novelle*. In his later autobiographical work, *Jugenderinnerungen und Bekenntnisse* . . . , he reiterates and expands this judgment. . . . In the course of [the chapter "Meine Novellistik,"] Heyse repeatedly praises Turgenev; particularly his *Sportsman's Sketches,* whose beauty and simplicity of description seem to Heyse to be in complete accordance with the basic nature of the *Novelle*. In view of the nature of the *Sketches* Heyse's willingness to regard them as an example of the *Novelle* would seem to indicate that the definition he had in mind at that time was rather vague. (pp. 435-36)

[Heyse] calls for works with an individual, specific character—works whose basic plots are clearly delineated (the term silhouette is at best shadowy), and capable of succinct summarization. Indeed, he says nothing [in the introduction to *Deutscher Novellenschatz*] which could not be considered valid for all other short literary forms, the epic poem and the ballad included. In order to further explain his meaning, Heyse cites Boccaccio's *Decameron*, ninth story, fifth day as an example.

Boccaccio's falcon, so ironically central in this short tale, bringing as it does both sorrow and happiness, is used by Heyse to exemplify his concept of simplicity and individuality in the *Novelle*. The fate of the hapless bird is the unique twist, "das Specifische," which lends mastery to what could have been a neither interesting nor original story. . . . That Heyse is formulating no rigid *Novellentheorie* here is indisputable, and yet from this short, innocuous statement, has arisen the prolonged debate over the merit, shortcomings and profound import of the "Falkentheorie." Heyse's bird has been alternately characterized as a "Dingsymbol" [physical sign], and as a concrete object or leit-motif. It was long the fashion, and still remains to a certain extent, to read a short prose work with net in hand, ready to trap the falcon, be it bird of flesh and feathers or merely a symbolic representation. (pp. 436-37)

It is the contention here that the so-called "Falkentheorie' is neither concerned with ferreting out any central "Dingsymbole" or leit-motifs from any particular *Novelle*, and that Heyse's remarks are anything but an iron-clad theory of the *Novelle;* he said only, "es könnte nicht schaden" [it couldn't hurt] if particular attention were paid by a prospective author to making the unique aspect of his work more outstanding. (p. 438)

What Heyse stated was simply that "es könnte nicht schaden" if the author of a Novelle would ask himself if he had fully exploited the unique character of his subject. This is merely a reiteration of the call for individuality which Heyse repeatedly makes, and not an attempt to establish a set of criteria for the genre. In point of fact, Heyse is always extremely careful to qualify any statements which he feels might be interpreted as dogma. He allows the greatest latitude both in choice of theme and form, to the extent that he does not even limit the *Novelle* to prose!

In view of the preceding study it is evident that Heyse had no intention of precipitating the great falcon hunt which ensued. This fact is further illustrated by the complete absence in any of his own *Novellen,* or in his critical observations on the *Novellen* of other authors, of reference to any specific "Falken." The bird which has occasioned such energetic search, praise and condemnation is not one of Heyse's creation, for he never claimed nor insinuated that he had written *the* theory of the *Novelle* to end all theories. Any judgment of Heyse on the basis that he did imply such a claim is therefore invalid. (p. 439)

Donald LoCicero, "Paul Heyse's Falkentheorie: 'Bird Thou Never Wert'," in MLN (© copyright 1967 by The Johns Hopkins University Press), Vol. 82, No. 4, October, 1967, pp. 434-39.

JOHN ADRIAN   (essay date 1972)

Theodor Fontane, Gottfried Keller, and Theodor Storm carried on an active correspondence with Paul Heyse, in which they discussed many of the works that he wrote. . . .

Fontane was mainly concerned with Heyse's *Novellen* and dramas. He became more and more critical in the course of the years. He objected to Heyse's works on stylistic grounds and complained that there were frequent discrepancies in narrative perspective. He thought that Heyse's *Novellen* often lacked a clear outline and that in the dramas, actions were often not well motivated. According to Fontane, Heyse constantly created improbable situations and at times was too pessimistic in his outlook.

Keller did not discuss Heyse's work in great detail, but usually merely thanked him with a few words of praise for the books he was sent. He believed in the talent of the young Heyse and defended his lyrics when Storm criticized them. Keller approved of most of Heyse's plays, with some reservations, and complimented him on some of his *Novellen*. In particular, he admired Heyse's portrayal of the heroines in the *Novellen* set in Italy and felt that with them Heyse had created something new in the genre. He greatly admired Heyse's powers of invention and congratulated him from time to time on the plots that he was able to create. He often complimented Heyse on his clear style and his use of language, but implied that Heyse was pompous in his dramatic presentation.

Storm discussed Heyse's works in greater detail and sometimes offered suggestions for improving what he considered to be a weak point in a given work. He disliked Heyse's lyrics, pointing out that they often read like formal exercises. On the whole he liked Heyse's dramas, although he felt that those where Heyse's personal feelings on a given subject came to the surface were better than the others. He was most receptive to Heyse's novels and *Novellen*, and frequently praised the lifelike characters and the logical development of the plot. His main objections were to those parts of Heyse's work where the writer expounded his anti-clerical bias or advocated sensuality.

All of Heyse's critics agreed that he wrote gracefully and with seeming ease, but that his works were sometimes poorly constructed. They also objected to the extent to which he idealized his characters and they found some of them unconvincing. Their attitude is due partly to the fact that they themselves wrote in a more realistic vein than Heyse.

Since Heyse rarely rewrote anything, almost all of Fontane's, Keller's, and Storm's suggestions for improving a certain work were ignored and no direct influence of their ideas can be traced in Heyse's work.

John Adrian, in an extract from his, Paul Heyse and Three of His Critics: Theodor Fontane, Gottfried Keller, and Theodor Storm; *a dissertation presented at National Library of Canada at Ottawa, in 1972, in* Dissertation Abstracts International, Sec. A *(copyright © 1972 by University Microfilms International; reprinted with permission), Vol. XXXII, No. 11, May-June, 1972, p. 6640-A.*

CHRISTIANE ULLMANN   (essay date 1976)

The chief reason for the neglect of Heyse's literary works may well be found in the emphasis that has been placed on the so-called *Falkentheorie*. This theory of the Novelle is deduced from Heyse's own writings; it has led in the few attempts at evaluating Heyse's *Novellen* to a preoccupation with the form and with hunting for a *Dingsymbol*. The content of the tales was frequently overlooked. (p. 111)

It is obvious that an attempt to re-evaluate the literary merits of Heyse's own writings must be based on his works. But in the light of these critical writings and the importance that is attached to the theory, sometimes to the detriment of the author's actual literary works, it is important to consider carefully what Heyse wants us to understand by the falcon and the *Grundmotiv* [basic theme] . . . . Heyse demands that the plot of the Novelle must be capable of being summed up in a few short lines. In order to have a strong silhouette, this outline has to have something characteristic and specific. In Boccacio's Novelle the falcon may be a symbol, but it is the action of butchering and serving the falcon which clearly and definitely strikes the reader as unique in the précis of the story. Therefore, when Heyse states that a modern writer of a Novelle should ask himself where the 'falcon' is, he does not necessarily speak of a symbol, to which Heyse's *Falke* has been consistently limited, but of an occurrence which clearly and definitely impresses the reader as unique in the précis of the Novelle. . . . Heyse's contribution to the German *Novellentheorie* is found in his insistence that a précis should form the basis of a Novelle, and for this concept he turns to the introduction of Boccacio's *novellas*. Heyse's emphasis upon a startling occurrence, one which can be retold in a few sentences, occurs again and more succinctly in his *Jugenderinnerungen und Bekenntnisse*. Heyse here really speaks of a device in narrative technique. He points out that a short tale has a particularly impressive impact if it is told around a clearly defined centre of happening, a real 'piece of news.' But Heyse clearly states that not each newsworthy case is usable for a Novelle. . . . [The] précis, the clearly defined case, is the narrative device and it ought to be specific. The spiritual problem brought out by this device should, however, have universal application. . . . It seems, therefore, a much better critical undertaking, instead of hunting for symbolic falcons, to look for the silhouette, the précis, of Heyse's Novellen, and then to investigate how far this well-defined case of a sensational kind expresses a spiritual or psychological problem of general application.

We can see this pattern of story development quite clearly in Heyse's own extremely compact Novelle **Andrea Delfin,** provided that we keep in mind the distinction between the narrative device of the précis and the universal application of the story. An analysis of Heyse's Novelle ought first to give the précis, before a more detailed analysis is attempted. Care must be taken here that the *silhouette* is brought out as a short summation of the sensational and specific aspects of the story, unhampered by a pre-occupation with symbolic meaning. (pp. 111-13)

Let us first try to find the précis, the *case* stated in a few sentences. This case should itself give a statement of a sensational kind, like the short introductions of Boccacio; it should also suggest some universally applicable idea. Thus the *silhouette* or précis of **Andrea Delfin** may be stated as follows: *A man, whose whole family has been destroyed by a tyrannical government, returns to destroy the same government. He commits three murders, but by an unfortunate coincidence kills his* *only friend and thereupon commits suicide.* The specific and characteristic turning-point that strikes the reader as unusual in the précis is the protagonist's killing of his own friend. The short statement of the case indicates also that the universal problem expressed in the story must be sociological, because of the tyrannical government, and psychological, because of the suicide of the murderer. But the universal problem does not yield quite that easily to interpretation. In order to find the psychological problem, which is expressed by the sensational case, the inner and outer developments surrounding the three murders have to be seen as they relate to the central character of Andrea Delfin. The full sociological and psychological problem can, however, be understood only if the many other characters of this complex and concentrated Novelle are taken into account.

Quite early in the Novelle the historical figure Querini, leader of a revolt against the Venetian government, receives a letter from the eponymous hero of the Novelle, Candiano, a nobleman exiled by the Venetian government, who has now returned to Venice under the name of Andrea Delfin. This letter gives his pre-history. After the murder of his family Andrea had lived for a while in a state of depression. Only after Querini's abortive coup against the tyrannical government of Venice is he shaken into action. At this point, and before he commits his first murder, Andrea is completely convinced that he is a chosen instrument of justice. That he may labour under a misconception is shown quite early in the Novelle, where the reaction of Querini to the letter is contrasted with the quiet sleep of Andrea. (p. 114)

The first inquisitor murdered by Andrea is the very one on whom Andrea has spied at the countess's palace, and who, he now knows, is directly responsible for the murder of his brother. The reaction of Andrea to this overheard conversation arouses the reader's suspicion that the first murder is more in the nature of revenge than justice. After this action Andrea also learns that the men he seeks to murder have been elected to the position of inquisitors without any choice of refusing or avoiding such social roles. Not only Andrea, but also the reader realizes that his victims are not free agents, but men forced into their positions by a complex situation. In the Novelle there is only a short remark to indicate that Andrea here has his first doubts concerning the justice of his actions. . . . We are led to suspect that Andrea's calm conviction is being shaken.

The next murder is that of a newly chosen inquisitor who had recognized Andrea as Candiano and spoken with special coldness of the murder of the noble house of Candiano. Here, too, the suspicion arises that the motive for the murder of this inquisitor is blood-revenge to which the motive of the personal security of the hero is added. Before he commits the third murder, Andrea admits to himself that this time his purpose is not only justice. He has just heard of a plot against his friend, and he decides to act on the spur of the moment. . . . The mental condition of the murderer, described here in great detail, is different from his reaction to the earlier two murders. Until now Andrea has managed to preserve an outward calm. This time he holds the dagger in a trembling hand; he has to tell himself to hold firm one more time. It is precisely at this moment, when a psychological crisis is imminent, that he makes his fatal error and kills his friend Rosenberg. After this mistake he is no longer able to act, although it would be an easy matter to kill the last inquisitor, who comes by alone and unguarded. Andrea recognizes that having shed innocent blood, he has become as guilty as the inquisitors. This is the overt reason

for his failure to act. Yet in spite of the outward similarities there remains a great difference between Andrea and the inquisitors. . . . The great inner difference is that the inquisitors are coldly inhuman, incapable of change, while Andrea, acting out of human impulses rather than from coldly reasoned motives of justice, is shaken into full self-realization. It is not only the shock at murdering his friend that renders him inactive but also the awareness that he has laboured under a self-deception in believing himself the chosen instrument of justice. For this reason he gives up the task of killing the last inquisitor. . . . *Frevelwahn,* guilty self-deception, appears to be the main 'idea-content' of Andrea's character. But, as Andrea writes in his letter, guilt and suffering are so mixed in his life that no man can judge him, only God.

If we ask how Andrea could fall into his *Frevelwahn,* the case widens into a social rather than a purely personal, psychological problem. The *Frevelwahn,* the self-deception that makes murder for justice possible, is only the final outcome of the whole atmosphere of deceit that prevails in Venice. Reading the Novelle with this sociological motive in mind, it becomes clear that not only Andrea Delfin, but the whole of Venice contributes and falls victim to the deception. Even Rosenburg, who, as the outsider, is the most open character, finally takes part in the general lie and *plays* a role, thereby deceiving Andrea and destroying both himself and his friend. . . . Paul Heyse stresses the atmosphere of deceit by changing the point of view of the narrative continuously. The reader is well aware that Andrea Delfin is Candiano from the beginning of the story, although Heyse tells us directly only at the end. By this generally half-veiled narrative we become conscious of the irony of the manifold deceptions and are taken through the maze of the social atmosphere of Venice. Thus, when Rosenberg, knowing Andrea only as Andrea Delfin, believes him incapable of working for the inquisitors, the reader knows that Andrea has accepted a position as a spy from the inquisitors and has been given the task of observing Rosenberg. Yet the deception at this point is at least threefold. Andrea is deceiving Rosenberg and also the inquisition, so that Rosenberg's estimation of his friend is at a deeper level true. Rosenberg in a more straightforward manner gives us his estimate of the social condition that produces the corrupt nature of Venetian society: the attempt to rule through error and deceit has so undermined the morale of the citizens that there is no basis left on which a renewal of society can be built. By his explanation Rosenberg unknowingly shows Andrea how self-deceiving his, Andrea-Candiano's, action is. In the absence of a moral foundation on which society can be rebuilt, the attempt to overthrow a corrupt government by terror and deceit can only lead to more terror. . . .

The opinion of Rosenberg can be accepted as Heyse's own estimate of the situation, because earlier in the Novelle the landlady has introduced a similar topic. Indeed, the history of the landlady and her daughter illustrates in its simple fashion Rosenberg's more intellectual view of a hopeless situation. The landlady's husband, who might well have been part of the basis from which a renewal of society would have been possible, was terrorized and finally killed by the Venetian government, because he tried to escape the whole atmosphere of deception and terror. . . . There remains no trust in justice and the law among rulers or people; all believe in the supremacy of deceit and terror.

This society, which has been ruled by fear and deceit, cannot be changed by more terror and deceit, for indeed the human foundation for an uncorrupted society has been destroyed. As Rosenberg points out, only complete destruction of this society by an outside force could lead to a reform. . . . Fear and deceit form the atmosphere that stalks the streets of Venice, not hope for an improvement of conditions. There is hardly a sentence or a figure which does not contribute to the atmosphere of deception and terror in Venice. Even the bats, flying over the canal after being disturbed by Andrea, deceive the widow into believing that her husband's avenging spirit has returned to murder the inquisitors.

As the Novelle progresses, this atmosphere develops and widens: from the first appearance of the grey stranger and the comic figure of the widow, through the meeting of Rosenberg and Andrea, to the last disappearance of Candiano, watched helplessly by a monk. But Andrea's transformation from the grey, sick stranger to Candiano, last member of a noble Venetian house, is not the only change: the widow also becomes a victim of suffering and guilt. Her belief in the action of the avenging spirit of her husband makes her ill. . . . Her daughter changes from the happily singing girl to the pale co-conspirator. She acknowledges in the end that she has known for some time that Andrea is the murderer. The *nobili* [nobility], who are not afraid to appear at the funeral of the first inquisitor, flee at the second murder to avoid contamination with the conspirators and lock themselves in their houses. Even the simple people, who at first looked on unconcerned, feeling that it served the *nobili* right, cannot escape a sense of fear when their taverns are closed and police supervision steadily increases. The extent to which Heyse wanted to generalize the theme of growing terror is shown by the comparison of the fear at the recurrent murders with the fear engandered by a recurring earthquake. . . . It is the sickness of Venice that is generalized, the terror that ensues from deceit, the *Frevelwahn* on which the whole of Venetian society has been built. This *Frevelwahn* of absolute power must of necessity end in the destruction of that society. Only an acceptance of this fate can finally cure the sickness of this society.

If we look at the silhouette of the Novelle again, we can see how much is concentrated in the sharply defined *case* of Andrea's experience. For the problem of society is also expressed in Andrea's character himself, if one keeps in mind his strange double appearance. He is more human than the inquisitors in his friendship with Rosenberg and in his pity for his landlady and her daughter. Here the mask of the helpless bourgeois Andrea Delfin becomes ironically the true face of Andrea. But he has also the typical coldness, the ability to deceive and terrorize, of the Venetian nobility. The calm he forces on himself makes it possible for him to deceive the citizens of Venice and to terrorize the inquisitors . Andrea is here the true *nobile* Candiano. In the end, when he realizes his own self-deception, he accepts dispassionately that the murder of his friend may indeed lead to the end of the reign of terror. As long as it is not known that Andrea murdered Rosenberg, the murder of an innocent man will be placed at the door of the inquisitors, and, since Rosenberg was an Austrian diplomat, outside intervention may well help to overthrow the government of Venice. It is this last desperate hope that is at least one of the motives for Andrea-Candiano's suicide in obscurity . . . .

The *idea content* of the Novelle that has universal application may be summed up as follows: *The claim of absolute power to rule by deceit and terror corrupts and eventually destroys not only that power, but also its antagonist and society as a whole.* Only realization and acceptance of this fate may lead

to a renewal. The general idea is in some respects related to the hybris of classical antiquity. But the modern psychological approach of the Novelle does not show so much its effect on the rulers as the corruption and destruction even of society's most ordinary and innocent members, the widow and her daughter. The outsider Rosenberg, an ideal human figure, sees the situation clearly, but he is totally unequipped to deal with it. The Novelle moves uncompromisingly and relentlessly to its tragic end. Looking at the *specific case*, the seemingly purely coincidental killing of a friend and the resulting suicide, then the close relationship of the specific case to the general idea content becomes obvious. Not only does the specific case make it possible to describe the decay of Venice through the psychological problems of one man, but the singular case of Andrea Delfin with his double character, his coldness as well as his humanity, his deceit and his final self-realization and self-destruction, becomes representative of the whole problematic society of Venice. Far from being unrelated, specific case and general idea content complement and illuminate each other. Thus the Novelle fuses its singular tale of horror with its tragic content in an unrelenting atmosphere of deceit.

The theory of the précis as a narrative device has proved itself as a technique of great possibilities. But it is the working out of these possibilities that makes a writer noteworthy. Heyse's exceptional ability to create a social atmosphere around his central case must be taken into account if his position in literature is to be taken seriously. Heyse creates this atmosphere not through his presence as omniscient author and commentator; instead he continuously shifts the point of view and lets his characters speak, move, and react. It is by such detailed and realistic observations as Andrea's moodily looking out over the canal, the reporting of the landlady's seemingly inconsequential chatter, the description of the restless movement of the disturbed bats, that the characters are given depth and the atmosphere is created. This method of creating a social background indicates that Heyse must be considered a writer of the Realist school. The fact that the social atmosphere is created to point up the social lie in its most destructive and negative form places this Novelle even more definitely into the Realist tradition of the later nineteenth century. Not only in *Andrea Delfin* but in all of Heyse's Novellen the central characters are embedded in, and act out of, their social condition.

For a modern reader the Novellen that deal with the colour bar may be the most interesting. Both Heyse's retelling of the French story *Urica* and his own prose Novelle *Cleopatra* delineate, possibly for the first time in German literature, the character of the 'good' liberal society, which is nevertheless entangled in its own prejudices. But even in such a seemingly trivial Novelle as *San Vigilio* there is a serious social background. In plot and content this Novelle seems nothing more than a lighthearted spoof of Storm's Novelle *Immensee*. The social atmosphere surrounding the not so star-crossed lovers is created through detailed, often satiric descriptions of a holiday resort and its seemingly unimportant chit-chat. But the social atmosphere that is here depicted grows into a serious indictment of the sentimentality, bigotry, and class-consciousness of Prussian society at the turn of the century. There is indeed much in Heyse's literary work, apart from the Novelle *Andrea Delfin,* that ought to be read again, not just for its technical brilliance, but as the work of a notable writer of the later nineteenth century, whose delineation of the *condition humaine* belongs to the great Realist tradition of Balzac and Keller. (pp. 115-20)

Christiane Ullmann, "Form and Content of Paul Heyse's Novelle 'Andrea Delfin'," in Seminar (© The Canadian Association of University Teachers of German 1976), Vol. XII, No. 2, May, 1976, pp. 109-20.

ADDITIONAL BIBLIOGRAPHY

Corwin, Robert N. Introduction to *Vetter Gabriel,* by Paul Heyse, pp. iii-xi. New York: Henry Holt and Co., 1911.
>   Biocritical essay. Corwin states that Heyse's works are "intense rather than profound."

King, Henry Safford. "The Status of Woman in Heyse's Novellen." *The German Quarterly* XI, No. 2 (March 1938): 95-7.
>   Reviews Heyse's theme, the self-determination of woman, in the novellas *L'arrabbiata, Er soll dein Herr sein,* and *Vetter Gabriel.*

Negus, Kenneth. "Paul Heyse's *Novellentheorie:* A Revaluation." *The Germanic Review* XL, No. 3 (May 1965): 173-91.
>   Reexamines Heyse's texts in which the *Falkentheorie* was developed, finding it a narrow theory, applicable to only a small segment of the genre in which he worked.

Rodgers, Anita M. "Fourteen Letters by Paul Heyse Discovered in Melbourne." *Journal of the Australasian Universities Language and Literature Association,* No. 28 (November 1967): 215-26.
>   Letters primarily from Heyse's university days. The actual correspondence is quoted in the German.

Robert E(rvin) Howard

1906-1936

(Also wrote under pseudonyms of Patrick Ervin, John Taverel, Sam Walser, Robert Ward, among others) American short story writer, novelist, poet, and essayist.

An influential writer of heroic fantasy, Howard is primarily known for his creation of Conan the Barbarian, who first appeared in the short stories "By This Ax I Rule!" and "The Phoenix on the Sword." Apart from this sword-and-sorcery primitive, Howard's other literary heroes include King Kull of Valusia; Solomon Kane, sixteenth-century Puritan; sailor Steve Costigan; Steve Harrison, detective; and Bran Mak Morn, a Pictish chieftain featured in "Worms of the Earth," possibly Howard's best tale in the supernatural genre. According to critics, Howard identified intensely with his fictional heroes. H. P. Lovecraft has stated, "the real secret is that *he was in every one of them*," and Howard himself wrote, "always I am the barbarian."

Howard was born in the small Texas town of Peaster. His father was a physician who settled in Cross Plains, Texas, with his wife and only child. A small, bookish youngster, Howard was often threatened by gangs as he grew up, until he became a sports and exercise fanatic. Since he could not afford a liberal arts education, Howard took commercial courses, such as shorthand, typing, and business arithmetic. He was in his teens when he decided to write fiction. This decision was prompted by an intense need for personal freedom, which Howard believed he could best satisfy by becoming a writer. In 1924 Howard sold his first story, "Spear and Fang," to *Weird Tales*, a pulp magazine which became his primary source of income.

Howard displayed the best qualities of a pulp writer with his fast narrative pace and direct style. In 1928 he introduced Solomon Kane in "Red Shadows." Kane was a somber character, seeking danger and fighting injustice. Like most of Howard's fiction involving a series character, the Kane stories are uneven. From 1929 to 1930 Howard wrote stories about a prizefighting roughneck sailor named Steve Costigan. As early as 1926 Howard presented Kull of Atlantis, possibly the most interesting of his characters, in a series of heroic fantasies, the first entitled "The Shadow Kingdom." Another, "The Mirrors of Tuzun Thune," is considered one of Howard's best and involves Kull in a fantasy of poetic atmosphere rather than high adventure. "Kings of the Night" introduces Kull to Bran Mak Morn, an anti-Roman Pictish hero whose unimposing size masks his extraordinary physical prowess. Howard's greatest creation nevertheless remains the invincible Conan, a character of unrestrained vitality and universal appeal. Some critics contend that this fantastic character represents an escape for an age with few ideals, and provides an echo for the voice of the socially alienated.

In addition to his vast output of fiction, Howard also wrote poetry. His poems are described by L. Sprague de Camp as "vigorous, colorful, strongly rhythmic, and technically adroit." Howard claimed, however, that he lacked a poetic sense, and when poetry writing proved unprofitable he abandoned it. Toward the end of his life Howard concentrated on tales of

the Old West, and such collections as *A Gent from Bear Creek*, according to some critics, contain his best work. Though personally troubled, Howard was professionally successful at the time of his suicide. Critics often stress the intelligence and perceptiveness apparent in his writings and the promise they indicated.

Howard's novels and short stories did not appear in book form during his lifetime. Beginning ten years after his death and from then on Howard's works have continued to appear in both deluxe limited editions and mass market printings. The adventures of his barbarian heroes, primarily Conan, have been perpetuated by such prominent fantasy authors as L. Sprague de Camp, Lin Carter, and Karl Edward Wagner. The fictional subgenre of "heroic fantasy," so termed by de Camp, was given one of its earliest and most exhaustive treatments in Howard's tales. His fantastic legends of sorcery and swordplay have inspired legions of imitators, but Howard himself remains the major figure in this expanding field.

PRINCIPAL WORKS

Skull-face, and Others   (novels and short stories)   1946
Conan the Conqueror   (novel)   1950; also published as
   The Hour of the Dragon, 1977

ROBERT E. HOWARD (essay date 1936)

There is no literary work, to me, half as zestful as rewriting history in the guise of fiction. I wish I was able to devote the rest of my life to that kind of work. I could write a hundred years and still there would be stories clamoring to be written, by the scores. Every page of history teems with dramas that should be put on paper. A single paragraph may be packed with action and drama enough to fill a whole volume of fiction work. . . . I try to write as true to the actual facts as possible; at least I try to commit as few errors as possible. I like to have my background and setting as accurate and realistic as I can, with my limited knowledge; if I twist too much, alter dates as some writers do, or present a character out of keeping with my impressions of the time and place, I lose my sense of reality, and my characters cease to be living and vital things; and my stories center entirely on my conceptions of my characters. Once I lose the "feel" of my characters, I might as well tear up what I have written. And once I have a definite conception of a character in my mind, it destroys the feeling of reality to have that individual act in any manner inconsistent with the character in which I have visualized him. My characters do and say illogical and inconsistent things—inconsistent as far as general things go—but they are consistent to my conception of them.

I really should use Texas settings more in my stories, since Texas is the only region I know by first hand experience. Three of my yarns in *Weird Tales* have been laid in Texas: **"The Horror From the Mound," "The Man on the Ground,"** and **"Old Garfield's Heart."** Sometimes too thorough a knowledge of a subject is a handicap for fiction writing (not that I claim to be an authority on the Southwest, or anything like that; but I was born here and have lived here all my life.)

While I don't go so far as to believe that stories are inspired by actually existent spirits or powers (though I am rather opposed to flatly denying anything) I have sometimes wondered if it were possible that unrecognized forces of the past or present—or even the future—work through the thoughts and actions of living men. This occurred to me, especially, when I was writing the first stories of the Conan series. I know that for months I had been absolutely barren of ideas, completely unable to work up anything salable. Then the man Conan seemed suddenly to grow up in my mind without much labor on my part and immediately a stream of stories flowed off my pen— or rather, off my typewriter—almost without effort on my part. I did not seem to be creating, but rather relating events that had occurred. Episode crowded episode so fast that I could scarcely keep up with them. For weeks I did nothing but write of the adventures of Conan. The character took complete possession of my mind and crowded out everything else in the way of storytelling. When I deliberately tried to write something else, I couldn't do it. I do not attempt to explain this by esoteric or occult means, but the fact remains. I still write of Conan more powerfully and with more understanding than any of my other characters. But the time will probably come when I will suddenly find myself unable to write convincingly of him at all. That has happened in the past with nearly all my rather numerous characters; suddenly I find myself out of contact with the conception, as if the man himself had been standing at my shoulder directing my efforts, and had suddenly turned and gone away, leaving me to search for another character.

The last yarn I sold to *Weird Tales*—and it well may be the last fantasy I'll ever write—was a three-part Conan serial (**"Red Nails"**) which was the bloodiest and most sexy weird story I ever wrote. I have been dissatisfied with my handling of decaying races in stories, for the reason that degeneracy is so prevalent in such races that even in fiction it can not be ignored as a motive and as a fact if the fiction is to have any claim to realism. I have ignored it in all other stories, as one of the taboos, but I did not ignore it in this story. Too much raw meat, maybe, but I merely portrayed what I honestly believe would be the reactions of certain types of people in the situations on which the plot of the story hung. It may sound fantastic to link the term "realism" with Conan; but as a matter of fact—his supernatural adventures aside—he is the most realistic character I ever evolved. He is simply a combination of a number of men I have known, and I think that's why he seemed to step full-grown into my consciousness when I wrote the first yarn of the series. Some mechanism in my sub-consciousness took the dominant characteristics of various prize-fighters, gunmen, bootleggers, oil field bullies, gamblers, and honest workmen I had come in contact with, and combining them all, produced the amalgamation I call Conan the Cimmerian. (pp. 56-8)

What I feel is one of the best stories I've ever written was a 30,000 word western (**"Vultures of Whapeton"**), the first draft of which I knocked off in two and a half days. . . . Yet I feel that if I ever do write anything of lasting merit it will be fiction laid in the early West. Some day I hope to be able to use the life of John Wesley Hardin, either as a biography or a basis for a historical novel. I rate Hardin, along with Billy the Kid and Wild Bill Hickok, as the three greatest gunmen who ever lived. I use the word "great" advisedly. A gunman of their type had to be more than merely a man whose hand was quicker and whose eye was truer than the average man. He had to be a man of extraordinary intelligence, a practical student of psychology and of human nature, and the owner of a keen analytical mind. I made this point clear in that latest western I mentioned above, though my main character was drawn from Hendry Brown rather than Hardin in that case. Gunmanship was more than a matter of muscular superiority.

I find it more and more difficult to write anything but western yarns. I have definitely abandoned the detective field, where I never had any success anyway, and which represents a type of story I actively detest. I can scarcely endure to read one, much less write one. (p. 59)

> *Robert E. Howard, "On Reading—And Writing"*
> *(1936), in* The Last Celt: A Bio-bibliography of Robert Ervin Howard, *edited by Glenn Lord (copyright*
> *© 1976, Glenn Lord; reprinted by permission of Glenn Lord), Berkley Publishing Corporation, 1976, pp. 41-60.*

H. P. LOVECRAFT   (essay date 1936)

[REH] had the fundamental honesty, simplicity, sincerity, and directness—the preëminently Aryan qualities—which have become so distressingly rare in modern urban life. While I basically disagreed with him regarding the superiority of barbarism over civilisation—and argued endlessly with him on that point—I respected his personality to a tremendous extent, and placed it miles above the "sophisticated" type of character. Indeed, I used him as a sort of model and example in arguing with persons like [Frank Belknap] Long and [Donald] Wandrei, who uphold a more disillusioned and decadent tradition. I told him how often I held him and his position up to extremists on the other side, so that he undoubtedly realised the depth and sincerity of my respect, even when I tore most vigorously into his pro-barbarian arguments. (p. 276)

As for his work—while the King Kull series probably forms a weird peak, I do not think the *best* of the Conan tales involve any radical falling-off. Some were pure adventure-yarns with the touch of weirdness rather extraneous, but that is not the case with *Hour of the Dragon*. His best work would probably have been regional and historical, and I was greatly pleased by his recent tendency to employ his own southwestern background in fiction. As a poet, too, he was phenomenally gifted. . . . His scholarship in certain lines was truly remarkable. I always gasped at his profound knowledge of history—including some of its more obscure corners—and admired still more his really astonishing *assimilation* and *vitalisation* of it. He was almost unique in his ability to *understand* and *mentally inhabit* past ages—including many without any resemblances to our own. He had the imagination to go beyond mere names and dates and get at the *actual texture of life* in the bygone periods which he studied. He could visualise all the details of every-day existence in these periods, and subjectively enter into the feelings of their inhabitants. As a result, the past was as alive for him as the present—while his grasp of *general* historical and anthropological principles enabled him to construct from pure imagination those prehistoric worlds of mystery and adventure and necromancy whose lifelife convincingness and consistent substance won such universal praise. No matter how assiduously the profit-motivated critics and editors tried to warp him, he was always a step ahead of them—and

a step ahead of himself when he seemed to listen to them. He had something to say—and all the hackneyed patterns and conventional technique in the world couldn't stop him from saying it. Nothing could squeeze the life and zest out of his work. (pp. 278-79)

> *H. P. Lovecraft, in his letter to E. Hoffmann Price on July 5, 1936, in his* Selected Letters: 1934-1937, *edited by August Derleth and James Turner (copyright © 1976, by Arkham House Publishers, Inc.; reprinted by permission of Arkham House Publishers, Inc.),* Arkham House, 1976, pp. 275-79.

H. R. HAYS   (essay date 1946)

The collected stories of Robert E. Howard range from the standard "weird tales" pattern (the monster unloosed and its final destruction, or the destruction of the dabbler in the occult) to a kind of action story in costume set in a prehistoric world of Lemuria and Atlantis invented by the author. Howard used a good deal of the Lovecraft cosmogony and demonology, but his own contribution was a sadistic conquerer who, when cracking heads did not solve his difficulties, had recourse to magic and the aid of Lovecraft's Elder Gods. The stories are written on a competent pulp level (a higher level, by the way, than that of some best sellers) and are allied to the Superman genre which pours forth in countless comic books and radio serials. Since this genre commands an incredibly large audience in the United States and seems to be an American phenomenon, its sociological and psychological significance cannot be lightly brushed away. . . .

[Howard's heroes were] wish-projections of himself. All of the frustrations of his own life were conquered in a dream world of magic and heroic carnage. In exactly the same way Superman compensates for all the bewilderment and frustration in which the semi-literate product of the industrial age finds himself enmeshed. The problem of evil is solved by an impossibly omnipotent hero.

Now if anything like democracy is to prevail in modern life it means that a heavy burden of responsibility is thrown upon the average citizen. It means that he must take a realistic interest in the difficulties of living. But the prevalence of Superman as reading matter for adults indicates a complete evasion of this responsibility.

Howard's life is like a fable illustrating the sad consequences of this situation. Living in the never-never land of Conan and King Kull, he slaughtered enemies by the dozen. He was fearless, inscrutable, desired by all women. Single-handed he toppled rulers from their thrones and built empires of oriental splendor. Even the menace of the supernatural was vanquished by magic that he alone was able to control. In the real world, however, he had no resources. When he was faced with the loss of maternal protection he took the way of self-destruction.

Thus the hero-literature of the pulps and the comics is symptomatic of a profound contradiction. On the one hand it is testimony to insecurity and apprehension, and on the other it is a degraded echo of the epic. But the ancient hero story was a glorification of significant elements in the culture that produced it. Mr. Howard's heroes project the immature fantasy of a split mind and logically pave the way to schizophrenia.

> *H. R. Hays, "Superman on a Psychotic Bender,"*
> *in* The New York Times Book Review *(© 1946 by*

The New York Times Company; reprinted by permission), May 29, 1946, p. 34.

FRITZ LEIBER (essay date 1961)

[After reading "**The Moon of Skulls**" and "**Red Shadows**" for the first time,] I'm once more impressed with Howard's simple, youthful, melodramatic power.

He painted in about the broadest strokes imaginable. A mass of glimmering black for the menace, an ice-blue cascade for the hero, between them a swathe of crimson for battle, passion, blood—and that was the picture, or story, rather, except where a vivid detail might chance to spring to life, or a swift thought-arabesque be added.

He knew the words and phrases of power and sought to use them as soon and often as possible, the words and phrases that the writer with literary aspirations usually avoids (sometimes quite mechanically) because they're clichés, words and phrases alike (I select from "**The Moon of Skulls**") black, dark, death, volcanic, ghost, great black shadow, symbol of death and horror, menace brooding and terrible, shrubs which crouched like short dark ghosts, outposts of the kingdom of fear, black spires of wizards' castles, ju-ju city, grim black crags of the fetish hills, henchmen of death, the Tower of Death, the Black Altar. . . .

These aren't bad words and phrases really. In fact, they are the same general sort that still make some Americans embarrassed about Edgar Allan Poe and his European reputation and influence. And Howard didn't use them like a hack writer, he used them like a poet. (Who but Howard could work into a good poem and make effective a pulpish bit like, "Jets of agony lance my brain"?) Yet his boyish, sincere, poetic use of the words and phrases of power will always make it difficult for us to demonstrate to literary people unsympathetic to the swordplay-and-sorcery field what it is we see in Howard.

The landscape, plan, diagram, or microcosm of each of Howard's earlier stories is as simple, limited, and complete as that of a boy's daydream, a hewn-out stage setting that can be held in the mind while the story progresses. It has no more parts than a good diagram. There is no worry at all how it intersects the real world. It is an inner world for a boy's solemn adventuring. In most fantasy there are only traces of this boyish stage in the development of the dream world (Eddison naming his rival nations in [*The Worm Ouroboros*] Demons, Witches, Pixies, Goblins, Imps, and Ghouls) but in Howard (especially, to my mind, in the King Kull and Solomon Kane stories) it is dominant.

Most of us, I imagine, create in childhood starkly simple landscapes for adventuring. I spent a lot of time on a rope bridge over a dark chasm; often there was a tiger at one end and a lion at the other. But it took Howard's unique talent and intensity to make powerful, genuine stories directly out of these materials with almost no disguise at all.

Broad strokes, stark landscapes, near-clichés of power—like I said.

I'm not belittling Howard when I denominate his writing as boyish. I'm thinking of his freshness, sincerity, and exuberance as much as anything else, and there is an undeniably boyish element in all swordplay-and-sorcery fiction, even the most sophisticated or wickedly decadent. (pp. 26-8)

Nor am I saying that Howard used clichés of the order of stony silence, iron will, morbid curiosity seekers, and rapier-like wit—but rather the near-clichés of the horror story, such as words like strange, weird, and eerie. (If something is strange, a good writer ought to be able to spot wherein the strangeness lies, and surely his description will be more effective if he can.) Howard generally didn't over-use those particular words, but he leaned heavily on such cousin-words as grim, black, dark, ghostly.

The landscape of the Conan stories shows a definite growth from the Kull and Kane tales. (Interesting, those three K-sounds; Kull, Kane, Conan.) No longer do we find so many hosts of killers inhabiting giant rooms, ancient cyclopean ruins, and impenetrable forests—hosts whose means of sustenance is hard to comprehend and whose day-to-day life down the centuries hardly picturable. In the Conan stories there are usually hewers-of-wood and drawers-of-water, merchants, sailors, farmers, scholars, priests, along with the fighters and magicians—even if the wolves do seem at times to outnumber the sheep.

The girl-whipping-girl references in "**The Moon of Skulls**"—which became girl-whipping-girl scenes in several of the Conan stories—remind me that Howard must have early discovered what a potent sexual stimulus this particular image is, along with the more-or-less veiled lesbianism that is frequently linked with it. (pp. 28-9)

Once again, I'm not criticizing Howard by harping on this matter. Spicy scenes fit as naturally into the sword-play-and-sorcery story as they do into the related, larger category of the picaresque—though they are by no means a necessary part of it: several of the best Conan stories have no sex scenes at all—notably my own favorite, "**Beyond the Black River.**"

Although it was one of his first long stories, "**Red Shadows**" is a wonderful compendium of Howard. Kane and Le Loup, developed with almost equal fullness, present the twin good and evil sides of one adventurous man's nature, there is a magnificent hymn to the jungle running through the prose, the African witchcraft is superb, and even the Giant Ape (which appears so often as a stock menace in Howard's subsequent tales) is handled with sympathy as well as power. (p. 30)

Fritz Leiber, "Howard's Style," in Amra *(copyright © 1961 by George H. Scithers), Vol. II, No. 17, 1961 (and reprinted in* The Spell of Conan, *edited by L. Sprague deCamp, Ace Books, 1980, pp. 26-31).*

L. SPRAGUE de CAMP (essay date 1976)

In 1928, Howard set down on paper a fictional character whom he had long borne in mind: Solomon Kane, an English Puritan of the late sixteenth century. The story, "**Red Shadows,**" appeared in *Weird Tales*. . . . Kane differs from most of Howard's heroes, who are brawny, brawling, belligerent adventurers. Kane is somber of dress, dour of manner, rigid of principles, and driven by a demonic urge to wander, to seek danger, and to right wrongs. In the Kane stories, some of which are set in Europe and some in Africa, Kane undergoes gory adventures and overcomes supernatural menaces. In these stories first appears Howard's distinctive intensity—a curious sense of total emotional commitment, which hypnotically drags the reader along willy-nilly. (p. 141)

Howard produced a sizable volume of poetry, nearly all of which has been published. Two of his poems appeared in *Modern American Poetry* for 1933. Like his prose, his verse is vigorous, colorful, strongly rhythmic, and technically adroit. He was modest about his talent, saying that, while he was born with the knack of "making little words rattle together," "I know nothing at all about the mechanics of poetry—I couldn't tell you whether a verse was anapestic or trochaic to save my neck. I write the stuff by ear, so to speak, and my musical ear is full of flaws."

Howard's models were the major Anglo-American poets of the late nineteenth and early twentieth centuries, such as Benét, Chesterton, Dunsany, Flecker, Harte, Kipling, Masefield, Noyes, Swinburne, Tennyson, and Wilde. Howard's clanging, colorful verse, while not quite so brilliant as that of Clark Ashton Smith, is better than the rather pedestrian poetry of Dunsany or Tolkien and far superior to Lovecraft's leaden Georgian couplets.

Howard was untouched by the revolution then beginning in Anglophone poetry, which, led by Pound, Eliot, and others, resulted in the almost complete abandonment of fixed forms in favor of free verse. Where Howard used simple language and fixed forms, most contemporary poets use turgid language and no form at all. Opinions differ as to whether this is an improvement.

Since, however, poetry paid little or nothing, and Howard, however unrealistic in some phases of human relationships, had a sound sense of economic reality, he wrote very little verse after 1930. (p. 142)

With so voracious a reader [as Howard], it is hard to be sure that he was *not* influenced by any given predecessor. Jack London was one of Howard's favorite writers. Howard esteemed Sir Richard F. Burton's narratives of travel and adventure, although he was skeptical of Burton's truthfulness. In Howard's stories, the influence of Edgar Rice Burroughs, Robert W. Chambers, Harold Lamb, H. P. Lovecraft, Talbot Mundy, Sax Rohmer, and Arthur D. Howden Smith is plain to be seen.

An alert reader can also pick up echoes of other, older writings in Howard's stories, or in individual scenes and passages. One of his rewritten and posthumously published stories was, in its various incarnations, titled **"The Black Stranger," "Swords of the Red Brotherhood,"** and **"The Treasure of Tranicos."** I suspect that Howard got the idea of the little colony (French in one version, Zingaran in another) on a wild, distant coast from "The Lady Ursula," in Charles M. Skinner's *Myths and Legends of Our Own Land.* . . . Howard's story **"The Frost Giant's Daughter"** (also published as **"Gods of the North"**) may have come either from "The Home of Thunder" in Skinner's book or from a similar incident in William Morris's *The Roots of the Mountains* . . .—or from both.

Other examples are the death throes of Khosatral Khel in **"The Devil in Iron,"** where the phraseology echoes Arthur Machen's "The Great God Pan"; the incident of the poisoned prong of Zorathus' iron box, in *Conan the Conqueror* . . . , which could have come from Sax Rohmer's *The Hand of Fu-Manchu* . . . or A. Conan Doyle's "The Adventure of the Dying Detective" . . . ; and the attacks on the king in **"By This Ax I Rule!"** and **"The Phoenix on the Sword,"** which closely resemble the death of Francesco Pizarro as described by William H. Prescott in *The History of the Conquest of Peru.* Where Gustave Flaubert, in *Salammbô*, described Hamilcar Barca driving his chariot "up the whole Mappalian Way," Howard, in **"The God

in the Bowl,"** has Kallian Publico driving his chariot "along the Palian Way."

Still, the man had much more than mere imitativeness. A young writer often imitates admired predecessors. Many have thus passed through a Hemingway or a Lovecraft period. If the writer is good, he assimilates these influences so that the derivations are no longer obvious. Howard, I think, was reaching this stage when he perished.

Three strong influences on Howard's fiction were, first, the romantic primitivism of London and Burroughs; second, a fascination with Celtic history and legend; and third, the racial beliefs then current. Howard's primitivism is summed up by a remark made by a character at the end of the story **"Beyond the Black River":** "Barbarism is the natural state of mankind. Civilization is unnatural. It is a whim of circumstance. And barbarism must always ultimately triumph." (pp. 145-47)

The ancient Celts fascinated Howard. Where Lovecraft was an Anglophile, Howard was a Celtophile. Of largely Irish descent, Howard made an affectation of his Celticism, sometimes signing himself "Raibeard Eiarbhin hui Howard." One St. Patrick's Day, he appeared in a green bow tie two feet across. Howard was more objective toward the Celts than Lovecraft ever was towards the Anglo-Saxons. Nevertheless, Howard harbored, throughout his life, a burning interest in Celtic history, anthropology, and mythology.

This interest appears in Howard's fantasies of Turlogh O'Brien, in his historical stories of Cormac Mac Art, and in other historical and contemporary tales with heroes of Irish names: Costigan, Dorgan, Kirowan, O'Donnell, and so on. He wrote fantasies and historical tales laid in the British Isles, of the struggle of Pict against Briton, of Briton against Roman, and of Irishman against Norseman. He read Donn Byrne's Irish novels but resented Byrne's making heroes of Ulstermen and Anglo-Normans. He studied the eccentric phonology and orthography of the Irish language. He took part in the arguments as to which of the two branches of the British Celts—the Goidels, Gaels, or Q-Celts and the Cymry, Britons, or P-Celts—reached the islands first. (p. 148)

Like Lovecraft, Howard was still under the spell of the Aryanist doctrine. This dogma identified the horse-taming Aryans, the original spreaders of the Indo-European languages, with the tall, blond, blue-eyed Nordic racial type—which seems unlikely in the light of present knowledge. Hence Howard wrote of the conquest, in Britain, of small, dark aborigines of Mediterranean type by "blond, blue-eyed giants"—the supposed Aryan Celts. According to present evidence, the conquering was probably the other way round. The Nordic aborigines were at least twice conquered by swarthy little Southerners, first by the prehistoric Beaker Folk from Spain and secondly by the Romans. Howard himself had black hair and blue eyes, a genetic combination that seems commoner in Ireland than elsewhere. Hence he was less englamorated by mere blondness than Lovecraft. Most of his heroes, in fact, are brunets. (p. 149)

During 1929-32, with the opening of wider markets for his fiction, [Howard] wrote several weird stories in the frame of Lovecraft's Cthulhu Mythos. He sold sport, adventure, Western, oriental, and historical stories. Most of his stories belonged to one or another of the score of series that he wrote, each series built around one character. . . .

Howard's novel **"Skull-Face"** ran as a serial in *Weird Tales*. It is an obvious imitation of Sax Rohmer, with an immortal Atlantean sorcerer, Kathulos, substituted for the insidious Doctor Fu-Manchu. Howard denied that "Kathulos" was derived from Lovecraft's "Cthulhu"; he said he had made up the name himself. (p. 51)

Although Howard was a versatile writer throughout his career, writing in several genres at once, his writing falls into three definite if overlapping periods. In each period, stories of one kind dominate his output. The first period, after he became an established writer, was that of boxing stories, from 1929 to 1932. The second, from 1932 to 1935, was that of fantasy. The third and last, from 1934 to 1936, was that of Westerns.

Howard's main writing, from 1929 to 1932, consisted of stories of prizefighting. He published twenty tales about a pugilistic sailor named Steve Costigan. Over half of these were sold to *Fight Stories* and the rest to *Action Stories* and *Jack Dempsey's Fight Magazine*.

Costigan, an able-bodied seaman and prizefighter, is an invincible roughneck with fists of iron, a heart of gold, and a head of ivory. These stories are comedies, full of broad, slapstick humor, of a sort that those who know only Howard's serious stories would never expect of him. The tales deal with prizefights, usually in port cities. There are plots, skullduggery, and virtue finally triumphant. The hero is an incorrigible sucker for a hard-luck story, especially from a fair but designing female. Howard explained his preference for heroes of mighty thews and feeble minds:

"They're simpler. You get them in a jam, and no one expects you to rack your brains inventing clever ways for them to extricate themselves. They are too stupid to do anything but cut, shoot or slug themselves into the clear." (pp. 51-2)

These stories would never have been [collected as *The Incredible Adventures of Dennis Dorgan*] but for Conan's popularity in the last decade. Still, they have ingenuity, action, and broad humor. Even at his corniest and pulpiest, Howard is fun to read.

The stories also show Howard's limitations. His knowledge of seafaring, for example, was second-hand. The closest he had come to going to sea was a motorboat ride in the Gulf of Mexico. Tales of Shanghai, Singapore, and other exotic ports are obviously by one who had never been there. But Howard had neither time nor facilities profoundly to research the *ambiance* of these places.

A couple of Dorgan stories, laid in San Francisco, give a picture of "high society" by one who likewise had never been there. The Societarians flutter limp paws, stare through lorgnettes and monocles, say "my deah" and "rawthah," and swoon at the sight of blood. But then, the class of readers for whom Howard was writing had never been there, either. (pp. 52-3)

Ever since he had begun the Solomon Kane stories, Howard had worked on and off at heroic fantasy. In 1926, he started **"The Shadow Kingdom,"** the first story in a new series about Kull of Atlantis. In these tales, Howard gave full vent to his primitivism. . . .

In 1932, at the beginning of his main spurt of fantasy fiction, Howard conceived his most popular character: Conan the Cimmerian. (p. 157)

Conan first surfaced as the hero of a rewritten Kull story, **"By This Ax I Rule!"** Howard changed the names and introduced a supernatural element to create **"The Phoenix on the Sword."** . . .

Conan was not only a development of King Kull but also an idealization of Howard himself. He is a gigantic barbarian adventurer from backward northern Cimmeria. After a lifetime of wading through rivers of gore and overcoming foes both natural and supernatural, Conan becomes king of Aquilonia. Dr. John D. Clark, in an introduction to a book edition of *Conan the Conqueror* (originally a *Weird Tales* serial, **"The Hour of the Dragon"**) said: "Conan, the hero of all of Howard's heroes, is the armored swashbuckler, indestructible and irresistible, that we've all wanted to be at one time or another."

Actually, Howard had more in common with Kull than with Conan. Kull is given to mystical broodings on the meaning of it all. Conan, on the other hand, is more the pure extrovert, much more interested in wine, women, and battle than in abstract questions. (p. 158)

Howard envisaged the entire life of Conan, from birth to old age, and made him grow and develop as a real man does. At the start, Conan is merely a lawless, reckless, irresponsible, predatory youth with few virtues save courage, loyalty to his few friends, and a rough-and-ready chivalry toward women. In time he learns caution, prudence, duty, and responsibility, until by middle age he has matured enough to make a reasonably good king. On the contrary, many heroes of heroic fantasy seem, like the characters of Homer and of P. G. Wodehouse, to have the enviable faculty of staying the same age for half a century at a stretch.

Although self-taught, Howard achieved a sound, taut, unobtrusive prose style. He wrote in sentences of short to medium length and simple construction, as became general after the Hemingway revolution of the thirties. He could give the impression of a highly colorful scene while making only sparing use of action-slowing modifiers. . . .

Some contemporary writers, who try to make up for lack of an interesting story by stylistic eccentricities, could profit from a study of Howard. (p. 162)

Howard was a devotee of the "well-wrought tale" as opposed to the "slice-of-life" school of fiction. Stories of either kind have their place; but for pure escapist entertainment, which Howard's stories were meant to be, the well-wrought tale usually works better.

As a writer, Howard had faults as well as virtues. His faults arose mainly from haste. Like his pulp-writing colleagues, he had to turn out a large volume to make a living. He rarely wrote more than two drafts and sometimes only one. Hence his stories have many inconsistencies, anachronisms, and other examples of careless craftsmanship. (p. 163)

Critics have blamed Howard for his fictional violence and for his immaturity in human relationships. Conan swaggers about the Hyborian stage, bedding one willing wench after another; but he views women as mere toys. True, he at last takes a legitimate queen, but as an afterthought. Howard was evidently as uncomfortable with love as the small boy who, viewing a Western, is loudly disgusted when the hero kisses the heroine instead of his horse. Furthermore, one critic was so staggered by the splashing of gore that he said Howard's stories "project the immature fantasy of a split mind and logically pave the way to schizophrenia.''

What seem like excessive bloodshed and emotional immaturity, however, were normal in the pulp fiction of Howard's time. Writers did not then deem it their duty to endow their heroes with social consciousness, to sympathize with disadvantaged ethnics, or to show their devotion to peace, equality, and social justice. A story that displayed these now-esteemed qualities would not have gotten far in the pulps.

Withal, Howard was a natural storyteller, and this is the *sine qua non* of fiction-writing. With this talent, many of a writer's faults may be overlooked; without it, no other virtues make up for the lack. (pp. 163-64)

Whatever their shortcomings, Howard's writings will long be enjoyed for their zest, vigor, furious action, and headlong narrative drive; for his ''purple and golden and crimson universe where anything can happen—except the tedious,'' spangled with ''vast megalithic cities of the elder world, around whose dark towers and labyrinthine nether vaults linger[s] an aura of pre-human fear and necromancy which no other writer could duplicate.'' (p. 164)

All through Howard's fantasy period, when he was writing tales of Kull and Conan, he kept pushing out into other areas of fiction. He wrote many stories of weird fantasy along conventional *Weird Tales* lines. In a couple of these, such as **"The Thing on the Roof,"** he used elements from Lovecraft's Cthulhu Mythos, to which he contributed the sinister volume *Nameless Cults*, by ''Friedrich von Junzt.''

Howard also wrote several detective stories. All have fantastic elements, like sinister oriental cults and African leopardmen. They were no great success, even though he sold them. Howard disliked the meticulous, intricate plotting called for in that genre. Moreover, never having lived in a big city, he found it hard to present the urban atmosphere convincingly.

He wrote his only interplanetary novel, **Almuric**. This was the nearest he came to science fiction proper, although he sometimes put super-scientific elements into his fantasies. **Almuric** is an obvious imitation of Burroughs. (pp. 165-66)

Howard also wrote tales of ancient, medieval, and modern adventure. Some brought in fantastic elements—magic, racial memory, monsters, lost cities, or prehistoric races—while others did not. . . .

Of Howard's many series of stories, built around a single character, one series has a Texan hero, Francis X. Gordon, adventuring in modern Afghanistan. Rifles crack, scimitars swish, and everybody kills everybody with gusto. These tales are derived from those that [Harold] Lamb and [Talbot] Mundy had been publishing in *Adventure*. (p. 166)

Howard early began work on Western stories, since he knew this milieu at first hand. He found the going hard. Knowing a setting too well, he said, could be a handicap. . . .

Many of Howard's Westerns are filled with a broad frontier humor, close to burlesque. . . .

Howard also wrote many non-humorous Westerns: grim, somber tales like most of his stories. To judge from those I have read, these are merely competent pulp. They are harmless amusement, with adequate dialogue and fair suspense. (p. 168)

When Howard's virtues and faults as a writer have been set forth, however, there remains that curiously hypnotic grip that his narratives have upon many readers. Apart from the headlong pace and verve and zest of Howard's storytelling, as Lovecraft put it, ''the real secret is that he himself is in every one of them.''

The ''self'' that Howard wrote into his stories with such burning intensity was a very—in fact fatally—flawed human being. He suffered from abnormal devotion to his mother, paranoid delusions of persecution, and a fascination with suicide. This somber self, with its nightmarish view of a hostile, menacing universe, its irrational fears, hatreds, and grudges, and its love affair with death, comes across in his fiction. It grips the reader whether he will or no, somewhat as do Lovecraft's fictional versions of his nightmares and neuroses. Thus the very traits that help to give Howard's fiction lasting interest are those that in the end destroyed him.

In any case, Howard's stories, despite their patent faults, bid fair to be enjoyed for their action, color, and furious narrative drive for many years to come. (pp. 169-70)

L. Sprague de Camp, "The Miscast Barbarian: Robert E. Howard," in his Literary Swordsmen and Sorcerers: The Makers of Heroic Fantasy *(copyright © 1976, by L. Sprague de Camp; reprinted by permission of Arkham House Publishers, Inc.), Arkham House, 1976, pp. 135-77.*

RAY WALTERS   (essay date 1978)

What explains Robert E. Howard's great life after death? All of his tales that are alive today are fantasies: sword-and-sorcery tales. Their heroes are indomitable males—King Kull, Solomon Kane, Bram Mak Morn and, greatest of all, Conan swaggering through faraway lands and times. Although they vary greatly in quality, all are written with compulsive, raw energy in a style that's a cross between Hemingway and the King James Bible.

Ray Walters, "Paperback Talk," in The New York Times Book Review *(© 1978 by The New York Times Company; reprinted by permission), April 30, 1978, p. 75.*

DARRELL SCHWEITZER   (essay date 1978)

Howard wrote a wide variety of adventure, pirate, western, historical, fantasy, and even detective fiction, though his mysteries were resoundingly bad, since he had little interest in the form. He wrote largely what he wanted to write, but also made an attempt to produce what the market demanded. (p. 5)

Howard's reputation depends primarily on his Conan stories; his other fiction has been reprinted solely because of their popularity. (p. 6)

The Conan canon proper consists of these stories: **"The Phoenix On The Sword," "The Scarlet Citadel," "The Tower of The Elephant," "Black Colossus," "The Slithering Shadow," "The Pool of the Black One," "Rogues In The House," "Shadows in The Moonlight," "Queen of The Black Coast," "The People of The Black Circle," "A Witch Shall Be Born," "Jewels of Gwahlur," "Beyond The Black River," "Shadows In Zamboula,"** *Conan The Conquerer* (a novel originally serialized in *Weird Tales* as *The Hour of The Dragon*), **"Red**

Nails,'' "The God in the Bowl,'' "The Black Stranger'' (edited by de Camp in all published versions), **"The Frost Giant's Daughter,''** and "The Vale of Lost Women.'' In the 1950s L. Sprague de Camp rewrote some unpublished non-Conan stories of Howard into Conan stories, very much as Howard would surely have done had he lived until the time of the Conan boom. . . . The collaborations generally lack the force of the completed tales, for several reasons. First, they are obviously stories Howard abandoned—false starts. They weren't working for him, so he never finished them. When a writer knows he is writing badly, he'll often set the story aside. Also, de Camp and [Lin] Carter are not Howard, nor is Bjorn Nyberg, who co-authored a pastiche novel with de Camp, *Conan The Avenger.* None of the pastiches have the same drive as the originals; they lack the headlong emotional intensity. Howard could sometimes get himself into a frenzied state, and carry the reader through by the sheer force of it, whether the story made any sense or not. De Camp's natural writing style is far from Howard's—he is clever, scholarly, frequently very witty, a good observer of human foibles. His characters in his own fantasies (e.g., *The Tritonian Ring*) have a wider variety of interests than a Howard barbarian, and generally behave like more ordinary human beings (they like safety and leisure). But de Camp's writing lacks the fury of Howard, and so do his pastiches. Not only do de Camp, Carter, and Nyberg lack Howard's more limited (and neurotic) point of view, but none of them are as crazy as he was. (pp. 7-8)

Conan, at about age seventeen, is first introduced to the Hyborian age in **"The Tower of The Elephant."** . . . The boy is very new to civilization when he arrives in The City of Thieves in Zamora, an appropriate setting, since he is a thief himself (most of the early stories are about burglaries that go wrong). Conan is presented not only as a ferocious barbarian warrior, but also as an adolescent, complete with a trace of adolescent insecurity and inexperience. He doesn't yet understand the subtleties of civilization, including the custom of laughing at people who seem ignorant. He commits a few gaffes among the tavern riff-raff, and: "The Cimmerian glared about, embarrassed at the roar of mocking laughter that greeted his remark. He saw no particular humor in it and was too new to civilization to understand its discourtesies. Civilized men are more discourteous than savages because they know they can be impolite without having their skulls split, as a general thing. He was bewildered and chagrined and doubtless would have slunk away, abashed, but the Kothian chose to goad him further." . . . (p. 11)

This is a very *human* scene. An older, more experienced man wouldn't be upset by such a thing, but a boy would. This is one of the secrets of Howard's success. The characters of his imitators seem to act the same way, whether they are seventeen or seventy. They don't grow and change. But Conan does. An older Conan wouldn't have reacted in this way, or seem at all inclined to slink away. More confident, he would have done what Conan did anyway, skewer the bastard with the nearest broadsword. Conan, like Howard himself, is always impulsive, but the young Conan is sufficiently unsure of himself to hesitate.

On impulse, and to soothe his wounded pride (not to mention his empty purse and scanty wardrobe—one loincloth) Conan proceeds to break into the Tower of The Elephant, where he intends to steal a fabled jewel from the sorcerer-priest who lives there. He had been laughed at for asking why so valuable a bauble remains secure in the middle of the aptly-named City

of Thieves. Everyone assumes that *of course* it is impossible to steal the thing. Conan is out to prove them wrong. But this burglary, like most of the ones Howard chronicles, has unexpected complications. Inside the priest's garden he meets Taurus of Nemedia, a master thief who's after the same prize, and he is able to teach the young Cimmerian a trick or two before getting killed by a giant spider. The two had agreed to work together—in Conan stories at least, there is honor among thieves—but now Conan has the prize all to himself. However, if Conan were to make off with a fabulous treasure, buy a palace, and settle down, the series would be a lot less interesting. So he always seems to lose what he's after. This time, it turns out that the source of the priest's power is an extracosmic thing being held prisoner in the tower, blinded, and subdued by torture. This thing grants powers and reveals arcane secrets, and is finally slain by Conan, not in a typical man-vs.-monster battle, but without struggle, as an act of mercy. Conan puts the creature out of its misery, at the same time bringing about the wizard-priest's destruction. He squeezes the thing's heart over the jewel he has come for, and then, as the creature had instructed him before it died, delivers it to the wizard, who is magically shrunk down and absorbed into the gem, where the spirit of the alien being takes its revenge. Conan escapes just before the tower collapses (it had been held up by the priest's magic), apparently without booty. Again he shows more than a one-dimensional nature. To help another intelligent being, he gives up his loot.

The story is one which has become standard in recent years—the barbarian invades the variously-defended castle, slaying monsters, destroying supernatural menaces, killing the wizard, and exiting, usually without the treasure he had come for. But it was new with Howard, and his version is vivid, deftly written, and more humanly believeable than most. (pp. 11-12)

Conan is usually depicted as a total extrovert with a very limited range of interests, primarily sex, violence, and booze; he is not very bright, except, perhaps, in a cunning sort of way, and not really very interesting as a personality. But he does have a knack for getting into—and out of—interesting situations. (p. 18)

Conan's approach to life is one of grim, live-for-the-moment fatalism: "In this world men struggle and suffer vainly, finding pleasure only in the bright madness of battle; dying, their souls enter a gray, misty realm of clouds and icy winds, to wander cheerlessly throughout eternity." . . .

The idea of finding pleasure only in battle is hardly new—the barbarians of the past frequently fought just for the love of killing. The Vikings are a typical example. And in Tacitus' *Germanicus* we read that Germanic warriors in Roman times became slovenly and bored when there was no battle to fight; when things got too tedious they went out and made one. Just like Conan.

Conan is not really interested in metaphysical speculation. On such subjects he says: "I know not, nor do I care. Let me live deep while I live; let me know the rich juices of red meat and stinging wine on my palate, the hot embrace of white arms, the mad exultation of battle when blue blades flame crimson, and I am content. Let teachers and priests and philosophers brood over questions of reality and illusion. I know this: if life is illusion, then I am no less an illusion, and being thus, the illusion is real to me. I live. I burn with life, I love, I slay, and am content." . . .

This attitude is one of the causes for Conan's popularity, I think. It has wide appeal in an age lacking ideals and devoted to hedonism. It especially echoes the sentiments of the alienated young. (p. 19)

What were Howard's racial ideas? According to de Camp, and also according to Howard's own letters, he was relatively liberal for his time and place, in direct contrast to H. P. Lovecraft. Howard never indulged in long racial harangues, damning everyone who wasn't an old-time Texan, the way HPL did with those who weren't old New Englanders. However, his time and place were far different than our own. No Black man was allowed to stay out past sundown in Howard's county, let alone live there. Thus he couldn't have had much contact with them, and any depiction would have been drawn more from popular stereotype than real life experiences. Such stereotypes were not only permitted in most pulp magazines; they were expected.

Howard viewed Blacks as incurably savage and primitive, but to him this might not be the worst thing in the world. He sympathized with the primitive and savage himself. Personal freedom was his one driving obsession (as he admitted in letters), and he saw civilization as unbearably restrictive. He overlooked, of course, the fact that real barbarians are more bound by tribal taboos, customs, and a sheer lack of opportunity than any civilized man. His romanticized version of the barbarian was strong, noble, uninhibited, and free—so the eternally primitive Black might live better and have more of the virtues he respected than a civilized White. He did, at times, depict them favorably in his fiction. He may have felt, like the typical Southerner, that races shouldn't mix, but he doesn't seem to have actively hated Blacks. (pp. 27-8)

What did Howard think of the sadism in his stories? He understood the climate of the times as well as anyone. He was more interested in making his stories ''as bloody and brutal as the ages and the incidents I was trying to depict actually were.'' But there were limits: ''I don't know how much slaughter and butchery the readers will endure. Their capacity for grisly details seems unlimited, when the cruelty is the torturing of some naked girl, such as Seabury Quinn's stories abound in—no reflection intended on Quinn; he knows what they want and gives it to them. The torture of a naked writhing wretch, utterly helpless—and especially when of the feminine sex amid voluptuous surroundings—seems to excite keen pleasure in some people who have a distaste for wholesale butchery in the heat and fury of a battlefield. Well, to me the former seems much more abominable than the cutting down of armed men—even the slaughter of prisoners in the madness of fighting lust.'' . . . (p. 33)

Clearly Howard started out in a flash of inspiration, mustering his considerable literary skills as he wrote, but how well did he keep it up? Did he exhaust the [Conan] series by the time he was done? Let's take a quick look at how the stories stack up in the order written, which presumably is very close to the order published: . . .

"The Phoenix On The Sword." . . . A reworked Kull tale, which means he had something to use as a springboard. Quite good, but hinged on coincidence. . . .

"The Frost Giant's Daughter." . . . This is rather slight, but what there is of it works. Conan encounters an interesting supernatural menace and prevails by sheer animal strength, as he often does. One might ask how the supernatural Frost Giants, who may or may not be illusory, and can clearly vanish at will, are material enough to be carved into hamburger, but Conan always insisted that anything solid enough to hurt you can feel the bit of steel. It's just as well they didn't have poison gas in his day. . . .

"The Scarlet Citadel." . . . An evil and vaguely motivated wizard, coincidental rescue, lots of blood. Probably the feud between the two sorcerers is the most interesting part. Fairly good. . . .

"The Tower of The Elephant." . . . Excellent! The perfect barbarian/burglar story. Contains a good portrait of the teenaged Conan. . . .

"Black Colossus." . . . Quite good. One of the most satisfactory versions of the resurrected-nemesis-from-the-past routine, even if the ending is a bit perfunctory. . . .

"The Slithering Shadow." . . . Fairly good. Conan has a sensible reason (dire desperation) for venturing into the standard-issue lost city of green stone. The picture of the decadent inhabitants apathetically awaiting their doom has more life in it than the many permutations wrought by Clark Ashton Smith, a fellow *WT* contributor who used this plot in about half his total output. (p. 50)

"The Pool of The Black One." . . . The pits. A bare vestige of a plot and lots of mindless butchery. Violence for its own sake. Presumably by the time this one came along Conan had already proven popular, so [Farnsworth Wright, editor of *Weird Tales*] bought a story inferior to **"Frost Giant"** because he knew the readers wouldn't care. (pp. 50-1)

"Rogues In The House." . . . Quite good. Civilized treachery contrasted with simple, clean-cut, barbaric chivalry (as Howard imagined it). This time Conan has a sound reason for indulging in his favorite pastime of battling giant apes. . . .

"Shadows In The Moonlight." . . . This time he does not. One wishes he had left the ape for Tarzan, the pirate stuff for a painting by Howard Pyle, and the pseudo-Cossackisms for Harold Lamb. A rather dismal hodgepodge. It seems that while Howard had hit his stride by this point, he also stumbled frequently. . . .

"The Black Stranger/Treasure of Tranicos." . . . Inferior Conan, and not much Conan at that, since he appears mostly at the end, as a device to resolve the plot and get everybody skewered as most of them richly deserve. By this time Howard was losing his grip on his original vision, and just went through the motions. It is the nature of a mass-production professional to compose fiction whether he is inspired or not. Here he wasn't. . . .

"Queen of The Black Coast." . . . Top-drawer material. Belit is one of Howard's few interesting female characters—too bad he killed her off so quickly. This is also one of the best treatments of the lost city motif. There is an excuse for its being there and an excuse for it being haunted. . . .

"The Devil In Iron." . . . Above average. The godlike being is a first-rate creation, but some of the plot convolutions are a bit contrived. . . .

"The People of The Black Circle." . . . Longer, less limited in scope than most of the series. Quite good. Achieves the considerable technical feat of changing scenes and situations a large number of times without seeming silly. (p. 51)

"A Witch Shall Be Born." . . . Pretty bad. Conan is just a prop in this one, but there is the famous crucifixion scene in which he shows incredible physical stamina, again without seeming silly. I don't think anybody but Howard could have even momentarily convinced the reader that Conan could pull nails out of his feet with his pierced hands, which presumably have broken bones and cut tendons, and then walk to a horse and climb into the saddle. (pp. 51-2)

"Beyond The Black River." . . . The Balthus/Conan friendship is interesting, but otherwise it's cowboys and Indians. Pretty poor. . . .

"Shadows In Zamboula." . . . Fair, with stereotyped characters. Not one of the more memorable stories. . . .

The Hour of The Dragon/Conan The Conquerer. . . . Well above average. A demonstration of all the strengths and only a moderate amount of the weaknesses of the series. But it does show Howard's inability to actually *plot* (rather than merely string together) the incidents in a longer story. . . .

"Red Nails." . . . Above average. All Howard's stories seem to be about hate; this is one of the few to examine the consequences. . . .

"The God In The Bowl." . . . A reject because it's too talky. Some good writing here, but the "shock" ending is too contrived to be effective. One of the few times Howard tries to go opaque about a story element so he can reveal it at the end. . . .

"The Vale of Lost Women." . . . Rejected for obvious reasons. Certainly this is the worst Conan story, with the possible exception of **"Pool of The Black One."** But it does shed some light on Conan's career as a chief of the Blacks.

If you look at the stories in this order, you see, I think, a general level of quality maintained, but with increasingly frequent slips. One can speculate that Howard wouldn't have maintained the series indefinitely. . . . (p. 52)

Although it may shock some afficianados, the Conan stories do not hold up at all as a series. Individual stories remain readable—Howard had a good sense of vast historical movements, the rise and fall of nations, and the like, as his essay **"The Hyborian Age"** reveals. He was not a very good creator of imaginary places. History he could handle; customs, culture, geography, religion, he couldn't. The Hyborian Age is simply a mishmash of various historical and quasi-historical (i.e., history considerably distorted) places and eras, to the point that if you know where a character is heading, you know what to expect even before he gets there. There are few geographical/social surprises in the series.

This is particularly obvious in **"The People of The Black Circle,"** which may be a rousing good story, but is simply set in Talbot Mundy's India with some of the names changed. Thus, after passing through Turan (Turkey) by the Vilayet (Caspian) Sea, one comes to Iranistan (Persia) and then reaches the Himelian (Himalayan) Mountains, which are inhabited by wild Afghuli (Afghan) tribesmen, and then goes through the Zhaibar (Kyber) Pass into Vendhya (India), in which the warrior caste is called the Kshatriya, as it really was in pre-modern India.

Howard was taken to task for this by his correspondents Lovecraft and [E. Hoffmann] Price, but he defended the practice on the grounds that his stories were set in an earlier age on our planet, and thus all the peoples are ancestors of those of historic times, accounting for the resemblances. This is fine to a point, but Howard goes well beyond that point. It is true that the folk of the European Renaissance are descended from those of Alexander the Great's time, but there are vast differences in language, culture, religion, politics, etc. And Howard is talking about a far greater span of time, in the course of which cataclysms erased all traces of the past. It would seem he was treading the thin line between acceptable license and sheer laziness, and fell off. The problem is that his desert tribesmen are stock pulp fiction Arabs, minus any reference to Islam, of course. His "Afghuli" mountain warriors are the same types who populate his stories of modern Afghanistan (*Swords of Shahrazar, The Lost Valley of Iskander*). No wonder it was so easy for de Camp to turn some of these historicals into Conan stories. . . . Aside from the vengeance-obsessed folk of **"Red Nails,"** Howard never came up with an interesting, original society, or anything that was more than a superficial version of some genuine one. (pp. 52-4)

It is to Howard's credit, however, that he bothered to mention the ways in which his peoples made their livings. Thus there are all sorts of common folk, sailors, fishermen, woodcutters, inn-keepers, and so on, especially in the longer and more detailed *Conan The Conquerer.* This is a huge stride beyond many of the Conan imitations, in which society seems to consist of but three classes: wandering swordsmen, evil wizards, and wenches.

Howard was, in my opinion, a writer of superior ability who only sometimes wrote as well as he could, due mainly to haste and sheer laziness. (p. 56)

This brings us to the subject of Howard's other works. The Conan series represents the merest tip of his literary iceberg: he wrote a huge quantity of fiction, and it would require five such volumes to discuss it at length. Most of his other fantasy works strike the same notes as the Conan stories, so it is fair to judge him on those. They are typical. Not quite so typical are the stories assembled into the book *King Kull.* . . . These were a series about a barbarian adventurer from Atlantis who becomes king of the rich land of Valusia. He was very much a prototype of Conan, but with differences. Conan is interested in little more than satisfying his appetites. Kull is one of the few Howard characters to show any intellect. The savage Kull is of a philosophical bent, and often ponders the ultimate questions. He explores (sometimes inadvertently) the supernatural universe around him. One story simply consists of Kull waking up in the land of the dead and talking with Old Man Death; and then returning home to find he had been merely stunned by a would-be assassin and not killed. **"The Mirrors of Tuzun Thune"** is one of Howard's best stories, and one of the least orthodox. It is basically a brooding mood piece, with little action. Tired of his life, Kull gazes into a wizard's mystic mirrors, seeking wisdom, something which seldom concerns most Howard characters. He is almost absorbed into another reality before someone kills the wizard and calls him back. This was a plot to do the king in, but forever after he still ponders the mysteries which have been revealed. Other Kull stories contain more typical swordly-and-sorcerous adventure, but even so Kull is the most interesting of Howard's characters. Because many of the stories go so far into the supernatural and metaphysical, the Kull series might appeal even to the fantasy lover who normally doesn't read Howard, and perhaps a little less to the action adventure fan who normally doesn't read fantasy. Although far different stylistically, **"The Mirrors of Tuzun Thune"** bears resemblance to the famous early fantasies of Lord Dunsany. . . . (pp. 58-9)

King Kull also appears in **"Kings of The Night,"** which is essentially a part of the Bran Mak Morn series, and may be found in the volume *Worms of The Earth.* . . . Bran Mak Morn is a Pict as history knows Picts, but also a descendent of those mentioned in both the Kull and Conan stories, which suggests these people are *eternally* savage, since they have been fiercely primitive for over a hundred thousand years. Across such a chasm of time, King Kull is summoned up by a Pictish wizard to help Bran fight the Romans in what is now Scotland, circa 200 A.D. The Romans never got very far north of Hadrian's Wall, the remoter Antonine Wall having been abandoned shortly after it was built. Howard attributed this to the heroic valor of the northern barbarians, and since they had so successfully resisted the constraining authority of Rome, his heart was with them. **"Kings of The Night"** and **"Worms of The Earth,"** which immediately follows it, are among his most vivid and passionate tales. The latter is also one of his best treatments of the supernatural. Bran asks the aid of the dread Little People (ideas for whom are largely borrowed from Arthur Machen, and openly acknowledged in a posthumously published tale **"The Little People,"** in which somebody is reading *The Shining Pyramid* shortly before *outre* things start happening), and they are so horrific both in aspect and personality that he long regrets it. His Roman enemy is carried off by them unharmed, but driven mad by what he has seen beneath the ground, and Bran kills him out of mercy, when he had planned on revenge. These same little people, pre-Pictish Picts (i.e., the *original* dwarfish Picts, with whom the later ones interbred in ages long gone), are seen more closely in **"The Lost Race."** This is an early, rather awkward piece, in which Howard for once does resort to lecturing, though not for very long. (pp. 59-60)

[The book **Red Shadows**] contains all the tales of Solomon Kane, an Elizabethan Puritan adventurer who travels about the world righting wrongs, seeking danger, killing sorcerers, and the like. Some of these stories are very good, some no good at all. Kane is even more of a somber, brooding giant than the usual Howard hero.

There were even Howard forays into the Lovecraftian Cthulhu Mythos. These stories, of which **"The Black Stone"** is probably the best known, tend to be written in a slightly less arthritic style than most of the type, but with all of their faults. There is a vast amount of exposition, although Howard manages to convey more experience than most Mythos writers, and the first half of the story isn't *quite* an essay. In **"The Black Stone"** the hero seeks the secret of that edifice, and discovers it to be associated with a rather routine cult of Macrocosmic Nasties. Howard soon realized this was not his *forte* and gave it up. (p. 61)

There are also a lot of westerns. Howard wanted to write a serious epic of the Southwest, and was sure that his career was headed that way in the last year of his life, but it never quite did. Surprisingly, he never used the land in which he lived all his life as effectively as he did those he imagined. Most of the westerns are strictly routine, but of interest are those collected in *A Gent From Bear Creek.* . . . Also of note is *The Pride of Bear Creek.* . . . These show a completely unsuspected side of Howard's writing—*humor,* a broad, raucous, slapsticky kind

of humor, rather like that of the traditional American tall tale. Some critics hold these to be his very best work, but I must agree with Karl Edward Wagner who said (in the introduction to *The Hour of The Dragon*) that this sort of thing tends to wear thin after a while, and that had he continued in this vein, Howard would have soon exhausted it. This is probably true. Mark Twain could write a lot more folksy humor because he was good enough. A work like *Huckleberry Finn* also had genuine substance, real characters, astute social observations, and much else. Howard never got beyond the "Aw shucks. We's jes here fer larfs" stage. (pp. 61-2)

Darrell Schweitzer, in his Conan's World and Robert
E. Howard *(copyright © 1978 by Darrell Schweitzer),
The Borgo Press, 1978, 64 p.*

STEVE ENG   (essay date 1981)

[*Always Comes Evening* was an initial] gathering of the then-known Howard poems. . . . [It is] a representative volume, capturing Howard's intense, somber poetic talent. As in his fiction, there is color and clamor and storytelling zest. Like Clark Ashton Smith, Howard may have been more instinctively a poet than a prose writer; and as with Smith—and to some extent Lovecraft, [Frank Belknap] Long, [Donald] Wandrei, and [Joseph Payne] Brennan—the power of his prose had its origin in his verse. Like much *Weird Tales* poetry, Howard's was often merely exotic or fanciful, yet much was supernatural-horrific, too. Howard's mother read him poetry from earliest childhood, and he later visited his many influences—the first three being Robert W. Service, Kipling, and Masefield; their drumming cadences and active verbs certainly resound in his verse. He named over two dozen other poets whom he liked, including Siegfried Sasson (whose war poetry may have inspired him), George Sylvester Viereck (whose pagen pomp evokes Howard), Alfred Noyes, Villon (whom he commemorated in a poem), Coleridge (after two readings, he is said to have memorized *The Ancient Mariner*), Swinburne, and Poe. A paraphrased couplet from Ernest Dowson was left as Howard's suicide note. (p. 443)

Steve Eng, "Supernatural Verse in English," in Horror Literature: A Core Collection and Reference Guide, *edited by Marshall B. Tymn (reprinted with permission of the R. R. Bowker Company; copyright © 1981 by Xerox Corporation), Bowker, 1981, pp. 434-52.*

JESSICA AMANDA SALMONSON   (essay date 1982)

Robert E. Howard was a great storyteller. Perhaps not a skilled writer in technical terms, but nonetheless, his ficiton is powerful in an awkward, honest, direct manner—not unlike many of his heros. Certainly his style is appealing, as his popularity continues in spite of his imitators' every effort to bury his genius with insipid copies—though even this may be his fans' fault, demanding "more" from someone too long dead to provide it.

It is indicative of his talent that he could do what few adventure writers can do even today: that is, depict a strong woman. Further, he did it in an atmosphere of rank misogyny: the male-defined pulp era of writing. He created Belit, at whose feet even mighty Conan had to sit; and he created Agnes de Chastillon, a Frenchwoman whose swordskill was unmatched in her time.

Rarely have women been portrayed as positively and strongly as Dark Agnes. I've no idea what Howard's ideas about women were; through much of his fiction, he seems fundamentally naive about women, yet comparatively far less exploitative in the way his female characters are depicted. Possibly he knew a rough, hard, endearing Texas woman who influenced him; possibly his love of history uncovered too many amazon figures to ignore. Perhaps he even gave thought to issues we consider modern and feminist. Maybe none of these things approached his thinking at all—but he saw, as lesser storytellers rarely see, that tales about whining, meek, abused chatels and sex objects are not as entertaining as stories about a woman loath of those positions. . . .

The first story, *Sword Woman*, tells the origin of Dark Agnes. It is a tough, angry story about a girl who could not be tamed, not even by a father who beat her regularly. She slays her disgusting husband-to-be with wicked delight, and sets off to adventure. She is a woman of moral character, however, living by a code of her own. (p. 4)

Intense, pointed, true—Agnes has sworn herself to celibacy, aware that even to share a bed with man, in her society and ours, is to be bridled. Howard captures the essence of a politic few men dare realize—a concept usually dismissed by men as the madness of man-hating lesbians, or whoever else can be blamed for men's own limited comprehension. This aspect of Agnes' character is important to both of the stories [*Sword Woman* and *Blades for France*] Howard wrote, so one would guess it a concept Howard was consciously exploring. In the third story [*Mistress of Death*], however, it is absent as a theme— which is one reason I strongly suspect he did not write much of that one at all. (pp. 4-5)

Blades for France is a less eloquent story with rougher edges, too obviously written by a history buff, but still very satisfying. It has some truly rare moments, as when chaste Agnes receives her first kiss—from another woman! In the end, when Agnes' comrade is moony over having held that noblewoman in his arms, Agnes is silent. But a wise reader will know what's in Agnes' mind: Ah, but she *kissed* me.

This second story is a bit less insistent than the first in establishing and re-establishing that Agnes is shapely and beautiful. This is the one failing common to most adventure writers' depictions of presumably strong women. However, though other writers seem to include this aspect because they can't help but eroticise women at the expense of their humanity, with Howard it seemed to be the only way he knew to establish the fundamental normalcy and logic to Agnes' choices.

He never conceived the notion of androgynous beauty, nor seemed to realize "beauty" itself is cultural. He felt compelled to establish that Agnes was traditionally beautiful in spite of herself, as if to say, "See—she *is* a woman despite her choices." It adds nothing of character or realism, though it establishes, in the only way the author knew, that Agnes is not a warrior because she was too ugly or too stupid or too abnormal to be a wife.

In this story Howard somewhat overcomes the need to beautify Agnes in typical terms. Had he written more stories of Agnes, surely he'd have been done with "excusing" her strength with her beauty. . . .

In both *Blades for France* and *Sword Woman* Agnes is repeatedly confronted by men who want only to bed her, by force

if necessary. She answers each with her sword, saying, "Must I slay half the men in France to teach them respect?" The reader knows her frustration; and the message is clear to Agnes: the men of the world *still* want her to be a broodmare and a drudge. But Agnes remembers her pitiful sister, and all the other women who had not escaped their restricting roles—and she kills the men who would not let a woman grow.

Once again Howard has proven capable of appreciating the type of woman most men fear to confront even as an archetype, much less as a fictional character or a real-life feminist freedom fighter.

Had a woman written of Agnes, the author would have been charged with man-hating, frigidity, being a castrating bitch, a crazy radical. But it was written by a man—a man who was a wonderful storyteller—a man whose vision far exceeded the imagination of his imitators and of detractors from feminist ideals. (p. 5)

Jessica Amanda Salmonson, "Dark Agnes: A Critical Look at Robert E. Howard's 'Swordswoman'," in American Fantasy (© 1982 by Robert Garcia), Vol. 1, No. 1, February, 1982, pp. 4-6.

ED SUMMER (essay date 1982)

The original Howard stories were very much of their time, of the 1930s. They were magical tales of a very powerful hero characterized by a wonderful kind of purple prose.

The stories stood out because they were a little tougher than the rest of that type of fiction, a little more risque. By today's standards, however, I think we'd find Conan a bit Victorian. He's as moral as a boy scout in some ways. He's very protective of his women. He never takes advantage of anybody.

But part of his appeal, even in modern times, is that he takes very direct action. We live in a world that's becoming increasingly complex, where the decision making process is getting more and more convoluted. Look at the modern court systems. Taking legal action against someone is an exceedingly complex, expensive and time consuming process.

Conan deals with things head-on. In one Howard story, Conan finds himself before a judge after killing one of the King's guards. The guard was about to do in one of Conan's friends, someone who'd saved his life, and Conan, naturally, defended his friend. The judge gives him a big speech about how immoral it was of Conan to kill the guard. Conan just stands there. 'Here was a friend of mine, someone who had fed me and sheltered me and saved my life. His life was in danger. I saved his life. Now, a judge tells me that my actions were wrong. Obviously everyone in this courtroom is mad. I seized my sword and slew them all.'

I find that a very appealing story. It's like cutting through red tape literally.

Conan's morality runs very much in that direction. He makes decisions based upon expediency and devotion. He has a god that doesn't help him, that doesn't care. That's a very existential situation, similar to what Camus wrote about in *The Myth of Sisyphus*. Conan can't find the meaning in life. He lives to fight, to feel the blood pounding in his veins, to drink good wine, to be with lusty women. That's what he lives for. He has no hope for an afterlife. (p. 65)

Ed Summer, "Conan the Barbarian," an interview with Ed Naha, in Starlog *(© copyright 1982 by O'Quinn Studios, Inc.), Vol. 5, No. 59, June, 1982, pp. 16-21, 65.*

ADDITIONAL BIBLIOGRAPHY

De Camp, L. Sprague, ed. *The Spell of Conan*. New York: Ace Books, 1980, 244 p.
> Collection of essays on heroic fantasy by Poul Anderson, George H. Scithers, L. Sprague de Camp, Avram Davidson, and others.

Lord, Glenn, ed. *The Last Celt: A Bio-bibliography of Robert Ervin Howard*. New York: Berkley Pub. Corp., 1977, 415 p.
> Extensive background material to Howard's writings, including a 247-page bibliography.

Wagner, Karl Edward. Foreword to *The Hour of the Dragon*, by Robert E. Howard, pp. 1-12. New York: G. P. Putnam's Sons, 1977.
> The evolution of Conan and some publication facts about *The Hour of the Dragon*.

Henrik (Johan) Ibsen

1828-1906

(Also wrote under pseudonym of Brynjolf Bjarme) Norwegian dramatist and poet.

Regarded as the father of modern drama, Ibsen brought realism and social concerns to a European theater that had been circumscribed by romanticism. He perfected the conversation drama and brought to his plays techniques of classic Greek tragedy. Employing techniques the "well-made-play" of Eugene Scribe and the realism of various other French and Russian authors of the time, Ibsen created a national drama distinctly Norwegian—something previously absent in his country's literature.

Ibsen was born in Skien to wealthy parents. The family was reduced to poverty when his father's business failed in 1834. Ibsen left home at fifteen, and after six years as a pharmacist's assistant in Grimstadt, he went to Christiana, now Oslo, hoping to enter the university. Although he failed several preliminary exams and was not admitted, his studies led him to the classical history that formed the basis of his first drama, *Catilina (Catiline)*, which was not produced for many years. This otherwise undistinguished first work contains the seeds of what later developed into Ibsen's primary themes: the importance of the individual and the search for self-realization. In this play, Aurelia and Furia are representative of two female types which recur in nearly all of Ibsen's dramas: one dull and domestic, the other fascinating but potentially dangerous. In Christiana, Ibsen met Bjørnstjerne Bjørnson, who was to become Norway's other great nineteenth-century dramatist. While the two men shared a lifelong relationship of mutual respect, serious misunderstandings became the cause of years-long rifts in their friendship. They were ultimately reconciled by the marriage of Ibsen's only son to Bjørnson's daughter.

In 1851 Ibsen took the post of assistant stage manager of the Norwegian theater in Bergen. One of his duties was to write and produce an original drama each year. These early plays, in verse, are for the most part derived from Norwegian history and legend. Though slight, they indicate the direction Ibsen's drama was to take, especially in their presentation of a strong individual who confronts a society that does not encourage individualism. In 1862, verging on a breakdown from overwork, Ibsen began to petition the government for a grant to travel and write. He was given a stipend in 1864, and various scholarships and pensions subsequently followed. For the next twenty-seven years he lived abroad in self-imposed exile, revisiting Norway only twice. Bitter memories of his father's financial failure, and of his own lack of success as a theater manager, in part account for this long absence. Also, Ibsen felt that only by distancing himself from his homeland could he obtain the perspective necessary to write truly Norwegian drama. He did not share in the cultural life of his host countries; rather, he kept himself apart and devoted himself almost fanatically to the writing of his intensely nationalistic dramas.

The massive body of Ibsen's work is generally divided by critics into three phases. The first consists of his early works written in verse, which were influenced by the prevailing romanticism of the European theater, and drew heavily from traditional

folk tales, songs, and the Norse sagas for subject matter. The second phase of Ibsen's work is made up of the plays of prose realism for which the dramatist is most famous. In his final phase, Ibsen continued to deal with modern, realistic themes, but made increasing use of symbol and metaphor.

Ibsen's earliest plays, including *Haermaendene på Helgeland (The Vikings at Helgeland)* and *Kjaerlighedens komedie (Love's Comedy)*, are notable primarily for their idiosyncratically Norwegian characters, and for those elements of gentle satire and not-so-gentle social criticism that were to distinguish Ibsen's later dramas. The first two plays Ibsen wrote after leaving Norway were the vast epic verse dramas *Brand* and *Peer Gynt*. *Brand* extolles the duty of the individual to be true to his own convictions and at the same time exposes the dangers of such an approach. *Peer Gynt* reflects Ibsen's disillusionment with what he saw as Norway's national character. This was the last drama he wrote in verse. The immense two-part "world-historical drama" *Kejser og Galilaeer (Emperor and Galilean)* was the last play Ibsen set in the past.

Ibsen entered his second phase in 1877, producing at two-year intervals those works of modern realism which initially shocked theater patrons and critics alike. The frank treatment of controversial subjects in *Samfundets støtter (The Pillars of Society)*, *Et dukkehjem (A Doll's House)*, *Gengangere (Ghosts)*, and *En folkefiende (An Enemy of the People)* aroused virulent criticism in Norway and throughout Europe. Bernard Shaw, Georg Brandes, along with Ibsen's early English translators Edmund Gosse and William Archer, were among the first to defend these works. They were instrumental in bringing the theater-going public to an acceptance of drama not merely as entertainment but as social commentary. These dramas are now recognized as sincere and highly moral indictments of the flaws in modern society.

With *Vildanden (The Wild Duck)* and *Hedda Gabler* Ibsen began a period of transition characterized by an emphasis on symbolic elements. Ibsen returned to Norway in 1891 and there wrote his last four plays: *Bygmester Solness (The Master Builder)*, *Lille Eyolf (Little Eyolf)*, *John Gabriel Borkman*, and *Når vi døde vågner (When We Dead Awaken)*, all dealing with the conflict of art with life. In these final works symbolism plays an increasingly large part, and Ibsen's focus shifts from the individual in society to the individual alone and isolated. The subjectivism and elusive symbolism of these last plays have led to critical conjecture that they are founded in autobiography.

Ibsen is credited with the introduction of the social problem play, which changed the form of nineteenth-century theater. Even his greatest detractor, August Strindberg, in reacting against Ibsen was forced to acknowledge his significance. Despite occasionally dated theatrical conventions and subject matter, his range, powerful imagination, great technical skill, and depth of moral vision combine to make Ibsen a continued influence on modern drama.

(See also *TCLC*, Vol. 2.)

PRINCIPAL WORKS

Fru Inger til Østraat   (drama)   1855
  [*Lady Inger of Østraat* published in *The Collected Works of Henrik Ibsen*, 1906-12]
Gildet på Solhaug   (drama)   1856
  [*The Feast at Solhaug*, 1909]
Haermaendene på Helgeland   (drama)   1858
  [*The Vikings at Helgeland* published in *The Collected Works of Henrik Ibsen*, 1906-12]
Kongs emnerne   (drama)   1864
  [*The Pretenders*, 1907]
De unges forbund   (drama)   1869
  [*The League of Youth* published in *Ibsen's Prose Dramas*, 1890]
Digte af Henrik Ibsen   (poetry)   1871
  [*Lyrics and Poems from Ibsen*, 1912]
Kjaerlighedens komedie   (drama)   1873
  [*Love's Comedy*, 1898]
Peer Gynt   (drama)   1876
  [*Peer Gynt*, 1902]
Samfundets støtter   (drama)   1878
  [*The Pillars of Society* published in *The Pillars of Society, and Other Plays*, 1888]
Et dukkehjem   (drama)   1879
  [*Nora*, 1882; also published as *A Doll Home*, 1882; also published as *A Doll's House*, 1889]
Catilina [as Brynjolf Bjarme]   (drama)   1881
  [*Catiline* published in *Early Plays: Catiline, The Warrior's Barrow, Olaf Liljekrans*, 1921]
Gengangere   (drama)   1882
  [*Ghosts*, 1890]

En folkefiende   (drama)   1883
  [*An Enemy of Society* published in *The Pillars of Society, and Other Plays*, 1888; also published as *An Enemy of the People*, 1939]
Brand   (drama)   1885
  [*Brand*, 1891]
Vildanden   (drama)   1885
  [*The Wild Duck* published in *Ibsen's Prose Dramas*, 1890]
Rosmersholm   (drama)   1887
  [*Rosmersholm*, 1889]
Fruen fra havet   (drama)   1889
  [*The Lady from the Sea*, 1890]
Hedda Gabler   (drama)   1891
  [*Hedda Gabler*, 1891]
Terje Vigne   (poetry)   1891
  [*Terje Vigne*, 1917]
Bygmester Solness   (drama)   1893
  [*The Master Builder*, 1893]
Lille Eyolf   (drama)   1895
  [*Little Eyolf*, 1894]
Kejser og Galilaeer   (drama)   1896
  [*Emperor and Galilean*, 1876]
John Gabriel Borkman   (drama)   1897
  [*John Gabriel Borkman*, 1897]
Samlede Vaerker. 10 vols.   (dramas, poetry, and scenarios) 1898-1902
Når vi døde vågner   (drama)   1900
  [*When We Dead Awaken*, 1900]
Breve udg Henrik Ibsen   (letters)   1904
  [*Letters of Henrik Ibsen*, 1905]
The Collected Works of Henrik Ibsen. 12 vols.   (dramas, poetry, and scenarios)   1906-12

[EDMUND W. GOSSE]   (essay date 1872)

It is not too much to say that [in *Peer Gynt*] the Norwegian language received a fuller and more splendid expression than in any previous work. It comes from the hand of Henrik Ibsen, a poet who is fast gaining for himself that European fame which nothing but the remoteness of his mother-tongue has hitherto denied him; his *Brand* . . . produced a great sensation in Scandinavia, and paved the way for this later drama, which surpasses it in vigour and fire, if it does not rival its spiritual sweetness.

Peer Gynt takes its name from its hero, and the germ of him is to be found in an old legend preserved by [Peter Christen] Asbjörnsen. Peer Gynt was an idle fellow, whose aim was to live his own life, and whose chief characteristics were a knack for story-telling and a dominant passion for lies. Out of this legendary waif Ibsen has evolved a character of wonderful subtlety and liveliness, and hung round it draperies of allegorical satire. *Peer Gynt* is an epigram on the Norway of to-day; it satirises, as in a nutshell, everything vapid, or maudlin, or febrile in the temper of the nation; in sparkling verse it lashes the extravagances of the various parties that divide the social world. It is the opposite of its predecessor, *Brand,* for while that poem strove to wake the nation into earnestness by holding up before it an ideal of stainless nobility, *Peer Gynt* idealises in the character of its hero the selfishness and mean cunning of the worst of ambitious men. In form, the poem is indebted to [Goethe's] *Faust;* but the style and execution are original and masterly: it is written in a variety of lyrical measures, in short rhyming lines. With such a prelude, we proceed to examine it.

The first act opens with a briskness worthy of the famous opening scene in [Ben Jonson's] the *Alchemist.* Peer Gynt, a strong, lazy young peasant, is in high dispute with his mother, Aase, a credulous, irritable, affectionate little woman, whose character is finely drawn throughout the piece. . . . To say that Ibsen describes scenery in his plays would be to do his judgment and taste a great wrong; but it is one of his greatest powers, and a manifest mark of genius, that by small and imperceptible touches he enables the reader to see the surroundings of his dialogues, and gather a distinct and lovely impression. In this act it is strikingly so; the narrow green valley, the buttresses of pine, the cloudy mountain-ridges, are never distinctly alluded to, and yet one is fully conscious of their presence; in this act, too, the simple humour of the dialogue is not interrupted or overlaid by any allegorical writing. (pp. 922-23)

Peer Gynt is the incarnation of that cowardly egotism that lives only for itself, and sneers at all exalted sentiment,—a vice that may be considered the special growth of our own time. Against this selfishness the poem is a powerful protest. . . . Against one thing we would protest, the flippant judgment some Scandinavian critics have passed on Ibsen as a merely "negative" satirist. A man who pours out the vials of scorn upon vice, and recommends virtue with such winning sweetness as does the author of *Peer Gynt* and *Brand,* is anything rather than negative.

We have said enough to show that this is a great and powerful work. It would be rash to pronounce anything impossible to the author of the third act of *Peer Gynt,* but it would seem that his very power and fluency are dangerous to him; the book is not without marks of haste, and there is a general sense of incongruity and disjointedness. The African act exemplifies this mixture of brilliant and crude elements; one is alternately delighted and scandalised. (p. 923)

> [*Edmund W. Gosse,*] *"A Norwegian Drama," in* The Spectator *(© 1872 by The Spectator), Vol. 45, No. 2299, July 20, 1872, pp. 922-23.*

THE SPECTATOR (essay date 1893)

It is useless to attempt a criticism of Ibsen's work, and at the same time ignore the fierce controversy that is waged over his merits by his admirers, and those who fail to appreciate him. One cannot remain blind to the fact that the Norwegian dramatist is regarded by a small section of the reading public as one of the greatest writers of the day, almost, indeed, as a prophet with a divine message, and by another—and rather larger section—as a half-crazed impostor, whose writings, if they have any meaning at all, can only be looked upon as the lamentable ravings of criminal lunacy; nor, unfortunately, can we remain deaf to the vehemence with which these contrary opinions are expressed, for the dramatist seems to possess the unfortunate gift of provoking both his enemies and his friends into quite unreasonable excesses of violence or civility. We, for our part, have as little wish to be over-civil as we have to be over-violent; still, we confess that we cannot quite believe in the good faith of some of the hostility that has been displayed towards Henrik Ibsen. That his critics should abhor both his matter and his method, is more than possible; but that they should fail to discover any meaning in the man at all, and can really look upon his plays as sheer drivelling rubbish, is hardly

credible. . . . Ibsen, indeed, is intelligible enough to any one who takes the pains to understand—often quite too disagreeably intelligible—and it is not by shutting one's own eyes that one can blind the rest of the world to his real powers. It is useless to deny that the man is possessed of a strange dramatic force and intensity, a weird and startling imagination, and an unrivalled power of laying bare and dissecting the evil side of human nature, or the accidental disease of a single human soul; and not only that, but that he has also the secret of presenting the problems of human doubt and misery in such a form as to arrest irresistibly the attention and set to work the imagination of his readers. That much an impartial critic, who neither likes nor admires him, is fain to concede. Unfortunately, the fanaticism of those who do admire, demands much more. And here we may remark that these admirers have done the object of their worship a singular dis-service in advancing the plea of symbolism. Ibsen's plays, they say, are all more or less symbolical; his plots, his characters, with all their horrible incidents and occasionally grotesque absurdities—which to the ignorant and uninitiated seem but the nonsensical dreams of a madman—are symbols of eternal truths. Of what are his plays symbolical, and who shall read their hidden meaning? Why, the same might be said of a nursery-rhyme. . . . What is the hidden meaning of *The Master-Builder*? One of its translators says that it has none in particular; the other translator declares that it describes the life and aims of the dramatist himself. . . . To taunt those who are not of Ibsen's following with stupidity because they cannot fathom a meaning upon which his followers themselves are not agreed, is a very doubtful way of strengthening the dramatist's reputation. The Ibsen school would do better to leave these symbolical meanings alone, and devote their defence to those doctrines with which their master's work is plentifully sprinkled, and of which the meaning is not obscure.

[*The Master-Builder*] is, perhaps, from either the literary or the dramatic point of view, quite the worst play that Ibsen has yet produced. From another point of view, it is far less disagreeable than *Ghosts* or *Hedda Gabler,* though we are not sure if it does not contain a moral more hopelessly wretched than even those dreary productions. (pp. 285-86)

If one could only fancy that the castle which Hilda and Solness contemplated building together was really a castle in the air, an ideal edifice which should harbour no earthly passion, then one might forgive much of the sordid tale that led to their resolve and its tragic ending. But the dramatist destroys all escape that way, and makes it only too clear in what spirit the two chief actors part for the last time. As Solness says of his own life, it is all "hopeless, hopeless! Never a ray of sunlight! Not so much as a gleam of brightness to light it!" The whole play seems to us to be nothing but one desperate, raging cry of revolt against human destiny. The builder starts well in life, "a boy from a pious home in the country," whose one idea is to please the great Master Builder of the Universe, in whose honour his churches are built. No happiness comes to him as a reward, nothing but the emptiest vanity of success, which success, he sees to his dismay, is only gained at the expense of another's failure and his own peace of mind. His crowning victory is only won at the cost of his crowning unhappiness. Recklessly he defies the Great Builder, and becomes himself a "Free Builder," to shape his life after his own fashion; only to find that he is clogged by chains everywhere,—chained by marriage to a dead wife, chained to a living conscience which he cannot kill. Still, the impossible, the idea of an impossible happiness on earth, beckons him on; and in his last desperate effort to attain it, his "dizzy conscience" once more asserts itself, and he is crushed for ever. *Vanitas vanitatum,*—one knows the text well enough, many have preached from it; but none have brought their sermons to a more hateful ending, we think, than Henrik Ibsen. There is no good on earth, he seems to say; its conventions and its morality are equally rotten and useless,—neither beyond the earth is there any happiness. (p. 286)

"Ibsen's Last Play," in The Spectator *(© 1893 by The Spectator), Vol. 70, No. 3375, March 4, 1893, pp. 285-86.*

BERNARD SHAW   (essay date 1897)

At last I am beginning to understand anti-Ibsenism. It must be that I am growing old and weak and sentimental and foolish; for I cannot stand up to reality as I did once. Eight years ago, when ["**A Doll's House**" was first performed in England, it] struck the decisive blow for Ibsen—perhaps the only one that has really got home in England as yet—I rejoiced in it, and watched the ruin and havoc it made among the idols and temples of the idealists as a young war correspondent watches the bombardment of the unhealthy quarters of a city. But now I understand better what it means to the unhappy wretches who can conceive no other life as possible to them except the Doll's House life. The master of the Doll's House may endure and even admire himself as long as he is called King Arthur and prodigiously flattered; but to paint a Torvald Helmer for him, and leave his conscience and his ever-gnawing secret diffidence to whisper "Thou art the man" when he has perhaps outlived all chance of being any other sort of man, must be bitter and dreadful to him. Dr Rank, too, with his rickets and his scrofula, no longer an example, like Herod, of the wrath of God, or a curiosity to be stared at as villagers stare at a sheep with two heads, but a matter-of-fact completion of the typical picture of family life by one of the inevitable congenital invalids, or drunkards, or lunatics whose teeth are set on edge because their fathers have eaten sour grapes: this also is a horror against which an agony of protest may well be excused.

It will be remarked that I no longer dwell on the awakening of the woman, which was once the central point of the controversy as it is the central point of the drama. Why should I? The play solves that problem just as it is being solved in real life. The woman's eyes are opened; and instantly her doll's dress is thrown off and her husband left staring at her, helpless, bound thenceforth either to do without her (an alternative which makes short work of his fancied independence) or else treat her as a human being like himself, fully recognizing that he is not a creature of one superior species, Man, living with a creature of another and inferior species, Woman, but that Mankind is male and female, like other kinds, and that the inequality of the sexes is literally a cock and bull story, certain to end in such unbearable humiliation as that which our suburban King Arthurs suffer at the hands of Ibsen. The ending of the play is not on the face of it particularly tragic: the alleged "note of interrogation" is a sentimental fancy; for it is clear that Helmer is brought to his senses, and that Nora's departure is no claptrap "Farewell for ever," but a journey in search of self-respect and apprenticeship to life. Yet there is an underlying solemnity caused by a fact that the popular instinct has divined: to wit, that Nora's revolt is the end of a chapter of human history. The slam of the door behind her is more momentous than the cannon of Waterloo or Sedan, because when she comes back, it will not be to the old home; for when the patriarch no longer

rules, and the "breadwinner" acknowledges his dependence, there is an end of the old order; and an institution upon which so much human affection and suffering have been lavished, and about which so much experience of the holiest right and bitterest wrong has gathered, cannot fall without moving even its destroyers, much more those who believe that its extirpation is a mortal wound to society. This moment of awe and remorse in "**A Doll's House**" was at first lightened by the mere Women's Rights question. Now that this no longer distracts us, we feel the full weight of the unsolved destiny of our Helmers, our Krogstads, our Ranks and our Rank ancestors. . . . (pp. 539-40)

Bernard Shaw, "A Doll's House Again" (reprinted by permission of The Society of Authors on behalf of The Bernard Shaw Estate), in The Saturday Review, *London, Vol. 83, No. 2168, May 15, 1897, pp. 539-41.**

MAX BEERBOHM   (essay date 1901)

[Ibsen has a] genius for dramaturgy and [an] inalienable power of filling us at the moment with a kind of intellectual excitement for which, analysing it later, we may or may not discover adequate cause.

"**The Pillars of Society,**" the earliest play of his final period, is interesting rather as a story than as a philosophic reflection of life. Ibsen here is, first and foremost, the rattling good playwright. . . . Thought, of course (with propagandism) comes into the play; but it is wholly subordinate to the conceived story. Hatred of idealism and respectability, hatred of Man and love of Woman, and all the rest of Ibsen's "fads," may be found in it, but never for one moment do they make or mar the story itself. Thus they would not incommode the public. As an attack on social institutions the play is quite negligible. It ought to have been called, not "**The Pillars of Society,**" but "The Skeleton in the Cupboard." Consul Bernick is essentially the man with a guilty secret and a predisposition to villainy. Ibsen, by presenting him as an average type of the class that he wished (incidentally) to attack, made nonsense of his incidental motive. But this matters little. The man is projected with great vitality, and is (except as the pretended type) a very impressive figure. Nor is it so much on what he is as on what happens that the excitement of the play depends. Will the noble young man who became his scapegoat unmask him now in all his hideousness to the world? Will his attempt to murder this young man be crowned with success? Will his little boy, whom he dearly loves, be drowned? Oh no, no! Do not harrow us too much! Let there be a happy ending! And there is. The young man is saved; so is the little boy; and the wicked man (this is the one impossible thing that Ibsen makes him do) atones for his sins by confessing them to his fellow-citizens, and so inaugurates his perfect reformation. Superior persons may sneer at the play (especially its last act) as melodrama; but it is melodrama of the very best kind. It is a hustle of ingenious and exciting chances around strongly and truly delineated characters, and the comic relief (of which there is much) is real straightforward fun. (p. 631)

Max Beerbohm, "Three Plays" (reprinted by permission of Mrs. Eva Reichmann), in The Saturday Review, *London, Vol. 91, No. 2377, May 18, 1901, pp. 631-32.**

HERMANN J. WEIGAND (essay date 1925)

The objectivity of treatment in "Hedda Gabler" is such that to call the play a tragedy or a comedy falls equally wide of the mark. Tragedy presupposes the dominance of sympathy, comedy the dominance of a mood of elation, if not laughter. We experience neither in sufficiently strong measure to count. In place of sympathy we feel cold curiosity; for laughter we feel contempt. Nor is there the blending of strong emotions that makes tragi-comedy. "Hedda Gabler" is simply a spectacle of life from which we retire with a shock.

The technical organization of the play is so lucid as to require little comment. The conflict is clearly delineated from the outset, and the grouping of the characters around Hedda, as the central figure, is readily perceived. The situation which forms the basis for the catastrophe is the maladjustment between Hedda and her environment; it is complicated by the unresolved dissonances of Hedda's own nature. By the end of Act I the tension resulting from this maladjustment is exposed from a great variety of angles. The repugnance of the aristocratically reared girl for the petty bourgeois family with which she has become affiliated through marriage; her contemptuous dislike of her husband; her shudder at the thought of approaching motherhood; the toning down of her social expectations, owing to the dubious financial outlook: all this warns of the approach of a crisis.

"Hedda Gabler" is thus what is called a drama of ripe condition. It is not analytical, however, in the sense of "Ghosts" or "Rosmersholm." Whereas in those dramas the crisis is preformed in the past, and the exposure of events antedating the dramatic action automatically precipitates the catastrophe, we have nothing of the sort here. In this play the ground is merely prepared by the past for an eventual crisis; the form which this crisis takes, however, and the moment of its appearance are conditioned by the spontaneous actions of Hedda in the space of time occupied by the Drama. In "Hedda Gabler" we witness no "revelations" that by the act of their exposure exert pressure upon the shaping of the future. . . . [It] is only to the reader and not to the participating characters that new facts are thereby brought to light.

What gives this method, however, the stamp of Ibsen's personal genius, is the degree of concentration with which the crisis is brought to a head and followed by the catastrophe. "Hedda Gabler" is the sort of theme which Hauptmann would have developed in a series of intervals extending perhaps over a year's time, like his "Fuhrmann Henschel" or "Rose Bernd." Ibsen completes the cycle of the action in thirty-six hours' time, without a change of setting. For all the extreme naturalism of his psychology, Ibsen resorts without stint to a degree of foreshortening that cuts down the intervals between succeeding stages of development to an almost irreducible minimum.

"Hedda Gabler" is the last of Ibsen's plays to have the dramatic interest centered on a complex woman character. The heroine, as usual, requires the closest kind of study. Her nature, shallow though it is, contrives to harbor so many contradictions that it is no easy matter to form a balanced view of her personality. Abject slavery to convention, coupled with an acute sense of personal freedom; cowardice and courage; crass materialism alongside of a pathetic idealism; candor and dissimulation;—these and other traits are interwoven into the strange pattern of her character. (pp. 245-46)

Of Hedda's development we are given sparse glimpses. Of aristocratic birth and traditions, the daughter of General Gabler,

Hedda grew up motherless. . . . Her later life also we have only in outline sketch. She was a popular ball-room belle, and the horsemanship of the proud beauty in her black habit and feathered hat attracted admiring attention. The only foreign element in her life of sport and social engagements was her clandestine intimacy with the brilliant and dissolute Eilert Lövborg, and this was terminated abruptly when it threatened to grow beyond the confines of conversation.

The old General died, leaving her impecunious. Hedda began to look around for a suitable match. . . . Among the suitors who showed serious intentions the most acceptable seemed Jörgen Tesman, and she chose him.

The six weary months of their wedding trip more than sufficed to make Hedda realize the colossal mistake of her choice. She had entered into the match without any feeling, expecting as a matter of course to find Tesman tolerable. Instead, she found him not only boring but disgustingly ridiculous. Herself a creature of perfect aristocratic breeding, everything about him offended her aesthetic sensibilities. (pp. 246-47)

For a nature like Hedda's the possibilities of realizing happiness in life were very limited. Could she have married a man of wealth and influence and of a personality that did not offend her aesthetic sensibilities, she might have gone through life without ever becoming aware that she had missed anything. As mistress of a salon, surrounded by admirers, the expression of the social talents which she undoubtedly possessed would have been given free play. She would not have had time to be bored; the craving for the power to mold a human destiny might have been diverted into the innocuous channels of petty intrigue. But with that one avenue to happiness closed, it is difficult, if not impossible, to conceive for Hedda a life that would not have exposed the dearth of substance and the absolute poverty of her nature.

For in the last instance the cause of her deadly boredom lay in herself. Hedda was self-centered to a degree that absolutely excluded any vigorously stimulating contact with life in any form. It would be conceivable that a person so completely self-centered as Hedda should be at the same time self-sufficient. That, however, would presuppose an unusually resourceful personality. Now, what characterizes Hedda more than anything else is a complete dearth of inner resources. Hers is a barren nature on which no seed has been able to thrive. The rudiments of sympathetic imagination, on which the expansion of personality depends, must have become atrophied long before she reached maturity. Her interests are of the very narrowest. Ideas in any form are distasteful to her. To Lövborg's intellectual side she is as coldly indifferent as to Tesman's special problems of research. To her a book is a book, regardless of contents, and boring as such. Her complete lack of imagination is instanced by the naïve question: "Can such a thing not be reproduced? Written over again?" . . . In revealing the boredom of her wedding trip to Brack, she lays particular stress on the fact that she had to go for six whole months without meeting a soul that knew anything of her circle or could talk about the things they were interested in. To judge by all signs, including her relation to Lövborg, even her sex life had never been developed beyond the point where desire finds satisfaction in conversation.

Without taking into account Hedda's complete self-centeredness, the atrophy in her of sympathetic imagination and the impoverishment of her inner life, it would be impossible to understand her marriage to Tesman. In taking the step she was completely blind as to what it involved. . . . What Hedda sought was a conventionally presentable husband; his individuality did not interest her in the slightest degree, she never gave it a thought of her own. The interests and the activities of men generally, except for the ball-room, were a closed world to her. Of the world at large she was as ignorant as a child, and far more indifferent. Without doubt their courtship was an entirely formal affair. Of Tesman's intimate self, when he felt at his ease, Hedda probably got the first glimpse the morning after the wedding.

No single relationship illuminates so many sides of Hedda's nature as her clandestine comradeship with Lövborg. The hardness, the incapacity for sympathetic expansion, the self-centeredness of her nature comes out in the glimpses that we get of this chapter of her past, and it reveals in addition her conventionality, her cowardice and a curious, unsubstantial idealism, manifested in a thin, pseudo-classic cult of beauty.

Hedda did not love Lövborg. She would have loved him had she been capable of either sympathy or genuine passion. As it was, the immediate basis of their comradeship was her curiosity about the forbidden side of life. Her veiled questions, prompted by a desire for thrills, but mistaken for sympathy by Lövborg, were designed to draw him out on the subject of his nightly dissipations, and in this she succeeded. Hedda's sensuality was attenuated to the point where suggestive images, conjured up by words, replaced physical passion and afforded a vicarious gratification. But with this prurient curiosity was blended a higher motive for their comradeship—the highest that her impoverished nature was capable of. Physically cold and incapable of love as she was, Hedda nevertheless idealized Lövborg. Because she was a cowardly slave to convention herself, she admired his courage in flying in the face of convention, in living his life to suit himself. She idealized his life of dissipation. It seemed a grand and bold and beautiful thing to her. She pictured him at the bacchanal with vine leaves in his hair; and that image, gleaned from some book about classical antiquity which she may have read in her school days, became to her, in the absence of a richer background, the sole symbol of a beautiful life of free abandon. Years later, when she tampers with his life, she clings with pathetic tenacity, as long as she can, to this last bit of wreckage of her one ideal.

Hedda suffers from the incongruity between her cowardly conventionality and her idealization of reckless abandon. She attempts to unite these two irreconcilable opposites in her own self by persuading herself that there is something courageous in her clandestine comradeship with the dissolute genius.

On superficial view, Hedda's low-voiced conversation with Lövborg in the second act may seem to contradict my assertion of her coldness. When there was danger of their friendship developing into something more serious, Hedda threatened Lövborg with her pistol and broke with him. But, as she confesses now, the fact that she did not dare to shoot him was not her worst act of cowardice that evening. More cowardly, as the context compels us to infer, was her refusal to yield to his passion. The contradiction, however, is more apparent than real. Her longing for the courage to do the unconventional thing and plunge into the life of dissipation is quite intelligible even in the absence of physical passion. Had she yielded to him, her gratification would have consisted in the consciousness of doing something wickedly unconventional, hence beautiful. Hedda's relation to Brack also substantiates her physical coldness. She knows perfectly well what sort of triangle the Judge has set his heart upon, hence there lies for her a peculiarly

racy zest in the thought of maneuvering the situation so dexterously as to keep it within the limits of Platonic vice.

It is difficult to keep free of the idea that there should not have been an element of genuine sympathy—of imaginative projection into his point of view—in Hedda's relation to Lövborg. As one keeps in mind the fact, furtively revealed in momentary glimpses, that Lövborg was the one individual who stood to Hedda for an ideal, one is tempted to attribute her challenge of his manhood, by sending him to Brack's party, in some measure to sympathy. It looks as if she had done it in part for his sake, to cleanse him of a stain that sullied his life. For her feeling there is something unaesthetic about the reclaimed rake, the total abstainer. He is no longer a free man. So it looks as though an essentially unselfish desire to restore his freedom to him were blended with her other motives in sending him to the banquet. One need become disabused of that idea, however, by her reaction to Brack's preliminary report of his suicide. "At last a deed worth doing," she exclaims in a clear tone of voice, and when Tesman and Thea have retired to the other room she reiterates the same idea:

> *Hedda.* (In a low voice.) Oh, what liberation there is in this act of Eilert Lövborg's.
>
> *Brack.* Liberation, Mrs. Hedda? Yes, for him it is liberation true enough.
>
> *Hedda.* I mean for me. It gives me a sense of freedom to know that a deed of deliberate courage is still possible in this world,—a deed of spontaneous beauty.

There is no mistaking the meaning of these words, "I mean for me." They show with dazzling clearness that Lövborg's life had significance for her only as a means to the accomplishment of wholly egotistical ends. In using him as a means for bolstering her ideal, and as nothing else, she shows that even in her relation to ideal values she was incapable of transcending the most narrowly possessive attitude. Having gotten from his life the one thrill it could give her—the sensation which she mistakes for an experience—she scrapped the rest that did not personally concern her without the least touch of sentiment. (pp. 248-53)

The conflict leading to the catastrophe is in substance the contest of two women striving each to control the destiny of a man. Hedda's is the aggressive rôle, while Thea, lacking the wits to sense her opponent's wiles, is purely on the defensive, and Eilert's is the subordinate part of being the object of the contest. Three times the action rises to a peak, with Hedda scoring three successive triumphs over her rival: The first, gained in the open, when Lövborg goes to Brack's party despite Thea's pleading; the second, a clandestine victory, when Hedda burns the precious manuscript; the third, when Hedda exults in the news of Lövborg's suicide. But each time her triumph is premature; time after time the fruit of her victories becomes vile and loathsome as she puts it to her mouth; so that at last, overcome with nausea and a sense of futility, she plays her final trump by making a spectacular and horrifying exit. (pp. 253-54)

To account for Hedda's suicide there is such a cumulation of motives as can scarcely be grasped in a single act of intuition. There is her terror of the prospect of eking out a miserable life of genteel poverty as the wife of the impossible Jörgen Tesman. There is her dread of motherhood. There is her sense of abject, crushing defeat maneuvered by fate rather than by a rival too stupid to sense the meaning of either the struggle or her victory. There is her feeling of nausea on beholding the one ideal that she could call her own befouled by life and irreparably defiled. There is her exhaustion, psychical and physical, after a supreme effort of will and a night and a day of acute nervous tension. Superadded to it all is her dismay upon finding herself at Brack's mercy as an alternative to becoming involved in scandal, and her revolt against being coerced into physical surrender to the sleek libertine as the price of his silence.

Death offered escape from all that was ugly and loathsome; but in addition, as shown by the manner of her death, the thought of suicide exercised a positive fascination as well. By dying in beauty, as she conceived it, she could vindicate her ideal and fling a final, unanswerable challenge at the world. Voluntary death, moreover, effaced the stigma of cowardice under which she had all her life smarted. Finally, the diabolical delight she experienced in anticipating how her deed would shock the survivors out of their wits, lent a positive zest to her act of self-annihilation.

Despite all these factors exerting pressure in the direction of suicide, the nervous shock we sustain from Hedda's deed is scarcely less than that of the half-fainting Brack, as instanced by his outcry: "Good God!—people don't do such things." There is always an element of the miraculous in voluntary death; it is the greater if the impulse for the deed has ripened underground. Not that she should want to kill herself is what shocks us, but that she should have the nerve, without warning, to convert impulse into action. The real crux of the matter is that until she has actually fired the fatal shot, we do not, in our hearts, believe her capable of committing such a deed. We have seen too much of her cowardice to reckon seriously with the idea that she should find the courage to put an end to her pitiful existence.

Yet, upon reflection, we can understand her singular act of courage as much as we can understand the rest of her actions. Her suicide finds analogies in her previous conduct. On two occasions we saw the bored and cynical expression of her eyes yield suddenly to a flaming animation that betokened an absolute concentration of her whole personality upon a single act of willing. In both cases that innervation, transforming her, was short-lived and spent itself in vain, but it betrayed for the moment the mettle of the heroine, albeit the quixotic heroine. In conceiving the impulse to suicide, her self is gathered up for the third time into a single concentrated current of will, and this time her will culminates in the action willed, because for this once both the act of willing and its execution lie in her own hand.

Cold as Hedda leaves us, her self-chosen death, for all the quixotic idealism which it betrays, strikes a finer note than we were prepared for. Her nature being what it was, warped beyond hope, narrow and self-centered to the point of complete isolation, Hedda's exit is at any rate in keeping with the best that is in her. We don't regret her passing, but neither do we scoff over her corpse. (pp. 260-62)

> *Hermann J. Weigand, "'Hedda Gabler'," in* The Guardian *(© Guardian and Manchester Evening News Ltd, 1925), July, 1925 (and reprinted in his* The Modern Ibsen: A Reconsideration, *Holt, Rinehart and Winston, 1925, pp. 242-73).*

BRIAN W. DOWNS (essay date 1950)

In *A Doll's House,* for all that play's slight awkwardness, Ibsen had worked out the characteristic dramatic formula of his later plays. The plan of [*Love's Comedy, Brand,* and *Peer Gynt*] is relatively straightforward: the point of *Peer Gynt* is, in a way, driven home by the way the action now glides, now jumps, from episode to episode with no taut linkage or causation, and the chronicle of Brand's life unfolds in natural and uncomplicated sequence from the moment that he sets foot in his native parish; similarly, the characters once granted, it needs but Lind's engagement to Anna and Falk's declaration to Svanhild to start *Love's Comedy* on the way that it follows unbrokenly and logically. Yet even through these plays there sounds, faintly, an echo of things long past: a glimpse of Peer Gynt's childhood explains his irresponsible fantasy, and there is a similar brief illumination of Brand's psychological 'pre-history'; Pastor Straamand, in *Love's Comedy,* serves not alone for a butt in the present, but he is a portent from the past too, a warning example of the deformation of character and destiny to which Lind and Falk may fall victims.

Elsewhere in his early work Ibsen had made more use of 'pre-history'. The melodramatic complications of *Lady Inger of Østraat* and their tragic outcome proceed from the sin of the heroine's youth and from her efforts to keep it concealed. In *The Vikings in Helgeland* one drama is, as it were, exhumed while the ostensible one is in progress, and it shapes the latter's end when Hjørdis, fomenting strife with her husband's guests, discovers that she ought rightly to have been the prize and wife of one of them, since it was Sigurd, and not her husband Gunnar, who fulfilled the condition demanded of her suitors, the killing of the polar bear on guard outside her virgin bower. (The utilisation of a gradually disclosed secret in drama is, of course, almost as old as drama itself, and two supreme tragedies, *Oedipus Rex* and *Hamlet,* owe their peculiar force and fascination partly to the manner in which the secret comes to light and partly to its operating as a still active virus. Ibsen certainly knew *Hamlet* and very probably *Oedipus Rex* too, but was probably put in the way of this particular device by the ingenuities of Scribe and by certain authors of the Romantic Revival, such as the Norwegian Mauritz Hansen.) (pp. 114-15)

Pillars of Society, again, embodied the process of exhumation, as I have called it—though from the purely dramatic point of view perhaps with not quite so great an effect as *The Vikings in Helgeland.* (p. 116)

In a twofold manner the reconstruction or exhumation has a deep bearing also on the *moral* drama embodied in the outward action of *Pillars of Society.* For it firmly connects the Consul's change of heart with the awakening of his conscience, which the sharer of his brother-in-law's secret, Lona Hessel, has deliberately come to undertake; and the awakening of his conscience forms part of her programme of letting in light and air on the Society of which he is the product, the victim and the exponent as well as the Pillar. (In any technical comparison, the contrast between *Pillars of Society* and *Hamlet* is plain enough; for the occult crime which comes to light in *Hamlet* is one with which the hero himself has had nothing to do. On the other hand, the parallel with *Oedipus Rex* is fairly complete; in Sophocles's play, as in Ibsen's, there is *both* a past offence of the hero's to be disclosed and expiated—the murder of Laius—*and* a present crime to be punished—Oedipus's defiance of the divine.)

The blending of past and present in *A Doll's House* closely resembles that of *Pillars of Society.* The focus throughout is on the present. It is not the expiation of Nora's forgery, let alone the perpetration of it years ago, it is her marital *malaise* that is at issue, and the discovery of the crime serves to transform vague *malaise* into acute crisis. Nevertheless, there is in *A Doll's House* more of the past than a scrap of doubtful paper. I do not refer to Krogstad's own crime and to his old sentimental relations with Fru Linde—though these things serve to build up that firm nexus between passing events and their forerunners by means of which Ibsen contrived to give an extraordinary relief and perspective to his mature works; I have in mind the allusions to, and the demonstrable effects of, Nora's upbringing, which heighten the moral drama. Her father, it transpires, an irresponsible spendthrift, brought her up with no sense of social obligation or serious thought for the morrow, while her husband, finding her a delightful companion like this, did nothing to repair the omission and, indeed, continued to treat her with the condescending playfulness less appropriate to a mother of three children than to a girl in her 'teens. Nora's overgrown irresponsibility, on the one hand, permitted the forgery. The way in which it was regarded, on the other hand, only encouraged her in chicane and bred the uneasiness of a stifled, guilty conscience. (pp. 116-17)

In *A Doll's House*, the psychological implications set aside, the reconstructed past is fairly simple: Thorvald Helmer fell seriously ill and needed a long holiday abroad; Nora forged her father's name on a promissory note and raised the funds required for that holiday, then slaved and saved enough behind her husband's back to pay to Krogstad the instalments of the debt as they fell due. (p. 119)

[What] drove this somewhat feather-headed, but sound and home-loving young woman to the grave act of abandoning home, husband and children? The term 'home-loving', liberally interpreted, may point to the answer. Though apparently unstayed by religion, Nora's is a deeply passionate and devoted heart. The keynote is firmly struck before we know anything about her crime, which after all was committed from unreflecting passionate love of her husband: Helmer aks where Nora would be financially if a tile blew off the roof and knocked his brains out, and she replies that she cares not where she would be if he were not with her. It is inconceivable to her that her feelings should not be absolutely reciprocated. Helmer may have his funny ways in pulling her up short when she looked like outrunning the constable; he could, no doubt, on occasions be cross with her; but there was a horror she had never so much as dreamed of, the distorted mask of fury and aversion that he turned upon her after opening Korgstad's fatal letter. It *was* the face of a strange man with whom she had been living.

An equally deadly shaft had already pierced her heart. Krogstad, she learns, once did what she had done, committed forgery and evaded the consequences; and Helmer—the fount of wisdom for Nora—gives it as his opinion that such a man must be the poisoner of his own children. By implication, he adjudges her unworthy to be a mother. It shows the seriousness with which she accepts this judgement that thereafter she keeps her children away from her as much as possible.

These two blows, the conviction of her unworthiness to be a mother and the knowledge that Helmer's love for her was fallible, have completely shattered the vital basis of Nora's life. To leave the hearth on which the fire has gone out can give her no further pangs.

The instinctive grounds of Nora's final act are thus abundantly justified. But that does not constitute a complete defence. It might have been so if, on Helmer's outburst of recrimination,

Nora had, in panic horror, thrown a wrap over her fancy dress and fled incontinently into the night. But then the great settling of accounts between husband and wife would have fallen away. And that Nora walks out of her doll's house offends some observers less than that she should dally to argue about it. An unthinking creature, they feel, takes to rationalising an instinctive impulse and begins talking as if she had swallowed John Stuart Mill's *The Subjection of Women* whole.

In endeavouring to account for the change in Nora's demeanour, besides the double shock, we must not overlook something a trifle febrile and morbid which her manner portrays from the start—her irresistible longing, for instance, to use strong language—which disquiets her friend Fru Linde. The long strain imposed by the repayment of her debt to Krogstad cannot entirely account for it, since it is just about to be removed. There seems to be something more. Nora tells her husband that she has been merry but never happy. That, no doubt, is an exaggeration, which profound disillusionment readily explains. Nora was probably quite happy most of the time. But there has been a small, lurking residuum of dissatisfaction, a waiting for something that does not happen. . . . (pp. 128-30)

The gap between Nora, the solemn defender of individuality, and Nora, the squirrel and the lark, has generally been felt too wide to explain away, though the magic of a great actress's art has on occasion conjured it away. There is, similarly, another flaw at the other end of the career which we are permitted to follow. Frankly incredible it seems that Nora should have failed to recognise her forgery as a crime. 'People like me don't get found out or else bluff their way through', is just a possible attitude for the spoiled and feather-brained, but Nora's very uneasiness *vis-à-vis* Krogstad and her desire to have the dubious IOU returned to her plead against her ignorance of the nature of her act.

One may observe too that in reality a Korgstad must have known his threats to be mainly bluff. But here the dramatic situation needed something 'strong': the dangerous blackmailer confronting the inexperienced woman who committed a crime from ignorance and love—and the position he takes up easily passes muster with theatre-audiences. In the same way the moral situation demands something 'strong' in the third act, and Ibsen opined with less justification that Nora's *volte-face* and last words would just carry conviction.

Le sérieux in Nora, such as it is, guarantees *le sérieux* of her last exit, and of the entire drama. But it also, I think, admits a ray of hope. Thorvald is sobered and impressed by it; it is not at all impossible that he has, if dimly, apprehended where the real rift between his wife and himself lies. . . . The summing-up of all this may well be that Nora's character is more consistent, that the tragedy which befalls her is deeper and that, at the same time, the conclusion comes rather nearer a reconciliation than these things are often thought to be. (pp. 130-31)

It was a testimony to the sympathetic interest in his heroine which Ibsen had aroused that her particular case should be so hotly disputed. But the arguments at once ranged much further. The bang of the Helmers' front door would not have alarmed so many people had they not been fearful that it might bring down on their heads nothing less than the whole fabric of marriage. . . .

It is always tempting to build up a generalisation from a concrete case, a generalisation not of necessity universally valid, but at any rate embodying a definite doctrine. Soberly considering the point, most people would agree that it is indefensible to hold an artist responsible for an ethical tenet, apparently justified in a single imaginary instance. . . . Ibsen believed that the age of relativity had come in, admitting of no general rules. He would never wish it to be claimed, for instance, on the evidence of *Pillars of Society* and *John Gabriel Borkman* that all big business is barratry, or, on the strength of *An Enemy of the People,* that every man who stands alone is in the right. (p. 132)

His very ingenuity in presenting an individual case so that it should convince logically and be dramatically moving, together with his choice of themes, did none the less lay Ibsen open to the charge that he was playing the advocate and presenting theses, not problems. The impression was particularly strong in *A Doll's House* by reason of the heavy-handedness with which Fru Linde's schoolmarmish proclivities drive Nora to an *éclaircissement.* At all costs, it appeared, the author was intent to stage a debate on matrimonial relations leading to a predetermined conclusion. The improbable argument at the end between the heroine and her husband confirms the impression that the play was largely written for its sake—otherwise it would not have been necessary to wrench probability so ruthlessly. Nora arraigns, not Thorvald only, but every husband; not the Helmer *ménage* is criticised, but marriage as an institution. (p. 133)

Even if the early plays are admitted to the count, Ibsen portrays, to be sure, more unsatisfactory than satisfactory marriages. It would be otiose to give the catalogue. Yet he does allow of happy marriages; that of Dr Thomas Stockmann provides an excellent case in point: so the institutions is not condemned root and branch. And what Ibsen does *not* hold up is equally important to remember. His works contain no defence of celibacy direct or implied. Nor is there any glorification of unlawful or transitory unions. (pp. 133-34)

The absence of candour and mutual knowledge, the failure to face common problems jointly and seriously, are seen to be the root defects in the Helmers's marriage, the main fault lying with the husband and his 'superior' attitude. The diagnosis closely resembles that made in *The Subjection of Women,* where Mill traces the 'slave mentality' of women back to the legal privileges reserved to the husband and the male, a point not directly made in *A Doll's House* itself, though it is implied in *Pillars of Society* and made one of the guiding notes for *A Doll's House,* in which Ibsen remarked that women are judged and condemned according to laws which they have had no hand in making. (pp. 134-35)

In his criticism of marriage, Ibsen was seen to be joining in that disturbing modern movement of looking in general upon man and his social arrangements from the factual, scientific, unsentimental and antitraditional point of view which was turning *belles lettres* into a branch of natural history. *A Doll's House* afforded support for this apprehension outside the treatment of the Helmer marriage.

Nora is irresponsible and frivolous, not only because the serious elements in her nature have never received encouragement, but also because she has inherited from her father a disposition towards frivolity and irresponsibility. In *Peer Gynt* and *Brand,* as was pointed out, Ibsen invoked childish memories as formative elements in the characters of his heroes, who, moreover, have a great deal in common with their respective mothers, the formidable Fru Brand and the feckless Aase. But the insistence on inherited characteristics in Nora's case is something novel. (p. 135)

A Doll's House harvested where *Pillars of Society* had already prepared the soil, and became in course of time the most popular of Ibsen's plays generally, and the agent by which more often than not his fame was propagated to parts of the world previously in ignorance of it. (pp. 144-45)

Brian W. Downs, *in his* A Study of Six Plays by Ibsen, *Cambridge at the University Press, 1950, 212 p.*

GEORGE STEINER   (essay date (1961)

With Ibsen, the history of drama begins anew. This alone makes of him the most important playwright after Shakespeare and Racine. The modern theatre can be dated from *Pillars of Society.* . . . But like most great artists, Ibsen worked from within the available conventions. The four plays of his early maturity—*Pillars of Society, A Doll's House, Ghosts,* and *An Enemy of the People*—are marvels of construction in the prevailing manner of the late nineteenth-century drawing-room play. The joints are as closely fitted as in the domestic melodramas of [Guillaume] Augier and [Alexandre] Dumas. What is revolutionary is the orientation of such shopworn devices as the hidden past, the purloined letter, or the deathbed disclosure toward social problems of urgent seriousness. The elements of melodrama are made responsible to a deliberate, intellectual purpose. These are the plays in which Ibsen is the dramatist Shaw tried to make of him: the pedagogue and the reformer. No theatre has ever had behind it a stronger impulse of will and explicit social philosophy. (p. 290)

But these tracts, enduring as they may prove to be by virtue of their theatrical vigour, are not tragedies. In tragedy, there are no temporal remedies. The point cannot be stressed too often. Tragedy speaks not of secular dilemmas, which may be resolved by rational innovation, but of the unaltering bias toward inhumanity and destruction in the drift of the world. But in these plays of Ibsen's radical period, such is not the issue. There are specific remedies to the disasters which befall the characters, and it is Ibsen's purpose to make us see these remedies and bring them about. *A Doll's House* and *Ghosts* are founded on the belief that society can move toward a sane, adult conception of sexual life and that woman can and must be raised to the dignity of man. *Pillars of Society* and *An Enemy of the People* are denunciations of the hypocrisies and oppressions concealed behind the mask of middle-class gentility. They tell us of the way in which money interests poison the springs of emotional life and intellectual integrity. They cry out for explicit radicalism and reform. As Shaw rightly says: "No more tragedy for the sake of tears." Indeed, no tragedy at all, but dramatic rhetoric summoning us to action in the conviction that truth of conduct can be defined and that it will liberate society.

These programmatic aims extend into Ibsen's middle period. But with *The Wild Duck* . . . , the dramatic form deepens. The limitations of the well-made play and its deliberate flatness of perspective began crowding in on Ibsen. While retaining the prose form and outward conventions of realism, he went back to the lyric voice and allegoric means of his early experimental plays, *Brand* and *Peer Gynt.* With the toy forest and imaginary hunt of old Ekdal in *The Wild Duck,* drama returns to a use of effective myth and symbolic action which had disappeared from the theatre since the late plays of Shakespeare. In *Rosmersholm, The Lady from the Sea,* and *Hedda Gabler,* Ibsen succeeded in doing what every major playwright had attempted after the end of the seventeenth century and what even Goethe and Wagner had not wholly accomplished: he created a new mythology and the theatrical conventions with which to express it. That is the foremost achievement of Ibsen's genius, and it is, as yet, not fully understood. (pp. 290-92)

Ibsen's late plays represent the kind of inward motion that we find also in the late plays of Shakespeare. *Cymbeline, The Winter's Tale,* and *The Tempest* retain the conventions of Jacobean tragicomedy. But these conventions act as signposts pointing toward interior meanings. The storms, the music, the allegoric masques have implications which belong less to the common imaginative repertoire than they do to a most private understanding of the world. The current theatrical forms are a mere scaffold to the inner shape. That is exactly the case in *The Master Builder, Little Eyolf, John Gabriel Borkman,* and *When We Dead Awaken.* These dramas give an appearance of belonging to the realistic tradition and of observing the conventions of the three-walled stage. But, in fact, this is not so. The setting is thinned out so as to become bleakly transparent, and it leads into a strange landscape appropriate to Ibsen's mythology of death and resurrection.

It is in these four plays—and they are among the summits of drama—that Ibsen comes nearest tragedy. But it is tragedy of a peculiar, limited order. These are fables of the dead, set in a cold purgatory. (pp. 295-96)

These are dramas of afterlife, engaging vivid shadows such as animate the lower regions of the *Purgatorio.* But even in these late works, there is a purpose which goes beyond tragedy. Ibsen is telling us that one need not live in premature burial. He is reading the lesson of meaningful life. (p. 297)

> *George Steiner, in a chapter in his* The Death of Tragedy *(reprinted by permission of Georges Borchardt Inc.; copyright © 1961 by George Steiner), Alfred A. Knopf, 1961, pp. 284-302.**

ROBERT BRUSTEIN (essay date 1964)

[Ibsen] is a Romantic rebel with a Classical alter ego which restrains his headier impulses towards total liberation, self-expression, and moral idealism by inhibiting his freedom, restricting his rebellion, and testing his ideals in the world of accommodation and compromise. . . . Ibsen's self-imposed discipline results in certain vertical conflicts within the individual plays. It can be seen, from another angle, in the horizontal development of his art and his changing concepts of dramatic form. The progression of Ibsen's career, in fact, is as dialectical as any of his plays. Works like *Brand, Peer Gynt,* and *Emperor and Galilean,* are relatively overt expressions of the author's early Romanticism in which he creates an architecture of poetry and metaphysics out of huge, irregular blocks of stone. But beginning with *The League of Youth,* and continuing through his "modern" phase (an eleven-year period, ending with *Hedda Gabler* in 1890), Ibsen suppresses his Romanticism—along with his poetry, his mysticism, and his concern with man in nature—to satisfy a pull towards prose, objective reality, and the problems of modern civilization. This Classical counterrhythm gives one the impression that Ibsen's art has been totally transformed. The rebel against God is domesticated into a rebel against society; the scene focusses on the collective as well as on the individual; the humanistic medical doctor becomes an important character, as Darwinist notions of heredity and environment begin to impinge on the action; the language becomes more thin and chastened; the

characterization more specific; the themes more contemporary; and the entire drama takes on, first, that manipulated quality we remember from the well-made play, then, that precision of form we associate with Sophoclean tragedy. Actually, Ibsen's art has changed much less radically than is first apparent, for, in his realistic plays, he has merely contained his rebellious spirit within a new form. As if to prove that this spirit has remained unsullied, Ibsen returns, in his last great plays, to his early prophetic, autobiographical, and metaphysical concerns, dramatizing them in a way which combines the Romantic freedom of his youth with the Classical restraint of his middle years. (pp. 49-50)

Any discussion of Ibsen's mature art must start with *Brand,* since this monolithic masterpiece is not only the first play he completed after leaving his native country, but his first, and possibly his greatest, work of enduring power. Nothing in Ibsen's previous writings prepares us for a play of this scope, Not even the substantial talent he displays in *The Vikings at Helgeland* and *The Pretenders,* for *Brand* is like a sudden revelation from the depths of an original mind. It is highly probable that Ibsen's achievement in *Brand* was intimately connected with his departure from Norway, for he seemed to find an important source of creative power in his self-imposed exile: "I had to escape the swinishness up there to feel fully cleansed," he wrote to his mother-in-law from Rome. "I could never lead a consistent spiritual life there. I was one man in my work and another outside—and for that reason my work failed in consistency too." . . . It was a period of the most exquisite freedom Ibsen had ever known, and his nostalgia for these years was later to find expression [in *Ghosts*] in Oswald's enthusiastic descriptions of the buoyant *livsglaede* (joy of life) to be found in the Paris artist community.

On the surface, *Brand*—an epic of snow and ice with a glacial Northern atmosphere and a forbidding central figure—would seem to have little in common with this warm, sunny Italian world. Yet the sense of abandon which Ibsen was experiencing is reflected in the play's openness of form and richness of inspiration. . . . Although in *The Pretenders* Ibsen had dramatized the conflicts in his own soul through a fictional external action, *Brand* was the most thoroughgoing revelation of his rebellious interior life that Ibsen had yet attempted, an act of total purgation, in which he exorcised the troll battle within his heart and mind by transforming it into art. With *Brand,* Ibsen confronted for the first time and in combination the great subjects which were to occupy him successively during the course of his career: the state of man in the universe, the state of modern society, and the state of his own feverish, divided soul.

The play, a storage house for all of Ibsen's future themes and conflicts, is constructed like a series of interlocking arches, each ascending higher than the last. The lowest arch is a domestic drama, in which Ibsen examines the relationship of the idealist to his family (the basis for later plays like *The Wild Duck*); the middle arch is a social-political drama, in which he analyzes the effect of the aristocratic individual on a democratic community (the basis for plays like *An Enemy of the People*); and the highest arch is a religious drama, in which he shows the rivalry between the messianic rebel and the nineteenth-century God (the basis for plays like *The Master Builder*). Pastor Brand—a reforming minister of extraordinary zeal (his very name means "sword and fire")—is the hero of all three dramas, and Ibsen's supreme idealist, individualist, and rebel. (pp. 50-2)

Brand introduced Ibsen into worldwide fame; and exhilarated by his success, he decided to have another try at the episodic poetic play with *Peer Gynt*. If Brand's character reflects Ibsen in his best moments (which is to say, at his most morally elevated), then Peer's reflects Ibsen in his most irresponsible moments (which is to say, at his most morally lax); yet, it is Peer who charms and ingratiates. It is likely that Ibsen, after punishing his own fanatical idealism, is here trying to discipline the more permissive side of his nature, the seeker after pleasure in the Italian sun. The play—with its folk quality, its satirical touches, and its occasionally tropical atmosphere—would seem to be the very obverse of *Brand*. Actually, it is a dramatization of the same themes, treated from a comic-ironic angle. Peer, the embodiment of modern compromise, hypocrisy, irresponsibility, and self-delusion, is very much like those feckless citizens whom Brand had come to reform. And while the play has no rebel or idealist to urge him towards the heights, the playwright himself acts in this capacity, assuming the function of Brand and exposing the extent to which Peer falls short of the ideal. Ibsen is here working out the negative technique he will use in most of his realistic plays, in which not the rebel but the characters rebelled against move to the foreground of the action. (p. 59)

[In *The League of Youth,* a] clumsy play about political maneuvering in a southern Norwegian town, Ibsen's decision to embark on a radically new career is immediately apparent. It is a work without a single line of verse—without a trace of poetic feeling—concerned with the details and problems of contemporary life, and corseted in a tight five-act structure which recalls the well-made play. Despite its inartistry and banality, *The League of Youth* is, in many ways, quite typical of the new phase of Ibsen's art. In later years, he is to find another form of expression for his poetic impulses, but verse is gone forever. Gone too is the extravagant sweep of his poetic masterpieces, and their self-expressive freedom. Ibsen has entered a period of extreme self-denial, which is even signified—considering his affection for Italy and general distaste for the Germans—by his move [from Rome] to Dresden. But it is German order, clarity, and restraint, rather than Italian ebullience, warmth, and intoxication which have now become essential to his art.

Before suppressing his Romanticism completely, however, Ibsen publishes his last great messianic epic, *Emperor and Galilean*. . . . This monumental double drama in ten acts is obviously designed as Ibsen's philosophical testament: "The positive world-philosophy which critics have so long demanded from me," he writes, "they will find here." In trying to resolve his own contradictions and assume an affirmative posture, Ibsen borrows freely from Hegel. The play even has a Hegelian subtitle: "A World-Historical Drama"—and Hegel's pattern of thesis-antithesis-synthesis is the pattern of its thematic development. While Ibsen's thesis and antithesis are brilliantly conceived and interpreted, however, his synthesis is much too cloudy to qualify as a "positive world-philosophy." Even when he wants to, Ibsen cannot codify his revolt, and his contradictions remain unresolved. Nevertheless, Ibsen was inordinately fond of this play, and thought it his masterpiece. Written in a luminous prose, modeled on the synoptic gospels, and informed by a strange visionary power, it is offered as a prophetic book for the world of the future.

Ibsen's hero, with whom he is quick to admit his affinities, is the fourth-century Roman Emperor Julian—called the Apostate because of his efforts to overthrow the state religion of Chris-

tianity. . . . Julian vacillates between the conflicting empires of Caesar and Christ, the conflicting claims of flesh and spirit, the conflicting demands of freedom and necessity, the conflicting values of self-realization and self-abnegation—both Peer Gynt and Brand inhabit his soul and tear him apart. (pp. 61-2)

In *The Emperor Julian,* the second part of the drama, Ibsen reveals Julian to be a false Messiah. Having misunderstood the oracle and pursued his will-to-power, Julian is persecuting Christians and declaring himself the only God, at the same time reviving the rites of Apollo and Dionysus. Julian's apostasy, and his war against Christ, however, have only strengthened Christianity: miracles are once again abounding, and the faithful are embracing martyrdom with the old joy. Julian even helps, unwittingly, to fulfill an ancient Christian prophecy when, having rebuilt the temple of Apollo, which Christ once threatened to destroy, he sees it annihilated by a whirlwind. Cursed by the bishops, resisted by the people, Julian is learning what has hitherto been obscure: "Jesus Christ was the greatest rebel that ever lived. . . . He lives in the rebellious minds of men; he lives in their scorn and defiance of all visible authority." (p. 63)

Emperor and Galilean contains many stunning dramatic passages, as well as being an extraordinary anticipation of Nietzsche's later attitudes towards Christianity, Dionysus, and the Superman. But the play does not succeed in formulating that "positive world-philosophy" that the author promised: the Third Empire remains a vague and misty dream. Nevertheless, *Emperor and Galilean* is a fine illustration of Ibsen's messianic demands, and the religious strain which always lies at the bottom of his thought. Furthermore, in the conflicting empires of Caesar and Christ, Ibsen has embodied in his own irreconcilable conflicts—between flesh and spirit, free will and necessity, realism and idealism—contradictions which will always be present, in one way or another, in his mind. (p. 64)

But after *Emperor and Galilean,* Ibsen has finished with the messianic drama. Having cast his lot with "the art of the future," he has decided to create not sprawling epics about man on the top of the world but rather well-constructed realistic prose works about man in the depths of the community. (p. 65)

[While] Ibsen's formal approach has changed, his themes remain substantially the same; and while his style is now more objective, his drama remains essentially the history of his revolt.

Ibsen's prose realism, then, is primarily a new surface manner beneath which the old thematic obsessions still obtrude. In transforming his art, Ibsen has not been able to destroy his Romantic rebellion; he has simply found another way to express it. He has turned his attention to the life of the community not to affirm it but to scourge and purify it, vindicating the rights of the individual against its compromising claims; and he has adapted the language of prose in order to discover a modern stage poetry, expressible through means other than speech. (p. 66)

In *Ghosts,* the culminating work of Ibsen's "realistic" period, the fjords and mountains are out of reach, but they can just be seen through the conservatory windows, providing a healthy contrast to the fetid atmosphere within. With *Ghosts,* Ibsen has at last gained control over his new drama, after the experimental bungles of *The League of Youth, Pillars of Society,* and *A Doll's House,* for he has finally achieved a perfect wedding of form and subject matter. His success is the result of substantial technical experimentation; after careful study of the Greeks, he has junked the techniques of the well-made play in favor of the more integrated structure of Sophoclean tragedy. As a result, one is no longer bothered by the noise of Scribean machinery in the wings. Plotted without sensational reversals and unconvincing conversions, *Ghosts* contains no surprise marriages (as in *The League of Youth*), no death ships prevented from sailing at the last minute (as in *Pillars of Society*), no incriminating letters rattling around in the mailbox (as in *A Doll's House*). . . . [Instead] the work is constructed on the pattern of *Oedipus,* beginning at a point right before the catastrophe, and proceeding, like a detective story, by digging up evidence from the past, to a terrible and inevitable conclusion. Because of this perfection of form, one no longer senses a structural incompatibility between the drama of ideas and the drama of action—as one does, for example, in *A Doll's House,* where a long discussion follows after the play has, for all intents and purposes, concluded. Idea and action are perfectly unified in the central image of the work.

The importance of this image is suggested by the fact that it is embodied in the title: Ghosts haunt the atmosphere—ghosts, as Mrs. Alving indicates, in a crucial passage, of two distinct kinds:

> I am half inclined to think we are all ghosts, Mr. Manders. It is not only what we have inherited from our fathers and mothers that exists in us, but all sorts of old dead ideas and all kinds of dead beliefs and things of that kind. . . . And we are so miserably afraid of the light.

Mrs. Alving's ghosts, then, are (1) *an intellectual inheritance*—the specters of beliefs which continue to prevail long after they have lost their meaning, and (2) *a spiritual inheritance*—the spirits of the dead which inhabit the bodies of the living, controlling their lives and destinies. (pp. 67-8)

"The whole of mankind is on the wrong track," wrote Ibsen in his notes to the play, thus indicating that *Ghosts* was not simply the tragedy of the Alving household, but the tragedy of nineteenth-century bourgeois Europe. For his underlying purpose here was to demonstrate how a series of withered conventions, unthinkingly perpetuated, could result in the annihilation not only of a conventional family but, by extension, the whole modern world. Thus, Mrs. Alving's weakness, Oswald's disease, Captain Alving's profligacy, Engstrand's hypocrisy, and Pastor Mander's stupidity are all merely cankered buds sent up by the dying roots of modern society. . . . [*Ghosts*] while closely patterned on Sophoclean tragedy, lacks one Sophoclean essential: a fatalistic acceptance of human doom. Sophocles ascribes the destruction of his heroes to the will of the gods; Ibsen ascribes it to the stupidity and inhumanity of generation after generation of men. And so the implications of Ibsen's position are the very opposite of Greek fatalism: even his belief in determinism implies a belief in will. For behind his conviction that mankind is on the wrong track is hidden his secret desire for a moral revolution through which mankind can once again be redeemed. Ibsen's task, in these realistic plays, is not to champion this revolution but rather to show the need for it by exposing the corpse that infects the cargo of modern life. (pp. 70-1)

[*An Enemy of the People* followed *Ghosts* within a year], propelled by [Ibsen's] fury over the hostile reception tendered to *Ghosts.* Since he published the play before he had an opportunity to cool his anger or complicate his theme, *An Enemy of the People* is the most straightforwardly polemical work Ibsen ever wrote. He had said of *Ghosts,* with much pride and some accuracy, that "in the whole book there is not a single opinion, not a single remark to be found that is there on the dramatist's account," but all of *An Enemy of the People* is there "on the dramatist's account." His self-discipline momentarily weakened by his hurt pride, Ibsen has invested this play with the quality of a revolutionary pamphlet; and Stockmann, despite some perfunctory gestures towards giving him a life of his own, is very much like an author's sounding board, echoing Ibsen's private convictions about the filth and disease of modern municipal life, the tyranny of the compact majority, the mediocrity of parliamentary democracy, the cupidity of the Conservatives, and the hypocrisy of the Liberal press.

As a result, *An Enemy of the People* is both an inferior work of art and an invaluable example of Ibsen's naked rebellion. Unlike Brand, who begins as a messianic rebel, Stockmann is converted to messianism through his growing awareness of the imperfections of modern humanity. And at the end of the play, his family gathered admiringly about him, he is preparing to reform the world through selective breeding, identifying himself with Luther and Christ. Because of Stockmann's late development, the drama of action is almost completely subordinated to the drama of ideas; and Stockmann emerges as the only rebel in Ibsen's drama whose defiant idealism is never tested in its effect on the happiness of others. The play shows Ibsen with his guard down, permitting his reformist tendencies to triumph momentarily over his self-critical dualism; and thus exposing his aristocratic idealism, the messianic quality which always lies at the bottom of his art.

Despite the crudeness, the vague hysteria, and the hollow posturing that sometimes characterize *An Enemy of the People,* it possesses a dynamism and energy which no other Ibsen prose work can boast, as if the author, unshackled by artistic complexity, were once more breathing the heady, exhilarating air of freedom. Actually, the play is a transitional work, which anticipates Ibsen's later development. Apparently having grown dissatisfied with the restricting pseudo-impartiality of the objective mode, Ibsen is already preparing to forge a more personal, vigorous, and direct expression of his revolt. As it is, Stockmann is probably the first really positive hero that Ibsen has created since Julian the Apostate—but he is too simplistically heroic to satisfy the author's dualism. In *The Wild Duck,* Ibsen pauses to punish himself severely for this self-indulgence by launching a murderous satirical attack on the messianic idealist. But after this, Ibsen is finished with the drama of the community. *Hedda Gabler* and *Rosmersholm* follow, each dominated by a strong central character; and then comes the last phase of his career, in which the messianism of Brand is adapted to the realism of *Ghosts,* and the works are centered once again on the divided, semi-autobiographical hero.

Even *The Wild Duck* can probably be considered as a semi-autobiographical work, though it contains the harshest criticism Ibsen ever directed against himself, and is almost a repudiation of everything he had written thus far. In its more open form, its harshly satirical tone, and its unresolved conclusion, *The Wild Duck* bears out Ibsen's contention that "in some ways this new play occupies a position by itself among my dramatic works." But its novelty is especially clear in its intellectual stance, for it is the only play in which Ibsen completely denies the validity of revolt. Stockmann had declared, obviously with the author's approval, that "all who live on lies must be exterminated like vermin." Yet Gregers Werle—a fanatical Ibsenite, whose metaphors, attitudes, and symbol-mongering suggest he has carefully read each of the master's works—exposes the lies of the Ekdal family, and succeeds only in mutilating everybody in it. In trying to follow Ibsenite principles, Gregers is, furthermore, excoriated so mercilessly that he almost seems a scapegoat. To use Ibsen's angry descriptive images, he is a "quacksalver," "mad, demented, crack-brained," a neurotic busybody suffering from "an acute attack of integrity," "morbid, overstrained," a superfluity seeking a mission, "thirteenth at table"—in short, an ugly, unwanted, unattractive man.

Yet *The Wild Duck* must be interpreted less as a repudiation of Ibsenism than a corrective to it. For while Gregers seems to be a typical Ibsenite, he is actually a sadly unbalanced one—almost a caricature of Stockmann or Brand. His commitment to the ideal, for example, comes from without, not from within, since it is the consequence of his conscience pangs over his father's sordid behavior; and he tries to realize the ideal not through his own heroic striving but through urging exemplary behavior on others. It is a sign of Gregers's intellectual inadequacy that he should mistake that latter-day Peer Gynt, Hjalmar Ekdal, for a superior being; but it is also a sign that he is a very incomplete rebel. For while Gregers may possess Brand's destructive fanaticism (his deadly effect on the Ekdals recalls Brand's effect on his family), he lacks Brand's heroic virtues, particularly his individualism and aristocratic will; Gregers is not a hero but a hero-worshiper. Ibsen is attacking the negative side of rebellion without bothering to affirm its positive side—an imbalance probably designed to correct the reverse imbalance in *An Enemy of the People*. Thus, Ibsen—who has suggested before, with much indignation, that the average man feeds on illusions—treats this insight now with a good deal more equanimity—not because he has grown more tolerant of the average man, but because he is more interested in attacking the inadequate idealist. It is doubtful that Ibsen has grown indifferent to the heroic claims of idealism and rebellion, since he continues to treat these with his usual respect in all his later plays. He is simply refusing to be institutionalized by slavish followers. Most important, in satirizing the Ibsenite who tries to codify his principles into rigid formulae, Ibsen is satirizing the ideologist in himself—that indignant moralist who would smash human happiness for the sake of ennobling mankind. (pp. 71-4)

Subtitled "A Dramatic Epilogue," [*When We Dead Awaken*] is clearly designed as the playwright's final statement, even though he is to speak, right before his stroke, of entering the battlefield again "with new weapons and in new armor." . . . *When We Dead Awaken* is not so much a new departure as a continuation and intensification of all his old themes, in which his mysticism, no longer concealed under an authenticated surface, has become more rampant and overt. In many ways, the play can be compared with Shakespeare's late romances or Beethoven's last quartets: the experimentation of an artist who is prepared to fall into excesses in order to expand the possibilities of his art. Like *The Winter's Tale*, for example, the play is full of minor flaws, and often inconsistent in plot and character. But it shows no falling off at all in dramatic power. Quite the contrary, it is one of the most valuable testaments we have to Ibsen's extraordinary mind and vision. And it suggests that, had he lived, Ibsen might have developed in the same direction as Strindberg or Maeterlinck, creating a drama of the soul to which the physical events of everyday life have been completely subordinated. (pp. 78-9)

In *When We Dead Awaken*, the spiritual exile has found his homeland; the messianic prophet has found his ultimate truth; the tired artist has found his resting place. And Ibsen, the rebel, has found his release, after a lifetime of ceaseless aspiration. (p. 83)

Robert Brustein, "Ibsen and Revolt" (copyright ©, 1962, Robert Brustein; reprinted by permission of the author), in The Tulane Drama Review, *Vol. 7, No. 1, Fall, 1962 (and reprinted in a slightly altered form as "Henrik Ibsen," in his* The Theatre of Revolt: An Approach to the Modern Drama, *Atlantic-Little, Brown, 1964, pp. 37-83).*

HAROLD CLURMAN (essay date 1977)

[*A Doll's House*] is perhaps more often produced than any other Ibsen play. It was certainly the most socially influential of his plays. Nora's slamming of the door in farewell to her husband—a highly theatrical device since we hear no door open or shut in the course of the play—is a door slam which reverberated around the world. Largely on this account, Ibsen is commonly regarded in the theater, at any rate, as a pioneer spirit of what today goes by the name of "women's lib."

In his *History of Modern Norway*, G. Derry takes pains to note that "within five years of the publication of *A Doll's House,* women were being admitted to the private Liberal Club in the tradition bound city of Oslo!" Yet it is remarkable that in his 1888 speech at a banquet for the Norwegian League of Women's Rights, Ibsen should have said, "I am not a member of the Women's Rights League. Whatever I have written has been without any conscious thought of making propaganda."

This seems a paradox. But in view of his central conviction that there is little hope for humankind unless every individual becomes an authentic person all of whose acts must stem from the deeper self, it is natural that Ibsen should have taken it for granted that this applied to men as well as to women. Or, to put it as Shaw does in *The Philanderer*, "If Ibsen's sauce is good for the goose, it is good for the gander as well."

If *A Doll's House* is read without preconceptions the implication is clear that men cannot be "free" (or authentic) persons unless women are equally free. It should be evident at the final curtain that while Nora is in a state of bewilderment, and she knows herself to be ignorant about everything except the necessity of her leavetaking, Torvald (Helmer), her husband, is even more bewildered. He does not quite understand what she means when she says that neither can lead an honest life unless the "miracle—the most wonderful thing of all" occurs. And if he did understand her, it would no doubt take as long for him to act on his understanding as it would take Nora to live by what she has yet to learn. Nora's abandonment of her home is not an act of defiance so much as a gesture of despair. (pp. 108-09)

The disaster of Nora's and Torvald's marriage is a possible prelude to a future education and, only remotely possible, a reunion. Both have begun as "dolls"; at the slamming of the door, their future soundness is still only a supposition.

From the first we observe that Nora and Torvald do not know each other, though of the two Nora is certainly the more aware. What is Nora to Torvald? In the opening scene we hear Torvald, by way of endearment, call Nora "a lark," "a squirrel," "a spendthrift," "a featherbrain," "a little woman" and "a little liar." He has forgotten that she persuaded him to go on the trip to Italy which saved his life; he barely inquires how she procured the money for it. . . . He can't possibly know that she saved most of her allowance for clothes, engaged in needlework and crocheting for others, working far into the night as a means of earning enough money to pay back the debt incurred for Torvald's sake. . . . Torvald owes his blissful domestic life to his thoughtlessness. In all essentials, he is more ignorant than she, for she has already faced and survived a crisis, taken difficult and dangerous action on his behalf.

Strindberg detested the play—he would! In a self-interview he took pleasure in pointing out that Torvald Helmer is an honest man—as a lawyer he never accepted a shady case—while Nora is a liar; worse still, a flirt, almost a hussy. Nora flirts, indulges in what she herself calls "pretty tricks." But this is her way, aside from an originally lighthearted nature, to penetrate the cuirass of Torvald's stuffy rectitude, his rigorous middle-class code of proper conduct. She can hardly reason with him because the heart has reasons that reason does not know. She wants above all to please him, she loves him, he is her knight. She constantly play-acts for him, and no doubt enjoys doing so. She is his baby. Why wrangle when you get your own way by sweet cajolery? If Torvald treats Nora like a "doll," she treats him like a child. Nora's coquetry, in short, is for the most part inspired by her husband's appetite for it. If this is "insincerity" it is something even more important for the actress playing the part than for the reader to notice.

Torvald at thirty is still a boob, but certainly no "villain" as he often appears in stage performances. His preachments as to the evil effect on children of a bad mother, shocking as they may sound to contemporary audiences, are by no means untrue. He concedes that fathers too may be held responsible for similar unfortunate influences. But what is most obtuse in his moralizing is not its substance but that it is hardly the result of any felt experience; it is largely bookish. What he says is the doctrine of his day; closely examined it is hardly very different from our own.

In the crisis of his life—Nora's announced determination to leave him—after he has been literally frightened out of his wits by the prospect of dismissal from his position and said unkind and stupid things, he begs her not to believe he seriously meant them. He was so dismayed at the thought of public disgrace. Nora reacts not to the explosiveness of his vituperation, but to the realization that he has thought only of himself. In the impending calamity he neither considers its causes nor is governed by the impulse to protect her. Just before he discovers her crime, he passionately declares—with brilliant theatrical effect—"I often wish you were in some great danger, so I could risk body and soul, my whole life, everything, everything for your sake."

She to whom love is everything, above the letter of the law, public opinion, even religion, of which she knows as little as most things learned by rote, discovers that his love is a convenience, not a commitment of the self. Thus her love for him is destroyed. (pp. 110-11)

When William Archer, the English theater critic and one of Ibsen's earliest translators, saw two performances of *A Doll's House* in 1883, he wrote his brother that "Nora requires an actress of even more uncommon physical and mental gifts than I imagined." This is especially necessary to render Nora's emotional coming of age convincing as well as clear. If the actress is unaware of the hazard in the scene, her "change" of character may appear too sudden and arbitrary. The director must call her attention to it.

In *reading* the play one may easily overlook the play's internal logic. After Torvald has been apprised of Nora's forgery, he bursts forth with "Do you know what you have done?" Almost as vehemently she attempts to prevent him from doing what she expects him to do. She cries out, "I won't have you suffer for it. I won't have you take the blame." He charges her with "play-acting," and after locking the door, repeats, "Answer me. Do you understand it?"

As readers we rush on without a break, to hear her reply; the play's turning point. On the *stage,* between his challenge and her answer, "I'm beginning to understand for the first time," there should be a protracted pause, or more exactly a strongly stressed silent *action* should follow, to mark her recognition of his attitude. We must *see* the terrible wrench she suffers here and the gradually mounting realization of what she must do. All she says as he continues his diatribe is, "I see." Her speeches until the moment she explains her resolve to leave are equally terse.

Most audiences now are familiar with the play's final passages. Those who have succumbed to the faddish presumptions of our day take Nora's leaving her husband and children as a matter of course or a banality; others—perhaps a minority—still consider her act foolish, cruel or dissolute. For such people she has, as Torvald says, "no religion, no moral code, no sense of duty," and possibly no common sense! Early on she tells Krogstad she doesn't know what "society" is, and to Torvald she confesses she hasn't fathomed the meaning of "religion." As for her darling children, she agrees, as she had been indirectly warned, that she is no fit mother for them. What can she teach them if she herself knows so little?

To his not wholly unreasonable protestations she very candidly replies, "It's hard to answer you. Torvald, I don't think I know—all these things bewilder me . . . I'm going to try to learn!" "Remember," he tells her, "before all else you are a mother, a wife and a mother," to which she answers, "I believe that before all else, I am a human being . . . or at least I should try to become one."

It is imperative for the understanding of the final scene to know that it is not one in which Nora as the "new woman" is mouthing portentous verities. She is groping sadly in a maze of confused feeling toward a way of life and a destiny of which she is most uncertain. And Torvald, after his first vociferous expression of indignation, arguments and pleas, is as much at sea as she is. Does he not say in a manner almost as pathetic as funny, "Just you lean on me; let me guide you and advise you; I'm not a man for nothing! There's something very endearing about a woman's helplessness."

If there is anything sure and steadfast in Nora's final posture it is that she "must take steps to educate herself" if she is ever to reach any understanding of herself and "the things around her." She "must learn to stand alone." As we have discovered in the earlier plays, and as we shall be more emphatically advised in the later ones, "to stand alone" is not Ibsen's prescription solely for women but for men as well. Perhaps, let us say, to begin with, that standing alone is a most problematic matter; that it is not in every respect possible or even desirable is something that his future plays in their alternation will demonstrate. . . . Nora's telling Torvald that she no longer loves him is not a cold but a heartbroken declaration. The ebbing of love is always profoundly painful.

What readers, audiences, actors and directors must keep in mind for a fuller comprehension of *A Doll's House* is that all its characters are bent on maintaining or achieving *worthiness,* what the Germans call *Anständigkeit.* (The same is probably true in most of Ibsen's plays.) The catch is that "worthiness" is different for each person. For Torvald Helmer as with most of the people of his class, to be worthy is to be in the "right." . . . His sense of "rightness" is dictated by society. . . . He is not petty, only petty bourgeois. In that class, the appearance of virtue is almost as important as the possession of it. Hence blindness or hypocrisy.

For Nora worthiness means to *do* right by everyone. She protected her father, she tries to shield Helmer in every way, she cares for her children, she gets a job for Mrs. Linde, she is generous with money, she won't take advantage of Dr. Rank's love for her and borrow money from him (it would be a kind of deceit in regard to her husband), and when her image of herself and her domestic life is shattered she does what she feels she must to become a true person.

Worthiness, "like individualism," has two faces: one demands responsibility to others out of deep selfhood; the other sets social propriety up as the norm of conduct—and leads willy-nilly to corruption. (pp. 113-15)

> Harold Clurman, in his Ibsen *(reprinted with permission of Macmillan Publishing Co. Inc.; copyright © 1977 by Harold Clurman), Macmillan, 1977, 223 p.*

DAVID THOMAS (essay date 1979)

Like other last plays by great writers, *When we dead awaken* . . . is an elusive work. It is not a play that yields easily to interpretation. The tissue of experience is so complex, the pattern of thought so intricate that even the dramatist has clearly found it difficult to shape his material into a cohesive whole. Michael Meyer, in his biography of Ibsen, likened the play to the flawed and unfinished masterpieces of Michelangelo's old age. Flawed it may be, unfinished it certainly is not. Nevertheless the comparison with Michelangelo is thought-provoking. Not for nothing is the main character in the play a sculptor; for with a sculptor's artistic economy Ibsen here chiselled out a work of complex substance in a classically simple form. In 1864 he had written to Bjørnson:

> I have not yet been able to come to terms with antiquity; I do not properly understand its relationship to our own age; I miss a sense of illusion and, above all, a sense of personal and individual expression both in the work of art itself and in the artist. And I still cannot help seeing—so far at least—conventions where others claim there are laws.

By the time he wrote *When we dead awaken* Ibsen had mastered the problem of fusing the Classical and Neo-classical concern for general nature with his own essentially Romantic concern for personal and private nature. With its sculptured tautness, *When we dead awaken* is an austere work but at the same time it is resonant with an emotive poetry of strange beauty. . . . [The] substance of this poetry may be seen to lie in the fusion of reality and myth that lies at the heart of the work.

The play begins at the level of lived-out and acted-out reality. Briefly, succinctly Ibsen sketches in emblematic images of the social environment (a late nineteenth-century, *haut bourgeois* environment) in which the characters live and from which they derive their values and life-styles. The main body of the action

then traces out the way the four major characters interact with each other; an ageing sculptor called Rubek, his young wife Maja, his former model Irene and a hunter called Squire Ulfhejm. The patterns of interaction traced out between these various characters are complex and richly facetted. But they acquire an added richness and depth when seen at the mythical and liturgical level at which the play also operates. Gradually, as the action of the play progresses, it becomes apparent that these various characters are linked quite explicitly with mythic figures in such a way as to add complex resonances to their patterns of behaviour in the play. In terms of theme and structure it also becomes gradually apparent that the play is concerned with tracing out a pattern of action that is not only realistically but also mythically and even liturgically complete. Thematically the play explores the polarized opposites of sin and expiation, life and death, death and resurrection: structurally it relies on classical archetypes while at the same time drawing strength from the liturgical pattern of the mass. *When we dead awaken* is therefore, at one and the same time, a play about living, a play that explores live relationships in a given social environment, and also a play about life, tracing out in mythical terms a complete cycle of love, suffering, death and transcendence. Throughout it operates at a level of concrete specificity, in terms of immediately particularized experience, and at a level of mythical, universalized experience. Only at the very end of the play are the various levels drawn together.

Viewed dramaturgically, the play follows a simple, dreamlike, almost musically determined pattern. Both Acts 1 and 2 open with scenes in which Rubek and Maja explore respectively their boredom in marriage and their decision to break with each other. These opening scenes are then followed in each Act by a decisive encounter between Rubek and Irene. Act 1 explores Irene's past, after she left Rubek, and her state of mind now; Act 2 explores Rubek's life in the intervening years and his spiritual malaise now. Only when the past has in this way been laid bare and in some sense brought to rest is the ground cleared for the final Act which takes Rubek and Irene to a *Liebestod* in the mountains and leads Maja back down to earth, where she belongs, with Squire Ulfhejm.

Themes are thus introduced in Act 1, only to be explored in a different key in Act 2, until the final chromatic ascent of the mountain in Act 3 leads to a vibrating and triumphant resolution of all the discordant stages in the progressions that have been traversed. (pp. 1-2)

The physical setting of the play echoes this progression. Act 1 is set in the grounds of a hotel at a coastal spa town. (p. 3)

Act 2 moves from the boredom of this emblematically suggested *haut bourgeois* environment to an austere but challenging mountain landscape. In a conversation with Gunnar Heiberg Ibsen suggested that he was thinking of the Hardangervidda as the setting for Acts 2 and 3, a desolate, forbidding and yet imposing mountain landscape conveying an overwhelming sense of isolation in which man is up against the most extreme forces of nature. Act 2 is set in the 'dead country' as Irene calls it, 'a vast treeless plateau' that 'stretches away towards a long mountain lake. Beyond the lake towers a range of mountain peaks, with bluish snow in their crevasses.' The dead country is a place in which the masks and subterfuges of everyday reality can be stripped away; it is a place of spiritual reckoning in which the ground is prepared for the mythical level at which the play now gradually begins to operate.

Act 3 moves to the mountain peaks, glimpsed in the distance in Act 2. In the stage directions for this Act Ibsen seems to anticipate the analogic stage settings of the expressionist theatre in which spiritual landscapes are chiselled out of the darkness with the help of expressive lighting and architecturally structured stage space:

> A wild jagged mountain top, with a sheer precipice behind. To the right tower snow-covered peaks, vanishing into drifting mist. To the left, on a scree, stands an old, tumbledown hut. It is early morning. Dawn is breaking: the sun has not yet risen.

This is a landscape in which myth predominates over reality. What Ibsen describes here is not a literal but a spiritual landscape, a visual correlative for mythical experience. As Rubek and Irene climb through the mists and the snow towards their mountain peak at the end of the Act, the visual imagery echoes and re-inforces their spiritual progression through the mists of perception to self-knowledge, self-fulfillment and self-transcendence. (pp. 3-4)

By the end of **When we dead awaken** we have witnessed an action that is complete in terms of lived-out relationships and also in terms of myth and liturgy. It is a play that leads us through a spiritual landscape as in a dream. It is an intensely personal work—Ibsen's searing reckoning with his own life—and at the same time a play that in its various images and situations anticipates some of the recurring themes of twentieth-century art. The loss of meaning in life, the corrosive effect of bourgeois materialism, the lack of genuine reciprocity in relationships, the reduction of people to the status of objects—all of this finds expression in Ibsen's play. And yet the vision that emerges from the play is ultimately life-affirming. For it is only when life has been faced with the kind of uncompromising honesty Ibsen applies in this play that its real meaning and worth can be appreciated.

What Rubek discovers by the end of **When we dead awaken** is that a life of unthinking materialism is a cancer that gnaws at the heart of human creativity. Commitment to materialist values can offer the promise of economic and social success; but the price to be paid in terms of exploitation of, and isolation from, others is spiritual death. The relevance of this insight to our present world hardly needs stressing, a world dominated by bourgeois capitalist and state capitalist versions of acquisitive materialism: with varying degrees of subtlety, the artist, in both systems, is pressured into mortgaging his creativity for the sake of social and material advancement.

Rubek also discovers that an art without love, the kind of *agape* of which Paul writes in I Cor 13:1-3, is as empty and devoid of humanly significant meaning as 'a sounding brass, or a tinkling cymbal'. Again the relevance to today's world is obvious, a world in which both the self-loathing of writers like Samuel Beckett and the congratulatory self-esteem of writers like Alan Ayckbourn and Neil Simon expresses itself, with almost mechanical predictability, in pointlessly hollow and cynical versions of human relationships. By contrast with the reactionary pessimism of absurdist writing or the equally reactionary nihilism of, say, Ingmar Bergman's more recent films, **When we dead awaken** emerges, despite its sombre tonality, as a hymn to life, 'that beautiful, miraculous life so full of riddles'. The vision inspiring it, I would argue, is both humanistic *and* religious. Its critique of bourgeois materialism is inspired by the same commitment to humane values one finds in the work of Marxist playwrights such as Brecht and Peter Weiss. But the equally deep religious commitment in the play (in-

volving a religiosity that accepts myth and liturgical symbolism but rejects mystification by repeatedly emphasizing authenticity of response to others as the only way to find purpose and meaning in life) seems to me inspired by essentially the same Christian existentialist insight one finds in plays such as *The Devils* by John Whiting or *The Business of Good Government* by John Arden and Margaretta D'Arcy.

When **Peer Gynt** was savaged by a malicious and short-sighted contemporary critic, Ibsen commented: 'My book *is* poetry: and if it isn't, then it shall be. The very concept of poetry in our country, in Norway, shall be made to come into line with my book.' The same might be said of **When we dead awaken.** When it was written, it baffled even some of Ibsen's most ardent admirers, especially his English admirers William Archer and Edmund Gosse. Today, when our analytic insight has begun to catch up with Ibsen's intuitive insight, it is understandably easier to appreciate the implications of a play in which the worlds of reality and myth are so complexly and so subtly intertwined. In **When we dead awaken,** written at the turn of the century, Ibsen combines reality and myth in a way that seems to anticipate the bridge that has yet to be built between the sociological insight of Marx and the spiritual insights of Christian existentialist theologians and philosophers such as [Paul] Tillich and [Karl] Jaspers. In so doing he offers, by implication, a vision of the Third Empire far richer, far more exciting and far more challenging than the essentially backward-looking, romantic vision with which he had unsuccessfully wrestled for so many years in writing **Emperor and Galilean. When we dead awaken** was a fitting epilogue for a great dramatist who, in his best work, wrote, and knew that he wrote, for the future. (pp. 117-18)

> *David Thomas, ''All the Glory of the World: Reality and Myth in 'When We Dead Awaken','' in* Scandinavia *(copyright © 1979 by Editor,* Scandinavica; *reprinted with permission), Vol. 18, No. 1, May, 1979, pp. 1-19.*

ADDITIONAL BIBLIOGRAPHY

Bradbrook, M. C. *Ibsen the Norwegian: A Revaluation.* London: Chatto & Windus, 1948, 150 p.
> Places Ibsen in relation to contemporary European dramatists. The critic also traces early literary influences on Ibsen.

Downs, Brian W. *Ibsen: The Intellectual Background.* Cambridge: Cambridge University Press, 1946, 187 p.
> An account of the artistic conventions and historical events which influenced Ibsen's dramas.

Downs, Brian W. ''Ibsen Before 1884.'' In his *Modern Norwegian Literature: 1860-1918,* pp. 43-64. Cambridge: Cambridge University Press, 1966.
> Critical overview of Ibsen's early plays.

Franc, Miriam Alice. *Ibsen in England.* Boston: The Four Seas Co., 1919, 195 p.
> Study of the popular and critical reactions to Ibsen's plays as they were first performed in England.

Gosse, Edmund W. ''Ibsen, the Norwegian Satirist.'' *The Fortnightly Review* XIX, No. LXXIII (1 January 1873): 74-88.
> Early review of Ibsen's ''great satiric trilogy'': *Love's Comedy, Brand,* and *Peer Gynt.* Gosse prefaces his critical remarks with the contention that ''Henrik Ibsen, the representative of a land unknown in the literary annals of Europe'' is the ''single accredited world-poet'' of his age.

Gosse, Edmund [W]. *Henrik Ibsen*. New York: Charles Scribner's Sons, 1926, 244 p.
Biography of Ibsen, with plot outlines and character descriptions from the plays.

Henderson, Archibald. "Henrik Ibsen." In his *European Dramatists*, pp. 75-198. New York: D. Appleton & Co., 1913.
Critical survey of Ibsen's work, with some biographical information.

Ibsen, Bergliot. *The Three Ibsens: Memories of Henrik Ibsen, Suzannah Ibsen and Sigurd Ibsen*. London: Hutchinson & Co., 1951, 184 p.*
Reminiscences of the Ibsen family by Henrik Ibsen's daughter-in-law.

Jaeger, Henrik. *Henrik Ibsen: A Critical Biography*. Translated by William Morton Payne. Rev. ed. 1901. Reprint. New York: Hasken House Publishers, 1972, 320 p.
Early biography recounting critical reaction to Ibsen plays; contains little actual criticism.

Koht, Halvdan. *The Life of Ibsen*. Translated by Ruth Lima McMahon and Hanna Astrup Larsen. 2 vols. New York: W. W. Norton & Co., 1931.
Noncritical biography.

Lucas, F. L. *The Drama of Ibsen and Strindberg*. New York: The Macmillan Co., 1962, 484 p.*
Contains a brief biographical sketch of Ibsen and an analysis of his character. This study also includes plot synopses and analyses of the major plays which draw heavily on biographical incidents.

Meyer, Michael. *Ibsen: A Biography*. New York: Doubleday & Co., 1971, 865 p.
Biography designed to supply information about Ibsen's years as a theater director and about his old age, periods Meyer feels were neglected in Halvdan Koht's earlier biography.

Northam, John Richard. *Ibsen's Dramatic Method: A Study of the Prose Dramas*. London: Faber and Faber, 1953, 232 p.
Examines Ibsen's stage directions and use of visual symbolism as an aid to the delineation of character.

Payne, William Morton. "Henrik Ibsen." *The Dial* XVI, No. 188 (16 April 1894): 236-40.
Review of *Brand*, prefaced by a discussion of Ibsen as "a poet with a message": that of individualism.

Scandinavian Studies: Henrik Ibsen Issue 51, No. 4 (Autumn 1979): 343-519.
Contains articles by Einer Haugen, Evert Sprinchorn, and Yvonne L. Sandstroem, among others.

Symons, Arthur. "Henrik Ibsen." In his *Figures of Several Centuries*, pp. 222-267. London: Constable and Co., 1916.
Study of Ibsen's character as revealed in the published volumes of his letters, along with a brief summary of his work.

Tennant, P.F.D. *Ibsen's Dramatic Technique*. New York: Humanities Press, 1965, 135 p.
Study of Ibsen's stage techniques.

James (Augustine Aloysius) Joyce

1882-1941

Irish novelist, short story writer, poet, dramatist, and critic.

Joyce is considered the most prominent literary figure of the first half of the twentieth century. His virtuoso experiments in prose both redefined the limits of language and recreated the form of the modern novel. Joyce's prose is often praised for its richness and many critics feel that his verbal facility equals that of Shakespeare or Milton.

Joyce was born in a suburb of Dublin to middle-class parents. Like Stephen Dedalus in *Portrait of the Artist As a Young Man,* he was educated by the Jesuits and underwent much the same emotional hardship and intellectual discipline as the hero of his first published novel. After graduating from University College in 1902, Joyce left Ireland, consciously abandoning the restrictive milieu which the short stories of *Dubliners* depict in harshly naturalistic detail. In 1903 his mother's serious illness brought Joyce back to Ireland. Following her death in 1904, Joyce moved permanently to the continent with his future wife, Nora Barnacle. In France and Italy, where the couple's two children were born, Joyce struggled to support himself and family by working as a language instructor. For a time they lived in Zurich, where Joyce wrote most of *Ulysses.* In 1920 Joyce and his family moved to Paris. Among the expatriate Americans living there between the wars was Sylvia Beach, who published *Ulysses* under the imprint of her bookstore, Shakespeare and Co. Following the international renown accorded *Ulysses,* Joyce gained the financial patronship of Harriet Shaw and afterward was able to devote himself exclusively to writing. Joyce spent nearly all of his remaining years composing his final work, *Finnegans Wake.* Though free from poverty, these years were darkened by the worsening insanity of Joyce's daughter Lucia and by several surgical attempts to save his failing eyesight. After the publication of *Finnegans Wake,* Joyce fled Paris and the approaching turmoil of the Second World War. He died in Zurich of a perforated ulcer.

Joyce's work spans the extremes of naturalism and symbolism, from the spare style of *Dubliners* to the verbal richness of *Finnegans Wake. Dubliners,* a group of naturalistic stories concerned with the intellectual and spiritual torpor of Ireland, is the first product of his lifelong preoccupation with Dublin life. Though so disgusted by the narrowness and provincialism of Ireland that he spent most of his life in self-imposed exile, Joyce nevertheless made Ireland and the Irish the subject of all his fiction. These stories are also important as examples of his theory of epiphany in fiction: each is concerned with a sudden revelation of truth about life inspired by a seemingly trivial incident.

Joyce's first novel, *A Portrait of the Artist as a Young Man,* is at once a portrayal of the maturation of the artist, a study of the vanity of rebelliousness, and an examination of the self-deception of adolescent ego. The novel is often considered a study of the author's early life. Originally entitled *Stephen Hero* and conceived as an epic of autobiography, *Portrait* was thoroughly rewritten to provide an objective account of its protagonist's consciousness. Many critics feel that structurally

it is Joyce's strongest work. However, most critics agree that *Ulysses* is the novel in which all of Joyce's considerable talents are fully realized. Fashioned after Homer's *Odyssey,* Joyce utilized the structure of that epic to universalize Dublin life and to serve as an heroic counterpart to its antiheroic protagonist, Leopold Bloom. Joyce created *Ulysses* from a complex of various techniques and experiments, one chapter, for example, being a parody of every English prose style from the Anglo-Saxon to the present. In *Ulysses,* and later in *Finnegans Wake,* he developed the stream of consciousness technique further than any previous novelist.

Using *Ulysses* as a case in point, many critics have remarked on Joyce's limitations of thought and concluded that his talent was essentially technical. But Joyce is not concerned with presenting a consistent vision of life. In lieu of a philosophy, he explores the interrelationships of life and literature in extremely allusive prose. His comic sense of life saves his work from being merely pedantic; in fact, his comic gift and stylistic experiments place *Ulysses* in the same category as the works of Rabelais and Laurence Sterne. Like the work of those predecessors, *Ulysses* is frequently bawdy. Published in Paris, it was banned in the United States due to its alleged pornographic content. The subsequent trial led to a landmark interpretation of the first amendment which allowed publication in 1933.

Joyce worked on his next book, *Finnegans Wake,* for seventeen years. Throughout that time portions of the book appeared in magazines as "Work in Progress." Unable to agree upon a formal classification for the completed work, critics hesitantly call it a novel. Meant to be the subconscious flow of thought of H. C. Earwicker, a character both real and allegorical, *Finnegans Wake* is literally a recreation of the English language. In this masterpiece of allusions, puns, foreign languages, and word combinations, Joyce attempted to compress all of human history into one night's dream. Admittedly a work for a select few, it has inspired a mass of critical exegesis. The author was probably serious when he remarked that a person should spend a lifetime reading it.

Joyce devoted his life to his art, overcoming hardships of poverty, reluctant publishers, and near blindness. His life has come to be a symbol for the spiritual alienation of the modern artist, and his work has spawned numerous imitations. A complicated artistic genius, he created a body of work worthy of comparison with the masterpieces of English literature.

(See also *TCLC*, Vol. 3, and *Dictionary of Literary Biography*, Vol. 10: *Modern British Dramatists, 1900-1945*.)

PRINCIPAL WORKS

Chamber Music   (poetry)   1907
Dubliners   (short stories)   1914
A Portrait of the Artist as a Young Man   (novel)   1916
Exiles   (drama)   1918
Ulysses   (novel)   1922
Pomes Penyeach   (poetry)   1927
Collected Poems   (poetry)   1936
Finnegans Wake   (novel)   1939
*Stephen Hero   (unfinished novel)   1944
Critical Writings of James Joyce   (criticism)   1959

*This work was written in 1901-06.

ARTHUR SYMONS   (essay date 1906)

Would you care to have, for your Vigo Cabinet, a book of verse which is of the most genuine lyric quality of any new work I have read for many years? It is called *A Book of Thirty Songs for Lovers* [the title was subsequently changed to *Chamber Music*], and the lyrics are almost Elizabethan in their freshness, but quite personal. They are by a young Irishman called J. A. Joyce. He is *not* in the Celtic Movement, and though Yeats admits his ability he is rather against him because Joyce has attacked the movement . . . I am offering you a book which cannot fail to attract notice from everyone capable of knowing poetry when he sees it. . . .

> *Arthur Symons, in an extract from his letter to Elkin Mathews on October 9, 1906, in* James Joyce Quarterly *(copyright, 1967, The University of Tulsa), Vol. 4, No. 2, Winter, 1967 (and reprinted in* James Joyce: The Critical Heritage, 1902-1927, *Vol. 1, edited by Robert H. Deming, Routledge & Kegan Paul, 1970, p. 36).*

THE ATHENAEUM   (essay date 1914)

[The fifteen short stories] given under the collective title of *Dubliners* are nothing if not naturalistic. In some ways, indeed, they are unduly so: at least three would have been better buried in oblivion. Life has so much that is beautiful, interesting, educative, amusing, that we do not readily pardon those who insist upon its more sordid and baser aspects. The condemnation is the greater if their skill is of any high degree, since in that case they might use it to better purpose.

Mr. Joyce undoubtedly possesses great skill both of observation and of technique. He has humour, as is shown by the sketch of Mrs. Kearney and her views on religion, her faith 'bounded by her kitchen, but if she was put to it, she could believe also in the banshee and in the Holy Ghost.' He has also knowledge of the beauty of words, of mental landscapes (if we may use such a phrase): the last page of the final story ['**The Dead**'] is full evidence thereto. His characterization is exact: speaking with reserve as to the conditions of certain sides of the social life of Dublin we should say that it is beyond criticism. All the personages are living realities.

But Mr. Joyce has his own specialized outlook on life—on that life in particular; and here we may, perhaps, find the explanation of much that displeases and that puzzles us. That outlook is evidently sombre: he is struck by certain types, certain scenes, by the dark shadows of a low street or the lurid flare of an ignoble tavern, and he reproduces these in crude, strong sketches scarcely relieved by the least touch of joy or repose. Again, his outlook is self-centred, absorbed in itself rather; he ends his sketch abruptly time after time, satisfied with what he has done, brushing aside any intention of explaining what is set down or supplementing what is omitted.

All the stories are worth reading for the work that is in them, for the pictures they present; the best are undoubtedly the last four, especially '**Ivy Day in the Committee Room.**' The last of all, '**The Dead,**' far longer than the rest, and tinged with a softer tone of pathos and sympathy, leads us to hope that Mr. Joyce may attempt larger and broader work, in which the necessity of asserting the proportions of life may compel him to enlarge his outlook and eliminate such scenes and details as can only shock, without in any useful way impressing or elevating, the reader. . . . (pp. 61-2)

> *"Short Stories: 'Dubliners',," in* The Athenaeum, *No. 4521, June 20, 1914 (and reprinted in* James Joyce: The Critical Heritage, 1902-1927, *Vol. I, edited by Robert H. Deming, Routledge & Kegan Paul, 1970, pp. 61-2).*

VLADIMIR NABOKOV   (essay date 1958?)

In composing the figure of Bloom, Joyce's intention was to place among endemic Irishmen in his native Dublin someone who was as Irish as he, Joyce, was, but who also was an exile, a black sheep in the fold, as he, Joyce, was. Joyce evolved the rational plan, therefore, of selecting for the type of an outsider, the type of the Wandering Jew, the type of the exile. However, . . . Joyce is sometimes crude in the way he accumulates and stresses so-called racial traits. Another consideration in relation to Bloom: those so many who have written so much about *Ulysses* are either very pure men or very depraved men. They are inclined to regard Bloom as a very ordinary nature, and apparently Joyce himself intended to portray an ordinary person. It is obvious, however, that in the sexual department Bloom is, if not on the verge of insanity, at least a good clinical example of extreme sexual preoccupation and perversity with all kinds of curious complications. His case is strictly heterosexual, of course—not homosexual as most of the ladies and gentlemen are in Proust (*homo* is Greek for same, not Latin for man as some students think)— but within the wide limits of Bloom's love for the opposite sex he indulges in acts and dreams that are definitely subnormal in the zoological, evolutional sense. I shall not bore you with a list of his curious desires, but this I will say: in Bloom's mind and in Joyce's book the theme of sex is continually mixed and intertwined with the theme of the latrine. God knows I have no objection whatsoever to so-called frankness in novels. On the contrary, we have too little of it, and what there is has become in its turn conventional and trite, as used by so-called tough writers, the darlings of the book clubs, the pets of club-women. But I do object to the following: Bloom is supposed to be a rather ordinary citizen. Now it is not true that the mind of an ordinary citizen continuously dwells on physiological things. I object to the continuously, not to the disgusting. All this very special pathological stuff seems artificial and unnecessary in this particular context. I suggest that the squeamish among you regard the special preoccupation of Joyce with perfect detachment.

Ulysses is a splendid and permanent structure, but it has been slightly overrated by the kind of critic who is more interested in ideas and generalities and human aspects than in the work of art itself. I must especially warn against seeing in Leopold Bloom's humdrum wanderings and minor adventures on a summer day in Dublin a close parody of the *Odyssey,* with the adman Bloom acting the part of Odysseus, otherwise Ulysses, man of many devices, and Bloom's adulterous wife representing chaste Penelope while Stephen Dedalus is given the part of Telemachus. That there is a very vague and very general Homeric echo of the theme of wanderings in Bloom's case is obvious, as the title of the novel suggests, and there are a number of classical allusions among the many other allusions in the course of the book; but it would be a complete waste of time to look for close parallels in every character and every scene of the book. There is nothing more tedious than a protracted and sustained allegory based on a well-worn myth; and after the work had appeared in parts, Joyce promptly deleted the pseudo-Homeric titles of his chapters when he saw what scholarly and pseudoscholarly bores were up to. Another thing. One bore, a man called Stuart Gilbert, misled by a tongue-in-cheek list compiled by Joyce himself, found in every chapter the domination of one particular organ—the ear, the eye, the stomach, etc.—but we shall ignore that dull nonsense too. All art is in a sense symbolic; but we say ''stop, thief'' to the critic who deliberately transforms an artist's subtle symbol into a pedant's stale allegory—a thousand and one nights into a convention of Shriners.

What then is the main theme of the book? It is very simple.

1. The hopeless past. Bloom's infant son has died long ago, but the vision remains in his blood and brain.

2. The ridiculous and tragic present. Bloom still loves his wife Molly, but he lets Fate have its way. He knows that in the afternoon at 4:30 of this mid-June day Boylan, her dashing impresario, concert agent, will visit Molly—and Bloom does nothing to prevent it. He tries fastidiously to keep out of Fate's way, but actually throughout the day is continuously on the point of running into Boylan.

3. The pathetic future. Bloom also keeps running into another young man—Stephen Dedalus. Bloom gradually realizes that this may be another little attention on the part of Fate. If his wife *must* have lovers then sensitive, artistic Stephen would be a better one than vulgar Boylan. In fact, Stephen could give Molly lessons, could help her with her Italian pronunciations in her profession as a singer, could be in short a refining influence, as Bloom pathetically thinks.

This is the main theme: Bloom and Fate.

Each chapter is written in a different style, or rather with a different style predominating. There is no special reason why this should be—why one chapter should be told straight, another through a stream-of-consciousness gurgle, a third through the prism of a parody. There is no special reason, but it may be argued that this constant shift of the viewpoint conveys a more varied knowledge, fresh vivid glimpses from this or that side. (pp. 286-89)

The characters are constantly brought together during their peregrinations through a Dublin day. Joyce never loses control over them. Indeed, they come and go and meet and separate, and meet again as the live parts of a careful composition in a kind of slow dance of fate. The recurrence of a number of themes is one of the most striking features of the book. These themes are much more clear-cut, much more deliberately followed, than the themes we pick up in Tolstoy or in Kafka. The whole of *Ulysses* . . . is a deliberate pattern of recurrent themes and synchronization of trivial events.

Joyce writes in three main styles:

1. The original Joyce: straightforward, lucid and logical and leisurely. This is the backbone of chapter 1 of the first part and of chapters 1 and 3 of the second part; and lucid, logical, and leisurely parts occur in other chapters

2. Incomplete, rapid, broken wording rendering the so-called stream of consciousness, or better say the stepping stones of consciousness. Samples may be found in most chapters, though ordinarily associated only with major characters. A discussion of this device will be found in connection with its most famous example, Molly's final soliloquy, part three, chapter 3; but one can comment here that it exaggerates the verbal side of thought. Man thinks not always in words but also in images, whereas the stream of consciousness presupposes a flow of words that can be notated: it is difficult, however, to believe that Bloom was continuously talking to himself.

3. Parodies of various nonnovelistic forms. . . . (p. 289)

The technique of this stream of thought has, of course, the advantage of brevity. It is a series of brief messages jotted down by the brain. But it does demand from the reader more attention and sympathy than an ordinary description. . . .

Inner thoughts rising to the surface and prompted to do so by an outside impression lead to significant word connections, verbal links, in the mind of the thinker. For instance, look at the way the notion of the sea leads to the most hidden thoughts within Stephen's tortured soul. As he is shaving Mulligan gazes out over Dublin Bay and remarks quietly: "God. . . . Isn't the sea what Algy [*that is, Algernon Swinburne, an English postromantic minor poet*] calls it: a grey sweet mother?'' (Mark the word *sweet.*) Our great sweet mother, he adds, improving as it were on the *grey* by adding the *t.*—Our mighty mother, he goes on, polishing up a nice alliteration. Then he refers to Stephen's mother, to Stephen's sinister sin. My aunt thinks you killed your mother, he says.—But what a lovely mummer (that is, mime) you are, he murmurs (look at the coils of the alliterating dragging up sense after sense: mighty mother, mummer, murmur). And Stephen listens to the well-fed voice; and mother and murmuring mighty sweet bitter sea merge, as it were, and there are other mergings. "The ring of bay and skyline held a dull green mass of liquid." This is inwardly transposed by Stephen's thought into the "bowl of white china [that] had stood beside her deathbed holding the green sluggish bile which she had torn up from her rotting liver by fits of loud groaning vomiting." The sweet mother becomes the bitter mother, bitter bile, bitter remorse. Then Buck Mulligan wipes his razor blade on Stephen's handkerchief: "—Ah, poor dogsbody, he said in a kind voice. I must give you a shirt and a few noserags." This links up the snotgreen sea with Stephen's filthy handkerchief and the green bile in the bowl; and the bowl of bile and the shaving bowl and the bowl of the sea, bitter tears and salty mucous, all fuse for a second into one image. This is Joyce at his best. (p. 297)

Synchronization is a device rather than a theme. Throughout [*Ulysses*] people keep running into each other—paths meet, diverge, and meet again. . . .

The Man in the Brown Macintosh is, however, a theme. Among the incidental characters of the book there is one of very special interest to the Joycean reader, for I need not repeat that every new type of writer evolves a new type of reader; every genius produces a legion of young insomniacs. The very special incidental character I have in mind is the so-called Man in the Brown Macintosh, who is alluded to in one way or another eleven times in the course of the book but is never named. Commentators have, as far as I know, not understood his identity. Let us see if we can identify him. (p. 316)

[Who] is he—he who appears at crucial points of the book— is he death, oppression, persecution, life, love? (p. 318)

> What selfinvolved enigma did Bloom [as he undressed and gathered his garments] voluntarily apprehending, not comprehend?
>
> Who was M'Intosh?

This is the last we hear of the Man in the Brown Macintosh.

Do we know who he is? I think we do. The clue comes in chapter 4 of part two, the scene at the library. Stephen is discussing Shakespeare and affirms that Shakespeare himself is present in his, Shakespeare's, works. Shakespeare, he says, tensely: "He has hidden his own name, a fair name, William, in the plays, a super here, a clown there, as a painter of old Italy set his face in a dark corner of his canvas. . . ." and this is exactly what Joyce has done—setting his face in a dark corner of this canvas. The Man in the Brown Macintosh who passes through the dream of the book is no other than the author himself. Bloom glimpses his maker! (pp. 319-20)

I do not know of any commentator who has correctly understood (the Nighttown) chapter. The psychoanalytical interpretation I, of course, dismiss completely and absolutely, since I do not belong to the Freudian denomination with its borrowed myths, shabby umbrellas, and dark backstairs. To regard this chapter as the reactions of intoxication or lust on Bloom's subconscious is impossible for the following reasons:

1. Bloom is perfectly sober and for the moment impotent.

2. Bloom cannot possibly know of a number of events, characters, and facts that appear as visions in this chapter.

I propose to regard this chapter 12 as an hallucination on the author's part, an amusing distortion of his various themes. The book is itself dreaming and having visions; this chapter is merely an exaggeration, a nightmare evolution of its characters, objects, and themes. (p. 350)

Readers are unduly impressed by the stream-of-thought device. I want to submit the following considerations. First, the device is not more "realistic" or more "scientific" than any other. In fact if some of Molly's thoughts [in the last section of *Ulysses*] were described instead of all of them being recorded, their expression would strike one as more "realistic," more natural. The point is that the stream of consciousness is a stylistic convention because obviously we do not think continuously in words—we think also in images; but the switch from words to images can be recorded in direct words only if description is eliminated as it is here. Another thing: some of our reflections come and go, others stay; they stop as it were, amorphous and sluggish, and it takes some time for the flowing thoughts and thoughtlets to run around those rocks of thought. The drawback of simulating a recording of thought is the blurring of the time element and too great a reliance on typography.

These Joycean pages have had a tremendous influence. In this typographical broth many a minor poet has been generated: the typesetter of the great James Joyce is the godfather of tiny Mr. Cummings. We must not see in the stream of consciousness as rendered by Joyce a natural event. It is a reality only insofar as it reflects Joyce's cerebration, the mind of the book. This book is a new world invented by Joyce. In that world people think by means of words, sentences. Their mental associations are mainly dictated by the structural needs of the book, by the author's artistic purposes and plans. I should also add that if punctuation marks be inserted by an editor into the text, Molly's musings would not really become less amusing or less musical. (p. 363)

In the course of her soliloquy, Molly's thought shuttles between the images of various people, men and women, but one thing we shall mark at once, namely, that the amount of retrospective meditation that she devotes to her newly acquired lover Boylan is much inferior to the quality and quantity of the thoughts she devotes to her husband and to other people. Here is a woman who has had a brutal but more or less satisfactory physical experience a few hours ago, but her thoughts are occupied by humdrum recollecting that reverts constantly to her husband. She does not love Boylan: if she loves anyone it is Bloom. (p. 364)

Vladimir Nabokov, "James Joyce: 'Ulysses'" (1958?), in his Lectures on Literature, *edited by Fredson Bowers (copyright © 1980 by the Estate of Vladimir Nabokov; reprinted by permission of Harcourt Brace Jovanovich, Inc.), Harcourt Brace Jovanovich, 1980, pp. 285-370.*

S. L. GOLDBERG (essay date 1962)

Let me say at the outset that I do not believe *Finnegans Wake* is worth detailed exegesis. . . . Undoubtedly it will always be a happy hunting-ground for what passes as "scholarship" and "research," and some of the results may even prove relevant enough to help explain what Joyce was about. Nevertheless, the work itself seems to me an artistic failure; and despite the enthusiastic assertions of its admirers, the questions it prompts the ordinary reader to ask remain, I believe, still the most important—questions concerned less with its verbal "meaning'' or its machinery than with its value: why Joyce ever undertook it, why it seems so laborious and, more particularly, so unrewarding to read through.

One thing we must grant is the seriousness of its intention. It arose not from mere *avant-garde* intoxication but from one of the central problems of our age: to discover what a fully unified, fully human vitality might be. . . . The artist and thinker alike have sought to ''see into the life of things,'' to apprehend a Reality in which the ''dissociations'' of our world—between nature and man, for example, or fact and value, or thinking and feeling, or necessity and freedom—will be healed, and in which both the individual and society can find the sustaining source and pattern of their life. (pp. 103-04)

Joyce's career offers almost a model of this whole process. From his early Romantic egoism he came eventually to discover the meaning of ''life,'' first in the creative understanding wherein he defined himself *as* a creative artist, and then in the more complex act wherein he defined the social and moral nature of his world and of himself. The critical exploration of the self led, with an exemplary logic, to the critical exploration of society. By the end of *Ulysses,* however, he came to a further problem. It was clear that the only forms of moral, social, and artistic life available in the modern world could not contain, or even sanction, the whole potential life of a Bloom, much less that of his creator. If, as the [*Portrait of the Artist as a Young Man*] and *Ulysses* subtly insist, the individual realises himself only as he discovers his life-values in the shape and meaning he finds-and-creates in his experience, the end result is a radical scepticism about any society, any institution, and indeed any artistic creation. The search for ''life'' must now proceed beyond all these—to what the individual (artist or citizen) and the particular ''now and here'' (Dublin—1904 or Paris—1922) share with all men and all societies, what the individual work of art shares with every human ''Word.'' In what reality does *mankind* find the source and pattern of its life? The answer could only be the meaning of human history itself. And so Joyce was led to the aspiration announced at the beginning of the nineteenth century and lurking ever since beneath the relativism of our age, beneath its historicism, its concern with psychology, anthropology, myth, symbolic form, language itself. He would confront Life directly, beyond the provisional forms of fiction, and write a comprehensive epic of Humanity, a ''monomyth'' of all the myths, the ''Words,'' by which Man has ordered his experience and therein ''understood'' reality and realised himself *as* Man.

Such a work would take both Joyce's career and his art to their logical conclusion. . . . [For Joyce, his ''monomyth'' would] express the crisis of modern civilisation and also reach the ultimate goal of Symbolistic art. Being both a comprehensive portrayal and a comprehensive example of the creative understanding of Man, it would become one with the reality it represented. It would be both a reflexion and a part of its own subject—as the *Portrait* had been—but now expressing a ''universal'' self-understanding, the author discovering in his experience of the world the pattern not only of the Romantic artist or the modern citizen, but of *homo sapiens*. It would (if we may describe one aspect of the form of *Finnegans Wake* in the manner of another) achieve the Symbolist bliss of being swallowed by its own tale.

There is no mystery, therefore, about the ''argument'' of *Finnegans Wake*. Indeed, it tells us, quite clearly, again and again: It portrays the course of history, which seems at first sight only a meaningless ''collideorscape,'' a chaotic, ''undivided reawl-

ity'' or a ''one-horse'' performance by ''Messrs. Thud and Blunder. . . . Promptings by Elanio Vitale.'' Nevertheless, we can apprehend recurrent patterns in the flux, ''the same tale'' told differently of all men, all societies, all civilisations. For all of us come into our world like little pigs ''in a poke''; we express our sense of our destiny in religious beliefs (as children do in make-believe games); marriages have to be made, property established, work performed; we obey, and we create, the never very satisfactory institutions of our world; life declines and yet renews itself; through the perpetual ''wake'' of life we enjoy what we can of ''these secret workings of natures.'' . . . Any one epiphany reflects the whole ''macromass,'' for it is not merely representative of, but a necessary step in, the process of life's self-comprehension. Perhaps the clearest and greatest of such epiphanies is the creation (or discovery) of the symbolic instrument of the alphabet—''allforabit''; it enables life to realise itself further in the development of language, in the highly self-conscious traditions of literature, and even, we must add, in the mass degeneration of language in our own decaying Civil Age.

In apprehending the substance of Life, personal identity appears merely accidental. . . . By shamming, by being ''not a man,'' he answers the first and last ''riddle of the universe'': what is man? He discovers himself, as Bloom and Stephen did, in traversing the ''Heroes' Highway'' where our fleshers leave their bonings.'' To ask why life takes the patterns it does, unfolds in the process it does, can only be answered in one way: ''Such me.'' Such (search) Everybody.

Thus the ''autobiographical'' Shem-the-Penman chapter, like all the others, reflects the universal pattern from its particular position within it. It focuses on the implications of the creative act, the *felix culpa* in which man both disrupts an existing order and fulfils the order of his becoming: on the necessary self-division of the ''celves,'' the doubt, the obloquy; the unfolding of the familial and other possibilities of man; the expense of energy that simultaneously carries him a step towards both life and death. Like all mankind's creative activity, *Finnegans Wake* is a ''letter selfpenned to one's other . . . neverperfect everplanned . . . [a] nonday diary . . . allnights newseryreel.'' As a work of art, however, it claims to represent that activity in its purest form: in our everyday space-world, only the Gracehoper's song can ''beat time.'' Shem, the artist who can make the dead awaken and speak, is ''the shining keyman of the wilds of change''; and we can see why the book ends with: ''The keys to. Given! A way a lone a last a loved a long the'' specifying no conclusion except the necessary repetition of the same enterprise, and none of the innumerable worlds in which it has been or may be performed.

Finnegans Wake is thus a ''Book of Lief''—written by Joyce (''authordux'') in one sense, but in another written by the language of everybody. . . . It is a language composed of, and reflecting, as many ''scriptsigns'' as possible—a language to represent (in both senses of that word) its own significance *as* language. It finds its artistic programme in exploiting its own symbolic status.

This, briefly, is the structure of Joyce's intentions, the reality he tries to ''render'' to us and to shape as he does so. The result, however, is so dubious that it raises doubts about the whole logic out of which the work arose. (pp. 104-08)

The central trouble with the work . . . derives from the very nature of its intention, from the universe it presents for us to imagine. That universe could briefly be described in the terms of another Symbolistic writer, Emerson: man is no more than "the faculty of reporting," the world no more than "the possibility of being reported." Joyce himself said that the debate between Bishop Berkeley and St Patrick expressed the defence and the indictment of his book; and the central issue there is precisely that of Emerson's doctrine: the identity of the artistic symbol (*i.e.* the work) with the world it constitutes and with the person through whom it is realised, so that the artist, his act of "meaning," and the meaning of things are finally indistinguishable. In the act of expressing his symbol, man himself becomes a symbol of a wholly organic, wholly symbolic universe. "There is no fact in nature," said Emerson, "which does not carry the whole sense of nature"; "the entire system of things gets represented in every particle"; in an ideal language, every word would be "million-faced." Life is an infinite potentiality of meaning. (p. 109)

[Joyce] was convinced that his reasons were sufficient; and by adopting the criticisms as his own and writing them into the work itself he fell back on the old tactic of defensive self-mockery. What he could not afford to recognise was the self-defeating nature of his ambition. For if he succeeded in expressing *all* that could be expressed, if he included *all* the potentialities of Life, if his work did become one with himself and with Reality, his art would supersede itself. This, of course, has been the haunting "death wish" of art at least since the Romantics—the desire (which has taken many forms) not merely "to see into the life of things" but to *become* the life of things. Joyce's own insistence on "the classical temper," his tortuously evolved aesthetic, his mature conception of "drama," exemplify the forces that held this desire in check, though its pressure can be detected in all his works. In the end, however, it seems to have escaped, or rather to have converted his very defences to its own use. The more comprehensively he tried to see "life," the less potent his work became as art; the "drama of the whole" turned into the death of "drama."

All the objections to *Finnegans Wake*—both those Joyce recognised and those he did not—arise, I think, from this absence of "drama." In the universe of the *Wake,* elements like precise observation and characterisation, consistent conventions, narrative structure, economy or inevitability of style, are necessarily insignificant. The various "selves" (or "characters" or "voices") are only "cells" of one gigantic whole; they do not enact drama, but exemplify laws, necessities beyond purpose, responsibility, victory, or defeat. There can be no discrimination between the actual and the possible; things, as we know them in everyday life, are only one symbolic fiction among others. It is impossible to call any of the wordplay pointless. In the absence of "drama," of any real "now and here," there is no way of denying the relevance, or even the existence, of any meaning any commentator cares to find in the words. Language is infinitely exploited and exploitable, for nothing creates any limit to its capacity to mean.

When Joyce asks, "It was life but was it fair? It was free but was it art?" we can respond only from our own sense of what life is; and whether *Finnegans Wake* is free or fair, whatever its value as autobiography or verbal experimentation or anything else, it is for me neither life nor art. Indeed, I would invoke the support both of *Ulysses* and of the insight on which its achievement rests: that we understand life (or imagine truly) only as individuals, necessarily living in and by means of our particular circumstances. Our physical limitations (being "ineluctable") may be seen as the grounds of comedy or tragedy or, as in the *Portrait* and *Ulysses,* a complex kind of irony

involving both. Nevertheless, without those limits we could not apprehend any true meaning in our experience because we could not engage the whole of our being in the act of apprehension. To imagine *truly,* to understand *reality,* involves us in choices. We have to decide about the presence, and nature, and relative status, of any "meaning" we confront. Our values, like those of Bloom or Stephen, are what we make of the world. And truly to imagine, really to understand, the whole History of Man or the Nature of Life can only be a theoretical possibility, a quite notional experience. To apprehend *everything* is to express mere potentiality as such—an enterprise in which the idea of error or distortion must lose its meaning, and with it, too, the possibility of choice and value. In the quasi-divine contemplation of *Finnegans Wake,* therefore, language and form can only freewheel in a boundless empyrean. With *Ulysses* it is not absurd to use the same terms as we might apply to *The Divine Comedy:* that it holds to, even as it transcends, all the specific choices, the enacted values, in which we discover our selves, or "life," or art. That transcending is its "drama." *Finnegans Wake,* on the other hand, merely assumes its "vision" and so it merely supersedes choice and value from the start.

The result is the most fundamental weakness of all: the book can only tell us its "argument"; it cannot realise it imaginatively. The language—despite its air of tremendous activity, despite the odd occasions when it does manage to relate disparate experiences—is generally *inert.* (pp. 110-12)

Finnegans Wake is obviously the response of a "cunning artist" to "the breakdown of public standards of value and significance." But the word "response" is ambiguous. To suppose (as Joyce and his admirers were occasionally wont to do) that it is a nonce-work, so to speak, a unique experiment that need not affect the language or art of anyone else, is to evade the question of why art matters at all. *Finnegans Wake* is not merely a personal reaction to an abstract situation, one which we ought to accept on a blind faith in Literature (or in Joyce as a Great Writer). It is a particular instance of that situation, a situation of which we ourselves are part, and we cannot avoid judging it and pondering the implications of our judgment. Perhaps Joyce always loved people and things too little. Certainly his imagination seems to have withered among rootless abstractions: most of the over-elaborate "schema" was added to *Ulysses* after 1920, the year in which he also moved to Paris, and *Finnegans Wake* almost confesses his own sense of tiredness, withdrawal, approaching exhaustion. But perhaps it also reveals a weakness in modern thinking—a tendency to take the medium of life for the substance, to expect too much of art or language or even of consciousness itself. In our desire to know more and more of life, and to possess even ourselves in complete and perfect selfconsciousness, we tend to forget (as Joyce perhaps forgot) that we can never see behind our own heads, and that, as we have finally to choose what we are, so we have finally to choose what we really know among all possible "truths" and "meanings." Similarly, we can dream of mastering the whole of life (as Joyce perhaps dreamed of doing) by surrendering to language or art, only if we forget the values necessarily engaged in them. *Finnegans Wake* fails to heal the dissociation of our experience in an all-embracing vision of Life; but what possibly could do so?

Joyce's career offers us the image of a dilemma far wider than his own. From Stephen to Bloom to Molly to *Finnegans Wake;* and at the end he is said to have been contemplating a book about the Sea, the Ultimate towards which *Finnegans Wake* flows: perhaps an even more abstract work, to which someone like Darwin or Teilhard de Chardin might have been the Vice? On the other hand, there is his remark in a letter to his daughter: "In my opinion *How Much Land Does a Man Need* is the greatest story that the literature of the world knows." He would not have been Joyce if he had failed to see the bearing on his own case either of Tolstoy's story or of his judgment of it, and we might allow it to stand as the final comment not only on his lifelong theme, but on both the achievement and the limitations of his work. (pp. 113-14)

S. L. Goldberg, in his James Joyce *(reprinted by permission of Grove Press, Inc.; copyright © 1962 by S. L. Goldberg), Grove Press, 1962, 120 p.*

MAURICE BEEBE (essay date 1964)

James Joyce's *A Portrait of the Artist as a Young Man* has been imitated so often since it appeared in 1915 that we are likely to think of it as the beginning of a literary movement rather than its climax. But if many a young writer or would-be artist has found a mirror in the *Portrait,* it is because Joyce succeeded in giving definitive treatment to an archetype that was firmly established long before the twentieth century. The first of the many sensitive young men who have followed Stephen Dedalus into exile was Joyce himself, who, like Proust, discovered that "he could become an artist by writing about the process of becoming an artist." (p. 260)

One reason why the *Portrait* still seems revolutionary to the young is that it argues for the necessary alienation of the artist from God, home, and country. "Alienation," an overworked word in modern criticism, is not synonymous with "detachment," for the former implies estrangement from something previously accepted, whereas detachment, as in [Henry] James, may be an innate quality in temperament. Joyce's insistence that the artist must withdraw from life, using it in his art but isolating himself from its interests, has been encountered frequently. . . . But just as James and Proust, for instance, disagree with Joyce on the purpose of detachment—James making the artist aloof so that he may observe life more objectively; Proust, that he may penetrate into his own subjectivity—another distinction may be made between Joyce and these two writers. Detachment from life was easier for James and Proust than it was for Joyce. . . . [Joyce, unlike Proust and James,] came into the world encumbered with religious and domestic obligations. Reared in strict Irish Catholicism, in a large middle-class family devoted to Irish nationalism, he had to shed imposed loyalties so that he might develop in his own way. For Joyce, alienation had to precede detachment.

Although the *Portrait* has been traditionally and, I think, correctly read as a novel which defends the need of the artist to withdraw from the normal commitments of life, this does not mean that Stephen rejects life itself. The artist dies to a certain kind of life that he may be reborn into another. (pp. 260-61)

[An] alternative to deciding whether Joyce champions or repudiates Stephen is to fall back on the convenient critical doctrine of the irony of noncommittal. In his later works, certainly, Joyce is free of opinions and judgments, and it may well be that in the *Portrait,* too, he attempted to avoid either favoring Stephen or making him the object of ridicule. Whether deliberate or not, much of the author's seeming aloofness from his subject is the inevitable detachment of time. The Joyce writing is a different person from the Joyce depicted. If Stephen's life parallels Joyce's, the story ends in 1902. Joyce did not finish writing the novel until 1915. The mixture of irony and sympathy may be explained as the half-apologetic, half-proud attitude of an older man looking back on the foibles of his youth. . . . The objectivity of the picture demonstrates Joyce's artistic ideal of the author's detachment from his subject, even when that subject is the author's self. (p. 265)

One way in which Joyce sought to detach himself from his hero was to depict not James Joyce, but the universal, representative, archetypal artist, the ideal which Joyce could achieve only partially in reality. Thus he had to omit certain features of his personality that seemed to him out of keeping with the conventional idea of the artist. In terms of the stereotype available to Joyce, a well-rounded, athletic poet would have seemed an anomaly, and everyone knows that poets are supposed to be gloomy rather than sunny. The Stephen haters may recognize that he is the stereotyped artist, but they err in assuming that he therefore cannot be a true artist. The cumulative weight of the stereotype, the frequency with which it appears in other portraits of the artist, may, on the contrary, actually convince us that whether we like the type or not, it may well characterize the essential, universal qualities of the artistic temperament. Byron, Baudelaire, Rimbaud, Baron Corvo, and many other artists of distinction had unbalanced and disagreeable personalities; and to dislike Stephen because of his lack of human roundness does not justify the opinion that he cannot therefore be an artist. (p. 266)

It would seem therefore that in depicting Stephen, Joyce drew not only on his own character and experience, modified by the artistic need for selection and economy, but also on the artist-heroes of life and fiction. (p. 267)

A Portrait of the Artist is written in the indirect first person. Everything is seen through the eyes of Stephen, but he does not narrate his autobiography nor describe his perceptions. Joyce's method is similar to James's center of consciousness, and Stephen's character, like that of James's sensitive observers, can be determined only by noting his subjective reactions to the world about him. . . . The mingling of auctorial description with character reponse allows Joyce to suggest precocious powers of observation and verbalization in his young hero. It is a method well adapted to the depiction of a child whose most characteristic feature is extreme sensitivity. (p. 269)

Joyce grants to the artist the right, even the need, to form at least a partial compact with life. But he also extends and intensifies Stephen's alienation, for the partial compact releases the artist from the man and provides him with the conditions under which he can best work. Just as there is the life that ends with death and the All-Life that transcends death and time, the River Liffey and Alph the Sacred River, every true artist is both the mortal man whose name is on his works and the godlike creator whose art world, like Keat's Grecian Urn, is universal in time and place. The young Stephen, denying this inevitable split, thought that he could be a Shelley or a Shakespeare only by not being a Bodkin. Joyce realized that Shelley and Shakespeare were Bodkins—men who loved and lived and died—as well as artists whose art became "the sea's voice." When Joyce learned this, he could write triumphantly, "In the convent they called her the man-killer: . . . I live in soul and body." Stephen may well be the drowned Icarus, but if he stands for Joyce, then he too, like Daedalus, may as artist fly high above the sea of life as he makes his way back from exile. (p. 295)

Maurice Beebe, "James Joyce: The Return from Exile," in his Ivory Towers and Sacred Founts: The

Artist As Hero in Fiction from Goethe to Joyce *(reprinted by permission of New York University Press; copyright © 1964 by New York University), New York University Press, 1964, pp. 260-95.*

ANTHONY BURGESS (essay date 1965)

There are a lot of things to marvel at [in *Ulysses*] but, first, a lot of questions to ask. Most of these questions are assumed in one fundamental question: Why did Joyce write the book at all?

Ulysses is a big book (933 pages in the 1960 Bodley Head edition), and its bigness is one answer. Every novelist wishes to prove to himself and to others that he can tackle a large canvas. (p. 83)

Starting with this vague and general and traditional intention, Joyce then (or simultaneously, or before) conceived another ambition—make a modern novel not merely rival classical achievement but contain it. Classical epic was expansive; classical drama was contractive. Homer covers heaven, earth, the sea and a great slab of time; Sophocles stays in one small place and confines the time of his action to twenty-four hours. And so Joyce stays in Dublin on June 16th, 1904, but also uses delirium and imagination to encompass a great deal of human history and even the End of the World. Greek epic and Greek drama are both contained within the framework of a modern bourgeois novel.

Epic length and the strictures of dramatic form can be reconciled not merely by imaginative 'loops' but by a more detailed examination of the characters' acts and motives than traditional novelists thought either necessary or decent. Bloom must not only eat but defecate; Molly Bloom must meditate not only on her lovers but also on what her lovers are like in bed. With so large a canvas, no human detail may be left out. But the traditional techniques for expressing unspoken thoughts are bound to be insufficient. Hence the 'stream of consciousness' of the 'interior monologue'—an endless commentary from the main characters on the data thrown at them by life, but unspoken, often chaotic, sometimes reaching the thresholds of the unconscious mind. This device had been used before—by Dickens and Samuel Butler, even by that great primitive Jane Austen—but never on the scale or to the limits employed by Joyce. (p. 84)

There are two artistic problems raised by the extensive use of interior monologue. The first is concerned with characterisation: how does one make one person's interior monologue sound different from another's, so that we instantly recognise which character is thinking without tiresome mechanical pointers like 'Stephen thought' or 'Bloom thought'? Part of the problem here lies in the fact that the 'stream of consciousness' is essentially pre-verbal: we do not say to ourselves: 'Where's light-switch? Very dark in here. Must be careful. Chair over there, I know. Damn. Barked shin on it'—rather we react without words to stimuli and memories, and any attempt to set down such a process in words is highly conventional. Joyce solves the problem by assigning a characteristic rhythm to the thought-stream of each of his three main personages. Stephen's is lyrical, subtle, somewhat clotted, and, since Stephen is a poet, his interior monologue is much more aware of words—not words as conventional signs for images but words as data for meditation—than that of either Bloom or his wife. Bloom's own rhythm is quick, jaunty, jerky, darting, clipped—appropriate for a man more given to pub-talk than to aesthetic dis-

quisitions, expressive of the very soul of an intelligent, but not over-educated, advertising canvasser. As for Molly Bloom's rhythm, it somehow combines the practical and the poetical, short words organised into long flowing phrases which—as we are made to take her mind all in one piece, not in instalments—coalesce into a single mammoth sentence which makes up the last chapter of the book.

The other problem is concerned with what the characters shall think about. The mind naturally strays and wanders, holding to nothing very long, coming back frequently to the same point again and again but rarely staying there. A naturalistic representation of the human mind monologuising to itself may be of scientific interest, but it has nothing to do with art. Themes must be imposed on the three main minds of the novel, and these themes must move in towards each other, suggesting purposeful movement and the unity proper to a work of literature. The main subject of the book—the creative relationship between spiritual father, spiritual son, and nonspiritual mother-wife—will clamp the consciousness of each member of the main trio down, preventing over-much free flight, but—in so spacious a book—more than that is needed. We have to consider not only the theme of the book but its structure.

We are back to Joyce's epic intention. He is not only emulating Homer but taking him over. The title *Ulysses* is no mere ironical reference to the decline of the heroic as exemplified in the emergence of the bourgeois novel from the original epic form: the title is the key to the structure. Bloom is Ulysses having his little adventures in Dublin; Stephen Dedalus is Telemachus in search of a father; Molly Bloom is both the beguiling Calypso and the faithful Penelope. These identifications would be merely fanciful if there were not a more solid parallel with the Odyssey built into the structure of the work itself: a little study shows the parallel to be both profound and detailed. Each episode of *Ulysses* corresponds to an episode of the Odyssey, and the correspondence proliferates in a mass of subtle references. (pp. 84-5)

But the Homeric parallel is only the beginning. Shape and direction are primarily imposed on each chapter by means of an Odyssean reference, but that reference suggests related references, sub-references, and these have much to do with not only the direction and subject-matter of the interior monologue but the action itself, and even the technique used to present that action. Thus, a Dublin newspaper-office is a reasonable parallel to the cave of Æolus—the god of the winds whose enmity Ulysses earned—and, so that the scriptures may be fulfilled, Bloom goes to the office of the *Freeman's Journal and National Press*. It is appropriate that the scene should be wind-swept, galleys flying about the place, but also appropriate that wind should suggest the lungs, the windiness of newspaper rhetoric, the art of rhetoric itself, the wind-swift transmission of news, the history of the art of the presentation of news (expressed in headlines which punctuate the text) and the technique through which the action, talk, and thought are presented. We end up with a formidable battery of clamps—the scene, the art, the presiding physical organ, the technique. Above everything puffs and blows the wind-god himself—the Editor. If we look deepest of all we shall find that the episode even has a predominant colour—red. Red is right for the art of inflaming passions through words and the journalistic cult of the sensational.

What applies in this chapter applies nearly everywhere in the book: to the Homeric parallel we add a presiding organ, art, colour, symbol, and an appropriate technique. (p. 86)

So far we have answered the question about Joyce's purpose in writing *Ulysses* purely in terms of a kind of technical ambition. There is always the danger that, bemused by the sheer skill of the book, we may ignore what the book is about. It is difficult in any work of art to fillet subject-matter from the presentation of subject-matter, and we may find in Joyce's attempt to make a sort of encyclopaedia with a heart, as well as a rainbow, a sufficient artistic, as opposed to technical, intention. The fundamental purpose of any work of art is to impose order on the chaos of life as it comes to us; in imparting a vision of order the artist is doing what the religious teacher also does (this is one of the senses in which truth and beauty are the same thing). But the religious teacher's revelation is less a creation than a discovery, whereas the artist feels that— God rather than God's servant—he is the author of order. I have already said that the creation of a human community in fiction is the closest the novelist can get to the creation of a cosmos, but Joyce is ambitious enough to want to create a human body (chapter by chapter, organ by organ) which is a sort of configuration (as in Blake or Swedenborg) of the ultimate celestial order. This is perhaps less blasphemous than it looks: it may even be taken as a gesture of piety. It may certainly be taken as Joyce's attempt to build for himself an order which is a substitute for the order he abandoned when he abandoned the Church. (p. 87)

> *Anthony Burgess, in his* Re Joyce *(reprinted by permission of W. W. Norton & Company, Inc.; in Canada by Faber and Faber Ltd; copyright © 1965 by Anthony Burgess), Norton, 1965, 272 p. (also published in Britain as* Here Comes Everybody: An Introduction to James Joyce for the Ordinary Reader, *Faber and Faber, 1965).*

BERNARD BENSTOCK (essay date 1969)

The motif of death is solidly established in the coda story of *Dubliners* ['The Dead'], not only with Joyce's succinct title, but with the various rhetorical devices embedded in the terse opening sentence: 'Lily, the caretaker's daughter, was literally run off her feet'. Lily's tagname, that of the funereal flower, serves as a symbol of death—as well as an ironic allusion to purity; the connotation of 'caretaker' is mere innuendo, since we later realize that he is custodian of the estate, rather than of a cemetery, but by then the effect is unalterable, and the smell of the graveyard is in our nostrils; and the hyperbolic figure of speech ('run off her feet'), which although figurative, is offered to the reader to be accepted 'literally'. Yet this early impregnation of death symbolism is soon belied ostensibly by the pleasant Christmas setting. . . .

The dead are very much in evidence, however, and death hovers over the feast at all times, emerging triumphant by the end. Three levels of these dead become apparent upon close examination: the deceased, the moribund, and the living-dead, the composition of the last group expanding with the progression of the story. (p. 153)

Those obviously close to death are the three old women, Aunts Kate and Julia and Mrs Malins. . . . [There is enough evidence,] from Joyce's capsule descriptions of them, for the reader to realize, even before Gabriel's awareness late in 'The Dead' of the imminence of Julia's death, that these old and sickly women are reminders of the final gasp of life.

But old age is not the only requisite for inclusion among the moribund, as Gabriel also comes to realize, since time brings all men towards death: 'One by one they were all becoming shades. Better pass boldly into that other world, in the full glory of some passion, than fade and wither dismally with age.' Such passionate glory is denied to the living-dead, those who remain alive, but fail to live: the disillusioned, the self-destructive, the blighted and wasted lives. It is with these that 'The Dead' is most concerned. First there is the servant girl Lily, just out of school and already cynically world-weary, presumably because of a prematurely unpleasant experience with a man. . . . Less serious reminders are seen in Mary Jane, in her thirties and unmarried, who plays 'Academy pieces' on the piano that no one listens to; Freddy Malins and Browne have their obvious vices; and Bartell D'Arcy, the much-praised tenor, is hoarse and consequently rather grouchy. Most important of course is the revelation that Gretta has been living a dead life in contrast to the remembered and cherished romance of her youth, a revelation that destroys the bubble of her husband's unreal existence, permanently deflating the self-assurance of his artificially bolstered world.

Even for those who are quick to perceive 'the skull beneath the skin' of most of the characters in 'The Dead', the Conroys at first seem to be a healthy contrast. Had there not been so much dynamic spontaneity associated with them, as they came in out of the snow much anticipated and warmly welcomed (Gabriel scrapes the snow from his shoes 'vigorously'; his clothes emit 'a cold fragrant air from out-of-doors', while Gretta goes upstairs with the aunts 'laughing'), perhaps we might have been more suspicious of their poses. (pp. 154-55)

The destruction of the superficial harmony of the married Conroys is well anticipated. And what are we to assume about the names Tom and Eva for the Conroy children? In 'Counterparts' Farrington has a son named Tom whom he beats for letting the fire go out; by way of contrast, Gabriel, a very different sort of father, is concerned about his son's muscles and eyes. (Two adults are also named Thomas: Chandler and Kernan.) And is Eva to remind us of Eveline Hill? Her relationship with her father has certainly soured. With the reference to Kathleen Kearney in 'The Dead' we find the first instance in which a previous *Dubliners* character is mentioned, the beginning of a process that Joyce went on to exploit fully, as both Kathleen and Gretta figure in Molly Bloom's thoughts.

The key words of the first paragraph of the first *Dubliners* tale (paralysis, simony, gnomon) are significant in varying degrees for every one of the fifteen stories, and reach their culmination in 'The Dead'. The whole process of the Morkans' soirée is a repeated one, so that even the reader (for whom this is a fresh experience) soon begins to feel an aura of *déjà vu* (Gretta caught cold after last year's party; Freddy can be expected to be drunk again). The participants themselves know the formula, as can be seen when Bartell D'Arcy, apparently a newcomer, at first refuses to allow his glass to be filled, until 'one of his neighbours nudged him and whispered something at him'—the ceremonial toast is next on the programme. The 'never-to-be-forgotten Johnny' is almost a parody of the theme of paralysis, and one might suspect that Daniel O'Connell, frozen in stone and covered with snow, is still another. The instances of simony are perhaps subtler, but the birth that took place in a manger among shepherds is being celebrated here in high style with the best of everything among the comfortable bourgeoisie, while irresponsible Freddy pays his debts after having cashed in on the Nativity by way of a Christmas-card shop. Even Gabriel is guilty of simony when, unnerved by his awkward conversation with Lily, he gives her a coin in order to cover his embarrassment, and when her attempt at refusal further discomfits him, he credits Christ as a precendent: '—Christmastime! Christmas-time! said Gabriel, almost trotting to the stairs and waving his hand to her in deprecation.' The Euclidian gnomon, however, has drawn little notice from commentators on *Dubliners,* yet that 'part of the parallelogram that remains after a similar parallelogram is taken away from one of its corners' (*O.E.D.*) offers us an insight into the author's technique in the book, where we come to understand the nature of the substance from its shadow. Father Flynn is that removed entity in **'The Sisters'**, Mrs Hill in **'Eveline'**, Mrs Sinico in **'A Painful Case'** (where the title itself is gnomonic), Parnell in **'Ivy Day in the Committee Room',** and of course Michael Furey in **'The Dead'**.

Gabriel Conroy no more escapes the paralysis of Dublin than any of the other protagonists in the *Dubliners* stories, as he himself comes to realize during his epiphany. As a man of sensitivity and intelligence he becomes aware of the significance of the epiphany. . . . Material comfort, intellectual superiority, an important position, and distinction as a reviewer of books do not qualify him for exemption from the paralytic situation: he remains rooted in the centre of the paralysis. At best he is a part-time tourist, not an exile; a continental cyclist, not a 'hawklike man'. He has reached the prime of life without realizing that he too shares the fate of the Freddy Malinses and Mr Brownes. Yet the surface evidence is at first deceptive. . . . But the literary critic and the teacher of literature are poor substitutes for the creative artist, and vacationing on the continent is but temporary escape. Gabriel's self-deception is as serious as Chandler's or Duffy's and has been far more successful until the night of the Morkan party. We never learn whether Gabriel's epiphany redeems him, but we can assume that he is redeemable: he is a younger man than James Duffy and has not cut off all avenues of contact with the outside world; unlike the adolescent in **'Araby'** he is mature enough to cope with 'anguish and anger'; and he is spared the intellectual pretention of Chandler, while country-cute Gretta will obviously prove less of a burden than the pretty-faced Annie. (pp. 159-60)

The contrast between cold and warmth hints at a symbolic understructure in **'The Dead'** that is far more complex than in any of the previous stories [in *Dubliners*]. . . . If we tend to conclude that Gabriel's self-betrayal is mechanically mirrored in his acceptance of warmth and gaslight in lieu of the cold outdoors, we overlook the significance of the most persuasive symbol in the story, the snow (which has evoked the most confusing range of interpretation from critics). Joyce employs the snow for double service in **'The Dead'**: what begins as representative of Life and of Gabriel's view of himself as standing apart from others modulates into a symbol of Death and of Gabriel included among the living dead ('Yes, the newspapers were right: snow was general all over Ireland').

The seed of self-destruction is as inherent in Gabriel himself as the suggestions of death are throughout the weave of the story. . . . Yet it is difficult to see much fault in Gabriel Conroy: what sin has he committed that he should be punished by a lifelong awareness of a rival he can never conquer or even combat? (pp. 163-64)

Actually, it is to the future that Gabriel has been disloyal: although he considers himself an advocate of liberal and advanced ideas, he allows his wounded ego to cause him to betray the future and sell out to a dying past. If he had gone ahead and quoted Browning over the heads of his audience, he would at least have been faithful to his own values. But injured pride sidetracks him into attempting to retaliate against Molly Ivors (who does keep faith with at least *her* idea of the future). They have clashed over Irish nationalism and the language question, areas in which Gabriel assumes that Molly is reactionary, attempting to revive a dead past, and he is progressive in looking forward to an international and cosmopolitan future. Despite the nature of his approach to these questions, he master-plans a speech to demolish Miss Ivors, a speech of sentimental clichés of reverence to the past. He denounces the 'new generation' and opts for the qualities of 'an older day'. He himself reveals the danger of his approach ('were we to brook upon them always we could not find the heart to go on bravely with our work among the living'), and claims to avoid that danger ('Therefore, I will not linger on the past'); but linger on the past he does, until that past in the figure of Michael Furey rises up to destroy him. Until this evening Gabriel has had no idea how limited his ability to embrace life has been; he actually saw himself as a passionate man, and maintained a faith with what he saw and believed. When he betrays that faith, he is vulnerable to the blinding revelation. The Christ of the future, of renewal and resurrection, is repeatedly betrayed during this Irish Christmas celebration.

There has been some speculation about the Christmas setting for **'The Dead'**, but little of it has been germane to this central idea of betrayal and self-awareness. . . . The Day of the Epiphany is a perfect Joycean choice for the final story of a volume in which climactic situations give way instead to a technique Joyce labelled 'epiphanies'. What should disturb us about **'The Dead'** is the total absence of Christianity from the Christmas festivities. (pp. 164-66)

If Joyce is obliquely paralleling the journey of the Magi to the crèche of the Christ child, he has probably meant that Gabriel Conroy should represent all three kings—his name Conroy has already attracted attention as containing *roi,* the French for king.

That Gabriel, a single magus, should be pressed into service to represent all three Magi seems as commonplace as St. Patrick's shamrock, but Joyce probably had a more esoteric source for his whimsical condensation. Joyce was probably well aware that the tradition of a trio of Magi comes from an Irish source. . . . Among the several "trilingual" sets of names of the magi in the Irish commentaries on St. Matthew we find Melchio, Aspar, Patisara.' These stem from the reverence for the three 'sacred' languages, Hebrew, Greek, and Latin. Joyce's magus has only two names, Gabriel Conroy, which metrically scan like Melchoir and Caspar, but Lily's low Dublin accent gives him a third: 'Gabriel smiled at the three syllables she had given his surname'—so that Con-o-roy parallels Balthasar. (p. 167)

Such parallels, if actually intended at all, are certainly sardonic and tangential, although the Joycean method allows for this sort of speculation, particularly at this point in his development, when the approach was becoming highly refined and was still quite unself-conscious. . . . More germane and far more serious is the revelation of Michael Furey that is brought to Gabriel during the later part of the evening, a Christ figure who sacrifices himself for his ideal. It would certainly be concomitant with Joyce's oft-quoted criticism of Christ as having shirked the major burden of life by not living with a woman, so that manly Gabriel, who has accepted that burden but is embarrassingly naïve in his contact with women, is again a parodic figure. The important point of such an investigation of **'The Dead'** is that Joyce is holding up Irish religious practices and theory for scrutiny, that he chooses to pit his latter-day archangels Gabriel and Michael against each other, revealing Michael as the traditional victor—though belated and retroactive—and Gabriel much deflated. Even the structure of the story is suspect from this point of approach. We have been informed that Joyce intended that '**Grace**', the penultimate story and originally the last one in *Dubliners,* parallel the three sections of Dante's *Commedia.* The horizontal structure of '**Grace**' conforms to that of a triptych, with the central segment of *Purgatorio* as the major section. This three-part structure is also available in '**Clay**', with the *Dublin by Lamplight* laundry as the *Inferno,* the Dublin streets as *Purgatorio,* and the Donnelly's home as an ironic *Paradiso*—as ironic as the Gardiner Street Jesuit Church of '**Grace**'. If '**The Dead**' follows this pattern—and there are definite space breaks indicated in the text—the Morkan household at Christmas-time is Hell indeed for Gabriel, while the carriage trip to the Gresham serves as a period of purgations, and the hotel scene of revelation is a third ironic paradise. The three portions in this case diminish in size as the story progresses.

In viewing '**The Dead**' as a tale of the Epiphany, we see Joyce at an interestingly close juncture with Yeats's attitude in 'The Second Coming'. Christianity as a dynamic force has dwindled to a mockery of itself: self-contradictory, as Gabriel belatedly and effetely opposes Michael, and self-betrayed, as simoniac symptoms of the commercialization of Christmas become apparent. . . . But on the Night of the Epiphany Gabriel Conroy follows his star to the Morkans' house on Usher's Island—not a new star, but the same one that has brought him there so often—expecting in his reconquest of Gretta to renew himself and sharpen the distinction and privilege which keep him safe from the doomed, the unbaptized, the unanointed. But on this night he comes face to face with his predecessor and with his own self, with the past that has claimed all the others and the future that he has betrayed in order to maintain his comfortable position on the outside. The enigmatic sentence that has bothered so many readers of '**The Dead**' ('The time had come for him to set out on his journey westward') indicates his awareness of his new responsibility: Gabriel must begin the quest of self-discovery to arrive at the real epiphany, to follow his star. After many false starts of self-deception, the 'rough beast, its hour come round at last, slouches toward Bethlehem to be born'. (pp. 168-69)

> Bernard Benstock, "The Dead," in James Joyce's "Dubliners": Critical Essays, edited by Clive Hart (copyright © 1969 by Faber and Faber Ltd.; reprinted by permission of Viking Penguin Inc.; in Canada by Faber and Faber Ltd.), Faber and Faber, 1969, Viking Penguin, 1969, pp. 153-70.

WILL DURANT and ARIEL DURANT   (essay date 1970)

Ulysses had described the vagaries of the conscious mind during a waking day; [*Finnegans Wake*] tried to reproduce the chaos of an unconscious mind during a night of uncontrolled fancies. In dreams the mind not only ignores the bounds of possibility and the restraints of morality, it also transcends the relations of past, present, and future, the limits of time and space, the barriers of matter, and it is utterly without respect for the rules of logic, grammar, or punctuation. It takes words apart into their syllables and recombines the syllables, it takes memories and persons apart and recombines their elements, according to marginal resemblances or fortuitous association. To find some sense in the phantasmagoria of dreams had challenged Freud

and now tempted Joyce; both undertakings were faulted by the tendency of the conscious mind, recalling a distorted dream, to distort it further by unwittingly remolding it according to canons of logic, sequence, and significance. (p. 86)

The title of the book is itself a play on words: with an apostrophe it would mean the mourning of a dead Finnegan by his convivial relatives; but the title has no apostrophe, and can mean "Finnegans wake up"; furthermore, it could mean *fin* (the end) plus again; so the insatiable prankster suggests not only indestructible generations of Finnegans, but the rhythmic recurrence of life, death, life, death, life. . . . The mythology of the volume stems from Tim Finnegan, a building laborer, who, too fond of the bottle, falls drunk from his ladder, and dies; but at his wake some spray or fragrance of whiskey brings him rushing avidly back to life. He is told to lie down like a good corpse, and await a proper resurrection in due theological time. He obeys, and resumes his interrupted dream. It transforms him into Finn MacCool, the giant leader of the Fenians in Ossianic legend; then, leaping over centuries, it reshapes Finn into H C E—i.e., Humphrey Chimpden Earwicker, keeper of a public house at Chapelizod (a suburb of Dublin). (p. 87)

Having read Giambattista Vico, Joyce followed him in conceiving history as a cycle of four stages: (1) theocratic, in which government is by priests, (2) aristocratic, in which government is by an elite of birth, (3) democratic, (4) anarchic, in which democracy crumbles into chaos; thereafter, in a grand *ricorso,* society seeks order through religion, theocracy is restored, and the cycle begins anew. Joyce divided *Finnegans Wake* into four sections corresponding to Vico's stages in history; so in the final section Saint Patrick comes to Ireland (A.D. 432), establishes Christianity, ends disorder, and sets Ireland upon another turn of the Viconian wheel.

On this wheel Earwicker is Everyman, and represents all men His sons Shem and Penman (=James Joyce) and Shaun the Post (= Stanislaus Joyce) represent the opposite and conflicting principles of thought and action, which are finally reconciled and unified (Joyce had read Giordano Bruno, and perhaps a little Hegel too). Their mother, Anna Livia Plurabelle, is all women—daughter, wife, mother, widow; she is also the stream of life, bearing all humanity and its woes; she is one with the river Liffey, which carries all its soiled and burdened waters into extinction in the sea, where they will be lifted up as mist to fall as rain into the rivers in another cycle symbolizing the resurrection of life and the eternal recurrence of history. Here, as in *Ulysses,* woman has the last word. In a lyric chapter that almost forgets puzzles and puns, Joyce pictures Anna Livia as looking back forgivingly upon life, accepting death without resistance, hoping that she will be cleansed of her sins as the oceans purify the effluvia of the streams, and dreaming of being reborn as fresh as water from the skies. The final sentence is cut short, suggesting both death and continuance; to complete it we must turn back to the beginning, as life does with each new birth; the last line of the book is finished by the first; the cycle is renewed.

Sometimes, as I hurried through this maze of philosophy, etymology, and history, I asked myself, Why couldn't Joyce say all this intelligibly, instead of hiding it under a hundred bushels of dreams, word mutilations, and puns? . . . Actually he answered: I was reporting a dream, not a Ph.D. thesis, and I had to use the confused memories, irrational combinations, and mangled speech of dreams. But do we mangle speech in our dreams, and do we then summarize summaries of history and cosmology?

In truth Joyce was drunk with dictionaries, and bursting with pilferings; he was infatuated with philology, and aspired to philosophy. He suffered from—enjoyed—an autoerotism of words, manipulating them, fondling them, squeezing every drop of juice out of them, in the ecstasy of imagination and privacy. It delighted him to break up a word into its components and varied meanings; to throw these pieces into the air, and to watch them fall into new and hilarious combinations. He was a man of sardonic humor, bearing pains and indignities impatiently, and revenging himself upon life by pricking its inflated actors, from prostitutes to popes, with the acid point of his impish pen. . . . [The] book, he said, is "a great joke, and is meant to make you laugh." In any case, he felt, it sounded well; read it aloud, and you will find some music in it; "Heaven knows what my prose means, but it is pleasing to the ear." In many ways it corresponded to the abstract painting that was beginning to rear its disheveled head. (pp. 87-8)

> *Will Durant and Ariel Durant, "James Joyce," in their* Interpretations of Life: A Survey of Contemporary Literature *(copyright © 1970 by Will and Ariel Durant; reprinted by permission of Simon & Schuster, a Division of Gulf & Western Corporation), Simon & Schuster, 1970, pp. 77-89.*

SAUL BELLOW (essay date 1972-73)

Unlike Huxley's *Brave New World* or George Orwell's *Nineteen Eighty-four,* Joyce's *Ulysses* is not directly concerned with technology. It remains nevertheless the twentieth century's most modern novel—it is *the* account of human life in an age of artifacts. Things in *Ulysses* are not nature's things. Here the material world is wholly man's world, and all its objects are human inventions. It is made in the image of the conscious mind. Nature governs physiologically, and of course the unconscious remains nature's stronghold, but the external world is a world of ideas made concrete. Between these two powers, nature within, artifacts without, the life of Mr. Leopold Bloom is comically divided. The time is 1904. No one in Dublin has seen Mr. Arthur C. Clarke's ultra-intelligent machine [in *2001: A Space Odyssey*] even in a dream, but the age of technology has begun and *Ulysses* is literature's outstanding response to it.

Now what is *Ulysses*? In *Ulysses* two men, Dedalus and Bloom, wander about the city of Dublin on a June day. Mrs. Bloom, a singer, lies in bed, reading, misbehaving, musing and remembering. But nothing that can be thought or said about human beings is left out of this account of two pedestrians and an adulteress. No zoologist could be more explicit or complete than Joyce. Mr. Bloom first thing in the morning, brews the tea, gives milk to the cat, goes to the pork butcher to get meat for his breakfast, carries a tray up to his wife, eats a slightly scorched kidney, goes out to the privy with his newspaper, relieves himself while reading a prize-winning story, wipes his bottom with a piece of the same paper, and then goes out to the funeral of Paddy Dignam. Matters could not be more real.

Now realism in literature is a convention, and this convention postulates that human beings are not what everyone for long centuries conceived them to be. They are something different, and they live in a disenchanted world that exists for no particular purpose that science can show. Still, people continue to try to lead a human life. And this is rather quaint, because man is not the comparatively distinguished creature he thinks himself to be. The commonness of common life was a great burden to nineteenth-century writers. The best of them tried to salvage something from the new set of appalling facts. Coleridge tells us how Wordsworth intended to redeem the everyday by purging the mind of "the lethargy of custom" and showing us the beauty and power of what we call commonplace. He did not do this to the satisfaction of his successors. English writers of the second half of the century were much more impressed by the weight given to the evil component of the commonplace by their French contemporaries. A novelist like Flaubert saw nothing in the banal average that did not disgust him. But art, virtuosity, language, the famous objectivity, these, after painful struggle, would make commonplace reality yield gold.

Joyce, a Flaubertian to begin with, gives in *Ulysses* the novel's fullest account of human life—within this realistic convention. As he sees it, the material world is now entirely human. Everything about us—clothing, beds, tableware, streets, privies, newspapers, language, thought—is man-made. All artifacts originate in thought. They are thoughts practically extended into matter.

Joyce is the complete naturalist, the artist-zoologist, the poet-ethnographer. His account of Bloom's life includes everything. Everything seems to demand inclusion. No trivialities or absurdities are omitted. Old bourgeois reticences are overrun zigzag. For what, after all, is the important information? No one knows. Anything at all may be important. Freud taught, in *The Psychopathology of Everyday Life,* that the unconscious did not distinguish between major and minor matters, as conscious judgment did, and that the junk of the psyche had the deepest things to tell us. Joyce is the greatest psychic junkman of our age, after Freud. For the last of the facts may be the first. Thus we know the lining of Bloom's hat, and the contents of his pockets; one knows his genitals and his guts, and we are thoroughly familiar with Molly, too, how she feels before her period, and how she smells. And with so much knowledge, we are close to chaos. For what are we to do with such a burden of information? *Ulysses* is a comedy of information. Leopold Bloom lies submerged in an ocean of random facts: textbook tags, items of news, bits of history, slogans, clichés, ditties, operatic arias, saws and jokes, scraps of popular science, and a great volume of superstitions, fantasies, technical accounts of the Dublin water supply, observations about hanged men, recollections of copulating dogs. The debris of learning, epic, faith, and enlightenment pour over him. In this circumambient ocean, he seems at times to dwell like a coelenterate or a sponge. The man-made world begins, like the physical world, to suggest infinity. The mind is endangered by the multitude of accounts that it can give of all matters. It is threatened with inanity or disintegration. (pp. 11-14)

At all events, Bloom's mind is assailed and drowned by facts. He appears to acknowledge a sort of responsibility to these facts, and he goes about Dublin doing his facts. This suggests that our scientific, industrial, technical, urban world has a life of its own and that it borrows our minds and souls for its own purposes. In this sense, civilization lives upon Bloom. His mind is overcome by its data. He is the bearer, the servant, the slave of involuntary or random cognitions. But he is also the poet of distractions. If Bloom were only the *homme moyen sensuel,* or everyman, nothing but the sort of person realism describes as "ordinary," he would not be the Bloom we adore. The truth is that Bloom is a wit, a comedian. In the depths of his passivity, Bloom resists. He is said in Dublin to be "something of an artist." To be an artist in the ocean of modern information is certainly no blessing. The artist has less power to resist the facts than other men. He is obliged to note the particulars. One may even say that he is condemned to see them. In the cemetery, Bloom can't help seeing the gravedigger's spade and noting that it is "blueglancing." He is therefore receptively, artistically, painfully immersed in his mental ocean. The fact that he is "something of an artist" aggravates the problems of information. He seeks relief in digression, in evasion, and in wit.

Why is the diversity of data so dazzling and powerful in *Ulysses*? The data are potent because the story itself is negligible. *Ulysses*, as Gertrude Stein once said, is not a "what-happens-next?" sort of book. A "what-happens next?" story would, like a nervous system, screen out distractions and maintain order.

It is the absence of a story that makes Bloom what he is. By injecting him with purpose, a story would put the world in order and concentrate his mind. But perhaps Bloom's mind is better not ordered. Why should he, the son of a suicide, the father who mourns a dead child, a cuckold, and a Jew in Catholic Dublin, desire moral and intellectual clarity? If his mind were clear, he would be another man entirely. No, the plan of Bloom's life is to be planless. He palpitates among the phenomena and moves vaguely toward resolution. Oh, he gets there, but *there* is a region, not a point. At one of the low hours of his day he thinks, "Nothing is anything." He feels his servitude to the conditions of being. When there is no story, those conditions have it all their own way and one is delivered to despair. The artifact civilization, Joyce seems to tell us, atrophies the will. The stream of consciousness flows full and wide through the will-less. The romantic heroes of powerful will, the Rastignacs and the Raskolnikovs, are gone. The truth of the present day is in the little Blooms, whose wills offer no hindrance to the stream of consciousness. And this stream has no stories. It has themes. Bloom does not, however, disintegrate in the thematic flow. Total examination of a single human being discloses a most extraordinary entity, a comic subject, a Bloom. Through him we begin to see that anything can be something.

But the burden of being a Bloom is nevertheless frightful. It is not clear exactly how Joyce would like us to see the Bloom problem. Long passages of *Ulysses* are bound together by slurs (in the musical sense of the word) of ambiguous laughter. It does, however, appear that Joyce expected the individual who has gone beyond the fictions and postures of "individuality" (romantic will, etc.) to be sustained by suprapersonal powers of myth. Myth, rising from the unconscious, is superior to mere "story," but myth will not come near while ordinary, trivial ideas of self remain. The powers of myth can be raised up only when the discredited pretensions of selfhood are surrendered. Therefore consciousness must abase itself, and every hidden thing must be exhumed. Hence Bloom's moments in the privy, his corpse fantasies at Paddy's funeral, his ejaculation as he watches crippled Gerty, his masochistic hallucinations in Nighttown. The old dignities must take a terrific beating in this new version of "the first shall be last and the last first."

How is the power of the modern age to be answered? By an equal and opposite power within us, tapped and interpreted by a man of genius. Joyce performs the part of the modern genius to perfection. This sort of genius, as I see it, comes from the mass without external advantages. Everything he needs is within him. By interpreting his own dreams, he creates a scientific system. By musical spells extracted from his own personality, he hypnotizes the world with his Siegfrieds and Wotans. He

is, as [R. G.] Collingwood calls him, the "mystagogue leading his audience . . . along the dark and difficult places of his own mind . . . the great man who (as Hegel says) imposes upon the world the task of understanding him." This task of understanding has certainly been imposed by Joyce. These men of genius take you in their embrace and propose to be everything to you. They are your *Heimat,* your church. You need no other music than theirs, no other ideas, no other analysis of dreams, no other manna. They are indeed stirring and charming. Their charms are hard to get away from. Theirs are the voices under which other voices sink. Once initiated into their mysteries, we do not easily free ourselves.

It is now seventy years since Bloom walked the streets of Dublin. In those seventy years the noise of life has increased a thousandfold. And already at the beginning of the nineteenth century Wordsworth was alarmed by the increase of distractions. The world was too much with us. The clatter of machinery, business, the roar of revolution would damage the inmost part of the mind and make poetry impossible. A century after Wordsworth, ingenious Joyce proposed to convert the threat itself into literature.

What you feel when you read *Ulysses* today is the extent to which a modern society imposes itself upon everyone. The common man, who, in the past, knew little about the great world, now stands in the middle of it. (pp. 14-17)

> *Saul Bellow, "Literature in the Age of Technology"* *(originally a lecture delivered in 1972-73), in* Technology and the Frontiers of Knowledge *by Saul Bellow and others (copyright © 1974, by Doubleday & Company, Inc.; reprinted by permission of the publisher), Doubleday, 1975, pp. 1-22.**

JACKSON I. COPE　(essay date 1981)

Joyce was the father of modern literature. He remade the short story in *Dubliners* and redimensioned the novel repeatedly in three successive experimental masterpieces. To demonstrate the nature of these powerful renewals . . . must be the primary aim of all critical assessments of Joyce. But to see properly the nature of Joyce's modernist revolution, one must not lose sight of Joyce the Victorian. He planted his fictions firmly in the novelistic tradition of his great predecessors by unquestioningly assuming that the matrix of the psyche's conflicting alienation and need was the family. This conception of the primal social unit, so foreign to the couples, the strangers, the dangling men of later fiction, provides the narrative thread of all Joyce's fiction from **"The Sisters"** through *Exiles* and the Dedalian histories in myth into the incestuous labyrinths of *Finnegans Wake.* Further, Joyce followed his great predecessors in embedding both the individual and the family in the yet larger social (or antisocial) network of the city, a metaphor for the disparateness and lonely sterility of modern life from Dickens through [John] Hawkes. (pp. 1-2)

Most readers now are willing to believe that the gradually elaborated and expanded stories that became *Dubliners* represent a carefully orchestrated unity rather than a loosely gathered sheaf of glimpses into modern urban decadence. But the nature of the unity and the ultimate perspective of judgment it offers upon the society of Dublin are not agreed upon. And this is owing in very large part to Joyce's late decision to close *Dubliners* with **"The Dead."** Detached from the collection, as it has so often been in anthologies, **"The Dead"** has been viewed as the annunciatory birth of feeling as frequently as it is seen as Gabriel's epiphanic realization that he has passed through life without living. The crux of debate has been, of course, the complex religious symbolism and the ambivalent shifts of tone in Gabriel Conroy's own assessments of himself and the evening's events. To argue a sense of the ending, we must, I think, work backwards and consider it as the ending of *Dubliners,* drawing the book together circularly from last sentence to first as we draw together *Finnegans Wake.* And to do so satisfactorily we must center *Dubliners* in that matrix of Dantesque cities of dreadful night of which [James Thomson's poem *The City of Dreadful Night*] offers such a superbly sophisticated example.

That Joyce conceived the book as a vision of a dead "city" is clear enough. . . . How much Dante's poem was in Joyce's mind as he was structuring *Dubliners* as a whole, though, can perhaps best be seen from the long letter he wrote to his brother in the fall of 1905 in which he outlined the order of the stories as he contemplated it in his penultimate version, beginning with **"The Sisters"** and concluding with **"Grace."** He was at the moment completely obsessed with *Dubliners.* (pp. 8-9)

It was in this mood that Joyce had decided to conclude the. volume with **"Grace."** Had he persisted in this plan, the book would have stood as a complicated parody of Dante expressing Joyce's disdain for a Dublin in which Father Purdon's religiosity was indistinguishable from Joe Hynes's patriotism. It would have been a parody on a large scale, like the "mystery play in half an act" in an early notebook that Joyce ironically labled "Dr. Doherty and the Holy City." But within the next two years Joyce's mood changed, and in 1907 his more developed sensibilities demanded modest emulation rather than parody of the great Italian. And in this new mood **"The Dead"** was written and added to redefine the structure of *Dubliners* as a whole. (pp. 9-10)

The larger significant movements of *Dubliners* have been rendered familiar by a multitude of critics: the boy at the beginning looks eastward toward Persia, the Pigeon House, Araby, while Gabriel Conroy at the end accepts the inevitability of his journey westward. The boy of **"The Sisters"** peers at a lighted window to discern an old man's death: Gabriel Conroy peers out of a darkened window at the universality of death symbolized by a boy long dead. The concinnity has its epicycles, too, making the progress of the first three stories a gnomon or *pars pro toto* of the whole. As the hope and spirit of childhood are abandoned to the paralysis of "adolescence" in the second grouping of stories, the lighted window of **"The Sisters"** is finally dimmed to extinction for the boy in **"Araby"** who "with anguish and anger" "heard a voice call from one end of the gallery that the light was out". . . . Both the largest and the enclosed metaphoric patterns constitute an anti-Dantesque movement, from light to dark, as the *Commedia* opens in "una selva oscura" and closes looking into that "somma luce" which moves, in the final line and version, "il sole e l'altre stelle."

And while **"The Sisters"** and **"An Encounter"** are stories of early summer (the one at the beginning of July and the other "in the first week of June"), the last story of the first group is set in "the short days of winter" when "Dusk fell" so early . . . , when "the air was pitilessly raw" and "the dark house" seems made up of "cold empty gloomy rooms". . . . The epicyclic seasonal pattern of the boy narrator's dying hopes confirms the darkness pattern, moving toward year's end from its burgeoning. This is the more striking in that **"Araby"** is the only story in *Dubliners* in which the season is not appro-

priate to the protagonist's age. Those which Joyce called "stories of adolescence," **"After the Race," "Two Gallants"** and **"The Boarding House,"** are all set in summer. . . . The one exception in this group is **"Eveline,"** which contains no indications of the season. But this omission itself appears to be part of the pattern. **"The Sisters"** opens with the boy speculating upon his relationship with the paralyzed priest who dies. When **"Araby"** closes upon its wintry darkness, the boy narrator has himself reached that "pleasant and vicious region" represented by the opulent "Persia" of the nightmare; and in finding that East the others had sought, finds it empty of hope or renewal: "Gazing up into the darkness I saw myself as a creature driven and derided by vanity; and my eyes burned with anguish and anger". . . . Following these words, **"Eveline"** opens with the first young adult also watching the darkness close over her world, but her quiescence is monitory of her ultimate failure: "She sat at the window watching the evening invade the avenue". . . . For all of Frank's efforts to move her, she is the most vividly, literally paralyzed of the long roll call of Dubliners whose psychic frustration parallels her own. Gazing upon "the black mass of the boat," she feels herself drowning: "Her hands clutched the iron [railing] in frenzy. Amid the seas she sent a cry of anguish". . . . It is the anguish of the young who have joined the priest in his paralysis, the "anguish" that burned in the eyes of the boy in the bazaar, but with the "anger" spent, all passion spent: "She set her white face to him, passive, like a helpless animal. Her eyes gave him no sign of love or farewell or recognition." There is no season attached to **"Eveline"** because Eveline is a symbol of the state of all the figures who follow, a state recognized by the narrator in **"Araby"**: they are the paralyzed living dead in a dark world of stasis where change and movement are illusion.

Joyce spoke of the other stories as "stories of mature life" and "stories of public life," but one must not allow these categories to displace the fact that all of the protagonists in both groups are entering or passing out of middle age. In keeping with this aging, the seasonal settings are all autumnal or hibernal. (pp. 10-12)

The winter darkness [in **"Araby"**] that settles over the bazaar of youthful hopes in the epicyclic series when the boy recognizes life and love as the vanity of vanities is strategically positioned to prepare *us* to recognize the seasonal decline of the later stories as a dying fall rather than a cyclical renewal (although, as I have said, the stories are connected circularly, the boy of **"The Sisters"** unsuccessfully trying to conjure up brave visions of Christmas to ward off the vision of the dead priest, as Gabriel attempts to ward off the universal dance of death with the ritual of Christmas celebrations).

These patterns can be discerned cutting a swathe through the entirety of *Dubliners.* Other internal echoings and positioning of stories, though, can be at least as helpful in revealing the movement and thesis of the whole. If **"Grace"** is a parodic, Dantesque journey toward the pinpoint of red light ("la somma luce") over a brothel on Purdon Street, **"The Boarding House"** (which would have corresponded in the first half to **"Grace"** closing the whole should **"The Dead"** not have been added), the middle story and last of those designated by Joyce as an account of "adolescence," is constructed upon a counter falling pattern into a modern urban *Inferno.* As a despairing descent from romantic aspiration into the death of Dublin it parallels the death of the spirit recognized in **"Araby"** (the final story of youth) and mocked in **"Grace."**

Twinned parodies of Dante's *Commedia*, then: the first, closing out the cycle of youth, presents a hopeless prisoner who mistook hell for heaven and (like the narrator of **"Araby"**) was disabused; the second, closing the original *Dubliners,* presents a spiritual whore mocking the salvation at the center of "la somma luce" while complacently aging Dubliners look on. And these peaks of traditional metaphoric action punctuate the darkening and dying structures of the entire series.

The whole was recapitulated and humanized in that magnificent afterthought, **"The Dead."** (pp. 14-15)

Joyce wrote to Grant Richards late in their disastrous negotiations about the publication of *Dubliners,* "It is not my fault that the odour of ashpits and old weeds and offal hangs round my stories" because, he explains, he was merely preparing "a nicely polished looking-glass" for his fellow citizens. . . . He was probably recollecting the "dark muddy lanes behind the houses . . . the back doors of the dark dripping gardens where odours rose from the ashpits . . . the dark odorous stables" that the boy of **"Araby"** contemplated. . . . Such descriptions of the sterile decadence of the city are familiar to readers of Dickens or Gissing, and it is this tradition that doubtless tempered Joyce's imagination. But because he was from the beginning intent upon portraying a psychological rather than physical waste land such as that which Thomson's despairing protagonist traversed, Joyce presents few such scenes. From *Dubliners* through *Ulysses* he chose to let a realistically detailed Dublin stand as its own denunciation. (pp. 16-17)

[It] is in **"A Little Cloud"** that the most sustained visions of a stunted Dublin waste land occur, as if Joyce felt that he had to "place" his volume in yet another way within the Victorian urban desert. . . . And Joyce teases his own structure with the admission that he has "put in allusions" by titling the story after that little cloud no bigger than a man's hand which arose that Elijah the rain-maker might make Israel fruitful once more in spite of King Ahab's defection to heathen gods under the influence of the foreign Queen Jezebel. . . . In Joyce's allusive little waste land poem Ignatius Gallaher plays Ahab-Solomon to Chandler's Elijah. Returned to Ireland from such foreign fleshpots as London, Paris, and Berlin, Gallaher is full of tales of their immorality, tales of "when the *cocottes* begin to let themselves loose" . . . , tales of "thousands of rich Germans and Jews" eager to marry him . . . , and full of "many of the secrets of religious houses on the Continent". . . . At first caught up with wonder and admiration at his former friend's glamorous life, soon Chandler begins "to feel somewhat disillusioned. Gallaher's accent and way of expressing himself did not please him. There was something vulgar in his friend which he had not observed before. . . . As the whiskey warms the timid man to a sense of his own superiority, Chandler passes from his praise of monogamous wedded bliss to a challenge that is also a prophecy: "'You'll put your head in the sack,' repeated Little Chandler stoutly, 'like everyone else if you can find the girl'". . . . The king of the bedroom sought by those "thousands of rich Germans and Jews" scoffs at the prophet: "'But I'm in no hurry. They can wait. I don't fancy tying myself up to one woman, you know'". . . .

Righteous and defeated, Chandler returns home. Far from writing a poem, he has never even read one aloud to his prim, sterile wife, out of timidity. Holding his infant son in his arms, however, he now reads to himself a poem (of subconscious choice) concerning the death of a formerly beloved woman. . . . Then the child begins to cry, spilling ironic rain upon the land whose sin is infertility of the soul, and evokes futile tears of

remorse from his father as the bawling infant inspires the one passion yet possible in Little Chandler and in his accusing wife: anger, not life. "Stop!" he shouts. "The child stopped for an instant, had a spasm of fright and began to scream". . . . But in replacing Elijah's growing cloud with these hopeless tears, the Joyce who renamed Gogarty as Malachi Mulligan could scarcely have failed to intend that this little story incorporate still another ironic scriptural parody that would take its much more serious, prophetic place in the allusive economy of *Ulysses.* It was the final assertion that the Dublin of *Dubliners* was the waste land. As Chandler/Elijah shouts at his son in despair, one hears those closing words of the Old Testament: "Behold, I will send you Elijah the prophet before the coming of the great and dreadful day of the Lord: And he shall turn the heart of the fathers to the children, and the heart of the children to their fathers, lest I come and smite the earth with a curse" (Malachi 4:5-6). (pp. 17-20)

> *Jackson I. Cope, "The Waste Land," in his* Joyce's Cities: Archeologies of the Soul *(copyright © 1981 by The Johns Hopkins University Press), The Johns Hopkins University Press, 1981, pp. 1-28.*

RICHARD ELLMANN   (essay date 1982)

What were Joyce's attitudes toward Church and state? To what extent was he shaped by the Catholicism he forswore? How committed was he to the liberation of Ireland? These questions haunt his hundredth birthday. . . .

He wrote to Nora Barnacle on August 29, 1904, "Six years ago [at 22] I left the Catholic Church, hating it most fervently. I found it impossible for me to remain in it on account of the impulses of my nature." The Church's attitude to sexuality was particularly repugnant to him. His letter went on, "I made secret war upon it when I was a student and declined to accept the positions it offered me." These positions, according to his brother Stanislaus, included that of priest. "By doing this I made myself a beggar but I retained my pride," Joyce wrote to Nora. "Now I make open war upon it by what I write and say and do."

His actions accorded with this policy. (p. 28)

Critics have sometimes contended that his books should not be taken as opposed to the Church. Of course no frontal attack is made in them. Joyce spoke in an early autobiographical essay of having adopted "urbanity in warfare" as his strategy. He was anxious that his books should not commit propaganda, even against institutions of which he disapproved. (p. 29)

Stephen's apostasy [in *Portrait of the Artist as a Young Man*] accordingly is presented as a choice for himself, and not necessarily one for others. On the other hand, he is an exemplum, not only in his capacity as artist, but in his character of emancipated man. His initial submission, in fear and remorse, to the terrifying sermons about death, judgment, and punishment, changes to revulsion at their cruelty. Yet Joyce is careful not to overstate his case. If Father Dolan, who in the first chapter pandies Stephen unjustly, is sadistic, the priest who hears the boy's confession after the retreat in the third chapter is kind and gentle.

Apart from such sporadic concessions, the Church is regularly presented in terms of darkness, constriction, and thwart. Stephen finds that its emphasis on the soul is as lopsided as the prostitute's emphasis on the body. His most adroit maneuver is taking over its vocabulary for his own secular purposes. He receives a *call,* hears "a voice from beyond the world," but what it summons him to is not the priesthood but life, including sexual love, and an art that would content body and soul alike. The word *sin* is modified to error, to *fall* is only to experience: Stephen ecstatically contemplates "To live, to err, to fall, to triumph, to recreate life out of life." He himself achieves *resurrection:* "His soul had risen from the grave of boyhood, spurning her graveclothes." He is ordained into a new priest-craft of his own devising: he imagines himself "a priest of eternal imagination, transmuting the daily bread of experience into the radiant body of everliving life." At the book's end he even takes over from the Church the care of *conscience;* it is he and not the Church who will forge a conscience for his race.

Just what this new conscience was to be Joyce clarifies in *Ulysses.* Neither Bloom nor Stephen could be described as pagan, though neither acknowledges any institutional belief. Bloom, in offering his conception of love as against the Citizen's hatred and violence, is voicing a humanist ethic. He also fulfills the role of the Good Samaritan when Stephen is knocked down. So far as Catholicism is concerned, he ruminates humorously about confession, communion, resurrection, marveling at the hold these strange conceptions have. Stephen, reared among them, but unwilling to accept Catholic limitations of his independence, is in active rebellion. His climactic moment comes as his mother's ghost, like that of the Commendatore in *Don Giovanni,* thrice summons him to repent. His anguished retort is "Shite!" when the true pagan would neither see the ghost nor recognize any inclination to repent. Stephen is never insouciant. When he points to his head and quotes Blake, who in turn was alluding to Dante, "But in here it is I must kill the priest and the king," Joyce at once sanctions his "mental fight" and accepts the responsibility for this rebellion.

In *Finnegans Wake* Joyce seems more relaxed about the Church and about rebellion. Shaun, as a hypocritical do-gooder with a claim to piety, is steadily mocked, but so is his errant and agnostic brother. Catholicism has its place in the book, a pervasive one that involves Saint Patrick, countless popes, church history, and theological squabbles. In terms of universal history, which the *Wake* presents, the Church's punctilio about forgotten issues adds to the joyful polyphony. In the night world shot through with dreams, religion appears no better and no worse than other human obsessions.

To be opposed to the Church as an institution is one thing; to be opposed to all religious feeling is another. At moments Joyce surprised his atheistical brother Stanislaus by unexpected concessions. . . . That this was not just a passing fancy appears to be borne out in *Ulysses*—less in Stephen and Bloom, who disclaim faith, than in Molly. She, while contemptuous of piety, is also contemputous of impiety, and approves a vague theism. . . . Although in May 1905 Joyce pronounced himself to be incapable of belief of any kind, he evidently had more than a few grains left. But any approach to orthodoxy repelled him. (pp. 29-30)

He had much the same feelings of intransigence toward the British state, as the occupying power in Ireland, that he had toward the Catholic Church. "Political awareness" was a quality he valued in writers. Joyce was politically aware without being political. That is, day-to-day politics did not interest him, but he thought of his writing as subsuming politics within it. His earliest recorded work was his lost poem about the man who had tried to lead Ireland to independence, Parnell. Flag-waving nationalism was not to his taste, but he regarded po-

litical independence as an aspect of the larger independence he was seeking. His brother records a conversation they had in April 1907. Stanislaus urged that an independent Ireland would be intolerable. "What the devil are your politics?" asked James. "Do you not think Ireland has a right to govern itself and is capable of doing so?" During his ten years in Trieste Joyce wrote nine articles setting forth the Irish "problem" for a local newspaper, and in 1914 he offered them as a book to an Italian publisher. They were not accepted: a pity, because they would have demonstrated that Joyce was altogether aware of and concerned about the political situation of his country.

Joyce is sometimes said to have been a lifelong Parnellite, but he was opposed to turning great dead men into stone effigies. In *Ulysses* he mocks the idea that Parnell is still alive and will return. The one post-Parnellite politician whom Joyce felt he could endorse was Arthur Griffith, who pleased him by being "unassuming" and "not indulging in flights." . . .

In *Ulysses* he acknowledged Griffith's political importance by making many references to him, alone among politicians of the day. And he called attention to the ultimately political direction of his own work by having Irish Stephen, at the end of the brothel scene, beaten up by a *British* soldier, whom he defies as "the uninvited." (p. 30)

[Indifference] was not a characteristic of a man who made a point of reading Irish newspapers every day, and who took a passionate interest in every detail of his native land. However skeptical he became of political progress, he endeavored in all his books to achieve something superpolitical, by disclosing sharply what life in Ireland was, and dimly what it might be. This was his higher politics. (p. 31)

Richard Ellmann, "On Joyce's Centennial," in The New Republic *(reprinted by permission of* The New Republic; © *1982 The New Republic, Inc.),* Vol. 186, No. 7, February 17, 1982, pp. 28-31.

ADDITIONAL BIBLIOGRAPHY

Bandler, Bernard, II. "Joyce's *Exiles.*" *Hound & Horn* VI, No. 2 (January-March 1933): 266-85.
> Study of *Exiles* concerned with the absence of God in the characters' world and the resulting epistemological quests.

Beja, Morris. "James Joyce: The Bread of Everyday Life." In his *Epiphany in the Modern Novel,* pp. 71-111. Seattle: University of Washington Press, 1971.
> Study of the development of Joyce's theory of epiphany and of the various types of epiphanies used in his fiction.

Blackmur, R. P. "The Jew in Search of a Son: Joyce's *Ulysses.*" In his *Eleven Essays in the European Novel,* pp. 27-47. New York: Harcourt, Brace & World, 1964.
> Discusses the inaccessibility of the modern novel to the common reader, utilizing an exegesis of *Ulysses* to demonstrate the obstacles in the path of an uninformed reader.

Connolly, Thomas E., ed. *Joyce's "Portrait": Criticisms and Critiques.* New York: Appleton-Century-Crofts, 1962, 335 p.
> Very good retrospective of criticism on *Portrait* including among others, Geddes MacGregor on Joyce's artistic theory, Grant Redford on the novel's structure, and Irene Hendry Chayes on Joyce's use of epiphanies.

Eckley, Grace. "Shem Is a Sham but Shaun Is a Ham, or Samuraising the Twins in *Finnegans Wake.*" *Modern Fiction Studies* 20, No. 4 (Winter 1974-75): 469-81.

Discussion of Joyce's characterization of the twins Shem and Shaun which disagrees with critical theories of a mergence of identity between the two characters.

Edel, Leon. "James Joyce and His New Work." *University of Toronto Quarterly* IX, No. 1 (October 1939): 68-81.
Argues that Joyce's use of language in *Finnegans Wake* is so intricate that only Joyce himself can fully understand his own achievement.

Ellmann, Richard. *James Joyce.* Rev. ed. New York: Oxford University Press, 1982, 928 p.
Comprehensive biography of Joyce which has become the standard work on his life.

Givens, Seon, ed. *James Joyce: Two Decades of Criticism.* New York: Vanguard Press, 1963, 486 p.
A retrospective of primary criticism on various aspects of Joyce's work, including essays by Hugh Kenner, Stuart Gilbert, and Edmund Wilson, among others.

Goldberg, S. L. *The Classical Temper: A Study of James Joyce's "Ulysses."* London: Chatto and Windus, 1961, 346 p.
Discussion of Joyce's aesthetic theories, his use of irony, and his reliance upon classical models for the structure of *Ulysses*.

Gross, John. *James Joyce.* Edited by Frank Kermode. New York: The Viking Press, 1970, 102 p.
Discusses the development of Joyce as poet, dramatist, and novelist within a chronological study of his works.

Halper, Hathan. *The Early James Joyce.* New York: Columbia University Press, 1973, 48 p.
Good survey of Joyce's work through *Portrait*.

Hart, Clive, ed. *James Joyce's "Dubliners": Critical Essays.* New York: Viking Press, 1969, 183 p.
Valuable collection in which an entire essay is devoted to each story in *Dubliners*.

Hayman, David. "Daedalian Imagery in *A Portrait of the Artist as a Young Man*." In *Hereditas: Seven Essays on the Modern Experience of the Classical,* edited by Frederic Will, pp. 33-54. Austin: University of Texas Press, 1964.
Examines the manner in which the Daedalus symbol functions in *Portrait* and *Ulysses* and leads to Stephen's understanding of the labyrinthine nature of life.

Kaplan, Harold. "Stroom: The Universal Comedy of James Joyce." In his *The Passive Voice: An Approach to Modern Fiction,* pp. 43-91. Athens: Ohio University Press, 1966.
How Joyce's comic vision of life informs *Ulysses*.

Kenner, Hugh. *Ulysses.* London: George Allen & Unwin, 1980, 182 p.

Critical guidebook designed to assist the serious student of *Ulysses*.

Levin, Richard, and Shattuck, Charles. "First Flight to Ithaca: A New Reading of Joyce's *Dubliners*." *Accent* IV, No. 2 (Winter 1944): 75-99.
Study which examines the thematic and structural resemblances of *Dubliners* to Homer's *Odyssey*.

Manganiello, Dominic. *Joyce's Politics:* London: Routledge & Kegan Paul, 1980, 260 p.
Political motifs in Joyce's works.

Mercier, Vivian. "James Joyce and the Irish Tradition of Parody." In his *The Irish Comic Tradition,* pp. 210-36. Oxford: Clarendon Press, 1962.*
How Joyce parodied epic literature, both Greek and Irish, to create his novels of modern antiheroes.

Prescott, Joseph. *Exploring James Joyce.* Carbondale: Southern Illinois University Press, 1964, 182 p.
Essays discussing Joyce's characterizations, his use of allusion, his verbal facility, and stylistic techniques.

Raisor, Philip. "Grist for the Mill: James Joyce and the Naturalists." *Contemporary Literature* 15, No. 4 (Autumn 1974): 457-73.
Argues that a naturalistic appreciation for detail was as important a component of Joyce's style and vision of life as his classicist appreciation for the universals of human experience.

Senn, Fritz, ed. *New Light on Joyce from the Dublin Symposium.* Bloomington: Indiana University Press, 1972, 208 p.
Papers collected from an international symposium, including, among others, essays by Leslie Fiedler on the nature of Bloom and Darcy O'Brien on Joyce's conception of love.

Tindall, W[illiam] Y[ork]. "Dante and Mrs. Bloom." *Accent* IX, No. 2 (Spring 1951): 85-92.
Discusses the importance of allusions to Dante's *Divine Comedy* in *Ulysses*.

Tindall, William York. *A Reader's Guide to "Finnegans Wake."* New York: Farrar, Straus and Giroux, 1969, 339 p.
Introduction to *Finnegans Wake* that delineates arrangement, allusion, and meaning in the work, though often in a very obscure manner.

Wilder, Thorton. "Joyce and the Modern Novel." In his *American Characteristics and Other Essays,* edited by Donald Gallup, pp. 172-80. New York: Harper & Row, Publishers, 1979.
Explains the method behind Joyce's often difficult style.

(Joseph) Rudyard Kipling

1865-1936

English short story writer, poet, novelist, essayist, and autobiographer.

Kipling is one of the most popular authors of all time and one of the finest short story writers in world literature. His critical reputation, however, has suffered because attention has often been paid not to his frequently flawless technique, but to the jingoistic political beliefs expressed in his work. It is only since Kipling's death that a major reassessment of his talents has begun. Critics for the most part agree that Kipling was a masterful storyteller who possessed profound insights into the role of "beneficent imperialism," though these insights were often clouded by a chauvinistic patriotism.

Born in Bombay, India, to English parents, Kipling was sent to school in England at the age of six. At first he lived with harsh and unsympathetic relatives, an unhappy experience he later wrote about in "Baa Baa, Black Sheep" and *The Light That Failed*. At twelve he went to the second-rate boarding school described, and somewhat embellished, in *Stalky and Co.* Just before his seventeenth birthday Kipling returned to India to work as a journalist on the Lahore *Civil and Military Gazette* and the Allahabad *Pioneer*. The verses and short stories he wrote as filler for these two newspapers were eventually published in books, and the successful sales of *Departmental Ditties* and *Plain Tales from the Hills* enabled Kipling to spend three years traveling. He married an American woman, the sister of his one-time collaborator Wolcott Balestier, and lived on her family's estate in Vermont for four years. During this time, Kipling wrote some of his best children's stories, including the two *Jungle Books*, and began work on *Kim*, critically regarded as his finest work. A lawsuit brought by another of his wife's brothers, and an attack of influenza which struck the entire family and caused his elder daughter's death, left Kipling disenchanted with life in the United States. In 1896 he returned to England and settled in the Sussex countryside, which figures prominently as the setting for many of his subsequent works. He was awarded the Nobel Prize in literature in 1907, the first English author to be so honored.

Kipling was an admirer of the French *conte*, and he brought this finely crafted short story form to English literature. He frequently narrated the action of his early stories in a tone of cynical worldliness which prompted J. M. Barrie's often-quoted remark that Kipling "must have been born blasé." These stories, brief, concise, and vigorous, display little depth of characterization, but are remarkable for their innovative plots and deceptively simple structure. Kipling's tendency to concision is sometimes overdone in his later stories. "Mrs. Bathurst," for example, is so compressed and elliptical that many critics admit they do not know what happens in the narrative. Kipling's stories for children are perhaps the most widely known and read of his works. Kipling had a gift for anthropomorphism, and he presented his animal characters, in works like the *Jungle Books*, with simplicity, humor, and dignity, marred only occasionally by excessive cuteness. Kipling also tended to anthropomorphize machinery. This tendency, together with his overuse of technical jargon, flaws such works as ".007" and "The Ship That Found Herself."

Of Kipling's four novel-length works, only *Kim* proved successful. Critics attributed the poor plotting and weak characterization of his first novel, *The Light That Failed*, to his youth and inexperience. His second novel, *The Naulahka*, written with Wolcott Balestier, exhibited the same shortcomings. *Captains Courageous*, still a popular children's book, is "really just a long short story," as Hilton Brown has noted. *Kim* shared with *Captains Courageous* what is essentially a short story structure; this "plotless picaresque," in Kipling's words, remains his most popular work with both readers and critics, most of whom concur with Nirad C. Chaudhuri in calling it "the finest story about India in English." Some critics, among them Edmund Wilson, have pointed out that the elements of conflict and resolution, essential to a novel's structure, are absent from *Kim* and from Kipling's other novels. The lack of introspection on the part of the protagonist of *Kim* has been cited as the primary fault in a potentially great work, and of Kipling's work in general.

In his poetry Kipling broke new ground by taking as subject matter the life of the common soldier and sailor in such off-duty activities as drinking, looting, and brawling. Most critical comment centered at first on Kipling's ignominious choice of topics for his verses and on his insistent, often-times offensive, imperialism. Then, in 1942, T. S. Eliot prefaced a new collection of Kipling's poetry and verse with a lengthy, and favorable, reassessment of Kipling as a poet. Eliot's study has been the starting point of many subsequent analyses of Kipling's poetic accomplishment, which is still in contention.

Although he is generally accepted as one of the masters of the short story form, Kipling's literary stature is still in flux. "During the later years of his life and even at the time of his death, the logic of his artistic development attracted no intelligent notice," Edmund Wilson noted. Some critics, perhaps most especially Eliot, have made the mistake "of defending him where he is not defensible," as George Orwell said. Critical consensus, however, is that despite his faults, Kipling's final place in English literature will be a prominent one.

PRINCIPAL WORKS

Schoolboy Lyrics (poetry and verse) 1881
Departmental Ditties (poetry and verse) 1886
In Black and White (short stories) 1888
The Phantom 'Rickshaw (short stories) 1888
Plain Tales from the Hills (short stories) 1888
Soldiers Three (short stories) 1888
The Story of the Gadsbys (short stories) 1888
Under the Deodars (short stories) 1888
Wee Willie Winkie (short stories) 1888
The Courting of Dinah Shadd (short stories) 1890
The Light That Failed (novel) 1890
Life's Handicap (short stories) 1891
Barrack-Room Ballads (poetry and verse) 1892
The Naulahka [with Wolcott Balestier] (novel) 1892
Many Inventions (short stories) 1893
The Jungle Book (short stories and verse) 1894
The Second Jungle Book (short stories and verse) 1895
The Seven Seas (poetry and verse) 1896
Captains Courageous (novel) 1897
The Day's Work (short stories) 1898
From Sea to Sea. 2 vols. (sketches) 1899
Stalky and Co. (short stories) 1899
Kim (novel) 1901
Just-So Stories (short stories and verse) 1902
The Five Nations (poetry and verse) 1903
Traffics and Discoveries (short stories and verse) 1904
Puck of Pook's Hill (short stories and verse) 1906
Abaft the Funnel (short stories) 1909
Actions and Reactions (short stories and verse) 1909
Rewards and Fairies (short stories and verse) 1910
Songs from Books (poetry and verse) 1912
A Diversity of Creatures (short stories and verse) 1917
The Years Between (poetry) 1919
Letters of Travel, 1892-1913 (sketches) 1920
Debits and Credits (short stories and verse) 1926
A Book of Words (speeches) 1928
Thy Servant a Dog (short stories) 1930
Limits and Renewals (short stories and verse) 1932
Souvenirs of France (essays) 1933
Something of Myself (unfinished autobiography) 1937
Complete Works. 35 vols. (short stories, poetry, verse, novels, essays, sketches, speeches, and unfinished autobiography) 1937-39

THE SPECTATOR (essay date 1889)

As a wholesome corrective to what may be called the oleographic style of depicting military life, now so much in vogue, Mr. Kipling's brilliant sketches of the barrack-room [in **'Soldiers Three'**], realistic in the best sense of the word, deserve a hearty welcome. Here be no inanities of the officers' mess, no apotheosis of the gilded and tawny moustachioed dragoon, no languid and lisping lancer, no child-sweethearts—none, in fact, of the sentimental paraphernalia familiar to readers of modern military fiction. Here, instead, we have Tommy Atkins as the central figure: and not Tommy on parade, but in those moods when the natural man finds freest expression—amorous, pugnacious, and thievish—a somewhat earthy personage on the whole, but with occasional gleams of chivalry and devotion lighting up his cloudy humanity. Too many so-called realists seem to aim at representing man as continuously animal, without any intervals in which his higher nature emerges at all. But Mr. Kipling happily does not belong to this school. The actualities of barrack-room life are not extenuated, but the tone of the whole is sound and manly. The author does not gloss over the animal tendencies of the British private, but he shows how in the grossest natures sparks of nobility may lie hid.

He has taken three widely different types of British soldier, a Yorkshireman, a Cockney, and a 'Paddy from Cork', and in spite of the savagery of the first, the cynicism of the second, and the thrasonical complacency of the third, we can fully comprehend the attractions which their company is supposed to have offered to the narrator. (pp. 41-2)

Mr. Kipling has a genius for reproducing quaint and characteristic Hibernicisms. How expressive for example are the words in which Mulvaney describes the court paid by an unscrupulous officer to a girl whom he wished to elope with him: 'So he went menowderin', and minanderin', and blandandherin' round an' about the Colonel's daughter.' In another place he speaks of some men who 'can swear so as to make green turf crack'. Who but an Irishman again would think of addressing a ghost as 'ye frozen thief of Genesis', or who would speak of a 'little squidgereen' of an officer?

Some of the stories in this collection introduce us to the realities of warfare in a surprisingly vivid fashion. . . . (p. 42)

The perusal of these stories cannot fail to inspire the reader with the desire to make further acquaintance with the other writings of the author. They are brimfull of humanity and a drollery that never degenerates into burlesque. In many places a note of genuine pathos is heard. Mr. Kipling is so gifted and versatile, that one would gladly see him at work on a larger canvas. But to be so brilliant a teller of short stories is in itself no small distinction. (p. 43)

> "'Soldiers Three'," in The Spectator, *Vol. 62, No. 3169, March 23, 1889 (and reprinted in* Kipling: The Critical Heritage, *edited by Roger Lancelyn Green, Barnes & Noble, 1971, pp. 41-3).*

OSCAR WILDE (essay date 1890)

He who would stir us now by fiction must either give us an entirely new background or reveal to us the soul of man in its innermost workings. The first is for the moment being done for us by Mr. Rudyard Kipling. As one turns over the pages of his ***Plain Tales from the Hills,*** one feels as if one were seated under a palm-tree reading life by superb flashes of vulgarity. The jaded, second-rate Anglo-Indians are in exquisite incongruity with their surroundings. The mere lack of style in the story-teller gives an odd journalistic realism to what he tells us. From the point of view of literature Mr. Kipling is a genius who drops his aspirates. From the point of view of life, he is a reporter who knows vulgarity better than any one has ever known it. Dickens knew its clothes and its comedy. Mr. Kipling knows its essence and its seriousness. He is our first authority on the second-rate, and has seen marvelous things through keyholes, and his backgrounds are real works of art. (p. 7)

> Oscar Wilde, "The True Function and Value of Criticism," in The Nineteenth Century, Vol. 28, No. 163, September, 1890 (and reprinted in Kipling and the Critics, edited by Elliot L. Gilbert, New York University Press, 1965, pp. 7-8).

ANDREW LANG (essay date 1890)

Some years ago, among the books which came in battalions to a reviewer, I found an odd little volume of verses, bound like an official report, Where is that volume now? It has gone the way of first editions; a thing to regret, as it was an example of Mr. Rudyard Kipling's **"Departmental Ditties."** They were light pieces of rhyme on Anglo-Indian life and society; they were lively, sad, cynical, and very unlike most poetry. Mr. Kipling's name was new to me, and, much as I had admired his verses, I heard no more of him till I received **"The Story of the Gadsbys,"** **"Studies in Black and White,"** and **"Under the Deodars."** They were all unpretending little tomes, clad in gray paper, and published in India. Then, on reading them, one saw that a new star in literature had swum into one's ken. Here was extraordinary brightness, brevity, observation, humor; unusual, perhaps unexampled, knowledge of life in India—life of the people, of their white rulers, of men and women, and of the private soldiers. Mr. Kipling had the unusual art of telling a short story: he cut it down almost to anecdote in his hatred of the prolix and the superfluous. This is always a rare art in English; in French it is more common, and is made far more welcome. (p. vii)

Mr. Kipling appears to myself to possess a very original genius, nor is this an original opinion. His **"Plain Tales [from the Hills"]** have been called "The best book ever written on India," by an authority of very great experience in life, in government, and in literature. For the first time he has shown English readers what India is like; how full of infinitely various life and romance. He seems to have seen and known, and been able to make real and vivid, the existence of all classes in that continent. For my own part, I least like his tales about official life, about flirtations and jobs, "appointments" of all kinds at Simla. The descriptions may be very true; they are not very pleasing. His married flirts, his frivolous ladies, his people who "play tennis with the Seventh Commandment," are melancholy, and, no doubt, admonitory spectacles. . . .

To my own taste—after all, it is a question of taste—his tales of native life in many ranks, castes, religions, and nations are his best. There is a wonderful horror, mixed with vulgar magic, in the story called **"The House of Suddhoo."** The confessions of an opium-smoker, in **"The Gate of a Hundred Sorrows,"** defeat De Quincey on his own ground. **"On the City Wall"** is a romance that is real, and an amazing glimpse into the true mind of Orientals, hidden from us often by a veneer of Western culture. **"The Strange Ride of Morrowbe Jukes,"** who fell into a village of thieves who should be dead but yet live, is a nightmare more perfect and terrible, I think, than anything of Edgar Poe's. There is a scene of passion at a midnight picnic,

and in a nocturnal dust-storm, which is purely magical, a revelation of things possible. The story of a little Indian child is a mere sketch, but it brings tears even into critical eyes. There is an astonishing variety in Mr. Kipling's powers. In the **"Phantom 'Rickshaw,"** his tale of the dead wife's appointment with her husband moves one like a vivid dream of the beloved dead. Then we have a handsome piece of witchery in the **"Bisara of Pooree,"** where the impossible becomes real to fancy. From these tales it is a long step to the military humors of **"Soldiers Three,"** the magnificent, daring, vain, and generous Irish Hercules, Mulvaney; the little cockney who shoots so well and has a madness of homesickness; Ortheris, and the large Yorkshireman who is their comrade. **"How They Took the Town of Lungtungpen"** and **"With the Rear Guard"** are tales of as good fighting as ever was transcribed. . . . The last story in **"Plain Tales"** promises, not a conclusion, but a beginning, to the legend of an English scholar sunk in drink, in Islam, and the dirt of a bazaar. All this would be entirely new, and we may trust that Mr. Kipling will give us a longer narrative on the subject. Whether he can write a long novel, or a novel, rather, of the usual proportions, remains to be seen. Very few men have excelled in both forms of the art fictitious, and he certainly excels in one. At a passage, a picture, an incident, a character, he is already, perhaps, all but unrivalled among his contemporaries. Can he weave many of these into a consistent fable? This remains to be tried.

I do not anticipate for Mr. Kipling a very popular popularity. He does not compete with Miss Braddon or Mr. E. P. Roe. His favorite subjects are too remote and unfamiliar for a world that likes to be amused with matters near home and passions that do not stray far from the drawing-room or the parlor. In style, as has been said, he has brevity, brilliance, selection; he is always at the centre of the interest; he wastes no words, he knows not padding. He can understand passion, and makes us understand it. He has sympathies unusually wide, and can find the rare strange thing in the midst of the commonplace. He has energy, spirit, vision. Refinement he has not in an equal measure; perhaps he is too abrupt, too easily taken by a piece of slang, and one or two little mannerisms become provoking. It does not seem, as yet, that he very well understands, or can write very well about, ordinary English life. But he has so much to say that he might well afford to leave the ordinary to other writers. He has the alacrity of the French intellect, and often displays its literary moderation and reserve. . . . To myself Mr. Kipling seems one of two, three, or four young men, and he is far the youngest, who flash out genius from some unexpected place, who are not academic, nor children of the old literature of the world, but of their own works. What seems cynical, flighty, too brusque, and too familiar in him should mellow with years. (pp. iv-xi)

> Andrew Lang, "Rudyard Kipling," in The Courting of Dinah Shadd and Other Stories by Rudyard Kipling, Harper & Brothers, 1890 (and reprinted by Books for Libraries Press, 1971), pp. vii-xii.

LIONEL JOHNSON (essay date 1892)

The two divisions of [Barrack-Room Ballads and Other Verses] disclose the strength and the weakness of Mr Kipling: triumphant success and disastrous failure. Certainly, there are weak things among the strong, and strong things among the weak; but the good and the bad, for the most part, are separated, the wheat from the tares. The **Barrack-Room Ballads** are fine and true; the **Other Verses,** too many of them, are rhetorical and only half true. It is more important, then, as it is more pleasant, to consider first, and at the greater length, the *Barrack-Room Ballads.*

They are written in the dialect of "the common soldier," of "Tommy Atkins"; they are composed in his spirit also. It is a curious reflection that the British army at large, and the British soldier in particular, have received so little attention in literature of any excellence. We have plenty of heroic poems, as Mr Henley and many others know well; plenty of verse alive with the martial spirit, with the "pomp and circumstance of glorious war"; plenty of things hardly less great than Wordsworth's "Happy Warrior," or the Laureate's "Ode on Wellington." But of the British army, as a way of daily life, as composed of individual men, as full of marked personal characteristics and peculiarities, our poets great and small have had little conception. . . . Certain criticisms which I have read of these *Ballads* have dwelt upon the technical difficulty of their dialect. Such criticism is of a piece with the prevailing apathy and ignorance concerning the army. . . . [So] many critics of literature, whose pride and business it is to be omniscient, are baffled by the technical terms or the appropriate slang of these *Ballads.* Poems thick with archaeological terms, with foreign phrases, with recondite learning and allusions, are accepted without demur. Mr Kipling's Indian stories have aroused no protest; but when he sings the common soldier in a common way, these omnivorous critics are aghast at the uncouth and mysterious language.

There are twenty of these *Ballads;* and there can hardly be said to be one failure among them, although two or three are of marked inferiority to the rest, and although the greater number look poor by the side of the four or five masterpieces. The most noticeable thing about them, on a first reading, is their swinging, marching music. The accents and beat of the verse fall true and full, like the rhythmical tramp of men's feet. (pp. 32-3)

They go with a swing and a march, an emphasis and a roll, which may delude the inexperienced into thinking them easy to "rattle off." I should be greatly surprised to hear that Mr Kipling thought the same.

The *Ballads* deal with a few marked incidents, experiences, and emotions from the private soldier's point of view; some general and unlocalised, but most peculiar to military life in the East. All Mr Kipling's undiverted and undiluted strength has gone into these vivid *Ballads;* phrase follows phrase, instinct with life, quivering and vibrating with the writer's intensity. No superfluity, no misplaced condescension to sentiment, no disguising of things ludicrous or ugly or unpleasant; Tommy Atkins is presented to the ordinary reader, with no apologies and with no adornments.

> We aren't no thin red 'eroes, nor we aren't no
>   blackguards too,
> But single men in barricks, most remarkable like you,

he sings: in a genial and, at the same time, an acute expostulation with the people, who exalt him in war but despise him in peace. . . . But no panegyrics could give the civilian a truer sense of the soldier's life, in its rough and ready hardships, than the experiences of camp and battle in these pages. . . . (p. 34)

There is plenty of matter in these *Ballads* to which "inquisiturient" critics, to use Milton's word, can take objection: the moral and dogmatic theology of the soldier, as indicated by

Mr Kipling, is somewhat unauthorised and lax. But Mr Kipling has no ambition to paint him, except in his own colours; and, very seriously contemplated, these *Ballads* give a picture of life and character more estimable and praiseworthy for many rugged virtues of generosity, endurance, heartiness, and simplicity, than are the lives and characters of many "gentlemen of England, who stay at home at ease."

Mr Kipling's *Other Verses* are less pleasant reading. Their rhetorical energy is splendid. At times they ring true to nature; but for the most part they are spasmodic, ranting, overstrained. (pp. 35-6)

Yet, like all that he writes with any degree of excellence, these lines have fine things in them: witness the description of him who walked from his birth "in simpleness and gentleness and honour and clean mirth": a just and noble praise.

Mr Kipling has run riot in chaunting the glories of action. . . . [But] he takes delight in other things also; and this glorification of the Strong, the Virile, the Robust, the Vigorous is fast becoming as great a nuisance and an affectation as were the True and the Beautiful years ago. It is so easy to bluster and to brag; so hard to remember that "they also serve who only stand and wait." Indeed, there seems to be no virtue which Mr Kipling would not put under the head of valour; virtue, to him, is *virtus,* and all the good qualities of man are valorous. From that point of view, saints and sinners, soldiers and poets, men of science and men of art, if they excel in their chosen works, are all Strong Men. That may be fair enough as a view of the matter to be sometimes emphasized; but we can have too much of it.

In some of his finest pieces Mr Kipling is a prey to the grandiose aspect of things. **"The English Flag,"** for example, in which the Winds of the World witness to England's greatness, is grievously spoiled by exaggeration of tone. We know that England is great, that Englishmen have done great things, that the fame of her glory has filled the corners of the earth; but we have no occasion to shriek about it, to wax hysterically wroth with those who deny it. . . . "What should they know of England, who only England know?" cries Mr Kipling; as though nothing short of ocular demonstration and a tourist's ticket could make the "poor little streetbred people" believe in the greatness of England by North, South, East and West. The occasion upon which the verses were written may justify some of this agitated declamation; but the tone is habitual with Mr Kipling. . . . I am in Mr Kipling's debt for so great a number of delights that I am the more moved to exclaim against his defects. I want to enjoy all that he writes. All that he urges against the effeminate, miserable people who take their whole standard of life and conduct from the opinions that they meet, and the society that surrounds them, is admirable; but it is not the whole truth. Perhaps, as Mr Stevenson suggests, there is no such thing as the whole truth.

Of the remaining poems, far the best are the **"Ballad of East and West,"** a thing to stir the blood like a trumpet; the **"Conundrum of the Workshops,"** a charming satire upon critics and criticism; and the ballads of the **"Clampherdown"** and the **"Bolivar."** The fierce and stinging verses against the Irish members concerned in the famous Commission are too virulent in their partisanship to be quite successful, even in the eyes of those who agree with them in the main. Of the Indian legends and ballads, we may say nothing; most of them have some force and spirit, but they do not equal the similar work of Sir Alfred Lyall.

Let me conclude by expressing my thanks once more for the *Barrack-Room Ballads;* in them, their unforced vigour and unexaggerated truth, I can forget all excesses of rhetoric, all extravagances of tone. (pp. 37-9)

> Lionel Johnson, " 'Barrack-Room Ballads and Other Verses' by Rudyard Kipling" (originally published in The Academy, Vol. XLI, No. 1047, May 28, 1892), in his Reviews and Critical Papers, edited by Robert Schafer, Elkin Mathews, 1921, pp. 32-9.

ROBERT BUCHANAN (essay date 1899)

The English public's first knowledge of Mr. Rudyard Kipling was gathered from certain brief anecdotal stories and occasional verses which began to be quoted about a decade ago in England, and which were speedily followed by cheap reprints of the originals, sold on every bookstall. They possessed one not inconsiderable attraction, in so far as they dealt with a naturally romantic country, looming very far off to English readers, and doubly interesting as one of our own great national possessions. We had had many works about India—works of description and works of fiction; and a passionate interest in them and in all that pertained to things Anglo-Indian, had been awakened by the Mutiny; but few writers had dealt with the ignobler details of military and civilian life, with the gossip of the messroom and the scandal of the governmental departments. Mr. Kipling's little Kodak-glimpses, therefore, seemed unusually fresh and new; nor would it be just to deny them the merits of great liveliness, intimate personal knowledge, and a certain unmistakable, though obviously cockney, humour. Although they dealt almost entirely with the baser aspects of our civilization, being chiefly devoted to the affairs of idle military men, savage soldiers, frisky wives and widows, and flippant civilians, they were indubitably bright and clever, and in the background of them we perceived, faintly but distinctly, the shadow of the great and wonderful national life of India. At any rate, whatever their merits were—and I hold their merits to be indisputable—they became rapidly popular, especially with the newspaper press, which hailed the writer as a new and quite amazing force in literature. So far as the lazy public was concerned, they had the one delightful merit of extreme brevity; he that ran might read them, just as he read *Tit-bits* and the society newspapers, and then treat them like the rose in Browning's poem:

> Smell, kiss, wear it—at last throw away!

Two factors contributed to their vogue; first, the utter apathy of general readers, too idle and uninstructed to study works of any length or demanding any contribution of serious thought on the reader's part, and eager for any amusement which did not remind them of the eternal problems which once beset humanity; and, second, the rapid growth in every direction of the military or militant spirit, of the Primrose League, of aggression abroad, and indifference at home to all religious ideals—in a word, of Greater Englandism, or Imperialism. For a considerable time Mr. Kipling poured out a rapid succession of these little tales and smoking-room anecdotes, to the great satisfaction of those who loved to listen to banalities about the English flag, seasoned with strong suggestions of social impropriety, as revealed in camps and barracks and the boudoirs of officers' mistresses and wives. The things seemed harmless enough, if not very elevating or ennobling. Encouraged by his success, the author attempted longer flights, with very indifferent results; though in the *Jungle Books,* for example, he got near to a really imaginative presentment of fine material, and,

if he had continued his work in that direction, criticism might have had little or nothing to say against him. But in an unfortunate moment, encouraged by the journalistic praise lavished on certain fragments of verse with which he had ornamented his prose effusions, he elected to challenge criticism as a poet—as, indeed, the approved and authoritative poet of the British empire; and the first result of this election, or, as I prefer to call it, this delusion and hallucination, was the publication of the volume of poems, partly new and partly reprinted, called *Barrack-Room Ballads*. (pp. 236-38)

The best of them is a ballad called '**Mandalay**', describing the feelings of a soldier who regrets the heroine of a little amour out in India, and it certainly possesses a real melody and a certain pathos. But in all the ballads, with scarcely an exception, the tone is one of absolute vulgarity and triviality, unredeemed by a touch of human tenderness and pity. Even the little piece called '**Soldier, Soldier**', which begins quite naturally and tenderly, ends with the cynical suggestion that the lady who mourns her old love had better take up at once with the party who brings the news of his death. . . . (p. 239)

With such touching sweetness and tender verisimilitude are these ballads of the barrack filled from end to end. Seriously, the picture they present is one of unmitigated barbarism. The Tommy Atkins they introduce is a drunken, swearing, coarse-minded Hooligan, for whom, nevertheless, our sympathy is eagerly entreated. Yet these pieces were accepted on their publication, not as cruel libel on the British soldier, but as a perfect and splendid representation of the red-coated patriot on whom our national security chiefly depended, and who was spreading abroad in every country the glory of our Imperial flag! (pp. 239-40)

Before proceeding further to estimate Mr. Kipling's contributions to literature, let me glance for a moment at his second book of verse, *The Seven Seas*. . . . It may be granted at once that it was a distinct advance on its predecessor, more restrained, less vulgar, and much more varied; here and there, indeed, as in the opening '**Song of the English**', it struck a note of distinct and absolute poetry. (p. 240)

The truth is, however, that [Mr. Kipling's] lamentable productions were concocted, not for sane men or self-respecting soldiers, not even for those who are merely ignorant and uninstructed, but for the 'mean whites' of our eastern civilization, the idle and loafing men in the street, and for such women, the well-dressed Doll Tearsheets of our cities, as shriek at their heels. Mr. Kipling's very vocabulary is a purely cockney vocabulary, even his Irishmen speaking a dialect which would cause amazement in the Emerald Isle, but is familiar enough in Seven Dials. Turning over the leaves of his poems, one is transported at once to the region of low-drinking dens and gin-palaces, of dirty dissipation and drunken brawls; and the voice we hear is always the voice of the soldier whose God is a cockney 'Gawd', and who is ignorant of the aspirate in either heaven or hell. Are there no Scotchmen in the ranks, no Highlanders, no men from Dublin or Tipperary, no Lancashire or Yorkshire men, no Welshmen, and no men of any kind who speak the Queen's English? It would seem not, if, the poet of '**The Sergeant's Weddin'** ' is to be trusted. Nor have our mercenaries, from the ranks upwards, any one thing, except brute courage, to distinguish them from the beasts of the field. This, at least, appears to be Mr. Kipling's contention, and even in the Service itself it seems to be undisputed. (p. 242)

But even a straw may indicate the direction in which the wind is blowing, and the vogue of Mr. Kipling, the cheerful acceptance of his banalities by even educated people, is so sure a sign of the times that it deserves and needs a passing consideration (p. 246)

Robert Buchanan, ''The Voice of the Hooligan?'' in Contemporary Review, *Vol. 76, December, 1899 (and reprinted in* Kipling: The Critical Heritage, *edited by Roger Lancelyn Green, Barnes & Noble, 1971, pp. 233-49).*

RICHARD Le GALLIENNE (essay date 1900)

Were Mr. Kipling to be considered as a writer of ballads and a teller of tales, and nothing besides, it had hardly seemed necessary to write a book about him; at all events, in the present stage of his career. Since the **"Recessional,"** however, he has been definitely more than that; while, long before it, if less explicitly, he was no less virtually a national influence. His Indian stories and songs did just that service for the Imperialistic idea which the imaginative man can do. They made us realise, as we had never done before, what a great dependency like India means, and what it means to maintain it; and, by this extensive object-lesson, made us sensitive as never before of the organic relation between us and our possessions in the furthest seas. Mr. Kipling, so to speak, roused the sleeping nerve centres of Imperialism. (pp. 127-28)

A certain amount of jingoism was naturally—and properly—inseparable from such work as the **"Barrack-Room Ballads"** and the Indian tales. A certain amount of jingoism, or chauvinism, or what you will, is inseparable from national existence. A nation could hardly go on existing if it did not believe itself the finest nation on earth, and in England's case, it is obviously something more than a private opinion. (pp. 128-29)

It may be said that the **"Recessional"** is symbolical, but, when using the terms of the Christian tradition for Englishmen, and in so momentous a connection, a poet has hardly more right to be symbolic than a clergyman in using those terms. Englishmen either don't understand, or are further strengthened in their natural hypocrisy; and the use of Christian terminology in England is sufficiently charged with hypocrisy without poets adding to it. Why not speak the truth? (p. 130)

I have not meant to imply for a moment that Mr. Kipling is consciously insincere in his vein of sacred Imperialism. At the same time one must be allowed to criticise an attitude so at variance with the temper of the bulk of his work. Heretofore he has always been cynically, even brutally, realistic about the facts and methods of empire. (p. 134)

On one side he is a sad-hearted pessimist, much given to that ''cold rage'' that

> seizes one at whiles
> To show the bitter old and wrinkled truth,

—and one may note his fondness for quoting James Thomson—on the other he reveals a strong vein of religious mysticism, now and again finding beautiful convincing expression, but at others degenerating into . . . clap-trap mysticism . . . , and into a religious sentimentalism which we may, not impertinently, trace to the Wesleyanism known to be in his blood.

It is quite possible for a man to believe two or more different things at once, or to think he believes them—which is about as deep as the roots of belief really go. He may, perhaps, give expression to the two or more beliefs side by side, without any insincerity. It is impossible, however, that the value of his utterances should not be diminished; and in spite of their great popular reception, and of their use politically, the **"Recessional"** and **"The White Man's Burden"** mark not an increase, but a decrease of Mr. Kipling's real authority. They are reactionary in the direction of sentimental superstition, and, however sincerely Mr. Kipling meant them, are serious reinforcements of British national hypocrisy.

But, of course, Mr. Kipling is nothing if not reactionary. If, on the one hand, he belongs to the age that invented the cinematograph and discovered the Röntgen rays, he is no less a product of the age that has produced the Dreyfus Case; an age that has looked on cold-eyed at the massacre of the Armenians and the suppression of the Finns; an age that is to see the reopening of a bull-ring at Havre. . . . At the present moment, as I have before had occasion to remark, in England—in fact, all over the world—the things of the mind are at a discount. There is in England just now a public opinion corresponding in no small degree to the present contempt in France for the ''intellectuels''; that is, for those who regard human life as something more than brute force, brutal rivalries, and brutal pleasures. We are in the thick of one of the most cynically impudent triumphs of the Philistines the world has seen. All that should be meant by civilisation is a mock. The once kindly fields of literature are beneath the heels of a set of literary rough-riders. All the nobler and gentler instincts of men and women are ridiculed as sentimentality. (pp. 137-39)

For this state of things in England Mr. Kipling is the most responsible voice. Of course, he did not create it. Such tidal moods of mankind go deeper than the influence of single personalities; or, indeed, if such cause them, they are usually long since dead, and the final effect springs from the cumulative power of their influence. Mr. Kipling's is not a lonely voice crying to-day what all will feel to-morrow. He is the voice of the tide at its height. Yet if the mood creates the voice, the voice powerfully reinforces the mood. There is a captaincy in expression, and such is the responsibility of the voice. And, at all events, if the voice has no real responsibility, one is obliged to treat it as though it had. Mr. Kipling stands for a certain view of life which some regret, and, as spokesman, is responsible for that view.

More than any other writer he has given expression to the physical force ideal at present fashionable, and the brutality inseparable from that ideal. (pp. 140-41)

One may recall Mr. Kipling's **"On Greenhow Hill."** . . . A native deserter had been troubling the camp at nights, and doubtless it was necessary that he should be caught and shot. However, entirely without instructions, Ortheris makes it known to his two friends that the game is to be his, and invites them to spend the day with him over against a valley along which every afternoon the deserter is known to make his way towards the camp. It is to be a sort of picnic. . . . (p. 142)

Now one understands that deserters have got to be shot, and that soldiers have no time to faint at the sight of blood, or shed tears upon their fallen foes. . . . But it is one thing to accept a hideous fact, and another to glorify it. Though in this story Mr. Kipling makes no overt comment, presenting the picture simply and nakedly as a piece of life, there has yet crept into the telling, as in all his stories of the kind, a certain tone of approval, even gusto, which leaves one in little doubt of his own feeling. It is murder as one of the fine arts, and the victim is—hardly a dog. And if he does not exactly glorify this particular example, he certainly has done his best to glorify the barbarous system in which it is but a minor episode. He is unmistakably the drum and fife in modern literature. (p. 144)

Richard Le Gallienne, in his Rudyard Kipling *(copyright, 1900, by John Lane; reprinted by permission of Dodd, Mead & Company), John Lane, 1900, 163 p.*

MAX BEERBOHM   (essay date 1903)

"George Fleming" is, as we know, a lady. Should the name Rudyard Kipling, too, be put between inverted commas? Is it, too, the veil of a feminine identity? If of Mr. Kipling we knew nothing except his work, we should assuredly make that conjecture. A lady who writes fiction reveals her sex clearlier through her portrayal of men than through any other of her lapses. And in Mr. Kipling's short stories, especially in **"The Light that Failed"** (that elongated short story which "George Fleming" has now adapted to the stage), men are portrayed in an essentially feminine manner, and from an essentially feminine point of view. They are men seen from the outside, or rather, not seen at all, but feverishly imagined. If to a lady who writes fiction you declare that men are not as she draws them, she will say (or, at least, think) that if they are not they ought to be. Mr. Kipling would say or think likewise about his own men. . . . [To Mr. Kipling the military typifies], in its brightest colours, the notion of manhood, manliness, man. And by this notion Mr. Kipling is permanently and joyously obsessed. That is why I say that his standpoint is feminine. The ordinary male fictionist has a knowledge of men as they are, but is preoccupied by a sentiment for women as he supposes them to be. The ordinary female fictionist has a knowledge of women as they are, but is preoccupied by a sentiment for men as she supposes them to be. (Between these two propositions lies the reason why so little of our fiction can be taken seriously.) Mr. Kipling is so far masculine that he has never displayed a knowledge of women as they are; but the unreality of his male creatures, with his worship of them, makes his name ring quaintly like a pseudonym.

In men's novels you will find, for the most part, that virility is taken for granted. The male characters are men, and, so far as their creator can see, there's an end of the matter. But, for a creatrix, there's only just the beginning of the matter. She *insists* that her male characters are men. That is a lurid fact which she herself constantly remembers, "and don't you," she seems to say to her reader, "forget it." The point is laboured by her both in the first person and through the lips of the male characters themselves. Into whatever circumstances of joy or sorrow she cast them, always they are acutely conscious of their manhood and acutely nervous of being mistaken for women. However urgent the other calls made by Fate on their attention, always they keep the corners of their eyes on the mirror, to assure themselves that their moustaches are bristling, and their chests expanding, and their pipes "drawing," satisfactorily. . . . In real life, men are not like that. At least, only the effeminate men are like that. The others have no preoccupation with manliness. They don't bother about it. That is the difference between them and the male creatures of female writers. It is, also, precisely, the difference between them and the male creatures of Mr. Kipling. Manliness on the one hand, manlydom on the other. Manlydom: find for me, if you can, a word more apt to Mr. Kipling's heroes.

Strange that these heroes, with their self-conscious blurtings of oaths and slang, their cheap cynicism about the female sex, their mutual admiration for one another's display of all those qualities which women admire in men, were not, as they so obviously seem to have been, fondly created out of the inner consciousness of a lady-novelist. There are, however, some respects wherein they differ from the heroes whom the average lady-novelist has made so painfully familiar to us. Women are rather squeamish, for the most part, and, though they idolise in men the strength which has been denied to themselves, they shrink from the notion of its excess. . . . Mr. Kipling is nothing—never was anything—if not unsqueamish. The ugly word, the ugly action, the ugly atmosphere—for all these he has an inevitable scent; and the uglier they be, the keener seems his relish of them. Strength, mere strength, is not enough to make a hero for him: his hero must be also a brute and a bounder. Writing of George Sand, Mr. Henry James once suggested that she, though she may have been to all intents and purposes a man, was not a gentleman. Conversely, it might be said that Mr. Kipling, as revealed to us in his fiction, is no lady. But he is not the less essentially feminine for that. (pp. 245-47)

Max Beerbohm, "Kipling's Entire" (originally published in The Saturday Review, *London, Vol. 95, No. 2468, February 14, 1903), in his* Around Theatres *(reprinted by permission of Mrs. Eva Reichmann), revised edition, Rupert Hart-Davis, 1953, pp. 245-48.*

FRANK MOORE COLBY   (essay date 1904)

There is no sign in Kipling's writings that he has ever learned anything from his critics or made any concessions to his public's demands. Take it or leave it, has been his attitude from the first. In his own good time, after people had despaired of him, he wrote **Kim**. We then told him distinctly that was the kind of thing we wanted of him, and asked him to do it again; whereupon he undertook the conduct of the British Government through the agency of bad verse. *The Islanders* may be true and statesmanlike, and rifle clubs may be founded on the strength of it, and cricketers may hang their heads for shame. Some say poetry is as poetry does; but not if it save the British Empire shall we ever admit the goodness of this poem or that it is a poem at all. It will be classed in the long run with Kipling's rhymed journalism, effective but transitory, a matter of a few fiery phrases, much overstraining and many flat lines. As mere literary pleasure-lovers, his readers have a right to complain. Bother his prophecies and devil take his reforms and all those ballads with a purpose, and letters on South Africa, and allegories on steam engines, and monodies on quartermaster's supplies. That is the way they feel about it, blaming not so much the subjects as Kipling's way with them. Critics who praise Kipling's faculty of throwing himself into a subject forget that one unfortunate result has been his total disappearance in it. He paints himself in with his local color. It has happened again and again. A man among men, but also a piston-rod among piston-rods. . . . From Kipling, as from a Tammany water main, we must take things as they come, knowing that protests are in vain.

He will not repent, or conform, or edit himself, or study how to please. But there is about him a sort of surly sincerity even at his worst. He at least is interested if you are not. He is pleased with each sudden new intimacy and exasperatingly glib in its jargon and would as lief lose readers as not. Bridge-building or whatever it may be—down he goes in it with a horrid splash of terminology and remains defiantly uninteresting for months at a time. It is not as if he tried to please and failed. It is his mood, not yours. He is merely muttering to himself the technicalities of his hobby, and criticism cannot shake it out of him. In the intervals of something like genius he is merely a pig-headed man. But the course has some advantages. He never does what is expected of him, but he sometimes does more. Whatever his sins are, they are not sins of subservience, and meanwhile he lives his own life. (pp. 25-7)

> *Frank Moore Colby, "The Writer Who Does Not Care," in his* Imaginary Obligations *(copyright, 1904 by Dodd, Mead and Company), Dodd, Mead, 1904 (and reprinted by Dodd, Mead & Company, 1913, pp. 25-32).*

GILBERT K. CHESTERTON (essay date 1905)

Now, the first and fairest thing to say about Rudyard Kipling is that he has borne a brilliant part in thus recovering the lost provinces of poetry. He has not been frightened by that brutal materialistic air which clings only to words; he has pierced through to the romantic, imaginative matter of the things themselves. He has perceived the significance and philosophy of steam and of slang. Steam may be, if you like, a dirty by-product of science. Slang may be, if you like, a dirty by-product of language. But at least he has been among the few who saw the divine parentage of these things, and knew that where there is smoke there is fire—that is, that wherever there is the foulest of things, there also is the purest. Above all, he has had something to say, a definite view of things to utter, and that always means that a man is fearless and faces everything. For the moment we have a view of the universe, we possess it.

Now, the message of Rudyard Kipling, that upon which he has really concentrated, is the only thing worth worrying about in him or in any other man. He has often written bad poetry, like Wordsworth. He has often said silly things, like Plato. He has often given way to mere political hysteria, like Gladstone. But no one can reasonably doubt that he means steadily and sincerely to say something, and the only serious question is, What is that which he has tried to say? Perhaps the best way of stating this fairly will be to begin with that element which has been most insisted by himself and by his opponents—I mean his interest in militarism. But when we are seeking for the real merits of a man it is unwise to go to his enemies, and much more foolish to go to himself.

Now, Mr. Kipling is certainly wrong in his worship of militarism, but his opponents are, generally speaking, quite as wrong as he. The evil of militarism is not that it shows certain men to be fierce and haughty and excessively warlike. The evil of militarism is that it shows most men to be tame and timid and excessively peaceable. The professional soldier gains more and more power as the general courage of a community declines. Thus the Pretorian guard became more and more important in Rome as Rome became more and more luxurious and feeble. . . . And as it was in ancient Rome so it is in contemporary Europe. (pp. 42-4)

And unconsciously Mr. Kipling has proved this, and proved it admirably. For in so far as his work is earnestly understood the military trade does not by any means emerge as the most important or attractive. He has not written so well about soldiers as he has about railway men or bridge builders, or even journalists. The fact is that what attracts Mr. Kipling to militarism is not the idea of courage, but the idea of discipline. . . . The modern army is not a miracle of courage; it has not enough opportunities, owing to the cowardice of everybody else. But

it is really a miracle of organization, and that is the truly Kiplingite ideal. Kipling's subject is not that valour which properly belongs to war, but that interdependence and efficiency which belongs quite as much to engineers, or sailors, or mules, or railway engines. And thus it is that when he writes of engineers, or sailors, or mules, or steam-engines, he writes at his best. The real poetry, the "true romance" which Mr. Kipling has taught, is the romance of the division of labour and the discipline of all the trades. He sings the arts of peace much more accurately than the arts of war. And his main contention is vital and valuable. Everything is military in the sense that everything depends upon obedience. (pp. 44-6)

Being devoted to this multitudinous vision of duty, Mr. Kipling is naturally a cosmopolitan. He happens to find his examples in the British Empire, but almost any other empire would do as well, or, indeed, any other highly civilized country. That which he admires in the British army he would find even more apparent in the German army; that which he desires in the British police he would find flourishing in the French police. The ideal of discipline is not the whole of life, but it is spread over the whole of the world. And the worship of it tends to confirm in Mr. Kipling a certain note of worldly wisdom, of the experience of the wanderer, which is one of the genuine charms of his best work.

The great gap in his mind is what may be roughly called the lack of patriotism—that is to say, he lacks altogether the faculty of attaching himself to any cause or community finally and tragically; for all finality must be tragic. He admires England, but he does not love her; for we admire things with reasons, but love them without reasons. He admires England because she is strong, not because she is English. There is no harshness in saying this, for, to do him justice, he avows it with his usual picturesque candour. In a very interesting poem, he says that—

> If England was what England seems

—that is, weak and inefficient; if England were not what (as he believes) she is—that is, powerful and practical—

> How quick we'd chuck 'er! But she ain't!

He admits, that is, that his devotion is the result of a criticism, and this is quite enough to put it in another category altogether from the patriotism of the Boers, whom he hounded down in South Africa. In speaking of the really patriotic peoples, such as the Irish, he has some difficulty in keeping a shrill irritation out of his language. The frame of mind which he really describes with beauty and nobility is the frame of mind of the cosmopolitan man who has seen men and cities.

> For to admire and for to see,
> For to be'old this world so wide.

He is a perfect master of that light melancholy with which a man looks back on having been the citizen of many communities, of that light melancholy with which a man looks back on having been the lover of many women. He is the philanderer of the nations. But a man may have learnt much about women in flirtations, and still be ignorant of first love; a man may have known as many lands as Ulysses, and still be ignorant of patriotism.

Mr. Rudyard Kipling has asked in a celebrated epigram what they can know of England who know England only. It is a far deeper and sharper question to ask, "What can they know of England who know only the world?" for the world does not include England any more than it includes the Church. The moment we care for anything deeply, the world—that is, all the other miscellaneous interests—becomes our enemy. Christians showed it when they talked of keeping one's self "unspotted from the world"; but lovers talk of it just as much when they talk of the "world well lost." Astronomically speaking, I understand that England is situated on the world; similarly, I suppose that the Church was a part of the world, and even the lovers inhabitants of that orb. But they all felt a certain truth—the truth that the moment you love anything the world becomes your foe. Thus Mr. Kipling does certainly know the world; he is a man of the world, with all the narrowness that belongs to those imprisoned in that planet. He knows England as an intelligent English gentleman knows Venice. He has been to England a great many times; he has stopped there for long visits. But he does not belong to it, or to any place; and the proof of it is this, that he thinks of England as a place. The moment we are rooted in a place, the place vanishes. We live like a tree with the whole strength of the universe. (pp. 46-9)

> Gilbert K. Chesterton, "On Mr. Rudyard Kipling and Making the World Small," in his Heretics (reprinted in Canada by permission of The Bodley Head), John Lane Company, 1905, pp. 38-53.

[ARTHUR] CONAN DOYLE (essay date 1907)

Which are the greatest short stories of the English language? . . . If it be not an impertinence to mention a contemporary I should certainly have a brace from Rudyard Kipling. His power, his compression, his dramatic sense, his way of glowing suddenly into a vivid flame, all mark him as a great master. But which are we to choose from that long and varied collection, many of which have claims to the highest? Speaking from memory, I should say that the stories of his which have impressed me most are 'The Drums of the Fore and Aft', 'The Man Who Would be King', 'The Man who Was', and 'The Brushwood Boy'. Perhaps, on the whole, it is the first two which I should choose to add to my list of masterpieces.

They are stories which invite criticism and yet defy it. The great batsman at cricket is the man who can play an unorthodox game, take every liberty which is denied to inferior players, and yet succeed brilliantly in the face of his disregard of law. So it is here. I should think the model of these stories is the most dangerous that any young writer could follow. There is digression, that most deadly fault in the short narrative; there is incoherence, there is want of proportion which makes the story stand still for pages and bound forward in a few sentences. But genius overrides all that, just as the great cricketer hooks the off ball and glides the straight one to leg. There is a dash, an exuberance, a full-blooded confident mastery which carries everything before it. Yes, no team of immortals would be complete which did not contain at least two representatives of Kipling. (pp. 302-03)

> [Arthur] Conan Doyle, "Kipling's Best Story," in his Through the Magic Door, Smith, Elder & Co., 1907 (and reprinted in Kipling: The Critical Heritage, edited by Roger Lancelyn Green, Barnes & Noble, Inc., 1971, pp. 302-03).

WALTER MORRIS HART (essay date 1918)

[The critic of Kipling's early stories] is impressed with the variety, with the richness, with the profusion and confusion of Kipling's methods. An attempt to give an orderly and reasonable account of it all may very properly be based on an analysis of the personality and training of Kipling himself. These can, I think, be shown to have developed naturally, if not inevitably, the prevailing characteristics of his technique. And these characteristics can, I think, be summed up in three adjectives: Kipling's technique is realistic, romantic, and intense.

The causes of Kipling's realism are not far to seek. He had, by nature, a certain clearness of vision; he had rather marvelous powers of observation; and he had an insatiable curiosity, a desire to turn all the pages of the book of life dwelling not too long upon any one of them. . . . Separated from his parents Kipling found himself at an early age face to face with the real and unfriendly world outside. It is not to be assumed that all of *Baa Baa, Black Sheep* is literaally true; but it may be safely regarded as an accurate summary of Kipling's own impression of this period of his life. He saw the seamy side of human nature—narrow religiosity, hypocrisy, jealousy; he "drank deep of the bitter waters of Hate, Suspicion, and Despair." We may read the later stories of school life, *Stalky and Company*, in the same way. Kipling is manifestly the spectacled Beetle of these tales, in the last one he is, indeed, no longer Beetle, but "I." He is not writing accurate autobiography; but he does give us many clews as to his own nature, his early tastes, his likes and dislikes, the kind of training he received in the United Services College. . . . Seventy-five per cent of its students were sons of officers. It did not set out to make scholars; and in pure scholarship Kipling—or Beetle—had no interest whatever. (pp. 111-112)

The result of [this early] training was Realism, realism of the peculiar type practised by Kipling, a realism essentially original. His originality as realist—not his originality as romancer, which is quite a different matter—is of the sort advocated by Flaubert in his famous advice to the young Maupassant, an originality which consists wholly in seeing things for oneself and expressing what one really sees. This realism of Kipling's is reflected in the representative character of his work, in the wealth of details of time and place and people. Yet Kipling never collects details as a scientist does; he is not seeking classified or classifiable knowledge; he is not a meteorologist, or a geographer, or an ethnologist. . . . He seeks, as he had sought as schoolboy and as journalist, facts that are in themselves humanly interesting or have some bearing upon a possible plot. He feels under no obligation to give us a complete or a precisely accurate picture of human life. "Get your facts first," Mark Twain once told him, ". . . and then you can distort 'em as much as you please." He seems to follow this advice. He limits himself to superlative characters; he takes no interest in the commonplace ones, nor yet in the queer or the problematic. His representative quality is thus limited and a matter of accident. He did not set out to cover his field with scientific thoroughness and system. You cannot imagine his stories, like Balzac's novels, classified as Scenes from Private Life, Scenes from Parisian Life, from Country Life, from Military Life, and so on. You cannot imagine Kipling conceiving a large plan and working it out on a large scale, in a thoroughgoing manner. He has rather the journalist-novelist's desire for what will make interesting copy; hence his superlative characters, and his picturesquely evil one as well. Hence his social satire—for what is social satire, after all, but a kind of glorified gossip, of artistic scandal? Yet for all his preoccupation with the scandalous side of human nature, Kipling's art is never naturalism; his characters are always something more than animals, they have human motives and ideals; and Kipling is too much the Anglo-Saxon, to follow Zola or Maupassant in their relentless pictures of the animal aspect of man.

In the psychology of these characters Kipling is never interested for its own sake. It is with him, though always present, yet never the chief element in the story. Its purpose is rather to increase the intensity of the whole. He does not deal with difficult psychological problems, with peculiar or unusual motives. And he emphasizes the external expression of emotion by word and gesture. Here again his method is not the result of analysis or of introspection but of observation.

In Structure, the result of this observation is a wealth of minor incidents which crowd in too rapidly to permit themselves to be gathered up and organized into great scenes. A further result is a certain incoherence. For Kipling, from the present point of view, may be classed with those realists who do not impress themselves much upon the structure of their stories, who prefer rather to follow the waywardness of events in real life. It is because of the brevity of his stories that Kipling does not wander very far. If they are not distinguished examples of proportion and coherence, they fulfil the other requirement of short-story structure, they are admirably concrete. (pp. 115-17)

Kipling's Moral Interpretations keep close to the facts; he is not given to speculation, to discovering new duties. He delights to emphasize *the fact* that many respectable people are bad (as many respectable people are aware). It is well that they should be reminded of their own shortcomings in order that they may judge less harshly the openly and honestly wicked. Doubtless his criticism of the English administration of India is sound enough; in any case it is concerned wholly with practical problems, not with such general questions as the duties of powerful nations with reference to the weak, for example. . . . (p. 117)

So much for Kipling the realist. He is also a romancer. And though his training seems to have pushed him mainly in the direction of realism, it pushed him somewhat in the direction of romance as well. (p. 118)

In *Stalky and Company* it appears that Beetle—that is the schoolboy Kipling—more fortunate than Black Sheep, has friends and is feared or respected. But he and Stalky and McTurk withdraw from the school activities to read and loaf and smoke in secret places of their own, often places which charm by pure beauty of landscape. The three are not understood by schoolfellows or masters, except the Head and the school chaplain; and here again there are hours of solitude with books. . . . It is clear, then, that beside the realistic impulse there existed a romantic impulse, less powerful, indeed, yet capable of putting its mark on the young author's work. The India, too, which he saw, was not without romance. The accounts of his actual journeys in *From Sea to Sea* show that he was sensitive to its beauty, its age, and its mystery.

As result of this romantic impulse there is, inevitably, an element of romance in Kipling's work; but it is much less pronounced than the realistic element. . . . Only now and then, in such stories as *The Strange Ride of Morrowbie Jukes,* in *The Man Who Would be King,* or in *Without Benefit of Clergy* and stories of its class, does he seem to offer an escape—manifestly not always an agreeable escape—from fact.

His own "problematic" personality, his early lack of adjustment to the world about him, is reflected in certain of the character-types which he creates. Mulvaney and Company have much the same relation to officers and fellow-soldiers that Stalky and Company have to masters and school-fellows. Only the Colonel understands one group; only the Head, the other. Both groups are irregular, highly individualized; their social functions are not easily classified. Yet they are not "queer" characters; they are merely superlative, idealized superstructure resting upon a solid basis of fact. This basis of fact is largely conveyed by vividly conjured up mental images, by a kind of imagination which is close to memory.

In the variety of races represented there is something of that exotism which not uncommonly accompanies the romantic tendency. A phase or extension of the same principle is involved in Kipling's power of tempering his own mind to enter another's soul, be that other English officer or official or child, or native, man or woman.

In the matter of Structure, it is manifest that the imagination of the journalist and writer of fiction has been at work in the perception and selection of facts, of such facts as are humanly interesting. The results of this imaginative observation are combined with imaginative spontaneity, with an unconsidered naturalness, which does not permit the reader's perception of form to stand in the way of his seeing, hearing, feeling with the writer, reflecting the mood of the story, answering not to an intellectual but to an emotional appeal. And while, in the invention of plot, the imagination as a rule runs close to what may well have happened, it breaks free, now and again, from the world of observed or observable events and creates astounding adventures—serious or tragic, like those of the Man Who Would be King—comic, like those of Krishna Mulvaney.

The third quality of Kipling's work, its intensity, is more striking than the other two, and perhaps more influential in the determination of his technique. Like his imaginative or romantic quality, it springs primarily from personality, from the problematic character of the writer. His early ill adjustment to the world about him led, as always with the strong and courageous, to vigorous self-assertion. (pp. 118-21)

This intense personality, intensified by the vicissitudes of his training, Kipling was able to project into his work, so that one may quite safely affirm that of all short-stories in the English language Kipling's are the most intense.

In every paragraph that he wrote you feel his vital energy. It reveals itself in the general air of spontaneity, in a certain scorn of the conventionalities of form, in the spontaneous overflow of feelings evoked by the story, in the vigorous appeal to the reader's sympathy. When Kipling is realistic or romantic he is intensely realistic or romantic. That is, it is the quality of intensity that raises realism and romance to a degree so high; intensity that seems to compel the elaboration and determine the nature of every one of the elements of narration. The time of action must be the present, for the situation must be new and vital, not such as to call up tender regret for the past, or any of the milder emotions with which we contemplate what is finished and put away. It is significant that there is in *Baa Baa, Black Sheep* no delight, no regret, no sentiment, in memories of childhood, but only present indignation. . . . (pp. 121-22)

Kipling's intensity expresses itself in the choice of characters—intensely living, active, effective, self-assertive. The reader, again, is conscious of Kipling's sympathy with these persons, even in defiance of accepted morals; and of his delight in his discovery of their characteristic gestures and their slang or jargon. Though, here, at times, one intensity clashes with another: Kipling's own personality shines too clearly through that of his creatures.

Kipling delights to depict intense emotion—tragic or comic or sentimental; elemental emotions, which stand out clearly, require no hair-splitting analysis. Here his intensity often takes the peculiarly Anglo-Saxon form of repression or belittling of emotion, resulting in those breaks in mood which are his chief defect. These are due also to an intense conviction of the reality of emotion, to a strong personal prejudice against anything like sentiment, which would permit the enjoyment or the inducing of emotion for its own sake. (pp. 122-23)

It is this same intensity of conviction that chiefly distinguishes the moral interpretations and comments of the stories. You get the impression that Kipling has observed widely and felt deeply, not that he has reasoned carefully. His cocksureness whether right or wrong is prejudice, not science. His satire is marked by intense antipathies, as to missionaries, M.P.'s, and respectable hypocrites. His humor, similarly, is marked by intense tolerance, as of Thomas Atkins, the junior subaltern, or the woman of the world. In a philosophy which is felt rather than reasoned, there are naturally contradictions; it is not surprising that Kipling should appear as advocate of The System, and at the same time glorify the self-assertion of the individual in conflict with it.

Manifestly, then, in spite of the strong tendency to moralize, in spite of the variety and certainty of opinion which we found to be characteristics of Kipling's work, the main strength of his stories does not, by any means, lie in the moral significance. He has transcribed a vast deal of life, but he has found no clue to its meaning. The natural bent of his genius is observation, imagination, intensity, not thought, not intellect. This is not, of course, to say that he is lacking in intellectual powers. He is a genius. But he is not a genius as thinker, or even as poet or novelist of the primarily intellectual type. This is merely to state the sufficiently obvious fact that he is not a Carlyle, an Emerson, a Goethe, a George Eliot. His genius does not run to abstract reasoning; nor does it run to that other expression of intellect and judgment, to sense of form. I mean simply that his *special strength* does not lie in form; I mean that he is not for style, an Addison; that he is not for structural technique, a Poe or a Stevenson or a Mérimée or a Maupassant. (pp. 125-26)

Kipling remains to the end what his training and his personality made him at the beginning of his career. His greatness still lies, not in his reasoning powers, not in his moral interpretation or criticism of life, not in his sense of form, but rather in his sense of fact, vivid, concrete, and humanly interesting; in a power of imagination closely related to this sense of fact; in an emotional or even sensational appeal; and in intensity, in vital energy. With the single exception of Chaucer, he is the most powerful personality of all those who have expressed themselves in the short-story. (p. 220)

> *Walter Morris Hart, in his* Kipling: The Story-Writer *(reprinted by permission of the University of California Press), University of California Press, 1918, 225 p.*

H. G. WELLS (essay date 1920)

It was quite characteristic of the times [the late nineties] that Mr. Kipling should lead the children of the middle and upper-class British public back to the Jungle, to learn 'the law', and that in his book *Stalky & Co.* he should give an appreciative description of the torture of two boys by three others, who have by a subterfuge tied up their victims helplessly before revealing their hostile intentions.

It is worth while to give a little attention to this incident in *Stalky & Co.,* because it lights up the political psychology of the British Empire at the close of the nineteenth century very vividly. The history of the last half-century is not to be understood without an understanding of the mental twist which this story exemplifies. The two boys who are tortured are 'bullies', that is the excuse of their tormentors, and these latter have further been excited to this orgy by a clergyman. Nothing can restrain the gusto with which they (and Mr. Kipling) set about the job. Before resorting to torture, the teaching seems to be, see that you pump up a little justifiable moral indignation, and all will be well. If you have the authorities on your side, then you cannot be to blame. Such, apparently, is the simple doctrine of this typical imperialist. But every bully has to the best of his ability followed that doctrine since the human animal developed sufficient intelligence to be consciously cruel.

Another point in the story is very significant indeed. The headmaster and his clerical assistant are both represented as being privy to the affair. They want this bullying to occur. Instead of exercising their own authority, they use these boys, who are Mr. Kipling's heroes, to punish the two victims. Headmaster and clergyman turn a deaf ear to the complaints of an indignant mother. All this Mr. Kipling represents as a most desirable state of affairs. In this we have the key to the ugliest, most retrogressive, and finally fatal idea of modern imperialism; the idea of a *tacit conspiracy between the law and illegal violence.* . . . (pp. 306-07)

> *H. G. Wells, "The Realities and Imagination of the Nineteenth Century," in his* The Outline of History: Being a Plain History of Life and Mankind, *Vol. II (© 1920 by H. G. Wells; reprinted with permission of Professor G. P. Wells),* The Macmillan Company, *1920 (and reprinted as "H. G. Wells on Kipling: 1920," in* Kipling: The Critical Heritage, *edited by Roger Lancelyn Green, Barnes & Noble, Inc., pp. 306-07).*

BHUPAL SINGH (essay date 1934)

Kipling's work relating to India was mainly done between 1888 and 1891 and is embodied in *Plain Tales from the Hills, Soldiers Three and other Stories, Wee Willie Winkie and other Stories,* and *Life's Handicap.* These four volumes cover ninety-six stories, taking the eight scenes of the story of the Gadsbys as a single story. All these stories have a genuine Indian atmosphere about them, and deal with Kipling's own time and 'own people'. They are the product of a vividly realized personal experience, shrewd observation and sympathy. In most of the stories, remarkable for their variety both of treatment and subject-matter, Kipling celebrates and perpetuates a certain type of Anglo-Indian character with which he was thoroughly familiar, that is, the hard-working and self-sacrificing civil servant, or the subaltern doing his duty under difficult conditions. In some stories he shows a sympathetic understanding of the British soldier in India, full of humour and tolerance. A large group gives a picture of Anglo-Indian society in holiday mood, its main occupation being 'playing tennis with the seventh commandment'. A smaller group deals with Indians in their contact with the English. (p. 68)

Out of the ninety-six stories mentioned above only twenty-eight may be said to be Indian as distinguished from Kipling's Anglo-Indian stories. These stories may again be divided into two groups, one consisting of anecdotes, sketches and stories in which Indians alone play the chief part, and the second comprising those in which Indians are minor characters: a khan-saman, a khitmatgar, a sais, or a subordinate. In many of the Anglo-Indian stories, Indian characters who are introduced are members of an Anglo-Indian household (menials); they do not contribute anything of importance to the development of the plot or its denouement. To the purely Indian group of Kipling's stories belong, *In the House of Suddhoo, The Gate of a Hundred Sorrows, The Story of Muhammad Din,* and *To be Filed for Reference* from the *Plain Tales from the Hills;* the eight stories that make up *In Black and White;* and *The Head of the District, Through the Fire, Finance of the Gods, Bubbling Well Road,* and *The City of Dreadful Night,* from *Life's Handicap.* Even the most ardent admirer of Kipling will not claim any extraordinary merit for these stories (possibly excepting two). They neither show much knowledge of, nor sympathy for, Indian life and character. They at best touch the outskirts of Indian life, often in its abnormal, crude and unimportant aspects. . . . The life of an ordinary Indian is as little mysterious as that of an ordinary European, which Kipling, having lived in India, must have known. Yet it is the abnormal and the mysterious element in our life which Kipling constantly emphasizes. *The Return of Imray* is not convincing. The motive is not adequate. A servant may kill his English master, but only from a stronger motive than that mentioned in the story. Similarly little Tobrah, vOwho pushes his helpless blind sister into the water to save her from starvation, is not a representative character. It is a cynical treatment of a heart-rending situation. Tobrah is not a normal Indian child, nor Bisesa a normal Hindu widow, nor Bahadur Khan a typical servant. (pp. 70-2)

Four stories, *The Judgment of Dungara, At Howli Thana, Gemini,* and *The Sending of Dara Da,* are satirical in intent. Satire, as distinguished from humour, skims the surface of life; it never goes deep enough. *The Judgment of Dungara* is a satire on missionaries labouring to win the millions of India for Christ. But they do not know the clever native priests they have to deal with. Just as in *The Naulahka* all the work of American doctors is rendered futile in a day, similarly in this story the leading converts of the Tübingen Mission revert to the worship of the great God Dungara, 'the God of Things as They Are'. . . . The same cynical attitude of Kipling towards missionaries is illustrated in the return of the heart-broken Lispeth to her ancestral gods. The satire, however, spoils this story, which is essentially tragic. *At Howli Thana* is a satire on native police who are in collusion with the dacoits against whom they are supposed to operate. *Gemini* is meant to illustrate the native proverb quoted by Kipling at the beginning of the story: 'Great is the justice of the White Man—greater the power of a lie.' . . . It is not often that Kipling travels beyond the borders of the India that he knew, the India of Pathan servants and orderlies, of scamps and cut-throats, of superstitious Suddhoos and fanatical lepers; but whenever he attempts to do so, as in this story, the result is disappointing. The common belief among Englishmen that Indians think very lightly of perjury is thus expressed in *The Bronckhorst Divorce Case:*

> No jury, we knew, would convict a man on the
> criminal count on native evidence in a land
> where you can buy a murder charge, including
> the corpse, all complete for fifty-four rupees.

There is no justification for sweeping statements of this character. *The Head of the District* propagates the view that the martial races of India would most strongly object to Indianization of the administration, that they would sooner accept sweepers as their rulers than, for example, Bengalees. . . .

Such stories leave a very unpleasant impression on the mind. They encourage racial pride and engender racial ill-will.

There is a group of short stories dealing with Eurasian and Christian life, and mixed marriages. This group contains some of the best of Kipling's purely Indian stories. *His Chance in Life* and *To be Filed for Reference* deal with what Kipling calls the 'Borderline where the last drop of white blood ends and the full tide of black sets in'. (pp. 72-4)

No treatment of Kipling as a writer of Indian stories would be complete without an examination of *Kim* and *The Naulahka*. These novels may be so called because each covers more than four hundred pages. Mr. Edward Farley Oaten would even go so far as to say that to 'call it [*Kim*] a work of fiction is a little misleading'. He regards it as 'the greatest masterpiece of journalism by the greatest living journalist'. . . . *Kim* cannot be dismissed as journalism. It is a work of high art. But so far as the 'magic of the East' is concerned, there is not more of it in *Kim* than in Kipling's other stories dealing with India, if the magic of the East is taken to mean real and normal India. Both Kim and the Lama, the chief characters in the story, are not Indians at all. Kim's father was an Irish soldier. . . . As an orphaned half-caste, Kim wanders in the streets of Lahore, and has special opportunities of learning the native language and of becoming familiar with scenes and places unknown to Englishmen in India. In his precocious sharpness he is the half-brother of Becky Sharp [in William Thackeray's *Vanity Fair*]; moreover he was brought up in the same school of poverty as Becky. But in spite of his stealthy prowls through the dark gullies and lanes of Lahore, his knowledge of India is confined to the 'Ajaib Ghur', the serais, the scenes and sights on the roads, cantonments of British soldiers, a Eurasian school, the house of Huneefa in Lucknow, a curio-dealer's shop in Simla, and the hills where he wandered in the Secret Service. Such experiences are not enough to give him a knowledge of real India. Kim's India, in spite of its picturesqueness, is the superficial India as an outsider sees it.

An examination of Kipling's other characters discloses the range of Kipling. In *Kim* we see the clever but unscrupulous border Pathan, Mahbub Ali of the Secret Service, who drinks brandy against the law of the Prophet and pursues 'the Flower of Delight with the feet of intoxication' in the gate of Harpies; the old Sikh Rissaldar, who had been in nineteen pitched battles and who is fond of singing the song of Nikal Seyn before Delhi; the spruce scribe, the young Kayeth letter-writer of Umballa, who writes a letter to Mahbub Ali on a promise of double payment; Colonel Creighton of the Survey Department, who takes a keen interest in the education of Kim; the wonderful Lurgan Sahib of Simla, who heals sick pearls; the talkative Babu Hurree Chunder Mookerjee, heavy-haunched, bull-necked, and an M.A. of Calcutta University, whose life's ambition was to be able to write F.R.S. after his name; the simple Jat from Jandiala; the bruised Mahratta E 23 of the Secret Service whom Kim helps to become a sadhu; and many other persons who do not play any part either in the Game or the Quest but appear and disappear like figures on the screen.

In spite of the variety and range of Kipling's characters and scenes, in spite of his great descriptive power, keen observation, and vivid imagination, the soul of India remains hidden from his eyes. What Kipling saw and understood, he has reproduced cleverly; what he loved he has recreated with the skill and vigour of an imaginative artist. But Kipling's range of observation, like that of most other Anglo-Indian writers, was limited to what could be seen on the surface. The heat of the plains in summer, scenes on a railway platform, life in a Roman Catholic School, or people jostling one another in crowded bazaars of a city like Benares, do not, however, make the whole of India.

Kipling has caught and reproduced the picturesqueness of India, but he is more conscious of her 'inherent rottenness'. India has 'the merit of being two-thirds sham; looking pretty on paper only'. He is painfully conscious of 'the want of atmosphere in the painter's sense'. There are no half tints worth noticing. Men stand out all crude and raw, 'with nothing to tone them down and nothing to scale them against'. India is a place beyond all others where one must not take things too seriously—the midday sun always excepted. Kipling himself did not take India seriously. In *By Word of Mouth* he says that it is best to know nothing. Unlike the Law Member of the Viceroy's Council, he knows that no one can tell what the natives think unless one mixes with them 'with the varnish off'. Kipling seems to have made some efforts to understand India with the varnish off. He visited the house of Suddhoo near Taxali Gate, he talked with Janoo and Azizun, the ladies of the city, in the recess of carved bow windows . . . ; he took interest in the intrigues of the sleek and shiny young men of fashion for whom Kim executed commissions. But all this is not enough to understand India. It is like trying to understand Europe from its night clubs, music halls, and Latin or Chinese quarters. (pp. 77-80)

Kipling's merits as an artist are great. He occupies an immortal place in the history of English literature, both as a poet and a story-teller. His portraiture of English and Anglo-Indian life and character has won universal approbation. But our examination of his Indian stories does not show that he has been more successful in coming nearer the soul of India than most of his countrymen. (p. 82)

> *Bhupal Singh, "Rudyard Kipling: A Survey of His Indian Stories," in his* A Survey of Anglo-Indian Fiction *(reprinted by permission of Oxford University Press), Oxford University Press, Oxford, 1934 (and reprinted by Rowman and Littlefield, 1974, pp. 68-82).*

ANDRÉ MAUROIS (essay date 1935)

Between 1900 and 1920, Kipling appealed to the rising generations in France as few French writers were able to do. His mannerisms ("but that is another story . . .") became French mannerisms. His legends inspired the games and moulded the ideas of French children. (p. 3)

It is curious to observe how Kipling's fame, as it grew and spread over the whole world, found a considerable body of opponents in England itself. What had happened? Three things. First came the usual reaction of the critics against the public, when the public has adopted their first favourable judgements with excessive unanimity. A second was something more subtle, a kind of shrinking modesty which the Kiplingesque heroes were bound to develop on seeing the machinery of their virtues thus taken to pieces. It is a peculiarity of the Kipling hero not to know that he is either a brave man or a wise man. He is silent, especially concerning his own actions. In reading Kipling, who unveiled him to others, and doubtless also to himself, he may have felt faintly vexed. And thirdly, there was the fact that in England Kipling's work was for a time associated with a political doctrine, and party spirit is often unable to distinguish between genius and incidentals. When the passage of time has stripped his work clear of associations, it will be seen that Kipling was not only the greatest English writer of our generation, but the only modern writer who has created enduring myths. (p. 4)

[Kipling has been spoken of] as the literary aspect of the British Empire. But the phrase hardly suffices to explain the intensity of feeling which Kipling's work gave to so many young Frenchmen at the time when the first translations were published. *Kim, Stalky and Co.,* and *The Jungle Book* were then our favourite books. In the letters of Riviere and Alain Fournier I find echoes of my own enthusiasm, which I shared with my fellow schoolboys at Rouen. How little we thought of British imperialism, as we read *City of Sleep,* or *The Bridge Builders!* What we sought in Kipling, apart from the admirable stories, was first and foremost *an heroic conception of life.*

That conception was neither exclusively British, nor exclusively imperial. Kipling has shown that it was one and the same for the Roman official on the Welsh Marches and for the British officer isolated in the Himalaya, or for the French officer isolated in the Atlas. Again, it was neither exclusively military, nor colonial. Whatever the milieu he described, Kipling discerned amongst men a constant and necessary hierarchy, the framework of an heroic society which takes shape whenever a human group has a difficult task to accomplish.

At the summit are the heroes, who dominate its elements of idleness, envy, fear, ambition and desire, or at least drive these passions under a cloak of silence, and so obviate that disorder which, unless the heroes take matters in hand, will reduce any society to a state of impotence. When the heroes are exhausted and order is virtually restored, it is the turn of the great administrators. These "great sahibs" are strong, cautious, and silent. They use few words among themselves in their concerns, a native sage is made to remark, and fewer still when they talk about them to an outsider. By skill and self-control the statesmen, for a certain time, maintain the societies created by the heroes. Then the self-seekers and talkers, encouraged by the apparent solidity of the established order, come to the forefront, and then begins the reign of the politicians and exploiters, destroyers of any society, and the cycle starts again.

Kipling has depicted those three classes of men. With the men of action, the pioneering heroes, he was familiar at an early age, in India. . . . The man of action is omnipresent in Kipling's work, whether he is building bridges or fighting famine, a Gurkhas' officer or a cotton-planter. His character is of the simplest. Neither love nor family counts for him so long as his day's work is not accomplished. He trusts nobody to take his place, unless it be other men of action, younger perhaps, but like himself, whom he treats as sons, as can be seen from the fact that he chooses the hardest tasks for them. But none others would he honour by subjecting them to the ceaseless toil which he imposes on himself.

The man of action matches himself against the fierce resistance of the forces of nature. To think out a bridge and design it—this is comparatively easy: a man is alone with his drawing-paper. But when he is building a bridge, he must reckon with chains that give, pulleys that snap, workmen who mutiny, not to mention the anger of the river and the ever-present wrath of the gods. For the gods hold in horror the victories of men, as the Greeks well knew. The hero accepts these strokes of fate with perfect equanimity. And to this Kipling gave full expression in the four closely packed stanzas of his famous poem, *If.* (pp. 15-17)

The hero gives his service neither for fame nor for coin, but for the honour of serving. (p. 18)

[The] heroic society, in the Roman legion or the Anglo-Indian regiment, amongst administrators or engineers, has always been built on a model which is practically unique. At the head is the Chief, who conceives, commands and controls—the real chief, for Kipling has no fondness or indulgence for the man who has the function without the virtues. He enjoys showing us, in *Tod's Amendment,* the ignorance of certain legal members and how a child can instruct them. In *Puck of Pook's Hill* he delights to show Maximus, the all-powerful general, soon perhaps to be a Roman Emperor, being quietly threatened by a centurion. And he is merciless towards the apoplectic colonel who pays attention to the wives of his junior officers. But it is because he appreciates the worth of the real chief that Kipling is so stern to the unworthy.

Beside the chief, the subaltern. The subaltern does heroic deeds, but changes the subject of conversation if anyone ventures to mention it. Some day he will be the chief's successor, but he never thinks of that day and would be outraged if anyone else raised the question. . . . (pp. 18-19)

In the next grade one finds, in the Army, the non-commissioned officer, or in the engineering shops, the foreman. He too, in his way, is a chief. Kipling has great respect for the N.C.O. . . . If the chief rules by his heroic virtues, the N.C.O. imposes his authority by his respect for discipline and by his amazing efficiency.

And in the last grade of the race of heroes (last, that is, in order, not in worth or importance), come the good soldier and the good workman. It is about them that Kipling wrote one of his finest poems, *The Sons of Martha.* . . . (pp. 19-20)

A born writer of books, reared by "the Famous Men" in a respect for the life that is not in books, finds himself at an early age, in India, in close touch with the life of men of action and the life of the native races. From these contacts he draws not only the subject-matter of stories which illustrate a Western philosophy of action, but also a truly Oriental sense of the marvellous. Thanks to him, the imagination of men bereft of the miracles of the East has been enabled suddenly to plunge into very deep layers of ancestral memory. Scratching at the surface of mere talk, he has been able to rediscover, underneath the man of the machine age, the man of the Bible and of Homer, underneath the subaltern of Gurkhas, the centurion of the legions. This doctrine has resulted in giving the British Empire "a mystico-literary justification." This is a historic fact, but an ephemeral accident: his enduring qualities are more deeply rooted. The things which he has described and sung are the eternal virtues which give a man the faculty of leadership and give a race the power of survival. . . . (p. 55)

André Maurois, "Rudyard Kipling," in his Prophets and Poets, *translated by Hamish Miles (copyright © 1935 by Harper & Brothers; reprinted by permission of the author and the author's agents, Scott Meredith Literary Agency, Inc., 845 Third Avenue, New York, New York 10022), Harper & Brothers Publishers, 1935, pp. 1-55.*

EDMUND WILSON (essay date 1941)

The eclipse of the reputation of Kipling, which began about 1910, twenty-five years before Kipling's death and when he was still only forty-five, has been of a peculiar kind. Through this period he has remained, from the point of view of sales, an immensely popular writer. The children still read his children's books; the college students still read his poetry; the men and women of his own generation still reread his early work. But he has in a sense been dropped out of modern literature. The more serious-minded young people do *not* read him; the critics do not take him into account. During the later years of his life and even at the time of his death, the logic of his artistic development attracted no intelligent attention. (p. 86)

The publication of Kipling's posthumous memoirs—*Something of Myself for My Friends Known and Unknown*—has enabled us to see more clearly the causes for the anomalies of Kipling's career.

First of all, he was born in India, the son of an English artist and scholar, who had gone out to teach architectural sculpture at the Fine Arts School in Bombay and who afterwards became curator of the museum at Lahore. (p. 87)

The second important influence in Kipling's early life has not hitherto been generally known, though it figures in the first chapter of *The Light That Failed* and furnished the subject of *Baa, Baa, Black Sheep,* one of the most powerful things he ever wrote. This story had always seemed rather unaccountably to stand apart from the rest of Kipling's work by reason of its sympathy with the victims rather than with the inflictors of a severely repressive discipline; and its animus is now explained by a chapter in Kipling's autobiography and by a memoir recently published by his sister. When Rudyard Kipling was six and his sister three and a half, they were farmed out for six years in England with a relative of Kipling's father. John Lockwood Kipling was the son of a Methodist minister, and this woman was a religious domestic tyrant in the worst English tradition of Dickens and Samuel Butler. (pp. 87-8)

He was next sent to a public school in England. This school, the United Services College, at a place called Westward Ho!, had been founded by Army and Navy officers who could not afford to send their sons to the more expensive schools. The four and a half years that Kipling spent there gave him *Stalky & Co.* . . . (pp. 90-1)

[At sixteen Kipling] went back to his family in India, and there he remained for seven years. . . . [He] started right in on a newspaper in Lahore as sole assistant to the editor, and worked his head off for a chief he detested. . . . He wrote short stories called *Plain Tales from the Hills,* which were run to fill up space in the paper, and he brought out a book of verse. His superiors disapproved of his flippancy, and when he finally succeeded in leaving India, the managing director of the paper, who had considered him overpaid, told the young man that he could take it from him that he would never be worth anything more than four hundred rupees a month.

The Kipling of these early years is a lively and sympathetic figure. A newspaper man who has access to everything, the son of a scholar who has studied the natives, he sees the community, like Asmodeus, with all the roofs removed. He is interested in the British of all classes and ranks—the bored English ladies, the vagabond adventurers, the officers and the soldiers both. 'Having no position to consider,' he writes, 'and my trade enforcing it, I could move at will in the fourth dimension. I came to realize the bare horrors of the private's life, and the unnecessary torments he endured. . . . Lord Roberts, at that time, Commander-in-chief of India, who knew my people, was interested in the men, and—I had by then written one or two stories about soldiers—the proudest moment of my young life was when I rode up Simla Mall beside him on his usual explosive red Arab, while he asked me what the men thought about their accommodations, entertainment-rooms, and the like. I told him, and he thanked me as gravely as though I had been a full Colonel.' He is already tending to think about people in terms of social and racial categories; but his interest in them at this time is also personal. . . . And he gives us in his soldier stories, along with the triumphs of discipline and the exploits of the native wars, the hunger of Private Ortheris for London when the horror of exile seizes him; the vanities and vices of Mulvaney which prevent him from rising in the service (*The Courting of Dinah Shadd,* admired by Henry James, is one of the stories of Kipling which sticks closest to unregenerate humanity); even the lunatic obsessions and the crack-up of the rotter gentleman ranker in *Love-o'-Women.* (pp. 93-5)

The natives Kipling probably understood as few Englishmen did in his time; certainly he presented them in literature as nobody had ever done. That Hindu other self of his childhood takes us through into its other world. The voices of alien traditions—in the monologues of *In Black and White*—talk an English which translates their own idiom; and we hear of great lovers and revengers who live by an alien code; young men who have been educated in England and, half-dissociated from native life, find themselves impotent between two civilizations; fierce Afghan tribesmen of the mountains, humble people who have been broken to the mines; loyal Sikhs and untamed mutineers. It is true that there is always the implication that the British are bringing to India modern improvements and sounder standards of behavior. But Kipling is obviously enjoying for its own sake the presentation of the native point of view, and the whole Anglo-Indian situation is studied with a certain objectivity.

He is even able to handle without horror the mixture of the black and the white. 'The "railway folk,"' says Mr. E. Kay Robinson, who worked with him on the paper in Lahore, 'that queer colony of white, half white and three-quarters black, which remains an uncared-for and discreditable excrescence upon British rule in India, seemed to have unburdened their souls to Kipling of all their grievances, their poor pride, and their hopes. Some of the best of Kipling's work is drawn from the lives of these people.' . . . (pp. 95-6)

Through all [his] years of school and of newspaper work, with their warping and thwarting influences, Kipling worked staunchly at mastering his craft. For he had been subjected to yet another influence which has not been mentioned here. His father was a painter and sculptor, and two of his mother's sisters were married to artists—one to Edward Poynter, the Academician, and the other to the pre-Raphaelite, Burne-Jones. . . . He had had from his childhood the example of men who loved the arts for their own sake and who were particularly concerned about craftsmanship. . . . Kipling evidently owes his superiority as a craftsman to most of even the ablest English writers of fiction of the end of the century and the early nineteen hundreds, to this inspiration and training. Just as the ballad of *Danny Deever* derives directly from the ballad of *Sister Helen,* so the ideal of an artistic workmanship which shall revert to earlier standards of soundness has the stamp of William Morris and his circle. In 1878, when Rudyard was twelve years old, his father had taken him to the Paris Exhibition and insisted that he learn to read French. The boy had then conceived an admiration for the civilization of the French which evidently contributed later to his interest in perfecting the short story in English. (pp. 96-7)

With such a combination of elements, what might one not expect? It is not surprising to learn that the young Kipling contemplated, after his return to England, writing a colonial *Comédie Humaine.* 'Bit by bit, my original notion,' he writes, 'grew into a vast, vague conspectus—Army and Navy List, if you like—of the whole sweep and meaning of things and efforts and origins throughout the Empire.' Henry James, who wrote an appreciative preface for a collection of Kipling's early stories, said afterwards that he had thought at that time that it might perhaps be true that Kipling 'contained the seeds of an English Balzac.'

What became of this English Balzac? Why did the author of the brilliant short stories never develop into an important novelist?

Let us return to *Baa, Baa, Black Sheep* and the situation with which it deals. Kipling says that his Burne-Jones aunt was never able to understand why he had never told anyone in the family about how badly he and his sister were being treated, and he tries to explain this on the principle that 'children tell little more than animals, for what comes to them they accept as eternally established,' and says that 'badly-treated children have a clear notion of what they are likely to get if they betray the secrets of a prison-house before they are clear of it.' But *is* this inevitably true? Even young children do sometimes run away. And, in any case, Kipling's reaction to this experience seems an abnormally docile one. After all, Dickens made David Copperfield bite Mr. Murdstone's hand and escape; and he makes war on Mr. Murdstone through the whole of his literary career. But though the anguish of these years had given Kipling a certain sympathy with the neglected and persecuted, and caused him to write this one moving short story, it left him—whether as the result of the experience itself or because he was already so conditioned—with a fundamental submissiveness to authority.

Let us examine the two books in which Kipling deals, respectively, with his schooldays and with his youth in India: *Stalky & Co.* and *Kim.* These works are the products of the author's thirties, and *Kim,* at any rate, represents Kipling's most serious attempt to allow himself to grow to the stature of a first-rate creative artist. Each of these books begins with an antagonism which in the work of a greater writer would have developed into a fundamental conflict; but in neither *Stalky* nor *Kim* is the conflict ever permitted to mount to a real crisis. Nor can it even be said to be resolved: it simply ceases to figure as a conflict. In *Stalky,* we are at first made to sympathize with the baiting of the masters by the schoolboys as their rebellion against a system which is an offense against human dignity; but then we are immediately shown that all the ragging and flogging are justified by their usefulness as a training for the military caste which is to govern the British Empire. The boys are finally made to recognize that their headmaster not only knows how to dish it out but is also able to take it, and the book culminates in the ridiculous scene—which may perhaps have its foundation in fact but is certainly flushed by a hectic imagination—in which the Head, in his inflexible justice, undertakes personally to cane the whole school while the boys stand by cheering him wildly.

There is a real subject in *Stalky & Co.,* but Kipling has not had the intelligence to deal with it. He cannot see around his characters and criticize them, he is not even able properly to dramatize; he simply allows the emotions of the weaker side, the side that is getting the worst of it, to go over to the side of the stronger. You can watch the process all too clearly in the episode in which Stalky and his companions turn the tables on the cads from the crammers' school. These cads have been maltreating a fag, and a clergyman who is represented by Kipling as one of the more sensible and decent of the masters suggests to Stalky & Co. that they teach the bullies a lesson. The former proceed to clean up on the latter in a scene which goes on for pages, to the reckless violation of proportion and taste. The oppressors, true enough, are taught a lesson, but the cruelty with which we have already been made disgusted has now passed over to the castigators' side, and there is a disagreeable implication that, though it is caddish for the cads to be cruel, it is all right for the sons of English gentlemen to be cruel to the cads. (pp. 97-100)

The fiction of Kipling, then, does not dramatize any fundamental conflict because Kipling would never face one. This is probably one of the causes of his lack of success with long novels. You can make an effective short story, as Kipling so often does, about somebody's scoring off somebody else; but this is not enough for a great novelist, who must show us large social forces, or uncontrollable lines of destiny, or antagonistic impulses of the human spirit, struggling with one another. With Kipling, the right and the wrong of any opposition of forces is usually quite plain at the start; and there is not even the suspense which makes possible the excitement of melodrama. There is never any doubt as to the outcome. The Wrong is made a guy from the beginning, and the high point of the story comes when the Right gives it a kick in the pants. (p. 103)

Edmund Wilson, "The Kipling That Nobody Read," in his The Wound and the Bow: Seven Studies in Literature *(reprinted by permission of Farrar, Straus and Giroux, Inc.; copyright 1929, 1932, 1938, 1939, 1940, 1941 by Edmund Wilson; copyright renewed © 1966, 1968, 1970 by Edmund Wilson), Houghton Mifflin Company, 1941 (and reprinted by Farrar, Straus and Giroux, 1978, pp. 86-147).*

W. H. AUDEN (essay date 1943)

[What is it] that makes Kipling so extraordinary? Is it not that while virtually every other European writer since the fall of the Roman empire has felt that the dangers threatening civilization came from *inside* that civilization (or from inside the individual consciousness), Kipling is obsessed by a sense of dangers threatening from *outside?*

Others have been concerned with the corruptions of the big city, the *ennui* of the cultured mind; some sought a remedy in a return to Nature, to childhood, to Classical Antiquity; others looked forward to a brigher future of liberty, equality and fraternity: they called on the powers of the subconscious, or prayed for the grace of God to interrupt and save their souls; they called on the oppressed to arise and save the world. In Kipling there is none of this, no nostalgia for a Golden Age, no belief in Progress. For him civilization (and consciousness) is a little citadel of light surrounded by a great darkness full of malignant forces and only maintained through the centuries by everlasting vigilance, will-power and self-sacrifice. The philosophers of the Enlightenment shared his civilization-barbarism antithesis, but their weapon was reason, i.e., coming to consciousness, whereas for Kipling too much thinking is highly dangerous, an opening of the gates to the barbarians of melancholia and doubt. For him the gates are guarded by the conscious Will (not unlike the Inner Check of Irving Babbitt). (p. 260)

Poem after poem, under different symbolic disguises, presents this same situation of the danger without, the anxiety of encirclement—by inanimate forces, the Picts beyond the Roman Wall. . . .

The Danes, the Dutch, the Huns, the "new-caught sullen peoples, half devil and half child," even the Female of the Species—by inanimate forces, Karela, the club-footed vine, the sea . . . the ice . . . and by Spiritual Powers. . . .

It is noteworthy that the *interested* spirits are all demonic; the Divine Law is aloof.

Given such a situation, the important figure in society is, of course, the man on guard, and it is he who, in one form or another . . . is the Kipling hero. Unlike the epic hero, he is always on the *defensive*. Thus Kipling is interested in engineering, in the weapons which protect man against the chaotic violence of nature, but not in physics, in the intellectual *discovery* that made the weapons possible. (p. 261)

His ethics and his politics are those of a critical emergency, which is why it is impossible to classify them under conventional party labels, for they presuppose a state where differences of opinion are as irrelevant as they are to a soldier in a foxhole, and, in so far as they apply at all, apply to everyone, Democrat, Nazi or Communist.

Of the guardians, Kipling has profound understanding. He knows that most of them are prodigal sons, given to drink and fornication, acquainted with post-dated checks, now cruel, now sentimental, and he does not try to present them as nice people. But when he turns from them to the Sons of Mary whom they are paid to guard (the shift from religious to social meaning is significant), his vision becomes dim and his touch uncertain, for his interest is not really in them, but only in their relation to the sons of Martha, so that what he sees is either too soft, the exile's nostalgic daydream of Mom and the roses round the door, or too hard, the sentry's resentful nightmare of the sleek and slack stay-at-homes dining and wining while he and his sufferings are forgotten.

Kipling has been rightly praised for his historical imagination, but it is questionable if historical is the right word. If by history we mean *irreversible* temporal changes as contrasted with the cyclical and reversible changes of Nature, then Kipling's imaginative treatment of the past is an affirmation of Nature and a denial of History, for his whole concern is to show that the moment of special emergency is everlasting. . . .

But if Nature and History are the same, how can Nature and Man, the Jungle and the City, be opposed to each other, as Kipling is clearly certain that they are? If one asks him "What is civilization?" he answers, "The People living under the Law, who were taught by their fathers to discipline their natural impulses and will teach their children to do the same" . . . in contrast to the barbarian who is at the mercy of his selfish appetites. But if one asks him "What is this Law and where does it come from?" he refers one back to Nature, to the Darwinian law of the Jungle, "Be Fit," or to the Newtonian law of the Machine. . . . (p. 262)

One might almost say that Kipling had to concentrate his attention and ours upon the special emergency in order to avoid the embarrassment of this paradox, for it is precisely when We are threatened by Them that we can naturally think of the ethical relation between Me and You as one of self-sacrifice, and the ethical relation between Us and Them as one of self-interest. It is precisely when civilization is in mortal danger that the immediate necessity to defend it has a right to override the question of just what it is we are defending.

It may not be too fanciful, either, to see in the kind of poetry Kipling wrote, the esthetic corollary of his conception of life. His virtuosity with language is not unlike that of one of his sergeants with an awkward squad. . . .

Under his will, the vulgarest words learn to wash behind their ears and to execute complicated movements at the word of command, but they can hardly be said to learn to think for themselves. His poetry is arid; personally, I prefer this to the damp poetry of self-expression, but both are excesses.

His poems in their quantity, their limitation to one feeling at a time, have the air of brilliant tactical improvisations to overcome sudden unforeseen obstacles, as if, for Kipling, experience were not a seed to cultivate patiently and lovingly, but an unending stream of dangerous feelings to be immediately mastered as they appear.

No doubt his early experiences of India gave him a sense of the danger of Nature which it is hard for a European to realize (though easier perhaps for an American), but these are not sufficient to explain the terror of demons, visible and invisible, which gives his work its peculiar excitement, any more than the English Civil War expresses Hobbes's terror of political disorder. Nor does it matter particularly what the real cause may have been. The ''mirror'' that Kipling holds out to us is one in which, if we see anything, we see vague, menacing shapes which can be kept away by incessant action but can never be finally overcome. . . . (p. 263)

W.H. Auden, "The Poet of the Encirclement" (reprinted by permission of Curtis Brown, Ltd.; copyright ©1943 by W.H. Auden), in The New Republic, *Vol. 109, No. 17, October 25, 1943 (and reprinted in* Literary Opinion in America: Essays Illustrating the Status, Methods, and Problems of Criticism in the United States in the Twentieth Century, *edited by Morton Dauwen Zabel, revised edition, Harper & Row, Publishers, Inc., 1951, pp. 259-63).*

T. S. ELIOT　(essay date 1943)

There are several reasons for our not knowing Kipling's poems so well as we think we do. When a man is primarily known as a writer of prose fiction we are inclined—and usually, I think, justly—to regard his verse as a by-product. I am, I confess, always doubtful whether any man can so divide himself as to be able to make the most of two such very different forms of expression as poetry and imaginative prose. I am willing to pay due respect, for instance, to the poetry of George Meredith, of Thomas Hardy, of D. H. Lawrence as part of their *oeuvre*, without conceding that it is as good as it might have been had they chosen to dedicate their whole lives to that form of art. If I make an exception in the case of Kipling, it is not because I think he succeeded in making the division successfully, but because I think that . . . his verse and his prose are inseparable; that we must finally judge him, not separately as a poet and as a writer of prose fiction, but as the inventor of a mixed form. So a knowledge of his prose is essential to the understanding of his verse, and a knowledge of his verse is essential to the understanding of his prose. (p. 5)

The starting point for Kipling's verse is the motive of the ballad-maker; and the modern ballad is a type of verse for the appreciation of which we are not provided with the proper

critical tools. We are therefore inclined to dismiss the poems, by reference to poetic criteria which do not apply. It must therefore be our task to understand the type to which they belong, before attempting to value them: we must consider what Kipling was trying to do and what he was not trying to do. The task is the opposite of that with which we are ordinarily faced when attempting to defend contemporary verse. We expect to have to defend a poet against the charge of obscurity: we have to defend Kipling against the charge of excessive lucidity. We expect a poet to be reproached for lack of respect for the intelligence of the common man, or even for deliberately flouting the intelligence of the common man: we have to defend Kipling against the charge of being a 'journalist' appealing only to the commonest collective emotions. We expect a poet to be ridiculed because his verse does not appear to scan: we must defend Kipling against the charge of writing jingles. In short, people are exasperated by poetry which they do not understand, and contemptuous of poetry which they understand without effort. . . . (p. 6)

What is unusual about Kipling's ballads is his singleness of intention in attempting to convey no more to the simple minded than can be taken in on one reading or hearing. They are best when read aloud, and the ear requires no training to follow them easily. With this simplicity of purpose goes a consummate gift of word, phrase, and rhythm. There is no poet who is less open to the charge of repeating himself. In the ballad, the stanza must not be too long and the rhyme scheme must not be too complicated; the stanza must be immediately apprehensible as a whole; a refrain can help to insist upon the identity within which a limited range of variation is possible. The variety of form which Kipling manages to devise for his ballads is remarkable: each is distinct, and perfectly fitted to the content and the mood which the poem has to convey. Nor is the versification too regular: there is the monotonous beat only when the monotonous is what is required; and the irregularities of scansion have a wide scope. One of the most interesting exercises in the combination of heavy beat and variation of pace is found in *Danny Deever*, a poem which is technically (as well as in content) remarkable. The regular recurrence of the same end-words, which gain immensely by imperfect rhyme (*parade* and *said*) gives the feeling of marching feet and the movement of men in disciplined formation—in a unity of movement which enhances the horror of the occasion and the sickness which seizes the men as individuals; and the slightly quickened pace of the final lines marks the change in movement and in music. There is no single word or phrase which calls too much attention to itself, or which is not there for the sake of the total effect; so that when the climax comes—

'What's that that whimpers over'ead?' said Files-on-Parade,
'It's Danny's soul that's passin' now,' the Colour-Sergeant said.

(the word *whimper* being exactly right) the atmosphere has been prepared for a complete suspension of disbelief. (pp. 10-12)

[If] I call particular attention to *Danny Deever* as a barrack-room ballad which somehow attains the intensity of poetry, it is not with the purpose of isolating it from the other ballads of the same type, but with the reminder that with Kipling you cannot draw a line beyond which some of the verse becomes 'poetry'; and that the poetry, when it comes, owes the gravity of its impact to being something over and above the bargain, something more than the writer undertook to give you; and that the matter is never simply a pretext, an occasion for poetry. There are other poems in which the element of poetry is more difficult to put one's finger on, than in *Danny Deever.* Two poems which belong together are *McAndrew's Hymn* and *The 'Mary Gloster'.* They are dramatic monologues, obviously . . . owing something to Browning's invention, though metrically and intrinsically ballads. The popular verdict has chosen the first as the more memorable: I think that the popular verdict is right, but just what it is that raises *McAndrew's Hymn* above *The 'Mary Gloster'* is not easy to say. The rapacious old ship owner of the latter is not easily dismissed, and the presence of the silent son gives a dramatic quality absent from Mc-Andrew's soliloquy. One poem is no less successful than the other. If the McAndrew poem is the more memorable, it is not because Kipling is more inspired by the contemplation of the success of failure than by that of the failure of success, but because there is greater poetry in the subject matter. It is McAndrew who creates the poetry of Steam, and Kipling who creates the poetry of McAndrew. (pp. 13-14)

Kipling's craftsmanship is more reliable than that of some greater poets, and that there is hardly any poem, even in the collected works, in which he fails to do what he has set out to do. The great poet's craft may sometimes fail him: but at his greatest moments he is doing what Kipling is usually doing on a lower plane—writing transparently, so that our attention is directed to the object and not to the medium. Such a result is not simply attained by absence of decoration—for even the absence of decoration may err in calling attention to itself—but by never using decoration for its own sake, though, again, the apparently superfluous may be what is really important. Now one of the problems which arise concerning Kipling is related to that skill of craftsmanship which seems to enable him to pass from form to form, though always in an identifiable idiom, and from subject to subject, so that we are aware of no inner compulsion to write about this rather than that—a versatility which may make us suspect him of being no more than a performer. We look, in a poet as well as in a novelist, for what Henry James called the Figure in the Carpet. With the greatest of modern poets this Figure is perfectly manifest (for we can be sure of the existence of the Figure without perfectly understanding it): I mention Yeats at this point because of the contrast between his development, which is very apparent in the way he writes, and Kipling's development, which is only apparent in what he writes about. We expect to feel, with a great writer, that he *had* to write about the subject he took, and in that way. With no writer of equal eminence to Kipling is this inner compulsion, this unity in variety more difficult to discern.

I pass from the earlier ballads to mention a second category of Kipling's verse: those poems which arise out of, or comment upon topical events. Some of these, such as *The Truce of the Bear,* in the form of an apologue, do not aim very high. But to be able to write good verse to occasion is a very rare gift indeed: Kipling had the gift, and he took the obligation to employ it very seriously. Of this type of poem I should put *Gehazi*—a poem inspired by the Marconi scandals—very high, as a passionate invective rising to real eloquence (and a poem which illustrates, incidentally, the important influence of Biblical imagery and the Authorised Version language upon his writing). The poems on Canada and Australia, and the exequy on King Edward VII, are excellent in their kind, though not very memorable individually. And the gift for occasional verse is allied to the gift for two other kinds of verse in which Kipling excelled: the epigram and the hymn. Good epigrams in English

are very few: and the great hymn writer is very rare. Both are extremely objective types of verse: they can and should be charged with intense feeling, but it must be a feeling that can be completely shared. They are possible to a writer so impersonal as Kipling: and I should like the reader to look attentively at the *Epitaphs of the War.* I call Kipling a great hymn writer on the strength of *Recessional.* It is a poem almost too well known to need to have the reader's attention called to it, except to point out that it is one of the poems in which something breaks through from a deeper level than that of the mind of the conscious observer of political and social affairs—something which has the true prophetic inspiration. Kipling might have been one of the most notable of hymn writers. The same gift of prophecy appears, on the political plane, in other poems, such as *The Storm Cone,* but nowhere with greater authority than in *Recessional.*

It is impossible, however, to fit all of Kipling's poems into one or another of several distinct classes. There is the poem *Gethsemane,* which I do not think I understand, and which is the more mysterious because of the author's having chosen to place it so early in his collected edition, since it bears the sub-heading '1914-1918'. And there are the poems of the later period.

The verse of the later period shows an even greater diversity than the early poems. The word 'experimentation' may be applied, and honourably applied, to the work of many poets who develop and change in maturity. . . . But just as, with Kipling, the term 'development' does not seem quite right, so neither does the term 'experimentation'. There is great variety, and there are some very remarkable innovations indeed, as in *The Way Through The Woods* and in *The Harp Song of the Dane Women* . . . and in the very fine *Runes on Weland's Sword.* But there were equally original inventions earlier (*Danny Deever*); and there are too, among the later poems, some very fine ones cast in more conventional form, such as *Cold Iron, The Land, The Children's Song.* (pp. 14-17)

Kipling is the most elusive of subjects: no writer has been more reticent about himself, or given fewer openings for curiosity, for personal adoration or dislike. (p. 19)

One might expect that a poet who appeared to communicate so little of his private ecstasies and despairs would be dull; one might expect that a poet who had given so much of his time to the service of the political imagination would be ephemeral; one might expect that a poet so constantly occupied with the appearances of things would be shallow. We know that he is not dull, because we have all, at one time or another, by one poem or another, been thrilled; we know that he is not ephemeral, because we remember so much of what we have read. As for shallowness, that is a charge which can only be brought by those who have continued to read him only with a boyish interest. At times Kipling is not merely possessed of penetration, but almost 'possessed' of a kind of second sight. It is a trifling curiosity in itself that he was reproved for having placed in defence of the Wall a Roman Legion which historians declared had never been near it, and that later discoveries proved to have indeed been stationed there: that is the sort of thing one comes to expect of Kipling. There are deeper and darker caverns which he penetrated, whether through experience or through imagination does not matter: there are hints in *The End of the Passage,* and later in *The Woman in His Life* and *In the Same Boat:* oddly enough, these stories are foreshadowed by an early poem . . . , *La Nuit Blanche,* which introduces one image which reappears in *The End of the Passage.* Kipling knew something of the things which are underneath, and of the things which are beyond the frontier (pp. 19-20)

The notion of Kipling as a popular entertainer is due to the fact that his works have been popular and that they entertain. However, it is permitted to express popular views of the moment in an unpopular style: it is not approved when a man holds unpopular views and expresses them in something very readable. I do not wish to argue . . . over Kipling's early 'imperialism', because there is need to speak of the development of his views. It should be said at this point, before passing on, that Kipling is not a doctrinaire or a man with a programme. His opinions are not to be considered as the antithesis of those of Mr. H. G. Wells. Mr. Wells's imagination is one thing and his political opinions another: the latter change but do not mature. But Kipling did not, in the sense in which that activity can be ascribed to Mr. Wells, think: his aim, and his gift, is to make people see—for the first condition of right thought is right sensation—the first condition of understanding a foreign country is to smell it, as you smell India in **Kim**. If you have seen and felt truly, then if God has given you the power you may be able to think rightly. (p. 30)

[Kipling's late poems] are sometimes more obscure, because they are trying to express something more difficult than the early poems. They are the poems of a wiser and more mature writer. But they do not show any movement from 'verse' to 'poetry': they are just as instrumental as the early work, but now instruments for a matured purpose. Kipling could handle, from the beginning to the end, a considerable variety of metres and stanza forms with perfect competence; he introduces remarkable variations of his own; but as a poet he does not revolutionize. He is not one of those writers of whom one can say, that the *form* of English poetry will always be different from what it would have been if they had not written. What fundamentally differentiates his 'verse' from 'poetry' is the subordination of musical interest. Many of the poems give, indeed, judged by the ear, an impression of the mood, some are distinctly onomatopoeic: but there is a harmonics of poetry which is not merely beyond their range—it would interfere with the intention. It is possible to argue exceptions; but I am speaking of his work as a whole, and I maintain that without understanding the purpose which animates his verse as a whole, one is not prepared to understand the exceptions.

I make no apology for having used the terms 'verse' and 'poetry' in a loose way: so that while I speak of Kipling's work as verse and not as poetry, I am still able to speak of individual compositions as poems, and also to maintain that there is 'poetry' in the 'verse'. Where terminology is loose, where we have not the vocabulary for distinctions which we feel, our only precision is found in being aware of the imperfection of our tools, and of the different senses in which we are using the same words. It should be clear that when I contrast 'verse' with 'poetry' I am not, *in this context,* implying a value judgement. I do not mean, here, by verse, the work of a man who would write poetry if he could: I mean by it something which does what 'poetry' could not do. The difference which would turn Kipling's verse into poetry, does not represent a failure or deficiency: he knew perfectly well what he was doing; and from his point of view more 'poetry' would interfere with his purpose. And I make the claim, that in speaking of Kipling we are entitled to say '*great* verse'. (pp. 34-5)

T. S. Eliot, "Rudyard Kipling," in A Choice of Kipling's Verse Made by T. S. Eliot with an Essay on Rudyard Kipling *by Rudyard Kipling, edited by*

T. S. Eliot (copyright © 1943 Charles Scribner's Sons; reprinted by permission of Faber and Faber Ltd), Charles Scribner's Sons, 1943, pp. 5-36.

C. S. LEWIS   (essay date 1948)

Kipling is intensely loved and hated. Hardly any reader likes him a little. Those who admire him will defend him tooth and nail, and resent unfavourable criticism of him as if he were a mistress or a country rather than a writer. The other side reject him with something like personal hatred. . . . For the moment, I will only say that I do not fully belong to either side.

I have been reading him off and on all my life, and I never return to him without renewed admiration. I have never at any time been able to understand how a man of taste could doubt that Kipling is a very great artist. On the other hand, I have never quite taken him to my heart. He is not one of my indispensables; life would go on much the same if the last copy of his works disappeared. I can go even further than this. Not only is my allegiance imperfect, it is also inconstant. . . . One moment I am filled with delight at the variety and solidity of his imagination; and then, at the very next moment, I am sick, sick to death, of the whole Kipling world. (p. 232)

The first cause for my sudden recoil from Kipling, I take to be not the defect but the excess of his art. He himself has told us how he licked every story into its final shape. He dipped a brush in Indian ink and then re-read the manuscript 'in an auspicious hour', considering faithfully 'every paragraph, sentence and word' and 'blacking out where requisite'. After a time he re-read the story and usually found that it would bear 'a second shortening'. Finally there came a third reading at which still more deletion might or might not be found necessary. It is a magnificent example of self-discipline, which Horace would have approved. But I suggest that even an athlete can be over-trained. Superfluous flesh should be sweated off; but a cruel trainer may be too severe in judging what is superfluous. I think Kipling used the Indian ink too much. Sometimes the story has been so compressed that in the completed version it is not quite told—at least, I still do not know exactly what happened in **"Mrs Bathurst"**. But even when this is not so, the art overreaches itself in another way. Every sentence that did not seem to Kipling perfectly and triumphantly good has been removed. As a result the style tends to be too continuously and obtrusively brilliant. The result is a little fatiguing. Our author gives us no rest: we are bombarded with felicities till they deafen us. There is no elbow room, no leisureliness. We need roughage as well as nourishment in a diet; but there is no roughage in a Kipling story—it is all unrelieved vitamins from the first word to the last.

To this criticism I think Kipling could make an almost perfectly satisfactory answer. He might say that he was writing short stories and short poems, each of which was to be the only specimen of Kipling in some number of a periodical. His work was meant to be taken in small doses. The man who gobbles down one story after another at a sitting has no more right to complain if the result is disastrous than the man who swills liqueurs as if they were beer. This answer, I have said, seems to me almost complete. Almost—because even inside a single story the brilliance of the parts, in my opinion, sometimes damages the effect of the whole. I am thinking of **"My Sunday at Home"**. The fancied situation is excellent; one ought to remember the story with chuckles as one remembers *The Wrong Box* [by Robert Louis Stevenson and Lloyd Osbourne]. But I know I am not alone in finding that one actually laughed less than one would have thought possible in the reading of it and that in remembering it one always reverts to the summer drowsiness of the Wiltshire country around the railway station. That superb piece of scene painting has almost blotted out the comic action. Yet I suppose it was originally introduced for no other purpose than to emphasize the solitude of the place.

The fault of which I am here accusing Kipling is one which only a great artist could commit. For most of us the old rule of cutting out every word that can be spared is still a safe one: there is no danger that even after this process the result will be too vivid and too full of sense. And, as far as mere art is concerned, I think this is almost the only fault I can find in Kipling's mature work; I say his mature work for, of course, like all men he made some unsuccessful experiments before he found his true vein. It is when I turn to his matter that my serious discontents begin. (pp. 233-34)

To put the thing in the shortest possible way, Kipling is first and foremost the poet of work. It is really remarkable how poetry and fiction before his time had avoided this subject. They had dealt almost exclusively with men in their 'private hours'—with love-affairs, crimes, sport, illness and changes of fortune. . . . With a few exceptions imaginative literature in the eighteenth and nineteenth centuries had quietly omitted, or at least thrust into the background, the sort of thing which in fact occupies most of the waking hours of most men. And this did not merely mean that certain technical aspects of life were unrepresented. A whole range of strong sentiments and emotions—for many men, the strongest of all—went with them. For, as Pepys once noted with surprise, there is a great pleasure in talking of business. It was Kipling who first reclaimed for literature this enormous territory.

His early stories of Anglo-Indian society still conform to the older convention. They are about love-affairs, elopements, intrigues and domestic quarrels. . . . The **'Departmental Ditties'** are much more typical of the author's real interests. . . . The whole bitter little collection presents a corrupt society, not in its leisure, but in its official corruption. In his later work this preference for depicting men at their jobs becomes his most obvious characteristic. Findlayson's hopes and fears about his bridge, McPhee's attitude both to engines and owners, William the Conqueror's work in the famine district, a lighthouse-keeper at his post on a foggy night, Gisborne and his chief in the forest, McAndrew standing his watch—these are the things that come back to us when we remember Kipling; and there had really been nothing like them in literature before. The poems again and again strike the same note. (pp. 235-36)

This spirit of the profession is everywhere shown in Kipling as a ruthless master. That is why Chesterton got in a very large part of the truth when he fixed on discipline as Kipling's main subject [see excerpt above]. There is nothing Kipling describes with more relish than the process whereby the trade-spirit licks some raw cub into shape. That is the whole theme of one of his few full-length novels, *Captains Courageous*. It is the theme of **'The Centaurs'**, and of **'Pharaoh and the Sergeant'**, and of **'The 'Eathen'**. It is allegorically expressed in **"The Ship that Found Herself"**. It is implicit in all the army stories and the sea-stories. . . . (p. 238)

This is one of the most important things Kipling has to say and one which he means very seriously, and it is also one of the things which has aroused hatred against him. It amounts to something like a doctrine of original sin, and it is antipathetic to many modern modes of thought. Perhaps even more antipathetic is Kipling's presentation of the 'breaking' and 'rawhiding' process. In **"His Private Honour"** it turns out to consist of prolonged bullying and incessant abuse. . . . (pp. 238-39)

Now there is no good whatever in dismissing this part of Kipling's message as if it were not worth powder and shot. There is a truth in it which must be faced before we attempt to find any larger truths which it may exclude. Many who hate Kipling have omitted this preliminary. They feel instinctively that they themselves are just the unlicked or unbroken men whom Kipling condemns; they find the picture intolerable, and the picture of the cure more intolerable still. To escape, they dismiss the whole thing as a mere Fascist or 'public school' brutality. But there is no solution along those lines. It may (or may not) be possible to get beyond Kipling's harsh wisdom; but there is no getting beyond a thing without first getting as far. It is a brutal truth about the world that the whole everlasting business of keeping the human race protected and clothed and fed could not go on for twenty-four hours without the vast legion of hard-bitten, technically efficient, not-over-sympathetic men, and without the harsh processes of discipline by which this legion is made. It is a brutal truth that unless a great many people practised the Kipling *ethos* there would be neither security nor leisure for any people to practise a finer *ethos*. (p. 239)

> C. S. Lewis, "Kipling's World," in Literature and Life: Addresses to the English Association, *G. G. Harrap, 1948 (and reprinted in his* Selected Literary Essays, *edited by Walter Hooper, Cambridge at the University Press, 1969, pp. 232-50).*

W. SOMERSET MAUGHAM   (essay date 1952)

[In the Indian stories Kipling] was at his best. When he wrote stories about Indians and about the British in India he felt himself at home and he wrote with an ease, a freedom, a variety of invention which gave them a quality which in stories in which the subject matter was different he did not always attain. Even the slightest of them are readable. They give you the tang of the East, the smell of the bazaars, the torpor of the rains, the heat of the sun-scorched earth, the rough life of the barracks in which the occupying troops were quartered, and the other life, so English and yet so alien to the English way, led by the officers, the Indian Civilians and the swarm of minor officials who combined to administer that vast territory. (p. vii)

[We] should not be surprised that Kipling sometimes wrote stories which were poor, unconvincing or trivial; we should wonder rather that he wrote so many of such excellence. He was wonderfully various.

In the essay Mr. T. S. Eliot wrote to preface his selection of Kipling's verse [see excerpt above] he seems to suggest that variety is not a laudable quality in a poet. I would not venture to dispute any opinion of Mr. Eliot's on a question in which poetry is concerned, but though variety may not be a merit in a poet, it surely is in a writer of fiction. The good writer of fiction has the peculiarity, shared to a degree by all men, but in him more abundant, that he has not only one self, but is a queer mixture of several, or, if that seems an extravagant way of putting it, that there are several, often discordant aspects of his personality. The critics could not understand how the same man could write **'Brugglesmith'** and *Recessional,* and so accused him of insincerity. They were unjust. It was the self called Beetle who wrote **'Brugglesmith'** and the self called Yardley-Orde who wrote *Recessional.* When most of us look back on ourselves we can sometimes find consolation in believing that a self in us which we can only deplore has, generally through no merit of ours, perished. The strange thing about Kipling is that the self called Beetle which one would have thought increasing age and the experience of life would have caused to disintegrate, remained alive in all its strength almost to his dying day. (p. xiii)

[My] opinion that Kipling's best stories are those of which the scene is laid in India is by no means shared by eminent critics. They think those Kipling wrote in what they call his third period show a depth, an insight and a compassion of which they deplore the lack in his Indian tales. For them the height of his achievement is to be found in such stories as *An Habitation Enforced, A Madonna of the Trenches, The Wish House* and *Friendly Brook. An Habitation Enforced* is a charming story, but surely rather obvious; and though the other three are good enough they do not seem to me remarkable. It did not need an author of Kipling's great gifts to write them. *Just So Stories, Puck of Pook's Hill* and *Rewards and Fairies* are children's books and their worth must be judged by the pleasure they afforded children. This *Just So Stories* must have done. One can almost hear the squeals of laughter with which they listened to the story of how the elephant got his trunk. In the two other books Puck appears to a little boy and a little girl and produces for their instruction various characters by means of whom they may gain an elementary and romantic acquaintance with English history. I don't think this was a happy device. The stories are of course well contrived; I like best *On the Great Wall,* in which Parnesius, the Roman legionary, appears, but I should have liked it better if it had been a straightforward reconstruction of an episode in the Roman occupation of Britain. (p. xxii)

Kipling's [early] critics were wrong to blame him for introducing his personality into his stories. What they meant of course was that they did not like the personality he presented to them; and that is understandable. In his early work he exhibited characteristics which were offensive. You received the impression of a bumptious, arrogant young man, extravagantly cock-sure and knowing; and this necessarily excited the antagonism of his critics. For such an assumption of superiority as these rather unamiable traits indicate affronts one's self-esteem.

Kipling was widely accused of vulgarity: so were Balzac and Dickens; I think only because they dealt with aspects of life that offended persons of refinement. We are tougher now: when we call someone refined we do not think we are paying him a compliment. But one of the most absurd charges brought against him was that his stories were anecdotes, which the critics who made it thought was to condemn him (as they sometimes still do); but if they had troubled to consult the Oxford Dictionary they would have seen that a meaning it gives to the word is: 'The narration of a detached incident, or of a single event, told as being in itself interesting or striking.' That is a perfect definition of a short story. . . . No one is obliged to read stories, and if you don't like them unless there is something in them more than a story, there is nothing to do about it. You may not like oysters, no one can blame you for that, but it is unreasonable to condemn them because they don't possess the emotional quality of a beefsteak and kidney pudding. It is equally unreasonable to find fault with a story because it is only a story. That is just what some of Kipling's detractors have done. He was a very talented man, but not a profound thinker—indeed I cannot think of any great novelist who was; he had a consummate gift for telling a certain kind

of story and he enjoyed telling it. He was wise enough for the most part to do what he could do best. As he was a sensible man, he was no doubt pleased when people liked his stories and took it with a shrug of the shoulders when they didn't.

Another fault found with him was that he had little power of characterization. I don't think the critics who did this quite understood the place of characterization in a short story. Of course you can write a story with the intention of displaying a character. Flaubert did it in *Un Coeur Simple* and Chekhov in *The Darling,* which Tolstoi thought so well of; though a purist might object that they are not short stories, but potted novels. Kipling was concerned with incident. In a tale so concerned you need only tell enough about the persons who take part in it to bring them to life; you show them at the moment you are occupied with; they are inevitably static. To show the development of character an author needs the passage of time and the elbow-room of a novel. . . . Now, I suggest that Kipling drew his characters quite firmly enough for his purpose. There is a distinction to be made between 'characters' and character. Mulvaney, Ortheris and Learoyd are 'characters.' It is easy enough to create them. Findlayson in *The Bridge-Builders,* and Scott and William in *William the Conqueror* have character; and to delineate that is much more difficult. It is true that they are very ordinary, commonplace people, but that gives point to the narrative, and surely Kipling was well aware of it. (pp. xxv-xxvii)

Kipling wrote in shorter sentences than were at that time usual. That can no longer surprise us, and since the lexicographers tell us that a sentence is a series of words, forming the grammatically complete expression of a single thought, there seems no reason why, when an author has done just this, he should not point the fact with a full stop. He is indeed right to do so. George Moore, no lenient critic of his contemporaries, admired Kipling's style for its sonority and its rhythm. 'Others have written more beautifully, but no one that I can call to mind has written so copiously. . . . He writes with the whole language, with the language of the Bible, and with the language of the streets.' Kipling's vocabulary was rich. He chose his words, often very unexpected words, for their colour, their precision, their cadence. He knew what he wanted to say and said it incisively. His prose, with which alone I am concerned, had pace and vigour. Like every other author he had his mannerisms. Some, like his unseemly addiction to biblical phrases, he quickly discarded; others he retained. He continued throughout his life to begin a sentence with a relative. Which was a pity. He continued to make deplorable use of the poetic *ere* when it would have been more natural to say *before*. Once at least he wrote *e'en* for *even*. These are minor points. Kipling has so made his style his own that I don't suppose anyone today would care to write like him, even if he could, but I don't see how one can deny that the instrument he constructed was admirably suited to the purpose to which he put it. He seldom indulged in long descriptions, but with his seeing eye and quick perception he was able by means of this instrument to put before the reader with extreme vividness the crowded Indian scene in all its fantastic variety. (pp. xxvii-xxviii)

[If] I have not hesitated to point out what seemed to me Kipling's defects, I hope I have made it plain how great I think were his merits. The short story is not a form of fiction in which the English have on the whole excelled. The English, as their novels show, are inclined to diffuseness. They have never been much interested in form. Succinctness goes against their grain. But the short story demands form. It demands succinctness. Diffuseness kills it. It depends on construction. It does not admit of loose ends. It must be complete in itself. All these qualities you will find in Kipling's stories when he was at his magnificent best, and this, happily for us, he was in story after story. Rudyard Kipling is the only writer of short stories our country has produced who can stand comparison with Guy de Maupassant and Chekhov. He is our greatest story writer. I can't believe he will ever be equalled. I am sure he can never be excelled. (p. xxviii)

> *W. Somerset Maugham, "Introduction" (copyright, 1952, by W. Somerset Maugham; reprinted by permission of Doubleday & Company, Inc.; in Canada by the Estate of the late W. Somerset Maugham), in* A Choice of Kipling's Prose *by Rudyard Kipling, edited by W. Somerset Maugham, Macmillan, 1952 (and reprinted in* Maugham's Choice of Kipling's Best *by Rudyard Kipling, edited by W. Somerset Maugham, Doubleday & Company, Inc., 1953, pp. vii-xxviii).*

C. E. CARRINGTON   (essay date 1956)

[*Debits and Credits*] was at first received coolly by the critics, though rapturously by the Kipling fans. It has had the experience, rare in the chronicle of his career, of steadily rising in favour with students of literature. I would venture the assertion that if Kipling had published nothing but **'The Bull that Thought'**, **'The Eye of Allah'**, **'The Janeites'**, **'The Wish House'**, **'A Madonna of the Trenches'**, and **'The Gardener'**, his name would stand high among the world's story-tellers. It would be hard to find such variety of subject, such richness of treatment, in the work of any contemporary, and, when compared with his own earlier work, these stories will be found to express a more delicate sensibility and a deeper penetration of motive. The other stories in the book, and even these six, display also Kipling's characteristic faults; some passages which gave offence to the thin-skinned, some almost incomprehensible jargon, and some lapses into obscurity. **'A Madonna of the Trenches'** must be grouped among his 'difficult' stories. It was typical of his indifference to public opinion that he began the book with an allegorical tale (**'The Enemies to Each Other'**) that seemed to be a kind of private joke. In form it is a version of the legend of Adam and Eve expanded at great length in a pseudo-oriental style like a stilted version of the *Koran*. It is remarkable that he published it, not that he wrote it. (p. 362)

Kipling's stories are sometimes cryptic, sometimes obscure, sometimes allegorical. Quite early in his career he developed a technique of leaving the story half-told and so maintaining the suspense. This is the traditional method of the ghost-story, which is spoiled if an explanation is offered, a method used by Poe in *Tales of Mystery and Imagination* which Kipling imitated as a young man.

He was not, strictly speaking, a writer of adventure-stories except in his books for children. The form of his stories for adults is usually a descriptive comment on a group of characters in a dramatic situation. For example, even so romantic a tale as **'The Man who Was'** tells next to nothing of the hero's adventures, which are left to the reader's imagination; but presents, almost visually, the effect of his sudden reappearance. In this instance enough is revealed, though in some others the narrative never emerges. **'At the End of the Passage'**, for example, is a problem-story in the same mode as the problem-pictures which were so popular at the Academy in Kipling's younger days. This is all I am going to tell you, says the author.

Make what you can of it. His 'knowingness' which infuriated some critics, his hints that he could say a great deal more if he chose to, were marks of juvenility which he grew out of. In later life, the hints were of what he did not know, the esoteric, the subliminal, the occult. There are cryptic elements in **'They'**, in **'The House Surgeon'**, in **'A Madonna of the Trenches'**, in **'The Gardener'**, but here they are dictated by humility in presence of the uncomprehended.

Other stories are found difficult for the reason that they seem to be wilfully obscure, through strangeness of vocabulary or complexity of construction. His love of jargon for its own sake (delightfully exhibited in *Just So Stories*) sometimes betrayed him, as it betrayed Rabelais, into mere avalanches of words. Sometimes the composition of his narrative, partially and gradually revealed in dialogue, is confusing. **'The Devil and the Deep Sea'** appears to have been written out of sheer delight in the terminology of marine engineering. Those parts of the narrative which concentrate upon this main theme are, in their way, a triumph of virtuosity, while the rest of it is so compressed, so pruned and cut, chopped off so short, that I, for one, have never been able to discover what happens at the end. The sea stories in general are the most technical, and **'Sea-Constables'**, a dialogue between four characters, all of them talking naval 'shop', is, if not the most obscure, perhaps the most difficult story Kipling ever wrote. By contrast, **'The Bonds of Discipline'**, also told in dialogue by two characters alternately speaking different jargons, is quite clear.

The cryptic and the obscure styles are combined in several stories and are carried to their greatest length in **'The Dog Hervey'**, which presents more puzzles the more it is examined; it abounds in literary, masonic, psychological, and canine clues which lead nowhere. Like **'Mrs. Bathurst'**, **'The Dog Hervey'** seems to have been made incomprehensible by ruthless cutting. Perhaps the themes of both are too complex for treatment within the limits of a short story.

Yet another group of difficult stories are the allegories or fables. . . . [**'The Children of the Zodiac'** is] a long fable of which no satisfactory explanation has been offered by any commentator. All that can be said about it with conviction is that it deals with the marriage of a young poet who dreads death by cancer of the throat, and that in 1891 Kipling was a young poet contemplating marriage, and ill with an affliction of the throat. We have his word for it elsewhere that he regarded cancer of the throat as the 'family complaint'. The fable, then, is personal—something between himself and the woman he was about to marry.

A problem piece in which the obscurity is gradually and skilfully made plain, is **'The Gardener'**, his story of the unmarried mother and the war-graves in Flanders. It is told with such tenderness as to efface the memory of the parallel tale of **'Mary Postgate'**. This is quite another view of the soul of a hard, efficient, loveless woman. All these war-stories—as the name *Debits and Credits* implies—turn upon loyalties, the part played in love or friendship by the one who gives and the one who takes, a relation often seen in reverse when seen with intimate understanding. In war who bears the greater burden, the one who lives or the one who dies? Kipling's obsession with the war-dead dwelt upon his understanding that the soldiers were initiates, admitted to a higher degree of the suffering which is the law of life, and so separated from their lovers at home.

The strongest continuing motive in his work throughout his whole career was the sense of comradeship among men who share a common allegiance because committed to a common duty. His love of technical jargon, though partly a mere delight in the richness of language, was strengthened by a conviction that the best talk is 'talking shop', the kind of conversation which lives and is genuine because it is based upon a secret shared between those who know how something is done, a secret conveying that kind of knowledge which is power. Freemasonry, with its cult of common action, its masculine self-sufficiency, its language of symbols, and its hierarchy of secret grades, provided him with a natural setting for his social ideals. In India, when very young, he had been a keen and loyal mason, and the ritual of masonry had first revealed to him the underlying unity of Indian life in the one context where race, religion, and caste were overlooked. Even a nonmason can point out scores of allusions to masonic ritual, dispersed through the whole of Kipling's verse and prose, proving how deeply the cult affected his mode of thought. (pp. 363-65)

His avowedly masonic episode, **'In the Interests of the Brethren'**, . . . was a demonstration to his brother-masons of what they might do to help soldiers on leave from the front, if they would take some liberties with masonic rules; and whether they accepted this advice his fellow-masons will know best. To the general reader **'Lodge Faith and Works, 5837'** is merely the scene set for the narration of some powerful stories in his later manner, notably [**'The Janeites'** and **'A Madonna of the Trenches'**]. . . . (p. 365)

[Kipling's last volume, however, *Limits and Renewals*,] shows some falling away in the author's skill; it is the book of a tired and ageing invalid. . . . A theme in all the war-stories was the 'breaking-strain', the amount of pressure human beings can stand from physical tortures and mental terrors without a psychological collapse; and his favourite treatment of this problem is the salvation of a personality by devotion to another personality, by loving rather than by being loved. Yet love may seem too strong a word for a mere clinging to life at whatever point an emotional attachment can be secured. It may be simply gratitude as in **'A Friend of the Family'**, or love of animals as in the story significantly named **'The Woman in His Life'**. The fear of fear, the knowledge that mental hells are more racking than physical hells, the unwillingness of even the bravest to face ultimate and hideous realities, may even reduce wretched mortals to a state where physical pain brings relief by numbing the mind. . . .

That last shrinking from the ultimate and the inevitable is the subject of the war-poem **'Gethsemane'** which many readers have found difficult. (p. 367)

His **'Epitaphs of the Great War'**, 'naked cribs of the Greek Anthology' he called them, include much comment on this theme; one that Rudyard Kipling thought good of its kind was **'The Coward'**. . . . (p. 368)

These were his final comments on the First World War: to every man his own private terror, his own vein of courage, his own breaking-strain, his own salvation by a loving attachment to life; and the other aspect of the picture may be seen in the strange, elaborate—not quite successful—allegories of the after-life, **'On the Gate'** and **'Uncovenanted Mercies'**. The reader is not expected to believe in them unreservedly.

Limits and Renewals includes one *comédie humaine* in Rudyard's happier style, the study of the village *curé* and the village atheist which he called **'The Miracle of Saint Jubanus'**, based upon an incident he had once seen when visiting a Spanish Cathedral. The book also includes an ill-natured anecdote, **'The Tie'**, written long since and dredged up from the bottom of his notebooks where it might better have been allowed to stay. But the strength of the book lies in the stories about doctors and disease, topics which now meant more to him than the life of soldiers and sailors that he had written about in his youth.

On any count, **'Dayspring Mishandled'** is an astonishing performance, a profound, obscure, and singularly unpleasant story about a vindictive feud between two expert bibliophiles, or rather the vindictive persecution of a sham expert by a genuine expert. Revenge goes so far that the victim is not spared further taunts and triumphings when dying of a painful disease. But more engaging than the revenge-motive is the virtuosity with which a spurious poem by Chaucer is composed, a fifteenth-century manuscript faked, and the specious scholar is deceived. As if this involution were not enough, the progress of the plot is contrasted with the degeneration of the victim, as disease wears him down, until the combined assaults of pain and disillusion reveal his breaking-strain.

The progress of an incurable disease is also the subject of **'Unprofessional'**, a story that repays study. Sir John Bland-Sutton said Kipling had here foretold the course of medical research, as far ahead as his **'Easy as A B C'** had foretold the progress of aviation. An early draft had borne the name **'Stars in their Courses'**, which suggested its theme, the revival of an old notion that had stimulated the astrologers in antiquity but had led them astray. When reconsidered in a modern laboratory, this notion might reveal, or so the author's fancy suggests, recurrent and rhythmical changes in the cells of the body—'tides' in the tissues produced by influences from without, 'the main tide in all matter'.

Rudyard's later writing, even more involved, compressed, and elaborate, had lost nothing in force or in range. While he reached out continually to master new technologies and to bring them within the scope of his art, he seemed less able to visualize a scene in a few unforgettable words. We are given situations rather than scenes, conversations rather than characters. The faking of the manuscript in **'Dayspring Mishandled'** is not likely to be forgotten, but one cares little about the two bibliophiles, and less about the victim's wife who is given an illicit love affair, by way of underplot.

It was an old joke in the book trade that two classes of books will always find a market in England, books about doctors and books about dogs. After his medical stories Rudyard indeed turned to the other category and enjoyed his last success with dog stories, in a new mode. He had always been a dog-lover and, from his earliest days as a writer, had introduced some favourite dogs into his stories about people. In **'Garm, a Hostage'** and **'The Dog Hervey'**, the dogs had been among the leading characters, but dogs seen through the human eye. His beasts, in the *Jungle Books* and elsewhere, had been treated allegorically, in another traditional style, as characters personified appropriately, like Circe's swine, in some animal garb that suited them. [*Thy Servant a Dog*] . . . was not a beast fable in the conventional form, but a genuine attempt to present a dog's point of view, in a simplified vocabulary which seemed adequate to a dog's intelligence, an experiment in the rudiments of language. (pp. 368-69)

C. E. Carrington, in his The Life of Rudyard Kipling *(copyright © 1955 by C. E. Carrington; reprinted by permission of C. E. Carrington and Macmillan London Limited), Doubleday & Company, Inc., 1956, 433 p.*

NIRAD C. CHAUDHURI (essay date 1957)

[In *Kim,* Kipling] wrote not only the finest novel in the English language with an Indian theme, but also one of the greatest of English novels in spite of the theme. This rider is necessary, because the association of anything in English literature with India suggests a qualified excellence, an achievement which is to be judged by its special standards, or even a work which in form and content has in it more than a shade of the second-rate. But *Kim* is great by any standards that ever obtained in any age of English literature.

This will come as a surprise from a Bengali, Kipling's *bête noire,* who heartily returned the compliment, and I shall add shock to surprise by confessing that I had not read *Kim* till about three years ago. The only work by Kipling which I had read before was *The Jungle Book.* I read it first when I was only ten years old, and I have never ceased reading it. It is now as much a part of me as are the Arabian Nights, Grimm's Fairy Tales, and Aesop's Fables, or for that matter the Ramayana and the Mahabharata. But I never had the courage or inclination to pass on to Kipling's other books, for I had heard of his 'imperialism' and contempt for Bengalis. I thought I should be hurt by an aggressive display of Anglo-Saxon pride, and while British rule lasted I should have been, because the contempt was both real and outspoken. Anyone curious to sample its expression might as well read a story called **'The Head of the District'**. . . .

There was no originality in Kipling's rudeness to us, but only a repetition, in the forthright Kiplingian manner, of what was being said in every mess and club. His political fads were explicit, and he was never sheepish about them. But his politics were the characteristic politics of the *epigoni,* when the epic age of British world politics was already past, and the British people had ceased to bring about great mutations in the history of the world. (p. 28)

Kipling's politics, which even now are something of a hurdle in the way of giving him a secure place in English literature, and which certainly brought him under a cloud during the last years of his life, are no essential ingredient of his writings. Kipling the writer is always able to rise above Kipling the political man. His imagination soared above his political opinions as Tolstoy's presentation of human character transcended his pet military and historical theories in *War and Peace.* Of course, quite a large number of his themes are drawn from what might legitimately be called political life, but these have been personalized and transformed into equally legitimate artistic themes. It is the easiest thing to wash out the free acid of Kiplingian politics from his finished goods.

Coming to particulars, *Kim* would never have been a great book if it had to depend for its validity and appeal on the spy story, and we really are not called upon to judge it as an exposition in fiction of the Anglo-Russian rivalry in Asia. Kipling's attitude to war and diplomacy had a streak of naïveté and even claptrap in it, which made Lord Cromer, in whom high politics ran in the blood, once call him, if I remember rightly, a cheeky beggar.

The spy story in *Kim* is nothing more than the diplomatic conceit of an age of peace, in which people enjoyed all kinds of scares, including war scares, and even invented them, in order to have an excuse for letting off some jingoistic steam, to ring a change on the boredom of living in piping times of peace. India in the last decades of the nineteenth century was full of all sorts of fanciful misgivings about Russian intrigues and the machinations of the Rajas and Maharajas, which the clever darkly hinted at and the simple credulously believed in. There is an echo of this even in one of Tagore's stories in Bengali.

But in *Kim* this political mode, which Kipling seems to have taken more seriously than it deserved to be, is only a peg to hang a wholly different story, the real story of the book. (p. 29)

[*Kim*] is the product of Kipling's vision of a much bigger India, a vision whose profundity we Indians would be hard put to it to match even in an Indian language, not to speak of English. He had arrived at a true and moving sense of that India which is almost timeless, and had come to love it.

This India pervades all his books in greater or lesser degree and constitutes the foundation on which he weaves his contrapuntal patterns. In certain books this foundation is virtually the real theme, and so it is in *Kim.* But the book is specially important in this that through it Kipling projects not only his vision of the basic India he knew so well, but also his feeling for the core and the most significant part of this basic India. (pp. 30-1)

Kipling was equally at home in our plains, hills, and mountains, and like all great novelists he remains firmly ecological. There are in *Kim* not only entrancing descriptions of the Himalayas but a picture of the green phase on the great plain that is uncanny in its combination of romance and actuality. We Indians shall never cease to be grateful to Kipling for having shown the many faces of our country in all their beauty, power, and truth.

As regards the human material the best choice in India is always the simplest choice, namely, the people and their religion. . . .

Kipling's artistic and spiritual instincts led him to these elemental and inexhaustible themes, although he may not have been wholly original in his choice, for in this as in many other things he was controlled by the general bias of British rule in India towards the commonalty. But whether completely original or not he stands supreme among Western writers for his treatment of the biggest reality in India, which is made up of the life of people and religion in the twin setting of the mountains and the plain. These four are the main and real characters in *Kim.* (p. 32)

> *Nirad C. Chaudhuri, ''Kim—The Finest Story about India in English,'' in* Encounter *(© 1957 by Encounter Ltd.), Vol. VIII, No. 4, April, 1957 (and reprinted as ''The Finest Story about India—in English,'' in* The Age of Kipling, *edited by John Gross, Simon & Schuster, 1972, pp. 27-36).*

J.I.M. STEWART (essay date 1963)

Of [Kipling's] Indian stories those concerning private soldiers are not quite the earliest. But they are the first coherent group with which Kipling startled and held a large public, and sufficiently characteristic to give us a good start. (p. 229)

'My Lord the Elephant' tells how [Private Mulvaney] restrained and quieted an elephant which had become enraged through being required to work in an elephant-battery, and how he later fell in with the same beast when it was holding up traffic in a pass. The merit here is all in the vividness and vigour of the evocation—and in that sort of boldness in claiming to know what it is like to be an elephant which D. H. Lawrence was later to show in regard to snakes and tortoises.

There is almost nothing that the young Kipling does not know—his knowingness was from the first a point of irritation with his critics—unless it be a few of the minor canons of good taste. (p. 230)

['His Private Honour'] is the story of an ordeal, or rather of a double ordeal. Private Ortheris is struck by a young officer, Ouless, on parade. Ouless instantly confesses the act to his captain; Ortheris as instantly protects Ouless by lying. Each man remains with his honour to rescue. Ouless, having thought the matter over, takes Ortheris on a private shooting-expedition. They fight with fists; Ortheris plasters his adversary but is fairly beaten; and thus the incident is purged. 'The boy was proven', we read of Ouless in the last sentence. And Ortheris, the mature soldier, has needed no proving:

> 'It was your right to get him cashiered if you chose,' I insisted.
>
> 'My right!' Ortheris answered with deep scorn. 'My right! I ain't a recruity to go whinin' about my rights to this an' my rights to that, just as if I couldn't look after myself. My rights! 'Strewth A'mighty! I'm a man.'

But if Ortheris, as well as being a man, is a public-school boy under his skin, it is a public-school boy of the decidedly un-redeemed sort that we are to meet in *Stalky & Co*. . . . The ethic, which is to run strongly and harshly through much of Kipling's work, is explicitly stated: 'First a man must suffer, then he must learn his work, and the self-respect that that knowledge brings.' In the foreground we have Ortheris who has learned and Ouless who has been learning; in the background we are shown the process at its most naked among the new men. (p. 231)

'His Private Honour' is an impressive performance. Within the same group come four tales which would alone establish Kipling as among the greatest writers of short stories—and the first of them, **'The Man who would be King'**, must have been written well before his twenty-third birthday. Carefully set in the kind of frame or induction to which he was to give much attention, it tells of two low-class English adventurers possessed by the wild dream of making their way to Kafiristan and there establishing their own empire. In fact they succeed, dominating and drilling whole tribes and achieving quasi-divine status before the determination of the dominant partner to break a vow and take a native wife brings their position crashing down, so that one is hurled to death in a ravine and the other must survive crucifixion before telling the story. The surface narrative is rich, vigorous, and convincing. The deploying of it is already full of a skilled craftsman's subtleties. There is a play of unobtrusive symbols, and a psychological realism so economically achieved that it serves to give glimpses of the two principal characters in depth without ever holding up the sheer sustained excitement of the action. Carnehan and Dravot have more of nature than do some answering characters in the maturest Conrad. Nor can Conrad—although so powerful an atmospheric writer—ever give body and sharp actuality to exotic scenes with the speed and spareness Kipling here achieves. Moreover, while the lesser symbolisms are designed artifice, we are aware of the sort of richness that comes from the pressure of less conscious significances. Dravot's *raj* might be a greater one in which analogous perils lurk, and the specific occasion of its downfall reverberates with a fear and horror lying very deep in Kipling's sexual nature.

In **'The Courting of Dinah Shadd'** Mulvaney courts Dinah and is accepted. He celebrates, flirts with another girl, Judy Sheehy,

and is presently confronted by the two mothers and their daughters. Almost before we know that this is anything other than coarse comedy, Judy's mother is pronouncing a tremendous curse upon Mulvaney, and the story turns perfectly upon the strong pivot of Dinah's response. . . . This is in essence a *short* story; it has the speed and power of a traditional ballad, with all its active virtue in the extreme concentration of its crisis. It ends with a ballad of Kipling's own, and it has been prefaced with a vivid and bustling description of the man-oeuvres during which Mulvaney tells his tale. We may doubt here whether the frame enhances the effect. Admirable in itself, it may yet strike us as a display of useless facile vigour when surrounding an action which commands so surely depths of primitive feeling and drives so straight at tragedy. (pp. 233-35)

Kipling's officer-class stories (as they may be called) of this early period are not so good, but a few may be mentioned as characteristic. In **'A Bank Fraud'** Reggie Burke, the genial and competent manager of an up-country branch of an Indian bank, is landed with an intolerably inefficient and censorious accountant. Notice of the man's dismissal comes when he is mortally ill, and Burke conceals it from him and pays his salary out of his own pocket till he dies. This is a sentimental tale on a simple gentleman-versus-cad formula which Kipling was never entirely to cease to exploit. **'Only a Subaltern'** is decidedly better. **'Thrown Away'** is the story of a boy reared under what parents call the 'sheltered-life system'—which Kipling knows is 'not wise'. The boy passes high into Sandhurst, not so high out—and then in India takes things too seriously. (This is unwise too.) He 'fretted over women not worth saddling a pony to call upon', made various mistakes, received a common 'Colonel's wigging', and then got leave to go hunting and in fact shot himself after writing despairing letters to his parents and a girl in England. An apprehensive major and the narrator arrive only in time to bury the body, burn the letters, and put up a story of death by cholera. They are much affected as they do all the right things—including chopping off a lock f330of the major's hair to send home, since the boy's hair is in no state for exhibition. At the same time they find themselves convulsed with laughter as they work 'at the grotesqueness of the affair'. There is to be much strange laughter in Kipling. . . . There is a strong antagonism to women in many of these stories. And all hold the same encyclopedic assuredness. . . . But Kipling was twenty or thereabouts, and perhaps the cleverest man in India. A phase of delusion may be forgiven him. Yet if his was a brilliant mind it was in some ways an obstinately naïve one. **'The Tomb of his Ancestors'** is a rather later story, but it exhibits his myth of Anglo-India still in its archetypal simplicity. . . . The myth, of course, is not wholly Kipling's. If we turn, for instance, to *Eothen* we find that [Alexander] King-lake's 'English gentleman among Orientals' exemplifies it in rudimentary form. (pp. 237-38)

Kipling's is essentially not a speculative mind, and this limits, now and later, the scope and effectiveness of his dealings with the starkest intimations of experience. **'At the End of the Passage'** begins with an elaborate and effective evocation of the strains endured by Englishmen whose duties tie them to unbearable places during the rigours of an Indian summer. Hummil suffers first from insomnia and then from what appear to be hallucinations. Eventually he is found dead, and 'in the staring eyes was written terror beyond the expression of any pen'. But in the eyes—it is intimated—there can be seen something else as well: the lingering images of substantial and objective horrors susceptible of record by a Kodak. This is not a very good way of suggesting that there can be more to a vision of evil than a disordered liver as sworn to by the obtuse doctor of **'The Phantom Rickshaw'**. And if as we read the story we happen to think of Conrad's 'Heart of Darkness' or James's 'The Turn of the Screw' we shall scarcely feel that Kipling can challenge either on this ground. Yet it has all Conrad's power—and far more than James's power—of actually sticking to the skin and pricking at the nerves and pounding in the head as it evokes the physical conditions prelusive of its dubious mystery. Moreover this story, even if not wholly successful, has importance as looking forward to one of Kipling's most mature themes. Hummil has been 'seven fathom deep in hell' and has there met despair and horror of which there can be no rational account. That we inhabit a universe in which this can happen is to remain Kipling's grand problem long after the tumult and the shouting dies.

A distinguished American critic, Mr. Lionel Trilling, has declared Kipling to retain some interest at least on account of his 'effect upon us in that obscure and important part of our minds where literary feeling and political attitude meet'. This, as far as it goes, is certainly true, and in **'The Man who Was'** we come upon a story in which this meeting may render the effect of violent collision. Here we have an English army officer who, captured by the Russians in the Crimea and for some unjust reason long held in barbarous captivity as a criminal, staggers into his old regimental mess in India, the manhood flogged out of him, to expire after having his identity revealed in a moment of high drama which is in itself one of the finest bravura things in Kipling. There is no mischief in the large improbability of the fable, for the writer realizes his situation irresistibly. The mischief is rather in an incidental intrusive chauvinism. We have seen that the basis of Kipling's political attitude is a just and Miltonic patriotism and a down-to-earth knowledge, such as he judged dangerously neglected, that powder had better be kept dry and sentinels vigilant. But a perversion of this feeling sometimes mars his most vivid imaginative achievements. In **'The Man who Was'** we have it strikingly. For being resolved to give his feelings rein, he goes about the job with ruthless impetus and resource. Over against Dirkovitch, the disagreeable Russian guest, is set Rissaldar Hira Singh, 'the son of a king's son' and a sort of well-affected Hotspur of a native regiment—and this to effects so crude that they could appeal, one would suppose, to the taste only of an inebriated subaltern. Indeed the appeal is not soldierly at all, and not even masculine. Mr. Trilling remarks, with some acid truth, that although Kipling makes much to-do about manliness he is not manly. (pp. 242-43)

The Light that Failed may be said—although this is a simplification—to exist in two forms the precedence between which is uncertain, but which were given to the world within three months of each other. . . . One of these has an ending, commonly admitted as of unbelievable badness, in which the hero and heroine become happily engaged. . . . The other and longer version, declared by Kipling to be the story 'as it was originally conceived by the Writer', is fairly called by Mr. Carrington 'an anti-feminist tract'. And a dramatization, produced in 1903, was to elicit from Kipling's inveterate enemy Max Beerbohm the conjecture that matter which so 'doted on the military' and so abounded in 'cheap cynicism about the female sex' had perhaps been 'fondly created out of the inner consciousness of a female novelist' [see excerpt above]. But in fact *The Light that Failed* is a painful rather than a merely embarrassing book. Like Lawrence's *Sons and Lovers* it is written out of experiences still bearing hard upon the novelist as he works. And

Kipling, who could see so brilliantly both places and people he had known and battles he had never witnessed, has no power to see himself—but only to see a press of his own angers and frustrations and fears. Some expression of these he contrives, and ekes it out with episodes of irrelevant robust *rapportage* surprising in a writer who believes himself to be here following *Manon Lescaut*. Yet the comparison is not quite absurd. It is possible to feel that had Kipling broken through some remaining barrier—or even given adequate time and artistic consideration to his task—he might have achieved a powerful presentation of the destructiveness of sexual passion. (pp. 247-48)

Whether or not there be irony in the fact, Kipling came nearest to a successful novel in a book for young people—for we lose contact with *Kim* . . . when we regard this story of an orphan white boy gone native, and using his native cloak of invisibility to become a peerless Secret Service agent, as other than essentially that. For Mr. Wilson, indeed, the story 'deals with the gradual dawning of his consciousness that he is really a Sahib. . . . What the reader tends to expect is that Kim will come eventually to realize that he is delivering into bondage to the British invaders those whom he has always considered his own people, and that a struggle between allegiances will result.' It is true that there is such a dawn of consciousness in Kim, but not quite true that the story 'deals' with it. And an alert grown-up reader will not in fact come to expect what Mr. Wilson supposes, any more than a juvenile reader will. The book would have to open on the note of [Henry James's] *The Princess Casamassima*, with Kim a potential Hyacinth Robinson, for any such legitimate expectation to be built up. And Kim is—sheerly and superbly—a boy's dream-boy: the kind who since a toddler has been 'hand in hand with men who led lives stranger than anything Haroun al Raschid dreamed of', whose infant ears are privileged to thrill to such words as 'Warn the Pindi and Peshawur brigades', who at a deliciously early age acquires playthings like 'a mother-of-pearl, nickel-plated, self-extracting 450 revolver', and who is equally adept at driving calving cows from a mountain hut and Russian emissaries from the forbidden valleys of Chini and Bushahr. Certainly Kim's growing sense of himself as a Sahib is unaccompanied—however reprehensible this may be—by the slightest persuasion that he is an invader bringing bondage. (p. 259)

Kim, completed long after Kipling's Indian days were over, is a genial book largely because so richly and nostalgically sympathetic, at once acknowledging and softening that potentially tragic conflict of races and faiths that was British India. But if that was a conflict which was to be, in the end, harmoniously resolved after all, there was certainly little in Kipling's later mind that could have contributed to anything of the sort. Over *Kim* we must suppose the influence of Lockwood Kipling, a wiser and more dispassionate man than his son, with whom it was much discussed during the years of its composition. . . . Kipling's own brilliant powers of memory and evocation are here enlisted, as too rarely, in what is entirely a labour of love. The result is a book that knits a lavishly achieved picaresque narrative to a central figure who almost brings off the ultimate feat of escaping from the pages in which he is created. Kim is scarcely either a social or a psychological possibility. But he is quite as real as Jim Hawkins, Bevis, or Huckleberry Finn, and is master of a terrain as irresistible as any these know.

Kim was published at about the mid-point of a substantial period of years in which it would have been reasonable to regard Kipling as having become primarily a writer for children. . . .

[*The Jungle Books* and the later *Just So Stories*] are perhaps best left unburdened with adult appreciation. Their punch lies, no doubt, in their manner of penetrating to genuinely primitive layers of feeling, and we may little have suspected in our nurseries how consistently this was being exploited in the interest of a didactic intention. Mowgli is one of Kim's immediate ancestors; the animal world in which he learns his own variety of the Great Game is somewhat overstaffed with father-figures; and the whole fantasy is open to the charge that, under cover of a seeming-great deal of freedom and wildness, it makes most play with the concept of submission. . . . (pp. 261-62)

[*Captains Courageous*] is a far less interesting book, overloaded with efficient second-hand descriptive writing, and dedicated to the mild proposition that judicious adventure and moderate hardship benefit spoilt children. . . . [*Puck of Pook's Hill* and *Rewards and Fairies*] are ingeniously instructive books in which Puck appears to a small boy and a small girl and acts as presenter of a succession of characters whose stories constitute a pageant of English history. Here again Kipling's historical sense is often finely at play, and many of the narratives notably approximate the remote and the wonderful. (p. 262)

Stalky & Co. is the title given to a collection of school stories brought together in 1899. Every now and then throughout his life Kipling added to the Stalky mythology, and it has received further accretions, not overtly fictional, from persons fortunate or unfortunate enough to have been his schoolfellows. It is clear that the United Services College was a horrible place. There is nothing out of the way in this. Much better-reputed schools have often been so. . . . What has struck his critics as strange, reprehensible, and probably neurotic, is the fact that Kipling seized upon the quite ordinary beastlinesses of the place, joyously inflated them, and then gave them to the world as hugely edifying. . . . There are, in fact, two elements making up the disconcertingness of the Stalky stories. In the first place, Kipling accepts quite whole-heartedly the theory of ritual suffering. Schoolboys—even quite small ones—may, like other initiates, be both proved and taught by the endurance of pain. And as the world will bring them plenty of suffering that is not their own fault, it may be held a sound preparatory discipline to see that a liberal allowance of pain comes to them in a completely arbitrary and savage way. Kipling's offence here is only that he takes this primitive doctrine out of the Victorian headmaster's study and hands it over, in dayrooms and boot-cupboards, to any lout who has the brute strength or the cunning to propagate it in a practical manner. Anybody who thus goes to work boisterously and joyously is a good chap, and well on the way to becoming a *pukka Sahib* too. In all this Kipling is scarcely being more than coarse-grained and emphatic; the doctrine has just enough harsh truth to disinfect it tolerably as we go along. The second cause of offence is much more genuine and serious. Roughly, it consists in the assumption that when Insiders flog Outsiders there can be no darkness in the Insider's hearts. . . . And yet the majority of the stories about these boys are surely puerile rather than vicious. . . . [The later Stalky] stories, at least, surely exhibit a Kipling who has drifted much out of the current of his time. That the sort of institution represented was a place of wise and beneficent training, presided over by persons deeply read in the philosophy of education, was an idea moribund long before Kipling had finished with Stalky and his friends. (pp. 262-64)

[Kipling's stories prompted by the South African War] are full of evidences of . . . perfected craft. But they are streaked, too, with a blind groping malice likely to make them uncomfortable

reading when these campaigns are as distant as Julius Caesar's. In *Traffics and Discoveries* . . . 'A Sahibs' War' is bad and 'The Comprehension of Private Copper' is very much worse—chiefly because of the really ugly way in which the writer's mood is palmed off as the villain's. . . . (p. 265)

The best of [Kipling's World War I] stories is perhaps '**A Madonna of the Trenches**'. . . . [There] is some facile pioneering with abreaction therapy, but the core of the story is supernatural rather than psychological. What has shattered the lad who relates it is not the horror of trench-warfare, with the dead piled up six deep to keep the mud back. It is his glimpse of the ghost of a woman—she has just died of cancer—and a living man facing each other in the last extremity of passion. . . . Kipling has little power over sexual feeling at close range and in detail. But he can bring it almost blindingly in, and this story ranks with '**Love-o'-Women**', '**Mrs. Bathurst**', and '**The Wish House**'. Set beside it, a good many of these stories seen unconvincing and contrived. In '**The Miracle of Saint Jubanus**' the cure of a French soldier—'blasted, withered, dumb, a ghost that gnawed itself'—is ascribed to a fit of immoderate laughter occasioned by a ludicrous incident in his parish church. France, which Kipling loved, deserved a better story than this one. (p. 282)

Kipling's verse is not so good as his prose. . . . For words do not come to Kipling in that sharply fresh interaction alike of their sensuous and their associative components which distinguishes good poetry. In his best verse he has nearly always to make do with being vigorously rhetorical and variously eloquent, and when falling short of this he is seldom very far from a mere jingling and spouting by rote. . . . Yet Kipling's range will be much obscured if we allow ourselves, without further exploration, to be deafened by his predominant tone. A first reading, or a reconsideration, may usefully begin with some quiet things: '**The Way through the Woods**', for example, and '**My Boy Jack**', '**A St. Helena Lullaby**', '**Buddha at Kamakura**', '**Heriot's Ford**', '**Mesopotamia 1917**', the finely cut '**General Joubert**', the enigmatic and haunting '**Gethsemane 1914-18**', and '**Rebirth**', which might be by Hardy. (pp. 283-84)

Kipling appears never himself to have claimed to be a poet. Yet the claim, when considered by others, is seldom turned down quite flat. George Orwell offered the view that Kipling is 'a good bad poet.' . . . Mr. Eliot [see excerpt above], arguing that poetry was something aside from Kipling's deliberate intentions which did nevertheless sometimes come to him, has pointed to the significant fact that any aspiration to the writing of it is absent from even Kipling's early verse. That such an ambition should be eschewed by a young man of powerful imagination and brilliant literary endowment is indeed remarkable, and we may see in it an impressive vindication of his stature as an artist. He himself knows the worth of his bays, has the born artist's knowledge of what it is not his to attempt. He cannot charge language with that sort of meaning which results in the creation of the great autonomous and self-subsistent things.

But this is not a technical matter. There have been few better technicians than Kipling. The deficiency comes from deep down. His language lacks the particularity and precision of poetry because his thought and feeling lack these qualities too. In verse—for some reason far more than in prose—he remains the young man who started into a rich imaginative creation while equipped with very little that intellect, reflection, and even education may provide. That he has a meagre stock of ideas—and that, while some of these are strong and true, a good many are simply superstitions and prejudices—is something that shows through more sharply in a body of work which could indeed conceivably be perused in a single evening. For the achieving of poetry, Kipling works on too small a basis alike of self-scrutiny and of contemplative habit. Although often strikingly original, he brings us nothing from a unique world. He touches us only on the side of our most common responses—this in every sense. But what territory is his, he commands. There was never a greater master of 'Common tunes that make you choke and blow your nose.' . . . (pp. 284-85)

Kipling's patriotic verse has some peaks that are unquestioned. **'For All We Have and Are'** is adequate to its grave occasion in 1914, and G. K. Chesterton was never more singularly foolish than when he wrote a parody of **'Recessional'**. (pp. 285-86)

The patriotic verse is certainly best when it is admonitory and minatory rather than celebrative. . . . (p. 287)

[With Kipling's verse] we are at least in some danger of feeling in the presence of what Keats calls a careless hectorer in proud bad verse. We may connect it—although the coincidence is far from entire—with one of the three main sources of Kipling's craft as criticism commonly distinguishes them: that of popular hymnology. But it is to the other of these sources, those in music-hall song and popular balladry, that what is really the more original part of his work may be traced back. (pp. 289-90)

Occasionally we may have to concede that the note [Kipling struck in his verse] is false—there is perhaps an example in **'The Return'**. Sometimes, as in **'The Ballad of East and West'**, it is certainly a highly romantic imagination that is at work. Yet the soldier's fundamental business is not romanticized. . . . [The] soldier-poems open out a new and vivid world of the imagination. **'The Ladies'** and **'Mandalay'** and **'Danny Deever'** and **'Fuzzy-Wuzzy'** and **'Gunga Din'** are all in their different ways splendid achievements.

A different facet of Kipling's verse is presented in those poems—many of them connected with **Puck of Pook's Hill** and **Rewards and Fairies**—in which the theme is the historical continuity of an English consciousness such as, in Kipling's view, must first have grown up in civilized people among the long-service legionaries and established settlers of the Roman Empire. For Kipling as much as for Hardy the English soil has history engraved upon it—quite literally so for the informed and seeing eye. . . . (pp. 291-92)

Kipling's verse does not interest us more as Kipling's own maturity grows. There is no equivalent in it to **'The Wish House'** or **'The Gardener'**. He does, indeed, consider in the verse of his later years a good many hard matters. **'En-Dor'** contains the whole of **'They'**, and **'Hymn of Breaking Strain'** expresses the full burden of **'Unconvenanted Mercies'** and a good deal else. But his tools remain the same and his medium scarcely enriches or subtilizes itself. In verse there is no earlier and later Kipling, as there is an earlier and later Shakespeare, an earlier and later Eliot.

But there is—working always carefully within his apprehended compass—a dedicated artist. (p. 293)

J.I.M. Stewart, "Kipling," in his Eight Modern Writers *(© Oxford University Press 1963; reprinted*

by permission of Oxford University Press), Oxford University Press, Oxford, 1963, pp. 223-93.

RANDALL JARRELL   (essay date 1963)

To most of us Kipling means India. Kipling's masterpiece, **Kim**, is an Indian story; so are the **Jungle Books;** so are the stories that made Kipling, in his thirties, the best-known writer in the world. It was this Indian Kipling whom Henry James called "the most complete man of genius (as distinct from fine intelligence) that I have ever known." Yet many, even most, of Kipling's best stories are stories of the English in England; the stories of Kipling's old age or late middle age—work that shows the easy and decisive mastery that was the result of a lifetime of imaginative realization—are with a few exceptions stories about England. (p. 279)

Baa Baa, Black Sheep is the one purely autobiographical story of a reticent and private-spirited author (his story of the future, **As Easy as A.B.C.,** makes "invasion of privacy" the sin upon which his new society is based). . . . **The Vortex** is one of the funnier examples of a compulsive form, Kipling's practical-joke story; the reader may feel, as I do, that he enjoys Kipling's farce for its charm and landscape, and is indifferent to its point. As for **"In the Interests of the Brethren,"** it is pure charm—who would have supposed that you could make, of the meeting of an imaginary Masonic lodge, one of the most winning of sketches? I imagine that, except for **The Magic Flute**, it is the most attractive work of art Masonry has produced.

But at this point the reader may feel like remarking, "Autobiography, compulsive practical jokes, Masonry—do the subjects of the stories keep on like this?" Well, yes. (pp. 279-80)

Revenge, love, disease and death, the supernatural, extreme situations, practical jokes, country ways, literature: these are some of the things that keep recurring in the stories. Yet the list of subjects seems to me, as I imagine it seems to the reader, a surprisingly varied and unusual one. Kipling is one of the most effectively realistic of writers—his stories are dazzling in their verisimilitude, their extraordinarily broad and detailed knowledge of special ways of speech and life, of a hundred varieties of local color; yet they are never mere slices of life, and are even more notable for their imagination than for their realism. If the reality principle has pruned and clipped them into plausibility, it is the pleasure principle out of which they first rankly and satisfyingly flowered. Kipling is far closer to Gogol than to a normal realist or naturalist: in Kipling the pressure of the imagination has forced facts over into the supernatural, into personally satisfying jokes or revenges, into personally compulsive fantasies or neuroses. Then too, like Gogol, Kipling is one of the great stylists of his language, one of those writers who can make a list more interesting than an ordinary writer's murder. (pp. 281-82)

A farm laborer whom Kipling knew particularly well said to someone, after Kipling's death, that the old fool did nothing but ask you questions; [his short stories] are the result of many asked and many unasked questions. The primary pleasure of a story like **Friendly Brook** is the atmosphere ("so choked with fog that one could scarcely see a cow's length across a field") through which it comes to us; grim, plain, warped through work and workaday speech. . . . (pp. 285-86)

There are few stories that seem, first of all and last of all, beautiful; **"They"** is one. It is almost as if the story's extraordinary beauty of picturing, and of the style which pictures, came out of Kipling's desire to have the story a memorial to his own dead daughter. It is a memorial in three tapestries, an early-summer, a late-summer, and an autumn day; the days themselves are hardly more beautiful than the story's movement through the days. . . . (p. 287)

It is interesting to compare the naturally beautiful *"They"* with the harshly and uncannily colorful *"Wireless,"* a story that leaves a sort of stained-glass deposit in the memory. It is seen and felt and heard as few stories are: if genius is the ability to perceive (and to make us perceive) likenesses never before seen, in concise hallucinatory form, then *"Wireless"* is a work of genius. It is certainly a work of astonishing originality, of the most extraordinary professional skill. (pp. 287-88)

As he got older, Kipling found it necessary to write more and more elaborately farcical practical-joke stories—stories of revenge, often; the confirmed reader will immediately think of pieces like *"Brugglesmith," My Sunday at Home, The Puzzler, The Vortex, The Village That Voted the Earth Was Flat, The Bonds of Discipline, Steam Tactics, "Their Lawful Occasions," Aunt Ellen, The Miracle of St. Jubanus, Beauty Spots.* I myself can read these stories with pleasure. (But if Kipling had written instructions on how to make a bed with hospital corners, or how to can gooseberries, I could read them with pleasure: as one of his characters exclaims, "It was the tone, man, the tone!") Most of these farces are stories for the confirmed reader only, since they have been written by the writer for the writer: in them, often, the writer tells us how he laughs so hard that he cannot speak or see or stand up, and how that luckiest of all winds, the dawn wind, comes and whispers to him that the next day everything is going to be even better. *The Village That Voted the Earth Was Flat* quite overcomes these humble, compulsive beginnings: a little of it is a little too good to be true, but what a knowing ingenuity of invention it has, how extraordinarily it is imagined! (pp. 289-90)

If you compare one of the best of Kipling's early stories (*Without Benefit of Clergy,* say) with some of the best of his late stories, you realize that the late stories are specialized in their moral and human attitudes—in their subject matter, even—in a way in which the early story is not. The early story's subject is a general subject that will repay any amount of general skill or general talent: you can imagine a greater writer's rewriting *Without Benefit of Clergy* and making a much better story out of it. But this is precisely what you cannot imagine with Kipling's later stories: Chekhov and Tolstoy and Turgenev together couldn't improve *"They"* or *"Wireless,"* since in each a highly specialized subject has received an exactly appropriate, extraordinarily skilled and talented treatment. These later stories of Kipling's don't compete, really, with *Gusev* and *The Death of Ivan Ilych* and *A Sportsman's Sketches,* but have set up a kingdom of their own, a little off to the side of things, in which they are incomparable: their reader feels, "You can write better stories than Kipling's, but not better Kipling stories." This kingdom of theirs is a strange, disquieting, but quite wonderful place, as if some of the Douanier Rousseau's subjects had been repainted by Degas. If we cannot make the very greatest claims for the stories, it would be absurd not to make great ones: as long as readers enjoy style and skill, originality and imagination—in a word, genius—they will take delight in Kipling's stories. (pp. 291-92)

Randall Jarrell, in his introduction to The English in England: Short Stories *by Rudyard Kipling, edited by Randall Jarrell (copyright © 1963 by Doubleday & Company, Inc.; reprinted by permission of the publisher), Anchor Press, 1963 (and reprinted in his* The Third Book of Criticism, *Farrar, Straus & Giroux, 1969, pp. 270-92).*

C. A. BODELSEN (essay date 1964)

Farcical tales are common in Kipling, they are found in nearly all the volumes of stories from every period of his life, but the great majority of them have no reference to his philosophy of mirth. Some of the *Plain Tales from the Hills,* for example *The Rout of the White Hussars* and *His Wedded Wife,* are merely accounts of somewhat primitive practical jokes. An example of a practical joke story from his later work on quite another scale is afforded by *The Bonds of Discipline* . . . , which describes in great detail a fantastic hoax staged by the whole complement of a British man-of-war for the benefit of a French spy.

But among the farcical tales there is a group that is different from those mentioned above, for one thing because Kipling here puts much of his usual reticence aside and tells the reader more about his private feelings, hopes and disappointments than elsewhere; but chiefly because, in contrast to the run of his farces, their real point is not the sequence of fantastic happenings that constitutes the action, but a spiritual experience which they are an attempt to express, and which is akin to that for which he uses the phrase 'the night got into my head' in *Something of Myself.* The following are the stories in question in chronological order:

> (*'Brugglesmith'*) (1891)
> *My Sunday at Home* (1895)
> *The Puzzler* (1906)
> *The Vortex* (1914)
> *The Prophet and the Country* (1924)
> *Aunt Ellen* (1932)

(pp. 6-7)

[The critic adds in a footnote that: *'Brugglesmith'* is in brackets because it is only halfway to belonging in the group. I have not included *Steam Tactics* . . . because there is no resolution of the tension in laughter, and because, unlike the others, it is a revenge story. . . . *The Prophet and the Country* definitely belongs to the stories that deal with the Revelation of Mirth, though it differs from the rest in that the sequence of grotesque events is not experienced by the 'I', but constitutes a story told him by somebody else.] (p. 7)

The list does not include *The Village That Voted the Earth Was Flat, Little Foxes* and *Beauty Spots,* nor those *Stalky* tales which contain descriptions of semi-hysterical hilarity, because all these belong in a different category. In the first three the laughter is part of a revenge or retribution, and this also in some measure holds good of the *Stalky* stories. When that is the case, Kipling invariably avoids any reference to his creed of laughter as a cosmic revelation. Nor have I included the stories where laughter figures as a healing power. There are several of these, the most important being the very late story *The Miracle of Saint Jubanus.* . . . These too belong to a group by themselves, for one thing because the laughter has not the character of a 'revelation', and for another because they are not farces.

The relevant stories thus constitute a well-defined group of six. Beginning in 1891 and ending in 1932, they are spread fairly evenly over some forty years of Kipling's literary career, and the recurrence of their basic theme bears witness to his continued preoccupation with the transcendental experience they describe. All these (as also the late revenge stories, with the exception of *Little Foxes*) are told in the first person. The reader is left in no doubt that the 'I' is Kipling himself, or rather the *persona* he consistently assumes whenever he makes an appearance in his own books. But with one exception, *'Brugglesmith'*—the first of them, and one in which he has not yet quite found the pattern characteristic of the rest—he is not the principal character, and he is always represented as sufficiently detached from the events that he witnesses to enjoy them as a kind of observer, for whose benefit the whole fantastic show might have been staged.

The actual events of these tales are clearly fictitious. Indeed, they are so egregious that they could not very well have happened in real life. But one is left in no doubt that Kipling believes he has experienced the emotional quality that they embody, and the story has the appearance of being a vision of a perfection glimpsed in felicitous moments, or a wish dream to meet with something like it in reality.

These stories are highly 'private', in so far as they deal with emotions that most readers cannot be expected to know, whether from themselves or from literature, and into which they must find it difficult to enter. It is not easy to give a straightforward account of something that is told indirectly or symbolically. . . . What happens, then, may be described as follows:

The familiar scene is exposed to a kind of shock which for a brief while makes it settle down into a pattern other than the accustomed one. The narrator suddenly finds himself in a universe governed by an internal logic other than that of his normal world, whose laws are earnestness, order and duty. The cosmic powers have discarded their severe mask, and their inmost essence is shown, at least for the moment, to be comic. The menaces and the sinister forces so often sensed at the back of Kipling's world are banned on this transfigured stage, where embarrassments and mishaps are merely laughable, and one can abandon oneself blissfully to happenings that become more and more outrageous as the story moves along. And this abandonment is felt as a release, or at least a respite, from the burdens and stresses of life.

He who experiences this is vouchsafed a glimpse of a comic cosmos, and at the same time a revelation of hidden meanings that have escaped him in his more sober moments. The process takes place, of course, inside his own mind, which undergoes a kind of enlargement, enabling him to discover new and exciting qualities in things that used to appear prosaic; and it is implied that what he perceives in this way is *a truth* that otherwise eludes one.

The experiences these stories try to describe involve, as it were, a pause in the inexorable regularity of the world. They have the effect of a private Saturnalia that produces a catharsis by the suspension of rules and distinctions that one normally has to observe. That for Kipling, who otherwise regards order as the basic principle of the universe, this should be a symbol of bliss, is a remarkable evidence of the complexity of his character. It is a complete contradiction of his usual philosophy, according to which it is only by working, doing one's duty, and meeting the challenges of fate with courage and patience that one can lead a tolerable life and preserve one's human dignity. Those who look for logic in such matters can perhaps find it in the explanation that this *is* after all only a Saturnalia, a few hours' holiday from the burden and the dust, and not applicable as a guide to ordinary conduct. It is, however, much

more likely that the explanation must be sought in the contradictions of the writer's personality: a tautness, sometimes a crampedness, that is occasionally reflected in his style and in his sudden outbreaks of intolerant anger, caused him to make a cult of the only effective form of relaxation he knew, and to identify memories of a more carefree period of his life with remembered scenes of hilarity. (pp. 8-11)

[When Kipling] deals with a comic experience he describes his characters, including himself, as displaying their emotions with a physical violence of which the gesticulations of Frenchmen and Italians, so despised by the Victorians, are only a pale reflection.

The action that precedes the release in laughter follows roughly the same scheme in all the stories in question. The characters are exposed to some comic accident, whose consequences deploy from one farcical scene to the next.

As an example one may take *Aunt Ellen,* the last of this kind of story Kipling wrote. The following is only a very brief synopsis, which leaves out many details. The narrator, who is clearly meant to be Kipling himself, has been on a visit to Cambridge and drives towards London in the evening. An old lady has given him a commission: a jar of jam and an eiderdown, which he ties on to his car. The bundle falls off and is run over by two undergraduates, who are on their way to a dance in London in a state of considerable elevation. Run over, the eiderdown soaked in red jam looks much like the victim of a traffic accident, and Kipling allows the undergraduate at the wheel to remain in the belief that it is in fact a mangled body. (This use of a macabre subject for comic effect probably owes something to R. L. Stevenson's *The Wrong Box.*) Both cars continue their way after the 'body' has been stowed into one of them. After a number of wayside adventures, they reach the outskirts of London in the early dawn. There they are stopped by a policeman. When he opens the bonnet of the car the down is blown out by the ventilator and sticks to the constable and one of the undergraduates, so that they look like two monstrous birds. Then follows the usual laughter motif.

All this may not strike the reader who does not know the story as an example of the grand tradition of humour. Nor is it. The action of these stories is not really humorous, it is comic. They are not meant to be humorous in the traditional sense, and one might even be tempted to ask if they are meant to be amusing. The author would no doubt reply that they were, but the question is really without meaning, because in that case he would not mean quite the same thing by 'amusing' as a good many of his readers. The writer's attitude to the bizarre events is of an oddly private kind, and the reader may find it difficult to share it. Sometimes, as in *Aunt Ellen,* there are overtones that are vaguely troubling or even sinister, as if this was a dream from which one would rather wake up. And in this there is nothing surprising: an atmosphere of unrest and tension is being built up to be resolved again in the laughter scene, and it communicates some of its quality to the reader.

But whether one finds them amusing or not, the comic events are not what the story is really about: it is about an adventure on the borderland of the normal, and, however important they may have been to the writer, they are slightly disconcerting to the reader who has had no experiences of that kind himself. Incidentally, I believe that a good many people do have similar accesses of a hilarity felt as a sudden expansion of the spirit. What makes Kipling stand apart is that he bases a philosophy, almost a creed, on them. (pp. 12-14)

If one reads the six stories in question in chronological order, one gets some idea of the stages by which his philosophy of Mirth developed. The first of them, *'Brugglesmith'*, represents only a half-way stage. It has nearly all the elements on which the philosophy is based, but gives no indication of the metaphysical implications which he was to read into them in later life. There is the whole apparatus of comic incidents that mount towards a climax—the narrator's wanderings through the sleeping city in the early hours of the morning, accompanied by a drunken man who involves him in more and more preposterous adventures. Underlying this comic theme there is a slightly sinister effect, as of a nightmare. The story even has something of the dawn atmosphere that in the later tales heralds the culmination: the release of tension in a storm of uncontrollable laughter. But the latter motif is absent here, and the narrator remains alone on the scene without anybody to share his mirth with. This is exceptional—it is only the case in *'Brugglesmith'* and *My Sunday at Home,* the two earliest stories of this type. In the others the hilarity is always shared; and this seems more true to life: hilarity in complete isolation is surely something that very few people experience. Or perhaps the young Kipling was an exception in that respect, and the need for companions to share his mirth was a measure of his waning animal spirits as he grew older. (p. 22)

> *C. A. Bodelsen, in his* Aspects of Kipling's Art *(©*
> *C. A. Bodelsen 1964; by permission of Barnes &*
> *Noble Books, a Division of Littlefield, Adams & Co.,*
> *Inc.), Barnes & Noble, 1964, 169 p.*

BONAMY DOBRÉE (essay date 1967)

[Rudyard Kipling] is a writer who can compel your imagination to accompany him from arid villages in Afghanistan to the rich downs of Sussex, from the plains of India to the wildest of Atlantic seas, from Arctic ice to the sweltering African forests. He can impart the chatter of journalists in London, the energy of pioneers in Canada, or the terrible isolation of a lighthouse-keeper. Here is a man who can horrifyingly reveal shocking depths of humanity, show it at its most tender and compassionate, or flash to you a queer vision of an archangelic world. He can go back to ancient Rome, even to pre-history, and forward to the year 2065. His variety is astonishing. It is of no use to read a few stories of one kind and put him in a certain category: you cannot pigeon-hole Kipling—he will catch you unaware. . . . What seizes you continually is the overflowing vitality that gives you the sense of being just there. And through the fiction, the lectures and the letters, there run threads of certain dominating ideas or intuitions, each, perhaps, simple in itself, but which woven together form an intricate, patterned tapestry.

He was temperamentally imbued with an exuberant zest for life, which he found to be "curious—and sudden and mixed", and an inexhaustible interest and delight in men. To use his own phrases, he found naught common on the earth, and more than once thanked Allah for the infinite diversity of His creatures in His adorable world. He had unceasing curiosity about what men do, and how they do it. (pp. 3-4)

Nor was it material facts alone that he gleaned from the people he bewitched into talking to him: he picked up stories from all sources. . . . We know the source of a few of his stories. **'The Finances of the Gods'**, for example, comes from his father's *Beast and Man in India:* **'Little Foxes'** was told him—in raw outline, obviously—by an army officer whom he met on board ship, when he "expected no such jewel". (pp. 4-5)

Added to these sources were the stories or ideas he got from previous writers, for naturally he was something of a plagiarist, as all good writers of necessity are. (p. 5)

The substance of his stories grew more and more throughout the years to be "the eternal mystery of personality", as one of the characters in **'A Friend of the Family'** phrases it—the vulnerable personality of man. . . . What fascinated him most, especially in his early maturity, was the character and being of the people who did things, for it was what they did that gave them individuality in the Great Game of 'To Be or Not to be' that they played in the face of an indifferent, timeless universe. His individuals had to have an integrity proud and secure in its own fortress—even an integrity of which others might not be proud; they had to be people of action of some kind (women differently from men) because it is through action alone that people reveal what they are, and arrive at a sense of themselves. (p. 6)

One might reverse Henry James's dictum on Turgenev, and say that there was in Kipling "an impalpable union of the democratic temperament with an aristocratic mind". He could apply to himself the saying "I met a hundred men on the road to Delhi, and they were all my brothers", but what he sought for were the aristocrats. An aristocrat for Kipling was one who, whatever his race, or caste, or creed, had a full man within him, who kept himself whole, and did not set too much value upon his feelings. Those who did this last were always objects of his contempt. . . . [As] we read in **'His Private Honour'**, "First a man must suffer, then he must learn his work, and the self-respect that that knowledge brings." Those who have his approval are the Ordes and Tallantires of the frontier districts, McAndrew the engineer, the doctors of his later stories, and among women, William the Conqueror in the tale of that name. Then again, there were in *Kim,* Mahbub Ali and Hurree Chunder Mookerjie, besides the Englishmen (the Lama is another matter—one of the contradictions in Kipling): there were Peachey Carnehan and Daniel Dravot in **'The Man Who Would be King'**, there were forgotten toilers in out-stations . . . : it did not matter if they were failures, or tramps, or 'wilful-missings', so long as they kept themselves whole, though sometimes only partly, as Dowse the lighthouse-keeper who went mad because of the infernal streakiness of the tides and so became 'A Disturber of Traffic', and Love o' Women who suffered the reward his name implies.

None were obviously successful in the worldly sense, for Kipling despised success; he has little to say for the high-ups, the administrators, the people in authority, who as a general rule . . . knew nothing of the matters they were dealing with. (pp. 7-8)

When talking to men about their work he learnt also about their characters—what better way could there be since a man's work is his character? Yet there is a difficulty here, for there is a limit to men's communication with each other. . . . (p. 8)

[Kipling's] tireless curiosity, his zest in all he saw, gave him abundant material. Some he got from his father, but most of the matter for his Indian tales came from his night-wanderings (the night had 'got into his head' from very early days) about remote quarters of the cities he got to know, hidden corners of the bazaars and so on, where he met the strangest people. . . . (p. 10)

Passages scattered throughout *Something of Myself* give a vivid picture of his growth as a professional writer soon to become the dedicated artist, a Maker, possessed by a Personal Daemon. (p. 11)

The Daemon is in charge: he cannot be dictated to, and will not work where he does not wish to, as Kipling found when he chose a brickyard in which to set a tale about Defoe. But, as he makes Shakespeare say to Ben Jonson in **'Proofs of Holy Writ'**, ''My Demon never betrayed me yet, while I trusted him.'' Moreover, ''Never follow up 'a success'.'' There was, also, the old Law, ''As soon as you find that you can do anything, do something you can't.'' For it is as John of Burgos said in **'The Eye of Allah'**: ''In my craft, a thing done with is done with. We go on to new shapes after that.'' It may be noticed that Kipling always had this in mind. In **'The Bull that Thought'**, the boys in the cattle-yard, playing with Apis, desired him to repeat himself, ''which'', the narrator says, ''no true artist will tolerate''.

But though he depended on what might ordinarily be called 'inspiration', Kipling gave a good deal of thought to what the Daemon provided; he by no means let the pen do the writing for him. (pp. 12-13)

He found writing and all that pertained to it 'glorious fun'; but from the beginning he laboured enormously to be worthy of the guidance he was given. (p. 13)

We see, then, the man enthralled by his imagination, letting it strike out into invented realism; for Kipling was primarily an artist, feeling and seeing by intuition, creating as he let his formative sensibilities wander. But—adding to the dimension—in common with his own Aurelian McGoggin, ''his grandfathers on both sides had been Wesleyan preachers, and the preaching strain came out in his mind''. In varying degrees there was always this duality giving substance to his tales. He was eager to *show* raw, naked humanity, from its horror to its near-angelic qualities, but also to suggest, or even state, a moral. (pp. 14-15)

[That kind of duality] serves in part to account for the structured complexity of the later tales, though even in the earlier stories there is usually more than one level. Kipling could always see, and feel, both sides of a question—or more if there were such. . . . He may be the prophet of work, the priest of discipline; but he is also the poet of love, and poet laureate of laughter. (pp. 15-16)

Bonamy Dobrée, in his Rudyard Kipling: Realist and Fabulist *(© Oxford University Press 1967; reprinted by permission of Oxford University Press), Oxford University Press, London, 1967, 244 p.*

ANGUS WILSON   (essay date 1977)

It is [his] Indian vision that Kipling will surely above all be remembered by, for the British Indian scene (native and Anglo-Indian) is a composition of relationships that no one else has ever put on paper, and no one else has ever made into a consistent social metaphor for human existence. A very strange man expressed himself here through a very strange, now historical, phenomenon. Against this, the obvious imperfections of the young Kipling's mind and the crudities of his craftsmanship in the early stories seem of little importance. The brashness, the assumed man-of-the-world voice, the club-gossip, the know-all ''I'' narrator, the occasional puritan's leer, the arch Biblical pastiche language and the even more arch

forays into pseudo-Arabian Nights narration—all these are minor flaws in a great East Window that shines and glints and darkens and dazzles as nothing else in any literature. There are some truly inferior stories among the scores of his Indian tales and more mediocre ones, and enough masterpieces—but the vision should be taken as a whole from the first tale, **''Lispeth''** in *Plain Tales from the Hills* to her reappearance in *Kim*—should be taken good and bad alike, with *Departmental Ditties* and *Barrack Room Ballads* thrown in. . . .

The *Jungle Books,* I think, need a short explanation, for they are very odd. And, of course, *Kim,* his most magical work, one of the oddest masterpieces ever written, demands our full scrutiny.

Three of the seven stories in *The First Jungle Book* and five out of the eight in *The Second Jungle Book* concern Mowgli and his jungle empire. For many people Mowgli, Baloo, Bagheera, Kaa and Co. *are* the *Jungle Books*—a kind of Greyfriars. But the merits of the individual Mowgli stories vary very much. Only a few, and perhaps only parts of these, show Kipling at his very top form.

The interest in the Mowgli group as a whole cannot really be a literary one. It is connected with his pervasive idea of the Law which is expressed in them more continuously than in the rest of his work, although hardly less obscurely. (p. 122)

The chief glory of [Kipling's] art in the Mowgli stories lies in his extraordinary combination of the natural and animal world with the world of the humans. Baloo is a bear and a housemaster; Bagheera is chiefly a leopard but a wise, sensual man more worldly than the bear; Kaa is primarily a python, delighting in his coils and glistening skin, lusting to chase and kill, but he is also an exceptional and clever man, knowing himself yet accepting The Law, perhaps a true intellectual as opposed to the Bandar-log who are monkeys and ''intellectuals''; the jackal is Mussolini's forerunner, and Shere Khan Hitler's, as wartime telegrams between the Kipling Society and General Wavell rightly suggested.

It is a strange achievement, a brilliant artistic bluff, where words and thoughts veer towards the human and movements, vision and feeling are as near to animal as a writer can hope to guess. And, of course, the whole is made credible by the extraordinary evocation of the jungle itself. . . . The law in this world is exact but far from Darwinian; we need note only that no animal will attack another at the pool in time of drought.

Into this world comes the lovable, strong, highly intelligent wolfcub boy, Mowgli, who learns the simple Law which in more complicated form he will have later to follow in human society. And, by his superior human intelligence and compassion, eventually also wins mastery in the animal world. The Law of the jungle is absolute and can be followed by the animals with comparative ease, for they do not know tears or laughter, the things that make man's life both more glorious and more complex and far more painfully burdensome among human beings than has ever been known in the Eden of Kaa and Baloo, however bloody and terrible many of the deeds that happen in the jungle.

All this about The Law is interesting, but as far as Kipling's art goes, it often gets in the way, with too much didactic moralising. In *The First Jungle Book,* only one story is reasonably free from it and that doesn't really get going until halfway through. **''Kaa's Hunting''** contains one of the most horrible scenes in all Kipling's work—and that work contains many such. It is the picture of the Bandar Log monkeys swaying helplessly towards their doom in the great ruins of the King's palace in a hypnotic trance induced by the coiling and looping of Kaa, the python's body and his "never stopping, low humming song". It is made more terrible by the jungle fact that, were it not for Mowgli's human unsusceptibility to the snake's enchantment, Baloo and Bagheera, Kaa's erstwhile co-hunters, would inevitably sway towards their death with the monkeys. For, in the jungle, all alliances—and bear, python and leopard have hunted together to rescue Mowgli—break up when the kill is on. It is made, indeed, even a little too horrible by a certain relish with which Kipling recites the awful fate of the frivolous, mischievous monkey folk.

The best Mowgli stories come in *The Second Jungle Book*. The manoeuvres by which Mowgli lures the ravening hordes of dholes, the red dogs from the South, to their death and the battle between the dholes and the wolves is one of the best action narratives in fiction. (pp. 125-26)

It is rare to find readers, Kipling fans or others, who are not captivated by *Kim;* it is equally rare to find many who can offer any detailed account of their enjoyment of the book. "Oh! *Kim,* of course, is a magical book," is the usual general account that follows a detailed discussion of his other works. And so it is. (p. 128)

I know of no other English novel that so celebrates the human urban scene (for English novelists are all touched by the Romantic country worship) except for that utterly dissimilar book, *Mrs Dalloway;* and when one reads of Kim's thoughts, "this adventure, though he did not know the English word, was a stupendous lark", one is reminded of the opening passage of Virginia Woolf's novel (Clarissa's thoughts as she steps out into the streets of London): "What a lark! What a plunge!" It is a note of delight in life, of openness to people and things that is maintained throughout the novel and is the essence of its magic.

Kipling's passionate interest in people and their vocabularies and their crafts is, of course, the essence of the magic of all his work. But in all the other books it tends to be marred by aspects of his social ethic—by caution, reserve, distrust, mastered emotion, stiff upper lips, direct puritanism or the occasional puritan's leer, retributive consequences, cruelty masquerading as justifiable restraint or bullying as the assertion of superiority. None of these is present in *Kim.*

Kipling's social ethic, it is true, is there in Kim's apprenticeship to "The Game", the British Secret Service in India. This is the way that, as a sahib's son, he will serve the British cause. This has stuck in the gullet of many liberal critics. . . . (p. 130)

True, Kim will be serving British rule, but this must be read within the context of Kipling's belief that the two higher values in this book—the richness and variety of Indian life and the divine and spiritual idiocy of the Lama—can only be preserved from destruction by anarchic chaos or from despotic tyranny by that rule. . . . Kim, by his involvement in The Game, can help to preserve that holy man whose spirituality he can glimpse and love but never hope to achieve. And let us note, it is a game, however terrible a one, in which Kim, by his strange street-arab status of friend of all the world and night climber across rooftops, is peculiarly associated—a game in which he must be able to carry maps in his head and remember a hundred objects seen and be able to pass disguised as twenty or so other people. These powers make him perfect material for a spy; the same powers made Kipling a great writer of fiction.

But, if the moralising side of Kipling is only lightly present in *Kim,* implicit in The Game, the corruption of Kim's world is always implicit rather than stated. The world Kim moves in is no ideal one. Only the Lama in his innocence mistakes the generous prostitute for a nun. It is a world of lies—Kim knows the Lama for a rarity because he tells the truth to strangers. Physical danger is constant and real. Human life is not held in high regard—Mahbub Ali is prepared to sacrifice Kim's life to get his message to Creighton, yet he loves Kim strongly and jealously. Few of the fifty or so vividly realised characters are without his or her faults, but most are made generous and loving by contact with Kim and the Lama. Yet Kim is never above the ordinary dishonesties and tricks of daily life. As the Lama says, "I have known many men in my long life, and disciples not a few. But to none among men, if so be thou art woman-born, has my heart gone out as it has to thee—thoughtful, wise and courteous; but something of a small imp."

And it is not Kim's virtues alone that win him the friendship of all the world. He is remarkably physically beautiful and, in a way that is successfully kept by Kipling from being fully sexual, flirtatious with all and sundry. It is part of his worldly guile. The prostitute in the train is won over by him as is the other prostitute who dresses him up when he escapes from St Xavier's School; the Sahiba's motherliness has an earthy tinge; the woman of Shamlegh yearns for him. In Lurgan's shop, as I have said, the jealousy of the Hindu boy has obvious sexual overtones; as I think does the jealousy of the horsedealer, Mahbub Ali, for Kim's overriding devotion to the Lama. Yet all this sensuality is without an explicit sexual tinge. I do not believe that this is Victorian self-censorship upon the part of Kipling. It is certainly not an avoidance of the subject in a book ostensibly intended for the young, for the scene where a prostitute tries to steal from Mahbub Ali is quite explicit. It is, I think, one more aspect of the purposeful attempt by Kiplinq in this novel to create a world that is real and ideal at one and the same time. Nor is the absence of overt sex offensively evasive as a modern critic might think. It is just a natural part of the innocent-corrupt world in which Kim lives.

As to evil it is strikingly absent, as may be measured by the unimportance of the "villains", the Russian and French spies. They are bad men, we know, for they offer violence to a very good man, the Lama. But their retribution is not the savoured brutal one of so many of Kipling's stories. They merely pass out of the novel, mocked by all the Himalayan villagers as they make off with their tails between their legs. Their humiliation is like that of Trinculo and Stephano on Prospero's magic island in *The Tempest* and we bless the babu Hurree Singh, who mocks them, as we bless Ariel. In default of true evil, we must judge the English chaplain, Bennett, as the villain, for he lacks all concern for freedom and variety, virtues so surprisingly celebrated by Kipling in this book. It could be said that this absence of real evil prevents *Kim* from vying with the great novels of the past as a "mature" book; but, in compensation, it must surely be said that this creation of an innocent world of guile makes it an unequalled novel.

Nirad Chaudhuri has said that *Kim* is the very best picture of India by an English author [see excerpt above], and I am sure he is right. But rich and convincing though the varied Indian characters are, and splendid though the evocations of the Indian scenes are from the Jain Temple outside Benares to the Himalayan foothills, it is yet Kipling's own India as Kim is Kipling's own street-arab and the Lama Kipling's own Buddhist. Many Indian critics, notably K. Jamiluddin in *The Tropic*

Sun, have pointed out that Buddhism is a very strange choice of religion to represent India, from which it has been absent for centuries. No doubt, Kipling was a bit influenced in his choice by his desire to draw on his father's special knowledge; but I think he was even more concerned to pose his own version of self-abnegation against his own version of commitment to the world as represented by Kim. The Lama and Kim make a most delectable Prospero and Ariel. And it is no sparring partnership for either, since the Lama's greatest erring from The Way is in his attachment to his Chela, and Kim comes close to exhausting his adolescent physical strength in bringing his master down from the mountains. The story of Kim and the Lama is, in the last resort, beneath all its superbly realised human and topical detain an allegory of that seldom portrayed ideal, the world in the service of spiritual goodness, and, even less usual, spiritual goodness recognising its debt to the world's protection. It is the culmination and essence of all the transcendence that Kipling gained from his Indian experience. In it alone of all his works he does ask, "Who is Kim?", although he cannot answer the question. In a sense, his answer is the book itself, for it is the best thing he ever wrote. (pp. 130-32)

> *Angus Wilson, in his* The Strange Ride of Rudyard Kipling: His Life and Works *(copyright © 1977 by Angus Wilson; reprinted by permission of Viking Penguin Inc.; in Canada by Secker and Warburg),* Secker and Warburg, 1977 *(and reprinted by The Viking Press, 1978), 370 p.*

IRVING HOWE (essay date 1982)

Encountering his stories of Indian life, with their high, even garish, coloring, Kipling's early readers delighted in his crude energy, his air of manly assertion, his ration of exotica, his touches of "barbarism" which seemed so bracing to a culture suspecting itself of decadence. It was precisely his "difference" that brought Kipling a quick and enormous popularity, enchanting even such unlikely admirers as Henry James and Oscar Wilde. Later generations, with the presumed advantages of historical distance, have been much more inclined to place Kipling in the moral setting of his time, as a writer who shared with Freud, as with many others, a deepening anxiety over the fate of civilization.

These two quite different men, starting from quite different premises of belief, shared—together with many of their contemporaries—a growing skepticism about the life of Europe, the durability of civilization, the future of the human enterprise. They shared a persuasion that civilization, if it was to survive at all, would require strict modes of discipline. Freud spoke gloomily of "repression" and its costs; Kipling wrote that "for the pain of the soul there is, outside God's Grace, but one drug; and that is a man's craft, learning, or other helpful motions of his mind." And perhaps because they did take so uncompromising a view of the cost in repression that we pay for every advantage of civilization, both men appreciated—Kipling drew his best work out of—those yearnings we all have to cast away the commands of authority and somehow return to the freedom and comeliness of childhood.

Both Freud and Kipling were inclined to see religion primarily as a mode of social discipline, an order and solace for the chafings of self-denial. Kipling did not theorize about this, but his feelings come through in a number of stories. **"The Church That Was at Antioch,"** a late story, is a sophisticated, occasionally biting account of primitive Christianity, with Peter and Paul not saintly presences but decidedly human figures not yet

able to contain the enthusiasms of their coarse followers. Civilization rests here largely with the hard, skeptical Romans. In **"The Eye of Allah,"** a charming story, Kipling shows religion in its disciplinary narrowness, holding back the scientific enthusiasms of Roger Bacon, checking the spirit of inquiry in behalf of social peace. Civilization requires here an acceptance of irksome constraints.

Both Freud and Kipling placed a heavy emphasis on the role of aggression in the human economy. For Kipling it was a theme so urgent it sometimes escaped his control. And both Freud and Kipling could not suppress a recurrent shudder before the final emptiness of things, a pang of dismay before the helplessness of man and the feebleness of his comforts. "When a man has come to the turnstiles of Night, all the creeds in the world seem to him wonderfully alike and colorless." The words are Kipling's, but they could stand as an epigraph for *Civilization and Its Discontents.*

Kipling is a writer with an astonishing variety of voices, some of them livelier and others more shallow than Freud's stoical gravity. Nor is Kipling the sort of writer who envelops one with a large, harmonious vision of life which, if only in the experience of reading, seems sufficient as a reading of experience. He often breaks, or breaks down, into a multiplicity of selves, and one of the problems critics have faced with him has been to align these selves with one another. Still, to notice the anxiety at the center of his work is to enable a singling out of that portion of his work which remains valuable. It is to rescue him a little from his reputation as bullyboy of empire, declaimer of manliness, preening toughie of combat. (pp. 27-8)

Kipling did not have a supple or reflective mind. He had only a small gift for self-doubt and not much more for contemplativeness. Only occasionally could he show that largeness of spirit we like to associate with the greatest writers. His work keeps dropping to a display of values likely to repel civilized readers.

And yet. . . . He was blessed with a rare abundance of natural talent. . . . Leave aside for the moment the later and more difficult Kipling, sufficiently aspirated, a brilliant if unacknowledged fellow-traveler of literary modernism. It is the early Kipling, the one people think they know, who solicits astonishment, not only in his own day but among such later writers as Brecht and Hemingway, Babel and Borges.

The early Kipling glows with gifts of a primary brightness. He gathers up details of Indian life that are completely fresh to English literature. He knows intuitively how to prod and halt a narrative so that it will pulse with tension—as in the wonderful **"The Man Who Would Be King,"** written in his early twenties. His language is strong but not yet sufficiently modulated, perhaps because at this age literary intelligence cannot keep pace with such exceptional gifts. Anyone opening himself to these early Indian stories—**"The Strange Ride of Morrowbie Jukes," "The Story of Mohammed Din," "Lispeth," "Without Benefit of Clergy"**—must be struck by the sheer energy of rendering. Kipling's gifts break past an evident crudeness of mind and many falsities of taste. Sometimes—and here criticism must retire baffled—they are gifts that reveal themselves *through* Kipling's crudeness of mind and falsities of taste. For Kipling is one of the great performers of English literature, in this respect at least a successor to Dickens. These brightly colored early stories must always raise in one's mind uneasy questions about the relation between literature as spectacle and literature as vision, questions about how to value works in which the spectacle is far more striking than the vision is steady.

The matter is more complicated still. There is not a single one of Kipling's deplorable values that is not balanced in his work by a countervalue. The blimpish authoritarianism of a story like **"The Head of the District"** is subtly controverted by the savoring of free personality in **"The Miracle of Purun Bhagat."** The schoolboy coarseness of *Stalky & Co.* is matched by delicacy of feeling in the treatment of such diverse characters as English soldiers in **"Black Jack,"** ailing old ladies in **"The Wish House,"** and a wide assortment of Indians, both Hindu and Moslem, in *Kim* and the stories. The brutality of some war poems is overshadowed by the compassion of a story like **"The Gardener,"** as well as by a number of poems that speak unaffectedly about the suffering of soldiers. And the sidling up to established power is complicated by solidarity with plebeian victims, as in the stories from the underrated *Soldiers Three* and poems like **"The Harp Song of the Dane Woman"** and **"The Last of the Light Brigade."**

Throughout his lifetime Kipling was savaged by liberals who could see only his faults and praised by jingoes who found comfort in his posturings. It has taken time to sort things out, and the job is by no means finished—for there are stories and poems in which the detestable values and undeniable talents interweave so completely that one is at a loss for a secure response. By and large, however, Kipling's career seems to confirm the truth of Yeats's observation that "we make out of the quarrel with others rhetoric, but of the quarrel with ourselves poetry." Kipling's best work—I take it to be *Kim*, parts of *Soldiers Three* and *The Jungle Books*, perhaps a dozen stories and two dozen poems—constitute a quarrel of inner self with outer mind, of precarious sensibility with blunt opinions. His enduring work was written apart from—it was written despite and sometimes against—his asserted beliefs.

A specter haunted Kipling's imagination, the specter of a breakdown of authority: at first the authority of public life, but in his later work that of private life as well. (p. 28)

[Kipling sees authority as] an earned and measured conservatism that has reckoned the costs of civilization and takes them to be worth paying.

It is out of this moderate conservatism—the best Kipling's mind (though not his imagination) could do—that he built his notion of "the Law" in *The Jungle Books*. (p. 29)

[In] his fascination with authority Kipling shows no interest whatever in profit or power, those motives that a later, disenchanted age would see as the underlying design of imperialism. He is touchingly innocent of debunking theories. It is the *claims* of imperialism that grip him, the claims of service and construction. And because he takes these claims with much seriousness, he can show—what at times must have been true—that there were numerous English administrators in India who also took seriously the code of service. (Indeed, in Kipling's devotion to the technocrats and soldiers who "get things done," he can be quite savage with the idle rich, "flanneled fools at the wicket and muddied oafs at the goal.") When Kipling describes the readiness of a certain kind of Anglo-Indian to work and sacrifice, often under conditions of hardship, we can respond with at least partial assent. We think, "Well, there's more to it than *that;* but still, that's how it must have felt to them." When Kipling exploits his innocence about the economic grounds and moral wrongs of imperialism, then we can

no longer suspend disbelief and find ourselves doing what sophisticated readers have been told not to do: we find ourselves "arguing" with works of fiction.

But how hard, in truth, do we now "argue"? Not quite with the heat, I think, that his work would have aroused several decades ago. Perhaps time does have some healing powers. . . . The political issues raised by Kipling's Indian stories, though still troubling, are slowly fading into the historical background, and the way is now clearer for the vibrancy of Kipling's language, the richness of his imaginings. (p. 30)

He seems a cousin to a number of 19th-century American writers, notably Twain and the young Melville, who find their creative powers stimulated by visions of a harmonious life, friendly and fraternal, in which no one can, or need, hold power over anyone else.

And this I take to be the great Kipling: a poet of odd sublimities and patches of transcendence, who yields himself to the voices of the helpless. He appears fully in *Kim,* but is also visible in some of the stories and poems. By the time he reaches his last writings Kipling can no more sustain his visions of bliss than Twain or Melville could sustain theirs; but like Melville, if not Twain, he settles on a stubbled plain of compassion, writing stories like **"The Wish House"** and **"The Gardener,"** which indicate, if not a resolution of, then a human resignation before, the problems of authority, the quandary of civilization.

That sense of evil which for cultivated people has become a mark of wisdom and source of pride, indeed, the very sun of their sunless world, is not a frequent presence in the pages of *Kim;* and when it does appear it can rarely trouble us with either its violence or grasp. (pp. 30-1)

Though in much of his work Kipling shows a quite sufficient awareness of evil, even at some points an obsessive concern, he seems really to want to persuade us through *Kim,* his most serious book, that in the freshness of a boy's discoveries and the penetration of an old man's vision, evil can become ultimately insignificant, almost as nothing before the unsubdued elation of existence, almost as nothing before the idea of moral beauty. Others, long before Kipling, have said as much, though few have embodied it with the plastic vividness that Kipling has. . . . (p. 32)

As imaginative renderings of an unfamiliar world, the early Indian stories still keep their vitality and charm. It is in the sense of history that they are weak, at the point where Kipling's fear for the survival of authority gets in his way. Intuitively he foresees the end of empire, but intellectually he will not let himself foresee another India. The step he cannot finally take is the one that E. M. Forster does take in *Passage to India,* when Aziz tells Fielding, "We shall drive every blasted Englishman into the sea, and then . . . you and I shall be friends."

Kipling's later stories—which means roughly those written after about 1905—have in recent years won an increasing critical reputation; some of these stories are indeed masterpieces, though it is by no means a settled judgment that they are superior to the fiction set in India.

The later stories are, in Henry James's phrase, elaborately "done." They are full of complicated observation and ingenious plotting. Kipling's themes now become veiled, diffused, mixed. The theme of authority, for example, is largely shifted from public to private relationships, and as it comes to be treated in more subtle ways, in a voice no longer ringing with assurance, it also acquires unexpected emotional resonance, strange breakthroughs of feeling. Anger, hatred, and revenge manifest themselves in devious, sometimes unpleasant ways. The later Kipling often seems an uncentered writer, without that obsessive relation to subject or place which can be a writer's blessing. He seems also a deracinated figure, despite his enormous prestige in English society and his association with the political leaders of the "radical right." Yet his craft, already formidable, grows still finer; he becomes a master of one of the purest English prose styles—incisive, flexible, a model of what might be called the demotic middle-style. Curiously, he also picks up many of the devices, and fragments of the sensibility, we associate with literary modernism. Though without sympathy for its declared ends, he comes intuitively to share the modernist stress upon doubt, division, anxiety, and depression—in short, upon the problematic. (pp. 32-3)

These later stories are sometimes marred by a tremulous spirituality, a hovering over otherworldly emanations, which Kipling makes more of than he can do with. They are also marred by an excess of "technique," beyond any visible need in the material at hand. It's as if Kipling were struggling to grasp perceptions beyond his usual reach, or his virtuosity were spinning off freely on its own. The much-admired **"Mrs. Bathurst,"** for example, tends to reduce its matter to a puzzle; for while it is easy enough to discern Kipling's intended theme—the destructiveness of overreaching love—few readers are likely to be clear in their minds about the way the story's conclusion realizes this theme.

But a handful of Kipling's late stories rank with the great short fictions of our century, if not quite with those of Joyce and Lawrence, then certainly with those of Hemingway and Flannery O'Connor. Both **"The Wish House"** and **"The Gardener"** graze perfection. They show the mature Kipling as master of English plebeian settings and figures, but more important, as a sensibility matured and ripened, one that has worked its way out of the traps of enmity and touched compassion. **"Friendly Brook,"** also a story of English plebeian life, though this time in the countryside, strongly recalls Hardy in its folklike matching of naturalist detail and a touch of the eerie. And the *tour de force* **"Dayspring Mishandled"** figures crucially in the Kipling canon as evidence of a struggle against hardened judgments, in this instance, a struggle to shed earlier dispositions toward the savoring of revenge. (p. 33)

I have been making high claims for Kipling in the hope that my reader will find them largely justified. But an honest appraisal must also speak of limits and that means ending with a recognition that in the main Kipling cannot be placed among the very greatest writers of the modern era. He is not in the company of Chekhov and Melville, Joyce and Proust, Eliot and Lawrence.

This is not for lack of skill. Kipling's prose is a superbly vigorous and supple instrument; his imaginings or fables are usually cogent and frequently vivid. Yet some element is too often missing. One does not feel regularly in reading Kipling the presence of an enlarging, liberating sensibility. One does not encounter a world view embracing at once the glories and shames of humanity and reconciling us, insofar as we can be, to the limits of our existence. Nor does one meet a mind which, agree with its conclusions or not, changes deeply and forever our way of looking at the world. Yet, in the portion of his work that lives, there are both peaks of greatness and extended plateaus of high accomplishment. There are intimations of a harmonious life short of the corruptions of maturity, and when Kipling reaches these, his work can rightly be called sublime.

And, as with every writer, he must be read and remembered for his best work. (p. 34)

Irving Howe, "Reconsideration: Rudyard Kipling," in The New Republic *(reprinted by permission of* The New Republic; © *1982 The New Republic, Inc.),* Vol. 186, No. 6, February 10, 1982, pp. 27-34.

ADDITIONAL BIBLIOGRAPHY

Birkenhead, Lord. *Rudyard Kipling*. New York: Random House, 1978, 421 p.
　　Critical biography, making extensive use of previously unpublished material, including letters, diaries, and dictated memoirs.

Braddy, Nella. *Rudyard Kipling: Son of Empire*. New York: Julian Messner, 1941, 278 p.
　　Anecdotal biography.

Braybrooke, Patrick. *Kipling and His Soldiers*. Philadelphia: J. B. Lippincott Co., 1926, 180 p.
　　Study of Kipling's stories and poems about soldiers and war. Braybrooke states that "Kipling has drawn a picture of the British soldier with an accuracy that can only come from a perfect combination of knowledge and sympathy."

Brown, Hilton. *Rudyard Kipling*. New York: Harper & Brothers Publishers, 1945, 237 p.
　　Study of Kipling's life and work. Brown devotes the first half of his book to biographical facts, and the second half to critical comment on Kipling's work.

Chevrillon, André. "Rudyard Kipling's Poetry." In his *Three Studies in English Literature: Kipling, Galsworthy, Shakespeare*, translated by Florence Simmonds, pp. 1-152. London: William Heinemann, 1923.
　　Study of Kipling's critical reception in France.

Cook, Richard. "Rudyard Kipling and George Orwell." *Modern Fiction Studies* VII, No. 2 (Summer 1961): 125-35.*
　　Discusses the similarities in the lives and philosophies of Kipling and Orwell.

Cornell, Louis L. *Kipling in India*. New York: St. Martin's Press, 1966, 224 p.
　　Study of Kipling's literary apprenticeship, his early years of journalistic work in India and the subsequent effect of this work on his later writing.

Croft-Cook, Rupert. *Rudyard Kipling*. Denver: Allan Swallow, 1948, 107 p.
　　Critical study of Kipling's works, with introductory and concluding chapters summarizing his life.

Fido, Martin. *Rudyard Kipling*. New York: The Viking Press, 1974, 144 p.
　　Biography, profusely illustrated with photographs.

Gilbert, Elliot L. *The Good Kipling: Studies in the Short Story*. Oberlin: Ohio University Press, 1970, 216 p.
　　Analysis of Kipling's approach to the short story.

Griswold, Hattie Tyng. "Rudyard Kipling." In her *Personal Sketches of Recent Authors*, pp. 266-80. Chicago: A. C. McClurg and Co., 1899.
　　Early biographical sketch in which the critic predicts that "it is as a storyteller, and not as a poet, that Kipling is best known, and probably will be in the future."

Gross, John, ed. *The Age of Kipling*. New York: Simon and Schuster, 1972, 178 p.
　　Collection of essays about Kipling's life and art by Leon Edel, Roger Lancelyn Green, Bernard Bergonzi, J.I.M. Stewart, and others, including many illustrations and photographs.

Henn, T. R. *Kipling*. London: Oliver and Boyd, 1967, 141 p.
    Critical study of Kipling's short stories, poems, novels, travel literature, and literary criticism. An extensive bibliography is included.

Matthews, Brander. "Cervantes, Zola, Kipling & Co." In his *Aspects of Fiction and Other Ventures in Criticism,* pp. 162-81. New York: Harper & Brothers Publishers, 1896.*
    Contrasts *Don Quixote,* "La Débâcle," and *The Naulahka.*

Norris, Faith G. "Rudyard Kipling." In *British Winners of the Nobel Literary Prize,* edited by Walter E. Kidd, pp. 14-43. Norman: University of Oklahoma Press, 1973.
    Discusses the reasons for the choice of Kipling as the recipient of the 1907 Nobel Prize in literature. The critic also examines all of Kipling's work published prior to this date.

Pritchett, V. S. "Kipling's Short Stories." In his *The Living Novel and Later Appreciations,* pp. 175-82. New York: Random House, 1964.
    Characterizes Kipling as "the only considerable English writer of fiction to have been popular in the most popular sense and to excite the claim to genius."

Rao, K. Bhaskara. *Rudyard Kipling's India.* Norman: University of Oklahoma Press, 1967, 190 p.
    Reevaluation of Kipling's stature as a writer about India. Rao concludes that "Kipling managed successfully to create the illusion that he knew and understood India."

Rutherford, Andrew, ed. *Kipling's Mind and Art: Selected Critical Essays.* Stanford: Stanford University Press, 1964, 278 p.
    Includes essays on Kipling by Rutherford, Lionel Trilling, Alan Sandison, and others.

Shanks, Edward. "Mr. Rudyard Kipling." *The London Mercury VII,* No. 39 (January 1923): 273-84.
    Brief critical overview of Kipling's career. Shanks concludes, "It does not happen very often in English literature that the political opinions of a writer interfere with critical judgement of his work," but that such is the case with Kipling.

Tompkins, J.M.S. *The Art of Rudyard Kipling.* London: Methuen & Co., 1959, 277 p.
    Study of some of Kipling's major themes.

C(yril) M. Kornbluth

1923-1958

(Also wrote under pseudonyms of Cyril Judd, Cecil Corwin, Walter C. Davies, Simon Eisner, Kenneth Falconer, S. D. Gottesman, Paul Dennis Lavond, Scott Mariner, Ivar Towers, among others) American novelist, short story writer, and editor.

Kornbluth was one of the earliest science fiction authors to extrapolate dystopian futures from existing social, political, and economic trends. His negative opinion of human nature led him to present a grim future as inevitable. His pessimism is evident in "The Little Black Bag" and "The Marching Morons," which arc considered classics in the genre. Kornbluth's greatest fame, however, came with the short stories and novels he coauthored with Frederik Pohl. Kornbluth and Pohl have often been called the finest science fiction collaborating team, and their first novel, *The Space Merchants*, remains one of the most highly regarded and widely read novels in science fiction.

Kornbluth sold his first story at sixteen and was an early member of the Futurians, a group of science fiction fans-turned-authors living in New York in the 1930s. Until he enlisted in the army in 1943, Kornbluth's short story output was prodigious. The exact number of stories he wrote is unknown, because of the many pseudonyms he applied to both his own work and to stories he wrote with fellow Futurians, including Pohl, Richard Wilson, Robert A. W. Lowndes, and Donald A. Wollheim. During World War II, Kornbluth fought in the Battle of the Bulge and won the Bronze Star. After the war he worked for Trans-Radio Press and began publishing stories, under his own name, in *The Magazine of Fantasy and Science Fiction, Startling Stories,* and John W. Campbell's *Astounding Science Fiction.* Kornbluth's acerbic wit and his mordant approach to scientific orthodoxy attracted the notice of editor Horace Gold, whose projected new magazine, *Galaxy Science Fiction*, was intended as a departure from the more traditional "space opera" stories promulgated by most other science fiction magazines. Kornbluth's first appearance in *Galaxy* was with "The Marching Morons," his most famous, much-anthologized short story positing a future in which birth control by the intelligentsia has led to a population of subnormal intellect. "The Little Black Bag," considered typically Kornbluthian, displays a similar lack of optimism. The little black bag of the title is a medical bag containing advanced curative discoveries from the future which allow the least fit to thrive and reproduce, again leading to a world populated by masses of morons. When the bag travels backward in time, human greed and selfishness result in its misuse and eventual destruction.

After collaborating with Judith Merril on two novels, *Gunner Cade* and *Outpost Mars,* Kornbluth wrote the novel *Takeoff* independent of a coauthor. He then teamed up with Pohl to produce a novel about a future world "solidly in the malignant grip" of big business and advertising agencies. Serialized in *Galaxy* as *Gravy Planet,* the novel appeared two years later as *The Space Merchants,* and has not been out of print since. *The Space Merchants* gained an unusually wide readership outside

Drawing from a photograph; reproduced by permission of David Kornbluth

of the science fiction community, and was eventually translated into nearly forty languages, even attracting comment in *Tide,* the advertising industry's trade journal. The success of *The Space Merchants* provided the impetus for subsequent collaborations between Kornbluth and Pohl. They wrote three more science fiction novels, *Search the Sky, Gladiator-at-Law,* and *Wolfbane,* as well as three mainstream fiction novels. Pohl completed most of the story fragments Kornbluth left at his early death by heart attack. These posthumous "collaborations" are gathered in *The Wonder Effect* and *Critical Mass;* one of them, "The Meeting," won the Hugo Award for best short story in 1972.

In a time when all technological advances were regarded as desirable, Kornbluth and Pohl were among the first to display increasing skepticism about the ultimate value of boundless progress, recognizing possible harmful consequences. This attitude was evident in their individual works, which were promoted by the popularity of their joint efforts. In between collaboration with Pohl, Kornbluth wrote *The Syndic,* a satiric novel of a future United States run by a benevolent dictatorship of gangsters. Kornbluth's third solo novel, *Not This August,* was written in the early part of the Cold War and is considered among the best of the cautionary tales about a Soviet takeover of the United States.

Kornbluth's novels were never quite as good as his short stories—a common failing in science fiction authors of the era. For the considerable skill and elegance of construction they display, B. A. Young has stated that Kornbluth's short stories should "be judged purely by the best literary standards." Notable among Kornbluth's later short stories are "Shark Ship," an early overpopulation horror story; "Two Dooms," an alternate-world story; and "With These Hands," a fresh treatment of a venerable science fiction theme: the growing disregard for handcrafted goods.

Kornbluth was one of the first science fiction authors to turn from contemplating outer space to the finite space of Earth. In his stories and novels, he depicted the horrors humankind is capable of perpetrating upon itself as infinitely more devastating than that of any extraterrestrial invader. The works of Kornbluth helped to bring a new level of sophistication to the genre of science fiction.

(See also *Dictionary of Literary Biography*, Vol. 8: *Twentieth-Century American Science Fiction Writers*.)

PRINCIPAL WORKS

Gunner Cade [with Judith Merril under the joint pseudonym of Cyril Judd] (novel) 1952
Outpost Mars [with Judith Merril under the joint pseudonym of Cyril Judd] (novel) 1952
Takeoff (novel) 1952
The Space Merchants [with Frederik Pohl] (novel) 1953
The Syndic (novel) 1953
The Explorers (short stories) 1954
Search the Sky [with Frederik Pohl] (novel) 1954
Gladiator-at-Law [with Frederik Pohl] (novel) 1955
Not This August (novel) 1955; also published as *Christmas Eve*, 1956
The Marching Morons (short stories) 1959
Wolfbane [with Frederik Pohl] (novel) 1959
The Wonder Effect [with Frederik Pohl] (short stories) 1962
Best SF Stories of C. M. Kornbluth (short stories) 1968
Thirteen O'Clock and Other Zero Hours (short stories) 1970
Before the Universe [with Frederik Pohl] (short stories) 1980

J. FRANCIS McCOMAS (essay date 1952)

An impressively successful integration of thoughtful science fiction with an expertly constructed espionage melodrama is the achievement of [*Takeoff*]. The science fiction element of Cyril Kornbluth's story is a projection of America as it could be not too many years from right now. Mr. Kornbluth's carefully detailed future is a grim thing to behold. Taking the Atomic Energy Commission as his prime example, this perceptive writer demonstrates that the smear tactics of contemporary "Patriots" can easily result in that commission (or any other government agency) becoming nothing more than a bumbling bureaucracy of scared second-raters, huddling under a blanket of red tape while true scientific progress goes by the board.

Such an environment of futility and fear would certainly nullify any hope of Americans ever reaching the moon. Who would dare to offer facilities for research and materials for constructing a rocket that might make the trip? If there were enough capable scientists and technicians with sufficient courage to buck native hysteria, where and how would they start? Finding the answers to these bitter questions is the problem faced by the protagonist, Michael Novak, ceramic engineer and plain, ordinary citizen.

Plagued by the self-doubts we all know, confused by friends and enemies alike, Novak stubbornly tries to do his duty as he sees it. Inevitably, his efforts to convince his uncaring countrymen that a moon rocket can be built bring him to the attention of an espionage ring. Of course these aren't the spies of the headlines, but quiet, murderous business men. Novak's fight against malice domestic and foreign is marked by intrigue, violence—and his own tenacity and faith. The pattern of his struggle is a skillful interweaving of murder mystery and science fiction adventure.

> J. Francis McComas, "Moon the Hard Way," in The New York Times Book Review (© 1952 by The New York Times Company; reprinted by permission), August 10, 1952, p. 15.

H. H. HOLMES (essay date 1953)

[Frederik Pohl and C. M. Kornbluth] combine to produce a book so rewarding that it should henceforth show up on all lists of science fiction "classics." As H. L. Gold wrote in introducing [*The Space Merchants*] in "Galaxy" . . . , it represents the type of future fiction which takes one given contemporary situation and carries it "to the utmost extremes we are capable of imagining." Here Pohl and Kornbluth create a civilization of the near future in which a world of serf-like "consumers" is dominated by the aristocracy of the advertising agencies; and the result, oddly, is not so much satire as a horrifyingly convincing reality. The story is of the war between the agencies and the underground "subversive" organization of Conservationists for control of the as yet unexploited planet of Venus; you'll have to go to the best work of Robert A. Heinlein for any comparable integration of melodramatic plot with an infinitely detailed depiction of a logically developed world.

> H. H. Holmes, "Science and Fantasy: 'The Space Merchants'," in New York Herald Tribune Book Review (© I.H.T. Corporation; reprinted by permission), July 5, 1953, p. 8.*

J. FRANCIS McCOMAS (essay date 1953)

In his personal formula for successful science fiction, C. M. Kornbluth stages a supercharged melodrama against the background of a crazily wonderful future. The world projected in [*The Syndic*] is, by current standards, a completely amoral affair wherein "legitimate" government has long since fled the United States for a pirates' base in British Isles gone Celtic primitive. The Atlantic seaboard is ruled by the Syndic, the end result of a long line of racketeers mellowed by the passing of generations. Despite their antecedents and their government by formalized corruption, the members of the Syndic are a likable lot of cultured cynics.

This account of the Syndic is complicated by a variety of curious factors that only a writer of Mr. Kornbluth's skill could conceive of and handle. He has concocted such coexistent phenomena as British clans led by priestesses with unlimited extrasensory powers and the Mob that rules the Middle West (out of Chicago naturally) with tactics considerably less benevolent than Syndic procedures. He has made it seem eminently reasonable that psychiatric alteration of personality should be developed primarily for purposes of espionage. All in all, this vastly entertaining book is a merry gibe at some of our most stubborn beliefs.

> *J. Francis McComas, "The Spaceman's Realm: Psychiatric Espionage," in* The New York Times Book Review *(© 1953 by The New York Times Company; reprinted by permission), November 15, 1953, p. 37.*

VILLIERS GERSON (essay date 1955)

The world-of-tomorrow envisioned by [Frederik Pohl and C. M. Kornbluth in "Gladiator-at-Law"] is a strange and frightening one, the more so because its seeds can be seen in today's society. Charles Mundin, a young lawyer whose practice and future are limited because he has not been born into one of the great hereditary legal families, faces a world in which cruelty is commonplace. Gladiators fight in arenas with scientific weapons; the fine suburbs of the twentieth century have become decaying slums in which roam gangs of frightening juvenile delinquents. The middle class man no longer owns his home. If he is lucky, he rents a totipotent machine for living owned by the great corporations who rule the world. If he offends these rulers, he is banished to such ghettos as "Belly Rave"; if still offensive, he meets his end in the arena. . . .

"Gladiator-at-Law" is a fast-moving novel of adventure and idea, possessed of a bite and savage vigor which makes it one of the outstanding science fiction novels of the year.

> *Villiers Gerson, "In the Realm of the Spaceman: Seeds of Tomorrow," in* The New York Times Book Review *(© 1955 by The New York Times Company; reprinted by permission), July 31, 1955, p. 15.**

C. M. KORNBLUTH (essay date 1957)

Apparently [*The Space Merchants*] is accepted as an outstanding example in recent science fiction of the department of social criticism called satire. The characteristic quality of satire in symbolic terms seems to be that it offers the reader a great quantity of symbols each of which is rather close to the object symbolized. As I leaf through the book I see that Pohl and I left virtually nothing in American life untransformed, from breakfast food to the Presidency of the United States. I see that with almost lunatic single-mindedness we made everything in our future America that could be touched, tasted, smelled, heard, seen or talked about bear witness to the dishonesty of the concepts and methods of today's advertising.

I don't claim any high literary merit for the book; if I were asked to rewrite it today it would come out a much less plotty job, and Pohl agrees with me on this. But it did have some effect. It stimulated thinking in a lot of places, some of them quite unlikely ones. There was a full-page review, for instance, in *The Industrial Worker*, the organ of such I.W.W. members, or Wobblies, as survive. I have reason to believe it was read by a lot of people who do not normally read science fiction. It had a vogue in the New York City theatrical crowd, an actor has told me, and I know it was read by broadcasting men across the country. It was read, of course, by the hypersensitive ad-

vertising people. In their trade paper *Tide* a reviewer wanted to know whether it was supposed to be good, clean fun or the most vicious, underhanded attack on the advertising profession yet. (If he had asked me, I would have told him "Both.") It is not dead yet, either, A radio version has been given and it may one day appear as a musical comedy. It is too soon to write off *The Space Merchants* as just another science fiction book which has shot its wad and been forgotten. Naturally I hope that it will have some real influence on American advertising, and I do state that the probability of this is not, as of today, 0.0000.

Arthur Clarke has complained of science fiction books like *The Space Merchants* that they are too ugly, that they should contain elements of love and beauty counterpoising the elements of ugliness and death. In this, as I have told him, he is perfectly correct. I think the book is flawed at least to that extent. What love there is in the book keeps turning into hate. There is a marked hostility to women throughout. This seems to be an unexpected and unwanted by-product of its collaborative authorship, since hostility to women does not turn up to that degree in my solo work or Pohl's. This essentially unrealistic concentration on the seamy side, I believe, made it impossible for us to bring off our happy ending. By the time the reader has gone through 178 pages of misery, animosity, squalor and violence, he is understandably reluctant to believe that on Page 179 everything can suddenly be patched up so that these savage creatures can live happily ever after.

There is some discussion in science fiction circles at this time about sadism in literature. I think a character in *The Space Merchants* can throw light on the subject. The arguments go as follows: Critic says, stop portraying ugly, meaningless violence in your stories; that is sadism and it breeds sadism. Writer replies: Ugly, meaningless violence is a part of life and I am portraying life.

The character Hedy, the skinny girl with the needle, might be described as a sadist's sadist. She is shown practicing sadism and getting a bang out of it. Yet there have been no complaints that I know of about her. I think this is because she is specifically labelled as a sick, deranged person. In this case the writers have been able to present ugly, meaningless violence and thus round out the reality of their story, and yet nobody seems to feel that sadism is being taught to or urged on the predisposed reader. There is a poison label firmly pasted on the sadistic episode and it seems to have done its job. (pp. 72-4)

> *C. M. Kornbluth, "The Failure of the Science Fiction Novel As Social Criticism" (originally a lecture delivered at University College, The University of Chicago on January 11, 1957), in* The Science Fiction Novel: Imagination and Social Criticism *by Basil Davenport, Robert A. Heinlein, C. M. Kornbluth, Alfred Bester, and Robert Bloch (copyright © 1959, by Advent:Publishers; reprinted by courtesy of Advent:Publishers, Inc.), third edition, Advent, 1969, pp. 49-76.**

KINGSLEY AMIS (essay date 1960)

Range of effect is uncommon in science-fiction writers, who show a depressing tendency to re-till their own small plot of ground: one thinks of Clifford Simak with his pastoral pieties, A. E. van Vogt with his superman fantasies, and almost anyone you like (Eric Frank Russell is the least unimaginative example) with his bright adventure stories and incuriosity about human character. Variety that goes beyond mere rearrangement is seldom to be found outside the works of [James Blish, Ray Bradbury, Arthur C. Clarke, Robert Sheckley, and Frederik Pohl], and variety of mood within a single work is rarer still. It does appear, however, in *The Space Merchants,* which has many claims to being the best science-fiction novel so far. It is one of several which Pohl wrote in collaboration with C. M. Kornbluth, a prolific and competent author. . . . Kornbluth's individual work—*Not This August,* in which America retrieves a total defeat by Russia and China, or *Syndic,* a chronicle of minor wars following upon a major one—soon suggests that his part in *The Space Merchants* was roughly to provide the more violent action while Pohl filled in the social background and the satire. Both sets of interests are appropriate to the construction of a utopia in which the economic system has swallowed the political, with power wielded immediately as well as ultimately by the large companies, the forms of the administration retained for their usefulness as a "clearing house for pressures," and society rigidly stratified into producers, executives, and consumers. The opening is pure Pohl: the hero, Mitchell Courtenay, copy-smith star class, attends a top-level conference of Fowler Schocken Associates, the advertising agency he works for, one of the most puissant and formidable in all Madison Avenue, billing "a megabuck a year more than anybody else around." The reader is introduced, casually and by degrees, to representative features of the society imagined: the industrial anthropology expert reports that while schoolchildren east of the Mississippi are having their lunches—soyaburgers and regenerated steak—packed according to the prescription of a rival firm, their candy, ice cream, and Kiddiebutt cigarette ration have been decisively cornered by a Fowler Schocken client, so that the children's future is assured. Similarly, the Coffiest account is mentioned and the cost of the cure from this habit-forming beverage estimated at a nice round five thousand dollars. Finally we come to the Venus project and a preview of the relevant television commercial. . . . (pp. 124-26)

One can see there the basic ingredients of the method: the detail, the casualness, the use of scattered hints which will cohere as the story progresses. The commercial itself provides that compound of the familiar with the unfamiliar which, as usual, serves the double purpose of inducing the reader to accept an imaginary world while offering him satire on the world he knows, a duality of present and future which is fundamental to good science fiction and is here neatly summarised in the title of the novel. Satirical treatment of the advertising profession as it now is extends some way into the treatment of character, so that the chief is a man of huge lyrical complacency, enmeshing all his subordinates in a web of self-congratulation and gazing round the conference room "with the air of a day-tripper in Xanadu"; similarly the Director of Market Research interrupts to say he just wants "to go on record as agreeing with Mr. Schocken—one hundred per cent—all the way!" These stock types are handled with wit and imagination, but they are stock types, and it is necessary that they should be so. In this type of story, which must consistently stop a good deal short of what is no more than barely possible, an added reference-point or reassurance to the reader can be furnished by treating character conservatively and limiting interest in it; it must be shown quickly that the familiar categories of human behaviour persist in an unfamiliar environment, and the book's whole tenor would be set awry by the kind of specifying, distinguishing, questioning form of characterisation to which general fiction has accustomed us. A mariner out of Conrad or Melville would be no use to us in Lilliput or Brob-

dingnag, for the point at which specialisation of character becomes a narrowing and a weakening is reached much sooner in science fiction than elsewhere. (pp. 126-27)

True to prescription, Mitchell is a generic kind of person, acquiescent in the earlier stages and thus able to provide denigrations of his society unconsciously and from within. It is through him that we learn of the development of advertising "from the simple handmaiden task of selling already manufactured goods to its present role of creating industries and redesigning a world's folkways to meet the needs of commerce"; through Mitchell we are progressively acquainted with a utopia of the comic-inferno type built on a complex of assumptions. This is not merely a world in which the advertiser is king, it also combines luxury with scarcity, fantastic gadgetry with an absence of fuel whereby Fowler Schocken runs a pedal-Cadillac, all manner of drinks and chewing gums with an extreme shortage of protein foods. To this extent, it enacts a remark of George Orwell's to the effect that luxuries are on the way to becoming less expensive and easier to obtain than necessities. This future America of 800 million people has top-level executives living in tiny two-room apartments and clerical workers occupying single stairs, separated by grilles that lift automatically at getting-up time, in the large office blocks. Here as much as anywhere else that science-fictional uneasiness appears, attaching itself to an existent or incipient neurosis about overcrowded streets and buildings as well as to the rational fear of global overpopulation. The social picture resulting from all this is filled in with remarkable completeness: the foulness of the atmosphere which shuts off the open air as a normal element, the disappearance of poetry that follows the immense expansion of verbal outlets via copywriting, and such splendid isolated touches as Mitchell's visit to the Metropolitan Museum of Art. He doesn't go much for religion, partly because a rival agency is covering that, but there is a "grave, ennobling air about the grand old masterpieces in the Met" that gives him "a feeling of peace and reverence." This he is able to glut to the full by contemplating a "big, late-period" effort, "I Dreamed I was Ice-Fishing in my Maidenform Bra." One point about this last stroke is that . . . it connects only generally with the initial assumptions, not specifically with actual current trends. Such elements, free from any loading of significance, are combined with others that concretise some familiar and vague nightmares about the ruthlessness of large combines and the various possibilities of violence increasing to the point where it becomes institutionalised: industrial feuds are legal if officially notified and "there are still bloodstains on the steps of the General Post Office where Western Union and American Railway Express fought it out for the mail contract."

After due advantage has been taken of Mitchell's vantage point as a hypnotised supporter of the system, and of the comic possibilities of his considering himself a free critical intelligence within it, he is made to change sides. This justifiable unoriginality is brought about not through any spontaneous conversion, but as a delayed result of personal suffering and danger; with the same lack of optimism as is perceptible in Bradbury's treatment of Montag [in *Fahrenheit 451*], Mitchell does not begin to hate his society until after it has begun to hate him. In this case it is long after: Mitchell is kidnapped by a rival's trick and sent to a nasty labour camp full of uncultured and violent consumers, and here the revolutionary movement makes contact with him, but he uses it for his own ends rather than becoming a part of it, escaping finally to a Venus uncontaminated by Fowler Schocken and his friends from an Earth that is still largely under the sway of the old régime. The closing scenes, on which I suspect the hand of Kornbluth lies heavy, offer little but adequate excitement and are not altogether a conclusion to the issues raised in the opening chapters. (pp. 128-31)

The Space Merchants, clearly, is an admonitory satire on certain aspects of our own society, mainly economic, but it is not only that. It does not simply show the already impending consequences of the growth of industrial and commercial power, and it does more than simply satirise or criticise existing habits in the advertising profession, though to its work in this direction it adds some effective parody: Mitchell's handout on the Venus pioneers is a capsule anthology of the ordinary-guy approach, the reverence for experts combined with hostility, the down-to-earth idioms and grammar, the comradely seriousness. Beyond all this, the book seems to be interested in the future as such, to inquire what might result from turns of events that are possible and are not invalidated by being unlikely, to confront men and women with a thing, as I put it, which may put them into a situation without precedent in our experience. That situation, both in this novel and in science fiction as a whole, will be an uncomfortable one by our standards, and it may be used to subject human beings to a kind of insecurity that is both new in itself and novel in the sense that it renders general and public what in the present context is only piecemeal and private. . . . The science-fiction utopia, political or economic, has a kind of relevance which no other sub-category can match, attracts some of the best minds in the field, and incidentally can perform a valuable introductory service for those who blench at the sight of a BEM ["bug-eyed monster"]; but it is a difficult form, often revealing a damagingly simple scale of values and taxing its authors' invention to the point where a cops-and-robbers interest may fill the picture after the first few chapters. Even *The Space Merchants* relies, as it goes on, more and more heavily upon Kornbluthain elements—there is a quite gratuitous scene with a female sadistic maniac who totes a sharpened knitting needle. Anyway, no worthy successor to it has come along in the half-dozen years since it was published, and meanwhile many an addict must have heaved a sigh for some fearful menace of the old-fashioned type, lethal instead of merely undesirable, and originating on Mars, not Madison Avenue. (pp. 131-33)

> *Kingsley Amis, "Utopias 2," in his* New Maps of Hell: A Survey of Science Fiction *(© 1960 by Kingsley Amis; reprinted by permission of Harcourt Brace Jovanovich, Inc.; in Canada by Jonathan Clowes Limited),* Harcourt Brace Jovanovich, 1960 *(and reprinted by Arno Press, 1975), pp. 111-33.**

FREDERIK POHL (essay date 1962)

Cyril Kornbluth, who was my good friend as well as my collaborator over a period of two decades, was seventeen years old when we first began writing stories together. I was not quite twenty. Neither of us was entirely an amateur—I was editing two science-fiction magazines, long since perished, and Cyril had already published three or four science-fiction stories—but we were so near to it as made no difference, and many of our writing habits were formed at the same time, writing the same stories.

In all, we wrote together seven published novels and perhaps thirty-five short stories. The short stories were what we did first, and most of them are awful. Of the thirty or so of these which we wrote from 1939 to 1943 at least twenty-five will

forever remain buried under the pseudonyms under which they were first published, if I have anything to say about it; but a few of them do seem to be worth another look, and they are included in [*The Wonder Effect*]. . . .

I recently came across a letter Cyril wrote to me while he was a machine-gunner in Belgium and I was a weatherman near Foggia in which he said, "I'm afraid science fiction has had it, killed by radar and the sniperscope." I don't remember whether I agreed with or not. Certainly it seemed like a logical point of view at the time. Science had caught up with science fiction and there didn't seem to be much future for the art . . . Less than a year later we were both civilians and both writing science fiction again. . . . (p. vii)

A number of reviewers have speculated, and readers from time to time ask, what the mechanics of collaboration were between us. I take this to condone the vanity of supplying an answer. There isn't one single answer, though, because we tried everything. At first I made up plots, Cyril fleshed out the stories and I rewrote them in final form for publication. That was the technique that produced the bulk of the early stories which I now hope to see forgotten. It was not a very good way of writing a story, and we never wrote a complete story that way after 1942. (I do retain some fondness for a few stories produced under that scheme. *Best Friend, Marstube* and *Trouble in Time* were written that way.)

The Space Merchants was written on an entirely different basis. I had written the first twenty thousand words of this story with the intention of doing it all by myself; but I showed it to Horace Gold, editing *Galaxy Magazine,* who wanted to publish it as a serial—not in ten years or when I got around to finishing it, but soon. Cyril had just come East. I showed him the part I had written and asked if he wanted to come in on it; he did; he went home and wrote the next twenty thousand words or so and then, turn and turn about, we wrote the last third of the book together.

That turned out to be a remarkably pleasant way to write a book. As we ultimately refined the process, we would spend a day or two talking out ideas and plot and then go on a concentrated, around-the-clock schedule, one working while the other slept, of producing manuscript in five-page chunks. What emerged was a good, healthy first draft. There were always revisions, which I usually did; but the changes were mostly cosmetic. The watch-on watch-off writing was generally done at my house in New Jersey, where Cyril had a room permanently set aside for him, and thus, in alternate increments of 1500 words or so, we constructed *Search the Sky, Gladiator-at-Law* and most of our three novels which were outside the science-fiction field. (Two of these were done wholly in this way. The third was like *The Space Merchants* in reverse; Cyril had begun a novel and was behind schedule and we finished it together.)

I don't know how well this system would work for anyone else. We had the advantage of long practice—and of having done some of our growing up together, so that our attitudes were more or less similar. Quite often a species of telepathy seemed to come into it. Several times I ended a page in the middle of a sentence and discovered, when it came my turn again, that Cyril had used the exact wording I had had in mind to complete it.

Wolfbane was a different sort of story. We planned it as a 15,000 word novelette—and wrote it that way, too, turn and about. But it was almost unreadable, far too telegraphic and compressed; and I opened it out to about 40,000 words, in which form it was published as a magazine serial; whereafter Cyril expanded it to about 60,000 words for the final book version. This was almost the last writing Cyril did before his death.

Of the stories in [*The Wonder Effect*], *The Engineer* was the only short we wrote together in the period between *The Space Merchants* and *Wolfbane,* and it was an accident. (In a different form, it was intended to have been a sequence in one of the novels.) *A Gentle Dying,* which was one of the last of our stories to be published, was actually almost the first we wrote. The manuscript was misplaced for years and did not turn up again until Cyril had died. The remaining stories in this book are all projects which were incomplete at his death, and which I subsequently completed. . . . (pp. viii-ix)

As this is not an obituary for Cyril Kornbluth but only a note on some of the stories we wrote together, I do not suppose it fitting to dwell on personal matters. But Cyril was a good man: intelligent, able, illuminating every gathering in which he took part. It was a pleasure to work with him. (p. ix)

> *Frederik Pohl, in his introduction to* The Wonder Effect *by Frederik Pohl and C. M. Kornbluth (copyright © 1962 by Frederik Pohl; reprinted by permission of the author), Ballantine Books, 1962, pp. vii-ix.*

DAMON KNIGHT   (essay date 1967)

[Kornbluth's] first novel was *Mars Child,* written in collaboration with Judith Merril; his second, *Gunner Cade,* also with Miss Merril; his third, *The Space Merchants* ("Gravy Planet"), with Frederik Pohl. All three, judging by style and manner, were at least three-quarters Kornbluth [In a footnote to the revised edition of *In Search of Wonder,* Knight reconsiders his previous statement, commenting that: This is probably unfair. A more recent novel on which Pohl and another writer collaborated seems to me full of the distinctive flavor of *The Space Merchants.*]; each was better than the last; but none of them has one-half the stature of *Takeoff.*

Takeoff is a science fiction novel about the building of the first Moon ship. It is also a contemporary novel of science and bureaucracy, and a tough, realistic murder mystery. It functions brilliantly on all three levels; Kornbluth's Midas touch makes the engineering of the spaceship as fascinating as the mystery behind it, and the devious workings of governmental intrigue as engrossing as either. The incidental love story is less effective, but this is a hindsight criticism.

Other hindsights: I regret the plot necessity that killed off the book's most engaging and believable character less than halfway through, and altered another, barely believably, to a villainess. In the protagonist himself there are traces of pulp characterization not evident elsewhere.

These are all minor cavils. If there is any serious complaint to be made to Kornbluth at this point, it must be based, oddly enough, on the very prodigality of his talent. Kornbluth's career is like that of a very bright schoolboy in a dull class; he discovered early that he could do the things the others struggled to accomplish a great deal better and with much less effort; he has been doing them ever since, with his tongue in his cheek.

Brilliant as it is, there is not an idea or an attitude in *Takeoff* that is original with its author. It is simply the standard material

of modern popular fiction, compounded with more skill than most of us can muster.

A still better book—Kornbluth's best novel, I think—is *The Syndic.* This is sociological science fiction, the exasperatingly difficult type of which more is talked and less written than any other. What passes for genuine sociological speculation is mostly counterfeit: crude analogy, gimmicked-up history, burlesque or parody. Kornbluth has written those, too, but this is the real thing—an imagined society that meets the test of a real one: that it's based on its own unique premises and has its own rationale; and this—wherein lies the trick—with such conviction that the reader can, indeed, must imagine himself living in it.

In *Not This August,* Kornbluth returns to the careful, workmanlike, and somehow disappointing style of *Takeoff.* (pp. 146-47)

[In] *Not This August,* (1) the United States has been conquered and occupied by Communist armies; (2) the people are starved and oppressed; (3) the active part of the plot concerns the hero's efforts to make contact with the underground opposition; and (4) the solution . . . involves a spaceship built in a secret cavern by the Good Guys.

Of these points, (1) is obvious fictional material and would have had to come from somewhere; remember the gleet of "Yellow Peril" stories—about an America conquered by Chinese or Japanese—that ended just before World War I? Item (2) is equally obvious; any other extrapolation would have been extremely odd as well as unsaleable; (3) is a stock novelistic device which I hope has not outlived its usefulness, and (4) is a Hollywood (or Madison Avenue) idiocy.

Kornbluth's treatment of all these things, even the ship-in-a-cavern, is . . . intelligent, factual, detailed and convincing. . . . The author's remarkable talent for producing the inside dope or a reasonable facsimile on anything at all, from dairy farming to Red Army methods, is here evidenced on nearly every page. Heaven forbid this story should ever become actuality; but if it did, the chances are, no fictional forecast would be more accurate (up to Chapter 15) than this.

Further, the book is tightly constructed and continuously readable; it has several vivid characters, a lot of equally vivid dialogue and action, and the same taut, hard-boiled excitement that made *Takeoff* so successful.

But this novel is written almost entirely in Kornbluth's extensive Working Stiff and Slob vocabularies, acquired (evidently) in an effort to reduce the gap between that oddfish, the writer, and the rest of humanity. Like everything else Kornbluth does, the effort has been thorough: Kornbluth has the words; but he hasn't got the tune.

No working stiff, or slob either, he has had deliberately to suppress the sensitive, cynical, philosophical, irreverent top slice of his mind in order to counterfeit the tribal conventions of the boobs around him. The result is as craftsmanlike, well polished and hollow-sounding as a tin dollar. It satisfies, even in a limited way, only until you compare it with the same author's short stories.

"Gomez," which leads off Kornbluth's Ballantine collection, *The Explorers,* was written especially for it; "**The Rocket of 1955**" and "**Thirteen O'Clock**" first appeared as long ago as 1941. In between come "**The Mindworm,**" "**The Altar at Midnight,**" "**The Goodly Creatures,**" "**Friend to Man,**" "**With**

These Hands'' and "That Share of Glory." All of them are written with distinction, even the cut-and-dried potboiler, "Friend to Man."

The remarkable thing is not that these nine stories, written over a thirteen-year period, are uniform in quality—they aren't—but that the earliest and slightest of them will stand comparison today with the average product of our best magazines. Kornbluth starts there, and goes up.

Three of the best are the result of a serious attempt to graft the mainstream short story onto science fiction. I dislike these three on principle. The very best of the lot, **"The Goodly Creatures,"** flunks the key clause of [Theodore] Sturgeon's definition of science fiction—"[a story] which would not have happened at all without its scientific content." The other two pass, barely, but are so close to mundane stories that they make me almost equally uncomfortable. **"The Altar at Midnight"** is about the gulf between generations, and the lure of destructive, well-paid occupations, and the guilt of scientists, and similar things, all of which strike familiar chords. The center of attention is a young spaceman, hideously deformed by his craft; I might have missed the mundane parallel, though I felt it, if Kornbluth himself hadn't spelled it out for me—the old used-up railroad men who congregate in a dismal bar in **"Gandytown."** **"With These Hands"** is merely the lament for hand-craftsmanship, already a cliché in the mainstream story, which Kornbluth has translated from book-binding to sculpture. But when I say "merely," I lie. Each of these stories represents the triumph of a master technician over an inappropriate form—as if, on a somewhat grander scale, Milton had written "Paradise Lost" in limericks, and made you like it.

I think these three stories explore a dangerous dead end in science fiction; but I'm unable to wish they had not been written. (pp. 147-49)

> Damon Knight, "Kornbluth and the Silver Lexicon," in his In Search of Wonder: Essays on Modern Science Fiction (copyright © 1956, 1967, by Damon Knight; reprinted by courtesy of Advent:Publishers, Inc.), revised edition, Advent, 1967, pp. 146-49.*

EDMUND CRISPIN (essay date 1968)

C. M. Kornbluth—the public C. M. Kornbluth—is remembered as having been buoyant, kind, cheerful and mischievous; and occasionally, as in the wholly light-hearted *I Never Ast No Favours,* this side of him would spill over into his writing. Most of his best stories, however, were conceived under a darker, colder star; there is in many of them a great bleakness, and not only a bleakness, but a blackness: Kornbluth in the privacy of his workroom looked at life and judged it wanting. The resultant steely pessimism is his justification as well as his trademark, for it has nothing in common with the merely atmospheric, expedient pessimism which so much other science fiction affects. Moreover, Kornbluth held it under tight control, knowing it to be an attitude which if too lavishly displayed will dilute to a mere incurable fit of the sulks. To put the point in another way, Kornbluth's pessimism is effective largely because it is specific. It does not try to latch on to everything in sight. It is not omnivorous. It selects.

The topics which it chiefly, recurringly selects are two: treachery and punishment.

Betrayal bulks large in Kornbluth's tales. Of the twelve [in *Best SF Stories of C. M. Kornbluth*], half are about betrayal in one form or another. But punishment bulks larger still. For to Kornbluth (as a writer) it seemed simply not true that the ungodly flourishes like a green bay-tree. Retribution, in Kornbluth's fiction, may be delayed. It may—as with young Foster in *Theory of Rocketry*—even be suffered in advance. But it can never be avoided. And if the sorry scheme of things by any chance fails to provide it, then it will be compulsively self-imposed: Bowman in *The Altar at Midnight,* like Dr. Full in *The Little Black Bag,* is committing slow suicide by alcohol.

Preoccupation with punishment is not, however, in itself sufficient to explain the impression of ruthlessness which Kornbluth's work conveys. To account for that we must look to the fact that in Kornbluth, not only the ungodly are mangled by the machine, but also the inadvertent; and not only the inadvertent, but the innocent too. Halvorsen the artist, in *With These Hands,* is doing nothing that a man may not honourably do, yet he is as doomed, from the start, as if he were a criminal—doomed because he is too unrealistic to see that the gimcrack juggernaut of technological advance will crush him and his ideals just as effortlessly and finally as it will crush anything else that happens to get under its wheels. ("There was the heroic, tragic central figure that looked mighty enough to battle with the gods, but battle wasn't any good against the grinning, knowing, hateful three-headed dog it stood on. You don't battle the pavement where you walk or the floor of the house you're in; you can't.") In short, the universe too is a betrayer: that final "chord from the lyre" twangs out of tune.

It was rare, though, for Kornbluth to miscalculate, even by a hair's breadth. As a technician he was superb, calling in aid a Mozartian sense of form, a natural talent for dialogue and for people, and a skill in metaphor which is all the more effective because never irrelevantly indulged. A polymath, he kept that factor too under iron discipline. Despite knowing so much about so many things, he declined to use his knowledge for decorative edging: if it had nothing significant to do with the matter in hand, he left it out. (This may sound easy and inevitable, but the example of other fiction-writing polymaths demonstrates that in fact it is not.) Finally, above all, he bore always in mind that imaginings must be *good* imaginings; that a good story must be a good *story.*

When he died—in 1958, aged 35—he left an unmendable gap not just in science fiction, but in literature at large. (pp. 12-13)

> Edmund Crispin, "Introduction" (© 1968 by Edmund Crispin; reprinted by permission of Faber and Faber Ltd.), in Best SF Stories of C. M. Kornbluth by C. M. Kornbluth, Faber and Faber, 1968, pp. 11-13.

DENNIS LIVINGSTON (essay date 1971)

While much of science fiction literature indicates little concern for the complexities of international relations, there does exist a significant substratum of stories, of varying literary quality to be sure, which does have something to say on this subject. (p. 255)

The social systems which may be found in science fiction usually take one of two broad forms. The first involves a traditional, three-class, hierarchically stratified society and consists of a mass of workers and peasants at the bottom, salaried personnel and lower echelon managers at the middle level, and a small group with ultimate decisionmaking authority at the top level. The highest and lowest class members may be called by different names—in [George Orwell's] *1984* they are the Party and the proles, in [Fritz Leiber's] *Gather, Darkness!* they are the Hierarchy and the commoners, and in *The Space Merchants* they are the heads of the largest advertising agencies and the consumers. This pattern has appeared with remarkable consistency in science fiction.

These stratified societies are distinguished from historical examples by the efficiency and ruthlessness with which the elite managers use modern techniques of psychosocial manipulation to induce mass conformity to the prevailing belief system and by the fact that membership in the elite is usually not hereditary. (pp. 255-56)

[In *The Space Merchants*] government continues to exist as the ostensible source of rulemaking, but the actual nexus of power is maintained by private individuals who direct the mass media.

Specifically, it is the heads of the top advertising companies who effectively rule the world in *The Space Merchants*. The motivating philosophy of the executive class is nothing more complicated than corporate greed buttressed by firm belief in the value of ever-higher standards of consumption and rising population levels. The individual citizen is continually subjected to a barrage of both subliminal and overt advertising messages and, if he should fall into debt, enters perforce into the lowest ranks of the consumer class, the contract laborers, from which he is unlikely to emerge. Industrialization has resulted in smog so bad that one must wear a nose-filter on the city streets although pedicabs have replaced fuel-powered vehicles. Formal organs of government are used as convenient meeting grounds for corporate leaders to hammer out bargaining positions. For example, United States Senators directly represent commercial interests and vote in proportion to the economic power of their clients. As in many science fiction stories of this kind there is a small band of conspirators, organized here into the World Conservationist Association, who do not see continually increasing consumption as the only way to maintain a viable economy and who are prepared to sabotage the system to propagate their beliefs. However, there is little they can do except escape to Venus and try to build a sane society there. This rather cynical and satirical view of the moral bankruptcy of society's leaders is a classic example of the use of science fiction as a medium for criticism of major contemporary trends and for warning us about the state we may be in if these trends are allowed to continue unchecked. (pp. 259-60)

> *Dennis Livingston, "Science Fiction Models of Future World Order Systems," in* International Organization *(copyright 1971, World Peace Foundation), Vol. 25, No. 2, Spring, 1971, pp. 254-70.**

SAM J. LUNDWALL   (essay date 1971)

No more than five years after the first publication of *1984*, the brilliant U.S. writer duo Frederik Pohl and Cyril M. Kornbluth brought out another sf novel, in which the new totalitarian state was shown in its fullest and most horrible detail. . . . (pp. 60-1)

Pohl/Kornbluth's brilliant novel [*The Space Merchants*] . . . tells about a not too distant future in which the big corporations have taken power and Money is king. The New York of *The Space Merchants* is diametrically opposite the London of *1984*, but in the end the slavery is all the same. Big Brother kicks his subjects into obedience; the new industrial tycoons drug

them. "If you want a picture of the future," O'Brien says in *1984*, "imagine a boot stamping on a human face—forever." It hardly matters much to the victim if the boot bears the sign of a Swastika or a Coca Cola bottle. The difference is that in the latter case the victim can even be made to pay for the privilege of being trampled upon.

Pohl/Kornbluth have written a number of sf novels on this theme, among others *Gladiator-at-Law* . . . , which is an acid settlement with the multi-national corporations like Philips, General Electric, Kodak and so on. The distance of Orwell's boot-state is enormous. Here the world is ruled by a number of giant corporations which write their own laws, fight regular battles with competitive companies and unite only in the idea of the holy profit.

In Orwell's dictatorship the citizen can revolt, as Winston does, by escaping the system for a time, away from the spy eyes and the Thought Police. . . . But in *Gladiator-at-Law* there is no Thought Police, no Ministry of Love. The industry doesn't need any executioners, it needs consumers. (p. 62)

[The theme is] widely used in anti-Utopian science fiction of today, and it seems as if the sf writers more and more now have turned from the earlier war and natural catastrophe themes to the results of our economic and environmental (mis)management and its impact on man. (p. 63)

> *Sam J. Lundwall, "The Air-Conditioned Nightmare," in his* Science Fiction: What It's All About, *translated by Sam J. Lundwall (copyright © 1969, 1971, by Sam J. Lundwall), revised edition, Ace Books, 1971, pp. 58-73.**

HAROLD L. BERGER   (essay date 1976)

In *Gladiator-at-Law,* Pohl and Kornbluth depict an America brutalized by commercial factions. The masses, violent, lawless, and depraved, live in gang-ruled, crumbling cities, while the "bubble-house class" luxuriates in the surrounding suburbia. The sense of nationhood and government itself have virtually dissolved, the country being little more than a playing field for competing corporate giants. Savage ironies expose a society in a state of moral collapse: vastly wealthy commercial interests heedless of rotting core cities and their canaille; a sophisticated legal system functioning in openly predatory conditions; an advanced technology co-existing with barbaric tastes— the highest art form being the bloody theatrical extravaganza on Field Days. A highwire stunt over a tank of piranha, a roller derby race between contestants fitted with elbow spikes, a broken-field run over barbed wire and castrator mines—such spectacles, according to a director, provide

> healthful entertainment, satisfying the needs of every man for some form of artistic expression. . . .

Pohl and Kornbluth pass sentence on that society and its foundations when, in the last moments of the novel, the rotted city of New York spontaneously crashes into rubble. From the debris a huge cloud rises and drifts seaward. . . . (p. 120)

For writers disposed to dip their pens in acid, America in the two decades following the Second World War seemed an orchard of quince. A nation throwing itself into an orgy of production and consumption unparalleled in history must look not a little ridiculous and dangerous. Not just a class but a whole people were the stuff of wonder and dismay. Pohl and Kornbluth could not lack subject matter nor could the spill of subject matter lack its Pohls and Kornbluths. (p. 121)

Harold L. Berger, "The New Tyrannies," in his Science Fiction and the New Dark Age *(copyright © 1976 by The Popular Press), Bowling Green University Popular Press, 1976, pp. 86-146.**

DONALD WEST (essay date 1981)

Within the genre [of science fiction, **"The Marching Morons"**] is generally regarded as a classic: one of those works which cannot be left out of any historical survey, and which even today can be put forward as an example of the kind of sf that is to be admired and emulated. Indeed, **"The Marching Morons"** is a very readable story. It is written with all Kornbluth's customary pace, dash and wit: a tight and fast-moving narrative that wastes scarcely a word and holds the reader's attention from beginning to end. However, such good, solid commercial readability is scarcely unique, and **"The Marching Morons"** has no unusual or outstanding features from a purely literary point of view. Yet for thirty years it has been widely admired, despite the fact that the science content is grossly inaccurate or completely implausible, the internal logic is faulty, the basic situation is impossible, the resolution is preposterous, and the overall outlook is indicative of a pathologically morbid mental condition. Kornbluth's story certainly deserves a place in any history of sf—but only as one of the clearest possible examples of what can go wrong with the genre: of dark, miserable, fear-ridden fantasies of revenge and power masquerading as the triumph of scientific objectivity over emotion and the victory of reason and logic over irrationality.

"The Marching Morons" tells how the tomb of one Honest John Barlow, a real-estate salesman from late twentieth century America, is discovered in the far future. Thanks to an accident with a new anaesthetic Barlow has survived in a state of suspended animation and he is duly brought back to life—mainly in the hope that he might be of some use in solving "The Problem". Taken to a nearby city, Barlow marvels at the wonders of futuristic buildings, cars which apparently travel at 250 Kph, garish animated advertising and inter-urban rocket ships. However, he suspects he is being tricked in some way and he flees, only to be refound and given some franker explanations. The cars, the rocket ships and the rest are indeed fakes: toys to fool a population whose average IQ has declined to 45. A world of five billion is run by a high-intelligence group of only three million (for convenience referred to in this article as the Elite) and The Problem is how to find some way of reducing this vast population, since the Morons breed uncontrollably. The story's title comes from an analogy cited by Barlow: "If all the Chinese in the world were to line up four abreast, I think it was, and start marching past a given point, they'd never stop because of the babies that would be born and grow up before they passed the point". In other words, the Morons can't be sterilized fast enough. Barlow immediately conceives a solution, but being a sharp (and greedy) businessman he refuses to reveal his plan until he is assured of rewards up to and including World Dictatorship. His terms being accepted, he sets the Elite to work on a vast campaign to persuade the Morons to emigrate to Venus. The colonization of Venus is of course a complete fake, since there are no real spaceships capable of travelling further than the Moon, but by advertising, undercover propaganda and manipulation of political and national rivalries Barlow successfully instils the Morons with what he calls "the lemming urge". Cities are torn down for

their steel and vast fleets of spaceships are built and take off for the promised land. Finally, when The Problem is solved, Barlow himself is paid off: put in a ship of his own and shot off into the graveyard of space . . . like all the others.

(There are casual mentions of Hitler's death camps, but exactly how the Morons are exterminated is not made explicit. Presumably they are simply dumped in space or on the Moon. Writing so soon after World War II and its mass atrocities Kornbluth probably felt that a hint was quite enough.)

The concentration camps of the Nazis are estimated to have claimed the lives of about six million people. That modern men could systematically and cold-bloodedly commit murder on such a scale was scarcely conceivable until the example was provided. Kornbluth's extrapolation pushes the millions up to billions—a quantum jump that strains credibility all over again. However, it is probably true that human nastiness knows no mathematical limits; atrocity on a grand scale is limited only by the logistics. In fact, Kornbluth scores his one hit here: in almost every other area his premises are frankly impossible. (pp. 17-18)

Kornbluth uses the term "moron" rather loosely. In medical terminology three degree of mental deficiency are usually recognized: *Morons* (IQ50-70) can learn useful tasks and adjust under supervision; *Imbeciles* (IQ25-50) can care for simple personal needs but must live in institutions; *Idiots* (IQ too low for measurement) are wholly incapable of looking after themselves. In Kornbluth's world the Morons are the comparatively bright ones; more than half the population would be Imbeciles or Idiots—persons who (if they were significantly mobile at all) would have considerable trouble tying their shoelace or crossing the street. (p. 19)

The real morons in Kornbluth's story seem to be [the] "geneticists". Kornbluth was writing well before several major advances in knowledge, but even so, heredity was not entirely a closed book in his time. . . . [Human] genetics is rather more than a simple matter of addition or subtraction. A tall man and a tall woman will have children who are tall—but not quite so tall as the parents. (Were it otherwise one could expect a race of giants by now, given the strong tendency for tall women to marry tall men.) More to the point: the children of very intelligent parents will probably be rather less intelligent, and the children of very stupid parents will probably be rather less stupid. In other words, the rule is regression to the mean. Even with controlled breeding there is a tendency to move back to the average, and where there is *no* control the tendency is a certainty. To establish—and maintain—a *new* average requires either an enormous effort or an enormous disaster, and a large gene pool makes either of these a little unlikely. In fact, short of the assumption that possession of any IQ over 60 automatically conferred sterility there is no way that the huge shift in the distribution of intelligence postulated in Kornbluth's story could have come about. Kornbluth seems to view intelligence as a sort of Capital: in the deserving Elite it mounts up from generation to generation by genetic compound interest, while among the shiftless Morons it is speedily and recklessly dissipated away. Unfortunately for this notion Nature is more of a Communist, and in the long run intelligence (and other qualities) dodges from high to low through average and back again in a way that is truly impartial. "Good Breeding" is very largely a myth maintained by social and environmental sanctions.

Enough has been said by now to indicate that the "science" in this particular piece of science fiction is distinctly shaky.

The situation is arbitrarily declared to exist—and therefore it exists, in defiance of all reason and knowledge. The author has a casual way with figures; neither statistics nor logistics seem to strike him as matters requiring too much attention. For instance, he is able to work out (when Barlow asks why the Morons are not left to kill themselves off) that "Five billion corpses mean about five hundred million tons of rotting flesh", but the very same five hundred million tons is subsequently packed into spaceships and shot off into space without any consideration of the (impossible) amounts of steel, fuel and sundries that would be required.

Still, while it is no doubt desirable for the science in sf to have at least a glancing connection with known realities it is not altogether and absolutely essential. Where the point of the story is not directly implicated, errors and improbabilities can be overlooked out of regard for merits elsewhere. However, the most glaring improbability of all is rather too obvious to be set aside: the inability of the superintelligent Elite to come up with any answers to the Problem. As Barlow himself puts it: "You're the great brains and you can't think of any?"

The given reason is that "Poprob had exhausted every rational attempt and the new Poprob attacklines would have to be irrational or subrational. This creature from the past . . . would be a foundation of precious vicious self-interest." The real reason, of course, is that without the unsolved problem and Barlow's solution there would be no story. However, this raises the second question: why does it have to be *this* solution?

Without stretching the imagination too much one can think of several possibilities not too foreign to a man of Barlow's stamp. He could market a contraceptive candy bar of irresistible attractiveness. He could start a fashion for suntan lamps emitting enough hard radiation to sterilize the users. . . . And so on and so forth. In fact, given a different preoccupation, this is a problem that would be settled out of hand. Kornbluth was writing before oral contraceptives, but the old sf standby of the miracle pill must have occurred to him. The conclusion has to be that the story was created for the sake of its solution: mass murder. The whole thing is a barely rational excuse for a particularly nasty piece of wish-fulfillment.

"**The Marching Morons**" is a fantasy of fear and revenge. The fear comes from an insecure sense of superiority which feels itself threatened by those who care nothing for its values. The revenge manifests itself as the sulky desire to strike back at those who (inadvertently or purposely) might infringe the privileges of selfishness. The Morons are an intolerable burden to be cast aside: "The actual truth is that millions of workers live in luxury on the sweat of a handful of artistocrats. I shall probably die before my time of overwork . . ." These are the descendants of the "migrant workers, slum-dwellers and tenant farmers" who so shiftlessly and inconsiderately bred and bred again while real-estate dealer Barlow remained childless and was ". . . a blind stupid ass to tolerate economic and social conditions which penalized childbearing by the prudent and foresighted."

Here is the true and authentic whine of Middle Class martyrdom, the voice which frets and moans over taxes and complains bitterly at the unfairness of a world which asks more from those who have than from those who have little. The poor and stupid are to be hated because, being poor and stupid, they lack the prudence and foresight of those who are richer and cleverer; they are to be feared because they are too numerous and might want too much, unreasonably and unaccountably failing to recognize that only those who are powerful and intelligent have the right to be selfish. These miserable creatures—all five billion of them—are scarcely human at all; only the Elite are "People—real people". (A phrase used twice.) The Morons are just five hundred million tons of meat: mumbling illiterates chewing candy bars and watching idiotic TV quiz shows, driving flash faked-up automobiles and visiting Moron psychiatrists. (The "Family Freud"—a neat little satirical vignette.) It is the "real people" who have the monopoly on art and science: Hawkins the potter, who has to listen in resigned disgust while the Moron storebuyer burbles on about the "est'etic" values of his wares, and Ryan-Ngana, who "between interruptions . . . was slowly constructing an n-dimensional geometry whose foundations and superstructure owed no debt whatsoever to intuition".

Smart boys, these—even if they couldn't quite solve the Problem without Barlow's "vicious self-interest". But that, of course, was strictly necessary: an intermediary was needed to distance the Great Brains from their dirty work. Not that they seem at all squeamish about it. One member of Barlow's team does commit suicide out of remorse, but the others manage to carry on bravely enough. Presumably once Barlow has been disposed of and everyone has given their hands a good wash they can cheerfully settle down to an idyllic future of aesthetic pleasures and intellectual joys, quite unencumbered by billions of tiresome Morons.

It could be argued that "**The Marching Morons**" is meant as irony. This is a rather dubious proposition, since it argues an extraordinary degree of disinguenuousness and cynicism on the part of the author. Still, speculation on the motives and intentions of authors is always difficult and dangerous, particularly when the work in question was written for commercial publication. . . . [Kornbluth] once described his novel *The Syndic* as "sick". "**The Marching Morons**" deserves some much harsher word—and Kornbluth may have thought so himself, if not at the time of writing them later. His story "**The Meeting**" (completed by Frederik Pohl) indicates that there was a good deal of ambivalence (at the last) in his attitudes.

But whatever the author's intentions, it seems fairly certain that "**The Marching Morons**" is not *read* as irony—nor, indeed, that it can be so read without making quite exceptional and unreasonable allowance. So while there may be some excuses to be made for the author, there is no excuse at all for the praise of the readers, the editors and the critics. For thirty years "**The Marching Morons**" has been Great sf, endlessly reprinted, whereas it should have been greeted with a yell of execration on its very appearance. The reason is discreditable and distasteful, but not too hard to find. Whether with conscious cynicism or purely by instinct Kornbluth has given expression to a whole series of the murky prejudices and atavistic impulses which lie beneath science fiction's facade of scientific sweet reason. (pp. 20-3)

Even as a metaphorical rendering of reality "**The Marching Morons**" is grotesquely distorted, but it does provide a very accurate evocation of a certain sort of class fear and hatred. A piece of straightforward class-distinction or racism would obviously be difficult to justify, but by taking intelligence (an objectively measurable quality) as his standard Kornbluth is able to cloak prejudice in a superficial veneer of rationality. In fact, any discrimination on grounds of IQ is inevitably going to involve class as well. In any society which is at all socially mobile class will follow intelligence: the clever rise while the less clever fall away. The greater the demands that are made on intelligence—as in a technological society—the more certain and swift this polarization becomes. Like fascism, the attraction of Kornbluth's story is the relief it offers from an abiding sense of social insecurity. It appeals to the lower middle classes of the intellect: those who are just far enough above the average to covet what they glimpse above and to fear and despise those below. The great terror of any elite is that *despite* its superiority it will somehow be dragged down to the level of the masses. Getting rid of the masses is one fantasy-solution. (p. 25)

Obviously there are considerable openings here for debate on the nature and extent of social obligations. It is sufficient to note that Kornbluth's story simply begs all the questions—it never rises out of its resentful fantasies of frustrated ambition. Fascism is really a kind of snobbery—and vice versa—and the members of the high-intelligence Elite are the ultimate fascist snobs: high IQ puts them up with the right sort of people, and that is that. They are beyond morality. They are also beyond rationality. **"The Marching Morons"** is not so much sf in the gutter as sf in the sewers, and those who have praised the story for so long would do well to consider on what basis their admiration rests. (p. 26)

> Donald West, "The Right Sort of People," in Foundation *(copyright © 1981 by the Science Fiction Foundation), No. 21, February, 1981, pp. 17-26.*

DAVID I. MASSON   (essay date 1981)

D. West has mounted a brilliant attack [see excerpt above] on **"The Marching Morons"**. But Kornbluth's story is no futurological warning: it is a fable. Of course its science is nonsense: Kornbluth cannot have expected readers to take seriously Black-Kupperman's Svengalization (from the distance of the North Pole) of a Senator and a President of the United States, respectively into a complete speech, and a decision for the whole government to take to spaceship. *The Marching Morons* is a piece of blackest irony about the insane, the Gadarene, human race, and the extent to which it is doomed to supercrises, to lying control, and to the toleration of cruelty, murder and genocide. (Its insanities are indeed as rife in those of high intelligence as in the less intelligent.)

Charles Galton Darwin's *The Next Million Years*, 1953, chapter VII, saw Man as a wild animal who will never be anything else (will never be domesticated by a Master Breed): I cannot imagine that any reasonable reader will seriously identify with Kornbluth's hyper-intelligent few. The absurdly extreme dysgenic development has, as in Kornbluth's **"The Little Black Bag"**, been invented for the sake of the fable and his familiar motif of betrayal. (p. 90)

> David I. Masson, in his letter to David Pringle (Editor) in April, 1981, in Foundation *(copyright © 1981 by the Science Fiction Foundation), No. 22, June, 1981, p. 90.*

FREDERIK POHL   (essay date 1981)

Not This August is cautionary science fiction, in the great tradition of *1984*—and of [Aldous Huxley's] *Brave New World*, [Nevil Shute's] *On the Beach* and many others. It is not meant as prediction. It is only meant as a warning. It doesn't say what will happen, positively, but what *may* happen, *if*—

Not This August was first published a quarter of a century ago and, until this new edition was in preparation, I had not read it since it first came out. I didn't know if it would stand up after all those years; but when I took it up again it gripped me from the first page, and kept me turning pages until the end, and left me wishing for more when it was done. History did not go the way Cyril Kornbluth outlined in this book when he was writing in the gritty, mean 1950s. But the essence of the novel is still true. (p. 8)

One could object to *Not This August* as a failed prediction, but of course it was never meant that way. That is one of the great virtues of cautionary science fiction. The story need not come true to be valuable—in fact, no one wants it to come true, the author least of all. What Cyril Kornbluth wanted us to know when he wrote *Not This August* was that there were grave dangers in the world—there still are, and much the same dangers; and that averting or rectifying those dangers presented graver dangers still, as the ending shows. And those, too, are unfortunately still present, and still need to be guarded against.

But it is not for the heuristic and normative values of science fiction that most people read it—thank heaven! We read it for fun, especially for the ironical, surprising insights that illuminate the world we live in.

Cyril Kornbluth was about as good at giving us those startling insights as any science fiction writer who ever lived. *Not This August* is vintage Kornbluth—witty, powerful and illuminating. . . . (pp. 11-12)

> Frederik Pohl, in his introduction to Not This August *by C. M. Kornbluth (copyright © 1981 by Tom Doherty Associates), revised edition, Tor Books, 1981, pp. 7-12.*

ADDITIONAL BIBLIOGRAPHY

Atheling, William Jr. [pseudonym of James Blish]. "A Question of Content." In his *The Issue at Hand,* edited by James Blish, pp. 121-30. Chicago: Advent Publishers, 1964.

> Differentiates between the "ikon-smashing" science fiction novel "ably exemplified by Pohl's and Kornbluth's *The Space Merchants,*" and the science fiction novel of ideas that "finds its way into the mainstream."

Pohl, Frederik. "Reminiscence: Cyril M. Kornbluth." *Extrapolation* 17, No. 2 (May 1976): 102-09.

> Personal recollection of Kornbluth's and Pohl's early membership in the Futurians, and the various methods they employed during their long history of collaborations.

Amy Lowell

1874-1925

American poet, critic, biographer, and essayist.

The leading proponent of imagism in American poetry, Lowell is remembered for her forceful theorizing on poetics, her eccentric, outspoken personality, and her massive biography of John Keats. With John Gould Fletcher, she was a pioneer in experimenting with polyphonic prose, an intermittently rhymed form of free verse. Although she was Ezra Pound's successor as the chief proponent of imagism—a movement which Pound later dubbed "Amygism"—Lowell is herself generally categorized as a minor, though versatile poet, whose work displayed occasional bursts of brilliance. She sought to liberate poetry from the strictures of meter, using as her vehicles free verse, polyphonic prose, and haiku in such volumes as *Pictures of the Floating World, Sword Blades and Poppy Seed*, and *What's O'Clock*. The last-named book, containing the best of Lowell's later work, was posthumously published and awarded the Pulitzer Prize in poetry in 1926.

A cousin of James Russell Lowell, whose literary reputation dogged her throughout her career, Lowell was born of a distinguished New England family. The Lowells' wealth and position provided Amy with opportunities for travel in Europe and a good education. In later years, the proper, conservative values acquired in her youth clashed with Lowell's naturally independent and domineering personality, forming an unresolved dialectic reflected throughout her life and work. In her late twenties Lowell decided to become a poet, and during the next few years she used her wealth, intimidating personality, and tireless industry to accomplish that end. Her first volume, discounting a childish vanity press publication, appeared in 1912. *A Dome of Many-Coloured Glass* is conventional and undistinguished, exhibiting nothing of the form characterizing Lowell's later volumes. She met Pound in 1913 and immediately embraced imagism, a style applied successfully in her next—and one of her best—volumes, *Sword Blades and Poppy Seed*. With this widely acclaimed collection, Lowell moved to the forefront of American poetry, a position from which she lent support to other writers, among them D. H. Lawrence. During the next decade, she wrote several books of criticism and over six hundred poems, edited three imagist anthologies, and became a popular speaker at American universities. Accompanying Lowell during her last years was Ada Russell, a former actress who became Lowell's secretary, close friend, and inspiration for several moving love poems. Lowell died shortly after completing her master work, a biography of her greatest influence, John Keats.

As Malcolm Cowley has noted, Lowell's "creative ability, critical integrity, and . . . powerful personality" enabled her to assume the leadership of America's New Poetry movement. She counseled other poets on their work, recommended and sold their manuscripts, harried recalcitrant editors, and wrote many articles and speeches promoting poetry's newest developments. Her critical theory is demonstrated in four books. The first, *Six French Poets*, introduced American readers to the chief post-symbolist artists. *Tendencies in Modern American Poetry* performed a similar service for Carl Sandburg,

H.D., and several other pioneers in modern verse, delineating their theories and offering surprisingly accurate appraisals of the future reception of their work. Lowell wrote a flawed, but definitely barbed, satirical parody of contemporary poetry in *A Critical Fable*, styled after her famous cousin's classic, *A Fable for Critics*. The fourth, *John Keats*, is valued as a landmark work for its wealth of previously unpublished material gathered from Lowell's private collection of Keatsiana. Keats and the English Romantics, as well as the French decadent Paul Fort, are considered the prime influences on Lowell's poetry.

Characteristic of her poetry is sensuous imagery, a precise economy of words, and delight in texture and color. Her verse ranges from tender love lyrics to dramatic monologues written in the rustic New England vernacular. An interest in Oriental literature is evident throughout Lowell's canon, reaching its height in the "Lacquer Prints" in *Pictures of the Floating World* and in the interpolated Chinese poetry of *Fir-Flower Tablets*, written with the aid of translator Florence Ayscough. A free verse dramatic monologue examining the clash between duty and desire, "Patterns" is considered by many to be Lowell's most important poem. "Lilacs," an imagistic descriptive poem, and "The Bronze Horses" from *Can Grande's Castle*, are also considered among her strongest works.

Although Lowell's poetry has been praised for its vitality and exoticism, it has also been dismissed as superficial, unoriginal, and pretentious. According to Oscar Cargill, Lowell "went in, mainly, for the pretty-pretty." Other critics cite a lack of firmness and concision which true imagism demands. But Louis Untermeyer, like most critics, finds Lowell's redemption in her role as an "awakener," claiming that she "invigorated the old forms while affecting the new techniques."

(See also *TCLC*, Vol. 1.)

PRINCIPAL WORKS

Dream Drops; or, Stories from Fairy Land, by a Dreamer (poetry) 1887
A Dome of Many-Coloured Glass (poetry) 1912
Sword Blades and Poppy Seed (poetry) 1914
Six French Poets (criticism) 1915
Men, Women and Ghosts (poetry) 1916
Tendencies in Modern American Poetry (criticism) 1917
Can Grande's Castle (poetry) 1918
Pictures of the Floating World (poetry) 1919
Fir-Flower Tablets (poetry) 1921
Legends (poetry) 1921
A Critical Fable (poetry) 1922
John Keats (biography) 1925
What's O'Clock (poetry) 1925
East Wind (poetry) 1926
Ballads for Sale (poetry) 1927
Fool o' the Moon (poetry) 1927
Poetry and Poets (essays) 1930

AMY LOWELL (essay date 1914)

In the first place, I wish to state my firm belief that poetry should not try to teach, that it should exist simply because it is a created beauty, even if sometimes the beauty of a gothic grotesque. We do not ask the trees to teach us moral lessons, and only the Salvation Army feels it necessary to pin texts upon them. We know that these texts are ridiculous, but many of us do not yet see that to write an obvious moral all over a work of art, picture, statue, or poem, is not only ridiculous, but timid and vulgar. (pp. vii-viii)

For the purely technical side I must state my immense debt to the French, and perhaps above all to the, so-called, Parnassian School, although some of the writers who have influenced me most do not belong to it. High-minded and untiring workmen, they have spared no pains to produce a poetry finer than that of any other country in our time. . . . Before the works of Parnassians like Leconte de Lisle, and José-Maria de Heredia, or those of Henri de Régnier, Albert Samain, Francis Jammes, Remy de Gourmont, and Paul Fort, of the more modern school, we [Anglo-Saxons] stand rebuked. (pp. viii-ix)

The poet with originality and power is always seeking to give his readers the same poignant feeling which he has himself. To do this he must constantly find new and striking images, delightful and unexpected forms. Take the word "daybreak," for instance. What a remarkable picture it must once have conjured up! The great, round sun, like the yolk of some mighty egg, *breaking* through cracked and splintered clouds. But we have said "daybreak" so often that we do not see the picture any more, it has become only another word for dawn. The poet must be constantly seeking new pictures to make his readers feel the vitality of his thought.

Many of the poems in [*Sword Blades and Poppy Seed*] are written in what the French call "Vers Libre," a nomenclature more suited to French use and to French versification than to ours. I prefer to call them poems in "unrhymed cadence," for that conveys their exact meaning to an English ear. They are built upon "organic rhythm," or the rhythm of the speaking voice with its necessity for breathing, rather than upon a strict metrical system. They differ from ordinary prose rhythms by being more curved, and containing more stress. The stress, and exceedingly marked curve, of any regular metre is easily perceived. These poems, built upon cadence, are more subtle, but the laws they follow are not less fixed. Merely chopping prose lines into lengths does not produce cadence, it is constructed upon mathematical and absolute laws of balance and time. In the preface to his "Poems," Henley speaks of "those unrhyming rhythms in which I had tried to quintessentialize, as (I believe) one scarce can do in rhyme." The desire to "quintessentialize," to head-up an emotion until it burns white-hot, seems to be an integral part of the modern temper, and certainly "unrhymed cadence" is unique in its power of expressing this.

Three of these poems are written in a form which, so far as I know, has never before been attempted in English. M. Paul Fort is its inventor, and the results it has yielded to him are most beautiful and satisfactory. Perhaps it is more suited to the French language than to English. But I found it the only medium in which these particular poems could be written. It is a fluid and changing form, now prose, now verse, and permitting a great variety of treatment.

But the reader will see that I have not entirely abandoned the more classic English metres. I cannot see why, because certain manners suit certain emotions and subjects, it should be considered imperative for an author to employ no others. Schools are for those who can confine themselves within them. Perhaps it is a weakness in me that I cannot. (pp. x-xii)

> *Amy Lowell, in her preface to her* Sword Blades and Poppy Seed *(© 1914 by Amy Lowell), The Macmillan Company, 1914 (and reprinted by Houghton Mifflin Company, 1925), pp. vii-xiii.*

WALTER LIPPMANN (essay date 1916)

Ever since Miss Amy Lowell explained the "new manner" in poetry [in a recent *New Republic* article,] I have been trying to imagine life lived as she describes it. For she says that there has been a changed attitude towards life which compels a poet to paint landscapes because they are beautiful and not because they suit his mood, to tell stories because they are interesting and not because they prove a thesis. I don't understand this "externality"; I don't know what it means to be interested in "things for themselves."

Let Miss Lowell try it some morning and see what happens. . . . [She] arrives at breakfast, and beholds a sliced orange. It fascinates her. She "never tires of finding colors in it," and sometimes the colors so occupy her that she takes them separately, unrelated to the sliced orange, as it were. She goes on gazing at "colors, and light and shade, in planes and cubes with practically no insistence on the substance which produces them." Says someone at the table, disconcerted: "Eat your orange, Miss Lowell.'' ''Impossible,'' is the unhesitating reply. ''I am interested in things for themselves. It is an inevitable change, my dear, reflecting the evolution of life.''

My guess is that Miss Lowell does not live at this pitch of externality. I imagine that among the thousand objects which might attract her attention—oranges, eggs, umbrellas, dust-heaps—she chooses some one about which to write a poem. And I imagine that she chooses it because it interests her for the particular mood she happens to be in. And I imagine that she feels she has written a good poem when her mood has got itself expressed about the object. I imagine she is external when it interests her to be external. To be sure, if she doesn't choose to be interested in her own feelings about the objects she selects, that is her affair. But she shouldn't ask us to believe that she has transcended them, and is now contemplating the world with the detachment of Aristotle's God. Nobody has ever yet succeeded in being external to himself, and I doubt whether Miss Lowell will succeed.

She speaks in her article about the universality of life, and then tells us that ''noble thoughts'' are anathema to the modern poet. Of course they are, if you put them in quotation marks. But there are noble thoughts which poets have not always ruled out of the universality of life, and those thoughts expressing the depth and variety of human desire are the elements which Miss Lowell's school somehow seems to avoid.

Much of their work often reminds me of the art collections which museums put in the basement—Persian pottery, a choice array of Egyptian beetles, six hundred and fifty specimens of Roman drinking cups, and a fascinating group of curious watches made at Nueremberg in the sixteenth century. All interesting enough if you have the time to look at them, and if properly distributed, amusing and delightful. A few specialists may be seen poring over the showcases, and an occasional party of tourists comes through bent on seeing all there is to see. But upstairs there is a crowd in front of the Madonna and Child, the famous Venus, and somebody's battle picture. Those are the art works the people remember, and hang photographs of in the parlor. It is the art with which they live.

And I wonder whether they're not more right than Miss Lowell, when they ask the artist to express human responses to the central issues of life and death. If art is a solace and a stimulus to men, are they such utter philistines in saying that the significant artist is not he who deals with things for themselves, but with things in relation to human need? I grant Miss Lowell that there are colors in the dustheaps, but what I'm afraid of is that her horror of noble thoughts has frightened her away from the effort to find color and significance in those more difficult objects about which human life revolves. I'm afraid that Miss Lowell calls a preoccupation with incidentals a brave attempt to be external and universal. (pp. 178-79)

Walter Lippmann, ''Miss Lowell and Things'' in The New Republic *(© 1916 The New Republic, Inc.; used with permission of the President and Fellows of Harvard College), Vol. 6, No. 72, March 18, 1916, pp. 178-79.*

WILLIAM LYON PHELPS (essay date 1921)

[Amy Lowell] is an experimentalist, delighting in new forms and modes of expression. Everything she writes shows vitality and her independent prefaces seem to indicate artistic ideals held with such conviction, not to say ferocity, that if people

were tortured, imprisoned or slain for heretical opinions in the field of art, she would go singing to the stake. . . .

But although I believe that Amy Lowell has now reached an enviable position in contemporary literature, and that she is regarded by many readers and many critics as a true poet, I by no means share all her theories, nor do I especially admire that part of her work which is perhaps most admired by her. Frankly, I am bored by her ''polyphonic prose,'' and I will not admit that it is poetry at all. With the exception of her first book, ''**A Dome of Many-Coloured Glass**,'' I think ''**Can Grande's Castle**'' is the least interesting and the least important of her works. If it can be judged as poetry, it is certainly inferior to that of the chief living poets; if it be judged as prose, it does not compare with the prose of Carlyle. It is really nothing but rhetoric and declamation, gorgeous, florid, ornate, horrendous; instead of being full of orchestral harmonies, which was her intention, I find its glare and racket merely nerve-shaking. The monotony of noise is worse than the monotony of silence. I am aware, of course, that this is an individual view; that many critics and many readers apparently love these sounds and colors; but the business of a reviewer is not to tell what other people think, but to give his own opinion.

Amy Lowell is a poet in spite of herself. I mean that, leaving out much of her free verse, her polyphonic prose and the work she has written to illustrate her theories, we have a sufficient amount of beautiful and original poetry. I like her best where she is most conventional.

Many writers of free verse could not write poetry to save their souls, but Amy Lowell, thoroughly trained in the great tradition of British poetry, has the right to experiment, founded on a mastery of correct technique. . . . So, if any one had either the ignorance or the hardihood to say of Amy Lowell, ''She writes free verse because it is easy,'' her success in couplets and stanzas is the answer. She is a poet; the real thing, not an impostor. . . .

If there are still those who doubt Amy Lowell's ability to write poetry, I advise them to look through her volumes and read the following: ''**Sword Blades and Poppy Seed**,'' in octosyllabics; ''**Patterns**,'' in lines of irregular length with frequent rimes; ''**The Cremona Violin**,'' in stanzas. Many other works might be cited, but I have chosen these three because they are to me proof positive—proof beyond all controversy—that she is, in every sense of the word, a poet. She is a poet of imagination and passion, with a remarkable gift for melody, a sound technique, and an acute perception of the color and tone of words. . . .

[I admire] her candor in the preface to the volume called ''**Sword Blades and Poppy Seed**,'' in expressing her belief that poetry cannot be written without a deliberate mastery of the craft and without continuous hard work. This whole preface should be read carefully by those who wish to understand and to appreciate her verse, for she states her creed unmistakably, and makes it clear that she belongs to no school. She will write in free verse when she feels like it; and she will write in conventional meters for the same reason.

The latest book, ''**Legends**,'' also contains an interesting preface. . . .

From the general aspect of the subject [of legends] in this preface she passes to an individual prefatory note on each one of eleven legends. They represent England, New England, Europe, Peru, Yucatan, China. Although they are all written with fervor and with absorption in the story, they are not all equally interesting. I regret to say I found some of them dull. She puts her worst foot forward, and as there may be some readers who will have the same impressions as my own, I hereby warn them not to drop the book because they do not like the first four poems: the last six seem to me quite superior both in interest and in beauty.

"The Ring and the Castle" is a splendid ballad, told in spirited and even thrilling fashion. **"The Statue in the Garden"** has magnificent passages, with truly dramatic suspense. There is an especial reason for reading **"Dried Marjoram,"** one of the best pieces in the book. In the preface she says that the theme "has been a favorite one with poets since time was. I stumbled across it in a history, or guide-book, of Hampshire County, England, but I need have gone no farther than the Bible and the story of Rizpah." She does not mention Tennyson; but what chiefly interested me was the difference from Tennyson in her manner of handling exactly the same theme. The difference is eloquent not only as between Alfred Tennyson and Amy Lowell, but between the Victorian and our age. Now, although I like the Victorian literature better than ours, and Tennyson's poetry more than Miss Lowell's, I think in this particular instance she has distinctly surpassed Tennyson. I like her treatment of the subject better, and I like her style much better. I think in every way and from every point of view **"Dried Marjoram"** is a finer poem than Tennyson's "Rizpah."

Amy Lowell is developing in a way that ought to cause general satisfaction. There is simply no comparison in excellence between **"Dried Marjoram"** and **"The Ring and the Castle,"** in this volume, and the best pages of her first book. While her chief forte is description, owing to her extraordinary sensitiveness to sounds, colors, and smells, she has given in **"Legends"** such a variety of beauty as to delight her friends and to bewilder her enemies.

William Lyon Phelps, "Amy Lowell, Poet in Spite of Herself," in The New York Times Book Review and Magazine *(© 1921 by The New York Times Company; reprinted by permission), June 12, 1921, p. 19.*

LEONARD WOOLF (essay date 1925)

["**John Keats,**" by Amy Lowell] has just been published in two volumes. It is a book which I have been looking forward to with considerable eagerness. . . . Sir Sidney Colvin, it is true, had only eight years ago produced his scholarly biography, but under the circumstances it seemed that there was obviously a place for a new "Life," and that everything had conspired to make it a work of great importance.

The promise has, in my opinion, not been fulfilled. It is, of course, impossible that any "Life" of Keats, told in the minute detail and with the profuse quotations from letters and poems which Miss Lowell gives in her 1,300 pages, could be anything but an intensely interesting and moving book. But these qualities are implicit in Keats's letters and in the terrific tragedy of his life. There emerges, too, out of the mere "documents" a figure of such charm, passion, and intelligence as the biographer, in search of raw material, can find nowhere else among the illustrious dead. Nor do I wish to imply, in what follows, that Miss Lowell has not got some new "material" which was worth publishing. There are a certain number of letters, some complete letters which had hitherto been published only in part, a few poems, and the fragment of a play which Miss Lowell

is inclined to ascribe to Keats. Many of these are of considerable interest, but none of them are of first-class importance.

And now for the criticism. The book is a failure because, as it seems to me, Miss Lowell has lost her sense of proportion. She is—and no blame to her—a Keats enthusiast; for years she has been collecting "Keatsiana," and it is clear that for years she has been studying the poems, letters, and documents with an almost scholastic minuteness. Enthusiasm is a good servant, but for a critic and biographer the worst master. It has landed Miss Lowell and her reader in a maze, or rather a series of mazes, from which, as one reads, escape into fresh air seems to be impossible. The first maze into which enthusiasm led Miss Lowell was useless verbosity. If she had only had the heart to cut her book down ruthlessly to half its present length, she would have improved it enormously. In the first place, she would have cut out all those passages which begin with "we can easily imagine," or words to that effect. Miss Lowell is continually suggesting to us what must or might have passed through Keats's head when he first went to call on Leigh Hunt or when he was wandering about the country at Burford Bridge or on similar important and unimportant occasions. This is an ancient biographical convention which eventually wraps the reader's brain in coil upon coil of psychological conjecture. It is a convention which hardly ever escapes the Scylla of banality or the Charybdis of picturesqueness. Closely connected with this convention is Miss Lowell's passion for filling in the details of a picture. This leads her into every kind of irrelevancy; it defeats her purpose and obscures the lines of the picture, presumably the portrait of Keats, which she intended her book to draw for us. For instance, she is not content to tell us that at 3 p.m. on Monday, April 14th, 1817, Keats took the boat from Southampton "bound ostensibly for Cowes, but in reality for solitary contemplation, and the beginning of that great work already determined upon, and already christened 'Endymion'"; she must go on to tell us that "the sixteen miles of water from Southampton to Cowes is minutely described in a guide-book to the Isle of Wight, the second edition of which was published in 1811"—and then for a page we are given extracts which Keats read, if he "fell in with this beguiling volume." Surely this is a kind of biographical running to seed!

Miss Lowell's book is, naturally and rightly in the case of Keats, half biography and half criticism. It is impossible to separate Keats's poems from his life, or his life from his poems. Miss Lowell describes the poems and goes into every critical problem connected with them in the same minute detail which she employs in her account of the days and hours of Keats's life. That there is often great interest in these problems and in what she has to say about them, I do not deny. And yet again and again I find in this part of the book the lack of proportion, the inability to distinguish between the important and trivial, which spoils the biographical portion. The perpetual searching for "sources" is one example of this. Critics like Miss Lowell seem to find it almost impossible to believe that the poet ever wrote a line without being "indebted to" some other writer for something in it. . . . [She] tries to prove that Keats was, in his "La Belle Dame Sans Merci," largely indebted to "Palmerin of England," and that the famous lines about the "magic casements" in the "Ode to a Nightingale" owe their existence to "Palmerin" and not to Diodorus Siculus, as, apparently, Professor Lowes holds. It is true that in this case Keats had read "Palmerin," and that, being about knights and ladies, it may have had the faintest and vaguest of influences at the very back of his mind while he was writing "La Belle Dame." But to argue, as Miss Lowell does and on the evidence which she produces, that it had detailed influence on that poem, or that the "perilous seas" of the "Ode" have anything to do with a "Perilous Isle" in "Palmerin," seems to me, I confess, criticism run fantastically mad.

Leonard Woolf, "The Life of Keats," in The Nation and the Athenaeum, Vol. XXXVI, No. 22, February 28, 1925, p. 749.

JOHN LIVINGSTON LOWES   (essay date 1925)

When an eager intellectual curiosity is coupled with a spirit of adventure and an indomitable will, things will happen. And when with these qualities there is conjoined a no less eager sense of beauty as revealed in line and light and colour and the potentialities of words and rhythms, the thing that happens will be poetry. And the poetry so engendered will be apt to add to the sum of beauty and to enrich our sense of it in unexpected and sometimes disconcerting ways. And it will also inevitably, in common with all adventuring (and with most things else), fail twice to once that it triumphantly succeeds. Those are the glories—attainment and attempts alike—of the spirit of adventure, and in that inextinguishable spirit the poetry of Amy Lowell is steeped.

I am not sure that this is not indeed its most distinctive characteristic. It flashes like a banner through the pages of *Can Grande's Castle*, and *Legends*, and *Men, Women and Ghosts*. But I suspect that its even more significant expression is found in poems which to all seeming are utterly bare of it. . . . [Consider **"Dawn Adventure"**—high] white stillness, cut suddenly by a falling curve of black; then a wind in the whiteness, and the friendly signal of the earthborn height, set over against the slow, indifferent movement of the higher height out toward a kindred deep: first a picture, succinct and sparing as a Chinese print; then all at once a touch which opens vistas—in that moment at the window is the sudden thrill of unforeseen experience which is at the heart of all adventure. And the poem is typical of a hundred others. At any moment the familiar may assume one of a thousand fleeting aspects of freshness or surprise. To catch this evanescence, above all to fix it, is perennial adventure and an endless quest. Often enough the swift irradiation is uncaptured, or it dims beneath the intractable medium of words, or in the effort to escape that dulling its intensity is overwrought. But all that is part of the adventure. And more than any recent poet Amy Lowell sought and missed and won triumphantly experience and expression of those flashes of sudden beauty which pass before most of us can say: 'Lo! there!'—which pass before many of us even know they *are*.

For she has been for years enlarging our boundaries through her own keen, clear perceptions of beauty that most of us have missed, and through her fearlessness in saying precisely what she saw. . . . No poet writing today, I think, save Thomas Hardy, saw and heard with more acute perception, or saw and heard and felt so many shades and tones and shapes of things—brilliant and subtle and fugitive and firm. And joined with this quick sensitiveness to physical impressions was an intellectual honesty as sensitive—a passion for truth which never knowingly falsified the report of what was seen. And that alert and vivid sense of beauty, restless with a poet's craving for expression, yet in expression lucidly exact, has schooled us, skeptical and reluctant scholars, to a quickened vision of strange loveliness in familiar things.

I know that to some this emphasis on the familiar will seem capriciously misplaced. But Amy Lowell lived with equal intensity in two worlds. One was the world of the crowded pages of 'The Bronze Horses,' and 'Sea-Blue and Blood-Red,' and 'Guns as Keys; and the Great Gate Swings' . . . : the world of the Orient, and of strange legends and superstitions, and of a Past which lay as in a mirror before her, dazzling in its brilliancy and tumultuous with movement—a world as remote as the planet Mars from Brookline Village, Massachusetts. The other was rooted deep in those things which were to her the centre—the things which were *her own*. And the poems which are touched with perhaps the most enduring beauty are those at the heart of which are the objects of her passionate attachment: her garden, the great room in which from sunset till sunrise she lived and talked and wrote, the shifting play of light and colour on trees and birds and sky outside her window, and (merged with all and crowning all) she to whom was dedicated, in *John Keats*, 'This, and all my books.' (pp. 159-63)

[The] poems of *Fir-Flower Tablets* are, in their exquisite art, among the masterpieces of their kind. . . . [In] nothing that Miss Lowell did are the finest qualities of her art more unerringly displayed. Its clarity is no less luminous, but its incised sharpness of line is softened, and its vividness acquires a purer tone. It is as if the mellow serenity of the age-old Orient had descended upon the more restless, keen-edged beauty of a newer world:

> The village is hazy, hazy,
> And mist sucks over the open moor. . . .
> My private rooms are quiet,
> And calm with the leisure of moonlight through an open
>   door.

Something of the magic of that tranquil line pervades the volume. (p. 164)

I have dwelt on the later lyrics because I believe that among them are the poems which are most surely marked for immortality. But these moments when swift, penetrating vision is subdued to keeping with the mood which it has stirred are but one element in an astonishing profusion. Those of us who have followed the rapid sequence of Miss Lowell's books—or rather, the succession of absorbing interests out of which they sprang—have marvelled at the unabated zest with which fresh fields were entered, searchingly explored, and then annexed. For Amy Lowell had to a high degree the instincts of the scholar bound up, in a nature of singular complexity, with the spirit of adventure and the artist's compelling bent. Sometimes one quality was uppermost, sometimes another; custom never staled her infinite variety. But in the longer, more ambitious poems the student in her, for both good and ill, walked *pari passu* with the adventurer and the poet. . . . Read side by side with 'Many Swans' the stark, primitive Kathlemet legend which so kindled Amy Lowell's imagination; compare with the 'Legend of Porcelain' the books on Chinese pottery which gave to it its lavishness of exquisite detail—do this (to take no more examples), and there will come fresh understanding of the ways of the imagination with its delved and garnered stuff. 'Not that exact knowledge could help the act of creation,' wrote Miss Lowell of Keats, 'but that, with knowledge as a spring-board, imagination could leap with more certainty of aim.' One could reconstruct Amy Lowell's ripest *Ars Poetica* from passages scattered through the pages of *John Keats*, and that last sentence reflects her own experience.

Heaven forbid, however, that I should convey to anyone (if such there be!) who does not know *Can Grande's Castle* or

Legends the notion that they are academic. They exhaust, on the contrary, one's adjectives (Miss Lowell's were inexhaustible) even to suggest their flashing, impetuous movement, the gaiety and gusto with which their bright, pure, sharply cut images pour along, their combined sweep and concentration, the dramatic contrasts and the stir and tumult of their incidents. I know no writer of English whose command of the rich vocabulary of sensuous impressions approaches Amy Lowell's; the almost physical impact of it startles one each time one turns her pages. But just these qualities which I have mentioned constitute, and always have, a peril to the artist.

There is in Miss Lowell's *Critical Fable* a *tour de force* of self-portraiture—or rather, a gay, sparkling, whimsical portrait of herself as she knew that others saw her. It was not meant to be taken too seriously. But behind its 'gorgeous nonsense' (to use a phrase of Coleridge's) is the humorous detachment of a keen intellect turned with disarming candour upon itself. (pp. 166-68)

It was Coleridge, as it happens, who, in 'The Rime of the Ancient Mariner' and 'Christabel' and 'Kubla Khan,' was to Amy Lowell the supreme artist of them all; and both he and she were clear-sighted enough to recognize, the one in his conversation and the other in her verse, the common defect of their quality, which was a too free spending of their affluence—an excess sometimes magnificent, but still excess. And one feels this in Miss Lowell's poetry, I think, precisely where the check of the familiar is withdrawn, and her intensely pictorial imagination revels at will in the exercise of its visualizing energy upon objects and events which (as she says in the Preface to *Can Grande's Castle*) she 'cannot have experienced,' yet which 'seem as actual as [her] own existence.' Of their vivid actuality there can be no question, but we are often dazzled by the unrelieved profusion of brilliant imagery, and instead of the sense of a large simplicity which the Chinese poems leave, we carry away that other impression of the 'great blaze of colours all about something,' which succeeded the most amazing talk of modern times. (pp. 169-70)

[Miss Lowell's] past work spoke for itself; there were endless fresh experiences to capture and interpret; and her invincible alacrity of spirit turned to those. The period of dashing swordplay . . . served its turn. The thing that matters now is the beauty which has emerged serenely from the practice of the theories which once evoked the flashing of so many harmless blades. And this peculiar beauty at its rarest (for perfection is an angel visitant) suggests the clarity of radiant air, and the pure lines of a pattern cut in polished stone—'clear, reticent, superbly final.' . . . Every volume is packed with undetachable examples, succinct, crisp, often trenchant; bright and brief (in the words of a poet whom Miss Lowell did not love!)—bright as 'the flashing of a shield.' But for renewed assurance one need only turn, in *What's O'Clock,* to 'The Anniversary,' and 'Twenty-Four Hokku on a Modern Theme,' and (for that matter) 'Evelyn Ray.' Moreover, the exactness which Miss Lowell loved is nowhere more remarkable than in her sense of the savour and 'feel' of words. (pp. 170-72)

[In] this last book one feels, I think, a deepening of experience, and a beauty less dependent on the eye. The poignant susceptibilty to sense impressions is still there. . . . There is still the delight in words that are carven and vivid and luminous as gems; the delight in rhythms as free as poised as the flight of a gull. And at times there is prodigality in each. But there has been nothing before in Miss Lowell's poetry quite like the 'half quizzical, half wistful,' altogether winning self-revelation

in 'The Sisters'; or the mocking lightness of touch and ironic suggestion of 'The Slippers of the Goddess of Beauty'; or the breadth and warmth and (in its true sense) homeliness of 'Lilacs,' or the sheer lyric intensity of 'Fool o' the Moon.' I am not forgetting 'Meeting-House Hill'; 'Purple Grackles'; that buoyant skit on John Keats which bears the title 'View of Teignmouth in Devonshire'; the 'Summer Night Piece' which, like 'Madonna of the Evening Flowers,' is a dedication; 'Prime' and 'Vespers'; the lines 'To Carl Sandburg'; the sonnets to Eleanora Duse. But these bear, some in rare degree, the stamp of a familiar loveliness. It is the new paths broken that are significant—now sadly so. For the ripest years, with disciplined powers and deepening experience behind them and fresh fields before, were yet to come. *Dis aliter visum.* She has added new beauty to English poetry. (pp. 173-74)

John Livingston Lowes, "The Poetry of Amy Lowell," in The Saturday Review of Literature (copyright © 1925 by Saturday Review; all rights reserved; reprinted by permission), Vol. II, No. 10, October 3, 1925 (and reprinted in his Essays in Appreciation, Houghton Mifflin Company, 1936, pp. 157-74).

JOHN DRINKWATER (essay date 1926)

I must be honest about this. The Editor of *The Yale Review* sent me Miss Lowell's [*John Keats*] early in the year, asking me to write about it. The review was not to be a long one, but in order to write it the book had to be read, and that is a very long task indeed. (p. 381)

I cannot form a final opinion as to how much or how little of the immense mass of her material in detail Miss Lowell was able to enlighten. She says many questionable things, and sometimes says them unattractively, but she also frequently achieves perfect critical insight as this, to quote one instance—"All poetry consists of flashes of the subconscious mind and herculean efforts on the part of the conscious mind to equal them." While, however, I may be doubtful as to whether or no in the aggregate her good moments are in excess of her bad ones, I have by now read a considerable part of her work, enough I think to form a clear opinion of its prevalent quality. And in the first place, I am convinced that no poet has ever been honored by homage so faithful and unsparing as Keats here receives from this latest prophet of an experimental school. Whatever Miss Lowell's book may or may not be, it is important. It is the record of a devotion that lost none of its freshness in the daily exercise of twenty years. Mr. Heywood Broun, in a beautiful obituary notice, said that he thought Amy Lowell was in love with John Keats, and this in no figurative sense. The idea is as shrewd as it is charming, and it is strongly supported by the evidence of this infinitely painstaking study. Miss Lowell's biography of Keats, sustained by a relentless determination to realize his personality and an impassioned desire to project herself into the secrets of his verse, is in effect the epic of an ardor as profound and personal as any that could possess a lover. And yet that is not quite the truth, and it is here that critical opinion is likely to find its quarrel with the work. In her biography of Keats, Amy Lowell has left us not the epic—the shaped and significant chronicle of a supreme emotion, an emotion that was clearly a governing influence in her life—but the very being of the emotion itself, with its multiplicity of gestures, its caprices, its wide variety of moods, its hesitancies no less than its assurances. And so criticism will sometimes say that this is not so much a great book as a body of living and splendid experience out of which a great book was crying to be made.

It is this view that I should have liked to defend in those discussions that were to be so sadly forbidden. I know the vehement yet generous disdain with which any heresy would have been dismissed, but I should have made my protest encouraged by Amy Lowell's own admirable fearlessness. It was, I suspect, some such impression as this that provoked less than just treatment of the book in some quarters in England. To approach the work sympathetically is at once to be aware of its very unusual emotional momentum; and if at the end some dissatisfaction is still felt, it is with a deep reverence, indeed with affection, for the passionate lifetime of experience that informed it. But without such enlightening sympathy, even acute critics were apt to see here twelve hundred pages on a subject that had already been exhaustively treated and that could not possibly repay further labor on such a scale. Such an attitude was gravely at fault, but it was not unintelligible. In one essential respect it coincides with our own, which certainly suffers from no antagonism. Unfriendly critics of the book may fail altogether to perceive the essential vitality that inspires it, the vigorous beauty of its emotion, but its warmest friends may reluctantly agree that whatever the material may be it has not finally been brought into expressive proportions. Disparagement will see but a vast accumulation of facts, some old and some new, that have not been properly subjected to processes of elimination and arrangement; it will complain that to read the book attentively is to undertake a labor equal to Miss Lowell's own, which is seriously more than the reader should be asked to do. Admiration, on the other hand, will be aware of the experience that absorbed a rich and original temperament, but it too may sometimes question whether it is not being asked to follow that experience moment by moment in a way ultimately impossible to anyone but Amy Lowell herself, instead of being given the significant design of that experience, which is the only way in which full impact could be made. But when this has been said, of the durable importance of the book there can be no doubt. It must affect all considered criticism of Keats hereafter. (pp. 382-84)

John Drinkwater, ''Amy Lowell's Keats,'' in The Yale Review *(© 1926 by Yale University; reprinted by permission of the editors), n.s. Vol. XV, No. 2, January, 1926, pp. 381-84.*

WILLIAM LEONARD SCHWARTZ (essay date 1928)

After the appearance of *East Wind* and *Ballads for Sale,* two posthumous volumes of poems by Amy Lowell, it now seems possible to attempt a special study of her treatment of Far Eastern themes from the point of view of a student of comparative literature. In this place, I propose to discuss the genesis of her interest in these motifs, to make a running commentary upon her Far Eastern poetry, to show how far her art was influenced by the Japanese and Chinese poets, and to indicate her merits as an interpreter of the Far East. (p. 145)

Amy Lowell went to London in 1913, where she fell in with a group of writers who were then cultivating an acquaintance with Chinese and Japanese poetry and art, under the influence of British scholars. This was the year of Tagore's first visit to the West. Amy Lowell met Ezra Pound in London and was influenced by him, I believe. Pound, the inventor of the name ''Imagist,'' was also the literary executor of Ernest Fenollosa, who left unpublished several manuscripts concerning the Jap-

anese Nō drama, and many notes on Chinese poetry. These essays and translations appealed strongly to Pound, and he perhaps communicated his enthusiasm for Far Eastern poetry to Amy Lowell. (p. 146)

Yet Miss Lowell was slow in attempting to express herself in the manner of the Japanese poet or painter. In her next books [*Sword Blades and Poppy Seed* and *Men, Women and Ghosts*] . . . , the only thing that is specifically Japanese is perhaps the perspective of some of the landscapes or some of the imagery. In her lectures called *Six French Poets* . . . , she did not enlarge upon Francis Jammes's curious interest in China, nor is there anything definitely Japanese in the anthologies entitled *Some Imagist Poets,* which she published for the reorganized Imagist school in 1915, 1916 and 1917, except the series of ''Lacquer Prints'' to be found in the last volume, which were reprinted in *Pictures of the Floating World.* . . . (pp. 146-47)

From 1916 to 1919, however, Miss Lowell grew more interested in Japan. Her acquaintance with the art and thought of that country was at first decidedly superficial, if it be judged by her special praise, in her *Tendencies in Modern American Poetry* . . . , of John Gould Fletcher's lines entitled ''A Young Daimyo,'' of which she wrote . . . : ''This to an occidental mind certainly has the charm of Japan.'' . . . There is a greater fund of accurate information in Amy Lowell's poem on Commodore Perry's expedition to Japan, entitled **''Guns as Keys and the Great Gate Swings''** . . . , found in *Can Grande's Castle.* . . . The parts of the poem that tell of the movements of Perry's squadron are written in ''polyphonic prose,'' while the passages in cadence depict scenes in Japan at that date. In this poem, as it seems to me, Amy Lowell adopted the technique, not of the Japanese poet, but of the Japanese designer of color prints or painter of illustrated scrolls,—the *makimono.* In support of this assertion, let me adduce the evidence that several lyrics in this poem are manifestly verse reproductions of well known color prints. The often quoted lines:

> At Mishima in the province of Kai,
> Three men are trying to measure a pine-tree
> By the length of their out-stretched arms. . . .

are an exact reproduction of one of Hokusai's ''Thirty-Six Views of Fuji.''

But the publication of her fifth volume of poetry, *Pictures of the Floating World* . . . , showed Amy Lowell as now adopting ''the *hokku* pattern'' for certain of the poems called ''Lacquer Prints.'' The volume also contains seven ''Chinoiseries,'' ''written in a quasi-Oriental idiom.'' Indeed, as the preface said, many of these poems also ''owe their inception to the vivid colour-prints of the Japanese masters.'' Here again, two poems are once more reminiscent of Edmond de Goncourt's prose. But of the 59 compositions in the Japanese series, only seven are cast in the tripartite arrangement that is characteristic of the *hokku.* Perhaps this was the reason why the Japanese poet Jun Fujita . . . was led to say that Amy Lowell ''missed the essential quality of the Japanese in her *hokkus.*'' I also hear many false notes in this pseudo-Oriental poetry, and I have found that when critics praise these ''Lacquer Prints'' they always select the same four or five pieces for our admiration.

Disregarding chronology for a moment, in order to complete the study of the Japanese themes in Amy Lowell's work, I call attention to the attempt that she made to adopt the strict *hokku* metre of 5, 7 and 5 syllables in a suite called **''Twenty-Four Hokku on a Modern Theme''** which appeared in *What's O'Clock.*

This volume also contains a later poem entitled **"The Anniversary,"** which has all of its twenty-four stanzas in the *hokku* metre. To me, it seems that these poems reveal more Japanese influence than all the rest of Amy Lowell's work, since the adoption of a foreign form of verse surely marks a deeper, more vital influence than the mere poetical interpretation of an Eastern work of art or the re-telling of a legend. Miss Lowell's Far Eastern writings, up to this time, may be fairly called a "Free Fantasia on Japanese Themes," to borrow the title which she herself gave to one of her earlier poems. Now at last she made a supreme and final effort to forget herself and write original verse like a Japanese poet, and this with a fair measure of success.

Miss Lowell's life of John Keats and a plan to revise for publication the translations which Mrs. Ayscough proposed to make from Chinese poetry began to absorb the poet's attention about 1918. (pp. 147-49)

Her collaboration with Mrs. Ayscough led Miss Lowell to the adoption of a special theory for the rendering of Chinese poetry which is stated in the Introduction to *Fir-Flower Tablets* and in Mrs. Ayscough's article "Amy Lowell and the Far East" in the *Bookman* for March, 1926. In a word, this was to express in English, whenever the rhythm allowed, the component parts of the pictographs found in the Chinese texts. This method of translation leads inevitably to some questionable interpretations, for which it seems that Amy Lowell was herself responsible. For instance, the Chinese character meaning "green" is also regularly applied to blue objects. But whenever a Chinese poet thought of the blue skies, Miss Lowell and Mrs. Ayscough make him speak of "green heavens." *T'ien shan*, a common Chinese phrase, refers to the celestial mountains, suggesting their purity, and not to any "heaven-high hills" with a suggestion of altitude. In practice, therefore, their theory of literal or pictural analysis of the Chinese character merely intensifies the latent queerness of these versions. Another criticism, made by a competent judge, is that there is "too much pomp and color" in Miss Lowell's renderings.

One regrets especially that *Fir-Flower Tablets* do not give a better idea of Chinese poetical form. Miss Lowell stated in her preface that she had "as a rule, strictly adhered" to the lines of the original stanza, and yet she allowed herself much liberty in this respect "solely in the interest of cadence." Professor Pelliot and the Chinese critic Hsin-Hai Chang also point out that some of the poems were not placed by Mrs. Ayscough in the mouth of the proper speaker. Thus, as Archibald Macleish so aptly put it. "Nowhere in the book does one come upon that spurious air of similitude which in portrait painting produces the impression, even upon those who do not know the original, that the picture is an excellent likeness. These translations are poems, they are as much Miss Lowell's as they are Li T'ai Po's."

Let me now take up the more general subjects of influence and esthetic doctrines. . . . We know that she considered, with John Gould Fletcher, that the modern poets are more and more indebted to the Japanese for a realization of the value of psychological suggestion. Her general method of poetical composition became curiously like the technique of the Japanese painters of "pictures of the floating world," a school which is famous for skill in design and pattern-making. A list might easily be prepared of the motifs common to Amy Lowell and to this school of Japanese art, including, for instance, the willow tree, the peony, cats and fire-works. Curiously enough, three-fourths of these very motifs are entirely absent from clas-

sical Japanese poetry. On the other hand, as a New Englander, Amy Lowell could not forget to commemorate, in such poems as **"Lilacs"** and **"Meetinghouse Hill,"** the China trade of her forefathers. But the Chinese influence was far weaker, for she was seldom moved to the composition of such fragments after the Chinese manner as **"Wind and Silver."** One cannot but regret therefore that Amy Lowell could not visit the Far East when we compare some of the renderings in *Fir-Flower Tablets* and the *hokku* in *What's O'Clock* with her earlier "chinoiseries" and "Lacquer Prints."

In conclusion, it seems to me that Amy Lowell is less important as a mere interpreter of the Far East than as a propagandist, practitioner and theorizer who drew attention to the poetry and art of China and Japan, as she chose to do even in writing her life of John Keats. . . . [If] we ever graft Far Eastern branches upon the stock of English poetry, we will turn back to Amy Lowell's Oriental verse with the gratitude and respect due to an inspired explorer. (pp. 150-52)

> *William Leonard Schwartz, "A Study of Amy Lowell's Far Eastern Verse," in* Modern Language Notes *(© copyright 1928 by The Johns Hopkins University Press), Vol. XLIII, No. 3, March, 1928, pp. 145-52.*

HARRIET MONROE (essay date 1932)

One may as well begin by granting Miss Lowell everything but genius. There is a rumor, probably too plausible to be true, that she once said, "I made myself a poet, but the Lord made me a business man." Did I say everything but genius?—but she has genius, only not of the kind we usually imply when we talk of the few fortunate poets who possess it. Her genius is that of the commander, the organizer; and she has chosen to organize herself as well as the world, and bring to bear all the resources of her imagination, temperament and scholarship in the service of a varied and practicable literary talent. (p. 78)

It has interested Miss Lowell to explore many fields and study all forms. . . . In her six books of verse are lyrics, grotesques, narratives; in rhyme, blank verse, free verse and the "polyphonic prose" which, with scholarly intuition of values, she adapted and modified from the French. And two other books, *Six French Poets* and *Fir-flower Tablets,* prove her skill in adapting to English the elusive meanings of modern French poets, and even, with the aid of her friend Mrs. Ayscough, of old Chinese. Also, in *A Fable for Critics,* she has tried her hand, like Byron, at a lightly running satirical handling of her contemporaries.

In all this astonishing variety one feels power. Behind it all is the drive and urge of a rich and strong personality. (p. 79)

Certain of her poems might survive even if someone else stood behind them: *Patterns,* for example, says a true thing, a thing close to people's lives and hearts, with beauty and concentrated force; and a few lyrics are delicately wrought on a motive of poignant wistfulness. But backed as they are by her magnificent authority, not only these will be cherished, but also enough others to round out and complete the portrait for the next age. People will feel the sweep and luxury of her brilliant passage through a sober world, and will keep in touch with it through the gaudy colors of *Can Grande's Castle,* which, whether or not it proves her case for polyphonic prose, presents to the limit its author's commanding audacity and love of color and drama. And they will admire the cosmopolitan intelligence which breaks through New England boundaries of mood and method, and searches the earth from Peru to China for gorgeous exotic flowers, in *Legends* and other sumptuous "pictures of a floating world." (p. 80)

One detects a certain scientific rapture in many of Miss Lowell's interesting experiments in technique. She delights in the rush and clatter of sounds, in the kaleidoscopic glitter of colors, even though the emotional or intellectual motive goes somewhat astray among them. In a few poems in the imagist anthologies—*Spring Day,* for example—one's ears and eyes feel fairly battered; still more in the *Can Grande* essays in polyphonic prose. She is most definitely true to the imagist technique in brief poems like some of the *Lacquer Prints*—the *Fuji* one, or *Paper Fishes. Patterns,* while not slavishly in that method, benefits by its exacting discipline; and such lyrics as *Venus Transiens, A Gift, Solitaire* owe to it their fine precision and fragile beauty. (p. 81)

But imagism could not hold her in, nor any other system of technique. She has used for her own purposes the training it gave her, just as she has used her study of prosody, and her wide reading of poetry in English and French, and, through translation, in other languages. No doubt it has sharpened her style, made it more direct and firm, even in the long narratives in *Legends,* and the picture-stories, if one may so call them, in *Can Grande.* Of these two books, I get more fun personally out of *Legends. Can Grande* seems too explanatory, too much a literary exercise, an effort to see what may be done with polyphonics in presenting characters, scenes, impressions, stories. Its colors and sounds hurtle against the mind with kaleidoscopic intensity from beginning to end of each narrative, so that one gets tired and loses all sense of climax. Also the form itself become monotonous with its teasing internal rhymes and assonances; it is ingeniously effective in the direction of virtuosity rather than beauty.

But in *Legends* she is less absorbed with technique, and so more free in the handling of her various methods. Her presentation of the stories selected from folk-lore and legendry here, there and everywhere may not be so mediaeval as the old ballads, so oriental as Lafcadio Hearn, . . . but it is a clever and effective interpretation by modern poet-scholar accomplished in the study of literature and rhythms. And the book is immensely entertaining. The stories are told with gusto by an up-to-date enthusiast, an artist who does not dawdle or grow weary or lose control of her method. And they are full of astonishingly good figures and picturesquely vivid descriptive passages; one is carried along with a sense of swift and expert movement.

The best of these "tales of peoples," in my opinion, are *Many Swans,* derived from our own aboriginal folk-lore, the knightly ballad *The Ring and the Castle,* the pretty Chinese *Legend of Porcelain,* and the New England murder-story *Four Sides to a House.*

A number of Miss Lowell's New England narratives are in the form of monologues in dialect—mostly character-sketches of lonely souls, pushed by a bitter fate to extremes of agony. The people in these poems seem to me authentically alive, and certain ones—*Reaping, Off the Turnpike,* the clock poem, *Number 3 on the Docket*—suggest strongly the weirdness of isolation on some of those decaying farms—human beings with nerves drawn tense to the verge of insanity. The free-verse rhythms may be rather ragged, but it is a harsh unmusical habit of speech which the poet is trying to suggest, and more flowing measures would destroy, rather than express, whatever poetry

is inherent in the situation. If some of them touch on the grotesque, they are all the more expressive of their author, for her sense of humor takes that direction.

In fact, Miss Lowell, as well as certain other modern poets—W. C. Williams, Alfred Kreymborg, Marianne Moore *et al*—have reminded us that the grotesque, even in poetry, is an authentic artistic motive. If a Japanese ivory-carver may put his sense of absurd incongruities into a netsuke, or a Gothic stone-cutter into a gargoyle, there is no reason why a poet should not take and give similar delight in such a grotesque as *Red Slippers,* which [is] . . . one of Miss Lowell's most brilliant successes. . . . (pp. 82-4)

One finds a similar quality in *Balls, Fireworks,* the *Stravinsky Trilogy* and other poems. In fact it colors her work generally, for it is one of her vital and controlling characteristics.

In summing up, one might inquire whether Miss Lowell has gone further as a lyric or a narrative poet, using *narrative* to cover all her various presentations of episodes of historic, legendary or more individual human adventure. Probably the latter direction has given more scope to her fecundity and energy, her love of color and sound and drama. The richness and luxury of her product in this kind contrasts strangely with the delicacy of her personal lyrics, which are mostly in a minor key of wistful sadness. On the whole she has been generously expressive. Her six volumes of verse and three of prose present, with singular completeness, a commanding—nay, enthralling—personality. Such energy, fecundity, persistence, intelligence, appearing in this world of compromises and half-successes, rebukes people less forceful, less unified, by achieving to the very limit of its power. And, as we suggested above, her books are only one element of the drama which she has impressed upon the literary history of our time. (pp. 84-5)

> *Harriet Monroe, "Amy Lowell" (originally published in a slightly different form in* Poetry, *Vol. XXV, No. 1, October, 1924), in her* Poets and Their Art *(© 1926 and 1932 by Macmillan Publishing Co., Inc.; reprinted by permission of the Literary Estate of Harriet Monroe), revised edition, Macmillan, 1932, pp. 78-85.**

WINFIELD TOWNLEY SCOTT (essay date 1935)

Amy Lowell's ultimate fame, as far as her own work is concerned, will rest on a dozen short poems and her biography of Keats. Such a record would not be bad, by any means, but this radical subtraction from the whole seems remarkable only to us who are near enough to be aware of the vast bulk of her writings—most of which later generations will easily forget.

The majority of Amy Lowell's poems are poetry of the present tense: the poem and the events seem to be simultaneous. Reflection is generally rapid and casual. It is a spoken poetry and, because much of it is in the cadence which Miss Lowell closely allied to natural human breathing, these qualities are appropriate to the case. It is, consistently enough, a poetry of pictures, and therefore it is not surprising that it is rarely, if ever, a profound poetry. At its best—such as "Lilacs," or "To Carl Sandburg," or "Meeting-House Hill"—it is a poetry of feelings and moods; never is it a poetry of thought and ideas. It is not static or dull at any given point, for Miss Lowell observed keenly and recorded sharply. After the period of her first two books she was almost invariably expert in craftsmanship.

Unfortunately, however, what is not dull at any given point may become dull in the aggregate. Much of Amy Lowell's work suffers in just this way. It is, indeed, something like seeing too many fireworks. When we can no longer be surprised and held by novelty of form, we must be held (if at all) by deeper qualities. Enduring poetry informs us, and with seemingly recurrent freshness of perception and expression. On the other hand, the freshness in Miss Lowell's poetry is not self-sustaining—it is a method of stunts and a matter of surfaces. Once familiarity penetrates these, the residue is seen to be amazingly poor, thin, and third-rate. At the same time, the nervous, continual plunging and taking of the breath in much of her versification becomes harrowingly monotonous. The small kernels of meaning (if they are there at all) are swathed, to scramble metaphors, in bandages of words, words, words. Contrary to the dicta of imagists, the work of Amy Lowell was too often not concentrated when it should have been. She could not (as Keats advised Shelley) load every rift with ore. She painted the rifts with a dazzling play of word-pictures. Such paint does not last.

If this is true of her briefer poems, it is even truer of her longer, more ambitious work—and there is much of the latter. The "polyphonic prose" narratives in *Can Grande's Castle* are, like most of Miss Lowell's work, remarkable *tours de force*. They have vigor and verve and great sounding splashes of variation, but they can not possibly last except as the phenomena of a genuinely noble experiment certain to fail. In allying all forms, they become formless. In relying completely upon the taste of the author, they seem to have no touchstone. And finally, instead of emerging as a free and supple expression, they strain and posture in complete artificiality. They do much and they say little. They labor, these mountainous poems, and again and again bring forth nothing more than mice.

The other narratives in rhymed and cadenced verse succeed no better. Sometimes, as in **"The Great Adventure of Max Breuck,"** the versification is simply amateurish; again, as in the New England narratives of *East Wind,* the capable verse (and not even capable in the choppy dialect stories) achieves only melodrama. . . . [In] **"Still Life,"** and, most explicitly of all, in **"Footing Up a Total,"** she bared her terrible fear—even her conviction—that her work was a glittering shell that contained nothing of permanent worth.

In many ways, Amy Lowell was a good critic. In her prose we come near to her as she was, a person of great gusto, of invigorating spirit, of emphatic pronouncements. Her collected volumes of essays serve, no doubt, merely transitory purposes. She was capable of glaring misjudgments which more careful thought would have intercepted. These faults aside, her reviews and lectures tingle with a commanding, provocative voice, a dogmatic and abrupt common sense. They served their purposes well. In the gigantic biography, *John Keats,* Miss Lowell set out to portray a man's life in its day-by-day progress. The merits of her success have never been fully acknowledged. The book stands four-square; its numerous triumphs will not let it be forgotten.

Unremitting years of labor on the *John Keats,* labor which certainly killed Amy Lowell, may have brought her some satisfaction. It is to be hoped so, for she had a nagging feeling of her own incompleteness—if one may safely rely on the evidence of the poems. In them, so she said, a heart could be found for the seeking. It requires no preconceived suspicion to find there the heart of a girlish, pathetic, and lonely woman. Underneath the ringing verbosity, the fuming cigars, and bump-

tious manner lies disappointment. **"Behind Time"** is simply a version of love, or security, in a cottage. **"To a Gentleman Who Wanted to See the First Drafts . . ."** is merely the virulence of an angry, flattered girl. **"On Looking at a Copy of Alice Meynell's Poems . . . ,"** one of Miss Lowell's most exquisitely finished and thoroughly authentic pieces—one of the fine poems of our time, indeed—is a woman's determined bravery in the face of personal tragedy: the expressed resolve to put away grief, which, by its very expression, reveals the fact that grief will not ever be put away. (pp. 326-29)

Her poems are the work of a woman who would have shown an extraordinary energy in any career; they are, even at their most expert, remarkable in the very light of their weakness—for Amy Lowell was not essentially a poet at all.

"God made me a business woman," she said, "and I made myself a poet." In a limited sense she did; but the poet is not quite the genuine article. . . . Her most famous poem, **"Patterns,"** illustrates her most characteristic abilities: vivid picturization, verse beautifully handled, and the symbolism of an idea. But the pictures outweigh the idea, the verse is better than the pictures, and the whole poem does not fuse into fine art. It remains embroidery work.

"Patterns," to be frank, is artificial and theatrical. Much of Amy Lowell's verse—and most of it, of course, is less well done than **"Patterns"**—must share the oblivion of all writing that has never really lived. As a poet Miss Lowell lacked the profound and vital power of penetration. She never said anything undeniably important about life. She never even implied as much. Her frequent use of symbolism had a varying success. With it, she occasionally secured a fine, macabre effect—as in **"Time's Acre"** and **"Four Sides of a House"**; but, altogether, her symbolism has neither the simple profundity of Yeats's poems nor the involved profundity of Blake at his best; it increases the turgid making of pictures.

A few of her things, however, give promise of long life. A dozen times or so—in the poems already cited, in the **"Madonna of the Evening Flowers,"** in **"Garden by Moonlight,"** and one or two more—she wrote not to hide but to reveal herself. She shows a little of what she actually felt, of what she was really like. These are poems of moods, of feelings; yet the author of them had learned how to use words with astonishing effect. Here is not display, but expression; and the very earnestness, the very sincerity, of her feeling matches her command of image, of cadence, and vocabulary. Qualities of technique, in turn, are strengthened and assured. These are not great poems: at best, they put her name a little below such poets as Whittier and Longfellow. (pp. 329-30)

Winfield Townley Scott, "Amy Lowell after Ten Years," in The New England Quarterly *(copyright 1935 by The New England Quarterly), Vol. VIII, No. 3, September, 1935, pp. 320-30.*

VAN WYCK BROOKS (essay date 1940)

For literary soldiership, or literary statesmanship, America had never seen Miss Lowell's equal. Literary politicians had always abounded, but she was the prime minister of the republic of poets; and under her control this republic rose from the status of Haiti and became an imperial republic of the calibre of France. . . . She touched a fuse wherever she went, and fireworks rose in the air; and there were no set-pieces more brilliant than hers, no Catherine-wheels or girandoles or fountains. There was no still, small voice in Amy Lowell. Her bombs exploded with a bang and came down in a shower of stars; and she whizzed and she whirred, and she rustled and rumbled, and she glistened and sparkled and blazed and blared. If, at the end, it seemed like the Fourth of July, it was a famous victory, none the less, though the fields and the trees were littered with the sticks and the debris, with charred frames and burnt-out cases.

Besides, much more was left than people felt on the morning after. Miss Lowell was a pyrotechnist, but some of her scenic effects were permanent; and when she was not permanent she was salutary. Her theory of "externality" was undoubtedly fallacious, and much of her work was factitious, the fruit of the will. As if poetry could ever be "external"! Yet her actual externality was good for the moment. It was a challenge to internality at a time when the "internal" poets were so often sentimental, derivative and soft. (p. 265)

No doubt, her externality reflected her own extroversion. It was an escape as well from a troubled psyche, for Miss Lowell's inner life knew no repose. She had solved none of her vital problems, and she remained the conventional child that expressed itself in the first of her volumes of poems. Indeed, she was never a poet, properly speaking,—the poet in her never struggled through,—so she seized on the outsides of things as her only chance of effectuality, and her dramatic instinct achieved the rest. . . . Among her treasures she was always the child, a Gargantuan child with the avidity of a Khan or a brigand; and she pillaged books,—she tore the entrails out of them,— and she used in the composition of her rockets and pin-wheels the *alchimie du verbe* of Rimbaud, Verhaeren, Mallarmé and various others. She wrote free verse after Debussy's piano-pieces; she stole the show at aquariums, with their "swirling, looping patterns of fish"; and every place she read about and every place she visited—whether Mexico, China, Peru, Saint Louis or Charleston,—left in her hand some scrap of a rhythm or a picture. She found a mine in Keats, whom she admired for his fearlessness, straightforwardness, directness, for all he had in common with herself; but everything served her purpose that gave her a little gold or brass, a beam of sandalwood or a bolt of silk, a flag, a trumpet, a tuba or a box of spices. (pp. 267-68)

Well, was it all for show? Was it merely a night of the Fourth of July? Was it only a parade and swagger of Boston fashion? There was surely enough of the material in Miss Lowell's talent, too much noise, too much excitement; and yet how much remained that was new and crisp, what vividness of colour, what joy of action. One could say much for externals that enlivened the senses; and, when one had given up to time the bric-a-brac, the petals of Chinese flowers whose roots were somewhere else around the planet, one came back to Miss Lowell's story-telling. She was a story-teller, if not a poet, who had studied her art in Chaucer, in Keats and in Browning, and who, in some of her best tales, followed Miss Jewett and Miss Wilkins, when she was not touched by Robert Frost. Perhaps this deep Yankee in her was to live the longest, the Yankee whose tales in *East Wind* and the ballad of *Evelyn Ray* refurbished this old New England *genre* with a note of her own that was wholly fresh. Her colours here were browns and greys, but some of her blues and reds were fast; and, among other pieces, *Can Grande's Castle*, with its cinematographic style, remained her most characteristic. Perhaps its excess of vivacity wore one out. It was charged with enough electricity to burn one's hand off: it was like a third rail, it was like a power-

line, and one had to touch the wires with circumspection. But there Amy Lowell exulted in her strength; and her feeling for ships and battles, for barbarism and heroism, for pageantry, pomp, dash and fanfaronade, for the theatre of history and the clash of peoples boiled up and bubbled over with a splendid brio. She was Lady Hamilton, she was Nelson, she was Commodore Perry in Japan, with his sailor-chanties; and no New England writer since the great days of Prescott and Motley had given the world such brilliant historical scenes. (pp. 268-69)

Van Wyck Brooks, "Amy Lowell," in his New England: Indian Summer, 1865-1915 *(copyright, 1940, by Van Wyck Brooks; copyright renewed © 1968 by Gladys Brooks; reprinted by permission of the publisher, E. P. Dutton, Inc.), Dutton, 1940 (and reprinted in his* A Chilmark Miscellany, *Dutton, 1948, pp. 262-69).*

GLENN RICHARD RUIHLEY (essay date 1975)

After her adoption of Imagist practices in 1913, the poetry of Amy Lowell centered in the treatment of the numinous scene or object with increasing refinement and flexibility. It was not, of course, her only interest, nor could it ever be a formula for writing poetry. Had this been true, Miss Lowell would have been reduced, like Wallace Stevens in the latter part of his career, to the writing of illustrations for a set of reasoned positions subject to the limitations of abstract thought. But the very opposite was true. As we see in her critical essays, systematic thought was uncongenial to Amy Lowell's mind and so she saw the more deeply. Her mind, absorbed by some impression of interest to her, an object, a person, a scene in a garden, would be suddenly illuminated so that its hidden nature was disclosed. But the process has nothing to do with reasoning in the usual sense, nor was the poet always aware of the meaning of her intuitions. (p. 109)

For those reading *Sword Blades and Poppy Seed* in 1914 and coming upon "**The Captured Goddess**," the most striking feature of the poem would have been its highly irregular form. There was no rhyme-scheme and almost no rhyme. Some lines consisted of but one or two words and the length of the stanzas varied from one line to twelve. Compared to the tidy quatrains of the Victorians or their sonnets and blank verse, such a poem gives an impression of lawlessness and the use of this form aroused great hostility in Amy Lowell's time among the defenders of the safe, old ways. (p. 122)

Miss Lowell used her freedom to create rhythms that give a sense of airy, unfettered movement; what she is envisioning is preternatural and it is afloat in the air. (p. 125)

Having created this vision of a divine beauty which transfigures the world, the poet proceeds to deepen her effect by describing the emotions which it produced—and the manifestation of the divinity in varied physical forms. . . . She is drawn forward tirelessly by her hypnotic absorption in a Presence glimpsed innumerable times on earth in the allure of color, flower forms, and even in precious stones. Her list is followed by an abrupt return to the goddess herself, the source and meaning of all this beauty.

In the last section of the poem, the poet treats one of the central paradoxes of life. Though divine in nature like the goddess, a thing may still be left unprotected in the divine scheme of things, subject to shipwreck. . . . There is a sensible withdrawal of feeling as the poet recoils before the vision of the

Goddess bound over to the hands of men and offered as an item of sale in the marketplace.

In this celebration of a divine beauty accompanied by the emotions of religious worship, the poem recalls "Before The Altar" and can be seen as a variant of a major theme that Miss Lowell treats in "The Slippers of the Goddess of Beauty" . . . and in "Fool O' The Moon," another poem from the end of her career. . . . "The Captured Goddess" appears to be the best of this group. It presents the mystical experience itself instead of the general statements about it we find in the poems before her Imagist phase. It has this same advantage over "The Slippers," although this is effective as a long-meditated and deeply felt restatement of her attitude written at the end of her life. As for "Fool O' The Moon," the feeling here is also intense and immediate, but the emotions of religious adoration are mixed with those of sexual desire.

This is clearly not the case in "The Captured Goddess." The emotion and its expression are self-contained and austere, the effect of a deep-seated attitude of mind revealed in these poems of her early Imagist phase. Nowhere is it expressed to better effect than in her sonnet, "Irony," a composition in wavering monochrome. . . . This poem has almost the air of clinical analysis and part of its effect consists in the refusal to flinch before so desolating a vision. What she offers in "Irony" is the Zen garden of gravel, sand, and rock, and like those gardens in Japan, it is a vision of the eternal frame of things. If such a scheme makes no allowance for the finite living thing and refreshes stones and shells only, it still contains an undeniable magnificence. The mid-day sun not only scorches the jellyfish, it also fills the beach with light, and there is an implication of grandeur in the unusual formal harmony of this poem. Aside from the consistency in tone and image, the harmony is due to the rhythms which transcend the rigid iambic pattern to form a single unbroken curve. It is also due to the consistency in language and, within that, an unobtrusive skein of s, b, and p sounds which draws together the poem as a whole. Taste in poetry differs with each reader, but with a poem such as this, one must concede at least the perfection of the style. In "Irony" the mood of the poet and the severity of the sonnet form she chose have combined to produce a poem of remarkable expressive force.

The same quality of expression applied to a related theme can be found in the poem, "Convalescence," which also appeared in *Sword Blades and Poppy Seed*. In this poem the victim who suffers is as solitary and abandoned as the sea creatures in "Irony," but here we have the adequate response. The swimmer who toils toward the "rounding beach" is the equal, in Miss Lowell's vision, of the ocean, an idea implied by the juxtaposition of his perfect silhouette against the ocean waters. Moreover, he succeeds in his struggle, and her account of this and the various luminosities of the seashore is one of the most vivid passages in her poetry. (pp. 125-28)

The life that thawed in "Convalescence" and warmed briefly in "A Tulip Garden" is as exposed as ever in "The Temple," but here it has discovered its inner nature and has achieved an equilibrium with the forces that would assail it. This sonnet, admirable for the force and expressiveness of its rhythms, is a dramatic image of the mysterious birth of an attachment which transforms two lives. Its subject is the friendship between Mrs. Russell and Amy Lowell, but the poem is far from being either intimate in feeling or sentimental. It is, rather, the revelation of an elemental force no less tremendous because we have diluted it into many unmeaning forms. . . . These lines leave

no doubt as to the spirituality of a love which sweeps irresistibly upward. But the paradox implied in "The Captured Goddess" continues in force. The flame which rose instantly to its source in heaven must be closely guarded from the scheme of things on earth, and in the remaining half of the poem we have the image of the building of a temple-fortress where man's art and determination are able to hold off the forces inimical to a divine attachment.

Miss Lowell's relationship with Ada Russell is also the subject of two admirable free verse lyrics, "Anticipation" and "The Taxi," which appear in this same volume. All three of these poems illustrate Amy Lowell's characteristic mode as dramatic lyricist. Though her lyrical impulse was strong, her short poems of personal feeling do not ordinarily sing. There were few occasions in her life for simple feeling, nor would a pure lyric utterance do justice to her exploratory vision. For these reasons she drew on her sense of the dramatic to produce a hybrid form. By this I mean that her personal emotions are usually objectified to some extent by translation into picture and narrative elements. While this sometimes led to diffuseness, a besetting sin in Amy Lowell, in other instances it gives unusual force and concreteness to the expression of intangible inner states. An example of this, both in its sharply focused images and the use of story to develop emotion, can be found in "The Taxi." Here, as in "The Captured Goddess," the free verse of Miss Lowell is so purely conceived and lithe that it has a plastic, statuesque character. . . . (pp. 129-30)

Even more affecting, perhaps, but less even in quality of writing, is her poem, "Patience," which was written about Ada a short time after their relationship had been established on a permanent basis. Here, more directly than in the other poems of this collection, Miss Lowell has given the sense of an awakening to spring in some Alpine fastness. . . .

[By the time that *Pictures of the Floating World* was published], Mrs. Russell had served with Amy for five years, her first close human tie in a life of more than forty years. In this same period of time Miss Lowell had also won belated success as a poet. As the result the character of her emotions changed. The poet had become more fully herself. Her feelings and so the forms which expressed them in her poetry became more extended, often swelling in outline, at times even serene.

There is also the difference in outlook occasioned by her Oriental studies. (p. 131)

Through her choice of an epigraph for *Sword Blades and Poppy Seed* Miss Lowell confides that she has been concerned to produce images of the Divinity, the "invisible face," which looks out of all nature. In the poems described above the individual is set against a Supernatural primarily hostile to man's desires, though it clothes itself in awesome beauty. In the poems of the Oriental phase, the power of art appears to mediate between the solitary individual and the Absolute. This is still essentially hostile to man, but now his life is dignified with ritual that ennobles it and sets him in the scheme of the Divine. This is what we see in "Reflections," a poem equally divided between attention to a transcendent beauty which invests the garden landscape and tragic unfulfillment expressed in the figure seated by the lake. . . . Though Miss Lowell was often a romantic, this poem is evidence that she could summon the restraint necessary to the control of tragic emotions. Nothing could be more reticent than these lines. The broken life is expressed only through the jarring of the water lilies, and the drops which stain the dress of the victim come from the lake, not her eyes.

Much of the effectiveness of **"Reflections"** depends on a sparseness of detail allowing the reader to build the symbolic images which are the real content of Miss Lowell's poetry. Taken simply as description, such pictures would signally fail. Close attention shows an incompleteness in this respect, exemplified here by the presentation of this elaborate garden-scene in four short lines. In place of an approximation of reality the effect that Miss Lowell achieves with her economy of language, the use of suspended rhythms that have the static quality of the lake and her few, well chosen details is the evocation of the spirit of the scene, the Numinous in the forms of the flowers, in the sound of the temple bells, and the unmelting figure at the side of the lake. Clothed in this way in these congenial Oriental forms, it is a more resonant image and a more delicate one than anything in the earlier poems. The crimson peonies glow brightly against the rain-blue dress, and the architecture of the verse has relaxed from the angularity found in **"Irony."**

The rise to organic form and the fullest extension of emotion are to be found in **"Free Fantasia on Japanese Themes,"** a brilliant treatment of the theme of deprivation. Here, the self is no longer shattered as in some of the poems collected in *A Dome.* It is triumphant in self-assertion, but the powerful energies released have no emotional outlet except in fantasy. The fulfillment of the poet's desires is entirely imaginary, and it is represented in a picturesque, Oriental setting. (pp. 132-33)

The powerful rhythms generated by the emotions of this poem contrast with the suavity of expression found in **"Solitaire,"** a free verse poem of closely related theme. (p. 134)

The meaning of **"Solitaire"** is contained in its implied statements on human imagination. Miss Lowell suggests that this offers not only a substitute for real-life events but experiences possible only to the spirit itself, hence the delicate texture of the poem. Like the lines of **"The Captured Goddess"** intended to evoke Divinity, this is a tissue of words which floats free of ordinary physical moorings. The poem resembles **"Free Fantasia"** in that both are treatments of Miss Lowell's life of fantasy, and they show the refinement of sensation gained by her study of the Orient. Free of the weight of the body and the limits of place, the mind rejoices in its ability to encompass essences for which the images in these poems are emblems.

Very like **"Solitaire"** in its brevity and precision, the surrealist **"Haunted"** is a dream-vision of another kind. . . . A terrifying account of sexual violation, it is Amy Lowell's involuntary witness to what is sinister and predacious in nature. That the poet intended to generalize her narrative in this way is shown in the imagery which concludes the poem with its links to all experience of covert evil and terror:

> Hark! A hare is strangling in the forest,
> And the wind tears a shutter from the wall.

The sexual imagery of **"Haunted"** prepares us to some extent for one of the most exuberant and effective of Miss Lowell's visions. In its cumbrous title, **"Little Ivory Figures Pulled With A String,"** Miss Lowell impugns the intellectual who would deny the Dionysian sources of human vitality, which she prefigures in the imagery of the opening stanza. . . . The strategy of the poem is to move alternately between the image of this dionysian revel and that of the constrained intellectual. In the concluding part, there is a direct reproof to one who "would drink" only from his brains, and finally the fusion of the two motifs in a passage of climactic intensity. . . . (pp. 135-36)

"Penumbra," another lyric from this period, is the very reverse of this orgiastic vision. One of the most tenuous of Miss Lowell's poems, it is an extended meditation which builds beautiful effects from a verse pattern that all but duplicates an unadorned, conversational speech. It is marked off from prose by the nice balance of phrasing in long cadences which seem to move to a rarefied music of the inner ear. The subject of the poem is the attachment between Ada Russell and Miss Lowell, a poignant emotion on both sides. In this poem the emotional bond not only unites the two women but it insinuates itself through their physical setting, drawing everything together into the single harmony which is the essence of the poem. . . . An emotion such as this is fragile, as are the circumstances upon which it depends. Acknowledging this in the very cadences of her verse, she has yet had the art to recreate its wistful, diaphanous beauty.

The account of the poems of Miss Lowell's middle phase could be extended indefinitely. *Pictures of the Floating World* contains a variety of vividly conceived subjects, but their power usually resides in suggestion rather than paraphraseable statement. So we may conclude with a comment made by the poet herself to explain her highly elusive **"Violin Sonata by Vincent D' Indy"** inscribed to her musician friend, Charles Martin Loeffler. . . . For many readers the poem would only be a description of Loeffler playing the violin in his home, though the atmosphere is eerie and there is a reference to the sawing of flesh "against the cold blue gates of the sky." In discussing her poem in the Boston *Transcript,* Miss Lowell remarked, "I meant to give the limits of humanity seeking to spiritualize itself to accord with its conception of Deity, which is D' Indy's very idiom, it seems to me." . . . This comment along with the epigraphs she chose for her first two books of poems show that Miss Lowell was aware of the pattern of symbolic meanings. . . . After giving her novel interpretation of the music of D' Indy, which she sees as expressive of man's upward reach toward God, she adds the telling phrase, "it seems to me." The fact that art and man showed themselves in these terms to her imagination *would seem to be* her best claim to survival as a poet. (pp. 137-38)

> *Glenn Richard Ruihley, in his* The Thorn of a Rose: Amy Lowell Reconsidered *(© 1975 by Glenn Richard Ruihley), Archon Books (The Shoe String Press, Inc.), Hamden, Connecticut, 1975, 191 p.*

JEAN GOULD (essay date 1975)

[*What's O'Clock* appeared] only a few months after the poet's death. This volume contained (with the exception of the sequence, **"Two Speak Together"**) some of her most personal, and moving, poems of love. Here was a whole sheaf of poems obviously written with Ada in mind: **"The Anniversary,"** marking ten years of a shared life, with a hint of her oncoming fate—"Blowing asunder, / Yet we shall be as the air / Still undivided." Then comes the **"Song for a Viola d'Amore"**; a seven-line lyric, **"Prime"**; and the extraordinary **"In Excelsis,"** with the lines . . . immortalizing the beloved's hands. And, though she spelled it differently, Amy was writing the seventeen-syllable, three-line poems (haiku) so popular today: **"Twenty-Four Hokku on a Modern Theme,"** carefully structured, anticipates **"The Anniversary,"** also in seventeen-syllable, three-line stanzas. The theme is the brevity of life. . . . (pp. 346-47)

These, along with such poems as **"Lilacs," "Purple Grackles,"** and the lately anthologized, symbolic poem, with the provocative title, "**Which, Being Interpreted, Is As May Be, or Otherwise,**" suggests a fantasy or deviate love (a frequent theme in Amy Lowell's work), represent her personal feelings. They precede "**The Sisters**" (the "queer lot" of women poets) and "**Fool o' the Moon,**" a moon-cult poem, and one of the numerous lyrics glorifying the naked body of a woman. "**The Green Parrakeet**" is still another of these, a fascinating, perplexing poem. The volume closes with the six sonnets to Eleonora Duse. Certainly one of the most consistently valid of all of Amy Lowell's volumes, *What's O'Clock* was awarded the Pulitzer Prize on May 3, 1926, nearly a year after her death. It was not, as her detractors like to imply, merely a gesture of posthumous honor to her position as an important figure in the poetry movement. *What's O'Clock* itself included enough good poetry to warrant the award. (p. 347)

> *Jean Gould, in her* Amy: The World of Amy Lowell and the Imagist Movement *(copyright © 1975 by Jean Gould), Dodd, Mead & Company, 1975, 372 p.*

C. DAVID HEYMANN (essay date 1980)

[Aside from a few poems, Amy Lowell's *A Dome of Many-Coloured Glass*] was of minimal interest; it contained an assortment of sentimental lyrics, jejune moralizing, undistinctive landscapes and still lifes, several tributes to Oriental themes and artifacts, some sonnets, Amy's wordy toast to the Athenaeum, and finally, a farrago of "verses for children." . . .

The poems worth considering include "**Before the Altar,**" a lively sequence showing the infuence of Keats, and "**A Fairy Tale,**" notable for its autobiographical content. The first contains the lines: ". . . the moon / Swings slow across the sky, / Athwart a waving pine tree, / And soon / Tips all the needles there / With silver sparkles. . . ." The second recalls the unhappiness of the poet in adolescence. . . .

Although Amy had not yet mastered the poetic line, she wrote candidly of what she knew and had seen. Scenes from her childhood appear and reappear: *Dome* is filled with memories of her grandfather's house at Roxbury; of the gardens at Brookline; of a field of blue gentians from a summer spent in the country; of climbing in trees; of watching fish swim in a pond. Occasionally her nature poems wax too poetic, as in a dithyrambic exercise entitled "**Song.**" . . . (p. 182)

In his poetry column for the *Chicago Evening Post* [Louis Untermeyer] concluded a review by saying that Miss Lowell's volume "to be brief, in spite of its lifeless classicism, can never rouse one's anger. But, to be briefer still, it cannot rouse one at all." (p. 183)

Sword Blades and Poppy Seed, Amy Lowell's second volume of verse, appeared in the autumn of 1914. Although about three-fourths of the manuscript consisted of poems written in meter, the richest samples were those in vers libre, or free verse. (p. 200)

[Amy's] second book showed considerable technical improvement over the first, although her themes and subject matter remained basically unchanged. People and places constituted one major focus; nature in all its phases represented another. The weather and seasons were described in a profusion of lights, shades, colors. Amy was obsessed with hues, weaving lists of them into the tapestry of her creations. (p. 201)

["**The Captured Goddess**"] composed in vers libre, was among the volume's highly regarded lyrics; equally popular were "**A Lady**" and "**The Taxi,**" both in free verse. In these poems the poet employs a touch of the dramatic to lend impact to sharply focused images, utilizing a story-line to heighten and develop the theme. (p. 202)

Amy was convinced that poetry was both a spoken as well as a written craft, best heard not only by the physical but by an interior ear. This theory was fundamentally a contradiction of the largely visual function of Imagism, of the Imagistic movement in poetry, and was based on Amy's conviction that poetry was a total experience, meant to appeal to all the senses. Such was the bulwark of still another form of verse invented by Amy—"polyphonic prose"—of which there were three samples in her second volume—"**The Basket,**" "**In a Castle,**" and "**The Forsaken.**" . . . (pp. 203-04)

[Miss Lowell's book *Six French Poets* consists of] essays based on lectures presented before sundry literary clubs and societies on a half-dozen Symbolists: Emile Verhaeren, Albert Semain, Remy de Gourmont, Henri de Régnier, Francis Jammes, and Paul Fort. . . . The essays were written in a colloquial and readily comprehensible style, placing the six postdecadent authors in a literary and critical framework that the average reader could easily appreciate. (p. 221)

[A number of the poems in Amy's third poetry collection, *Men, Women and Ghosts,*] were sheathed in a mist of passion, while other poems suffered from literary pretentiousness and emotional self-indulgence. In keeping with her previous collection, the present volume combined a variety of poetic modes: rhymed meter, free verse, polyphonic prose. It included the frequently anthologized dramatic monologue, "**Patterns,**" and a block of four dramatic monologues spoken by rural New England dwellers and grouped under the heading "**The Overgrown Pasture.**" A dozen poems, including the raucous "**Bombardment,**" were devoted to military battles, past and present (five, in one section called "War Pictures," were evoked by World War I); four, collectively entitled "**Bronze Tablets,**" presented anecdotal scenes dating back to Napoleon, although Bonaparte himself appears only in passing. (p. 230)

The best-remembered of the offerings in *Men, Women and Ghosts* is surely "**Patterns,**" with its famous epitaphic last line: "Christ! What are patterns for?" In the poem a British noblewoman, strolling through her garden bedecked in Queen Anne finery, receives a letter stating that the Duke, whom she is about to marry, has been killed at the Battle of Waterloo. Hiding her tears, the lady completes her walk until, at poem's climax, the thought of his mutilation "In a pattern called a war" brings on her final cry of anguish, coupled with her resolve to live the remainder of her life alone. The poem has frequently been attacked on the grounds that the highly stylized setting seems inappropriately summarized by an outburst in an idiom too contemporary with our own feelings to suit its generating episode. According to critics, the temptation is thus to use the exclamation "Christ! What are patterns for?" to delve psychoanalytically into Amy Lowell's personal life. It is true, for instance, that Amy often conceived of herself as an American version of a titled European lady and frequently portrayed herself as one in her poems. (p. 233)

Miss Lowell adopted the tactic of alternating books composed primarily of brief lyrics, such as *Men, Women and Ghosts,* with books of longer narratives. Her next volume of poetry, *Can Grande's Castle* . . . , was named for the refuge where Dante, the Florentine exile, wrote portions of his *Divine Comedy*. The new volume contained only four poems, each penned in polyphonic prose, each depicting a grand and sweeping panorama, the type of setting that best suits this genre.

The book's first narrative, **"Sea-Blue and Blood-Red,"** paints impasto war scenes in Italy, Egypt, England, and at Trafalgar, the drama revolving around Lord Nelson and his mistress, Lady Emma Hamilton. The motif "red" is created by the excessive wartime spilling of blood and by the incandescent bursting of Mt. Vesuvius. **"Guns as Keys: And the Great Gate Swings"** follows a similar pattern. The poet contrasts Commodore Perry's expedition to force open the ports of Japan to international trade, to the countermeasures adopted by the Japanese to prevent the invasion. In this oratorio Amy measures two alien cultures, the gallant heroism of Japan versus the extroverted self-confidence of America—Eastern stoicism versus Western fortitude. **"Hedge Island,"** the shortest and least workable of these poems, views England before and after its industrial revolution by zeroing in on the English mail and stagecoach system; it investigates the development of contemporary British manners and mannerisms and touches on the interaction between English town and country—overcrowded London as opposed to the sparsely populated, desolate countryside. The last and longest poem, **"The Bronze Horses,"** portrays war scenes witnessed in Rome, Constantinople, and Venice over a span of centuries by the four bronze horses that adorn the façade of St. Mark's Cathedral in Venice. The poem ends with the basic bloodletting theme of **"Sea-Blue and Blood-Red"**; it reproduces a terrifying Austrian air raid on Venice early in World War I. . . . (p. 234)

Although wordiness and confusion obscured these multivoiced prose poems, nothing impaired the prose contained in *Tendencies in Modern American Poetry* . . . , a muster of six essays on six contemporary poets grouped in pairs as literary Evolutionists, Revolutionists, and Imagists. Robinson and Frost, the Evolutionists, represented the inception of the new poetry in their return to realism and natural speech. Masters and Sandburg, the Revolutionists, represented the breakdown of linguistic patterns, an attack on "literary environment," including the liberation of the line from meter. H. D. and Fletcher, the Imagists, represented the realization of the modern point of view, the creation of a contemporary artistic creed, a substantial break with the etymologic past. Amy remained convinced that modernism was the trend of the future, not only in poetry but in all the arts. *Tendencies* attempted to explain the interpenetration of American culture with the modernist sensibility and argued sensibly that modernism was not as dogmatically antisocial and antibourgeois as many tended then to believe. The author presented her ideas with a direct, intimate forthrightness that made clear the differences in the development of these three successive phases of the new poetry. The half-dozen poets in this study are further illuminated by the inclusion of a fair amount of biographical data, including material on childhood and family. The collection is enhanced by long excerpts of key poems. Its chief deterrent is Miss Lowell's stubborn belligerence, her nagging insistence that she was right and everyone else, no matter what they believed, wrong. Too frequently one gets her dogmatic, sometimes unorthodox views practically shoveled down one's throat. John Gould Fletcher, for one, is described as "a more original poet than Arthur Rimbaud." (pp. 234-35)

[The title *Pictures of the Floating World*] was a translation of the Japanese word *ukiyo-e,* a term commonly associated with

a form of eighteenth-century Japanese painting that delighted in capturing the passing frivolities, the small pleasures of life. The book consisted of 174 short, free-verse lyrics compiled from some thirty journals and magazines and Amy's three Imagist anthologies. (pp. 248-49)

The opening section is a series of fifty-nine "Lacquer Prints," renditions of the Japanese hokku, a fixed lyric form consisting of three short, unrhymed lines of five, seven, and five syllables that are typically epigrammatic or suggestive. By juxtaposing two or three details that coalesce in the reader's mind to form a clear, whole picture, the hokku attempts to rouse the reader's emotion and thereby stimulate spiritual insight. . . .

The mechanics of the hokku forced Amy to preserve the conciseness of Imagism which her longer poems often lacked. Although she captured the rock-hard and crystal-clear quality of Japanese verse, she lost a good deal of its elliptic impressionism. Miss Lowell's aim, in the majority of her hokku renditions, was simply to record descriptive detail. . . . (p. 249)

The seven "Chinoiseries" that follow "Lacquer Prints" are longer, less illusory and evanescent; they depend on fewer concentrated images and contain plot as opposed to mere description. Consequently, they are less captivating than the hokku versions. The remainder of the book, the bulk of the volume, departs radically from the Oriental theme suggested by its title. Instead it takes its inspiration from the volume's opening epigraph, a lengthy quotation from Whitman's poem "With Antecedents," which begins: "With antecedents, / With my fathers and mothers and the accumulation of past ages, / With all which, had it not been, I would not now be here, as I am." We are apparently meant to infer from this that Whitman was Amy's antecedent, an appraisal further borne out by the section's Whitmanesque title, "Planes of Personality," itself divided into six subheadings: **"Two Speak Together"**; **"Eyes, and Ears, and Walking"**; **"As Toward One's Self"**; **"Plummets to Circumstance"**; **"As Toward War"**; and **"As Toward Immortality."**

The first plane, **"Two Speak Together,"** is, as its title suggests, partially autobiographical. We may safely assume that the "two" in question in these fifty or so poems are Amy Lowell and Ada Dwyer. The poems themselves are rhapsodies, love songs, sensuous dream-visions in which Amy, the lover of beauty, frankly and provocatively apostrophizes her companion. (p. 250)

The second of the **"Planes of Personality"** consists of poems that are chiefly sensorial and which take up Amy's old but memorable infatuation with Mother Nature. Here we find poems with titles such as **"The Back Bay Fens," "Winter's Turning,"** and **"Trees."** (p. 251)

The third plane contains a group of poems reflective of the psychological makeup of the poet and her metaphysical relationship to the world. The most notable of these is the poem **"In a Time of Dearth,"** which describes, symbolically, a period in which the poet is unable to create. In many respects it is reminiscent of several of T. S. Eliot's early poems, particularly his "Portrait of a Lady." Despite his seeming influence, Amy demonstrated little affection either for Eliot or his work. (pp. 251-52)

Of the remaining poems in "Planes of Personality," only two demand attention. **"Appuldurcombe Park"** is a tearful ballad about a woman denied physical love by the invalidism of her husband and her subsequent affair with a cousin, later killed at war. The poem's refrain, "I am a woman, sick for passion," struck some readers as Miss Lowell's true confession, a painful, self-analytic revelation based on actual want. The other, **"On a Certain Critic,"** the volume's final poem, is an informal, talky salute to the carefree spirit of the Romantic poets, concentrating on Keats and his passion for the moon; as it progresses, the sequence gradually takes up the question of the critical reception accorded Keats following his early demise. If nothing else, the poem demonstrates that the figure of Keats was still central to Amy's thoughts. . . . (pp. 252-53)

In holding to her theory of thematically unified volumes, the poet published her longer poems, eleven of them, in 1921, in a collection called *Legends.* The term applied loosely; the volume was constructed around a group of popular folktales and fables, from which Amy created her own legends, abridging, expanding, collating various drafts and fragments. She drew generously from a wide spectrum for her mythopoeic tales, hoping thereby to create a single interwoven legend that would link the various provenances of her poems: New England, England, Central Europe, China, North America, Yucatán, Peru. (p. 253)

Despite certain continuities, the poem fails to achieve a sense of wholeness or unification of vision.

The same year another volume misted into print, *Fir-Flower Tablets,* a collection of translations of ancient Chinese verse. The essential difficulty here was that Amy read no Chinese and was therefore dependent on the English versions provided her by Florence Wheelock Ayscough. . . . (p. 254)

Amy was determined . . . to "knock a hole" in Pound's *Cathay.* She proposed to stun the readers of Harriet Monroe's *Poetry* with renditions of eleven Chinese poems, which would surely set Ezra Pound straight and ward off any of his constituents by demonstrating "for the first time how Chinese poetry really worked." . . .

Pound read Chinese not much better than Amy, but the freshness, the tang of his imagery and language, the suppleness of his line in *Cathay,* far outclassed the thick-wristed, iron-lung efforts of the two ladies. (p. 255)

One of Amy Lowell's lighter poetry projects was her pamphlet, *A Critical Fable* . . . modeled after "Cousin James's" *A Fable for Critics.* (p. 262)

In varying meter and jestful rhyme, she surveyed the efforts of her poetic contemporaries as James Russell Lowell had surveyed his, not with the same impact of wit and learning, but with a fair measure of energy and boldness. (pp. 262-63)

Although an amusing romp, Amy's parody is not as clever as it might have been. If anything, it proves the value of James Russell Lowell's *Fable,* showing his skill as well as the innate difficulty of the form. Amy's version, despite the ease with which some of it is written, suffers from a convoluted format. The shape it assumes—a dialogue between a young bon vivant about Cambridge and an elderly gentleman who turns out to be James Russell Lowell—does not take the reader far. The most commendable aspect of the poem is its author's recognition of Stevens's talent, a discovery she had actually made earlier, and her incisive remarks on the hidden "madness" of the characters in Frost's *North of Boston.* She has also, in her account, given Poe, Whitman, and Emily Dickinson their proper due as the leading American poets of the nineteenth century. But there are plenty of weaknesses, such as the perfunctory way Pound and Eliot are dismissed. . . . (p. 263)

The 1,300-page, two-volume biography [of John Keats] was no work of genius, but Miss Lowell made some important discoveries and corrected several lingering misconceptions concerning the poet's life. Her one notable contribution to Keats scholarship was her reevaluation of Keats's relationship with Fanny Brawne, his mistress—previously depicted by biographers as an unfit mate for Keats, incapable by nature of understanding him or of valuing him at his true worth. Amy Lowell became the first biographer to paint Miss Brawne in a favorable, even sympathetic light. Her analysis altered substantially the views of future Keats-Brawne appraisers and provided critics with new evidence for evaluation of his work. (p. 269)

Three volumes of Miss Lowell's verse were published posthumously [*What's O'Clock, East Wing, Ballads for Sale*]. . . . In 1930, *Poetry and Poets,* a selection of Amy's prose writings, appeared. *The Collected Poems,* containing some 650 titles, was published in 1955, a compilation of eleven volumes composed over a twelve-year span. (p. 275)

What's O'Clock, whose central theme is the reciprocation and completion of love, was the last volume Amy had prepared for publication; it contains several of her best known and most mature poems: **"Lilacs," "Purple Grackles," "Meeting-House Hill," "Nuit Blanche," "In Excelsis,"** and a half-dozen worshipful sonnets for Eleonora Duse. **"Lilacs"** and **"Purple Grackles"** are samples of literary naturalism, odes to the beauty and divinity of flowers and birds, poems laced with reflective descriptions of small moments amid the grand outdoors. The next two are compositions of a vaguer, more subjective nature. In **"Meeting-House Hill"** a church spire is imagistically transposed into the mast of a ship afloat in a blue sea of a sky, the poet imagining herself transported back in time. In **"Nuit Blanche"** the poet uses Keats's favorite symbol—"A red moon leers beyond the lily-tank. / A drunken moon ogling a sycamore, / Running long fingers down its shining flank . . ."— to depict the passing of a mood: "Music, you are pitiless tonight. / And I so old, so cold, so languorously white."

"In Excelsis," written for Ada Dwyer, arises out of the poet's sense of incompletion, her search for totality and sexual fulfillment. It is endowed with the Sapphic touch that pervaded much of the verse being written in Paris at this time by the pagan cultists: Renée Vivien, Colette, and Nathalie Barney; as such it is highly imitative and in ways extremely artificial. . . . (p. 276)

Several other poems in the same collection follow a similar pattern. **"Which, Being Interpreted, Is As May Be, or Otherwise,"** is, according to Jean Gould, a symbolic and provocative sequence that deals with the autobiographical theme of deviate love; it substantiates the fashionable tenet that it is not who or what one loves but the emotion itself that counts. **"The Sisters"** looks at the subject of female poets ("a queer lot"), while **"Fool o' the Moon"** deifies both the lunar surface and the naked female form, pointing indirectly to Amy's sexual awakening and rejuvenation in middle life. **"The Green Parakeet"** is an understated, ironic, figurative study of guilty love, the death of purity, the ruination of nature. (pp. 276-77)

Amy's second posthumous collection, *East Wind,* featured a total of thirteen longish narratives, among them **"The Doll"** and **"The Day That Was That Day,"** poems that continued Amy's informal competition with Robert Frost for laurels as recorder of native New England dialect. On the whole, the volume is only of peripheral interest. It was not until her third title, *Ballads for Sale,* a selection of descriptive lyrics and brief tributes to persons and places, that the poet expressed a new sentiment—self-distrust and doubt. Such are the circumstances that surround a poem such as **"On Looking at a Copy of Alice Meynell's Poems, Given Me, Years Ago, by a Friend."** . . . (p. 277)

Another sequence in the same volume, **"Still Life: Moonlight Striking Upon a Chess-Board,"** strikes the same chord and like other of her late poems is a return to a more regular form of verse, a retreat beyond the experimental:

> I might have been a poet, but where is the adventure to
> explode me into flame.
> Cousin Moon, our kinship is curiously demonstrated,
> For I, too, am a bright, cold corpse
> Perpetually circling above a living world.

These lines serve as a last, perhaps fitting epitaph for Amy Lowell, although D. H. Lawrence furnished an equally evocative memorial in a letter addressed to the poet: "How much nicer, finer, bigger you are, intrinsically, than your poetry." (p. 278)

> C. David Heymann, "Amy Lowell: Last of the Barons (1874-1925)," in his American Aristocracy: The Lives and Times of James Russell, Amy, and Robert Lowell *(reprinted by permission of Dodd, Mead & Company, Inc.; copyright © 1980 by C. David Heymann), Dodd, Mead & Company, 1980, pp. 157-282.*

ADDITIONAL BIBLIOGRAPHY

Aiken, Conrad. "Miss Lowell Abides Our Question." *The Dial,* LXVII, No. 801 (18 October 1919): 331-33.
    Attacks Lowell's reputation, judging *Pictures of the Floating World* to contain her worst work to date.

Aiken, Conrad. "Amy Lowell as Critic." In his *Scepticisms: Notes on Contemporary Poetry,* pp. 251-57. New York: Alfred A. Knopf, 1919.
    A critical rending of *Tendencies in Modern American Poetry.*

Allen, Hervey. "Amy Lowell As a Poet." *The Saturday Review of Literature* III, No. 28 (5 February 1927): 557-59.
    A survey of Lowell's poetry, and a discussion of her poetic style and theories.

Ayscough, Florence. "Amy Lowell and the Far East." *The Bookman,* New York LXIII, No. 1 (March 1926): 11-18.
    Overview of Lowell's Oriental poems. Ayscough recounts the experiments in technique Lowell conducted during their collaboration.

Benét, William Rose. "Amy Lowell: 1874-1925." *The Saturday Review of Literature* I, No. 43 (23 May 1925): 774-75.
    High praise for Lowell's talent and character.

Fuller, Henry Blake. *"Tendencies in Modern American Poetry."* The *Dial* LXIII, No. 753 (8 November 1917): 444-45.
    Reviews Lowell's second book of criticism. Fuller discusses the six poets Lowell includes, and questions the omission of Vachel Lindsay as a significant new talent.

Gregory, Horace. *Amy Lowell: Portrait of the Poet in Her Time.* New York: Thomas Nelson & Sons, 1958, 271 p.
    Biography that emphasizes Lowell's formidable personality.

Hicks, Granville. "The Poets: Amy Lowell, Lindsay, Sandburg, Robinson, Frost." In his *The Great Tradition: An Interpretation of American Literature since the Civil War,* pp. 237-46. New York: The Macmillan Co., 1933.*
    A short appraisal of Lowell as a poet driven by every new influence of her day and hampered by her own stubborn individualism, an artist who "left no body of work that we can point to as purely her own, the complete and distinct record of a unique vision of life."

Kilmer, Joyce. "The New Spirit in Poetry: Amy Lowell." In his *Literature in the Making by Some of Its Makers,* pp. 253-62. New York, London: Harper & Brothers, 1917.
    An interview with Lowell in which Kilmer elicits Lowell's theories of poetry.

Lucas, F. L. "A New Life of Keats." *The New Statesman* XXIV, No. 623 (4 April 1925): 748-49.
    A review of *John Keats,* attacking the book for many of the same reasons as did Leonard Woolf (see excerpt above).

Phelps, William Lyon. "Amy Lowell, Anna Branch, Edgar Lee Masters, Louis Untermeyer." In his *The Advance of English Poetry in the Twentieth Century,* pp. 245-76. New York: Dodd, Mead and Co., 1918.*
    A discussion of free verse and a survey of Lowell's career up until *Men, Women and Ghosts.*

Scott, Winfield Townley. "Amy Lowell of Brookline, Mass." In his *Exiles and Fabrications,* pp. 114-123. Garden City, N.Y.: Doubleday & Co., 1961.
    An informative biocritical essay.

Sedgwick, Ellery, III. " 'Fireworks': Amy Lowell and the *Atlantic Monthly.*" *The New England Quarterly* LI, No. 4 (December 1978): 489-508.
    Reprints and comments upon the correspondence of Lowell and *Atlantic* editor Ellery Sedgwick.

Self, Robert T. "The Correspondence of Amy Lowell and Barrett Wendell: 1915-1919." *The New England Quarterly* XLVII, No. 1 (March 1974): 65-86.*
    Collected letters, revealing "a profound mutual respect and professional interaction between the older New England tradition and twentieth-century American literature."

Sergeant, Elizabeth Shepley. "Amy Lowell." In her *Fire under the Andes: A Group of Literary Portraits,* pp. 11-32. 1927. Reprint. Port Washington, N.Y.: Kennikat Press, 1966.
    Fascinating memoir of Lowell's day-to-day life, by one of her friends.

Wood, Clement. *Amy Lowell.* New York: Harold Vinal, 1926, 185 p.
    A critical study which reveals a consistent contempt for Lowell's work.

Roger Mais

1905-1955

Jamaican novelist, short story writer, dramatist, poet, and journalist.

Many critics consider Mais an important pioneer of West Indian fiction. He was one of the first Jamaican authors to present a realistic picture of the urban slum-dweller. He also elevated the "cult of the folk" to a literary status unheard of in the Caribbean before his time. Mais is best remembered for his three novels—*The Hills Were Joyful Together, Brother Man,* and *Black Lightning*—each of which portrays the individual's struggle to retain a sense of humanness in a hostile environment. Though he has often been criticized for a tendency to overwrite, Mais created a language which was both mystical and poetic. He combined the prose of the King James Bible (which had a profound influence on Jamaican culture) with his own native Creole speech, thus achieving a regional, yet universal, style. Mais was deeply concerned with the social questions of his day, but his fiction goes beyond sociopolitical commentary in its exploration of the individual's relationship to all of existence.

Mais was born in Kingston, the son of middle-class parents. At the age of seven he moved with his family to the parish of St. Thomas in the Blue Mountains. There he received a formal education from his mother, who was a teacher, and eventually attended a local high school. Upon graduating Mais entered the civil service, but he felt confined as a public servant and left within a year. A number of jobs followed; he was a painter, a farmer, a horticulturist, a photographer, and eventually a journalist for the *Daily Gleaner* and, later, the *Public Opinion*. A socialist and a member of Norman Manley's nationalist movement of the 1930s and 40s, Mais was imprisoned for six months in 1944 for publishing the famous article "Now We Know," a perceptive attack on English colonialism during World War II. While in prison he began writing his first novel, *The Hills Were Joyful Together,* which took nine years to complete. The work was both praised and attacked for its stark presentation of the dreadful conditions inflicted upon the working class. *The Hills* was soon followed by *Brother Man* and *Black Lightning*. In these, Mais refined his style and continued to demonstrate his deep awareness of the conflict between human frailty and the harsh Jamaican environment. Disturbed over the state of the arts in his native land, Mais left Jamaica for Europe in 1951. He was working on a fourth novel when he returned three years later, ill with cancer. Mais's condition worsened and he died within a year, his novel left uncompleted.

Mais's fiction is marked by a commitment to the poor, to the working class, and to all individuals who seek to dignify their existence. This commitment is best exemplified by the three novels on which his reputation rests. Though *The Hills Were Joyful Together* is essentially concerned with victimization, it is not only social protest. In it Mais also dealt with such questions as human destiny, individual freedom, social responsibility, and human suffering. The novel's protagonist, Surjue, is a failure within his society. Nevertheless, he attains heroic dimensions as the embodiment of an integrity which is inten-

Lee Hunt

sified rather than forfeited by his conflict with a brutal world. Similarly, Bra Man in *Brother Man* fails to accomplish his goal and is defeated by his own people, but, like Surjue, his heroic stature is salvaged by his nobility, compassion, and moral strength. Mais intended the story of Bra Man to parallel the life of Jesus, but this similarity has been criticized as too close to establish Bra Man as a character in his own right. However, despite its failings, *Brother Man* succeeds both stylistically and as an examination of the distance between the actualities of human existence and the ideal. In his last work, *Black Lightning*, Mais shifts his focus to treat the struggle between the artist and society. Jake, a blacksmith and sculptor, cannot find meaning in the external world, though he is dependent upon it. His final act of suicide is Mais's most extreme example of the individual who seeks to define his own existence, even at the price of death. This theme is apparent in Mais's plays and poetry as well, although in these genres he never achieved the high standard set by his novels.

Initial criticism of Mais's work tended to follow sociological and ethical analyses of his fundamental themes. Recently critics have begun to treat his literature as art, rather than social propaganda. Many have praised his unique, rhythmical use of native speech. Other critics have attacked his sentimentality and his presentation of character. His plots are often uneven and episodic and his symbolism weak. Still others have questioned his choice of themes, suggesting that, as a writer, Mais was unable to successfully express his ideas in universal terms. Most have concluded that he was an artist who was aware of the complexities of human life.

Despite its faults, Mais's work represents an important step in the development of Caribbean literature. Mais's intense vision and concern for humanity have influenced the people and literature of a country striving for national identity.

PRINCIPAL WORKS

And Most of All Man   (short stories and verse)   1939
Face and Other Stories   (short stories)   1942
Hurricane   (drama)   1943
Masks and Paper Hats   (drama)   1943
Atalanta in Calydon   (drama)   1950
The Potter's Field [first publication]   (drama)   1950; published in journal *Public Opinion*
The Hills Were Joyful Together   (novel)   1953
Brother Man   (novel)   1954
Black Lightning   (novel)   1955
The First Sacrifice [first publication]   (drama)   1956; published in journal *Focus*

*These works were published as *The Three Novels of Roger Mais* in 1966.

KARINA WILLIAMSON   (essay date 1966)

Roger Mais by-passes the West Indian racial issue in his novels by writing about a stratum of society in which colour is of minimal importance: the predominantly black lower classes of Jamaica. He differs in an important respect from most other West Indian novelists: nearly all his career as a man, and most of it as a writer, was spent in Jamaica, and hence he writes about Jamaican society from *inside:* not merely from inside knowledge, but from continuing participation. . . . [This] was in itself an assertion of nationalism. A West Indian culture could come only when West Indians ceased to regard 'culture' as an imported luxury and could take for granted the propriety of relating their own experience from their own point of view. It is a painful reflection on the thoroughness of the colonial process in the West Indies that this was a right which needed to be won. Writer after writer has testified to the struggle to win acceptance for West Indian arts from the West Indian public against the prevalent assumption that 'culture' was something which only grew abroad. (pp. 139-40)

The unfavourable conditions with which the writer or artist had to contend in Jamaica, the frustration of seeing his assaults spend themselves against a wall of apathy, may in part explain the ferocity of Mais's first novel, [*The Hills Were Joyful Together*]. Part of his intention, no doubt, was to puncture the complacency of his countrymen. But his anger was directed more immediately against a system which permitted the miseries and evils he observed among the masses in Jamaica.

It was thus in a spirit of vigorous polemic that Mais launched his first novel. . . . The focus is on a 'yard' in Kingston, a microcosm of Jamaican working class society. All the members of this society-in-miniature make an appearance, but the novel is mainly built round the stories of three groups: Shag, Eu-

phemia, and her lover, Bajun Man; Bedosa and his family; Surjue and Rema. Violence and misery is their common lot. Shag murders Euphemia for her faithlessness; Bedosa is hunted down by a man he has wronged and falls beneath a train while trying to escape; Surjue joins in a robbery, is arrested after being left in the lurch by his partner and finally dies in an attempt to break out of prison; in his absence Rema goes mad and is burnt to death. The root of the evils epitomized in these stories is in society itself [a theme often voiced by the prison chaplain]. . . . If there were nothing in the book beside this simple determinism we should be justified in regarding it as a tract rather than a novel. But none of the characters is shown to act *simply* in response to social pressures, and their lives are very much richer and more complex than this outline suggests. (pp. 141-42)

We may judge from [his notes to the novel] that Mais was aiming at a sort of Jamaican tragedy on Dreiserian lines. . . . [But can he call] his book 'realistic' and yet invoke tragedy by its classical formula, 'terror and pity'? Can a story of such violence—murder, suicide, madness, brutality—be 'realistic'?

The truthfulness of **The Hills Were Joyful Together** as a record of Jamaican life has been vouched for by critics in Jamaica itself. . . . 'A slice of real life' was the phrase used by N. J. Marr, inviting sceptics to check its fidelity against newspaper reports. Certainly it came under fire from some people in Jamaica, not (significantly) because it was untrue but because the kind of truth it exposed was damaging to Jamaica's reputation; these protests were a back-handed tribute to Mais's veracity.

His novel, however, is not a sociological treatise. Beyond anything it may be held to 'prove' about conditions among the working classes, it conveys Mais's feeling for the tragic quality of their lives.

The central image is the prison, both physical and figurative. A large portion of the story is concerned with Surjue's experiences in prison and his attempt to escape. He must escape, not so much because of the physical brutalities, but because of the threat to his manhood and integrity. . . . The prison image is expanded in one of the quasi-choric passages which intersperse the narrative. . . . This passage is the key to the tragedy. Like the comments of the chaplain it makes explicit what is implicit in the action, a claustrophobic sense of being caught up in events beyond individual volition, a web of inescapable misfortune. There is no suggestion of a pattern in events based on justice or revenge; innocent and guilty suffer or prosper indiscriminately. Chance is the only arbiter, and Mais's ironies make it clear that one of the few certainties of life is that if you trust to luck it will let you down. (pp. 142-44)

Mais's attitude, however, is ultimately neither cynical nor defeatist. Although his novel envisages life at this level as a vain struggle against oppressive social forces and the malignity of chance, it also pays tribute to the qualities which survive: Surjue's courage and integrity, uncorrupted by misery or temptation; the love between him and Rema, shown in one brief flowering before disaster catches up with them both; the tenderness and sympathy of three of the subsidiary characters, Zephyr, Mass Mose and Ras; and above all the common capacity for gaiety and goodwill shown on the night of 'the big fish-fry'. This episode (described in a passage of sustained and superbly emotive writing) is the essential counterpoise to the scenes of brutality and suffering which dominate the latter part of the book. It illustrates Mais's point that even lives hemmed in by social evils, as these are, can have an affirmative quality. (p. 144)

Mais expended himself heavily in *The Hills*. 'It was conceived out of a desire, that grew ultimately to a compulsion, lean and hungry and remorseless until it was fulfilled', he wrote in his notes. Although his two other novels show no slackening of energy, neither has this fierce involvement. On the other hand, they show an advance in technique, and carry the dramatic tendencies of *The Hills* a stage further.

All Mais's novels lean towards drama in the sense that they represent the clash of personalities mainly from the outside through dialogue and action. But *The Hills* is presented through a blend of narrative and dramatic techniques that is not wholly successful. It is prefaced by a stage direction and a list of *dramatis personae*, but, choric passages apart, the main body of the novel is transmitted in straightforward narrative style. The choric passages (that I think is intended to be their character) are in a kind of prose-poetry charged with symbolism, and their function seems to be to direct the reader to the wider significance of events, to hint at a 'universal' dimension to the story. The weakness of the device is its arbitrariness. Mais does not succeed here, as he was to later, in *Brother Man*, in integrating such passages, and they seem to be nudging us too palpably in the direction the author wants us to go. (pp. 144-45)

Mais broke away from urban society in his third novel. *Black Lightning* is set in a self-sufficient community in the hills, evidently based on memories of the holding in the Blue Mountains where Mais lived as a child. Yet it is the least local of the three novels because it deals with human relationships at their most unsophisticated; the characters are almost as well insulated from the 'artificial' pressures of society as if they were on a desert island. The central figure is Jake, a blacksmith, and the story tells of his struggle to keep clear of dependence on other people: 'he resented, with all a strong, whole man's resentment, any thought of being dependent upon anyone for anything.' His need for independence destroys his marriage and leads him to withdraw more and more into solitariness, concentrating everything on his carving of Samson which becomes the image of his own conflict. To him, the notion of dependence is inseparably associated with weakness and deficiency. (p. 146)

There is nothing exclusively Jamaican about Jake's situation, yet it is easy to see how much it reflects a Jamaican consciousness. For that reason *Black Lightning*, more than either of Mais's other novels, seems to me a landmark in the development of the West Indian novel. It is rooted in a way of life that is both local and universal, and although its central predicament is of special relevance to West Indians, it is also of fundamental human concern. (p. 147)

> *Karina Williamson, "Roger Mais: West Indian Novelist" (copyright Karina Williamson; by permission of Hans Zell (Publishers) Limited), in* Journal of Commonwealth Literature, *No. 2, December, 1966, pp. 138-47.*

NORMAN WASHINGTON MANLEY   (essay date 1966)

[Roger Mais was] by nature a genuine original, widely read, profoundly curious about experience and with a vast capacity for anger and passion. For years he had been shaping and sharpening his own tools and his weapons of war. He experimented with plays, with poetry, with short stories—he wrote a great amount that never was seen except by his closest friends.

Then he plunged as an artist and a writer into the national movement and when he went to prison in 1944 for a famous denunciation of one of Churchill's imperialistic hangovers so often expressed during the war, life and fate gave him the final twist that made him so fine an instrument for the major work of his life—[the fiction collected in *The Three Novels of Roger Mais*]. (p. 111)

I am sure these books have tremendous literary merit. As good writing about strange experiences and human beings fully alive, everyone will delight in them. They are in a long and famous stream of realism but the realism is not done by a cold perfectionist nor by a philosophical mind but by a human being who shared to the full in the colour and vitality that shine through all these pages.

The writing is spare and lucid, the use of words is sheer delight, and the sense of character and scene and the feel for the dramatic encounter are superb. But beneath all that two things stand out. First a love of human beings and an acceptance of their diversity and of all that is strange and unexpected in their make-up. And next an abiding faith in the common man and a deep and urgent personal concern in their problems, in what life denies them and how life destroys them or how they triumph over life.

Roger Mais did not write about the products of leisure and the cultivated life, he wrote about raw humanity and how it suffers in the framework of hardship and in the face of authority. He wrote about a world that is the real world still for most of those who dwell on earth. The patterns and the lights reflect from different surfaces but beneath, the reality is the same. (p. 112)

> *Norman Washington Manley, in his foreword to* The Three Novels of Roger Mais *by Roger Mais (reprinted by permission of the Executrix of the Roger Mais Estate), Jonathan Cape Ltd., 1966 (and reprinted as "The Creative Artist and the National Movement," in his* Manley and the New Jamaica: Selected Speeches and Writings 1938-68, *Longman Caribbean, 1971, pp. 110-12).*

JEAN CREARY   (essay date 1968)

I remember the outcry that greeted the appearance of *The Hills were Joyful Together*. . . . The reader was thrown straight into a world everyone in Jamaica knew existed, and yet which the middle classes were united in a conspiracy of silence to ignore and reject. (p. 52)

Yet within and behind this human underworld lies beauty and pattern. Ackee, lime, mango trees of the Jamaican countryside, still live, though stunted, within the yard, continuing the cosmic pattern. Sun and moon continue to create for Mais's painter's eye their timeless rhythms of beauty. . . . The characters move to the rhythms of a community as in a dance drama, and we are reminded of Mais's work as a dramatist. . . . [All] Mais's works have elements of dramatic form in them. Persons move towards each other and away in their relationships, they come to the foreground in a moment of action, and then fade back. While in the background we hear the chorus of the Sisters of Charity, of the wise, compassionate Rastafarian brother. These rhythms, both communal and within Mais's artistic eye, culminate in the choreographed meeting point of the fish fry, where the imprisoned spirits of the slum-dwellers erupt into a rhythmic celebration of life and fellowship. (pp. 53-4)

But the pattern is asserted so that it may be denied. There is no ultimate escape from the disintegrating forces of poverty. (p. 54)

The book has its grave weaknesses. There is a sameness in the exploration of character. The dramatic forms do not always heighten and direct the inner drama; they are used in a hap-hazard manner. Mais overwrites, is too prolix and, at times, sentimental. . . . Mais did not know when to cut, understate. But his weaknesses come from the same source where lie his strengths—from his innocent yet potent awareness of himself and of his environment. There is no cautious glancing at other models, no anxiety to conform to decorum. He wrote what he felt, urgently. His style had been largely formed by the time he visited England and France in 1952. There are a few literary influences: D. H. Lawrence, the English classical poets, Shake-speare, Turgenev, a little of Dostoyevsky and Conrad, and above all, the Authorized Version of the Bible. This last was a cultural influence as much as a literary one, for sixteenth-century prose of King James's Bible is part of Jamaican Creole speech itself. And Mais drew the mystical element in his writing from the rhythmical, figurative style of both Bible and Jamaican *patois*. He used words to reach behind the symbols of language and objects to the nameless reality beyond symbols, the timeless Word of St John's gospel. So that when in Mais words fail, the reader is usually left not with a sense of emptiness, but of vision outreaching vocabulary.

This is true of both the language and the main character of *Brother Man.* Here, Mais is again exploring the microcosm of the slums. But he is concerned with a wider concept and the enclosed yard gives place to a Kingston slum street. Surjue was destroyed against both tenement and prison wall. Is there any way for human values to survive in the modern human predicament? His answer is one of the utmost daring. He developed Ras, the figure of the gentle Good Samaritan and observer in *The Hills,* and created Brother Man, John Power. John Power has human features. He is the focal point of the community, the healer of mind and body, the religious leader and the helpful undemanding neighbour. . . . Yet Mais uses his portrait of a Rastafarian cultist—the Rastafarian greeting, 'Peace and Love, Brother Man', comes at once to mind—only as a fulcrum between the human and the ideal. We learn something of John Power's thoughts, but very little of his motivation, because as his name implies, he unites in himself Every-man—hence the common name, John—with the ultimate motivation, Power. In him the humanity that gleams fitfully, fragmented, in the various characters of *The Hills,* comes together. And his significance moves beyond that of John Power the Healer and Leader, to that he assumes in the final confrontation with the hysterical, violent mob that cannot endure his goodness. He is Mais's vision of the reincarnate Christ. This is no escape into sentimental mysticism from the political realities. Mais's conviction of spiritual values was too absolute. . . . This Gospel Presence fuses with Mais's writing in the rhythmical, Biblical prose.

As with *The Hills,* sociological or ethical values are inadequate for a criticism of *Brother Man,* because physical conditions are interpreted under the eye of the artist. Human and artistic values, for Mais, meet, each illuminating the other. In a sense, the personality of Brother Man is a work of art beyond the levels of normal literature, exploring the artistic pattern of life itself. And so the artistic faults in the book also imply a lim-itation of the vision. At times the physical, human presence of Brother Man loses its definition. The Word is no longer incarnate. The plot, too, is uneven and episodic, diverted by a multiplicity of subsidiary characters. When moving on a plane of such heightened symbolism, any deviation into mechanical narration or portraiture jars heavily. But at its key points the novel is usually successful. . . . Unlike *The Hills were Joyful Together, Brother Man* ends in triumph, with more than a hope for the future. For Roger Mais did not hold the orthodox Christian faith in the hereafter; his gospel was for the here and now. The joyful peace implicit in the ending is its own fulfilment.

Brother Man must be set against the vision of his last published novel, *Black Lightning*. . . . This novel is concerned with the predicament not of man in society, but with the artist. It is set not in Kingston, but in the lush, quiet countryside Mais knew in his boyhood. Jake, the blacksmith, is the centre of a small but complete world consisting of his family and a few friends. His relations with his beautiful mare, his fussy housekeeper, the deformed, bitter accordion-playing Amos, his books, his smithy, his sculpture—these and more indicate his potential fulfilment. He is prosperous, busy, respected, loved. In his workshop a statue [of Samson], the work of a life-time, is giving form to his deepest aspirations. The statue is both self-expression and self-exploration. (pp. 55-9)

Yet as it takes shape, the figure of Samson becomes increasingly identified with Jake himself; and the boy on whom he leans, with Amos the blind accordionist. The implications of this are profoundly pessimistic. For Jake has his own Delilah. His wife, Estella, leaves him to elope with another man. Worse, this is not a simple case of unfaithfulness. Betrayal lies for Jake in the very fact of the human sexual relationship. He cannot survive without Estella, yet he cannot tolerate the loss of his individual will and personality that a relationship demands. Estella is equally destructive whether she stays or goes. As Estella tells Amos in the final, chorus-like discussion of Jake's predicament, 'we got on fine, until he found out that he was leaning on me too much'. And she explains further, 'he could never forgive you that he had to be dependent on you for something. It's in him. He just can't help it.'

The basic betrayal implicit for Jake in human relationships reaches outwards to cosmic implications. For the statue stands for more than Jake's suffering for Estella. . . . Above all, [it] embodies the agony of the artist. For Jake, the normal world outside—Bess the housekeeper, Miriam her daughter, his apprentice Glen, and George, errand-boy and mischief maker, even the countryside with its moods, scents and burgeoning life—all inspire and torment him. They form his life and give him joy, yet their ultimate meaning eludes him. They are everything, and nothing. . . . Jake's statue is also in one sense of Jake himself, and at the moment of Jake's illumination, lightning strikes him blind. No interpretation can more than hint at the implications of this awe-inspiring image, which reaches out beyond the book to the bright darkness of Mais's own vision. Mother Croly, the village crone who serves at times as a chorus to the action, sees Jake's blinding as God's punishment for blasphemy. . . . But is not this blasphemy implicit in any human aspiration to understand man's condition? We are reminded of Faustus. And of Tiresias, blinded for his moment of vision. And of Oedipus, who understood, and put out his eyes. The paradox of the title 'Black Lightning', enlightenment that brings darkness, is deliberate, fully realized in the book. And it is tragic. Jake now destroys his statue and withdraws into his world of darkness. (pp. 59-61)

The ending has a sense of Greek tragedy about it. When Jake goes out to die in the flowering wood, we are reminded of the tragic peace of Sophocles's *Oedipus at Colonus,* where another blinded man went out to shake off the burden of his flesh in a sacred grove. And against the particular, personal tragedy of Jake the artist, Mais is careful to counterpoint the fecund beauty of pastoral nature, the idyllic scenes of George and the mare, the unclouded love affair between Miriam and the apprentice Glen, with whom the book ends. (p. 61)

> Jean Creary, "A Prophet Armed: The Novels of Roger Mais," in The Islands in Between: Essays on West Indian Literature, *edited by Louis James (© Oxford University Press 1968; reprinted by permission of Oxford University Press), Oxford University Press, London, 1968, pp. 50-63.*

KENNETH RAMCHAND (essay date 1969)

Shortly after the publication of his first novel *The Hills Were Joyful Together* . . . , Roger Mais declared that his intention had been 'to give the world a true picture of the real Jamaica and the dreadful condition of the working classes'. We find in the work, accordingly, a stark and realistic picture of impoverished people trapped in a squalid slum that is identifiably Jamaican. The work has been received in the spirit in which it was passionately submitted, and Mais's second novel, *Brother Man,* consolidated the author's reputation as a novelist of social protest. The reputation has persisted in spite of his third novel, *Black Lightning* . . . , in which there are no signs of organized society and not the slightest expression of a protesting attitude. The work has been virtually disregarded in the West Indies, but I would like to contend that it is in *Black Lightning* that Mais's art and understanding are in greatest harmony, and that it is upon this his last published novel that his reputation must rest.

I do not wish to imply that *Black Lightning* must be kept separate from the other novels, nor would it be proper to take the view that it is unrelated to the Jamaican social situation. But there is a progressive movement from novel to novel of a kind that can only be described as exploratory, and I would like to trace this movement as a way of showing how *Black Lightning* develops out of, and imaginatively transcends the local situation.

The first novel, *The Hills Were Joyful Together,* is set in a yard which is a microcosm of Jamaican slum life. The characters are differentiated from one another, but the author is more interested in projecting the life of the yard as a whole than in creating individual characters. Supplementing what we make of the expressed life of the yard are authorial intrusions of two kinds, advancing two main 'philosophies'. The first has to do with Mais's social protest intention, and may be described as materialistic determinism. It is usually put in the mouth of the prison chaplain. . . . The second philosophy declared in the novel occurs in authorial choruses at the beginnings of chapters. It is a philosophy of Chance, or the indifference of the Universe. . . . As Mais declares them, however, these philosophies clash, and his art is at its least convincing when he tries to show them working together. The episode dealing with the death of Surjue at the end of the novel is illustrative. Surjue is just about to make good his escape from prison. It is a dark and cloudy night, but just as the escaping character reaches the top of the prison wall, the wind parts the clouds and the moon shines through. Mais also contrives that at this precise moment, Surjue's enemy, warder Nickoll, writhing with toothache, should lift his head, see Surjue, and bring him down with the one gunshot that would have been possible in the circumstances. As Surjue falls to the ground on the free side of the wall, the perverse clouds return to cover the moon, and a seemingly disconsolate dog bays in the distance. Mais's over-deliberate manipulation at this emphatic point in the novel is neither in keeping with the life-qualities he expresses in his character, nor does it do justice to his intuitions about life suspended in expressive scene and image.

In contrast to Mais's self-conscious demonstrations, there are images of distress and vulnerability which *express* more than the author can state. These appear notably in his presentation of the women, Rema and Euphemia. Then there are scenes in which the sheer perplexity of being human and not in control of the inner heartland is in evidence. . . . Mais's recurrent expressive quality works to great effect in *Black Lightning,* not least in the section dealing with Estella's crucial elopement. On the story level, Estella leaves Jake because she prefers Steve. We have to wait till the end of the novel to realize that she still loves the hero, and had left him only because his unconscious resentment of his dependence upon her had begun to show. The scene in which Estella tries to choose between Steve and Jake, however, prepares us for complications by showing Estella as a creature pained and baffled not simply about what choice ought to be made, but bewildered by the strange contrarieties that exist within. . . . These are the dilemmas Mais is really interested in as an artist, and as he develops, he finds they are attributable neither to society nor to an external and malignant Chance.

In *Brother Man,* the setting is again the Kingston slums, and the theme is still an obviously social one, but there are significant shifts of emphasis. The authorial intrusions are not only reduced in frequency, they are disciplined into the form of a Chorus placed at the beginning of each act in a five-act novel. While the details in each act are identifiably local, the Chorus neither insists upon the specialness of the Jamaican yard-dwellers' situation nor offers indignant 'philosophical' generalizations. Rueful and detached, it abstracts the essential repetitive humanity of what goes on among the urban proletariat. . . . Mais is clearly standing back from his 'case', but his commitment is no less than in the previous novel.

To some extent, the pessimism and pathos of *The Hills Were Joyful Together* were modified by a number of un-emphasized positives in the novel: charity, embodied in Mass Mose the clarinet-player, the kindly Zephyr, and Ras, the serene and compassionate cultist; the healing power of *eros,* seen in the relationship between Surjue and Rema, and recalled with idyllic force by Surjue at the time of greatest despair . . . ; and an elemental and rhythmic energy which binds the yard-dwellers in community, as on the night of the fish-fry . . . when they enact in song and dance the miracle of catastrophe overcome— the crossing of a swollen river. In *Brother Man,* Mais gives prominence to one of the positives latent in *The Hills Were Joyful Together:* the novel hopefully explores the protective possibility of Messianic leadership. It differs further from its predecessor in being guilt around a central character. But in the presentation of Bra' Man, Mais fails.

The extended parallel between the life and crucifixion of Christ and that of Bra' Man shows Mais's determination to universalize his work, but it leads to the introduction of arbitrary visions and apparitions, miracles, naïve moralizing as in the incident of the crab and the little boy, and an unfortunate pseudo-Biblical prose. . . . Mais tries to make Bra' Man viable as a separate character, not a copy of Jesus, but the parallels are too strong for the differences to make any impact on the reader. (pp. 179-183)

A consideration of the relationship between Bra' Man and the girl Minette throws further light on Mais's failure with the central character. Bra' Man rescues Minette from the desperate beginnings of prostitution and brings her to live in his house. Certain episodes suggest that Minette has been introduced as a sleeping temptation to the prophet. . . . Although clearly worried about the sexlessness of his hero, Mais feels it necessary to keep him Christlike and chaste. . . . Mais will not allow intercourse by passion, but intercourse through compassion is allowable for the Christ-character. Mais's failure with Bra' Man as a fictional character lies in this: the conflict which ought to have been located in the character registers only as an uncertainty of intention in the author.

With the inevitable 'crucifixion' of Bra' Man . . . Mais's exploration of the redeeming power of a secular Messiah comes to a disappointed end. Yet Mais does not allow disillusionment to be registered in this novel. The shock of Bra' Man's failure is plastered over by an ambiguous 'vision of certitude'. . . . The only certitude . . . , however, is that Bra' Man and Minette love each other. Unless we are meant to imagine that Bra' Man is indulging in a superior irony over Minette's understanding, the novel ends over-optimistically as far as Bra' Man's public prospects are concerned.

The rejection of Bra' Man by his followers, like the crucifixion of Christ, was a revelation of human contrareity. The wild impulse by which they become a mob to destroy the one upon whom they found themselves dependent was the result of inner, not outer pressures. It is the inner, private world that Mais explores in *Black Lightning*. There is no social density; the setting of the novel is remote, self-contained, rural.

In a small cast, the central character is Jake, an artist-blacksmith, and the central symbol is Samson. But whereas the parallel between Bra' Man and Christ had been imposed externally by the author, Mais now invests in the consciousness of his fictional character; it is Jake who fastens upon Samson as a model of man's independence. . . . It is ironic that Jake should identify with Samson, for Samson is a symbol of both strength and weakness, an archetype of the human person. Mais is able to unfold Jake's growing awareness of this irony as the dramatic, disconcerting process of the novel.

When the novel begins, Jake is at work on a carving of Samson in solid mahogany, but progress is slow because his artist's hands are struggling to express a truth not in accordance with his preconception of Samson. After Estella leaves him, Jake's complacency starts to crumble, the carving begins to take 'its own end into its hands', becoming 'what it wants to be . . .'. The finished work Jake contemptuously reveals to Amos is not Samson in his prime, but the blinded Samson, a figure of ruined strength leaning on a little boy. . . . The lesson of Samson is driven home when Jake is blinded by lightning and he is brought to depend upon Amos and Bess. Although Mais does not see the sense of purpose which now comes into these characters' lives as negligible, he makes us share Jake's contempt for the shabby process of salvage to which men must resort in the world. It satisfies our sense of the protagonist's stature that with the tragic discovery of his own and Samson's dependent humanity Jake should move inevitably to an aristocratic suicide.

Through his central character, Mais expresses a tragic view of life, and a dignified response to it. In the developing relationship between Glen and Miriam which he runs alongside the story of Jake, a more practical positive merges.

The prevalence of concubinage in the social milieu from which his characters derived, and Mais's uninhibited and realistic transfers into *The Hills Were Joyful Together* and *Brother Man* must have made it easier for the writer from Jamaica to observe the natural conflicts and instinctive compacts that are constituents in sexual love. And the drawing together of Bra' Man and Minette after Bra' Man's public failure in *Brother Man* must have led the author to wonder about the possibilities of men and women coming to terms with their world through sexual relationships. However all this may be, the relationship between Glen and Miriam is presented as a wayward succession of approaches and retreats until Jake's suicide drives them to the final step of accepting the need to be dependent upon each other.

By combining the suicide of Jake with the growth of love between Glen and Miriam, Mais discovers a pattern of renewal after destruction. The natural setting of the novel reinforces this impression. For Jake's alienation occurs in a world which includes George's spontaneous affinity with nature (climaxed by the youth's exulting ride on the mare Beauty), and the human crises in the novel are made to coincide with phenomena in nature. All these motifs are caught up in the final movement of the novel. (pp. 183-87)

It is by a strict logic to the situation and the character that for Jake as for Samson the [end] should be self-destruction. Jake must pull down his own self and hostile temple to be whole again. A more generalized sense of renewal is suggested by Jake's suicide taking place in a burgeoning wood after the flood. . . . At the same time as Jake embraces his death, moreover, Amos and Estella make their compact in the wood; George and Beauty are exulting in that gallop across the common; and Glen and Miriam draw together. . . . As Jake's suicide shot sounds from one part of the wood, life asserts itself in another. This is a long way from the death of Surjue in *The Hills Were Joyful Together*. . . . And there is more conviction in Glen's and Miriam's tentative embrace than in the 'vision of certitude' of *Brother Man*.

Mais's sense of the tragic in life, and his compassionate understanding were stimulated by the society in which he lived. In his most assured fiction he attained to a genuine tragic vision by separating the stimulus from its special social context. (pp. 187-88)

Kenneth Ramchand, "The Achievement of Roger Mais" (originally published in Caribbean Quarterly, *Vol. 15, No. 4, December, 1969), in his* The West Indian Novel and Its Background *(copyright © 1970 by Kenneth Ramchand; by permission of Barnes & Noble Books, a Division of Littlefield, Adams & Co., Inc.), Barnes & Noble, 1970, pp. 179-88.*

OSCAR R. DATHORNE (essay date 1972)

Self-seeking martyrdom is one aspect of the social background that has seemingly plagued West Indian writers. It has been mentioned by both Samuel Selvon and V. S. Naipaul, with characteristic levity, but in other writers it is treated with the sanctity of its Christian prototype. Roger Mais begins to deal with it in his very first novel, *The Hills Were Joyful Together* . . . , where Surjue endures the horrors of political martyrdom, but his most touching and thorough study of this theme was in *Brother Man* . . . , where Bra Man experiences all of the agonies of a latter-day Christ. To some extent Jake's pride and ultimate suicide make *Black Lightning* . . . also the story of a martyr. A consideration of the works of Roger Mais will reveal these paramount interests.

Even before he had written a novel, Mais had published two volumes of short stories: *Face and Other Stories* . . . , in which he had employed poems to show changes from one mood to another (much as he was to employ a chorus later in *Brother Man*) and *And Most of All Man* . . . , in which the main story was about "Man, the eternal protagonist amid eternal processes." The latter was to be a theme to which Mais was socially committed in most of his work. . . . *The Hills Were Joyful Together* is written in the tradition of *Black Fauns* . . . by the Trinidadian writer Alfred Mendes. Twenty-five people live in the same yard and discuss religion, sex, and politics. As in Mendes's book, all action is set in the yard. But this is not just "a panoramic picture of West Indian lower class life," as Arthur Seymour, the West Indian poet and editor of the now defunct *Kyk-over-al* has called it; it demonstrates the tragedy of humans, living amongst passions they vainly try to grapple with and which they cannot fully understand. By the end of the story six people are dead, because death and violence are always present amongst them and Surjue has experienced police torture.

Mais had himself been sent to prison during the war for writing a well-known article said at the time to be subversive to the war effort. [The article, **"Now We Know,"**] was a bold attack on colonialism and adopted a caustic tone in describing some of its evils. . . . He had written this in 1944, and *The Hills Were Joyful Together* took up the same aggressive tone, which, although disturbing and passionate, was nevertheless too close to a document to succeed as a novel. When, for instance, Mais writes about Surjue and police brutality, he is describing what he had himself experienced. . . . Mais is far too close to the details of the events he is describing, and his readers are let in for too great an amount of detail. The way that the character reflects on the meaning and significance of punishment is unnatural under the circumstances. . . . [It] is simply Mais thinking out loud, and his first novel is little more than a dramatization of the **"Now We Know"** article.

Not only was it unconvincing from this standpoint but from the viewpoint of the dialect as well. . . . Mais had as yet not come close enough to the feel of Jamaican speech, and words like "nuttin'," "doin'," "say" to introduce a sentence, "bloke," and so on abound. At one stage a character even ejaculates. "Lawd Jesus." The reproduction of dialect was to improve, and by the time Mais wrote his last novel, he was considerably better. (pp. 275-77)

Some redeeming features help the first novel. There is a tripartite arrangement of character and incident; Shag is quiet; Euphemia (Shag's girl friend) is seductive; Bajun Man (a West Indianism for a man from Barbados) is her lover. In the second group is Bedosa, who bullies his wife. One of his children, Tansy, cannot go to school because he has to help run the laundry. The third group of characters is Surjue, a gambler and his attractive wife, ma. The lives of the characters crisscross—their common link is the tragic lot of the peasantry. (p. 278)

Of course the novel is melodramatic. But Mais says that it is "the vengeance nature exacts from them for being poor." As a resut these people are imprisoned, and Surjue's imprisonment and his attempts at escaping, symbolize the "captivity" of all the three groups. The end of the novel seems to suggest that death is the only way out, although indications throughout point to the validity of the folk-culture. Corruption is the real prison, Mais suggests: the corruption that comes about from the absence of myth and the denial of legacy.

It is perhaps a little difficult to realize that, though Roger Mais was a contemporary of C.L.R. James and Claude McKay, he belonged in spirit to George Lamming, Edgar Mittelholzer, and Samuel Selvon. Therefore, although he might have been a chronicler of peasant life, he was still very much a novelist interested in the novel-form. His first novel demonstrated a style that he was to make his own and which he was to use in all three novels, in particular the device of telling a number of stories together and having them all link up ephemerally but convincingly. . . . It is a device that is seen best in the second novel, where he concerns himself with the theme of the religious martyr—at one stage two pictures are placed one over the other; a girl comes home after a night out, and as she reflects, all that she thinks about is as real and as *present* as what happens to her at that moment.

In *Brother Man,* Bra Man preaches "peace and love," and Bra Ambo is equated with the powers of evil and darkness—he practices a perverted form of *obeah* (magic). In many ways the parallel between Christ and Bra Man is followed almost too carefully; so Bra Man first has his years of preparation, fasts and heals the sick, goes up to the hills to meditate, is betrayed by one of his own people, and finally dies. But interlaced with this story are a number of [others, such as the relationships of Girlie and Papacita and Jesmina and Shine]. (pp. 278-79)

Although the central story remains centered on Bra Man (as *The Hills Were Joyful Together* was on Surjue), the other characters, far from emphasizing Bra Man's worthiness, distract from his role. Here then is not the neat arrangement as before. There are a number of minor characters like Corporal Jennings, Shine, and Assistant Superintendent Crawley who are all given the full treatment one would expect of major characters. As a result there is some confusion in the reader's mind; the characters are all too "bright"—everyone is involved in some way with the police and gaol; everyone has committed or eventually commits a criminal act of one kind or another. In the midst of this Bra Man becomes a pious bore, writing his autobiography, meditating by the seashore, performing miracles, and speaking in parables to the young—at one stage he lectures a boy on the evils of catching crabs ("Crab feel pain, feel 'fraid, same like you an' me").

In spite of all this, Bra Man is convincing, not only as a messianic Christ-figure but as a person. There are parts of his life that border on the absurd as when he tries to nurse a sick bird back to life, but his relationship with Minette, the prostitute he had reformed, shows his powers of determination and his own firm faith in himself. However, at one stage of the novel this relationship is not at all clear; Minette has been trying to seduce Bra Man for the greater part of the novel, and his resistance testifies to his strength of character. But Mais delights in the obvious description of the sexual act—there are unreserved descriptions devoted to Girlie and Papacita, Jesmina and Shine, and then finally the scene with Bra Man and Minette. . . . But they continue to live as if they are still "spiritual" companions. People refer to them in the rest of the book in this way; Mais, by leaving one in doubt with regard to their relationship, has alienated the reader's defence that is so necessary later on when Bra Man is labelled a hypocrite.

Finally, it is technique, however, that convinces the reader, for people remain very much themselves. Mais is not so much interested in narrative progression as in psychological revelation; the story takes a long time to unfold between incidents, but the characters build up their own form in the process. At one stage, when Bra Man sees a vision, Mais does not call him by name, but it is obvious to whom he is alluding. The language helps to identify Bra Man, and the rhythm of the Bible is reserved for him, almost blatantly so at some stages; as for example: "And he fasted those three days and three nights, hiding himself in a cave; and after that he came again, and lodged in his own house."

At other stages it is the dialect which gives authenticity to the scenes; there are fewer cases of Americanisms here, although the boy with the crab does reply "Gee!" to Bra Man's parable. The language of the love scenes is especially tender, . . . [as in] the first meeting between Minette and Papacita on the street. . . . (pp. 279-80)

Mais's last book was *Black Lightning,* and its point of association with the previous one is in the portrayal of the chief character; just as Bra Man was like Christ, so is Jake like Samson; Samson had an unfaithful wife, so has Jake; Samson went blind, so does Jake, and finally they both destroy themselves. Jake is strongly individualistic, even proud, and when he realizes that a man cannot face the world alone, he commits suicide. But *Black Lightning* is a mere shadow of *Brother Man;* the technique of telling parallel stories is followed, and again it detracts from the main story. Here it is the story of Glen and Miriam which is related, but parts of it read simply like an exercise in the most effeminate type of effete pastoralism which Mais often betrays in his verse. . . . (p. 281)

The writing is unsuccessful, because the strong masculinity that was apparent in the descriptions of slum life in Mais's first novel, the vigour of the sexual descriptions of the second, are absent here. Jake is, however, a realistic and convincing human being; his loss of his wife, his artistic vision, and his sight are all in some way connected, and . . . [an artificial use of language] is found only in the scene in which Miriam and Glen are introduced. There is an element of the ridiculous in the two old cronies, Massa Butty and Tatta Joe, who come to see Jake, for their conversation is not genuine Jamaican English, and they contribute nothing to the action of the novel.

In many ways *Black Lightning* is a very personal novel about the life of the artist; both Jake and his companion Amos are artists: Jake is a woodcarver engaged on a statue of Samson and Amos is a musician. . . . Jake's inner life keeps him intensely interested in the statue on which he is working, because it comes to represent a noble side to himself, that he had the power of God. When he decides to destroy the statue, the realization has come to him that the artist is not a god. . . . The destruction of Samson is really the impending destruction of Jake himself.

A suitable way of summing up the three important works of Roger Mais is to say that he was interested in the human condition and its reflection in the lives of the socially outcast in the West Indies. He drew heavily on his own experiences, and he said of his first novel in an interview in the Jamaican *Daily Gleaner* that he had been intimate with the material he described for forty-seven years. His importance is that he shows this human situation at its worst and that those who inflict like those who endure are involved in a curious agent/victim relationship that links them both to a final condemnation. His

novels tell of this inescapable reckoning that awaits all, and he draws heavily from the Bible to give his "message" universal implications. But the hope is there—in the powerful evocations of physical and spiritual love, in the intense delineation of the perception of the artist who endures with the society, in the figure of the man on the cross (Surjue, Bra Man, and Jake) condemned to death but living, dead but with intense visions of the pure, good life. Or as Mais says of Bra Man in *Brother Man* after his stoning, he recovers consciousness after three days, and at sunset he "saw all things that lay before him in a vision of certitude." (pp. 281-83)

> Oscar R. Dathorne, "Roger Mais: The Man on the Cross," in Studies in the Novel *(copyright 1972 by North Texas State University), Vol. IV, No. 2, Summer, 1972, pp. 275-83.*

EDWARD [KAMAU] BRATHWAITE   (essay date 1974)

[*Brother Man*] is Mais' 'best' published work because it brings together in one minor classic, all the aspects of his instincts and talents. . . . The shoemaker, Brother Man (John Power), hero of this novel, is a member of [the Rastafarian religious sect]. (pp. x-xi)

[Here] we have to remark on Mais's individualism and extraordinary perception. In the late 1940s and 1950s when he was getting to know his Kingston, the Rastafari, as is demonstrated by the crowd-beating of Brother Man towards the end of the book, were a feared, despised, and rejected group. Not until the [1960s] . . . did this group begin to get a fair hearing. Yet ten years before . . . we find Mais making a Rasta the centre of his novel—in fact transferring the character Ras from the original version of *The Hills Were Joyful Together* into the Brother Man of the second novel. And for Mais, Brother Man did not represent violence, drug abuse, and criminal mentality, as John Public then thought; but rather, as the Rastas themselves had always averred, Peace and Love. In fact, Mais goes to the other extreme and romanticizes the elements of goodness in his Rastafari. For the contemporary reader, Brother Man is perhaps too Christ-like to be always 'true'; unlike the ideal of the Rastas, he is not fully enough grounded in reality. But this is a tendency Mais shows in all his novels. What he does achieve in *Brother Man,* however, is the depolarization of his rural and urban norms into a single equator, and the condensation of his moralizing tendency into a single mask. The novel is in this sense a 'humanist' triumph, if by this term we understand an emphasis on humane elements within an alienating environment. Had Mais not limited so severely his characterization and the matic variations, we might have had a major novel by any standard. (pp. xi-xii)

Yet in writing this novel, Mais moved towards certain important formal and stylistic interventions which make it far more important than its limitations would suggest. In fact, as we begin to examine *Brother Man,* the first thing that strikes us is the remarkable coincidence of 'style' and 'formal structure'; a coincidence, indeed, which we associate more with poetry than with prose fiction. By 'style' I mean the way—action flow—the book is written; its use and movement of language. By 'form', I refer to how the work is built: its 'archi-structure'. Both these are unusually clear in *Brother Man.*

The book is about people in a particular anonymous society, and about particular named persons within that society. The people and persons are, for the most part, members of the urban proletariat: simple, uneducated sufferers, still full of peasant. Stylistically, Mais makes these points with a Chorus of People, followed by narrative, and an almost dramatic presentation of characters. The Chorus is divided into two phases, each having a specific function and point. In phase one, it is the author himself who speaks, describing the qualities of the people, introducing us to them, leading us into the novel. . . . Phase two of the Chorus, on the other hand, introduces us, through change of language, to the cardiograph of the people themselves. . . . These two language-styles also set the novel firmly in its cultural context, where bi- and inter-lingualism is a feature of our culturation. Composed from two worlds, European settler and African slave, we reflect this in our speech. . . . But it is when we come to examine the sections of the narrative which follow, that we realize how inextricably bound up is style and structure in this book. The flow of language takes us into formal structures [similar] . . . to black urbanized folk music. Book and music both have a common mother in the life-style of the people. We can therefore learn something about the book by knowing something about its music and vice versa. Mais's Choruses, for instance, which are about people, are also like musical ensembles . . . , while his dialogues, which deal with persons, are not only significantly rhythmic, they produce an effect similar to the 'trading' between soloists during a jazz performance. . . . But all this has to be seen and felt in conjunction with Mais's sense of structure for this musical point to be properly taken. In this respect, we should note the formal patterning of the book. It is divided into five major parts, each of which is preceded by a short chorus—'Chorus of People in the Lane'. In addition, these parts are divided into sections, each representing a distinctive mood or movement and containing a particular configuration: people to persons; perhaps in pairs: male/female, female/female, child/adult; persons in accord, persons in conflict; persons alone; persons in crowds; good/evil, love/friendship/hate . . . all within a fluid structure/style similar to New Orleans jazz. (pp. xii-xiv)

[Mais] also introduces improvisation—variations on a theme. In Part One, for instance, the stated theme is love. But each section introduces a variation of meaning and quality, stage and mood. For Girlie and Papacita, for example, love is hot/sensual/carnal: a love/hate process. For Jesmina and Cordy, it is sisterly/domestic, with undertones of the sensual. Between Bra' Man and Minette it is more complex. She is an aspect of *eros* (sensual love), he of *caritas* (more impersonal love). In later sections of the novel we have variations on attitude and response to superstition . . . fear, loneliness, and family to death. . . . (p. xvi)

This musical form and metaphor also helps us to understand how Mais conceives of and treats the central principle of all his books. Bra' Man (Life) is structurally opposed to Bra' Ambo (Evil). But Mais treats Life and Evil in this book not in moral but in *social* terms, as the human action between what we might call 'interlates' (goodies: those whose function it is to join or make things) and *isolates* (baddies, loners: those whose tendency is to hurt or destroy). Symbolically in the novel, therefore, Brother Man is the healer, Bra' Ambo the destroyer, though at the (anti)-climax of the story it appears that the roles have been reversed . . . , bringing the plot to its denouement. Until then, however, the movement of the novel is concerned with the pressure of accident and circumstance on its three central interlate pairs: Girlie-Papacita, Jesmina-Cordy and Brother Man-Minette. Defects in the first two groups cause them to deteriorate into isolates, resulting in the love-craziness of Girlie which leads her to kill Papacity . . . ; insanity of Cordy which leads her to kill her infant child . . .

then hang herself. . . . The third group, as befits its importance, comes under wider attack. Minette is under pressure from Papacity to desert Brother Man and come with him. Her resistance to his sexual temptation . . . is what preserves this interlate, and in the end she (and Jesmina who has come to stay in the household after Cordy's death) are ready for the final test of their group's integrity, when the community turns upon Brother Man during a wave of anti-Rastafarian feeling. (pp. xvi-xvii)

The ensuing 'crucifixion' and resurrection of Brother Man make him more 'human' and result in a neat and finally poignant end to the novel. But by this time, one feels, Mais had become a prisoner of the very structure that I praised above. You can see, for instance, that since Bra' Man's 'crucifixion' comes about through the action of the until then structurally passive Chorus/public, rather than through the actions of the personae of the plot, it is in a sense a weakness: a result of not asking *why*. But by the time he came to write **Brother Man,** Mais appears to have lost that acute sense of political protest that made him write **'Now we know'.** Consequently, he never seems to link the condition of his Kingston poor with the persistent poverty of colonial underdevelopment, or even with the disillusionment of the historical struggle for independence. . . . And this is perhaps why his style, apart from its function in the Choruses, fails to remain active and autonomous within its structure. Characterization, while not becoming caricature, was becoming, like the Chorus, anonymous.

But failure on this level of conventional criticism is marginal compared to the aesthetic discoveries Mais was beginning to make in this novel. Anonymity, for instance, may be seen as failure or as artistic alternative to individuation. Much of modern jazz, for instance . . . , has returned to the essence and origins of black music in the gospel, work-song, rhythm and blues, and is therefore relevant to our discussion, since Mais' emphasis was also on the community and the way the community expressed itself. . . . Mais' Choruses have this communal function and when Brother Man, subtly tempted by pride of individuation . . . loses beat with this, the Chorus becomes 'tuneless' . . . and he is struck down by the multitude.

Brother Man, in other words, is pointing not to the development of the Faustian novel, where individual characteristics triumph and are stressed; but towards the alternative tradition of inter-related perceptions, as is now being explored by George Lamming, Wilson Harris and Lindsay Barrett, for example, (in *Song for Mumu*). But Mais was himself, paradoxically enough, moving towards individuation and away from the folk/urban expression of his first two published novels. The drift of his work generally, culminating in **Black Lightning** . . . , reveals this. It is a radical West Indian problem. Can we say with the tropical drought, or do we emigrate? Do we sing the pebble or the whole revolving globe? Like so many West Indian writers before and since Mais decided to try for the latter. (pp. xvii-xix)

Edward [Kamau] Brathwaite, "Introduction" (© Edward [Kamau] Brathwaite 1974; reprinted by permission of the author), in Brother Man *by Roger Mais, Heinemann, 1974, pp. v-xxi.*

JEAN D'COSTA   (essay date 1978)

The Hills Were Joyful Together and *Brother Man* form a single component in Roger Mais's literary achievement. It is difficult to speak of one without reference to the other; knowledge of one is incomplete without the contrasts and balance supplied by the other. The two novels treat of the same world and the same kinds of people, but with important differences. The yard of *The Hills Were Joyful Together* with its broken cistern, its rotting garbage and its twisted trees is located on just such a street as the 'cracked and patched asphalt strip' of lane that is the setting of *Brother Man.* Many of the protagonists of the earlier novel can be recognised in *Brother Man,* with significant changes. These two books together established Roger Mais's reputation as a novelist fiercely dedicated to the exposure of social ills in contemporary Jamaica. Apart from H. Orlando Patterson with *The Children of Sisyphus,* no other Jamaican novelist has matched Mais's detailed, vivid portrayal of urban slum life, and none has brought to this exercise such a compelling visionary interpretation.

The world of the two novels provides a haunting picture of slum life in Kingston in the last decades of the colonial period. Character and situation are blended delicately, mysteriously, as Mais unfolds the human panorama of broken families, rootless men, women and children imprisoned in a common insecurity. The names of the characters express the alienation and social vacuum into which they are born: Buju, Crawfish, Manny, Girlie, Puss-Jook and Flitters. . . . Their names are type-markers rather than identifiers: labels for those cut off from past and future, lacking the supportive ties of stable family and social structure. (p. 2)

In both novels Mais shows the daily pattern of slum life: the borrowed coal-pot on which Ras's woman prepares a meagre breakfast, Brother Man at his cobbler's bench, the small, stiflingly hot rooms where Rema and Cordelia lie ill, the smells of garbage, the little shops with 'the dustings of cornmeal and flour under the smirking two-faced scale' where neighbours gather to gossip, the physical drudgery of washing and cleaning which keeps thirteen-year old Tansy from school and the constant scavenging in gully and dump which occupies Manny. (p. 3)

This, then, is the raw material of *The Hills Were Joyful Together* and *Brother Man.* The earlier novel treats of the lives of a group of people living in a tenement yard 'in Kingston, Jamaica. Time: Today.' The affairs of three couples—Rema and Surjue, Shag and Euphemia, Charlotta and Bedosa—make up the greater part of the action. Through them the reader sees into the psychology of unemployment, law-breaking, religious neurosis, grinding poverty and its frustrations, as well as sickness of body and mind. Death and madness haunt this world. The forces of life exist, but in a posture of defeat. In *Brother Man* the pattern is altered. Life is seen to be that which contains death: its imagery is triumphant and transcendental while that of *The Hills Were Joyful Together* is pessimistic and deliberately ambivalent. Three couples form the action of this novel too, and here too disease of body and mind is shown at work in individuals as well as in the group. But these characters differ from their counterparts in *The Hills Were Joyful Together* in ways that suggest a deepening wisdom in Mais himself. (p. 4)

A shorter, tighter novel, *Brother Man* is no less realistic, no less harsh in representing the lives of the under-privileged poor than is *The Hills Were Joyful Together.* Structurally similar to the earlier novel in that it treats of the group rather than of a hero or heroine, *Brother Man* alters this pattern significantly with the role of John Power, Brother Man, who is a major figure set in a group of interwoven lives balancing him in interest and importance. Yet in both the group is unquestion-

ably the centre of interest, the true hero: open-ended, its boundaries those of street and tenement, its circumstances rigidly set by poverty, the group of yard and lane forms a classical pattern of interconnected lives which determines the shape of the novels. Through this framework Mais explores the nature of time, eternity, fate, free will, joy, sorrow, death and life.

The task which he sets himself is that of tracing the motive forces which affect the lives of individuals in terms of group interaction and personal destiny. The structure is thus deliberately employed to bring out the fluidity of the world he portrays; chorus and choric figures (such as Zephyr) counterbalance the potentially heroic characters such as Surjue and John Power, Brother Man. All of the major characters function as foils for each other, and even minor characters are allowed a degree of introspection which prevents the reader from accepting any one character as the central viewpoint of either novel, as the group of yard and lane journey through time and space together. For convenience I shall refer to this structural pattern as 'the group-as-hero' to differentiate Mais's experiments in form from those of other writers.

In practical terms this kind of structure can lead to diffuseness. The problems of handling so large a number of characters as those of *Brother Man* are great, and the group in *The Hills Were Joyful Together* is even larger. Mais is successful mainly because his interest in the individual is as keen as it is in the group itself. This is a skill which dramatists and painters must possess: to grasp the whole through articulation of the parts. Thus dialogue and dancelike movement against a vivid backdrop play an important part in revealing character and situation. Looking with the painter's eye, Mais brings out the shapes, colours, tones and linear patterns of this world: crazing minds are suggested in the crazed plaster and cracked walls, the patterns of decay expressed by seamed bricks, splintering wood, and shards of broken glass lying in street and gully. (pp. 5-6)

Mais's use of outer and inner landscapes owes nothing to the pathetic fallacy of the Romantic Movement. Nature and physical background complement human attitudes, but there is no simple one-to-one correspondence, no allegory or comfortable chain of meaning. (p. 6)

Funerary imagery of coffin, skeleton and shroud expand individual experience into a mystical humanism that is as characteristic of Mais as the social realism for which he is commonly remembered. The treatment of death and life in the two novels puts forward a view of life which encompasses the sharp delineation of individuals caught up in an historical moment, and relates them and their time to all men and all time. It might be argued that this is no more than any piece of art should do. The special significance of Mais's achievement is simply its pioneering novelty: working largely without models of any kind (save to a limited extent in poetry), he had to give form and language to his peculiar world. He had to do this and uphold at one and the same time the uniqueness of this world and its essential humanity. In many ways this demands the treatment of contraries, and paradox is one of the major stylistic and visionary modes used in the two novels. Hence the blending of opposites: light and darkness, growth and decay, love and hate, joy and sorrow, grace and damnation. In the authorial commentaries of *The Hills Were Joyful Together* and the choric passages of *Brother Man,* the tension of opposite poised against opposite gives depth and sharpness to the unfolding drama. (p. 7)

Despite the fact that elements of Biblical story have plainly influenced the plot and characters of the two novels it would be a mistake to see Mais as a simplistic exponent of Christianity. Out of the influences of a Christian childhood and a lasting fascination with the myth and diction of the Authorised Version of the Bible comes a religious sensibility that uses all available stimulation to grasp the mystery of human existence. . . . (p. 9)

Both novels are exploratory in a very real sense: the search for 'somewhere in the world' is as much a quest by the writer as it is for the reader following him. The sense of quest is strongest in that area which most displays the visionary shift that sets *Brother Man* apart from the first novel: the treatment of the themes of Death and Life. In both novels Death is a constant: it is one of the elemental forces at work in man and universe. Many of the human actors are simply masks for Death as is emphasised by choric statements and certain stereotyped characters. But an all-powerful Death makes for no quest at all; the mystic in Mais reaches equally towards Life. In *The Hills Were Joyful Together* these forces are shown as cyclic, moving constantly to cancel each other or existing in some kind of secret alliance beyond human comprehension. (pp. 9-10)

The final difference between *The Hills Were Joyful Together* and *Brother Man* lies in Mais's exploration of choice and chance. In sometimes painful detail he traces the inter-twining of circumstance, coincidence and outer influences on the willpower and personality of individuals. Many are destroyed in this web of varied forces, but all have one final right that cannot be abrogated up to the moment of death: the right to choose their attitude towards experience. . . . This freedom is upheld in different ways by all of the characters in the two novels: by Zephyr the prostitute, generous and enigmatic, by Charlotta in her heroic response to Bedosa's death, by the three adolescents groping for some meaning to life, by Ras who pursues peace, and by Shag, Euphemia, Rema and Surjue pursued by the guardian demons of their own personalities. In *Brother Man* this last freedom becomes the major key of a hymn of praise to the duality of existence. (pp. 10-11)

With no tradition of his own to fall back on, Mais experimented as freely with style as with structure, using whatever he happened to fancy with more than poetic licence. His style is copious, undisciplined, at times calculatedly vulgar, at others unconsciously banal, very often poetic in sound as well as in imagery, sometimes elegantly simple and sometimes a discord of ill-chosen modes.

Part of Mais's difficulty certainly arises from the wealth of styles available to the West Indian writer. He can select several distinctive oral styles from within his own culture, ranging from creole to varieties of spoken standard English, and he can hardly remain unaffected by the literary traditions of English and American culture. The writer whose community affords him many varieties of language benefits perceptually and artistically from the linguistic abundance. . . . Equally, this abundance can lead to confusion or hesitancy in adapting an oral style into written form. In Mais's work no one style predominates: his use of different styles shows the richness of his literary and linguistic background as well as his own uninhibited manipulation of this cultural wealth for his own ends.

Perhaps only a mystic could show at once such sensitivity and such indifference to language forms and literary traditions. *The Hills Were Joyful Together* makes free use of dialects and jargons, mingling oral varieties with surreal symbolist poetry, with brash journalistic prose or flat academic discourse and then breaking suddenly into the romantic-realistic style of writ-

ers such as Hemingway. However the reader always remains conscious of a central vision that dictates every shift of style; the fault is that of imperfect control of the experiments, not that of imitation. In *Brother Man* many of these irregularities have disappeared, and shifts of style are consistently functional rather than arbitrary or uncontrolled.

Dialogue and stream-of-consciousness episodes form such an important part of these novels that special attention must be paid to the styles used here. The technical problem is that of representing Jamaican speech-forms in a written style. . . . Mais does not avoid the problem. Lacking both a suitable spelling system and the specialised training to devise one, Mais uses abbreviations of standard spellings to suggest creole forms: 'Po' li' Papa-Joe', 'fo'get', 'et'. At other times he attempts phonetic spellings such as 'somep'n', 'ketch', 'waan' and 'yuh'. Sometimes spelling is used to give the appearance of dialect rather than dialect itself: 'lissen', 'laff' and 'likker' are no more useful than 'listen', 'laugh' and 'liquor'. The grammatical forms of creole are treated in the same way. At times the correct form will be used, at others the standard English variant (note 'dem' and 'them' in Charlotta's speech). In certain characters however, greater care is shown in reproducing creole usage as exactly as possible. Charlotta's speech is in fact more consistent in this respect than that of Euphemia, for example. But all display inconsistencies in varying degrees. (pp. 59-61)

Apart from oral styles, many other literary styles are used in the novels. *The Hills Were Joyful Together* displays four broad types: the romantic-realistic, the dramatic (which overlaps with the oral in dialogue and inner thought-stream), the poetic-meditative and the academic-journalistic. Uniting all of these is functional tone-shift, which ultimately derives from the habit of code-switching described above. Shifts may be ironic (as the hymns are), or used to bring out contrasts of personality or situation (as between Ras, Surjue, Flitters and Bajun Man). Often the tonal change alters the perspective of the situation: the poetic meditations withdraw the reader's consciousness from the immediate and the particular to focus on the transcendental and the universal. (p. 62)

However, these different styles do not show different world-views proceeding side by side. The experiment does no more than to take us into simple contrast, even when the lyrical prose echoing the meditations redresses the clumsiness of the other styles used. In *Brother Man* varieties of style are organically as well as structurally related. A striking example of this real functional unity of contrasting styles can be found in the Testament of John Power. . . . The sentence pattern and vocabulary are those of formal legal writing, but it is a simpler style lacking the scientific jargon and laboured latinisms of the opening of the fish-fry episode. It also reads aloud well, which many such passages from the earlier novel do not. The rhythms of the Testament are those of ritual language: the cadences of Biblical prose and seventeenth century devotional literature fuse with the formal academic style, deepening our view of John Power's character while evoking a sense of the mystery and complexity of the world in which he lives. (pp. 64-5)

Mais's use of figurative language is as striking as his mixture of styles and is of equal structural importance in both novels. The poetic meditations of *The Hills Were Joyful Together* and the choric interludes of *Brother Man* [display] a haunting, subtle play with words. . . . [Throughout these works we can see] three of the most characteristic features of Mais's figurative language: his painter's eye for rhythms of shape and outline, his unconventional gift for seeing one experience in terms of some other apparently unrelated aspect of life, and his heightened awareness of the interdependence of life and death. (pp. 65-6)

Again and again in *The Hills Were Joyful Together* some startling image breaks the surface of caustic realism, modifying our view of the immediate situation and its universal references. . . .

To a far greater extent than in *Brother Man*, systems of imagery and symbolism are used in *The Hills Were Joyful Together* to define the qualities of relationships and the nature of certain connected events. For Shag and Euphemia there is a pattern of images centred on death and realised in terms of disease, decay, vermin and nameless snake-like nightmare horrors; the value of these images is expanded by the extension of the system to enclose other seemingly uninvolved protagonists [such as] Ditty and Wilfie. (p. 66)

[A certain] bias in Mais's approach probably accounts for the heavy didacticism of parts of this novel. The authorial voice intrudes all too often to tell us what to feel and why. In addition instances of unintentional vulgarity and bad taste occur, especially in passages where Biblical language is used for situations inadequate to carry such high intensity, or where metrical language is made to supply atmosphere that should have arisen from the meaning of the actual words. (p. 68)

These faults present the negative side of experiment and innovation. In any case *Brother Man* does not repeat the mistakes of *The Hills Were Joyful Together*. . . . [There are many] examples from that novel of highly successful writing, such as the visionary moments in John Power's career and the descriptions of Cordelia's disintegration. In these Mais synthesises the technicalities of craft with the world-view which supplies the raw materials of the craft. His language demands emotional involvement from the reader: the burden of feeling with character and situation is forced upon the reader by the play upon his sensibility and imagination. Intellectual and ideological appeals play a secondary role, just as derivative elements of style and structure are secondary to the search for workable modes of expression. From a study of the language of the novels emerges an image of a complex, restless, fiery imagination deeply moved with compassion for man the individual caught up in history, and equally moved with awe for man linked to man in the timeless stream of universal life. (pp. 69-70)

I see Roger Mais as the spokesman of emergent Jamaica. . . . [*The Hills Were Joyful Together* and *Brother Man*] reveal those aspects of Jamaican life which preyed most upon a sensitive, rebellious nature: they possess a sharp, sensuous imagining of a place and a time, and they are concerned with the agony and desperation of man, and the nature of fate and responsibility. Mais's fascination with the relationship of circumstance, choice, chance and fate emerges most clearly in the imagery and associative language in which certain events are presented: the moment of death, the onset of insanity, the crisis of an illness, an instant of intense communication between protagonists or of blinding insight into the meaning of experience are expressed in mystical terms. Each of these is an attempt to express the inexpressible. This is always insisted upon; the moment is far more than its surface suggests. The contrast between this mystery and the harsh realism of the setting is the special originality of Roger Mais. Whatever the technical faults of his writing, or the limits of his personal experience, Roger Mais's two novels offer the opportunity to look back into our past and beyond our own history into the illimitable flow of life stretching out from the sharp particular moment. (pp. 71-2)

Jean D'Costa, "Introduction" and "Style and Worldview in 'The Hills Were Joyful Together' and 'Brother Man'," in her Roger Mais: "The Hills Were Joyful Together" and "Brother Man" *(© Longman Group Ltd 1978), Longman, 1978, pp. 1-12, 59-72.*

KARINA WILLIAMSON   (essay date 1981)

Roger Mais came to novel-writing late in life. His first book, a collection of short stories, was published in Kingston, Jamaica, in 1942, but it was not until 1953, when he was forty-seven, that his first novel, *The Hills Were Joyful Together,* was published in London, thereby enabling his work to reach a wider public. It was followed in quick succession by [*Brother Man* and *Black Lightning*]. . . . A fourth, unfinished novel has never been printed. His first two novels [reveal his concern over the social ills in contemporary Jamaica], and they remain his most popular novels in the West Indies; but their very success as novels of protest has had a damaging effect on his reputation in the long run by focusing attention too much on the documentary and polemical elements in his work at the expense of its more durable qualities. That is probably why, in spite of the reissue of his three novels in 1966, Mais is the least known of the major West Indian writers outside the Caribbean. (p. 245)

[The structural pattern of his first two novels is based on] a set of characters inhabiting a Kingston 'yard' (in *The Hills Were Joyful Together*) or lane (in *Brother Man*), whose interwoven fortunes during the limited time-span of the novels form the substance of the narrative. . . . (pp. 245-46)

Because Mais's compassionate interest in individual lives is as deep as his interest in group-dynamics, the vitality and diversity of his characters is not sacrificed to the exigencies of the scheme, though the strains it imposes are sometimes visible in weaknesses of style or plot. Nevertheless, Mais successfully creates a world that is both true to the historical situation (Jamaica in the period of emergence from colonial bondage) and yet transcends it. . . . [It] is through his local vision . . . that Mais succeeds in transcending the historical moment. . . . (p. 246)

Karina Williamson, "Reviews: 'The Hills Were Joyful Together' and 'Brother Man'," in The Review of English Studies, *Vol. 32, No. 126, May, 1981, pp. 245-46.*

ADDITIONAL BIBLIOGRAPHY

Harris, Wilson. *"Black Lightning." Journal of Canadian Fiction* III, No. 4 (1975): 41-4.
    Examination of the characters in *Black Lightning*. Harris discusses the folk element in Mais's novel as expressed through the main characters Jake, Estella, and Amos.

Lacovia, R. M. "Roger Mais: An Approach to Suffering and Freedom." *Black Images* I, No. 2 (Summer 1972): 7-11.
    Thematic study of Mais's fiction. Lacovia discusses the novelist's concept of freedom and his philosophy of suffering as an "enlightening approach to faith."

Moore, Gerald. "Outcasts." In his *The Chosen Tongue: English Writing in the Tropical World*, pp. 85-96. New York: Harper & Row, 1969.*
    Discussion of *The Hills Were Joyful Together* and *Brother Man*. Moore focuses his study on the setting in each of these novels and how it affects character and action.

Thomas Mann

1875-1955

German novelist, short story and novella writer, essayist, and critic.

Mann is one of the greatest novelists of the twentieth century. Singlehandedly he raised the German novel to an international stature which it had not enjoyed since the time of the Romantics. Like his contemporaries Joyce and Proust, Mann keenly reflected the intellectual currents of his age, particularly the belief that European realism was no longer viable for the inhabitants of a sophisticated and complex century. Yet, while Joyce and Proust expressed this predicament through the form of their writing, Mann maintained the outward conventions of realistic fiction, emphasizing an ironic vision of life and a deep, often humorous, sympathy for humanity. His novels and stories demonstrate a great narrative gift and are shaped by a number of recurring themes: the isolation of the artist in society, the nature of time, and the seduction of the individual by disease and death. Along with a fascination with evil and decay in Mann's work, there also exists a constructive unity and sincerity in his work. In the words of Ignace Feuerlicht, he desired "not to bewilder, but to satisfy his readers," to make them fully aware of "man's spirit and his possibilities."

Born in Lübeck, Germany, Mann was the son of a successful grain merchant and the younger brother of Heinrich Mann, who also became a noted novelist. His mother, an accomplished musician, was born and raised in South America. A bourgeois background, and the conflicting natures of his parents, were to figure predominantly in much of his fiction, most notably *Buddenbrooks*. Mann's first story, *Gefallen*, published when he was nineteen, showed a marked Romantic influence. However, he soon abandoned the tenets of Romanticism and developed an ironic sensibility that became the signature of his art. Although he did not serve in World War I, due to health problems, Mann remained involved in the conflict through his nationalistic political essays. Following the war he cultivated his interests in Goethe, Freud, Nietzsche, and Schopenhauer, publishing *Der Zauberberg (The Magic Mountain)*, for which he was awarded the Nobel Prize in literature in 1929. Despite his nationalism during World War I, Mann fervently opposed the growth of national socialism and fascism in the 1930s. In 1933 he left Germany and went into self-imposed exile, eventually settling in the United States. There he published the complex and often misinterpreted novel *Doktor Faustus (Doctor Faustus)*. An imaginative reworking of the Faust myth, *Doctor Faustus* achieved greatness both as the tragic story of the fictional composer Adrian Leverkuhn and as a metaphorical depiction of the decline of modern Germany. In 1952 Mann left the United States and spent the remaining years of his life in Switzerland.

Mann won immediate recognition with the publication of his first novel, *Buddenbrooks*. Written in the manner of the Scandinavian genealogical novel, *Buddenbrooks* traces the rise and fall, through four generations, of a wealthy Hanseatic family. Its central theme is the emerging relationship between the bourgeois life of the nineteenth century and the precarious

modern sensibility of the artist. *Buddenbrooks* foreshadows many characteristics of Mann's later work: the focus on disease, the isolation of the artist, the opposition of spirit to life, even the degenerative effects of art on the individual psyche, as seen in Tom and Hanno. In a limited sense, *Buddenbrooks* is Mann's most successful novel, a late masterpiece in the nineteenth-century realistic tradition. *Der Tod in Venedig (Death in Venice)* is the most representative of the decadent, poetic, and ironic stories Mann wrote throughout his career. Often considered one of the best novellas in world literature, *Death in Venice* poignantly reflects the artist's struggle to reconcile inherited discipline with the impulses of a sensitive nature.

The Magic Mountain was Mann's first major novel after *Buddenbrooks,* and it marked a new direction in his career. The novel was his attempt to overcome the dualism of his youthful stories—to resolve the enmity of life and spirit that dominated those works. Molded after the German *Bildungsroman,* of which it is both a parody and an affirmation, *The Magic Mountain* follows the education of its protagonist, Hans Castorp, from his initial flirtation with disease and death to his eventual reaffirmation of life. It also presents another of Mann's central themes: the conflict of the intellectual and emotional natures within each human being. The tetralogy *Joseph und seine Brüder (Joseph and His Brothers)* is, in both length and scope,

Mann's most ambitious work. Full of irony and humor, the cycle evolves as a Biblical commentary written from the perspective of modern liberalism. Mann reinterpreted the Joseph story as the emergence of the individual out of the tribal collective; of history out of myth; of a personal God out of the unknowable. His concern was to provide a myth for his own times, capable of sustaining and directing his generation, and of restoring faith in the power of humane reason. *Doctor Faustus* is considered Mann's most complex novel. In contrast to the optimistic tone of the Joseph tetralogy, *Faustus* is a deeply pessimistic, somber book. Here, once again, Mann demonstrated his belief in the relationship between art, in this case music, and decay, disease, decadence, and finally death. Though it has been criticized for its failure to solve the problems it raises, *Doctor Faustus* represents the climax of Mann's literary career.

Critical opinion of Mann's work has been consistently high. He has been praised for the depth of his vision and the sheer vastness of his intellect. He has also been lauded as the greatest "ironist" of the twentieth century, though he preferred to call himself a humorist, suggesting a more sympathetic approach to humanity than most critics have acknowledged. He has been called a master of style, and his compositions, brilliantly realistic on one level yet deeply symbolic on many others, have rarely failed to reach both the critical and the less sophisticated reader. Mann has been attacked for an inability to resolve the predicament of the artist in modern society. Some critics have also suggested that his work suffered from pretentiousness, a verbose rhetoric, overly ambiguous ironies, and over-exploitation of parody and other stylistic techniques within conventional frameworks. The most common criticism, however, is that his characters are often cold and distant and that Mann himself did not truly empathize with their plight. But in general, most critics agree that beneath the complexity of his work Mann expressed a commitment to humanity and a desire to resolve the dualities of life.

Though the exact nature of Mann's greatness is still debated, Mann's success has been universal; he was a superb observer, craftsman, creator, thinker, and ironist. Through his art he offered a remarkable understanding of his times. In the words of Martin Swales, the "twentieth century found no more eloquent representative *and* critic than Thomas Mann."

(See also *TCLC*, Vol. 2.)

PRINCIPAL WORKS

Gefallen (short story) 1894; published in journal *Die
    Gesellschaft*
Der kleine Herr Friedemann (short stories) 1898
    ["Little Herr Friedemann" published in *Children and
    Fools*, 1928]
Buddenbrooks (novel) 1901
    [*Buddenbrooks*, 1924]
Tonio Kröger (novella) 1903; published in *Tristan*
    [*Tonio Kröger* published in *Death in Venice*, 1925]
Tristan (novella) 1903
    [*Tristan* published in *Death in Venice*, 1925]
Königliche Hoheit (novel) 1909
    [*Royal Highness*, 1916]
Der Tod in Venedig (novella) 1913
    [*Death in Venice*, 1925]
Friedrich und die grosse Koalition (essay) 1915
    [*Frederick the Great and the Grand Coalition* published
    in *Three Essays*, 1929]

Betrachtungen eines Unpolitischen (essays) 1918
Der Zauberberg (novel) 1924
    [*The Magic Mountain*, 1927]
Mario und der Zauberer (novella) 1930
    [*Mario and the Magician*, 1931]
Die Geschichten Jaakobs (novel) 1933
    *[*The Tales of Jacob*, 1934]
Der junge Joseph (novel) 1934
    *[*Young Joseph*, 1935]
Joseph in Ägypten (novel) 1936
    *[*Joseph in Egypt*, 1938]
Stories of Three Decades (short stories and novellas)
    1936
Lotte in Weimar (novel) 1939
    [*The Beloved Returns*, 1940]
Die vertauschten Köpfe (novel) 1940
    [*The Transposed Heads*, 1941]
Joseph der Ernahrer (novel) 1943
    *[*Joseph the Provider*, 1944]
Doktor Faustus (novel) 1947
    [*Doctor Faustus*, 1948]
Der Erwahlte (novel) 1951
    [*The Holy Sinner*, 1951]
Die Betrogene (novella) 1953
    [*The Black Swan*, 1954]
Bekenntnisse des Hochstaplers Felix Krull (novel) 1954
    [*Confessions of Felix Krull, Confidence Man*, 1955]

*These works were published as *Joseph and His Brothers* in 1948.

RAINER MARIA RILKE (essay date 1902)

[In *Buddenbrooks*] Thomas Mann has given evidence of a capacity and an ability that cannot be ignored. It was his intention to write the history of a family that is going under—the "decline of a family." Only a few years ago a modern author would have been content to show the last stage of this decline, the last heir, dying of himself and of his fathers. Thomas Mann felt that it would be unjust to concentrate in a last chapter on the catastrophe to which generations in fact contributed; and conscientious as he is, he begins at the point when the family's fortunes have reached their peak. He knows that beyond this peak the inevitable decline sets in: at first in a barely perceptible dissolution, becoming more and more marked, until at last nothing remains.

Thus he was faced with the necessity of narrating the life of four generations, and Thomas Mann's way of solving this unusual problem is so surprising and interesting that, though it takes days, one reads these two weighty volumes with attention and suspense, without tiring or skipping anything, without the least sign of impatience or haste. One has time, one must have time for narration of the calm and natural succession of these happenings, precisely because nothing else in the book seems to be there for the reader, because there is no point at which—over the head of events as it were—a writer superior [to his material] bends down to an [equally] superior reader, in order to persuade him and carry him along. For that very reason one is wholly involved and almost personally engaged, quite as if one had found in some secret drawer old family papers and letters, in which one slowly read ahead, to the limit of one's own memories.

Thomas Mann felt quite rightly that he had to become a chronicler, that is, a calm and unexcited reporter of events, to narrate the history of the Buddenbrooks; and that it would nevertheless be his task to be a poet, and to imbue many figures with convincing vitality, with warmth and substance. He has combined both aims most happily by interpreting his role as chronicler in a modern way and endeavoring, not simply to record salient data, but to include conscientiously everything apparently unimportant and slight, a thousand particulars and details; for after all, everything actual has its value, is a tiny bit of that life that it was his purpose to describe. And in this manner, by this deeply felt absorption in particular events, by a grand (*grosse*) justice vis-à-vis all happenings, he attains a liveliness of representation which is due less to the material itself than to the continuous materialization of all things. Here something of [the painter Giovanni] Segantini's technique has been transformed to another milieu: the thorough and impartial management of every passage, the careful compilation of the material, causing everything to appear important and essential; the surface traversed by a hundred furrows, which seems unified, informed with life to the observer; and finally the objective element, the epic manner of narration, which gives even cruel and frightening matters a certain character of necessity and of being ordained by law. (pp. 7-8)

The story shows the calm, unself-conscious life of an older generation and the nervous, self-observing haste of its descendants; it shows small and ridiculous people violently thrashing about in the tangled nets of their destinies. It reveals also that even those who are somewhat more far-seeing are not in control of their good fortune or disaster, both of which arise from a hundred small movements and spread out and draw back, almost impersonal and anonymous in their origin, while life goes forward like a wave. It is shown with particular subtlety how the decadence of the family manifests itself above all in the fact that the individual members have changed the direction of their lives, as it were: no longer is it natural for them to live [with their energies directed] toward the exterior world; rather, the tendency toward introversion becomes more and more apparent   The last of them too, Little Hanno, walks about with his glance turned inward, listening attentively to the inner world of his soul, from which his music streams forth. In him there exists the potentiality of another ascent (of a different sort, to be sure, from the one the Buddenbrooks hope for)—the potentiality, infinitely endangered, of becoming a great artist; it is not realized. The sickly boy is ruined by the banality and ruthlessness of his school, and dies of typhus.

His life, a day of his life, takes up considerable space in the second volume. And however cruelly fate seems to be treating the boy, here too we hear only the excellent chronicler who supplies a thousand matters of fact without permitting himself to be swept away into anger, or into acquiescence.

And besides the colossal labor and the poet's gift of seeing, this noble objectivity deserves praise; it is a book in which there is no trace of arrogance on the author's part. An act of reverence toward life—life that is good and just in its enactment. (pp. 8-9)

> *Rainer Maria Rilke, "Thomas Mann's 'Buddenbrooks'," translated by Henry Hatfield (1902; originally published under a different title in his* Rainer Maria Rilke: Bücher Theater Kunst, *edited by Richard von Mises, Jahoda und Siegel, 1934), in* Thomas Mann: A Collection of Critical Essays, *edited by Henry Hatfield (reprinted by permission of Prentice-*

Hall, Inc., Englewood Cliffs, New Jersey 07632), Prentice-Hall, 1964, pp. 7-9.

BRUNO FRANK   (essay date 1913)

If the France of today had a writer like Thomas Mann, so deeply in love with the language and so beloved by it—a writer armed besides with such form-giving strength and such a wealth of understanding—it would have a spiritual throne prepared for him. There, the literary art is not regarded as a rather superfluous ornament on the edifice of national consciousness. As strong cement it is admixed to the mortar which holds the structure together. I think of the intellectual tremors evident there during the publication days of a new work by Anatole France, for instance—who is not half so new, so significant and forward-looking as, for us, the German Thomas Mann whose story, *Death in Venice,* his most profound work and, so far, his work of highest artistry, is in these days brought to light, not without evoking murmurs of approval from the experts.

But there should be shouts—not murmurs. There should be shouts: hats off, bow deeply, deeply to the ground—for here, and this time in his most princely garb, comes Europe's ranking epic poet of the day, the writer of what linguistically is the most powerful prose written by a German since Schopenhauer closed his eyes.

No injustice! The German public has certainly not been shabby in its treatment of the great figure of Thomas Mann. Tens of thousands have bought his books. Hundreds of thousands have read them. And yet, in the consciousness of the German intellectuals of today, he seems like just one more excellent author and not many know that in spiritual history it was a great year which gave him to us.

No man before Thomas Mann (let this be stated aloud, for once) has written so fully animated a German—a German, to be sure, which refrains from all the word-forming excesses that are now commonplace, but a German full of awareness and breathing force, down to the very last particles. It is not highly selective taste alone which so expresses itself; the real source of such peculiarity can be only quite an egregious earnestness, quite an egregious sincerity of thought and feeling. And as water returns to the cloud from which it descended, one psychic state will here, *via* art, turn back somewhere into the same psychic state. (pp. 119-20)

Serving art, in the higher sense, is a service for heroes, and this, for the first time quite extensively and candidly, is the subject of the new story by Thomas Mann. It is not as if here he were speaking of himself for the first time; fundamentally, like every poet, he never did anything else. But the disguises in which he used to appear were too convincingly genuine and too sumptuous for people to look underneath. Today one cannot think without amusement of the time when the novel, *Royal Highness,* appeared and one member of certain court circles lifted his voice in defense of the modernity of his class, against that picture of courtly, disciplined serfdom and representative asceticism—while the writer really was just speaking fraternally and parabolically of the lonely dignity of him who also "represents" himself, and thereby the world in the forms of beauty.

The struggle which such an artist wages against himself, against the chaos erupting within him, his heroic struggle and his heroic defeat are related in the novella, *Death in Venice.* It describes the passing of a senescent individual enjoying great and well-deserved fame—his end on a southern journey taken for his health, an all but fugitive interruption of the artistic slavery at home, with which he felt no longer able to cope. Formlessness, dissolution, nothingness overtake him in the disguise of a late, strange, sensual adventure, a love story experienced fully and exclusively within, tingling his every nerve although he does not even dare address a single word to the object of his tender feelings. It is as though he were no longer able to speak to her. It is as though there were no longer the figure of a living, truly desired woman but a congealed fever-vision, a dream-product. But in the main—some eerily two-faced spectres notwithstanding—the dreams which the sinking one dreams and weaves into the light, clear, sunny oceanic landscape of the South are rather unlike the frightening spooks to which we have been accustomed by Germans and Scandinavians: they are bright, light, Greek dreams; and walking therein, softly calling to each other, are Plato's beautiful and knowing figures. Until the black cavern yawns and the shadowy abyss devours the world. The world—that is to say, here, this one man alone. For while Thomas Mann again has us walking in radiantly clear surroundings, while a ride in a gondola or a mass in San Marco or a summer morning on the sand of the Lido were surely never shown with such convincing veracity, while this epic master's absorption of all the virtues and capabilities of the naturalist way of presentation is not denied at any point here, either—yet it is, and ought to be, as though all characters of the novella except the hero himself were soaring, a hand's-breadth above the ground. They are phantoms, even though radiant phantoms. They are dream creatures, and Aschenbach, the poet, has brought them along with him. Moreover, he has brought the very cholera that he will die of along with him to Venice. Not in the real, medical sense, of course. We are told quite plainly how Syrian traders bring the cholera from overseas, how it simultaneously shows up in several Mediterranean ports, while Europe still trembles with fear lest it might come overland, from East Asia, by way of the Russian plains. . . . This is what happened in fact, two years ago, and so we find it admitted. And yet, somehow the disease seems linked to the great failing spirit who came down in flight from the North. He really is finished already; he really has been submerged in darkness and dissolution at the moment when a nauseous inability to work seized him at home and put him to flight. In a sense, his Venetian experiences are phases after death.

In point of style, of the technique of language, this new work also is unmistakeably the child of its masterful creator. It resembles its elder brothers and sisters and yet is plainly distinguishable from them, in accordance with its destined end. After all, to the experts the fascination of Thomas Mann's epical writing has always lain in his employment of style to characterize divers events and persons, while remaining wholly true to his own. This time, a significant change occurs even within one and the same work—from the Nordically severe, dogmatic manner of the early chapters (in which the formalistic, the somewhat "officiously didactic" traits attributed to Aschenbach the artist are apparent) to the sensuous wealth of the later ones, when the soft, well-rounded sentences flow as if waves were rolling on a blue Southern sea. Or as if ringing beneath the beautiful words were the gentle melody of a Greek pastoral flute.

Aschenbach the artist perishes. Not, of course, like the typical representative of the literate *literati*, who at some point has failed to make the grade and now quits and decamps, or is redeemed from his sterility. On the contrary: as one who has

given his greatest, Aschenbach pays for a fertile life based on the spirit alone with an eruption of the repressed and proudly denied sensual forces—an eruption with which he can cope no longer.

The problem of artistry in our time which has become so conscious is here fearlessly handled. Whoever is great today—so states a man who is in a position to know—owes his greatness less than ever before to an inspired, quickly grasping naiveté; the sap of his artistry has passed through a filter of the most painful knowledge, and a tenacious will has formed the vessel. But today, as ever, all creative powers rise in the end from the well of spurned sensuality.

Aschenbach perishes; but Thomas Mann lives and gives his scarcely veiled pledges for his own future. We learn that the coming years may expect a great work from him, a work in which he will recreate the figure of Frederick of Prussia—out of a feeling, proudly and modestly indicated, of fraternal familiarity with this great genius of discipline and duty. And we learn more: a bright vista opens to those who love our language and our poetic art.

But why does Aschenbach perish, since his creator and brother lives and promises so much? Because more than a mere human, an entire moral condition is to die in him. For Thomas Mann, despite all his intelligence and insight, is like all poets something of a Utopian. Of those who come after us he longingly expects what the living generation still lacks: the conciliation of the ancient struggle of senses and spirit, the completely easy conscience. If today the best have still so hard a time of it, if to be able to accomplish their work they cannot relax their grip upon themselves for even a poor instant, if today their "reborn ingenuousness" (their "superficiality from depth," to speak with Thomas Mann's ethical forebear) still resembles a heavily assaulted fortress—the grandsons will dwell in it as in a flowering garden, under Greek skies, no longer knowing that it could be otherwise. The great artists who then are on earth will be able to live more easily than Aschenbach, the hero who succumbs.

Will they? Will human greatness, will artistic greatness ever grow on any soil other than struggle and suffering? No matter—there is no poetry without faith: Pan's flute, whose sound we hear, faithfully leads our march into the future. (pp. 120-23)

Bruno Frank, "'Death in Venice'," translated by E. B. Ashton (originally under a different title in Wuerttemberger Zeitung, *1913; reprinted by permission of Charles Neider), in* The Stature of Thomas Mann, *edited by Charles Neider, New Directions, 1947, pp. 119-23.*

ERIKA MANN and KLAUS MANN (essay date 1939)

It is difficult, perhaps almost impossible, to see and judge as a public figure one to whom we are closely attached by human ties. It seems hardly possible to separate the man from his work, particularly in a case like Thomas Mann, whose work is so intimately bound up with his personality. All his books, and even the great literary essays, are autobiographical in character, a trait clearly recognizable in *Buddenbrooks* and in *Tonio Kröger*, which can be discerned as it were under a mask in *His Royal Highness, Death in Venice* and *The Confessions of Felix Krull*, and which, for the keen-sighted, is even to be divined in *The Magic Mountain*. Not until *Joseph and His Brothers* does the autobiographical and confessional element seem quite to fade into the background. Yet what a thrill of surprise it gives us to discover and recognize it even here. For those characters from a far-distant time and an alien scene take on strangely familiar traits. Young Joseph is not unlike Tonio Kröger; at the same time he has a vague resemblance to Tadzio, the lovely Polish boy, whose charm laid so mortal a spell, in Venice, on Gustav Aschenbach, the aging man weary of his own dignity. The torments of hopeless love which Joseph causes Potiphar's wife, the priestess and *femme du monde,* who is, in her way, as dignified as Gustav Aschenbach in his, and who, like him, suffers degradation in that mortal enchantment, not only recall the bitter-sweet end of the German writer in Venice, but also the dubious delights into which a certain Hans Castorp sank with a guilty conscience when he suffered his heart to be overwhelmed with love for Madame Chauchat. That love for a sick woman, that forbidden adventure on the magic mountain, was 'hopeless,' like Aschenbach's passion, like Madame Chauchat's desire, like that rather contemptuous yet very powerful attraction which Tonio Kröger, the brooder, felt for the 'fair and commonplace,' the frivolous and harmless. And yet again, the motive of a love which burns the more unquenchably just because it is hopeless returns, like some great, sorrowful musical theme recurring throughout a composer's work, in the novel now in the process of writing, centred round the aged Goethe, *Lotte in Weimar.* For Goethe too loved hopelessly, and wanted to love hopelessly, when he loved Lotte, the betrothed of his friend. All these torments and ecstasies are interwoven, all these figures bear faces which are akin, and in all these faces we recognize, with reverence and love, the poet who created them. It is the face of Jacob, the thoughtful face of the father watching his son, young Joseph, with anxious yearning. Then a mysterious and comical change passes over it, and it melts into the features of Felix Krull, that genius at 'making faces,' and when it settles again, it takes on the lineaments of upper middle-class dignity, the likeness of Thomas Buddenbrook, the last patrician, who indulged in Schopenhauer like a drug fiend, then simply fell dead in the street because a dentist had hurt him—or because he would not put up with life any longer. But then again there is a change; the face turns more solemn on the one hand, smoother and more callow on the other. It is the face of Prince Klaus Heinrich, the beloved and secretly melancholy Royal Highness, who had to keep at a severe ceremonial distance from 'ordinary people' and in the end found happiness all the same, an 'austere' happiness, when the sweet and capricious betrothed, the strange girl Imma came. (pp. 90-2)

Given such a wealth of memories and associations, of touching relationships, it is not easy to remain 'detached.' On the other hand, we should not wish to turn our personal intimacy with the author's life into a fatal handicap by regarding his work merely as a complex of family allusions, and hence losing the power to appreciate it as one of the fullest manifestations of the German, of the human spirit which our time has seen.

The range of problems and human affairs which has entered into this creation, and formed its artistic and spiritual themes, has grown gradually but steadily wider until it has attained the magnitude we know today. It is characteristic that the great essays, that is, the writings of a more general and social nature, have played a preponderating part in Thomas Mann's work only since the World War. The complex of problems which preoccupied and exercised his mind for years, almost exclusively and with painful insistence, could find concrete artistic form in the ironic sadness of the confessional novels. The problem that dominated Thomas Mann's work solely and uniquely, up to the war, was the problem of the creative spirit.

The problem of decadence, which gave the great chronicle of the decline and fall of an upper middle-class family, the Buddenbrooks, its spiritual content, was only a part, a section of the problem of the creative mind. For the artistic temperament already afflicts the last of the Buddenbrooks, not only the oversensitive, over-affectionate boy Hanno, but his father too, who was, to all appearances, still sound. They are estranged from the solid business life of their family; they have been touched by the dangerous breath of the spirit.

The last, and actually the first great bourgeois epic of Germans, *Buddenbrooks,* is the story of bourgeois decay. In its decadence, the race of great merchants gives birth to the artist. It is true that he still harbours a yearning for the 'ecstasies of the commonplace,' the soothing solidity of bourgeois life. This longing is also the fate of Tonio Kröger, who weaves his nostalgic monologues between two worlds—the bourgeois and the bohemian. In a way that gives one pause, the notions 'bourgeoisie' and 'strong, simple life' are here identified. Tonio Kröger is estranged from life because he is estranged from the bourgeoisie.

'The creative spirit' after that appears in many guises and under many masks, for he is, after all, an actor too and likes to wear all kinds of strange costumes; but we can always recognize him as the man standing aloof from life, and isolated, the man who does not really 'belong.' Once we find him under the mask of the Prince, who merely represents instead of living; once in the disguise of the swindler who, for his own dubious purposes, apes the respectability which is the genuine lot of other 'bourgeois' human beings. And between the two spheres, between 'mind' and 'life,' Eros hovers, a graceful, cunning go-between. (pp. 92-4)

'Whoever has looked upon beauty is dedicated to death,' said a German poet whose knowledge of all things concerning death, beauty and love was profound. That poet was August von Platen, to whom Thomas Mann has paid homage in a great study: *Platen, Tristan and Don Quixote.* For Eros can also appear in the likeness of the angel of death. His seduction is at times the seduction of annihilation—that very fascination which so ensnared poor Thomas Buddenbrooks as he sat reading Schopenhauer in the summerhouse and to which Hans Castorp, in *The Magic Mountain,* owed so many strange experiences, physical and spiritual. The most cunning and equivocal of all gods—thus Plato describes Eros—is revealed in that feeling of which Platen sang, and which Thomas Mann has described as 'the bias towards death.'

This formula, 'the bias towards death,' is one of the intellectual *leit-motifs* which run through a long critical and philosophical study, *Reflections of an Unpolitical Mind,* on which Thomas Mann worked during the four war years, 1914-1918. This book marks a turning-point in his inner life and in his work. For the first time the problem of the creative spirit recedes. The antithesis 'mind' and 'life,' which had predominated in all Thomas Mann's creative work from *Tonio Kröger* to *Death in Venice,* is replaced by other antitheses, other spiritual polarities.

Rather paradoxically, the author's interest in social and political matters is earliest manifested in the *Reflections of an Unpolitical Mind.* It is true that this interest at first takes the form of a long and bitterly angry attack on that type of intellectual who concentrates his efforts and interests primarily on social and political matters—that is, the western, democratic type most clearly represented in Germany by Heinrich Mann. This 'literary prophet of civilization,' with his optimism and his belief in progress, is thrown into contrast with the conservative, non-political German Romantic; French rhetoric is contrasted with German musicality, the western idea of civilization with the German ideal of *Kultur* (ostentatiously spelt with a capital K instead of a small c). The *Reflections* are a pamphlet in the grand style, written with passion and grief against the spirit of the Entente Cordiale, the spirit of the democracies with which the Germany of Luther and Bismarck was at war. The author of this strange and at times movingly beautiful book has long since outgrown all the *opinions* expressed in it. All the same, within the whole compass of his work, it is of decisive importance. (pp. 94-5)

The patriotism of this strange war book is by no means the hearty, flag-flapping kind; it is a melancholy patriotism, a kind of suspicious enthusiasm, familiar not only with all the greatness of Germany, but also with all her evil potentialities. It is a pessimistic enthusiasm which lends the book its almost musical charm and its vibrant but dubious verve. It is not mere chance that one of the *leitmotifs* of the book should be the recurring phrase 'the bias towards death.'

It is that very bias which had to be overcome. As Nietzsche overcame in suffering his love for Schopenhauer, Wagner and romanticism, thereby winning a brighter, austerer happiness, the author of the *Reflections* overcame the melancholy conservatism, the secretly rather sceptical enthusiasm for what is already doomed and marked by death. *The Magic Mountain* is the epic record of a process which leads from the interest in sickness, death and decay to the interest in life and finally to an all-embracing sympathy with life and the living. But through this new and brigther melody other notes run, the old notes rising from the depths. The experiences that were gathered 'down there,' in the depths, are not to be forgotten up in the light. It is the man who knows darkness who loves the light most. (pp. 96-7)

> *Erika Mann and Klaus Mann, "Portrait of Our Father," in their* Escape to Life *(copyright, 1939, by Erika Mann Auden and Klaus Mann; copyright © renewed 1967 by Erika Mann Auden; reprinted by permission of Houghton Mifflin Company), Houghton Mifflin, 1939, pp. 76-100.*

THOMAS MANN (essay date 1953)

[What] is there that I can say about [*The Magic Mountain*], and the best way to read it? I shall begin with a very arrogant request that it be read not once but twice. A request not to be heeded, of course, if one has been bored at the first reading. A work of art must not be a task or an effort; it must not be undertaken against one's will. It is meant to give pleasure, to entertain and enliven. If it does not have this effect on a reader, he must put it down and turn to something else. But if you have read *The Magic Mountain* once, I recommend that you read it twice. The way in which the book is composed results in the reader's getting a deeper enjoyment from the second reading. Just as in music one needs to know a piece to enjoy it properly, I intentionally used the word "composed" in referring to the writing of a book. I mean it in the sense we more commonly apply to the writing of music. For music has always had a strong formative influence upon the style of my writing. Writers are very often "really" something else; they are transplanted painters or sculptors or architects or what not. To me the novel was always like a symphony, a work in counterpoint, a thematic fabric; the idea of the musical motif plays a great role in it.

People have pointed out the influence of Wagner's music on my work. Certainly I do not disclaim this influence. In particular, I followed Wagner in the use of the leitmotiv, which I carried over into the work of language. Not as Tolstoy and Zola use it, or as I used it myself in *Buddenbrooks,* naturalistically and as a means of characterization—so to speak, mechanically. I sought to employ it in its musical sense. My first attempts were in *Tonio Kröger.* But the technique I there employed is in *The Magic Mountain* greatly expanded; it is used in a very much more complicated and all-pervasive way. That is why I make my presumptuous plea to my readers to read the book twice. Only so can one really penetrate and enjoy its musical association of ideas. The first time, the reader learns the thematic material; he is then in a position to read the symbolic and allusive formulas both forwards and backwards. (pp. 724-25)

[*The Magic Mountain*] is in a double sense a time-romance. First in a historical sense, in that it seeks to present the inner significance of an epoch, the pre-war period of European history. And secondly, because time is one of its themes: time, dealt with not only as a part of the hero's experience, but also in and through itself. The book itself is the substance of that which it relates: it depicts the hermetic enchantment of its young hero within the timeless, and thus seeks to abrogate time itself by means of the technical device that attempts to give complete presentness at any given moment to the entire world of ideas that it comprises. It tries, in other words, to establish a magical *nunc stans,* to use a formula of the scholastics. It pretends to give perfect consistency to content and form, to the apparent and the essential; its aim is always and consistently to *be* that of which it speaks.

But its pretensions are even more far-reaching, for the book deals with yet another fundamental theme, that of "heightening," enhancement (*Steigerung*). This *Steigerung* is always referred to as alchemistic. You will remember that my Hans is really a simple-minded hero, the young scion of good Hamburg society, and an indifferent engineer. But in the hermetic, feverish atmosphere of the enchanted mountain, the ordinary stuff of which he is made undergoes a heightening process that makes him capable of adventures in sensual, moral, intellectual spheres he would never have dreamed of in the "flatland." His story is the story of a heightening process, but also as a narrative it is the heightening process itself. It employs the methods of the realistic novel, but actually it is not one. It passes beyond realism by means of symbolism, and makes realism a vehicle for intellectual and ideal elements.

All the characters suffer this same process; they appear to the reader as something more than themselves—in effect they are nothing but exponents, representatives, emissaries from worlds, principalities, domains of the spirit. I hope this does not mean that they are mere shadow figures and walking parables. And I have been reassured on this score; for many readers have told me that they have found Joachim, Claudia Chauchat, Peeperkorn, Settembrini, very real people indeed.

The book, then, both spatially and intellectually, outgrew the limits its author had set. [What was to have been a] short story became a thumping two-volume novel—a misfortune that would not have happened if *The Magic Mountain* had remained, as many people even today still see it, a satire on life in a sanatorium for tubercular patients. When it appeared, it made a stir in professional circles, partly of approval, partly of the opposite, and there was a little tempest in the medical journals. But the critique of sanatorium therapeutic methods is only the foreground of the novel. Its actuality lies in the quality of its backgrounds. Settembrini, the rhetorical rationalist and humanist, remains the protagonist of the protest against the moral perils of the Liegekur and the entire unwholesome milieu. He is but one figure among many, however—a sympathetic figure, indeed, with a humorous side; sometimes a mouthpiece for the author, but by no means the author himself. For the author, sickness and death, and all the macabre adventures his hero passes through, are just the pedagogic instrument used to accomplish the enormous heightening and enhancement of the simple hero to a point far beyond his original competence. And precisely as a pedagogic method they are extensively justified; for even Hans Castorp, in the course of his experiences, overcomes his inborn attraction to death and arrives at an understanding of a humanity that does not, indeed, rationalistically ignore death, nor scorn the dark, mysterious side of life, but takes account of it, without letting it get control over his mind.

What he comes to understand is that one must go through the deep experience of sickness and death to arrive at a higher sanity and health; in just the same way that one must have a knowledge of sin in order to find redemption. "There are," Hans Castorp once says, "two ways to life: one is the regular, direct and good way; the other is bad, it leads through death, and that is the way of genius." It is this notion of disease and death as a necessary route to knowledge, health, and life that makes *The Magic Mountain* a novel of *initiation*.

That description is not original with me. I got it recently from a critic and make use of it in discussing *The Magic Mountain* because I have been much helped by foreign criticism and I consider it a mistake to think that the author himself is the best judge of his work. He may be that while he is still at work on it and living in it. But once done, it tends to be something he has got rid of, something foreign to him; others, as time goes on, will know more and better about it than he. (pp. 725-27)

I read a manuscript by a young scholar of Harvard University, Howard Nemerov, called "The Quester Hero. Myth as Universal Symbol in the Works of Thomas Mann," and it considerably refreshed my memory and my consciousness of myself. The author places *The Magic Mountain* and its simple hero in the line of a great tradition that is not only German but universal. He classifies it as an art that he calls "The Quester Legend," which reaches very far back in tradition and folklore. *Faust* is of course the most famous German representative of the form, but behind Faust, the eternal seeker, is a group of compositions generally known as the *Sangraal* or Holy Grail romances. Their hero, be it Gawain or Galahad or Perceval, is the seeker, the quester, who ranges heaven and hell, makes terms with them, and strikes a pact with the unknown, with sickness and evil, with death and the other world, with the supernatural, the world that in *The Magic Mountain* is called "questionable." (p. 727)

The writer declares that Hans Castorp is one of those seekers. Perhaps he is right. The Quester of the Grail legend, at the beginning of his wanderings, is often called a fool, a great fool, a guileless fool. That corresponds to the naïveté and simplicity of my hero. It is as though a dim awareness of the traditional had made me insist on this quality of his. . . .

In *The Magic Mountain* there is a great deal said of an alchemistic, hermetic pedagogy, of *transubstantiation*. And I, myself a guileless fool, was guided by a mysterious tradition, for it is those very words that are always used in connection with the mysteries of the Grail. Not for nothing do Freemasonry

and its rites play a role in *The Magic Mountain,* for Freemasonry is the direct descendant of initiatory rites. In a word, the magic mountain is a variant of the shrine of the initiatory rites, a place of adventurous investigation into the mystery of life. And my Hans Castorp, the *Bildungsreisende,* has a very distinguished knightly and mystical ancestry: he is the typical curious neophyte—curious in a high sense of the word—who voluntarily, all too voluntarily, embraces disease and death, because his very first contact with them gives promise of extraordinary enlightenment and adventurous advancement, bound up, of course, with correspondingly great risks. (p. 728)

Hans Castorp is a searcher after the Holy Grail. You would never have thought it when you read his story—if I did myself, it was both more and less than thinking. Perhaps you will read the book again from this point of view. And perhaps you will find out what the Grail is: the knowledge and the wisdom, the consecration, the highest reward, for which not only the foolish hero but the book itself is seeking. You will find it in the chapter called "Snow," where Hans Castorp, lost on the perilous heights, dreams his dream of humanity. If he does not find the Grail, yet he divines it, in his deathly dream, before he is snatched downwards from his heights into the European catastrophe. It is the idea of the human being, the conception of a future humanity that has passed through and survived the profoundest knowledge of disease and death. The Grail is a mystery, but humanity is a mystery too. For man himself is a mystery, and all humanity rests upon reverence before the mystery that is man. (pp. 728-29)

> *Thomas Mann, "The Making of 'The Magic Mountain'" (originally published in* The Atlantic Monthly, *Vol. 191, No. 1, January, 1953), in his* The Magic Mountain, *translated by H. T. Lowe-Porter (copyright 1927 and renewed 1955 by Alfred A. Knopf, Inc.; copyright 1952 by Thomas Mann; reprinted by permission of the publisher), Knopf, 1958, pp. 719-29.*

ANNA HELLERSBERG-WENDRINER (essay date 1955)

In Thomas Mann the thinker, the mystic, the poet, we see the phenomenon of a man so powerful as an artist that his works gained the admiration of five continents without revealing to the average reader, or to the average critic, the meaning of their contents.

Mann was aware of this fact. In a letter written to me in the spring of 1953 he expressed his agreement with my conviction that the critics have failed to discover the essence of his novels. . . . What then is the hidden meaning of Thomas Mann? He has only one theme: the separation of man from the fertile grounds which condition his existence. His whole vision is of the majestic darkness, the immutable monotony of a mind estranged from truth by a long genealogy of error. He felt that truth exists. He never ceased his search for it. And he died at the age of eighty years without realizing that he had expressed it in his art. (p. 583)

In spite of his failure to understand the ontological scope of his own majestic structures, however, Mann sometimes had lightning-like intuitions of their profundity, especially when he tried to explain to his readers what had emerged from the unconscious regions of his lonely God-bound soul. One day, for instance, he spoke in the Library of Congress in Washington on the leading idea of his biblical novel: *Joseph and his Brothers.* He pointed to the universal, the theological, tendency of this work. "What I had in mind," he said, "was the gradually unfolding detachment from the idea of God as it manifests itself in the succession of several generations."

Abraham's form of inner reality seemed to Mann identical with his nearness to God. The patriarch cherished the ideal that it was of all-embracing significance to discover a Highest Being whom he could serve. The vision of this Supreme Being was not given to him without personal efforts. His longing to recognize it, to approach it, was the reason for his soul's relentless strife. Jacob, representing the second stage of development, appeared to Mann as half-detached. He compared him with the figures of Rodin, still embraced by stone, but slowly emerging to reach out to open space. The subjectivity, the sentimentality, the egocentricity of Jacob's piety stood between him and the object of his reverence.

This sentimental father, with his expansive individualism and the pompous glory of his religious self, clouded the perspectives of his son Joseph, who was endowed with the power of a genius to discover the nakedness, the divine economy in the structure of existence. His genealogy threw him into the void of uncertainty. Here he moved without ground under his feet, with all the might of his eagle-like soul caught up in the storms of fate. He was betrayed by a tradition which had lost its sacred roots. He is the very symbol of twentieth-century man. Mann's Joseph in Egypt, therefore, had to lose himself in the cult of practicality. Cut off from spiritual creativity, he had to exhaust his engineering talents in the realm of economic organization: he became "Joseph the Provider."

Unconsciously or consciously, Thomas Mann represented here different stages in the history of Western thought. The age of the Fathers of the Church, the age of the Protestant revolt, and our present age of anxiety in which the great forces shaping the world are not inside but outside of organized religion—in the religious energies of existentialism, the Te Deum of expatriated Christian souls. (p. 584)

Thomas Mann ascribed to his *Doktor Faustus* an identity of form and content. This judgment is valid not only for this novel: it was the sign under which all of his creations were born. And it is the fundamental criterion of art in its absolute form. The epic technique, which Mann used in his biblical novel, as well as his other works, can be described as an application of the principle of expressionistic abstraction. The design of each of the leading figures has as its functional center one quality of unifying might: namely, the awareness or lack of awareness of its relation to a Supreme Being. Thus we have here the unique example of a poetic power devoted to a single idea as the structural principle of an epic edifice. Perhaps we are able to find in this unique integrity the explanation and justification for the universal success of works which nobody understood.

In the epic technique of reducing the existential pattern of his characters to the nucleus of one unifying quality, Mann found an artistic principle to express the secret functioning of the "Gestalt" of the human soul. . . . Consequently, in his desire to make form and content identical, Mann tried unconsciously to write the eternal poem of the image of God in man. (pp. 584-85)

Most of his critics have seen in him a writer who stands for "Art" in contrast to "Life." . . . Their statement has a certain surface truth but failed to uncover those depths which give Mann his whole meaning.

Life is indeed the object of the poet. But as in all great poetry it is life in its ultimate sense—the Life of the Eternal Mover, the Creator of stars and mountains and men. Art is indeed here in opposition to life. It is not art as such—but the art of our own epoch which has lost the grounds of reality. The hero of *Doktor Faustus* discovered that the decline of modern art was caused by the loss of the protecting and inspiring framework of the Liturgy.

Interest in the structure of being was already awake in the untaught author of *Buddenbrooks,* who, in spite of his external culture, was an intellectually neglected, spiritually starved youth. As in his later biblical novel, the young Mann saw his ancestors in the light of their distance from God. The most impressive characters in *Buddenbrooks,* the third generation—Thomas, Antonie and Christian—clearly represent variations on Mann's one and all-embracing theme, the distortion of reality through the loss of an awareness of ultimate things. Mann interrelated their various deviations from the order of Being to an existential pattern of time-less significance. (p. 585)

The death of Thomas Buddenbrook stands-out in the landscape of modern literature, a symbol of universal significance. It proclaims what Berdyaev calls the fallen image of modern man, and in this image we find the key to Thomas Mann's work. (p. 586)

Anna Hellersberg-Wendriner, "The Essence of Thomas Mann," in Commonweal *(copyright © 1955 Commonweal Publishing Co., Inc.; reprinted by permission of Commonweal Publishing Co., Inc.), Vol. LXII, No. 24, September 16, 1955, pp. 583-86.*

GLENWAY WESCOTT (essay date 1963)

[*The Magic Mountain* has been Mann's] most popular novel (in the United States), and though surely its main theme and setting are unforgettable—pulmonary disease as an exemplification of the human condition in general, Alpine sanatorium as a macrocosm—you may not have kept in mind various details that I attach importance to, or see meaning in; perhaps you have scarcely noticed them, with so much else to notice on every page. It is one of the most minute and florid compositions in all literature, with a forceful sort of homogeneity made up of many small contrasts, with every thread drawn tight, every bit of the colorfulness and the highlights and the shadows in keeping and in order; yet never quite three-dimensional, like an immense millefleurs tapestry.

Do you remember how it starts, in medias res, with the arrival at the International Sanatorium Berghof of a young everyman, Hans Castorp, to visit his tuberculous soldier-cousin, Joachim? Immediately we are provided with a symbol of transitoriness and a suggestion of the disgust of death: he has to wait for his room to be fumigated, because an American lady has just died in it. Swiss altitude and the stimulation of the environment of sick people affect him with a certain inverse hilarity, something like a mardi gras, but with a hint of witches' sabbath. He keeps blushing, and perhaps it is fever; he laughs more than ever, and has bad dreams.

Then in Chapter II the strong skillful narrator turns us around and bids us look at Hans's family background and childhood, a small world of the upper bourgeoisie, rather like that of his first novel, *Buddenbrooks,* presumably not unlike that of the Mann family in Luebeck; in which, however, disquieting themes of the present work as a whole are predicated, foreshadowed: bygone time, which has a tragic or at least harrowing aspect (certainly it must be bad for one, if one ponders it too constantly and intensely); a sense of the relatedness of love and disease;

vaguely homosexual feelings; and a good many inklings of death, death mystical and universal!

For example, there drifts up in Hans's mind, from that half-forgotten life, the similarity, noticed by him at the time, between the odor of his grandfather's corpse laid out in the coffin and the body odor of one of his schoolmates, a somewhat sickly boy; and not many pages later, when Frau Chauchat, the female protagonist of the work, makes her entrance, very exciting to the young bourgeois, what attracts him particularly is her resemblance to another schoolmate, one named Pribislav Hippe. Hippe means scythe, emblem and implement of the Grim Reaper. Liebestod, love-death? No, principally, in this book, it is Liebeskrankheit, love-sickness. For the idea and the point of a sanatorium is to get well, isn't it? This Berghof of Mann's imagination is the very abode of the will to live; simply fatuous and physical in some cases, hopeless in some, systematic and feasible in a few. It is as churning and writhing and jumping with life as a fishpond or a snake pit or a monkey house. (pp. 175-76)

Before we have read twenty pages we realize that despite a Tolstoian gift for details of the human condition, for the texture and pattern of ordinary assorted everyday existence, this is not going to be anything like an eighteenth- or a nineteenth-century novel. In the "Lebensabriss" [biographical sketch], with reference to these preliminary chapters, Mann speaks of "the comfortable English key I began in." Comfortable? English? Sometimes in comments on his own work like this, whether in commendation or the opposite, he seems almost to be joking, enjoying the thought that his readers were apt to believe anything that happened to come into his head. But if this is a joke, it is one that he persisted in year after year; and he would always buttress and back himself up in any whimsicality about his writing by referring to his forerunners in fiction, the blessed hierarchy and peck order of his chosen old masters of novel writing. (pp. 177-78)

Presumably he intended *The Magic Mountain* to satirize certain novels of the past, somewhat as Cervantes did in *Don Quixote;* Fielding and Jane Austen likewise, here and there. Mann's touch in the satirical way is delicate, almost too delicate. Some of his best pages are colored by sophistication and implicit bookishness. In so far as he gives himself English airs, he compensates for this soon enough, with deliberately, self-consciously German effects. When he has waxed lyrical or epical, he offsets it with a sentimental passage or a slight parody or a farcical turn. Though surely nothing in the entire great novel is exactly a laughing matter—with grief and disease ubiquitous, even morbidly glamorous in it—again and again, by the above means and other devices, he induces in us something in the nature of hilarity; a mood corresponding to his young hero's when he first arrives on the mountaintop and is influenced by the altitude: jocund, mystical, slightly hysterical.

In the way of a little further extension of his dualistic habit of mind, he was inclined to a kind of double entendre, but not in the ribald sense. The scene of the love-making of Hans and Frau Chauchat when they have had too much to drink is just a little ribald. Note that during it they converse in French, very Teutonic French.

As a rule the effect of Mann's dichotomousness in his way of writing was merely mockery showing through the earnestness, pathos and gruesomeness interspersed and blended with the pleasurable vitality; two tones at once, as in shot silk, or in certain fine composite minerals, which rather unifies the work, as to its mood and manner.

Its more important structural unity is just the portraiture, a constant comparison and contrast of the denizens of Berghof; crossbeams and cornerstones of the human nature there assembled. Of the mentality and character of his half dozen personages of greatest consequence in the sanatorium, Mann not only gives subtle and powerful, sometimes overpowering explanations, but lets us hear their own self-expression, explaining things to one another, haranguing one another, arguing. (pp. 178-79)

The most astonishing and prophetic of the creatures of Mann's imagination in this novel is an Eastern European Jew named Naphta, orphaned in a pogrom, in which local avengers of Christ crucified his father; adopted, after that, by Jesuits, and given every advantage of worldly and theological education. Despite this, and somewhat in consequence of it, he has become a type of crypto-Communist and proto-Nazi. Catholicism and terrorism mixed, blood lust and dialectics mixed, have made a veritable witches' brew in this man's head, which issues in pages and pages of frightening and sickening talk. "Liberation and development of the individual are not the key to our age," he declares. What it needs, what it is straining to bring about, what must happen to it in due course, is a "moral chaos" and a "radical sepsis" and, in due course, an "anointed Terror." Some such nasty combination of words issues every time he opens his mouth; prescriptions of gangrene, applications of maggots, lancings of things with a rusty knife.

He and Settembrini violently discuss all this for ten or fifteen pages at a time, about a hundred pages, all in Volume II. Political theory, history lessons biased in one way or the other, opposite views of the future of European humankind: their debate raises the tone of the work above the sensationalism and sometimes sordid hypochondria inherent in the subject matter of the tuberculosis life; but at the same time loads it down with what you might call editorializing, ideas that seemingly never develop, never move along with the chronology of the fiction, and cumulatively constitute the great fault of the novel as such, the work as a whole, the narrative per se: its abstraction, volubility, voluminousness.

Very specifically in two chapters, this baptized Jew and this idealistic agnostic Italian between them, conduct an important part of Hans's adult education, the development and expansion of everyman's mind, which is *The Magic Mountain*'s main theme, refrain, and gist: demoralizing devil on the one hand, guardian angel on the other, contending for his soul. (pp. 179-80)

Three quarters of the way through *The Magic Mountain,* Mann introduces a personage even more impressive than Settembrini or Naphta, though less intellectual, less inclined to serious conversation: Mynheer Peeperkorn, a "kingly, incoherent man," a giant and an immoderate drinker, almost an alcoholic. Both in and out of his cups, Peeperkorn personifies the love of life and the joy of living. Before long Frau Chauchat becomes his mistress; and after that he commits suicide, for a reason which Mann seems to find more respectable than the deathward urges of others of the Alpine society: a feeling of the onset of old age, which friendly frequentation of Hans along with their mutual beloved has intensified. (p. 182)

The Magic Mountain is what is (or was) known in German critical writing and textbooks as a "Bildungsroman" or an "Entwickelungsroman," a development novel. Hans does develop astonishingly. Almost at the end of the vast novel—on the penultimate page, to be exact—Mann refers to him as a *simple* soul. Simple, perhaps, in the old primary dictionary meaning: honest and uncunning, but by that time certainly not uncomplicated, not innocent, not ordinary. Mann in his determined way, with almost ostentatious skillfulness, has made him plausible, but hardly (as it seems to me) probable, having conferred upon him an intellect too far-ranging, spiritual interests too cosmic and esoteric. Is there any other protagonist in world literature so well educated, at least well informed, and indefatigably meditative and speculative? Mann's suggestion is that his basic indecisiveness, his inability or disinclination to make up his mind, only adds to the extent and importance of his intellectuality, verging on infinitude, or at any rate, constantly broaching infinite matters. As we read the closing chapters, were it not for the author's strong technique, somehow referring back to the opening chapters every little while, echoing what he has already said, jogging our memories, we might almost forget that this is the same boy who first came to the Berghof: full-fleshed, clean and soft, energetic though phlegmatic, rather sleepy when not excited, red-faced with inhibition and fever.

Frau Chauchat points out to him that, whereas she lives for life's sake, from moment to moment, impetuously and self-forgetfully, what he wants from life is the educative effect, self-realization, self-enrichment; and this difference between them rather vexes her. Within Mann's intellectual frame of reference, as gradually disclosed in the work as a whole, the reader finds this only natural: contrast between male and female, and between Teuton and Slav. Certainly, in the outcome of everything that happens to Hans during his sojourn at Berghof, the aggregate of everything that transpires about him, he gets what she has accused him of seeking.

Let me call your attention to the cultural sophistication of all this, not just a reviving and updating of old pagan religious traditions and myths, Prometheus, Orpheus, Theseus, Tiresias, Oedipus, which has gone on continually in European arts and letters since the Renaissance. In Germany, especially, this has been a more eclectically bookish and artistic epoch than the quattrocento or the cinquecento; also more theatrical and musical. The allusiveness and resonance in Mann's work derived from a whole shelfful of nineteenth-century writers as well as the ancients, and to half a lifetime of concerts and operas. Hans is a variant upon Wilhelm Meister, obviously; he is also Faust, with two Mephistos instead of just one; he is also Tannhäuser, as of Act I, in Venusberg; and once in a while, for a page or two, he is Parsifal. Does not the International Sanatorium Berghof also occasionally remind you of the *Decameron?* Except that the victims of Mann's plague are all up in the castle, not down below in the city; and they do very little of their storytelling themselves. Mann enjoyed his own copious aristocratic language, and would not have trusted any of his dramatis personae to bring out in a colloquial way the iridescent meaningfulness that he saw in them and in their various plights and crises. (pp. 183-84)

The Magic Mountain is an almost perfect example of its type of novel: the group portrait of a little world set apart. In form and structure it corresponds somewhat to Katherine Anne Porter's *Ship of Fools.* But naturally the German great man interprets his world in the philosophical way much more than the American woman of genius does, and sets his worldlings to philosophizing also, as in imitation of their creator. This results in the one notable imperfection of *The Magic Mountain:* its extreme length and looseness, in which one may see some self-indulgence on Mann's part, but which, for him, certainly,

was a matter of aesthetic principle, creative innovation. (pp. 184-85)

Nineteenth-century men and women of genius of the highest rank indulged in a vast amount of expository self-expression in their novels. Perhaps it was more important to Mann to feel that he was being a genius like them, to manifest genius in everything he wrote, than simply to master his form, and to be brief and evocative and expeditious. Indeed I know that there are worse faults than length and complexity. Mann's artistry never, never flagged or fell into ordinary stereotypes. In the totality of *The Magic Mountain,* nine hundred pages long, there are only a few slumps or anti-climaxes, a few pages of complicated violent action a little skimped, and some progressions and retrogressions just synopsized, not rendered; harmless little holes, inconspicuous little blemishes, in the massive construction. I complain of the too much, not the too little. (p. 186)

If, at that stage of his development as a novelist, which was, in fact, the turning point of his art, Mann had been obliged or persuaded or inspired to reduce *The Magic Mountain* to one volume instead of two, he would have . . . sacrificed a vast mass of his marginal, interpretational writing, and a good deal of the abstract arguing of his characters also, and kept every bit of definite time and three-dimensional location and lifelike humanity and interesting action: narrative pure and simple! It could not be reduced in any other way. The superfluity is all in the expository prose. There is not the least fat or gristle or roughage or padding in the story line or the portraiture or the intimate conversation or the passages of poetical or emotional expression. (p. 187)

> Glenway Wescott, "Thomas Mann: Will Power and Fiction," in his Images of Truth: Remembrances and Criticism (reprinted by permission of William Morris Agency, Inc. on behalf of author; copyright © 1963 by Glenway Wescott), Hamish Hamilton, 1963, pp. 164-241.

IGNACE FEUERLIGHT   (essay date 1968)

["Tonio Kröger"] consists of three parts. The first one begins in winter and ends in an "eternal spring" of creativity, the second takes place in spring, and the third in the fall of the same year. The first part is biographical; it extends from Tonio's fourteenth to about his eighteenth year, spent in his native town, and includes some general remarks on his subsequent life in the south. Most of this part is concerned with a walk and a dancing lesson. The second part is laid in Munich in Tonio's early thirties; but the author never explains when Tonio arrived there. What Mann called the lyrical-essayistic center piece is a rather nonlyrical essay in dialogue or monologue form. The third part is a description of Tonio's vacation trip to the north and ends with his letter to Lisaweta. There are no adventures, no plot, and no climax.

"Tonio Kröger" has neither the structure nor the content of a traditional novella. It is mainly concerned with the contrast between art and life, or rather between the artist and ordinary people. Some of Tonio's—that means Mann's—general assertions are contrary to widely held beliefs and open to argument. Art, according to Tonio, is not a profession but a curse. The artist feels that everybody sees in him a marked man. In order to represent human emotions effectively, one has to be extra-human, un-human. . . . As soon as one becomes a human being, one is finished as an artist. Warm and sincere feelings are useless; they only make dilettantes. The artist puts feelings on ice, analyzes them, and renders them calmly. Emotional impoverishment is a prerequisite for creative endeavor. Whenever Tonio's ''heart lives'' (which is not often), he cannot write well. For instance, when on his passage to Copenhagen the stormy sea arouses his old feelings for nature, his whole literary output consists of two verses, poorly rhymed at that. (p. 110)

However, the somewhat self-pitying view that art is self-sacrifice rather than self-fulfillment has nothing to do with social criticism, i.e., with the artist's precarious situation in modern materialistic society. Kröger does not attack society; he longs to be an integral part of it. He is a well-known and apparently well-paid writer and lecturer, and is invited to bourgeois parties. The conflict lies within himself. Not society but the bourgeois within himself causes Kröger's uneasiness, sadness, and bad conscience. His double nature springs from his origin. While his mother, of foreign blood, was sensuous and passionate, his father, the Nordic business man, was dignified, reflective, and puritanically correct. This origin corresponds to that of Thomas Mann's and is symbolized by Tonio Kröger's foreign-sounding first name, derived from his mother's family, and by his native last name.

His father's influence makes Tonio see another negative aspect in the artist's existence. Not only does the artist fail to live genuinely, but his work, so different from that of ordinary citizens, makes him suspect and disreputable. The repeated statement, ''After all, we are not gypsies in a green carriage,'' only proves that deep down Tonio is convinced or afraid that he is a gypsy. And when, in returning to his hometown, he is suspected of being a wanted criminal, he is neither surprised nor indignant.

One can hardly subscribe to Tonio's two charges against the artist; that he does not live and that he is suspect. Quite a few non-artists lack warm, exciting, genuine lives, and quite a few are not always as harmless and sincere as Tonio sees them. Ironically, the exemplar in life for Hans Hansen, the idolized model student, ended as a drunk. On the other hand, many artists—including Mann—found true self-expression and a full life in creativity. Many artists—again including Mann—were also rather conventional and respectable in their private lives and even sensitive and constructive moralists. (pp. 110-11)

Tonio has been wrongly considered a lonely Romantic outsider in search of a friend and a home. It is true that Hans Hansen prefers other boys, that Inge does not care about him at all, and that he tells Lisaweta that he would be proud and happy to have a genuine human friend among non-literary people. But first of all, Lisaweta herself is a non-literary, though artistic, friend. And he also could have any number of friends among the intellectuals, the sensitive, and the ''suffering.'' But for some reason, or, as he thinks, because of the bourgeois in him, he is only looking for the friendship of people who cannot or do not care to understand him, an unusual criterion for friendship. (p. 112)

Much of ''**Tonio Kröger**'' is autobiographical. The native town is not named but, as in **Buddenbrooks**, recognizable as Lübeck. There is, for instance, a Holsten promenade and the Baltic (wrongly the translation has the North Sea . . .). The father is a respected grain merchant, the foreign-born mother plays musical instruments and leaves for the south after her husband's death. Tonio despises school and writes poems. His love of the sea is mystical. His love of Hans and Inge has parallels in

Mann's life, too. He lives first in the south and then in Munich. His vacation trip to Denmark, some of the experiences during the trip, the public library in the old family home, the threat of arrest, the stay at the beach of Aalsgaard, all are taken from Mann's life.

Lisaweta Iwanowna has no model in life and has, therefore, remained colorless. She only gives Tonio tea and cues for his long and all-too-literary talk on literature. The ''passionate and sinful'' years in the south are not autobiographical either. This period constitutes the weakest, at least the vaguest part of the whole story. The ''adventures'' are not specified, no details about the ''exhausting'' life, nor a single day or incident are given. Mann led no ''excessive'' life in Italy prior to the publication of **Buddenbrooks**.

Some elements of the story had already been used in **Buddenbrooks**; for instance the parents, the walnut tree, the fountain, the mystical love of the sea, the decay of the family, the artistic way of life as a sign of the decay . . . , the grandmother's prolonged agony, the river (Trave), the *Kurhaus* (in Travemünde) where little Tonio lives in the summer, the grocer Iwersen, the name Kröger, and the loneliness of the student. To some, Tonio looks like a more robust Hanno. Such a resumption of themes and names is quite common in Mann, especially in his early period. The dancing teacher and his name (Knaak) also occur in another story (''**The Fight between Jappe and Do Escobar**''); the homoerotic love of a fourteen-year old boy appears again in ''**Death in Venice**'' and in *The Magic Mountain*.

The style is often lyrical and rich in alliteration. Sometimes, as in the description of the raging sea, Mann uses onomatopoeia. Occasionally, however, we observe a certain verboseness and fuzziness. The use of the leitmotif, the literal or varied repetition of phrases and sentences, is even more pronounced than in **Buddenbrooks**. It is also felt to be more musical and is perhaps more justified, since the theme of return dominates the story. Tonio returns to his native town, he sees ''Hans and Inge'' again, is once more an outsider at a dance, and relives his old feelings. One of the symbols used in the story is the dance. The social dance means a simple, happy life. Tonio does the wrong thing and is excluded from it. He then has to dance alone the very difficult and dangerous sword dance of art. . . . (pp. 113-14)

''**Tonio Kröger**'' is one of the most popular of Mann's stories. It has endeared itself, especially to young people, because of its adolescent melancholy and yearning, its often provocative statements about art, and its musical lyricism. One of its strongest assets is the impressionist yet tender description of nature, of a wintry day, of trees, of light, and especially of the sea. It was particularly dear to Mann himself. He counted it among his important works. (p. 114)

[''**Tristan**''] is a beautiful and lively novella about the deadly lure of beauty. Gabriele Klöterjahn, the young and lovely wife of a businessman and mother of a vigorous baby, suffers from a respiratory ailment and seeks cure in a sanitarium. There she meets a writer, Detlev Spinell, learns to see things from his aesthetic point of view, is induced by him to play Wagner's *Tristan* on the piano, and dies shortly after. The action begins in January and ends two months later.

The playing of *Tristan* is the climax of the novella, but its title also has parodistic overtones. Spinell, in a way, resembles the legendary lover, since he is an artist and has an affair of sorts with a married woman. However, he does not feel Tristan's passionate love and, instead of being united in death with his Isolde, only brings about, or at least accelerates, her death.

This parody of "Liebestod" is coupled with a satire on the artist, or rather the aesthete. Spinell feels at home only in the realm of beauty; he hates the useful, the practical, the ordinary—in short, "life." At the end, he symbolically runs away from life. He consciously overlooks reality and triviality or "corrects" it in his imagination. He does not really love Gabriele. To him, she is not so much a woman, a human being, as a thing of beauty, which he adores almost mystically from a distance. (pp. 114-15)

Although ["Tristan"] is the main figure of the novella, he is referred to three times merely as "a writer" before the author gives his name and speaks of him as "the writer." Mann obviously treats him with unmitigated irony, which, in a way, is directed against himself. Together with Tonio Kröger, Gustav Aschenbach, and Adrian Leverkühn, Spinell belongs to the line of Mann's lonely artists. He is the only ridiculous and the least talented one. (p. 115)

The novella clearly shows the antitheses which are characteristic of the early Mann. On one side there is health, life, activity, normality, warmth, simplicity, business, usefulness, individuality, sunshine; on the other side there is sickness, death, beauty, dream, spirit, literature, sophistication, music, self-obliteration and night. Since Mrs. Klöterjahn is forbidden to play the piano for reasons of health, the music from *Tristan*, exalting the charms of night, death, and eternity, is the worst possible one for her to select. It is characteristic not only of Mann's musical taste but also of the antithesis night-day that she plays three Chopin nocturnes before *Tristan*.

The style is generally ironic and marked by the use of leitmotifs. The most obvious of these is the strange little vein that arches pale-blue and sickly across Mrs. Klöterjahn's brow. The most curious one, unfortunately lost in the translation, is the seemingly innocuous "übrigens" (by the way), that thrice introduces a sentence stating which of the two doctors is in charge.

There is a complete change in atmosphere and a break in style when Mrs. Klöterjahn plays *Tristan*. Mann has always been a master in knowingly analyzing, as well as poetically suggesting, music. The style becomes rhythmical, exalted, and contains exclamations, apostrophes ("O night of love!"), alliteration, onomatopoeia, rhymes, questions, repetitions, and metaphors. But even this ecstatic climax is used to produce ironic effects. Mrs. Spatz leaves the room because the beautiful music is a deadly bore to her; and the insane Mrs. Höhlenrauch interrupts the music by walking through the room "rigid and still."

The novella reminds the reader of *Buddenbrooks,* especially in the antitheses. Klöterjahn is also a business man from Lübeck, though, as in *Buddenbrooks* and "Tonio Kröger," the city is not named. Like Gerda Buddenbrook, Gabriele is the daughter of a merchant who plays the violin, and she herself is highly musical. *Buddenbrooks* as well as "Tristan" tell of a wintry day with its billions of atoms of light, of a nursemaid in red and gold, and of the transfiguration of an old and decaying bourgeois family through music. The novella shares with "Death in Venice" the connection between beauty and death, with *The Magic Mountain* the sanitarium in the mountains, the authoritarian chief doctor, and the fascination with death, and with *Doctor Faustus* the inhuman artist who is responsible for the death of an angelic person, the importance of music, and the parodistic title. (pp. 116-17)

["Death in Venice"] was first published . . . as a "Novelle" in two installments. Mann had interrupted his work on the humorous *Felix Krull* to write this tragic story.

Gustav Aschenbach, a greatly admired writer over fifty years of age, notices an exotic-looking man at the edge of a Munich cemetery and, out of a sudden yearning for distant scenes, goes to an Adriatic island, but, being disappointed, he leaves after ten days for Venice, where a strange gondolier takes him to the Lido. At the hotel, he sees Tadzio, a Polish boy of fourteen, whose "perfect, almost godlike" beauty he first admires with the "cool approval of a connoisseur" only. Because of an unpleasant wind, the constant sultriness and a foul smell, he decides to leave for a resort near Trieste. But when he learns at the station that his trunk was sent to a wrong place, he returns to the hotel and decides to stay there. He now enjoys the sea and the sun and falls madly in love with Tadzio. Although he later finds out that there is a cholera epidemic in Venice, which the authorities conceal from the public, he does not leave. No longer hiding his passion for the boy, he often follows him through the streets. On the day when Tadzio's family is scheduled to leave Venice, the writer dies on the beach. (p. 117)

Aschenbach's encounter with Tadzio signifies the encounter of intellect with beauty, or spirit with life, an encounter which, according to Mann's views, is bound to be short, unsatisfactory, and fruitless. . . . In "Death in Venice," spirit and beauty have confusing and perhaps conflicting claims, although Aschenbach's personal relationship with Tadzio seems to be unambiguous. Aschenbach offers himself up in spirit to create beauty while Tadzio is a possessor of beauty. . . . This seems to imply an identification of spirit and art. . . . Beauty is the artist's way to the spirit. . . . While this statement may be ascribed to Aschenbach's "dream logic," it must be said that Mann's own views on the relationship between art, life (often identified with beauty or symbolized by beauty), and spirit are rather confusing. In the course of his life, these three concepts seem to have played the game of musical chairs. Sometimes two of them sit on the same chair. (pp. 118-19)

Another relationship confusing to most readers of Mann is that between love and life. Biologically, love springs from life and leads to life; emotionally, it often is life at its liveliest and best. . . . Yet in German Romanticism, in a great part of Mann's *Magic Mountain,* and in "Death in Venice," love is tied up with disease and death. There are several reasons for this "perversion." First, both love and death shatter the frontiers of the individual. Second, Aschenbach's love for Tadzio, like Diane's love for Krull or Castorp's love for Clavdia, is "nothing for life," as Diane says; it has nothing to do with children and marriage.

Third and most important, Aschenbach's death is that combination of love and death which is so dear to some German Romantics and celebrated particularly in Wagner's *Tristan:* the "Liebestod." (p. 119)

Still another relationship which is perplexing to many readers is that between the sea and death. In a speech celebrating Gerhart Hauptmann's sixtieth birthday, Mann asserted that love of the sea is nothing but love of death. . . . One of the "profound sources" of Aschenbach's love of the sea is his "yearning for the unorganized, for nothingness." . . . His urge to go to a sea resort may, therefore, be taken as a symptom of his never completely suppressed yearning for chaos and death. Incidentally, Thomas Mann, Thomas and Hanno Buddenbrook,

Tonio Kröger, Hans Castorp, and Gustav Aschenbach love a land-locked sea—the Baltic, the North Sea, or the Adriatic—not an Ocean. Thomas Mann once said that neither the Atlantic nor the Pacific aroused him as much as a land-locked sea.

The novella or, as some prefer to call it, the small novel is written with consummate skill. There are no extraneous or accidental elements. Words, sentences, and persons often have several meanings, can be interpreted on several levels, and are interconnected in many ways. Mann himself asserted, probably with some exaggeration, that nothing had been invented in **"Death in Venice,"** but he also maintained that even insignificant details are symbolical and that the story has many facets.

Aschenbach himself, for instance, is first the artist per se, whose downfall and death exemplify the impossibility of an artist's ever achieving perfect beauty and dignity. He is also the special type of artist who forgets that art demands dissoluteness as well as discipline, who exerts rigid and cold discipline in the cult of form, and who, therefore, succumbs to frantic dissolution, as if life (or death) were cruelly taking revenge for being neglected. (p. 120)

Tadzio, the handsome but fragile Polish boy of fourteen, means many things, too. He represents perfect beauty, the tantalizing and unattainable goal of a classical writer, or again the projection of the narcissistic tendencies inherent in the artist. He is the boy-god Eros as well as Hermes, Thomas Mann's favorite Greek god, who, among many other things, leads the souls to the realm of death. At the end of the novella, Tadzio is called a *Psychagog*, a leader of souls. It is perhaps not accidental that three of the six letters in his name form the German word for death: *Tod*.

The man carrying the rucksack at the edge of the cemetery, the weird gondolier, and the street singer are, at first sight, different individuals and have different jobs. According to his short autobiography, Mann had actually seen them before or during one of his stays in Venice. But the three have a strange resemblance. With some allowance made for slight deviations, they are of medium height or undersized, thin, beardless, snub-nosed, red-haired, foreign looking; they wear something yellow, have two furrows on their forehead, bare their teeth, and have a strikingly large Adam's apple. They look bold, provocative, or even dangerous. The man whom Aschenbach sees at the cemetery, the man who handles the gondola . . . , and the singer with the strong smell of carbolic acid all suggest the traditional pictorial representation of death.

The three men do not belong to the place where they are seen. They are strangers. The man at the Munich cemetery is not from Munich, the gondolier and the singer are not Venetians. This fact is connected with Aschenbach's emotions. The man at the cemetery makes Aschenbach long for foreign countries. Aschenbach adores a foreign boy, experiences feelings which have been foreign to him, and his wild dream culminates in the homage to the "stranger god." This god, Dionysos, incidentally has some connection with India, from which the cholera came. The three men not only suggest the spell of that which is foreign but also lawlessness and chaos; the man at the cemetery has no visible aim, the gondolier has no "concession," and the singer laughs "as if possessed."

No wonder that the three have also been viewed as projections of Aschenbach's repressed yearning for death or his secret craving for the strange, the forbidden or the chaotic. It is perhaps not accidental that Aschenbach resembles the three

strangers. He is below middle height, beardless, bold ("heroic"), and a stranger. . . . Nor is it perhaps accidental that his name begins with *Aschen* (ashes), a symbol of death. (pp. 121-22)

The novella offers more or less overt connections, double and triple meanings, parallels, and identifications. The title itself is equivocal. It may refer to the death caused to many by the cholera, or solely to Aschenbach's death, or to both.

In spite of the many meanings, connections, and interpretations, and in spite of the richness of the vocabulary and the wealth of images, the style seems firm and direct. And in spite of the frenzied emotions and the terrible plague, the narration is controlled and objective. It is ironical or paradoxical that a story purported to show how low the artist can and must sink, is told with the most elevated art. (p. 122)

The mythology of **"Death in Venice"** is mainly based on the *Odyssey* and on Erwin Rohde's *Psyche*, one of the most influential books on Greek religion. In *Psyche* reference is made to the Dionysian frenzy in Euripides' *Bacchae*. *Bacchae* may have influenced Aschenbach's dream of the orgy and the "stranger God." In Euripides' play, Dionysus comes from Asia and is called a foreigner. The main theme of *Bacchae* is also an important one in **"Death in Venice"**: When a person fights against passions and denies them instead of recognizing them as the essence of life, they will become ugly and destroy him.

The use of Greek mythology, of a hexameter by Homer, of dactylic rhythm, internal Platonic dialogues or monologues in an otherwise realistic story of a twentieth-century writer may seem peculiar. There probably are three main reasons for it. First, Aschenbach . . . is a classical writer and, therefore, may be connected with classical antiquity. Second, the use of ancient Greek cultural elements widens and deepens the story and perhaps raises its conflict to a mythical level. And third, the allusions to antiquity and its different moral and religious standards definitely softened the blow that many readers felt at the time of the publication of the novella because of the theme of homosexuality. Few modern writers before Mann dared to deal with such a topic. (pp. 123-24)

In **"Death in Venice,"** Mann wants to show that the artist's striving toward dignity is doomed to failure. The highly disciplined, aristocratic, and intellectual Aschenbach succumbs to the "irresistible temptation of the abyss," of chaos and irresponsibility. Yet, though it is hardly the height of dignity for a man of fifty to follow a boy of fourteen in the streets for hours on end, or to lean his forehead on the door of the room where this boy lives, it should be noted that Aschenbach never makes a vulgar gesture, never utters a vulgar word, never expresses a vulgar thought to Tadzio. Indeed, he does not even talk to him. Even his last days seem to be ennobled by thoughts of Plato. And his death, unlike that of Thomas Buddenbrook, is marked by dignity: He dies painlessly in the beach chair looking at the beautiful sea and the beautiful boy.

In the *Neue Rundschau*, where it was originally published, and in the **Collected Works** . . . the novella is divided into five chapters. Many a reader might think of the five acts of the traditional German tragedy, since Aschenbach seems to succumb to an inexorably tragic fate. One should not overlook, however, that the aging and tired writer only half-heartedly fights against his doom, that he finally chooses his self-destruction and, above all, that his death and the weeks preceding it do not detract or destroy anything from the excellence of his works, which are the truly great Aschenbach and which will long survive the Aschenbach in the flesh.

"Death in Venice" stands out as Mann's greatest achievement in the genre and as one of the most accomplished German stories of all times. Written in a masterly style, relatively short, but full of ideas, meanings, and overtones, it is a superb narration of the rapid deterioration of a fine and disciplined mind, of love's progress in an aging person, a vivid description of the atmosphere and life in a resort, of mysterious Venice, of the impact of the plague, and an evocation of the ever-present lure and danger of evil and chaos. Though directed against art, it is a tribute to the beauty of the written word, the human body, and the ageless sea.

Mann wrote his short story "Mario and the Magician" . . . while vacationing at a Baltic resort. He utilized the experiences he had some time earlier in an Italian sea resort.

The narrator tells his story to a person who is neither named nor characterized. It is about a "tragic travel experience" which he had while vacationing with his wife and his two small children in Torre di Venere on the Tyrrhenian Sea. The style of the story, however, is never rambling, casual, informal, or hesitant, but literary throughout. The structure is clear and firm: the first part shows the irritating life at the resort; the second, an entertainment which continues and explains the general tenseness. The first paragraph points to the last. (pp. 125-26)

Mario, a shy, melancholy, but friendly waiter, who is known to the family from a garden café, only emerges toward the end, in the last eighth of the story. It is, therefore, remarkable that his name is the first component of the title, preceding even that of the magician. It is as if the author wanted to honor this modest young man, or at least the basic decency which he represents, and to raise him to the rank of a worthy or even superior antagonist of the powerful "illusionist."

It is useful to compare "Mario and the Magician" with the much earlier "Death in Venice." Both stories unfold exclusively, or for the most part, in an Italian resort during the holiday season. In both stories, the general atmosphere is unpleasant, and the stay at the resort should have been broken off. Both "artists" dies at the end. Aschenbach's homoeroticism brings about his downfall, and the kiss which Cipolla forces Mario to give him, perhaps because of a homosexual inclination, is shortly followed by his collapse. Aschenbach's death may be called a "Liebestod," since the beauty of the beloved boy leads him to his death. But Cipolla, who pays with his life for the kiss of a young man, also dies of a "Liebestod" of sorts. In "Mario and the Magician," there are, as in "Death in Venice," names reminding us of classical antiquity: Venere, Mario, Ganymed; there is also a "classic weather" and the "sun of Homer". . . . The inhabitants of Venice live under the threat of an infectious disease, and the Italians in "Mario," too, pass "through something like a disease" . . . , a highly infectious and dangerous one at that: fascism.

In "Death in Venice," the artist loses his extraordinary aristocratic dignity because of the impact of ordinary "life," sex, chaos, and irresponsibility. In "Mario and the Magician," ordinary citizens lose their dignity and their sense of responsibility and reality because of the illusions of extraordinary art. Both stories are indictments of art, although "Mario" is probably more an indictment of fascism. Both are devoid of humor and generally considered tragic; the original subtitle of "Mario" reads "Tragic Travel Experience."

Cipolla is a caricature of the artist, reminiscent of the "marked" men of Mann's earlier stories. He is a hunchback, drinks and smokes excessively, and suffers from an inferiority complex. (pp. 126-27)

But Cipolla is more than just another of Mann's representations of the lonely, unhappy artist who is "different" and who is distrusted by the ordinary citizens. He is violently and outspokenly nationalistic and fascist. He manages to turn almost any topic into a subject of political propaganda. . . . Thus Cipolla is an incarnation of the evil power which ugly fascism held over the masses—especially the young, many of whom were glad to escape from their personal freedom, their individual responsibility, and their sense of reality, in order to follow the commands of the leader and to act as the others did.

Mann may have had the prophetic feeling that the apparently irresistible attraction of fascism could only end in violence. Cipolla's "entertainment," that lasts much too long, as the narrator repeatedly stresses, only ends when he is shot by the young man whose deep and unhappy love he had mocked. The end is a genuine relief for the narrator. Five times he uses the word "end" in the last paragraph of the German original. (pp. 127-28)

[The] novella of a little mountebank's death of 1929 has connections with the short stories about marked men of the 1890's, with "Death in Venice," the great novella of a master's death of 1912, and with the Magic Mountain, the great novel about the education of an average man through disease and death of 1924; but "Mario and the Magician" is, above all, one of Mann's earliest pronouncements against the deadly menace of political mass hypnosis and an overheated and overbearing nationalism. (p. 129)

Ignace Feuerlight, in his Thomas Mann *(copyright ©1968 by Twayne Publishers, Inc.; reprinted with the permission of Twayne Publishers, a Division of G. K. Hall & Co., Boston), Twayne, 1968, 177 p.*

HARVEY GROSS (essay date 1971)

Doctor Faustus shows a great artist and the world he represents succumbing to radical evil. Mann's method, always complex, treats the story of Adrian Leverkühn on many levels; or, speaking musically, in many voices, rhythmic and melodic transformations, and instrumental textures. *Faustus* is biography and autobiography, personal confession, a textbook of musical theory, political and cultural allegory, apocalyptic myth, and high prophetic anguish. Three tercets from the *Inferno* (Canto II) stand on the title-page; we are reminded that we not only begin a journey through Hell but undertake a work which is, in Dante's sense, richly *polysemous*.

We shall keep in mind, then, Dante's scheme of four-fold interpretation: namely, that a text may be read on literal, allegoric, moral, and anagogic levels. The literal level concerns itself with what we read on the title-page, *The Life of the German Composer Adrian Leverkühn Told by a Friend.* The allegoric level concerns itself primarily with the intricate metaphoric implications of music: with Adrian's compositions as a complex symbol for modern cultural reality. The moral is hardly a "level" of *Faustus;* at myriad places Mann strikes through his narrator's mask, loses his cool, and calls down God's thunderbolts on the seducers and traducers of his country. Similarly, anagogy as the concern with typology and "last things,'' and with the relationship of past and present, permeates the book.

I mention Dante's scheme of interpretation but do not use it for lopping or stretching. Mann himself uses it to interpret his story as he tells it. No work of Mann is so agonizingly self-conscious; he writes the critique of Faustus simultaneously with the text. Dante's scheme also brings into prominence the medieval *cantus firmus* moving beneath the book's modern polyphony. Adrian is not Goethe's wide-eyed striver but Marlowe's persistent sinner, the Faust of the Lutheran Reformation. (pp. 178-79)

Adrian Leverkühn enters the musical world of the late nineteenth century and devises a radical restructuring of musical technique. He ''breaks through'' tonal and harmonic expressiveness to new contrapuntal discipline; he overturns the conventional affective symbolism of consonance and dissonance. . . . And in his ''breakthrough,'' in his revolutionary achievement of craft, Adrian returns music to the past. His techniques—his retrograde canons, his weaving of symbolic letters into the musical fabric, his strict forms of variation, and his uses of modal scales and organum—all derive from an earlier period in music history. (pp. 179-80)

Mann pushes and pulls on the question of freedom and determinism. If Adrian is not free to compose except in his radical atonal style, then he is a victim of History. History has used up the art-forms of the previous age; History has brought a hegemony of the word into musical work. From Beethoven's Ninth Symphony to Mahler's *Das Lied von der Erde,* from Wagner to Schönberg's *Gurrelieder,* the word exerted its determining influence on music. From Wagner's *Tristan* to Schönberg's *Verklärte Nacht,* traditional harmony moved through a process of chromatic dissolution toward the eventual abandonment of tonality and key relationships. These developments were required by the nature of music itself, by the demands of structure and technique and not, as the devil reminds us, ''by social conditions.'' Here Mann puts the questionable doctrine of aesthetic fatalism into the devil's mouth. . . . Echoing Nietzsche's prophecy that art in an age of excessive historical awareness becomes self-conscious and *critical,* the devil mockingly consoles Adrian: ''Art becomes critique—something very much worthy of respect, who denies it?'' Mann has, of course, practiced the art of stylistic and mythic parody; he has devoted many pages of his fictional work to exhaustive critique. Is Mann, then, of the devil's party and unaware of it?

We can firmly say that Mann is unaware of nothing. He understands the treacherous appeal to historical process and the supple confusions implicit in the doctrine that says because a thing happened it *had* to happen. (pp. 180-81)

Mann makes it easy for us to understand Adrian's music as the devil's invention, a symbol of totalitarian ideology and its demands for the renunciation of freedom. Mann also suggests Adrian's music is *his* music, a symbol for everything his work stands for: its elaborate thematic structure, its relentlessly critical treatment of culture, its parodistic style. Does Mann, in effect, indict himself in *Doctor Faustus*? Much critical confusion has resulted in attempts to answer this question. We can weakly say, ''yes and no''; invoke the principle of the identity of opposites; talk about Mann's dialectical inscrutability. We come to no secure conclusion if we remain frozen on the allegoric level. But on the moral level Adrian's life and art—that ambiguously savage and utterly spiritual music—may be viewed as expiations for what Germany inflicted on the world.

Evil of the Nazi kind cannot be forgotten, forgiven, or taken back: it can only be atoned for.

We hear Mann's agony on every page. . . . How could the land of Kant and Hegel, Schiller and Goethe, Bach and Beethoven spawn the regime of Hitler, Goebbels, and Streicher; promulgate the blood purges; maintain the ghastly death camps? Who or what was to blame for ''the dictatorship of the scum''? In desperation Mann applies hindsight in a most perilous undertaking: the fixing of historical guilt. The determinism informing Adrian's discussion of music history also torments Mann's arraignment of the German past. He sees the Reformation and its resurgence of medieval demonism making a permanent contribution to the underside of German religious life. He sees Luther's positive acceptance of secular authority contributing to the German passion for obedience, and establishing German political destiny, its drive toward the extremities of revolution and reaction. Mann examines other aspects of German history. *Blut und Boden* [blood and soil] emphasis on *das Volk* inflamed the German tendency toward political irrationalism. Nietzsche, who is everywhere present in *Doctor Faustus,* served the Nazis as an ideological hero. Wagner gave the Nazis a folk religion and a racial theory.

This historical evidence is ''strictly'' composed into the thematic texture of *Doctor Faustus.* On nearly any page we hear a familiar motif, or its expansion, diminution, or inversion. The cumulative effect leaves the reader protesting, as Zeitblom protests Adrian's twelve-tone method, that *Faustus* was already written before Mann wrote it; that he brought no freedom to the book but only followed the strict logic of his musical-dialectical method. And the implication is strong that there is no more freedom in history than in Adrian's music where every note falls into its necessary contrapuntal relationship, ''and no note is free.'' Luther and the Reformation, the German character, romantic-mythic emphasis on the folk, the hammer blows of Nietzsche's critique of all values: all fitted into a predetermined historical context and made the Nazi state an inevitable historical phenomenon.

Thus it appeared to Mann during the years 1943-1946. All the stresses of overwhelming guilt, shame, and despair shaped the apocalyptic fiction of *Doctor Faustus. The Magic Mountain* ends on the battlefields of the First World War; but Mann could imagine some mediation of the historical crisis, a further (although unglimpsed) turning of the dialectical process which would set the world moving toward love and community. The sacrifice of blood would be the necessary tribute men pay—through the release of destructive action—for controlling the demonic. In *The Magic Mountain* Mann stands with the biblical prophets, proclaiming expiation through suffering, tempering words of doom with tidings of possible redemption. After the testing of souls, a new historical chapter can begin. But in *Doctor Faustus* Mann stands with the biblical apocalyptists, facing a radically different situation. It is too late for history to change its course; the apocalyptic message announces ''Creation has grown old.'' The end of time and history is imminent or has already come to pass. In such a predicament men no longer make historical choices. History is now fatality; historical process a deadly movement toward the end of movement. (pp. 182-84)

Mann enforces the apocalyptic thrust of *Doctor Faustus* with three distinct endings. We watch with Serenus Zeitblom as Nazi Germany stumbles into its final abyss of horror; we watch with Adrian as he collapses into paralytic madness—at the end of his allotted twenty-four years; we listen to the end of *Dr.*

Fausti Weheklag, Adrian's last and greatest work, and its cello fermata on high G. Only in Adrian's music—the play within the play—does Mann suggest that the apocalypse might be transcended. This music divests itself of all parody and self-imposed "objectivity"; it returns to new (and old) expressiveness. Here we can say that Mann turns back from the apocalyptic to the prophetic. Here the hope beyond hope, "the miracle which goes beyond belief," offers itself: that turning away from History as irrational force breaking the necks of men, and toward history as the power reestablishing the world. For the true prophet receives those messages which assure men new beginnings are possible and new stages of existence attainable. He does not have foreknowledge of what the future holds, but he urges faith in "a significance for man's way in the world." Of all Mann's works, indeed, of all modern novels, *Doctor Faustus* most deeply questions this significance. But the answer, like Adrian's final cello tone, remains as a light in the darkness. (p. 184)

Harvey Gross, "Thomas Mann," in his The Contrived Corridor: History and Fatality in Modern Literature *(copyright © by The University of Michigan 1971), University of Michigan Press, 1971, pp. 155-84.*

R. J. HOLLINGDALE (essay date 1971)

[*Doctor Faustus*] is a monster: with the best will in the world one cannot love it. 'The great German novel', part melodrama, part collection of essays, part torture-chamber of language, *Doctor Faustus* is full of borrowings—so full I have come to suspect that it is only my ignorance which prevents me from recognizing the original of *every* incident in it. The book is *put together,* a product of the desk and the filing-cabinet. It is airless, horribly airless; it smells of the midnight, and worse of the *midday* lamp; one cannot breathe in it. The old Germany fails to live, it is only brought forth from a lumber room and it smells of must and mould. The worst result—I mean worst from a conventional point of view—is the way in which it cannot endure comparison with what it has borrowed: how Adrian's interview with the Devil cannot endure comparison with Ivan Karamazov's; how its borrowings from the Faust Book cannot endure comparison with the Faust Book itself. But one cannot, for reasons I shall give later, exclude the possibility that these effects were intentional—or at any rate that the pressure of his theme forced the author along just this path: the path of excessive borrowing, of degrading what has been borrowed, of lifeless characterization, and of everything else 'wrong' with *Doctor Faustus*. That it is a 'great' book, an enduring book; that it can justly take its place as the last of the four great monuments Mann erected to his existence—I do not doubt for a moment. It is faulty, to be sure, but it is part of the mystery of art that a work of art can be full of faults and yet worth ten thousand petty 'successes'.

There are signs in the text of *Doctor Faustus* that Mann would have liked to make the *political* implications of his novel simple and direct; but by this date—long before this date—he had become incapable of a simple and direct response to that which was moving towards its conclusion in Europe. If we did not already know something of the complexity of his mind, of its fundamental inability to give a univocal verdict on anything—or at least its inability to do so without having first voiced *other* verdicts, even *counter*-verdicts: if we did not already know that, we should find it very paradoxical that a work apparently intended as a forthright attack and condemnation should be so extremely complicated in structure. *Doctor Faustus* is famously a novel with four or five levels of meaning: a circumstance which would, even if these levels of meaning were totally integrated one with another, militate against any sort of simplicity, directness or forthrightness. But these four- and five-fold significances are *not* thus integrated, they are *put together,* laid one on top of another: is it surprising therefore that, instead of seconding and supporting one another, they are sometimes mutually contradictory? so that, far from being direct and forthright, the novel is thoroughly and fundamentally ambiguous?

The prime cause of this contradiction and confusion is, as is only proper, the Devil—the nihilistic principle, *'der Geist, der stets verneint'*—and the role he plays in *Doctor Faustus*.

On one level, Adrian Leverkühn, the central figure of the novel, is a German composer whose life and career is described by his friend Serenus Zeitblom; on another, he is Nietzsche, inasmuch as the course of his life and that of Nietzsche's are in general and in a very large number of details identical (but he also borrows events from the lives of others, e.g. Tchaikovsky and Hugo Wolf); on a third level, he is the legendary Faustus, who sold his soul to the Devil in exchange for superhuman powers and was at the last taken to Hell; and on the final level, he is Germany, the German people. Now Mann assures us that the fits of rather cold and mirthless laughter of which Leverkühn is sometimes the victim indicate the presence of the Devil. (pp. 45-6)

This is very confusing—quite apart from the question whether Thomas Mann joins with the author of *The Song of Bernadette* [Franz Werfel] in believing in the existence of the Devil. I cannot say that the diabolical presence in Leverkühn's laughter is something that leaps to the eye: but if the Devil *is* intended to be present there, he is going to play the Devil with the 'levels of meaning'! Leverkühn's laughter belongs on level one, the literal level: it is a characteristic of the German composer Adrian Leverkühn. It also belongs on level two, inasmuch as it recalls Nietzsche's exortations to laugh even when there is not very much to laugh about. The Devil, however, belongs only on level three, the Faust level: on levels one and two he does not exist. On the literal level the Devil is something imagined by Leverkühn after his brain has become infected by syphilis. Adrian believes, with Hans Castorp and Naphta, that genius and illness are the same thing, and in that conviction he deliberately infects himself. His subsequent dialogue with the Devil is, as in the parallel case of Ivan Karamazov, a monologue in which he speaks out to himself his own most secret thoughts. The rationale of this aspect of the novel is that the supernatural events of the Faust legend are in reality imaginings, they belong to the mind, and in the life of Leverkühn they are restored to the mind and are all the product of disease. So long as *Doctor Faustus* is faithful to this idea it is not involved in any ambiguity, but is on the contrary very solid work and very imaginative. But this is not nearly enough for Mann. He wants the fictional Leverkühn to represent, not only the legendary Faust, but also the *real* Germany: and this involves him in making Leverkühn the victim of *real* forces, that is forces outside his own mind, with the consequence that the Devil and other elements of the Faust legend are introduced into his biography (the literal level) as real events and in circumstances under which they cannot be merely a product of his mind. Is the Devil in *Doctor Faustus* a real personage, the 'secret hero of the book'? If he is, he can appear during Leverkühn's boyhood—disguised as mocking laughter, inorganic growths, the eccentrics of Kaisersaschern, or in any other disguise—and at any other time or place, and the sense of the novel is that Leverkühn-Faust has literally sold his soul and Germany has done literally the same thing: in this event, however, all those passages in the novel inspired by the idea of restoring the events of the Faust legend to the mind are fundamentally misleading as to the novel's meaning. If the Devil is not a real personage, he cannot appear during Leverkühn's boyhood or at any other time before Leverkühn is infected, nor can he embody himself in anything which is not a product of Leverkühn's imagination, and the sense of the novel is that Leverkühn-Faust has *symbolically* sold his soul and Germany has done symbolically the same thing: in *this* event, however, it is all those passages which suggest the independent existence of the Devil which are fundamentally misleading. The fact of the matter is that the Devil in *Doctor Faustus* is both an independent personage *and* the product of Adrian's diseased brain: which is as much as to say that his role in the novel is fundamentally ambiguous.

The ambiguity and contradictoriness of the 'secret' hero spreads its influence over the whole book, the reason being that one does not know whether the ostensible hero Leverkühn is to be regarded as the author of the catastrophe which strikes him or as merely its victim. If the Devil is a real personage, then Leverkühn (Nietzsche-Faust-Germany) is seduced and destroyed by a force stronger than he and is to be pitied; if the Devil is a figment of Leverkühn's imagination, then Leverkühn (Nietzsche-Faust-Germany) is *himself the Devil*. The point is crucial because it involves the narrator, whose love and admiration for Leverkühn is the supposed reason for the book's existence, in mutually contradictory attitudes towards his subject. Serenus—who when Adrian is Faust is Faust's Wagner, and when Adrian is Germany is Thomas Mann himself—has a hard fight indeed to sort out in his mind whether his hero is the Devil's victim or the Devil himself: in fact, he does not and cannot do it, because his hero is *both at once.* . . . What is the reason for this confusion? It is that Leverkühn's character is framed in accordance with the idea that the Devil is a product of his imagination, i.e. that he is himself the Devil, whereas [certain passages are] consistent only with the idea that the Devil is real, i.e. that Leverkühn is his victim. . . . (pp. 46-9)

The ambiguity of Mann's feelings towards Cipolla is indeed as nothing compared with the ambiguity of his feelings towards Adrian Leverkühn, the very genius of ambiguity. That he exercises fascination is not merely not concealed, it is emphatically insisted on: Dr Watson is not more completely prostrate before the genius of Sherlock Holmes than Zeitblom is before that of Leverkühn. And yet Adrian is entirely possessed and obsessed by 'daemonic powers', lives a life to which, it is hinted, no kind of filthiness is foreign, is incapable of most normal human relationships, sacrifices his friends to his own ego without the smallest tincture of regret, and ends by being transported to a 'private hospital for nervous diseases' where, to judge from his own account of himself, he should have taken up residence long before: and all this is given the character of 'necessity' so that he may compose a number of works which, if Zeitblom's account of them is to be trusted, are of the most questionable quality and whose human and spiritual content is in any case limited to a reflection and repetition of the sickness of soul that has made their production possible. This double image—transcendent genius and spiritual idiot—never coalesces into a single, three-dimensional one: the narrative brings now this into focus and now that, and the reader is left with the conviction that the author's attitude towards this composite figure is altogether indecisive—in short, ambiguous.

What is the implication of all this for the ideological aspect of *Doctor Faustus*? It is, of course, that as social criticism too the novel is thoroughly ambiguous; that Mann's assertion in his book on its origin that 'Hitler had the great merit of . . . calling forth a wholly unequivocal No' is in fact untrue: not, of course, in the sense that Mann was lying, but in the sense that what he says in his book on how he wrote *Doctor Faustus* misreports what he says in *Doctor Faustus* itself; and in that event the novel must, on the ground that what the artist says he said is not evidence, be accounted the more trustworthy witness. As a politician, Mann did say No to Hitler, and said it firmly and often; but as an artist whose subject was the nihilism of contemporary Europe in all its aspects his feelings towards the final expression of that nihilism could not be unequivocal. In any event, they *were* not. (pp. 49-50)

[Mann's] huge mythological novel *Joseph and his Brothers,* which occupied [him] for sixteen years, explains itself over and over again: far from posing as the inventor of the story he is telling, the author speaks as if he were a lecturer addressing a class. It is a tone unlike that of any other novel I have read. The reader is assumed throughout to be completely familiar with the Genesis story of Jacob and his sons: the author's self-imposed task is to elucidate it. The elucidation is so extensive one might suppose that nothing was left unexplained, that the author had forestalled any commentator. Yet, in all this mass of explanation and commentary, he nowhere answers in plain words the two questions which loom largest and which, considering the way in which the novel is written, might have been answered most clearly: what myth? and why Joseph? What myth?—that is to say, what is the meaning imposed on the events described? Why Joseph?—that is to say, what attracted Mann to precisely this legendary figure and his history? (pp. 113-14)

[In all respects] Joseph is a typical Mann artist-nature—but in one respect he differs from all the others except the parodistic Felix: he knows he is inevitably destined for victory. The agonizings of Tonio, Adrian's devil-pact, the despairings of Gregory, are not for him: he is born 'chosen', he inherits 'the blessing' and he lives blithely on in the consciousness that, whatever accidents may befall him, he must in the long run come out on top. Even at the bottom of the pit he experiences no doubts on this head: he merely comes to think he has misjudged the speed of his success because he has underrated—or, perhaps failed to take into account at all—the effect his evident superiority and self-confidence would have on other people. As a result of this experience he learns to exercise a degree of cunning and concealment; and thereafter he never suffers a comparable reverse again. When he is sent down into the pit a second time—his removal to prison at the instance of Potiphar's wife—his mood is one of perfect composure: he knows quite well that nothing can really harm him. For this reason—and herein lies the key to him—he is irrepressibly cheerful, and thus the whole book too is cheerful.

Joseph, 'the man of the blessing', is the light side of Mynheer Peeperkorn, just as Cipolla had been his dark side: the self-sufficient force of personality which on the magic mountain was able effortlessly to dominate exhausted reason and virtue and for a time to raise the other inhabitants of that domain above their normal level of existence. As such, he is the type of mythological hero understood today by the term 'superman'; the genius of light to whom everything is easy. It is a myth which received great impetus from Nietzsche, although he, of course, did not invent it, and his 'superman' is a precisely defined conception differing in essential respects from the popular idea of it. Joseph resembles Nietzsche's superman only in so far as he resembles Goethe—a point we shall come to in a moment. As an individual his 'herodom' consists in his being an instrument of the Divine Purpose: it is this which ensures his eventual triumph. God is a major personage in the novel, but he is not recognizably the God of any known religion: perhaps he resembles the Lord of the Book of Job and thus the Lord of the prologue to *Faust,* who is modelled on him, more than he does any other God; but his relationship with the Heavenly Host and with mankind is so peculiar and, in the last resort, so lacking in anything 'godlike', that one is driven into regarding him as an intellectual construct put together by a very ingenious mind which is seeking to reconcile and represent contemporaneously in one person the differing, conflicting and evolving ideas of God present in Biblical and Egyptian mythology. Since his author also introduces the idea of evolution itself into him, so that, in addition to being an amalgam of differing conceptions of godhead, he is also and at the same time evolving into the God of Abraham, Isaac and Jacob; and since it is in addition suggested that these human actors are in some sense the creators of the God they subsequently worship, who, after they have created him, assumes discrete existence—I leave it to you how much credibility is left to him. As theology the novel is fantasy and phantasmagoria; and what 'purpose' this literally unbelievable divinity is working out through his 'Chosen Seed' I, at any rate, am unable to reveal. But does that matter? Only in so far as the elaborate but in the end unconvincing mythological machinery serves to obscure the actual myth. 'Divine Purpose' can here only be the mode in which the hero, the 'superman', expresses to himself his sense of invincibility. Of any coherent, comprehensible 'purpose' in God's behaviour there is not the remotest sign; God himself is neither coherent nor comprehensible; what *is* clear, comprehensible and consistent is the hero's sureness of step and certainty of victory, his inner poise, the security and infallibility of his instincts, and, as a consequence of this, his enjoyment of existence. Joseph's *cheerfulness* is the key to his conception of Divine Purpose: he trusts in the goodness of God, and believes he is chosen by God, because he feels happy on earth—he explains his happiness by a myth. This method of explanation is, of course, the one adopted throughout the Old Testament: when the nation prospers, it means God is pleased; when the nation suffers, it means God is displeased. That is how the Jews gave meaning to their prospering and suffering; and this, in a novel which ransacks Old Testament myth for both its machinery and its meaning, is how the hero gives meaning to his state of permanent well-being. The myth of *Joseph and his Brothers*—the meaning manufactured by that novel—is the myth of Divine Purpose, the brute fact which the myth seeks to give meaning to is the hero's cheerful invincibility. Joseph, as Mann discovered and interpreted him, is the artist happy and victorious; the huge dramatized lecture in which the story of Joseph is simultaneously unfolded and commented on, is a celebration and explanation of this state of being. (pp. 115-17)

> *R. J. Hollingdale, in his* Thomas Mann: A Critical Study *(copyright © 1971 by R. J. Hollingdale), Bucknell University Press, 1971, 203 p.*

MARTIN SWALES (essay date 1980)

Buddenbrooks has as its subtitle 'Verfall einer Familie'. This decline consists in an ever-increasing incapacity for practical affairs, for energy, for self-assertion, which is accompanied by a growing inwardness, by a susceptibility for experiences that obliterate—or at least challenge—the social (religious scruple, philosophy in the Schopenhauerian mode, music in the Wagnerian mode). The narrative voice conveys both the substantiality of the social world, and the sheer urgency of the awakening inner life. And the narrative stance is a particular mixture of sympathy and detachment which involves showing and comprehending—rather than judging. All of which is not to imply the withholding of criticism. For Mann, through his narrator, is able to imply a critique both of the family brutality and of the unfocused voluptuousness of the rootless inner life. Such narrative judgment—and the balance that goes with it—is central to the whole novel, to its historicity in aesthetic terms (as marking a vital transition from the realistic mode to the more inward mode of the twentieth-century novel) and to its historicity in thematic terms (as achieving a profound historical understanding of the decline of a whole 'bürgerlich' ethos).

T. J. Reed has shown in his superlative book that this notion of 'Decline'—'Verfall'—partakes of that psychology of decadence which was current at the time when Mann was writing. Moreover, it has specifically to do with Nietzsche whom Mann was later to describe as 'der unvergleichlich größte und erfahrenste Psychologe der Dekadenz' (incomparably the greatest and most experienced psychologist of decadence). . . . Nietzsche stridently defended life against knowing, and it is one of the quirky yet strangely moving aspects of his philosophy that he desperately attempted to subdue the thinking mind, to drown his lucid, aphoristic, irreverent prose in the heavy organ-notes of conviction and affirmation. *Buddenbrooks* is, then, permeated with Nietzsche: not only in its theme ('Verfall') but also in the handling of that theme, in that ambivalence which notes the mindlessness *and* the admirable vitality of the early Buddenbrooks, which notes the critical intelligence *and* the dreadful debility of, say, Christian and Hanno.

Now, to comment on the philosophical 'content' of the novel as I have done is to discuss an aspect which clearly is of major importance in the understanding of this text. But one must not conclude that *Buddenbrooks* is, as it were, concerned simply to put across a philosophical message or system by the (didactic) means of the novel form. For the importance of the 'philosophy' in this novel—of its whole intellectual framework—is not that it raises questions of timeless (i.e. universal) import, but that, for Thomas Mann, the changes in the Buddenbrook family are changes in the historically evolving capacity for consciousness of a German burgher family, and in this sense the reflectivity, the 'philosophy' interlocks with the psychology of the characters, with the epic, leisurely, circumstantial depiction of family life. . . . [In *Buddenbrooks*], the metaphysics are profoundly to do with the kind of thinking, the kind of mind, that was possible in nineteenth-century German society. (pp. 18-21)

Moreover, the 'philosophy' in Mann's novel is not simply expressed in moments of thoughtfulness, of narrative reflection: it is present in so much of the novel's specificity, in Tony's phrase about 'die Dehors wahren' (keeping up appearances), in the details of Thomas's dress and outward behaviour, in the corrosive tension between Thomas and Christian, in the latter's almost erotic relationship to his own bodily disorders, in the deliberate incomprehension with which Thomas treats Hanno. (p. 21)

How much, then, does this novel tell us about history and society? One thing is clear: Mann did not set out to write about social and political change. We know that the initial project was for a brief story about Hanno, and that it was an approach from the great German publisher, Samuel Fischer, which converted the account of the 'sensitiven Spätlings' (sensitive latecomer) . . . into a weighty novel about the family, the prehistory of that latecomer. *Buddenbrooks* would seem, then, to be located in Thomas Mann's personal concerns (with art, with his own family background). Yet generations of readers have felt that the novel was not 'merely' about local, private concerns. What Mann captures is the waning, not just of one family, but of a whole complex social ethos. For the notion of 'being a Buddenbrook' involves a number of things: a sense of family dynasty, a capacity for business acumen, a position within the civic life of the community (as Consul or Senator), and a respect for moral and religious values. Now, for the early Buddenbrooks, these various strands interlock in unproblematic harmony. But the inwardness of later generations is both the expression—and in part the perception—of the unworkability of this ethos. And the attempts of later Buddenbrooks to maintain the continuity prove ever more doomed (as the repeated 'Leitmotive' in the text show: their recurrence expresses both the continuity and the growing hollowness of the attempts at maintaining such a continuity). . . . [This social ethos] expresses a consonance between effective commercial effort, money-making on the one hand, and the moral conscience, the life of the inward spiritual man on the other. But the 'Decline', the growing inwardness of the Buddenbrook family, derives from and helps to create the gulf between these two spheres. (pp. 25-6)

Buddenbrooks is magnificently all of a piece: the metaphysical theme *is* also the social and historical theme. The ideas are inseparable from the substantial existence which they lead in the social and psychological lives of the characters. (p. 28)

In its first conception, *Der Zauberberg (The Magic Mountain)* . . . was intended as a brief, humorous counterpart to *Der Tod in Venedig* [(*Death in Venice*)]. Gradually, however, the material expanded in weight and implication under the impact of the war years. (p. 47)

Der Zauberberg tells the story of a somewhat ordinary young man, Hans Castorp, who leaves his home in North Germany in order to spend three weeks with his cousin Joachim who is a patient in a Swiss sanatorium. Castorp prolongs his stay on being told that he himself is suffering from a mild tubercular condition, and he finally becomes so fascinated with life in the sanatorium that he stays on for seven years. (p. 52)

One particular problem confronts us [when reading *Der Zauberberg*]: what, precisely, happens to Hans Castorp during his seven-year stay at the sanatorium, does he get anywhere, does he develop? On closer examination, we seem to be dealing with contradictory evidence. On the one hand, there are undeniably moments of insight, high points where Castorp seems to grow and mature; on the other hand, these moments of achievement seem to disappear without trace. We must look, then, in detail at the process of interaction between the hero and the world of the sanatorium which yields the narrative substance of this novel. (p. 53)

The sense in which the sanatorium represents a world of extremes is suggested at several points in the novel: it is a world that makes the intellectual more purely cerebral because there are no everyday practicalities which deflect the patients from their endlessly pursued thoughts. The 'Berghof' is also a world which makes the physical more purely physical in that sickness tends to foster an unremitting interest in the workings of the body as vital arbiter of character and destiny. The 'Berghof' is, then, for Castorp a rarefied world which allows extreme positions to exist in the hermetic ambience of an—as it were—experimental situation. It is this invitation to experiment with values, ideologies, principles, which provides our hero with a sense of discovery, of openness to varieties of experience which the practical world of the 'flatlands' cannot vouchsafe him. (p. 54)

When Hans Castorp arrives on the 'Berghof', he is confronted by extreme figures, extreme in the sense that they stand for one particular, circumscribed human possibility. As Castorp falls under their sway, he reflects on the values which they represent, values which are latent within him. Yet in the process of confronting these various values, he comes, strangely, to apprehend not the rightness of one value-scheme, but the human totality of which such schemes are but a part. These glimpses of wholeness—they are intimations and no more—constitute the moments of insight and growth to which I have already referred. There are at least four such moments which are important. The first grows out of Castorp's interest in medicine (in the chapter entitled 'Forschungen'—Researches). Castorp gains in answer to his question 'what is man?' a number of insights: that the living process is, in chemical terms, identical with the process of death and decay (it is oxidation in both cases, except that, in the living process, the organic form renews itself). Castorp reflects that this chemical process is the necessary precondition of man's being—and of his whole capacity for thinking, speculating, philosophizing. . . . Insight, intellectual understanding, then, is a function of the material constitution of man: it can, in consequence, never fully understand the process of which it is a part, because it cannot stand outside the context of its own functioning. What Hans Castorp perceives is the complex totality of man's being and experience. And this perception relativizes the 'extreme' positions of so many of the 'Berghof' mentors: it illuminates the partialness of Peeperkorn's vitalism that cannot acknowledge death, it reveals the hollowness of Settembrini's monolithic rationalism and optimism, the untenability of Naphta's attempt to divorce mind, consciousness from the physical living process. Yet this insight, for all its importance, fades from Castorp's mind.

The second—thematically similar—moment of insight comes in the chapter 'Totentanz' (Dance of Death) where Castorp decides to take an interest in the dying patients in the sanatorium, to visit them, to offer formal expressions of sympathy and condolence. Form itself is one of the key themes of the novel: Castorp has learnt in his medical inquiries that the preservation of organic form is what distinguishes living from dying. Form is also central to the medical profession itself—doctors formalize by means of latinate categorizations the multifarious possibilities of sickness. Thereby they answer the process of dissolution, decay and loss of form by strict formality. Form, Castorp learns, is at the heart of any humane morality, for human dignity resides in the ability to know of the abyss and to answer it with form, with ceremony and observances.

Once again, however, Castorp fails to hold fast to what he has learnt. Moreover, the theme of form itself does not remain a stable value, an unambiguous key to human wholeness. For the notion of humane form is relativized by the references to Spanish Court etiquette where form is seen to imply a schematization of human behaviour to the point of lifelessness. Moreover, as Hans Castorp blunders through the swirling snowflakes in the chapter 'Schnee' (Snow) he reflects that the snowflake in its total formal perfection represents a *deathly* perfection, an order to which all dynamics and flux have been sacrificed.

It is in the chapter 'Schnee' that we find one of the major points of insight of the novel. Castorp loses his way in a blizzard, and as he sinks into a slumber, close to death, he has a dream of perfect humanity, of the 'Sun People' who live a life of sensuous beauty and ordered, serene social intercourse, while yet knowing of the dark, mysterious horrors embedded in the very heart of man. From this vision Castorp concludes that all the warring opposites, all the antagonistic values which have been so much part of his 'Berghof' experience hitherto, do not prove the fragmentariness and dislocation of man: rather, all these opposites are the function of—and hence are encompassed by—what is ultimately a coherent human wholeness. . . . Here, then, we come to the italicized message of the 'Schnee' chapter, one which involves the all-important vision not only of human but of *humane* wholeness. Strangely, however, when Hans Castorp does manage to find his way back to the 'hochzivilisierte Atmosphäre des "Berghofs"' . . . (the highly civilized atmosphere of the 'Berghof'), he forgets both the substance and the import of his dream of humanity.

The fourth point of insight comes in the chapter 'Fülle des Wohllauts' (Richness of Harmony) where we learn of Castorp's fascination with certain pieces of music of which there are gramophone records available in the sanatorium. There is one piece which he cherishes with a particularly intense and yet also sceptical love. It is a song, the 'Lindenbaum'. The song, we learn, has a simple strength, a kind of folksy sturdiness. But it is a song in praise of death, for it centres upon that peace which promises ultimate release from care and stress. . . . Here, clearly, we sense Hans Castorp's significance as a representative German. . . . For what is at issue is the powerful hold of the irrational, of longing for death, over the German imagination. Hans Castorp is in part in love with this spiritual attitude—hence his fascination with the sanatorium, but he is also sceptical about it. The 'Lindenbaum' represents *a* world: but it is not *the* world. Death, Castorp has recognized before, should not be allowed to possess man's thoughts: goodness and love should be affirmed as the necessary (moral) concomitant of human wholeness and distinction. . . . And yet, as before, the lesson is allowed to evaporate as Hans Castorp stays on in the increasingly petty, irritable atmosphere of the sanatorium. And in the closing scene of the novel, he goes into battle with the 'Lindenbaum' on his lips: of critical reserve there seems to be no trace. Does death assert its hold over Castorp's mind at the last? Is the humane love, which he has glimpsed, a utopian vision, apostrophized by the narrator in the closing sentence, yet nowhere near being realized?

All of this is, of course, to raise again the question of Castorp's development (or lack of it). Our narrator frequently asserts that Hans Castorp is 'mittelmäßig'—mediocre. But we must understand this epithet not only in a negative, i.e. patronizing, sense. The hero is mediocre in that he is the 'middle way' (the 'Mittel-maß') in which all extremes, all exclusive values, ideologies are present. This gives Castorp his curiously dominant stature in the novel; his very indeterminacy makes him the 'Sorgenkind des Lebens' (problem child of life). It also explains why he—more than any of other characters—should occasionally glimpse the truth of human and humane wholeness.

But *Der Zauberberg* shows that such a truth cannot be possessed as a once-and-for-all insight, as a convenient recipe for right

living. Moreover, it is also suggested that man cannot achieve a straightforwardly definable goal which would allow him to enact this wholeness in outward, palpable terms. And this remains true on two levels: in a philosophical sense, activity is seen by definition to involve a restriction of the complex, potential self (the 'middle way') to a series of finite, circumscribed deeds and choices; and in a practical sense, the world which Castorp inhabits, the sanatorium, and ultimately the carnage of the First World War, is anything but an experiential context which allows the wholeness of man to be externalized in action. Hans Castorp, like so many 'mediocre'—i.e. average—men of his generation, ends his life as cannon fodder.

There is one final aspect of *Der Zauberberg* which needs to be clarified, and this is its whole relationship to the German tradition. [*Der Zauberberg*] was first conceived within the context of Mann's allegiance to that Romantic, anti-Western tradition which he had explored and vindicated in the *Betrachtungen eines Unpolitischen*. But in the course of writing the novel, Mann's awareness of his own intellectual roots changed in response to changing historical circumstances. What began as a validation of the 'magic mountain' of the mind yields to the urgent sense that its inherent values had dangerous political implications. Yet what Mann offers is not simply a repudiation of his own intellectual traditions, not simply a didactic novel. Instead, he takes up a particular artistic mode which will allow him to argue that, in cultural terms, the humane thoughts about man were demonstrably embedded in the German cultural tradition, just as he also suggests, in the vision of the 'Sun People', that the kind of human possibility which he is affirming is a legacy from the most illustrious and ancient of sources, from the classical world—hence the mediterranean landscape, the classical temple. This is Mann's answer . . . to Nietzsche's darker, more stressful vision of Greek humanity in the closing paragraph of *Die Geburt der Tragödie*. The particular novel mode which Mann employs is that of the *Bildungsroman*. This is a type of novel which has its roots in the late eighteenth century, in the 'Humanität' that is linked with Goethe's Weimar. It is a novel concerned with the leisurely growth and cultivation of the individual, with the animating force of concepts involving the whole man, human totality. The *Bildungsroman* is by no means an unproblematic genre: it is concerned with the elusiveness of the complex self, with the tensions between activity and cognition. In one sense, Mann operates with superb, probing subtlety within this tradition—in his concern for the protagonist as 'middle way', in his insistent awareness of the volatility and impermanence of moments of insight and understanding. But this is not all: for Thomas Mann also implies a critique of the German tradition of the *Bildungsroman,* he implies that its 'humanity', while an admirable legacy, has paid too little attention to practical affairs, to politics, to society. . . . It also implies that 'ideas' are to do with 'things', that man's consciousness is vitally interlocked with the society he inhabits. From this it follows that the spokesmen on the magic mountain express values (the on occasion facile liberalism and rationalism of Settembrini with his progressive projects to eliminate human suffering, the sickly mysticism of Naphta with its sinister, cultic overtones, the pathetic, overheated vitalism of Peeperkorn) which are not timeless, freefloating intellectual concepts, but which are part and parcel of a historical world—of pre-1914 Germany. Such values, it is implied, were articulated with a kind of hermetic insouciance, without any real awareness of that social world which moulded them and which was, in its turn, moulded by them. Both the kind of values and the way in which they were debated had to do with that society which moved headlong into the carnage of the 1914-18 war. This is Mann's criticism of his cultural heritage, then, a criticism which, like Castorp's doubts about the 'Lindenbaum', involves scruple, conscience—but also, of course, a profound love. . . . *Der Zauberberg* exploits all the subtlety, the elusiveness and the allusiveness of the *Bildungs-roman,* while seeking to make it support certain commitments to which it had been less than responsive. The result is not a cautionary tale about the dangers of German inwardness, nor is it an exercise in cultural self-congratulation. It offers both allegiance and critique: and this gives the novel its historicity within the German tradition. Moreover, that historicity is the correlative of Mann's growing awareness of his own culture's responsibility for (and before) history. (pp. 55-63)

Thomas Mann's creative output during the 1930s is dominated by two major works, by the Goethe novel *Lotte in Weimar,* and by the sequence of four novels known as *Joseph and seine Brüder (Joseph and his Brethren).* What is remarkable about both projects is that they offer humane, conciliatory, indeed friendly variations on Mann's characteristic themes—and this at a time of great personal distress and of ever deepening political horror in Germany. Viewed in this context, both projects emerge clearly as an answer to the inhumanity rife in Germany. (p. 65)

In the *Joseph* novels . . . we have a hero who is a 'Künstler-Ich', an artist figure. Joseph has the unease, the disquiet, the self-awareness of 'Geist', all the handmarks of spiritual election in Mann's work, yet it is a distinction that co-exists with an ability to engage in practical work, in politics. . . . [In this figure,] we have a man of spiritual distinction who does not disdain the demands of progressive work in the service of society, we have awareness, 'Geist', without the curse of in-activity and metaphysical attrition. (pp. 66-7)

[Volume I of the tetralogy, *Die Geschichten (The Tales of Jaa-kob),*] tells how Jaakob manages to win the birth-right from Esau, how he lives for seven years in a foreign land, serving Laban in order to acquire Rahel as his wife. On the day of his marriage he is tricked, and finds that he is married to Leah. But he manages to get his own back by stealing Rahel, and she it is who is Joseph's mother. At one point Jaakob speaks to Joseph of his uncertainty about God's purposes, and he recounts a fearful vision he has had of himself failing to meet God's demands: God has demanded that he, Jaakob, sacrifice his son Joseph, but Jaakob's nerve fails him at the last minute. Joseph coolly says that his father should not have stopped when he did, because he already knew what the outcome would be—because it all happened before in the story of Abraham and Isaac. . . . But Jaakob lacks the serenity of his son and continues to feel that he has failed in some sacred test of spiritual courage. Joseph renews the attempt to console his father, pointing out that he (Jaakob) was in a different position from Abraham precisely because he knew the terms and outcome of the test—he knew the myth, he knew God's purposes. Moreover God knew that he knew all this. . . . Here we reach the centre of Joseph's character, and the centre of the novel tetralogy. Joseph is a uniquely self-conscious hero in the sense that he knows the plot in advance of the events that befall him. Yet his sophistication does not blight his ability to enact the 'Kreis-läufe', the recurring patterns that form his destiny. Part of him is, as it were, narrator to his own selfhood, divine onlooker on his own experience. And the narrator, with a self-con-sciousness worthy of his protagonist comments on his own God-like presence in the tale he unfolds. . . . God is a benev-olent novelist who has taken the main character into His con-

fidence. And the main character is indeed blessed from the heavens above and the depths below: he can accept his allotted role because it is, by any standards, a good part that is written for him, a particularly engaging mixture of divinity and ef-frontery. There is no sense that such a life is somehow too inauthentic, too unstrenuous to be of significance. And the narrator, in telling his story, will maintain a tone of high, urbane irony: that of latter-day (post-Freudian, post-Jungian) myth-maker whose knowingness enhances rather than devalues the experiences he has to recount. . . . (pp. 70-2)

Volume II of the novel sequence, *Der junge Joseph (The Young Joseph),* tells of the enmity that develops between Joseph and his brothers: the latter vent their hatred by beating their brother and casting him into a pit. Joseph realizes how egocentric he has been, but he also notices the Hebrew word used by his brother Reuben to designate the pit: Bôr. It can mean a number of things—well, prison, underworld, the Kingdom of the Dead. Joseph knows with all the promptings of his mythical con-sciousness that he will rise again after three days and be reborn into a new life. This knowingness is inseparable from his grief, and it makes possible its transcendence at the moment he is experiencing it. . . . What was anguish to Tonio is a source of comfort to Joseph. Joseph's tears . . . in the pit prefigure the tear he will shed much later in his story when he is finally reunited with his brothers. Joseph is, of course, rescued from the pit by Ishmael: his emergence, stained and befouled, is like a birth, and once again the mythical pattern repeats itself. (pp. 72-3)

The third volume of the tetralogy, *Joseph in Ägypten (Joseph in Egypt),* tells the story of Joseph's coming to Egypt. He becomes the servant of Potiphar, and gradually advances in favour. But Mut, Potiphar's wife, falls desperately in love with him: as she is unable to seduce him, she incriminates him by grabbing his coat and then bringing a public accusation of attempted rape. Joseph is sent to prison once again. The hero descends—but only to rise again. It is spring when he is sen-tenced: just as the seed is put into the ground and dies in order to be reborn, so Joseph eventually is released and rises higher than before. In the final part of the cycle, *Joseph der Ernährer (Joseph the Provider),* he interprets Pharaoh's dream of the seven cattle and the seven ears of corn, and is rewarded for his prophetic skill by being appointed to the principal admin-istrative office in Pharaoh's kingdom. His brothers arrive from Canaan to buy corn: Joseph makes them go back for Benjamin, the youngest. Finally, in an extraordinary moment, com-pounded equally of theatricality and tenderness, Joseph reveals himself to his brothers. (pp. 73-4)

So ends Thomas Mann's largest fictional work. It is an ex-traordinary achievement, learned, circumstantial, serene, comic, a conciliatory epic of mankind. When, in the last volume, our hero consoles Benjamin for the loss of his brother, he says that the grave is not so final: . . .

the stone has been rolled away.

The reference to Christ's resurrection is, of course, unmistak-able. On frequent occasions the narrator does what Joseph does at this moment: he makes the link between the Old Testament story and Christianity. He does so with the knowingness of a Christian narrator, of a voice which, as it were, knows the sequel. And to know the sequel, in these novels, is the par-ticular attribute of Joseph *and* of the narrating voice. God turns out to be a novelist with a monopoly of the good stories. [The passage where] Joseph, on his way to Egypt, reflects that Jaakob will believe the blood on the coat of many colours to be his son's . . . is characteristic of the *Joseph* novels in that it attempts to close the gap between particular experience (what something is) and general patterns of significance (what something means). What it also does, of course, is to associate with the great Judaic story of Joseph the Christian story of Our Lord's Passion. It associates them and seeks to conciliate between them. Moreover, it also mediates between the two principal strands of Western European Christianity, between Catholicism and Protestantism by suggesting that one of the profound doctrinal issues that divides them (whether in the eucharist the bread and wine *are* the body and blood of Christ, or whether they *represent* the body and blood of Christ) is ultimately—within the univ·rse of *this* divine novelist—a non-issue.

I have dwelt on the references to Christianity because I think it is important to remember the time in which these novels were written. . . . This is the period when the Jews suffered the most appalling persecution at the hands of a Christian country, Germany. It is striking that when Mann at this time seeks to write a conciliatory epic of mankind he should take up as the vessel for this sophisticated, ironic humanity a Jewish story. Moreover, we must remember that in his treatment of the Joseph story Mann attempts to reconcile the individual and the typical, the interesting and the recurrent, modernity and prehistory, psychology and myth. Once again one must recall the 1930s in Germany with their repudiation of the intellect as 'zersetzend', of psychology as decadent, with their archaizing, regressive use of myth and mythical consciousness. In Nazi Germany myth was synonymous with primitivism. In the *Joseph* novels myth is married to sophistication, urbanity, self-consciousness. In Nazi Germany myth was nationalist, exclusive, suffused with cultic irrationalism: in Mann's novel sequence myth makes possible a universal, tolerant, syncretic consciousness and intelligence. Above all, in [the *Joseph* novels] . . . Mann creates, as I have already implied, [a figure] whose spiritual distinction is not bought at the price of repudiating the friendlier thoughts about man and his destiny. (pp. 74-6)

Martin Swales, in his Thomas Mann: A Study *(© 1980 by Martin Swales), Rowman and Littlefield, 1980, 117 p.*

ALFRED KAZIN (essay date 1981)

Thomas Mann was not just one of the greatest writers of our time; he was also one of its luckiest, most honored, best rewarded—and stuffiest. He was the most famous German novelist of the century, and as he said with typical modesty and accuracy when his famous first novel, *Buddenbrooks,* was published in 1900 (he was 25), he alone brought the German novel into world literature. . . .

It was in America that the already towering author of *The Magic Mountain* went on to perhaps his most significant work—the tetralogy *Joseph and His Brothers.* The complicated often profound *Doctor Faustus,* although not readily admired here, was a penetrating allegory both of the "superior" artist (like Thomas Mann) and Germany's own pact with the devil. Mann wrote me that he was astonished that the book elicited "so many yawns." (p. 70)

[This] immensely dignified personage, born into a wealthy North German merchant family whose decline he so unforgettably detailed in *Buddenbrooks,* this devoted husband and father of six children wrote the most famous story in modern times of homosexual attraction, *Death in Venice.* Mann claimed that for Gustav von Aschenbach—the much honored and haughtily solitary man of letters who dies of cholera in Venice because he is too obsessed with a Polish boy seen playing on the beach to leave the plague-ridden city—he borrowed some traits from the composer Gustav Mahler. He borrowed even more from his own public persona and the fascination with prepubescent boys that appears in several early stories. And if *Buddenbrooks* was about "decline," Mann's most famous novel, *The Magic Mountain,* was about sickness and the catastrophe looming over Western civilization just before 1914. His long preoccupation with sickness, morbidity, and death was to come to some sort of crisis with *Doctor Faustus*—a work too much about the "German sickness" to be easily understood in other countries, and too close to German guilt to be welcome in Germany. Clearly, Mann was the most Prussian of writers and yet anti-German in many important particulars, stuffy *and* ironic at the same time, a paradox of personality, and one who drew some of his best work from his own doubleness. (pp. 70-2)

Thomas Mann developed into an extraordinarily confident, poised writer who despite his laughing disclaimers and deft ironies notoriously thought of himself as occupying for Germans something like Goethe's authority. The Imperial Germany of Wilhelm II lent itself to this kind of self-importance. Mann never ceased to benefit from the *hoch* bourgeois status provided him by his father's family wealth and position in Lübeck. . . . Mann also benefited—and thoroughly relished—his exceptional position as a *novelist* in a culture whose heroes were poets, philosophers, composers. He was good at manipulating writers into his personal claque, angrily rejected criticism. Even in America he kept up his lifelong practice of public readings from his work in order (like Dickens) to bind an audience more firmly to himself. . . .

[These] traits of irony and mockery were deeply woven into Mann's great creative work. Mann said of *Death in Venice* that the meaning of the passion described there was really "confusion and a stripping of dignity." Himself often psychosomatically ill, he was fascinated all his creative life with sickness as a form of withdrawal and with death as the resolution of a culture that proud Germans thought would last forever. No one understood better than Mann how easily whole cultures—not just families—can die. As Germans have observed better than anyone else, "civilization" may be just pretense. The tubercular Hans Castorp in *The Magic Mountain* has to become ill and withdraw to a sanatorium on a mountaintop in order to recognize that life in the valley below is not what it seems.

No one but Mann in the long agony of the Hitler years could have occupied himself with a magnificent fiction woven out of the biblical Joseph. Probably no other writer has turned the Bible to such imaginative, opulently mythical yet witty use. Perhaps the publicly stuffy Mann was also a creation. As a writer he was endlessly resourceful and *solid*. He endures. (p. 72)

Alfred Kazin, "The Double Life of Thomas Mann," in Saturday Review *(copyright © 1981 by Saturday Review; all rights reserved; reprinted by permission), Vol. 8, No. 12, December, 1981, pp. 70, 72.*

ADDITIONAL BIBLIOGRAPHY

Apter, T. E. *Thomas Mann: The Devil's Advocate.* New York: New York University Press, 1979, 165 p.

Thematic and philosophical examination. Apter focuses on Mann's fascination with evil as demonstrated in his work.

Björkman, Edwin. "Thomas Mann." In his *The Borzoi 1925: Being a Sort of Record of Ten Years of Publishing*, pp. 31-6. New York: Alfred A. Knopf, 1925.
Brief studies of *Buddenbrooks, Death in Venice,* and *The Magic Mountain*. Björkman concludes that "Mann's greatest worth lies undoubtedly in the challenge to free, clear thought which every line of his work contains."

Bolkosky, Sidney. "Thomas Mann's 'Disorder and Early Sorrow': The Writer As Social Critic." *Contemporary Literature* XXII, No. 2 (Spring 1981): 218-33.
Interpretation of "Disorder and Early Sorrow." Bolkosky argues that in this short story Mann abandoned his typical presentation of the apolitical scholar-artist "and embarked on a reassessment not only of his values but of his view of life and history."

Brennan, Joseph Gerard. *Thomas Mann's World.* New York: Russell & Russell, 1962, 206 p.
Thematic study. Brennan examines Mann's attitude toward art and the artist and analyzes Mann's artistic personality "as it stands revealed in his work."

Burkhard, Arthur. "Thomas Mann's Appraisal of the Poet." *PMLA* XLVI, No. 3 (September 1931): 880-916.
Detailed examination of Mann's early fiction. Burkhard focuses on the conflict between Mann's "bourgeois origins and his artistic profession" as developed in the artist-heroes of his stories.

Hatfield, Henry C. "Thomas Mann's *Mario und der Zauberer:* An Interpretation." *The Germanic Review* XXI, No. 4 (December 1946): 306-12.
In-depth examination of *Mario and the Magician.* Hatfield argues that *Mario and the Magician* is symbolic rather than allegorical, and that its symbolism is not limited to the political realm, as many critics have determined, but that it is philosophical as well.

Heller, Peter. "Some Functions of the Leitmotiv in Thomas Mann's Joseph Tetralogy." *The Germanic Review* XXII, No. 2 (April 1947): 126-41.
Structural analysis of the Joseph tetralogy. Heller argues that Mann's development of the leitmotiv in the Joseph story "manifests itself on all levels of the work," and that it is this device which gives the novels their mythical quality.

Kaufmann, Fritz. *Thomas Mann: The World As Will and Representation.* Boston: Beacon Press, 1957, 322 p.
Analysis of Mann's major fiction. Kaufmann focuses on "the convergence between artistic vision and truth, on the one hand, and metaphysical vision and truth, on the other," as realized in Mann's art.

Levin, Harry. "Dialectical Siblings: Heinrich and Thomas Mann" and "Traveling Companions: Hermann Hesse and Thomas Mann." In his *Memories of the Moderns,* pp. 65-73, 74-9. New York: New Directions Books, 1980.*
Biographical commentary. In the first essay, Levin discusses the dialectical personalities of Thomas and Heinrich Mann. In the second he reconstructs the relationship between Mann and Hermann Hesse.

Lovett, Robert Morss. "*Buddenbrooks.*" In his *Preface to Fiction: A Discussion of Great Modern Novels,* pp. 81-96. Chicago: Thomas S. Rockwell Co., 1931.
In-depth examination of *Buddenbrooks.* Lovett praises Mann's artistic control and calls him "a craftsman who accomplished his effects by means so subtle as to seem only a happy accident."

Schilling, Bernard N. "Tränen-Trieschke . . . Grünlich . . . Permaneder." In his *The Comic Spirit: Boccaccio to Thomas Mann,* pp. 194-216. Detroit: Wayne State University Press, 1965.
In-depth study of *Buddenbrooks,* focusing on its comic elements.

Slochower, Harry. "Bourgeois Liberalism: Thomas Mann's *The Magic Mountain.*" In his *Three Ways of Modern Man,* pp. 50-104. New York: International Publishers, 1937.
Study of *The Magic Mountain.* Slochower argues that Mann's epic novel is the most complete expression of German liberalism, "the last great statement of the vacillating liberalism of the German middle class."

Slochower, Harry. "The Use of Myth in Kafka and Mann." In his *Spiritual Problems in Contemporary Literature,* edited by Stanley Romaine Hopper, pp. 117-26. New York: The Institute for Religious and Social Studies, 1952.*
Brief structural analysis of *Doctor Faustus* and *The Magic Mountain.* Slochower argues that both *Doctor Faustus* and *The Magic Mountain* were organically structured by Mann according to mythic and religious motifs.

Stock, Irvin. "'The Holy Sinner', Thomas Mann." In his *Fiction As Wisdom: From Goethe to Bellow,* pp. 86-101. University Park: The Pennsylvania State University Press, 1980.
Analysis of *The Holy Sinner.* Stock attempts to demonstrate an intended parallel in Mann's novel between Gregorius and Christ.

Thomas, R. Hinton. *Thomas Mann: The Mediation of Art.* London: Oxford University Press, 1963, 188 p.
Detailed examination of selected works. Thomas utilizes a number of different methods—critical, political, historical, and others—in an attempt to present a more encompassing view of Mann's work.

Van Doren, Mark. "*Joseph and His Brothers:* A Comedy in Four Parts." *The American Scholar* 26, No. 3 (Summer 1957): 289-302.
Calls Mann's Joseph story a "comic work," and states that the author himself possessed a "comic genius" because he was able to annihilate time and present us with a picture of human nature in eternity.

Katherine Mansfield (Murry)

1888-1923

(Born Kathleen Mansfield Beauchamp; also wrote under the pseudonym of Boris Petrovsky) New Zealand short story writer, critic, and poet.

During her brief career, Mansfield's innovative style helped shape the modern short story form. She is a forerunner in the use of stream-of-consciousness and is among the first English authors whose stories depend upon incident rather than plot. In addition to her stature as a literary influence, such stories as "Bliss," "The Garden Party," and "Prelude" assure Mansfield a continued readership.

Born in Wellington, New Zealand, Mansfield went to London in her early teens to complete her education at Queen's College, and was thereafter dissatisfied with colonial life. At nineteen, after two restless years at home, she returned to London with prospects of a musical career which, despite her talent as a cellist, did not develop. Mansfield lived a bohemian existence in London, eventually marrying a young musician whom she immediately left, later claiming she had undergone the marriage to gain material for a story. During the period following this first marriage, Mansfield wrote the bitter short stories published in *In a German Pension*. Unlike her later work, these stories are told from the point of view of a first-person narrator. Between 1911 and 1915 Mansfield published stories in *The New Age, The Open Window, Rhythm*, and other literary periodicals. These stories, including "The Woman at the Store" and "Violet," are more strongly plotted and sympathetic than those of *In a German Pension;* there are fewer comic touches than in the earlier stories, and the sarcasm is softened. In 1912 Mansfield met editor and critic John Middleton Murry, who had already published some of her work, and she began to assist him in editing the magazines *Rhythm* and *The Blue Review*. Through Murry, whom she later married, she gained access to the exclusive literary circles of London. His editorial advice was sought, if not always followed, for the rest of her life.

Mansfield's brief reunion with her only brother just before his death in World War I released childhood memories which found expression in her short stories set in New Zealand, such as "Prelude," "A Doll's House," "The Apple Tree," and "At the Bay," which are among her finest works. They feature lush description and evidence remarkable insight into the minds of children. Some of the New Zealand stories were collected in *Bliss, and Other Stories,* and these established Mansfield as a major talent. Though plagued by illness, she wrote at a feverish pace during her final two years of life, her mature work appearing in *The Garden Party, and Other Stories*. This collection and *Bliss* remain her two most popular books. Much of Mansfield's work was posthumously published, including her last stories, early magazine fiction, letters, journals, and poetry. For the most part, however, this work is considered inferior to her earlier collections.

Mansfield enjoyed both popular and critical success in her lifetime. She was meticulous in her craft, expressing her dominant themes of loneliness and isolation in restrained and controlled prose. At its best, her writing is notable for clarity of

Culver Pictures

visualized detail. Her avowed intention was to intensify "the so-called small things so that everything is significant." Although she was greatly successful in accomplishing this aim, the tendency to characterize objects, events, and characters alike as "dear" and "tiny," flawed some of her later work. Mansfield's technique has been likened to that of her greatest influence, Anton Chekhov, although a few critics place less credence in the theory that she patterned her style on his. Certainly she was an admirer of his work. Critics have also noted similarities between Mansfield's poetic prose style and that of A. E. Coppard, as well as the treatment of everyday themes she shared with Virginia Woolf.

Mansfield was in the forefront of those writers who treated "the so-called small" rather than the epic, and, according to H. E. Bates, many have followed her "in squeezing the significance out of the apparently commonplace, trivial behavior of their fellow men."

(See also *TCLC*, Vol. 2)

PRINCIPAL WORKS

In a German Pension   (short stories)   1911
Prelude   (short story)   1918
Bliss, and Other Stories   (short stories)   1920

Je ne parle pas Français (short story) 1920
The Garden Party, and Other Stories (short stories) 1922
The Doves' Nest, and Other Stories (short stories) 1923
Poems (poetry) 1923
The Little Girl, and Other Stories (short stories) 1924;
 also published as *Something Childish and Other Stories*,
 1924
Journals of Katherine Mansfield (journals) 1927
The Letters of Katherine Mansfield. 2 vols. (letters) 1928
*The Aloe (short story) 1930
Novels and Novelists (criticism) 1930

*This work is a revision of the earlier Prelude.

REBECCA WEST (essay date 1922)

One result of the conquest of prose by the logic of poetry is
that many writers who would in any past age have written verse
are now just as pleased to say what they want to in prose; and
Katherine Mansfield is one of these. There is at the end of *At
the Bay* something that in any other age would have been a
lyric, where the young girl, dreaming desperately of love in
her moonlit room, hears a call from the wood beyond the garden
that sends her, still half dreaming, out into the moonlight to
answer it; where she encounters such an unpleasing substitute
as the world often offers to such dreamers, from which only
her young strength rescues her, but afterwards it does not seem
to matter, in spite of the ugliness, in spite of the disappointment, because there are still the clouds and the moon in the
sky, and the deep sound of the sea. How one admires Miss
Mansfield for conceiving that moment, as well as for insisting
on working under conditions that make it possible for her to
conceive such beauty. For *At the Bay* is a continuation of
Prelude, that section of a work of genius which was the best
thing in *Bliss.* In other words, Miss Mansfield is writing a
novel, but it is coming to her slowly. There is, after all, no
reason why creation in art should take only an infinitesimal
fraction of the time that is taken by creation in life. Abandonment to the leisurely rhythm of her own imagination, and refusal to conform to the common custom and finish her book
in a year's session, has enabled her to bring her inventions
right over the threshold of art. They are extraordinarily solid;
they have lived so long in her mind that she knows all about
them and can ransack them for the difficult, rare, essential
points. Thus she produces such attenuated yet powerful sketches
as the scene in the garden, when Linda thinks of her husband
with love and disgust and fatigue and at the same time is forced
by the personality of her new baby, to whom she thought she
was indifferent, to recognise that she loves it. And to deal with
those visions born of her deliberations she brings a technique
that has been sharpened on the products of her swifter and more
immediate work. Her choice of the incident that will completely
and economically prove her point is astonishing, and only not
invariable because she is occasionally betrayed into excessive
use of her power of grotesque invention. . . .

One of the results of Miss Mansfield's poetic temperament is
that beauty is the general condition of her story. Most of her
tales are laid in the glowing setting of the sub-tropics: *Marriage
à la Mode* is acted in a midsummer countryside: even the miserable *Miss Brill* sits in a pleasant springtide day. Even in the
lamentable *Life of Ma Parker* there is a kind of sensuous beauty

in the description of the love of the old charwoman for her
grandson. The mind takes pleasure in merely moving in such
an atmosphere, apart from the meanings it may find there.

> Rebecca West, *"Notes on Novels: 'The Garden
> Party',"* in New Statesman *(© 1922 The Statesman
> Publishing Co. Ltd.), Vol. XVIII, No. 466, March
> 18, 1922, p. 678.*

J. C. SQUIRE (essay date 1922)

Books of short stories are now rare; books of short stories in
which one can be at all interested are exceedingly rare. (p. 9)

Miss Mansfield's collection, *Bliss,* boldly labelled "stories,"
is, therefore, remarkable for not being tedious. It is far from
tedious. She has so penetrating a mind and such a talent for
expression that she would be interesting whatever form she
were using and whatever subject she were writing about. It is
not that she has a markedly personal view of things, a passionate or a philosophical attitude; she is restrained, and leaves
her affections and her admirations too much to be guessed and
deduced. It is not that she has a rich prose style; she checks
the natural music in herself, and contents herself with a perpetual stream of exact statements as terse as she can make
them. Every word counts to the intelligence and the eye, but
none to the ear. But the fabric of her writing has no weak or
dull places. She beats all the writers of dyspeptic "economical" "realistic" "studies" on their own ground. Every story
is a tissue of accurate observations accurately expressed. Miss
Mansfield has an extraordinary visual, and, if one may say so,
olfactory, memory; her stories may vary in reality, but her
material settings—in which one includes everything from vegetation to the human garment of flesh—never. Almost every
page contains minor felicities which a man with the pencilling
habit would be inclined to mark.

The first few pages are crowded with them. (pp. 10-11)

Miss Mansfield can bring before one's eyes any visible object,
from the perspiration marks on a maid's bodice to the summer
lightning fluttering "like a broken bird that tries to fly and
sinks again and again struggles." And the accuracy and simplicity of her statement extends beyond this to whatever non-
material state she may wish to describe. She continually delights with images such as that in which she sets down the
silence between bachelor friend and spinster friend over teacup
and fire in **"Psychology":** "That silence could be contained
in the circle of warm, delightful fire and lamplight. How many
times hadn't they flung something into it just for the fun of
watching the ripples break on the easy shores?" . . . How
satisfying the descriptions of mind and of matter are blended
might be illustrated from any of these stories. . . . The trouble
is that, generally speaking, one remembers little more than
pictures, large or small. One has looked at a series of these.
They have dawned on the darkness, grown bright, and quietly
faded. But very seldom has one been moved. Very seldom has
one felt the faintest impulse to laugh, cheer, or cry. Why? The
people are not quite real enough and not quite enough happens
to them.

It isn't that Miss Mansfield is naturally a mere quiet note-taker,
or that she belongs temperamentally to that depressing class
of people who think they have done the finest thing in the
world when they have described several articles of furniture
and exhibited a phantom "he" or "she" incapably yearning,
frustrate, or disillusioned. **"Sun and Moon"** is a delicious, a

pathetic, and beautiful story, which might have resulted from a collaboration of Tchekov and Hans Andersen. In **"The Man Without a Temperament"** her detail is at its best, and she uses the most inconspicuous "events" to produce a beautiful and exalting impression. Generally, however, interested as one is, one doesn't much care what happens, and very little does happen. In the first long story, very remarkable as a series of photographs, the people are, except at moments, seen clear but out of contact with us, through a glass. We leave them where they started. Either this was meant to be the beginning of a novel, or else the author was under the influence of the theory that it is cheap and vulgar to let anything happen in a narrative. Sometimes she seems to remember the other theory that if anything does happen it ought to be unpleasant. The conclusions of **"Bliss"** and **"The Little Governess"** are illustrations of that. It is not that the episodes are in themselves unlikely or uncommon. Girls often are assaulted, and husbands often are unfaithful; but these stories (the indications given of these characters) do not prepare one for the endings. Had Miss Mansfield changed the last page of each, and prevented the catastrophes, we should never have suspected that Harry was a disloyal husband, or the old German an old satyr. It is a pity that **"Bliss"** thus fails to come completely off. The scenes are drawn with consummate precision, the wife is less shadowy than usual, and there are moments lyric in their intense beauty. Everything powders when we have the feeling that a realist is playing tricks with reality.

But, with all its limitations, this is a book one is bound to respect, if, possibly, one is not certain to re-read it. The author's powers have greatly matured since she wrote her first book. Her outlook, too, has modified: she is no longer at her best, and most enthusiastic, when writing of what she hates. We may hope that in the future she may be inclined to write more about the things she loves. Let there be calamity, but let us at least be moved by it; it is depressing to read of miseries and never turn a hair at them because the author has refused to abandon herself in sympathy. Let Miss Mansfield's materials remain what they are. One does not ask her to write of pirates or cowboys, murders, burglaries, or financial ramps. Childhood and the domestic interior are her favourite haunts, and her imagination will always take her back to them. But she can afford to let herself go more, to abandon a theoretic restraint which is foreign to her, to reflect on the truth that the literature which obtains and keeps a hold on people does not makes its principal appeal to the recognising eye or even to the understanding. . . . And what happens to people who rely too exclusively on the treatment, however masterly, of incidental detail may be illustrated from this volume. Three times in the course of the book "a piece of iron banged" meets the eye, and from two several stories I make these two extracts:

> . . . he began to do his exercises. Deep breathing, bending and squatting like a frog and shooting out his legs.

> . . . he began to do his exercises—deep breathing, bending forward and back, squatting like a frog and shooting out his legs.

The better it is done the more one remembers it and the less effect it has the second time. (pp. 12-16)

> *J. C. Squire, "Miss Mansfield's Stories," in his* Books Reviewed *(reprinted by kind permission of J. C. Squire's son, Mr. Raglan Squire), Hodder & Stoughton Limited, 1922, pp. 9-16.*

VIRGINIA WOOLF   (essay date 1927)

The most distinguished writers of short stories in England are agreed, says Mr. Murry, that as a writer of short stories Katherine Mansfield was *hors concours.* No one has succeeded her, and no critic has been able to define her quality. But the reader of her journal is well content to let such questions be. It is not the quality of her writing or the degree of her fame that interest us in her diary, but the spectacle of a mind—a terribly sensitive mind—receiving one after another the haphazard impressions of eight years of life. Her diary was a mystical companion. 'Come my unseen, my unknown, let us talk together', she says on beginning a new volume. In it she noted facts—the weather, an engagement; she sketched scenes; she analyzed her character; she described a pigeon or a dream or a conversation. Nothing could be more fragmentary; nothing more private. We feel that we are watching a mind which is alone with itself; a mind which has so little thought of an audience that it will make use of a shorthand of its own now and then, or, as the mind in its loneliness tends to do, divide into two and talk to itself. Katherine Mansfield about Katherine Mansfield.

But then as the scraps accumulate we find ourselves giving them, or more probably receiving from Katherine Mansfield herself, a direction. From what point of view is she looking at life as she sits there, terribly sensitive, registering one after another such diverse impressions? She is a writer; a born writer. Everything she feels and hears and sees is not fragmentary and separate; it belongs together as writing. Sometimes the note is directly made for a story. 'Let me remember when I write about that fiddle how it runs up lightly and swings down sorrowful; how it *searches*', she notes. Or, '*Lumbago.* This is a very queer thing. So sudden, so painful, I must remember it when I write about an old man. The start to get up, the pause, the look of fury, and how, lying at night, one seems to get locked". . . . (pp. 73-4)

In all this we seem to be in the midst of unfinished stories; here is a beginning; here an end. They only need a loop of words thrown round them to be complete.

But then the diary is so private and so instinctive that it allows another self to break off from the self that writes and to stand a little apart watching it write. The writing self was a queer self; sometimes nothing would induce it to write. 'There is so much to do and I do so little. Life would be almost perfect here if only when I was *pretending* to work I always was working. Look at the stories that wait and wait just at the threshold . . .'. (p. 74)

No one felt more seriously the importance of writing than she did. In all the pages of her journal, instinctive, rapid as they are, her attitude toward her work is admirable, sane, caustic, and austere. There is no literary gossip; no vanity; no jealousy. Although during her last years she must have been aware of her success she makes no allusion to it. Her own comments upon her work are always penetrating and disparaging. Her stories wanted richness and depth; she was only 'skimming the top—no more.' But writing, the mere expression of things adequately and sensitively, is not enough. It is founded upon something unexpressed; and this something must be solid and entire. Under the desperate pressure of increasing illness she began a curious and difficult search, of which we catch glimpses only and those hard to interpret, after the crystal clearness which is needed if one is to write truthfully. 'Nothing of any worth can come of a disunited being', she wrote. One must have health in one's self. After five years of struggle she gave up the search after physical health not in despair, but because she thought the malady was of the soul and that the cure lay not in any physical treatment, but in some such 'spiritual brotherhood' as that at Fontainebleau, in which the last months of her life were spent. (pp. 74-5)

Virginia Woolf, "A Terribly Sensitive Mind" (originally published in New York Herald Tribune, September 18, 1927), in her Granite and Rainbow (© 1958 by Leonard Woolf; reprinted by permission of Harcourt Brace Jovanovich, Inc.; in Canada by the Author's Literary Estate and the Hogarth Press Ltd), Harcourt Brace Jovanovich, 1958, pp. 73-5.

ANDRÉ MAUROIS (essay date 1935)

[Katherine Mansfield's method] is not that of those English novelists who take up a story at the moment of the hero's birth and slowly conduct it through a consecutive series of incidents towards a final catastrophe or into the luminous deltas of contentment. What [she] does is to select a family, a setting, and there make a deep cut into time, describing the impressions of the people during the brief chosen moment, and telling us nothing about them except through their own thoughts and remarks at that moment. From the opening lines, she makes them speak, and mentions them by name, without making any effort to instruct us about them. We come to know her heroes rather as we know our fellow-passengers in a railway carriage, or our neighbours in a restaurant: that is to say, by building them up from their conversation.

Nor is Katherine Mansfield's method that of the French novelists, such as that of François Mauriac in *Genitrix* or *La Fin de La Nuit*, which likewise make an incision in time. The French novelists, like the French tragedians, choose for such a process a moment of crisis, whereas one particular feature of Katherine Mansfield's art is that, for the theme of her composition she chooses an ordinary day, a day marked only by some small family event—the Burnells' removal, a garden party, a child's journey with her grandmother, an episode after a bereavement. It is precisely the intensity of this commonplace day which quickens our emotion or our sense of wonder, just as is done by those artists who can convey a sense of all the beauty of the world by painting a plate of fruit and a white table-cloth.

Crisis it may be, for everything is a crisis in life, but a crisis in miniature. . . . That a short story can contain and suggest as much truth about the world as a long novel, had been shown by Tchekov and Mérimée, whom Katherine Mansfield held in passionate admiration. But it is doubtful whether Tchekov himself would have dared to build up anything on a foundation so fragile as that of *Prelude*. . . . [Here] Katherine Mansfield parts company with her master. "Tchekov made a mistake," she says, "in thinking that if he had had more time he would have written more fully, described the rain, and the midwife and the doctor having tea. The truth is one can only get *so much* into a story; there is always a sacrifice. One has to leave out what one knows and longs to use. Why? I haven't any idea, but there it is. It's always a kind of race to get in as much as one can before it *disappears*."

The more skilled her artistry becomes, the more she is freed from the superstition of subject-matter. Some of her early stories, those preceding what may be called her "mystical" period, which begins in 1915, with the death of her brother, are as carefully contrived as the stories of Maupassant. Others are reminiscent of Villiers de l'Isle-Adam. But these stories are far from being her best. It is only when Katherine Mansfield is no longer herself that she is saved. She is right in believing that her very brevity helps her. A story of hers will often remind one of those mutilated sculptures, which become all the more beautiful in our eyes as it is our own genius which roused and quickened by that of the artist, reconstructs its missing head or limbs. (pp. 334-36)

The world of Tchekov is a male world: the thoughts and the conversations of its inhabitants are filled with ideas and activities. The world of Katherine Mansfield is primarily a feminine world. The house, clothes, children, women's cares—and more exactly, those of well-to-do women—are the things that matter. With the household cares she likes to mingle the feelings of women, their judgements of people, their musings. The men in Katherine Mansfield's pictures scarcely seem to have any work to do: that does not interest her. What is Stanley Burnell's job in life? Does she tell us? I have forgotten. What we do know, is what his wife thinks of him.

In the universe of women, the truth about people is discovered slowly, though the accidents of long talks. In *New Dresses,* Mrs Carsfield and her mother are finishing off certain green cashmere dresses with apple-green belts. The husband has gone out and the two women are talking about children. Through their remarks, which are inextricably connected with their womanly occupations, the characters of the children and all the relationships of the family are revealed to us. . . . (pp. 337-38)

Women and their moods, their secret alliances against the male, that particular voice in which they talk together in the evening, the long conversations of a mother and daughter, their mysterious bonds of union with certain objects. . . . About all such things nobody has ever spoken better. (p. 339)

Cross-sections of the feminine universe, very finely cut—this might serve as a first definition of the work we are examining; but it is one which still lacks the essential. The virtue of Katherine Mansfield's stories lies not merely in their truthfulness, but in their poetry. The characters are plunged in a real world, where their actions are controlled by the great natural rhythms—the hours of the day, the seasons, the tides, the courses of the stars. "I feel always trembling on the brink of poetry," she wrote.

The idea, in her work, is never explicitly stated. There are no formal metaphors, but they are suggested. One of the characters in *Prelude* lets drop the remark that the aloe flowers only once in a hundred years, and Linda Burnell fancies that it is flowering on that day. The symbol is not explained, but need it be? The blossoming pear-tree is linked up with the happiness of Bertha Young. A tiny lamp in a doll's house, a fly killed by a banker—these small things become centres for stories. . . . Incarnations of this kind bring about a mystical communion between man and nature.

As a method of diagnosing a writer's philosophy, it would not be altogether useless to discover what words he uses most frequently. In the case of Katherine Mansfield one would find *beautiful . . . delightful . . . exquisitely . . .* It is the beauty of the world that impresses her more than anything else. (pp. 340-42)

To Katherine Mansfield's heroines the world is harsh and frightening. Nearly all her stories are of moments of beauty suddenly broken by contact with ugliness, cruelty, or death.

But things must be accepted thus. Life is just this mixture, as Laura divines so clearly at the end of *The Garden Party.*

The diversity, and the way in which we try to crowd everything into it, even death itself, is exactly what is so disturbing to a girl of Laura's age. She feels that things should be different, but life is like that, and we did not make it so. In life the garden party and the death of the workman happen on the same day, at the same time of day. Laura may protest that things like that *ought* not to happen at the same time, but Life answers: "Why not? In what way do they differ?" They happen, and it is inevitable. But there is beauty in the inevitability. (pp. 342-43)

To make oneself worthy of being a writer, one has to become purified and detached. And in the closing pages of [Katherine Mansfield's] journals we feel that she has attained this purification: "But now that I have wrestled with it, it's no longer so. I feel happy—deep down. *All is well.*"

And "all is well," we might echo, whenever we finish one of Katherine Mansfield's finest stories. All is well, or more precisely, all is exactly thus. Before the greatest art, which is also the simplest, silence is the only expression of delight. (pp. 344-45)

> *André Maurois, "Katherine Mansfield," in his* Prophets and Poets, *translated by Hamish Miles (translation copyright © 1935 by Harper & Brothers; reprinted by permission of the author and the author's agents, Scott Meredith Literary Agency, Inc., 845 Third Avenue, New York, New York 10022; originally published as* Magiciens et logiciens, *B. Grasset, 1935), Harper & Brothers Publishers, 1935, pp. 313-45.*

H. E. BATES (essay date 1941)

[It is] not too much to say, I think, that Katherine Mansfield and A. E. Coppard, for all their faults and their debt to Tchehov, succeeded more than any other writers of their day in assisting the English short story to a state of adult emancipation. Before their time the short story in English had known imagination, as in Poe, ingenuity, as in Wells, masculinity, as in Kipling, humour and trickery, as in O. Henry, colour and irony, as in Crane, together with most of the virtues and vices of the novel; but with the possible exception of Conrad, himself only just coming into his own, it had been very little touched by poetry. Lyricism was kept outside it; poets, having their own medium, left it alone. But it will remain eternally to the credit of Katherine Mansfield and A. E. Coppard that both attempted to bring to the short story some of the fancy, delicacy, shape, and coloured conceit of the Elizabethan lyric, . . . [and] when they left it the short story had gained new vitality and new design and above all, perhaps, a certain quality of transparency. (p. 124)

[Both] are the meeting-places of Russian and English influences—Katherine Mansfield combining Tchehov and Virginia Woolf (by way, perhaps, of Dorothy Richardson), Coppard combining Tchehov and, rather surprisingly, Henry James. Both had the satisfaction of being acclaimed, in the early twenties, as highly original writers—yet it would be truer to say, I think, that both were more remarkable as the means of transmitting certain influences than originating them. Neither disrupted, as Joyce did, the prose of their time; neither excited the moral and mystical controversies of *Ulysses* and *The Rainbow;* neither shook the foundations of society, like Samuel

Butler. Yet after them, as after Joyce, Lawrence, and Butler, the things they touched could never be quite the same again. (pp. 124-25)

[Katherine Mansfield's] art, and her particular application of it to the short story, was intensely personal. She is a writer with a flavour. Just as D. H. Lawrence can be detected as the central figure of most of his work, so Katherine Mansfield is the unseen and unspeaking personality behind every page she wrote. From her letters she will be seen as a personality capable of spontaneous but unenduring responses; her mind is quick, nervous, in a state of constant receptive flutter; her eye takes in the imagery of surrounding life in a series of wonderfully vivid and excited impressions; all these receptions and responses are, in the first place, emotional, only secondarily to be analysed, if at all, at some later moment of personal catechism and distrust. All this is heightened and aggravated by the complaint from which she suffered—so that she is either very much up or very much down. Such a state of personal tension, alternately exultant and despondent, inevitably shapes and colours her work; but behind it lies a strong force of personal courage, finding its expression in a gaiety that is exuberant, slightly ironical, and sometimes quite schoolgirlish in its eagerness to demonstrate how she can triumph over suffering.

All this is the woman emotionally shaping the writer. This is the secret, the genius if you care to put it so, that cannot be copied. But a state of consumptive emotional tension cannot, of itself, shape short stories, and it would be surprising if so receptive a personality as Katherine Mansfield's were to have been wholly uninfluenced by other practitioners.

Katherine Mansfield read widely, and was in fact so influenced. The key influence to her work has always been regarded as Tchehov. (pp. 126-27)

From Tchehov, it seems to me, Katherine Mansfield learned, or had her attention drawn to, two important things that had hitherto found no place in the English short story: casual and oblique narration. Like Tchehov, Katherine Mansfield saw the possibilities of telling the story by what was left out as much as by what was left in, or alternately of describing one set of events and consequences while really indicating another. Her shades of tone and meaning are subtle; but they differ from Tchehov's in one important thing. Tchehov's stories have a certain greyness of tone—he works in pencil and pastel. Katherine Mansfield's are vivid and clearly coloured—the light shines through them as it shines through a picture of stained glass. That side of her art, though enriched primarily by her remarkable natural gifts of observation, has much in common with the art of two of her contemporaries, Virginia Woolf and Miss Dorothy Richardson. Like theirs also, her art is essentially feminine; she delights in making her characters show their thoughts by a kind of mental soliloquy, fluttering, gossipy, breathless with question and answer. . . . (pp. 128-29)

But the dangers of such a style are clear. There is the danger that the voice of the narrator may become confused, even though wrongly, with the voice of the character; and one feels in certain of Katherine Mansfield's stories that this has happened, and that the girlish, chattering voice is the voice of the writer thinly disguised. Then there is the danger of monotony—of becoming bored, as one does in life, by a voice talking constantly of itself and answering all its own questions before anyone else has a chance. Lastly, as the method is repeated, it tends to give even very different characters a touch of sameness, until they are all chattering overgrown schoolgirls busy asking and answering breathless facile questions about love and life and happiness.

Character indeed, that is, the building up of character, was not Katherine Mansfield's strong point. She catches at people— very ordinary, very lonely, very happy, very pathetic people— as they pass; she succeeds in extracting from each, as it were, a moment or two of self-revelation, gives them her blessing and lets them slip through her kindly, sympathetic fingers. They pass into the mist of crowds and remain there: interesting memories which gradually fade as the reader's sense of pity for them fades, until they become negative and remote again. It is here in fact that the popular comparison with Tchehov must begin to break down—for where in Tchehov we both feel and know more about a character as it steps beyond the story than we did in the beginning, in Katherine Mansfield we have an impression only of feeling, and not of knowing, more. It is our hearts that have been the object of attack. Tchehov's characters, for all their pencil greyness of tone, step beyond the boundaries of his stories firmly as characters, forming in their immense variation a whole Russian national portrait gallery. Katherine Mansfield, catching at a couple of dozen types, these mostly young girls and women, can nowhere challenge the greatness of Tchehov's range. Her art in fact lacked— because she was ill, because her personality was never fully resolved, because she died young—the Russian's final objective strength. Time and circumstance limited its development, leaving it supremely personal, as it were soft-boned, with a certain rosy delicacy, but in all final tests of comparison immature.

Yet Katherine Mansfield became known and talked of, in the nineteen-twenties and perhaps even in the early 'thirties, as the greatest of all new influences on the short story. Many good writers of stories were writing at about that time, among them Maugham, Galsworthy, Conrad, and George Moore, to say nothing of the person who wrote that supreme but unwanted volume, *Dubliners,* and their work has so far stood the time-test as well as, in some cases much better than, her own. Why did she put the short-story world into a flutter? Was it because, almost for the first time, the English short story stopped being concerned with set situations, improbabilities, facile action, artificial dilemmas? . . . Was [it because] someone had at last shown that ordinary lives, unmanipulated into highly dramatic emotional entanglements, could be interesting? She turned away from much of contemporary literature for an illuminating reason—it lacked both truth, her own "devouring passion," and humility. Somewhere here, I think, in the freshness of her approach to life and in the freshness of her casual, apparently scrappy, vivid and beautifully coloured method, may be found the reason for her popular and influential success.

At her instigation, indeed, the short story suddenly turned round, as it were, and had a look at life—not Life with a capital letter, but the very ordinary yet very extraordinary life going on in suburban homes, poor streets, villages, back bedrooms, barbers' shops, cafés, hotels, in every place. The war had not only struck down the social barriers everywhere, but it had struck down the social barriers for writers especially. Katherine Mansfield stands at the beginning, though she is by no means responsible for it, of a new era of democratic literature, in which the short story was to find an exceptionally happy place. . . . Writers, after the Great War of 1914-18, found themselves less fettered than at any time in history. They had suddenly a free pass to say and see and do and describe anything

they wanted. No subject was now barred to a writer, to the last limit of physical experience.

To the short-story writer, therefore, perhaps even more than to the novelist, a world of immense new possibilities was opened up. Katherine Mansfield, showing that by freshness of approach even the most trivial aspect or incident could become vitally interesting, has her share in the opening up of that world. Her importance lies less perhaps in what she did than in the fact that she indicated what could be done. Few writers have successfully imitated her extremely personal method; many have followed her example in squeezing the significance out of the apparently commonplace, trivial behaviour of their fellow-men. (pp. 130-33)

> *H. E. Bates, "Katherine Mansfield and A. E. Coppard," in his* The Modern Short Story: A Critical Survey *(Canadian rights by permission of Laurence Pollinger Limited, as agents for the Estate of H. E. Bates), T. Nelson and Sons Ltd, 1941 (and reprinted by Michael Joseph Ltd, 1972), pp. 122-47.**

ELIZABETH BOWEN (essay date 1956)

"Katherine Mansfield's death, by coming so early, left her work still at the experimental stage." This could be said—but would it be true? To me, such a verdict would be misleading. First, her writing already *had* touched perfection a recognizable number of times; second, she would have been bound to go on experimenting up to the end, however late that had come. One cannot imagine her settling down to any one fixed concept of the short story—her art was, by its very nature, tentative, responsive, exploratory. There are no signs that she was casting about to find a formula: a formula would, in fact, have been what she fled from. Her sense of the possibilities of the story was bounded by no hard-and-fast horizons: she grasped that it is imperative for the writer to expand his range, never contract his method. Perception and language could not be kept too fresh, too alert, too fluid. Each story entailed a beginning right from the start, unknown demands, new risks, unforeseeable developments. Often, she worked by trial-and-error.

So, ever on the move, she has left with us no "typical" Katherine Mansfield story to anatomize. Concentrated afresh, each time, upon expression, she did not envisage "technique" in the abstract. As it reached her, each idea for a story had inherent within it its own shape: there could be for it no other. That shape, it was for her to perceive, then outline—she thought (we learn from her letters and journal) far more of perception than of construction. The story *is* there, but she has yet to come at it. One has the impression of a water-diviner, pacing, halting, awaiting the twitch of the hazel twig. Also, to judge from her writings about her writing, there were times when Katherine Mansfield believed a story to have a volition of its own—she seems to stand back, watching it take form. Yet this could happen apart from her; the story drew her steadily into itself.

Yet all of her pieces, it seems clear, did not originate in the same order. Not in all cases was there that premonitory stirring of an idea; sometimes the external picture came to her first. She found herself seized upon by a scene, an isolated incident or a face which, something told her, must *have* meaning, though she had yet to divine what the meaning was. Appearances could in themselves touch alight her creative power. It is then that we see her moving into the story, from its visual periphery to its heart, recognizing the "why" as she penetrates. (p. 89)

Katherine Mansfield's masterpiece stories cover their tracks; they have an air of serene inevitability, almost a touch of the miraculous. (p. 90)

Of love for experiment for its own sake, Katherine Mansfield shows not a sign. Conscious artist, she carries none of the marks of the self-consciously "experimental" writer. Nothing in her approach to people or nature is revolutionary; her story-telling is, on its own plane, not much less straightforward than Jane Austen's. She uses no literary shock tactics. The singular beauty of her language consists, partly, in its hardly seeming to *be* language at all, so glass-transparent is it to her meaning. Words had but one appeal for her, that of speakingness. . . . She was to evolve from noun, verb, adjective, a marvelous sensory notation hitherto undreamed of outside poetry; nonetheless, she stayed subject to prose discipline. And her style, when the story-context requires, can be curt, decisive, factual. It is a style generated by subject and tuned to mood—so flexible as to be hardly *a* style at all. One would recognize a passage from Katherine Mansfield not by the manner but by the content. There are no eccentricities.

Katherine Mansfield was not a rebel, she was an innovator. Born into the English traditions of prose narrative, she neither revolted against these nor broke with them—simply, she passed beyond them. And now tradition, extending, has followed her. Had she not written, written as she did, one form of art might be still in infancy. One cannot attribute to Katherine Mansfield the entire growth, in our century, of the short story. . . . We owe to her the prosperity of the "free" story: she untrammeled it from conventions and, still more, gained for it a prestige till then unthought of. How much ground Katherine Mansfield broke for her successors may not be realized. Her imagination kindled unlikely matter; she was to alter for good and all our idea of what goes to make a story. . . . (pp. 90-1)

How good is Katherine Mansfield's character-drawing? I have heard this named as her weak point. I feel one cannot insist enough upon what she instinctively grasped—that the short story, by reason of its aesthetics, is not and is not intended to be the medium either for exploration or long-term development of character. Character cannot be more than *shown*—it is there for use, the use is dramatic. Foreshortening is not only unavoidable, it is right. And with Katherine Mansfield there was another factor—her "stranger" outlook on so much of society. I revert to the restrictedness of her life in England, the eclecticism of her personal circle. She saw few people, saw them sometimes too often. This could account for her tendency to repeat certain types of character. This restless New Zealand woman writing of London deals with what was more than half a synthetic world: its denizens *are* types, and they remain so—to the impoverishment of the London stories. . . . Her sophisticates are cut out sharply, with satire; they are animated, expressive but two-dimensional.

In the South of France stories, characters are subsidiary to their environment; they drift like semi-transparent fish through the brilliantly lighted colours of an aquarium. Here, Katherine Mansfield's lovely crystallization of place and hour steals attention away from men and women. . . . [The] South of France stories are about moods.

Katherine Mansfield, we notice, seldom outlines and never dissects a character: instead, she causes the person to expose himself—and devastating may be the effect. The author's nominal impassivity is telling. I should not in the main call her a kind writer, though so often she is a pitiful one. Wholly be-

nevolent are her comedies: high spirits, good humour no less than exquisite funniness endear to us "**The Daughters of the Late Colonel**," "**The Doves' Nest**," "**The Singing Lesson**." Nor is the laugh ever against a daydreamer.

The New Zealand characters are on a quite other, supreme level. They lack no dimension. Their living-and-breathing reality at once astonishes and calms us: they belong to life, not in any book—they existed before stories began. In their company we are no longer in Katherine Mansfield's; we forget her as she forgot herself. The Burnells of "**Prelude**," "**At the Bay**," and "**The Doll's House**" are a dynasty. Related, though showing no too striking family likeness, are the conversational Sheridans of "**The Garden Party**." Of Burnell stock, graver and simplified, are elderly Mr. and Mrs. Hammond of "**The Stranger**"—Katherine Mansfield's equivalent of James Joyce's "The Dead." Alike in Burnells, Sheridans, and Hammonds we feel the almost mystic family integration. . . . I do not claim that the New Zealand stories vindicate Katherine Mansfield's character-drawing—the *drawing* is not (to my mind) elsewhere at fault. What she fails at in the European stories is full, adult character-*realization*—or, should one say, materialization? (pp. 91-2)

The New Zealand stories are timeless. Do the rest of the Katherine Mansfield stories "date"? I find there is some impression that they do—an impression not, I think, very closely checked on. To an extent, her work shows the intellectual imprint of her day, many of whose theories, tenets, preoccupations seem now faded. It is the more nearly *mondaine*, the "cleverer" of her stories which wear least well. Her psychology may seem naive and at times shallow—after all, she *was* young; but apart from that much water has flowed under bridges in thirty years. "**Bliss**," "**Psychology**" and "**Je ne parle pas français**" (technically one of her masterpieces) give out a faintly untrue ring. And one effect of her writing has told against her: it was her fate to set up a fashion in hyper-sensitivity, in vibratingness: it is her work in this vein which has been most heavily imitated, and travesties curdle one's feeling for the original. (pp. 92-3)

She wrote few love stories; those she did today seem distant, dissatisfying. Staking her life on love, she was least happy (I think) with love in fiction. Her passionate faith shows elsewhere. *Finesses,* subtleties, restless analysis, cerebral wary guardedness hallmark the Katherine Mansfield lovers. Was this, perhaps, how it was in London, or is this how Londoners' *amours* struck young New Zealand? She had left at the other side of the world a girlhood not unlike young Aunt Beryl's: beaux, waltzes, muslin, moonlight, murmuring sea. . . .

The stories are more than moments, instants, gleams: she has given them touches of eternity. The dauntless artist accomplished, if less than she hoped, more than she knew. Almost no writer's art has not its perishable fringes: light dust may settle on that margin. But against the core, the integrity, what can time do? Katherine Mansfield's deathless expectations set up a mark for us: no one has yet fulfilled them. Still at work, her genius rekindles faith; she is on our side in every further attempt. The effort she was involved in involves us—how can we feel her other than a contemporary? (p. 93)

Elizabeth Bowen, "Katherine Mansfield" (1956), in her Seven Winters: Memories of a Dublin Childhood and Afterthoughts *(copyright © 1956, 1962 by Elizabeth Bowen; reprinted by permission of Curtis Brown Limited, London, as Literary Executors of the Estate of Elizabeth Bowen), Alfred A. Knopf, 1962 (and reprinted in* Discussions of the Short Story, *edited by Hollis Summers, D. C. Heath and Company, 1963, pp. 89-93).*

J. MIDDLETON MURRY (essay date 1959)

[In February 1918 Katherine Mansfield] began to write a long, beautiful and strange story *Je ne parle pas français.* In sending it to me she wrote to explain its nature.

> I've two kick-offs in the writing game. One is joy—real joy—the thing that made me write when we lived at Pauline, and that sort of writing I could only do in just that state of being in some perfectly blissful way at peace. Then something delicate and lovely seems to open before my eyes, like a flower without thought of a frost or a cold breath, knowing that all about it is warm and tender and 'ready'. And that I try, ever so humbly, to express.
>
> The other kick-off is my old original one, and *had I not known love* it would have been my all. Not hate or destruction (both are beneath contempt as real motives) but an extremely deep sense of hopelessness, of everything doomed to disaster. There! I got it exactly—a cry against corruption—that is absolutely the nail on the head. Not a protest—a cry.
>
> (p. 86)

That passage from her *Letters* is vital to any true understanding of Katherine Mansfield. First we need to remember that the months at the Villa Pauline when she could, and did, write out of a state of being in some perfectly blissful way at peace—was the time when she was writing *Prelude.* . . . [It] was a time of pure joy: of the self-effacement of love in writing and living.

But there was that other creative condition in Katherine Mansfield—what she calls an extremely deep sense of hopelessness: and this she says would have been her only creative condition, if she had not known love. The most astonishing examples of creation from this state are her stories *Je ne parle pas français* and the unduly neglected *The Married Man's Story.* There is nothing strained or forced in them: they spring naturally from a like attitude of self-effacement: only there is in them no joy.

These two conditions alternated incessantly in Katherine Mansfield. She goes out to the world in the self-abandonment of joy and love: or she withdraws into herself in despair and hopelessness. I do not think it is possible to choose between them, or to say that one more than the other is characteristic of Katherine Mansfield. It is the alternation itself which is characteristic of her: and above all characteristic of her letters.

But I think that as her work reached its final stage, before she gave up writing altogether, these two conditions became somehow blended together in her art. I have, myself, not much doubt that her two most perfect stories are two of her very last, written less than a year before her death: *The Doll's House* and *The Fly.* They are both very short: and they have, to my sense, an absolute finality about them. I can define their quality only in a phrase of Keats: they have in them 'a sorrow more beautiful than beauty's self'.

How was this achieved? . . . I think it can only be understood as following some such pattern as this: (1) a sort of bitter revulsion from life—which is characteristic of her work prior to *Prelude;* (2) a joyous and loving acceptance of life—which finds its first complete expression in *Prelude;* (3) then a far more poignant disillusion with and revulsion from life—'nessum maggior dolore'—which found its first complete expression in *Bliss,* and gradually deepened through experience into the very profound sense of hopelessness which finds expression in *Je ne parle pas;* and, finally, (4) an acceptance even of this hopelessness: and out of this acceptance comes the last perfection of her work. (pp. 86-8)

In the last resort, if we are not content with superficial understanding, Katherine Mansfield can only be comprehended, or the comprehension of her expressed, in some such terms as William Blake used to express his experience. His effort towards self-annihilation—the sole condition, as he believed, of the true, the Divine Imagination—was renewed in her. By 1921 it had become the burden of all her thinking on her purpose and herself. . . . Her one concern was to be the pure vehicle of experience. . . . Then, suddenly in her effort to write *At the Bay* she achieves the condition.

> There's my Grandmother, back in her chair with her pink knitting, there stalks my Uncle over the grass; I feel as I write, 'You are not dead, my darlings. All is remembered. I bow down to you. I efface myself so that you may live again through me in your richness and beauty.' And one is *possessed.*
>
> (pp. 89-90)

[Now] we see out of what a condition of soul that perfect and profound simplicity was created. There is the doctrine, there is the experience, there is Art. That in the last resort is what the supreme achievement of art is—the utterance of Life through a completely submissive being. (p. 90)

And so it is that if I had to choose one adjective to describe the essential quality of what she did and what she became, it would be the adjective 'serene'. And it seems to me that those who are responsive to her writing recognise this serenity—the serenity of a rainbow that shines through tears—and know that it comes from a heart at peace 'in spite of all'. . . . In spite of all, the little lamp glows gently and eternally in *The Doll's House;* in spite of all, the sleeping face of the dead man in *The Garden Party* murmurs that All is well; and though Ma Parker has nowhere to cry out her misery, she is beautiful for ever, in spite of all. (p. 91)

J. Middleton Murry, "Katherine Mansfield" (originally a lecture delivered in a slightly different form in 1935), in his Katherine Mansfield and Other Literary Studies *(© 1959 by Mary Middleton Murry; reprinted by permission of The Society of Authors as the literary representative of the Estate of John Middleton Murry), Constable, 1959, pp. 69-93.*

IAN A. GORDON (essay date 1963)

Within a year of her arrival in London [in 1908, Katherine Mansfield] was pregnant; married, and not to the father of her child; had left her husband, and been packed off by an unsuspecting mother to recuperate in a Bavarian village. The child miscarried; the incident was closed. But all of this lay behind the snarling ill-humour of her stories of this period. They . . . form the first seven stories in her 1911 volume, *In a German Pension.* The Germans are observed with loathing. But the Germans are not the real target. What she is depicting is the grossness of the male, guzzling and drinking, pressing his unwanted attentions on the young girl in *At Lehmann's* and on the middle-aged wife in *Frau Brechenmacher Attends a Wedding*. . . . For all their German background and variety of characters, these stories are almost autobiography. (p. 8)

[The stories Mansfield wrote in 1911] show a mellower spirit than the 1910 stories. There is a certain genial and kindly humour in *The Advanced Lady;* and love, in *The Swing of the Pendulum,* in spite of the intrusion of a predatory male, leads to a conclusion acceptable to the central woman character. But nothing shows the change of attitude so clearly as *A Birthday.* The theme is the birth of a child, and the father, Andreas Binzer, is shown as (being a male, inevitably) selfish, but sensitive, nervous and finally overjoyed. There is nothing of the disgust with childbirth so clearly enunciated in *At Lehmann's* of the previous year. (p. 9)

[During 1914 and 1915], Katherine Mansfield wrote two of her best stories to date, *Something Childish, but very Natural,* a love-story which is evidently the Murry's love-in-a-cottage situation projected back to a couple of youngsters, and *An Indiscreet Journey,* based on a visit she paid to Paris in early 1915 to renew acquaintance with an old admirer. To these months also belongs *The Little Governess,* a longer story on several of her recurring themes—the young woman alone in the world, the predatory male, the unsympathetic foreign official. Katherine Mansfield had known them all. The story represents a technical advance. For the first time she is inside her character. We are at the beginning of that sensitive feeling for characters portrayed through their own fleeting thoughts which lies at the basis of all her mature work. (pp. 10-11)

[*Prelude*] is the story that set the standard and established the pattern for all her later work. The 'Burnell' family are evoked in their early days, the little girls still small children, Stanley Burnell at the opening of his prosperous career, the whole told 'in a kind of special prose' (the phrase is her own) that is one of the secrets of her originality. (p. 11)

Her writing of 1918 includes two New Zealand stories, *Sun and Moon,* on the surface an allegory but in fact a 'Burnell' family story of the *Prelude* group, and the unfinished *A Married Man's Story,* an 'interior' narrative in a Wellington setting. Her best two stories of the year are *Bliss,* with its innocently happy wife who recognizes in a moment of horrified insight her successful rival, and the polished *Je ne Parle pas Français.* This last represents a return to old experiences, handled with a technical competence which is approaching its peak. (p. 12)

After arranging for the publication of a volume of her stories of the last few years—they were published as *Bliss, and Other Stories* in late 1920, and included the subtle and evocative *Prelude*—she left [London] for the south of France. (p. 13)

At Mentone she wrote six stories. . . . Three are on her *leitmotiv* of the woman on her own in an unfriendly world. The central situations in *The Lady's Maid, Miss Brill,* and *The Life of Ma Parker* are variations on this theme, with the lonely woman now slipping into middle-age. *The Daughters of the Late Colonel* is a magnificently envisaged story of two women devastated by the death of their father. . . . *The Young Girl,* a slight but sensitive sketch of adolescence, and *The Stranger* complete the group written at Mentone. (pp. 13-14)

When she moved to Switzerland, the pressure of work mounted: 1921 was the busiest year of her life. . . . This is the great year of the 'Burnell' family sequence, lovingly remembered at various periods of their lives. (p. 14)

All of this group and the six Mentone stories were published in *The Garden Party and Other Stories*. . . . They do not exhaust its contents. Along with some earlier work there was the love-story, *Mr. and Mrs. Dove,* delicately poised between mockery and sentiment, and a vicious delineation of a brittle woman rejecting the love of a devoted husband, *Marriage à la Mode,* written perhaps in contrition to make her peace with the writer of *The Man With a Temperament.* (p. 15)

[The strength of her final volume, *The Dove's Nest,*] lies once again in the stories of her own town, pre-eminently in the classic re-creation of childhood, *The Doll's House.* (pp. 15-16)

The Fly, written in early 1922, when she knew that the finish was not far off, is often asserted to be her 'indictment of life'. It is, rather, her clear-eyed admission that life goes on. (p. 16)

Ian A. Gordon, in his Katherine Mansfield *(© Profile Books Ltd. 1963), revised edition, British Council, 1963, 35 p.*

ROBERT MURRAY DAVIS   (essay date 1964)

The incidents of **"The Garden Party"** repeat in varying degrees of complexity one basic situation as a framework for the symbols, parallels, and contrasts. At the core of most scenes is Laura's attempt first to deal with other people or with experience on a mature level in a style—whether verbal or physical—learned from her mother; then her loss of confidence in that style; and finally her retreat to childish responses. The first challenge, dealing with the workmen come to erect the marquee, establishes this situation most clearly: "'Good morning,' she said, copying her mother's voice. But that sounded so fearfully affected that she was ashamed, and stammered like a little girl, 'Oh—er—have you come—is it about the marquee?'" She attempts briefly to maintain the adult role, avoiding mention of the morning's beauty because "she must be businesslike." . . . But with her admission that "she did quite follow him" comes a release from the stiffness of the adult role she has learned from her mother. She is now free to wonder what the workmen are thinking; in the pre-sexual curiosity of childhood, she can contrast the workman's sensitivity to the lavender sprig with the silliness of her dancing partners; and, taking a bite of the piece of bread and butter which had spoiled her portrayal of a mature woman, she is able to feel "just like a work-girl," matey and comfortable with the workmen.

It is as a child that Laura hugs her brother, speaks on the telephone, and, with a child's impulsive sentimentality, responds to the "darling little spots" of sunlight, "Especially the one on the inkpot lid. It was quite warm. A warm little silver star. She could have kissed it." But it is as a girl on the verge of physical and emotional maturity that she responds to the lilies. . . . (pp. 61-2)

These flowers are also the basis of Laura's renewed contact with her mother. At the beginning of the story, Mrs. Sheridan's garden is full of roses: "You could not help feeling that they understood that roses are the only flowers that impress people at garden parties; the only flowers that everybody is certain of knowing." It is with this view of flowers as socially useful that the workman's spontaneous appreciation of the lavender is contrasted. Now, confronted with the lilies that her mother has bought on impulse and her mother's admission that she is not logical, that is, not wholly governed by her conventional views, Laura accepts her mother on a deeper level. In the first episode, she tried on her mother's verbal style and physical mannerisms like a little girl scuffling along in mother's high heels; now she has discovered a shared enthusiasm, a sympathy, so that she is not merely imitating but becoming.

When Laura and Jose learn of the accident, their ensuing quarrel about canceling the party descends to childish irrelevance. (p. 62)

In her confrontation with her mother, Laura is also rendered speechless by her mother's logic: hearing about the death is itself accidental and should therefore make no difference; furthermore, Laura's prating about sympathy is itself unsympathetic, Mrs. Sheridan implies, to the only people that matter. Having made sympathy seem childish, Mrs. Sheridan bestows on Laura the hat which temporarily reconciles her to the party and to the social, logical view of life. . . . [The hat's] immediate effect is to block communication with Laurie. Further examination reveals an even more complex set of meanings. For one thing, it presents Laura with a new life-style: as a "charming girl" Laura is bemused by the hat because it represents not merely social position or rank—which she need not accept at her mother's valuation, though she does not yet know it—but also her transformation from child to woman, a condition she cannot avoid. Therefore, the hat is difficult for her to reject because it meets her own needs and even, as the scene with the lilies shows, her latent desires. Yet the style is for her unsatisfactory; though she "looks a picture" (a key phrase), it is the picture of a woman in her mother's image; and it is to this altered version of his sister rather than to the sensitive child—who despite her hat and her new role still needs sympathetic human contact—that Laurie responds.

Laura's acceptance of the role imposed by her mother persists until she begins to descend the hill into the darkening lane of cottages. In the darkness, dressed in white lace and "the big hat with the velvet streamer," she feels cut off from the "dark people" around her. . . . As in the morning episode, where she felt like a work-girl, she wishes to assume a disguise, "to be covered up in anything, one of those women's shawls even," but she can no longer dismiss class distinctions because here she is different.

Critics have assumed that Laura's response to seeing the dead workman indicates a new maturity or an accession of knowledge. That this is by no means certain is clear when we examine the language of the episode in the context of the whole story. When Em's sister leads Laura towards the body, she reassures Laura with the words "'e looks a picture. There's nothing to show." The language recalls Mrs. Sheridan's use of "picture" to describe Laura and Laura's thoughts, after seeing herself in the hat, "of that poor woman and those little children, and the body being carried into the house. But it all seemed blurred, unreal, like a picture in the newspaper." Even if one does not accept the argument that the term "picture" has become synonymous with "untrustworthy, unreal, artificial," the description of Laura's response to the body indicates that she is once again retreating from the real world. . . . (pp. 63-4)

Yet Laura has in a way matured, in a way reconciled herself to her situation and to life. When she says, with "a loud childish sob, "Forgive my hat," she becomes more mature than her mother and Jose ever can be. She has earlier feared and retreated from her mother's kind of maturity—the only kind she knows—because it insists upon a view of life that carefully restricts sympathy and almost precludes it. Yet her own childish position, impulsive and thoughtless, cannot suffice because it cannot endure. It is in subconscious recognition of these facts that she says "Forgive my hat." Not "the hat," as it had been when she first entered the dark lane, but "*my* hat."

In accepting the hat—it is "a black hat trimmed with gold daisies"—she accepts intuitively its symbolic components: the blackness representing the fact of death and suffering and division of humanity which in the morning she had rejected; the gold the beauty that there is in life, in light, even in garden parties where one can "be with people who are all happy, to press hands, press cheeks, smile into eyes"; the flowers not the roses or the arum lilies that are socially impressive, but the daisies that had been displaced (as unworthy the company of roses?) at the story's beginning, which like the canna lilies symbolize necessary and instinctive maturing. The way lies open for her to accept maturity without accepting her mother's version of it.

All of this is, of course, implicit, for at the end of the story she stammers, as she had after her first attempt to play an adult role. This time, however, she is not ashamed, but awed, and her recognition of the complexity of experience is her first step towards maturity. (p. 65)

Robert Murray Davis, "The Unity of 'The Garden Party'," in Studies in Short Fiction *(copyright 1964 by Newberry College), Vol. 11, No. 1, Fall, 1964, pp. 61-5.*

JAMES H. JUSTUS (essay date 1973)

Katherine Mansfield is known chiefly for two kinds of stories, both frothy. One group, best illustrated by **"Marriage à la Mode,"** concerns young couples (married or otherwise) who, despite their slightly down-at-heels chic, egotistically doubt each other's capacity to measure up to their private notions of worth, sophistication, fidelity, and so on. They are not concerned with social issues and indeed are only perfunctorily concerned about anything or anyone outside themselves. The second kind of story commonly deals with the well-to-do young innocent whose romantic dreams are shattered abruptly by the realism of the actual world, a realism most often represented by poor people or cynical men. This is the Katherine Mansfield of **"Her First Ball"** and **"The Garden Party,"** two stories which have been popular in the last two decades.

But a third kind of story, not much favored now, suggests as true a side of Katherine Mansfield as the other two: the study of eccentric, pathetic old ladies. Inexplicably, many early reviewers considered such stories as **"The Daughters of the Late Colonel"** and **"Miss Brill"** not merely ineffective portraits but heartless and snobbish caricatures. These are in fact the most enduring stories which Katherine Mansfield wrote, partly because they depend upon neither a topicality in which smart talk and fashionable attitudes soon become dated (as in **"Marriage à la Mode"**) nor a jejune innocence which becomes cloying naïveté (as in **"Her First Ball"**).

The very existence of these three kinds of stories by a talented writer suggests a somewhat broader range than Katherine Mansfield is usually credited with having. (These groupings do not include the early sketches and stories collected in her first book, *In a German Pension* . . . , the strength of which lies in the author's brittle observations of customs, manners, and cultural nuances and biases rather than in formal narrative art.) This range also suggests that there is no single paradigm Mansfield story just as there is no single such story in Lawrence, Joyce, or even Conrad. Our impulse to find paradigmatic patterns, however, remains particularly strong in Katherine Mansfield's case, and the texts of her stories lend some justification to it. For the nature of recurring scenes, overlapping characters and character types, and echoing moments of discovery, her first real story, **"The Tiredness of Rosabel"** . . . , is instructive.

The story is too accomplished to be called juvenilia—its author was twenty shen she wrote it—though it is slighter in substance and thematic development than later similar pieces. But this story of a millinery clerk who dreams romantically after work in her shabby flat contains characters which Katherine Mansfield was to return to again and again. As the spirited ingénue, Rosabel shows healthy flashes of exasperation in her dealings with a wealthy young woman and her handsome escort, an overfamiliar gentleman with a "disdainful" mouth. And though here they are mostly the stuff of Rosabel's dreams, *things* of the social world are inventoried, and their specificity in this slight narrative is the same quality which gives the later stories their remarkable air of physical solidity. . . . Even the outright authorial intrusion is to show up, considerably refined, in the mature work.

Despite her working-class status, it is easy to see how Rosabel becomes Leila (**"Her First Ball"**), Laura (**"The Garden Party"**), Kezia (**"The Doll's House"**), Fanny (**"Honeymoon"**), Bertha (**"Bliss"**), and all those other sensitive, well-bred young ladies who strike us as being the most patently autobiographical of the heroines, at least at one stage in their development. But at another stage, the spoiled, wealthy, unnamed lady of **"The Tiredness of Rosabel"** must also be autobiographical. She is repeated, most notably, in Monica Tyrell of **"Revelations,"** Anne Proctor of **"Mr. and Mrs. Dove,"** and Rosemary Fell of **"A Cup of Tea."** If Rosabel suffers from tiredness, all of these are threatened by ennui. Faintly dissatisfied, and fleetingly entertaining charitable thoughts about the working classes, they show up again, with some variation in elegance, in such stories as **"A Dill Pickle," "The Escape," "The Stranger,"** and **"Poison,"** all of which are studies of couples who have lost any sense of Rosabel's "tragic optimism" and whose marriage is marked by the refusal of a mate to give himself fully and unreservedly to his spouse.

In what is perhaps Katherine Mansfield's most famous (and certainly the most facile) story, **"Marriage à la Mode,"** these two feminine types merge in Isabel, who with some pangs of regret, nevertheless accepts the offer implied in her husband's parting letter: *"God forbid, my darling, that I should be a drag on your happiness."* The words used to describe her— "shallow, tinkling, vain"—are from the heroine's own point of view, a maneuver which supplies both self-knowledge on the character's part and perspective on the reader's; though modest, a kind of pervasive *bovaryisme* permits sympathy for, as well as disapproval of, the protagonist. This double level of perspective, carried forward by the tension between humble affection and vulgar affectation, is one of Katherine Mansfield's hallmarks.

These Isabels, Kezias, Lauras, and Rosemarys are stunningly alive to nuances, not despite the paraphernalia of the world which they inhabit and dominate, but because of it. It is a rich, textural world in which things themselves take on the kind of sentient significance that in another writer, Forster or Lawrence or James, would be supplied by society, the intricate network of people interacting on specific consciousnesses. In no other writer of her day, with the possible exception of Proust, do

things matter so much. . . . And the situations, precisely placed—meetings at seaside retreats and out-of-the-way flats, in lengthy cab-rides and brief sea voyages, at parties and entertainments and public tea—are socially restricted and are conceived almost wholly in terms of *talk*. Outright quarrels almost never occur in a Mansfield story; more often, bittersweet banter is chillingly premonitory of future separations. With the quiet dropping of suggestions and the half-serious queries and evasive declarations, in domesticated scenes in which opposing familiarities intersect, we are given the portentous clues to the death of love.

Yet if ingénues and smart matrons, sisters to certain heroines out of Maugham and early Noel Coward, seem the representative Mansfield protagonists, there is also the sizeable group of lonely older women, shabby, proud, some of them genteel, who have proceeded about as far as possible from the "tragic optimism" of their youthful counterparts. **"The Tiredness of Rosabel"** is again instructive. In this earliest story, *dreams* of romance—pegged inevitably to affluence—can be only that. Rosabel scorns the reading tastes of a fellow bus passenger, cheap advertisements, shoppers who only browse, and the "sickening smell of warm humanity," but she nevertheless lives in a room four flights up, where the inadequate heat must be supplemented by an old flannel dressing gown, a calico nightdress, and a grimy quilt. If Rosabel the dreamer anticipates the Leilas and Kezias of later stories, what Katherine Mansfield calls "the real Rosabel, the girl crouched on the floor in the dark," anticipates the pathetic older creatures who have no hopes for a future and who exist perilously, mentally as well as physically, in a locked-in present.

Such a person is the speaker in **"The Canary,"** probably the last story Katherine Mansfield completed before her death. . . . **"The Canary,"** a prose dramatic monologue, is hardly a story at all, but its bleak statement on man's lonely fate is presumably Katherine Mansfield's final word. "Perhaps it does not matter so very much what it is one loves in this world," says the speaker. "But love something one must." Through sheer force of will she can isolate and elevate objects of her love, but the effort outweighs the apparent benefits. Loss, sadness, sorrow are still there, waiting.

In most stories, this fate is evoked quietly, without a trace of Modernist experimentation. It is as if the worlds of Chekhov and Hardy had been evoked but stripped of their social configurations, leaving only psychological and spiritual inevitability. And yet not quite stripped. There is a kind of poetics of poverty at work in most of the stories, blatant in some (like **"Pictures"**) and covert in others (like **"A Cup of Tea"**), which threads the psychological shocks and reminds us that a grim economic unease is very much a part of the configurations of the societies which this "comfortable" New Zealander chose to depict. Fate in a Mansfield story is too impacted, too felt, to admit the kind of fashionable despair that we detect in some of the fiction of George Moore. The fragile order of routine, the occasional treating of oneself to a modest luxury, the magnifying significance of a cherished treasure, all the tics and gestures which, representing a minimal purchase on solid reality, prevent for a while longer an acceleration in the slow slide into the abyss: these are the qualities which give a sense of psychological movement even in those stories which have little narrative action.

"Miss Brill" is perhaps the best known and the best of these. The treasure is a fur necklace—a cunning, roguish "Dear little thing!" to Miss Brill, a funny, out-of-date "fried whiting" to a young girl and her boy friend in the park; and the Sunday treat is a slice of honey-cake which might or might not contain an almond. Her sudden realization of another perspective puts Miss Brill's own into shadow. The fragile arrangement of her life is disordered—perhaps permanently—and the day that begins "so brilliantly fine" ends in her dark little room, "like a cupboard," where Miss Brill sits quietly with her hurt.

No other story is as effectively understated as **"Miss Brill,"** but something of the same psychological movement can be seen in several other pieces. **"The Daughters of the Late Colonel"** is high comedy. (pp. 13-17)

[Behind] the technical élan of the comedy—the precisely heard dialogue and skilfully built scenes, the almost imperceptible leaking of past causes into effects of the present—is the spiritual death that Katherine Mansfield so brilliantly and horrifyingly traces in the vague gestures, the magnification of the trivial, the indecisions, the fear of a former authority which continues to drain away all will and purpose. The story dramatizes a state that from the beginning of her career to its end obsessed Katherine Mansfield.

"The Daughters" is also her most extreme statement on the assertive male who subordinates and shapes to his own ends the lives around him. . . . Such a specific threat to individuality accounts, I think, for Katherine Mansfield's warm response to Joyce's Molly Bloom, who so handily rejects such threats, and her general enthusiasm for Lawrentian vitality. *Aaron's Rod*, she declared in 1922, was "written by a living man, with *conviction*." She then generalizes:

> In youth most of us are, for various reasons, slaves. And then, when we are able to throw off our chains, we prefer to keep them. Freedom is dangerous, is frightening.

> If only I can be [a] good enough writer to strike a blow for freedom! It is the one axe I want to grind. Be free—and you can afford to give yourself to life! Even to believe in life.

Being free is merely a luxurious yearning for the protagonists of **"Life of Ma Parker"** and **"The Lady's Maid,"** two grim, and less successful, variations on **"The Daughters."** What the narrator in **"The Canary"** refers to as sorrow "that we all know"—illness, poverty, death—is not occasional but the very measure of the lives of both Ma Parker (whose crises simply depress "the literary gentleman" for whom she works) and the maid (whose mistress shows only mild curiosity about her disappointments). Believing in life is a strenuous task for Miss Ada Moss of **"Pictures,"** which with both fullness and delicacy describes a day in the life of a former singer. (pp. 17-18)

Like **"The Daughters,"** these three protagonists suffer from an inability to "be free," from the leeching away of individuality. The maid has merged her own life with that of her former mistress; Ma Parker has devoted all her energies to the welfare of various members of her family; Miss Moss, having survived her modest talent, is now willing to accept any role offered her, including the real-life one of aging prostitute. By the merging of economic disrepairs and psychological dislocations, Katherine Mansfield seems to suggest that individuality is not even a quality that can be earned. Well-to-do young innocents may be momentarily addled by the casual onslaught of an actuality harshly alien to their dreams, but they *are* young and well-to-do. The Miss Brills and Miss Mosses are neither. For them it is not a matter of deciding to buy a plumed hat or

an exquisite enameled box for twenty-eight guineas, but whether to spend "one and thrippence" at a tea-room.

Moreover, the harshness and disappointment of these characters impinge on the lives of the custodians of comfort considerably more frequently than might at first appear. (p. 18)

An adulterous affair puts the young woman of **"This Flower"** into the hands of a shady doctor. Her tolerance and courage contrast sharply with her lover's concern for appearances, and his cowardice makes this story one of Katherine Mansfield's sharper critiques of the aggressive male.

Charity—or at least charitable thoughts—often wins in the struggle between the shallow urge to demonstrate patrician responsibility and the self-indulgent satisfaction in one's own comfort. But the victory is always brief. In a household of Sheridans, Laura can be the "sensitive one" in only limited ways and for a limited time; the working class can be "ever so nice" only so long as its members work for her pleasure and in her context. Once away from the banked flowers, trellises, shimmering lights and colors of a manicured garden, their life is trailed by dingy footpaths, soot and grime, cramped houses, and sudden death. (pp. 18-19)

I have said that these three types of narrative demonstrate a wider range in her art than Katherine Mansfield is usually credited with having. But in another sense there is a quality of the writing which does alert us, which makes us realize that there *is* something called "a Mansfield story," and its defining resonance makes the operable range even more restricted than that of her contemporaries. Whatever the status of its characters, each story projects an emotional context which cuts across social and economic boundaries. In fashionable houses or shabby flats, the great common emotion is loneliness; when it is in fact not a present and realized state, it is not far away, potential and richly threatening.

The pervasiveness of this emotional context is, I think, a clue—perhaps an obvious one—to the problem of autobiography in Katherine Mansfield's career: the extent, that is, to which the art is transposed life, and the nature of that transposition. It accounts, in other words, for not only the basically egoistic character of the stories but also their control, the hard disinterestedness, which prevents the infections of her life from invading her art.

From the beginning, even her less astute critics were quick to point out an apparent lack of sympathy behind the stories. As a rhetorical device, radical disinterestedness was a perfectly acceptable, even conventional, authorial attitude in satiric sketches such as those found in *In a German Pension;* her more developed narratives, however, suggested a critical detachment so pronounced as to render suspect those emotional moments of self-discovery toward which all aspects of the stories moved. (p. 19)

[If] the socially insulated Burnells seem self-sufficient to a fault in **"At the Bay"** and other stories transparently drawn from Katherine Mansfield's family, those who dominate **"Bliss,"** **"Marriage à la Mode,"** and other studies of husbands and wives are even further detached from a supportive society. Such couples are self-sufficient in a chilling, almost pre-Existential way. In the moment of crisis—and it can be spontaneous joy as well as sudden despair—the illumination breaks upon the reader's consciousness even before it comes to the heroine's: she is alone. This is as true of Bertha in **"Bliss"** as it is of the protagonists of **"Revelations"** or **"The Escape"** or **"Je ne**

parle pas français.'' And what these narratives assert is the inevitability of further loneliness, deeper estrangement. Deterioration in human relationships assumes almost the status of natural law in **"Ma Parker," "The Lady's Maid," "Pictures,"** and **"Miss Brill."** A notable paradox, then, of Katherine Mansfield's fiction, dealing as it does with domestic relationships, is the absence of trusting friends or spouses. Prefigured as early as **"The Woman at the Store,"** a muted melodramatic piece done in the naturalistic manner, and most starkly and interestingly rendered in **"Je ne parle,"** the Mansfield heroine is spiritually cut loose from nourishing human ties.

But out of the stresses of abandonment comes resilience, a strength created by the embattled self. In a sense, Katherine Mansfield is the most egocentric writer of her time. . . . There are considerably more crises in Katherine Mansfield's life than in her art, and each one is apparently recorded—somewhere— in relentless detail. Although it is sometimes strident, her own recording more often than not shows a matter-of-factness, almost as if the act of cataloging symptoms, reactions, moods becomes an aid for coming to terms with her illness. But the fiction, however close to real or imagined moments in her life, has little explicit relationship to such crises. By the miracle of imaginative transformation, the fiction is purified of blatant hates, fears, and despairs. (p. 20)

Though she may have been a wistful, despairing woman for most of her brief life, she was also a willful, undespairing artist, whose contributions to our knowledge of the heart are finally about the conduct not of social classes but of human beings, caught in small moments charged with implications rippling through and beyond the boundaries of a single consciousness. Her stories, even some of the frailer ones, can still be read with both interest and admiration, partly because Katherine Mansfield learned that egocentricity in life is not the same thing as creative egoism. The first is oppressively demonstrated in the private utterances; the second constitutes a minor triumph of the romantic sensibility. (p. 22)

> *James H. Justus, "Katherine Mansfield: The Triumph of Egoism," in* MOSAIC: A Journal for the Comparative Study of Literature and Ideas *(copyright © 1973 by the University of Manitoba; acknowledgment of previous publication is herewith made), Vol. VI, No. 3 (Spring, 1973), pp. 13-22.*

PAUL DELANY (essay date 1976)

The subject of **"The Doll's House"** is class prejudice: two innocents are persecuted only because they are poor. The story owes its special tone and poignancy to the circumstance that the oppression it describes is strictly psychological—that is, inflicted by emotional rather than material brutality—and that the main characters are children. Isabel, Kezia, and Lottie Burnell are three sisters who are given a magnificent doll's house by a family friend. They are already among the social elite of their small New Zealand settlement, but their prestige now rises even higher as their schoolmates vie for invitations to see the house. All are at length granted the favor except the two Kelvey girls, who are ostracised by their schoolmates because their mother is the local washer-woman. Kezia, however, defies convention by showing the house to the Kelveys. She is caught in the act by her aunt, who indignantly drives the Kelveys away, though not quickly enough to prevent their catching a glimpse of the house's wonders—of which the most

wonderful, to Kezia, is a tiny lamp on the dining room table. (p. 8)

It is obvious that the plot of **"The Doll's House"** turns on the Kelveys' exclusion from the society of their schoolmates; what is less prominent is that Kezia has in certain ways chosen to be excluded too. In the life of her creator that choice led her in adolescence to the vocation of artist; but in the world of the story Kezia knows only that she is an outsider. She shares the outlook of Stephen Dedalus, loitering "on the fringes of his line," though, like him, she cannot know yet where her instinctual aloofness will lead. The story suggests two reasons for her isolation: she is emotionally more sensitive than her peers, and she reflexively opposes her older sister Isabel, who has taken her stand for hierarchy and the established order. It is Isabel, for example, who claims the prerogative of being first to tell about the doll's house at school. . . . (p. 9)

A number of incidental details in the story imply that Kezia and the Kelveys are natural allies because of similarities in situation and temperament. As Kezia and Lottie respond to their sister's self-assertiveness by walking silently at the edge of the road, so do the Kelveys silently "hover at the edge" when their schoolmates exclude them from a discussion of the doll's house. Later, when the Burnells expect visitors, "Isabel and Lottie, who liked visitors, went upstairs to change their pinafores. But Kezia thieved out at the back." The expression "thieved" (i.e. stole away) hints at Kezia's kinship with the outcast Kelveys, whose father is rumored to be in prison, and anticipates the "crime" she is about to commit against the proprieties of her class. (p. 10)

[The moral scheme of **"The Doll's House"**] allows for three styles of action. On one side we have the snobbish pack of schoolgirls whose cruelty has a monstrous and absolute quality, in the mode of a William Golding fantasy. Opposed to them are the Kelveys, passive and inarticulate victims—yet dignified by their touching devotion to each other (which contrasts with the invidious distinctions that obsess the other girls). . . . Between these somewhat one-dimensional opponents stands Kezia, the moral fulcrum of the story since she alone seems able to understand and evaluate the compulsions of both sides. She also is free to choose which side to ally herself with, though her decision becomes evident only towards the end of the story, and even then it seems at first that her kindness to the Kelveys may be no more than an impulsive gesture of support. It shows her to be morally superior to her schoolmates, but this in itself would be a trite conclusion, one that would justify the critic in dismissing the story as a rather patronising variation on the theme of *noblesse oblige*. However, the story has a further, symbolic dimension—it is suffused, one might say, with the imagined light of "the little lamp" in the doll's house. This gives a subtler meaning to what would otherwise be a straightforward episode of class snobbery and injustice.

We learn early in the story that the lamp has a special attraction for Kezia: "what [she] liked more than anything, what she liked frightfully, was the lamp. . . . The lamp was perfect. It seemed to smile at Kezia, to say, 'I live here.' The lamp was real." Her passion remains exclusive since Isabel and the other girls fail to appreciate the unique appeal of the lamp, despite Kezia's prompting. But in what, precisely, does that appeal consist?

One interpretation of the lamp would be that it epitomizes, for Kezia, those qualities of warmth, brightness, and security that make a house into a home. Her less sensitive schoolmates,

Isabel especially, are taken with the miniature carpets, the beds with real bedclothes, in short, all the material comforts of bourgeois domesticity. The appeal of the doll's house, for these girls, lies in its being the replica of a style of life that they accept without question. We note that Isabel and Lottie welcome visitors (though Kezia evades them), and do not think of challenging their Aunt Beryl's right to decide whom they shall associate with. But Kezia has a double vision. One side of her nature seems uneasy with the stresses and limitations of conventional family life. This theme is barely touched on in **"The Doll's House,"** though another story about the Burnells, **"Prelude,"** focuses on the tension between the delicate, melancholy Mrs. Burnell and her ebulliently self-centered husband. The title **"The Doll's House"** may therefore suggest an affinity with the vacuous and oppressive domestic life in Ibsen's play of similar name; it is a "perfect" house, but one that seems to stifle its occupants. . . . (pp. 12-13)

Still, Kezia has a child's absolute need for the security of a home and family. . . . (p. 13)

[The lamp is a symbol] in **"The Doll's House,"** of everything about family life that warms and sustains, whatever discords may accompany these gifts. When the lamp is given this meaning, the final words of **"The Doll's House"** create a mood of pure pathos, as the Kelveys rest by the road after Aunt Beryl has driven them out like vermin:

> Presently our Else nudged up close to her sister. But now she had forgotten the cross lady. She put out a finger and stroked her sister's quill; she smiled her rare smile.
>
> "I seen the little lamp," she said softly.
>
> Then both were silent once more.

These are the disinherited of their society, children of an absent father and a mother who "[goes] about from house to house by the day." Nor can they expect a better future, since their schoolmates already taunt them by demanding: "Is it true you're going to be a servant when you grow up, Lil Kelvey?" The pathos of the ending is that the Kelveys, who are only allowed to glimpse the doll's house and the lamp, are the children best able to appreciate the value of what is denied them.

The lamp thus contributes to the theme of class opposition in the story, insofar as it symbolises the comforts that the middle class children enjoy and that the Kelveys are deprived of. But it lends itself to a further interpretation not purely domestic. . . . The artist's one responsibility, in Mansfield's view, is to bear true witness to his time, and he can only do so by first purging himself of personal doctrine or prejudice. This is the implication of her remark to Sylvia Lynd: "I find my great difficulty in writing is to learn to submit." . . . The artist must lose himself in the object of his attention for it to become radiant, a "bright breathing thing" displayed to the reader in its fullness of being. The artistic power is thus, in the first instance, the power of vision; though *from* that vision there may flow the weightiest moral or even political consequences. (pp. 13-14)

The artist, in this tradition, is the person who can single out from a scene or episode that "something central that permeates," and can then render the special quality of that essence in a way that permits others to perceive it too. In **"The Doll's House"** that essential thing is the little lamp, appreciated at first only by Kezia, the child-artist. Yet the conclusion of the story implies a further revelation. When Lil Kelvey fears to enter the Burnells' yard at Kezia's invitation, "Suddenly there was a twitch, a tug at [her] skirt. . . . Our Else was looking at her with big, imploring eyes; she was frowning; she wanted to go." On first reading, we would naturally take this silent appeal as a further stroke of pathos which underlines Else's backwardness and deprivation. But Else's words at the end of the story—"I seen the little lamp"—are an epiphany: we suddenly realise that Else alone had shared Kezia's vision of that "perfect" and "real" thing. She, who until the end of the story speaks no word and seems barely human, is an artist too.

It remains to assess the moral scheme governing Mansfield's handling of her subject. On one level, the story emphasizes what is *different* about the Kelveys: they have been excluded from the society of their schoolmates because they are poor, and can expect no better treatment for the rest of their lives (we can imagine Lil, in old age, as someone like the much-abused charwoman in **"Life of Ma Parker"**). The brevity of their view of the doll's house therefore evokes pathos, because it prefigures a lifetime of dispossession. Then, at the end of the story, we have an assertion of *similarity:* Else, in spite of her humble origin, can share with Kezia the vision of the lamp and thus be exalted in the reader's eyes.

"Life of Ma Parker" describes the world as it appears to a charwoman who must do her work while grieving for her favorite grandson; but in **"The Doll's House"** the narrative viewpoint is reversed, so that we are restricted almost entirely to an external view of the Kelveys. We can assume that they suffer when mistreated by the other girls, but this suffering is not directly expressed or described. The Kelveys speak a total of sixteen words, though much is said to them and about them; the story's focus is usually on how their superiors respond to their mere presence, since their only actions are to listen, to look, and to run away. Once Kezia has shown her moral worth by inviting them to see the doll's house her role is complete, and we learn nothing of her response to the Kelveys' expulsion by Aunt Beryl. The final scene in which Else blissfully recalls her glimpse of the lamp is a kind of coda. She is now alone with Lil, so her words can be heard neither by her persecutors nor by Kezia. They are a revelation, with an implied moral, addressed directly to the reader by the narrator.

This moral closely resembles the one expressed in a famous quatrain from [Thomas] Gray's *Elegy:*

> Full many a gem of purest ray serene
> The dark, unfathomed caves of ocean bear;
> Full many a flower is born to blush unseen
> And waste its sweetness on the desert air. . . .

By accepting without complaint the hardships of their lot, the lower classes acquire, in Gray's eyes, a moral dignity that those above them lack.

Similar attitudes are implicit in the action and characterisation of **"The Doll's House,"** though Mansfield adds, as we have seen, a typically modern third term: Kezia, the future artist who has a foot in each camp. Whereas Gray is content to gaze soulfully at the poor across the sundering gulf of class privilege, Mansfield conceives of the artist as one who can enter imaginatively into the experience of both sides and distil that experience into a pure artistic form. On the face of it, **"The Doll's House"** shows the strong crushing the weak; Mansfield sees the brutality of this oppression, but endows the Kelveys with a spiritual radiance that compensates for their defeat. This quality is different from Gray's traditional Tory sentimentality about his sturdy rustics; it is closer in spirit to Dostoevsky and Chekhov. (pp. 15-16)

Through the symbolism of the lamp, ["**The Doll's House**"] suggests that the artist has a natural affinity with the poor and humble insofar as both must *"learn to accept,"* and that this acceptance is the source of their spiritual and creative powers. Conversely, the artist who rebels against "what life is" descends from art to propaganda and thereby betrays his calling; while the rebellious peasant or worker becomes simply horrifying. . . .

[The way Mansfield] presents the Kelveys in **"The Doll's House"** amounts to a sentimental distortion of lower-class experience, and an emotional exploitation of it for the author's benefit. That this exploitation is accomplished with remarkable literary finesse does not change its essential nature. (p. 17)

> Paul Delany, "Short and Simple Annals of the Poor: Katherine Mansfield's 'The Doll's House'," in MOSAIC: A Journal for the Comparative Study of Literature and Ideas (copyright © 1976 by the University of Manitoba; acknowledgment of previous publication is herewith made), Vol. X, No. 1 (Fall, 1976), pp. 7-17.

MARILYN ZORN (essay date 1980)

It is perhaps inevitable, given our cultural bias, that Bertha Young [of **"Bliss"**], who yearned to share her feelings of "bliss" with her husband and friends and failed to find the language that would communicate it, has been misunderstood and misrepresented by the critics of this most popular of Katherine Mansfield's stories. . . .

Poor Bertha! According to these critics, she is quintessentially a female stereotype: timid, sentimental, childish, frigid, naive, self-deluding. Such a figure (no matter how self-contradictory some of those qualities might be) of course deserves the disillusionment which comes to her at the end of the story when she discovers her husband's and friend's affair. Perhaps her worst fault . . . is that she has thought herself happy. Even her bliss is suspect. . . . (p. 141)

But to strip Bertha of her human dignity and to make the story into an unpleasant little exposé of a social group and of a child-woman is to fail to recognize the author's state of mind during the writing of the story and her hopes and intentions for her art. For Katherine Mansfield was not thinking small or smart at the time **"Bliss"** was composed. The story was written a week after the hemorrhage which signalled the seriousness of her lung condition. Like Keats in a similar situation she was henceforward convinced that she did not have enough time left to seal the accomplishment her work had promised. . . . [There] is in her letter to Murry at the conclusion of the first draft of **"Bliss"** the conviction that the stories are crowding up on her, that the writing is a matter of necessity and that her powers are sufficient to her inspiration: "One extraordinary thing has happened to me since I came out here. Once I start them they haunt me and plague me until they are finished and as good as I can do." In accord with that sense of power comes also a heightened sensitivity to nature which Katherine Mansfield ascribes to her illness. On February 20, 1918, the day after she hemorrhaged, she wrote to Murry: "Since this little attack I've had, a queer thing has happened. I feel that my love and longing for the external world—I mean the world of *nature*—has suddenly increased a million times." It is this awareness of the signatory aspect of nature which links Katherine Mans-

field to the Romantic poets. Like Keats and Shelley, she sees nature as a veil for the ideal world, offering intimations of a beauty and state of being which are transcendent, never possible except in hints and brief glimpses offered in the natural beauty of the world. It is the poet's task to testify to the visionary world's possibility, but he or she is continually aware that such insight also includes its transcendence. Hence to be a messenger of such a world also means that one must speak of its corruption in the real world. When Katherine Mansfield tells Murry that she has two starting points for writing—the sense of joy and the "cry against corruption,"—she is being as true to Shelley's vision that life "Stains the white radiance of Eternity" as any twentieth-century writer can be. Moreover, **"Bliss's"** theme encompasses exactly the visionary joy and the cry against corruption which we associate with the Romantics. One of the unacknowledged sources for the story is Shelley's poem "The Question." . . . The silver blossoms offered by Pearl and Bertha in the moment with the pear tree are an echo of the poem's speaker offering "visionary flowers" to his lover in the fifth stanza. Finally, the poem's last line asks the question which troubles Bertha throughout the story: "Oh, to Whom" can the vision be communicated? A year later, the season, the emotion, and Shelley's poem are still linked together in the author's mind. (pp. 142-43)

A major assumption about the story must be, then, that Bertha's state of mind and her need to share it with her friends and husband are seen as perfectly valid by the author. The lack of awareness on the part of those close to her is seen as their incapacity, not Bertha's. Her intuition of the new life which might grow out of her awareness, her brief glimpse of ideal womanhood, and her awakened sexual desire are genuine in the story—not fraudulent and not sentimental. The failure of the vision is the result of those elements in the society and in the individual which Katherine Mansfield identified as corrupting.

Since it would be difficult to speak of Bertha, the most childlike of the story's characters, as corrupt, it is better to ask what has caused Bertha's vision to falter. There is no denying the irony with which the author views her character. She chips away at the illusory nature of Bertha's happiness until at the end nothing seems to be left of it. Still, there she is throughout the story with her "bliss," the only character who is so graced. Moreover, Katherine Mansfield gives her the two central metaphors of the story: the vision of the pear tree and the analogy for art, "playing." . . . Bertha shows [an] aesthetic sense in her remark about the piano: "What a pity someone does not play; what a pity someone does not play." The remark must be taken symbolically. Bertha's intuitions about love and her child have used the same analogy: what good is the rare violin if it is shut up in a case and never played? . . . It is obviously not enough for the artist to have the vision; there must be a language to communicate it and a community of listeners who speak the language to understand it when it is spoken. It is Shelley's question again: "Oh to Whom?"

Yet supposing Bertha had the tongues of angels to aid her, it has traditionally been her language which has drawn most criticism from her readers. One might suggest that that is so, not because Bertha's speech is so empty and vacuous, but because she sounds like a woman, or our concept of how a particular kind of middle-class woman sounds. . . . She uses "so" and "such" as intensifiers. She has a range of adjectives which only women use, like "divine" and "little precious" and "incredibly beautiful." She uses the tag question to avoid self-assertion; she hedges; she speaks in italics. Further, the author has for her a variety of sentence forms to imply elevated emotion and sensitivity: the rhetorical question, the exclamation, repetition, the abrupt shift in syntax signalled by the dash, the unfinished sentence. When Bertha's breathless, exclamatory perceptions are contrasted with Harry's talk about digestion or the small talk of the dinner guests, the distance between their sensibilities is emphasized. Also emphasized is the difference in female and male speech.

Thus, a major effect of Bertha's speech is to reinforce her sad awareness that she will not be able to communicate her vision, unless a sympathetic woman friend will share it. Because her language for experience must stress its affective and subjective qualities, there will be few reference points in such a language beyond the self unless there is congruence of emotion. Yet Harry's response to Bertha's emotion is to deny it and to hood his own. Bertha, in trying to tell her husband about her "bliss" during the phone conversation, recognizes that it will seem absurd to him and breaks off their exchange. Her very sensitivity to her husband's insensitivity, her secret admiration for his deflating jokes about her enthusiasms, insures that she will not ask for intimate communication with him. Thus she will remain the impersonal "good pal" she perceives he wishes her to be in their marriage.

Bertha's set generally seems to discount the language of emotion and enthusiasm or to parody it by exaggerating the banal until genuine emotion seems suspect. Bertha feels her estrangement from them throughout the dinner party with the result that she grows more and more tense. The woman who felt "bliss" earlier now feels a kind of hysteria at her inability to communicate with them. Because Pearl has seemed sympathetic, she desperately waits for a "sign" that she has shared her emotion. But she is unable to distinguish true intimacy from false, and so the moment at the window before the pear tree turns out to be one more imposture. "Your lovely pear tree" thus becomes a symbol of the desirability of human intimacy and the betrayal of it.

It is important that the reader not undervalue Bertha's vision, although in terms of the story it is unrealized. For it is one of the poles of feeling in the story. Without it, Bertha's disillusionment is empty of significance, as empty as one of her guest's stories. Since it is the pear tree that draws together the characters and their emotions in the story, it is well to look more closely at the images the author associates with the tree. By the time Bertha and Pearl stand before the pear tree in their moment of intimacy, both of the women have been identified with it. Moreover, Bertha's bliss, supposedly enveloping both the women at this moment, has also been identified with it. The earlier imagery for the bliss has been a series of sun images, which Bertha internalizes. Now the sun image is linked with the moon through the candle metaphor, which seems to project an ideal order of relationship in nature: "Although it was so still it seemed, like the flame of a candle, to stretch up, to point, to quiver in the bright air, to grow taller and taller as they gazed . . . almost to the rim of the moon." . . . Images which link the sun and the moon are for Katherine Mansfield holistic. They suggest the earthly paradise, the condition of pre-lapsarian innocence. . . . In their ideal selves there is no distinction between [Bertha and Pearl]. They equally bear treasures of bliss and offer visionary flowers. What Bertha has discovered is the potential life all women possess. What the vision suggests is that there are possibilities of relationships which are gracious and free.

Finally the story shows that these potential relationships are corrupted and thwarted by the character of human interaction in the world. For against Bertha's momentary glimpse of Pearl's and her own ideal self is projected another demonic vision of the world and its way with women.

Beginning with Face, the women in the real world of the story are threatened with actual and imagined acts of violence. In counterpoint to Bertha's vision, the talk at the party is a continuous barrage of horror stories. . . . Art itself gives expression to the violence: they talk about the poem about a "girl who was violated by a beggar without a nose." . . . Indeed, Harry's passion for the white flesh of lobster and green pistachio ices makes erotic love exactly like eating, and together with Face's experiences, vaguely cannibalistic. His vulgarity is given a sinister turn by the double entendre in the joke about his daughter: "My dear Mrs. Knight, I shan't feel the slightest interest in her until she has a lover." . . . At that point in the story, both of the male guests show by their actions that they know, if Bertha doesn't, about the affair with Pearl. Even Pearl, who might seem to have come off the winner in the real world of the story, is shown as vulnerable to the questionable ethics of relationships between men and women. For it seems she will be eaten, after all, in Harry's terms. Her blindness is subtly expressed. Along with the Gioconda smile, she is described as one who "lived by listening rather than seeing." . . . It is clear she is caught up in the force which Bertha imagines as "blind and smiling" when she imagines desire. In these circumstances, the image is ambiguous and even terrible. The only person who seems to have responded to the ideal Pearl is Bertha, and in their world, they must be rivals.

Katherine Mansfield, then, has not written a satire of a foolish woman who overvalues her life's happiness; nor has she written a satire of the pretensions to art of a group of Philistines. What she has done is to write a somber story about the potential for love and beauty in human relationships which can be glimpsed but not realized. Certainly, a woman like Bertha, condemned to inarticulateness by her female language, cannot realize it. Yet her openness to "bliss" and the potential in life, and her desire to share the vision, do make her the heroine of the story. The question with which Bertha ends the story is not unhopeful. She has been questioning all day. Her "Oh what is going to happen now?" is certainly resigned, certainly an admittal of powerlessness at this final moment. But it does look forward to the future. It acknowledges her losses. It propels her forward into the life she must lead. (pp. 144-47)

Marilyn Zorn, "Visionary Flowers: Another Study of Katherine Mansfield's 'Bliss'," in Studies in Short Fiction *(copyright 1980 by Newberry College), Vol. 17, No. 2, Spring, 1980, pp. 141-47.*

J. F. KOBLER   (essay date 1980)

"The Young Girl" deserves greater recognition among Katherine Mansfield's stories not only because it is probably the minor masterpiece [Antony] Alpers has called it, but also because of its unusual narrative point of view. Although the story of an innocent young girl facing the "evils" of the adult world is a Mansfield staple, this version is the only one told by a sexless first person narrator. (p. 269)

Clearly this fact about the narration of **"The Young Girl"** raises a number of questions, the first of which must concern the author's intentions. Did Mansfield leave out or obfuscate the narrator's sex on purpose? Indeed so! No authorial accident exists here. The sex of each of her other first person narrators is so naturally given through a name, a title of address, or a personal pronoun that the absence of such talismen in **"The Young Girl"** indicates conscious intention. In addition, the internal evidence of the story, as I shall show, strongly argues for textual manipulation to make the narrator's sex not only not given but actively ambiguous.

A corollary to the missing facts but supplied ambiguities about the sex of the narrator is the absence of information about the relationship between the narrator and Mrs. Raddick, the mother of the 17-year-old, unnamed girl. What relationship empowers Mrs. Raddick to ask " 'You don't mind taking Hennie?' " Later this narrator, observing Mrs. Raddick's desperate need to get to her gambling but her much less pressing need to have her daughter chaperoned, says " 'I seized my courage' " and then speaks to the daughter, " 'Would you—do you care to come to tea with—us?' " The dash-marked hesitations in this dialogue indicate the wariness with which the narrator assumes the role of chaperon to Mrs. Raddick's son and daughter. Why it is assumed at all remains even more of a mystery than does the sex. However, a declared sex would lead to possible definitions of the relationship. The following close examination of some of Mansfield's "tricks" shows how she avoids defining her narrator sexually; it conjectures as to how thematic concerns are enhanced through her narrative manipulation.

For example, in the car on the way to tea, the girl says she loathes " 'being stared at by old fat men. Beasts!' " The narrator reports that "Hennie gave her a quick look and then peered out of the window." Hennie's response suggests that he is worried about a male narrator's feelings being hurt, especially if he is old and fat. The story is already one-third completed at the point of this minor and hardly conclusive action; nothing prior has given any clue to the narrator's sex. (pp. 269-70)

Another tantalizing bit of dialogue occurs when the narrator asks "if I might smoke." The girl responds, " 'Of course,' said she. 'I always expect people to.' " In a story otherwise loaded with pregnant pauses in the dialogue, the girl does not hesitate on the word "people." At this time, even in upper levels of European society, one did not "always expect" women to smoke. Therefore, if Mansfield had inserted one of those pauses in dialogue here, it surely would have suggested maleness to the reader. But the absence of the pause suggests little, and the word "people" tells us a great deal about the girl's attitude. Of course, either a man or a woman in an inferior social position (employed as nanny or tutor by Mrs. Raddick) might ask permission of these children to smoke. On the other hand, if the narrator is not a social inferior, then the girl is being treated as a young lady in the narrator's asking her permission to smoke, whatever the sex.

Although this episode provides no tangible evidence about the narrator, it says a great deal about Mansfield's intention to withhold evidence. The hypothetical sentence "I always expect men to," rather than the actual one in the story, would have settled the whole issue. But it would also destroy one of the essential thematic elements. "People" may seem like an artificial word, but the choice is right for this girl in her present state of mind. She is at war with the entire adult world, both sexes. She expects people, that is, adults, to smoke. But children, of which she is still one, of course, do not smoke. Because she currently despises all adult people, she will not restrict her contemptuous response to men or women, regardless of which this smoker happens to be. (pp. 270-71)

However, two other events may incline readers slightly toward femaleness. In one, the narrator is urged by the girl to complete a sentence suggesting that the girl likes Monte Carlo better than London because it is more—" '*Enfin*—gayer,' I cried, waving my cigarette." If not feminine, that at least seems effeminate. Later, returning to the Casino from the tea shop, the narrator says the automobile "tore through the black-and-gold town like a pair of scissors tearing through brocade." Can anyone argue with much success that images drawn from the world of sewing are inherently feminine, that a male narrator would only be given such a simile by an unsuccessful author? I think not. (p. 271)

Taken all in all, then, the factual evidence about the sex of the narrator remains ambiguous and contradictory, if not quite balanced. Nor do the narrator's attitudes reveal the sex. Nothing in the story remotely suggests the arousal of male emotions of sexual conquest or fatherly affection. Nor do any envious or competitive emotional waves emanate from a jealous female. Motherly emotions are not visible. Mansfield has done a remarkable job of constructing a neutral, or neuter, point of view in this story. The consciousness of the narrator is objective even though it is a first person story. But the result is not a bland nothing; the result is a story which elicits a marvelous aesthetic blending of sympathy and antipathy for the girl. But not just for this one girl; rather for the condition, for a world in which children must grow up, in which the pain of reaching adulthood is inflicted not only upon the child herself but also upon those around her. This young girl is not yet ready to become the young woman her mother tries to create by getting her into the Casino and having her hair put up.

That theme is hardly a new one, but it is individualized in this story through the sexless narrator and other related contradictions, conflicts, and ambiguities. For example, the approaching painful end of a seventeen-year-old's adolescence is balanced by the entrance of her twelve-year-old brother into the experience. Hennie does not know he is beginning to feel those pains, but his actions are already not totally those of an innocent child. He reacts to adult social concerns. The already mentioned reproachful look he gives his sister represents an adult awareness that feelings can be hurt. At another point, Hennie calls the narrator's attention to an English bulldog, about which he exclaims: " 'He's a ripping chap, isn't he? I wish I had one. They're such fun. They frighten people so, and they're never fierce with their—the people they belong to.' " The dash to indicate the speaker's hesitation and his fumbling for the proper word indicate that Hennie knows there is something he should not say at this point. The expected word from Hennie is probably either "owners" or "masters," but he shifts to the clumsy and forced " 'the people they belong to.' " Although the shift might be read as protective of the feelings of the narrator who may be "owned" in some sense by Mrs. Raddick (especially if, like the bulldog, the narrator is a "chap"), a more likely interpretation is that Hennie is embarrassed by his sister's actions. Neither children nor dogs are allowed in the casino, but Mrs. Raddick's effort to get her daughter inside has resulted in that daughter's saying to her " 'Oh, shut up, mother.' " Unlike the bulldog, the girl has indeed been fierce with the person she belongs to. Hennie's hesitation, then, may be caused not by his desire to protect someone's feelings, but by his awareness that the actions of his mother and sister are improper. The phrase he finally chooses is no more important in itself than are the words he might have used; the real point lies in the hesitation as such. Thus the acute pain of the seventeen-year-old girl is reflected in the incipient coming-to-awareness of her twelve-year-old brother, without taking the story away from her. (pp. 272-73)

Although these depictions of complex human and societal relationships and the emotional ambivalence which results in large part from them are similar to those in other successful and often better known Mansfield stories, **"The Young Girl"** is outside Mansfield's mature style. **"The Young Girl"** is one of only six first person narratives among the last fifty-eight pieces written by Mansfield. Of the other three finished stories, two are narrated by males, one by a female. Most of Mansfield's later stories are not technically first person narratives, but these omniscient stories are not really omniscient; they are told through the consciousness of the main character. It is difficult to imagine this young girl being seen largely through her own eyes, as **"The Garden Party"** is seen through Laura's eyes or **"The Fly"** depicts almost entirely the consciousness of the boss. This girl is one who must be seen from outside looking in. Few principal characters in Mansfield stories are as sullen, as audibly and visibly nasty as she is; still the reader is supposed to have at least a balance of sympathy and antipathy, perhaps even, in the long run, greater sympathy. The story honestly depicts the momentary little witch she is, while saying at the same time, she has reasons for being that way. And those reasons are more universal than particular. Mrs. Raddick may be a bad mother, but the girl is not what she is because of parental abandonment, or worse. In fact, the absence of her name and the presence of the definite article in the title combine with the more subtle elements discussed here to suggest that Mansfield sees this girl as the prototypical seventeen-year-old, caught in perhaps the most painful of all life's transitions, from child to adult. The sympathy is supposed to be universally felt for every young girl, "like a flower that is just emerging from its dark bud."

In order to depict this sympathy, Mansfield needed a neutral narrator whose attitudes are not based on sex. If most readers do, in fact, feel the maleness of the narrator, that may suggest only that no character can be depicted totally apart from manifestations of sexual differences. However, this narrator in no way directly colors the depiction of the girl with male or female emotions. At the very least, the story is sexually unbiased. Perhaps the opening and closing sentences mostly clearly illustrate this sexually neutral narration.

The story begins with this sentence: "In her blue dress, with her cheeks lightly flushed, her blue, blue eyes, and her gold curls pinned up as though for the first time—pinned up to be out of the way for her flight—Mrs. Raddick's daughter might have just dropped from this radiant heaven." The final sentence reads: "Her dark coat fell open, and her white throat—all her soft young body in the blue dress—was like a flower that is just emerging from its dark bud."

Not only sexually neutral, those two descriptions in terms of imagery seem exceedingly bland, ordinary, common, perhaps even trite. Images of beauty dropped from a "radiant heaven" and "like a flower . . . emerging from its dark bud" are by no means strikingly fresh. But they work here because the rest of the story justifies their presence and explains their emotional blandness or neutrality.

Katherine Mansfield risked a great deal in using those sentences, as she also did in giving her story to a sexless narrator. But if she intended for the person who takes the children to tea to remain sexually unidentified, then she had to produce a first person story. No third person point of view could hide

the sex of such a character. Her accomplishment was worth the risks. This is an intriguing, aesthetically satisfying story, a minor masterpiece. **"The Young Girl"** allows its readers to realize in completely unsexual terms the universal pain of being aged twelve going on seventeen. (pp. 273-74)

> *J. F. Kobler, "The Sexless Narrator of Mansfield's 'The Young Girl'," in* Studies in Short Fiction *(copyright 1980 by Newberry College), Vol. 17, No. 3, Summer, 1980, pp. 269-74.*

ANTONY ALPERS (essay date 1980)

[*Je ne parle pas français* was Katherine Mansfield's] first major story to be written through a persona not her own. Its method is simply a total impersonation of its cynical narrator, and the fact that Katherine was reading so much Dickens at the time . . . is not without significance. Always impersonating, as she was, she had now found a way to use that faculty throughout a major piece. One other, more visible influence, is that of Dostoevsky: in the story's tone, and in the self-revelation of its seedy narrator, there is more than a trace of the *Notes from Underground*. (p. 270)

Je ne parle pas français is the story which Katherine called her "cry against corruption," and it prompted one of her most revealing general statements of artistic aim. The paragraphs that follow have been quoted rather often, but we need them here for an understanding of what she was about. They were written before she had completed half of the story:

> I've two "kick offs" in the writing game. *One* is joy—real joy—the thing that made me write when we lived at Pauline, and that sort of writing I could only do in just that state of being in some perfectly blissful way *at peace*. Then something delicate and lovely seems to open before my eyes, like a flower without thought of a frost or a cold breath—knowing that all about it is warm and tender and "ready." And *that* I try, ever so humbly, to express.
>
> The other "kick off" is my old original one, and (had I not known love) it would have been my all. Not hate or destruction (both are beneath contempt as real motives) but an *extremely* deep sense of hopelessness, of everything doomed to disaster, almost wilfully, stupidly, like the almond tree and "pas de nougat pour le noël." There! as I took out a cigarette paper I got it exactly—*a cry against corruption*—that is *absolutely* the nail on the head. Not a protest—a *cry*, and I mean corruption in the widest sense of the word, of course.
> I am at present fully launched, right out in the deep sea, with this second state. . . .

Since, after *Prelude, Je ne parle pas français* was the longest piece in *Bliss and Other Stories,* it must have contributed to the stir which that book caused in 1920. Yet criticism has largely overlooked it, perhaps because it has only been known, through all these years, in an expurgated version, with cuts that have blunted its meaning. The little private-press edition in which it first appeared is very rare. It has never since been reprinted, and few know the story in its intended form.

Its narrator, through whose mind the whole of it passes while he sits musing in a café, is a cynical young Parisian called

Raoul Duquette, a "little perfumed fox-terrier of a French-man." He writes for two newspapers, but is going in for serious literature (he is the author so far of *False Coins, Wrong Doors,* and *Left Umbrellas*) and he has a taste for English things of quality: he wears an English overcoat, and has an English desk in his flat; he likes that ridiculous song about "One fishball"; and he has a homo-erotic liking for the young English writer, Dick Harmon, whom he met in Paris once and who was far too fond of his mother.

In the café Duquette picks up a writing-pad, to find that some-one has written there "that stupid, stale little phrase, *je ne parle pas français,*" and it is this that suddenly brings back the whole tragic tale of Dick and the helpless pretty English girl whom he brought across to Paris and at once deserted there. (pp. 270-71)

The story was, obviously, in some measure a riposte to [Francis] Carco's *Les Innocents*. . . . (p. 272)

There is not much difficulty in seeing that Dick Harmon "partly is Murry" . . . ; and that Mouse, with her muff, is partly the Katherine he took to Paris in 1912 and partly the one who had left Waterloo six weeks before; though also, surely, the Mar-guéritte whom he deserted in Paris in 1911 and allowed to think his mother was to blame. While Raoul Duquette, like Scott Fitzgerald's Nick Carraway, is Katherine seeing herself see herself. His part is full of implied self-condemnation for her clever self—for the copy-hunting Winnie of *Les Innocents*. Of course it is not on that plane that the story endures.

Two years later, when Constables were about to publish the collected volume that included *Je ne parle pas français,* Michael Sadleir insisted that certain passages be cut. They were all to do with sex misused, and their purpose was to make Duquette's self-portrayal explicit and evil. To examine them in detail here would be tiresome, but it is only in the light of their harsh ironies that the story's full intention can be seen. In a sense, it was really Katherine's *Waste Land*. (p. 273)

If the story has a weakening fault, it lies in the slightness of the character of Mouse. Not quite enough is known of her, and she can hardly bear the intended weight of "a tribute to Love." (pp. 273-74)

[The uncompleted *A Married Man's Story* represents] her only use, after *Je ne parle pas français,* of a male narrator on such a scale, unmistakeably a "cry against corruption," and the only thing of hers that could be described in the terms she used.

Once again it is a piece that critics, and even fellow writers such as Elizabeth Bowen, have overlooked when attempting what André Maurois once called "the difficult task of analysing Katherine Mansfield's talent." Because it is incomplete? But its five thousand words of tensely compact writing make it longer and more substantial than most of her best-known sto-ries, and for other reasons too it is an important one to examine for signs of what its author was moving toward.

Neither nostalgic nor satirical, it has the sharp concreteness found only in the best of her later work. Its self-centred nar-rator, the son of a chemist who has poisoned his wife, is a new invention. The child's recollections of the dying mother's visit to his bed, of a battered harlot lurching into the shop for his father's famous pick-me-up, and the domestic scene of frozen hatred in which the tale itself is written—all are signs of an intention to strike out in new directions. (pp. 281-82)

At the Bay depicts the passage of a single summer's day, from sunrise to night, and from necessity to dream, in the lives of all the Burnell family at their summer cottage in "Crescent Bay." Aunt Beryl and the grandmother are with them, and Alice the maid, while Uncle Jonathan has taken a cottage there as well, so that we meet again the extended family which was Harold Beauchamp's richest gift to his daughter's art. The baby boy that Linda was expecting in the time of *Prelude* has been born; down at the beach we encounter the tribe of the Samuel Josephs, dragooned by the whistle of their "lady-help"; and the "fast" Mrs. Harry Kember, who smokes and is vulgar, and plays bridge on a summer afternoon. She and her equally hasty husband, whose crude advances will horrify Beryl after nightfall, stand for such evil as obtrudes upon the after-Christ-mas pastoral. To remind us of town and of necessity there is Stanley Burnell, blustering and practical and bossy, who must dash off to the office in a stiff collar, leaving the women and children—their relief is immense—to enjoy what he provides.

The story is given outward shape by the ancient universals, sun and moon and tide, and by the "sleepy sea," which is heard before sunrise and in the moonlit, Debussyan close. The cycle of the day affects the lives at first of sheep and sheepdog and the shepherd with his pipe (it is one that smokes), but in due course of every living thing that is present in the story, not least the flowers, nearly all of which are little insignificant invaders, like the human colonists—who, as in *Prelude,* are colonists come out from a Colonial town. Their sense of iso-lation in time and place is implied by numerous local details, wonderfully remembered, and made explicit by Alice's thoughts as she walks along the empty road.

Though outwardly shaped by the ancient rhythms, more pro-foundly the story is structured within by something else. As *Prelude* shows the family's move to a new home and their thoughts as they go to sleep, *At the Bay* contrives for most of them to reflect, in their different ways, on the mysteries of birth and love and death, and in the process we notice that some are capable of dream or of deep reflection, and some are not. The story opens in the freshness of a dewy sunrise, its prose all alert and free of symbol. It ends, with a little envoi of a mere five lines, in the poetry of night and sea and moon. By then the littoral is symbolic.

The events of the day provide contrasting glimpses of the char-acters' thoughts on love and death. For some, this is done through their daydreams. Some wear masks, which are re-moved for us; others, like Stanley Burnell, wear none. Death makes at first a comic entry to the story, when the lewd Mrs. Kember (whose husband will surely have to murder her some-day) is imagined by the other women, "stretched as she lay on the beach: but cold, bloody, and still with a cigarette stuck in the corner of her mouth." It tinges with sadness the siesta taken by Kezia with her grandmother, who has been drowsily thinking of the past and of her son who died; it returns in comic mode with Alice's visit to the widow Stubbs; it is a passing shadow over Jonathan's little talk with Linda in the garden about his wasted life, and over Linda's thoughts of her romantic youth. For the children, at their card game in the wash-house, it is reduced to the fear of spiders or Uncle Jonathan's sudden appearance at the darkening window. For Beryl, nightfall means the transformation of her romantic daydream into Harry Kem-ber's cat-like snatching by the garden gate; after all of which come these few lines to enclose the whole:

> A cloud, small, serene, floated across the moon.
> In that moment of darkness the sea sounded

deep, troubled. Then the cloud sailed away,
and the sound of the sea was a vague murmur,
as though it waked out of a dark dream. All
was still.

The little envoi, impeccably shaped, with its three-word close, returns the story to the tonality of its lovely opening, and restores its dominant symbol, the sleepy sea.

Let us turn back to that opening, to its effects and purposes. This story with a three-word title and a three-word close has also a three-word beginning—in effect a stage direction:

> Very early morning. The sun was not yet risen,
> and the whole of Crescent Bay was hidden un-
> der a white sea-mist. The big bush-covered hills
> at the back were smothered. You could not see
> where they ended and the paddocks and bun-
> galows began. The sandy road was gone and
> the paddocks and bungalows the other side of
> it. . . .
>
> (p. 343)

That is fresh and enticing for many reasons—perhaps chiefly because of its underlying assumption that the scene is already part of our experience. There is no narrator telling us of things we do not know. The sudden raising of the curtain has made us feel that we are the sole observer and it governs all that follows, making one bright wakeful instant of the whole first paragraph: an enchanting pop-up, sharp and specific, yet full of mystery to a child, in which adjectives are few and of the simplest sort. . . .

There is at first no sound. The author, refined almost out of existence, only sees. But then when sounds take over, deep in the bush we only hear a clear cold stream, not a *writer*. When something disturbs the quiet, it is not the predictable bird that twenty other authors would produce, but the "snapping of a twig," and then, "such silence." (p. 344)

At the Bay has indeed its weak moments, and it does not improve on *Prelude* at every point. The scene in the water between Stanley and Jonathan is flawed, the portrayal of Jonathan being worthy of the young James Joyce, but that of Stanley more like something out of Galsworthy. A more serious defect occurs in the portrayal of Alice: the dislike of her which Beryl feels becomes the author's too, and distracts attention from her important role.

It is Alice who gives overt expression to the sense of isolation of the little summer colony, the sense of there being no "others" in the background. . . . (p. 346)

[One] of the things that Katherine Mansfield wished to do, and did do in *At the Bay,* with art that conceals if not with intellect that obtrudes, was to give expression in symbolic form to a Colonial experience, now passed and not to be known again,

which might perplex an old-world mind, but which still holds good as material for literature. Yet this is one of the least of its aims. (p. 347)

> *Antony Alpers, in his* The Life of Katherine Mans-
> field *(copyright © 1980 by Antony Alpers; reprinted
> by permission of Viking Penguin Inc.; in Canada by
> Jonathan Cape Ltd.), Viking Penguin, 1980, 466 p.*

ADDITIONAL BIBLIOGRAPHY

Brophy, Brigid. "Katherine Mansfield." In her *Don't Never Forget: Collected Views and Reviews,* pp. 255-63. New York: Rinehart and Winston, 1966.
    Biographical portrait of Mansfield.

Ellman, Mary. "Katherine Mansfield." *The Yale Review* 70, No. 2 (January 1981): 300-04.
    Compares three current books about Mansfield. The critic briefly outlines Mansfield's life and characterizes her as "one of the archetypes of the daring would-be liberated women" of the early 1900s.

Hanson, Clare, and Gurr, Andrew. *Katherine Mansfield.* New York: St. Martin's Press, 1981, 146 p.
    An analysis of Mansfield's stories, focussing on "the solidity of the structure of her stories and on their weight of implication."

Iverson, Anders. "A Reading of Katherine Mansfield's 'The Garden Party'." *Orbis Litterarum* XXIII (1968): 5-34.
    Detailed analysis of "The Garden Party" in terms of classical and Biblical mythology: Laura "leaves her own people to walk in the valley of the shadow of death; after a narrow passage through the nether world she returns to the upper world, but changed, reborn as it were."

Murry, John Middleton. Introduction to *The Critical Bibliography of Katherine Mansfield,* by Ruth Elvish Mantz, pp. xiii-xvii. London: Constable, 1931.
    Brief reminiscence of Mansfield's literary career and her life.

Pritchett, V. S. "Katherine Mansfield." *The New Yorker* LVII, No 36 (26 October 1981): 196-200.
    Biographical outline, with emphasis on those people—John Middleton Murry, Virginia Woolf, D. H. Lawrence—who affected Mansfield's life and work.

Stanley, C. W. "The Art of Katherine Mansfield." *Dalhousie Review* X, No. 1 (April 1930): 26-41.
    Approbatory overview of Mansfield's work, citing her "exceedingly fine, artistic writing," which the critic feels makes her "a greater artist than almost any of the writers of English fiction in recent times."

Whitridge, Arnold. "Katherine Mansfield." *Sewanee Review* XLVIII, No. 1 (January-March 1940): 256-72.
    Biographical essay, concentrating on those events in Mansfield's life that inspired the main themes of her writing.

Charlotte (Mary) Mew

1870-1928

English poet, short story writer, and essayist.

Mew's reputation rests on two volumes of poems: *The Farmer's Bride* and *The Rambling Sailor*. In verse noted for its original use of traditional metrical forms, its economy of language, and its controlled passion, Mew wrote of the sorrows and joys inherent in life and love. Her most anthologized poem, "The Farmer's Bride," shares critical acclaim with two dramatic monologues, "The Fête" and "Madeline in Church."

Mew grew up in genteel poverty in London, where she acquired a limited formal education. After her brother and sister were confined to mental institutions, Charlotte and her remaining sister pledged themselves to celibacy, to prevent the spread of insanity to future generations. Mew published short stories and essays in *The Yellow Book* and *Temple Bar* in the 1890s, turning to lyric poetry around 1900. She reached the peak of her poetic powers during the five years leading up to 1916, when she published *The Farmer's Bride,* which was a critical success. Mew wrote very little thereafter, devoting herself to the care and support of her sister and ailing mother. Physically and emotionally drained by their long illnesses and subsequent deaths, Mew entered a hospital for minor surgery in 1928 and, while there, took her life.

Mew frequently used dialect and dramatic monologue to express her elemental themes of love, spiritual longing, natural beauty, and death. "The Farmer's Bride" has for the most part been praised for its effective use of dialect and concentration of emotion. Some critics, however, have questioned Mew's wisdom in using dialect, due to the marked contrast between the farmer's rustic speech and the tone of the poem's remaining sections. Mew's religious and nature poems are filled with clear, palpable images, with impressions layered upon impressions, phrased in simple, conversational language. The short poem "Sea Love" expresses in a simple melodic song the poet's theme of the transience of love. In "Madeline in Church," a work called uneven but powerful, Mew portrays a protagonist torn between a search for spiritual or physical love. Most critics contend that Mew created from her imagination rather than her personal life, though a few perceive the poetic personae of the many nuns and harlots in her poems as artistically transmuted desires.

Some critics cite Thomas Hardy as Mew's most notable influence, noting similarities in theme, subject, and language between her "The Farmer's Bride" and his Wessex novels, particularly *Jude the Obscure*. Hardy himself spoke highly of Mew's poetry, and May Sinclair once wrote the poet, "I don't know any living writer (with, possibly, the exception of D. H. Lawrence) who is writing things with such profound vitality in them. And you have qualities of tenderness and subtlety that he has not." Although Mew's work is little known today, many readers share Louis Untermeyer's judgement that seldom has so little work held so much promise.

PRINCIPAL WORKS

The Farmer's Bride (poetry) 1916; also published as *The Farmer's Bride* [enlarged edition], 1921; also published as *Saturday Market* [enlarged edition] 1921

The Rambling Sailor (poetry) 1929
Collected Poems (poetry) 1953
Collected Poems and Prose (poetry and short stories) 1979

THE NATION (essay date 1916)

No touch of the amateur remains upon [Miss Charlotte Mew's *The Farmer's Bride*]. Strictly personal sighs and regretful yearnings have, no doubt, been felt, but they are resolutely suppressed, or thrown into concrete forms, appealing to wider sympathies. Perhaps this definiteness is due to an obviously intimate acquaintance with France. In many poems one hears echoes of the French language, and many more echoes of the French spirit. One also hears a dim echo of the peculiar and interesting time that we call "the 'Nineties." "The Farmer's Bride" is an excellent poem, except that the farmer is made so sympathetic and sensitive that a mere man can hardly imagine why the most sensitive woman should run out into the night to avoid him. "Fame," "The Narrow Door," "The Fête," "The Changeling," "The Quiet House," and "Madeleine in

Church,'' how excellent they all are, clearly realized, full of hard and definite vision! (p. 444)

"The Lyric," in The Nation, *Vol. XIX, No. 15, July 8, 1916, pp. 442, 444.**

WILFRID SCAWEN BLUNT   (essay date 1918)

I have been reading Miss Charlotte Mew's book of verses (*The Farmer's Bride*) which you brought me last time you were here and am a good deal interested by it, more so than by any of the poetry books which have been sent me for a long time—and I should be glad if you will let her know that it is so.

At the same time I should like to make several remarks which I think . . . may be of use to her.

She has the great merit, which few of her contemporaries possess, of making one feel in each piece that she has something to say which is worth saying and which she can say better in verse than in prose. Yet she generally leaves one in a puzzle as to what the situation of the lyric exactly is. This, if she does it on purpose, is not quite fair, and I cannot help suspecting that it is sometimes so. Also I am sure it is a mistake, as if it is repeated too often, the reader loses confidence and will not take the trouble to worry it out for fear it should prove after all a shadow without any material reality.

This difficulty of getting at a complete understanding of the position is increased in Miss Mew's case by her writing sometimes as a man, sometimes as a woman, which also I consider a great mistake as it always takes away something of the poem's full sincerity. A woman ought *always* to write like a woman notwithstanding the temptation there doubtless is to invert the roles—especially if she is writing anonymously for the newspapers—and I daresay many of hers were first published in this way. Only it is an axiom with me that sexual sincerity is the essential of good emotional work.

As to form, though I do not venture to say much about that to a poet who is a poet, I would suggest that her verse would be more effective if kept to a stricter metre. But I am old fashioned on this point. (pp. 202-03)

Wilfrid Scawen Blunt, in his letter to Sydney Carlyle Cockerell on July 17, 1918, in Friends of a Lifetime: Letters to Sydney Carlyle Cockerell, *edited by Viola Meynell (reprinted by permission of the Executors of the Viola Meynell Estate), Jonathan Cape, 1940, pp. 202-03.*

HAROLD MONRO   (essay date 1920)

[*The Farmer's Bride*] is told in forty-six lines, marred by no verbiage. It develops its own appropriate rhythm as it proceeds. It passes with the certainty of Fate to the tragical concluding lines. . . . (p. 76)

One of the peculiarities of the authoress of [*The Farmer's Bride*] is a projection of herself outside herself, so that a kindred personality seems walking with her through life, her own, yet not her own. (pp. 76-7)

She does not tire you with her personality; but continually interests you in its strange reflections. There is a rumour through the whole book of Death (that favourite subject of all poetry), as of a fact in the background, not to be forgotten, yet not a reality. It involves the parting of friends: otherwise it is not important. Grief is more terrible, far more absorbing, than

death. It is not a wringing of hands, or wailing. It quickens perception and excites compassion. (p. 77)

It is difficult to form any clear conception of the authoress of these poems. She only half surrenders the magic of her personality. . . .

Charlotte Mew's poem **"The Changeling"** is one of the most original of its kind in modern poetry. It has nothing in common with Christina Rossetti, Stevenson, Walter de la Mare, or any other writer of fairy poetry. It is neither written down or up: it is factful, not fanciful. It is not quaint or sweet, but hard and rather dreary. You do not smile; you shiver. (p. 78)

"Ken," described in the poem of that name, who "fidgets so, with his poor wits," who seemed, "an uncouth bird," . . . is another unfortunate. He is not taken by the fairies, but removed by human beings to the "gabled house facing the Castle wall." He has an unnatural understanding, and there is no possibility that he will ever conform to the herd-idea of what a man should be. Ken's removal is little different from his death. No words are wasted on describing its emotional effect. The method of this poem is to stir the reader to great apprehension and then abruptly leave his imagination to follow its own natural course. (p. 79)

The longest and least easy poem in the book is **"Madeleine in Church."** A first impression will be that it rambles, but closer examination shows that every detail is essential to the main structure. The study of the type *Madeleine* has provided a subject, of course, for many novelists. . . .

Swinburne in hundreds of flowing lines dropped few such stinging comments on the Galilean as Madeleine in her halting phrases. . . . Her grievance is personal and bitter, being that of a believer. . . . (p. 81)

No argument, or quotation, can prove that the poetry of Charlotte Mew is above the average of our day. She writes with the naturalness of one whom real passion has excited; her diction is free from artificial conceits, is inspired by the force of its subject, and creates its own direct intellectual contact with the reader. Her phraseology is hard and concentrated. To praise her poetry is to offer homage where it is due; and to recommend it is to desire for others the enjoyment one has oneself experienced. (pp. 81-2)

Harold Monro, "Poets and Poetasters of Our Time: Charlotte Mew," in his Some Contemporary Poets (1920), *Leonard Parsons, 1920, pp. 75-82.*

MARGUERITE WILKINSON   (essay date 1921)

I have found a book by an English woman who writes with intense vitality, with rare individuality. Charlotte Mew fills every line of her work with life. Her mind walks upright through her world. She is a person in literature.

The poems in **"Saturday Market"** are difficult to place and to describe. It might be a mistake to call them lyrical ballads, for the term suggests something quite alien to them in structure and atmosphere. Yet they are narratives in which the moods of men, women and children are dramatized in a strongly subjective way that makes them lyrical. It is as if the poet put on other lives as we put on garments. Or perhaps it would be truer to say that she lets other lives wear, for the nonce, the raiment of her words.

In this she is most obviously feminine. It is easy to imagine that she has listened, in womanly fashion, to these stories which she tells, or to others like them; that she has taken sorrow and doubt and wonder from the lips of other human beings into her own heart and made them her own; that she has carried these confessions about with her in her mind, day after day, brooding over them with an almost motherly thoughtfulness, seeking the why of them; and that she has set them down, finally, with her sympathy, her intuitive understanding added to them. I do not know how these poems could have been made in any other way. But, whether I am wrong or right in the conjecture, such is the effect that they give. . . .

Quite as remarkable as her broad and profound sympathy is the delicacy and sensitivity of her mind. **"The Farmer's Bride"** and **"Madeleine In Church"** are evidence of an exquisite intellectual accuracy. A crude mind, even with strength, would make these tales intolerable. Some things must be said perfectly, or not at all. Charlotte Mew's revelations are poignant, but not alarming. Although her characters have passion they do not rant.

A number of the poems, **"The Farmer's Bride,"** **"Arracombe Wood,"** and **"Sea Love"** are written in the homely and beautiful speech of English farmers and fishermen. **"Sea Love"** is a brief, convincing treatment of an old theme, the transitory nature of many loves. . . .

Other poems have a Parisian setting and in them French is shrewdly interwoven with English to give the atmosphere. **"Le Sacre Coeur"** is one of the most adroit. It uses a powerful symbolism that will displease many readers. Another is **"The Narrow Door,"** a brief, ironical, effective lyric. But whether she writes of the people of Paris or of the folk of the English countryside, Charlotte Mew's language is always close to the life that she is describing.

The same is true of her rhythms. They are the very echoes of the moods of her poems. She is one of a few living poets who understand organic rhythm, who know how to make every syllable, every catch of the breath contribute to verisimilitude of presentation and emotional tensity. Yet her art seems to be artless. There will be critics, perhaps, who will call it careless. The undiscerning may prefer to suppose that she could not use their level and dull iambics or the prim trochees of the metronome. But the discerning will find in these cadences a rich and subtly varied music.

It seems probable to me that she has been influenced, in the making of her rhythms, by her knowledge of French, for many of her lines flow out rapidly to an end, as the rhythm of French speech often does. Other qualities suggest French influence.

"Saturday Market" is not a book of slack, popular verse. It is for lovers of the best contemporary poetry. It asks something of readers—that they meet understanding with understanding, subtlety with subtlety. It will not please Pollyanna. It will frighten a few of the orthodox. But it is real as life is real. It has leaping lights in it to illumine the minds of the thoughtful. Of English poets recently introduced to us Charlotte Mew and Wilfred Owen . . . are the most interesting by far.

> *Marguerite Wilkinson, "Lyrics That Are Not for Pollyana," in* The New York Times Book Review *(© 1921 by The New York Times Company; reprinted by permission), June 19, 1921, p. 10.*

A. WILLIAMS-ELLIS (essay date 1922)

Those whom we may, with only a little exaggeration call adherents of the 'Flat School' of Poetry have gained a great deal by their renunciation. Their effects are achieved by a great economy of language—literal as well as metaphorical, for their poems are generally short—by a certain metrical chastity, and by reliance on the poignancy of the commonplace if the object be narrative, and by the beauty of the ordinary if the object be landscape or symbolical.

Miss Charlotte Mew is of this school, and her work shows a wonderful degree of craftsmanship: we shall hardly ever find a word out of place or weak. She very rarely either uses an inversion or allows her rhyme to steer the course of her ship. Occasionally her emotion is exceedingly poignant, especially when she treats the idea—it recurs in several of the poems— of the dreamlike spell which hangs about the death of those we love or who are familiar to us. The raw grave, the broken fragment of a flower, cannot be the reality and the sense of continued companionship the illusion! (pp. 270-71)

Very often she writes as [George] Crabbe might have written if he had been born in an age when free verse had loosed the bonds of narrative poetry; now and then as Pope might have written in the twentieth century.

There is a poem called **'Madeleine in Church'** which reminds one of the passages from his 'Eloisa and Abelard.' . . . (pp. 271-72)

The whole poem is a remarkable one, full of energy. Miss Mew seems to have caught exactly the point of view of the sort of woman she describes, and this is the more remarkable because in **'The Farmer's Bride,'** the name-piece of her book, she has mastered and understood a very different type of sex-reaction in a woman. The farmer—we are given him in a few lines—a kind, busy, practical man, marries a very young girl who is as shy as a levret. . . . But Miss Mew does not take up a conventional feminist 'gross male' attitude. At the end of the poem she contrives to show us the affair from the farmer's point of view. The poem is full of humanity and sympathy. The Nemesis of Miss Mew's style is that she is apt to become prosaic. Very often the reader feels that her thought could have been more easily expressed in prose. But to those who value strength, poignancy, and economy her poems will always be interesting. (pp. 272-73)

> *A. Williams-Ellis, "Short Studies of Some Modern Poets: Charlotte Mew," in her* An Anatomy of Poetry, *Basil Blackwell, 1922, pp. 270-73.*

THOMAS EDWARD LAWRENCE (essay date 1924)

Miss Mew: too much emotion for her art, for her intellect, for her will. Such intensity of feeling is a sign of weakness. She is a real poet—but a little one, for the incoherency, the violence of over-wrought nerves does much harm to her powers of expression.

It's good stuff—*Beside the Bed: On the Asylum Road: I have been through the Gates: On the Road to the Sea:* these are four excellent things—but only the passion is molten: the form, the thought, the music, these are unresolved, to be guessed at, or worse, to be supplied by the reader if his passion is set burning by sympathy with hers. (pp. 361-62)

> *Thomas Edward Lawrence, in his letter to Sydney Carlyle Cockerell on March 19, 1924, in* Friends of a Lifetime: Letters to Sydney Carlyle Cockerell, *edited by Viola Meynell (reprinted by permission of the Executors of the Viola Meynell Estate), Jonathan Cape, 1940, pp. 361-62.*

HAROLD MONRO (essay date 1928)

[The poetry of Charlotte Mew and that of Thomas Hardy have] various characteristics in common. His range is admittedly much wider, but imaginatively Charlotte Mew is hardly his inferior. Technically her poetry is of real significance, and her greatest gift was that rare one of compression which enabled her to condense into forty-six lines such a tale for instance as is told in the title piece of **"The Farmer's Bride,"** truly a masterly poem. . . .

There is in some of these poems an emotional intensity so powerful that indeed we may wonder at the self-discipline that must have been needed to control it within the intellectual bounds which she evidently set herself. At such moments however as in the last stanza of **"The Pedlar"** she is suddenly off her guard, and seems to be on the point of yielding a fragment of her personality:

> Give me the key that locks your tired eyes,
>   And I will lend you this one from my pack,
> Brighter than coloured beads and painted books that
>   make men wise:
> Take it. No, give it back!

With dramatic swiftness she recovers herself, and the impression given to the reader is one certainly of having seen, nearly of having felt, the movement that accompanied the words. (p. 113)

> *Harold Monro, "Charlotte Mew," in* The Bookman, *London, Vol. LXXIV, No. 440, May, 1928, pp. 112-13.*

VIRGINIA MOORE (essay date 1934)

[Charlotte Mew] was not quite great, but she had greatness in her, not in quantity, for she left only two small volumes, one posthumous, but in crystal and indubitable quality. The work is uneven. If she were alive she would no doubt destroy many published poems, and wise critics would applaud. Certainly the *Early Poems*, which foreshadow the later, should have been allowed to moulder. . . . (p. 192)

At least thirty poems out of some sixty in **The Farmer's Bride** and **The Rambling Sailor** (not counting the *Early Poems*) are beyond all description limpid and fine. They are intelligent but not intellectual; and though emotional, not heavily so. By the lightest means, the most wistful, the most poignant, the most circling and purposeless and yet the most sure, they break the heart. The short ones like **"Sea Love,"** evanescent finality, and *"Fin de Fête,"* mighty indirection, which Thomas Hardy kept among his papers, would be ruined by one off note; but the pitch is absolutely true. The long poems pile impression on impression, image on image, perhaps factually but never emotionally unrelated, so that they carry the greatest possible burden of meaning. Strange and opposite things are juxtaposed in a way which should sound jerky, in long lines which by all the rules should be unwieldy, and the effect is wonderful, is devastating. Compression was impossible: their essential meaning, like that of a life, is not single, but a subtle mingling of diverse elements. The separate ideas usually begin and end on the same line, they do not run over; yet the lines are extraordinarily flexible. (pp. 194-95)

It is as if, in her poetry, she were always protesting against the inert and lifeless, the alien thing which beckons us and rejects us. . . . **"Beside the Bed"** and **"To a Child in Death"**

are the more beautiful because they cannot be analyzed. Here is a desperation made gentle and still. . . . **"I Have Been Through the Gates"** is as solemn as Milton, but less pretentious. The "Go through, go through the gates" of Isaiah is answered in lofty mournfulness. . . . (pp. 195-98)

But it is the long **"Madeleine in Church"** which, by varying line and tempo, involves us the most deeply in her human questioning; for it is like the impetuous talk of someone with a heart too full to let the words come out slowly, with precision. (p. 199)

> *Virginia Moore, "Charlotte Mew" (originally published in a different form in* The Yale Review, *Vol. XXII, No. 2, December, 1932), in her* Distinguished Women Writers *(reprinted by permission of the publisher, E. P. Dutton, Inc.), Dutton, 1934, pp. 189-202.*

PATRIC DICKINSON (essay date 1948)

Charlotte Mew's are not the kind of poems you talk about. There is a ruthless, appalling, inexorable quality in them. (p. 44)

A verse taken from its context . . . cannot do more than hint, for her poems are very physically whole. Quotation is amputation. Meredith's 'words that bleed' is near. But Charlotte Mew's words do not bleed, they are 'burned, and not quite through,' raw; bruised; wept dry. Her style is laconic, unimpassioned, unimpeded by its words. She never uses a 'poetical' phrase. Her communication is naked to naked, and what she communicates is a painful woundful theme. A poem like *In Nunhead Cemetery* is so intense, so agonising that it does indeed burn into our sensibility. There is nothing left to *say* about it. There, in words and rhythms managed with a minute precision, a detached artistry, is an expression of grief so hopeless that one turns away speechless oneself, in compassion for the graveside lover. Her compassion too is for the speechless, the beyond speech: the frightened girl in the quiet house, or Ken the idiot, who was taken to the Asylum. . . . (pp. 44-5)

Her poems keep to the point with the insistence of a physical ache. Their immediacy hurts. There is no lapse of time, no change of feeling perceptible: the poem and the experience seem concurrent, the one creating the other. Of all woman poets Charlotte Mew has this faculty most pronounced: of the concentration of her whole life and self into the moment of each poem, so that it is impossible to tell when these poems came. That she was forty-six in the year of their publication is no clue at all, nor are the scenes or places. Did she ever visit France? Did she—but it does not matter. After reading her poems one does not want to know, would resist knowing, the circumstances of her life.

The circumstances of her poems, then: their outward dress, their style? Most important of all, their rhythms, for it is the originality of his rhythms that marks the poet. Form is secondary. (p. 45)

Charlotte Mew's rhythms are basically conversational. That is a crude way of saying it: but inside us often I think feelings and thoughts arising together compose a kind of inward monologue, a half-articulate soliloquy. (One of her most remarkable poems is **Madeleine in Church,** in which this invert confessional method is used overtly, dramatically.) This kind of rhythm is a fundamental of twentieth century poetry, and Charlotte Mew was using it at a time when the predominant practice of poetry was still nineteenth century. She was an innovator. These changes never happen as arbitrarily as the lecturers would like or the critics assume. *The Love Song of J. Alfred Prufrock* is very akin rhythmically to Charlotte Mew. No comparison with Mr. Eliot is postulated. But one is too inclined to regard him as an isolated phenomenon, rather than as one of many portents. He was quick to seize upon and to concentrate a rhythm, a way of using words, that was 'about.' . . .

> Tonight again the moon's white mat
> Stretches across the dormitory floor

So begins her poem *The Fête*. The use of the commonplace and the commonsense in poetic imagery is also of the times. It is extraordinary to find how little her poems date; for, again, her vocabulary is simple, conversational, the reverse of rhetorical. . . .

She was, I believe, an original poet of minor genius, perhaps a great minor, of whom there are few. Her range was limited, but within it she had a complete and freezing mastery. (p. 46)

> Patric Dickinson, *"A Note on Charlotte Mew,"* in The Nineteenth Century and After, *Vol. 144, No. 857, July, 1948, pp. 42-7.*

FRANK SWINNERTON (essay date 1950)

[As] far as I can tell, the volume called **"The Farmer's Bride"** contains much that is of quite personal and unmistakable beauty. It has, of course, some callow verses which are timidly inquiring or in the fashionable mode of impersonation, but the effect of it as a whole is deeply moving. I should like to quote here, for example, in full, two long poems called **"The Quiet House"** and **"The Forest Road,"** both of which achieve intense communication of feeling and reverie. I cannot do so, because of their length. The former, with its apparently inconclusive thoughts, by which a history is made plain to us, is the perplexity of a girl made manifest; the latter, a lover's dramatic apostrophe to a sleeping woman. . . . **"Madeleine in Church,"** another and at times acutely successful impersonation; the title poem, **"The Farmer's Bride"**; several pictures of children; and **"Arracombe Wood,"** in dialect, all have their individual effect; but all are raised by their surroundings and the associations with what has been read before. In whatever she wrote, she was always guiltless of calculated gesture, which to me is in itself a mark of quality. Her aim was to communicate with scrupulous truth that vision which had come with strong feeling as the result of a personal impression of life. Her use of language is admirable; its suppleness constantly enchants the ear; but what gives the poems perfection is a sincerity which finds fit words because the impulse to write, to tell, has been so intense. (pp. 259-60)

> Frank Swinnerton, *"The War-time Afflatus, 1914-1918,"* in his The Georgian Literary Scene, 1910-1935: A Panorama *(reprinted by permission of the author), Hutchinson, 1950, pp. 257-72.**

THE TIMES LITERARY SUPPLEMENT (essay date 1953)

It is difficult to quote from [Charlotte Mew's] work. Her best poems, **"Fame," "The Call," "On the Asylum Road,"** are remarkably close-knit. She is fond of using a very long line with a loose iambic movement. . . .

These she intersperses with shorter lines. Her sentences are long and her syntax sometimes as complicated as that of a Metaphysical poet. But her best effects are, unmistakably feminine; she has the rare gift of conveying great intensity of emotion in a simple and unassuming form. There is nothing in her poetry at the same pitch as "Fifteen wild Decembers . . .''; her note, like that of Mary Coleridge of whose poems (and particularly of "On such a Day") one is often reminded, is more subdued but none the less moving. . . .

There is a quality [in Charlotte Mew's work] which many good poets who are women have had in common—the presence of an emotion kept under restraint in daily life, and the absence of any wish to be striking and original. It is easy to see why Hardy so much admired Charlotte Mew's verse that he copied out the poem **"Fin de Fête"** on a slip of paper in the British Museum.

It must be admitted that her longer semi-dialect poems, even such well-known anthology pieces as **"The Farmer's Bride"** and **"The Rambling Sailor,"** are less distinguished. The latter, with its incongruous profanity in the Masefield manner, is quite untypical of her. These poems are spoilt by a professional element, and by the attempt to put herself in the place of other people and to describe an imagined scene dramatically. The section entitled "Poems from France," which are mostly *Dramatis Personae* like **"Madeline in Church,"** is the weakest in the book, though here, too, we catch glimpses of her quality.

> *"Emotion in Restraint,"* in The Times Literary Supplement (© *Times Newspapers Ltd. (London) 1953; reproduced from* The Times Literary Supplement *by permission), No. 2707, December 18, 1953, p. 814.*

HILARY CORKE (essay date 1954)

Charlotte Mew is one of the most original and inventive of poets, her forms strong and entirely individual; her forte is the long semi-dramatic poem, in which she shows a control and sense of balance and effect that are quite astonishing; and her most successful subjects are such matters as **"Madeleine in Church"** (a prostitute's colloquy with the Virgin) or **"The Fête"** (a boy's first sexual experience). A single poem by "queer lonely unhappy" Miss Mew tells us more about human beings and their relationships, one to another, more about this world we live in, more about "reality," than the whole corpus of Mr. [Wallace] Stevens' writings. Nor do her advantages stop there: I am not at all sure that she does not exceed in what might appear at first to be the other's own peculiar province, that is, "intelligence"—both negatively, in declining to ask the fundamental questions that it is more circumspect for the creative artist not to (if Coleridge had been this wise, we should have had another *Ancient Mariner* and the rest of *Christabel*); and positively, in that the construction of her poems displays an intuitional grasp of her material so much more logical than his mere logic. . . .

Most of Charlotte Mew's excellences are to be seen [in] the intricate ode-like stanzas, the subtle rhythms, the very characteristic "long lines," the gift for epigram ("Only the hair / Of any woman can belong to God"), the technique of juxtaposition of plain statements in such a way that the reader himself is lured into providing the poetic links between them.

Which is not to say that Charlotte Mew has not her faults. She has several, and they are all exceedingly plain ones—the weak phrases, the lapses into bathos or into sentimentality, the most unhappy attempts on contemporary slang. But I feel that as faults they are particularly unimportant, arising rather out of her circumstances than her nature; and if it is they that have so far prevented her from taking her proper place amongst this century's poets, I hope that their very obviousness may tend to disarm future criticism. (p. 80)

Hilary Corke, "Absence in Reality," in Encounter (©1954 by Encounter Ltd.), Vol. II, No. 6, June, 1954, pp. 78-81.*

HOXIE NEALE FAIRCHILD (essay date 1962)

It has long been customary to tag [Charlotte Mew] with a respectful "unduly neglected." All she needs to come fully alive today is a few people who will take the trouble to read her.

Much less overtly autobiographical than most women poets, she is resourceful in providing dramatic disguises for her personal difficulties. Few of the poems report actual circumstances of her life; we are not reading entries in a diary. Nevertheless her objective correlatives group themselves in patterns which indicate that she is almost always thinking of one or both of two inhibited personal desires. She wants a man; she wants a nonromantic religion; she is unable to obtain either on terms acceptable to her. (p. 333)

Almost never does she associate love with complete happiness. There is one seemingly confident affirmation of the power of love to transcend old age and death, but the wistful title is *À Quoi Bon Dire?* The horrified revulsion of *I Have Been Through the Gates* and *Ne Me Tangito* is much more typical. On the other side of her conflict, poems suggesting full sympathy with Christianity are somewhat more numerous. At the last moment, a novice about to leave the convent with her lover joyfully turns back to Christ, her heart's *true* love. *The Little Portress* is a tenderly sympathetic sketch of a saintly young nun. . . . *Le Sacré-Coeur,* another poem on God's judgment of the modern world, has more of her characteristic morbidity without ceasing to be thoroughly religious. On the *butte* all is dark and quiet. Far below blaze the lights of Paris, a pretty harlot to be bought and sold, "So old, so young and infinite and lost." Yet here atop Montmartre, the poet reminds the city, yearns "the Man who bought you first." . . . But the Harlot city shrugs her shoulders—why mourn for a lover who died so long ago?

In her most characteristic poems, however, sexual and religious longings are juxtaposed in agonized tension. *Pécheresse* (the title is a pun) is the monologue of a fishing-village girl who, "for love and not for gold," gave herself to a sailor from a foreign ship. After a night and a day he left her, never to return. She dreads damnation but cannot bring herself to confess as a sin her one brief glimpse of Paradise. (pp. 334-35)

There is no need to ask the name of Charlotte Mew's favorite saint. In *She Was a Sinner,* the Magdalene so tells her story as to suggest that in her love for Jesus, and perhaps even in His love for her, earthly and spiritual passion were reconciled. (p. 336)

Hoxie Neale Fairchild, "More Mavericks," in his Religious Trends in English Poetry: Gods of a Changing Poetry, 1880-1920, Vol. V (copyright © 1962 Columbia University Press; reprinted by permission of the publisher), Columbia University Press, 1962, pp. 296-346.*

BABETTE DEUTSCH (essay date 1963)

[A] deep sense of the cruelty intrinsic to human relationships, together with a feeling for the charm of country things, made congenial to Hardy the work of Charlotte Mew. She wrote several dramatic monologues in the vernacular, of which possibly the best known is the title poem of her first book, **"The Farmer's Bride."** Another touching piece is **"The Shepherd's Prayer,"** spoken by an old countryman, looking through the farmhouse window from his deathbed. A stanza may show something of the appeal that her work had for Hardy.

> Turning around like a falled-over sack
> I can see team plowin' in Whithy-bush field and meal
>   carts startin' up road to Church-Town;
> Saturday arternoon then men goin' back
> And the women from market, trapin' home over the
>   down.

The homely simile is one that he may well have envied, and the rolling cadence has a rightness that his formal metres did not always achieve. (p. 6)

Babette Deutsch, "A Look at the Worst," in her Poetry in Our Time: A Critical Survey of Poetry in the English-Speaking World, 1900 to 1960 (copyright © 1963 by Babette Deutsch; 1963 by Doubleday; reprinted by permission of Babette Deutsch), revised edition, Doubleday & Company, Inc., 1963, pp. 1-30.*

MARY C. DAVIDOW (essay date 1978)

Was there something rather special in Charlotte Mew's poetry which attracted Thomas Hardy? The title poem of the slender volume, **The Farmer's Bride,** represents Charlotte Mew at her best, a modest and authentic poet. . . . [She] tells her story dramatically and effectively in forty-six lines characterized by a precision of detail, restraint and felicity of diction, and a rhythm which admirably approaches the natural cadences of the bewildered farmer. The narrative movement of the poem advances through an uncluttered, brilliantly charted course to its inevitable conclusion. The dialect of the farmer links him with Hardy's rustics, for the dialect is that of the West Country. (p. 438)

What strikes the reader who is familiar with the poem and Hardy's *Jude the Obscure* is the strong resemblance between the farmer's *bride* and Sue *Bride*head. They are both epicene women. A careful examination of Hardy's novel reveals that Charlotte Mew, either consciously or unconsciously, was influenced by Hardy's presentation of Sue's abhorrence of the sexual act. In describing Sue's neurosis, Hardy carefully builds his case by narrating the lengths to which Sue goes to avoid the marriage act. . . . Charlotte Mew describes the farmer's "bride" as follows:

> All in a *shiver* and a scare
> We caught her, fetched her home at last
>   And turned the key upon her fast . . .

and later she adds:

> "Not near, not near!" her eyes beseech
> When one of us comes within reach.

(pp. 440-41)

[Sue and Charlotte Mew's farmer's "bride"] possess an inordinate *fear* of physical union, and as a result of their dread of the sexual act, each enforces continence upon her mate. Sue, according to Jude, was "on the whole, cold—*a sort of fay,* or a sprite—*not a woman!*". . . . Charlotte Mew's narrator—the farmer—describes his bride:

When us was wed she *turned afraid*
Of love and me and all things human;
Like the shut of a winter's day
Her smile went out, and *'twadn't a woman*—
More like *a frightened fay.*
       One night, in the Fall, she runned away.

A further example of similarity in diction and situation between the poem and the novel occurs in the last stanza of **"The Farmer's Bride":**

She sleeps up in the attic there
Alone, poor maid. *'Tis but a stair
Betwixt us.* Oh! my God! . . .

and in the novelist's comment about Jude and Sue following their agreement to refrain from sexual union:

After this the subject of marriage was not mentioned by them for several days, though living as they were, *with only a landing between them,* it was constantly in their minds.

Charlotte Mew follows a similar technique in her poem **"I Have Been Through the Gates."** . . . There is an intrinsic relationship between the poem and passages in *Jude* in which Hardy describes Christminster as it appeared to Jude when he entered its gates for the first time. (pp. 442-43)

Charlotte Mew's poem **"I Have Been Through the Gates"** is linked through its diction and imagery to Hardy's archetypal city of Christminster. The poem is infused with imagery and symbolism which ultimately transform "heart" and citadel into the holy city of Jerusalem. The opening line of her poem establishes at once the old wise man archetype. . . . (p. 444)

Just as Christminster is the symbolic representation of the formal education Jude yearned for in his youth but was denied by fate from acquiring, so the old wise man archetype discernible in Charlotte Mew's opening lines represents, I feel, some highly regarded individual who once exerted a powerful influence over the narrator. It is important to take into account the dramatic shift in tense from the past in the first several lines: "His heart, to me, *was* a place of palaces" to the present tense in line six: "His heart *is* a place with the lights gone out, forsaken by great winds and the heavenly rain. . . ." The lyric obviously celebrates a *return:* "I have groped, I have crept / Back, back." In the main the poem is a lyrical outpouring of the speaker's profound love, even veneration, for the ruler of the turreted and pinnacled citadel. It is at the same time an expression of grief for the loss of vitality and creativity in the wise old man: "His heart is a place with the lights gone out, forsaken by the great winds and the heavenly rain." Thus, while the majestic hymn-like quality of the lyric creates a mood of reverence, in the first part of the poem, the pervading note of sadness introduces and sustains to the end a tone of poignant melancholy.

Charlotte Mew, through the poetic device of transmuting abstractions, such as devotion, admiration, and love, into concrete terms—*palaces, pinnacles, shining towers*—is able to express the ineffable. Diction throughout the poem suggests an emotional link between the speaker and her subject, the presence within the gates. (p. 445)

[Several] of Charlotte Mew's poems are written in the West of England dialect or, as Hardy might call it, the Wessex dialect. Among them are **"The Farmer's Bride," "Arracombe Wood," "Sea Love,"** and **"Old Shepherd's Prayer."** In the latter poem the dying shepherd speaks and mentions the place-name "Church-Town," a name which appears in **"The Farmer's Bride."** But perhaps more to the point is the fact that in **"Old Shepherd's Prayer"** one encounters not the farmer's *bride* "too young maybe—," but a *Sue:* "And down in yard, fit to burst his chain, yapping out at *Sue* I do hear young Mac." Moreover, in *The Early Life of Thomas Hardy,* published when both Charlotte Mew and Hardy were deceased, the reader is informed that in 1886 "from the white entrance gate in the wall, a short drive, planted on the windward side with beech and sycamore leads up to the house, arrivals being notified to the inmates by the voice of a glossy black setter [Moss], who comes into view from the stable at the back *as far as his chain will allow him.*" (The italics are mine.) In Charlotte Mew's poem, Mac (is it really Moss?) is "fit to burst his chain, yapping out at Sue." All mere chance? I believe that the link between the poem and the biographical detail is clearly in evidence. (pp. 445-46)

In earlier attempts at writing poetry, Charlotte Mew experimented with turning some of her own prose into verse form. The best example in which she demonstrates a mastery of the technique is her essay, **"Notes in a Brittany Convent,"** published in 1901 in *Temple Bar,* and reprinted in the same year in *Living Age.* The following excerpt from the essay may clarify my position in this paper and throw some light on Charlotte Mew's ability to use this technique as early as 1903:

The little portress also will die young, whatever age they write up over her. She may be forty, but it is an ageless face which looks out through the open window by the gate, as you look in for letters. A face too thin and sensitive, but lovely with its look of dreams dismissed, passed on the way to some divine reality. She sits framed in the slit of window, reading, the black profile of her veil, with its white rim so still beneath the outline of the crucifix which hangs above it on the wall. As you pass, though she does not look up, you catch somehow the fragrance of that presence with its sense of benediction; know the smile which you may meet as you come back, so bright, so human, yet a little sad with all its sunshine, like a late spring day. . . .

(p. 446)

"The Little Portress" was printed in *Temple Bar* in 1903, and is subtitled: "St. Gilda de Rhuys." An atmosphere of quiet, of whispered sounds pervades the entire poem, as one might imagine it pervaded the cloister. The alchemistic transmutation of the sentence: "She seems to borrow something from the stillness of the sunshine in which, to memory she always sits" into its poetic form is startling.

The stillness of the sunshine lies
   Upon her spirit: silence seems
   To look out from its place of dreams. . . .

Then compare stanza four with the sentence: "She sits framed in the slit of window, reading, the black profile of her veil with its white rim so still beneath the outline of the crucifix which hangs above it on the wall."

That is her window, by the gate.
   Now and again her figure flits
   Across the wall. Long hours she sits
Within: on all who come to wait.

Her Saviour too is hanging there
A foot or so above her chair.

The point I wish to make here is simply that Charlotte Mew
was adept at transforming passages of prose into the stuff of
poetry, and that she more than likely knew what she was doing
when she chose to describe her farmer's bride as ''more like
a little frightened fay'' who '''twadn't a woman.'' (p. 447)

> *Mary C. Davidow, ''Charlotte Mew and the Shadow
> of Thomas Hardy,'' in* Bulletin of Research in the
> Humanities *(copyright © 1979 Readex Microprint
> Corporation), Vol. 81, No. 4, Winter, 1978, pp. 437-
> 47.*

MICHAEL SCHMIDT   (essay date 1979)

[Charlotte Mew] reached the peak of her poetic powers between
1909 and 1916 when—in her forties—she began writing verse
with confidence. Her short stories, which had appeared widely
before this time, came now with more originality and
fluency. . . . [She] began to develop a prose style that engaged
reality at its most intense; and from this style it was only a
small step to her poetry. The rhythms of her verse were present
in her mature stories.

Communication in her best stories is by gesture, facial expression, or through symbols—conversation is always secondary to *how* it is said. The ordering of the images is more
expressive than the story itself. Hence later, in her poems, the
forms are of crucial importance. There is as much eloquence
in the disrupted, dramatic syntax, the long fluent line, the
rhythmical emphasis and the quality of the objects rendered,
as in the plot and explicit statement of the poem, if it has one.
(pp. 58-9)

A letter Charlotte wrote to a friend tells us much about her
mode of composition and her ideas of form. She is writing
about **'In Nunhead Cemetery'** (note the punctuation—in dashes):
'The last verse which you find superfluous is to me the most
inevitable—(and was written first)—being a lapse from the
sanity and self-control of what precedes it—the mind—the
senses can stand no more—and that is to express their failure
and exhaustion.' She explains that she does not write the poem
straight out: she assembles it, fits it together. The artistry is
in the organization. The content, when under sufficient emotional pressure, must violate form, if the poem is to be true.
We will look in vain for formal perfection in her work: form
is servant, not master. The emotional content elbows out the
form, or pulls it in. This is deeply subjective poetry, resonant
and vivid because of the physical veracity of the observations,
the speaking quality of the voice, and the poet's intense response.

Her review of Emily Brontë's poems brings us a little closer
to her notion of form. She has been compared with Emily
Brontë, but apart from their shared intensity, the comparison
does damage to the integrity of each. They differ as much in
their use of forms as in the quality of passion they convey.
Charlotte Mew begins by remarking that Emily Brontë's forms
are 'curiously deficient'. 'They are melodies, rather than harmonies, many of a haunting and piercing sweetness, instinct
with a sweeping and mournful music peculiarly her own . . .
Everywhere, too, the note of pure passion is predominant, a
passion untouched by mortality and unappropriate by sex.'
Mew's own poems aim at a *harmonic* effect—in other words,
the combining of various elements in a single phrase or rhythmic
passage, an opacity; the poetry is built of phrases, not of cad-

ences, even in the long lines; and each phrase draws together
elements—sometimes conflicting—from several registers of
human sensation and emotion. It is not a poetry of developing
thought but of developing emotional experience in a physical
world. And nor can we find much sweetness in Charlotte Mew.
Her own poems are everywhere instinct with mortality, the
lament for the passing of beauty, passion, things and people
loved; and there is a profound sensuality about all her poetry
and explicit sexuality about some of it. It is the *impure* passion,
longing for purity (usually conceived in religious imagery—
she was much drawn to Roman Catholicism, though she was
never converted) since it cannot achieve any earthly permanence.

Mew's early poems explore religious suffering (in the form of
martyrdom), punishment, death, sorrow, loss and love. There
is one poem full of misanthropic humour, **'Afternoon Tea'**.
But the others, occasionally witty, are of a generally dramatic
and elegiac tone. Recurrent images—the stair, the rose, red
petals, dreams, and hair—relate the poems to one another. They
seem to illuminate one another. The traditional material is
heightened and made strange by her peculiar physicality of
response.

It was with **'Poems from France'** that she established her own
voice. **'The Fête'** was her first outstanding poem. A boy in a
French school experiences the fair—and love. His dramatic
monologue ends with an expression of loss—loss, in effect,
of purity, innocence, some intangible. . . . The pain and loss
implicit in intense pleasure are conveyed in the extremely complex verse form. The same power of expression characterizes
'Madeleine in Church', Mew's main achievement—uneven but
powerful. It too is a dramatic monologue, of a hundred and
forty lines, spoken by a woman who fails to re-establish religious faith after a life of intense sensuality. (pp. 59-61)

'Madeleine' reminds us of Mary Magdalen, whose redemption
was made possible only by the physical being of Christ. 'She
was a sinner, we are what we are: the spirit afterwards, but
first the touch.' The poem is about 'the touch', the inability
of the individual—without personal, incontrovertible revelation—to believe in anything beyond the physical world. Christ,
she avers, cannot understand the profound darkness of her soul.
She tries to explain herself to Him. . . . Her materialism is
not intellectual but an emotional disposition which cannot comprehend the metaphysical. 'We are what we are' recurs as a
refrain. She asks God, 'If it is Your will that we should be
content with the tame, bloodless things.' The poem is a celebration as much as a lament. She laments the ephemerality
of those physical experiences which seem all-important, and
yet as she laments she relives and celebrates. The power of
the poem is in the ambiguous way she at once prays to and
rejects Christ, in her ambivalence towards her own life. 'If
there were fifty heavens God could not give us back the child
who went or never came.' She cannot accede to Christ. . . .
For Madeleine, and indeed for Mew, if we can trust the evidence of the poems, the world is too richly physical to allow
belief in anything beyond the power bodies and objects and
their mute attraction have over the mind and heart: 'the spirit
afterwards, but first the touch.'

There are occasional echoes in her work—of Browning, Hardy,
and others—but 'influences' are transmuted by her own voice.
With Hardy she shares some themes—for instance, the unal-
terability of past experience, memory, and its effect on the
present; ephemerality of the passions, regret, the difficulty of
sustained love. Heaven is not 'to come' but in the past, in

youth and its spent intensities. The future is merely a termination of possibilities one by one, a putting out of candles. 'I remember rooms that have had their part / In the steady slowing down of the heart.' it is a difficult, unredeemed vision, thoroughly materialistic. . . . (pp. 61-3)

> *Michael Schmidt, "Charlotte Mew," in his* A Reader's Guide to Fifty Modern British Poets *(© Michael Schmidt 1979; by permission of Barnes & Noble Books, A Division of Littlefield, Adams & Co., Inc.), Barnes & Noble, 1979, pp. 57-63.*

ADDITIONAL BIBLIOGRAPHY

Boll, T.E.M. "The Mystery of Charlotte Mew and May Sinclair: An Inquiry." *Bulletin of the New York Public Library* 74, No. 7 (September 1970): 445-53.*

> Pieces together evidence of the Mew/Sinclair friendship. Boll produces correspondence proving that Sinclair encouraged Mew to write and to publish, and that Sinclair introduced Mew and her work to influential poets, publishers, and reviewers.

Davidow, Mary C. "The Charlotte Mew-May Sinclair Relationship: A Reply." *Bulletin of the New York Public Library* 75, No. 7 (September 1971): 295-300.*

> Refutes Boll's evidence and conclusion concerning the end of Mew's and Sinclair's friendship.

Monro, Alida. "Charlotte Mew: A Memoir." In *Collected Poems of Charlotte Mew,* by Charlotte Mew, pp. vii-xx. London: Duckworth, 1953.

> Biographical memoir. Monro cites Mew's professional disappointments and the years lost in caring for her family as possible reasons for her small literary canon.

Untermeyer, Louis. "Charlotte Mew." In his *Modern British Poetry,* pp. 158-65. New York: Harcourt Brace Jovanovich, 1962.

> A concise appraisal of Mew's career. Untermeyer reprints fifteen of Mew's poems after concluding that had she nothing but the original edition of *The Farmer's Bride*, "it would have been sufficient to rank her among the most distinct and intense of living poets."

Warner, Val. Introduction to *Collected Poems and Prose,* by Charlotte Mew, pp. ix-xxii. Manchester: Carcanet Press, 1981.

> Biocritical essay.

Christian (Otto Josef Wolfgang) Morgenstern

1871-1914

German poet, translator, essayist, and critic.

Though Morgenstern wished to be remembered for his serious and mystical poetry, he is best known for the nonsensical grotesques found in the *Galgenlieder (Gallows Songs)* and *Palmström*. In these humorous works Morgenstern alters the relation between things and words so that language proves itself to be unreliable, undermining the reader's confidence in the accepted meanings of words. Morgenstern is often compared with Lewis Carroll for his distinctive imaginary world, and with Edward Lear and Ogden Nash for his fanciful characters and coining of new words.

Morgenstern was born in Munich. He studied political science, philosophy, and art history at the University of Breslau. In 1894 Morgenstern moved to Berlin, establishing a reputation as a lyric poet and critic. After learning Norwegian and Swedish, he supplemented his income by translating works of Ibsen, Strindberg, and others. Morgenstern's first volume of poetry, *In Phanta's Schloss*, was praised by Rilke. His most popular work, *Gallows Songs*, was originally written for the private amusement of friends. However, the poet's playfulness and humor extended the work's appeal to a large number of educated Germans and to a German-language audience in Austria and Bohemia. The publication of *Melancholie* and a long-developing religious crisis marked the end of what is regarded as Morgenstern's worldly period. Thereafter he wrote only serious philosophical and religious poetry and prose. In 1909 Morgenstern met Rudolf Steiner, a leading proponent of the esoteric religious system of anthroposophy, whose teachings contributed to the mysticism of Morgenstern's later poems. Morgenstern's final volume of poetry, *Wir fanden einen Pfad*, was dedicated to Steiner.

Morgenstern intended his poems to express both humor and profound spirituality, and he objected to having his humorous verse labeled metaphysical nonsense. In his most important poems collected in *Gallows Songs* and *Palmström*, Morgenstern distorts syntax, coins new words, and twists normal meanings of familiar words. Metaphors are brought to life as the poet plays with words and the things they name. Most critics agree that Morgenstern's grotesque poetry presents translators with considerable challenges. The poet uses the idiosyncracies of the German language, making it difficult to convey in English both the sense and nonsense of his work. Some of his most successful pieces are in the form of epigrams, which became more and more philosophical and mystical after 1906. Critics point out that his philosophical and religious poetry collected in *Melancholie, Einkehr,* and *Wir fanden einen Pfad* suffers from its very seriousness of intent. Less critical mention is made of these later works, though when discussed they are usually described as poetry diluted with the abstractions of mysticism. These works, while technically competent, are generally considered uninspiring. They stress the love element of Morgenstern's philosophy without the playfulness of his early verse.

Morgenstern's reputation rests with his humorous poetry. Critics liken his play with language to the techniques of the dadaists

and surrealists. Like these artistic rebels, he manipulated language and image to defy conventional bourgeois logic. He contributed humor and a new perspective on life to a German-language audience. Morgenstern's unique blend of love and humor and his perception of the mystical union of all living things, pervades his best works.

PRINCIPAL WORKS

In Phanta's Schloss (poetry) 1895
Auf viele Wegen (poetry) 1897
Ich und die Welt (poetry) 1897
Ein Sommer (poetry) 1900
Galgenlieder (poetry) 1905
  [*Christian Morgenstern's "Galgenlieder"* [partial
    translation], 1963; also published as *Gallows Songs*
    [partial translation], 1964]
Melancholie (poetry) 1906
Einkehr (poetry) 1910
Palmström (poetry) 1910
Ich und Du (poetry) 1911
Wir fanden einen Pfad (poetry) 1914
Stufen (aphorisms, essays, and diaries) 1918
Epigramme und Sprüche (aphorisms) 1919
Mensch Wanderer (poetry) 1927

The Moon Sheep   (poetry) 1953
Gesammelte Werke   (poetry, aphorisms, and essays) 1965
The Great Lalula and Other Nonsense Rhymes   (poetry)
   1969
The Daynight Lamp and Other Poems   (poetry) 1973
Selected Poems of Christian Morgenstern   (poetry) 1973

FRANZ KAFKA   (essay date 1920?)

[*The following excerpt is taken from Gustav Janouch's conversations with Franz Kafka.*]

I was with Kafka in his office. I had with me Christian Morgenstern's *Songs of the Gallows*.

'Do you know his serious poems?' Kafka asked me. *'Time and Eternity? Steps?'*

'No, I had no idea that he wrote serious poems.'

'Morgenstern is a terribly serious poet. His poems are so serious that in *Songs of the Gallows* he has to save himself from his own inhuman seriousness.' (p. 78)

> *Franz Kafka, in an excerpt (1920?), in* Gesprache mit Kafka *by Gustave Janouch (copyright © 1968 by Fischer Verlag GmbH, Frankfurt-am Main; reprinted by permission of New Directions Publishing Corporation; in Canada by Joan Daves), S. Fischer, 1968 (and reprinted in* Conversations with Kafka *by Gustave Janouch, translated by Goronwy Rees, revised edition, New Directions, 1971, p. 78).*

BABETTE DEUTSCH and AVRAHM YARMOLINSKY   (essay date 1923)

[A religious bias is visible in the work of] Christian Morgenstern, more especially in his later books. Morgenstern is, however, best known as the author of grotesque poems, some of which caricature the prevalent positivist philosophy. His light verse, even when it is serious in intent, is as full of delicious folly as "Alice in Wonderland." His poetic evolution was from a smiling skepticism to a God-intoxicated affirmation of the world. (p. xxi)

> *Babette Deutsch and Avrahm Yarmolinsky, in their introduction to* Contemporary German Poetry: An Anthology, *edited and translated by Babette Deutsch and Avrahm Yarmolinsky, John Lane The Bodley Head Ltd., 1923, pp. xiii-xxvii.*

L.A. WILLOUGHBY   (essay date 1937)

[Where], the Englishman asks, are the equivalents in modern Germany of Lewis Carroll, W. S. Gilbert, A. A. Milne, E. V. Knox, A. P. Herbert, of that type of intellectual, clean, social humour which makes *Punch* the best comic paper in the world? The answer is to be found in the **'Grotesques'** of Christian Morgenstern. (p. 148)

Like our own Lewis Carroll he is convinced that the child mind contains the very essence of humour. From Nietzsche he derives his sceptical views on language, its inability really to express in words the thoughts at the back of the mind. It is this inadequacy of human speech which provides him with the

basis of his humour. . . . As a mathematician Lewis Carroll must similarly have felt that words did not reflect reason in the way that mathematical signs represent the values underlying them, that words, on the contrary, had a life of their own, independent of their origin. And so, like his English brother, Morgenstern proceeds on philological lines: as Alice meets a 'mock turtle' in Wonderland, so Morgenstern invents a 'Mondkalb' ['Moon calf'] and even a 'Mondschaf' ['Moon sheep']; as Alice recites a whole poem of meaningless words, so Morgenstern composes a musical nonsense poem entitled *Das grosse Lalula*. There are for him greater monsters in language than in all the oceans and forests of the world: he conjures up a 'Nasobem' which stalks along on its nose, and an 'Elef-ant' ['11-ant'] inevitably suggests the existence of a 'Zwölef-ant' ['12-ant']. If Lewis Carroll conceives of a grin without a cat, Morgenstern transcribes a fishes 'Nocturne' by indicating with the signs for short and long the dumb opening and shutting of their mouths. And sometimes he allows himself to be carried away by the mere music of his verse as in the *Schaukelstuhl* which just rocks on the terrace in the wind because it likes the sensation and the poet enjoys the rhythm.

Morgenstern imagines the most incongruous situations. . . . (pp. 148-49)

It would be wrong, however, to dismiss Morgenstern as a mere buffoon. There was another, very earnest side to his nature which comes out in his devotion to the mystic philosophy of Spinoza and to the theosophy of Rudolf Steiner. 'There is no way outside of us', he maintains, 'we merely go round in a circle. If we would go forward, the path leads inwards'. His chief poetry is inspired by the deep religious feelings of Angelus Silesius whose famous motto: 'Mensch, werde wesentlich!' ['Man, become essential!'] he makes into his own. He pours out his yearning for mystic union with God which will only be achieved in death when, too, the secret of the Universe shall be revealed to man. . . . (p. 149)

The volumes of lyrical verse collected under the title [*Melancholie, Einkehr,* and especially the posthumous *Wir pfanden einen Pfad*]. . . , have won for him an honourable place among the mystical poets in which Germany is so rich. (p. 150)

> *L. A. Willoughby, "Christian Morgenstern," in* German Life & Letters, *Vol. I, No. 2, January, 1937, pp. 148-56.*

BAYARD QUINCY MORGAN   (essay date 1938)

Germans have plenty of nonsense to their credit, but it was Morgenstern who first "fixed," so to speak, his highly sophisticated form of it, and it is to Morgenstern that one would naturally turn for an exemplification of it in German. To be sure, as we examine his grotesque and fantastic creations more closely, we hear underneath them, in many cases, a deep and earnest tone, some times almost a despairing one, as the poet records his rejection of the absurdities and inequities in the world about him. These comic poems are now gathered together in two slender volumes, one entitled *Palmström* from the fictitious character who serves as the principal protagonist of his quaint ideas, the other *Galgenlieder* (Songs of the Gallows), because one group of poems centers around weird pictures of a gallows which is supposed to have stood at one time on "Gallows Hill" at Werder near Potsdam.

Upon subjecting the hundred-odd short poems in these two collections to detailed scrutiny, I found that they began to arrange themselves in categories, which I classified: Sheer nonsense; Rhyme nonsense; Punning fancies; Sound effects; Printed shapes; Satires; Philosophic concepts; Sensible ideas grotesquely presented; Bizarre ideas; Superior nonsense. . . .

Largely untranslatable, in my opinion, are Morgenstern's punning fancies, some of which are among his most engaging inspirations. Such as *Die Oste* (by analogy with *Weste),* which is worn on the back as the vest is worn in front, [and] *Der Zwölf Elf,* who decided to call himself 23. . . . (p. 288)

In not a few cases [as in *The Stations*], the underlying idea is a perfectly sensible one, but the poet gives it one of his inimitable twists and carries it over into the world of mirth. . . .

Closely related to each other are the poems [*The Day-Night Lamp* and *The Odor-Organ*], which present what I have called bizarre ideas, philosophic concepts, and "superior nonsense," and these three groups comprise more than half of the entire number and include a good many of the verses that are most widely quoted and most gleefully cherished. (p. 289)

The poems of "superior nonsense" [such as *Korf's Clock*] are of great variety and resist collective characterization. They evidence an uncommon verbal, metrical, and unlogical ability, and charm us by their very lack of the sense they seem to possess. (p. 290)

Finally, as to the poems involving philosophic concepts [such as *The Impossible Fact*] it seems to me that they owe their distinctive character to a type of ideation that is on a definitely higher plane. (pp. 290-91)

All humor, we are told, is tragedy with the signs reversed; but humanity has reason to be grateful to those poets who can achieve that reversal with ease and grace. Morgenstern's success in this regard seems to me likely to constitute his chief claim to lasting commemoration. (p. 291)

> *Bayard Quincy Morgan, "The Superior Nonsense of Christian Morgenstern," in* Books Abroad *(copyright 1938 by the University of Oklahoma Press), Vol. 12, No. 3, Summer, 1938, pp. 288-91.*

A. CLOSS (essay date 1938)

[Christian Morgenstern] seeks to find a spiritual meaning in earthly life. His poetry and *pensées,* however, especially towards the end of his short life, turn more towards mysticism. . . . A great deal of Christian Morgenstern's work has . . . been ignored, yet who is not acquainted with the bizarre shapes mirrored by the prism of his wit in the famous '*Galgenlieder*' and '*Palmström*' poems? It is a world full of superreal senselessness in which the moon adapts itself to the shape of the German alphabet, waning in the form of *A* and waxing as *Z,* or we find some gem like the brilliant dialogue between earth and a cube. . . . (p. 407)

The '*Lattenzun mit Zwischenraum,*' the lonely '*Knie,*' '*Das ästhetische Wiesel,*' which stands on a *Kiesel* for the sake of the rhyme, the '*Perlhuhn,*' which counts the number of its pearls, or the '*Fisches Nachtgesang*' (without words) have become common property. But this word-comedy expresses in reality a profound earnestness and moral significance which was all too often lost on a hyper-intellectual generation. The consumptive author of '*Melancholie*' was an admirer of Walther von der Vogelweide, Goethe, Paul de Lagarde and Nietzsche. Like the last he struggles to discover the secret of life until, a few years before his death, Angelus Silesius's mystic utterance,

"*Mensch, werde wesentlich*" ["Man, become essential"], struck him as a revelation. . . . His heart yearns for the world beyond without, however, rejecting the earthly plane. (p. 408)

> *A. Closs, "Changing Views," in his* The Genius of the German Lyric: An Historic Survey of Its Formal and Metaphysical Values, *George Allen & Unwin Ltd, 1938, pp. 372-447.**

W. WITTE (essay date 1947-48)

Far from being in any way fortuitous, the partnership of the humorist and the mystic in Morgenstern's work is as close as it is permanent. It is not a case of one phase in his development succeeding another; both notes are sounded from the beginning, both go on reverberating until the very end, sometimes separately, sometimes in a chord. The poem *Das ist der Ast in deinem Holz* (from *Wir fanden einen Pfad*) shows how the two main forms of Morgenstern's art and thought tend to merge, his extraordinarily expressive grotesque style invading (and enlivening) a serious religious meditation on the subject of spiritual Pride. . . . (One may note, in passing, that in some of Morgenstern's poems the distinction between the serious and the mock-serious remains fluid. *Das Kirchlein,* from the volume *Mensch Wanderer,* a piece that would do credit to Palmström's whimsicality and to his tender heart, provides an example of this piquant ambiguity; *Die Eheringe* and *Vor dem Föhn* are others. All these could without incongruity be transferred to the *Galgenlieder.*)

Sometimes the mystical poet and his ally the humorist will produce variations on the same theme. In his life of Morgenstern, Michael Bauer prints a previously unpublished fragment which had originally been intended for Morgenstern's first volume of verse, *In Phanta's Schloss.* In this poem, the goddess Imagination grants the poet a glimpse of infinity, and he describes how the mind which has traversed the universe, journeying round the 'great Ring of pure and endless light', finally returns to its starting-point and is thrown back upon itself. What mortal man finds beyond the stars is his own self, it is in his own soul that he must seek the answer to the riddle of existence. Modulating from the mystical to the grotesque key, Morgenstern takes this theme up again in *Böhmischer Jahrmarkt,* one of the pieces in the posthumous collection *Die Schallmühle.* Here the conquest of interstellar space is achieved, not by the magic power of imagination, but by means of a mechanical aid: a super-telescope (symbolising the relentless 'progress' of modern science) directs the observer's glance all the way round the curved shape of the universe, back to (the back of) his own self again. . . . But alas!—by the time the cosmic circuit is completed, the observer will be in his grave. Having become an end in itself in our mechanised world, science marches on, not caring whether anyone benefits by its results or not. By elaborating the absurd consequences of his initial assumption, Morgenstern parodies the ruthless logic of scientific thinking. The theme must have attracted him, for we find him treating it yet again . . . in a pregnant and amusing miniature entitled *Letzte Fernsicht.* . . . (pp. 125-26)

The *reductio ad absurdum* of contemporary science is a task which offers welcome scope to the talents of the satirist, and Morgenstern sets about it with gusto: witness such poems as *Zukunftssorgen, Die Tagnachtlampe* (a new invention which at the turn of a switch changes day into night), *Der Aromat* (a kind of olfactory cafeteria), *Die Wissenschaft.* But he does not by any means confine himself to satire; and we shall not do justice to his humorous poems by interpreting them . . . in a merely negative sense, as substitutes for or distortions of a latent mysticism which had not yet found its full and proper expression. Morgenstern's humour has its positive side; it does not shrink from any of the fundamental questions with which contemplative minds have wrestled throughout the ages, and it is often no less illuminating than his mystical speculations. In his *Galgenlieder,* the most formidable problems of philosophy and theology are passed in review—the relation between man and the cosmos (*Das Lied vom blonden Korken; Schiff 'Erde'*); common sense and the supernatural (*Der Glaube*); the nature of time (*Die Korfsche Uhr; Vom Zeitunglesen*); life and matter (*Der durchgesetzte Baum; Das Butterbrotpapier*); the Platonic Idea (*Das Grab des Hunds*); the inadequacy of language, both as a means of self-expression and as a key to reality (*Der Purzelbaum; Die Westküsten; Die Nähe*); faith and dogma (*St. Expeditus*); the subjectivist view of perception—with its ontological implications—and the problem of error (*Der Meilenstein; Täuschung*); fate and the limitations of human knowledge (*Schicksal; Vice versa*).

On the face of it, all this seems rather unpromising material for humorous treatment; anyone unfamiliar with Morgenstern's work might well feel a trifle apprehensive, expecting to find 'humour' of a pedantic and unfunny kind. Let him but sample the poems, however, and his doubts will be dispelled. Morgenstern handles even the thorniest questions with such apparent ease and nonchalance, he blends logic and fantasy with such cunning, he makes his most devastating points with such a delightful show of wide-eyed innocence, he manipulates words and concepts with such dexterity, and at the same time with such genuinely creative imagination, that few readers find it in their heart to resist the subtle enchantment. To the philosophically-minded he offers a distinctly intellectual form of pleasure. The average reader, it is true, may not always be fully aware of the deep philosophic waters below the gaily rippling surface; but the fact that the *Galgenlieder* volume used to be something of a best seller proves that there is nothing unduly esoteric about its appeal. . . . [Who] could remain impervious to the charm of a poem like *Vice versa?* Disarmingly simple, full of tender sympathy, this little poem reveals the author's awareness of what might be called a fourth dimension of the spirit; it belongs to the borderland where humour and mysticism interpenetrate. . . . (pp. 126-27)

If, having found intellectual stimulus and aesthetic satisfaction in Morgenstern's humorous verse, the reader turns to his serious poems in a mystical vein [in *Ich und Du* and *Mensch Wanderer*], he must be prepared for disappointment, at any rate as far as their literary merits are concerned. Not that there can be any doubt about the sincerity of the feelings and convictions that inspire them; but as poems they are decidedly inferior. It is strange that this should be so, for Morgenstern attached the utmost importance to the spiritual lessons which these poems are intended to convey, and one might have expected him to be moved to poetic utterance by matters that meant so much to him. Certainly, in reading the poems in question, one feels that he is almost desperately eager to make his reader share the adventures of his mystical pilgrimage; but for all his eagerness, or perhaps because of it, he fails. He fails, not merely in the general sense in which all such attempts to express the ineffable are foredoomed to failure, but in the more specific sense that in his mystical verse he falls far short of his own best achievement in other *genres*. All the poetic graces which are so abundantly at his command in his humorous poems seem to have deserted him here: the remarkable ease

and flexibility of his diction, his originality, his mastery of the poetic *nuance*, his imaginative, creative use of language, his economy of expression—all are gone. Instead, we often find a diction which is stiff, involved, prosaic, and full of clichés. . . . We find pretentiousness, affected archaisms, ugly nonce-words, and deplorable lapses of taste. . . . We find colloquialisms incongruously inserted into high-flown passages. . . . We find instances of rather questionable punning. . . . Lastly, we find the irritating habit, so common among 'Spasmodics', of using hyphens, dashes, spaced type, and capitals in order to create the impression that there is more in a word or a line than meets the eye. . . . Everywhere in these poems one remains painfully conscious of a sense of strain; they speak of spiritual joys, but they do not succeed in re-creating any such experience in the reader.

The poems which relate to Rudolf Steiner and his anthroposophy are no less forced and unconvincing than the rest. . . . [Steiner's] influence maintained its hold on the poet to the end. Had Morgenstern found a secure anchorage at last, a doctrine which left no room for any further doubts (as Steiner himself asserts)—or are we perhaps entitled to surmise that in the poems about Steiner and Steiner's teaching, the repression of an unresolved mental conflict cramped the poetic faculty?

It goes without saying that any conjecture of this kind remains incapable of strict proof. What is certain is that the gift of poetic utterance, like the beatific vision of the mystic, is not to be attained simply by an effort of the will. However hard Morgenstern tried to make his mystical poems a worthy vehicle of his spiritual message, the result is undistinguished at its best; at its worst, a mere mockery of the author's noble intentions. But when he gives rein to his humorous play impulse, he carries us with him into a grotesquely charming Wonderland where we find ourselves released from the prisonhouse of contemporary materialism. Strange as it may appear, the humorist, in his humbler way, succeeds where the mystic fails—for a release of the spirit from its imprisonment in the material world is one of the prizes of the mystic's quest. He that shall humble himself shall be exalted: and humour (in the words of G. K. Chesterton) 'corresponds to the human virtue of humility, and is only more divine because it has, for the moment, more sense of the mysteries'. (pp. 127-30)

> *W. Witte, "Humour and Mysticism in Christian Morgenstern's Poetry," in* German Life & Letters, *Vol. 1, 1947-48, pp. 124-30.*

WOLFGANG KAYSER   (essay date 1957)

Morgenstern is widely known only as a poet of grotesques, which reminds one of the fate of Wilhelm Busch's pictorial humoresques. Busch and Morgenstern are often mentioned in one breath. But in spite of certain techniques they have in common, the difference between their works is easily verified. Busch consistently uses satire as his starting point. Satire is by no means absent from Morgenstern's *oeuvre*, which contains a number of parodies (of naturalistic drama, Gabriele d'Annunzio, [Paul] Scheerbart, and others). But Morgenstern himself repeatedly emphasized the difference between his parodies and his grotesques. Actually, even those grotesque poems which relate to literature are neither caricatures nor parodies. The world of these poems unfolds skillfully but does not present a distorted image of models selected for ridicule. An untrammeled imagination appears to be at work, which results in the kind of higher nonsense cultivated by Edward Lear rather than

Busch. Lear and Morgenstern also agree in the use of poetic conventions in order to produce a tension between form and content: meter, rhythm, sound, rhyme, and refrain are fully exploited with the aim of enhancing the striking contrast between words and meaning. (pp. 150-51)

Morgenstern's imagination was frequently engaged by "verbal invention" (*sprachlicher Einfall*). A sound, a word, a phrase provide the stimulus. . . . Morgenstern's imagination continued to operate in this manner by creating new characters and their milieu through the medium of language. The characters and their milieu established cyclic connections between the poems. Korf and Palmström [recurrent characters in Morgenstern's poems] acquired a life of their own, and among the nonhuman realms the sphere of the moon was given special attention. . . . Language suggested the creation of Tulemond (*tout le monde*) and Mondamin, and a whole host of mythical events were added. In Morgenstern's poems the mythmaking verbal fantasy can be seen at work. A word like *Schäfchenwolken* (fleecy or lambkin clouds) suffices to arouse Morgenstern's imagination. He has a passion for creating strange animals: the moon sheep, the night mare, the raven, the toad, the fish, etc. The place in language or reality to which they owe their lives can always be identified. In this way the nonsense seems to become meaningful and legitimate; several layers of meaning are created, between which the narrative oscillates without coming to rest on any one of them. With ludicrous pedantry Morgenstern makes his deeply learned commentator Dr. Jeremias Mueller stress the realistic elements. The *Tonmassage* (Sound Massage), for instance, with which the expiring air is to be treated, denotes the familiar phenomenon of articulate speech; and it is easy to see why a cork in an upright position cannot see its own reflection. Here pedantry makes nonsense out of sense.

The confusion increases in cases where inanimate objects are treated like living things. When language furnishes the cause, the hidden aspects of such objects are suddenly brought to light, and nonsense is manifested as verbal nonsense. . . . We enter a world in which parts of organic wholes have made themselves independent: "A knee walks lonely through the world." I do not want to spoil the fun engendered by this higher nonsense; but the attentive reader cannot help being puzzled or disconcerted. . . . There is something uncanny about these things. Morgenstern constantly questions language, which produces such oddities. (pp. 151-52)

One immediately spots the humorous technique at work in [*Die Nähe*]. Morgenstern is not interested in hiding it, since his procedure is not an arbitrary one but concerns the very principle of language. One of his favorite devices is that of personification. An abstract feminine noun becomes a woman, just as the Middle Ages had their Lady Honor, Lady World, Lady Love, etc. This is a process by means of which the obvious significance of the feminine article is heightened. The comparative appears as a new and, again, apparently legitimate force. Since we have reached the human level, the seamstress (*Näherin*) is the phonetically justified successor of proximity (*Nähe*), and her tendency to regard her well-attested origin as a joke seems very shortsighted. The reader's superior knowledge is skillfully and by no means unsuccessfully invoked; for who would be as simple-minded as Mrs. Nolte? One certainly cannot take the whole thing seriously, nor is one supposed to. The reader is slightly confused and may even seek to rediscover the humorous aspect of the seemingly correct grammatical situation. Morgenstern's intention would be fulfilled if he now

began to suspect language. As early as 1896 Morgenstern noted in his diary: "Often a word suddenly strikes me. The total arbitrariness of language, which encompasses our world view—and, consequently, the arbitrariness of the world view—is revealed". . . . In the same year he noted that "man is imprisoned in a cage of mirrors" (which we are perhaps justified in equating with language).

Between 1906 and 1908 the number of entries concerned with the duplicity of language increases. One comes upon phrases like "destroy language!" or "by bourgeois I mean those things in which man has hitherto felt at home, especially his language. To rid the latter of its bourgeois traits is the noblest task of the future." In 1907 he had written: "The older I grow the more one word comes to dominate my thinking—grotesque." We now know what he meant by "grotesque." Over and above the ridiculousness suggested by absurdity and distortion, the grotesque inspires a fear which grows out of the sudden recognition that man's position is precarious. In his grotesques, Morgenstern wants to shake our confidence in language and the image of the world which it supplies. He does so by using the principles of language itself—such as word formation, metaphor, rhyme, simile, intensification—for the creation of absurdities. The "basic idea" of the *Galgenlieder* is "more or less grotesque." (p. 154)

[Morgenstern] merely wanted to shake the naïve belief in language as a road to reality; but unlike the other contemporary writers of grotesques he firmly believed in its existence. "Destroy language," he quotes Master Ekkehart as saying, "and, with it, all things and concepts. The rest is silence," and adds: "This silence, however, is—God." (Morgenstern later thought he had found a path in Rudolf Steiner's anthroposophy.) He aimed at the destruction not of language as such but of the false sense of security it gives: "I do not want man to be shipwrecked; but he should realize that he is sailing an ocean." Morgenstern's grotesques are not as harmless as many people take them to be. If they leave too much room for humor, however, this may be due to their author's failure to eliminate the category of transcendence. (p. 155)

Wolfgang Kayser, "The Grotesque in the Twentieth Century," in his The Grotesque in Art and Literature, *translated by Ulrich Weisstein (translation copyright © 1963 by Indiana University Press; originally published as* Das Groteske: Seine Gestaltung in Malerei und Dichtung, *Gerhard Stalling Verlag, 1957), Indiana University Press, 1963, pp. 130-76.**

JETHRO BITHELL   (essay date 1959)

Morgenstern's humour owes nothing whatever to tradition or schools of any sort; it is *sui generis*, if ever anything was. His first book of humorous verse, *In Phanta's Schloss*. . . , shows the influence of Nietzsche, from whom he derived his questioning of the essentiality of words. The quaint and whimsical verse of [*Galgenlieder, Palmström, Palma Kunkel* and *Der Gingganz*—collected as *Alle Galgenlieder*] has to be labelled with a new term: *Sprachhumor,* a humour which flies like sparks from verbal quibbles. It is metaphysical humour: Gingganz, for instance, is Morgenstern's term for an ideologist. But Morgenstern was no ingenious punster: his wit is austerely intellectual, a diversion so to speak from his philosophical speculation on the relation of *nomen* [name] and *res* [thing], or *das Wort* [the word] and *das Ding an sich* [thing in itself]. To flippant laymen *das Ding an sich* has always seemed mirthful; and Morgenstern, though strictly philosophical, strikes a mirthful philosophy from the very impossibility of name and thing being identical. In other words, while the thing is of the eternal essence the name for it is illusory, as the hopeless disagreement of thinkers on the nature of things shows. One has only to think of all the systems of scholasticism—each thought out and nailed down idea by idea with the incontrovertible logic of the best minds of the Middle Ages: *Nominalismus, Universalismus, Konzeptualismus, Terminismus*, and so forth—to appreciate what may have been Morgenstern's point of view that metaphysically it cannot be proved to the satisfaction of everybody that the idea (or name—*logos, Wort*) is the thing, or that the thing is the idea. His wit, therefore, plays—and with how clear a flame!—round the idiocy of our faith in words—which possibly convey no ideas at all, or, if they do, problematic ideas. . . . Morality, the naturalists had proclaimed, is relative; Morgenstern, though less dogmatically, proclaims the relativity of knowledge. And miraculously into this spider's web of speculation the magic of poetry is caught: the mystical life that the *Volkslied* [folksong] gives to birds and beasts and fishes, surprises of rhythm and diction, and sometimes in the very things that the poet questions he finds those tears that moved the soul of Virgil. (pp. 65-6)

> Jethro Bithell, *"Humorists, Satirists, Satanists and Visionaries," in* Modern German Literature: 1880-1950 *(copyright © 1959 Jethro Bithell), revised edition, Methuen & Co Ltd, 1959, pp. 54-74.**

MAX KNIGHT (essay date 1963)

A large number of Morgenstern's **Galgenlieder** are based on visual pictures that fascinated him. He "saw" things like a painter—his father and both grandfathers, Josef Schertel and Christian E. B. Morgenstern whose work can be seen in German art galleries, were all landscape artists of the romantic school. Thus Christian Morgenstern is an heir of the romanticists, just as he is a precursor of the surrealists. When he sees, presumably in a zoo, a kangaroo watching a frightened sparrow on a fence post, this situation, and nothing more, is the poem. Nothing "happens." The poem could end after the first two lines: "Behind the fence, the kangaroo/has on a sparrow cast his view." But these lines are very suitable for book illustration, stick in the mind, and we are likely to remember them when we visit a zoo and see a chance sparrow there. The hen in the railroad station and the rocking chair on the terrace are also "visual verse." Morgenstern's grotesque animal world is a true heritage from his romantic-artist forebears; his creatures inhabit the German fairy-tale forest. The Nosobame is a cousin of [Arnold] Böcklin's unicorn in "Schweigen im Walde." (pp. 3-4)

Morgenstern plays with words as a child plays with blocks, piling them up, rearranging them, knocking them down. All his life he preserved the child's vision: to see words (and things) as though he had never seen them before; and he played with them as imaginatively as a child. Paraphrasing Nietzsche's "In any true man hides a child who wants to play," Morgenstern dedicated the **Galgenlieder** to "the child in man."

Some verbal quibbles had a special appeal for Morgenstern, because they enabled him to upset the "Philistine's" smug feeling of security. "To me," he said, "the term middle-class connotes a safe, comfortable, middle-of-the-road policy. Above all, our language is 'middle class,' in the middle of our road. To drive it to one side or the other, or even off the road, is the noblest task of the future." Applying himself to this noble task, Morgenstern took literally such untranslatable idioms as "die Flinte ins Korn werfen" and used them as subjects for his verses. Had he been an American he probably would have been tempted by the original flavor of "by the skin of one's teeth," "greased lighting," "dragging a red herring," or similar metaphors. He is likely to have chuckled over the wentle-trap shell (the shift of the association from Treppe to trap), and would perhaps have allowed himself some low-brow capers about an icicle envying a bicycle, a Hebrew chiding a Shebrew, an out-law wishing to be an in-law, or an egret missing his egress (and turning back as regret)—about any linguistic caprice or coincidence. (pp. 5-6)

Morgenstern felt that people use their familiar language unthinkingly, mouthing what they had heard before. "Most people do not talk—they quote. One feels tempted to put quotation marks around almost everything they say, because they have not themselves created the form of what they say, but merely followed habit." (p. 6)

Morgenstern said about man's unthinking use of language: "I don't want to see man shipwrecked, but he should be conscious of the fact that he's sailing on the high seas." But not all **Galgenlieder** had such "ulterior motives." Some were undoubtedly sparked simply by rhymes and some by those lucky verbal accidents which he loved to exploit and which resulted in a humor sui generis. The public and the critics repeatedly insisted on reading all kinds of interpretations even into that group of **Galgenlieder** that were purely fun. Morgenstern mildly chided these pedants in his mock explanations by "Dr. Jeremias Müller" printed in *Ueber die Galgenlieder*, a "commentary" to the **Galgenlieder.**

As though Morgenstern had anticipated contrived attempts to read more into his fancies than he had put into them, he made clear in his **"Aesthetic Weasel"** that the rhyme, and no "deeper meaning," caused him to write at least this particular jingle. The "Wiesel" sitting on a "Kiesel" in "Bachgeriesel" can justifiably be translated as a ferret nibbling a carrot in a garret, a mink sipping a drink in a kitchen sink, a hyena playing a concertina in an arena, or a lizard shaking its gizzard in a blizzard instead of the way chosen in this volume. In **"Das Böhmische Dorf,"** similarly, Morgenstern says in the poem itself that Korf appears in the poem merely "because of the rhyme" with Dorf. (p. 6-7)

During Morgenstern's time and later, the **Galgenlieder** were often classified as nonsense poetry. To this, Morgenstern, who was a mild-mannered, almost timid person, says, please don't, in a disarming plea to his critics: "One thing I beg of you. Should the terms 'nonsense' or 'gibberish' be included in the review—no matter how flattering the qualifying adjectives might be—kindly reconsider them in favor of something like 'folly' or 'craziness.' Surely you would not want to tag with these two evil German Philistine and tavern terms of thoughtlessness the very humor that aims at a certain kind of spirituality. 'Higher nonsense' 'fit to be classified as literature' is the cheapest and unwisest that can be said" about the **Galgenlieder**—a slogan used without doing justice to the evidence. (pp. 9-10)

> Max Knight, *"Introducing Christian Morgenstern," in* Galgenlieder *by Christian Morgenstern, translated by Max Knight (© 1963 by Max E. Knight; reprinted by permission of the University of California Press), University of California Press, 1963, pp. 1-12.*

CHARLES BISHOP (essay date 1978)

Like many another classic, Christian Morgenstern's *"Fisches Nachtgesang"* is more often alluded to (and reproduced) than actually read. . . . [The] work can indeed be "read", and . . . it has something poetic and interesting to say. A highly effective precursor of concrete poetry, it is a delightful and subtle little work with more to it than first meets the eye.

The body of the work, the "picture", is a playful set of visual puns, suggesting simultaneously a fish with scales, a pond with waves, and a metrical pattern. Looking at the individual units, one sees not only a pattern of accent marks, but childlike images of sleeping fish　and happy fish　which, in the manner of some illusionist and op art pictures, almost seem to move about and change places. The "tone" of the picture is light and sparkling.

The work is effective nonsense because it plays with language and meaning in a way which is both absurd and logical. Fish do not sing; therefore their nonexistent song is wordless—a picture, a logical and humorous synesthesia, and Morgenstern caps his visual puns by teasing us with a paradox, a poem which is not properly a poem at all, though it has all the elements of a poem: words, lines, meter and images.

Like the best nonsense poets, Morgenstern is able to move beyond the merely playful and into the realm of the mysterious. For perhaps fish *do* sing. By giving his fish a "nightsong" rather than just a song, the poet is able to hint at strange possibilities beyond the limits of rationality; dreams perhaps, or an underwater fairyland, or a mythic nightworld in which fish really do acquire voices and sing. But if so, it is a song that we shall never hear, for ours is a different world.

Who then can tell us what song the fish sang? Morgenstern has done it. It is witty, light and playful, but also secret and mysterious, hidden in night and water and silence. (pp. 11-12)

> *Charles Bishop, "Unheard Melodies: Morgenstern's 'Fisches Nachtgesang'," in* Germanic Notes, *Vol. 9, Nos. 1 & 2, 1978, pp. 11-12.*

ERICH P. HOFACKER　(essay date 1978)

In Phanta's Schloss (In Fancy's Castle) is the title of Morgenstern's first volume of poetry. . . . [Its] chief inspiration was Nietzsche. . . . [Morgenstern characterized the volume] as humorous and fantastic. Mythological, cosmic, and middle-class concepts surprise us here in their striking combination. (p. 24)

One of the best poems in this collection is called **"Auffahrt"** (**"Ascent"**). The relentless drive to the stars in the phantom chariot drawn by steeds of the night is described in effectively changing rhythm and a varied rhyme scheme. The sound of a distant waterfall is the last vanishing impression from the earth before the poet enters the deep solitude of his dream world that may reveal to him the mysteries of the universe. (p. 25)

[*Auf vielen Wegen (On Many Roads)*] was published in 1897 and subsequently enlarged and combined with another thin volume of lyrics called *Ich und die Welt (I and the World)*. As the original title indicates, the collection offers a large variety of themes, moods, and lyric forms. These lyrics range from a lighthearted song of sheer joy in life, written in unconventional stanzas, to the meditative free verse groping for the meaning of human existence. Frequently the earthbound and spirtual are contrasted, as in the poem **"Inmitten der grossen Stadt"** (**"In the Midst of the Large City"**). Here we see the silent river flowing through the metropolis at night, reflecting the thousands of stars above while man is lost in fleeting moments of pleasure and pain, unaware of himself as part of the universe.

"Morgenfahrt" (**"Morning Ride"**) describes a sunrise impressionistically in three four-line rhymed stanzas. This is quite different from the dithyrambic effusion of *In Phanta's Schloss* which Morgenstern composed in the same period. (pp. 27-8)

Morgenstern's charming humor—not the grotesque humor of the *Galgenlieder* but the kind we encounter in Gottfried Keller—is also represented in the collection *Auf vielen Wegen*. There is the **"Kleine Geschichte"** (**"Little Story"**) of the little flag that was in great distress because its red and yellow stripes wanted to unite. . . . The simple language of the folk song is apparent, just as it is in the other tale called **"Anmutiger Vertrag"** (**"Charming Pact"**), where the poet and the nightingale come to a charming agreement. We are reminded of a similar situation in Walther von der Vogelweide of whose lyrics Morgenstern compiled a small anthology in 1906. (pp. 29-30)

In the winter months of 1896-1897 Morgenstern had a number of significant dreams which he fashioned into a cycle of twelve lyrics forming part of *Auf vielen Wegen*. The best known of these is entitled **"Der Stern"** (**"The Star"**), symbolizing the poet's higher world. Just as daytime experiences are usually more concise and more sharply delineated than the imagined happenings of our dreams, Morgenstern's description of his dream is more extended than his portrayal of the physical world; it is presented in free verse in long unrhymed lines and slow rhythm. (p. 30)

Following the cycle of twelve dreams we find, in *Auf vielen Wegen*, some kind of Dance of Death, a sequence of poems under the caption **"Vom Tagewerk des Todes"** (**"On the Labor of Death"**). Death appears in the guise of the sower who in sowing wastes innumerable seeds, as the guest who turns into the solitary toper, as the reaper who comes to the blacksmith, as the ghostly pilot causing the boat to be shipwrecked, as the drunken switchman on the last trip, as the stranger who pushes the mountain climber into the abyss and, finally, as the visitor coming to the sick man in his delirious dream. Better known than these episodes in verse is the poem entitled **"Vöglein Schwermut"** (**"The Little Bird Melancholy"**) which belongs to the same group. The imaginary bird called melancholy flies across the world singing such a mournful song that anyone who hears it cannot hear anything else. He can no longer endure the light of day and does away with himself. Every midnight the bird takes its rest on the finger of death. He strokes it softly and says, "fly away, my little bird, fly away." And again it flies across the world singing. In its language this poem approaches the manner of the folk song. Its form is light-winged in spite of the deadly seriousness of its contents. (p. 32)

[In August, 1898, Morgenstern wrote] the collection *Ein Sommer (A Summer)* and dedicated it to Dagny Fett, his youthful friend. Its poems appear almost exactly in the order in which they were composed. They reflect a great joy in color and, at the same time, reveal a great tenderness and delicacy of feeling. (p. 36)

At the very beginning of this century, when Morgenstern had to seek refuge in the Swiss Alps because of the treacherous disease of his lungs, he had enough opportunity to ponder his fate as a human being. . . . At that time, he had no religious conviction in the traditional sense, but only an unfailing presentiment that his spiritual self in some way would outlast his earthly life. We find it expressed in his poem **"Unverlierbare Gewähr"** (**"Unbreakable Guarantee"**). . . . (p. 41)

[The *Galgenlieder*] are the product of a highly imaginative mind that gives full sway to its fancies which, however, have a coherence and organic development of their own. Here we get a different world. Morgenstern says: "From the gallows hill you see the world differently and you see different things than others do." An adult uses languages as a tool for communicating with others and describing the world as it is. In the gallows songs, language appears as a creative force. It links the empirical world with a world of fancy. Things of our daily life become animated: a boot, a funnel, a hall. As in fairy tales, animals have human feelings and can talk: a hack horse, a donkey, a porcupine, a hippopotamus. New creatures are created linguistically: a twelve nix, a moonsheep, a hawken chick, a nasobem. The Gingganz, Morgenstern explains to a puzzled critic, is a dreamer or ideologist. Abstract concepts take on bodily form: proximity philosophizes about its mission and is changed into a seamstress. A somersault is dissatisfied with himself, and a sigh goes skating. This language creates matter out of thin air: the open spaces between the pickets of a picket fence are used as building material. Thus Morgenstern describes not only a potential world, as we shall see in *Palmström,* but he also bestows existence upon the impossible. This is the magic attraction of the *Galgenlieder* and the secret source of their popularity. Morgenstern wanted to loosen up the dull, dismal seriousness to which man was tied in a materialistic contemporary world. He wanted to stimulate the imagination and spread a spirit of levity, cheerfulness, and freedom; and in this he was singularly successful. Although the authoritative literary critics of the day, with few exceptions, did not know what to do with the *Galgenlieder* and did not mind saying so, the general public took to them and gave them an enthusiastic reception. (pp. 62-3)

[*Palmström*] came out in the spring of 1910. Tenderhearted Palmström and his like-minded friend von Korf are not only imaginary but very imaginative characters. Unconcerned about the realities of life, they live in a world of their own. They share one feature with Till Eulenspiegel, the prankster in the old German folk tales: they often take metaphors literally. The best-known example is the poem **"Die weggeworfene Flinte"** (**"The Abandoned Rifle"**). It is based on the phrase "die Flinte ins Korn werfen" ("to throw one's rifle into the wheat field") indicating that a person abandons his undertaking. Roaming along a wheat field one evening, Palmström catches sight of a rifle that had been thrown away between the stalks. He stops his carefree singing and sadly sits down to examine his find. Picturing the despondent man who threw his rifle away, Palmström commiserates with him. He decorates the barrel and the butt with poppy and the spikes of the wheat and leans it against the nearest road sign, hoping that the fainthearted man would pass by again. A charming example of human sympathy and understanding for an unknown fellow man.

Linguistic imagination creates an odd garment in the poem **"Die Oste."** It is invented as a counterpart to *die Weste,* a waistcoat to be worn under the jacket and visible in front, sometimes made of fancy material with pockets for a watch and other valuables. Why should our stomach be privileged to be covered with flower patterns and fancy buttons and pockets? Let's have equality, Palmström argues, and wear such a garment on our back, an eastcoat. Lo and behold! The tailors take up the idea in no time and produce a hundred thousand such pieces of clothing before they go out of fashion. (pp. 63-4)

Morgenstern's search for his spiritual identity was fundamental to him. It continued for many years, had many aspects, and underwent several changes. It was expressed in verse and prose. (p. 74)

The ideas he had expressed in his pantheistic poems [published under the title *Melancholie (Melancholia)*] provided food for further meditations which were published after his death under the heading **"Tagebuch eines Mystikers"** (**"Diary of a Mystic"**). They constitute a highlight of *Stufen* and begin with these words: "I wrote this at the point where man coincides with God, where he ceases to experience himself as a separate being." (p. 77)

The idea of the identity of God and man sheds a new light on the role of evil and suffering among human beings. (p. 78)

When we remember that Morgenstern wrote the **"Diary of a Mystic"** at a sanitarium in Birkenwerder, we can understand his interest in the problem of death. (p. 80)

Morgenstern's evolutionary pantheism was a natural result of his way of experiencing of the world. (p. 81)

Now that the division between the physical world and the world of the spirit no longer existed for Morgenstern he could see the one reflected in the other. An inner experience could well be represented by an external situation. The feeling of being on the brink of death, when the longing for eternity and the natural shrinking back from it becomes an acute struggle, could well be pictured by mountain scenery. That is what we find in the second and third poems in the collection of lyrics entitled *Einkehr (Introspection).* . . . In response to this longing for eternity, mortal man shrinks from the imminent plunge. (pp. 84-5)

The realization of the precariousness of his health could not help but produce in the poet an undercurrent of anticipation of an early departure, reflected not only in his letters but also, now and then, in his poetry. (p. 85)

[The] poems included in *Einkehr* are characterized by their cosmic awareness and their religious overtones. (p. 88)

[Pantheism] which finds its key in Christ's awareness of His unity with God, is persistently expressed in Morgenstern's poetry. In **"Das Kornfeld"** (**"The Wheatfield"**), the poet observes a wheatfield swaying in the breeze and imagines each ear to be endowed with a soul and a spirit. (p. 92)

"Memento," the short form of *memento mori* ("think of death"), takes on a new meaning in Morgenstern's pantheism. Nature reminds him, rightly so, of the frailty of the human body. He is running a race with the steady pace of fate. Sometimes he seems to have gained on fate, but eventually they will arrive together at the little place called *Totenbrück* ("bridge of death"). Suddenly the poet stops and flings the pagan word "fate" into the face of his own time. He recalls his identity with God and is intent on his goals, moving through a thousand darknesses, decreeing life and death for himself. . . . *Einkehr* closes with an elaboration of John 14:6. . . . This is the last of five fragments from an uncompleted lyrical cycle on Christ. It is important to note that this cornerstone of Morgenstern's Christ-oriented pantheism was already developed before the poet met Margareta Gosebruch von Liechtenstern, his future wife. (pp. 92-3)

Morgenstern's love had taken on a religious connotation. Margareta had become a powerful spiritualizing force, and he hoped that this could also be said for him. In the prayer **"Getrennter Liebender Gebet zu einander"** (**"The Separated Lovers Pray to Each Other"**) contained in *Mensch Wanderer (Man the Pilgrim)* each plays the role of the guardian angel for the other. . . . The religious tenor of their togetherness is revealed in a short poem of ten lines published in *Ich und Du (I and You)*, the collection of lyrics which is primarily a testimony to the poet's love for Margareta. The poem describes a wishful dream in which on some star the lovers come to life again as a blooming rosebush. He is the root, she the bush, he will be the branches, she the leaves, he the rose, and she its fragrance. Thus their lives are united in every fiber, in every breath rising as a prayer of thanks.

Ich und Du, with the subtitle *Sonette, Ritornelle, Lieder*, published in 1911 has as its motto: "Wer nicht stirbt, vor er stirbt, der verdirbt, wenn er stirbt" ("he who does not die before his death will perish when he dies"). This points out the necessity of a spiritual rebirth during our lifetime. (pp. 100-02)

It is significant to note that, among the fourteen chapters of *Stufen, [eine Entwicklung in Aphorismen und Tagebuch-Notizen (Stages, a Development in Aphorisms and Diary Notes)]*, those dealing with ethical concerns, that is, *Ethisches, Erziehung, Selbst-Erziehung* ("discipline," self-discipline"), *Am Tor* ("at the gate") take up considerably more space (from five to twelve pages each) than do the others, written during the last three years of the poet's life. (p. 122)

[We have in *Wir Fanden einen Pfad (We Found the Path)*] Morgenstern's spiritual legacy reflecting the religious experience of his last years. Although many of these poems could not have been written without anthroposophical insight, almost all is expressed in such terms that it is readily accessible to any person, whatever his religious persuasion may be. We learn, for instance, that others can help us find the path to ultimate truth but that the last decisive steps must be taken by the individual himself. This involves rigorous training of our willpower, of our trains of thought, and of our moods. (p. 129)

Morgenstern did not feel disturbed by his approaching death. When, a short time before his death, someone inquired about his illness, he replied that he did not feel sick, that only a person who is a slave to his illness is actually ill. No really free human being could be sick. In his own case his works could bear this out. (p. 131)

> *Erich P. Hofacker, in his* Christian Morgenstern *(copyright © 1978 by Twayne Publishers, Inc.; reprinted with the permission of Twayne Publishers, a Division of G. K. Hall & Co., Boston), Twayne, 1978. 149 p.*

ADDITIONAL BIBLIOGRAPHY

Calder, W.M. "Translating Morgenstern." *Oxford German Studies* 4 (1969): 142-54.
    Finds that selecting appropriate gender and vocabulary and capturing the poet's intent are some of the difficulties faced when translating Morgenstern's nonsense poetry.

Carruth, Hayden. "Comment: *Gallows Songs*." *Poetry* CXII, No. 6 (September 1968): 421.
    Brief descriptive review concluding with the remark that Morgenstern is "a third-rate poet."

Keyser, Samuel Jay, and Prince, Alan. "Folk Etymology in Sigmund Freud, Christian Morgenstern, and Wallace Stevens." *Critical Inquiry* 6, No. 1 (Autumn 1979): 65-78.*
    Examines myth-making in Morgenstern's "Der Werwolf" and the way in which its meaning is preserved in Jerome Lettvin's English translation.

Roy, Albert. "Christian Morgenstern: Poet of the *Galgenlieder*." *The American-German Review* XXVII, No. 3 (February-March 1961): 4-7.
    Appreciation of Morgenstern, with several translations from his poetry.

(Sir) Charles G(eorge) D(ouglas) Roberts

1860-1943

Canadian poet, short story writer, novelist, historian, critic, and essayist.

An artist of emotion, originality, and color, Roberts is often called "the father of Canadian literature." He celebrated Canada's confederation in his work, and drew upon his maritime environment to create poetry and prose which is at once Canadian and universal. Roberts wrote verse pivotal to his country's poetic growth, achieving excellence with the elegiac "Ave," written in memory of Shelley, and with a long narrative poem in free verse, "The Iceberg." These are rivaled for preeminence only by "The Tantramar Revisited," describing New Brunswick's marshlands, and the sonnets included in his *Songs of the Common Day*. A master of short love lyrics, meditative pieces, and nature poems, Roberts is also recognized for his animal stories, in which he glorifies the primal struggle for life. Numerous tales of the wilderness, written throughout his career, are among Roberts's most popular works.

A native of Fredricton, New Brunswick, Roberts attended the University of New Brunswick. There, in 1880, he composed *Orion, and Other Poems*, a volume that won the praise of Matthew Arnold and Oliver Wendell Holmes. Roberts served as editor of the magazine *Week* until 1885, when he was appointed professor of English literature at King's College in Nova Scotia. For over a decade he published a steady flow of poems and novels. In 1897 he moved to New York. There he began a new phase in his career: the writing of short stories, most notable among them the animal stories contained in such collections as *The Watchers of the Trails* and *Kings in Exile*. Roberts lived in New York and London for thirty years, a period during which he wrote many volumes of stories but very little poetry, none of it up to his previous standard. He returned to Canada in 1927, a year after receiving the first Lorne Pierce medal for imaginative literature, awarded by the Royal Society of Canada. Upon his return Roberts began writing verse again, enjoying a poetic Indian summer that culminated in *The Iceberg and Other Poems* in 1934. A year later he was knighted by King George V.

Desmond Pacey calls poetry Roberts's first love. *Orion, and Other Poems* opened a new era in Canadian poetry, called by some critics the first Canadian Renaissance. This volume owes much to Greek mythology, the English epic, and to the nineteenth-century Romantics. The poems of *In Divers Tones*, Roberts's second collection, reveal a change of heart in their author. While *Orion* is idealistic and forceful, *In Divers Tones* tends toward melancholy. Roberts wrote: "The Hands of chance or change have marred, or moulded, or broken . . . all I have most adored." *Songs of the Common Day* continues to reflect growth in the artist, most notably in the tour-de-force "Ave" and in the better sonnets, which display Roberts's poetic mastery and precision; among these, "The Sower" is one of Roberts's most popular and artistically accomplished lyrics. Subsequent collections, including *The Book of the Native* and *The Book of the Rose*, mark a sharp decline in Roberts's poetic powers.

Surpassing these collections in artistry and importance, Roberts's animal stories are attempts to illustrate the crucial interdependence between natural and human life. In *Kindred of the Wild* Roberts's treatment of this theme neither sentimentalizes animal existence nor demeans human nature. In *Kings in Exile* he achieves the imaginative rendering of how the dull brain of a wild animal interprets its surroundings.

In 1927 Roberts's published *The Vagrant of Time*, which initiated a new period of inspiration and revived poetic excellence. The promise of *The Vagrant of Time* was fulfilled in the ensuing collection, *The Iceberg, and Other Poems*. While the predominant mood is nostalgic—to be expected from a late Romantic—Roberts also manages a masterpiece of objectivity in the title poem. In "The Iceberg" the poet "faces his fascination with the inhuman," according to Jean Mallinson, combining energy with a firmness uncommon to free verse. The next volume, *Canada Speaks of Britain*, includes "As Down the Woodland Ways," which states its author's belief in the timeless regeneration of life, and "Two Rivers," in which Roberts compares his own restlessness to the Tantramar's, with its ceaseless tide-driven motion.

During the nineteenth century, critics praised all of Roberts's work. Recent criticism tends to favor his poetry over his prose. Of his dozen volumes, the lyrics celebrating Canada's heritage and the landscape and rural life of the eastern tidewater are both critical and popular favorites. However, some critics have charged Roberts with modeling his poetry too closely on his literary forebears—notably Tennyson, Keats, Longfellow, and Shelley—in his effort to shield Canada's artistic reputation from charges of pioneer uncouthness and inelegance. Nonetheless, Roberts's best works are enduring contributions to Canadian poetry, and his patriotism, innovation, and counsel influenced an entire school of early twentieth-century Canadian writers. He is regarded today as one of the key founders of his country's literature.

PRINCIPAL WORKS

Orion, and Other Poems   (poetry)   1880
In Divers Tones   (poetry)   1886
Autochthon   (poetry)   1889
The Canadians of Old   (novel)   1890; also published as
       Cameron of Lochiel, 1905
*Ave: An Ode for the Centenary of the Birth of Percy Bysshe
       Shelley, August 4, 1792*   (poetry)   1892
*Songs of the Common Day, and Ave: An Ode for the Shelley
       Centenary*   (poetry)   1893
The Book of the Native   (poetry)   1896
The Forge in the Forest   (novel)   1896
History of Canada   (history)   1897
New York Nocturnes and Other Poems   (poetry)   1898
The Heart of the Ancient Wood   (novel)   1900
The Kindred of the Wild   (short stories)   1902
The Book of the Rose   (poetry)   1903
The Watchers of the Trails   (short stories)   1904
Red Fox   (novel)   1905
The Haunters of the Silences   (short stories)   1907
Kings in Exile   (short stories)   1909
New Poems   (poetry)   1919
The Vagrant of Time   (poetry)   1927
Eyes of the Wilderness   (short stories)   1933
The Iceberg and Other Poems   (poetry)   1934
Twilight over Shaugamauk and Three Other Poems
       (poetry)   1937
Canada Speaks of Britain   (poetry)   1941
The Last Barrier and Other Stories   (short stories)   1958
Selected Poetry and Critical Prose   (poetry and criticism)
       1974

---

*ROSE-BELFORD'S CANADIAN MONTHLY AND NATIONAL
REVIEW* (essay date 1880)

The readers of the *Canadian Monthly* are familiar with the name of Mr. C.G.D. Roberts, as the author of a beautiful lyric, **'The Ballad of the Poet's Thought,'** published in these columns. Most of us have also read with pleasure and pride as Canadians the lyrics contributed by this young Canadian poet to the pages of *Scribner's* Magazine, and high expectations were formed of the treat which lovers of genuine lyric poetry might expect from [*Orion and Other Poems*]. The volume takes its name from the longest poem, **"Orion,"** which is epic in form: the blank verse, vigorous and musical, bears the impress of no particular school, certainly not that of the prevalent Tennysonian rhythm. (pp. 552-53)

[It is] thoroughly Greek, and saturated with the spirit of the glorious Greek religious art. Surely it is like what Keats wrote and Shelley; that is to say, it is true poetry, unmarked by mannerism any more than Shelley is marked by it. Of equal beauty, but in lyric form, is **'Ariadne.'** A strain of mediaeval music clad in modern richness of expression is **'Launcelot and the Four Queens.' 'A Ballad of Three Mistresses'** is mystical and voluptuous. . . .

'Memnon' and **'Drowsyhood,'** are familiar to the readers of *Scribner*. Among the other lyric poems—all good, not one feeble or wanting in *verve,* and originality—we specially commend those which revive ancient classical forms, those in Sapphics and Choriambics. . . . [Does] not the publication of such a book as this by Mr. Roberts, of New Brunswick, justify us in auguring good things of the spread of a genuine literary spirit in Canada? Here is a writer whose power and originality it is impossible to deny—here is a book of which any literature might be proud. (p. 553)

> *"Book Reviews: 'Orion and Other Poems',"* in Rose-Belford's Canadian Monthly and National Review, *Vol. V, No. 5, November, 1880, pp. 552-53.*

ARCHIBALD LAMPMAN   (essay date 1891)

Mr Roberts was the first Canadian writer in verse who united a strong original genius with a high degree of culture and an acute literary judgement. He was the first to produce a style strongly individual in tone, and founded on the study of the best writers. (p. 411)

Mr Roberts' work, so far as it is available for purposes of criticism, is contained in two small volumes: the first, *Orion and Other Poems* published in 1880, when he was still an undergraduate of the University of New Brunswick, and not yet twenty years of age; the second, *In Divers Tones*, published in 1887, when he was in his twenty-seventh year. The first volume was of course immature, but it was an immaturity full of promise, and full of exhilaration for the poet's younger contemporaries. Some of the work in it is astonishing indeed for a Canadian schoolboy of eighteen or nineteen. . . . The second volume, that of 1887, may be considered the work of Mr Roberts' maturity, for he has published nothing as good since. In this the promise of the first was strengthened and in part fulfilled. A few of the poems were remarkable accomplishments, and the workmanship of them all excellent enough to secure Mr Roberts a high place among the writers of the continent.

All Mr Roberts' writing is of a very scholarly character; it is the work of an artist and a student, possessed of a decided original tone of feeling. In each of his volumes, the longest and most important work is a poem in blank verse, the subject chosen from Greek classic legend, **"Orion"** in the first and **"Actaeon"** in the second. In these poems Mr Roberts has won the rare distinction of having succeeded admirably in blank verse—a severe test. The blank verse of **"Orion"** and **"Actaeon"** is an interesting study. It has a highly original quality, and at the same time shows a curious mingling of many influences. It is the workmanship of a student of Homer, influenced largely by Milton and Tennyson, somewhat also by Keats and Matthew Arnold. I do not know of any writer, with the exception of Matthew Arnold in his **"Balder Dead,"** who has given to blank verse a more charming touch of Homer than Mr Roberts. His verse is not quite so Homeric in its lightness and swift movement as that of **"Balder Dead"** but it has more weight and a greater fulness of music. It is touched somewhat with the halt and restraint of Milton, corrected with a spice of the rich impulsiveness of Tennyson's "Œnone." On the whole it is very fine; probably no better has been done on this side of the Atlantic.

The style, which in its immaturity showed so much imagination and intellectual force in **"Orion,"** is developed, pruned and compacted in **"Actaeon."** Here the verse is full of strength and melody, cleanly wrought and excellently balanced. While reminding one of the Greek, of Tennyson, and of Matthew Arnold, it is so penetrated and coloured by Mr Roberts' own peculiar picturesque quality as to form an altogether original style. The **"Actaeon"** is certainly the best poem of that kind that has been written in America, and as regards workmanship I think it will stand comparison favourably with Tennyson's "Œnone." (pp. 411-12)

Mr Roberts' genius has in it a strongly pagan, earth-loving instinct, a delight in the mere presence of life and nature for their own sake, a delight half intellectual, half physical, touched with a passionate glow. This quality is most strongly marked in two poems which are also noticeable for their success in an unusual form of verse. The **"Tantramar Revisited"** and **"The Pipes of Pan"** are written in the elegiac distich of Tibullus and Ovid, a form which has been transferred into English with good effect. There is a certain passionate stress in it, which makes it specially applicable to descriptive writing of an emotionally meditative and reminiscent character. . . . ["**Tantramar Revisited"** illustrates] our poet's keen sympathy with nature and his strenuous and scholarly gift of expression. . . . What a vivid naturalistic expression there is in . . . the **"Pipes of Pan"**—a beautiful poem. . . . [What] artifice of phrase the poet uses to convey to all the senses of the reader the rank, warm, luxuriant aspect of the spot he is describing. . . . It is possible that some . . . lines are in a slight degree overdone, reminding one in that respect of the American poet Edgar Fawcett, who is very fond of reaching natural effects by artifices of this kind. . . . [There] is a sort of silvery joyousness in the movement of all the poem, which causes it to grow upon one's [taste] the more frequently it is read.

The ode is a kind of verse in which Mr Roberts is perhaps not qualified to be very successful. He has not sufficient ease and flow to work well in complicated stanzas. His talent applies itself best to blank verse for which a certain self-retardative, almost cumbrous tendency of movement, peculiar to him, is an excellent qualification. Nevertheless in his first volume there is a very good ode, that to **"Drowsihood."** It is a purely sensuous production and rests its claim to distinction entirely upon the beauty of its workmanship. Occasionally Mr Roberts' work is spoiled by an effect of strain and elaborate effort, the movement of the scarcely successful labourer. (pp. 413-15)

"In the Afternoon," a truly beautiful little poem, is an illustration of Mr Roberts' most noticeable faculty, the power of investing a bit of vivid landscape description with the musical pathos of some haunting reminiscence or connecting with it a comforting thought, some kindly suggested truth. . . . [There] follow many descriptive couplets, full of happy and life-like touches. . . . (p. 415)

As a sonnet writer Mr Roberts has been unevenly successful. Two or three of his sonnets are impressive in thought and excellently modulated: but others bear traces of effort and consequently do not thoroughly capture the ear. . . .

Amongst other things Mr Roberts has tried his hand at writing some rousing patriotic poems; with the degree of success which

usually attends deliberate efforts of that kind. They are clever, but heavy, pompous, more of the tongue [than] the heart. (p. 417)

It is always difficult to form an estimate of any contemporary writer; but I think that any one who has read through Mr Roberts' two volumes, particularly the second, will conclude that he has been in contact with a very clever man, a scholar, a man of wide culture, variously appreciative, evincing especially a sort of deep physical satisfaction in the contemplation of nature, united to a strenuous and original gift of expression. He will find in him passion, strong, though not of the finest ring, a rich and masterful imagination, the genuine faculty of verse, an ear intolerant of any failure, and a cool and subtle literary judgment, but I think he will also find him wanting in spontaneity, in elasticity, in genuine tenderness, and in delicacy of feeling. His want of tenderness and genuine delicacy appear most strongly in two love poems, included in his second volume, **"Tout ou rien"** and **"In Notre Dame,"** the first a declaration which could only proceed from the most boundless and pitiless egotism; the other, to me a still more disagreeable poem, an expression of brawny passion, pitched in an exaggerated and over-sensuous key.

In Mr Roberts' work, notwithstanding the great ability that has gone to the making of it, there is often a certain weightiness and deliberateness of phrase, which suggests too strongly the hand of the careful workman, and robs it of the fullest effect of spontaneity. Although his poems are written upon many various subjects and either of his books might appear upon a cursory glance to be somewhat remarkable for variety, only three or four really different notes are struck, and all the poems are found to be attuned to these. Mr Roberts is purely an emotional and artistic poet like Poe or Rosseti, and never attempts to lead us to any of the grander levels of thought and feeling. He has nothing to teach us beyond some new phases of the beauty of nature, which he has interpreted admirably; and altogether his work impresses us as the product of a strong artistic talent, rather than of a soul accustomed to the atmosphere of the nobler and severer beauty. (pp. 417-18)

Archibald Lampman, "Two Canadian Poets: A Lecture by Archibald Lampman" (originally a lecture delivered at the Library of the Literary and Scientific Society, Ottawa, on February 19, 1891), in University of Toronto Quarterly *(reprinted by permission of University of Toronto Press), Vol. XIII, No. 4, July, 1944, pp. 406-23.**

BLISS CARMAN (essay date 1895)

[The] every day aspect of country life and the common-place things of the Canadian landscape have moved Mr. Roberts to love and sympathetic expression. **"The Sower," "The Fir Woods," "Burnt Lands," "The Potato Harvest," "The Herring Weir,"**—such are the themes that he has treated in a series of sonnets and published, along with other poems, in his most recent volume, **"Songs of the Common Day."** (p. 164)

His hand is too heavy for bric-a-brac verse, but the most serious aspects and aspirations of life are plastic in his sure grasp. There is a dignity and fineness in his attitude towards the problems of this little earth, characteristic of the amplest-minded artists of all times. He is never petty and never vindictive. Without superstition of any sort, he is yet imbued with the ancient worship of Nature; the quiet of a northern pantheism pervades all his deeper work. (p. 165)

And yet, it is not in "common forms," and "unregarded things," that he touches his most consummate height of song. For the larger, more wondrous and dim, pulses of life beat through his imagination like the lift and fall of the sea. . . . This sums up the sentiment for nature, the sympathy with the outer world and passion for its perfection of loveliness, which make Mr. Roberts akin to Keats and the Greeks. . . . And then this sentiment for the beauty of the world is touched with pathos, with an unstrained ancient childlike pathos, in the **"Epitaph for a Sailor Buried Ashore,"** perhaps its author's finest and most appealing brief lyric. (pp. 166-67)

It is in a still higher flight, however, a still more ambitious sphere of poetry, that we shall find our author at his best. Matthew Arnold has said that poetry "interprets in two ways; it interprets by expressing with magical felicity the physiognomy and movement of the outward world, and it interprets by expressing, with inspired conviction, the ideas and laws of the inward world of man's moral and spiritual nature." . . . Mr. Roberts shows, as it seems to me, "the faculty of both kinds of interpretation, the naturalistic and the moral." (pp. 167-68)

It is no scant praise, then, and yet I think it is not unjust, to say that Mr. Roberts in the work he has so far done has shown power in both these directions, both as a loving prophet of Nature and as a critic of the human aspiration. It is just so, by devotion to both these aims, that he will come to earn a secure place in English poetry. (p. 169)

> *Bliss Carman, "Mr. Charles G.D. Roberts," in* The Chap-Book, *Vol. II, No. 4, January 1, 1895, pp. 163-71.*

CHARLES G.D. ROBERTS (essay date 1897)

[Nature-poetry] is not mere description of landscape in metrical form, but the expression of one or another of many vital relationships between external nature and "the deep heart of man." It may touch the subtlest chords of human emotion and human imagination not less masterfully than the verse which sets out to be a direct transcript from life. The most inaccessible truths are apt to be reached by indirection. The divinest mysteries of beauty are not possessed exclusively by the eye that loves, or by the lips of a child, but are also manifested in some bird-song's unforgotten cadence, some flower whose perfection pierces the heart, some ineffable hue of sunset or sunrise that makes the spirit cry out for it knows not what. And whosoever follows the inexplicable lure of beauty, in color, form, sound, perfume, or any other manifestation,—reaching out to it as perhaps a message from some unfathomable past, or a premonition of the future,—knows that the mystic signal beckons nowhere more imperiously than from the heights of nature-poetry. (p. 445)

> *Charles G.D. Roberts, "The Poetry of Nature," in* The Forum, *Vol. XXIV, No. 4, December, 1897, pp. 442-45.**

JOHN BURROUGHS (essay date 1903)

In Mr. Charles G.D. Roberts's *Kindred of the Wild* one finds much to admire and commend, and but little to take exception to. The volume is in many ways the most brilliant collection of animal stories that has appeared. It reaches a high order of literary merit. Many of the descriptive passages in it of winter in the Canadian woods are of great beauty. The story called

"A Treason of Nature," describing the betrayal and death of a bull moose by hunters who imitated the call of the cow moose, is most striking and effective. True it is that all the animals whose lives are portrayed—the bear, the panther, the lynx, the hare, the moose, and others—are simply human beings disguised as animals; they think, feel, plan, suffer, as we do; in fact, exhibit almost the entire human psychology. But in other respects they follow closely the facts of natural history, and the reader is not deceived; he knows where he stands. Of course it is mainly guesswork how far our psychology applies to the lower animals. That they experience many of our emotons there can be no doubt, but that they have intellectual and reasoning processes like our own, except in a very rudimentary form, admits of grave doubt. But I need not go into that vexed subject here. They are certainly in any broad generalization our kin, and Mr. Roberts's book is well named and well done.

Yet I question his right to make his porcupine roll himself into a ball when attacked, as he does in his story of the panther, and then on a nudge from the panther roll down a snowy incline into the water. I have tried all sorts of tricks with the porcupine and made all sorts of assaults upon him, at different times, and I have never yet seen him assume the globular form Mr. Roberts describes. (pp. 299-300)

> *John Burroughs, "Real and Sham Natural History," in* The Atlantic Monthly *(copyright © 1903, by The Atlantic Monthly Company, Boston, Mass.), Vol. XCI, No. DXLV, March, 1903, pp. 298-309.**

J. D. LOGAN (essay date 1924)

[Roberts] was the first native-born Canadian to take the leading role in making real and permanent, both by singular influences and by actual production in poetry and imaginative prose, a native and national literature in Canada. (p. 110)

Roberts' own poetry may be critically appreciated (1) as a recrudescence of the English classical idyll; (2) as poetry of nature, with special reference to its distinction from the nature-poetry of Lampman; (3) as elegiac poetry; and (4) as poetry of modern eroticism.

At the outset it is important to emphasize two singular facts. First, with the single notable exception of Roberts' spasmodic 'Call' to the Canadian people to achieve a national destiny, and with the further exception of a national or Canadian setting and color in some of his nature-poetry, Roberts' verse is anything but Canadian. Secondly, Roberts' poetry is signally an example of poetry which is not, to use Matthew Arnold's formula, 'a profound and beautiful application of ideas to life.' It is characteristic of the essential Canadian genius that its attitudes to the universe and to existence are moral and religious, that it values the fine arts, including literature, as a means for the ideal enhancement of life, and loves the Beautiful in the fine arts as the only visible instance of the union of the real and of the ideal, which is, philosophically viewed, our only pledge of the ultimate supremacy of the Good. The only really deadly criticism, therefore, that can be applied against the poetry of Roberts is that he has missed in his own verse the supreme ethical note or ideal which is in the poetry of one of his masters, Keats:—

> Beauty is truth, truth beauty,

and that he did not engage himself to write poetry, with the intent which was really the aim of Keats, as well as of Arnold, namely, as a profound and beautiful application of ideas to life. Aware now of the unethical intent and quality of Roberts' poetry, we can the better and more justly appreciate his development as a poet and his achievements in poetic substance and technique. (pp. 115-16)

Roberts' first volume *Orion and Other Poems* is a significant disclosure, both positively and negatively, of his essential genius and art. Positively, the bias or bend of his genius was towards English neo-classical idyllism and sensuous impressionism. Negatively, his genius lacked, and has continued to lack, original imagination or imaginative power. In his first volume, his 'properties,' to use a term borrowed from the stage and employed by Robert Bridges, Poet Laureate, are the same 'properties' as appear in the Keatsian idyll. In Roberts' earliest verse masquerade mythical Greek deities and heroes, sylvan demi-gods and demi-goddesses, Arcadian denizens and shepherds, painted with rich sensuous color against a background of pastoral or idyllic landscape, to the accompaniment of impressionistic verbal music; alliteration, consonance, assonance, and vowel harmony. All this is a recrudescence, unmistakably, of the same qualities in Keats, Tennyson, and Swinburne. In short, Roberts appears as an unoriginal or unimaginative nature-and-figure-painter and verbal melodist. (p. 117)

As yet, then, Roberts' poetry discloses only talent in him, nothing of genius, or originality, or imagination. His poetry is, after all, a cleverly sublimated academic exercise. . . . It is all Artifice; all artificial. (p. 118)

In his second volume of poems, *In Divers Tones,* there is an advance in variety of inspiration, in his forms and metres, and in finish of technique. Still, on the whole, the themes and properties, rhythms, metres, and color are those of English neo-classical idyllism and impressionism. There is, however, some suggestion of a change away from his former too imitative adherence to the subject, manner, and style of the English idyllists. There is, for instance, a suggestion of a structural, but not ethical, influence from Browning. There is, in this regard, a Browningesque coinage of unconventional or awkward diction, an adoption of a Browningesque metre and an introduction of 'medley' as when he inserts, after the Browning manner, a lyrical interlude, unexpectedly and with no logical justification, into the text of a broader, more serious movement and more ethically informed subject. His second volume of poetry, *In Divers Tones,* shows that Roberts has talent, but is still unimaginative and artificial. Yet his second volume is much more significant than his first, not by its being more various in its themes and forms, but by its exhibiting new tendencies in the bent of the poet's mind and imagination. There is a tendency towards ethical influences and to get away from his early pre-occupation with English neoclassical idyllism and impressionism. There is also the merest show of a tendency to occupy his imagination with ideas of the Canadian 'spirit' and the beauty and wonder of Nature in Canada. There is, however, no distinctive embodiment of inspirational ideas or moods awakened by the Great Dominion or the New World.

Notwithstanding, in his second volume Roberts is taking his first step on the way to the expression of the essential form and manner of his creative genius as a poet. He was born to lilt, in simple lyrical and descriptive verse, the aesthetic sensations and the emotional nuances of Canadian life and external nature. In short, Roberts was born to become, as he did become, the most engaging and artistic, though not the first, native-born Canadian idyllist. *In Divers Tones* he first appears as a really significant creative Canadian poet. But whenever, in his later literary career, Roberts forsakes his light or simple idyllic and impressionistic treatment of Canadian life and external nature, as he forsakes it in the monody, in his poetry of city life, and in his poetry of modern eroticism, he may be engaging or arresting or impressive, but in nowise is he creatively significant.

In the same volume, *In Divers Tones,* Roberts exhibits two manners. In some poems in the volume he clings to his old manner of English Classical Impressionism. In other poems in the same volume he essays his new manner of Canadian Impressionism. The first is distinguished by overweighted sensuousness, by over-burdened luxurious color of descriptive epithet and verbal music. An impressive example is *Off Pelorus*. . . . (pp. 118-20)

Roberts' strictly Canadian Impressionism is colorful and musical, but the structure of the verse is simple, as, for instance, *On the Creek,* an idyllic lyric, full of Canadian color, and highly alliterative. (p. 120)

Roberts developed other 'manners' or styles. But, unquestionably, this Canadian idyllic impressionism, simple in thought and form, yet colorful and musical, is his natural *forte*—his *natural, characteristic manner.* It is exemplified, in the same volume, by other Canadian idylls in the simple style of *On the Creek,* as, for instance, *In The Afternoon, Salt, Winter, Geraniums, Birch and Paddle;* by distinct and deliberate suffusions of Canadian Nature in dactylic hexameters, as in *The Tantramar Revisited,* and in the sonnet-form (somewhat anticipating the nature-poetry of Lampman), as in Roberts' genuinely noble sonnets *The Sower,* and *The Potato Harvest.*

We may turn now to a general consideration of Roberts' poetic treatment of Nature. In Roberts' first volume, in his strictly Arcadian poetry, there is nothing of Canadian Nature, nothing of Canadian scenery, nor the color and sentiment of Canadian life in the habitat of the distinctive Canadian spirit. In the second volume, *In Divers Tones,* there is a definitive engagement, on his part, with Canadian Nature, or with Canadian life and sentiment pictured against Canadian backgrounds; and also a change in the form and style of Roberts' poetic composition.

The natural forms of Roberts' art are light, simple, lyrical, and descriptive verse, which he treats with charming naturalness, almost *naiveté,* with simple tunefulness of ballad or folk rhythms, and which sometimes he delicately suffuses with a contemplative revery, a gentle melancholy, or a subdued sentimental reflection on the magic and mystery of Nature and life, somewhat in the manner of Herrick and Tennyson, and Longfellow. But Roberts' lyrical idyllism or nature-description is not always wholly soft or sentimental, pretty, or gentle, or charming, nor is his new manner always in folk rhythm in form. At times, even when simple, his verse is picturesque, even brusque, vigorous, and over-weighted with descriptive details as if, in the last matter, he must 'paint in' all the features and properties of Canadian Nature and leave nothing of its physiognomy to be added by the imagination of the reader.

Roberts, however, has one singular limitation, an innate defect of his genius. He cannot limn the human person or figure as one of the properties of his poetry of Canadian woodlands or pastoral scenery and life. In the matter of human portraiture against a background of Nature Roberts, as poet, is abstract and faltering in drawing, lifeless, unveracious, ineffective. Otherwise in the Canadian idyll or in nature-description he is concrete, veracious, simple but graphic, nearly always winningly musical and on the whole satisfying. In short, Roberts discloses in his new manner, in the' Canadian idyll and his Acadian nature-poetry, the sure possession of the secrets of color, movement and music, and of real Canadian national sentiment, in the presence of life and nature. He is an adroit nature-colorist and verbal melodist. (pp. 120-22)

Roberts' treatment of Nature may be illustrated by examples taken from his second volume, *In Divers Tones* . . . , and from *The Book of the Native* . . . , in the latter of which are some poems that really belong, in form, and spirit, to the time when he was changing his abstract *Arcadian* manner to his concrete *Arcadian* manner as in his *In Divers Tones*. Illustrative of Roberts' change to a Canadian theme and to the modern simple method of treating Nature, in the pseudo-classical style, an apt example is *The Tantramar Revisited,* composed in the dactylic hexameter, a form, suggested, no doubt, by Longfellow's pretty story of Evangeline. In this poem Roberts treats Canadian Nature with an impressive originality in properties, color, and sentiment, and certainly with a pervasive directness and veracity which prove his sincerity and which convince the reader that the poet was moved by the beauty and pathos of his Acadian subject. . . . (p. 122)

For an example of his colored realism or idyllic naturalism tinged with a sort of Wordsworthian plainness or austerity of style and ethical revery, consider his sonnet *The Sower.* It has been called Roberts' 'popular masterpiece.' As a sonnet, it is perfect in artistic structure, and is as faithful to Canadian Nature and sentiment as, say, Millet's paintings, *The Reapers* and *The Angelus,* are true to French pastoral life and religious sentiment.

But this sonnet is a good example of Roberts' ineffectiveness in human or spiritual portraiture. How effectively it pictures for us the land, the sky, the birds, the human properties of the Acadian landscape in Nova Scotia. The poem visualizes vividly for us all the features and elements of external Nature; yet it fails to visualize the Sower *himself,* to limn him effectively, graphically, impressively against the background of Nature as, on the other hand, Millet has graphically limned the human figures in his paintings against the French landscape.

Finally: a poem which is a really fine example of Roberts' characteristic genius and art in the authentic Canadian idyll and in nature-description, and which, perhaps, contains his nearest approach to graphic figure-poetry, namely, his lyric *The Solitary Woodsman,* is specially noteworthy. Though published in *The Book of the Native,* it really belongs to the period of *In Divers Tones* when Roberts was changing over to his natural and characteristic manner of Canadian idyllic impressionism. For it is a gentle, natural, and simple lyrical idyll of Canadian Nature and life, tinged with a delicate mood of contemplation and pathos. A touch more of 'personal detail,' of moral characterization, would have made *The Solitary Woodsman* as universal and popular a portrait as the genre picture of the hardy, happy village blacksmith in Longfellow's poem with that subject. Nevertheless, the poem has vigor, action, life-likeness; it is veracious and picturesque. In it Roberts is at his best in the Canadian lyrical idyll and in figure-portraiture.

Strict analysis of Roberts' nature-poetry reveals both the positive qualities and the defects of his genius and art. As a poet of Nature in Acadia he hardly more than effects *glimpses* of Canadian scenery and pastoral life, colorful, no doubt, and tinged with a homely or even tender naturalistic sentiment. His pictures of Canadian scenery and pastoral life are indeterminate *pastels* of the general features of Nature in Canada rather than

rich, broad paintings done with the forthright, broad brushwork of a master artist. It is all pretty, or charming, and faithful to Nature in Acadia. But it is all based on superficial observation and is devoid of poetic, that is to say, profound and beautiful application of ideas to life. It is not to be expected that the Canadian people will treasure these pastels of Canadian scenery and pastoral life. For though they be beautiful, simple, and realistic, the ethical element in them is always a reflection, a moral platitude, from the poet's own moralizing, or a recrudescence of some older poets' moralizings. (pp. 123-24)

His pure lyrical pastels, as for instance, *On the Creek,* and *The Solitary Woodsman,* are more likely to remain permanently popular than are his Nature poems in other forms, as, for example, the genuinely important sonnet-squence in his *Songs of the Common Day*. . . . In these sonnets, however, he shows no increase of descriptive power but only the variety of his word-painter's palette. Moreover, in these sonnets there is a felt insincerity of aim. Though fine in structure, faithful to Canadian Nature, variously treating the aspects of Canadian Nature, and often sentimental and moralistic, they impress the reader as having been designed and written deliberately to show forth the poet's powers in realistic or naturalistic impressionism, in the philosophical interpretation of Nature, and in technical artistry. Notwithstanding, it must be admitted that in these sonnets Roberts, as an impressionistic painter of Canadian Nature, is a master, and has his analogues, in the pictorial painting of Nature, in Corot and Millet, and in the tonal painting of Nature, in MacDowell and Debussy. These sonnets were consciously designed to be 'works of art,' and to impress the philosophically minded poets and critics of poetic form. Fine and masterful as they are in technical artistry, and impressive, too, with a resurgence of moral ideas, nevertheless they appeal neither to the popular heart nor to the philosophical imagination. For they create in the heart of the reader the sense only of a splendid achievement in poetic artistry, but never any sense of the poet's own enrichment of life from his interpretation of beauty in Canadian Nature, civilization, and life.

Summarily: as an original Poet, Roberts' *forte* is the treatment of Canadian Nature and pastoral life in impressionistic pastels, to an accompaniment of verbal music in folk rhythms or simple lyric forms. Thus accepted and appreciated he is a satisfying nature-colorist and melodist. But, impressive and magnificent, as he is, in more formal or larger poetic genres, as for instance, the sonnet and monody, he fails to give us in both a vital application of ideas to life.

Consideration of Roberts' poetry of modern eroticism reveals only what has been called a variety of Roberts' 'ethical heterogenity.' This, however, is a defect in the man rather than in the poet, and only negatively affects Roberts' significance in the literary history of Canada. Roberts' work as a threnodist, romantic novelist, and inventor of a species of animal psychology in the romance is considered elsewhere. It is, however, as the inaugurator of the First Renaissance in Canadian Literature, both poetry and prose, rather than as a poet of Canadian Nationality and Nature, that Roberts has a right to a supremely significant status in the literary history of Canada. (pp. 124-26)

J. D. Logan, "Charles G.D. Roberts," in Highways of Canadian Literature: A Synoptic Introduction to the Literary History of Canada (English) from 1760 to 1924 *by J. D. Logan and Donald G. French (copyright, 1924, by McClelland and Stewart, Limited; reprinted by permission of The Canadian Publishers,*

McClelland and Stewart Limited, Toronto), Mc-Clelland and Stewart, 1924, pp. 110-26.

PELHAM EDGAR (essay date 1943)

[The] future will recognize even more than we are willing to do that Roberts was a pivotal figure, a musical hinge around which our poetry first began to revolve. (p. 117)

His formal fiction, [however,] is not quite first-rate. His constructive skill is not of the highest order, and humanly speaking his power of invention is weak and his command of incident limited. But books that we might call "near novels," like *The Heart of the Ancient Wood* and *In the Morning of Time* have an enduring fascination. And some of the stories appearing in the animal volumes, but deviating from the theme, are works of the highest art. *The Perdu,* of *Earth's Enigmas,* is such a piece, and others might be named that possess the same haunting suggestiveness, and the same deftness of touch and unerring quality of observation.

As for the animal stories themselves it must be admitted that their never ending flow makes for monotony. While the vogue lasted their influence operated, but that influence is now dead and the modern short story has taken on a totally new character. Our concluding survey may more profitably deal with the poetry of Roberts which is destined to endure all the fluctuations of taste and time. Here is no question of the ephemeral, but of the inevitable, once said and said forever. (pp. 123-24)

The two poems which he has come to regard as his most significant utterances happen also to be the longest that he has written. They are the *Ave* of his early prime, and *The Iceberg* produced in the Indian summer of his career as evidence of recovery from a period of depression and physical weakness. . . .

Ave is Roberts' only effort of sustained magnificence. It is definitely in the tradition of the great odes when poets wrote with their singing robes upon them. Readers who prefer that poets should speak to them in their natural voice will find their preference in simpler examples of his art which may be met at almost every random turning of the page.

The Iceberg should meet their demand. There is magnificence here also, but it is projected with a more natural simplicity. Once we have accepted the fact that we are dealing with a very knowledgeable iceberg we can yield ourselves to the powerful stream of the poet's imagination. (p. 124)

Southward ever, and on to the tracks of the ocean ships the berg proceeds—a strange voyage that the poet has evidently taken and which we seem to share! The *Titanic* is sunk, the weeks pass, and now shrunk to "a little glancing globe of cold" the iceberg merges "forever in the all-solvent sea."

Other types of poetry of which Roberts has given us powerful examples are short lyrics of love or nature, and meditative pieces whether in stanzaic or sonnet form where he presents a philosophy of life that is prevailingly optimistic and tinged often by a mysticism which may have originally derived from Emerson and the transcendentalists, but which he has made characteristically his own.

His nature poems have exercised more influence on subsequent writers than any other portion of his work. They are fine without exception in their qualities of observation, and simple and vital in expression. A sonnet not often quoted, *When Milking Time*

Is Done, might readily have been written by Lampman at a later time. (p. 125)

Genuine magnificence finds scope in the tight-packed fourteen lines of *In the Wide Awe and Wisdom of the Night* and its often quoted companion piece *O Solitary of the Austere Sky.* The sonnet *The Empire Speaks of Britain* is proof that his fingers have not lost the magic touch upon the keys. It has the passion and the power of the sonnets that Wordsworth dedicated more than a century ago to the cause of independence and liberty. (p. 126)

Pelham Edgar, "Sir Charles G.D. Roberts and His Time," in University of Toronto Quarterly *(reprinted by permission of University of Toronto Press), Vol. XIII, No. 1, October, 1943, pp. 117-26.*

LORNE PIERCE (essay date 1943)

Thirteen years after Confederation, when [Roberts] was but twenty, his first book appeared, and he strode into his rightful place at the head of Canadian poets, and for sixty-six years has continued to write with distinction and power, with charm and with the unfailing colour and flavour of this Northern land. . . . He was for the new woman as well as the new man, because he was solidly for the new order when based upon ripe wisdom, vast sympathy and compassion. The Tory in Roberts loved great and noble traditions, and upon these other traditions in time would be built. The Churchman in him revered the dignity and solemnity that belonged to rubric and ritual, for out of them came an exalted pattern of life. . . . His confession of faith was not shouted, but it may be discovered in such poems as **"Autochthon," "Kinship," "The Heal-All"** and **"A Song of Growth,"** in which whatever is spiritually enduring in the Darwinian hypothesis finds a place, man's oneness with all living things and with the divine hand that made him also. He proclaimed no evangelical renewal in the manner of the revival movements, but the possibilities of man's infinite improvement he did not overlook in **"A Song of Growth," "At Tide Water," "Renewal," "Recessional," "Earth's Complines"** and **"Ascription."** Catholic and Protestant, Moslem and Hindu, were gathered into his cosmic vision in such poems as **"Beyond the Tops of Time," "Child of the Infinite," "The Aim,"** and similar verses. The whole universe was made divinely restless, until, in Augustine's words, it should at last find its rest and peace in Him who first conceived it all. Any conception of man's immortality must depend upon ideas regarding man's divinity, and here Roberts reached his own sublimest height. His crowning vision is that of man in mystical union with the cosmic mind and energy of the vast Over Soul. In **"The Unsleeping," "In the Wide Awe and Wisdom of the Night"** and **"O Solitary of the Austere Sky,"** he joins man to the godhead in a deathless enterprise. (pp. xx-xxi)

In his first great poem, **"Orion,"** he sang:

Then get thee up to the hills and thou shalt behold the morning.

It was of the morning time of a new nation in a new world that he resolved to sing. . . . There is no fanatical insistence upon a narrow Canadianism. He tells of the seasons, of ploughing and mowing, seedtime and harvest, log boom and flight of the wild geese, but it is mankind the world over that we see through Canadian eyes. The farmer "godlike, makes provision for mankind." There is nothing parochial and thin about this; there is something exactly right about a farmer anywhere making provision for mankind, and above all a Canadian farmer. . . . We do not claim for [Roberts] a place alongside Homer, but we do claim for him a place in the great tradition of English letters, and above all we claim for him a supreme place in the consideration of his own countrymen. (pp. xxi-xxii)

It has been said that Roberts' love songs lack passion and that his work wants humour. He has enough of both. Each is directed and controlled by a fine mind, and the unfailing note of each is joy. Like his patriotic verse, his love songs are best when he sings of home. Let him be judged and praised for what he intended, for this he grandly achieved, and occupies by right the highest place among all those who have served Canada by their pen. (pp. xxiii-xxiv)

> *Lorne Pierce, in his introduction to* Sir Charles G.D. Roberts: A Biography *by E. M. Pomeroy (copyright © McGraw-Hill Ryerson Limited, 1943; reprinted by permission), Ryerson Press, 1943, pp. xiii-xxiv.*

NORTHROP FRYE   (essay date 1956)

Roberts is a subjective and descriptive poet, not a mythical one, and the organizing formal principles which give both intellectual and emotional unity to his work come out of his personal life. The formal basis of his poetry is chiefly in the recollections and associations of his Maritime childhood. Being a late Romantic, this means that his central emotional quality is nostalgia. From there he expands to descriptive landscape poetry, still usually with a nostalgic emotional core, and from there the next logical step would be to intellectualized poetry. Roberts tried hard to attain to this third stage, but had nothing intellectual in his mind, . . . still, the pattern of a representational poet is complete in him. (pp. 45-6)

> *Northrop Frye, in an excerpt from "Letters in Canada," in* University of Toronto Quarterly *(reprinted by permission of University of Toronto Press), Vol. XXV, No. 3, April, 1956 (and reprinted in his* The Bush Garden: Essays on the Canadian Imagination, *Toronto: House of Anansi Press, 1971, pp. 1-128).*

DESMOND PACEY   (essay date 1958)

[Poetry was Roberts's] first and his last love. He wrote his stories and novels at least in part to please the public and to make money; he wrote his poems to express his real convictions and insights and to satisfy his own creative urge. (p. 35)

The poems for which Roberts is likely to be remembered were produced . . . in two periods of creative activity, one extending from the early eighteen-eighties to the early eighteen-nineties, and the other from the mid-nineteen-twenties to the mid-nineteen-thirties. There are minor differences in the poems of the two periods—the early poems are all in traditional metres, and especially in the form of sonnets and elegiac odes, the later ones are often in free verse—but their characteristics are basically the same. The best poems from both periods fall into three main classes: objective descriptive poems in which Roberts reveals his talent as a painter in words; lyrics in which he expresses his own moods of elation, depression, restlessness, or nostalgia; and more pretentious but less satisfying poems in which he seeks by means of symbols to convey his sense of the immensity, grandeur, and power of the cosmos.

Reading *Orion and Other Poems* . . . today, it is difficult for us to see why the book received such extravagant critical acclaim. Only when we remind ourselves that it was published when the poet was twenty, and that most of its contents were written when he was an undergraduate, do we realize that it is indeed a remarkable performance. It is imitative, naively romantic, defective in diction, the poetry of books rather than of life itself, but it is facile, clever, and occasionally distinctively beautiful.

The prefatory poem, **"To the Spirit of Song,"** states, in Shelleyan language and imagery, the romantic doctrine of inspiration. **"Orion,"** the title poem, is also Shelleyan in its choice of landscape, its imagery of fire and light, its colourful diction, and in its soaring lyrical flights; the death scene has touches which remind us of Tennyson's "Morte d'Arthur," and there are other passages which suggest Swinburne; but in spite of some good individual lines the poem as a whole is diffuse and cloying. Keats, however, is the obvious influence on **"Ariadne"**—the Keats of "Endymion" and "The Eve of Saint Agnes." . . . It is Tennyson's turn in **"Lancelot and the Four Queens,"** where the rhythm, the diction, and even the morality are his. As in Tennyson, the setting quite overshadows the story and the characters.

A series of undistinguished ballades and rondeaux follow—mere finger exercises—but then one's persistence is rewarded by discovering two poems of a quite different and much more original sort. Here, in **"The Flight"** and **"One Night,"** Roberts uncovers a vein which one wished he had chosen to explore again—the vein of the weird, the macabre, the nightmarish. (pp. 43-5)

But with **"A Song of Morning"** we are back to Shelley, and with **"An Ode to Drowsihood"** to Keats. In the central stanza of this latter poem, however, the unreality of the whole suddenly and fleetingly gives way to the particularity of a New Brunswick landscape, and we get a faint premonition of *Songs of the Common Day.* We get a further premonition a few poems further on, when in **"Iterumne"** and **"At Pozzuoli"** Roberts for the first time employs the sonnet form which he was later to make the vehicle for almost all his best poems. The rest of the volume, however, is quite unrewarding, with the possible exception of the rather pretty, lilting lyric **"The Maple."**

Orion is the work of a young poet thoroughly steeped in the legends of ancient Greece and the poetry of Keats, Shelley and Tennyson. Most of the poems are artificial in language and feeling, but in a few of them there are glimpses of genuine interior and exterior landscapes. What we hear above all is Roberts tuning his instrument—practising the sonnet, the ode, the ballade, the rondeau, the epistle, the elegy, and the narrative. The verse is always competent—smooth in rhythm, rich and suggestive in language, apt in imagery—but it is seldom very distinctive. It is the work of an apprentice, who is quite frankly serving under a sequence of masters from whom he hopes to learn his art.

In Divers Tones . . . is still the work of an apprentice, but of an apprentice who has gone a long way toward independent mastery. It opens with two poems that reveal Roberts' national consciousness—**"Collect for Dominion Day"** and **"Canada."** These poems, and especially the latter, are apt to seem much more conventional in thought to us than they did to his contemporaries. **"Canada"** is a quite explicit plea for Canadian independence at a time when the dispute between the advocates of Independence, Imperial Federation, and American Annexation was at its height and was indeed the chief political issue in the country. So passionately and unselfishly was Roberts dedicated to the Independent cause that he resigned the editorship of *The Week* early in 1884 rather than submit to the publisher's Annexationist policies. But even this knowledge does not redeem the poems from the charge of rhetoric, nor hide from us the bad taste of such lines as

> To stream on each remotest breeze
> The black smoke of thy pipes exhales.

The third poem, "**Actaeon**," is a further exercise in the classical narrative, and it has yet to have its due from the critics. This is a much better poem than "**Orion**," though the influence of Tennyson, in diction, and Browning, in form (the poem is a dramatic monologue), are rather too apparent. The blank verse is handled with greater dexterity, the diction is more disciplined, the description is not allowed so completely to eclipse the story. There is little of the lazy diffuseness of "**Orion**" or "**Ariadne**" here: the poem has a firm structure, a clear hard outline of story and theme. Some of the individual lines—for example, "Its high chill dawns, its long-drawn golden days"—are among the best that Roberts ever wrote, and the ending has a magic suggestiveness that he never surpassed. . . . (pp. 45-7)

But the really remarkable development evident in this book is not that Roberts has discovered Canadian nationalism nor improved his technique in the classical narrative, but that he has begun to recognize the poetic possibilities in his own environment. (p. 47)

The verse form of "**Tantramar Revisited**" is not original—it is virtually identical with that of Longfellow's *Evangeline*—but it is perfectly suited to the theme of nostalgic remembrance, and it is handled with masterly ease. (pp. 47-8)

A suitable verse-form, a definite structure, accurate visual detail—all these "**Tantramar Revisited**" displays. It also demonstrates that when he was at his very best, when he had selected a thoroughly congenial subject, Roberts could find the exact words in which to body forth his own vision. (p. 48)

But the poem has another claim on our attention. It satisfies us because Roberts has here been content to recognize his own limitations. Description of places was his strong point, description in which the scenes described are related to basic but simple human emotions and actions. Had he listened to his contemporary critics, he would have attempted to philosophize about the scene—and he would have betrayed his own honest vision.

"**Tantramar Revisited**," in other words, makes it clear that Roberts had found a matter and a manner ideally suited to his gifts. (pp. 48-9)

Unfortunately, the volume also contains a number of poems that foreshadow Roberts' later inferior work. There is a group of love lyrics which seem almost incredibly artificial and laboured. . . .

The few really good poems in *In Divers Tones* are so outnumbered by the derivative and weak ones that hardly anyone could have foreseen that Roberts' next volume, *Songs of the Common Day* . . . , would mark such a great advance in his art. (p. 49)

The best of the sonnets, with the partial exception of "**In the Wide Awe and Wisdom**," are those that deal most objectively and concretely with New Brunswick scenes. The worst are those in which Roberts ventures into overt didacticism, or employs an artificial diction that is not in keeping with the homely subject-matter.

It is obvious that in the thirteen years since the publication of *Orion* the influence of Keats and Shelley upon Roberts had receded, and that of Wordsworth had advanced. The strengths and the weaknesses of these sonnets may be attributed in large measure to Wordsworth's influence. The strengths are the fidelity to fact, the readiness to see beauty and significance in simple things, the steady sanity of vision, the sincerity of tone, and the greater, but still far from perfect, simplicity of diction. The weaknesses attributable to Wordsworth's influence are the tendency to become too overtly didactic—to state rather than to display the beauty of the commonplace—and the occasional too prosaic and too detailed catalogue of facts. But the chief weakness is Roberts' own, and results from his failure to take seriously enough Wordsworth's essay on poetic diction. Roberts has tried, in many of these sonnets, to graft some of Keats' ornateness of diction on to the stem of Wordsworthian realism. Even some of the best of the sonnets reveal this lack of decorum—for example in "**When Milking Time Is Done**," all is simple and in keeping until we suddenly come upon "the sky's pale dome"—a good enough phrase in itself, but out of place here. Expressions like "the samphire pipes," "mystic dream-dust of isle," "chemic ray," "unassuaged of rain or breeze," "comforting auguries," "a mystic rune," "the germ of ecstasy," "effluence rare"—these occur intermittently to mar our enjoyment.

But in the best sonnets these flaws of diction are rare, and are almost eclipsed by the virtues of clarity, exactness, sincerity, and restraint. We see the landscape clearly, we infer the importance of the scene to Roberts in particular and human beings in general, and we are impressed by the cunning fusion of fact and feeling into a poetic whole. Granted that predominantly descriptive sonnets of this sort are not of the very highest order of art, these are done so well that we accept them with much more pleasure than we would a less deft handling of more pretentious themes.

The miscellaneous section of *Songs of the Common Day* is far less rewarding. "**Autochthon**" is a not particularly memorable excursion into Emersonian monism; "**Marsyas**" is a belated example of Roberts' ability to handle classical legends skilfully; "**Grey Rocks and Greyer Sea**" is a pleasing elegy with rather too obvious Tennysonian echoes. The rest of the section is negligible, and one or two of the poems—"**Bringing Home the Cows**," for example—are ludicrous. The chief trouble with most of these poems is their ornateness of diction: Roberts' ballads, for example, have little of the stark simplicity they should have.

"**Ave**," however, is a much more considerable piece of work. Professor [James] Cappon put his finger on its chief weakness when he declared that the transition from the description of the Tantramar country to the study of Shelley himself is awkward and forced. Apart from this, and even this is not quite as serious a matter as Professor Cappon asserts, the poem is a very satisfying exercise in the elegiac form. That however is all it is—an exercise. Although he sincerely admired Shelley as a poet and a man, he could not identify Shelley's fate with his own, as Shelley was able to do with Keats in "Adonais" or Milton with [Edward] King in "Lycidas," nor pour out the personal grief which makes Arnold's elegy for [Arthur Hugh] Clough so moving. "**Ave**" is a very creditable *tour-de-force*, but it does not speak to the heart.

The Book of the Native . . . appeared when Roberts was at the height of his popular fame as a poet. . . . This book too is divided into three sections: "**The Book of the Native**," "**Lyr-**

ics,'' and ''**Ballads.**'' The first part contains poems in which Roberts explores farther the mystical path he had first trod in ''**Autochthon**'' and ''**In the Wide Awe and Wisdom**''; the second contains a number of simple, homely lyrics which might well have been included in *Songs of the Common Day;* and the third contains seven mediocre narrative poems. Much the best part of the book is the second: poems such as ''**The Brook in February,**'' ''**Butterflies,**'' and ''**An August Wood Road**'' have the descriptive clarity and emotional sincerity of the best poems in his previous volume. Some of the mystical poems are good as expressions of feeling but their thought is vague and derivative. Roberts can evoke a sense of mystery and wonder, but when he goes on to philosophize, as he too frequently does, he takes refuge in verbal evasions and comforting compromises. (pp. 50-2)

There is a decline in *The Book of the Native,* but there is a positive descent in *New York Nocturnes.* . . . Most of the poems in this book are completely lacking in distinctiveness of thought or expression. . . . It is significant that the best poems in the book—''**The Solitary Woodsman**'' and ''**Beyond the Tops of Time**''—represent reactions to the themes of *Songs of the Common Day* and *The Book of the Native* respectively. But the general trend of the volume is away from rural vignettes and mystical visions to lyrics of love and loneliness. The poems indicate that Roberts felt unable to write directly of city life, except as something to escape from, and turned to love and his memories for release. But the love poems, with the partial exceptions of ''**Presence**'' and ''**A Nocturne of Trysting,**'' do not have an authentic ring. They seem contrived and artificial, the products of fancy rather than imagination. The impression here, contrary to that of *Songs of the Common Day,* is of an art without substance, of an inspiration which has become attenuated, of a mind which has turned in upon itself without the moral strength or intellectual honesty to make a real ''confession of the ill.''

In 1901 Roberts published his collected *Poems,* but no new work appeared in book form until 1903, when *The Book of the Rose* was published. This book is no better and no worse than its immediate predecessor. It is divided into two parts, one containing love lyrics, the other miscellaneous poems. The love poems are derivative and artificial, perfervid and laboured. (pp. 52-3)

The second part of *The Book of the Rose* is better, but the best poems in it—''**The First Ploughing,**'' ''**Child of the Infinite,**'' ''**The Great and the Little Weavers**''—are reversions to his earlier matter and manner and do not suggest any real growth in his art. Some of the poems almost recapture the authenticity and particularity of *Songs of the Common Day,* others the mystic exaltation of *The Book of the Native.* One or two—''**The Stranded Ship,**'' for example, a vigorous ballad with a Kiplingesque swing to it, and ''**Heat in the City,**'' a vivid picture of urban squalor and sorrow—are interesting new departures, but the great bulk of the section is mediocre.

As if he recognized that his poetic inspiration had flagged, Roberts abandoned the craft almost entirely for the next twenty-five years. (p. 54)

In 1927 he published *The Vagrant of Time,* in 1934 *The Iceberg,* and in 1941 *Canada Speaks of Britain.* Although even the best of the poems in these volumes did not quite attain the level of the best in *Songs of the Common Day* and *The Book of the Native,* they came much nearer to that mark than the poems he had been publishing in the intervening decades.

The Vagrant of Time contains only about a dozen new poems—most of its contents are reprinted from *New Poems*—but they are almost all good, and they reveal a genuine development in Roberts' poetic technique. (pp. 54-5)

The Iceberg and Other Poems is chiefly memorable for its title poem, but it also contains ''**Taormina,**'' a haunting, vivid, nostalgic poem full of colour and rhythm, ''**Be Quiet, Wind,**'' a soft, sweet lyric, ''**The Squatter,**'' a fairly successful attempt to repeat, but in free verse form, the success of ''**The Solitary Woodsman,**'' and ''**Westcock Hill,**'' a poem nostalgic of his childhood home which communicates real emotion by means of precise but suggestive images.

But ''**The Iceberg**'' is the pride of the book. It is a long narrative poem in free verse, and reveals how economically and functionally Roberts had learned to use this treacherous form. . . . Some of the descriptive passages are magnificent, and the whole poem has life and movement on the one hand and a firm orderly structure on the other. Many of the metaphors are very striking. . . . (pp. 55-6)

But for all its virtues, ''**The Iceberg**'' does not quite reach the level of ''**Tantramar Revisited**'' or the best of the sonnets in *Songs of the Common Day.* Those early poems, though predominantly descriptive, were infused with warm human feeling, and at least implied man and his daily work. Implicitly, in spite of the contemporary charge that they lacked human interest, they did deal with human action and reflections upon human action. ''**The Iceberg,**'' on the other hand, is almost purely descriptive, objective, and impersonal; it lacks just that impingement on human destiny that makes [Edwin John] Pratt's *Titanic* so much more moving.

Roberts' last book of poems, *Canada Speaks of Britain,* was published early in the second World War as a patriotic offering. It contains eight new war poems, three old ones which had first been published during World War I, and three new miscellaneous poems. The war poems need not detain us: they express conventional ideas in conventional form. The miscellaneous poems—''**Two Rivers,**'' ''**Twilight over Shaugamauk,**'' and ''**As Down the Woodland Ways**''—do not add substantially to his reputation either. The last is the best—it is a clear, neat statement of the eighty-year-old Roberts' faith in resurrection and the persistence of life. ''**Twilight over Shaugamauk**'' is a fairly successful exercise in nostalgia. ''**Two Rivers,**'' Roberts' tribute to the Tantramar and the Saint John, is chiefly interesting on autobiographical grounds. Clear-sighted about his own character, Roberts sees his own restlessness reflected in the constant ebb and flow of the tide-driven Tantramar. . . . (pp. 56-7)

Roberts' enduring distinction as a Canadian poet is the fact that he was the first to realize the poetic possibilities of a straightforward description of the topography of his own land. He began where Sangster left off, writing imitations of the work of the English Romantics, but when he wrote the poems in *Songs of the Common Day* he really established an indigenous Canadian verse. (p. 58)

Desmond Pacey, ''Sir Charles G.D. Roberts'' (originally published in a modified form as the introduction to Selected Poems of Sir Charles G.D. Roberts, Ryerson Press, 1955), in his Ten Canadian Poets: A Group of Biographical and Critical Essays (copyright © McGraw-Hill Ryerson Limited, 1958; reprinted by permission), Ryerson Press, 1958, pp. 34-58.

JOSEPH GOLD (essay date 1965)

Roberts' animal stories constitute, as far as I can ascertain, the only sustained attempt to use the materials of the Canadian Wilderness for the purpose of expressing a coherent view of the world that man inhabits. Roberts has created a Canadian mythology, in which animals, rather than gods, play out a systematic drama of conflict and resolution. This is all done, of course, within the framework of an accurate survey of natural history, and it is a brave man who would casually question Roberts' knowledge of the wilderness. (p. 23)

This aura of design, pattern, structure, in a world peopled by creatures pursuing a highly dramatic and meaningful action pervades all the best Roberts' stories, and there are many of them. We will return to the question of meaning later, but for the moment let us pursue the question of the purposeful design in the stories and exactly what attitude Roberts brings to nature and why he writes of animals at all. . . . [He believes] that through the animal the writer can approach some larger vision of basic human drives and some understanding of the transcendent universal design to which all things contribute. [In his essay, **"The Animal Story,"** Roberts] says of the animal story:

> It leads us back to the old kinship of earth, without asking us to relinquish by way of toll any part of the wisdom of the ages, any fine essential of the 'large result of time'.

By this Roberts means that the artist can use animals to make sense of the world of which man is part and from which he grew, that we are given a detachment and perspective from which to examine the fundamental base on which we rest. Roberts' aim in his stories is to present his own vision of truth, a vision that, value judgments aside, reminds one first of William Wordsworth's and William Faulkner's. What could be more Faulknerian than "the old kinship of earth?" And Faulkner's "verities of the heart" are anticipated in Roberts' mythology as story after story presents the struggle of honour, dignity, courage, love, and hate symbolized in elemental struggle. . . . [In the same essay, Roberts speaks] of the need for the human mind to "bring" meaning to nature. The world man sees need not be a collection of disparate facts, but a world of potential significance realized and ordered by the artist's imagination. Its significance is more or less, depending on our degree of humanity. The word "humane" suggests human in a compassionate and accepting role. It is possible, says Roberts, to see in the world he presents "clear and candid life".

Roberts' animal world amounts then to an affirmative vision in which the conditions of a wilderness struggle for survival are accepted and confirmed. It remains to show the precise terms on which such an acceptance is possible and to illustrate this affirmation from the fiction itself. . . . Roberts brought his imagination to bear on nature and animals and produced his own Canadian mythology. The principal feature of this myth is that, while individual creatures constantly lose the struggle for survival, life itself persists. In the long run death itself has no sting and is ironically defeated by the uses nature makes of its processes. All things conspire to sustain life and the stories create a very strong sense of rhythmic pattern and cycle, of the seasons, of birth and death, of mating and separating, and these patterns persist no matter what the creatures, what the setting or what human interference is attempted. This may not seem like a great deal by which to celebrate some meaning to existence, but after all has man ever been honoured for doing more than living, to the best of his ability?

Roberts is, to my knowledge, the only writer who has used animals to illustrate such a vision. . . . "Human" and "animal" are labels earned by the quality of behaviour so that a writer may humanize an animal world or animalize a human one. Roberts is after all a poet, which is to say that his imagination makes definition and his human version of the animal world dignifies and enobles that world. Roberts celebrates courage and endurance and for this reason his stories of defeat and death produce not despair but a sense of elevation, and often something akin to catharsis. His animals and birds and fishes confront overwhelming odds. Every second is a challenge to life itself. The combatants in man's conflict, when not hunger and cold, are accident and disease. . . . Every moment wrenched from time is a major victory and every meal is a conquest over an indifferent universe. Roberts would agree with Blake that "everything that lives is holy" but he would add, I suspect, "And holy because it lives."

The techniques Roberts employs are simple and it is the retention of simplicity that is his greatest strength. There is no commentary, no moralizing, but a stark presentation of animal impulses and success or defeat. *The Last Barrier* is by no means a collection of the best of Roberts' stories, but since it is readily available we must confine ourselves to it. The title story illustrates the Roberts' theme and technique most clearly. The salmon is born, miraculously grows up and dies in the paws of a bear after a hopeless struggle to climb a waterfall. This is the archetypal pattern of the birth-death cycle for all living creatures. But Roberts conveys to the reader a clear sense of his own awe at the fact that the process takes place at all. Survival 1tself is a miracle and even before this, gestation and birth. (pp. 24-6)

The strong sense of the infinite scale of size in the universe, from the minute forces of energy to the unconquerable seasons, is characteristic of Roberts' awareness. The salmon is not only born but turns into something animate, complete, perfect and volatile and for the humanizing, poetic imagination of Roberts, this is a supreme and even divine achievement. . . .

The protagonist salmon of this story follows an almost classic pattern of development and is presented as a case history. . . . Roberts writes a history of one sample of myriad life that inevitably ends in defeat, and yet he writes it in such a way as to indicate, not a despairing or cynical view of the natural process, but a celebration of the struggle itself. . . . (p. 27)

The ending to the *The Last Barrier* is full of meaning. During one of the salmon's annual absences the falls of his stream have greatly changed by virtue of a shift in formation that makes them now insurmountable. The salmon ends itself in vain leaps and is finally injured and exhausted. . . .

When the fish can struggle no longer it is ready to give up its life, for life and struggle have become synonymous. Nature fulfills itself in many ways and the writer provides a curiously ironic ending in which the fish, unable to master the falls alive is carried to their summit in death, as food in the mouth of the bear. A greater harmony, accessible only to the human imagination, is thus illustrated by the writer. The final victory is paradoxically that of life itself, and many deaths go to its making. In spite of the reiterated patterns of the stronger eating the weaker and cunning or speed eluding the dull or slow, Roberts is not interested in labouring a cliché. He goes to some pains to indicate that not even the fittest survive. (p. 28)

It is interesting at this point to consider more precisely the basis for the inevitable discussion of Wordsworth's influence on Roberts. . . . [The] Mutability Sonnet is at the centre of Wordsworth's outlook, and it is curious that it reflects so accurately the themes illustrated everywhere in Roberts' prose,

> From low to high doth dissolution climb,
> And sink from high to low, along a scale
> Of awful notes, whose concord shall not fail. . . .

"Concord shall not fail," Wordsworth says, and later he writes "Truth fails not." Concord is Truth and Truth is Concord; that is all you know on earth and perhaps all you need to know, and this hypothetical dictum might stand as well for Roberts as for Wordsworth. The animal stories also amount to a hymn to concord and harmony, and this "scale of awful notes" along which life and death and change harmoniously run is to be perceived by the imagination of a detached artist, a man possessed of heightened sensibility, who is not confused by spiritual myopia. When this "scale" is heard it produces not despair but a transcendent understanding. (pp. 28-9)

"Truth fails not" and that truth for Roberts is the endless cycle, the supremacy of life, the drama of a struggle in which all things participate, each atom playing some meaningful role in a series of events that conspire to a harmony which the poet perceives and makes into art. . . . Roberts' animals never become pets, the reader is never allowed to lose his detachment and there is no compromise in the recorded events with the bloody processes of universal natural law. There is too, the mastery of perspective, the ability, almost Swiftian, to construct whole worlds scaled to the size of ants as in **"The Prisoners of the Pitcher-Plant"** or to the world of giant moose and bear as in **"The King of the Mamozekel"**. Nor is there space to pursue the brilliance of poetic description, always used for specific and often symbolic purposes, or to comment on the division of the whole work into groups or types that follow definable patterns. For instance, Roberts varies his stories so as to produce a strong sense of the individual animal personality. . . .

I know of no other Canadian writer who has left a body of work so consistently arranged about a clear idea of the order of life itself, or a writer of animal stories who has been at one and the same time so true to the characteristics of his actors and able to produce a genuine, unsentimentalized or dynamic fiction. (p. 31)

> *Joseph Gold, "The Precious Speck of Life" (reprinted by permission of the author), in* Canadian Literature, *No. 26, Fall, 1965, pp. 22-32.*

W. J. KEITH (essay date 1969)

Desmond Pacey has observed that "the favourite form of fiction in Canada in the late nineteenth century was the historical romance." . . . [It] is scarcely surprising to find that nearly all of [Roberts'] early fictional writings fall into this category.

The first of these was not, in fact, an original novel but a translation of *Les anciens canadiens*, a French-Canadian romance by Aubert de Gaspé that had originally appeared in 1862. Roberts' English version, *The Canadians of Old*, was published in 1890, and is worth examining with some care since it seems to have had a notable influence upon his later fictional output. (p. 60)

One of the major archetypes of historical romance is, of course, a love affair between members of opposing forces. This is an important element in *The Canadians of Old*—in the constant but unconsummated love between Cameron of Lochiel and Blanche, sister of Jules d'Haberville, and in the eventual marriage between Jules and the Englishwoman. . . .

But the Romeo-and-Juliet-type love affair is only a particular example of the more general problem of human relations between nations and races. One theme explored by Gaspé and later developed by Roberts involves the differing allegiances of generations in a period of rapid historical change. (p. 62)

Gaspé has provided a number of exciting episodes, such as Cameron of Lochiel's heroic rescue of the man trapped on the ice, but with Roberts the main plot invariably involves action and excitement. . . . The great weakness of Roberts as a writer of fiction is his apparent inability to realize that the art of the novel is not invariably linked to the creation of suspense. (p. 64)

The Forge in the Forest, which was compared at the time of its publication to Stevenson's *Kidnapped,* may be taken as representative. Ultimately it is of little value since it provides, with insufficient variety or subtlety, all the stock ingredients and clichés of the genre. . . . Ultimately—and here lies the essential difference between Roberts' historical romances and those of, say, Sir Walter Scott—the weaknesses of the fictional story detract from our appreciation of the historical setting. (pp. 64-5)

If, however, we read these early writings within the context of the rest of Roberts' work, there is one feature that deserves particular attention. This is the use of "woodcraft" as a significant element in the plot. We may find it difficult to provide the necessary suspension of disbelief as adventure relentlessly follows adventure, but the incidental circumstances are not without interest. In *The Forge in the Forest,* for example, we may well be intrigued by the ways in which the hero succeeds in tracking his enemies through the forest, by the sheer practical details of self-preservation in a wild and dangerous country. This, linked with the impressive beauty and grandeur of the external scene which is vividly described, looks forward to the theme of the struggle for existence within nature which is to be explored, much more subtly and profoundly, in the animal-stories. (pp. 65-6)

Roberts' later fiction (from 1900 onwards) is more ambitious and much more effective. True, there is no consistent development—we cannot point to a "typical" or "representative" Roberts novel. As in his poetry, he flits from one possibility to another without ever attaining complete mastery of any particular technique or approach. But in his fiction he is never guilty of obvious imitation. Indeed, he seems to go against the major trends of the novel in his own time, for Roberts is primarily a story-teller in the most literal sense of the word. Throughout these novels and romances, we get the feeling that we are listening to a yarn; the omniscient narrator is always Roberts with a story to tell. He does not seem interested in the techniques and subtleties of the serious novelist.

This has both advantages and disadvantages. Roberts is not afraid of strong plots or traditional situations. At the same time he does not always possess the vigour and confidence to carry them off. He certainly has an imaginative faculty—that is clear from *The Heart of the Ancient Wood* and *In the Morning of Time.* (pp. 66-7)

[*The Heart of the Ancient Wood*] is a book that eludes the normal categories. Its title might lead us to suppose that it belongs with the animal-stories for which Roberts was later to become popular, and indeed the "furtive folk" play important roles in the unravelling of the plot. But these are no ordinary wild animals. They include a she-bear who adopts and protects the human heroine and a marauding panther who responds obediently to human command. On the other hand, if these details suggest in turn a juvenile story of whimsy and sentiment, we are no nearer an accurate classification. Perhaps the least unsatisfactory way of approaching the book is to treat it as a moral fable, acknowledging literary relationships on one side to the beast-fable, and on the other to that species of serious romance of which W. H. Hudson's *Green Mansions* is a better-known (and later) example. (pp. 67-8)

The Heart of the Ancient Wood is an unusual story told with skill and acuteness. From the first chapter, which follows "old Dave" along the trail to the clearing, thus giving us the experience of penetrating physically into the heart of the wood, Roberts is in full control of his material. The human beings are characterized simply but effectively, and by the time Miranda and Kroof come together, we are prepared to accept the fabulous plane upon which much of the story moves. If Miranda, by her very name, reminds us of Prospero's daughter, she is faced with a very different "brave new world," and the eventual departure from her paradise recalls not so much the banishment from Eden as an inevitable progress out of a Blakean innocence that is no longer satisfying. Roberts, we might say, has created a backwoods myth, and the insights he provides are to be received on a mythic level. Unless we are unduly rigid in our requirements for prose fiction, *The Heart of the Ancient Wood* will be found a bold and by no means unsuccessful experiment.

Barbara Ladd . . . is set in New England at the time of the American War of Independence, and thus reflects Roberts' change of residence from Canada to the United States. It proved the most popular of Roberts' novels at the time of its first publication, but this is more likely to be explained by its setting than (as is sometimes suggested) by an awakening of American interest in Canadian literature in general or the work of Roberts in particular. Despite this change in location, however, there is much to link *Barbara Ladd* with the rest of Roberts' work. Its heroine, for instance, like Miranda and the later Mademoiselle de Biencourt, is one of his favourite children of nature. . . . And Robert Gault, the hero, is almost predictably "a skilled shot and keen huntsman." . . . As in *The Heart of the Ancient Wood,* the main theme of the novel is the growth of the heroine from a carefree girl to a mature young woman, and as in the romances of Acadia, a love affair is complicated and endangered by the political hostilities of the time. (pp. 72-4)

Unfortunately, Barbara's move from Second Westings to New York results in a decline in the quality of the novel which it is tempting to attribute to Roberts' imperfect familiarity with the world of the big city after his move south of the border. Her adventures in American high society, the uneven fortunes of her love for Robert Gault, are all stale and conventional compared with the freshness and originality of the early sections. While we may admit that frustration and uncertainty are vital to Roberts' intention, this does not excuse the decline in wit and inventiveness. The ending, when Robert returns wounded from the war and is protected by Barbara, certainly rounds off the plot, but in the process the "microcosmic image of the life of the nation" has been blurred. It is an ending in terms of wish-fulfilment, not in terms of reality. But if Roberts has failed to bring his novel to a satisfying conclusion, we can at least give him credit for exploring an intriguing and challenging idea. Although *Barbara Ladd* cannot be judged an unqualified success, it certainly displays a literary intelligence of a high order—and one that is not afraid of tackling something new.

If the Second Westings of *Barbara Ladd* often appears to be Westcock, New Brunswick, removed in both space and time, in *The Heart That Knows* . . . Roberts makes no such attempt at disguise. Here he returns to the village in which he grew up, and creates within it a story that belongs firmly in the tradition of the regional novel. (pp. 76-7)

[We] come to admire Roberts' skill in tracing the development of an individual mind, and the charity and honesty with which he presents his material. To the casual reader, indeed, this skill is self-disguising. There is nothing flamboyant about it, none of the literary self-consciousness that proudly draws attention to its own technique. The art consists in being completely at one with the immediate purpose. There is no barrier between the experience and the reader. It is an inconspicuous but none the less remarkable achievement. (p. 79)

Roberts, as we have seen, could never resist a "strong" plot, and here this becomes, ironically, an artistic weakness. But this should not blind us to the excellence of the central chapters, many of which, in their uncompromising and nerve-touching authenticity, would not have disgraced the pen of D. H. Lawrence. Had Roberts devoted the care and attention to his prose that he lavished on his poetry, he might even have produced that elusive spectre, a great Canadian novel.

Roberts' last full-length novel, *In the Morning of Time* . . . , experiments in yet another direction. It is a story of prehistoric man, and offers an imaginative account of Man's brave but perilous rise out of the world of Nature and the evolution of something approaching civilization. Although written towards the end of Roberts' writing life, its themes provide an excellent introduction to the animal-stories which we shall be considering in the final chapter. (pp. 79-80)

Roberts invites us to follow the fortunes of an early human tribe that he calls "The People of the Little Hills." Though recognizably men, they yet retain in heightened form many animal qualities, traces of which are still to be found in Roberts' backwoodsmen but are almost totally absent in the urbanized population of our own time. . . . By the same token, the tribe lacks many of the qualities that are now considered characteristically "human," and the chief interest in the novel lies in the gradual development of such qualities in the mind of the genius (and, later, leader) of the tribe, whose name is Grôm.

Like his creator, Grôm has a "restless spirit" and is continually "craving new knowledge, new adventure." . . . On his first recorded expedition, seeking a new home for the tribe which is threatened by an inferior but numerically stronger race, he stumbles upon a volcanic area and so first learns the properties of fire. . . . He is accompanied on this expedition by a girl, A-ya, who at first followed him without his knowledge. Gradually a romantic attachment is developed, and this too is a new discovery. . . . Throughout the book, new discoveries in weapons and skills develop alongside new feelings and patterns of behaviour. . . . [We] witness the parallel evolution of such states as maternal affection, monogamy and tolerance. (pp. 80-2)

This urge towards discovery dictates the form of *In the Morning of Time.* Indeed, it is less a novel than a series of individual adventures. Crisis follows crisis, and Grôm, who is presented as a sort of prehistoric Moses leading his people onward and upward in both space and time, continually works at finding a solution for the present dilemma while at the same time looking ahead in anticipation of the next onslaught. The novel was originally serialized, and its episodic structure becomes increasingly evident in the completed book. Once again, Roberts' penchant for high adventure endangers its ultimate effectiveness. Possibly influenced by Jack London's prehistoric suspense-story, *Before Adam,* Roberts spoils the later chapters of his novel by lapsing into the sensational. (p. 82)

At first sight, the gap between prehistoric man and the inhabitants of eighteenth- and nineteenth-century North America seems considerable. It is tempting to discount Roberts' range in time and space as another symptom of his restless instability and to explain any apparent resemblances as the result of deficient powers of inventiveness and discrimination. But Roberts is only too well aware that the primitiveness of the People of the Little Hills and the sophistication of New England are equally superficial. Links between them are provided by the Indians of the historical romances and the backwoodsmen of a later day. All depend, directly or indirectly, upon the world of nature, and the standards that separate them from the beast can be as easily underrated as exaggerated. The writing of *In The Morning of Time* was interrupted by the First World War, and the trenches of France must have seemed but a small remove from the ever-threatened life of prehistoric man or the perilous existence of wild animals in a state of nature. The book was published in 1919, the year in which W. B. Yeats likened modern man to nothing more dignified than "weasels fighting in a hole." The last few words of Roberts' novel offer a ray of hope as the tribe eventually arrives at the "sweetly wooded and rivulet watered hill" . . . towards which they have been striving; but they are still surrounded by jungle and wilderness inhabited by fierce and overpoweringly strong adversaries. Their only hope lies in their evolving qualities of intelligence and endurance. (pp. 83-4)

[In December 1892, Roberts] published his first animal-story, **"Do Seek Their Meat From God."** *Earth's Enigmas* followed in 1896, though it should be stressed that this volume contained tales of the lumber-camps, dream-fantasies and even (in the first edition) a short historical romance as well as stories of animal life. Two years later, [Ernest Thompson] Seton's first full-length book, *Wild Animals I Have Known,* became a best-seller, and Roberts has freely acknowledged that this work created the popular interest that encouraged him to develop his own gift for the animal-story. Subsequently, both writers produced numerous books portraying the lives of wild creatures. . . . (p. 87)

We may freely grant that [Roberts] wrote too much, that his weakness for both the sensational and the exotic is a blemish. In his prose, as in his verse, a winnowing process is required. But whereas we are left in his poetry with a number of skillful, satisfying but unallied poems, in his animal-stories we find a distinct body of work that can ultimately stand as representative of the "world" of Charles G.D. Roberts. This is a generally unrecognized but none the less substantial achievement that deserves to be accepted as a permanent contribution to a specifically Canadian literature. (p. 121)

W. J. Keith, in his Charles G.D. Roberts *(reprinted by permission of Douglas & McIntyre Ltd.; copyright © 1969 by The Copp Clark Publishing Company), Copp Clark Publishing Company, 1969, 136 p.*

D. G. JONES   (essay date 1970)

Roberts, Carman, Lampman, and Scott are conventionally regarded as the poets of nature. They were clearly influenced by the nineteenth-century Romantics. But they also reflect an authentic desire to get out of a garrison culture that was becoming increasingly oppressive. . . . Dissatisfied with the established culture, they clearly look to nature in the hope of discovering a larger and more vital conception of life. (p. 90)

In the title poem of his first volume, **Orion,** Roberts concludes his portrait of the great hunter on a highly affirmative note: cured of his blindness, Orion opens his eyes on a fresh and dynamic world and proceeds to give his heart up "straightway unto love." Six years later, with the volume *In Divers Tones,* Roberts' youthful optimism is gone. Here the story of Acteon, in which the hunter turned hunted is pursued by his own hounds, seems more prophetic. Roberts' personal disillusionment, something of his dismay arising from his experience of life during the intervening years, is evident in the well-known **"Tantramar Revisited,"** which appeared in the same volume.

The poem celebrates the speaker's return to the land of his boyhood and is largely descriptive; yet, despite the grandeur and tranquillity of the landscape, the poem is elegiac in tone. The speaker's mood is a mixture of relief and anxiety. Since he left the scene of his childhood, he tells us, the "Hands of chance and change have marred, or moulded, or broken, / Busy with spirit or flesh, all I have most adored." There is nothing to suggest that his experience will be any different in the future. Only the immediate moment offers him some sort of haven from the pressure of time. The world of his youth appears untouched by the erosion of the years; yet, even here, it may be no more than a "darling illusion" of distance, and he resolves not to test it by a nearer view. Meanwhile, as he moves back and forth in his mind between childhood memories of a sustaining activity and the hushed inactivity of the present, the landscape before him mirrors his own situation. Just as the speaker has arrived at a pause in his struggle with life, so has the world of the fishing villages. The boats are pulled up on the beaches; the nets have been hung up to dry; the hay waves golden on the hillsides; the sea sparkles in the distance, giving no hint of its potential menace. The speaker is nonetheless aware of the ever-present destructive power of the sea. For the moment, it is contained. The "green-rampired" point and the "long clay dikes" fencing the fields from the turbid "surge and flow of the tides vexing the Westmoreland shores" protect the land and the ordered life of the villagers. While the world is washed with wind and light and the grey hawk wheels above the haystack, the moment seems poised between the forces of creation and destruction, precarious but still.

Beginning with this volume, Roberts' poetry reveals a gradual withdrawal: an increasing inability to affirm the immediate moment, to celebrate action, or to look with confidence towards the future. It is the mutability and irrationality of life which he cannot account for and which continually take him by surprise. Roberts was aware of a division between culture and nature, and, as we [can see] in **"Beside the Winter Sea,"** his separation from the woman is also a separation from the land. Yet it is the land and the world of woman that alone seem capable of comprehending and healing the injuries of life. In **"At the Tidewater"** he appeals to the land to illumine the experience he brings. . . . (pp. 90-1)

It is in his animal stories that Roberts celebrates life with the greatest confidence. There his characters move in a Darwinian world—more broadly, in a world of Job. Writing of Roberts' animal stories, Joseph Gold maintains that the "strong sense of the infinite scale of size in the universe, from the minute forces of energy to the unconquerable seasons, is characteristic of Roberts' awareness" [see excerpt above]. Often, as in the opening pages of **"The Last Barrier,"** the story of a salmon, Roberts creates through a series of sharply observed details the picture of a universe everywhere dependent on the dynamic interplay of forces in conflict. Again and again in his stories, creature preys upon creature, the snake on the mouse, the hawk on the snake, in a continual struggle to survive. Yet, though the eagle preys on the lamb, as in **"The Young Ravens that Call Upon Him,"** Roberts obviously delights in the eagle as much as the lamb. As long as he is dealing with animals alone, he tends to rejoice in the energy and variety of life despite its indiscriminate violence. . . . What this acceptance may mean in terms of a purely human order is another and more complex question, one which Roberts does not appear to have worked out very clearly.

Mr Gold sees Roberts confronted with the problem of "man's apparent lonely helplessness" in an indifferent universe. For the solution of this problem, Mr Gold contends, "The terms of his clerical background were not acceptable, the raw materials of a New Brunswick wilderness were to hand, and so Roberts brought his imagination to bear on nature and animals and produced his own Canadian mythology. The principal feature of this myth is that, while individual creatures constantly lose the struggle for survival, life itself persists. In the long run death itself has no sting and is ironically defeated by the uses nature makes of its processes."

It is true that Roberts introduces this "myth" or evolutionary idealism into his poetry, but the poems in which it appears are not among his best work, precisely because, in the context, the baldly stated idealism is frequently not convincing. In the poem **"As Down the Woodland Ways,"** for example, after observing the crumbling stumps of trees, crushed beetles, mangled grubs, Roberts goes on to conclude:

> Through weed and world, through worm and star,
> The sequence ran the same—
> Death but the travail-pang of life,
> Destruction but a name.

In leaping from the particular concrete situation to a more distant abstraction, the poet manages to lose sight of the grubs and beetles and the actuality of their quite individual destruction. Death ceases to exist. That "darling illusion" is achieved by a logical distance or sleight-of-hand. The assertion fails to meet the questions posed by the preceding stanzas because it shifts to another level of discourse. A number of the later poems are weakened by just such a lack of integrity, by vagueness, or by an overly facile optimism.

To recognize that the life of the species continues at the expense of the individual is, in any case, cold comfort. The survival of the species is in itself an obscure good. It hardly answers the queries that grow out of Roberts' personal anxiety, the bewilderment so central to various of the poems. Roberts seems loath to accept the conditions of a wilderness struggle for survival as applicable in the realm of human affairs. Even in the animal stories, whenever the human point of view is introduced, the picture becomes troubled by conventional moral distinctions between just and unjust, guilty and innocent. (pp. 91-3)

It is the human point of view which prevails in the most personal of the poems, ["**Tantramar Revisited**", "**Beside the Winter Sea**", "**In the Night Watches**", "**Westcock Hill**"] . . . , which are all elegiac poems characterized by a poignant sense of loss, division, and death, the sense of the speaker's dismay. Typically Roberts escapes by withdrawing to a distance. In many of the sonnets, for example, he becomes the impersonal, passive observer. Even so, the picture of life which he presents is frequently sombre. Even in the gayest, **"The Pea-Fields,"** for instance, we encounter a certain frustration, a final check on the immediate enjoyment of life. Certain of the later lyrics are images of life's variety and potential vitality locked and frozen in ice. In **"Kinship"** the speaker withdraws to what he terms rather vaguely "the borderland of birth." In one of the best and most ambitious of the late poems, **"The Iceberg,"** the speaker's point of view is identified with the berg; and though he may celebrate the vast forces and teeming life of the world through which he moves, his own role is passive and resigned. It is a ruinous career in which the speaker is reduced to a "little glancing globe of cold," content, he tells us, to merge "forever in the all-solvent sea."

Roberts' poetry is informed by a stoic courage, that is, by a courage to suffer rather than a courage to act. In the animal stories, on the other hand, we are often impressed by the characters' capacity, not simply to endure, but to rejoice in life, however precarious or bitterly fought. There too Roberts tends to keep his eye much more steadily on the individual and the reality of the individual creature's suffering or joy. And the emphasis on the positive significance of struggle and suffering is there more convincing. Mr Gold makes the observation that the animals in these stories lead more dignified and meaningful lives than do the characters in the novels of such contemporaries of Roberts as Zola and Dreiser. He argues: . . .

> Roberts would agree with Blake that "everything that lives is holy" but he would add, I suspect, "And holy because it lives."

Such a philosophy has its dangers. Stated baldly, it may still seem little more than a stoic pessimism or the justification of a morality of power. It needs to be amplified before we can tell how significant or palatable it might be. Particularly we should like to know what its implications might be for life in human society. How does it bear on the individual human being? Is sheer survival to be his principal aim? Is survival in itself the supreme virtue and justification of the individual existence? Roberts never seemed to have answered these questions clearly, with the result that his poetic energies were sapped by indecision and anxiety. The stories may be his best work. After the promise of the early volumes, his later poetry emerges as a diminished thing. (pp. 93-4)

D. G. Jones, "The Problem of Job," in his Butterfly on Rock: A Study of Themes and Images in Canadian Literature *(© University of Toronto Press 1970), University of Toronto Press, 1970, pp. 83-110 [the excerpt of Charles G.D. Roberts' poetry used here was originally published as "As Down the Woodland Ways" (reprinted by permission of the Literary Estate of Charles G.D. Roberts), in his* Twilight over Shaugamauk and Three Other Poems, *Ryerson Press, 1937].*

JEAN MALLINSON (essay date 1976)

I agree with W. J. Keith, who recently edited the *Selected Poetry and Critical Prose* of Charles G.D. Roberts, that—with two exceptions, the early poem **"The Tantramar Revisited"** and the later **"The Iceberg"**—Roberts' best poems are the descriptive lyrics, mostly in sonnet form, which appeared in *Songs of the Common Day,* with a few scattered here and there in the earlier *In Diverse Tones* and the later *The Book of the Native.* (p. 31)

I wondered if the possible reason for his failure to achieve the promise of *Songs of the Common Day* is that he could not reconcile his critical theory with what he was in fact doing in the poems which we most admire. . . . [In his essay **"The Poetry of Nature,"** Roberts divides] "the poetry of earth" into "That which deals with pure description, and that which treats of nature in some one of its many relations with humanity." The argument of his essay is that purely descriptive poetry is scarcely worthy the name, and that the true poetry of nature, as seen in Keats and Wordsworth, is to be found only when nature has passed through "the alembic of the heart," when "man's heart and the heart of nature . . . [are] closely involved." (pp. 31-2)

It is evident to anyone reading Roberts' best poems that this Romantic view of the poetry of nature was suited neither to his temperament as it is revealed in his poems, nor to the landscapes to which he was drawn and in the midst of which he had grown. The more he removes himself and his temptation to relate or reflect, the more precise and objective and detailed his lines, the more we are moved. The two sonnets from *In Diverse Tones,* **"The Potato Harvest"** and **"Tides",** communicate a clairvoyant sensitivity to the nuances of colour and sound in the landscape. There are human figures in the first poem, but they are seen from a distance, almost heard rather than seen. . . . There is more projection of human feelings into landscape in **"Tides":** The ebbtide "sighs" "Reluctant for the reed-beds", "the winding channels grieve". The restrained melancholy and the evocation of water, tides, even the specific line "ebbing in the night-watches swift away", are very like Arnold, but the final line "And in parched channel still the shrunk stream mourns" has a grip and strength which is Roberts' own, at his best. (p. 32)

It is certainly true, as Cappon says, that for one who wrote so much, the range of Roberts' poetry is narrow; but it seems to me that it is precisely the almost absence of human figures from the landscapes in the poems that makes them interesting. . . . [It seems to me that the strength of the sonnet **"Mowing"**] lies in the sense it conveys of mowing not as something which is done, but as a relentless process which happens. The mowing machine is in a sense an intrusion in nature, but the imagery links it to nature. . . . (p. 33)

There is in these sonnets a range of times, seasons, vistas; but I get the impression that it was to "austerity and reticence" as he calls it in his essay that Roberts responded most authentically. (pp. 33-4)

I do not wish to suggest that Roberts wrote only about winter and the absence of things and people. Yet he seems most authentic when writing of these things. He is by temperament drawn to the bleak and the austere. Margaret Atwood's remark that "There is a sense in Canadian literature that the true and only season here is winter: the others are either preludes to it or mirages concealing it" is true of Roberts. Yet his emotional preference for stubble fields, deserted landscapes, grey sea and sky is often weakened by the poetic language in which it is expressed. His poem **"The Stillness of the Frost"** comes close to confronting his fascination with the negation of winter, though it is marred by the rhetoric of the closing lines. . . . Roberts . . . perceives the winter landscape like the world as it must

have been, at the dawn of time, when it lay "cold, / Unwaked to love".

These poems are only a handful among the hundreds that Roberts wrote; far more numerous are the fatuous and facile poems in which he fails to move aside, but rather places himself and his ideas in the landscape and the poem, and the result is usually the shallow rhetoric of what Roberts called "poems of aspiration".

It seems to me from a superficial acquaintance with Roberts' poetry that he possessed a modest talent for an easy mastery of verse form, and an acute and sensitive eye and ear, not for people but for landscape. The influences which led him to dissipate his poetic gifts were no doubt various but his central dilemma is one that is shared by all colonial writers. It is the problem of style in a context which has no indigenous literary tradition, and for which the only available models are old-world forms, not entirely appropriate to the novelty of experience in a new land. (pp. 34-5)

Most of Roberts' late attempts at free-verse are pale imitations of Whitman; but in [**"The Iceberg"**] he masters in his own way the irregular cadence of the free-verse line, and embodies—in the speaker, the great iceberg—his fascination with the inhuman, the negative, which has been tracking him through his poetic career. Now he turns and faces it, the landscape which is without love or hate, which is, so far as human values go, absence, indifference. . . . At the centre of the poem is a vision of the ocean—ecological, organic, indifferent to our concerns—and, in the midst of it, "the Alp afloat", "A shape pearl-pale and monstrous", which somehow becomes an organic part of it. . . . The iceberg waits, in the fog, "greatly incurious and unconcerned", as a ship approaches: it "towered, a dim immensity of doom". The cataclysmic destruction of a great ship and its passengers is simply one incident among the others that mark the voyage of the iceberg from the Arctic north to the southern seas where it becomes "A little glancing globe of cold" and then its "fragile, scintillating frame" merges "forever in the all-solvent sea".

In an essay published in 1886, **"The Outlook for Literature"**, Roberts has written with perception about the problems of creating a literature in a new country. He is aware of the powerful potential subjects, particularly in the landscape. . . . But Roberts, though he wanted to write what he called "that characteristically modern verse which is kindled where the outposts of an elaborate and highly self-conscious civilisation come in contact with crude humanity and primitive nature" too often harkened to what he called "the voice from the drawing room" rather than the "voice of the wilderness". He sensed and shared what he perceived as his countrymen's apprehension lest they be seen as uncultured, unconventional, rugged. His achievement as a poet is uneven, flawed, very short of first rate, yet when he was able to forget the ambiguous burden of late Romantic preconceptions and lose himself in that landscape which he called "stern, overwhelming, vast, weird" his work did not prove tame. (pp. 36-8)

Jean Mallinson, "Kingdom of Absence" (reprinted by permission of the author), in Canadian Literature, *No. 67, Winter, 1976, pp. 31-8.*

L. R. EARLY (essay date 1981)

The renewed interest of nineteenth-century poets in Greek culture had three facets which it is useful to distinguish: Romantic

Hellenism, which properly denotes a nostalgic regard for Greece as the fountainhead of Western values; the adaptation of classical meter and stanzas to English versification, notably by Tennyson and Swinburne; and the recourse to Greek myth as a potent source of symbolism and narrative design. All three concerns are represented in *Orion and Other Poems,* though the last remains of greatest interest in Roberts, as in his English predecessors.

Orion showcases its mythological narratives, five of them if we count Roberts' long poem on Sir Launcelot. **"Orion,"** **"Ariadne,"** **"Launcelot and the Four Queens,"** **"Memnon,"** and **"Sappho"** occupy roughly half the pages in the book. They represent Roberts' participation in an enormously popular nineteenth-century fashion which stems primarily from Shelley and Keats. . . . Though uneven in quality, **"Orion"** and the other mythological poems reflect a remarkable understanding by Roberts of his major precursors in the genre, as well as an ability to use both classical and nineteenth-century sources effectively. (p. 11)

Roberts' **"Orion"** is typical of early Confederation poetry in its predominantly Romantic form. In attempting to express a vision of human experience in mythological terms, it recalls *Endymion* and *Prometheus Unbound,* though it is neither on the same scale nor of the same rank. It is closer in scale to the classical poems of Tennyson and Arnold but lacks their characteristic focus on a specific moral issue, usually of highly personal relevance. **"Orion"** more closely parallels the works of Keats and Shelley in a number of ways. Like their narratives, it reinterprets classical myth as a reflection of the timeless spiritual forces which condition human life, and it implies a certain sympathy with "pagan" values in reaction to the ascetic element in Christianity. Structurally it subordinates simple narration to its symbolic and philosophical dimensions. The Romantic mythological narrative is not so much a sequence of events as a series of *places,* or an orchestration of symbols.

It is especially in its setting that **"Orion"** shows the "peculiar style of intense and comprehensive imagery" which Shelley noted as distinctive of Romantic poetry. The first thirty lines of **"Orion"** survey the rugged splendour of Chios. With its gorgeous imagery and stately cadence, this passage remains one of the few successful renderings of sublime landscape in Canadian poetry. . . . Although the mountain domain of eternal snow, sunshine, and tempest is the familiar locus of the Romantic sublime, it is impressively recreated in the opening of **"Orion."** Roberts' landscape is charged with contraries: storm and calm, love and death, youth and age. The scene displays traces of a former cataclysm now resolved in sensuous, rich serenity, and thereby epitomizes the action which follows: Orion's agony and its remission. (pp. 12-13)

Unlike Horne's heroic Builder, Roberts' Orion is a simple if awesome giant whose innocence seems to precipitate his fall. If there is a central weakness in Roberts' poem, it is an unwarranted ambiguity about Orion which leaves us uncertain whether or not he is partly responsible for his agony. This question turns upon his identity as the Hunter. If anything might be cited to explain his suffering as in some sense deserved, it is his ruthless extermination of the animals in Chios. I think that Roberts intends this point but badly muddles it. On the one hand Orion is identified throughout the poem with the grand forces of elemental nature and described as "kingly" like the beasts he slays . . . in ironic contrast to Œnopion's evil sovereignty. On the other hand he undertakes a wholesale slaughter at Œnopion's behest. In emphasizing Orion's "god-like" aspect when he appears bearing the skins of the slain animals, and in juxtaposing this entrance with the sacrifice of the wolf ("well-pleasing to Apollo"), Roberts implies approval of Orion's exploit. There are reasons, though, to think that we should nto approve, and ought to regard the slaughter as a crime for which the giant's blinding, however reprehensible on Œnopion's part, is moral retribution. This view of the poem will depend largely on how we read Orion's long report of his deeds. . . . I take it to be an unconscious self-indictment full of false assumptions and unintended irony. . . . As events prove, Orion is utterly mistaken in hoping to establish Arcadia through eliminating animal predation. Human wickedness remains, and human notions of "honor" . . . are subverted by malice and vengefulness. Orion's account of heroic toils undertaken in prospect of a blissful recompense employs the voyage metaphor typical of romance, but in fact the poem turns into an abortive quest-narrative. Furthermore, Orion describes the harmony he felt with nature and the gods during his great hunt, but adds that he was troubled at night by " 'phantoms . . . / Unfettered . . . / Fain to aghast me,' " which he ignored. And in the end he claims Merope that he " 'may drink deep draughts / Of Love's skilled mixing' ": another ironic metaphor, considering the drugged wine which shortly makes him vulnerable to Œnopion's cruelty.

In addition to internal evidence for regarding Orion's hunt as a crime in Roberts' treatment of the myth, there is the evidence in Roberts' later work of his sympathy with the "kindred of the wild" and his revulsion from any wanton slaying of animals. More to the point, though, is the eventual remission of Orion's suffering through his union with the dawn-goddess, granted because he maintains reverence for the gods despite his massacre of their creatures and even in the midst of his anguish. There is more ambiguity here, in that Œnopion is also shown observing sacred rites near the beginning of the poem; however, the king is later referred to as "he of gods forgotten" by Nereids who grieve over the prostrate Hunter. . . . Roberts may intend to discriminate between Orion's ignorant crime and Œnopion's cold-blooded treachery, though this is not certain. The importance of Orion's reverence *is* stressed repeatedly, and it is possible to see the poem's ultimate theme expressed in the contrast between the giant's "heroism" and his reverence. His heroic action (of a perfectly traditional kind) is shown to be meaningless, while his reverence (an attitude rather than an action) issues in his apotheosis. In the end his transformation is achieved through love, the creative principle, in antithesis to his murderous proficiency in confederacy with Œnopion at the outset. (pp. 14-16)

Our problem is understanding just what Roberts means by love. Evidently Eos embodies divine love in contrast to the earthly love of Merope and an intermediate kind represented in the Nereids. Earlier, when Orion claims Merope's hand, anticipating "sweet draughts / Of Love's skilled mixing," the implication is that she offers an oblivion like the drugged wine which he gets instead. And when the Nereids gather round the sightless giant, the narrator avers that "had he seen as grievous were his case, / Blinded with love and stricken with delight." . . . By contrast, the love of Eos renews Orion's vision. But if Roberts means to extend the long tradition in Western poetry by which divine love is symbolized in sexual terms, his meaning is inadequately conveyed. Eos is described in extremely sensuous detail and her retreat with Orion to a green bower has rather the effect of a line of dots after an embrace in an old-fashioned novel, or of the fade-out in movies before the era of open sexuality. (p. 17)

The second mythological narrative in Roberts' debut volume is much less successful. (p. 18)

["**Ariadne**"] is by far the poorest of Roberts' mythological pieces. Like "Orion," the poem concerns the union of a betrayed mortal with a god. Once more the contrast between corrupt human relations, as represented by Theseus, and the divine order, identified with Bacchus, is clearly drawn, and Ariadne's ultimate bliss is pictured in idyllic terms which recall the resolution of the longer poem. Bacchus charges his bride to "forget the Past's dumb misery," and the final stanza takes a parting glance at the flawed human world. In "**Ariadne**," however, the theme is hardly more than an occasion for word-painting, and unfortunately the poem is weak even at this level. A pictorial narrative with minimal plot, it altogether lacks the technical brilliance of "**Orion**." The descriptive opening stanzas are filled with abstractions which make little impression, and the remainder largely taken up with Bacchus' windy speech, at best a cliched pastoral invitation. Roberts' Ariadne is a lifeless figure artfully posed, and his Bacchus a bore; the one fails as completely to provoke sympathy as the other to inspire wonder.

The poem which follows is a different matter, in more ways than one. In "**Launcelot and the Four Queens**" Roberts resorts to Arthurian rather than classical mythology; the poem is, however, closely linked in theme to the other narratives. The story appears in the sixth book of Malory's *Le Morte d'Arthur,* which provides Roberts with a good deal of dialogue and imagery. His treatment and versification are Tennysonian, closer to the laureate's early work such as "Sir Launcelot and Queen Guinevere" and "The Lady of Shalott" than to the *Idylls,* and there are also echoes of Keats's "La Belle Dame" and "Eve of St. Agnes." In this case, however, Roberts is well in control of his sources. "**Launcelot and the Four Queens**" is one of the principal achievements of *Orion,* second only to the title poem in length, and more successfully executed. It also registers a crucial shift in the volume's poetic vision in turning from a myth of transcendence to a view of the world as beautiful but fallen and riddled with paradox. Again the plot involves the complications of *eros* and again the protagonist's deliverance is reflected in his heightened awareness of nature. But this time his deliverance is problematical, very far from suggesting anything like a divine marriage. The gods are conspicuous by their absence from a world where nature, her creatures, and human beings appear ambiguous and threatening, and where the supernatural appears to be malign. (pp. 18-19)

The poem creates a wonderful atmosphere of sensuous luxuriance and subtle menace made keen through tight construction and a brisk tempo. The one-line argument to Part 1—"Launcelot sleepeth under an apple-tree"—leaves little doubt about the archetypes Roberts will play upon. In contrast to the sublime panorama of "**Orion**" we are confronted with a landscape where creatures, vegetation, even the hour ("languid noon") are tinged with dubious moral significance. It is the landscape of enchantment, hinting everywhere at entrapment and captivity:

> A robin on a branch above
> Nodding by his dreaming love
> 　　Whose four blue eggs are hatched not yet,
> Winks, and watches unconcerned
> A spider o'er the helm upturned
> 　　Weaving his careful net. . . .

The robin mates only to advance the reproductive cycle and can afford to be unconcerned. But against the vision of redemptive love in "**Orion**" and "**Ariadne**" Roberts focuses in "**Launcelot**" upon the sinister aspect of human sexuality—the dark knot of carnal knowledge and moral dislocation at the heart of Genesis and *Paradise Lost.* For men and women, we are reminded, sex has spiritual meanings beyond the instinctive mating and generation in the natural world, and this condition of being human colours our perception of things around us. Later when the captive Launcelot notices the beams of a young moon "that from the sun, her paramour / Yet walketh not aloof," it is as though the whole cosmos is implicated in amorous intrigue.

As in Milton's treatment of the Genesis story, the central issue in "**Launcelot and the Four Queens**" is choice. Morgane le Fay, "enamored sore" of the sleeping knight, is challenged by one of her companions:

> "Faith! we the fairest knight have found
> That ever lady's arms enwound,
> Or ever lady's kisses crowned;
> 　　Myself can wish no royaller lover." . . .
> "Nay! Think you then to choose for him,"
> Quoth Eastland's queen, "while shadows dim
> His sheeny eyelids cover?" . . .

But the question of choice is not as simple as distinctions between sleeping and waking or freedom and force. The "shadows" which dim Launcelot's sleep have their counterparts in his waking consciousness, and the prison to which the queens carry him has its counterpart in his bondage to Guinevere. What Roberts conveys here is the ambiguity which clouds all choice in a world where motives remain ultimately obscure and realities shift place with illusions. (pp. 19-20)

"What Magic makes Truth mars," runs the line in Part 5 which we might take to crystallize the theme of the poem. Yet we would be wrong, considering its larger design and particularly the characterization of Launcelot. This narrative dramatizes nothing so simple as the triumph of truth over falsehood or virtue over vice. In Launcelot's devotion to Guinevere lies his self-knowledge and proof against sorcery. But of what does this devotion consist? We are told plainly at the real centre of the poem in Launcelot's song, which begins conventionally enough as a pretty lyric of tender longing, undergoes a startling modulation, and ends [on a note of accusation]. . . . Launcelot is indeed "the fairest knight" but he is also an errant knight in more than one sense, and Roberts' poem is full of hints about his corruption. There is the curious fact that his armour is black. There is his agreement with the damsel who releases him which, however courteously spoken, smacks of low bargaining rather than moral courage. And there is his final vulgar gesture when he turns in his saddle—at a safe distance—to jeer at the "witches." Roberts has written not a lesson about the power of Truth, but a parable about the paradoxes of human life. His Launcelot is at once fair and foul, enlightened and duped, bound and free. "**Launcelot and the Four Queens**" is a splendid reworking of the Arthurian episode: not a parody, but the sort of lightly ironic treatment of romance which Tennyson just missed bringing off in *The Princess.*

"**Memnon**," the next mythological narrative in *Orion and Other Poems,* follows several intervening lyrics. Roberts is virtually original in taking for his central figure the Trojan ally slain by Achilles and commemorated at Egyptian Thebes by a great statue said to produce a mournful sound when struck by the rays of the rising sun. (p. 21)

The structure of Roberts' poem is identical to that of Tennyson's "Oenone" . . . : a few introductory stanzas provide the setting for a long monologue in which the protagonist addresses a lament, in a refrain, to his mother, recalling past happiness and the events which have brought present woe. The traveller who appears in the opening stanzas supplies a viewpoint, which we are invited to share: as dawn rises over the Egyptian desert he is startled by the sound that breaks from the prostrate, half-buried statue. We are given a vivid picture, reminiscent of Shelley's "Ozymandias," of desolate reaches of rock, sand, and palm, strewn with the rubble of ancient idols. These ruins, with their aura of vast periods of time gone by, are echoed in the account of Troy's fall which the statue of Memnon gives in the ensuing monologue. In an effective manipulation of perspective and a finely condensed image, Memnon's spirit looks back on the origins of the Trojan catastrophe, to "the fatal Spartan woman wed / To Troy in flames." . . .

In Greek mythology Memnon is Aurora's son by Tithonus, and his plight as Roberts pictures it closely corresponds to the plight of his father in Tennyson's "Tithonus." . . . According to the myth, Aurora obtained from Zeus immortality for her human lover but forgot to ensure his immortal youth. Tennyson's poem memorably shows the despair of a decrepit Tithonus who yearns for death to release him from a shadowy, impotent existence. In Roberts' poem Memnon, like his father, is consigned to a limbo between mortality and immortality. (p. 22)

As the tale of a figure tormented by his link to divinity, **"Memnon"** ironically qualifies the vision of **"Orion"** and **"Ariadne."** Indeed the crucial role of the dawn-goddess in both **"Memnon"** and **"Orion"** invites us to consider them together; in the shorter poem the four spheres of existence depicted in **"Orion"** reappear in a melancholy light. In one sense **"Memnon"** is, like "Tithonus," a parable about the human spirit fated to grieve itself forever, caught between nature and divinity. While Roberts' cultivation of various poetic forms in *Orion and Other Poems* often appears merely self-conscious, his Spenserian stanzas here seem admirably suited to convey a sense of broad spaces and the long, slow lapse of time.

In **"Sappho"**, the last and briefest classical narrative in *Orion*, Roberts made only a mediocre contribution to the voluminous literature on this subject. (pp. 22-3)

[Roberts' poem,] whatever his intentions, falls short of the exquisite and scarcely avoids the indignity of crude melodrama. The first ninety-odd lines show Sappho on the cliff listening in anguish to Phaeon's song as his boat passes below, and describe her fatal plunge and her body's recovery. The rest of the poem consists of a dirge delivered by a "chorus of Lesbian youth, singing around the funeral pyre." The whole is operatic, uneven, and conventional in marking out the tragic contrast of the vulnerable mortal with her timeless poetry. As for details, fire and flowers are associated with Sappho by tradition, and praise of her as "the tenth muse" descends from an epigram of Plato. The rich colours which abound in her lyrics seem merely gaudy here. As represented by Roberts, perhaps she is the first of the many "drowned poets" in Canadian literature.

Apart from their individual merits and defects, the five mythological poems in *Orion* have a collective importance both thematically and for our assessment of the volume's place in our poetry. As a genuine expression of the mythopoetic impulse, the book does represent a breakthrough. Among Canadian poets, Roberts was the first to make effective use of one of the fundamental creative procedures of the Romantics; that he should echo Shelley, Keats, and Tennyson in realizing the poetic value of myth should be no cause for surprise or deprecation. A look at [Charles] Sangster's volumes of 1856 and 1860 or [Edward Hartley] Dewart's anthology of 1864 suggests that the primary "myths" of pre-Confederation verse were sentimental and pious cliches more aptly associated with eighteenth-century models. In this respect Roberts brought Canadian poetry *into* the nineteenth century, and the fact that he did it in the year 1880 only underscores the urgency of his contribution. (p. 23)

L. R. Early, "An Old-World Radiance: Roberts' 'Orion and Other Poems'," in Canadian Poetry: Studies, Documents, Reviews, *No. 8, Spring-Summer, 1981, pp. 8-32.*

ADDITIONAL BIBLIOGRAPHY

Archer, William. "Charles G.D. Roberts." In his *Poets of the Younger Generation*, pp. 362-72. 1902. Reprint. St. Clair Shores, Mich.: Scholarly Press, 1969.
    Traces Roberts's poetic growth.

Cappon, James. *Charles G.D. Roberts and the Influence of His Times.* 1905. Reprint. Ottawa: Tecumseh Press, 1975, 52 p.
    A reprint of the first lengthy critical study of Roberts's work, surveying his poetic canon through *The Rose of Life.*

Daniells, Roy. "Lampman and Roberts." In *Literary History of Canada: Canadian Literature in English,* edited by Carl F. Klinck, Alfred G. Bailey, Claude Bissell, Roy Daniells, Northrop Frye, and Desmond Pacey, pp. 389-405. Toronto: University of Toronto Press, 1965.*
    Chronicles Roberts's limitations, but deems him praiseworthy as "Canada's first man of letters."

Jackel, David. "Roberts' 'Tantramar Revisited': Another View." *Canadian Poetry,* No. 5 (Fall/Winter 1979): pp. 41-56.
    An indepth reappraisal of Roberts's "The Tantramar Revisited."

Keith, W. J. Introduction to *Selected Poetry and Critical Prose,* by Charles G.D. Roberts, edited by W. J. Keith, pp. xv-xxxix. Toronto: University of Toronto Press, 1974.
    Survey of the poetry and critical prose.

Polk, James. "Lives of the Hunted." *Canadian Literature,* No. 53 (Summer 1972): pp. 51-9.
    Describes attributes of the Canadian animal story, and compares Roberts's portrayal of animals to that of other writers in the genre.

Pomeroy, E. M. *Sir Charles G.D. Roberts: A Biography.* Toronto: Ryerson Press, 1943, 371 p.
    Informative biography.

Stephen, A. M. "The Poetry of Charles G.D. Roberts." *Queen's Quarterly* XXXVI (Winter 1929): 48-64.
    Surveys Roberts's works, assigning the poet a minor position in world literature because of his expatriation, his failure to pursue the cosmic enigmas posed in his first poetry collections, and his failure to apply the precepts of psychology to his art.

Strong, William. "Charles G.D. Roberts' 'The Tantramar Revisited.'" *Canadian Poetry,* No. 3 (Fall/Winter 1978): 26-37.
    An excellent indepth analysis of "The Tantramar Revisited."

White, Greenough. "A Pair of Canadian Poets." *The Sewanee Review* VII, No. XI (Winter 1899): 48-52.*
    Comments upon Roberts's poetic devices: his subject matter, tone, and phrasing.

Will(iam Penn Adair) Rogers

1879-1935

American humorist and journalist.

Rogers was the last of America's cracker-barrel philosophers and one of the most celebrated public figures of his day. Like his predecessors Artemus Ward and Mark Twain, he offered dry, whimsical commentaries on a plethora of political, social, and economic issues. Rogers's aphoristic, satirical observations, which he voiced in magazine articles and nationally syndicated columns, revealed the foibles and injustices of society and reaffirmed the humorist's role as the voice of the "average" American.

Rogers was an uniquely American phenomenon; he was a part-Cherokee cowboy who attained fame as a writer, lecturer, and stage and screen actor. Born in Oklahoma into a prosperous ranching family, the young Rogers was an expert rider and lariat stunt man. He appeared in Wild West shows throughout the world, and in 1905 he made his vaudeville debut. In vaudeville he enlivened his performances with off-the-cuff lectures on the art of roping. Rogers's humorous chatter, nonchalant delivery, and southwestern drawl proved a popular combination, resulting in an invitation to join the Ziegfeld Follies. His wife suggested that he vary and supplement his material with comments on contemporary personages and events. Following this advice, he delighted audiences with his homely philosophy and pungent remarks, becoming a renowned humorist and interpretor of the news. Rogers's first two books, *The Cowboy Philosopher on the Peace Conference* and *The Cowboy Philosopher on Prohibition*, were drawn from his Follies monologues. His subsequent works, such as *The Illiterate Digest*, *There's Not a Bathing Suit in Russia*, and *Letters of a Self-Made Diplomat to His President*, were garnered from the newspaper columns "Will Rogers Says," "The Worst Story I Ever Heard," "The Daily Telegram," and also from his serialized correspondence from abroad appearing in *The Saturday Evening Post*. Rogers's death in a 1935 plane crash sent the entire country into mourning, prompting Carl Sandburg to reflect, "There is a curious parallel between Will Rogers and Abraham Lincoln. They were rare figures whom we could call beloved without embarrassment."

In his writings, as on the stage, Rogers affected a pose of ignorance, emphasizing his simple, rural background and lack of formal education. In reality he was a well-informed and thoughtful commentator, skilled in the use of the pun, metaphor, and hyperbole. By assuming the stance of a good-natured, naive country boy, Rogers was able to lampoon Congress, presidents, and foreign heads of state without occasioning offense or indignation. His *The Cowboy Philosopher on the Peace Conference*, for example, mocks the diplomatic stratagems of the Versailles talks, while *The Cowboy Philosopher on Prohibition* treats the futility and hypocrisy of the Volstead Act. Rogers's shrewd, fundamentally pessimistic point of view has been compared to Twain's, as has his profound distrust of the motives and objectives of those in power. Unlike Twain, however, he was incapable of sustaining an idea at length. Rogers's forte was the pithy sentence—the short but highly suggestive statement calculated to effect an immediate response.

The Bettmann Archive

Today's reader finds much of Rogers's work dated. His topical humor is no longer relevant, and his intentional misspellings and grammatical errors seem excessive. Nevertheless, his writings are valued for the insight they provide into the concerns and opinions of the country during the tumultuous 1920s and 1930s. Damon Runyon offered this assessment: "Will Rogers was America's most complete human document. He reflected in many ways the heartbeat of America. In thought and manner of appearance and in his daily life he was probably our most typical native born, the closest living approach to what we like to call the true American."

(See also *Dictionary of Literary Biography*, Vol. II: *American Humorists, 1800-1950*.)

PRINCIPAL WORKS

The Cowboy Philosopher on Prohibition (aphorisms) 1919
The Cowboy Philosopher on the Peace Conference (aphorisms) 1919
The Illiterate Digest (sketches) 1924
Letters of a Self-Made Diplomat to His President (fictional letters) 1926
There's Not a Bathing Suit in Russia (sketches) 1927

The Autobiography of Will Rogers   (sketches and
    aphorisms) 1949
The Best of Will Rogers   (sketches and aphorisms) 1979

JOHN CRAWFORD (essay date 1924)

When Will Rogers comes on stage at the Follies, with his jaw
full of chewing gum and his arms loaded with ropes, he makes
you feel sorry for him. You know he is going to get tangled
up in the ropes or lose a stroke of his gum. . . . He begins
talking in his Oklahoma drawl, and all the while he is chewing
gum and playing with the ropes. You know you could do it
better than he. When he begins to make the ropes writhe like
snakes and strikes the bullseye again and again with his quaint,
homely wit, you are as proud of him as if you had done it
yourself. But those seemingly offhand remarks of his are neatly
timed to coincide with some spectacular stunt with the ropes.
It is not until afterward, when you try to tell it to some one
who has not seen the Follies that you realize two things: he
put it over in the only language and intonation possible, and
he said something keen and penetrating and true. All in the
name of gawky, innocent, country-jake, amateurishness.

This **"Illiterate Digest"** is goods off the same bolt. He is down
in black and white where you can watch him closely and go
back and see how he did it. He is just about as unsophisticated
in doing his work as a Russian toe dancer, and one job is as
intricate as the other. He gives the impression of being simply
the cross-roads general merchandise store talkers of a continent
rolled into one man. But the fact of the matter is that he knows
just what he wants to do, just how he wants to do it, and he
does it. He is an expert satirist masquerading as a helpless,
inoffensive, ineffectual zany. . . .

Rogers is always for the man beneath. He puts a pin into the
pompous and jeers at the self-righteous and the self-important.
He is non-partisan in politics, you can name the administration,
if you will let him crack jokes about it. . . . His chapter on
the grave problem of etiquette, or how to tell a butler, and
when, is as good as Donald Ogden Stewart, and much less
savage. The report of the Democratic National Convention is
a classic of exaggeration, in the good old Artemus Ward-Mark
Twain-Bill Nye tradition, but, like them, he works in a germ
of hard, cold truth. **"The World Tomorrow"** is a selection of
pithy, informing, moral paragraphs, after the fashion of a well-
known and well-paid editorial writer, it is hilarious nonsense.
But as a matter of fact, it is hard to find one part of the book
noticeably better than another part. It is all good.

> *John Crawford, "Will Rogers Knows More than He
> Pretends," in* The New York Times Book Review
> *(© 1924 by The New York Times Company; reprinted
> by permission), December 14, 1924, p. 2.*

THE NEW YORK TIMES BOOK REVIEW (essay date 1927)

Despite its alluring title, [**"There's Not a Bathing Suit in Russia"**] is really an appendix to Will Rogers's **"Letters of a Self-
Made Diplomat,"** a continuation of those racy and pithy observations on European politics which made the latter a notable
if informal contribution to international understanding. The
bathing-suit element in the book is very slight—a paragraph
or two in which Mr. Rogers observes, "If there is a bathing

suit in Russia, somebody is using it for an overcoat. . . . [I]
cabled my old friend Mr. Ziegfeld: 'Don't bring Follies to
Russia. You would starve to death.'" . . .

[He] proceeds to give Russia the once-over in terms intelligible
to children and Congressmen. "The real fellow that is running
the whole thing in there is a Bird named Stalin, a great big
two-fisted fighting egg from away down in the Caucasus. . . .
He don't hold any high position himself, but he tells the others
what ones they will hold." Proclaiming himself equipped with
an open—nay, an empty—mind, he thinks the trouble with
Bolshevism is that it is being administered by former news-
papermen, with a tendency to "make-up" the nation anew
every day. . . .

"There's Not a Bathing Suit in Russia" is written in a rather
more sparkling, if diluted, vein than the preceding volume of
which it is really a part. Take for example, his opening remark:
"I was passing through Paris looking for a good show and
somebody suggested the House of Deputies. It's a Satire on
our Congress"—it's a pity that he did not leave the sentence
stand but insisted on adding—"so that will set you laughing
right there." This is humor diluted. But here's another one,
sheer high-spirited horseplay. "They can pull the Cabinet Chairs
out from under that band of accomplices who plot against us
once a week: they will hit the floor but they will come back
up out of it with nothing hurt but their political pride." With
such squirts from the syphon of his carbonated wit does Will
Rogers enliven and make palatable the raw vodka of his political report to the American people on the state of Russia. It
is a fine achievement to succeed simultaneously in two such
difficult and mutually exclusive fields as humor and politics.
It takes more than queer spelling and tricky twists of wording
to accomplish that: it takes brains and common sense and an
open mind which, if admittedly empty, is not the non-refillable
variety.

> *"Will Rogers Takes to the Air," in* The New York
> Times Book Review *(© 1927 by The New York Times
> Company; reprinted by permission), June 26, 1927,
> p. 11.*

JAMES FEIBLEMAN (essay date 1939)

There are a number of comedians whose popularity is enormous. . . . Popularity of their sort is fleeting, of course, and
it is quite possible that although their names are on every tongue
in America, they will be almost forgotten in a few years. But
since they will be replaced by others who will be just as popular, it may be concluded that they do fill a certain function,
even though they have to be often changed. They evidently
reflect certain evanescent moods to which the public is susceptible, and they pass with the passing of these moods. (p. 260)

Will Rogers, the screen and radio comedian and columnist,
belongs to this class of popular idols. . . . Although he had
his limitations, he was a clever man, and did represent something in America. He came closer than anyone else in the
country to filling the rôle of official fool. The place he sought
was an official one indeed; for he wanted to be the Congressional and Presidential fool, corresponding to the court fool of
the Middle Ages. . . . That he had anti-democratic leanings
and admired power in whatever form, there can be little doubt.
His attacks, repeated again and again under the guise of humour, on the idiocies of Congressmen, were really aimed at
democracy and representative government. (p. 261)

From his envied coign of vantage as public comedian, Rogers was able to point out the truth about many things which might not otherwise have been accepted so pleasantly. In a letter to a friend, Rogers revealed that he saw the point, for he says, "Don't take what a comedian says to heart, if anyone ever starts taking me serious I am sunk." Will Rogers was full of contradictions. He was, for instance, a fearless critic at times. He attacked everything, from business ("Gentlemen, you are as fine a group of men as ever foreclosed a mortgage on a widow. I'm glad to be with you Shylocks.") to Christianity ("I tried to find out who the Barbarians were. From the best I could learn, Barbarians were people who stole from you. If you stole from the Barbarians you were indexed in your history as a Christian"). He observed the effect of the absence of liberalism in Soviet Russia in its proper perspective, when he said, upon the news of the execution of some public official, that "Russia doesn't have what you might call a constant critic," and he wrote an epitaph for the unfortunate:

Here lies the body of Nicholas Vimsky,
He tried to criticize Stalin, but Stalin outlasted himsky.

He was even keen enough to observe that fame and position were often the result of events, and that events continued to occasion the fortunes of the great. He observed that "Being great as President is not a matter of farsightedness; it's just a question of the weather, not only in your own country but in a dozen others. It's the elements that makes you great or that break you." The Rogers prose, however, was a pose, and so his words of wisdom had to be spoken in an ignorant language, abounding in grammatical errors. Rogers also said proudly that he was ignorant of art and disliked it. (pp. 261-62)

The Achilles heel of Will Rogers was his respect for big business and big business men. He spoke of the American Government as "the biggest business in the world," and intimated that the rich would make better Congressmen than the poor, on the grounds that only the rich were accustomed to dealing in large sums of money. Frequently in his syndicated newspaper paragraphs, Rogers had something good to say about some wealthy person whom he was visiting or knew. He wanted written on his epitaph, "I joked about every prominent man of my time, but I have never met a man I didn't like." Rogers might have been a wiser man, and therefore a more permanently valuable comedian, had he lived through the long years of the trade depression. As it is, there is little worth remembering, for his own ambition has been fulfilled: "I hope to be like a good bookkeeper: when my volumes are finished my accusations and denials will balance so even that I haven't really said a thing." (pp. 262-63)

> *James Feibleman, "The Popular Comedy: Idols of the Marketplace," in his* In Praise of Comedy: A Study in Its Theory and Practice *(reprinted by permission of the author), George Allen & Unwin Ltd, 1939, pp. 260-67.**

WALTER BLAIR   (essay date 1942)

"Ther's at least one instance," said Abe Martin, [humorist Kin Hubbard's character], "where havin' enough rope didn' end disastrously, an' that's Will Rogers." It was natural that Hubbard and the cowboy humorist should admire each other, because the success of the humor of Rogers as well as that of Hubbard was largely the result of an ability to squeeze a great deal of good sense into a funny sentence.

Rogers was the more successful of the two. (p. 262)

It is interesting to guess at the reasons for this great fame Rogers had. Undoubtedly, one thing that helped it a great deal was the novelty of a cowboy humorist. Perhaps even more important was the fact that he embodied for Americans a type which in some ways at that time seemed more representative of the life of the country than the farmer type did. And the way the screen plays of some decades had portrayed heroic western cowboys certainly had built up a friendly attitude—if not a worshipful one—toward the type. (p. 263)

The notion that Rogers wrote and thought like the great mass of philosophers in homespun before him had a solid basis. In several ways, of course, he was unique. His cowboy background, his experiences on the stage and in Hollywood, the fact that he lived in an age of airplanes and skyscrapers—all made him diverge somewhat from the exact pattern of earlier humor. But he had the old-fashioned horse-sense kind of a mind, and he won laughs in old ways.

Back of his humor, as almost everybody said who wrote about him, was a philosophy. (p. 265)

He himself thought that ideas made his humor what it was. When someone spoke to him about the poor grammar in his newspaper articles, he said, "Shucks, I didn't know they was buyin' grammar now. I'm just so dumb I had a notion it was thoughts and ideas." His feeling, he said, was that "A gag to be any good has to be fashioned about some truth. The rest you get by your slant on it and perhaps a wee bit of exaggeration, so's people won't miss the point." (pp. 265-66)

When he turned to writing, he often continued to use the old-fashioned device of acting like a fool. . . . He was in the habit of saying, "I studied the fourth reader for ten years." He dotted his pages with poorly spelled words, thus getting back to a device which had not been used by most humorists since the time of the Civil War. Another way he had of showing his illiteracy—one not often used by American humorists before him—was the lavish misuse of capital letters. His grammar was bad, and he let on that he had little respect for it. "Grammar and I," he said, "get along like a Russian and a bathtub" and, again, "Maybe ain't ain't so correct, but I notice that lots of folks who ain't usin' ain't, ain't eatin'."

He used many of the kinds of expression that had long been useful to humorists. The old habit of linking together in one sentence a group of queerly assorted articles—a habit useful to Ward, Twain, Nye, and others—made possible such a remark as "Russia's a country that used to have four exports—dukes, grand dukes, princesses and whiskers." He had a liking for puns and malapropisms, as hosts of humorists had had before him: "Now the President says we're going to recognize the Czecho-Slovaks. We may recognize them but we will never pronounce them." The old device of the comic simile cropped up in sentences like "Americans are getting like a Ford car—they all have the same parts, the same upholstery and make exactly the same noises" and like "Eskimos are thicker here [in Alaska] than rich men at a save-the-Constitution convention."

Most of the pains he took with his writing went on polishing his lines until they did two things, both important: (1) they phrased a humorous idea in a way that *seemed* very casual and (2) they phrased the idea in just the way to make it most amusing. . . . He used the same sort of care Josh Billings did on phrasing. Often he wrote eight or ten versions of a sentence before he got one that suited him. But his expressions, for all their working-over, had to seem offhand, spontaneous, accidental. (pp. 268-69)

[There were times] when the cowboy comedian took on, in his writings, a fictitious governmental job. Traveling abroad, he posed as "a self-made diplomat," writing reports to either the chairman of the Senate Committee on Foreign Affairs or to the President. . . . [What] he said about Europe had about as little diplomatic tactfulness as anyone could imagine. (pp. 271-72)

Rogers' suspicion of Europeans and his democratic way of sizing up things with his humble mind and confidently making known what he had decided carry back one's memory to a time when another Westerner, Mark Twain, had looked at Europeans and European things and had made unflattering remarks with just as much confidence. (pp. 272-73)

When Rogers died, not a few commentators thought of comparing him with Mark Twain. But there was one great difference between the two, a very significant one. The earlier humorist turned against whatever he disliked with a hate that was ferocious; Rogers had no hate. "When I die," he said, "my epitaph or whatever you call those signs on gravestones, is going to read, 'I joked about every prominent man of my time but I never met a man I didn't like.' I am proud of that. I can hardly wait to die so it can be carved." And again: "You folks know I never mean anything by the cracks I make on politics. I generally hit a fellow that's on top because it isn't fair to hit a fellow that's down." This meant that, though many people thought Rogers was a sort of unofficial preacher-at-large to the United States, the sermons he preached did not attack the popular sins of the day as ferociously as they might have done. Perhaps, though, more ferocity would have spoiled his humor—as it sometimes spoiled Mark Twain's; perhaps this funnyman, the latest of a long line of towering philosophers in homespun, went as far as anyone could who was as true to the traditions of his craft as Will Rogers was. (p. 273)

> *Walter Blair, "Abe Martin and Will Rogers," in his* Horse Sense in American Humor from Benjamin Franklin to Ogden Nash *(copyright 1942, 1970 by Walter Blair; reprinted by permission of the author), University of Chicago Press, 1942, pp. 256-73.*

JOHN T. WINTERICH   (essay date 1949)

[*The Autobiography of Will Rogers*] is a compilation of simon-pure Rogersana, with the column which Will wrote from the end of 1922 to his death in Alaska in 1935 providing, happily, the bulk of the text. The result will be compared to Poor Richard, Puddn'head Wilson, Maceus Aurelius, and Samuel Pepys, and it can stand up under that comparison without having to produce a passport.

Here, for instance, is superb documentation of the boom and of the bust—primary historical source material of high authenticity and importance. Nothing will give the soul of Will Rogers greater delight, or make him chuckle with deeper satisfaction, than for him to turn to some authoritative elucidatory text, fifty or 500 years from now, and find "Rogers, *op. cit.*" peppered throughout the footnotes.

Today's reader is not so likely to chuckle. The Rogers scraps which we used to read twenty years ago with rueful grins now take on a tartness and a mordancy which were there all the while, but were hidden under the laugh. We Americans have always held to the principle of when-you-say-that-comma-smile—it is all right with us if our most sacred institutions are

assaulted provided the attack is made in a spirit of good clean fun. Here it is not a case of the Rogers humor wearing off: rather has it mellowed into transparency and permitted us to look underneath. Thus:

> October 31, 1929: Sure must be a great consolation to the poor people who lost their stock in the late crash to know that it has fallen in the hands of Mr. Rockefeller, who will take care of it and see that it has a good home and never be allowed to wander around unprotected again. . . .

If Will Rogers were alive today and said some of those things without smiling, some unsmiling committee would have him under the Capitol Hill klieglights as quick as you could say subpoena. (p. 19)

> *John T. Winterich, "Simon-Pure Rogersana," in* The Saturday Review of Literature *(copyright © 1949, copyright renewed © 1975, by Saturday Review; all rights reserved; reprinted by permission), Vol. XXX, No. 42, October 15, 1949, pp. 19-20.*

ALISTAIR COOKE   (essay date 1949)

I suppose men will gravel their brains for a long time to say what is the secret of men like Mark Twain and Will Rogers. Horse sense, common sense, is a first dull stab at a quality which is an almost frightful gift, in people without a smitch of ill-will, of seeing how simply and ruthlessly the world turns. Will Rogers knew more about foreign policy than anyone I know at the United Nations, the fundamental way it works, the uncomfortable plain facts that irritate the professional diplomat but which cannot be explained away. (pp. 178-79)

Looking at the Abyssinian war and the rise of Hitler he wrote sadly and briefly, "As I see it, little nations has no business being little" and "Statesmen think they make history; but history makes itself and drags the statesmen along."

Many of these sound like fighting, even bitter, words. And so they are. Will Rogers would not be the first American to be worshipped for a myth based on a gentle exterior. Most Americans had to think of him as a kindly sentimentalist in the best of all possible worlds, because he opened up the grave beneath their feet, and if they had dared to take him seriously they would have had to lynch him. But when the molasses starts to flow over his grave, as it will for many years to come, it will be well to remember the honorable core of him, who met many men he despised, and many pretensions he exploded; who lived by compassion and friendliness, out of sheer desperation at the evil things his eyes and his honesty showed him. (pp. 179-80)

> *Alistair Cooke, "Will Rogers" (originally a radio broadcast on BBC, London, England, in 1949), in his* One Man's America *(copyright © 1951, 1952, copyright renewed © 1980, by Alistair Cooke; reprinted by permission of Alfred A. Knopf, Inc.), Knopf, 1952, pp. 173-80.*

NORRIS W. YATES   (essay date 1964)

Why did Rogers capture the public on a scale that probably surpassed even Mr. Dooley and Abe Martin? Blair has suggested that his cowboy origins helped [see excerpt above]. Through them he embodied a figure that people liked to feel was more representative of American life as a whole than was any farmer type; moreover (says Blair), he reached the public through more media than any other humorist had used. Other commentators have stressed that he was always just a little, but never too far, ahead of the main drifts of public opinion. (pp. 115-16)

Without an exhaustive and probably impossible study of public opinion during Rogers' career, it is not feasible to test the hypothesis that Rogers accurately voiced the immanent attitudes of the "big Honest Majority" in politics. If one goes ahead and assumes that he did so, Will's political opinions offer basic clues to what that majority were thinking and feeling. If one rejects the hypothesis, Will's public image and his views at least offer one more humorist's portrait, not only of the crackerbox oracle but of the solid citizen trying to think things through. This citizen shows traits of the man idealized by the conservative who distrusts reformers and asks only to be let alone, and traits also of his counterpart in the liberal mythology who participates in reform movements for the sake of getting the great corporations and militant unions to let him alone. Rogers tried to embody both images at once without sacrificing the approval of either faction. He declared once that, "I am just progressive enough to suit the dissatisfied. And lazy enough to be a standpatter." The pretense of laziness, a trait which is part of the stereotype of the wise oaf, helped to mask his inconsistency. (pp. 118-19)

On the whole, Will (because of his essential detachment from political strife) was closer to the conservative than to the liberal citizen, especially before the Great Slump. Aloofness toward factions was necessary if Will was indeed to speak for all the people, but it also stemmed from his real indifference to the outcome of party squabbles. His detachment was reflected in his view of politics as entertaining spectacle (an approach close to H. L. Mencken's). (pp. 119-20)

Outside the realm of party politics, Rogers' views were indeed neither conservative nor liberal, but composite. He walked in the middle of the road, holding a view commonly labeled conservative: that government is essentially a business; and holding another, commonly held to be part of the Progressive-New Deal ideology, that a powerful, centralized federal government is a good thing. Neither view changed much with the times. . . .

[Henry Ford was] for Rogers a symbol of administrative know-how and power. (p. 121)

Rogers also admired the personality and policies of Benito Mussolini, who, he thought, was like Ford in being an efficient business manager. Will reflected the views of many Americans during the nineteen-twenties; Abe Martin said in 1927, "Nearly ever'buddy I've talked to would like t' borrow Mussolini fer a day or two. . . ." (Perhaps the emphasis should fall on the final phrase.) (p. 122)

Will's respect for executive power is surprising in a man who could hit hard, in his role as presumptuous clown, at both big-businessmen and politicians: "I tell you, the more I hear these big men talk, the more I realize I am the only one that is trying to uphold the rights of the common people." But Will was used to the one-man rule of the cattle empire; his point of view was that of the lone entrepreneur who distrusts both corporate wealth and organized labor, and looks to the executive branch of the Federal Government as the only force capable of keeping both off his back. (p. 123)

Like most crackerbarrel philosophers, Rogers sometimes showed, under the mask of the wise fool, a mixture of shrewdness and

of genuine naïveté. He saw all too well the inability of Congress to act when action was needed, and he appreciated the potentialities for good of a strong executive. Yet he wanted that executive to rule a vast and complex nation by the simple code of the individual rancher, a code surviving from pioneer days. . . .

Other inconsistencies also stand out in Rogers' attitudes. Will was a crackerbox sage who had discarded the crackerbox for mass media rendered possible by modern technology. . . . (p. 125)

Not the least of Rogers' inconsistencies was the fact that under his approval of the welfare state ran a counter-current of skepticism about the liberal icon of progress. A letter of inquiry from Will Durant in 1931—when Rogers was anticipating the New Deal in his advocacy of farm relief and stricter regulation of banks—called forth one of Rogers' few statements of basic principle. He wrote to Durant, "Nothing don't mean anything. We are just here for a spell and pass on. Any man that thinks that Civilization has advanced is an egotist. Fords and bathtubs have moved you and cleaned you, but you was just as ignorant when you got there. We know lots of things we used to didnent know but we dont know any way to prevent em happening." Such a distrust of the common man's "progress" must have met with the approval of Mencken, who also had a letter to Durant in the same volume. Rogers added, "Indians and primitive races were the highest civilized, because they were more satisfied, and they depended less on each other, and took less from each other. We couldent live a day without depending on everybody. So our civilization has given us no Liberty or Independence." His skepticism became almost nihilistic:

> Suppose the other Guy quits feeding us. The whole thing is a "Racket," so get a few laughs, do the best you can, take nothing serious, for nothing is certainly depending on this generation. Each one lives in spite of the previous one and not because of it. And dont start "seeking knowledge" for the more you seek the nearer the "Booby Hatch" you get. And dont have an ideal to work for. Thats like riding towards a Mirage of a lake. When you get there it aint there. . . .

The philosophy indicated in this letter eliminates the significance of society; it is frontier individualism carried to the point of anarchy. In its denial of progress, knowledge, and ideals, it also clashes with the assumptions of the Progressive-New Deal tradition. Here, despite his humanitarian leanings, Will suggests the conservative rather than the liberal citizen.

The fact that Rogers' popularity reached new heights during the depression suggests that the public was in the mood for a strong if unstable mixture of New Dealism, wry humor, and grassroots skepticism. If one adds to this mixture a respect for the Man on Horseback (like a cattle king) who Gets Things Done; nostalgia for one's rural origins; an inconsistent readiness to make use of modern technology; a pungent, proverbial style; and most important, the elusive essence that makes a man Will Rogers rather than just another ranch-hand; then one has the combination for becoming the best-liked humorist of his generation. (pp. 126-27)

Norris W. Yates, "Will Rogers and Irvin S. Cobb,"
in his The American Humorist: Conscience of the
Twentieth Century *(© 1964 by The Iowa State University Press, Ames, Iowa 50010; reprinted by per-*

mission), Iowa State University Press, 1964, pp. 113-33.*

E. PAUL ALWORTH   (essay date 1974)

Although Will Rogers had been a successful humorist on the vaudeville platform for fourteen years, [*The Cowboy Philosopher on the Peace Conference*] was his first attempt at humorous writing. In an effort to project his stage personality on the printed page, he leaned heavily on ludicrous spellings and expressions, just as many American humorists before him had done. As to content, Will's humor in his first book centered largely on the diplomatic maneuvers of President Wilson and the American delegation at the conference. The humorist was a strong admirer of the President, and most of his quips are based upon President Wilson's experience in Europe. (pp. 33-4)

[Encouraged by the success of his first book,] the humorist collected some of his jokes about Prohibition and published a second volume . . . entitled, *The Cowboy Philosopher on Prohibition.* Since Prohibition was one of the highly controversial topics of postwar America, Will found it a rich source of humor. (p. 35)

Will's first two books show definite traces of his vaudeville technique. Since his quips are treated as separate jokes, there is no continuity in the writing. Some of them seem weak on the printed page, although they were successful when delivered on the stage in an Oklahoma drawl. Much of the material seems strained, as if he had been forced to extend a short quip to a paragraph to suit the requirements of a book. (p. 36)

Will's early humor was developed during his career on the variety stage of New York, and it reflected, for the most part, the viewpoint of the vaudeville comedian. Among New Yorkers the stock character of the "yokel" was always a source of humor; thus the apparent illiteracy of the cowboy philosopher enhanced his stage personality. The common-sense nature of his pronouncements made in this rural idiom provided an element of incongruity which his audiences found irresistible. . . .

In the transition from oral to written humor, Rogers carried with him the same devices, mannerisms, and pretenses. Although he could not transfer his grin and his drawl to the printed page, he employed in his written work the same homely and colorful mode of expression, the same characteristic qualities of simplicity and directness, and the same pretense of ignorance and illiteracy. (p. 96)

Will's books do not have any structural pattern. All of his books except one, *Ether and Me,* were collections of humorous material previously used by the cowboy philosopher either on the stage or in his column. His first two publications, *The Cowboy Philosopher on the Peace Conference* and *The Cowboy Philosopher on Prohibition,* are nothing more than a series of jokes which he had previously used in the Ziegfeld Follies; the quips are presented as paragraph units; and they are bound together only by concern for a common theme. . . . His third book, *The Illiterate Digest,* is a collection of his weekly columns for book publication, and the subjects range from the Tea Pot Dome political scandal to Will's comments on etiquette.

One of his most popular books was *Letters of a Self-Made Diplomat to His President,* a collection of articles written for the *Saturday Evening Post;* the articles are structurally related by their form, for the book purports to be a series of letters written to President Calvin Coolidge that describe Will's ob-

servations during his tour of Europe in 1926. In addition to describing the general European scene, the humorist sends advice to Coolidge about the farm problem and on the Congressional election of 1926. On the same trip, Will made his first visit to Russia, and *There's Not a Bathing Suit in Russia* is an account of this trip. *Ether and Me* is a short volume describing a gall-stone operation which Will underwent in 1929. Other than these books and his columns, Will's writing was confined to a few magazine articles, generally on political subjects, and to the introductions to books written by such friends as Eddie Cantor and Charles Russell. (p. 98)

In keeping with his pose of ignorance, Will's language, in both his written and oral expression, was nonliterary, to say the least. It may be termed a homely, low-colloquial expression characterized by misspellings, grammatical errors, weak punctuation, and excessive slang. The humorist seems to have written carelessly, almost slovenly at times, with a fine disregard for the rules of grammar, preferring to believe that it was his thought and his ideas that made his humor and not his manner of expression. Some of his most common errors were subject-verb-agreement, improper case, incorrect number or gender, misplaced modifiers, improper tense formation, and sentence fragments.

Some of Will's grammatical errors appear so frequently that they appear to be individual irregularities which characterize his style. For example, his sentence structure was often loose and inept; for he wrote exactly as he spoke, without any attempt to subordinate elements of his sentences. Thus his most common sin of punctuation was the run-on sentence; when he came to the end of a complete thought, he simply inserted a comma and wrote on. Likewise, the humorist made excessive use of capitalization; he indiscriminately capitalized nouns, pronouns, adjectives, verbs, prepositions, and conjunctions according to whim. Sometimes he capitalized only the first letter of a word, sometimes the whole word, and on occasions the whole sentence. Although liberal in his use of capitals in his prose, he went to the opposite extreme in omitting apostrophes in contractions and in the possessive case; thus "was not" is usually contracted to "wasnt" or "wasent" and the posessive case is formed by adding "s" or "es" to the nouns concerned.

Although Will did not make any serious attempt to record the speech of a particular region, he did utilize the slang and idiom of the Southwest. The highly colorful speech of the region gave an air of authenticity to his character as a cowboy philosopher. The humorist made considerable use of "aint" as well as other slang expressions such as "lickerty-split," "bust right out," "cuckoo," "buggered up," "a knockout," "hot dog," "nifty," "snooty," "hokum," "cockeyed," "sitting pretty," "jerky," "mooched up," "rumdum," "geezer," "skypiece," "rag money," "crow hopper," and a host of others. (pp. 99-100)

With a fine disregard for the conventions of grammar, he made no pretense of aiming at a literary style, nor did he consciously attempt to imitate the writing of other humorists. He did, in fact, nothing to improve his literary technique; and how much of his ungrammatical expression was willful, how much was ignorance, and how much was carelessness, no one can say.

The real basis of Will's humor lies in his expression of his ideas. Both the form and content of his jokes contribute to his humor, and it is difficult to say which of these elements is more important. Will himself liked to think that exaggeration was the foundation of his humor; but exaggeration is too loose a term to apply to all of his comedy since various degrees of exaggeration produce different reactions. For humorous purposes, it is usually the *too* much, not the much, that is funny. Hence effective exaggeration is based upon the incongruity between what the reader expects and what the humorist provides in an extension of the truth; the incongruity between what the reader thinks as the norm or average as against the humorist's interpretation makes for laughter.

Will's technique was to take the truth and extend it just beyond the realm of possibility, usually not far enough to produce burlesque, but to such an extent that his readers recognized the absurdity. His remarks on the London Naval Conference of 1930 demonstrated this method. As a result of the treaty, he wrote, ''Well, we got the treaty signed for the limitation of naval vessels. You hold a conference and decide to sink some vessals that would sink themselves if the conference was postponed for another week. England is to sink three battleships that competed against the Spanish Armada. Japan is raising two that the Russians sunk and will resink them for the treaty and the weeklies. We are building two to sink.''

The terms of the treaty announced are true, but the methods of carrying it out are exaggerated beyond the bounds of reason. Had the humorist said that England and Japan were sinking ships of World War I, the statement might be true but not funny. The humor lies in the incongruity between the truth and Will's interpretation of it which is so illogical and inappropriate that it obviously cannot be taken seriously. The incongruity is further heightened by the fact that the humorist pictures England and Japan as reaching into the past to comply with the agreement, which contrasts with the United States which will reach into the future. The idea that the United States will build two ships to sink is just enough of a distortion of the truth to throw the reader off balance and give him the momentary conviction that America has been bested in diplomacy again, which is probably what Will wanted his reader to think. Although the exaggeration of the American role is unpleasant, it is not painful because it is not true; thus it becomes a joke, and the humorist's reputation as a crackerbox philosopher who sees through diplomatic maneuvers is enhanced.

Often Will's remarks contain both perceptual and conceptual qualities which are homogeneous in comic feeling; the perceptual quality acts as a stimulant to the imagination, the creation of an image that looks funny, while the conceptual quality plays a trick upon the mind, a thought process that provokes laughter. Together these qualities provide a broad base for humor—as is evidenced by Mark Twain's book, *Huckleberry Finn*. Most readers find great delight in the visual picture of Huck and Jim, the runaway slave, floating down the river on a raft, as well as much humor in the conversations between the two. Will often used the same technique. When the American diplomats arrived in London for the naval conference, he wrote: ''The American delegation arrived this afternoon and went into conference at once at the American Bar and sank a fleet of schooners without warning.''

The reader's first reaction is to the perceptual quality of the quip: the picture of sober American diplomats coming to London for a disarmament conference, and immediately going to a bar distorts the importance of their mission. The incongruous picture of dignified diplomats with top hats and frock coats standing around a bar, not usually associated with dignity, is laughter-provoking. But then Will leads his readers on, until their minds abruptly realize that ''schooner'' is an ambiguous term which may refer to either a naval vessel or a glass of beer; and the obvious meaning is no longer so obvious. Al-

though the humorist has pretended to be heading in a certain direction, he has actually arrived somewhere else; the mind is momentarily tricked; and the consequence is a joke which is rich in flavor.

Although Will's frequent exaggerations and incongruities are genuinely funny, they never reach the colossal proportions of the ''tall tales'' of the Western humorists; for his objective was to provoke a quiet chuckle rather than boisterous laughter. (pp. 100-02)

Much of Will's humor is based upon the element of surprise, as when he inserts a ''shocker'' in the midst of apparently innocuous remarks. During the depression, he wrote: ''Now everybody has got a scheme to relieve unemployment, but there is just one way to do it and thats for everybody to go to work. 'Where?' Why right where you are, look around and you see lots of things to do, weeds to be cut, fences to be fixed, lawns to be mowed, filling stations to be robbed, gangsters to be catered to. . . . Course a man won't get paid for it but he won't get paid for not doing it either.'' The reader, who is reading and complacently agreeing with the humorist, suddenly comes to ''filling stations to be robbed, gangsters to be catered to.'' The incongruous relationship between the lawful and unlawful methods of work causes a momentary shock before the reader realizes that a practical joke has been played upon his mind, quickly and spontaneously. . . .

Because Will Rogers was so intimately connected with the political scene, he not infrequently used his humor, as did Mr. Dooley, to point to some deficiency in the political or social situation. In fact, political satire in America during the 1920's and 1930's was virtually the monopoly of Will Rogers. This form of humor has always been the weapon of the common man; and, although the cowboy humorist never brandished it as heavily as Finley Peter Dunne, he used it effectively in his attacks upon issues important to him. However, since Rogers had the role of satirist thrust upon him, his comments are only rarely as penetrating as Mr. Dooley's. He was at his best when he felt strongly about some action. On the question of Philippine independence, he wrote: ''You refuse to give the Philippines their independence. I am with you. Why should the Philippines have more than we do?''

There is no question about Will's real feeling about Philippine independence. What he is doing is simply tearing away the veil of American smugness and self-satisfaction which had developed through paying lip service to the idea of freedom while denying it to the Filipinos for political and economic reasons. (p. 105)

Another characteristic of Will's humor was his use of the ''punch line'' or ''snapper'' at the end of his columns. Almost invariably the final sentence summarizes the essence of his thought and expresses it in a thought-provoking manner. . . .

The ''punch line''not only serves to summarize the idea but is couched in such terms as to make it easy to remember. Writing about the amount of income tax paid by the wealthy families of America Will said, ''Don't feel discouraged if a lot of our well known men were not as wealthy according to their Tax as you thought they ought to be. They are just as rich as you thought. This publication of amounts had nothing to do with their wealth. It was only a test of their honesty, and gives you practically no idea of their wealth at all.'' (p. 107)

In the development of his humorous style, Will Rogers used many of the verbal devices made popular by American humorists in the nineteenth century; these include cacography, puns, and comic metaphors. Although cacography does not seem hilariously funny to the reader of today, Will's generation still found humor in the device so successfuly exploited by Artemus War, Josh Billings, and Abe Martin. (pp. 107-08)

Cacography in Will was never an art. In fact it is difficult, as has been observed, to tell where he deliberately misspelled either to maintain a pretense of ignorance or to be humorous; where he misspelled through carelessness or ignorance with no humor intended. Yet he recognized the value of word distortion in producing a comic effect, and there are many examples of what might properly be termed cacography in his work. . . .

Some of these distortions are more than simple misspellings. A few are obvious puns as in "poet lariat," "bee," and "doe." In some of the words, the peculiar spelling creates a meaning which is incongruous to the original meaning; the spelling of "passafist," for pacifist, for example, carries a negative impression of the real word. And "frater*noty*" suggests that fraternities are "not frater" or not brothers.

Sometimes Will's spelling seems to indicate that he is trying to record the idiom of the Southwest in his writing; thus many of his apparently misspelled words are not words at all but merley his attempt to reproduce the sound of oral English. The humorist normally uses "er" and "a" to represent the slurring together of two words: "Kinder" (kind of), "orter" (ought to), "sorter" (sort of), "woulda" (would have), and "coulda" (could have). (p. 108)

Among the lighter veins of humor, Will had a fondness for puns. Although he was not a punster in the extreme sense, he enjoyed playing with words when the opportunity presented itself. Most of his word play resulted in rather obvious puns where the shift of meaning seems frivolous rather than witty. For example, he once gave a radio speech in imitation of Calvin Coolidge: "I am proud to report that the condition of the country as a whole is prosperous. I dont mean that the whole country is prosperous, but that as a hole it is prosperous. That is, it is prosperous for a hole. There is not a whole lot of doubt about that." The length of the expression served as assurance that none of his listeners would miss the obvious shift in the word "whole." There is no real meaning involved in the change from "whole" (in general) to "whole" (total) thence to "hole" (excavation); the ambiguous nature of the word as it is pronounced, whether as an adjective or as a noun, whether abstract or concrete, is the basis for the pun.

Some of his puns, however, are packed with meaning. Writing of the relationship between the United States and Mexico, he said that "The difference in our exchange of people with Mexico is; they send workmen here to work, while we send Americans there to 'work' Mexico." (p. 109)

Will was also partial to the comic metaphor or simile. Reared in the Southwest, he had a habit of expressing himself in pungent figures of speech which reflected his background. His cowboy heritage combined with his interest in politics to create some incongruous metaphors which were both colorful and humorous. In speaking of a horseshoe tournament in Florida, he wrote, "The Champion Mule Slipper Slingers of the world are at St. Petersburg . . . They can take a pair of second hand Horses low quarters and hang'em on a peg more times than a dry Congressman can reach for his hip pocket." (p. 110)

The pattern of Will's technique, both in form and expression, reflected his personal philosophy of humor. Early in his career

as a vaudeville comedian, the humorist developed a formula for his jokes from which he seldom deviated. After he became successful, he was asked many times about his views on humor; and he always gave the same answer: he tried to make his jokes on up-to-date subjects; he preferred to keep his quips short; and he liked to base his remarks on some element of the truth.

For the topical humor which Will wrote, his concept of the importance of timeliness seems essential. Most humorists recognize that there are no new jokes, only old ones recast into new surroundings; consequently, Rogers seems to have learned early that old humorous material could be made effective by relating it to current topics of public interest. When he said over and over that his humor always related to the "now," he did not mean, however, that his comedy *depended* on timeliness for its effect since the form of his material is often funny in itself; but, because most of his humor was related to topical events which *at the time* were of great public interest, the impact of his jokes was reinforced. (pp. 110-11)

In the tradition of Franklin, Billings, and other nineteenth-century humorists, Will practiced terseness as an element of his humor. Few of his jokes ran over five or six lines, and his weekly column was a series of short jokes loosely connected together. The humorist once said, "Being brief somehow gives the impression of intelligence, and folks do admire intelligence. Brevity and clarity show that you have done some thinking, and that you know what you are talking about." Thus he liked to create sharp, terse phrases which could be easily remembered and which contained a great deal of common sense. . . .

The fundamental quality, however, of Will's humor—and the one he thought most important—was truth. He liked to think that all of his jokes were rooted deep in the subsoil of reality. Explaining his technique, he said, "I use only one set method in my little gags, and exaggerate it, but what you say must be based upon the truth." (p. 111)

When Will spoke of his jokes as being based on the truth, he did not mean factual truth but truth as he thought of it. Much of his reputation as a crackerbox philosopher rested on the fact that a majority of his readers usually agreed with him; they felt that most of what he said was true and more sensible than other pronouncements on the same subject.

By and large, the humor of Will Rogers reflected the same techniques employed by the old-time American humorists. As both a lecturer and a writer, he used the same expressions, the same devices, and the same manners as his predecessors. He used them so successfully that not a few of his readers thought of him as the greatest humorist the country had produced, for he embodied to many Americans a type of crackerbox philosopher which seemed more representative of the country than any humorist before him. (p. 112)

E. Paul Alworth, in his Will Rogers *(copyright © 1974 by Twayne Publishers, Inc.; reprinted with the permission of Twayne Publishers, a Division of G. K. Hall & Co., Boston), Twayne, 1974, 140 p.*

JOSEPH A. STOUT, JR. and PETER C. ROLLINS (essay date 1975)

The Cowboy Philosopher on the Peace Conference exhibited Will Rogers' earliest manner of comic delivery. Nevertheless, the book demonstrated that Rogers could say things clearly and humorously. It might well be also that Rogers did not write this book in the traditional sense; rather the work could have been assembled from notes Rogers sent to the publisher.

In 1915, Will Rogers was assigned to the Midnight Frolic portion of Ziegfeld's Follies. Because the audience included wealthy New Yorkers and visiting dignitaries, it provided a special challenge to a humorist, for many of those who attended could afford to return night after night. As a result, Rogers was forced to change his material every evening. One way of changing—suggested by his wife Betty—was to build gags around contemporary events. As the humorist stated in the introductory note to this book, he was always received well by men of real power: "you can always joke about a big Man that is really big." After Rogers became more adept at the satirical style, he applied his verbal lasso to bigger game. Instead of simply jesting at patrons who appeared at the Follies, he applied the same sort of familiar criticism to figures of national importance. This book demonstrated continuous evidence of the new, bolder style. For example, Rogers asserted that the President talked to him about traveling to Versailles with the Peace Commission: "I still wanted to go along, but he said: 'Wait till some other trip and I will take you'." Financier Bernard Baruch was just plain "Barney." Rogers stated that Josephus Daniels was allowed to travel to Europe, but that he would only behave himself "in a Crowd." And Secretary of War Newton Baker was described as returning to France because "Old Newt kinder likes Paris."

For Rogers' audience, there was a twofold appeal of this verbal assertion of familiarity. It indicated that Rogers knew these powerful figures and that he could discern their motives. Moreover, the fact that he spoke of them by nickname rather than their official titles reduced the sense of distance between Rogers' audience and these great men.

The humor of *The Cowboy Philosopher on the Peace Conference* was related to more than the failings of Woodrow Wilson's gallant peace efforts. On the most superficial level, Rogers' humor played upon the simple human comedy of such a polyglot gathering. These observations were concocted to delight rather than instruct. There was the familiar Rogers device of developing a parallel between politicians and show business celebrities. Speaking of Wilson's triumphal tour of Italy, Rogers explained that the President was well greeted not because he symbolized Europe's intense nationalistic aspirations, but simply because "He had a letter of recommendation from Caruso." Then there were the human problems entailed in the confrontation of vastly different cultures: "Let's hope the Turkish Delegation don't bring all their WIVES or we never will get PEACE." Finally, Rogers underscored how difficult it was for the average American to keep track of all of these complex European developments: "Now the Pres says we are going to recognize the CZECHO SLOVAKS. We may recognize them but we will never pronounce them."

But there was a dark side of Will Rogers' observations, one which emphasized that human viciousness rather than Wilsonian idealism was triumphing at the diplomatic tables. Rogers was especially caustic about the Japanese: "The Japanese have offered to protect Siberia if they have to stay there forever." Rogers was disappointed that the recognition of nationalism was not leading to greater harmony, but more conflict: "The Czechoslovaks have gotten their freedom, I see where they are at war." In what may have been the climax of this expression, Rogers summarized his sense of the tragic absurdity of the entire meeting: "And they call THAT A PEACE CONFER-

ENCE." Here he emphasized the unwillingness of mankind's official leaders to live up to their promises. (pp. xviii-xx)

Rogers believed that what really lay behind the facade of the "peace conference" was a rapacity which could be satisfied by neither well-meaning declarations nor presidential charisma. From Rogers' common sense point of view, Wilson's verbal fog invited more Machiavellian members of the Big Four to devour Europe. In these dark moments, Rogers revealed that he placed little faith in American idealism: "They agreed on one of the Fourteen Points that was that America went in for nothing and expects nothing. They are all unanimous WE GET IT." Rogers recognized that Wilson was surrendering on so many points because he hoped that a League of Nations somehow would transform the international jungle into a law-abiding community of nations, but the Oklahoman questioned constructing a world of peace on the foundations of reprisals and reparations.

Rogers in this book demonstrated a special ability to translate complex, impersonal problems into comprehensible metaphors. This translation clarified problems, and thereby postured the mind of his audience toward constructive thought. In a lighter vein, Rogers noted that even the announcement of an armistice could have comic, human results: "Of course, we got the word a couple of days before it was really signed. Making everybody have TWO DRUNKS where one would have done just as well." (p. xxi)

At more serious moments, Rogers attempted to penetrate the official rhetoric of world leaders to the timeless human motives at work. Late in this book, he swept all of the 800,000 words of the Versailles Treaty and all of Wilson's Fourteen Points aside in favor of a metaphor straight out of rural American experience. He stated simply that the Allies "could have settled the whole thing in one sentence. 'If you BIRDS START ANYTHING AGAIN WE WILL GIVE YOU THE OTHER BARREL.'" Speaking in equally familiar terms to the readers, Rogers translated the fundamental tragedy of Versailles. President Wilson may have hoped for a new Europe, but the treaty was a disaster for anyone capable of making a realistic assessment of the political future of the continent. In Rogers' unequivicable terms, "I thought the Armistice terms read like a second Mortgage. But this reads like a FORCLOSURE." While students of international politics could reasonably complain that Rogers oversimplified the complex issues, it is clear that the translations provided by his journalism helped Americans to confront their problems in human terms. Humor, of course, was his primary goal. But Rogers' journalism made pressing current issues clearly identifiable and manageable for his audience.

Finally, *The Cowboy Philosopher on the Peace Conference* not only marked a special moment in Will Rogers' career—his movement from stage comic to author—but the book revealed some of the basic ingredients of his humor: Rogers' humor helped close the gap between Americans and their leaders; Rogers' humor could entertain, but it served equally well to indict human selfishness; Rogers' employment of metaphors from everyday life brought abstract problems to the level of average comprehension. For these reasons, the audience for Will Rogers' journalism grew as his output increased. (pp. xxii-xxiii)

Joseph A. Stout, Jr. and Peter C. Rollins, in their introduction to The Cowboy Philosopher on the Peace Conference *by Will Rogers, edited by Joseph A. Stout, Jr. and Peter C. Rollins (© 1975 Oklahoma State*

University Press), Oklahoma State University Press, 1975, pp. xv-xxiii.

WILL ROGERS, JR.   (essay date 1979)

From 1926 to his death in 1935, Will Rogers wrote a daily column. Only a few paragraphs long, it was usually printed in a box with the title **"Will Rogers Says."** Appearing on the front page of over four hundred newspapers, it was easily the most read column of its day.

I thought, as most people thought (and probably Dad did, too), that its appeal was its timeliness. People would read the headline first, and what Will Rogers said about the headline, immediately thereafter. It was the instant insight, the instant gag that, I felt, gave the column its popularity and political power. . . .

It was my memory that while many of Will Rogers's remarks were lasting, most of them simply referred to long lost happenings. . . .

I was wrong. In fact I am surprised to see how relevant to current events are so many of the comments in [*The Best of Will Rogers*]. This, it seems to me, is because so many of the things we think of as referring to today's news are actually a human condition. Party politics, investigations, political pomposities, all have a way of repeating themselves. (p. xi)

In his lifetime the whole country knew who Will Rogers was and what he was. They respected him and his judgment. So read, not just for the gags, but for the kindly, tolerant, understanding, constructive attitude behind them. For that was the real Will Rogers. (p. xii)

> *Will Rogers, Jr., in his foreword to* The Best of Will Rogers *by Will Rogers, edited by Bryan B. Sterling (© 1979 by Bryan Sterling; used by permission of Crown Publishers, Inc.), Crown, 1979, pp. xi-xii.*

ADDITIONAL BIBLIOGRAPHY

Brown, William R. *Imagemaker: Will Rogers and the American Dream.* Columbia: University of Missouri Press, 1970, 304 p.
> Studies Rogers's public image and assesses his impact on the American conscience.

Cadenhead, Ivie E., Jr. "Will Rogers: Forgotten Man." *Midcontinent American Studies Journal* 4, No. 2 (Fall 1963): 49-57.
> Synthesis of criticism directed at Rogers and his influence on public opinion, focusing on his "antidemocratic" tendencies and his sometimes misinformed political statements.

Day, Donald. *Will Rogers: A Biography.* New York: David McKay Co., 1962, 370 p.
> Considered the definitive biography.

Karsner, David. "Will Rogers." In his *Sixteen Authors to One: Intimate Sketches of Leading American Story Tellers,* pp. 281-90. New York: Lewis Copeland Co., 1928.
> Overview of Rogers's career, with brief critical commentary on his writings.

Ketchum, Richard M. *Will Rogers: His Life and Times.* New York: American Heritage Publishing Co., 1973, 415 p.
> Well-illustrated, comprehensive biography.

Payne, William Howard, and Lyons, Jake G., eds. *Folks Say of Will Rogers: A Memorial Anecdotage.* New York: G. P. Putnam's Sons Publishers, 1936, 224 p.
> Collection of reminiscences by friends, family, and famous associates, including Cecil B. DeMille and Franklin Delano Roosevelt.

Rollins, Peter C. "Will Rogers and the Relevance of Nostalgia: 'Steamboat 'Round the Bend','" In *American History/American Film: Interpreting the Hollywood Image,* edited by John E. O'Conner and Martin A. Jackson, pp. 77-96. New York: Frederick Ungar Publishing Co., 1979.
> Discusses Rogers's "film persona," with special emphasis on his last role as Doc Pearly in "Steamboat 'Round the Bend."

Edgar (Evertson) Saltus

1855-1921

American novelist, essayist, short story writer, poet, biographer, historian, critic, and dramatist.

An innovative decadent in American literature, Saltus opposed with his ornamental prose style and intense pessimism the vapid sentimentality of the late nineteenth century. For the most part his eroticism, sensationalism, atheism, and rebellion against convention have hindered any enduring regard for his work outside a cult following of readers and critics. Criticism of Saltus's work varies dramatically, though a general consensus ranks *Imperial Purple,* nine essays on historic figures of the Roman empire, as his best work. Also highly acclaimed in their time were *The Truth about Tristrem Varick,* a novel whose protagonist seeks the ideal only to find himself in the electric chair, and *The Anatomy of Negation,* a history of antitheism. Historical chronicles with sophisticated subjects, such as apocryphal Bible history, eroticism, and religions, represent a significant part of Saltus's diverse work.

Saltus was twenty when he entered Yale, which he attended for only a year, afterward seeking education abroad, mostly in Heidelberg, Munich, and Paris. Granted a degree in law from Columbia in 1880, he chose not to practice, commencing instead a high society life in New York City. In 1883 Saltus married Helen Sturges Read, and in the same year he began his literary career with a study of Balzac. Saltus and his wife separated in 1893, and in the novel *Madam Sapphira,* a study of feminine unchastity, he disguises an attempt to justify the ensuing divorce. He subsequently married and then also divorced Elsie Walsh Smith. His third wife, Marie Giles, introduced him to theosophy, and themes derived from this occult philosophy may be found in his later works.

The companion volumes *The Philosophy of Disenchantment* and *The Anatomy of Negation* represent their author's pessimistic philosophy: the former is a popularized interpretation of Schopenhauer and the latter examines the relationship between spiritual negation and human value. They gained repute as highly readable manifestos of nihilism and the decadent sensibility.

Mr. Incoul's Misadventure, Saltus's first novel, exposes personal characteristics of the author, and reveals human malice as the *raison d'être* of pessimism. Saltus's next novel, *The Truth about Tristrem Varick,* concerns Varick's pursuit of the ideal and also his pursuit of Viola Raritan. Benjamin De Casseres considered it the "greatest novel to ever come from an American pen." *The Pace That Kills* introduces the character Alphabet Jones, a novelist who treks through society seeking ideas for his craft, and who serves as a mouthpiece for Saltus. The essays in *Imperial Purple* reveal the glory of Rome as lived by the powerful and wealthy—and by their victims. Although this is Saltus's masterpiece, its lurid subject is often considered offensive.

The Lords of the Ghostland is in the same vein as *The Anatomy of Negation,* a history of religions. Carl Van Vechten wrote that it "contains more absorbing information than any other volume on a similar subject." It is also critiqued as unequi-

From Dictionary of American Portraits, Dover Publications, Inc., 1967

vocal evidence that Saltus's literary efforts were sabotaged by a passionate love for his own words.

Commentators explain Saltus's pessimism as a reaction to the spiritual vacuum that remained after the optimistic tenets of the nineteenth century failed. In later works, such as *The Lords of the Ghostland,* Saltus seeks an answer in the doctrines of reincarnation and the transmigration of souls. However, as Claire Sprague points out, he never fixed on a stable philosophical viewpoint. Eric McKitrick states that Saltus's tragedy was "a gnawing fear of involvement, a terrible unwillingness to be spiritually, morally, or intellectually engaged, even in the simplest way." There have also been frequent critical observations of sadism in his work as he seems to savor death. Some critics contend that credit is due Saltus for seeing horror at a time when optimism reigned, while others claim that by adopting theosophy he merely lost his nerve. Overall, Saltus maintains a minor importance for his earlier challenge to an overly sentimental, stale society and the genteel literature it produced.

PRINCIPAL WORKS

Balzac (biography) 1884
The Philosophy of Disenchantment (essays) 1885

The Anatomy of Negation (essays) 1886
Mr. Incoul's Misadventure (novel) 1887
The Truth about Tristrem Varick (novel) 1888
The Pace That Kills (novel) 1889
A Transaction in Hearts (novel) 1889
A Transient Guest, and Other Episodes (short stories)
   1889
Love and Lore (essays) 1890
Mary Magdalen (novel) 1891
Imperial Purple (essays) 1892
Madam Sapphira (novel) 1893
Enthralled (novel) 1894
Purple and Fine Women (short stories) 1903
The Pomps of Satan (essays) 1904
The Perfume of Eros (novel) 1905
Historia Amoris (essay) 1906
Vanity Square (novel) 1906
The Lords of the Ghostland (history) 1907
Daughters of the Rich (novel) 1909
The Monster (novel) 1912
The Paliser Case (novel) 1919
The Imperial Orgy (history) 1920
The Ghost Girl (novel) 1922
The Uplands of Dream (essays and poetry) 1925
Poppies and Mandragora [with Marie Saltus] (poetry)
   1926

THE LITERARY WORLD (essay date 1887)

Mr. Saltus, who has heretofore distinguished himself as an amateur pessimist in two little books on *The Philosophy of Disenchantment* and *The Anatomy of Negation,* has lately made a theoretical application of his ideas to life by writing a novel wherein pessimism runs riot. *Mr. Incoul's Misadventure,* the production in question, is not an agreeable novel to read, and it leaves a bad taste in the mouth. Mr. Saltus, however, has bright ideas; he has a fair command of satire; he has a style of his own, and this style, while not free from affectations, is brilliant, subtle, abounding in color. Moreover, he can describe a landscape, a view in an old Spanish city, a scene in a gambling-den, a bull-fight, a love-meeting, a murder, and a suicide, with a great deal of spirit, a well-chosen variety of epithet, and a certain amount of refinement, the refinement being of that theatrical sort which depicts the unspeakable by calling attention to the fact that it is left unsaid.

When it comes to the portrayal of character, Mr. Saltus shows himself at once to be hopelessly wanting in creative power. The best thing we can say of the three leading personages in his story is that they are frankly and utterly impossible. The whole affair is like a performance of melodrama. The atmosphere is feverish and enervating; the actors come and go, and their epigrams and soliloquies afford passing entertainment; red and green lights are burned at intervals, and the consequent effects do not fail to impress the audience; finally, when one is a little fatigued with all this display of scenic art, the curtain rises on the last act, revealing the weak-brained hero of the performance in the course of delivering an impassioned address on the emptiness of existence, the malignity of fate, the cherished solitude of annihilation. To this sublime utterance he is inspired by the fact that he has been foiled in his attempt to carry on an intrigue with a married woman and has been pub-

licly disgraced by the man he has wronged. When the address is concluded, the hero gazes into a mirror and finds that the once black locks upon his temple have turned white through the intensity of his emotion. He seizes a hypodermic syringe, injects a dose of morphia into his arm, and expires to slow music, in an ecstasy of gorgeous visions. The curtain falls, and we come out into the fresh air of heaven and look once more upon the fadeless stars. Then the absurdity of the affair becomes fully evident, and we realize that the mock heroics and pessimistic fustian of the stage have no place in earnest, sincere, every-day life. They may, perhaps, afford passing entertainment in moments of *ennui,* but they must not be taken too seriously. Pessimism, to the majority of humanity, is, and will always remain, theatrical, and no amount of brilliant rhetoric can make it anything else.

> *"Mr. Incoul's Misadventure: A Romance of Pessimism," in* The Literary World, *Vol. XVIII, No. 21, October 15, 1887, p. 347.*

BEVERLEY E. WARNER (essay date 1888)

Pessimism, which may fairly be called the science of despair, has of late come into prominent notice again through the fashionable utterances of Mr. Edgar Saltus, the author of the *Anatomy of Negation,* the *Philosophy of Disenchantment,* and a novel or two of doubtful tendency. It is no new thing of course. Solomon was touched with it. The flower of the best philosophic Roman thought evolved its last analysis, when suicide was recommended as the only escape from a world of evil. Mr. Saltus is a devout disciple—although he would probably wearily deny the adjective as involving too much exertion—of [Arthur] Schopenhauer and [Eduard von] Hartmann who are the modern exponents of scientific pessimism, and his book, the *Philosophy of Disenchantment,* is a sort of digest of their respective philosophies—clarified of much of the original mystic verbiage, and strained into a moderate sized volume for the American market. (p. 432)

Fortunately for an intelligent discussion, Mr. Saltus has defined his science in unmistakable terms. We are not left to draw inferences, as to what he means by his hobby. He is bolder than his disciples, and braves discussion in this definition. "Broadly stated," he says, "scientific pessimism in its most advanced form, rests on a denial that happiness in any form ever has been or ever will be obtained, either by the individual as a unit or by the world as a whole." And this as the author goes on to state because life is not a 'pleasant gift,' but a "duty which must be performed by sheer force of labor."

Such a broad statement involves its upholder in a web of inconsistencies of course. But these are gaily discounted by Mr. Saltus either by passing them over entirely, or by giving up the whole question in an admission which never for a moment shakes his belief or stays his dogmatic conclusions. The essential Atheism of the pessimistic philosophy is contained in these words, which, according to Mr. Saltus, is the ground work of Schopenhauer's argument. "The question as to what the world is has been considered, and the answer conveyed, that Will, the essence of all things, is a blind, unconscious, force, which after irrupting in inorganic life, and passing therefrom through the vegetable and animal kingdoms, reaches its culmination in man, and that the only relief from its oppressive yoke, is found in art and in impersonal contemplation."

In view of this Mr. Saltus concludes—always as the channel of Schopenhauer's thought—that "The best use life can be put to is to pass it in a sort of dilletante quietism.'' He has the grace to make a sort of apology to the human race, that only a very few possess the ''refinement of sense and burnish of intellect'' necessary to this enviable state.

Happiness being denied, on the ground that it involves duty and labor, the pessimist finds himself in a difficulty as to how he is to endure this wretched planetary existence for any length of time. ''Where, then, it may be asked,'' he continues, ''for this malady of the refined, are the borderlands of happiness to be found? From the standpoint of this teacher (Schopenhauer) the answer is that they are discoverable simply and solely, in an unobtrusive culture of self; in a withdrawal from every aggressive influence and above all in a supreme indifference. (pp. 432-33)

But at this brutal conclusion even Mr. Saltus pauses, and although not in the context hedges upon its spirit. ''It may be remembered,'' says he of his Master, ''that beyond the surface of things here examined, he pointed in another essay to the influence of morality on general happiness, and recommended the practice of charity, forbearance, and good will to all men, as one of the first conditions of mental content.''

Here of course, visible to all eyes save those of a blind disciple, is a glaring and palpable contradiction of the substance of pessimistic teaching as quoted by Mr. Saltus himself. For ''the practice of charity, forbearance, and good will to all men,'' is not indulged in without effort, struggle, and sacrifice, which will keep even the burnished intellect of a scientific pessimist from the enjoyment of ''dilletante quietism.'' (pp. 433-34)

In violence of all philosophic calmness, and unprejudiced observations, the pessimist spends all his exertions upon the confessed evils of mankind, and blemishes of the world. Nobody disputes that both exist. No one claims perfection. Very high authority uttered the sentence, ''in the world ye shall have tribulation.'' We grant it. But while admitting, we protest, not as a theory, but as an experience, that life is a good, virtue is a practice, happiness is a fact. But the scientific pessimist turns his eyes away from the light, and roams through the dark recesses. He uncovers the festering sores, and points out the diseased spots. He dwells upon dishonor and weakness, failure and falsehood. A beam of sunlight falling across his path is not a messenger of life, it is a thing in which he discovers specks floating, and dust arising. And why? Not to alleviate misery, but to glory in it—to teach men to loath themselves and to despise their neighbors. To analyze horrors, to elevate the self-disgust of an hour, or a generation, into a science, and to prove that despair and hopelessness are the true solution of the problem of life. And this he persists in for some inscrutable reason, in spite of the protest of facts, which he will not consider. What he has written, he has written. In spite even of the intuition that he is building a house of cards, for as Mr. Saltus says, with sublime infallibility, ''*in spite of vagaries* [an admission which seems to me significant of conscious defeat], pessimism as expounded by Schopenhauer and Hartmann possesses a real and enduring value, which is difficult to take away.''

Surely, if Mr. Saltus is a true prophet, God the Father made a mistake in creating the world, God the Son failed in redeeming it, and God the Holy Ghost is a will-o'-the-wisp, instead of a spirit guiding into all truth. This is pessimism in its last analysis. Not a pretty sentiment for the pleasure of those who find joy in nursing a secret grief, but the negation of God, and a denial that this is God's world. (pp. 439-40)

Beverley E. Warner, ''Practical Pessimism,'' in New Englander and Yale Review, *No. CCXIX, June, 1888, pp. 432-42.*

G. F. MONKSHOOD and GEORGE GAMBLE   (essay date 1903)

[In *Mary Magdalen*] Edgar Saltus has combined the idea of the splendid casuist with two ideas of his own: that Judas Iscariot was in love with Mary Magdalen; and that out of the combination could be formed, with care, an original chronicle—half historical, half scriptural, and wholly the work of an articulate scholar. (p. viii)

Mary Magdalen is not a work devised for the use and abuse of the circulating library—is not a work intended for the railway-train, the country-house, the holiday-wild seashore. It has nothing to do with pastime; it is merely a piece of literature. In even the quiet study, however, a few may think it deplorable; but only a religious fanatic could term the work obnoxious. To some it may seem unpleasant; to others it may appear unnecessary. But there are persons who fully consider that a man has a right to reconstruct any particular scriptual story—just as a man has a right to explore its magic and mystery, to expound what he thinks its ''manifold meanings,'' in his own selected style and place. Many a man in a pulpit, many a theologian in print, has put a construction on portions of the Bible at which a novelist (unless his name were Renan or Farrar) would turn green with envy. Although invention is not confined to those whose calling is fiction, nevertheless the fact remains that any attempt to re-compose even a portion most minute of that exalted collection of compilations known to us as the New Testament, can be justified by one thing only—an artistic success. This the author of *Mary Magdalen* has achieved to the full. He has treated his subject with power, with poetry, and with tragical dignity. He frequently touches the sublime; he never approaches the ridiculous. There is no hysteria; there is no irreverence. The book may not be a thing of truth; it is certainly a thing of beauty. The publisher calls it a novel; the author names it a chronicle. And by the careful employment of a literary finesse common to the Latins but rare with the Anglo-Saxons, he has woven a spell of a long-dead time whose echoes will live for ever—he has upconjured a charm that none but a wizard of words could seek to attain or hope to achieve. (pp. ix-x)

[Edgar Saltus's] plots are brief; so are his books. Not one of the novels of Edgar Saltus runs to fifty thousand words; they average fewer than forty thousand: that is to say, not quite one-fifth of the number that go to erect an *Eternal City* or to sob the *Sorrows of Satan*. This hardly makes for his popularity. The brain of the ordinary reader is like to the stomach of a horse: both can bear with small nutrition provided the bulk is big. However—though Mr Saltus does not believe in piling above, beneath, and about an over-prolonged, off-trailing plot something approaching a million syllables—he yet is a master-builder. He can construct a story with the skill of a Frenchman; and the trail of the American is neither over all, nor even all over a part: in fine, he abstains from allowing his drama to happen off the stage.

He does not adopt the cyclic method—as did the elder Dumas; but he does transport his people from novel to novel—as did Balzac and Thackeray. The principal actor in one book may have only a line in another—or may merely make an appearance; but Tancred Ennever plays the part of *jeune première* in two; and in four or five, "Alphabet" Jones, the novelist, is either chorus or god *and* machine.

Mr Saltus's dialogues are brief but brilliant; and he never calls his characters witty—he makes them so. Often they talk like their author. This makes them talk alike. But because they are mostly drawn from the ranks of the great "four hundred," the similarity of style in their speech does not seem an artistic fault; and if we allow that it be a sin to make his characters talk like himself—well, Edgar Saltus sins in the company of Mr Meredith and the younger Dumas, as well as several others. (pp. xlvii-xlviii)

Edgar Saltus has no "message"—at least to quote Carlyle, he has "no Morison's pill" for us. But he is a man of such diversity that to neglect him any longer were to neglect to the edge of a folly a philosopher and psychologist, a poet and pessimist, an instructor and ironist, a scholar and satirist, a critic, a wit, and a writer. In addition, he is a novelist; and though far, at times, from being a great teller of tales, he is always that very rare thing in our populous world of laborious scribblers—a great writer of English. (p. lxiii)

> *G. F. Monkshood and George Gamble, in their introduction to* Wit & Wisdom from Edgar Saltus *by Edgar Saltus, edited by G. F. Monkshood and George Gamble, Greening & Co., Ltd., 1903, pp. v-lxiii.*

THE NEW YORK TIMES SATURDAY REVIEW OF BOOKS (essay date 1906)

[The] personages of Mr. Saltus's ["**Vanity Square**"] gossip and play bridge, yawn and quote poetry, wear fine clothes and trifle with the great passions.

Among them is presently projected a stranger from far away, a Canadian woman who might be from Mitylene, or medieval Florence. A trained nurse, this woman is, but one of commanding skill, the daughter of a famous bacteriologist admitted for his scientific fame into the peerage of England; a rare creature in the matters of personal charm and comprehension of human nature. One accepts her, in the beginning, as a veritable angel, and then finds himself condemning her, on purely circumstantial evidence, as a demon. Yet, one closes the book in doubt. . . .

[After we have finished the book] we cannot quite decide whether or not Miss Stella Sixsmith is a sinful woman. . . .

Mr. Saltus has attempted no large picture of fashionable New York life in the beginning of the twentieth century. He is not competing with [Edith Wharton's] "The House of Mirth." He deals with individuals and he works, as usual, like a cameo cutter. But he catches some of the superficial spirit of the time, and his story has to do only with people who have millions to spend, and spend them. It is as good a document as any for the reformer seeking a text for a denunciation of the useless rich. Yet he shows that they toil over their passions, their jealousies, their search for pleasure, their games of chance, though they do not spin.

Still one would no more accuse Mr. Saltus of coming to the front with a fresh indictment of New York society than one would accuse him of condemning the admirable and uplifting profession of the trained nurse because his woman that came from Canada, and might have come from Mitylene, is temporarily in the nursing business, to gratify her scientific yearnings, and to be doing something.

Mr. Saltus writes as well as ever—much better in this book, indeed, than in ["**Imperial Purple.**"] . . . Here is nothing overwrought, cryptic, or pretentious. Here is no trace of the cliché. . . . Mr. Saltus forms his own unhackneyed phrases of well-chosen words—always the right word, and one word at a time. . . . [It] would be difficult to find much fault with the writing of "**Vanity Square**," which is a smart and interesting story: no better, ethically, perhaps than the ordinary "society novel" but immeasurably better than most of that kind in its literary graces.

> *"'Vanity Square'," in* The New York Times Saturday Review of Books *(© 1906 by The New York Times Company), June 9, 1906, p. 365.*

ELBERT HUBBARD (essay date 1907)

[The] joy of Saltus lies in the fact that he gives you joy in yourself; you are all the time thinking how there are so precious few readers who have the subtle insight into the heart of things to understand a book by Edgar Saltus. You shake hands with yourself on being hand and glove with a man like Saltus, who is so big and witty and wise and charmingly indifferent to praise or blame.

The joy of reading consists in self-discovery. Any man who can read Saltus is different, peculiar, unique, and belongs to the Elect Few, the Illuminati—and inwardly acknowledges it. Saltus is confidential—a word, a look, raising of the eyebrow, a level stare—you understand because you are you—no one else does. We are all would-be monopolists—we like to know something that no one else knows. Saltus tells it to us. He is the wisest man in the world, at least I'd rather admit it, than to attempt to prove him wrong. He is a linguist, and tells you things in French, German, Arabic, Latin, Greek, Sanskrit. He tells you about the Indra, Agni, Maruts, Mitra, Yama, and Varuna, and dilates on izeds and amshes. He refers you to passages in Hindoostanee, and shows you now how Sargon and Khammurabi are unreliable and unworthy—things you always suspected, but preferred not to say for family reasons. His sentences are short, sharp, severe, yet simple, and cast purple shadows. He is always reverent, always deferential, always gentle, as gentle as [Joseph Ernest] Renan who tells you astounding things and then adds, "But of course I may be in error—all I do is to give my present view."

In [his] book "**The Lords of the Ghostland**," Saltus makes little journeys to the homes of the eight great deities who represent the great religions of the world.

Saltus believes in them all—worships them all—and without argument or animus allows you to discover for yourself that they are all very much alike, all had a common origin, and a common destiny awaits them. From the way Saltus writes of each, you might imagine that he is a priest piously upholding and explaining to you the greatness and goodness of his god. The title of the book is really what gives the clue, otherwise you might read one chapter, say on Ormuzd and think the author was trying to proselyte.

All of these gods dictated books and inscriptions, ordered tables of stone, and had immaculate sons and daughters born in a miraculous way, who performed miracles.

All did the things their creators did or would have liked to do were they able. All reveal the love, hope, ambition, aspiration, the hate and jealousy, the roguery and weakness of their many creators.

The book is superbly wise, divinely witty and yet touchingly pathetic because it deals with the dreams that filled the lives of millions upon millions of human beings, all now turned to dust, their books and temples existing only as the faint echoes of things that were. Their mysteries we fully understand—the Sphinx does not speak simply because she has nothing to say. Things explained cease to be mysteries; and miracles are simply things that never happened, save in the minds of poets. Believed as poetry they are charming, accepted as literal truth they make you something less than a man. (pp. 134-37)

Edgar Saltus is the best writer in America—with a few insignificant exceptions.

This does not mean that he is the greatest man in America. A man may be very great and still not know how to either read in public or write for the press.

Edgar Saltus is to prose what Swinburne is to poetry. He knows literature, political history, art, ancient mythology and that peculiar form of modern mythology called orthodoxy.

Yet as Carlyle said of a certain great man, he has his limitations.

He knows only one kind of a woman; he does not know the women who toil and drudge on the farm, the honest wife of an honest mechanic, the old woman of the simple ways left desolate save for the sustaining faith in a fetich, the children who tread country roads going to school, those children who toil in mills from daylight until dark, consigned to a living, lingering death. That is to say he is academic, bookish, and delves in a day that is dead. He of all men fishes the murex up, but he cannot tell you what porridge ate John Keats, because the economic value of food stuffs is as much out of his line as is their production. He knows Broadway, but he does not know trees, flowers, birds, bees and beetles. He is lost and undone excepting among decollette dames who make him dream of how burning Sappho loved and sang, and the Swan of Leda sailed. (pp. 139-40)

But, again I say, the man can write. He writes so well that he grows enamoured of his own style and is subdued like the dyer's hand; he becomes intoxicated on the lure of lines and the roll of phrases. He is woozy on words—locoed by syntax and prosody. The libation he pours is flavored with euphues. It is all like a cherry in a morning Martini.

I know Addison, Macaulay, Carlyle, Walter Pater, Robert Louis the Beloved, but not one of these wrote as faultlessly and filed down in the estimation of a hair, as does Edgar Saltus who is the Lord of Language, if not the Crown Prince of Ideas. He is a writer's writer, and writers read him not for what he says, but for the way he says it. (p. 141)

> Elbert Hubbard, *"Heart to Heart Talks with Philistines by the Pastor of His Flock,"* in The Philistine *(copyright by Elbert Hubbard, 1907; copyright renewed © 1934 by the Literary Estate of Elbert Hubbard), Vol. 25, No. 5, October 1907, pp. 129-43.*

PERCIVAL POLLARD (essay date 1909)

In the eighties Mr. Saltus was of those who spurred the general American interest in sex stories. His **"Tristrem Varick"** and **"Mr. Incoul"** . . . were, in their day, sensations. They were fused out of examples from the French and out of Mr. Saltus' passion for clever phrases. That passion, later, was to threaten his destruction. After the earlier novels he wrote essays, again novels,—some of them somewhat unpleasantly autobio-

graphic—stories that revived the glories of Rome, or gave of Mary of Magdala as vivid an image as Wilde gave of Salome. He gave us a popular and fascinating version of Schopenhauer. The years, in brief, delivered him of some fiction, of a little stately poetry, and of much prose in essay form, in which latter appeared the seed of what is now nothing less than a sacrifice made for style. (pp. 81-2)

Always addicted to the paradox, to the phrase for phrase's sake, to the sentence that glitters yet is not gold, this author had been gradually letting go the hold he had on logic, upon proportion, and upon the simple enunciation of simple things. By the time he compiled, from the dry and foreign documents in our libraries, his **"Historia Amoris"** and his **"Lords of the Ghostland,"** he was become hopelessly mazed by the clamant meaninglessness of his own too brilliant sentences. For some years past his most disinterested friends must often have asked whither this author's piling of phrase upon phrase, heedless of either sense or nonsense, must eventually tend. If we put ourselves upon Mr. Saltus' own plane; if we search the old and jog the new in an equally mad quest for a phrase; if we borrow the jargon of the advocate and the alienist to fit the case of a prosateur intoxicated with the froth of his own exuberance, we may declare that by the time he wrote **"The Lords of the Ghostland"** Mr. Saltus was a dervish dancing in his prose.

We had to go even farther. Perusal of the book paved the way for verbal vertigo in the reader. One found oneself juggling with syllables that meant nothing, though alliterative, coining phrases that sounded magnificent yet had nothing to do with the case, and propounding the obvious with an impertinent air of discovery.

Just as Mr. Saltus in previous volumes had made palatable various old philosophies and histories, including that of love, so this book, that marked the most tragic point reached by the preciosity of his prose, had vague intention to be a history of the divinities in history and legend. The ancient origins of ancient creeds were marshaled, commented on, and made backgrounds against which Mr. Saltus let off his alliterative and paradoxic fireworks. (pp. 82-3)

If that was what you liked—just a show of rhetorical contortionism—**"The Lords of the Ghostland"** was the book for your money. . . . But if you really wished to know the why and wherefore, if you wanted to pass beyond the portals of the temple, you had to leave Mr. Saltus, still babbling, musically, ceaselessly, enchantingly, but—babbling—at the gate. He stood there, reeling and babbling, the slave of his own syllables.

That book, was the final confession of his defeat by the defects of his virtuosity. What he had once done eloquently and admirably in his **"Philosophy of Disenchantment"** and his **"Anatomy of Negation"** he attempted again; as he had once given us popular and fascinating versions of Schopenhauer and other philosophers, so now he thought to give us an equally successful version of what legend or history have dryly told us of those things that men and gods believed when yet the world was warm in youth. Instead he had given us but sound and fury. . . . (pp. 83-4)

A history of the ideal, the sub-title told us, was what our author had conceived. It was a history of nothing save his own pathologic and phraseologic condition. His chapters on Brahma, Ormuzd, Ammon-Ra, Bel-Marduk, Jehovah, Zeus, Jupiter and The Ne Plus Ultra revealed only the diligence with which Mr. Saltus had searched the libraries, so that out of their most sibilant and trumpeting names he could concoct a medium through which to display his own virtuosity. Not one single chapter in the book could we read and assimilate a definite idea, nor yet the outline of a single spent ideal. (p. 85)

"Somnambulist of history?" Had not Mr. Saltus, in that phrase, with unconscious irony hit off his own method of walking through the paths blazed by other historians? Referring to legends used by Richard Wagner, Mr. Saltus wrote:

> Transformed by ages and by man, yet lifted at last from their secular slumber, the Persian myths achieved there their Occidental apotheosis, and, it may be, on steps of song, mounted to the ideal where Zeevan Akerene muses.

That was a typical sentence. (pp. 85-6)

As a "story of beautiful illusions" Mr. Saltus's protagonists presented the book. It robbed one, instead, of the illusion that Mr. Saltus might still be saved from the fate of being a prestidigitateur of prose. (p. 86)

> Percival Pollard, "Women, Womanists and Manners," in his Their Day in Court (copyright, 1909, The Neale Publishing Company; © 1969 by Johnson Reprint Corporation), Neale Publishing, 1909 (and reprinted by Johnson Reprint Corporation, 1969, pp. 62-87).*

CARL Van VECHTEN   (essay date 1918)

[Edgar Saltus] has written history, fiction, poetry, literary criticism, and philosophy, and to all of these forms, at least in some degree, he has brought sympathy, erudition, an intelligent point of view, and a personal style. He enjoys an imagination and he understands the potent art of arranging facts in kaleidoscopic patterns so that they may attract and not repel the reader. (pp. 89-90)

Saltus's style may be said to possess American characteristics. It is dashing and rapid, as clear as the water in southern seas. The fellow has a penchant for short and nervous sentences which explode like so many firecrackers and remind one of the great national holiday. . . . (p. 97)

His essays, whether they deal with literary criticism, history, religion (almost an obsession with this writer), devil-worship, or cooking, are pervaded by that rare quality—charm. . . . (pp. 97-8)

The Anatomy of Negation is Saltus's masterpiece in his earlier manner, which is as free from flamboyancy as early Gothic. This manual is a history of antitheism from Kapila to Leconte de Lisle and, while Saltus in a brief prefatory notice disavows all responsibility for the opinions of others expressed therein, it can readily be felt that the book represents love's labour, that the author's sympathy lies with the iconoclasts throughout the centuries. . . . Never was any book, so full of erudition and ideas, written by a true sceptic, so easy to read. (pp. 106-07)

Mr. Incoul's Misadventure, Saltus's first novel, is . . . superior to any of his later fiction. It, too, should be triple-starred. In it will be found, fastidiously distilled, the very essence of all the personal qualities of this writer. Mr. Incoul is composed with fine reserve; the fable holds the attention; the characters are unusually well observed, felt, and expressed. A mocking irony grins between the lines and the final cadence includes a murder and a suicide. . . . The pages are permeated with suspense, horror, information, cynicism, and an icy charm, about

evenly distributed, all of which qualities are suggested by the astounding title.

The Truth about Tristrem Varick is composed with the same restraint that informs the style of *Mr. Incoul's Misadventure,* a restraint seldom to be encountered in Saltus's later fictions. The book is a history of the pursuit of the ideal which lands the pursuer in the electric chair. (pp. 107-08)

Eden, the third of Saltus's fictions, marks a decided decline in his powers. (p. 109)

With *The Pace that Kills,* Saltus doffs his old coat and dons a new and gaudier garment. A hard, brilliant glitter informs the surface of this sordid melodrama. . . . (p. 110)

The slender pamphlet entitled *Love and Lore* assembles a series of slight papers, interrupted by slighter sonnets, on subjects which, for the most part, Saltus has treated at greater length and with greater effect elsewhere. (p. 111)

Mary Magdalen, on the whole, is disappointing. . . . Once the plot is under way Saltus seems to lose interest. He lazily quotes dialogue from the Bible, a pitfall George Moore cannily avoided in *The Brook Kerith*. The early chapters suggest *Imperial Purple,* published a year later, on which the author may well have been working at this time. (pp. 112-13)

Imperial Purple marks the high-tide of Edgar Saltus's peculiar and limited genius. (p. 115)

The sheer lyric throb of this book has remained unsurpassed by its author. Indeed, its peculiar sensational swing is rare in all literature. The man writes with invention, with sap, with urge. Our eyes are not delayed by footnotes and references. . . . Blood flows across the pages; gore and booty and lust are the principal themes; yet Beauty struts supreme through the horror. (pp. 115-16)

Madam Sapphira is a vivid study of unchastened womanhood. This novel, as a matter of fact, appears to be Saltus's chivalric version of the circumstances surrounding his first divorce. (p. 117)

Enthralled, a story of international life setting forth the curious circumstances concerning Lord Cloden and Oswald Quain: an insane phantasmagoria of crime, avarice, and murder. For the second time in this author's novels incest plays a rôle. (p. 118)

When Dreams Come True again brings us in touch with Tancred Ennever, the stupid protagonist of *The Transient Guest.* In the meantime he has become an almost intolerable prig. It is probable that Saltus meant more by this fable than he dared let appear. The roar of the waves on the coast of Lesbos is distinctly audible for a time and the solution appears to belong to quite another story. . . . Ennever has turned author. (pp. 118-19)

The first two stories in *Purple and Fine Women* are French in form. Paul Bourget himself is the hero of one of them. In **"The Princess of the Sun"** we are offered a revised version of the Coppelia theme. **"The Dear Departed"** exposes Saltus in a murderous, amorous mood again. In **"The Princess of the Golden Isles"** a new poison is introduced, muscarine. Alchemy furnishes the leitmotif for one tale; the experimenter seeks an alkahest, a human victim for his crucible. We are left in doubt as to whether he chooses his wife, who wears a diamond set in one of her teeth, or a gorilla. Metaphysics and spiritualism rise like dim vapour out of the melodrama of this book. (p. 119)

The Perfume of Eros is frenzied fiction again; amnesia, drunkenness, white slavery, sex, are its mingled themes. Romance and Realism consort lovingly together in these pages. (p. 120)

The Pomps of Satan is replete with grace and charm, a quality more valuable to its possessor than juvenility, the author informs us in a chapter concerning the lost elixir of youth. Neither form nor matter assumes ponderous shape in this volume. Satan's pomps are varied; the author exhibits his whims, his ideas, images the past, forecasts the future, deplores the present. . . . Hardly as evenly inspired as *Imperial Purple, The Pomps of Satan* is more witty. It is also more tired.

In Stella Sixmuth, *Vanity Square* boasts such a vampire as even Theda Bara is seldom called upon to portray. Not until the final chapter, however, do we discover that this suave adventuress has been poisoning a rich man's wife, with an eye on the husband's hand and purse. . . . Little more than an exciting story, this novel contains fewer references to the gods and the caesars than is customary in Saltus. In compensation, he discusses phobias, dual personalities (a girl with six is described), and theories about the life beyond. (pp. 120-22)

It will be recalled that Tancred Ennever was collecting notes for *Historia Amoris* in 1895, which would seem to indicate that Saltus had begun to sift material for it himself at that time. The title is a literal description of the contents. Such a work might have been made purely anecdotal or scientific, but Saltus's purpose, at once more serious and more graceful, has been to show how the love currents flowed through the centuries, to explain what effect period life had on love and what effect love had on period life. . . . Readers of *Love and Lore, The Pomps of Satan, Imperial Purple,* and *The Lords of the Ghostland* will find that much of the material of those books has gone into the making of this History of Love.

In *The Lords of the Ghostland,* a history of the ideal, Saltus returns to the theme of *The Anatomy of Negation.* The newer work is both more cynical and more charming. It is, as the title indicates, a comparative history of religions. . . . Mr. Saltus finds joy in writing about the gods, the joy of a poet, and if his chiefest pleasure is to extol the gods of Greece, that is only what might be expected of a truly pagan spirit. Students of comparative theology might learn much from these pages, but they will learn it unwittingly, for the artist supersedes the teacher. Saltus is never professorial. The scientific spirit never obtrudes; there is no marshalling of dull facts for their own sakes. Nevertheless, I suspect that the book contains more absorbing information than any other volume on a similar subject. (pp. 122-23)

The Monster is fiction, incredible, insane fiction. The beast of the title is incest, in this instance inceste manqué, because it doesn't come off. . . . (p. 124)

It is, you may perceive, as an essayist, a historian, an amateur philosopher that Saltus excels, but his fiction should not be underrated on that account. His novels, indeed, are half essays. Even the worst of them contains charming pages, delightful and unexpected digressions. His series of fables suggests a vast Comédie Inhumaine, but this statement must not be regarded as dispraise: it is an exact description of his morbid, erotic art, often inspiring dread and amazement, but never pity. Saltus was sufficiently inhuman so that he found himself incapable of creating a human character. All his figures are the inventions of an errant fancy; scarcely one of them has the lineaments of a living being, but they are none the less creations of art. (p. 127)

GORHAM B. MUNSON (essay date 1922)

On the title page of the extremely rare Curious Case of H. Hyrtl, Esq. . . . , a weekly dreadful he edited, Edgar Saltus described himself as the author of several attempts in history, philosophy and ornamental literature. In the seldom seen *Love and Lore* . . . he planted this paragraph:

> The pleasure which comes of a novel should be physical. It should put the reader in a state of tension sufficient to cause an evocation of fancies which without that influence would decline to appear. . . . The first duty of a novelist is to irritate the reader. The second duty is to be able to bone the dictionary as a chef bones a bird. The third duty is to have emotions, and to be so prompt in detaining them that the reader shares their effect. But, paramount of all, he should let no work go from him that does not instill some lesson and make men, and women too, the better and the wiser for his prose. If he fail in any one of these duties, then the Exact Representation of the Fugitive Impression is not his to convey.

The first instance names the genre, ornamental literature, to which the novels of Edgar Saltus, including the posthumous *Ghost Girl,* belong. The second states the aesthetic which *The Ghost Girl* most recently exemplifies. The rarity of the books containing these instances suggests the background for his career.

For to secure the majority of Saltus's thirty odd books, one must wage a prolonged and exciting hunt in the dusty twilight of second-hand book shops. And the reason is that Saltus was submerged in the limbo of American literature by a period whose stenogram follows. From the fall of the New England school (roughly 1860) to the rise of the present Young America (roughly 1910) the dominant American literary taste was Anglo-servile and embraced a moralism derived from the pioneer, the puritan, the industrialist and the Victorian, an amalgam now happily named genteelness. Critics of power with any interest in aesthetics were completely lacking. And so one giant, Mark Twain, was wrecked, and two others, Walt Whitman and Henry James, were largely dissociated from an American audience and their influence shunted to Europe.

At its best, this period permitted only the suave selected realism of Howells to function freely. At its worst, it created a cloudy limbo into which it cast its significant talents—Ambrose Bierce, Stephen Crane, Lafcadio Hearn, William Vaughn Moody, Frank Norris, Percival Pollard and many others, so that much of recent criticism has been devoted to their extrication. Naturally, Edgar Saltus, who was greatly affected by French literature and whose philosophy came from Buddhism, Schopenhauer and the more learned branches of occultism, and whose attitude was the dandy's, naturally Saltus too was obscured. It was customary for critics to lament that a man of his ability should have released to any other mark than the wastebasket his "muddy manuscripts."

Actually, his manuscripts glitter. He had a consummate ability to compress whole libraries of yawns into two hundred pages of excitement, as when he wrote his handbook on atheism, *The Anatomy of Negation,* or his little compendium of pessimism, *The Philosophy of Disenchantment,* or his history of the ideal, *The Lords of the Ghostland,* or his history of Rome, *The Imperial Purple*—the last considered by Arthur Symons his masterpiece. His erudition was wide but delightfully accessible; his pen was light, swift and sensuous and turned scores of epigrams that match with those of Wilde, who admired Saltus.

In fiction he baked "ornamental literature." First of all, he irritated. . . . Very quickly, he straps the reader into a rack of suspense—for he wrote "mystery" stories—but it is a suspense adorned with the most luxuriant flora from the dictionary. . . . In telling *The Ghost Girl* he detains surprises, shudders, horrors, tortures that are, if not provocative of deep contemplation, amazingly titillating. Finally, he does "instill a lesson"—and Saltus, of course, spoke as an artist—by energizing his well planned design with a pessimistic fatalism.

His materials were the temperamental choice of a sadist who experienced a furtive delight in viewing the sufferings of man. As far as they allow, he attains intensity. With materials, criticism cannot quarrel: it can only measure their power and estimate the artist's success with them. Saltus chose those that preclude depth but permit intensity, and so could not go beyond a decorative surface. But within the limits imposed by the "Exact Representation of the Fugitive Impression" as sole objective, he was a master.

Ghost stories as a rule pass as quickly as a cheap fiction fortnightly. They lack attitude, style and sophisticated plausibility. *The Ghost Girl* has them. What it purports to be, it admirably is. (pp. 23-4)

> Gorham B. Munson, "Mr. Huneker's 'Pet Author'," in The New Republic (reprinted by permission of The New Republic; © 1922 The New Republic, Inc.), Vol. 33, No. 417, November 29, 1922, pp. 23-4.

ARTHUR SYMONS   (essay date 1923)

[Saltus's] pages exhale a kind of exotic and often abnormal perfume of colors, color of sensations, of heats, of crowded atmospheres. He gives his women baneful and baleful names, such as Stella Sixmouth, Shom Wyvell; these vampires and wicked creatures who ruin men's lives as cruelly as they ruin their own. His men have prodigious nerves, even more than his women; they commit all sorts of crimes, assassinations, poisonings, out of sheer malice and out of over-excited imaginations.

Of that most terrible of tragedies, the tragedy of a soul, he is for the most part utterly unconscious; and the very abracadabra of his art is in a sense—a curious enough and ultra-modern sense—lifted from the Elizabethan dramatists. In them—as in many of his pages—a fine situation must have a murder in it, and some odious character removed by another more stealthy kind of obliteration. But, when he gives one a passing shudder, he leaves nothing behind it; yet in his perverted characters there can be found sensitiveness, hallucinations, obsessions; and some have that lassitude which is more than mere contempt. Some go solemnly on the path of blood, with no returning by a way so thronged with worse than memories. "No need for more

crime," such men have cried, and for such reasons reaped the bitter harvest of tormenting dreams. Some have imagination that stands in the place of virtue; some, as in the case of Lady Macbeth, still keep the sensation of blood on their guilty hands. . . .

[*Mary of Magdala*] is a vain attempt to do what Flaubert had done before Saltus in his *Hérodias,* and what Wilde has done after him in *Salome,* a drama that has a strange not easily defined fascination, which I can not dissociate from [Aubrey] Beardsley's illustrations, in which what is icily perverse in the dialogue (it can not be designated drama) becomes in the ironical designs pictorial, a series of poses. (pp. 263-64)

In one page of Saltus's *Oscar Wilde: An Idler's Impressions* . . . he evokes, with his cynical sense of the immense disproportion of things in this world and the next, the very innermost secret of Wilde. They dine in a restaurant in London and Wilde reads his MS. "Suddenly his eyes lifted, his mouth contracted, a spasm of pain—or was it dread?—had gripped him, a moment only. I had looked away. I looked again. Before me was a fat pauper, florid and over-dressed, who in the voice of an immortal, was reading the fantasies of the damned. In his hand was a manuscript, and we were supping on *Salome.*"

Mr. Incoul's Misfortune seems to have its origin in some strange story of Poe's; for it gives one the sense of a monster, diabolical, inhuman, malevolent and merciless, who, after a mock marriage, abnormally sets himself to the devil's business of ruining his wife's lover's life, and of giving his wife a sudden death in three hideous forms: a drug to make her sleep, the gas turned on, and the door locked with "a nameless instrument." . . .

[*The Truth about Tristrem Varick*] is based on social problems of the most unaccountable kind. It has something strangely convincing in both conception and execution; it has suspense, ugly enough and uglier crises; and that the unlucky Varick is supposed to be partially insane is part of the finely woven plot, which is concerned with strange and perilous incidents and accidents; and which is based on his passionate pursuit of the ravishing Viola Raritan; the pursuit, really, of the chimera of his imagination.

And among the hazards comes one, of an evil kind—such as I have often experienced in foreign cities—that, in turning down one street instead of the next, a man's existence, and not his only, may be thereby changed. To have stopped one's rival's lying mouth and his lying life at the same instant is to have done something original—it is done by a poisoned pin's point. Then, this Orestes having found no Electra to return his love, but finding her vile, he lets himself disappear out of life in an almost incredible fashion, leaving the woman who never loved him to say, "I will come to see him sentenced:" a sentence which writes her down a modern Clytemnestra.

What Saltus says of Gonfallon can almost be said of Saltus: "With a set of people that fancied themselves in possession of advanced views and were still in the Middle Ages, he achieved the impossible: he not only consoled, he flattered, he persuaded and fascinated as well." Saltus can not console, he can sometimes persuade; but he can flatter and fascinate his public. . . . The novelist is the comedian of the pen: it is his duty to amuse, to entertain—or else to hold his peace: to one in his trade nothing imaginable comes amiss. It is not sin that appals him, but the consequences of sin; such as the fact that few sinners have ever turned into saints. In a word, he writes with his nerves.

Take, for instance, *A Transaction of Hearts* . . . , one of the queerest novels ever written and written with a kind of deliberate malice. Gonfallon, who becomes a bishop, falls passionately in love with an ardent and insolent girl who is his wife's sister; and before her beauty everything vanishes: virtue, genius, everything. "For a second that was an eternity he was conscious of her emollient mouth on his, her fingers intertwined with his own. For that second he really lived—perhaps he really lived." One wonders why Saltus uses so many ugly phrases—a kind of decadent French fashion of transposing words; such as the one I have quoted, together with "Ruedelapaixia" (meant to describe a dress), "Rafflesia," "Mashed grasshoppers baked in saffron"; phrases chosen at random which are too frequently scattered in much too obvious a profusion over much too luxurious pages. I read somewhere that Oscar Wilde said to Amélie Rives: "In Edgar Saltus's work passion struggles with grammar on every page," which is certainly one of Wilde's finest paradoxes. (pp. 265-68)

[*Imperial Purple*] shows the zenith of Saltus's talent, not in conceiving imaginary beings, but in giving modern conceptions of the most amazing creatures in the Roman Decadence, and in lyrical prose. . . . (p. 268)

> Arthur Symons, "Edgar Saltus," in his Dramatis Personae *(copyright, 1923 by The Bobbs-Merrill Company; copyright renewed © 1951 by Arthur Symons; used with permission of the publisher; The Bobbs-Merrill Company, Inc.), Bobbs-Merrill Company, 1923, pp. 263-68.*

H. L. MENCKEN (essay date 1925)

Forty years ago Edgar Saltus was a shining star in the national literature, leading the way out of the Egyptian night of Victorian sentimentality. To-day he survives only as the favorite author of the late Warren Gamaliel Harding. I can recall, in the circle of Athene, no more complete collapse. Saltus plunged from the top of the world to the bottom of the sea. (p. 277)

The causes of the débâcle are certainly not hard to determine. . . . Saltus was simply a bright young fellow who succumbed to his own cleverness. The gaudy glittering phrase enchanted him. He found early in life that he had a hand for shaping it; he found soon afterward that it had a high capacity for getting him notice. So he devoted himself to its concoction—and presently he was lost. His life after that was simply one long intoxication. He was drunk on words. (pp. 277-78)

His wife's biography [*Edgar Saltus: The Man*] is encased in an orange slipcover which announces melodramatically that it is "an extraordinary revealing life." It is, but I doubt that what it reveals will serve to resuscitate poor Saltus. The man who emerges from it is simply a silly and hollow trifler—a mass of puerile pretensions and affectations, vain of his unsound knowledge and full of sentimentalities. (p. 278)

[He] plunged into writing at the precise moment when revolt against the New England Brahmins was rising; he attracted attention quickly, and was given a lavish welcome. No American author of 1885 was more talked about. When his first novel, **"The Truth About Tristrem Varick,"** came out in 1888 it made a genuine sensation. But the stick came down almost as fast as the rocket had gone up. His books set the nation agog for a short while, and were then quietly forgotten. He began as the hope of American letters, and ended as a writer of yellow-backs and a special correspondent for the Hearst papers. What ailed him was simply lack of solid substance.

He could be clever, as cleverness was understood during the first Cleveland administration, but he lacked dignity, information, sense. His books of "philosophy" were feeble and superficial, his novels were only facile improvisations, full of satanic melodrama and wooden marionettes. (pp. 281-82)

"The Anatomy of Negation" and **"The Philosophy of Disenchantment"** have been superseded by far better books; **"The Truth About Tristrem Varick"** reads like one of the shockers of Gertrude Atherton; **"Mary Magdalen"** is a dead shell; the essays and articles republished as **"Uplands of Dream"** are simply ninth-rate journalism. Of them all only **"Imperial Purple"** holds up. A certain fine glow is still in it; it has gusto if not profundity; Saltus's worst faults do not damage it appreciably. I find myself, indeed, agreeing thoroughly with the literary judgment of Dr. Harding. **"Imperial Purple"** remains Saltus's best book. It remains also, alas, his only good one! (p. 282)

> H. L. Mencken, "Edgar Saltus" *(originally published in* Chicago Tribune, *October 11, 1925), in his* Prejudices: Fifth Series *(copyright 1926 by Alfred A. Knopf, Inc. and renewed 1954 by H. L. Mencken; reprinted by permission of Alfred A. Knopf, Inc.), Knopf, 1926, pp. 277-82.*

W. L. GEORGE (essay date 1925)

[In the stories of *Purple and Fine Women*] we find Saltus taking naturally to France, and particularly to the *grand monde*. Saltus did not inherit from the nineties an impulse to realism. He has no kinship with Zola, whose soul, according to Mr Anatole France, was too completely concerned with zinc factories and flatirons. There are no flatirons in Saltus. He is essentially oriental and fantastic. Drink is served in a flask of gold. A party is given by the morganatic widow of an emperor. He makes a world about him, sensuous and aesthetic, a world of chinchilla, emeralds, and Malines lace, where evolve only people to whom work is an incident, and perhaps love an accident. In this world he evolves as a philosophical jester. He loves it, but he is not deceived by it, does not take it seriously. In many of the stories he plays a trick upon the reader. The conclusion is perhaps not so much a trick as a revelation that the story is not true. The reader has been taken in.

It may be that he describes himself on page one [of '**A Bouquet of Illusions**'], when he says: 'I had not a care on my mind, a regret on my conscience, a speck on my shoes.' One conceives him again when he remarks: 'Frequentation with Epictetus makes one very civil.' I am sure that Saltus was civil, providing one did not mind his being a little *distrait*. One imagines him hating a bore as Mrs F's aunt hated a fool. His mind is easily wearied; in the middle of a story, his attention wanders as he realizes with horror that the tale-teller is about to become pathetic. He is essentially negligent. Things are what they are, and things do happen: in the turmoil he sits, Olympian, but secretly watchful of anything that might amuse him.

Through Saltus runs strongly the cynical strain. When a lover relates his interview with the spirit of his dead beloved, Saltus remarks: 'He grows lyrical.' In the same story, he retorts to the haunted lover that his shoemaker was annoyed by apparitions of deceased customers. Of two lovers he observes that 'they had interchanged all those lovely vows which means so much and also so little.' He sums up a vulgar rich woman who got into society by saying that 'there was a sesame in her dollars.'

Thus Saltus, in the *grand monde*, remains unimpressed; he likes it as a show; he is never deceived by it. When he introduces characters he is apt to call them de Chose or de Machin. He does not give them magnificent names. He ironically calls them 'Chose' and 'Machin,' which is the French for Tom, Dick and Harry. And no doubt he gives them a 'de' only so that they may fit the atmosphere. To him they are 'de' because people are 'de,' and they are not de much. One feels this again whenever the story drifts across a duke, for in the mind of Saltus the duke is always amiable, but wholly aimless. He is not on his knees to dukes, normal features of the landscape. They merely provide him with merriment. A continuous trickle of humor passes through his pages. The dowager in **'The Top of the Heap'** is sister to the Oscar Wilde duchess. When Saltus causes the dowager to say of her son: 'He has a perfect mania for going to the dentist's, and that, I think shows so much conscientiousness,' we recognize that woman, and crave her acquaintance. Again, Saltus sums up a character as 'Alphabet Jones, a man of polite letters.'

Perhaps we strike the completely sincere Saltus whenever he talks about women. He has for them a perfectly French passion. He looks upon them, not only as utensils for reproduction, but angels fathered by demons; to an extent he agrees with Nietzsche in looking upon women as a reward, but he has a certain disdain for the warrior, and might say, parodying Nietzsche: 'Man is for art, and woman the reward of the artist.' Subject to an ironic outlook, Saltus loves women as they are, women as he sees them. He sees them in an atmosphere of light, color, scent, as exquisite phantoms which a kiss materializes. He speaks of 'the silk of her mouth.' A little further he gives an ideal description of his vision: 'Her eyes were pools of purple, her hair was a garland of flame, her mouth a scarlet thread.' He himself applies the *mot juste* to his own dream: Sultry. He defines when he says: 'Her hair made a garland of gold. Her eyes were sultry, her lips were scarlet.' (pp. vii-x)

It is not easy to sum up Saltus, nor is it necessary. I have lost the taste for classification, and I am not concerned to know what place posterity will assign to him. He may, in five hundred years, figure in the cyclopedias of literature, or again he may not. (p. x)

W. L. George, in his introduction to Purple and Fine Women *by Edgar Saltus, Pascal Covici, Publisher, 1925 (and reprinted by AMS Press, 1968), pp. v-x.*

ERIC McKITRICK (essay date 1951)

Today Edgar Saltus is all but forgotten; yet of all the fugitive colors in which [the 1890s were] painted, some of its deepest purples were laid on by him. Saltus was one of the few Americans of the Cleveland era who could give any cues to those coming out of adolescence with the bohemian urge for "liberation." Surrounded by a culture pointedly lacking in aesthetic stimulus, they found his novels, translations, and lurid "histories," with their glittering surface effects and perfumed depravity, very exciting. . . . (pp. 22-3)

Imperial Purple, which came out in 1892, was undoubtedly Edgar Saltus's masterpiece. Nothing he ever did, before or after, quite came up to it. "There was an hour," he had written in this same year, "when I hoped to be known as a novelist; I hope now to make at least a pencil-mark in history. To my thinking, of all pursuits it is the most aristocratic." Yet in few senses might *Imperial Purple* be called history. Using names and events that appear to have been dug up, for the most part,

out of Suetonius and [Jules] Michelet, Saltus unfurls a livid chronicle of Rome's imperial Caesars in the days of the Decadence; with bland equanimity he invests them in regalia more dazzling, with deeds more corrupt and tastes more depraved, than any novelist would ever have dared let appear in his fiction for fear of being stoned in derision from the marketplace. With sheer description Saltus achieves a brief *tour de force;* his images have a calculated flair, a knowing insolence, which compel, even now, a kind of surreptitious delight. . . . As bridges between one fantastic episode and the next, Saltus contents himself with cryptical suggestions, dreamily redolent of hidden obscenities, or with brief supercilious epigrams, and pirouettes away from them before incurring any commitments. . . . The book abounds in gross spectacle. Caesar, "in the attributes and attitude of Jupiter Capitolinus," sitting high in a jeweled car, "blinking his tired eyes," makes his triumphal return from Gaul with Vercingetorix in tow, to the accompaniment of "explosions of brass" from "twisted bugles" and swelling roars from the multitudes along the Via Sacra. Nero, "a bloated beast in a flowered gown, the hair done up in a chignon, the skin covered with eruptions, the eyes circled and yellow," plays impresario at sumptuous massacres in the amphitheatre. . . . While the effect is all rather outrageous, it is undeniably hypnotic. As long as there remains such material to hand, Saltus scintillates. There is an illusion of prodigal resources. Saturnalian pageantry and silken corruption are congenial to his temperament and the occasion afforded here allows free rein to his *forte*, a talent for description and evocation that exfoliates richly when nothing else is at stake. The curtain falls on *Imperial Purple* with such an impression remaining uppermost, and indeed, there is a sense in which this fascination with the opalescence of surface shimmer for its own sake—when we think of the contemporary setting of what Louise Bogan has called "a kind of psychic polar cold"—is all to Saltus' credit. (pp. 24-5)

There is, in *Imperial Purple,* a wanton, lyric buoyancy that cushions the real tragedy of Saltus' career. This, it seems, was a gnawing fear of involvement, a terrible unwillingness to be spiritually, morally, or intellectually engaged, even in the simplest way. It comes more into focus with such of the novels as *A Transaction in Hearts* . . .and *Mr. Incoul's Misadventure* . . . , probably his two best. Both of them might very well have turned out to be witty little set-pieces in the Oscar Wilde manner, contrived momentary visions of evil, artificial, perverse, and all, but in their special way perfect. They both start out promisingly. . . . The main theme of [*A Transaction in Hearts*] is supposed to be [the Reverend Christopher] Gonfallon's guilty lust for his sister-in-law; poor Saltus never once really approaches it. Over the first part of the book hovers the delicate odor of decomposition that he undoubtedly desired and intended but whose implications he never seemed to know how to exploit. . . . Yet eventually guile succumbs to melodrama and a panicky demoralization sets in, spoiling the whole carefully-prepared tone of the piece. It all ends in rather a rout, the author seeming to have lost control over his people and having hardly an idea of what he wants them to do from one page to the next. Something of the same sort happens to *Mr. Incoul's Misadventure,* whose bejeweled Fu Manchu type of charm is sustained by stage props like bullfights and libraries of erotica; situations potentially interesting are at once resolved and extinguished in suicide and murder.

This sort of thing demands a special kind of conviction and the literary milieu in which Saltus functioned was incapable of pointing out to him his simplest problems. There was too great a gulf between what was being done at the time and what Saltus might have done in the kind of hothouse he needed to work in; it gave him nothing to push against in the way of example, sympathy, or legitimate criticism. On the other hand it sustained him in his perversity of temperament by defaulting, open-mouthed, before his pretensions (which were never really very sure of themselves); the American literary public, by its indiscriminate outrage, allowed him for the moment an unhealthy *carte blanche* for sheer trifling. (pp. 25-7)

If the uncongenial artistic climate in which Edgar Saltus lived in the late eighties and nineties could be called the sole factor preventing his development then it would have to be said that the oblivion in which he now rests was a case of rank injustice. And yet the more one looks into his work, with all its showy talent and frequent flashes of virtuosity, the greater is the sense one gets of a kind of sheer empty dread that may well have been pathologically incurable. At the very outset of his career Saltus had struck an attitude. It was one which promised a forlorn kind of absolution from virtually any kind of involvements and constituted perhaps the only intellectual baggage he could ever hope to carry. With vestiges of Munich and Heidelberg discipline still clinging to him and free as yet from the flamboyance which infected his later style, he produced in 1885 *The Philosophy of Disenchantment,* a melancholy amalgam of ideas culled from Schopenhauer and Eduard von Hartmann announcing "a new school, which, in denying the possibility of any happiness, holds as first principle that the world is a theatre of misery in which, were the choice accorded, it would be preferable not to be born at all." The enlightened pessimist will decline to oppose life; he is aware that nothing in it is worth a struggle, that pain is its "inevitable concomitant," that its few pleasures will be unexpected and will have nothing to do with antecedent desire. He will have no great hopes and few regrets. Saltus followed *The Philosophy of Disenchantment* with a companion volume, *The Anatomy of Negation,* and with it he bade an early farewell to anything resembling formal polemic. "To avoid misconception," he writes in a prefatory note, "it may be added that no attempt has been made to prove anything."

The next stage was a version of the art for art's sake doctrine. From one of his early masters, Balzac, he appropriated the trick of having certain characters turn up again and again in his stories; one of these, "A. B. Fenwick Chisholm-Jones" ("Alphabet Jones") is an urbane and witty novelist who prowls through idle society in search of plots and serves Saltus as mouthpiece for his epigrams and other *obiter dicta* on art and life. . . . Even within the realm of art itself Saltus felt that one's activity ought to be strictly limited. He was sensitive to the roughness of contemporary prose (as well as of contemporary manners) and managed to persuade himself that something tolerable in the way of art might be achieved by concentrating on diction alone. "It may be noted," he wrote, "that in literature only three things count, style, style polished, style repolished; there imagination and the art of transition aid, but do not enhance."

Thus in a stroke the difficulties of art were reduced to a simple few. In Saltus' favor, of course, was the fact that these few problems were still the ones being neglected in American fiction. The readers of the day who could no longer endure the stylistic turgidity and prudery of what was being given them, who were ready at last for unabashed frivolity and were willing to follow Saltus' hints that most intellectual and moral commitments might as well be ignored as a sad and complicated

joke, were treated to a new and exciting kind of entertainment. (pp. 27-9)

If Saltus' novels could be said to have a setting, it was most often that of New York society, whose vulgarity was transformed, in his frenetic imagination, into a kind of fastidious and aristocratic immorality which it never really possessed. . . . [Their specialty], (aside from adultery), was murder—the kind of dénouement which Saltus preferred to any other. Here he insisted on aesthetic standards, and he derived them from the Florentine nobility. . . . Over themes of death he lingers with an almost pathetic savor. There are suicides by drowning, hypodermic injections, and blowing out of brains; there are killings by asphyxiation, duels, poisons, abortion, stabbing, shooting, and cutting of throats. A countess is discovered dead with a trunk containing the dried heads of former enemies. The hero of *The Monster,* Gulian Verplanck, is mangled by dogs. Even the Holy Crucifixion is described in part. There are several cases of near incest, which was even worse than death.

Edgar Saltus' reputation as an epigrammatist also had a certain basis. His most famous *mot* was made in answer to a woman who had asked him which character in fiction he admired most. "God," was his reply. (pp. 29-30)

Saltus in his heydey was most criticized for his "eroticism." It was a chilly kind of eroticism, lacking in flesh and blood. Vance Thompson, Saltus' contemporary, was a lush and incontinent pornographer; Saltus had a little too much tact for that. He worked in innuendo. . . . Edgar Saltus could not bring himself face to face either with sexual love or romantic sentiment and attempt to trace out any sort of implications from them. . . . To the British and French Decadents of the day, the perfumes, the exotic regalia, the depravity, the paradox, the *mot juste* represented a struggle toward deeper meanings in art and life. For all their exaggerated prominence these were still the epiphenomena of creativity; for Edgar Saltus they were its all. . . . [In] the end Saltus could not come to terms with experience on any level. . . . The characters in Saltus' cooked-up plots are soulless and wooden; they are guided listlessly by their creator through a mocking void of misery strewn with baubles, a hell peculiarly theirs and his—a hell of caprice without hopes or expectations. (pp. 30-1)

Eric McKitrick, "Edgar Saltus of the Obsolete," in American Quarterly *(copyright, Spring, 1951, copyright renewed © 1979, Trustees of the University of Pennsylvania), Vol. III, No. 1, Spring, 1951, pp. 22-35.*

VAN WYCK BROOKS (essay date 1952)

Edgar Saltus, a New Yorker born,—"with a gold spoon in his mouth," if not, like his Tancred Ennever, "with a gold pen as well,"—had gone to Heidelberg to study and picked up there the pessimism of Schopenhauer and Eduard von Hartmann. A lover of luxury, cats and pleasure, "a bad little boy, grown up," as someone said who should have known him well, he was prepared when he went to Paris to relate this phase of German thinking to the so-called decadent feeling that he found in France. He presented his own hedonism in two philosophical studies, *The Philosophy of Disenchantment* and *The Anatomy of Negation,* in which he handled his difficult themes with a lightness and lucidity that gave him a certain reputation as an admirable writer. It was one of his observations that only three qualities mattered in writing, style, style polished and style repolished, and, dandy that he was in prose as well as in appearance, he was at his best undoubtedly in these early books. As in the first two romances that rapidly followed his return to New York, *The Truth about Tristrem Varick* and *Mr. Incoul's Misadventure,* the style of these essays in philosophy was translucent and restrained, and it was later that he developed his liking for the purple patch, although purple was his favourite word already. (p. 114)

[In] Paris, Saltus had written *Mary Magdalene* and *Imperial Purple,* a pageant of Roman history beginning with the empire when Rome was "choked with gold and curious crime,"—picturesque studies that recalled the conquests of antiquity, on the one hand of Flaubert, on the other of Renan. Like the *Salome* of Oscar Wilde, whom Saltus knew in all his phases, these books owed almost everything to French examples, resembling George Moore's evocations of the Romano-Judaean world in their note of "ornamental disenchantment." Saltus expressed a fatalism that was characteristic of the *fin de siècle* and appeared in a dozen forms in such diverse writers as Mark Twain, Henry Adams and Ambrose Bierce.

In these and a few other books,—*Historia Amoris,* for one, a history of love ancient and modern,—Saltus the essayist was more interesting by far than he was in his role as the author of too-facile romances. For having, like one of his characters, a "reverence for good prose," he believed it was "the shudder that tells" in all types of writing, an idea that suited more or less the kind of history he chose to write but that led straight to melodrama when he wrote fiction. He was like the earlier Henry Harland in the often charming style that accompanied his burden of suicide, mystery and murder, the constant themes of the fantasy-world that he built on the New York "Upper Ten," the only sphere that existed for his imagination. The actual people who were soon to appear in Edith Wharton's novels were dimly suggested in Saltus's "gilded gang," who often bore old New York names like Varick and Gulian Verplanck and owned ancestral domains on the river or Canal Street. Their locale was sometimes Gramercy Park and oftener "Vanity Square," east of Central Park, approached by the Plaza, though they were on shipboard oftener still on their way to Cairo, Java, Japan or Pierre Loti's,—rather than Melville's,—Polynesian islands. Europe for them was too old a story and they were tired of friends who had "sent in their resignations to everything but the humdrum," for they had lost the ability to be shocked but not to be bored and for them New York knew too little of the art of living. Its principal art was "devising new ways to be dull." (pp. 115-16)

[In] Saltus's vision New York society appeared to be as decadent as the world he had found in Suetonius and pictured elsewhere. It was a kind of fairyland peopled with characters who had not been observed but had rather been dreamed by a mind shaped in France,—by certain romancers and poets and the books they had read,—for which even Gramercy Park at night was "pervaded with a suggestion of absinthe and vice," as if Verlaine himself had been reeling through it. (p. 117)

> Van Wyck Brooks, "New York: Up-Town," in his The Confident Years: 1885-1915 *(copyright, 1952, by Van Wyck Brooks; copyright renewed © 1980 by Mrs. Van Wyck Brooks; reprinted by permission of the publisher, E. P. Dutton, Inc.), Dutton, 1952, pp. 103-18.*

CLAIRE SPRAGUE (essay date 1968)

How strong the intellectual discontent between 1880 and 1915 was has yet to be fully measured. . . .

To the larger intellectual discontent of the period, the historian of ideas must add the Saltusian formulation of pessimism—one contained in two books and one essay. These works have a surer, if minor, place in American social and intellectual history than they have been given. In [*The Philosophy of Disenchantment, The Anatomy of Negation*] . . . , and "**What Pessimism is Not,**" Saltus stirred a post-war generation not yet situated in the robust imperialism and Naturalism more characteristic of the last decade of the nineteenth century. (p. 32)

That Saltus felt himself a pioneer, a vanguard proponent of a new religion not yet fully defined (and therefore so much the more attractive) deserves underlining. Although Mencken considered pessimism already old-fashioned by the time Saltus wrote about it, the evidence suggests otherwise. . . . Indeed, a better case might be made that Saltus was accepting or encouraging a point of view just becoming known. (p. 33)

In the modernists of his day—in Henry James, Emile Zola, the brothers Goncourt, Stendhal, Gustave Flaubert, Ivan Turgenev, Charles Baudelaire, and Edgar Allan Poe—he finds melancholy support of the pessimistic tenet that "life is an affliction."

The man in search of relief from the affliction of life and its attendant illusions of love and happiness may find it, Schopenhauer suggests, in art and contemplation, or in the more rigorous solutions of asceticism or absolute chastity. (pp. 33-4)

Von Hartmann's doctrine allowed for a mitigated pessimism which the example of his life supported, surrounded as he was by wife and children in contrast to Schopenhauer's misogynistic, solitary personal life. . . .

In contrast to his teacher, von Hartmann urges that man is "most happy when he is the unconscious dupe of his illusions." The Unconscious, therefore, permits illusion and the consequent individual mitigation of misery. Von Hartmann also uses the concept of the Unconscious to support his belief that the universe is evolving toward redemption from evil. Thus, he both has and has not Schopenhauer's Will, keeping it but making it unconscious and directive instead of irrational. (p. 34)

[We are left] with an energetic, vivacious presentation of a melancholy, apparently resigned doctrine, a surface paradox not uncommon in the history of human thought. . . .

[In *The Anatomy of Negation*] Saltus continues his work as an apostle and popularizer. [*The Philosophy of Disenchantment*] had examined the modern version of scientific or theoretic pessimism; this one ambitiously traces the "tableau of antitheism from Kapila to Leconte de Lisle." (p. 36)

Saltus manages to fit Jesus into a history of anti-theism: "He was the most entrancing of nihilists, but he was not an innovator," for he built upon Essene doctrine. Saltus warns us that Essene doctrine makes thorough sense only if we realize that it was preparing men for death, not life. The imminent end of the world underlines, perhaps explains, Christ's emphasis on renunciation of self, on voluntary poverty, on communal property, and on the celibate life. (p. 37)

Saltus, implicitly agnostic or anti-theist, is afraid to wound his readers' traditional theism. He therefore plays down the pessimist's rejection of ultra-mundane felicity. He introduces what is to be his lifelong concern with religion, here expressed negatively. He also presents his reader with an escape clause: "Life is not an affliction to those who are, and who can remain young.'' His escape into beauty or art may be foreshadowed. He demonstrates his obsession with the illusions of love and happiness and evinces not the irrelevancy of social action but an uneven, naïve political sensibility which later hardens into an acceptance of American imperial dreams.

In his last work on pessimism, an essay entitled **"What Pessimism Is Not,"** Saltus perfectly suits paradox to style and content. He shows the reader in effect that pessimism is the point of view of the paradoxist. He makes it clear that pessimism is not equal to its clichés, that it does not invite suicide, gloom, or pain. In fact, as the central paradox of the essay tells us, it is not the pessimist but the optimist who "takes everything amiss." For the optimist "has any number of big dolls, and their sawdust disconcerts him terribly." The image is excellent. The earnest optimist is, in his earnestness, discomfited by a great deal. He dislikes failure, which Saltus bravely avers is more salutary than success; and, when failure enters the optimist's world, "he dashes his head in the pillow."

What is at issue in this essay is surely an early effort to subvert the American philosophy of "uplift." The pessimist opens his eyes; the optimist shuts his. The latter expects the perfections of Paradise; the former accepts imperfection. The pessimist denies only "one thing . . . that happiness exists"; he knows that pain "is the inevitable concomitant of life." Therefore why accept a golden age of the past? If any such age exists, it is "not behind us, but beyond." Although by the end of the essay the pessimist has come dangerously close to accepting his opposing partner's whatever-is-is-good, the paradoxist remains by definition ambivalent, agile, cunning.

What Saltus masks in the serio-comic irony of paradox is his desire to believe. His denomination of pessimism as the "religion of the future" in his earlier books indicates what we would know anyway—that the rejection of traditional religion will involve the search for a replacement. By the time Saltus wrote his next book about religion the mask had dropped. In *The Lords of the Ghostland* . . . Saltus examines the major religions of the world through nine gods: Brahma, Ormuzd, Amon-Râ, Bel-Marduk, Jehovah, Zeus, Jupiter, and Christ. These "lords of the ghostland" are the gods of the various unseen heavens man has created, and Saltus bows to them. . . . (pp. 39-40)

What sharply distinguishes this book from his earlier works on pessimism is Saltus' concern with doctrines of reincarnation and transmigration. He is already more than tempted by the doctrines of theosophy. While pessimism had to be discussed within the context of society and history, theosophy permits Saltus to discuss the soul in relation to eternity and so to leave the temporal far behind. The ethics of Christianity he had never attacked. Not only in *The Anatomy of Negation* and in *The Philosophy of Disenchantment* but in the essay, **"What Pessimism Is Not,"** he had spoken of "the abnegation of self" which he traced as far back as Buddhism. His version of pessimism stresses the stoic side of Christianity.

Saltus has not changed from a non-believer into a believer; he is always a believer. He had expected pessimism to become the religion of the future; it had not. Moreover, pessimism could not serve a man who needed some divinity in his substitute religion, and that he chose theosophy is not entirely surprising. Yet no one could have been more sceptical of theosophy than Saltus or more ironic about its pretensions. (p. 41)

Theosophy represented a faith in the power of the unseen and the intangible, a faith in the supremacy of the imagination over the machine. The twentieth century may need to extricate itself from the reverse fallacy. It may need to relearn the power of the conscious in relation to the unconscious. But Saltus saw as any sensitive observer of the nineteenth century could not fail to see, that the data now partially subsumed in the pioneer disciplines of psychology and psychoanalysis were those his century ignored or suppressed.

What Saltus could not generate was a sufficient degree of commitment to either pessimism or theosophy or to a personal set of convictions. He needed a stronger inner demon than he had and a stronger, more intelligent response from his environment. But what he saw and what he needed other contemporaries had also seen and needed. Greater men, like William James and Henry Adams, had spoken from a basically similar sense of the special destructiveness of modern life. The Saltus visions and needs were not isolated. (p. 43)

"Doing it" [in the 1890s] meant having style. All of Saltus' critics unite in agreeing that Saltus had it. (p. 65)

Saltus, bred on Balzac, Flaubert, the brothers Goncourt, Leconte de Lisle, Baudelaire, and Hugo could hardly reject craftsmanship. Their example suffuses his strictures on style as they were to suffuse twentieth-century literary platforms. His stress on the precise, the exact word is recognizably Flaubert. (p. 67)

In a personal notebook Saltus adopts, predictably, the conviction that style is a jealous divinity. . . . (p. 68)

The jealous divinity sometimes relaxes, for at other times Saltus suggests that geniuses often write badly and are exempt from slavery to form as second-order writers are not. . . . Saltus comfortably sustained, however, the paradox of "freedom" for the genius and "slavery" in the form of discipline for the rest—and clearly places himself with the rest. (pp. 68-9)

A careful reader of Saltus may cull an adequate enough bouquet of rare and exotic words: "duscholia," "intussusception," "repercuted," "opopanax," "elenchicism." (p. 76)

Surprise was an effect Saltus desired to achieve. If both humor and paradox are "the commonplace in fancy dress," the fancy dress, or surprise, could come in the rare word. (pp. 76-7)

Epigrams and witty turns of phrase also occur in the novels. . . .

Saltus, like Wilde, did not want to be commonplace. When he defends inconsistency of character [in his fiction], he does so on the ground that human beings act inconsistently and unexpectedly. (p. 77)

We cannot say of him, as we can of Wilde in *The Importance of Being Earnest*, that "Whenever ordinary morality appears," he makes it seem ridiculous.

For "ordinary morality" is the base of the Saltus contribution, as it is of most of Wilde's work. The particular ways in which both constructed and used pun, epigram, and paradox; their inversions; and their wit are related to one another and to the world of Baudelaire, Barbey d'Aurevilly, Joris Karl Huysmans, and others. . . .

No "peacock phrases, glowing periods and verbal surprises" embellish every page of any single work by Edgar Saltus. His practice, by comparison with Wilde or with Huysmans, is more muted, soberer, less daring, less extravagant, less rich. (p. 78)

The ideal of style was an 1890's one that had its immediate origins in France—from the example of Flaubert, Baudelaire, and their successors. . . . [Saltus's] concern for dress, like the concern for the polished word, was a concern for form in life and art.

Saltus was theoretically committed to the polishing and repolishing of prose. The evidence of his practice is, however, incomplete and indecisive. (p. 79)

What abets the possibility that Saltus revised less than his legend has it is his remarkable productivity. If the dates that follow most of his novels are accepted as the beginning and end dates of composition, then Saltus wrote them with remarkable speed. . . .

He must have worked at a furious pace. Even his acknowledged "first" work, *Imperial Purple,* appears to have been written in three months. Although there is no special merit to works written slowly over several years, the combination of Saltus' great quantitative production and his minor status as a writer suggest less devotion to revision than he had advocated. A less attractive version of polishing and repolishing could include Saltus' habit of using and reusing his own material, favorite lines or paragraphs. . . . (p. 80)

Saltus was primarily a conscious carrier of post-Romantic theory, as his essays on fiction in *Love and Lore* adequately show. He never gave the fiction he discussed a name. He adopted neither the Realist nor the Naturalist label, but he does use a curious term which he seems to have coined himself. He refers in several places to "ornamental literature"—which may seem a perfect term for *fin-de-siècle* or "decadent" literature. Yet the contexts of the phrase suggest that "ornamental" is merely a synonym for imaginative literature—for fiction as distinct, for example, from history or from the essay.

Sometimes, however, it literally means ornate. . . . Ornate means here what we expect it to mean: the sensuous, the criminal, or the violent thrill or *frisson.* (pp. 80-1)

He could be bare; he could be baroque. It is unlikely that he found these two styles antipodal or contradictory. The trajectory of his career shows him moving gradually toward the baroque, toward an impressionist prose that did not necessarily discard the short line. . . . Saltus became desperately afraid of the commonplace in himself and in his style. In a classic substitution of frenzy for matter, he adulterated his very real talent. (pp. 81-2)

History, he had said, "is illuminated with crimes that have been applauded and absolved because of their inherent beauty." He had connected crime and beauty; in strife and love he had seen, like some of the early Greek philosophers, the dialectic that defines life, that creates act and change. Above that dialectic he had placed beauty as the unifying agent of the universe. Even in love, he had looked below pleasant surfaces and been fascinated by the work of Richard von Krafft-Ebing ("a scientist of real value"), Jean Charcot, Pierre Janet, Havelock Ellis. At his most exaggerated, Saltus seems a Sir Epicure Mammon, a comic would-be voluptuary in his fantasies of love and material delights. Like his esthetic contemporaries in England and France, a Wilde or a Huysmans, he suggests a libertinism he never actually practiced in his art or in his life. The suggestions were apparently enough for his audience—an unfortunate situation since a more astringent opposition, one more intelligent and involved, might have wrested a deeper response out of the writers of the 1880's and 1890's.

To have sensed the connection between obsessional love and crime required acumen in a layman of the later nineteenth century. Saltus did not develop the connection—less because he was a layman than because he characteristically did not develop and deepen his often acute insights. That he broached a new way of seeing the connection between love and war in terms of abnormal psychology and economic determinism is to his credit. That he functioned so frequently, therefore, as historian and amorist is not surprising since what was polar did interconnect. What more exquisite occupation than to examine and adjust the relationships between the shudders of pain and of pleasure, of Ares and Eros? That adjustment could focus on Rome, Russia, and contemporary wars as easily as upon historical lovers, *don juanisme,* and local examples of ideal and aberrational love. The focus was that of the cinematographer—sharp, fleeting, popular. Nevertheless it was there—right on what continues to absorb so many students of human behavior. (pp. 119-20)

Saltus was, with contemporaries like James Huneker, Vance Thompson, and Percival Pollard, at the very least, "a Service." In his role as a cultural middleman, he brought to the newer and growing middle-class audience news of French and other European literatures and habits. He helped to make American literary insularity impossible. The 1920's completed his job. He and his "decade of small things" anticipated other concerns and interests of the 1920's. His criticism of the American cultural environment included, for example, explicit use of the Puritan past as scapegoat and explicit awareness of the simplicities of the art-morality debates of the period. The Saltus who coined "Bourgeoisophobus" suggests some relationship with the Mencken who coined "booboisie." Both writers flourished when genius was more often equated with immorality than it is today. The existence of an avant-garde (now that it is dead, it is taken for granted) had its beginnings as an idea and as a fact in the American climate of opinion that included Saltus. This avant-garde insisted on craftsmanship and risked being called "esthetic" for that insistence. The bare, early Saltus style, departing radically from classic nineteenth-century American prose style, is closer to twentieth-century practice. Saltus also looked eagerly to discoveries in psychology; he was particularly fascinated with pathology. Pathology might describe, if not explain, what happened to his deluded lovers. He saw the dust beneath the gilt and accepted in pessimism a thin explanation for frustration and reality. But pessimism allowed him to become an early subverter of "uplift."

His novels are transparent footnotes to pessimistic doctrine in which he tries to remind his confident contemporaries that "Happiness is a myth invented by Satan for our despair." Although the novels are more ornamental than profoundly disenchanting, they are based on the discordance between idea and existence which erupts in disillusion and violence—a subject central to human experience that has had its special relevance in American literature. Saltus' interest in economics and politics, in the ecology of empire, and in the decay of the city was not accidental. He saw with Henry James that "nowhere else does pecuniary power so beat its wings in the void" as in the United States. But he lacked major talent, adequate allies, and the audience (it could be small; it had to be supportive) to make his nibbling at materialism and provincialism sufficiently telling.

His was not merely a general disaffection for life; he was convinced of the special destructiveness of modern life. His ennui was not peculiar. It joins a long tradition of laments characteristic of the Romantic temperament for the loss of enthusiasm, of joy, of creative power. In his search for a credo,

Saltus also joins other artists. He chose pessimism, theosophy, or elements of estheticism to supplant voids left by the failures of the dominant nineteenth-century systems of political and religious thought. His pessimism was more like stoicism or epicureanism than cynicism. He did not agree with Max Nordau, a preacher of dire decline before Spengler, that genius is morbid. For Saltus, not genius but pseudo-genius is morbid. (pp. 121-23)

When Saltus forgot, or could not follow, what he knew by virtue of his limited endowments, his own work lapsed. The fine art of shocking was an art worth cultivating in his time. When that art became for the later Saltus a desperate effort to rescue himself from the commonplace, it was no longer fine but fake. Thrill overthrew truth; the shudder became melodrama. (p. 123)

Although Saltus is more the eclectic than the eccentric he has generally been made out to be, he cannot be rescued from complicity in the corruptions that he had the courage to see but not to resist. He had a real gift for popular entertainment and comic exaggeration, but left no enduring single work which shows the combination and maturation of these gifts. In fact, his reputation rests rather lopsidedly on his "purples," his diabolisms, and his clever style. It ought to rest a little more evenly: on several novels and on a number of his essays on society, manners, and trivia. Indeed, were the essay as popular as it once was, more readers would be enjoying Saltus. There is a residue of vision and conviction in Saltus left, even when posterity has completed her ruthless excisions from his work. More than the first-order writer, he reveals direct reactions to specific literary, cultural, and political issues of his era. For the social and intellectual historian, Saltus is, therefore, a prolific, highly coruscated and frequently sensitive register of the period. (pp. 123-24)

His self-proffered conflict is suggestive; it speaks for so much in the Romantic and in the specifically American Romantic temperament: "I was born with a lot of vices that never put their nose to the window. I like wine and never drink—I would gamble perhaps but I don't know one card from another—I am a mystic at heart and believe in nothing. Debauchery attracts me and I live like a monk." His remarks make a specialized addition to the literature of America's fear and fascination for experience. The self-portrait is very likely a literary creation, but even its imagined accuracy or its very conception show that longing and frustration which made the man and the era "almost" decadent. If achievement does come back, as Henry James felt, to "the intensity with which we live," then Saltus' intensity is recorded for us only fitfully and during the brief span of some ten years. His pilgrimage was not sufficiently passionate. It could not, like his grandfather's, make "a wilderness a paradise"; but it could and did make a small and interesting garden. (pp. 124-25)

Claire Sprague, in her Edgar Saltus *(copyright ©1968 by Twayne Publishers, Inc.; reprinted with the permission of Twayne Publishers, a Division of G. K. Hall & Co., Boston), Twayne, 1968, 154 p.*

MORSE PECKHAM (essay date 1978)

Saltus's first book was a brief essay on Balzac. This first effort was not inappropriate to his interests in pessimism, for Balzac was a naive sociological novelist, while the Goncourts and Zola, who in the 1880's was publishing the first part of the Rougon-Macquart series, were examples of the ideologically self-conscious stage of sociological fiction, marked by an extreme social pessimism. Saltus' next two books, then, are fruitfully understood as the effort to get at the strain in the Romantic tradition which underlay Balzac and was obvious in the most important fiction of the 1880's. These two interests, the philosophical and the sociological, emerge in Saltus's third book. *The Philosophy of Disenchantment* was not a work of formal philosophy but rather a popularization—and a very good one—of a philosophical tradition of the 19th century, as found in the magnificent poetry of Leopardi, in Schopenhauer, and in Hartmann. *The Anatomy of Negation* is particularly interesting because it is an effort to study the pessimistic negation of the value of existence from ancient times, beginning with the Buddha, to the 1880's, and to study that tradition in terms of the religious and social human conditions from which it emerged. The climax is a passage on Leconte des Lisle, "perhaps the most perfect poet of France" and certainly the most austerely pessimistic.

The other step forward in this second study of pessimism was the appearance of Saltus's style, not yet perhaps in its full maturity, but certainly remarkable for its crispness and its vividness. . . . At this point it is enough to recognize the emergence of that style from an intense study of pessimism and negation. What lay in the future for Saltus at his best is the use of that style to relate historical circumstances which in their horror justified that pessimism. His novels, together with his extremely voluminous journalistic essays, are, with the exception of the first novel, *Mr. Incoul's Misadventure,* a commercialization of both his style and his philosophy, a condition that necessarily softened the latter. (A collection of some of these popular essays, *The Pomps of Satan* . . . , is an excellent demonstration of how his position could be made amusingly fit for popular consumption.) That first novel, however, is at least a fairly successful effort to present that inherent human viciousness which justifies pessimism and negation. For it is a story of how a proud American aristocrat revenges himself upon his wife and her lover, and is both undetected and unpunished.

A full justification for pessimism, however, is to be found in history; and in *Imperial Purple* Saltus used the history of the Julian and Claudian emperors to exemplify the human capacity for viciousness. Mr. Incoul is a worthy companion of these emperors, for he too is thoroughly protected from the consequences of his two murders by his wealth and his social position. The Caesars had unlimited power and wealth. There was no ideology capable of imposing a morality, nor any social power capable of controlling the pleasure to be found in exerting the most brutal and revolting subjection, exploitation, humiliation, torture, and murder on less powerful human beings. Saltus's point certainly seems to be that when human beings can do exactly as they wish, this is the way they are likely to behave. *Imperial Purple* was published in 1892. Nearly thirty years later the Russian Revolution gave him the opportunity to repeat his message. *Imperial Orgy,* an account of the horrors of Russian Czars, beginning with Ivan the Terrible, is even more powerful, though not so well written, than the first analysis of imperial pleasure-seeking; for it countered the point that the Caesars were pre-Christian. Russia was a Christian country, and the Russian czars were Orthodox Christians. Nevertheless, their autocratic viciousness was if anything even more spectacular than that of the Roman Caesars. Saltus had the prescience to perceive that, given the tradition of Russian rulers, the new intellectual and proletarian rulers would be little different, and they have not been, though certainly less imaginative, except in their steady continuance of the Czarist tradition of imperialistic expansionism.

The shudder of human history became Saltus's most serious interest, one which extends to the analysis of religion and its consequences in **The Lords of the Ghostland** and of the relation of sexuality to power in **Historia Amoris**. . . . Saltus was willing to face the horror of history, of religion, of sex—of human behavior, and for this reason I have used the word "heroic." For that willingness he shared with the other decadents. The term "decadence" was used by the decadents themselves. But does it mean they were living in a time of decadence, or that they were decadents in a time of social health? Certainly it has been the second meaning that has been used against them, and has justified both their denigration and the failure to comprehend the cultural significance of the movement. It was, I think, a moment within the larger movement which I have called Stylism, and exhibits the offensive and vandalistic potentialities of Stylism. I have called the decadents heroic, for at a time of sentimentality and bourgeois optimism, they had the courage to see the horror of humanity, evinced when it is not under social control, and the shudder of history.

Yet, much as we may regret it, Saltus himself was not able entirely to sustain his position. Like so many of the decadents he turned to an innovative transcendentalism, specifically, Theosophy, at the end of the **Lords of the Ghostland** and in several of his novels. "It would certainly be a species of snobbery to accept theosophy in Yeats and to reject it in Saltus," Claire Sprague writes. . . . I am not a snob; I reject it in Yeats. It is particularly depressing that Saltus was capable of conceiving of Russian Bolshevism as a force directed from transcendental realms and designed to cleanse the world for a redemptive rebirth. This failure of nerve on the part of Yeats and Saltus and other decadents, though by no means most of them, is indeed depressing. But it is not difficult to account for it. Religious belief, together with various forms of philosophical transcendentalism and idealism, was the enormous redundancy of the culture surrounding Saltus, and there is more excuse for him than for Yeats, who lived in a more intellectually sophisticated and realistic cultural environment. Saltus's failure, though not complete, nor so complete as Yeats's, nor so intellectually damaging, reveals the necessity for stylism and the "decadence," and shows the extreme importance of

style as a strategy for maintaining both protection against culturally redundant absurdities and for mounting heroically vandalistic attacks upon that culture and its untenable beliefs. But that failure also shows that style is not in itself enough, nor are art and beauty as instances of style. None of these turned out to be powerful enough to sustain a self-ascription of value. To find a more powerful strategy remained the problem of the next stage of the Romantic tradition of European culture. (pp. 66-8)

Morse Peckham, "Edgar Saltus and the Heroic Decadence," in TSE: Tulane Studies in English *(copyright © 1978 by Tulane University), Vol. 23, 1978, pp. 61-9.*

ADDITIONAL BIBLIOGRAPHY

De Casseres, Benjamin. "Edgar Saltus." In his *Forty Immortals*, pp. 88-93. New York: Joseph Lawren, 1926.
Describes Saltus and his works in terms of mysticism stating that "his contempt and disdain of 'merely human' things is beautiful. It is a gesture toward the Infinite."

Levin, Harry. "The Discovery of Bohemia." In *Literary History of the United States, Vol. II*, edited by Robert E. Spiller, Willard Thorp, Thomas H. Johnson, and Henry Seidel Canby, pp. 1065-79. New York: The Macmillan Co., 1948.*
Brief overview of Saltus's life and work.

McKitrick, Eric L. "A Pinch of Saltus." *The New York Review of Books* XV, No. 8 (5 November 1970): pp. 41-2.
Review of Claire Sprague's study of Saltus, which treats him as a problem of "disparity between promise and achievement [see excerpt above]." McKitrick devotes much of this review to his own insightful evaluations of Saltus.

Pattee, Fred Lewis. "The Émigré Writers." In his *The New American Literature: 1890-1930*, pp. 215-32. New York: Cooper Square Publishers, 1968.*
Assessment of Saltus as an émigré writer, educated in German universities and influenced by French literature.

Saltus, Marie. *Edgar Saltus: The Man*. Chicago: Pascal Covici, 1925, 324 p.
Biography by Saltus's third wife.

M(atthew) P(hipps) Shiel

1865-1947

(Also wrote under pseudonym of Gordon Holmes) English novelist, short story writer, essayist, and poet.

Though best known for his classic of fantasy literature, *The Purple Cloud,* Shiel wrote in a diversity of genres. In the various works of his long and prolific career he was in turn a writer of detective stories, a horror artist in the tradition of Poe, a pioneer of modern science fiction and fantasy, and in his final lost work, *Jesus,* a reinterpreter of the New Testament. Shiel's narratives are consistently extravagant in style and subject, appealing to afficionados of the offbeat in literature. Recognized as his masterpiece, *The Purple Cloud* is an example of Shiel's favorite theme of a world apocalypse out of which emerges an extraordinary individual who, like the character Adam Jeffson, is the first specimen of a new humanity.

Shiel was born in the West Indies and raised in a devoutly religious household. Later he attended Kings College in London and studied medicine at St. Bartholomew's Hospital, though he ultimately chose a literary career. His first book, a collection of short stories entitled *Prince Zaleski,* was originally brought out by John Lane, publisher of the *fin de siècle* magazine *The Yellow Book,* which was notorious as a symbol of 1890s decadence in English art and literature. This collection featured decorations by decadent artist Aubrey Beardsley; the protagonist of the stories, Prince Zaleski, is often described as a decadent version of Sherlock Holmes, a genius living exiled from humankind in his hermitage of exotic decor. The stories in Shiel's second collection, *Shapes in the Fire,* carry on a tradition of Poesque supernatural horror, including the macabre and atmospheric anthology pieces "Xelucha" and "The House of Sounds." Examples of some of Shiel's best short fiction can also be found in the later collection *The Pale Ape, and Other Pulses.*

In his first novel, *The Yellow Danger,* Shiel introduces one of his characteristic themes: that of the Nietzscheian superman. Like *The Yellow Wave* and *The Yellow Peril, The Yellow Danger* hails the technological and, to Shiel, moral superiority of the white race. The grandiose naval battles in this novel are typical of the large scale upheaval in which he prepares his main characters for their destinies as leaders in a new world. *The Lord of the Sea* again features a superman hero, and to critic Sam Moskowitz this book is the high point of an anti-Semitic ideology which runs throughout Shiel's works. More overtly, Shiel in his writings often attacked Christianity and all religious belief in general, preferring a faith in science and the progress of biological evolution. In *The Young Men Are Coming* he expresses his ethic of physical and intellectual superiority with the parodic proverb: "Cursed are the meek! For they shall *not* inherit the earth." The extermination of all but two members of the human race by a deadly mist is the basis for Shiel's best work, *The Purple Cloud.* For the most part this novel is admired as a tour de force in which narrative interest is maintained despite the presence of only a single character throughout almost the entire story.

Much of the fascination for Shiel's readers lies not in his bizarre plots and superhuman heroes but in his flamboyant style

From a drawing by Neil Austir; courtesy of A. Reynolds Morse

which employs a wealth of rare words, exotic images, and a vast knowledge of extraordinary subjects. A. Reynolds Morse calls him "one of the greatest writers ever to use the English language." Though most critics would consider this an obvious overstatement, Shiel's original imagination, his weird inventiveness, and his intense individuality qualify him as an important writer in the history of fantastic literature.

PRINCIPAL WORKS

Prince Zaleski   (short stories)   1895
Shapes in the Fire   (short stories)   1896
The Yellow Danger   (novel)   1898
Cold Steel   (novel)   1899
The Man-Stealers   (novel)   1900
The Lord of the Sea   (novel)   1901
The Purple Cloud   (novel)   1901
The Weird o' It   (novel)   1902
The Yellow Wave   (novel)   1905
The Last Miracle   (novel)   1906
The Isle of Lies   (novel)   1908
The Pale Ape, and Other Pulses   (short stories)   1911
The Dragon   (novel)   1913; also published as *The Yellow Peril,* 1929
How the Old Woman Got Home   (novel)   1927

THE ATHENAEUM (essay date 1895)

[In *Prince Zaleski*] Mr. M. P. Shiel seems to have aimed at a combination of the mysterious terror inspired by Poe's tales and of the sensational amazement which Mr. Sherlock Holmes's extraordinary perspicacity provokes. The ingenious prince who unravels these mysteries for the guileless Mr. Shiel bears a strong family resemblance to some of the well-known private detectives of fiction, in spite of his Oriental luxury, his mystical erudition, and his comparative politeness; but the stories are something more than surprising—they have distinctly the faculty of creating a creepy feeling and of making the reader feel genuinely uncomfortable. But Mr. Shiel does not yet make the best use of his very real talent for the terrible: he is not quite simple and direct enough. The most successful stories of this character attain their end by an almost bald clearness of plot; if any over-elaboration or superabundance of detail be introduced, the momentary pause given to the reader by the necessity of thinking over the circumstances detracts considerably from the impressiveness of the general effect. The fact is that where Mr. Shiel has failed is in his attempt to combine the detective story with the tale of horror; he would have been more successful if he had told the stories simply, without troubling about the prince's cleverness in elucidating them. The story which suffers most from the detective element is the first, which but for that is really the most terrible; the second is the simplest and most artistically perfect; the third is to some extent spoilt by a rather stupid pun. Mr. Shiel's style is original, and under the circumstances not ineffective; the occasional French words and French uses, such as "matinal" for *matutinal,* and the general preciosity of the language seem to suit the description of the mysterious prince who is the central figure. (pp. 375-76)

"Short Stories: 'Prince Zaleski'," in The Athenaeum, *No. 3517, March 23, 1895, pp. 375-76.*

THE BOOKMAN New York (essay date 1895)

Prince Zaleski was a glorified Sherlock Holmes. "The victim of a too importunate, too unfortunate love, which the fulgor of the throne could not abash," took to meditation on the past and future of mankind, and when some one brought him the chatter of the daily newspapers, which he scorned to read, he would deign to light up the mysteries of the present with his magnificent mind. If only he could have been wiled from his gloomy palace to watch the sordid wickedness of the world, not one crime would have gone undetected. But he was probably not much interested in the detection of crime; only in the philosophy of the motives, and in the illustration crime affords of the strange workings of the human soul. We can imagine him saying, with a yawn, to an ordinary baffled Scotland Yard officer, "Oh, there is nothing in that. Show me something more difficult." Indeed, Mr. Shiel had to invent impossibly

difficult puzzles for him, otherwise he would not have dared to approach so magnificent a creature at all. "He lay back on his couch, volumed in a Turkish *beneesh,* and listened to me, a little wearily perhaps at first, with woven fingers, and the pale inverted eyes of old anchorites and astrologers, the moony greenish light falling on his always wan features." His *mise en scène* is magnificent; an open sarcophagus with the mummy of an ancient Memphian, palaeolithic implements, gnostic gems, fretted gold lamps, fumes of *cannabis sativa* make part of it. Plainly, only crimes of a poetic order could be brought for detection here. . . . Mr. Shiel's mysteries are very good, if a trifle laboured, and he has put them into literary form. But as he has not quite got us under the mystic spell, we are not able to maintain a constant gravity before his gorgeous prince. (pp. 266-67)

"Novel Notes: 'Prince Zaleski'," in The Bookman, New York *(copyright, 1895, by George H. Doran Company), Vol. 1, No. 4, May, 1895, pp. 266-67.*

THE BOOKMAN London (essay date 1898)

Mr. Shiel is a marvellous man. His audacity is splendid. He foretells the future—a ghastly vision. He relates the history of Armageddon. He slaughters not regiments, but races; he blows up not ships, but fleets. He harrows our very souls with prophecies of horror. [In **"The Yellow Danger"** he] has written a remarkable, an extraordinary book, though its excellence is not literary—an extravaganza of unparalleled boldness that, whether we laugh or no, we cannot well help but read. It gratifies our national vanity, too, for England becomes the refuge of the distracted nations, and an English youth saves the world from ruin. Again and again throughout the pages there is a great complacent roaring of the British Lion. But—since we speak of roaring—the naval battles are really good—good reading, that is, for landsmen—we are no experts. And this at least seems true, that with our modern apparatus, so much stronger, as the writer points out, for attack than defence, the mutual destruction in a battle of ironclads would be appalling. On naval matters the book is interesting; when it imitates the statesmen and newspapers of the day it is clever; when it discourses of tortures it is creepy; and when it drowns Chinamen—millions of them, with outstanding pigtails—in the Maelstrom it crosses the limit of horror and becomes comical. Mr. Shiel, we repeat, is a marvelous man, and his book is a marvellous book. (p. 169)

"Novel Notes: 'The Yellow Danger'," in The Bookman, London, *Vol. XIV, No. 84, September, 1898, pp. 169-70.*

THE BOOKMAN London (essay date 1901)

[In **"The Lord of the Sea"** there] is so much confidence, such superfluous vigour, and such thundering eloquence in the book that not all those who throw it away as intolerable will throw it into the rubbish heap. Absurd it may be—and we think it is—but its absurdity has something sublime about it, and its audacity is magnificent. It is one of the "Strong Man" books. For the most part these are idealisations of Mr. Cecil Rhodes. But Richard Hogarth is not another Rhodes. His dominion extends—or is to extend, for it is a tale of the future—over land and sea. But Europe isn't quite ready for him. Poor Europe! It has indeed had little preparation for embracing so tremendous a saviour, and stabs and beats the regenerator, till he thinks he would like to go back to his blacksmith's forge.

(For he had been English yeoman and blacksmith ere Destiny found him.) But finding out that he is a full-blooded Jew, he elects rather to lead the chosen people in Palestine. This he does with extraordinary success, and we see him again there as an old man, like David before the Ark, dancing to the Lord. "With body and arms danced he; and with toe and heel he danced. And he sang a Song of Ages." But, no, we will not give that Song of Ages. Our readers might implicate us in Hogarth's madness. Oh, we haven't hinted at a thousandth part of his adventures or the wonderful things in his career. No cold-blooded Northerner this man, who was made to rule us all, and lead us to the real goal of humanity, but an Oriental; and Mr. Shiel seems to exult in making him as extravagantly Oriental as possible, and in defying all tame conventions in his picture of the man with the "hinnying laugh" and the three black moles on his cheek. Well, Orientals have their moments of exaltation. But they are mostly distinguished for their gravity. However, this isn't a book that admits of discussion for a moment. You must swallow it or cast it away—far away. Is it nightmare or inspiration?

> *"Nightmare or Inspiration," in* The Bookman, *London, Vol. XX, No. 119, August, 1901, p. 156.*

THE BOOKMAN London (essay date 1907)

Mr. M. P. Shiel has enough imagination to furnish forth a dozen novelists; if he had only an equal share of judgment and could control his imagination, instead of being controlled by it, he would be one of the greatest forces in modern fiction; for imagination is the one thing that is lacking in the majority of new novels. Mr. Shiel seems to be wanting in the powers of observation, judgment, reticence, that most of our leading modern novelists have, and to have that supreme gift of imaginative inventiveness that most of them want. His German Baron Kolar is a big and admirable piece of characterisation, but when you find the Baron kidnapping men who resemble facially the traditional portraits of Christ, starving and torturing them to get the right look of anguish into their expressions, then actually crucifying them and using the means that were adopted for producing the illusion of "Pepper's Ghost" to throw an apparition of the crucified man up into the dark arches of a crowded church, your belief in it all breaks down under the strain, and the whole thing becomes as grotesquely fantastic and impossible as a nightmare. The Baron's object is to avenge himself for a wrong he has suffered at the hands of a priest by working up a great religious revival on the strength of these miraculous appearances, and then by exposing the imposture and accusing the Church of aiding him in it to deal religion a death blow from which it will never recover. The daring originality of ["**The Last Miracle**"] fascinates you; its careless coincidences, the luridly melodramatic extravagance of some of its incidents exasperates you; but Mr. Shiel's triumph is that you are interested in spite of yourself, and once started cannot put the story aside till you have come to the end of it.

> *"Novel Notes: 'The Last Miracle," in* The Bookman, *London, Vol. XXXII, No. 192, September, 1907, p. 214.*

CARL VAN VECHTEN (essay date 1926)

My first impressions of Shiel were rather mixed. I think, indeed, that this might be anybody's experience, unless he happens to be lucky enough to hit first upon one of the better novels, *The Lord of the Sea*, for example, for the work of this imaginative adept is curiously uneven—not a little of it bearing the mark of undue haste in execution—and its intelligent perusal and appraisement is further complicated by the fact that this author from year to year has varied his "tone," style and form yielding to the mood of the new matter presented. Unfortunately, I did not start out with the best books. I began with *Prince Zaleski*, . . . and I could honestly say that I liked it, but the next two volumes that I read—I shall not mention their names here—almost caused me to forsake the quest. (pp. 150-51)

Nevertheless, even if they are lucky enough to begin with one of the better of Shiel's romances, most readers, I fancy, will find it necessary to acquaint themselves with several others before they can appreciate with any exactitude the magic of this writer or can capitulate to his special charm. Any novice in the matter, to be sure, should be perfectly aware at once of the vitality and glamour, the presence of the grand manner, in *The Lord of the Sea*, but whether he will see further than this, at first, I am not so sure, for Shiel, apparently, to an early reader, is a mere maker of plots, a manufacturer of wild romances in the manner of Jules Verne or of the Dumas of Monte-Cristo. It is only a little later that one perceives that here there is a philosophic consciousness, a sophisticated naïveté, an imaginative au delà, of which the plot is only the formal expression. Shiel, I feel convinced, will satisfy any admirer of *The Count of Monte-Cristo*, but, in the end, he will also satisfy any reader who cares for George Meredith or Herman Melville, two writers, as unlike as the Poles in themselves, with whom the author of *The Lord of the Sea* has a certain esoteric affinity, and gradually it will further become evident that Shiel may be compared more reasonably with the H. G. Wells of the early romances, and even with W. H. Mallock, than with the creator of *Twenty Thousand Leagues Under the Sea.* (pp. 151-52)

> *Carl Van Vechten, "Matthew Phipps Shiel," in his* Excavations: A Book of Advocacies *(copyright, 1926 and renewed 1954 by Carl Van Vechten; reprinted by permission of the publisher), Knopf, 1926, pp. 148-61.*

H. P. LOVECRAFT (essay date 1927)

Matthew Phipps Shiel, author of many weird, grotesque, and adventurous novels and tales, occasionally attains a high level of horrific magic. *Xelucha* is a noxiously hideous fragment, but is excelled by Mr. Shiel's undoubted masterpiece, *The House Of Sounds,* floridly written in the "yellow nineties," and recast with more artistic restraint in the early twentieth century. This story, in final form, deserves a place among the foremost things of its kind. It tells of a creeping horror and menace trickling down the centuries on a sub-arctic island off the coast of Norway; where, amidst the sweep of daemon winds and the ceaseless din of hellish waves and cataracts, a vengeful dead man built a brazen tower of terror. It is vaguely like, yet infinitely unlike, Poe's *Fall of the House of Usher.* In the novel *The Purple Cloud* Mr. Shiel describes with tremendous power a curse which came out of the arctic to destroy mankind, and which for a time appears to have left but a single inhabitant on our planet. The sensations of this lone survivor as he realises his position, and roams through the corpse-littered and treasure-strewn cities of the world as their absolute master, are delivered with a skill and artistry falling little short of actual majesty. Unfortunately the second half of the book, with its conventionally romantic element, involves a distinct letdown. (p. 392)

H. P. Lovecraft, "Supernatural Horror in Literature" (1927), in his Dagon and Other Macabre Tales, edited by August Derleth (copyright 1965, by August Derleth; reprinted by permission of Arkham House Publishers, Inc.), Arkham House, 1965, pp. 347-413.*

M. P. SHIEL (essay date 1935)

I have considered no music too sweet, nor wit too deep, to put into the sort of narrative of events that I have evolved. It seems to be considered in England that the one named *The Purple Cloud* is my "best," but in America they think better of my *How the Old Woman Got Home* . . . while I myself think best of one named *Children of the Wind*—or think best of the *memory* of the dream of it, for I shrink from re-reading it, lest I should find it less rich in wit and singing than I anticipate, as once happened to me. But the *Old Woman* one has this distinction, that in it is given, so to say, my political system. I first demonstrate what "*good*" means—and anyone who makes quite sure of this little thing will be astonished at the flood of light which it will throw into his thoughts on all sorts of subjects. I demonstrate, then, that the noun "*Good*" means pleasure, that the adjective "*good*" means pleasant—and nothing else. Then I demonstrate that *all* pleasure, *all* good, is the result of truth, of science—the science of the amoeba or of Newton. Then I demonstrate that the growth of truth, of science, of pleasure, of Good, depends (1) upon brains (a little), and (2) upon luck (much). Then I demonstrate that, though the luck of a million is exactly a millionfold more than the luck of one, the million must be *in the way* of truth, seeking truth, or no luck can accrue—must be scientists, men of leisure; but this they can't be, if they are slaves, i.e., "landless men", men without a country: so that any great growth of Good depends upon countries being owned by nations. (pp. 25-6)

M. P. Shiel, "Of Myself," in his Science, Life and Literature *(reprinted by permission of Dr. Jan van Loewen), Williams and Norgate Ltd, 1950, pp. 15-27.*

EDWARD SHANKS (essay date 1947)

[M. P. Shiel was] one of the most remarkable minds and imaginations of all time. (p. 469)

[*The Purple Cloud*] would appear to date itself with some definiteness. When it was written the North Pole was still unreached, and the recent failure of Nansen to reach it was still lively in the public mind. That failure did make credible the fancy which inspired Shiel, the idea that there was something mystically forbidden about this particular spot on the surface of the earth. Now not one but several men have trodden the ice of the Pole and we are told that it is destined to be the Clapham Junction of the airlines of the future. But who cares a rap about this when he reads Shiel's account of Adam Jeffson's journey or regards it as anything but a proper and adequate prelude to the tremendous fantasy which follows? This book was a legend, an apocalypse, out of space, out of time.

In speaking of Shiel, it is difficult to avoid giving the impression that he was a 'one-book' man. To some extent at any rate, that he must always be. There is a parallel case which is worth mentioning. Herman Melville will always first and foremost be the author of *Moby Dick*. For as many generations ahead as one can see critics and readers will continue to pay at any rate lip-service to that one book. But among the readers thus influenced some will always seek in other books the qualities however attenuated or frustrated which made that one great.

So it will be with Shiel. The gold which shows so richly in his finest work can be seen in all the others and there will always be readers anxious to seek it out. They will be rewarded. For the first and last thing to be said about him is that he had the character of a poet and a prophet—a prophet, I mean, in the Old Testament manner. His vision always approached the apocalyptic, just as his style often approached (sometimes, one has to own, too closely) the dithyrambic. He believed intensely in what he saw, whether it was a depopulated world or a world set right by the application of an economic theory. He may—I could not tell—have attempted to compromise with the demands made on authors who desire popular success. If he ever did, his own indomitable inner self kept on breaking in. I doubt whether it would be possible to read a whole page of any of his books without recognizing the author. (pp. 469-70)

Edward Shanks, "Epilogue" (originally his address at the funeral of Matthew Phipps Shiel on February 24, 1947), in The Works of M. P. Shiel: A Study in Bibliography *by A. Reynolds Morse, Fantasy Publishing Co., Inc., 1948 (and reprinted in* The Works of M. P. Shiel (1865-1947), A Resurgence: The Shielography Updated, Vol. III, *by A. Reynolds Morse, privately published by the author, 1980, 469-71).*

A. REYNOLDS MORSE (essay date 1947)

When reading Shiel I find myself in an enchanted world of refulgent, semi-scientific fantasy. I discover a pair of evanescent creatures with viscera of white fire who excrete pure carbon, a box emitting rays that blind the Chinese hordes invading England, and a vivisectionist who betrays himself by taking out insurance on his victims.

Shiel has been a master at romantic fantasy and unbounded invention from the beginning. His first published book, *Prince Zaleski* . . . is no less energetic and amazing than his last, *The Young Men Are Coming!* . . . He can always float a sunken ship, unravel a murder, or conjure creatures from the outer atmosphere to cause an earthly hurricane just at the crucial moment. He has no equal when it comes to accounting for extraneous objects found in a coffin; to killings by a pistol set off by the sun, or to catching a would-be slayer in his own electric trap. Indeed, in some tales he invents so freely and so rapidly that his details almost clog the story. Whatever he is talking about, he is always specific: a steam engine, antique architecture, medicine, or odd weapons. (pp. 481-82)

Shiel is at once so formidable, majestic and remote a citadel that it is difficult to decide just how to approach him. After one is exposed to the musical tumult of his rhythm, the surprising cacophony, the rapid irregular beat of his creative style, the once-dull ear becomes intensely sensitive, like Haco Harfager's in "**The House of Sounds.**" In the midst of an imposing storm (indeed there is hardly a single Shiel novel which does not somewhere involve a mighty tempest) Harfager could still hear the delicate tinkle of a silver bell buried deep in a remote crypt inside a coffin containing the corpse of his mother. As the rats chewed their way through special partitions set in the coffin which was open at the foot, they bit through strings which caused a series of bells to tinkle, signalling the progressive stages of his mother's physical disintegration.

The real problem is not only to get the uninitiated into this most ornate and romantic Gothic edifice, but to lure him on to explore it further; for there are admittedly many stumbling blocks in the pathway to Shiel's exotic kingdom. Quite apart from his reckless disregard of sentence and paragraph structure, his use of an apparently unlimited vocabulary, and all the other stylistic and literary problems he poses, there is the disturbing fact that his mind-wrenching stories often end not with a bang but a whimper: witness the tantalizing denouement of *The Last Miracle* . . . , in which Baron Gregor Kolar fights to overthrow the Church defended by a devout Christian. In a unique test of their credos the men meet to choose between two pills, one of which contains poison. The world turmoil over the Baron's fake miracles and the death throes of Christianity are almost ignored at the end, and the grim foe of the Church is left archly triumphant. Or in *Contraband of War* . . . , when the refined Spaniard Appadacca finds he cannot defeat the rough American Dick Hocking, after a struggle that is almost global in its implications, he joins forces with him. The book ends on a note of bathos, for the world would be literally at the feet of *two* such Overmen as these. But not all of Shiel's stories have this characteristic ending. There are several which are close to the conventional, like [*The Man-Stealers, Cold Steel, This Knot of Life,* or *The White Wedding*] . . . , wherein gamekeeper Shan O'Shannon, in a raging torment between loyalty and love marries a girl who is pledged to his master.

Shiel's characters often expound an infinite wisdom and then act as though they had none at all. (pp. 482-83)

Shiel is apt to try one's patience by having his characters overlook the obvious. They never take the shortest distance between points, invariably choosing the most round-about. In *The Evil that Men Do* . . . , Hartwell for five exciting years fails to piece together a note he found in the pocket of an overcoat which proves the man Drayton, whom he is impersonating, to be guilty of murder! . . . Wealthy Jack Hay, in *The Weird O' It* . . . , spends a miserable night in an infested London doss-house in the futile effort to impress on his stubborn consciousness the sin of a world which allows such vile places to exist. The end, the Overman concept, that Shiel has in mind for his people is admirable, but the other way thither is strewn with thorns.

One is also often tempted to inquire how any character can survive Shiel's abuse. One wonders how his women, [Margaret in *The Man-Stealers,* Laura in *Cold Steel,* or even Hannah in *The Lost Viol*] . . . , manage to outlive an adventurous pace that would undo a twentieth century man! It is obvious that his people can only draw their superior vitality from the author himself. (pp. 483-84)

I personally regard M. P. Shiel as one of the greatest writers ever to use the English language. . . . I have long been deeply conscious of the radiant glow of his inextinguishable genius. His profound knowledge, his immense vocabulary, his liquid light-bubbling poetic narrative, his vast vivid imaginings combine to lift him leagues above the other great novelists. (pp. 485-86)

> *A. Reynolds Morse, "Introduction" (1947), in his* The Works of M. P. Shiel: A Study in Bibliography, *Fantasy Publishing Co., Inc., 1948 (and reprinted in his* The Works of M. P. Shiel (1865-1947), A Resurgence: The Shielography Updated, Vol. III, *privately published by the author, 1980, pp. 481-86).*

SAM MOSKOWITZ　(essay date 1963)

[Shiel] produced three detective stories which were published . . . under the title *Prince Zaleski*. (p. 143)

Prince Zaleski, a mysterious Russian, solved difficult crimes by brilliant deduction. M. P. Shiel personally assumed the role of his "Dr. Watson," but instead of London's metropolitan Baker Street there was a Gothic castle furnished with partially unwrapped mummies. The stories are primarily of historical interest, actually being no more than pastiches falling into the same category as Maurice LeBlanc's Lupin or August Derleth's Solar Pons tales, take-offs on the Holmes stories. Nevertheless, this book caused renowned novelist Arnold Bennett to comment later: "I read, and was excited by, *Prince Zaleski* when it first appeared."

Shiel's next book was a rather ordinary romance, *The Rajah's Sapphire,* . . . and followed within months by *Shapes in the Fire,* a collection of short stories. The latter . . . [includes] a number of his most bizarre tales of horror, including *Xelucha, Tulsah,* and *Vaila,* the last later rewritten under the title of *The House of Sounds.* The style of all of them is berserk Poe with all genius spent. (pp. 143-44)

The thought that England might be conquered by the yellow men of Asia was Shiel's contribution to the literature of future wars. In later years, Shiel's publishers made the claim that the phrase "the yellow danger" was coined by him. (p. 145)

[*The Yellow Danger*] suited the mood of the times. . . . Through the lips of his Chinese strategist, Dr. Yen How, M. P. Shiel expresses his view of the inherent superiority of the white man over the yellow when he tells his compatriots: "Poh! Your Navy! Who built it for you? It was they. Your Navy is like a razor in the hands of an ape which has seen its master use it. The brute may or may not cut its own throat with it."

Yen How urges that the yellow races strike before the white man's progress has made the dream of yellow supremacy a forlorn hope. Uniting China and Japan, Yen How, through political manipulation in Asia (where the leading European nations were involved at the turn of the century), starts a frightful war on the continent. In chapter after chapter, Shiel spares no detail in describing the battle movements of every naval unit of the Great Powers of that period, even to the extent of drawing sketches of the battle formations, which are included in the book. (pp. 145-46)

The quality and importance of this work are on a part with the plot outline, but the book reached a wide audience.

Following this heartening success, Shiel's next science fiction novel . . . was again a future war tale, but with a difference. Frequently referred to as the second best of Shiel's novels, *The Lord of the Sea* reaches an intensity of anti-Semitism that provokes comparison with Hitler's *Mein Kampf,* for which it could have served as an inspiration.

This is the background: The Jews, after being systematically expelled from every nation in Europe for buying up half the land and holding mortgages on the rest (literally), flood into England, where they begin the process anew. One third of all members of Parliament are Jews. After initial prosperity, the poor British farmers, who must pay rent to the Jews, bend under the heavy yoke.

The prime Jewish villain, Frankl, is pictured as lewdly grasping for Irish girls with "phylacteried left arm." He also routinely forecloses mortgages as a prelude to Sabbath rites. Frankl, described by one of Shiel's characters as a "dirty-livered Jew," is interrupted at his prayers by the hero, Richard Hogarth, who whips him with a riding crop.

Tired from his exertions and bleeding from a stab wound in the shoulder inflicted by a servant attempting to save his master from the beating, Hogarth, whose physical description amazingly parallels that of Shiel, returns home to receive the staggering news from his Irish father that he was actually born of Jewish parents; therefore he should take pride in his people: "*They* are the people who've got the money." (pp. 146-47)

[Hogarth] makes public that he is a Jew. He is banished to Palestine where he is revealed to be a new incarnation of Jesus who, for the next sixty years, rules his people. During that period, Shiel says, his followers took the commandment "Thou shalt not steal" to heart, and "therefore, Israel with some little pain attained to this."

Only in his prediction that Palestine would flourish under the Jews does Shiel's novel show any merit, either in prophecy, prose, or decency. It need scarcely be emphasized that the only difference between his method and the Nazis' rests in the fact that he would have permitted the Jews to emigrate with their lives. (pp. 147-48)

[*The Purple Cloud*] is justifiably the most highly regarded of Shiel's works. . . . (p. 148)

The Purple Cloud shows strong influence of Mary Wollstonecraft Shelley's *The Last Man* in its seemingly interminable yet individually potent episodes describing a world from which virtually all human life has departed. . . . On reaching civilization [after an expedition to the North Pole, the protagonist, Adam Jeffson,] discovers that the entire earth is a vast graveyard. The cause, a purple gas issuing from fissures, has killed everyone.

On this device, H. G. Wells commented, "No one can dispute that some great emanation of vapour from the interior of the earth, such as Mr. Shiel has made a brilliant use of in his *Purple Cloud,* is consistent with every demonstrated fact in the world."

Jeffson's twenty-year, detailed search through the ruins of the world, since it is presented in synoptic diary form with frequent self-conscious flarings of rhetoric, is scarcely easy reading. Nor is the description particularly pleasant, of Jeffson's shift toward madness that causes him to burn city after city. Neither is his unreasonable brutality when he finally discovers, alive in Constantinople, a girl who was so young when the catastrophe occurred that she doesn't even know how to speak.

The reaction on finishing the novel is similar to that experienced on completing Franz Kafka's grim *Metamorphosis:* It was worth reading, but you would hate to do it again! (pp. 148-49)

Shiel, though weak at plotting, was a writer's writer stylistically. His mad literary rhythms, seemingly improvised, like a jazz artist's at a jam session, were a bubbling fountain at which new techniques of phrasing could be drunk. While the artistry was rarely sustained, it had flashes of splendor. For 1901, a passage like "Pour, pour, came the rain, raining as it can in this place, not long, but a torrent while it lasts, dripping in thick liquidity like a profuse sweat through the wood . . ." anticipated the method of innovators like Thomas Wolfe at a much later date.

Again Shiel turned to the theme of future war for *The Yellow Wave.* . . . This is really a love story projected against the background of a war between Russia and Japan which threatens to involve the other nations of the world, which have at last learned the ways of peace. Never one to coddle his lead characters, Shiel sacrifices the two lovers at the end to bring peace between the combatants.

In *The Last Miracle* . . . fiction is once more used to project one of Shiel's fanatical hatreds, one as violent as that against the Jews. Though he was the son of a minister, Shiel knew no bounds in his almost paranoid vilification of organized religion. He felt that the only true religion was science and that science was the only thing that uplifted a man, whereas to the great faiths he attributed most, if not all, of the blame for man's problems and ignorance.

In this novel, a scientist, through undisclosed means, causes the disappearance of people, and their various crucifixions appear as "visions" in churches throughout the world. The novel terminates so abruptly as to be virtually unfinished. Its purpose seems to be a vast orgy of antireligious diatribe, rather than the telling of a story. For the solution of men's problems, Shiel offers, in notes to the book, some deep-breathing exercises which resulted in unfavorable, but deserved, comparison with Bernarr Macfadden, who, even then, was promoting "physical culture" to commercial success.

Shiel's *style* in storytelling was so spectacular that many tend to think all his books are fantasies. Collectors read and collect his books for the bizarreness of his method, regardless of their literary classification. Therefore, while other books written during the same period as those outlined, such as *Contraband of War, Cold Steel, The Man-Stealers, The Weird o' It, Unto the Third Generation, The Evil That Men Do, The Lost Viol, The White Wedding,* and *This Knot of Life,* might interest the Shiel devotee, they are neither science fiction nor fantasy.

A borderline case is *The Isle of Lies* . . . , in which a youth is trained to virtual infallibility of memory and clear thinking, but fails in an attempt for political control of the globe because of his weakness for women.

One of the books listed, *This Knot of Life* . . . , is of special importance, inasmuch as it strengthens the certainty of Shiel's tendency to a Nazi-like anti-Semitism. In many of his books appears the superman, forerunner of the super race. Shiel has a new term for such men. He calls them "Overmen," and in *This Knot of Life* admits to having derived the term from the German "*Ubermensch.*" His villain here is a fiendish Jew named Sam Abrahams. Some student might, as an exercise, try to find a single Shiel book in which there is not a direct or implied slur at the Jews, usually accompanied by another at religion. *The Dragon* . . . reprinted as *The Yellow Peril* . . . is no exception—in it he classifies a group of English traitors as "pure Jews, only, with their bad heredity, lacking the brains of Jews."

As might be inferred from the title under which it was reprinted, *The Yellow Peril* is almost a paraphrase of *The Yellow Danger.* Again, a diabolical Chinese ("the only man who can outwit a Jew in business is a Chinaman—don't forget") sets the European nations at one another's throats so they are weakened for the poised Oriental invasion. The Chinese again come galloping across Asia and Europe, like a movie retake. Shiel heartily approves of this, because it will destroy Christianity and religion. "Good!" he says. "Now, the scientist denies that apes, Negroes, bishops, bouzis, dervishes, are religious."

In the nick of time, when England is about to be invaded, the Overman ("*Ubermensch*") comes up with a ray that blinds all the invaders. The Overman issues the following dictum, the epitome of Shiel's lifelong philosophy:

That Great Britain be considered my private property by right of Conquest.

That taxes (except "death-duties") be abolished; and "customs."

That citizens be liable to daily drill, including running and breathing.

At the age of seventy, Shiel claimed he was still running six miles a day for reasons of health.

That Research and Education be the nation's main activities.

That education, transport, power, médicine, and *publishing* be taken over by the government.

That Doctors be "consecrated"; and be Bachelors of Science; and be taught in "Consecration" that "To the pure, all things are pure."

That Clergymen now leave off uttering in public, for money, whatever comes to seem childish to average people.

With this book, Shiel ended a period of eighteen years of writing and did not resume again for ten years. The only other book worthy of serious attention in this era is the short story collection *The Pale Ape* . . . , which contains some of Shiel's better short stories, including *Huguenin's Wife* as well as a unique detective character, Cummings King Monk, who is adept at ventriloquism in addition to his deductive accomplishments. (pp. 149-52)

[A] great deal of energy and venom still remained in Shiel when he wrote *This Above All,* a fable of immortality. . . . Based on the idea of the eternal woman, possibly inspired by Karel Čapek's *The Makropoulos Secret,* Shiel's volume centers around a Jewess who has come down through the ages as an imperishable thirteen-year-old, and her efforts to get Lazarus (who is still alive after being touched by the hand of Christ centuries earlier) to marry her. In the meanwhile, so as not to get rusty while waiting, she has married a whole string of mortal men whom she discards as they age. The plot is constantly being interrupted by her blasts against Christianity and religion, her advocacy of science and research as well as long fasts, and her slow and silent eating (preferably honey and nuts).

It soon develops that Jesus is still alive and that Jesus, Lazarus, and the "young" girl are all members of a special race of long-lived human beings. Here, Shiel attempts to alter the theological picture of Jesus. While he concedes that the man was basically good and kind, he warns that he was also a Jew and, if alive, might favor his own people. He also retranslates from the original Greek and reinterprets New Testament passages, to the effect that Jesus may have occasionally imbibed too much wine and that he was really not against divorce. The reader is faced with a decision: Does Shiel hate the Jews because they created Christianity, or does he hate Christianity because it was created by Jews?

If the book has any worth-while message, it lies in the preachment that age/immortality does not mean wisdom. Shiel, himself, seems an excellent case in point.

Probably Shiel's single best short story is *The Place of Pain,* to be found in the collection *The Invisible Voices.* It deals with a Negro preacher in British Columbia, once highly respected in the community, who falls from grace and declines into drunkenness after apparently making an unusual discovery in the wilderness. This discovery he eventually confides to a white man who has been kind to him, when he feels he is dying from tuberculosis. It seems that he had by accident found that a rock placed in a mass of froth at the bottom of a waterfall would convert the water into a pool that acted as the convex lens of a telescope. Through this lens, he has seen, or so he implies, nightmarish and monstrous sights on the moon. He dies just as he wades out to place the stone in the correct spot to form a lens for the white man to look through.

The story is magnificently handled and Shiel exercises unaccustomed restraint in its telling. Though the Negro does not duplicate his discovery for the reader or actually describe what he saw on the moon, one is led to believe that he is telling the truth. If there is any flaw, it is that Shiel cannot excise his racial prejudice: "He had called them frankly a pack of apes, a band of black and babbling babies; said that he could pity them from his heart, they were so benighted, so lost in darkness; that what they knew in their wooly nuts was just nothing."

Shiel's last important work of fiction was *The Young Men Are Coming,* and it is at once one of his most imaginative and one of his most damning novels. A sort of super flying saucer lands in England and fantastic flaming-haired creatures whisk away an aging Dr. Warwick. (pp. 153-55)

Returned to earth and immortal, Dr. Warwick organizes the "young men" into a group of virtual storm troopers to defeat the "old men" who are planning a "fascistic" movement. The political goal of the "young men" is to overthrow religion and substitute science (reason) in its place.

A revolutionary war ensues. (p. 155)

As far as bloodshed is concerned, Shiel scoffs at the notion that "the next war will wreck civilization." Wars are merely "inconveniences," he avers, concluding, "*Cursed* are the meek! For they shall *not* inherit the earth."

If one were to assume the role of apologist for M. P. Shiel, what could be said for him? It could be said that while he made no impact on mainstream literature, he did make a minor, if flawed, contribution to science fiction. It might be said that faults aside, his work displayed unquestioned erudition and scholarship, and that there were honest flashes of power and brilliance in his writing.

It would have to be admitted that, in the psychiatrist's vernacular, the man had a "problem." Its manifestations were obvious, but its cause can only be speculated upon. Descriptively Richard Hogarth in *The Lord of the Sea* comes very close to being a replica of Shiel down to the three moles on the cheek and the Irish father. Somewhere along the line did Shiel learn something about his ancestry that he could not reconcile with his early religious training? Is there a link between this information and a mother of whom he never speaks? Was it really the ubiquitous Jewish villain, Dinka, speaking in *The Young Men Are Coming,* "If I am a bit of a Hebrew inside, isn't my coat as Christian as they make 'em?"—or is it Shiel? (pp. 155-56)

> Sam Moskowitz, "The World, the Devil, and M. P. Shiel," in his Explorers of the Infinite: Shapers of Science Fiction *(copyright © 1963, 1959, 1958, 1957 by Sam Moskowitz; copyright © 1960 by Ziff-Davis Publishing Co.; reprinted by permission of the author),* World Publishing Co., 1963, pp. 142-56.

J. MACLAREN-ROSS (essay date 1964)

Large conceptions came easily to Shiel: though sometimes docketed as a writer of Science Fiction, romantic or Gothic fantasies, he was built on the grand scale, and his best novels are Apocalyptic in scope. The themes of international conflict and world domination recur constantly: the latter was often attempted and achieved for the good of humanity by one of his 'Overman' characters—he eschewed 'the misbegotten term superman (latin and anglo-saxon) for Ubermensch'—but his ruthless and basically benevolent Overmen were different from the Teutonic variety: one of them, Richard Hogarth (*The Lord of the Sea,* . . .) was really a Jew whose father's name was Sir Solomon Spinoza. (p. 80)

Adam Jeffson in *The Purple Cloud* surpasses all other Overmen: finding himself alone in a world where everyone has been killed off by a wave of cyanogen gas, he imagines himself to be 'the Arch-one, the motive of the world', and sets out to 'ravage and riot' in his kingdom like the Caesars. It is typical of a Shiel creation that, in [A. Reynolds] Morse's words, Jeffson's 'fear that he will finally find someone else alive mounts page by page' and that when he does come upon his Eve by a streamlet in Istanbul, 'his first impulse is to kill and eat her'. (The Eve motif recurs in many of the novels, notably *The Isle of Lies:* Shiel's women—many of them Jewish, and one patterned after his first wife, 'a Parisian Spaniard' who resembled his mother—are extremely realistic, though wayward and contrary to an infuriating degree, and the course of true love is rarely permitted to have its run.)

Containing not only some of Shiel's most magnificent scenes and set-pieces, *The Purple Cloud* illustrates one of his greatest strengths: the ability to buttress his situations with selective and specific detail which—despite the melodramatic plots, missing wills, lost heiresses, hidden treasures, etc.—causes the reader to suspend disbelief. (p. 81)

It is as though [Shiel] had set himself to make literature out of the late Victorian romantic mystery, much as Stevenson did with Captain Marryat or Raymond Chandler with the material of the *Black Mask* novelette; and, as with the latter, an element of burlesque was perforce present in the result. But even in a short tale like *Monk Wakes an Echo* . . . , in which Shiel is consciously sending-up the sensational stories of his day, the realistic touch and odd detail is not omitted: the Scots baronet-vivisectionist ('the only exact biologist in the world') who, having trapped the Investigator, 'sat to a repast of potatoes, boiled cod, black bread, whisky' with a revolver beside him on the table, is almost a Hitchcockian figure, and in the story's mere sixteen pages, enough incident is packed to supply several episodes of a series like *The Avengers.* (p. 82)

[Shiel's *Best Short Stories*] offers a splendid cross-section of his macabre invention and literary progress; new readers will find there not only Zaleski (who knew 'forty-three—and in one island in the South Seas, forty-four—different methods of doing murder', all undetectable), but an Indian Maharajah who lives to 120, snatches his future wife from her husband's funeral pyre, and is consumed, finally, in a more horrid manner; a Cockney husband raped on the wedding night by his dead sister-in-law (another Rachel); an embalmed corpse which turns into a gigantic vermilion-feathered cat. . . . (p. 83)

But it is Shiel's journey as a stylist that can be charted through these tales: from the impassioned rococo eloquence and beautiful bizarrerie of the early examples to the cool—indeed, chilling—mosaic of words which makes up *The Primate of the Rose;* he had come a long way from Poe and the archaic adjective in his final phase. He took enormous pains, suiting his style to content: a scene of passion or pursuit is panted out in short

breathless gasps; his innumerable tempests . . . literally crackle; his vocabulary, already immense, was enriched by knowledge of many languages and his startling similes were sometimes direct translations from them. He accounted Job the greatest genius and greatest poet who ever lived, and M. P. Shiel the best living prose writer . . . ; many critics in his lifetime, however, endorsed the latter opinion, and certainly one has only to compare his best work with a sham modern-Gothic attempt at a 'powerful' or 'elemental' novel such as *Radcliffe* by David Storey, to see where the difference lies, or his one real piece of Science Fiction . . . *The Young Men Are Coming* (containing evenescent beings from outer space with body-temperature so high that they excrete sticks of carbon) with the modern product so highly praised. (pp. 83-4)

Enigmatic to the last, [Shiel] never revealed to even his closest disciples the full nature of his 'religion of science', designed to replace outmoded Christianity; but now that the missing MS notebooks which were a bar to the publication of *Jesus* have at last come to light, his message may shortly be deciphered. . . . But however important the message may prove, it would be a shocking waste if he were to remain the centre of a philosophical and private cult. A revival is in any case due, and it is as literature that his works are likely to be remembered, which is what he would most have wanted. (p. 84)

J. Maclaren-Ross, "The Strange Realm of M. P. Shiel," in London Magazine (© London Magazine 1964), Vol. 4, No. 6, September, 1964, pp. 76-84.

LIONEL STEVENSON   (essay date 1967)

Shiel's representative novels are obviously in the category of science fantasy, their closest analogues being Wells's *War of the Worlds* and Conan Doyle's *Lost World* and *The Poison Belt.* Shiel differs from such rivals by the subordination of plausible scientific evidence to the sensational elements of insanity, sadism, holocausts of destruction, and heroic death for virtuous characters. The recurrent themes of treasure hoards and autocratic power are the stuff of wishful adolescent dreams; but Shiel was able to give them a sort of demonic plausibility by the sheer audacity of his invention, the portentous philosophical digressions, and the grandiloquent metaphoric style, embroidered with alliteration and internal rhymes.

Many of Shiel's stories first came out as newspaper serials, and he also wrote routine detective fiction under the pseudonym of "Gordon Holmes"; but his work cannot be dismissed as run-of-the-mill thrillers. His overriding concern with style compelled him to make extensive revisions and excisions in such books as were republished in later editions. He seems to have been sincerely convinced that his fiction was contributing to a new philosophy that could reconcile religion and modern science. These artistic and intellectual impulses helped him to demonstrate that the full-blooded Gothic tradition could be revitalized in the twentieth century without lapsing into the ludicrous. (pp. 116-17)

Lionel Stevenson, "Purveyors of Myth and Magic," in his The History of the English Novel: Yesterday and After, Vol. XI (copyright ©, 1967 by Barnes & Noble, Inc.; by permission of Barnes & Noble Books, a Division of Littlefield, Adams & Co., Inc.), Barnes & Noble, 1967, pp. 111-54.*

ADDITIONAL BIBLIOGRAPHY

''A Record-Smashing Literary Resurrection.'' *The Literary Digest* CI, No. 3 (20 April 1929): 29.
> Overview of Shiel's critical reception.

Ross, Mary. ''A World for a Toy.'' *New York Herald Tribune Books* (4 May 1930): 14.
> Scientific background to *The Purple Cloud*.

Russell, D. C. ''In Praise of M. P. Shiel.'' *The New York Times Book Review* (8 April 1945): 3, 27.
> Praise for *The Purple Cloud*.

Shanks, Edward. '' 'The Purple Cloud' and Its Author.'' *The London Mercury* XX, No. 115 (May 1929): 62-9.
> Criticizes most of Shiel's fiction as over-elaborate in plot and style, while praising *The Purple Cloud, The Last Miracle,* and *Prince Zaleski* as his most successful works.

(William Adolf) Carl Sternheim
1878-1942

German dramatist, critic, novella and short story writer, novelist, essayist, poet, and autobiographer.

Sternheim is often regarded, and regarded himself, as "the German Molière." He is remembered for his satires examining middle-class materialism, smugness, and moral duplicity in Wilhemine Germany. These works feature stylized characters, elegant plotting, telegraphic dialogue, and a strict economy of form. Sternheim is also recognized as a forerunner of the expressionist playwrights, and his hectic, staccato dialogue is his contribution to the technique of literary expressionism. Rediscovered by German scholars in the sixties, Sternheim has been said to represent "the high point of social satire in the German theater during the first two decades of the twentieth century."

Sternheim grew up in Berlin. He studied law, philosophy, and psychology at various German universities, but his greatest love was literature. Due to both his family's wealth (his father was a prosperous Jewish banker) and to large settlements from his first two wives, Sternheim was not compelled to write for a living. He in fact lived in luxury residences throughout Europe, while writing his satires of the bourgeoisie and the lower classes. The apogee of Sternheim's career was reached in the period 1911-16, but after World War I his popularity declined. Hitler banned Sternheim's plays as "decadent" in 1933, and the author lived outside Germany for the remainder of his life.

Sternheim's early works include a number of standard romantic tragedies, such as *Ulrich und Brigitte* and *Don Juan*, which explore relations between the sexes. His next works are the first to display the dramatist's characteristic themes and style. In the ten-play cycle *Aus dem bürgerlichen Heldenleben (Scenes from the Heroic Life of the Middle Class)*, Sternheim analyzes bourgeois values and hypocrisies. Opening this drama-cycle is a trilogy of plays—*Die Hose (A Pair of Drawers)*, *Der Snob (The Snob)*, and *1913*—which feature the Maske family as they manipulate their way to social acceptance, material gain, and sexual satisfaction. Sternheim's one-dimensional characters operate in a materialistic society where everyone and everything has a price. His emphasis on individual will and personal freedom in defiance of social conventions derived from his studies of Neitzsche. Sternheim also shares thematic links with dramatist Frank Wedekind, though he avoids Wedekind's ponderous moralizing. In his plays Sternheim views sexuality as a means of personal freedom and presents the bourgeois male as a sexually repressed being obsessed with wealth and power, as seen in *Die Kasette (The Strong Box)*. Critics have mentioned the influence of Sternheim on Bertolt Brecht, a later dramatist who also penetrated bourgeois hypocrisy with humor.

In addition to his dramatic works, Sternheim wrote ironic experimental short stories, collected as *Chronik von des zwanzigsten Jahrhunderts Beginn*. In these pieces he portrays man's primitive drives and tries to reconcile morality and reason, psychological attributes which he found to be in perpetual conflict.

Sternheim's reputation has been reevaluated since the publication of his complete works in the mid-1960s. His comedies have been compared with George Grosz's caricatures—cynical, pessimistic, and satiric, characterizing the cool, detached spirit of the Weimar republic. Sternheim's self-imposed title, "the German Molière," has been variously considered by critics. Walter Sokel has noted that, unlike Molière, Sternheim presents no rounded or sympathetic characters, while Egbert Krispyn has described the Maskes as idealized rather than realistic bourgeois characters, contending that their creator considered the bourgeois "a person of estimable qualities." Sternheim's works have been both condemned as cynical and hailed as free of all illusion. The dramas and short stories explore the implications of freedom, responsibility, and action in middle-class society. Though Sternheim's works expose a narrow mentality in a particular time and place, they have retained their humor along with their significance as social satire.

PRINCIPAL WORKS

Ulrich und Brigitte [first publication]   (drama)   1907
Don Juan   (drama)   1910

Die Hose (drama) 1911
  [*A Pair of Drawers* published in journal *Transition*, 1927;
  also published as *The Underpants* in *The Modern
  Theatre*, 1957; and *The Bloomers* in *Scenes from the
  Heroic Life of the Middle Class*, 1970]
Die Kassette (drama) 1911
  [*The Strong Box* published in *An Anthology of German
  Expressionist Drama*, 1963]
Bürger Schippel (drama) 1913
  [*Paul Schippel, Esq.* published in *Scenes from the Heroic
  Life of the Middle Class*, 1970]
Der Snob (drama) 1914
  [*A Place in the World* published in *Eight European Plays*,
  1927; also published as *The Snob* in *From the Modern
  Repertoire*, 1958]
Chronik von des zwanzigsten Jahrhunderts Beginn. 2 vols.
  (short stories) 1918
Die deutsche Revolution (essay) 1919
Europa. 2 vols. (novel) 1919
Die Marquise von Arcis (drama) 1919
  [*The Mask of Virtue*, 1935]
1913 (drama) 1919
  [*1913* published in *Scenes from the Heroic Life of the
  Middle Class*, 1970]
Tabula Rasa (drama) 1919
Berlin oder Juste Milieu (criticism) 1920
Fairfax (novella) 1921
  [*Fairfax*, 1923]
Tasso oder Kunst des Juste Milieu (criticism) 1921
Aus dem bürgerlichen Heldenleben [first publication]
  (dramas) 1922
  [*Scenes from the Heroic Life of the Middle Class*, 1970]
Das Fossil (drama) 1923
  [*The Fossil* published in *Scenes from the Heroic Life of
  the Middle Class*, 1970]
Gauguin und Van Gogh (criticism) 1924
Die Schule von Uznach, oder Neue Sachlichkeit (drama)
  1926
Vorkriegs-Europa im Gleichnis meines Leben
  (autobiography, letters, and reminiscences) 1936
Gesamtwerk. 10 vols. (dramas, novel, novellas, short
  stories, essays, criticism, and autobiography) 1963-76

PIERRE LOVING (essay date 1924)

If you should ask the younger, the *sansculotte* dramatists of
Germany, what they owe to Carl Sternheim, who is now in
his silverish middle years, they would, one hazards, reply together as a junta, and warmly enough, that it is to him that
they are indebted above everything else for a due recognition
of the value of a dated style. By this is merely meant that they
wish to reflect the age in which they live, its tone, its color,
its rhythm, its dynamism, for it is from these elements that
they themselves, like Sternheim who only slightly precedes
them, draw their deepest sustenance. But the unconscious or
half-conscious dole of Sternheim to those who come after and
in part supersede him is something greater too: they have been
taught by him to flay the apeing conscience of the times. [Frank]
Wedekind accomplished something of this sort also, and Sternheim is in no small degree the worshipful follower of Wedekind.

One imagines in any case such men (taken at random) as [Wal-
ter] Hasenclever, Brecht, [Ivan] Goll, [Reinhard] Göring, [Ar-
nolt] Bronnen admitting without a qualm at least this much.
One imagines moreover that they regard him in the light of a
trail-blazer, a glittering advance courier—glittering like a dark
clouded jewel, however—of what they themselves in the fulness of their gifts hope to become. But to us with no high
incandescent mirage to cut off the far purer distance, because
we approach him and his work across a gulf of objectivity, he
is hardly more than a sharp disciple of the more pungent Wedekind, and what he has taken from both Wedekind and Strindberg stands fairly open on the page. Nevertheless it would be
most unwise and quite unjustifiable to underrate the debt which
almost every writer under thirty-five in Germany and Austria
owes him. Calculable or not, it cannot be easily put aside or
with impunity erased. Somewhere Franz Blei, the German critic
of Expressionism, has traced in characteristic opulent fashion
the whole new trend to Sternheim's plays—or it may be he
did not stop short in his level accusation until he came to the
imposing monument of bitter scorn and barbaric vengefulness
which Sternheim himself is.

One of the most remarkable elements in recent German drama
is its temper of withering satire. Satire is Sternheim's ripest
gift. It is as it were the birthmark by which we may always
know him, whatever his wanderings over years and seas of
change may chance to be. This satire of his is omnipresent,
however, and it is as blasting as the cartoons of George
Grosz. . . . At bottom that is what Sternheim's satire is: treatment, and criticism *pari passu,* of human life; this brings it
home to the nerve-ends and only few people can stand the
enormous strain. Even Germans have charged **"Die Hose"** and
"Bürger Schippel" with being damnably vulgar and grotesque.
In a sense they are so. The average (phantom) reader, if he
truthfully analyzed his emotions on seeing these plays, would
probably say that his scalp crawled or his flesh smarted or his
conscience—having slept serenely the longest of sleeps presumably—started to turn like a sluggish earth-colored worm
prisoned in a slimy furrow of after-rain mould. Of course he
would be only admitting a not too well-known truth, namely
that conscience is the eternal bourgeois in every man. And it
is conscience, to be exact, that Carl Sternheim takes huge
delight in prodding and gouging with his knobbly blunt stick.

Why, it may be asked, should Sternheim choose conscience?
The reason is fairly obvious if we don't scruple to face the
matter. When, say, you read a book of primitive African lore,
a book like [Blaise] Cendrars' "L'Anthologie Nègre" and find
that some half-naked savage, owing to the omission of a sacrifice to his god or to the spirit of his dead enemy, is sadly
thinning away, the flesh dropping from him in what is really
a famishment of the soul—call it interior anguish if you like—
you may put it down without much danger of overstatement
that he is somehow progressing very decently along the road
of eventual philistinism. Well, Sternheim strikes mercilessly
at the fat vine of philistinism inside all men. (Let us remember
that it was Heine who invented the word in its present connotation.) He strikes however hardest of all, most vigorously,
at the pettifogging trivialities of conscience. From this to the
actual middle-class of his nation is but a logical transition. The
middle class is therefore his butt. One observes in the end that
Sternheim is by way of being a humanist, a martyr even, but
a martyr whose love of god is all composed of the yeasty venom
which his soul brews darkly against the devil. He knows quite
well that the conscience of the dull-spirited small man ridic-
ulously imagines itself in the hidden places of its *amour-propre*

as nothing less than a fellow-trencher at the board of kings. The illusion is well worth deflating.

Thus it may be seen that Sternheim is a first-rate moralist and this is true of him even in his most flippant pieces like **"Der Snob"** or **"Fairfax."** But when I say that he is moral, profoundly so, I do not mean, since there is the possibility of confusion in the United States today, that he is a democrat. Let us at once put him down, then, as a moralist who is inveterately undemocratic. He prefers to play the aristocrat in life and is therefore cosmopolitan. His cosmopolitanism on the other hand is so fiercely uncompromising, so proud, that it verges very often on pure snobbishness. This charge would no doubt leave Sternheim quite cold because he is aware, none better, of the elastic meanings of words. He manages to lash and hurt precisely because he can use the words of his victims and twist their ordinary meanings into a harsh mockery of themselves. He does the same with quite commonplace situations. Snobbishness for him may, in consequence, take on the form of a fine art capable of the most exquisite perfection. In almost every one of his plays, from **"Der Marquis von Arcis"** to **"Bürger Schippel,"** he is the silent laughter behind the scenes and the spoken lines.

The young men in Germany and Austria, as I have already pointed out, owe a great deal to Sternheim's style which is—probed to its centre—just one way of looking at life, a distinctively modern way. They have absorbed from him both his flexibility and his offending chunky rawness. The language, however, is beaten—beaten that is, and made flexible thereby—and bullied almost, so that it approaches at times to the pitch of sheer travesty. In this fashion, it will be noted, modelling always the speech he deftly uses, he is able to keep his characters, as he goes along, moving unembarrassedly on the stage. It is so, without tormenting them in the interest of his sly themes, that he gives them true human scope. At the same time, by this very wilful use of language, he manages to steer the pliable mind of the audience. In this I believe—because he does not stint his resources of speech—he shows himself to be a new sort of dramatist in our own theatre. Situation there is a-plenty. But he keeps us amused or engaged by this fashion of wrenching dialogue in his own way. Indeed it is a method that has become nowadays almost traditional in Germany.

One may say with truth that he is an anatomist of human nature; but one thing, being a gentleman of high blood in the literary sense, he will not grant even his closest-limned characters; he will not grant, that is, that his philistine ever thinks, ever genuinely feels, ever imagines at an odd moment what life may be above or without his foaming beer stein, his crassness in love, his cloddish denial of beauty. That, too, is how he likes to regard his auditor. He broadly caricatures his playgoers believing no doubt that, when they laugh at his creations, they do not even know what they are laughing at themselves. Mass stupidity! They do not even know they are being victimized by the dramatist. They laugh as though at their neighbor's foibles. In truth it is they and their next neighbor and the next—the whole circular wall of bodies and lives and ambitions in the theatre—that are being devastatingly jeered at and brought low, crushed by the fattish laugh which comes indeed out of their own loose-lipped mouths. When they return home, when they inadvertently start doing something that faintly resembles a bit of action in the play they just witnessed, when they hear out of their own mouths the imbecilities of Sternheim's characters, then perhaps they are caught up for a brief instant by

a pointed thought that maybe the dramatist was actually mumming them and no one else right before their friends and intimates.

Pierre Loving, "Carl Sternheim," in The Saturday Review of Literature *(copyright © 1924 by* Saturday Review; *all rights reserved; reprinted by permission),* Vol. 1, No. 19, December 6, 1924, p. 360.

WILLIAM A. DRAKE   (essay date 1927)

We have his works before us, and in these we can see, not Carl Sternheim, but Carl Sternheim's Germany. In his fantastic comedies of the German bourgeois life, which he sarcastically terms "heroic," in *Europa, Die Deutsche Revolution, Berlin oder Juste Milieu, Tasso oder Kunst des Juste Milieu, Libussa,* and all the books which have come sputtering from his raucously laughing, iconoclastic pen, we have a panorama of decay and futility. It would be tragic, if Sternheim did not show it to be so inexpressibly ludicrous; desperate, if he did not present it, by means of an adroitly calculated art, in such a way as to leave us with the conviction that all is not yet lost, and that there is still time to bring this reeling world back to its straight course.

Sternheim's comedies, like the plays of Oskar Kokoschka, are not easy for Americans who have not lived intimately in Germany to understand. He has, however, perfected a more universally eloquent medium in what remains, so far, at least, as the world outside of Germany is concerned, his most solid work, the *Chronik von Zwanzigsten Jahrhunderts Beginn.* In the fourteen stories which make up this chronicle of follies and defeats, Sternheim has contrived to denude what he sees to be the soul of the German bourgeoisie, with all its inconsistencies, its virtues, its lusts, its lack of stamina, its frivolous ambitions, its empty pretensions, and its occasional substantial virtues. In **"Vanderbilt,"** for example, he ridicules that bourgeoisie as it reaches forward impudently to grasp a portion of life to which it ought not aspire; and in the more famous story of **"Napoleon,"** he shows the reverse of the medal in an almost tender tale of courageous and patient struggle against adverse circumstances, which is undaunted by every misfortune but, in the end, exasperated beyond endurance by the crassness of the newly rich.

The chief recipient of Sternheim's abuse is the bourgeois social "climber," who, he seems to feel, is especially responsible for the undermining of the structure of modern society. In his comedies, begun as long ago as 1908, he takes the destinies of the Maske family as an example. In the first [*Die Hose*], Theobald Maske is seen as an abject government employee, much disturbed by the fear that an embarrassing accident, which has happened to his wife in public, will endanger his position. In the second [*Der Snob*], Theobald's son, Christian, filled with a desire to rise in the world, follows the eminent example of Sir William Davenant, who claimed Shakespeare as his father, and, by cleverly sacrificing his mother's good fame, manages to convince his aristocratic beloved that his blood is sufficiently blue to mingle with her own. Finally, in *1913,* he appears as the great captain of industry, Christian Maske Freiherr von Buchow, Excellenz, a completed aristocrat. In another play, the whole life of a scholar is upset by the sudden expectation of inheriting a fortune of 140,000 marks. In *Burgher Schippel* and *Tabula Rasa,* the insolent rise of the bourgeoisie to financial prestige is again burlesqued. And the lesson, in each case, is that vaulting ambition makes the bourgeoisie fawning, unscrupulous, and cruel in the going, and leaves them restless and hypocritical anomalies in the end. It is Sternheim's wish, behind his brutal scorn, to bring them back to the simple humanity which they have so long forgotten. (pp. 154-56)

> *William A. Drake, "Carl Sternheim," in his* Contemporary European Writers *(copyright, 1927, by William A. Drake), John Day, 1928, pp. 152-56.*

ARTHUR ELOESSER   (essay date 1933)

Sternheim is important, and exerted considerable influence, on account of his attempt to reform the language of the stage, which was particularly successful in **Bürger Schippel**. Naturalism had tried to reproduce the speech of real life as found in everyday use, with all its falterings, hesitations, pauses, and imperfections. The neo-Romantic revival, which he also regarded as part of the "plush period" [the comfortable, tasteless bourgeois world of the closing decades of the nineteenth century], was, after all, no more than an inverted naturalism, which dressed up its verse and poetic prose in historical costume and made still greater demands upon the stage in the way of scenery and illusionist devices. Sternheim purified his grammar from all the accretions of everyday speech and created what has been called the "telegraphic style," which cuts down the phrase to its essentials, makes it hard and glittering, and lends steely wings to the dialogue. His talent, which, though ingenious, lacked the fostering warmth which would have brought his ideas to maturity, was haunted by visions of Latin comedy, in which the dialogue falls lightly from the tongue in a sort of verbal dagger-play which seeks to reach its mark by thrust and feint and parry. His process of overtraining ended by banting down his characters till they lost all vital colour; yet, all the same, during his best experimental period this method produced an acceleration and heightening of the pace of the action, in which the ideal world of the stage was dominated by the rhythmic movement of the characters. This was the second step towards expressionism, after Wedekind and contemporaneous with [Georg] Kaiser. (pp. 151-52)

> *Arthur Eloesser, "The Literary Revolution," in his* Modern German Literature, *translated by Catherine Alison Phillips (copyright 1933 by Alfred A. Knopf, Inc.; reprinted by permission of the publisher; originally published as* Die Deutsche Literatur vom Barock bis zur Gegenwart, *Bruno Cassirer, 1931), Knopf, 1933, pp. 57-155.**

RICHARD SAMUEL   (essay date 1939)

Sternheim applies elements of Expressionist technique especially in language, the style of which is peculiarly affected. His disillusionment led to cynicism and destructive criticism, but not to a discovery of new values or to humour. There is no character in his plays which attracts our sympathy. His method is caricature, by which it is easy to reveal the vulgarity, weakness and selfishness behind the 'bourgeois mask' though it is impossible thereby to achieve the true aim of Comedy which is to expose human weakness, but with kindliness and forgiveness. (p. 58)

[The 'Telegram Style'] becomes a mannerism with Sternheim who by his cynicism aims at the destruction of existing values. This is reflected in his method of writing; it is known that his original drafts showed the conventional grammatical usage, which was only afterwards distorted. It was the articles that became the particular victims of his pruning knife. (p. 161)

> *Richard Samuel, "The Search of Expressionism for a New Drama and a New Theatre" and "Expressionist Tendencies in Style and Language," in* Expressionism in German Life, Literature and the Theatre (1910-1924) *by Richard Samuel and R. Hinton Thomas, W. Heffer & Sons Ltd., 1939, pp. 38-68, 146-70.**

WALTER H. SOKEL   (essay date 1959)

Theobald Maske, in Sternheim's [**Die Hose** (**The Bloomers**)], is the common man who in the beginning of the common man's century is proud and sure in his commonness. Exaltation, eccentricity, and greatness of any kind are incomprehensible to him. His motto is "What is comfortable is right." He is ignorant of Shakespeare and has only vaguely heard of Goethe. His principle is not to read books, "because I am not interested in the opinions of other people." He is perfectly satisfied with the ideas formed in his own brain; reading would only interfere with his originality. He has not the least interest in politics or philosophy, nor in any issue outside his personal well-being. Maske's smug ignorance shocks the intellectual poet Scarron, who has always lived for ideas and ideals. (p. 121)

Frau Luise Maske, the young wife of the typical Philistine Theobald Maske, is attracted to the poet Scarron, who has rented a room in her apartment because he is in love with her. She makes only the slightest pretense of resistance to the romantic cavalier. The conventional development of this situation would show romantic young people getting together and putting horns on the bourgeois husband. But in the Expressionist comedy the reverse occurs. The bourgeois is the successful rival in love; the poet loses by default.

The poet's passion is verbal, not real. He is in love with the idea of being in love, not with a woman of flesh and blood. When Luise, slightly impatient with his ineffectual enthusiasm, expects him to make love to her, he rushes off to write about her. The artist's absorption in work is an effectual device for keeping him pure and untainted by life. It is the alibi of the man who cannot feel deeply and genuinely enough to engage in a human relationship. Afraid of real emotions, Scarron escapes to idealization and art. Like Mann's Malvolto, Sternheim's Scarron is unable to fulfill the romantic expectations which he has aroused; like Malvolto, he is a cheat.

When Luise's amorous and unhappy manner reminds him of his failure, he shifts his interest from the wife to the husband. For all his vulgarity, the solid bourgeois acts like a magnet on the weak and fickle intellectual. Scarron senses that this smug "little man," who is so proud of his littleness, is actually the great man to whom the future belongs. The poet is on the defensive, no longer believes in his romantic values; the bourgeois, perfectly at peace with himself, is on the offensive, cannot conceive of any values other than his own. (p. 122)

Maske is also victorious in that other human realm traditionally associated with the poet: love. Crude and egotistical though he is, Maske can love. In contrast to the poet, who promises so much and gives so little, the bourgeois promises little but accomplishes much. He may not speak of love with Scarron's eloquence but, on the most primitive and basic level, he loves and satisfies the women he desires. While his wife is in church seeking consolation for her disappointment in Scarron, Theobald Maske makes love to a spinster into whose lonely life he brings a ray of affection. And the rent money received from the unstable poet (who has paid a year's rent in advance for a room of which he tires after one day) enables Maske to afford to give his wife a child. Whereas Scarron will soon be nothing but a faded memory to a woman whose life has found a meaning in domesticity, Maske founds a powerful dynasty which is destined to rise to a ruling position in business and industry. The "heroic life of the *bourgeoisie,*" as Sternheim calls his cycle of middle-class comedies, has begun with Theobald Maske's total victory over the ephemeral values of literature and the intellect. The commonly held view that sees in Sternheim, and the Expressionists generally, mere rebels against the bourgeois way of life is likely to obscure the fascination which the ruthless self-confidence and vitality of the bourgeois hold for the early Expressionist, who keenly feels these qualities lacking in himself. The modern bourgeois passes the test of love which the modern poet fails. Sternheim's style demonizes the speech of the German *bourgeoisie.* Its effect is ambiguous. It is an aggressive parody of the bourgeois, to be sure; but, at the same time, it flatters him by exaggerating his ruthless forcefulness and cynical virility. It raises the bourgeois to the rank of a "blond beast." Thus, Sternheim's "telegram-style" dialogue expresses the typical Expressionist's ambivalence toward the bourgeois: he secretly admires him while overtly attacking him. (p. 123)

> *Walter H. Sokel, "The Impotence of the Heart," in his* The Writer in Extremis: Expressionism in Twentieth-Century German Literature *(reprinted with the permission of the publishers, Stanford University Press; © 1959 by the Board of Trustees of the Leland Stanford Junior University), Stanford University Press, 1959, pp. 119-40.**

WALTER H. SOKEL   (essay date 1963)

Carl Sternheim's comedies of "the heroic life of the bourgeoisie" lack the dreamlike distortions of much of Expressionist drama. Their hilarious caricatures and farcical situations remind one at first glance of conventional comedy. However, if we look a little closer, we discover qualities that profoundly distinguish Sternheim's comedies from the traditional type and make them the nearest counterpart to the grimly sardonic drawings of George Grosz.

There are not in Sternheim's comedies, as there are in Molière's, characters with moderate points of view, representing common sense—i.e., the common ground shared by author and audience. Sternheim fails to supply us with the convenient yardstick by which we can judge, while feeling comfortably above them, the comic characters as eccentrics. In Sternheim it is not the characters, but the world that has lost its center. His characters demonstrate a process that defines the whole of bourgeois society, and that might be called a quiet pandemonium of cold-blooded, insidious inhumanity. In *The Stronbox,* faith in securities, the new "soul of man," triumphs effortlessly over the older romantic, sensuous, and sentimental nature of man. But Sternheim does not weep for the lost glory of romantic man. He, too, is shown to be a self-drugging fraud. The aesthete and lover Silkenband is even phonier and more absurd than the tough-minded Professor Krull, with his monomaniac obsession with the securities contained in the strongbox. Sternheim's characters function grotesquely in a world become demonic through what is supposed to be most commonplace and sober in it—its monetary system. Instead of making love to his beautiful young wife, the materialistic professor locks himself in with the strongbox, counting the maiden aunt's securities, listing and relisting their numbers, and fig-

uring their values. Yet neither does Sternheim hold any brief for the neglected young beauty, who turns out to be engaged in a ruthless struggle for power with her shrewd and terrifying spinster aunt. No single value is more rational than any other; beauty and art, romantic love, sensuality, legacy-hunting, and financial fever—all are absurd.

Sternheim's characters are "soulless" in the literal sense—they have no stable permanent core of personality. They are completely identified with their maneuvers and obsessions—their "masks." Many of Sternheim's comedies deal with a bourgeois family called Maske. The name symbolizes modern man's essence, which Sternheim "unmasks." The modern bourgeois's essense is his mask—his veneer, as in Dickens' Mr. and Mrs. Veneering, who foreshadow Sternheim's ruthless characters not only in their go-getting cold-bloodedness but even in their peculiarly staccato baldness of diction, which perfectly expresses their cold-blooded spirit. Yet the obsessions of these characters are not the idiosyncrasies of individual eccentrics nor the embodiments of timeless vices familiar to us from Molière. They embody the obsessions of society and the absurdity of the human condition itself. Lacking a stable center at his core, man in Sternheim is denatured.

Sternheim's "comedy" has a mission as its plot—the old aunt's strongbox pulls all men away from sexuality and passion to its own cold self. Not plot, but theme, is the center of interest. If the plot were the main interest—in other words, if Sternheim had written a traditional comedy about greed—the question of whether or not Professor Krull would inherit the strongbox would be left in suspense until as near the end as possible. Instead, the disclosure of the aunt's will, which bequeaths the contents of the box to the Church, is put near the middle of the play. The play ends not with the ironic punishment and just comeuppance of a greedy and neglectful husband, but with a new convert to mammonism. Capitalism, as the modern truth, replaces the older "truths" of chivalrous mummery and romance, or bohemian idealism. However, the "mission" of capitalism is patently absurd, too, since we know that the securities in the strongbox will never belong to their worshipers. The strongbox becomes a symbol of absurdity, like the Mars machines "seen" by the Father in [Reinhard] Sorge's play. An absurd mission, seriously and consistently engaged in, reveals the absurdity of the world. (pp. xxiv-xxvi)

Carl Sternheim represents the sardonic and nihilistic spirit of Expressionist caricature and shows the influence of Frank Wedekind on the one hand and, on the other, points to future developments in literature and art (Dadaism, Bert Brecht, George Grosz). (p. xxxi)

> *Walter H. Sokel, in his introduction to* Anthology of German Expressionist Drama: A Prelude to the Absurd, *edited by Walter H. Sokel (copyright © 1963 by Walter H. Sokel; reprinted by permission of the author),* Anchor Press, 1963, pp. ix-xxxii.

ALEX NATAN   (essay date 1963)

Carl Sternheim was not interested in creating new forms of drama. As long as he could translate the contemporary scene into the grotesque, and thus could take revenge for the defeats and subsequent scandals which his first plays produced, he seemed to be content. His artistic atheism, his native wit and satirical vein, made it impossible to expect contributions from him which might solve the dilemma of his time. He too practised successfully the destruction of the shop-worn expressions of the German language. . . . Sternheim confessed to the intellect and discarded the substance. By trying to become a German Molière, he displayed an acute awareness for the comical and grotesque aspects of life. But his brilliant inspirations never achieved lasting effect, because Sternheim himself killed them through the artificiality of his own language. If God was dead, Sternheim certainly played the successful grave-digger when making his shallow ''juste milieu'' of German society the butt of his malicious satires. The playwright was often charged with his inability to create real characters. Reading his plays today one cannot but admit that this charge is unwarranted. On the contrary, the character Sternheim persiflaged grew into a prototype of general validity which dominated Germany and which the brush of the painter, George Grosz, has preserved. Sternheim, more pitiless than Ibsen, was much concerned with the debunking of ''Lebenslüge'' [''Life's lie''] and, in this process, laid bare unwittingly the isolation of the modern artist. . . . Sternheim's dramatic exposure of the ruling but stupid aristocracy, and of the down-trodden but ambitious bourgeoisie proved in the long run more dangerous in all its consequences than any other medium of communication then at the disposal of any German writer. (p. 5)

Alex Natan, in his introduction to German Men of Letters: Twelve Literary Essays, Vol. II, *edited by Alex Natan (© 1963 Oswald Wolff (Publishers) Limited), Wolff, 1963, pp. 1-10.**

R. BECKLEY (essay date 1963)

The vogue for epic surveys of social or political eras and family sagas running into several generations is typical of the period in which Sternheim was writing and natural to an age which was witnessing such spiritual change and upheaval. Thomas Mann's first novel, *Buddenbrooks,* which deals with the decline of a family over four generations, was written in 1901, almost ten years before the first part of Sternheim's trilogy of the Maske family appeared. On an even greater scale was Heinrich Mann's trilogy of novels, *Das Kaiserreich,* published between 1914 and 1925 and attempting to deal with all the main figures and events of the Wilhelmine era. Sternheim, however, seems to have been the first to present in dramatic form the history of a family of more than one generation. The great dramatic trilogies of the nineteenth century had tended on the whole to cover subject-matter too widely conceived to be confined within five acts, but with the interest concentrated on a single character, or pair of characters. . . . In Sternheim's trilogy, however, Christian Maske, the hero of the second play [*Der Snob*], is unborn at the end of the first [*Die Hose*], while his father, Theobald, is long since dead and not even a subject for passing reference in the third play [*1913*], in which his grandchildren appear on the scene for the first time.

Whether or not Sternheim was the innovator of this kind of dramatic trilogy, which seems to owe its peculiar form to the novel, his example was followed by two expressionist dramatists with varying success: by Georg Kaiser in the famous *Gas* trilogy, and by Fritz von Unruh in the unfinished *Dietrich* trilogy. Similarly, the technique of characterizing a whole era by emphasizing the same aspects of it in a series of different situations, which is Sternheim's method throughout this group of plays, may have influenced Bertolt Brecht's conception of *Furcht und Elend des dritten Reiches,* where twenty-two independent scenes form a play only by virtue of the common underlying theme indicated in the title.

Like Kaiser, Sternheim made many attempts at dramatic composition before he found where his true bent lay. His early failures are interesting for his development, if only because they are so utterly different in tone and choice of theme from the satiric comedy in which he afterwards excelled. *Ulrich und Brigitte,* a play written in blank verse of the ''Hiawatha'' kind about 1907 and described as a ''Dramatisches Gedicht'' [''Dramatic Poem''], deals with the romantic agonies of two young lovers who discover they are brother and sister. The added attraction of incest grafted on to the Romeo-and-Juliet theme marks the work as a product of the Impressionist or Neo-Romantic movement which had already celebrated its greatest triumphs with the plays of Maurice Maeterlinck, but was now in its decline. The verse of this play is not merely bad. Its prosaic tone and wilfully awkward staccato rhythms are a ready-made parody of the romantic metre from which they struggle to escape, as the closing lines of the drama clearly reveal. . . . (pp. 135-36)

Don Juan, a more grandiose work of the same period, is ambitiously called a tragedy and divided into two parts, like Goethe's *Faust.* Once again Sternheim chooses a hero who, like Bluebeard and Casanova, was dear to the hearts of the Impressionists for his neurotic obsession with sex, but in the more serious moments of the play the sentiments tend to be expressed in prose, while the verse (especially in the form of songs or stanzas) is reserved for certain caricatured figures such as the king of Spain, from whom the audience's sympathy has to be alienated. Unlike *Ulrich und Brigitte, Don Juan* ends on an almost casual note. As the Don, at the head of a cavalry charge (he is engaged in one of Philip the Second's wars), falls in the thick of the fighting, an onlooker cheers him *sotto voce,* then goes over to the carriage where the Don's mistress is waiting and laconically conveys the news of his death. . . . (p. 136)

The radical change from Romantic tragedy to comic satire only hinted at in the cool tone and occasional grotesque characters of *Don Juan* is complete in Sternheim's next play [*Die Hose*]. For a theatre-going public conditioned to the appearance in drama of monsters of human depravity, as long as they were dressed in historical costume, and prepared to accept the presentation of contemporary social evil only when seen with the passionate conviction and broad human sympathy of a Gerhart Hauptmann, the shock of encountering the cold passionless gaze with which Sternheim insolently views the older generation of his day in *Die Hose* must have been considerable. The potentiality of such satire to shock must depend on the seriousness with which it is taken. The effect of Gay's *Beggar's Opera* or Beaumarchais' *Mariage de Figaro* on the audiences they attacked was no doubt very different from the polite amusement these plays afford a modern audience, which does not feel itself personally attacked and whose sympathies in any case lie with the author. A recounting of the plot of *Die Hose* shows that, following the fortunes of all satire bound to a specific time and place, its power to make us laugh is greater than its power to arouse our indignation, righteous or otherwise. (p. 137)

It may be doubted whether Sternheim ever again arranged his subject so neatly or produced the maximum effect of irony with so light a touch. The offending garment which flutters so mockingly into the opening conversation of the play is never allowed to disappear from the imagination of the audience. Re-created with added magnificence under the assiduous fingers of the ageing spinster it takes on a malicious life of its own and directs the fates of the characters to the opposite conclusion of that which they had planned for themselves. . . .

The note on which Sternheim closes relies for its effect on a device much employed in the later propagandist phase of Expressionism. Like so much Expressionist technique it is an inconsistency or break in style which, while provoking a shock or protest as the audience's or reader's first reaction, enables a particular scene, situation or sentiment to be strikingly imprinted on the memory by means of its very incongruity. (p. 139)

In spite of some public displeasure, Sternheim undoubtedly found enough approval and encouragement to explore further the vein of comedy which he seems almost accidentally to have chanced upon. The second play of the Maske trilogy was not in fact the next work at which he tried his hand, but it is the next to reveal his development as an artist: the improved economy in his dramatic technique, the perfecting of his powers of characterization, and the increasing profundity of his critical insight. Moreover, it was quite a different kind of play, not a repetition of the earlier *succès de scandale*. *Der Snob* is a satirical study of the social entry of Theobald Maske's son, Christian, into the ranks of the aristocracy. Compared with *Die Hose,* the plot is simple, because Sternheim is here more concerned with the presentation and development of character. The opening of the new play is itself an ironic comment on Theobald's tender hope for a son, with which the earlier play had closed; for Christian has already, while still in his early childhood, worked his way up by sheer hard work, tenacity and ruthlessness, partly inherited from his father, to a position where, as a powerful business executive, he controls a considerable portion of the national wealth. (pp. 140-41)

Unlike his treatment of Luise and Scarron in *Die Hose,* both of whom he foils and unmasks before the end of the play, in *Der Snob* Sternheim seems to delight in leading his main character on to further folly until the measure he attains to is itself sufficient poetic justice. (p. 142)

It may be questioned whether Sternheim's view of the society of his day was ever produced with greater clarity or wit than in these two plays. He himself said that every play after *Die Hose* offered nothing fundamentally new. It merely repeated what he thought could not be stated too often: that the age was spiritually dead.

There seems little doubt, however, that Sternheim attempted to broaden his vision to extend over the whole of bourgeois society and to present an epic survey of the problems and conflicts of his time. It was not only his plays that he collected under one title and linked in such a way that the whole attempted to be more than the sum of its parts. His short stories, too, when they had reached a certain number, were published together as *Chronik von des XX Jahrhunderts Beginn,* and a long essay entitled *Berlin oder Juste Milieu* tries to trace the essential history of that city in relation to its time and the rest of Europe, "ab urbe condita". But Sternheim's talent was probably too exclusively satirical to produce a more comprehensive survey at this stage in his career, and later on his sympathies, and the new problems and needs of a changing society, modified his artistic aims and intentions.

The third play of the Maske trilogy *1913,* bears witness to his attempt and partial failure to succeed in giving to his presentation the dimensions of a true saga. His difficulty lay possibly in the fact that he was unwilling to concede that there was anything more than banal in the bourgeois scale of experience and yet wished to convey that for such a society the end, if not terrifying, must be grisly. Significantly enough, Sternheim calls this play a *Schauspiel* [spectacle], not a *Komödie;* the

comedy it contains has something of a sour quality, and the laughs it affords are rather bitter. Christian Maske as an old man has an enormous fortune and a vision of his family's glorious future to bequeath to three highly unsatisfactory grown-up children. The father appears to have unwittingly and unwillingly visited his sins upon them. (pp. 143-44)

[If this play fails to convince], it is perhaps because Sternheim was too honest to pretend to a vision more compelling than that which he possessed, for there is no doubt that the work is grand in its conception. But the courage with which he begins to present the degeneration of the house of Maske seems to desert him as the plot develops to its climax. His attitude to his characters becomes ambivalent. There are moments when Christian, in conversation with his secretary seems to have changed from the early self-seeker to a man whose position has taught him a serious sense of responsibility towards his fellow-countrymen. This impression is strengthened by Sternheim's intimation that Christian's secretary, Wilhelm Krey, has been seriously tempted and will be lured from his socialist cause by the wealth and success of his employer. This makes a mockery of young Germany's revolt against the materialism of its parents, which is symbolized by Friedrich Stadler's decisive exit from Maske's house at the end of the play, after his friend Krey has shown signs of going over to the enemy camp. Moreover, Christian's almost pathological hatred of his elder daughter, which has the important function of providing the motive for the external conflict of the play, is never very convincingly explained. Finally, *1913* does not sum up the underlying theme of the trilogy, as one expects it to do, because the trilogy was probably not conceived organically. It rather bears witness to Sternheim's realization that his vision needed constant modification.

All the plays of this period show signs of the mental struggle in which Sternheim's search for the truth underlying appearances involved him. In *Bürger Schippel,* the main character is again a man eager for acceptance in a higher social circle. (pp. 145-46)

Signs of a definite change in Sternheim's attitude to the world around him may be found in the play *Tabula Rasa*. . . . It is the last of the "sardonic" comedies, and represents a clean sweep in more ways than one. As the representative of a workers' union, who has sold out to the employers in exchange for an easy job and a high salary, Wilhelm Ständer, the main character of the play, is a creation which reveals Sternheim at the very limits of his cynicism, for it is by means of this same character that the playwright gives some intimation of a dawning interest in the problem of the social responsibility of the individual. When the director of the factory where Ständer works offers him an active partnership in the business, he declines, knowing that the position would require much more hard work and self-sacrifice than he has been used to, without an equal increase in financial gain. His decision is interpreted by everyone as a sign that he will not desert the cause of the workers, and as Ständer had cunningly foreseen, they agree to his being accorded a handsome pension equal to the salary from the partnership but without the work and the responsibility.

In an attempt to understand the play some critics have interpreted Ständer's actions as an illustration of Sternheim's assertion that every man must have "den Mut zu sich selbst"— "the courage to be himself". It is claimed that to be oneself, and be selfish, is better than to be afraid of being oneself. "Den Mut zu sich selbst haben" is certainly a theme which is central to all Sternheim's work, but the aspect of it which interests Sternheim varies from play to play. In *Die Hose* the main figure asserts himself in a world of shams, but if in the process he exploits everyone and every situation to his own advantage, he has the justification of being a real human being with a real problem—the need to find the wherewithal to support a family. Ständer has no such problems. The niece he spoils and pampers is, as he says himself, the luxury in which he likes to indulge himself. That Sternheim condemns Ständer for his selfishness seems clear from the opening and closing scenes of the play, which are made to comment on each other. At the opening of the play the woman who lives with Ständer as his wife and looks after him as his servant demands an increase in her weekly allowance. Ständer maintains she is not employed by him and does not receive pay, but chooses to help him of her own free will and is occasionally given unsolicited gifts. Ständer is in fact exploiting his housekeeper-cum-bedfellow under the pretence of refusing to enter into anything so ignoble with her as a master-servant relationship. However, when towards the close of the play the director of the factory calls on Ständer, Sternheim intimates by a repetition of certain expressions used earlier that Ständer is being offered the partnership on conditions similar to those he has forced on the woman he lives with. His refusal brands him as the kind of man who is the continual butt of Sternheim's satire—a hypocrite who propounds principals, but has none, and whose actions are in direct contrast to his expressed ideals.

Exactly what factors contributed to the change noticeable in Sternhcim's work after *Tabula Rasa* has not been investigated, but his position in relation to the other writers of Expressionism may not be without significance. Sternheim was older by at least a decade than the generation of young dramatists who called themselves Expressionists, and his early satires of bourgeois life reflect the mood of the preceding generation of the brothers Thomas and Heinrich Mann. The period of Expressionist drama with which the greater part of *Aus dem bürgerlichen Heldenleben* coincides, was, in contrast to the latter, impulsive, emotional and idealistic. It sought to establish the myth of "der neue Mensch"—the new generation that would bring about the spiritual rebirth of decadent Western civilization, and its normal vehicle of expression was certainly not the comic satire. (pp. 147-49)

The change comes, however, with *Die Marquise von Arcis*, written towards the end of the First World War and based on an idea from a story by Diderot. Conforming to the ideals of the Expressionist movement, it is yet an entirely original contribution, in that Sternheim develops further the themes which unite all his work.

Indicative of his desire to get away from contemporary social satire is his choice of a subject with an historical setting (Paris in the mid-eighteenth century), which enables him to give his theme greater universality. The play opens with a classic Sternheimian contrast. The Marquis d'Arcis and the Marquise de Pommeraye have been ardent lovers for many years, and their relationship is regarded by the whole of Paris as the ideal example of human constancy. The Marquise, however, has come to suspect that the Marquis' passion for her has cooled, and in order to trick him into confessing the truth she pretends to him that the intensity of her feelings has declined with the years. The Marquis swallows the bait, expresses his deep admiration for the Marquise's honesty, and suggests that from now on they should be as true in friendship as they were once constant in their love. The Marquise makes a show of accepting this new reality, but begins in secret to form a plan which will give her the revenge her wounded pride demands and also force the Marquis, disillusioned and contrite, to accept the continued validity of their old relationship. She is aided in her scheme by the Marquis' determination to discover a new mistress with whom he will be able to experience the spiritual rebirth that will once again give purpose and meaning to his life. The Marquise finds what she thinks will be the perfect tools for her stratagem in the figures of Madame Duquenoy and her daughter Henriette. Madame Duquenoy is a lady of gentle birth who has fallen upon evil times, and in order to maintain appearances and continue living in the standard of comfort to which she is accustomed, has sold her daughter to a series of noblemen. Henriette, who is notorious for her candour, has accepted the ugly truth of her position, finding her best defence in an assumed cynicism.

After paying mother and daughter a handsome sum to move to a part of Paris where they are not known, and to lead there for a while a life of unimpeachable respectability, the Marquise de Pommeraye introduces Henriette to the Marquis d'Arcis, who immediately falls in love with her. (pp. 149-50)

In rejecting the Marquise's and society's estimate of Henriette and refusing to react in the accepted way to the idea conveyed by the word "prostitute", the Marquis undergoes the first stage in his spiritual rebirth. In having the courage to meet a changing human situation with the new and unbiased attitude it requires he becomes the "neuer Mensch" of Expressionism. The Marquise's plan fails because it is based on an outmoded and ignoble conception of human nature. She had not reckoned with the Marquis' creative nobility of soul, which had enabled him to find the real human being behind the derogatory label. At the end of the play Sternheim stresses what might be considered his particular comment on the Expressionist ideal of the "neuer Mensch", for thc Marquis' moral struggle and subsequent victory not only save him from spiritual suicide, but create out of Henriette Duquenoy, the social outcast, a "new woman"—the "Marquise von Arcis" of Sternheim's title.

There is no more impressive or exciting sequence in the whole of Sternheim's work than the Marquis d'Arcis' triumph over the prejudice of his age. The author himself seems to take the lesson of the play to heart, for in his last important work for the stage, written five years later on the subject of Oscar Wilde's fall from public favour, he brings to the task of presenting the English dramatist the same fervent sincerity which the Marquis d'Arcis brings to his "reconception" of Henriette. Wilde's homosexual activities, on account of which, according to Sternheim, his age condemned him both as man and artist, are not unduly stressed. Neither are they ignored. They are seen positively as one small part of the overwhelming evidence that Wilde was a giant among his contemporaries—the one man who had the courage to be himself at a time when public opinion, narrow, self-righteous and ignorant, made moral cowards of all other men. Like the Marquis d'Arcis Wilde turns his back on the conventional world, as represented by the frigid Lord Alfred Douglas and his implacable father, and finds among the social outcasts of London's all-night cafés the essential humanity which he had sought in vain elsewhere. The subsequent trial and imprisonment of Wilde are seen as the hysterically vicious acts of an age unhealthily obsessed with the word "immorality".

The problem of the individual and his relation to society is all-important for the German drama of the twentieth century, but it is possible that Sternheim's personal circumstances contributed greatly to his particular formulation of it. His consciousness of his Jewish background, and the mingled suspicion and fear with which society regards the minority groups in its midst, may well have increased the feeling of isolation common to so many modern artists. Most of his plays deal with the socially unaccepted or unacceptable—in the later phase with those who refuse to accept society. Probably only someone who has experienced acutely as a basic element of his existence the feeling of "not belonging" could present the unsympathetic picture of society we find in the early plays, or conceive the importance of the individual who has the courage to be himself, regardless of contemporary opinion, which gives such unexpected dignity to his later work. (pp. 151-52)

R. Beckley, "Carl Sternheim," in German Men of Letters: Twelve Literary Essays, Vol. II, edited by Alex Natan (© 1963 Oswald Wolff (Publishers) Limited), Wolff, 1963, pp. 131-54.

EGBERT KRISPYN   (essay date 1964)

[A] confidence in the essential goodness of mankind motivates Carl Sternheim's satirical play *Die Hose*. In this so-called comedy the faults of the bourgeois world are illuminated through the contrast between those who have undergone its corroding influence on their personalities and the primitively vital Maske, who under the cloak of outward conformity has asserted his independence of the stifling code. Sternheim, in attacking the middle-class world, shows that basically the bourgeois is a person of estimable qualities which are prevented from coming to the surface because of the unpropitious spirit of the age.

This interpretation of *Die Hose* deviates from the view held by Carol Petersen, who sees in the comedy an ironically exaggerated exposé of the bourgeois vices as embodied in Maske. (pp. 35-6)

Sternheim's intentions with *Die Hose* have apparently always been subject to misunderstandings of this nature, for in the Foreword to the second edition he tried to correct them. According to Sternheim's own interpretation, borne out by the text, it is wrong to regard *Die Hose* as an ironical attack against the figure of Theobald Maske. The latter is not intended as a personification of the negative aspects of middle-class society. He is, on the contrary, an example with which the author intended to open the eyes of his bourgeois audience to their own fundamental virtues. Maske's basic qualities, such as the urges for self-preservation and for self-sufficiency which make him disregard literature and philosophy, are demonstrated to make him superior to the erudite Scarron and the latter's cheaper pendant Mandelstam.

These two are the main exponents of the bourgeois ideology in its various aspects; the barber, for instance, through his boundless admiration for the music of Wagner, who, at least in Sternheim's opinion, epitomized the worst aspects of the Zeitgeist. As Mandelstam reveals himself through his enthusiasm for this composer, so does Scarron through the opinions he voices in the debate with Maske. The crassest example is his reaction when Theobald refers to the role of the heart. "Das Herz ist ein Muskel, Maske." It is Scarron, not Maske, who adheres to the pedestrian materialism which pervaded the mental atmosphere of Wilhelmian Germany. In his other utterances Scarron indulges in empty phraseology which is intended to sound profound, but really only covers up his unwillingness to face the concrete facts of life. . . .

Another character who deliberately shuts out the world is the scholar Stengelhöh, who is usually disregarded in interpretations of *Die Hose*. He tries to arrange his life in such a way that he need not be reminded of the basic facts of sexuality, or of the existence of any living creatures such as small children, canaries, dogs, and cats. Maske, on the other hand, refuses to bother with the realms of science and the arts, and limits himself to the instinctual level of life. That level includes food and sex, but also an awareness of the nature of love and the ability to bring some happiness into the lives of his fellows. (pp. 36-7)

The portrayal of Maske serves to show the vast resources of vitality which the bourgeois unleashes in himself if he refuses to pay homage to the artistic, philosophical, and scholarly sacred cows of his environment and time, and discards professional ambitions. But this lonely rebellion against the prevailing system is only possible under the cover of outward conformism—hence Maske's name and his concern about the central incident of the play, which might have resulted in the loss of his protective anonymity. (p. 38)

Egbert Krispyn, "Expressionists and Expressionism," in his Style and Society in German Literary Expressionism (copyright © 1964 by The Board of Commissioners of State Institutions of Florida), University of Florida Press, 1964, pp. 25-43.*

H. MACLEAN   (essay date 1966)

[Scathing] in his treatment of characters with artistic and literary pretensions was Carl Sternheim. Both Scarron in *Die Hose* . . . and Seidenschnur in *Die Kassette* . . . are, like the weaklings in Wedekind's and Kaiser's plays, compulsive talkers. It is the poetry of cliché which Scarron adopts, compressed poetic cliché, in which the empty inflated phrases follow on one another with stunning rapidity, so that they are immensely funny when delivered with the staccato precision employed by actors in Sternheim plays. Seidenschnur's protestations of love, delivered with the same bombast, are deflated when they become entangled with the mechanics of the camera: "Your picture, Lydia, flows into the lens, into the chambers of my heart." Both Scarron and Seidenschnur are savage denunciations of the inadequacy of the romantic type, who claim to be preoccupied with their innermost selves, claim to be superior to bourgeois philistines, to which they, the artistic philistines, cling nevertheless like drowning men. They are in a way the false egotists, for they remain as empty at the end as they were at the start, they attach themselves to the body of the "shark", and seek not strength but only protection for themselves.

Sternheim's portrayal of the middle classes, annihilating as it is, is not intended, as [Wilhelm] Emrich forcefully reminds us, to be regarded as satire, it is not a "scourging" but a "recognition" of reality. His main characters, his Maskes, Krulls and Ständers, are not merely intended to show the emptiness of a life given over to materialism and middle class ambition. They are not there as warnings, but as signposts in a waste country. There is about them an aliveness, a vitality which is strangely attractive and survives dedication to a limited aim. Sternheim is therefore not sarcastic, but perfectly genuine when he describes them as heroes, for they have gained their freedom by overcoming the restraints which are imposed on them by society. This is very much the idea of freedom which activates the hero in Wedekind's *Der Marquis von Keith* . . . , who sets out to free himself from middle class society by dominating it. Keith fails, but Sternheim's characters have less inner life and more tenacity and grasp of reality than Wedekind's characters. Theobald Maske (in *Die Hose*) and in even more extreme fashion his son Christian Maske (in *Der Snob*) subordinate society to their own goals. Christian works quite cold-bloodedly and with exact machine-like calculation; he is the prince of the manipulators. In Christian and his other heroes, Sternheim has created characters who stand out as unique in Expressionism for two reasons: they are the only contrivers and manipulators to win their way to personal freedom and they are the only liberated personalities who do not represent some purpose greater than themselves. They are the pure egotists, egotists unsullied as it were by frustration on the one hand or by the intrusion of any moral, artistic or community ideal which transcends the individual and which Sternheim despised heartily. Yet these characters are not individuals in the orthodox sense. They achieve their power and urgency by the fact that the whole horrible world which Sternheim "recognizes", the wealth and status worshippers spread over all the rungs of the social ladder, is concentrated into them and shaped by them, or more accurately is shaped by the words that are spoken; for Sternheim's characters do not live by virtue of their individual fate or by their position in an unfolding story, but through their language.

Sternheim said of Gottfried Benn that he "destroys concepts from within, so that language totters and citizens lie flat on belly and nose"; like Benn, Sternheim was an uncompromising critic, not only of idealistic concepts, but also—and this is more characteristic of Expressionism in general—of the platitudes which are used to paper over unpalatable and unfamiliar realities. Conventional images are seen as masks concealing the essential attributes of a person or object, and the revolt against the lazy classification of people according to comfortable and familiar categories is a recurring theme. . . . (pp. 270-72)

> *H. Maclean, "Expressionism," in* Periods in German Literature, *edited by J. M. Ritchie (© 1966 Oswald Wolff), Wolff, 1966, pp. 257-80.**

J. M. RITCHIE (essay date 1970)

[Sternheim] has pulled off that combination rare in the German theatre; he has written successful comedies which have gained academic acclaim. . . . [This] acclaim has not been easily come by and study of the plays themselves does much to explain the embarrassment of earlier critics when faced with Sternheim. At first sight it is hard to reconcile the written texts of his plays with the general picture of the hectic world of theatrical experimentation one normally associates with German theatre of the 1920s in general and Expressionist theatre in particular. Yet when they are studied more closely it becomes clear that almost all the modern theatrical developments right through to Brecht are there already *potentially* in Sternheim. First of all one must remember the date: *The Bloomers* (1911), *The Snob* (1913)—this was over fifty years ago! Yet it is remarkable what Sternheim was already doing. He had realised that the naturalistic theatre *à la* Hauptmann was dead. He had realised that its contemporary opposite, the neo-romantic theatre *à la* Hofmannsthal/Hauptmann was also dead, particularly in comedy. And he had realised that the exquisite nuances of symbolism in the theatre were stone dead. These were avenues which the German theatre had already exhaustively explored. Hence in a Sternheim comedy the audience is never invited to 'hunt the symbol,' never supposed to feel that it is being transported onto a higher plane of 'poetic' truth; nor, however, does

Sternheim offer his audience a simple realistic picture of bourgeois reality. He had served a long apprenticeship in the theatre and had written eight plays exploring such theatrical possibilities—the realistic, neo-romantic and symbolic genres—before he found his own peculiar form in 1911 with *The Bloomers,* a middle-class comedy. . . . Many of the themes he tackled had already been attempted by contemporary dramatists and the creative process is reminiscent of Brecht's love of adaptations and popular successes. And like Brecht later, Sternheim too was fascinated by American capitalism and gangsterdom. His last works were called *Knockout* and *John Pierpoint Morgan. Paul Schippel Esq.,* was even set to music by Dohnanyi as *The Tenor,* a reminder of how close music and drama were in these days in Germany and yet another pointer to Brecht. Altogether Sternheim's total output numbered about thirty plays. Not all of these were of equal quality, nevertheless even disregarding the prose works, novels, short stories, critical essays, etc., he left behind on his death a considerable *oeuvre.*

As for the plays themselves, although he did turn them out remarkably quickly, it must not be thought that these were mere popular pot-boilers. For a start his peculiar theatrical language with its distortion, intentional starkness and avoidance of all metaphor and emotion was clearly not aimed at wide popular appeal. In effect it was this deliberately mannered unpoetic language which disturbed audiences and critics probably more than anything else in Sternheim. His language, like his plays, is constructed. This unnaturally mannered style can be taken as a foretaste of the expressionistic shorthand called 'telegraphese' or 'telegram style'; but much more significant is the force with which this style registers Sternheim's personal reaction against the melodic and psychological subtleties of the Hofmannsthal variety, and more, it is remarkably akin to Brecht's later rejection of the whole bourgeois aesthetic of beauty as the source of art. Sternheim is working towards something entirely different from the old ideal that the aim of art is beauty and the pleasure which beauty imparts. For Sternheim, as for Brecht later, Romanticism was the great error which contemporary man had to combat at all costs, and he does everything in his linguistic power to destroy it. Perhaps now that the language of Gottfried Benn has been accepted alongside that of Rilke as a possible form of literary expression the time is ripe at last for a proper appreciation of Sternheim's deliberately unnatural style. He himself has many affinities with Gottfried Benn and dedicated one of his plays to him, with the significant sub-title, New Objectivity!

The same process of reduction towards extreme precision and hard functionalism which can be observed in Sternheim's treatment of language can also be observed in his treatment of plot. As [Walter] Sokel has said of Expressionist drama in general, plot as such almost disappears and a more musical 'theme' takes its place. Sternheim simply selects typical situations and permutates them as required by the demands of his play. In Act I of *The Snob* the social climber gets rid of both of his parents. In Act II he gets one of them back. In Act III there is a dazzling reversal of the classic theatrical situation; in the Sternheim comedy the impostor is *not* exposed in the end, on the contrary he rises to even greater heights. Just as there is little plot so too there are no exquisite nuances in the psychological analysis of character, and no need for a long exposition to introduce the main characters and the situation. The characters, in as much as they are characters, describe themselves. For example, Christian, the Snob, tells in a long monologue how he has managed to 'arrive'. Characters like this are *typical* people in *typical* situations—typical, however, not in any crude naturalistic sense of the word. Nothing about the play is really naturalistic or realistic from the mannered language to the general shape of the play itself. The overall effect is one of shock—the shock of recognition. Already Sternheim has begun to exploit the theatrical tricks which Brecht was to exploit so much more extensively, such a short time afterwards, and like Brecht he is not afraid to break through the bonds of realism into drastic and grotesque extremes. The plays are, as has been suggested, unnaturally constructivistic and formalised. The stage settings, for example, are generally constant from act to act: always just one room, and into this one room stream all the right people and always at the right time. It is like a parody of the well-made play—'la pièce bien faite'—and this is exactly what it is: parody! A parody of the Ibsen drama of domestic interior, or the French society play or the Oscar Wilde variety of the conversation piece. Parody is the medium of nearly all modern literature of the Twenties, parody that often comes dangerously close to plagiarism. It is the medium of Brecht, a deliberate and conscious exploitation of all the technical possibilities to hand permitting of no restriction or limitation of scope from mere realism. This may be Expressionism but it is the cold side of Expressionism. Instead of the chaotic, poetic kind of Expressionist play Sternheim presents plays which are almost geometrically constructed, and pared down to the absolutely bare essentials. And all the unrealistic effects banished by the naturalistic school of drama are re-introduced, as for example, long monologues and asides. Altogether the effect is of actors *acting*. Audiences are never asked to believe that they are watching something real happening now before their very eyes. It is thereby possible to perform the plays in two main styles, either with the exaggerated overstatement of melodrama, stressing the deliberate unreality of the whole business, or with the very cool understatement of a brittle Noel Coward manner. Either way the play is the thing and its own curious dynamics must simply be accepted. Either way the result is extremely funny.

But Sternheim is more than just funny. He is the surgeon on the body of the age with a quick scalpel which penetrates through the protecting flesh to the very bone, exploring the servility, the philistinism, the hypocrisy, the empty idealism of the hated bourgeois who loves to wrap up even the most sordid negotiation in an aura of idealistic romanticism. This is the 'where-is-the-higher-significance-of-all-this-for-me' cry of Theobald in *The Snob,* when in reality as the play demonstrates, money and power are the only things that talk to him. The bourgeois is the hated enemy. Sternheim attempts to destroy him by making him ridiculous and there is no softening of the blow. Again this is a point which has disturbed many critics about Sternheim's plays. Sokel in the introduction to his *Anthology of German Expressionist Drama* [see excerpt above] has correctly described this essential difference between a Sternheim comedy and a normal comedy. (pp. 9-13)

[All of Sternheim's] characters are hateful or unsympathetic.

Sternheim saw himself as the German Molière and his *Snob* is the German Tartuffe, but now there is no king's messenger in the last scene to save the situation. Instead Christian goes on from strength to strength, climbing higher and higher in society. Theobald, the Count, Christian, even Marianne and Sybil—they all have the same will to power, the same egotism. And when one looks at the other plays this is all there seems to be on the surface: Nietzsche and Darwin. Nietzsche's will to power and the idea of the superman; Darwin's survival of the fittest by adaptation to circumstance and the struggle for

existence, the very phrases are exploited even in the starkly reduced text of a play like the *Snob,* though there is absolutely no philosophising except for purposes of ridicule. The result of all this is an almost Brechtian alienation. On the one hand the bourgeois is exposed as a mere climber with the will to power who is prepared even to suppress his own parents to get on in the world. On the other hand the emptiness of the struggle is revealed, a world without values is exposed. On the one hand we despise the snob for what he is doing; on the other hand we almost admire this superman for the enormous vitality, the *élan vital* he deploys in the doing of it. Here again we are very close to the Brechtian character like Mack the Knife, the bourgeois villain of immaculate appearance and enormous crimes and close to Sternheim himself, though Sternheim is perhaps even more like his eponymous hero Oscar Wilde. This again is in a powerful modern tradition. We are nowadays too prone perhaps to think of the artist as the social outcast, the outsider, the tramp with his dustbin perspective of society, thereby overlooking the strong trend in the opposite direction. Some modern artists have attempted to be insiders. They do not need to sink to the lower depths to look at society from below—they write from the top, dress in blindingly white linen like Baudelaire or Oscar Wilde, or the clinical cloak of a Gottfried Benn and cast a cold, contemptuous aristocratic gaze *down* on the middle classes. The modern artist can be a dandy like Sternheim; a German Noel Coward, only much more savage. This is again something that many critics have not been able to forgive Sternheim—the fact that he was so rich and lived in a castle with a butler, valet and servants to look after him even while they admit that it was this same wealth which gave him his extraordinary insight into the capitalistic money manipulations of his age. Yet Sternheim is an almost classical example of the dandy, that problem figure of the modern age. . . . (pp. 13-15)

This is the real source of Sternheim's heroic battle against the forces of his age, for he is like his own hero Christian the Snob, immaculate, clear-headed, calculating, rational, logical, but at the same time a wild man with a devouring fire in his guts. Sternheim cannot be dismissed as a sardonic rationalist or cynic, there is plenty that he feels strongly about, only this turns to hate expressed in cold language and strict form. He is a man with a mission but once again a mission which has been misunderstood—Sternheim believes quite simply that every man has somewhere within him a self all his own, and it is up to him to realise this self regardless of the various social, political, religious and other pressures of modern society which restrict this. He must have moral and civil courage, the courage of his own vices. The individual must accept his own peculiarities for good or evil and live them to the full. Only in this way can humanity be saved from the dead hand of uniformity and the capacity of man to produce infinitely new forms of humanity preserved. Hence there is no moral or spiritual ideal guiding the conduct of the individual, Sternheim is prepared to accept any 'so-called' vices provided they are the true expression of the self, the only question is which methods the individual must employ to escape the normalising, standardising pressure of society and this generally is the *mask* with which he conceals the true self until he is sufficiently powerful to live out his real life.

From this the reason for the embarrassment of Communist critics when dealing with Sternheim becomes apparent. It is true that Sternheim was a bitter enemy of the bourgeoisie; it is true that he claimed that all great art must be political and that he wielded his pen for extreme left-wing journals, apparently convinced of the energy of the Russian working class movement and the proletariat as compared with the decadence and debility of the Western middle classes. Yet where does he really stand? Mittenzwei, the Communist critic, sees him between conservative and progressive, mystic and rationalist, idealist and realist, between Nietzsche and Marx. And this is a fair description. Sternheim is essentially non-aligned. His criticism of the bourgeoisie is devastating yet he has no simple solution for society. He is an intellectual afflicted like Gottfried Benn with the curse of 'progressive cerebration' and the longing for escape. This escape he seeks like Gottfried Benn in a kind of primitive vitalism. Hence he is at the same time the destroyer of idealistic platitudes and the admirer of the American capitalist go-better.

His solution to the problems of the age is a form of extreme individualism. But this is an extremely private solution and explains the communist disquiet—formalism is bad enough, but such subjectivism is unforgivable. And yet it is perhaps this same subjectivism so typical of the expressionist generation which is the source of Sternheim's strength today. With ferocity and single-mindedness he exposes the problem of the individual in society—like Brecht he offers no simple solution and like Brecht he is very, very funny. In this way he is more than a mere social critic or satirist exposing the sins and excesses of the philistines, he is the true expressionist visionary. It has been simple for some critics to see in Sternheim's heroes the shadows of the cold-blood mediocrities of the future Hitler regime. But he goes more deeply even than this. His aim was to strike through appearances to the heart of the matter, to reveal the true nature of man. His art is 'the purest image possible for a shattering age like his own', his mission not the 'rebirth of society' but the 'rebirth of man'. Sternheim is not dated, for steeped though he is in the characteristics of the German world of a particular period this vision raises his art above the limitation of time and place. No-one will go to Sternheim for comfort as they would go to Goethe or Hölderlin, yet he remains a great artist—a literary figure, a theatrical figure of stature. (pp. 15-17)

> *J. M. Ritchie, in his introduction to* Scenes from the Heroic Life of the Middle Classes: Five Plays *by Carl Sternheim, translated by M.A.L. Brown, M. A. McHaffie, J. M. Ritchie, J. D. Stowell (reprinted by permission of John Calder (Publishers) Ltd), Calder and Boyars, 1970, pp. 7-22.*

DAVID MYERS (essay date 1973)

Carl Sternheim liked to see himself as a modern German Molière, a playwright-doctor operating on the social ills of his time. His satirical surgery is aggressive, stylish, and sophisticated in technique; in fact there is every justification for considering him one of twentieth-century Germany's most original and controversial comic playwrights. One of the many controversies and scandals that have raged around Sternheim since his cycle of comedies *Aus dem bürgerlichen Heldenleben* appeared in the second decade of this century is whether he created a new, ruthless, and egoistic race of heroes whom he worshipped for their snobbish triumphs over the bourgeoisie, or whether he meant to ridicule these "heroes" along with all his other characters and so consistently maintain an attitude of supercilious misanthropy.

Otto Mann answers this question in his essay on *Bürger Schippel* by comparing Sternheim to Aristophanes as dramatists who assume such a superior, godlike attitude to life that all human activity seems farcical and ludicrous to them. In particular,

Mann sees the proletarian bastard Paul Schippel not as a hero but as a poor devil who is mercilessly satirized for his belief that if he can just make it to the middle class, his life will have been fulfilled. Wilhelm Emrich, by way of contrast, considers this interpretation to be a misunderstanding of Sternheim's intentions. Relying heavily on Sternheim's own essayistic self-interpretations, Emrich refers us to the dramatist's allegedly positive heroes who, he explains, overcome the evils of conventionality and hypocrisy by being unabashedly egoistic individualists. They are contemptuous of all the social ideologies and altruistic moralities because they believe only in their duty to themselves, their duty to find self-fulfilment in independence and freedom. . . . This view of Sternheim's characters sounds very imposing, but becomes questionable when we see that "heroes" of Sternheim's comedies like Schippel, Krull, and the Maskes have no greater godgiven originality than money-grabbing and class-climbing. (pp. 39-40)

[In his essay *Das gerettete Bürgertum*] Sternheim goes on to recommend Schippel and the Maskes to us as heroes because they have seen through the hypocrisy of bourgeois society's preaching the ideology of altruism and are now fanatically possessed by their ruthless drive for power. This apotheosis of Nietzschean vitality is Sternheim's retort—or over-reaction?—to contemporary critics who tried to denigrate him as a "mere" satirist. . . . But if we try to apply this theoretical self-evaluation of Sternheim to his plays, we understand immediately why Otto Mann and Wilhelm Emrich interpret the heroes of these plays so radically differently. For Sternheim's essayistic paeans to originality and individualism become either ludicrously petty or morally contemptible when they are embodied as principles in his main dramatic characters. Emrich may have correctly interpreted the theory of some of Sternheim's essays, but Otto Mann has seen what happens when this theory becomes artistic reality in a play like *Bürger Schippel*. Actually, there is a discrepancy in Sternheim's works not only between essay and play, but also between essay and essay. We have already seen how Sternheim praised ruthless egoists in *Das gerettete Bürgertum;* but when these ruthless egoists expressed their ambitions, quite logically, in capitalist exploitation of the workers or imperialist expansion, Sternheim was very quick to condemn them, and even quicker to claim credit as a prophetic satirist for having exposed them. . . . [In] his essay of 1918, *"Die deutsche Revolution,"* he proclaimed his hatred of "a German imperialism which gradually threatened the world, and in particular an individualistic English world, with the cunning methods it had learnt from America." In the same essay he refers scornfully to the "capitalist circulus vitiosus that holds the whole of Germany in its grasp". But, and here is the point of self-contradiction, the heroes of Sternheim's plays, whom he is suggesting we admire for their energy and individualism, are social climbers and power-mongering capitalist entrepreneurs of the most ruthless sort! Christian Maske is a conniving parvenu capitalist in *Der Snob* and cold-bloodedly prepares his munitions factories for the coming war in *1913*. Schippel, the revolutionary proletarian, becomes a smooth-talking factory director in *Tabula Rasa*. Ständer in the same play lives off the dividends from his shares in this factory. Krull in *Die Kassette* hungers after nothing so much as capitalist shares. Need one go on? Sternheim has quite clearly contradicted himself. He morally condemned capitalism but admired capitalists. (pp. 40-1)

His plays are often marked by the same ambivalent division of sympathies that we see in the essays. In *1913* and *Tabula Rasa,* for example, he pits self-sacrificing socialists against power-mad capitalists. He sentimentalizes the socialist as a saint but then satirizes him; he caricatures the capitalist as a Machiavellian beast, but then involuntarily admires this beast.

In *1913* Friedrich Stadler is elevated to the role of socialist saint when he storms into the stronghold of capitalist corruption prophesying a spiritual rebirth for the nation. But his rhetoric is so inflated and his posturing so outrageous that we cannot take him seriously. As Stauch-v. Quitzow points out, Sternheim puts parodies of Schillerian idealism into Stadler's unwitting mouth and so ridicules his vague ecstasies about Germany's future. The only other socialist in the play, Wilhelm Krey, is also ridiculed by Sternheim because of the credibility gap between the highmindedness of his exhortations to others and the trivial vanity of his own personal behaviour. Krey's socialist revolution is hopelessly compromised by his submission to the whims of Ottilie, just as Ago von Bohna's communist idealism in *Das Fossil* is swept aside by his lust for Ursula, and Werner Sturm's revolutionary passions in *Tabula Rasa* seem tamed by his tender love for Nettel Flocke. Sternheim seems intent on demonstrating through these figures that man's sexual desire is a much stronger force than his political idealism, just as he wanted to show in *Die Kassette* and *Bürger Schippel* that sexual desire is in its turn much weaker than greed for money and social position.

The main conflict in *1913* is not between socialist and capitalist, but between capitalist and capitalist, namely between Freiherr Christian Maske von Buchow and his scheming daughter Sofie. They are both unashamed beasts of prey and they both fit Sternheim's essayistic definition of the hero. . . . Morally we can have no sympathies with either of them, nor did Sternheim mean us to. But seen aesthetically as personalities, they both have the fiery will-power and fierce joy in giving battle which Sternheim so obviously admired. The difference between them is that Sofie is driven on by a blind will to expand and control, whereas Christian in the last hours of his life has had a tragic insight into the ironic futility of everything he has built up: he had begun as an individualist storming the class barriers of convention and prizing the unique nuances of his own character, but he has ended by creating a society living off the stereotyped, shoddy products of technology and having lost all appreciation for the artistic nuances in the individual works of a craftsman. This is the reason why he considers joining Wilhelm's new cause, the chauvinist ecstasies of which, incidentally, sound decidedly like an unconscious anticipation of national-socialist propaganda. At bottom, however, he really only wants to resist decrepitude and what he feels to be the boredom of peace by standing at the hottest point of a fight, any fight. He is not morally concerned with the fact that his factories are churning out munitions that must be used in a war of some kind, but only with his determination to assert his will-power over his daughter Sofie and to educate his other daughter Ottilie to be an amoral animal of prey like himself. His final dance of vainglorious triumph over Sofie is grotesque and repulsive and presumably intended by Sternheim to be contrasted with the too noble rhetoric of the saintly Friedrich Stadler in the following and final scenes. It seems necessary to conclude that *1913* has no positive central character, but rather a complicated villain-hero and a satirized saint in a minor role. (pp. 41-2)

[Sternheim's] encouragement of the bourgeois to be his honest, repulsive self was tongue-in-cheek mockery. Audiences failing to realize this reacted with righteous indignation. Every time that they did this, Sternheim had the satisfaction of knowing that his play had been a success. The audience had been wounded in their smug self-esteem and their pretensions to the sacred ideals of love, friendship, and culture had been unmasked and made ludicrous. In other words, Sternheim's real intention was to taunt his public with satirical caricatures of themselves and thereby provoke them into an educative self-questioning.

There are no positively meant heroes to be found in Sternheim's best satirical comedies. For such unironically meant protagonists we must look to the flamboyant heroes of his later Romantic dramas, particularly Dietrich Brandt in *Das leidende Weib*, the Marquis of Arcis in *Die Marquise von Arcis*, and Chevalier des Grieux in *Manon Lescaut*. . . . It is true that Brandt, the Marquis, and des Grieux struggle against the conventions of bourgeois society, but Sternheim is deliberately overlooking the fact that they are very much noble, self-sacrificing heroes of the grand passion, whereas his Maskes, his Schippels, and Ständer are loveless egoists, scheming social climbers, and ruthless capitalists. Indeed it is against a society very much like that of Christian Maske von Buchow and Direktor Schippel that Sternheim's romantic heroes make their tragic protest. This distinction between the comic villain-hero and the tragic noble hero is very much in keeping with a key statement in Sternheim's aesthetic theory in which he distinguishes between comedy and tragedy. . . . [The] passage suggests that Sternheim does have an educative intention and that he is therefore neither an immoralist nor a nihilist. It also suggests that the preposterous heroes of his comedies are meant to be at least partly absurd in that they are fanatically and senselessly possessed of the very qualities which Sternheim wishes to operate on as the surgeon of his time.

Sternheim is thus not the creator of modern heroes who will form the basis of a new, more honest society, as Emrich and Wendler in particular have alleged. On the contrary. He is an ambivalent mixture of an arrogant cynic, who had an almost pathological need to mock and to satirize, and a sentimentalist with a decided weakness for the pathos of the romantic tragedy. His serious dramas of the later period are decidedly inferior to his cynical satires, and his reputation must stand or fall on his gift for farce, caricature, parody, and witty derision of human folly. (pp. 45-6)

David Myers, "Carl Sternheim: Satirist or Creator of Modern Heroes?" in Monatshefte (copyright © 1973 by The Board of Regents of the University of Wisconsin System), Vol. 65, No. 1, Spring, 1973, pp. 39-47.

SOL GITTLEMAN (essay date 1976)

How to deal with Carl Sternheim's sometimes heroic, sometimes preposterous bourgeoisie? Critics continue to debate this ambivalent dramatist's intention when he created his modern heroes for the cycle of plays *Aus dem bürgerlichen Heldenleben.* One group contends that Sternheim conceived of his middle-class patriarchs as intrepid and vital components of the New Society, embodiments of a Nietzschean dynamism which is ruthlessly triumphant. Others suggest that Sternheim intended to denigrate this Bürger-world and the hypocrisy of pre-war Imperial Germany. I should like to offer a possible model for Sternheim's *patresfamilias* in certain male types found in the plays of the dramatist who most significantly influenced Sternheim's ideas: Franz Wedekind, and in doing so, perhaps lend the weight of my argument to those who argue that Sternheim was primarily concerned with debunking the Wilhelminean society.

The relationship between Wedekind and Sternheim, in everything from linguistic idiosyncrasies to dramaturgy to philosophical speculation, has been discussed in some detail. Most important for Sternheim, however, is Wedekind's constant struggle against the forces of civilization which thwart man's basic drive to be free. It was Wedekind who first launched this all-out attack on institutional middle-class morality, and he gave to a female archetype, his Lulu of *Erdgeist* and *Die Büchse der Pandora,* the role of representing uninhibited pleasure and gratification in the face of society's need to control, to limit, and to restrain. . . . It is in the character of the unrepressed female that Wedekind finds the positive, dynamic strength of a free society, and he finds in the male, conversely, the restrictive, rational powers of a civilization which in order to survive had to control the threatening potency of Lulu and her kind. Throughout Wedekind's plays we encounter men who illustrate these counterforces of the established order, coolly rational, sexually totally in control, and motivated primarily by a classical, capitalist economic philosophy. In Wedekind, this is Economic Man, *homo economicus,* the enemy and ultimately the destroyer of Lulu. (p. 25)

Sternheim's idea of *homo economicus* is no less flattering and just as devastating with regard to the relationship between Eros and economics. Theobald Maske in *Die Hose* is the personification of the ordered, patriarchal civilization which keeps one eye on the accounts and the other on the wife. He has been married to the beautiful Luise for one year, but because his civil service position provides them with only modest means, they cannot afford any children and therefore abstain from sex. Ironically, Luise's innocent sexuality gives Maske the opportunity to add to his income. During an imperial parade, the visible disarray of her underclothing affects two bystanders so much that they eagerly rent rooms from Maske, in order to court the embarrassed Luise. But Luise's frustrations give way to excitement; she sees in the boarders two potential lovers, and both Scarron and Mandelstam are soon competing for her affections. Luise welcomes the opportunity for freedom and adventure, but, alas, the passions of the potential lovers prove to be empty. . . . Since Sternheim's dramatic invention is ultimately more comedic than Wedekind's, Luise's "tragedy" obviously makes a lesser impact than that of Lulu. But in both instances it is society that refuses to respond to the basic drives of the female. (p. 27)

In *Die Kassette,* the confrontation between female life force and *homo economicus* is more graphic and symbolically more concrete. Fanny is the highly desirable wife of the teacher Heinrich Krull, who hopes some day to inherit a fortune from his Aunt Elspeth. Elspeth understands the nature of Krull's greed, and in order to counteract Fanny's sexual control over him, she keeps the family fortune of stocks and bonds in a strongbox with which she constantly tempts him.

From the beginning, Sternheim juxtaposes the economic and the erotic. . . . Gradually, Krull's will is worn away by the attraction of the strongbox. He loses all interest in Fanny and transfers his sexual appetite to the money container itself. In order to distract him from Fanny, Aunt Elspeth cleverly allows him to take possession of the strongbox. As he carries it into bed with him, Heinrich speaks to the object of his economic greed the way he once spoke to the object of his erotic drive. . . . (p. 28)

In the end, Elspeth deceives Krull, and leaves her wealth to the church, but not before Fanny and her step-daughter are both reduced to lurking in the hallways, in search of husbands who have locked themselves in their rooms to count stock certificates.

These two plays suggest that a strong case can be made for a tragic view of Sternheim's women. Their primary tyrants are men who are incapable of a genuine, sustained eroticism. Like Wedekind before him, Sternheim connects this sexual inadequacy or abnormality to the males' economic preoccupations. Given Sternheim's own political and personal convictions on the nature of materialist capitalism, I find it difficult to advocate any interpretation other than that Sternheim's male protagonist, the *homo economicus,* is the destroyer of the life force, and in Sternheim's mind a consummate villain. (p. 29)

> *Sol Gittleman, "Sternheim, Wedekind, and 'Homo economicus'," in* The German Quarterly *(copyright © 1976 by the American Association of Teachers of German), Vol. XLIX, No. 1, January, 1976, pp. 25-30.**

RHYS W. WILLIAMS (essay date 1977)

Sternheim criticism has always been divided. His detractors have insisted that his dramatic work represents an idiosyncratic and wilful distortion of the social realities which confronted him, but his apologists have praised his unambiguous definition of social types and values. No critic has ever denied that Sternheim's method involves distortion. The question is how that distortion is used. Does it penetrate surface appearances and reveal hidden truth, or does it remain sterile mannerism?

Recent critics seem no more decided on this issue than were Sternheim's contemporaries. . . . What, however, has not been appreciated is that Sternheim himself was fully aware of the dilemma posed by his work and sought to contribute to the debate that surrounded it. In his various writings on Van Gogh he tried to clarify his own theoretical position and discuss problems inherent in his method. Indeed, his shifting image of Van Gogh serves as a correlate to his own artistic development and throws light on a problem which beset the writers of the Expressionist period.

Sternheim published three works concerning Van Gogh: an essay entitled *Vincent van Gogh,* which appeared in the periodical *Hyperion* in 1910; a fragment entitled *Legende von Vincent und Paul,* first published in *Die Aktion* in 1916, and *Gauguin und van Gogh,* completed in 1923 and published the following year, the first chapter of which was a revised version of the *Legende.* At each stage of Sternheim's own development it is Van Gogh who consistently embodies, for him, the highest creative qualities.

In the essay of 1910 the painter is presented as the practitioner of a theory which Sternheim derived from his reading of the works of the neo-Kantian philosopher, Heinrich Rickert. In *Die Grenzen der naturwissenschaftlichen Begriffsbildung* . . . Rickert's thesis was that the empirical world consisted of an infinite variety of things, both quantitatively and qualitatively; man's knowledge of the world depended on his capacity to overcome this variety quantitatively ('Überwindung extensiver Mannigfaltigkeit') and qualitatively ('Überwindung intensiver Mannigfaltigkeit'). Sternheim was clearly fascinated by the idea that the creative artist performed an analogous feat of conceptualization. His conviction that art could provide knowledge of the world in the form of concepts ('Begriffe') was set out in the Van Gogh essay. Here Sternheim isolates two possibilities. First, art can . . . [preserve] for posterity, by a process of selection and concentration, what is representative of a period in history or a landscape. The quality of the resulting work he terms 'Extensität' ['extensiveness'], a quality which Van Gogh demonstrates in his portrayal of the characteristic landscape of Provence. The second kind of Rickertian concept is illustrated by a quality which, in Sternheim's view, Van Gogh shares with Manet and Renoir: they all select objects at random and emphasize what is essential to all objects of that class. The resulting work of art has 'Intensität' ['intensity']; it gives the essence of an object. For Sternheim, then, Van Gogh's work embodies both types of 'Überwindung' ['overcoming'] postulated by Rickert.

Three other features of the Van Gogh essay of 1910 deserve mention. The first is Sternheim's desire to read into the creative work the personal experience of the artist. In his two subsequent portraits of Van Gogh Sternheim is attracted as much by the painter's life, his unconventional behaviour and social sympathies, as by his paintings. A second feature of the 1910 essay is the use of the 'heterocosmic analogue', the notion that the artist stands in the same relation to his work as God to the Creation. . . . There is a hint here of the artist's rivalry with God, but there are also pointers to the later view that the artist does not create a new world so much as reproduce the existing world in more concentrated form. . . . By 1916 all references to the heterocosmic analogue are dropped, and in 1923 any suggestion of the artist's autonomous will is totally rejected. Sternheim's evolving image of Van Gogh reflects his growing suspicion that his image for creativity implies an aestheticism from which he is anxious to distance himself. A third feature of the 1910 essay similarly recalls Sternheim's youthful neo-Romanticism: the confusion of the aesthetic and the erotic. . . . This feature, too, is deleted from Sternheim's later portraits of Van Gogh. (pp. 112-13)

[The *Legende von Vincent und Paul*] reveals that Sternheim's aesthetic theory, and consequently his image of Van Gogh, has undergone significant changes since 1910. After 1914 Sternheim came to regard the whole German cultural tradition, with only a handful of exceptions, as having shaped the bourgeois ideology which he held responsible for the outbreak of the war. Constrained, therefore, to narrow the scope of his original theory to exclude writers whom he now repudiated, Sternheim developed what he liked to consider a phenomenological theory. By this he meant that the artist should concentrate single-mindedly on the object before him, excluding all theoretical knowledge, all moral, political, social, and philosophical preconceptions, and admitting only what was given; he should disregard all tradition, all received wisdom. (p. 114)

Previously, as we have seen, Sternheim argued that art always involved 'Überwindung der Mannigfaltigkeit'. Now he stresses that this is a purely formal process. Bourgeois writers of the German idealist tradition may now be rejected wholesale, not because they fail to select, but because they select according to moral, metaphysical or ideological considerations, because they are not phenomenological in their approach. If selection is purely formal, it follows, for Sternheim, that outside art no selection should take place at all. . . . We are faced here not with a major internal contradiction in Sternheim's theory but with a major shift of emphasis.

The *Legende* of 1916 contains the first statement of a phenomenological approach which Sternheim advocated for the rest of his life. It is puzzling, at first sight, that Sternheim's new socio-political commitment should be so closely linked to an approach that purports to be disinterested. The Van Gogh of the *Legende* is vehemently anti-bourgeois; his whole life implies a rejection of the conformism and materialism which Sternheim held to be bourgeois traits. Van Gogh's aesthetic theory, his claim to view reality without metaphysical or moral preconceptions, is bound up with his attitude to society. His family background and education are shown to be riddled with moral imperatives, so that an art free from moral strictures, even implicit ones, is, at the same time, a protest against a bourgeois tradition. Van Gogh's naive, unbiased vision is both the prerequisite for 'Erkenntnis' ['perception'] and a contradiction of accepted values. It is in this sense that Sternheim's phenomenological approach can be said to imply a revolutionary stance. In perceiving the object, Van Gogh in the *Legende* puts out of his mind any associations it might have for him, when such associations persist in impinging on his consciousness. . . . The process is still akin to the Rickertian 'Überwindung intensiver Mannigfaltigkeit' of 1910, but is now more rigorous, requiring the exclusion of all traditional associations and accepted values. The artist still arrives at the essence of an object, the species within the individual, the universal within the concrete. But what is new is the socio-political dimension. The essence is now not merely what is characteristic of a class of objects, but what remains after the superficial bourgeois accretions have been stripped away. (pp. 114-15)

[A subject implicit in] *Gauguin und van Gogh* is the relationship between the individual and society, an issue which can never be completely divorced from the aesthetic theory. . . . Throughout the work Paris represents urban, industrial culture, with its depersonalized and aggressive materialism. Sternheim's repugnance for the mushrooming metropolis of Berlin, elaborated upon in *Berlin oder Juste milieu,* is here reiterated. The bourgeois evils—the worship of mediocrity, the acceptance of an absolute morality, and, most insidious of all, the prevailing conformism—are now transferred wholesale from Berlin to Paris. Only by flight from the capital is Van Gogh able to preserve the integrity of his personality. Thus the journey to Arles, the symbol of freshness and fecundity, implies a rejection of bourgeois values, a spiritual rebirth. . . .

Sternheim's Van Gogh does not advocate political or religious solutions to social evils, for both Marxism and Christianity appear to Sternheim to presuppose a collective consciousness, a single set of laws applicable to all human beings. Such notions he repudiates, and his Van Gogh is consequently made to proclaim a highly individual programme. . . .

In *Gauguin und van Gogh* Sternheim does not suggest that radical individualism is an end in itself. It is merely the prerequisite for a free community. (p. 118)

In *Gauguin und van Gogh,* then, the debate about modes of artistic representation encompasses a political argument. The crucial issue is the relationship between the artist and his world. (p. 119)

When due weight is attached to the polemical intention behind Sternheim's *Gauguin und van Gogh,* Sternheim himself seems to come down firmly on the side of Van Gogh. It is Van Gogh who is concerned with the relationship of art to the world it depicts, with its capacity for revealing the inner structure of things; Gauguin's interest, on the other hand, lies in the relationship of art to the creative artist, in its capacity for revealing a personal vision. Van Gogh's phenomenological theory contents itself with what is given, an approach devoid of appeal for Gauguin. . . . (pp. 122-23)

But the polemical intention is not the whole story. Gauguin is a powerful opponent. His art is accorded the highest praise.

And his aesthetic theory reminds us of Sternheim's own critical terminology, derived from Rickert. Indeed, it seems that Sternheim is actually giving us two perspectives on the same process. The very vehemence with which he makes Van Gogh defend his approach suggests that the attempt to dislocate the visible world to reveal its essential, inner structure, as he puts it, invariably lays the artist open to the charge of seeing what he wants to see, of projecting into the world his own private vision. . . . The phenomenological theory that the artist's vision should be determined by the object alone hardly seems borne out by Sternheim's own practice in *Gauguin und van Gogh.* He selects from Van Gogh's life incidents and theories which coincide with his own concerns, ignoring what does not. By contrast with Paris, for example, Arles is portrayed as an ideal community. . . . Yet, when [its inhabitants] later insist that Van Gogh be removed to an asylum, they are miraculously transformed into 'Spießburger' ['Philistines'] . . . and the ideal community is henceforth located in the asylum. Does this technique not involve wilful distortion and manipulation?

The debate between Gauguin and Van Gogh is not, we may conclude, a conflict between mutually exclusive points of view, with Sternheim coming down heavily on one side. Rather it is an exploration of two tendencies inherent in Sternheim's own work. Such debates are found elsewhere in Sternheim's writings, notably in the novel *Europa* . . . , where Carl Wundt advocates what I have called a phenomenological approach and is roundly attacked as a dilettante by the politically committed Eura Fuld, the mouthpiece of Sternheim's socio-political theories. Two *fictional* characters, then, Carl Wundt and Van Gogh, are the most consistent exponents of the phenomenological approach. Yet neither can be completely identified with Carl Sternheim. It is as if blatant 'Tendenz' ['trend'] and pure aestheticism were the dangers that beset him, so he drew between them a thin phenomenological line and sought in vain to tread it. Sternheim was clearly aware that, pushed to its logical conclusion, the phenomenological approach was unrealizable in practice. This is why it is only in fictional works that its potentialities and limitations can be explored.

At the outset I claimed that *Gauguin und van Gogh* was a representative work. First of all, it supplies ample evidence of the way in which Van Gogh appealed to the Expressionists: they could see in him not merely the formal distortion which coincided with their search for 'Wesen' behind the chaotic and confusing phenomena of the empirical world, but also the socially committed artist. . . . But Sternheim's story is representative in another sense: it embodies what most critics have seen as the central paradox of Expressionist writing, a paradox which some find stimulating and others regard as a major defect. [Georg] Lukács, for one, takes issue with the Expressionists' flight from reality, their desire to alter the way in which the world is perceived, rather than attempt to alter the world itself, by revolution. And certainly, while they saw themselves as revolutionary, their revolution was an artistic, or at most an epistemological one, though, it might be argued, no less valuable for that.

Sternheim was more aware of this paradox than many of his contemporaries. While he was unwilling to give his full support to political propaganda, as his strained relations with the *Aktion* circle illustrate, he could nevertheless regard art as political in the widest sense. . . . And while he extols the artist's unique skill, he is careful to stop short of aestheticism. Sternheim's own aspirations were to be a realist writer, in the sense that he wanted to deal in social types, to treat contemporary social

reality. He saw himself as heir to the French nineteenth-century realist tradition; his tributes to Flaubert in particular were frequent and generous. Yet his literary practice was founded on dislocation and distortion: the utmost concentration and economy—both conceptually and linguistically—which his theory demanded of him inevitably invited critics to view his work as manneristic. Fully aware of this ambiguity, Sternheim set out to embody it in an unresolved debate. In *Gauguin und van Gogh* there is polemic, but there is also self-examination. (pp. 123-24)

Rhys W. Williams, "Carl Sternheim's Image of Van Gogh," in The Modern Language Review *(© Modern Humanities Research Association 1977), Vol. 72, No. 1, January, 1977, pp. 112-24.*

MICHAEL HAYS (essay date 1978)

[Few critics] have made any serious effort to examine [*Don Juan*] or understand Sternheim's intellectual and artistic position prior to his "major" plays. . . . A closer look at the evolution of *Don Juan* can provide information about a crucial moment in Sternheim's development, a moment at which precisely those texts and ideas were available to him which, when brought to bear on his work, helped define the course of his later development.

The two earliest extant plot summaries indicate that, when Sternheim began working on *Don Juan* in May and June of 1905, he saw his subject mainly in terms of earlier tradition. Later the same year, he suddenly began to move away from a purely "literary" conception of his main character towards an examination of *Don Juan* in a concrete social context. Sternheim also decided to extend his play, giving it two parts, both based on historically verifiable material. . . . Why this shift took place is not immediately clear. Sternheim came to this decision in October, tore up his first draft and began to steep himself in historical and literary material from the sixteenth and seventeenth centuries. As [Wilhelm] Emrich indicates, Sternheim read Havermann's book on Don Juan of Austria and Mignet on Philipp II. Far more important, though, may have been . . . [B. Dietrich's] book entitled *Don Quijote und sein Dichter,* which had just appeared, and which seems to shed more light on Sternheim's change of attitude. . . . Although the *idealistisch-schwärmerische* [idealistic-enthusiastic qualities] remains a part of Don Juan's character, it is tempered by other material added in . . . other versions of the play that follow. In addition, the very fact of turning away from a literary ideal towards a real historical personage—Cervantes [author of *Don Quixote*] and not Don Juan of Austria—indicates that Sternheim's discovery is not of the way in which life emulates art, but rather of the fascination of observing an individual develop his creative potential in the face of adverse social conditions. It is not the rebel, Don Juan, but the socially conscious reformer-idealist Don Quixote/Cervantes that dominates in the second version of *Don Juan.* And it is historical reality—a real Don Juan—that serves as the starting point for Sternheim's youthful exploration of the notion of creative talent. Sternheim, in other words, has begun to move away from his own idealization of German neo-romantic aestheticism, but has not yet found another critical or artistic vocabulary with which to replace the first. (p. 115)

Particularly important for our understanding of both *Don Juan* and Sternheim's later work is the second, more sudden shift that took place in Sternheim's plans after January 1906. Between October and January Sternheim had rewritten and expanded his play in order to develop the new "quixotic" Don Juan and strengthen the social and historical foundations of the interaction with Juana, Philipp II and others. In late January and February this entire edifice is laid waste and a totally new notion of the play and its central character emerges. (p. 116)

[It seems] likely that Don Quixote served as a steppingstone in the transition from neo-romanticism to Sternheim's later "nietzschean" social and critical positions. (pp. 116-17)

Sternheim may have had some contact with George Bernard Shaw's *Man and Superman* and *Ceasar and Cleopatra*. In his prefaces to these plays Shaw draws attention to the importance of several artists who also turn up in Sternheim's correspondence: Cervantes, Goethe, Raphael, Carlyle, Wagner and Nietzsche. One can well believe that Sternheim had simply read works by or about these men, as did Shaw, because they were of general interest at the time. This would then be another example of their parallel development. I would, in fact, be inclined to think this the case were it not for the manner in which Sternheim's ideas about ethics, philosophy, romantic idealism, and even the characters he creates for his plays suddenly began to evolve in a manner similar to Shaw's credo on these subjects. The parallels are so numerous that one is led to speculate that Sternheim was programmatically following Shaw's lead. (p. 118)

In the early months of 1906, a period which was as important for him personally as it was for the development of his plays, Sternheim changed his mind about the significance of Don Quixote, rejected his earlier neo-romantic view of art almost completely, began discussing aesthetics, problems of morals and ethics and launched into a study of philosophy in general. A basic outline for all of these events can be culled from the prologue and the text of Shaw's Don Juan drama *Man and Superman*. In writing about the play Shaw not only suggests the possibility of a (Dona) Juana, but also insists that the modern Don Juan, "instead of pretending to read Ovid . . . does actually read Schopenhauer and Nietzsche, studies Westernmark. . . . In fact he is now more Hamlet than Don Duan . . . a true Promethean foe. . . ." Sternheim certainly began to conceive of his own Don Juan in Promethean terms. And he began himself to read Nietzsche and Schopenhauer. . . . [The] notion of an unquenchable creative drive, one that finally moves beyond what the earth has to offer, is . . . presented by Shaw in Act III, scene 3 of *Man and Superman*. Shaw's Don Juan is not tied to worldly pleasures. He is consumed with a passion for divine contemplation and creative activity which prevents him from having any permanent interest in love or sex. Sternheim's Juan takes on the same dimensions in the second part of his play.

For Shaw, the man of genius is "selected by nature to carry on the work of building up an intellectual consciousness of her own instinctive purpose." He "incarnates the philosophic con-

sciousness of life . . ." . . . . It is this same kind of natural selection and creative consciousness with which Sternheim first invests Don Juan and later elaborates a doctrine of individual creative energy much like Shaw's "life force" in the *Bürgerliches Heldenleben* series. (pp. 118-19)

In locating potential sources for the various stages in the development of *Don Juan,* I have tried to indicate what triggered the processes of intellectual and artistic development that led both to the final version of this play and to Sternheim's later dramatic and critical production. Those who categorize Sternheim as a neo-romantic as well as those who picture him as independently drawing together various aspects of art and philosophy at this time have relied too much on Sternheim's later statements or on a simple textual reading of *Don Juan.* It seems that Sternheim at this early stage is at once more complex and more straightforward and eclectic than he has been depicted. His struggle to create in himself both the artist and his art led him to dissemble many of his sources, particularly Shaw. At the same time, once Sternheim is located within this larger context, his work, especially that which comes after *Don Juan,* stands clearly within the dramatic and artistic consciousness of the era—not outside of or in opposition to it as a certain tradition has it. The final revisions of *Don Juan* were made in 1909. By then Sternheim was ready to move on to the *Bürgerliches Heldenleben* series, his "mature" work. It was the success of these later plays that led some of Sternheim's friends to refer to him as "the Moliere of the twentieth century"— shortly after [Augustin] Hamon's book on Shaw, *Le Molière du XXe siècle,* appeared in France. (p. 122)

Michael Hays, "Carl Sternheim's 'Don Juan': An Artist in Search of His Art," in The Germanic Review *(copyright 1978 by Helen Dwight Reed Foundation; reprinted by permission of the author), Vol. LIII, No. 3, Summer, 1978, pp. 115-23.*

ADDITIONAL BIBLIOGRAPHY

Garten, H. F. "Social Satire." In his *Modern German Drama*, pp. 87-101. London: Methuen & Co., 1964.
    Descriptive overview of Sternheim's major plays and their themes.

Rose, Margaret A. "The Sea-Serpent Topos in Daumier's *Les bons bourgeois* and in Sternheim's *Aus dem Buergerlichen Heldenleben*." *Arcadia* 10, No. 2 (1975): 184-89.
    Examines significance of the sea-serpent imagery in Sternheim's *Die Hose.*

Williams, Rhys W. "Carl Sternheim's Use of the Sea-Serpent Topos: An Amplification." *Arcadia* 11, No. 3 (1976): 288-90.
    Cites Sternheim's German and French predecessors in the use of the sea-serpent topos. This piece expands on points noted in the Rose essay [see entry above].

Bram (Abraham) Stoker

1847-1912

Irish novelist, short story writer, biographer, essayist, and critic.

Stoker is best known as the author of *Dracula,* "the most suspenseful and titillating piece of horror fiction ever written," as Daniel Farson characterizes it. He also wrote mediocre but well-received adventure novels and romances, several other horror novels, and a laudatory biography of his long-time friend and employer, the Shakespearean actor Sir Henry Irving. Despite his prolificacy, however, Stoker is regarded as a one-book author, his sole memorable contribution being the creation of the Transylvanian count whose name has become synonymous with vampirism.

Stoker was bedridden for the first seven years of his life. During this period of illness, which Stoker recalled made him "thoughtful," his mother told him stories of her own childhood during the cholera plague in Sligo, recounting instances of live interment and corpse burnings. At Trinity College, Stoker made up for his early invalidism by excelling in athletics as well as in his studies. He graduated with honors in mathematics in 1870 and followed his father into the Irish civil service, where he worked for ten years. During this time Stoker also was an unpaid drama critic for the Dublin *Mail,* contributing glowing reviews, more unabashed praise than criticism, of Henry Irving's theatrical performances. The two men became friends and, in 1879, Stoker left his job to become Irving's manager. He also discharged various managerial, secretarial, and even directorial functions at the Lyceum Theatre. Despite his extensive duties, Stoker wrote a number of novels, including *Dracula.* He also found time for a rich and varied social life, which was encouraged by his wife, Florence Balcombe, a childhood sweetheart for whom Stoker had competed with Oscar Wilde. Following Irving's death in 1905, Stoker was associated with the literary staff of the London *Telegraph* and wrote two more horror novels, *The Lady of the Shroud* and *The Lair of the White Worm.* In his final years, Stoker was afflicted with gout and Bright's Disease. Some biographers believe that he died of advanced syphilis, having contracted the disease about the time he was composing *Dracula.*

Critics generally regard *Dracula* as the culmination of the Gothic vampire story, preceded earlier in the nineteenth century by Dr. William Polidori's "The Vampyre," Thomas Prest's *Varney the Vampire,* J. S. Le Fanu's *Carmilla,* and Guy de Maupassant's "Le Horla." A large part of the novel's initial success was due, however, not to its Gothicism but to the fact that "to the Victorian reader it must have seemed daringly modern," as Daniel Farson notes. An early review of *Dracula* in the *Spectator* contains the comment that "the up-to-dateness of the book—the phonograph diaries, typewriters, and so on— hardly fits in with the mediaeval methods which ultimately secure the victory for Count Dracula's foes." Stoker utilized the epistolary style of narrative which was characteristic of Samuel Richardson and Tobias Smollett in the eighteenth century, and which Wilkie Collins further refined in the nineteenth. The narrative, comprising journal entries, letters, newspaper clippings, a ship's log, and phonograph recordings, allowed Stoker to contrast his characters' actions with their

own explications of their acts, as Carol Senf points out. Though Stoker's other novels were favorably reviewed when they appeared, they are dated by their stereotyped characters and romanticized Gothic plots; and except by afficionados of supernatural fiction they are rarely read today. Even the earliest reviews frequently decry the stiff characterization and tendency to melodrama which flaw Stoker's writing. Critics have universally praised, however, his beautifully precise place descriptions. Stoker's short stories, while sharing the faults of his novels, have fared better with modern readers. Anthologists frequently include Stoker's stories in collections of horror fiction. "Dracula's Guest," originally intended as a prefatory chapter to *Dracula,* is one of the best known.

Some early critics noted the "unnecessary number of hideous incidents" which could "shock and disgust" readers of *Dracula.* One critic even advised keeping the novel away from children and nervous adults. At first *Dracula* was not interpreted as anything but a straightforward horror novel. Then Dorothy Scarborough indicated the direction that future criticism would take when she wrote that "Bram Stoker furnished us with several interesting specimens of supernatural life always tangled with other uncanny motives." In 1931 Ernest Jones, in his *On the Nightmare,* drew attention to the theory that these "other uncanny motives" involve repressed sexuality. Critics have since tended to view *Dracula* from a Freudian psychosexual standpoint; however, the novel has also been interpreted from folkloric, political, feminist, medical, and religious points of view.

Today the name of Dracula is familiar to many people who may be wholly unaware of Stoker's identity, though the popularly held image of the vampire bears little resemblance to the demonic being that Stoker depicted. Adaptations of *Dracula* in plays and films have taken enormous liberties with Stoker's characterization. A resurgence of interest in traditional folklore has revealed that Stoker himself did not conform to established vampire legend. Yet *Dracula*, hastily written by a man who had studied mathematics and worked at primarily clerical jobs, has had tremendous impact on readers for almost ninety years. Whether Stoker evoked a universal fear, or as some modern critics would have it, gave form to a universal fantasy, he created a powerful and lasting image that has become a part of popular culture.

PRINCIPAL WORKS

The Duties of Clerks of Petty Sessions in Ireland
    (handbook) 1879
A Glimpse of America (essays) 1886
The Snake's Pass (novel) 1890
The Watter's Mou' (novel) 1894
Dracula (novel) 1897
The Jewel of Seven Stars (novel) 1903
Personal Reminiscences of Henry Irving (biography)
    1906
The Lady of the Shroud (novel) 1909
Famous Imposters (essays) 1910
The Lair of the White Worm (novel) ′1911; also published
    as *The Garden of Evil*, 1966
Dracula's Guest, and Other Weird Stories (short stories)
    1914
The Bram Stoker Bedside Companion (short stories) 1973

THE ATHENAEUM (essay date 1890)

The reader of **'The Snake's Pass'** is tempted to exclaim with Madame de Longueville, after a literary performance at the Hôtel Rambouillet, "Que cela est beau! et, mon Dieu, que cela est ennuyeux!" so long, so good, and so dull is Mr. Bram Stoker's new novel. The scene of action is laid in the west of Ireland, whose beautiful coast is as well described as the strange phenomenon of the shifting bog which plays so large a part in the story. The two heroes are almost equally high-minded, scrupulous, and self-sacrificing; in fact, they carry these virtues to a pitch which amounts to absurdity in their dealings with the villainous Murtagh Murdock. Andy, the car-driver, is quite the most amusing character in the book, and very good company as a rule. His dialect is occasionally oppressive, but possibly accurate. The writer shows himself so thoroughly capable of entering into the delightful humour and light-heartedness which constitute the charm of the Irish character to the benighted Saxon, that it is an additional pity he should have altogether denied Norah Joyce her birthright in this respect. The two young men also are quite overweighted by the burden of their solid virtues, without one redeeming weakness or the smallest sense of humour.

"Novels of the Week: 'The Snake's Pass'," in The Athenaeum, *No. 3295, December 20, 1890, p. 850.*

THE ATHENAEUM (essay date 1895)

There is some good descriptive writing in this little tale [*The Watter's Mou'*] about smuggling and love and duty nobly done. . . . The chief defect of the book, inevitable perhaps from the author's associations, is a tendency to melodramatic and stagey writing in some of the speeches and situations. . . . But in spite of a certain air of unreality about the whole tale, it has interest and movement enough to arouse and sustain the attention.

"New Novels: 'The Watter's Mou'," in The Athenaeum, *No. 3513, February 23, 1895, p. 246.*

THE ATHENAEUM (essay date 1897)

Stories and novels appear just now in plenty stamped with a more or less genuine air of belief in the visibility of supernatural agency. The strengthening of a bygone faith in the fantastic and magical view of things in lieu of the purely material is a feature of the hour, a reaction—artificial, perhaps, rather than natural—against late tendencies in thought. Mr. Stoker is the purveyor of so many strange wares that **'Dracula'** reads like a determined effort to go, as were, "one better" than others in the same field. How far the author is himself a believer in the phenomena described is not for the reviewer to say. He can but attempt to gauge how far the general faith in witches, warlocks, and vampires—supposing it to exist in any general and appreciable measure—is likely to be stimulated by this story. The vampire idea is very ancient indeed, and there are in nature, no doubt, mysterious powers to account for the vague belief in such beings. Mr. Stoker's way of presenting his matter, and still more the matter itself, are of too direct and uncompromising a kind. They lack the essential note of awful remoteness and at the same time subtle affinity that separates while it links our humanity with unknown beings and possibilities hovering on the confines of the known world. **'Dracula'** is highly sensational, but it is wanting in the constructive art as well as in the higher literary sense. It reads at times like a mere series of grotesquely incredible events; but there are better moments that show more power, though even these are never productive of the tremor such subjects evoke under the hand of a master. An immense amount of energy, a certain degree of imaginative faculty, and many ingenious and gruesome details are there. At times Mr. Stoker almost succeeds in creating the sense of possibility in impossibility; at others he merely commands an array of crude statements of incredible actions. The early part goes best, for it promises to unfold the roots of mystery and fear lying deep in human nature; but the want of skill and fancy grows more and more conspicuous. The people who band themselves together to run the vampire to earth have no real individuality or being. The German man of science is particularly poor, and indulges, like a German, in much weak sentiment. Still Mr. Stoker has got together a number of "horrid details," and his object, assuming it to be ghastliness, is fairly well fulfilled. Isolated scenes and touches are probably quite uncanny enough to please those for whom they are designed.

"'Dracula'," in The Athenaeum, *No. 3635, June 26, 1897, p. 235.*

THE BOOKMAN London   (essay date 1897)

Since Wilkie Collins left us we have had no tale of mystery so liberal in matter and so closely woven. But with the intricate plot, and the methods of the narrative, the resemblance to stories of the author of "The Woman in White" ceases; for the audacity and the horror of **"Dracula"** are Mr. Stoker's own. A summary of the book would shock and disgust; but we must own that, though here and there in the course of the tale we hurried over things with repulsion, we read nearly the whole with rapt attention. It is something of a triumph for the writer that neither the improbability, nor the unnecessary number of hideous incidents recounted of the man-vampire, are long foremost in the reader's mind, but that the interest of the danger, of the complications, of the pursuit of the villain, of human skill and courage pitted against inhuman wrong and superhuman strength, rises always to the top. Keep **"Dracula"** out of the way of nervous children, certainly; but a grown reader, unless he be of unserviceably delicate stuff, will both shudder and enjoy. . . .

"Novel Notes: 'Dracula'," in The Bookman, London, Vol. XII, No. 71, August, 1897, p. 129.

JAMES MacARTHUR   (essay date 1904)

Mr. Bram Stoker is a born story-teller. He has a knack of engaging your interest at the very outset and holding it through a series of exciting chapters until the dénouement. Perhaps he has never told a better story than *The Jewel of Seven Stars* . . . , although his stories always have something about them that leave an impression, and won't be forgotten. . . [*The Jewel of Seven Stars*] is a tale of wonder and mystery, and the reader who is already acquainted with Mr. Stoker's previous work, knows how well he can mystify his readers and keep them on tenter hooks of suspense until the end is reached. It is full of "thrills." There are pages in it which are capable of making the flesh of the most *blasé* reader creep. The story opens with the discovery of an attempted crime which at first glance might seem to have no further importance than that of some daily occurrence reported in the newspaper, but the circumstances that attend the trance into which the victim has fallen after being attacked by some unknown person become grave and complicated and mysterious. . . . It should be noted also that Mr. Stoker has very successfully surrounded his story with an atmosphere that impresses the mind and warms the imagination of the reader to the unusual and extraordinary character of the tale he is telling. Mr. Stoker has undoubtedly written a very clever and masterly story of thrilling interest which is likely to command a popular audience.

*James MacArthur, "Books and Bookmen," in Harper's Weekly, Vol. XLVII, No. 2461, February 20, 1904, p. 276.**

MONTAGUE SUMMERS   (essay date 1918)

[It] is well-nigh impossible for a story which deals with the supernatural or the horrible to be sustained to any great length. Elements which at first are almost unendurable will lose their effect if they are continued, for the reader's mind insensibly becomes inured to fresh emotions of awe and horror, and *Dracula* is by no means briefly told. . . . [It] extends to more than four hundred pages, nor does it escape the penalty of its prolixity. The first part, "Jonathan Harker's Journal," which consists of four chapters is most admirably done, and could the whole story have been sustained at so high a level we should have had a complete masterpiece. But that were scarcely possible. The description of the journey through Transylvania is interesting to a degree, and even has passages which attain to something like charm. "All day long we seemed to dawdle through a country which was full of beauty of every kind. Sometimes we saw little towns or castles on the top of steep hills such as we see in old missals; sometimes we ran by rivers and streams which seemed from the wide stony margin on each side of them to be subject to great floods. It takes a lot of water, and running strong, to sweep the outside edge of a river clear." Very effective is the arrival of the English traveller at the "vast ruined castle, from whose tall black windows came no ray of light, and whose broken battlements showed a jagged line against the moonlit sky." Very adroitly are the various incidents managed in their quick succession, those mysterious happenings which at last convince the matter-of-fact commonplace young solicitor of Exeter that he is a helpless prisoner in the power of a relentless and fearful being. The continual contrasts between business conversations, the most ordinary events of the dull listless days, and all the while the mantling of dark shadows in the background and the onrushing of some monstrous doom are in these opening chapters most excellently managed.

So tense a strain could not be preserved, and consequently when we are abruptly transported to Whitby and the rather tedious courtships of Lucy Westenra, who is a lay figure at best, we feel that a good deal of the interest has already begun to evaporate. I would hasten to add that before long it is again picked up, but it is never sustained in the same degree; and good sound sensational fare as we have set before us, fare which I have myself more than once thoroughly enjoyed, yet it is difficult not to feel that one's palate has been a little spoiled by the nonpareil of an antipast. This is not to say that the various complications are not sufficiently thrilling, but because of their very bounty now and again they most palpably fail of effect, and it can hardly escape notice that the author begins to avail himself of those more extravagant details of vampirism which frankly have no place outside the stories told round a winter's hearth. It would have been better had he confined himself to those particulars which are known and accepted, which indeed have been officially certified and definitely proved. But to have limited himself thus would have meant the shortening of his narrative, and here we return to the point which was made above.

If we review *Dracula* from a purely literary point of approach it must be acknowledged that there is much careless writing and many pages could have been compressed and something revised with considerable profit. It is hardly possible to feel any great interest in the characters, they are labels rather than individuals. As I have said, there are passages of graphic beauty, passages of graphic horror, but these again almost entirely occur within the first sixty pages. There are some capital incidents, for example the method by which Lord Godalming and his friend obtain admittance to No. 347 Piccadilly. Nor does this by any means stand alone.

However, when we have—quite fairly, I hope—thus criticized *Dracula,* the fact remains that it is a book of unwonted interest and fascination. Accordingly we are bound to acknowledge that the reason for the immense popularity of this romance,— the reason why, in spite of obvious faults it is read and re-read—lies in the choice of subject and for this the author deserves all praise. (pp. 333-35)

Montague Summers, "The Vampire in Literature" (1918), in his The Vampire: His Kith and Kin *(copyright © 1960 by University Books, Inc.; reprinted by permission of Mrs. L. Vyse and J. H. Porter) K. Paul, Trench, Trubner & Co., Ltd., 1928 (and reprinted by University Books, 1960), pp. 271-340.**

H. P. LOVECRAFT (essay date 1927)

[The] ingenious Bram Stoker . . . created many starkly horrific conceptions in a series of novels whose poor technique sadly impairs their net effect. *The Lair of the White Worm,* dealing with a gigantic primitive entity that lurks in a vault beneath an ancient castle, utterly ruins a magnificent idea by a development almost infantile. *The Jewel of Seven Stars,* touching on a strange Egyptian resurrection, is less crudely written. But best of all is the famous *Dracula,* which has become almost the standard modern exploitation of the frightful vampire myth. Count Dracula, a vampire, dwells in a horrible castle in the Carpathians, but finally migrates to England with the design of populating the country with fellow vampires. How an Englishman fares within Dracula's stronghold of terrors, and how the dead fiend's plot for domination is at last defeated, are elements which unite to form a tale now justly assigned a permanent place in English letters. *Dracula* evoked many similar novels of supernatural horror, among which the best are perhaps *The Beetle,* by Richard Marsh, *Brood of the Witch-Queen,* by "Sax Rohmer" (Arthur Sarsfield Ward), and *The Door of the Unreal,* by Gerald Bliss. (pp. 392-93)

H.P. Lovecraft, "Supernatural Horror in Literature" (1927), in his Dagon and Other Macabre Tales, *edited by August Derleth (copyright 1965, reprinted by permission of Arkham House Publishers, Inc.),* Arkham House, 1965, pp. 347-413.**

MAURICE RICHARDSON (essay date 1959)

Dracula, by Bram Stoker, the best known of all vampire stories, [is] almost the last of the Gothic romances. It was published first in 1897 and it still sells at the rate of several thousand copies a year, so it must have preserved powerful horripilatory properties for all its crudeness. (p. 426)

Dracula, I think, provides really striking confirmation of the Freudian interpretation . . . [The vampire superstition] embodies a particularly complex form of the interest, both natural and unnatural, which the living take in the dead. In ghoulism the necrophiliac traffic is one way, as it were, but in vampirism 'the dead first visits the living and then drags him into death being himself reanimated in the process'.

These are surface considerations. The starting point from which to investigate the hidden content of the superstition is . . . Freud's dictum that morbid dread always signifies repressed sexual wishes. In vampirism they become plainly visible. Here we enter a twilight borderland, a sort of homicidal lunatic's brothel in a crypt, where religious and psychopathological motives intermingle. Ambivalence is the keynote. Death wishes all round exist side by side with the desire for immortality. Frightful cruelty, aggression and greed is accompanied by a madly possessive kind of love. Guilt is everywhere and deep. Behaviour smacks of the unconscious world of infantile sexuality with what Freud called its polymorph perverse tendencies. There is an obvious fixation at the oral level, with all that sucking and biting, also a generous allowance of anality. We are left in no doubt about the origin of the frightful smell, compost of charnel house and cloaca, that attaches to the vampire.

It is very remarkable how in *Dracula,* Stoker makes use of all the traditional mythical properties and blends them with a family type of situation of his own contriving that turns out to be a quite blatant demonstration of the Oedipus complex. From a Freudian standpoint—and from no other does the story really make any sense—it is seen as a kind of incestuous, necrophilous, oral-anal-sadistic all-in wrestling match. And this is what gives the story its force. The vampire Count, centuries old, is a father-figure of huge potency. He is planning, from his ancestral lair in the Carpathians, a raid on England to set up a contemporary vampire empire. He has summoned Jonathan Harker, a young solicitor, to make the necessary arrangements concerning property. These, owing to the elaborate obsessional code of rules governing the vampire's existence, are extremely complicated. The vampire or 'undead' can only move about freely during the hours between sunset and sunrise. During that time he enjoys all the freedom of movement and change of a phantom. By day he is confined to his coffin.

Vampires are not very particular about their choice of object. When, on his first morning as a guest in Castle Dracula, Jonathan Harker cuts himself, the Count's eyes blaze with oral-sadism. He makes a sudden grab but just manages to restrain himself. That night when Dracula's daughters, who are themselves vampires, crowd into Jonathan's bedroom, the directly sexual nature of the phantasy underlying the superstition is revealed. (pp. 426-27)

Later on in the story, which is told by the multi-narrational method—'As I must do something or go mad, I write this diary'—used so successfully by Wilkie Collins—Dracula lands in England and the endogamous motif linking all the characters together as members of one family becomes apparent. Dracula's first English victim is Miss Lucy Westenra, beloved by a psychiatrist, Dr. Seward. (He has in his care a 'zoophagous maniac' who is forced to become Dracula's agent. This is a rather impressive piece of characterization and one that seems to show an intuitive insight into the oral nature of the manic depressive disposition.) The second victim is Lucy's bosom friend, Mina Harker, as dear if not dearer to her as any sister. She is the wife of Jonathan Harker.

Dracula's onslaughts on Mina are not fatal, because they are interrupted. The language in which Mina describes them leave you in little doubt about their sexual character and the incestuous guilt attaching to it. Note particularly the extrasanguinary symbolic significance attaching to blood:

> He placed his reeking lips upon my throat. . . . I felt my strength fading away, and I was in a half swoon. . . . With that he pulled open his shirt, and with his long sharp nails opened a vein in his breast. When the blood began to spurt out, he took my hands in one of his, holding them tight and with the other seized my neck and pressed my mouth to the wound, so that I must either suffocate or swallow some of the—Oh, my God, my God! what have I done?' . . . She began to rub her lips as though to cleanse them from pollution.

Mina is saved and Lucy avenged by a noble brotherly band led by Dr Van Helsing, Seward's old master, a Dutch psychiatrist. (If he were in practice to-day he would be a right-wing Catholic Jungian.) Van Helsing is up to all the vampire's tricks, though until the very end he is always a step or two behind. Apart from Van Helsing, who represents the good father figure, the set-up reminds one rather of the primal horde as pictured somewhat fantastically perhaps by Freud in *Totem and Taboo,* with the brothers banding together against the father who has tried to keep all the females to himself. Dracula himself seems almost conscious of this. When nearly cornered in his house at 'Carfax' after several of his mobile coffins have been destroyed, he snarls:

> You shall be sorry yet, each one of you! You think you have left me without a place to rest; but I have more. My revenge is just begun! I spread it over centuries and time is on my side! Your girls that you all love are mine already: and through them you and others shall yet be mine. . . .

One is tempted to add: 'mine. . . . in a vast polymorph perverse bisexual oral-anal-genital sado-masochistic timeless orgy'. There are several more passages in which the symbolism and the underlying incestuous complex stick out a mile. Often, especially during some of Van Helsing's lectures to Seward on the Count's psychology, Stoker shows insight into the infantile nature of the vampire's personality. When the great struggle is finally over, and virtue has triumphed over polymorph perversion in a last minute Lyceum melodrama rescue situation and the Count has been staked through the heart in his coffin, in the moment of final dissolution a look of peace comes over his face that is on a par for intensity with the raging fury that had preceded it.

I doubt whether Stoker had any inkling of the erotic content of the vampire superstition. . . . He wrote several other occult thrillers, but not one of them is a patch on *Dracula.* (pp. 428-29)

> *Maurice Richardson, "The Psychoanalysis of Ghost Stories," in* The Twentieth Century *(© The Twentieth Century, 1959), Vol. 166, No. 994, December, 1959, pp. 419-31.**

RICHARD WASSON   (essay date 1966)

From the time of its appearance in 1897, Bram Stoker's *Dracula* has never been out of print, has been translated into several languages (including Gaelic) and has been transformed into several versions for the theatre and movie-going public. No doubt numerous psychological and sociological explanations for the novel's popularity might be offered; among these possibilities is a political theme (perhaps "undertone" might be more exact) which would appeal to audiences throughout the series of crises presented by the two world and the cold wars. Count Dracula, if not always in the plays and movies, at least in the novel represents those forces in Eastern Europe which seek to overthrow, through violence and subversion, the more progressive democratic civilization of the West.

This claim might seem facetious to those inclined to regard the book as a hack job designed to titillate its audience. But even writers of popular novels have political opinions and Stoker is no exception. . . . In *Lady of the Shroud* (1909), one of the most entertaining bad novels ever written, he uses the Vampire theme to present a fantastic solution to the Balkan situation. Under the leadership of the heir of an English capitalist, "The Land of the Blue Mountains," a tiny state on the Adriatic, rings itself with cannon and battleships, protects its skies with

"aeros," the then ultimate weapon, and leads its neighbors into a confederation of states called "Balka," thus ordering the chaos which tempts the imperialistic ambitions of both the Turkish and the Austro-Hungarian empires. In that book Stoker abandons the vampire-horror techniques about half-way through to write what he undoubtedly thought was a political novel.

In *Dracula* the political theme is more covert and certainly less urgent; but it is nevertheless there and in the same peculiar way as in *Lady of the Shroud.* The locale of the novel, near the border of three Balkan territories in the center of Roumania, is suggestive enough. Jonathan Harker, whose journal begins the tale, describes it as a distinctly eastern portion of Europe where the laws and customs of the West do not apply. Harker describes the area as "certainly an imaginative whirlpool of races . . . where hardly a foot of soil has not been enriched by the blood of men, patriots, invaders." While the rest of Europe has been free to develop a culture, this area has been a bloody battle ground.

More interesting than the location, is Dracula's ancestry—he is a direct descendent of Atilla the Hun. . . . The Count sees himself as having performed an important political function for the West; through war and diplomacy he and his "race" kept the Turks at bay and finally defeated them. . . . He later acts the part of the betrayed and the sacrificed by telling Mina that "hundreds of years before they were born," he had intrigued and "fought" for the very men who are now seeking to destroy him . . . , a fact which Van Helsing, who, as we shall see in a moment, represents the assorted powers of the West, grudgingly acknowledges. . . . But his victory has rendered him historically obsolete and left his people exhausted. "The warlike days are over; blood is a precious thing in these days of dishonorable peace," he continues in language similar to that of other leaders associated with the decline of Austro-Hungarian power; "the glories of the great races are as a tale that is told". . . . The people are exhausted and "the walls of my castle are broken," he tells Harker. The Count, descendent of the Hun, feels himself cheated and deprived, and therefore like his ancestor, who, in a moment of victory over the Turks turned Westward, decides to move on England. His land a place of wars' excrement, he seeks his just rewards by reviving the Westward push of the "hooded hordes."

But the political motif becomes more complicated, for Stoker sees the Count as a threat to progress, which he conceives in terms of increasing democracy and improved technology. One line of thematic development asserts that whereas in the old days the Count had to exist on the primitive frontier of Western culture, his best chance for survival is now in England, the most progressive, rational and democratic nation in Europe. On another level, Stoker points out that modern victories can be better won by subversion than by invasion and that modern war depends upon the conversion of the citizens of democracy to a vampirish bloodlust. These themes add up to the idea that technological progress, having cut humanity off from the old superstitious, dark knowledge, makes itself increasingly vulnerable to the demonic powers like the Vampire, for, having written them off as unreal, civilized man has no defense against them. Since only doctors of the mind, Seward and Van Helsing, can cope with such monsters the novel carries the implication that demonish forces have been unloosed in the human psyche by technological and political progress.

Count Dracula's motives for coming to England make these themes clear. Becoming a vampire through his great lust for slaughter and his knowledge of alchemy, he seeks to perpetuate himself by changing his locale and his mode of operation. Van Helsing, in the unintentionally comic dialect Stoker gives him, provides an excellent summary of Dracula's plan: "He find out the place of all the world of most promise to him. . . . He learn new social life, new environment of old ways, the politic, the law, the finance and the science, the habit of a new land and a new people" . . . . England is the "place of most promise" because "its law, its social life, its politics and science will serve to protect him." . . . (pp. 24-5)

Initially the Count's plan meets with success. He gets into England, spreads the coffins, with the bloody dirt in which he must nightly lie, carefully around London and establishes contact with the mad Renfield. Moreover, he selects as his first victim Lucy Westenra (appropriately, as her name implies, she is the light of the West), a typical Victorian upper middle class woman who has known no evil. But though he turns her into a vampire, a group forms to save her and thwart his evil power.

If the Count's motives are political, the group's are even more so. They see themselves as an alliance of free men, qualified "by nationality, by heredity, or by possession of natural gifts" . . . and dedicated to setting the world free. . . . The group forms around Lucy Westenra's three lovers: Dr. Seward, the appropriately named Lord Godalming, Quincy P. Morris, an America; and Lucy's friend, Mina Harker. Coming to their aid are Dr. Van Helsing, Mina's husband, and Seward's patient, Renfield. Each contributes something specific. Lord Godalming, for example, gets favors unextended to commoners. . . . Van Helsing as a Catholic has an unlimited supply of the Host, a fine seal for door and window cracks through which the Count must vaporize himself. . . . Harker's legal knowledge enables the group to evade the law. . . . Madam Mina manages to get bitten by the vampire, but instead of deserting to the Count, she uses her new-found sympathy with his un-British East European habits to help the allies track him down.

More interesting perhaps is Quincy P. Morris, who is popular literature's archetypal Texas millionaire. Though the dialect Stoker has him speak is as bad as Van Helsing's, he serves an important political function. As we might suspect, the American is the most pragmatic campaigner. While Van Helsing is in charge of the long range plans, it is Morris who is always there with practical suggestions and who on the spur of the moment can make the best decisions. Once, when the group is surprised by the Count, Morris concocts a plan of action which almost traps him. More importantly, when the Count is on the run and Van Helsing is directing his efforts to trapping him, Morris points out that while the group is well prepared to exorcise evil spirits, they are virtually defenseless against more material threats from wolves and gypsy partizans. He therefore volunteers to supply the necessary military aid in the form of Winchesters. "I propose we add Winchesters to our armament. I have a kind of belief in a Winchester when there is any trouble. . . ." . . . Stoker not only suggests that America become the armorer of the West but argues that she cannot live up to her full promise until she gives up the Monroe Doctrine's restrictive measures against her participation in European affairs. . . .

Perhaps the most interesting character in the group is the madman Renfield, through whom Stoker builds up the pseudo-scientific theory of Vampirism. The man theorizes that by eating live flesh and consuming blood from living bodies he can stay alive forever . . . . Yet Renfield, unlike the Eastern European Count, recognizes the horror of his dream. He has himself committed and though it costs him his life, he resists

the Count's bribes of a repast of live rats and bats in order to warn the others of Dracula's strategy. . . . English reason is strong enough to counter Eastern European bloodlust, even in a lunatic.

This group proves that though progress makes England vulnerable, it also provides the means by which Dracula can finally be destroyed. While the Count can manipulate elements of English society to his advantage, he ultimately has to rely on tradition and habit. The defenders, however, "have the sources of science" and "are free to use them." They have "self devotion in a cause and an end to achieve which is not a selfish one". . . . The Austrian is limited by the narrowness of his purpose; he cannot operate during daylight hours; he cannot move freely over water; he cannot enter rooms or seduce a victim unless the person allows him to. Though he has the stubborn cunning of a secret purpose and superior powers of political and military maneuvering, he is limited by his lack of freedom.

The allies quickly rout the Austrian. Together they track him to his Transylvanian lair and ambush him on the road. Covered by American Winchesters in the hands of Seward, Godalming, and Van Helsing, Harker and Morris push through the army of defending gypsies and simultaneously plunge knives into Dracula's heart and sever his head, killing the Count forever. This act frees Mina from her own vampirism and restores peace to the world.

Thus the Count is controverted and his threat to the progress of Western Civilization brought to an end. While on the surface Stoker's gothic political romance affirms the progressive aspects of English and Western society, its final effect is to warn the twentieth century of the dangers which faced it, both in the years following *Dracula*'s publication and in the present. It is Dracula's meance that is most memorable, and that menace is only increased by the progress of the civilized world. One of the things Van Helsing most fears is that the Count will come to learn more of Western life, come ultimately to adopt a kind of scientific approach and to learn that he has freedom of choice. If blood lust of the vampire once links itself to modern politics, to modern science, there will be little if any defense against it, a fact which has been too vividly proven in our violent century. The popular imagination so stirred by the political horrors of our time, which turns again and again to the nightmares of the Nazi era and which reads the warnings of science fiction with great attention, cannot help but be stirred by the political implications of *Dracula*. (pp. 26-7)

Richard Wasson, "The Politics of Dracula," in English Literature in Transition (copyright © 1966 Helga S. Gerber), Vol. 9, No. 1, 1966, pp. 24-7.

C. F. BENTLEY (essay date 1972)

Dracula's great success cannot be attributed to conventional literary strengths, in which the work is deficient. The possibilities in a psychoanalytical approach to *Dracula* have been noted [see Richardson excerpt above], but no attempt has been made to investigate in detail the sexual implications of the story.

Ernest Jones, in the section entitled 'The Vampire' in his monograph *On The Nightmare*, states that the vampire superstition 'yields plain indications of most kinds of sexual perversions', and it would seem that such perversions, concealed by symbolism, are the dynamic of *Dracula*, and may largely account for the initial success and continued popularity of the work. Nothing in Stoker's other writings or in what is known of his life suggests that he would consciously write quasi-pornography, and it must be assumed that he was largely unaware of the sexual content of his book. In common with almost all respectable Victorian novelists, Stoker avoids any overt treatment of the sexuality of his characters. The obscenity laws, the tyranny of the circulating libraries, and the force of public opinion were, throughout the greater part of the nineteenth century, powerful constraints on any author who wrote for the general public, but it is probable that for many writers, including Stoker himself, an even stronger reason for avoiding sexual matters was a personal reticence amounting to repression. Stoker's 'living' characters (that is, those other than vampires) are, both the women and the men, models of chastity. One male-female relationship, that of Jonathan Harker and Mina Murray, is of primary importance to the story, and they marry at an early stage of the plot, but the sexual elements that presumably exist in their relationship are never revealed, much less discussed. However what is rejected or repressed on a conscious level appears in a covert and perverted form through the novel, the apparatus of the vampire superstition, described in almost obsessional detail in *Dracula,* providing the means for a symbolic presentation of human sexual relationships.

A close examination of certain episodes in the work shows that Stoker's vampires are permitted to assert their sexuality in a much more explicit manner than his 'living' characters. One of the three vampire women who attempt to attack Jonathan Harker at Dracula's castle assesses the potency of her intended victim with a surprising directness: '"He is young and strong; there are kisses for us all."' Although their nominal intention is to suck Harker's blood, the advances of the women and Harker's responses are, throughout this significant episode, consistently described in sexual terms. . . . The ambivalence of Harker's response, combining both 'longing' and 'deadly fear', is especially revelatory, as is his concern over the feelings of his fiancée, Mina: the vampire women offer immediate sexual gratification, though on illicit and dangerous terms, a tempting alternative to the socially imposed delays and frustrations of his relationship with the chaste but somewhat sexless Mina. The entire episode, including Harker's subsequent doubt as to whether he was awake or dreaming, has the irreal quality of a masturbatory fantasy or erotic dream. . . . With the exception of Dracula's brief and abortive assault on Harker when momentarily aroused by the sight of blood from a shaving cut trickling down the latter's chin, the prominent vampire attacks in the novel are always on members of the other sex: the female vampires attempt to make Harker their prey, and Dracula attacks Mina Harker and Lucy Westenra, suggesting that vampirism is a perversion of normal heterosexual activity. The relationships between the vampires themselves are rather more complicated; of the three vampire women, two resemble Dracula and so presumably are related to him, while the third is spoken of as their sister. Therefore it would appear that they are either Dracula's daughters or sisters, but when one of them taunts Dracula with the accusation: '"You yourself never loved; you never love!"', he rejoins meaningfully: '"Yes, I too can love; you yourselves can tell it from the past. Is it not so?"', implying that an incestuous relationship has existed between them. In this interchange Stoker seems to be consciously endowing his vampires with a sexual freedom that would be unthinkable in his 'living' characters. A remarkable heightening of sexuality occurs in the formerly virginal Lucy when she becomes a vampire, and, as in the episode of the three

vampire women, 'languorous' and 'voluptuous' are two of the terms that Stoker chooses from his rather limited vocabulary of the erotic to describe the new freedom of her behaviour.

The blood of the living, which the vampire craves, also has strong sexual undertones. . . . [Ernest Jones] equates the loss of blood to a vampire with the emission of semen, and this is undoubtedly what underlies the attempted attack on Harker by the vampire women, but even when no vampire is present, the giving and receiving of blood may still be charged with sexual meaning. Lucy Westenra, weakened by Dracula's nocturnal attacks, receives blood transfusions from, successively, Arthur Holmwood, John Seward, Dr. Van Helsing and Quincey Morris. . . . This sequence of blood transfusions symbolizes sexual intercourse, with Lucy of necessity acquiring a freedom and promiscuity that could not possibly be described in actual terms, especially when the central figure is a girl whose behaviour is as chaste and respectable as that of her friend Mina. (pp. 27-9)

The same symbolism would seem to be present in a curious episode later in the story, when Dracula has invaded the bedroom of Harker and his wife Mina.

> On the bed beside the window lay Jonathan Harker, his face flushed, and breathing heavily as though in a stupor. Kneeling on the rear edge of the bed facing outwards was the white-clad figure of his wife. By her side stood a tall, thin man, clad in black. His face was turned from us, but the instant we saw we all recognised the Count—in every way, even to the scar on his forehead. With his left hand he held both Mrs. Harker's hands, keeping them away with her arms at full tension; his right hand gripped her by the back of the neck, forcing her face down on his bosom. Her white nightdress was smeared with blood, and a thin stream trickled down the man's bare breast which was shown by his torn-open dress. The attitude of the two had a terrible resemblance to a child forcing a kitten's nose into a saucer of milk to compel it to drink. . . .

The episode contains a strange reversal of the usual relationship between vampire and victim, as Dracula is forcing Mina to drink his blood. Stoker is describing a symbolic act of enforced fellatio, where blood is again a substitute for semen, and where a chaste female suffers a violation that is essentially sexual. Of particular interest in the earlier passage is the striking image of 'a child forcing a kitten's nose into a saucer of milk to compel it to drink', suggesting an element of regressive infantilism in the vampire superstition.

The symbolic meanings of blood in *Dracula* are rendered more complex by an incident that occurs later in the same chapter. Mina, bleeding after Dracula's attack on her, is being comforted by her husband. . . . Although the reaction of horror, and its accompanying exclamation of 'Unclean', comes from Mina, and although Jonathan firmly refuses to share it ('"Nonsense, Mina. It is a shame to me to hear such a word. I would not hear it of you; and I shall not hear it from you"'), Mina's description of herself while the 'thin stream of blood' trickles from her recalls ancient primitive fears of menstruation. The mention of a 'thin open wound' is especially noteworthy: in *Dracula* the mark of the vampire's bite is usually described as two round punctures caused by the elongated canine teeth, whereas this phrase suggests a cut or slit similar to the vaginal orifice. . . . [Dracula has] bitten Mina, causing the 'unclean' flow of blood, and symbolically he has forced her to undergo sexual intercourse with him. In this incident veinous blood symbolizes not semen but menstrual discharge, suggesting that blood as a symbol has multiple meanings in *Dracula,* but that sexual significances predominante.

The methods used to destroy vampires also contain sexual implications, and revealingly, are modified according to the sex of the vampire. Lucy, who becomes a vampire after succumbing to Dracula's attacks, is released from her 'undead' state into true death by her erstwhile fiancé Arthur, who drives a hardened and sharply pointed wooden stake through her heart. The phallic symbolism in this process is evident, and Lucy's reactions are described in terms reminiscent of sexual intercourse and orgasm, and especially the painful deflowering of a virgin, which Lucy still is. . . . On the other hand, when Dracula himself is to be destroyed, although a stake driven through the heart remains part of the method, the emphasis is shifted to decapitation of the vampire. Now it has long been recognised that the head is a very common penis-substitute in dreams concerning the fear of castration. Dracula is rendered powerless, symbolically castrated, by having his head cut off: a sexual revenge is taken on the creature whose depredations have been basically sexual in character. Van Helsing, the novel's expert on vampirism, sometimes uses the term 'sterilize' when discussing means of defeating and destroying Dracula, implying that he entertains a castration fantasy based on fear and envy of the vampire's powerful sexuality.

Although vampirism is ostensibly presented as a supernatural phenomenon of evil, to be combated with the weapons of religion, such as the Cross and the Host, and those of superstition, such as garlic, it is in actuality treated as a shameful and terrible disease. Two physicians, Seward and Van Helsing, the former an authority on mental illness and the latter a polymath who has made a special study of vampirism, are omnipresent, and their medicoscientific techniques, including blood transfusions, hypnotism, and sedatives, are an important part of the fight against Dracula. The traditional view of vampirism as a species of demonic possession to be cured by spiritual means survives in the novel, but it has been partly displaced by a more modern attitude which sees vampirism as a disease and a perversion possibly amenable to medical treatment, recalling the Victorians' horror of masturbation and nocturnal emissions.

Details of the vampire's existence are rich in psychological implications. . . . Dracula's wooden coffins filled with earth, as necessary as blood for sustaining the vampire's life in death, since he must return to one of them during each day, are an obvious womb-substitute, and together with Van Helsing's repeated assertions that Dracula has a 'child-mind' or a 'child-brain', confirm the suggestion already advanced, namely that there is an element of infantile erotic regression in vampirism.

Though the vampire's attack symbolizes sexual intercourse, or more precisely, in view of the presumed chastity of the two female victims, loss of virginity, there is one important difference. Unlike actual defloration, the process is reversible, for the victim can be redeemed by the death of her seducer, the vampire; the burn-mark on Mina's forehead, caused by the touch of the Host when she was 'unclean', disappears as soon as Dracula is destroyed. The physical and spiritual degradation incurred by the victim of a vampire need not be permanent, and in any case to fall victim to a vampire does not, in this novel, involve social degradation; the vampire women who attack Harker at Dracula's castle are described as 'ladies by their dress and manner', and Dracula himself, though presented as a creature of infinite wickedness, is, as Stoker emphasizes, a European nobleman with an ancestral home, a distinguished lineage, and a 'courtly' manner. On occasions he displays a thoroughly aristocratic contempt for his somewhat *bourgeois* antagonists, while they, with a proper sense of his rank, customarily refer to him in their diaries and journals as 'the Count'. Dracula has much in common with the corrupt but gentlemanly seducers of popular fiction and drama whose archetype is Lovelace in Richardson's *Clarissa.* Just as they can attempt and sometimes succeed in the seduction of innocent females without forfeiting their claim to be gentlemen because of the freedom given them by society's double standard, and because of a received definition of the gentleman that includes licentiousness as one of his qualities, so Dracula appears curiously guiltless in his vampirism, for he is merely obeying the dictates of his corrupt nature, and, in choosing beautiful young women as his victims, is only exercising an admittedly perverted *droit de seigneur.* In particular his nocturnal visits to Lucy, pre-empting the claims of her fiancé, have a distinct echo of the medieval *jus primae noctis,* the more so as Dracula, who is several centuries old, once was a feudal lord, and certainly retains the outlook and behaviour of one. (pp. 30-2)

Stoker's work, in spite of its modern setting, is a fantasy using the materials of folklore, and its chief character is therefore permitted to force his way into the bedrooms of respectable young women and to exercise freedoms that would be surprising even in the avowedly 'fast' novelists of the day. (p. 33)

C. F. Bentley, "The Monster in the Bedroom: Sexual Symbolism in Bram Stoker's 'Dracula'," in Literature and Psychology *(© Morton Kaplan 1972), Vol. XXII, No. 1, 1972, pp. 27-34.*

ROYCE MacGILLIVRAY (essay date 1972)

Bram Stoker's *Dracula* has never been much praised for its literary merits. Yet this horror novel . . . survives today, after more than seventy years of popularity, as one of the little group of English language books from the nineties still read by more than scholars. Because of the succession of horror films based on it, whether *Dracula* would have achieved this success solely through its intrinsic merits is uncertain. Certainly without the films it is hard to believe that Dracula would be one of the few proper names from novels to have become a household word, known even to people who have never heard of the novel. Stoker created a myth comparable in vitality to that of the Wandering Jew, Faust, or Don Juan. This myth has not, so far, been crowned with respectability by its use in great literature, yet is it too much to suggest that in time even that may be achieved? Such a myth lives not merely because it has been skillfully marketed by entrepreneurs but because it expresses something that large numbers of people feel to be true about their own lives. (p. 518)

Stoker, who sets his narrative uncompromisingly in the framework of the technologically advanced and modern-minded Victorian civilization, weaves into it the commonplace details of everyday life precisely where we expect them least. It is absurd, and yet convincing, to find that Dracula has a sizeable library in his vampire castle, from which he has been quarrying information about the customs, laws, and so forth of England. Coming into the room one evening, Harker finds him lying on a sofa reading Bradshaw's railway guide. In the castle where no servants are ever seen, Harker glimpses Dracula making Harker's bed and setting his table. As we read of the meals which Harker was served ("an excellent roast chicken," "an excellent supper") we wonder, as Stoker robably intends we should, whether Dracula also did the cooking. It is touching that when the pursuers break into the house Dracula has bought in Piccadilly they find his clothes brush and brush and comb there—necessary implements, it seems, even for someone who lives in a coffin. While they wait at his house, Mrs. Harker, with pleasing impudence, sends them a telegram there to warn them that Dracula may be approaching. When Dracula, intent upon fleeing from England, meets a sea captain to commission him to ship his one remaining box of earth out of the country—the captain of course does not know that the stranger who is addressing him is a vampire and will be hiding in the box—Dracula is seen to be wearing a straw hat, which, as Van Helsing remarks in his imperfect English, "suit not him or the time." Perhaps this element of the incongruous in the novel is intended only as a gentle form of self-parody, or of mockery at tales of the supernatural. I think, however, that it plays a rather more important role than this. We live daily, Stoker seems to say, with the incongruous, with the ironies, contradictions, and wild absurdities of life. We have no reason then to be surprised if the most preposterous events should come upon us at the very moment when life seems most sober, rational, and humdrum.

Stoker created in Dracula a towering figure who dominates the novel and appears utterly convincing. It was unfortunate for Stoker that he did not live early enough to write his novel at the beginning rather than the end of the nineteenth century. Had Dracula come to literary life in the age of Romanticism and the Gothic novel, one imagines that he would have been received rapturously into the literary tradition of western Europe instead of being sternly restricted, as he has been, to the popular imagination. In view of the extraordinary pains Stoker took to make the geographical and social background of the novel as accurate as possible—his description of Whitby, where Dracula landed in England in the midst of an immense storm, is a reliable guide for tourists today—it is not surprising to find that he selected for his vampire a real historical figure, Vlad the Impaler, also known as Dracula, who was voivode or prince of Wallachia from 1456 to 1462, and again in 1476. In real life Dracula was known for his horrifying cruelty, but Stoker, who wanted a monster that his readers could both shudder at and identify with, omits all mention of the dark side of his reputation and emphasizes his greatness as a warrior chieftain. As Dracula entertains young Harker in his castle, he cannot refrain from reminiscing about the campaigns in which he took part. Though he pretends to be merely talking about the history of his part of Europe and conceals all personal involvement, a telltale sign appears: in his speaking of things and people, and especially of battles," Harker notes, "he spoke as if he had been present at them all." When Van Helsing has had a Budapest correspondent make enquiries into the identity of the historical figure whose living corpse they are pursuing, he is able to report: ,

> He must, indeed, have been that Voivode Dracula who won his name against the Turk, over the great river on the very frontier of Turkeyland. If it be so, then was he no common man; for in that time, and for centuries after, he was spoken of as the cleverest and the most cun-

ning, as well as the bravest of the sons of the "land beyond the forest."

(pp. 519-21)

Fixing himself on this biographical basis, Stoker gives his vampire story an unexpected and, in view of later exploitations of the Dracula theme in films, a remarkably sophisticated psychological interest, and even a degree of pathos. . . . Dracula, a polished and eloquent gentleman as well as a wily antagonist, is untypical. In their non-fictional existence, as described by tradition, vampires tend, it seems, to be squalid and animallike. But for the superiority of Dracula there is a reason beyond that of his superiority in life. Dracula, we are led to believe, has been slowly recovering his faculties since the time of his death, when they were partly destroyed. While the execution of his elaborate project for transferring himself to England, where multitudes exist to be his prey, is the highest achievement that his process of self-development has yet yielded, there are possibilities that if he survives he will become more dangerous still. "What more may he not do." Van Helsing asks, "when the greater world of thought is open to him?" Dracula's power to grow intellectually is, however, barren. No matter what he grows into, he must remain painfully and utterly separated from the surrounding world of men and all its values.

Dracula, though at a lower level of literary achievement, is—like [Hermann Hesse's *Steppenwolf* and Albert Camus's *L'Etranger* and *La Chute*]—a novel of alienation. The depiction of Dracula as an alienated figure derives from the traditional vampire legends, the Gothic novels, and the idea of the romantic hero, as well as from Stoker's psychological acumen. When we have seen Dracula in this light, we can grasp the double irony of his statement to Harker in the castle that "I long to go through the crowded streets of your mighty London, to be in the midst of the whirl and rush of humanity, to share its life, its change, its death, and all that makes it what it is." This touching sentimentality, which masks the fact that he wants to be among these people to prey on them, also masks his defeat. Though he has retained and recovered some human characteristics, he can no more share the people's "whirl and rush" and life and change than he can ever see again the armies he commanded so long ago. Dracula's disastrous expedition to England can even be seen as unconsciously suicidal, as his attempt to extinguish his anguish in a lasting death. (pp. 521-22)

The popularity of the Dracula myth in this century suggests that many persons find a resemblance between themselves and Dracula and between themselves and vampires in general. It is hard not to suggest that vampire stories, including *Dracula,* reflect, in a sensationalized but recognizable form, the truth that the close association of any two persons is almost certain to involve, however faintly, some "vampirish" exploitation, be it economic, intellectual, or emotional, of one of them by the other. (pp. 523-24)

One of the defects of the novel is the Victorian emotionalism which occasionally makes the modern reader wince. A far graver defect, however, is its weakness of characterization, a rule whose only exception is the magnificent and convincing figure of Dracula. This weakness is especially evident in all six of the little band of heroes pursuing Dracula. Harker is the most convincing, principally because Stoker has not tried to give him a distinct character but has been content to let him be a transparent object through which events are viewed. Part of the reason why the first fifty or sixty pages of the novel, which deal with Harker's experiences in Transylvania, are so much better than the remainder of the work is that no characters but the superior Dracula and Harker appear in them, except briefly. After these first pages, in which he is introduced in great detail, Dracula is removed almost completely from the direct view of the reader. In this way Stoker maintains in the reader a sense of the ominous—not, be it noted, a sense of the mysterious, which is little awakened because the approach which the heroes of the novel take to the reemergence of vampires in modern society is severely practical and rationalistic—but he deprives himself of the full use of his strongest creation.

The only character in the novel who comes close to being boring is, oddly enough, slightly better developed than most of Stoker's characters. This is Renfield, the zoophagous patient in Dr. Seward's lunatic asylum. Renfield's repulsive desire to eat flies, birds, and other small living creatures, and all the other details of his malady and daily life are described with surprising relentlessness. Eventually he is allowed to play a feeble part in the action by admitting Dracula into the asylum when his prospective victim, Mrs. Harker, is visiting there; according to the rules which tradition tells us govern a vampire's actions, he cannot enter a house until one of its occupants has admitted him, but thereafter he can come and go as he pleases. As Stoker is a story teller par excellence, it is strange that he does not enliven the sections which deal with Renfield by including more action, perhaps in the form of a subplot based on Renfield's past life. But if the treatment of Renfield is unsuccessful, that is not because he is irrelevant to the novel. I suggest we should regard him as a good idea which does not quite succeed. His simplest function is to tie together disparate parts of the narrative through his presence. Stoker may also have felt the need of a sluggishly unfolding account of Renfield to contrast with the usual swift pace of his narrative. But most importantly, Renfield joins Dracula and his pursuers in a traingular relationship in which he heightens our awareness of their character and position.

As we seek to define the most important role he plays in this relationship, it becomes evident that he is the sad anti-Dracula of the novel. Along with his desire to feed on living things, he has dim hopes of becoming a vampire. Meanwhile, his madness and his prison walls confine him as much as Dracula is confined by his alienation and the rules that restrict the actions of a vampire. We are constantly aware of Renfield's exclusion from the band of pursuers and thus see in him an echo of Dracula's alienation. In the same way, it may be mentioned in passing, Dracula's alienation is mocked by the clubbiness and family feeling of the pursuers. (pp. 524-26)

Dracula is a thoroughly unpolitical novel. This statement is true both in the sense that Dracula ignores the party issues of the day and in the more general sense that it ignores the strains of the class society of late Victorian England. To the historically minded, however, it is interesting for its expression of certain attitudes belonging to Stoker's part of the Victorian period, and for its anticipations of the intellectual climate of our century. The alienation theme in the novel is especially relevant to the twentieth century—indeed, is brought out in the novel with a sharpness which seems almost anachronistic and which deserves close examination by the historians of the development of the English novel—but the novel expresses also the disquiet of many Victorian intellectuals about the atomizing and dehumanizing effects of their own time. . . . The novel also reflects the foreboding with which some Victorians faced the new century. Surely some ill-fortune would take away the good things which had been so unstintingly poured upon Vic-

torian England? Dracula may have partially symbolized for contemporaries this nameless threat. The vampire theme has special relevance, too, to the Victorian problem of loss of faith. The abandonment of traditional Christianity reopened the whole question of what becomes of a person after death. In our time *Dracula* probably gains part of its impact from the intense fears which have clustered, more in this century than in any other, about the problem of growing old, a problem which vampires, who are capable of living forever, have solved.

But of all that is historically interesting in *Dracula,* nothing is more curious than its combination of the Victorian preoccupation with death and an almost twentieth-century preoccupation with sex. This combination is found, for example, in the hunting activities of the vampires, who belong to the dead but pursue the living in what often seems to be a spirit of blatant sexuality, and in the destruction of beautiful female vampires by driving stakes through their hearts as they sleep in their tombs.

I must not allow my remarks on the faults of this novel to conceal the remarkable skill with which it is written. It is hard to believe that anyone who has observed the power Stoker shows in *Dracula* of setting a scene and developing its action with a maximum of conciseness and vividness could dismiss him as a mere writer of thrillers. It is even harder to believe that anyone who has examined this novel's extraordinary richness of detail and Stoker's ability to subordinate this richness to a severely disciplined plot could regard him as deficient in inventiveness, intellectual power, or a sense of literary design. . . .

[His] language rises at times to a kind of poetry. Had Stoker been able to overcome the single problem of his weakness in characterization, there is no reason why *Dracula* should not have been one of the minor masterpieces of English fiction. Even in its imperfect form it deserves to be known to scholars as more than a source of sensational films. (pp. 526-27)

Royce MacGillivray, "'Dracula': Bram Stoker's Spoiled Masterpiece," in Queen's Quarterly, *Vol. LXXIX, No. 4, Winter, 1972, pp. 518-27.*

LEONARD WOLF   (essay date 1972)

[When] *Dracula* appeared, it was still recognizable as a Gothic novel in the tradition of Walpole, Lewis, Radcliffe and Maturin. There were the usual fearful dangers: a lustful villain, dark and mysterious mountains, crumbling architecture—a castle in Transylvania, a ruined chapel in London, a tumbling abbey in Whitby—the usual alarums and surprises along with vaults, stone walls and reverberating darkness in the holds of ships. A point of some importance is that the conflicts in the old fictions between antagonists were essentially physical and external. Stoker's achievement is that while he kept plenty of that machinery, thereby fulfilling an implied agreement with the literary past, he managed at the same time to make his vampire tale a gathering place for symbols of extraordinary internal meaning. In 1972, seventy-five years from the time of its publication, *Dracula* is fully visible as a visionary novel . . . whose allegorical power transcends the fairly narrow Christian work that Stoker made.

The Christian message is certainly there, but it is quiveringly entangled in matters that (sadly) seem to have more "modern" significance: the meaning of human energy; the concept of sanity; the nature of identity; and most intensively the awful powers of sexual repression and evasion. It is an entanglement, I hardly need add, that is probably unconscious on Stoker's part, and has been carefully unrecognized by a couple of generations of readers. For the most part, *Dracula* has been read as a rousing good thriller, rather than as the great contemporary allegory of blood it certainly is.

Even Montague Summers, who is prepared to dote on nearly anything vampiric, will only concede to Stoker the achievement of a brilliantly selected subject matter and occasionally "admirable" writing [see excerpt above]. But Summers, after praising the first four chapters, says of the book ". . .and could the whole story have been sustained at so high a level we should have had a complete masterpiece." In fact, we have a complete masterpiece. . . . (pp. 180-81)

A summary of the action of *Dracula,* useful as it is to remind us who does what to whom, can hardly explain why the story has domesticated itself in the contemporary imagination where, over a seventy-five-year period, it has taken on all the symbolic authority of a legend. How has this tale by a part-time hack writer managed to create in the minds of nearly three generations of readers a sense of an old memory recovered? Why does it inexhaustibly generate prose imitations of itself? Even more to the point, how does it happen that the film industry of all the world has been unable to let Stoker's vampire achieve, finally, the rest the novel itself has given him?

I have already given a simple answer to these complex questions by claiming that *Dracula* is a great book, and I have suggested that its greatness lies in the ways in which Stoker fuses the Christian allegory of his vampire tale with the other matters he exposes even as he tries to avoid knowing what they mean. (p. 205)

Dracula squirms with . . . primordial, dark or forbidden news from the abyss. More than that, much of its artistic strength comes from the intensity with which Stoker evades what he guesses—while he decks it out in the safer Christian truths that he repeats. (p. 206)

[It is] a piece of triumphant restraint which makes Dracula move through the book, when he does appear with a cold, dry, sinister largeness that befits a creature who is a "man or shade, / Shade more than man, more image than a shade." From the first moment that we see him, he stirs up those matters with which the book deals. He is strong, feral and old. If Van Helsing has energy with grace abounding, then Dracula is charged with the grandeur of satanic power. Their struggle is allegorical and instinctual, but in either case, it turns on blood, because the blood as it flows in mortal veins is life, at the same time as it represents life everlasting. The struggle between Van Helsing and Dracula is, however, more than religious, though Van Helsing pursues him with crosses, the Host and prayers. Those aids belong to the Church, but Van Helsing also uses garlic flowers, the woodrose and the stake—remedies that do not depend upon Christ because the vampire is an evil beyond theology, rooted in instincts not yet recognized, much less controlled. (p. 220)

Dracula is considerably more than a sexual danger. Stoker insists on his brooding, primordial animality—he is antirational, childlike, instinctual. His evil is related to the animal heat of that Ugric tribe which "bore down from Iceland the fighting spirit which Thor and Wodin gave them, which their Berserkers displayed to such fell intent on the seaboards of Europe. . . ." The blood of such peoples, mingled with that of "the Huns, whose warlike fury had swept the earth like a

living flame," is also in his veins. When he talks of his past, though he glows with his consciousness of inherited power, the vitality of which he boasts is above all bestial, as his features remind us. He is profusely hairy, with massive eyebrows, and hands that are "broad, with squat fingers" and pale pointed ears. . . . Even his cunning, slowly modifying itself toward intelligence, is the cunning of the animal that counts on swift physical motion to counter its errors in judgment. Van Helsing speaks of his "child-mind," and Dracula is dangerous because he is in the course of evolving it into a brain that will be devoted to the grandeur of evil.

So much for the beast. What sort of *person* is Dracula? The answer is that he is not a person—he is a presence; or, better, he is an absence that requires concealing. Stoker has not made Dracula's personality his problem, nor is trying to assess it ours. Beyond the physical descriptions of him that emphasize his power, there is little for us to turn to for character analysis, though I confess that there are a few sharp moments when something resembling a self passes before us; as, for instance, when we are given the suggestion that this quintessential monster whom the beasts and the very winds obey, sets the table, makes beds, cooks and cleans away the dishes in his castle. There is another moment when Van Helsing's band, searching Dracula's Fenchurch Street house, comes upon the vampire's personal effects which include "also a clothes brush, a brush and comb, and a jug and basin—the latter containing dirty water which was reddened as if with blood." This find strikes a note of loneliness, but we are still far distant from a Dracula who might be a tormented figure, more acted upon than acting. Despite a few pious Christian remarks by Mina Harker that Dracula is to be pitied, and the notation that in the moment of his death "there was in . . . [his] face a look of peace," Stoker has brilliantly avoided building *any* sympathy for him. He does nothing, ever, to entice compassion. Instead, he is a thoroughgoing evil creature who drinks the blood of his victims because he likes doing what, in any case, it is his destiny to do. Even in the instant before he is destroyed, his "red eyes glared with [a] horrible vindictive look. . . ." And, as "the eyes saw the sinking sun . . . the look of hate in them turned to triumph." We may well believe that Harker's great Kukri knife and Quincey Morris's bowie did not flash a moment too soon.

Dracula, then, is a novel that lurches toward greatness, stumbling over perceived and unperceived mysteries: Christianity, insanity, identity, a spectrum of incest possibilities, marriage, homosexuality, immortality and death. All of them are bound together in the inclusive meaning of blood. If I claim greatness for this strange book, it is because, after nearly three generations, it continues to pulse with sometimes coherent, more often dismembered symbolic material of the sort that makes up what Jung has called "primordial experience which surpasses man's understanding, and to which he is therefore in danger of succumbing." Stoker's achievement is that he put all this *stuff* into his book with such skill that a headlong reader as well as one capable of worrying over the signs and portents is always in the grip of the narrative line. To put it another way, Stoker, organizing the tale of the vampire and his enemies, did not create impediments to our appreciation of "the disturbing vision of monstrous and meaningless happenings that in every way exceed the grasp of human feeling." (pp. 220-22)

Leonard Wolf, "Dracula: The King Vampire," in his A Dream of Dracula: In Search of the Living Dead *(copyright © 1972 by Leonard Wolf; reprinted by permission of Little, Brown and Company), Little,*

Brown, 1972 (and reprinted by Popular Library, 1977, pp. 171-224).

DANIEL FARSON   (essay date 1975)

[Bram Stoker] wrote many short stories. Most of them have been forgotten like the majority of his novels, and are indeed forgettable. . . . (p. 97)

But Bram was a writer of extremes: he could wallow in the depths of sentimentality yet write two classic stories of the macabre. Both concerned rats. **'The Judge's House'** tells of a scholar, Malcom Malcomson, who is anxious to prepare for his examinations in an atmosphere of solitude, and rents a desolate house on the outskirts of a market town. The landlady of the local inn, where he is staying, is aghast. . . . (pp. 97-8)

Warned against staying there on his own, Malcom replies rather pompously, as Stoker's male characters tend to do:

> But, my dear Mrs Witham, indeed you need not be concerned about me! A man who is reading for the Mathematical Tripos has too much to think of to be disturbed by any of these mysterious ''somethings''.
>
> (p. 98)

The story is too good to disclose in . . . condensation for it has a dimension all its own. Like the greatest of horror stories, it is rendered straight, like the report of an accident or the committal to paper of a nightmare while it is still livid in the mind. His use of rats to enhance the reader's fear is brilliant—creatures we know to be real and commonplace, but strangely sinister. The setting of the lonely house is of no importance here; it is a product of Bram's imagination, but **'The Burial of the Rats'**, equally uncanny, was inspired by his early visits to Paris. It is set among the endless dust-heaps that lie outside the town at Montrouge. . . . (p. 99)

Bram writing in the first person, loses his way until he finds a dilapidated shanty occupied by an old woman, and asks the direction. . . .

The narrator conveys his terror to the reader. He continues:

> After a time I began to grow uneasy. I could not tell how or why, but somehow I did not feel satisfied. Uneasiness is an instinct and means warning. The psychic faculties are often the sentries of the intellect, and when they sound alarm the reason begins to act, although perhaps not consciously.
>
> (p. 100)

'Uneasiness is an instinct and means warning': Bram Stoker was a master of *unease*.

'The Secret of the Growing Gold', in which the hair of a murdered woman continues to grow until it finally traps the murderer, her husband, is no more far-fetched than **'The Judge's House'** but infinitely less compelling. A third story succeeds: **'The Squaw',** a straightforward horrific narrative, set in Nuremberg Castle. (pp. 100-01)

Candidly, most of [Stoker's novels] might have been written by another author. There is throughout the most surprising contrast between florid romance and lurid horror. . . .

[*Miss Betty*] is dedicated to 'My Wife' and opens at Cheyne Walk where they lived—and that is the most intriguing part of it. The rest is an old-fashioned romance about highwaymen, with Miss Betty herself making Pollyanna look like Jezebel by comparison. . . .

[*The Man*] has a final flourish that would be hard to surpass in mawkishness. . . .

Bram's tales of horror had far more conviction. *The Lady of the Shroud* . . . concludes with a prophetic ariel attack, a foretaste of air-raids to come—and has a faint echo of *Dracula* in a Balkan princess who *pretends* to be a vampire. But Bram's interest in the supernatural went far beyond vampires. *Jewel of the Seven Stars* concerns the resurrection of an Egyptian Queen who ruled twenty-five centuries before Christ. I should place this book next to *Dracula* for suspense and readability. The climax is grand. . . . (p. 205)

It has been said Heinemann's [Stoker's publisher] were so shocked by the original ending that Stoker toned it down in deference to them. Even so, it is compulsive reading. 'The great stake'—the resurrection of a woman—is an immense theme, while the sincerity of the loyal band of fanatics has echoes of the avengers in their pursuit of Count Dracula. (p. 206)

Bram had a feeling for history and mystery. *Famous Imposters* . . . contains the intriguing theory of 'The Bisley Boy'—that Queen Elizabeth had died as a baby and a boy had been substituted by her terrified guardians, who were expecting a visit from King Henry.

Another piece of non-fiction, Stoker's most bizarre publication of all, was ['' **The Censorship of Fiction**,''] one of several articles contributed to the *Nineteenth Century Magazine* in 1908. Advocating the censorship of fiction, Bram revealed how deeply disturbed he was. The diatribe starts gently: 'There is perhaps no branch of work among the arts so free at the present time as that of writing fiction.' Stoker adds sadly that this means that the author's 'duty' to the state 'appears to be nil'.

His argument is age-old and all too familiar today: that there must be some sort of give-and-take rules, that 'freedom contains in its very structure the forms of restraint.' This could take the form of the writer's own 'reticence' which Stoker acclaims as 'the highest quality of art; that which can be and is its chief and crowning glory'. He admits that this is an attribute which is virtually undefinable. The other restraint is some sort of censorship, something to be avoided if possible. 'But if no other adequate way can be found and if the plague-spot continues to enlarge, *a censorship there must be.*' Conceding that one form of censorship already existed—the police—he is, at least, disinclined to support 'repressive measures carried out by coarse officials . . . [though] . . . it is the coarseness and unscrupulousness of certain writers of fiction which has brought the evil; on their heads be it.' (pp. 207-08)

For once, and most revealingly, the 'fair sex' are included in the damnation of those with base appetites; indeed 'women are the worst offenders in this form of breach of moral law.'

Stoker's main attack concentrates on literature, or fiction as far as his purpose in concerned: 'What use is it, then, in the great scheme of national life, to guard against evil in one form whilst in another it is free to act? In all things of which suggestion is a part there is a possible element of evil. Even in imagination, of whose products the best known and most potent is perhaps fiction, there is a danger of corruption.' At this point he makes an extraordinary admission: '*A close analysis will show that the only emotions which in the long run harm are those arising from sex impulses, and when we have realised this we have put a finger on the actual point of danger.'* (pp. 208-09)

I have always felt that, when the Longfords of this world tell us what we should not read, they are more concerned with the danger of *their* corruption than our own. Most people can read pornography without such risk and can even benefit, but 'they' recognise the temptation and in trying to resist it, involve us too to prove them right. The subject has a salacious appeal which they find irresistible.

It is depressing to have to place my great-uncle [Bram Stoker] alongside Mrs Ormiston Chant, 'the prude on the prowl' and scourge of Marie Lloyd and music hall, in his own time, beside Lord Longford and Mary Whitehouse in ours.

Coming from the author of **Dracula** these views seem incredible. 'The only emotions which in the long run harm are those arising from sex impulses.' Is it possible that Stoker did not realise he had written one of the most erotic books in English literature? Is it possible that he was unaware of the sexual implications it contained?

The passages in **Dracula** speak for themselves. (pp. 209-10)

[Stoker's] last and strangest book [is] *The Lair of the White Worm.*

It might have been written under the influence of drugs, a 'trip', along 'the high road to mental disturbance', to use a phrase from the book. At one time I wondered if he was being treated with drugs to alleviate the painful Bright's Disease which corroded him in his last years.

At the very least, *The White Worm* is a literary curiosity. The plot is so bizarre, almost ludicrous, that it is hard to imagine anyone taking it seriously. But on a recent re-reading I became increasingly impressed by the way-out blend of Gothic surrealism; read on that level it is dazzling. Also, without a vestige of humour, it is immensely funny. Significantly, it is Stoker's most popular book after **Dracula**. . . . It too could become a cult, with its rampant symbolism and powerful sense of hallucination. (pp. 217-18)

[There are many] echoes of *Dracula*. The two heroines are Lilla and Mimi, as against Lucy and Mina. Lilla is the virtuous victim; Mimi becomes Adam's wife. Over tea, Lilla has staring-matches with Caswell, apparently tests of power between good and evil. Mimi comes to Lilla's rescue with her own flow of goodliness; Lady [Arabella] sides with Caswell. After one of these bouts, immense flocks of birds are summoned, presumably in response to Lilla's dove-like qualities. They arrive in tens of thousands, attracting ornithologists bewildered by this quirk of migration. The birds decimate the land, and so Caswell from his turret flies an immense kite in the shape of a hawk and the land falls quiet. The silence spreads to all the animals. . . . (pp. 219-20)

This strange though powerful theme of the birds is really irrelevant, and Stoker soon tired of it. Adam compares notes with Sir Nathaniel, who tells him the local legend of a monster that lives underground, the great white worm. With a remarkable prophecy of the Loch Ness Monster, Stoker refers to the original plains of England with 'holes of abysmal depth, where any kind and size of antediluvian monster could find a habitat. In places which now we can see from our windows, were mudholes a hundred or more feet deep. Who can tell us when

the age of the monsters which flourished in slime came to an end?' Just imagine if such a creature could assume human form! (p. 220)

'What was the real identity of the beautiful, reptile-like Lady Arabella March?'—asks the paperback cover. *She* is the great White Worm! They see, one night in the woods, an immense tower of snowy white, tall and thin, with the green light of her eyes above the trees, and vast coils of the serpent's body below. The white colour comes from the china clay in the cavernous soil. Like Count Dracula, the Worm moves with the vital protection of darkness. (p. 221)

One of the delights of the book is its rampant snobbery. After a wild tea-party during which Lady Arabella first tries to suck Mimi into the well-hole and then attempts to imprison the guests, Mimi's main objection is one of etiquette—'As a social matter, she was disgusted with her for following up the rich landowner—throwing herself at his head so shamelessly.' The landowner, meanwhile, is going mad in his turret. As the climax is reached, there is another of Stoker's great storms: the lightning is attracted by the great kite he is still flying, with a wire reel found in a chest that Mesmer had left to the family. He disappears from the novel, raging against the elements: 'I am greater than any other who is, or was, or shall be. When the Master of Evil took Christ up on a high place and showed Him all the kingdoms of earth, he was doing what he thought no other could do. He was wrong—he forgot ME.'

The prevalence of sexual symbols cannot be denied. 'The dread of snakes,' wrote Freud, 'is monstrously exaggerated in neurotics—all this has a definite sexual meaning.' Chests correspond to 'the female organ, with the obvious symbolism of the lock and key to open it'. Revealingly, Mesmer's chest has *no* lock or key, though Caswell seems to open it in his sleep. Winding stairs 'are symbolic representations of the sexual act', and the rising kite is one of the most famous and familiar symbols of all. Finally, Stoker's disturbance over sexual intercourse can be seen in his revulsion from the snake's hole, which has to be destroyed. (pp. 222-23)

Surely his obsession with horror and this repetition of sexual symbols indicate that Stoker was disturbed. . . .

The Lair of the White Worm was published three years after Stoker had written in the *Nineteenth Century* that 'the only emotions which in the long run harm are those arising from sex impulses.'

There is no deceiver like the self-deceiver. (p. 224)

> *Daniel Farson, in his* The Man Who Wrote "Dracula": A Biography of Bram Stoker *(copyright © 1975 by Daniel Farson; reprinted by permission of St. Martin's Press, Inc.; in Canada by Michael Joseph Ltd), Michael Joseph, 1975 (and reprinted by St. Martin's Press, 1976), 240 p.*

MARK M. HENNELLY, JR.   (essay date 1977)

[In **Dracula**], when Mina Harker reads her husband's Transylvanian journal and relates it to the recent enigmatic events in London, she discovers that "There seems to be through it all some thread of continuity"; and the attentive reader makes an identical discovery in Bram Stoker's long-neglected tale of two cultures. Until now there have been occasional folkloric, psycho-sexual, and even political readings of the novel; but such studies generally see this horror classic as a *sui generis* phenomenon and not as a sign of the times, not as a drama of conflicting epistemologies, which is so much a part of the Victorian tradition and which Dracula presents with brutal candor. Although the ''Gothic'' tradition is peripheral to this study, it is even more surprising that treatments of the Gothic or Romantic novel have almost totally neglected Stoker's most terrifying example of the genre. (p. 13)

[Besides] being a masterpiece of Gothicism (which itself is ultimately concerned with the problem of *belief* in the Demiurge), *Dracula* is an allegory of rival epistemologies in quest of a gnosis which will rehabilitate the Victorian wasteland; and . . . this rehabilitation demands a *transfusion*, the metaphor is inevitable, from the blood-knowledge of Dracula. Caught between two worlds, the now anemic nineteenth century all but dead, the twentieth powerless to be born without fertile, ideological conception, fin-de-siècle England desperately needs redemption. As Van Helsing announces: ''we go out as the old knights of the Cross to redeem. . . . we are pledged to set the world free''. . . .

Symbolizing the battleground between Ancients and Moderns, the Wasteland often provides a psychoscape for Victorian poetry and fiction; and the ''waste land'' of Tennyson's ''Morte d'Arthur,'' the ''ominous tract'' of Browning's ''Childe Roland,'' Arnold's ''darkling plain'' of ''Dover Beach,'' Dickens' Coketown, and Hardy's Egdon Heath are just some examples of its prevalent imagery. . . . In *Dracula*, Dr. Seward, alter-ego for the Victorian reader, makes clear the relationship between his wasted London, ''under brown fog'' like T. S. Eliot's, and his own blasted, scientific beliefs. ''It was a shock for me to turn from the wonderful smoky beauty of a sunset over London, with its lurid lights and inky shadows and all the marvellous tints that come on foul clouds even as on foul water, and to realize all the grim sternness of my own cold stone building, with its wealth of breathing misery, and my own desolate heart to endure it all''. . . . Here the oxymoron suggests that even naturally-wasted London is better than his own artificially-petrified, ''desolate heart.'' However, the most salient passage for the wasteland theme, and one of the more remarkable passages in Victorian literature, locates the ''waste of desolation'' . . . in London's geographic other-self, Transylvania—even the repeated *desolate* condition serves to link the two cultures. The broken-English here is characteristically Van Helsing's; and this description of Dracula's motivation and kingdom prompts his already mentioned pledge to ''set the world free'':

> I have told them how the measure of leaving his own barren land—barren of peoples—and coming to a new land where life of man teems till they are like the multitude of standing corn, was the work of centuries. Were another of the Un-Dead, like him, to try to do what he has done, perhaps not all the centuries of the world that have been, or that will be, could aid him. With this one, all the forces of nature that are occult and deep and strong must have worked together in some wondrous way. The very place, where he have been alive, Un-Dead for all these centuries, is full of strangeness of the geologic and chemical world. There are deep caverns and fissures that reach none know whither. There have been volcanoes, some of whose openings still send out waters of strange properties, and gases that kill or make to vivify. Doubtless, there is something magnetic or electric in some

of these combinations or occult forces which work for physical life in strange way; and in himself were from the first some great qualities.

(pp. 13-14)

The meaning of this lengthy passage is central to the understanding of *Dracula.* Both nocturnal-lunar Transylvania and diurnal-solar London are ''barren land[s]''; and each desperately needs the strength of the other to heal its own sterility. . . . [The] above excerpt reveals that Dracula is a kind of primitive Corn God who ''directs the elements'' . . . , a Fisher King (Stoker's dream of a ''vampire king rising from his tomb'' precipitated the novel) who has anachronistically as ''this man-that-was'' . . . lived long past his prime and rests in an unholy Perilous Chapel. . . . Now he must be slain and replaced by a viable, young, twentieth-century totem—at least he must be slain and his energy re-absorbed if the London wasteland is to be renewed and if Eliot's ''hooded hordes swarming'' are to be checked. Thus, although once a ''vital principle . . . symbolic of good,'' the Count's energy is now only malign. At the cosmic level of the ''geologic and chemical world,'' Dracula's *élan vital*, these ''gases,'' can either ''kill or make to vivify'' depending, at the personal level, on whether they are repressed as with Lucy, or honestly accepted as with Mina. (pp. 14-15)

[The] quest to redeem this wasteland is not a search for a literal grail or treasure, but as Van Helsing understands a search for redemptive knowledge: ''We shall go to make our search—if I can call it so, for it is not a search but knowing''. . . . Many literary historians have found this gnostic quest to be the central theme of nineteenth-century letters and of the Victorian arts in particular. (p. 15)

By dramatizing the intimate identity between Transylvania and London, between vampirism and civilization, the circular structure of *Dracula,* whose locale shifts from the Carpathians to England and then back to Transylvania, also reveals the thematic link between the epistemologies of the two wasted kingdoms. The central point, as Van Helsing understands, is: ''For it is not the least of its terrors that this evil thing is rooted deep in all good''. . . . Or in the cockney accents of Thomas Bilder, the London zoo-keeper: ''there's a deal of the same nature in us as in them theer animiles''. . . . For example, Dracula's castle is a schizoid dwelling with upper, fashionable apartments and even a Victorian library but also with lower crypts and vaults; while, analogously, Dr. Seward's Victorian mansion conceals a lunatic asylum, complete with fledgling vampire, beneath it. Dracula has three lovers; Lucy has three suitors. Dracula hypnotizes; Van Helsing hypnotizes. Dracula sucks blood; Van Helsing transfuses blood. . . . (p. 17)

[Armed] with his Catholic faith, so foreign to low-church Protestantism, and his ''open mind,'' [Van Helsing] is the primary savior of the wasteland. (p. 23)

Mark M. Hennelly, Jr., '''Dracula': The Gnostic Quest and Victorian Wasteland,'' in English Literature in Transition *(copyright © 1977 Helga S. Gerber), Vol. 20, No. 1, 1977, pp. 13-26.*

PHYLLIS A. ROTH   (essay date 1977)

[For] both the Victorians and twentieth century readers, much of [*Dracula*'s] great appeal derives from its hostility toward female sexuality. (p. 113)

The facile and stereotypical dichotomy between the dark woman and the fair, the fallen and the idealized, is obvious in *Dracula*. Indeed, among the more gratuitous passages in the novel are those in which the "New Woman" who is sexually aggressive is verbally assaulted. Mina Harker remarks that such a woman, whom she holds in contempt, "will do the proposing herself." Additionally, we must compare Van Helsing's hope "that there are good women still left to make life happy". . .with Mina's assertion that "the world seems full of good men—even if there *are* monsters in it.". . . A remarkable contrast!

Perhaps nowhere is the dichotomy of sensual and sexless woman more dramatic than it is in *Dracula* and nowhere is the suddenly sexual woman more violently and self-righteously persecuted than in Stoker's "thriller."

The equation of vampirism with sexuality is well established in the criticism. [Maurice] Richardson refers to Freud's observation that "morbid dread always signifies repressed sexual wishes" [see excerpt above]. We must agree that *Dracula* is permeated by "morbid dread." However, another tone interrupts the dread of impending doom throughout the novel; that note is one of lustful anticipation, certainly anticipation of catching and destroying forever the master vampire, Count Dracula, but additionally, lustful anticipation of a consummation one can only describe as sexual. (pp. 113-14)

[From] the novel's beginning, a marked rivalry among the men is evident. This rivalry is defended against by the constant, almost obsessive, assertion of the value of friendship and *agape* among members of the Van Helsing group. Specifically, the defense of overcompensation is employed, most often by Van Helsing in his assertions of esteem for Dr. Seward and his friends. The others, too, repeat expressions of mutual affection *ad* nauseum: they clearly protest too much. Perhaps this is most obviously symbolized, and unintentionally exposed, by the blood transfusions from Arthur, Seward, Quincey Morris, and Van Helsing to Lucy Westenra. The great friendship among rivals for Lucy's hand lacks credibility and is especially strained when Van Helsing makes it clear that the transfusions (merely the reverse of the vampire's blood-letting) are in their nature sexual. . . . Furthermore, Arthur himself feels that, as a result of having given Lucy his blood, they are in effect married. Thus, the friendships of the novel mask a deep-seated rivalry and hostility.

Dracula does then appear to enact the Oedipal rivalry among sons and between the son and the father for the affections of the mother. The fantasy of parricide and its acting out is obviously satisfying. . . . [Such] a threatening wish-fulfillment can be rewarding when properly defended against or associated with other pleasurable fantasies.

Among the other fantasies are those of life after death, the triumph of "good over evil," mere man over super-human forces, and the rational West over the mysterious East. Most likely not frightening and certainly intellectualized, these simplistic abstractions provide a diversion from more threatening material and assure the fantast that God's in his heaven; all's right with the world. On the surface, this is the moral of the end of the novel: Dracula is safely reduced to ashes, Mina is cleansed, the "boys" are triumphant. Were this all the theme of interest the novel presented, however, it would be neither so popular with Victorians and their successors nor worthy of scholarly concern.

Up to now my discussion has been taken from the point of view of reader identification with those who are doing battle against the evil in this world, against Count Dracula. On the surface of it, this is where one's sympathies lie in reading the novel and it is this level of analysis which has been explored by previous critics. However, what is far more significant in the interrelation of fantasy and defense is the duplication of characters and structure which betrays an identification with Dracula and a fantasy of matricide underlying the more obvious parricidal wishes. (pp. 115-16)

[The] split between the sexual vampire family and the asexual Van Helsing group is not at all clear-cut: Jonathan, Van Helsing, Seward and Holmwood are all overwhelmingly attracted to the vampires, to sexuality. Fearing this, they employ two defenses, projection and denial; it is not we who want the vampires, it is they who want us (to eat us, to seduce us, to kill us). Despite the projections, we should recall that almost all the on-stage killing is done by the "good guys": that of Lucy, the vampire women, and Dracula. The projection of the wish to kill onto the vampires wears thinnest perhaps when Dr. Seward, contemplating the condition of Lucy, asserts that "had she then to be killed I could have done it with savage delight.". . . Even earlier, when Dr. Seward is rejected by Lucy, he longs for a cause with which to distract himself from the pain of rejection. . . . Seward's wish is immediately fulfilled by Lucy's vampirism and the subsequent need to destroy her. Obviously, the acting out of such murderous impulses is threatening: in addition to the defenses mentioned above, the use of religion not only to exorcise the evil but to justify the murders is striking. In other words, Christianity is on our side, we *must* be right. . . . Correlated with the religious defense is one described by Freud in *Totem and Taboo* in which the violator of the taboo can avert disaster by Lady MacBeth-like compulsive rituals and renunciations. The repeated use of the Host, the complicated ritual of the slaying of the vampires, and the ostensible, though not necessarily conscious, renunciation of sexuality are the penance paid by those in *Dracula* who violate the taboos against incest and the murder of parents.

Since we now see that Dracula acts out the repressed fantasies of the others, since those others wish to do what he can do, we have no difficulty in recognizing an identification with the aggressor on the part of characters and reader alike. It is important, then, to see what it is that Dracula is after.

The novel tells of two major episodes, the seduction of Lucy and of Mina, to which the experience of Harker at Castle Dracula provides a preface, a hero, one whose narrative encloses the others and with whom, therefore, one might readily identify. This, however, is a defense against the central identification of the novel with Dracula and his attacks on the women. (pp. 116-17)

In accepting the notion of identification with the aggressor in *Dracula,* as I believe we must, what we accept is an understanding of the reader's identification with the aggressor's victimization of women. Dracula's desire is for the destruction of Lucy and Mina and what this means is obvious when we recall that his attacks on these two closest of friends seem incredibly coincidental on the narrative level. Only on a deeper level is there no coincidence at all: the level on which one recognizes that Lucy and Mina are essentially the same figure: the mother. Dracula is, in fact, the same story told twice with different outcomes. In the former, the mother is more desirable, more sexual, more threatening and must be destroyed. And the physical descriptions of Lucy reflect this greater ambivalence: early in the story, when Lucy is not yet completely vampirized, Dr. Seward describes her hair "in its usual sunny ripples" . . . ;

later, when the men watch her return to her tomb, Lucy is described as ''a dark-haired woman.''. . . The conventional fair/dark split, symbolic of respective moral casts, seems to be unconscious here, reflecting the ambivalence aroused by the sexualized female. Not only is Lucy the more sexualized figure, she is the more rejecting figure, rejecting two of the three ''sons'' in the novel. This section of the book ends with her destruction, not by Dracula but by the man whom she was to marry. The novel could not end here, though; the story had to be told again to assuage the anxiety occasioned by matricide. This time, the mother is much less sexually threatening and is ultimately saved. Moreover, Mina is never described physically and is the opposite of rejecting: all the men become her sons, symbolized by the naming of her actual son after them all. What remains constant is the attempt to destroy the mother. What changes is the way the fantasies are managed. To speak of the novel in terms of the child's ambivalence toward the mother is not just to speak psychoanalytically. We need only recall that Lucy, as ''bloofer lady,'' as well as the other vampire women, prey on children. In the case of Lucy, the children are as attracted to her as threatened by her.

I have already described the evidence that the Van Helsing men themselves desire to do away with Lucy. Perhaps the story needed to be retold because the desire was too close to the surface to be satisfying; certainly, the reader would not be satisifed had the novel ended with Arthur's murder of Lucy. What is perhaps not so clear is that the desire to destroy Mina is equally strong. Let us look first at the defenses against this desire. . . . [Mina] acts and is treated as both the saint and the mother (ironically, this is parcicularly clear when she comforts Arthur for the loss of Lucy). She is all good, all pure, all true. When, however, she is seduced away from the straight and narrow by Dracula, she is ''unclean,'' tainted and stained with a mark on her forehead immediately occasioned by Van Helsing's touching her forehead with the Host. Van Helsing's hostility toward Mina is further revealed when he cruelly reminds her of her ''intercourse'' with Dracula: '' 'Do you forget,' he said, with actually a smile, 'that last night he banqueted heavily and will sleep late?'''. . . This hostility is so obvious that the other men are shocked. Nevertheless, the ''sons,'' moreover, and the reader as well, identify with Dracula's attack on Mina; indeed, the men cause it, as indicated by the events which transpire when all the characters are at Seward's hospital-asylum. The members of the brotherhood go out at night to seek out Dracula's lairs, and they leave Mina undefended at the hospital. They claim that this insures her safety; in fact, it insures the reverse. Furthermore, this is the real purpose in leaving Mina out of the plans and in the hospital. They have clear indications in Renfield's warnings of what is to happen to her and they all, especially her husband, observe that she is not well and seems to be getting weaker. That they could rationalize these signs away while looking for and finding them everywhere else further indicates that they are avoiding seeing what they want to ignore; in other words, they want Dracula to get her. This is not to deny that they also want to save Mina; it is simply to claim that the ambivalence toward the mother is fully realized in the novel.

We can now return to that ambivalence and, I believe, with the understanding of the significance of the mother figure, comprehend the precise perspective of the novel. Several critics have correctly emphasized the regression to both orality and anality in *Dracula*. Certainly, the sexuality is perceived in oral terms. The primal scene [in which Dracula forces Mina to drink his blood] makes abundantly clear that intercourse is perceived in terms of nursing. . . . The scene referred to is, in several senses, the climax of the novel; it is the most explicit view of the act of vampirism and is, therefore, all the more significant as an expression of the nature of sexual intercourse as the novel depicts it. In it, the woman is doing the sucking. . . . While it is true that the reader may most often think of Dracula as the active partner, the fact is that the scenes of vampire sexuality are described from the male perspective, with the females as the active assailants. Only the acts of phallic aggression, the killings, involve the males in active roles. *Dracula,* then, dramatizes the child's view of intercourse insofar as it is seen as a wounding and a killing. But the primary preoccupation, as attested to by the primal scene, is with the role of the female in the act. Thus, it is not surprising that the central anxiety of the novel is the fear of the devouring woman and, in documenting this, we will find that all the pieces of the novel fall into place, most especially the Jonathan Harker prologue.

As mentioned, Harker's desire and primary anxiety is not with Dracula but with the female vampires. In his initial and aborted seduction by them, he describes his ambivalence. Interestingly, Harker seeks out this episode by violating the Count's (father's) injunction to remain in his room; ''let me warn you with all seriousness, that should you leave these rooms you will not by any chance go to sleep in any other part of the castle.''. . . This, of course, is what Harker promptly does. When Dracula breaks in and discovers Harker with the vampire women, he acts like both a jealous husband and an irate father: ''His eyes were positively blazing. The red light in them was lurid. . . 'How dare you touch him, any of you?'''. . . Jonathan's role as child here is reinforced by the fact that, when Dracula takes him away from the women, he gives them a child as substitute. But most interesting is Jonathan's perspective as he awaits, in a state of erotic arousal, the embraces of the vampire women, especially the fair one: ''The other was fair as fair can be, with great wavy masses of golden hair and eyes like pale sapphires. I seemed somehow to know her face and to know it in connection with some dreamy fear, but I could not recollect at the moment how or where.''. . . As far as we know, Jonathan never recollects, but we should be able to understand that the face is that of the mother (almost archetypally presented), she whom he desires yet fears, the temptress-seductress, Medusa. Moreover, this golden girl reappears in the early description of Lucy.

At the end of the following chapter, Jonathan exclaims, ''I am alone in the castle with those awful women. Faugh! Mina is a woman, and there is nought in common.'' Clearly, however, there is. Mina at the breast of Count Dracula is identical to the vampire women whose desire is to draw out of the male the fluid necessary for life. That this is viewed as an act of castration is clear from Jonathan's conclusion: ''At least God's mercy is better than that of these monsters, and the precipice is steep and high. At its foot a man may sleep—*as a man.* Good-bye, all! Mina!'' (. . . ; emphasis mine).

The threatening Oedipal fantasy, the regression to a primary oral obsession, the attraction and destruction of the vampires of *Dracula* are, then, interrelated and interdependent. What they spell out is a fusion of the memory of nursing at the mother's breast with a primal scene fantasy which results in the conviction that the sexually desirable woman will annihilate if she is not first destroyed. The fantasy of incest and matricide evokes the mythic image of the *vagina dentata* evident in so many folk tales in which the mouth and the vagina are identified with one another by the primitive mind and pose the threat of castration to all men until the teeth are extracted by the hero. The conclusion of *Dracula,* the "salvation" of Mina, is equivalent to such an "extraction": Mina will not remain the *vagina dentata* to threaten them all.

Central to the structure and unconscious theme of *Dracula* is, then, primarily the desire to destroy the threatening mother, she who threatens by being desirable. . . . Finally, the novel has it both ways: Dracula is destroyed and Van Helsing saved; Lucy is destroyed and Mina saved. (pp. 117-20)

> Phyllis A. Roth, "Suddenly Sexual Women in Bram Stoker's 'Dracula'," in Literature and Psychology (© Morton Kaplan 1977), Vol. XXVII, No. 3, 1977, pp. 113-21.

GLEN ST. JOHN BARCLAY   (essay date 1978)

Dracula was in many ways a triumph of eroticism over incompetence. It is not surprising that Stoker was never able to repeat it. His other occult novels are singular examples of his capacity to nullify potentially exciting plots by sheer bad writing. The most popular next to *Dracula* was *The Jewel of Seven Stars,* which had indeed an ideal motif for a story of high adventure. The hero, a young barrister, is summoned at midnight from his rooms in Jermyn Street; he hastens to Kensington Palace Road where a mysterious and apparently murderous assault has been made upon a famous Egyptologist, whose beautiful daughter is conveniently in love with him. The police are called in and the Egyptologist is found to be on the brink of completing an experiment to bring back to life the mummy of Queen Tera, a fabulous Egyptian beauty, somewhat over-endowed in the sense of possessing seven fingers on each hand, and seven toes on each foot. Unfortunately, literally nothing happens: there is almost no dialogue, no attempt at characterization, virtually no action and nothing but anti-climax at the end.

Nor oddly is there anything in the nature of erotic symbolism. The sweltering sexuality of *Dracula* is totally absent from *The Jewel of Seven Stars.* It does return, albeit very allusively, in *The Lady of The Shroud,* which in many ways is the best story that Stoker ever wrote, but which can hardly be considered as a novel of the occult, despite the ghoulishness of the title, since the whole point of the action turns on the hero's discovery that his lover is not the vampire he thought she was.

However sex and the occult provide the mainsprings of the plot of Stoker's last and by far his worst novel, *The Lair of the White Worm.* . . . Howard P. Lovecraft comments that this book 'utterly ruins a magnificent idea by a development almost infantile' [see excerpt above]. One may or may not agree with this valuation of the idea, but there is no doubt about Stoker's ability to ruin it. He does indeed lose control of the story to such an extent that it is really impossible to know what he actually thought he was writing about. The initial concept involves the hunt for a gigantic snake, surviving underground from what Stoker vaguely calls 'the geologic age—the great birth and growth of the world, when natural forces ran riot, and when the struggle for existence was so savage that no vitality which was not founded in a gigantic form could have even a possibility of survival'. . . . The dramatic possibilities of the situation should have been heightened by the suggestion that the snake or 'White Worm' has acquired occult powers over one of the local heiresses: 'if my theory is correct,' the hero's grand-uncle explains, 'the once beautiful human body of Lady Arabella is under the control of this ghastly White Worm.' Stoker presumably means 'once human' rather than

'once beautiful', since Lady Arabella is undoubtedly attractive, although in an emphatically serpentine manner. . . . (pp. 53-4)

Lady Arabella and the White Worm are only part of the story, however. There is also an objectionable landowner, Caswell, who is hated by the local farmers for apparently quite inconsistent reasons. . . . [Caswell] has a monstrous servant Oolanga, whose face 'was unreformed, unsoftened savage, and inherent in it were all the hideous possibilities of a lost, devil-ridden child of the forest and the swamp—the lowest of all created things that could be regarded as in some form ostensibly human.' Unfortunately after this promising introduction, Oolanga never actually does anything. Neither does Caswell, despite his having evil intentions towards two local girls, Lilla and Mima Watford, who are so far from being developed as characters that they are not even given any dialogue. Lilla Watford is however considered sufficiently important by Lady Arabella to require killing off, after which the snake-lady 'tore off her clothes with feverish fingers, and in full enjoyment of her natural freedom, stretched her slim figure in animal delight'. At the end of the story, Caswell's kite attracts a bolt of lightning which destroys the manor and its owner, and also presumably Lady Arabella, who has been lurking underneath in her capacity as the White Worm. It is really impossible to know what Stoker was trying to do in the story. All one can be sure of is that it could not possibly have been less competently written.

There is a brutally simple explanation for both the compelling eroticism of *Dracula* and the absolute nullity of his last story: as his great-nephew Daniel Farson discovered, Stoker actually died from the tertiary stage of syphilis before the *White Worm* was published, which would indicate that he contracted the disease some fifteen years before, or in 1897, the year in which *Dracula* was first published. Farson suggests further that Stoker had been driven into the company of 'other women, probably prostitutes among them', by the frigidity of his beautiful wife Florence, who appears to have refused to have sexual relations with Stoker after the first year of their marriage, during which their only child, Noel, was born. Florence undoubtedly seems to have been incredibly beautiful, incredibly vain and incredibly uninteresting. If she was also frigid, she could well have provided the model for Stoker's extremely boring heroines. By the same token, by driving Stoker into the arms of more accommodating and doubtless more adventurous ladies, she could also have indirectly provided him with models for his vastly more interesting vampires. The occult novel owes a substantial debt to Florence Stoker.

Farson's interpretation is certainly in accordance with all the known facts, chronologically and also psychologically. Stoker certainly contracted syphilis about the time that he wrote *Dracula;* he certainly had every reason to consort with prostitutes for at least a decade before that; and the tremendous eroticism of the book does indeed imply psychological stresses upon the author which would be consistent with the image of a highly conventional man driven by frustration and humiliation into unconventional ways. The vampires are presented as appallingly destructive demons incarnate; however they are also breathtakingly voluptuous and desirable; and their victims await their ministrations with ecstatic longing. The resulting commerce is disastrous for both parties: the victim dies and is corrupted into becoming a demon as well; and the demons are eventually exorcized by being decapitated if men, and impaled if women. The symbolism of guilt and frustration is well-nigh perfect.

The fact is that Stoker's achievement is a phenomenon of psychopathology rather than of literature. As a novelist, Stoker had almost no sense of characterization, no sense of prose style and no philosophical sense of the occult at all. What he did possess was a lively if hardly creative imagination and, on one memorable occasion at least, a remarkable mastery of the multinarrative technique of storytelling. He was able to put these qualities to the service of the vampire legend to which he was introduced quite fortuitously, at a time when he was emotionally harrowed by sensations of guilt and frustration, very possibly heightened by the symptoms of the primary stages of syphilis with their attendant feelings of anxiety and even horror. He was thus uniquely fitted by time and circumstances to give wings to the most effective image of erotic perversity that the western consciousness has ever frightened itself with. One should not of course exaggerate either the value or the extent of his achievement. . . . The vampire legend as developed by Stoker is after all born of sexual frustration and syphilis: it does not fascinate because it responds to anything in human experience, or because it tells us anything about the nature of existence: its appeal derives from its images of murder, exploitation, necrophilia, sadism, chauvinism and oral sex. Not many of these are actually the ingredients of a life-enriching myth. There is nothing the world needs less than a new vampire story. (pp. 55-7)

Glen St. John Barclay, *"Sex and Horror: Bram Stoker,"* in his Anatomy of Horror: The Masters of Occult Fiction *(copyright © 1978 by Glen St. J. Barclay; reprinted by permission of St. Martin's Press, Inc.; in Canada by Weidenfeld (Publishers) Limited), Weidenfeld and Nicholson, 1978 (and reprinted by St. Martin's Press, 1979), pp. 39-57.*

CAROL A. SENF (essay date 1979)

More familiar with the numerous film interpretations than with Stoker's novel, most modern readers are likely to be surprised by *Dracula* and its intensely topical themes; and both the setting and the method of narration which Stoker chose contribute to this sense of immediacy. Instead of taking place in a remote Transylvanian castle or a timeless and dreamlike "anywhere," most of the action occurs in nineteenth-century London. Furthermore, Stoker de-emphasizes the novel's mythic qualities by telling the story through a series of journal extracts, personal letters, and newspaper clippings—the very written record of everyday life. The narrative technique resembles a vast jigsaw puzzle of isolated and frequently trivial facts; and it is only when the novel is more than half over that the central characters piece these fragments together and, having concluded the Dracula is a threat to themselves and their society, band together to destroy him.

On the surface, the novel appears to be a mythic re-enactment of the opposition between Good and Evil because the narrators attribute their pursuit and ultimate defeat of Dracula to a high moral purpose. However, although his method of narration doesn't enable him to comment directly on his characters' failures in judgment or lack of self-knowledge, Stoker provides several clues to their unreliability and encourages the reader to see the frequent discrepancies between their professed beliefs and their actions. The first clue is an anonymous preface (unfortunately omitted in many modern editions) which gives the reader a distinct warning:

How these papers have been placed in sequence will be made manifest in the reading of them.

All needless matters have been eliminated, so that a history almost at variance with the possibilities of later-day belief may stand forth as simple fact. There is throughout no statement of past things wherein memory may err, for all the records chosen are exactly contemporary, *given from the standpoints and within the range of knowledge of those who made them.*

Writers of Victorian popular fiction frequently rely on the convention of the anonymous editor to introduce their tales and to provide additional comments throughout the text; and Stoker uses this convention to stress the subjective nature of the story which his narrators relate. The narrators themselves occasionally question the validity of their perceptions, but Stoker provides numerous additional clues to their unreliability. For example, at the conclusion, Jonathan Harker questions their interpretation of the events:

We were stuck with the fact, that in all the mass of material of which the record is composed, there is hardly one authentic document; nothing but a mass of typewriting, except the later notebooks of Mina and Seward and myself, and Van Helsing's memorandum. We could hardly ask any one, even did we wish to, to accept these as proofs of so wild a story.

The conclusion reinforces the subjective nature of their tale and casts doubts on everything that had preceded; however, because Stoker does not use an obvious framing device like Conrad in *Heart of Darkness* or James in *The Turn of the Screw* or employ an intrusive editor as Haggard does in *She* and because all the narrators come to similar conclusions about the nature of their opponent, the reader is likely to forget that these documents are subjective records, interpretations which are "given within the range of knowledge of those who made them."

While Stoker's choice of narrative technique does not permit him to comment directly on his characters, he suggests that they are particularly ill-equipped to judge the extraordinary events with which they are faced. The three central narrators are perfectly ordinary nineteenth-century Englishmen. . . . With the exception of Dr. Van Helsing, all the central characters are youthful and inexperienced—two dimensional characters whose only distinguishing characteristics are their names and their professions; and by maintaining a constancy of style throughout and emphasizing the beliefs which they hold in common, Stoker further diminishes any individualizing traits. The narrators appear to speak with one voice; and Stoker suggests that their opinions are perfectly acceptable so long as they remain within their limited fields of expertise. The problem, however, is that these perfectly ordinary people are confronted with the extraordinary character of Dracula.

Although Stoker did model Dracula on the historical Vlad V of Wallachia and the East European superstition of the vampire, he adds a number of humanizing touches to make Dracula appear noble and vulnerable as well as demonic and threatening; and it becomes difficult to determine whether he is a hideous bloodsucker whose touch breeds death or a lonely and silent figure who is hunted and persecuted. The difficulty in interpreting Dracula's character is compounded by the narrative technique, for the reader quickly recognizes that Dracula is *never* seen objectively and never permitted to speak for himself while his actions are recorded by people who have determined to destroy him and who, moreover, repeatedly question the sanity of their quest. (pp. 161-62)

Stoker reveals that what condemns Dracula are the English characters' subjective responses to his character and to the way of life which he represents. The reader is introduced to Dracula by Jonathan Harker's journal. His first realization that Dracula is different from himself occurs when he looks into the mirror and discovers that Dracula casts no reflection. . . . (p. 163)

Even before Harker begins to suspect that Dracula is a being totally unlike himself, Stoker reveals that he is troubled by everything that Dracula represents. . . . To Harker, Dracula initially appears to be an anachronism—an embodiment of the feudal past—rather than an innately evil being; and his journal entries at the beginning merely reproduce Dracula's pride and rugged individualism. . . . It is only when Harker realizes that he is assisting to take this anachronism to England that he becomes frightened.

Harker's later response indicates that he fears a kind of reverse imperialism, the threat of the primitive trying to colonize the civilized world, while the reader sees in his response a profound resemblance between Harker and Dracula:

> This was the being I was helping to transfer to London, where perhaps for centuries to come he might . . . satiate his lust for blood, and create a new and ever-widening circle of semi-demons to batten on the helpless. The very thought drove me mad. A terrible desire came upon me to rid the world of such a monster. There was no lethal weapon at hand, but I seized a shovel which the workmen had been using to fill the cases, and lifting it high, struck, with the edge downward, at the hateful face.

This scene reinforces Harker's earlier inability to see Dracula in the mirror. Taken out of context, it would be difficult to distinguish the man from the monster. Behavior generally attributed to the vampire—the habit of attacking a sleeping victim, violence, and irrational behavior—is revealed to be the behavior of the civilized Englishman also. The sole difference is that Stoker's narrative technique does not permit the reader to enter Dracula's thoughts as he stands over his victims. The reversal of roles here is important because it establishes the subjective nature of the narrators' beliefs, suggests their lack of self-knowledge, and serves to focus on the similarities between the narrators and their opponent. . . . In fact, Stoker implies that the only difference between Dracula and his opponents is the narrators' ability to state individual desire in terms of what they believe is a common good. For example, the above scene shows that Harker can justify his violent attack on Dracula because he pictures himself as the protector of helpless millions; and the narrators insist on the duty to defend the innocents.

The necessity of protecting the innocent is called into question, however, when Dr. Van Helsing informs the other characters about the vampire's nature. While most of his discussion concerns the vampire's susceptibility to garlic, silver bullets, and religious artifacts, Van Helsing also admits that the vampire cannot enter a dwelling unless he is first invited by one of the inhabitants. In other words, a vampire cannot influence a human being without that person's consent. Dracula's behavior confirms that he is an internal, not an external, threat. Although perfectly capable of using superior strength when he must defend himself, he usually employs seduction, relying on the

others' desires to emulate his freedom from external constraints: Renfield's desire for immortality, Lucy's wish to escape the repressive existence of an upper-class woman, and the desires of all the characters to overcome the restraints placed on them by their religion and their law. As the spokesman for civilization, Van Helsing appears to understand that the others might be tempted by their desires to become like Dracula and he warns them against the temptation. . . . Becoming like Dracula, they too would be laws unto themselves—primitive, violent, irrational—with nothing to justify their actions except the force of their desires. No longer would they need to rationalize their "preying on the bodies and souls of their loved ones" by concealing their lust for power under the rubric of religion, their love of violence under the names of imperialism and progress, their sexual desires within an elaborate courtship ritual.

The narrators attribute their hatred of Dracula to a variety of causes. Harker's journal introduces a being whose way of life is antithetical to theirs—a warlord, a representative of the feudal past and the leader of a primitive cult who he fears will attempt to establish a vampire colony in England. Mina Harker views him as a criminal and as the murderer of her best friend; and Van Helsing sees him as a moral threat, a kind of Anti-Christ. Yet, in spite of the narrators' moral and political language, Stoker reveals that Dracula is primarily a sexual threat, a missionary of desire whose only true kingdom will be the human body. Although he flaunts his independence of social restraints and proclaims himself a master over all he sees, Dracula adheres more closely to English law than his opponents in every area except his sexual behavior. (In fact, Dracula admits to Harker that he invited him to Transylvania so he could learn the subtle nuances of English law and business.) Neither a thief, rapist, nor an overtly political threat, Dracula is dangerous because he expresses his contempt for authority in the most individualistic of ways—through his sexuality. In fact, his thirst for blood and the manner in which he satisfies this thirst can be interpreted as sexual desire which fails to observe any of society's attempts to control it—prohibitions against polygamy, promiscuity, and homosexuality. Furthermore, Stoker suggests that it is generally through sexuality that the vampire gains control over human beings. Van Helsing recognizes this temptation when he prevents Arthur from kissing Lucy right before her death; and even the staid and morally upright Harker momentarily succumbs to the sensuality of the three vampire-women in Dracula's castle. . . . For one brief moment, Harker does appear to recognize the truth about sexual desire; it is totally irrational and has nothing to do with monogamy, love, or even respect for the beloved. It is Dracula, however, who clearly articulates the characters' most intense fears of sexuality: "Your girls that you all love are mine already; and through them you and others shall yet be mine—my creatures, to do my bidding and to be my jackals when I want to feed." . . . Implicit in Dracula's warning is the similarity between vampire and opponents. Despite rare moments of comprehension, however, the narrators generally choose to ignore this similarity; and their lack of self-knowledge permits them to hunt down and kill not only Dracula and the three women in his castle, but their friend Lucy Westenra as well.

The scene in which Arthur drives the stake through Lucy's body while the other men watch thoughtfully is filled with a violent sexuality which again connects vampire and opponents. . . . [The] scene resembles nothing so much as the combined group rape and murder of an unconscious woman; and this kind of violent attack on a helpless victim is precisely the kind of behavior which condemns Dracula in the narrators' eyes. Moreover, Lucy is not the only woman to be subjected to this violence. At the conclusion, in a scene which is only slightly less explicit, Dr. Van Helsing destroys the three women in Dracula's castle. Again Dr. Van Helsing admits that he is fascinated by the beautiful visages of the "wanton Un-Dead" but he never acknowledges that his violent attack is simply a role reversal or that he becomes the vampire as he stands over their unconscious bodies.

By the conclusion of the novel, all the characters who have been accused of expressing individual desire have been appropriately punished: Dracula, Lucy Westenra, and the three vampire-women have been killed; and even Mina Harker is ostracized for her momentary indiscretion. All that remains after the primitive, the passionate, and the individualistic qualities that were associated with the vampire have been destroyed is a small group of wealthy men who return after a period of one year to the site of their victory over the vampire. The surviving characters remain unchanged by the events in their lives and never come to the realization that their commitment to social values merely masks their violence and their sexuality; and the only significant difference in their condition is the birth of the Harkers' son who is appropriately named for all the men who had participated in the conquest of Dracula. Individual sexual desire has apparently been so absolutely effaced that the narrators see this child as the result of their social union rather than the product of a sexual union between one man and one woman.

The narrators insist that they are agents of God and are able to ignore their similiarity to the vampire because their commitment to social values such as monogamy, proper English behavior, and the will of the majority enables them to conceal their violence and their sexual desires from each other and even from themselves. Stoker, however, reveals that these characteristics are merely masked by social convention. Instead of being eliminated, violence and sexuality emerge in particularly perverted forms. (pp. 164-68)

> Carol A. Senf, " 'Dracula': The Unseen Face in the Mirror," in The Journal of Narrative Technique (copyright © 1979 by The Journal of Narrative Technique), Vol. 9, No. 3, Fall, 1979, pp. 160-70.

ROSEMARY JACKSON (essay date 1981)

[Bram Stoker's *Dracula* follows the horrific tales of Stevenson and Wells, *Dr. Jekyll and Mr. Hyde* and *The Island of Dr. Moreau*], to provide a culmination of nineteenth-century English Gothic. It engages with a similar desire for and dismissal of transgressive energies. The consequences of a longing for immortality from a merely human contest are horrifically realized by Dracula, who is not content with a promise of eternal life elsewhere. He dissolves the life/death boundary, returning from an otherworld to prey upon the living. He occupies a paraxial realm, neither wholly dead nor wholly alive. He is a present absence, an unreal substance. Dr. Van Helsing points out that Dracula produces no mirror image. (p. 118)

Dracula's victims share his un-dead quality. They become parasites, feeding off the real and living, condemned to an eternal interstitial existence, *in between* things: 'We all looked on in horrified amazement as we saw the woman, with a corporeal body as real at that moment as our own, pass in through the interstice where scarce a knife-blade could have gone!' Like the elusive demon of [James Hogg's *Confessions of a Justified*

Sinner], Dracula has no fixed form. He metamorphoses as bat, rat, rodent, man. He is without scruple, without form. His appearance means that chaos is come again, for he is *before* good or evil, outside human categorization. The text is never completely 'naturalized' as a moral allegory. Van Helsing realizes that Dracula is the inverse side of his legality, that only a thin line separates them. (pp. 118-19)

The vampire myth is perhaps the highest symbolic representation of eroticism. Its return in Victorian England (drawing upon legendary material, Polidori's *Vampyr,* the popular *Varney the Vampire* and implicit vampiric elements of *Frankenstein*) points to it as a myth born out of extreme repression. It is during his period of engagement to [Mina] that Harker enters the world of Dracula and vampirism: a bourgeois family structure, to which his engagement is the key, gives rise to its own undead, suggesting that the law contains, through repression, its 'other'. The fantasy of vampirism is generated at the moment of maximum social repression: on the eve of marriage. . . . It introduces all that is 'kept in the dark': the vampires are active *at night,* when light/vision/the power of the *look* are suspended.

What is represented in the vampiric myth in *Dracula* is a symbolic *reversal* of the Oedipal stage and of the subject's cultural formation in that stage. . . . [It] could be claimed that the act of vampirism is the most violent and extreme attempt to negate, or reverse, the subject's insertion into the symbolic. The vampiric act is divided into two: firstly, a penetration of the victim with canine (phallic) teeth; secondly, a sucking of the victim's (life-supporting) blood. The first re-enacts the subject's insertion into the order of the phallus (father), through reversal; the second implies that through such negation, a return has been established to the pre-Oedipal stage, replacing the subject in a symbiotic relation to the mother (the blood sucking repeats sucking at the breast as well as the condition of being provided with life-as-blood inside the womb). With each penetration and 'return' to the unity of the imaginary, a new vampire is produced: further objects of desire are endlessly generated, creating an 'other' order of beings, for whom desire never dies and whose desire prevents them from dying—hence the subversive power of the vampire myth and a consequent recourse to magic and mechanical religious rites (the stake through the heart, the crucifix) to fix and defeat desire. The sadistic piercing of the vampire with the stake re-asserts the rule of the father, re-enacting the original act of symbolic castration visited upon the subject for desiring union with the mother. Stoker's version of the myth repeats this castration, and rids the world at the same time of all non-bourgeois elements.

The ideological implications of having Lucy and Mina as the vulnerable bodies of the text hardly need spelling out. Stoker's sexual and political position is rather more conspicuous in his less successful fantasies, such as *The Lair of the White Worm*. . . . This exorcises evil incarnated in a black servant, Oolanga, and a violent female, Arabella, both being sadistically destroyed. Arabella *is* the white worm, interestingly both snake-like and without colour (i.e. life); threatening an aristocratic and male-dominated world, she/it is necessarily sacrificed for the preservation of patriarchy.

Very clearly with *The Lair of the White Worm,* but equally so with *Dracula,* Stoker reinforces social, class, racial and sexual prejudices. His fantasies betray the same tendency as many Victorian texts: they manipulate apparently non-political issues into forms which would serve the dominant ideology. Like Wells, Stevenson, Lytton and mainstream novelists, Stoker identifies the protean shadow of the 'other' as evil. In the guise of its 'unnameable' absolute otherness, social realities are deformed and dismissed. The shadow on the edges of bourgeois culture is variously identified, as black, mad, primitive, criminal, socially deprived, deviant, crippled, or (when sexually assertive) female. Difficult or unpalatable social realities are distorted through many literary fantasies to emerge as melodramatic shapes: monsters, snakes, bats, vampires, dwarfs, hybrid beasts, devils, reflections, *femmes fatales*. Through this identification, troublesome social elements can be destroyed in the name of exorcising the demonic. Many fantasies play upon a *natural* fear of formlessness, absence, 'death', to reinforce an *apparently 'natural'* order of life—but that order is in effect an arbitrary one which identifies the 'norm' as a middle-class, monogamous and male-dominated culture. In the name of defeating the 'inhuman', such fantasies attempt to dismiss forces inimical to a bourgeois ideology. (pp. 121-22)

> Rosemary Jackson, "Gothic Tales and Novels," in
> her Fantasy: The Literature of Subversion (© 1981
> by Rosemary Jackson), Methuen, 1981, pp. 95-122.*

ADDITIONAL BIBLIOGRAPHY

Bierman, Joseph S. "*Dracula:* Prolonged Childhood Illness, and the Oral Triad." *American Imago* 29, No. 2 (Summer 1972): 186-98.
> Interprets *Dracula* as a retelling of Stoker's early invalidism "in that it is essentially a tale of medical detection of puzzling illnesses, of obscure diagnoses, and unusual cures. . . ."

Carlson, M. M. "What Stoker Saw: An Introduction to the History of the Literary Vampire." *Folklore Forum* X, No. 2 (Fall 1977): 26-32.
> Discussion of the vampires preceding *Dracula* in literature, and of the differences between the literary and the folkloric vampire.

Fry, Carol L. "Fictional Conventions and Sexuality in *Dracula.*" *Victorian Newsletter*, No. 42 (Fall 1972): 20-2.
> Brief equation of *Dracula* with the classic Gothic melodramatic plot of a rake pursuing and seducing a virgin. Fry touches on some of the parallels between vampirism and sexuality.

Gide, André. "Journal 1928." In his *The Journal of André Gide, Vol. III: 1928-1939,* translated by Justin O'Brien, pp. 3-29. New York: Alfred A. Knopf, 1949.*
> Journal entry of February 27, 1928. Gide details his reaction to F. W. Murnau's *Nosferatu,* the first film based on Stoker's novel *Dracula,* primarily noting the faults he found in the portrayal of the vampire.

Kirtley, Bacil F. "*Dracula,* the Monastic Chronicles and Slavic Folklore." *Midwest Folklore* VI, No. 1 (Spring 1956): 133-39.
> Cites the "surprisingly deliberate authenticity" Stoker attained in *Dracula* with the use of folk themes concerning vampirism.

Masters, Anthony. *The Natural History of the Vampire.* New York: G. P. Putnam's Sons, 1972, 258 p.*
> Explores myths and beliefs surrounding vampires. Masters recounts documented instances of vampire activity from the eleventh century, and devotes a chapter to the vampire in literature.

McNally, Raymond T., and Florescu, Radu. "Bram Stoker and the Search for Dracula" and "Bram Stoker and the Vampire in Fiction and Film." In their *Dracula: A True History of Dracula and Vampire Legends,* pp. 18-33, 161-81. Greenwich, Conn.: New York Graphic Society, 1972.*
> Informal account of contemporary sources available to Stoker at the time he researched *Dracula.* The second chapter cited is a recounting of appearances of Dracula and the vampire figure in film and literature.

Nandris, Grigore. "The Historical Dracula: The Theme of His Legend in the Western and in the Eastern Literature of Europe." In *Comparative Literature: Matter and Method,* edited by A. Owen Aldridge, pp. 109-43. Urbana: University of Illinois Press, 1969.
> Extensively researched study of the Dracula theme in European literature. Nandris prefaces his article with a synopsis of the plot of *Dracula,* gives the etymology of the name Dracula, and traces the life of the historical Dracula.

Ronay, Gabriel. *The Truth about Dracula.* New York: Stein and Day, 1972, 180 p.
> Examination of the vampire myth, which the critic sees as symptomatic of the inability to accept death.

Roth, Phyllis A. *Bram Stoker.* Boston: Twayne Publishers, 1982, 167 p.
> Critical study of most of Stoker's work, omitting discussion of the short horror stories. Roth includes a biographical chapter and an extensive bibliography.

Scarborough, Dorothy. "The Devil and His Allies." In her *The Supernatural in Modern Fiction,* pp. 130-73. 1916. Reprint. New York: Octagon Books, 1967.*
> Passing description of *Dracula* as "the tensest, most dreadful modern story of vampirism," while also commenting that the book "loses in effect toward the last, for the mind cannot endure four hundred pages of vampiric outrage and respond to fresh impressions of horror."

Shuster, Seymour. "*Dracula* and Surgically Induced Trauma in Children." *British Journal of Medical Psychology* 46, No. 259 (1973): 259-70.
> Posits a connection between Stoker's childhood illness and his conception of the plot of *Dracula.* Shuster assumes that Stoker was hospitalized in his childhood.

Stade, George. Introduction to *Dracula,* by Bram Stoker, pp. v-xiv. New York: Bantam Books, 1981.
> Brief recapitulation of the modern critical tendency to interpret the "prevailing emotion" of *Dracula* as "a screaming horror of female sexuality."

Sullivan, Jack. "Psychological, Antiquarian, and Cosmic Horror, 1872-1919." In *Horror Literature: A Core Collection and Reference Guide,* edited by Marshall B. Tymn, pp. 230-75. New York: R. R. Bowker, 1981.*
> Includes a brief outline of *Dracula* and a discussion of the character of Van Helsing. Sullivan mentions changing critical reactions to *Dracula* and summarizes some of Stoker's other horror stories and novels.

Weissman, Judith. "Women as Vampires: *Dracula* as a Victorian Novel." *The Midwest Quarterly* XVIII, No. 4 (July 1977): 392-405.
> Interprets *Dracula* as a novel of "sexual terror." Weissman sees the female vampire as a symbol of "the sexually straighforward and insatiable woman" who is threatening to the sexually insecure man.

(Johan) August Strindberg
1849-1912

(Also wrote under pseudonym of Härved Ulf) Swedish dramatist, novelist, short story writer, poet, essayist, and journalist.

Strindberg is considered one of the greatest dramatists in modern literature. He has been called the "father of expressionism" and his *Ett Drömspel (The Dream Play)* and the trilogy *Till Damaskus (To Damascus)* are recognized as forerunners of surrealism and the theater of the absurd. With the dramas *Fadren (The Father)* and *Fröken Julie (Miss Julie)*, he proved himself an important and innovative exponent of naturalism. Strindberg wrote prolifically in several other genres. His novels, poems, and essays continue to command critical attention, although his dramatic achievements overshadow the significance of these works.

Strindberg was born in Stockholm; his father was an impoverished aristocrat and his mother a former servant. A sensitive child, Strindberg felt unwanted and unloved. He chronicled his unhappy childhood in the novel *Tränstekvinnans son (The Son of a Servant)*, describing his sense of abandonment upon the death of his mother, his fear and dislike of his father, and the humiliations and injustices he encountered at school. According to the author, his early years held little but misery and conflict. His adult life brought further anguish: he failed at careers in acting, teaching, and journalism, and entered into three unsuccessful marriages. The first, to Siri von Essen, is bitterly recorded in *Le Plaidoyer d'un fou (The Confession of a Fool)*. Their love-hate relationship is also recounted in the short story collection *Giftas (Married)* and in the dramas *The Father, Kamraterna (Comrades)*, and *Dödsdansen, första delen (The Dance of Death)*. The marriage ended in 1891. Two years later, Strindberg married Frida Uhl. During this marriage he experienced five distinct psychotic episodes—marked by deep depression and hallucinatory visions—which he later termed his Inferno Crisis. Strindberg abandoned writing and concentrated on the occult and alchemy. The Crisis ended in 1896, when he sought psychiatric help, and a year later, this marriage also ended. His third marriage was far less traumatic, but also failed.

The Inferno experience had a profound effect on Strindberg's life and work. He began studying the philosophies of Emanuel Swedenborg and the Indian mystics, seeking the source of human suffering. He concluded that suffering is the result of sin and a prerequisite to salvation and atonement. Strindberg's last years were relatively peaceful and productive. He returned to the theater to transform the horrors of the Inferno Crisis and his new-found religious mysticism into dramatic images, cofounding the Intimate Theater which was dedicated to staging his dramas. Although he continued to write plays and novels, he devoted most of his energy to composing *En blå bok (Zones of the Spirit)*, a prodigious collection of essays on a variety of opinions and ideas. Strindberg died in self-imposed isolation, greatly admired by the people of Sweden. International acclaim came later, as translations of his work appeared.

Critics divide Strindberg's work into two phases, citing the Inferno Crisis as the fulcrum of the dramatist's career. The

satirical novel *Röda Rummet (The Red Room)*, the historical drama *Mäster Olof (Master Olof)*, and the naturalistic plays *The Father* and *Miss Julie* are examples of his pre-Inferno writings. *The Red Room*, an episodic satire on Stockholm's bohemian circle, is based on the author's own experiences as a member of that coterie. His impressions of the artists, journalists, and intellectuals who comprised this circle have been praised, as has his vivid and picturesque prose style. *Master Olof*, Strindberg's first theatrical success, is also first in a cycle of twelve chronicle plays concerning Swedish rulers. Like Shakespeare, Strindberg dramatized a series of historic events that embodied the social and political issues of the day.

While *Master Olof* introduced Strindberg as a leading Scandinavian playwright, *The Father*, produced six years later, and *Miss Julie* secured his reputation as a brilliant, innovative dramatist. In these works Strindberg developed a new, intense form of naturalism. Influenced by Émile Zola, Strindberg depicted his characters and their lives with scientific objectivity. However, he furthered this concept by focusing solely on the "moment of struggle," the immediate conflict or crisis affecting his characters. Dialogue and incidents not pertaining to this "moment" were eliminated, removing all vestiges of the well-made play. The theme of *The Father, Miss Julie, Comrades*, and *The Dance of Death* is based on Nietzsche's concept of life as a succession of contests between stronger and weaker wills. Strindberg applied this theory to his recurring theme of sexual conflict, a battle between the sexes for intellectual and psychological supremacy. It was in his naturalistic dramas, composed during the last, stormy years of his marriage to Siri von Essen, that Strindberg demonstrated his distorted and misogynistic view of women. His female characters are diabolic usurpers of man's "naturally" dominant role: with infinite cunning and cruelty, they eventually shatter his "superior" psyche and drain his creative and intellectual powers. These alienated and abused male characters reflect the author's self-image, that of the perennial outcast and victim. Strindberg's sexist approach has been widely censured but has not detracted from the importance of these works.

The stylistic experiments of Strindberg's post-Inferno period proved a turning point in modern dramaturgy. From his studies, Strindberg concluded that earthly life is a hell which men and women are forced to endure; their experience of reality is a nightmare in which they suffer for sins committed in a previous life. *To Damascus*, *The Dream Play*, and *Spöksonaten (The Spook Sonata)* are based on this premise, presenting a fragmented and highly subjective view of reality that approximates the Inferno Crisis. To achieve this effect, Strindberg employed the symbolism and framework of dreams, creating a grotesque and ludicrous world that is believable and frightening: individuals appear and disappear at random; scenes and images change at the slightest provocation; and characters encounter their worst fears and fantasies. With *To Damascus* and *The Dream Play*, Strindberg prefigured the major dramatic movements of the twentieth century. His influence can be seen in the work of Samuel Beckett, Eugene O'Neill, and Eugène Ionesco.

Because Strindberg was an intensely autobiographical and self-analytical writer, a few critics, such as Desmond MacCarthy, have dismissed his plays as "products of the unfortunate 'cathartic' type of creation, which purges no one but the creator." The majority of commentators, however, regard Strindberg as a major literary force. O'Neill believed that Strindberg "was the precursor of all modernity in our present theatre." Most critics agree that, despite its virulent subjectivity, his work augured, in both content and form, the dramatic methods of the modern theater.

(See also *TCLC*, Vol. 1.)

PRINCIPAL WORKS

Fritankaren [first publication]   (drama)   1870
I Rom   (drama)   1870
Fråan Fjärdingen och Svartbäcken   (short stories)   1877
Röda Rummet   (novel)   1879
    [*The Red Room*, 1913]
Mäster Olof   (drama)   1881
    [*Master Olof*, 1915]
Dikter på vers och prosa   (poetry)   1883
Lycko-Pers resa   (drama)   1883
    [*Lucky Pehr*, 1912; also published as *Lucky Peter's
      Travels* in *Lucky Peter's Travels and Other Plays*,
      1930]
Giftas. 2 vols.   (short stories)   1884-86
    [*Married*, 1913]
Sömngångarnåtter på vakna dagar   (poetry)   1884
Tränstekvinnans son   (novel)   1886
    [*The Son of a Servant*, 1913]

Fadren   (drama)   1887
    [*The Father*, 1899]
Hemsöborna   (novel)   1887
    [*The People of Hemsö*, 1959]
Fröken Julie   (drama)   1889
    [*Countess Julia*, 1912; also published as *Miss Julia* in
      Plays by August Strindberg, second series, 1913; and
      Miss Julie in *Miss Julie and Other Plays*, 1918]
Den starkare   (drama)   1889
    [*The Stronger* published in *Plays by August Strindberg,
      second series*, 1913]
Le Plaidoyer d'un fou   (novel)   1895
    [*The Confession of a Fool*, 1912]
Inferno   (novel)   1897
    [*The Inferno*, 1912]
Till Damaskus. 3 vols. [first publication]   (drama)   1898-
    1904
    [*To Damascus*, 1913; also published as *The Road to
      Damascus*, 1939]
Folkungasagan   (drama)   1899
    [*The Saga of the Folkungs* published in *The Saga of the
      Folkungs. Engelbrekt*, 1959]
Gustave Vasa   (drama)   1899
    [*Gustavus Vasa* published in *Plays by August Strindberg,
      fourth series*, 1916]
Påsk   (drama)   1901
    [*Easter* published in *Easter, and Stories*, 1912]
Dödsdansen, första delen   (drama)   1905
    [*The Dance of Death* published in *Plays by August
      Strindberg, first series*, 1912]
Kamraterna [with Axel Lundegard]   (drama)   1905
    [*Comrades* published in *Plays*, 1912]
En blå bok. 4 vols.   (essays)   1907-12
    [*Zones of the Spirit*, 1913]
Ett Drömspel   (drama)   1907
    [*The Dream Play* published in *Plays by August
      Strindberg, first series*, 1912]
Spöksonaten   (drama)   1908
    [*The Spook Sonata* published in *Plays by August
      Strindberg, fourth series*, 1916; also published as *The
      Ghost Sonata* in *Chamber Plays*, 1962]
Stora landsvägen   (drama)   1910
    [*The Great Highway* published in *Modern Scandinavian
      Plays*, 1954]
Plays by August Strindberg. 4 Vols.   (dramas)   1912-16

FRIEDRICH NIETZSCHE   (essay date 1888)

I read your tragedy [*The Father*] twice with the greatest emotion. I was astonished beyond all measure to find a work in which my own conception of love—war with regard to its means and in its fundamental laws, nothing less than the deadly hatred of the sexes,—had been expressed in so splendid a manner. This play is really destined to be performed at M. Antoine's Théâtre Libre in Paris! (p. 200)

*Friedrich Nietzsche, in his letter to August Strindberg
on November 27, 1888, in "A Correspondence between Nietzsche and Strindberg" by Herman Schef-
fauer, in* The North American Review *(reprinted by
permission from* The North American Review; *copyright © 1913 by the University of Northern Iowa),
Vol. 198, No. DCXCII, July, 1913, pp. 197-205.*

JUSTIN HUNTLY McCARTHY   (essay date 1892)

A new star has arisen in the North. Scandinavia, which has given us the greatest dramatist of our generation, is not exhausted by a single name. Norway says Henrik Ibsen. Sweden says August Strindberg. The Swedish dramatist is not the peer of the Norwegian dramatist, but he is in his degree a remarkable personality, a potent factor in that deeply interesting problem, the future of the modern drama. . . . [The] drama of the North is very active, very much alive, and Strindberg is its most powerful force after Ibsen. . . Ibsen has been accused by some of his critics of painting life in too sombre colours; his pictures of life are joy and brightness, mere hilarity, when contrasted with the plays of Strindberg. (p. 326)

Strindberg has worked in many forms of literary art; he has written novels, stories, verses, sketches of travel, even an autobiography, and has worked hard at all of them. . . . He is intensely impulsive, passionately following high ideals, passionately fighting all that he held unjust and evil in the world's business, and all he has written is written to express his ideas. . . . Here and now it is his dramatic work that I am going to consider, for it is his dramatic work that I hold of most importance; it is his dramatic work that is making him a force in Europe at this moment. . . . [*Mäster Olof*] deals with the dissensions that arose in the ranks of the disciples of the Reformation when Lutheranism was introduced into Sweden. Its chief interest is in showing how Strindberg studies the modern problems of humanity in an historical subject. It bears the same relation to his later work that Ibsen's *Kongs-emnerne* does to his later comedies.

Mäster Olof was followed . . . by *Gillets Hemlighet, The Secret of the Guild,* a four-act comedy of love, mystery, and terror, the scene of which is laid in Upsala in the beginning of the fifteenth century. This was followed by *Herr Bengts Hustru,* or *Bengt's Wife,* which, though it is laid in the time of the Reformation, deals with the question of marriage in a very modern spirit. I have only space to mention these plays thus briefly. They are merely the steps which lead us to . . . the Strindberg of the modern plays of *Fadren,* and *Fröken Julie,* and *Kamraterna.*

[The first of these plays, *Fadren,* a tragedy in three acts,] is, perhaps, the most profoundly tragic play that the literature of the North has yet produced, *Ghosts* not excepted. (pp. 328-29)

The Father is, in brief, the story of the struggle for supremacy between two persons, between a man and a woman, between a husband and a wife. . . . The woman, the wife, Laura, is, as it were, the outcome of the modern theories of women, the theories that have found what may be called their romantic interpretation in Nora Helmer [of *A Doll's House*] and in the heroine of *The Lady from the Sea.* The doctrines of feminine equality which lead Ellida Wangel to insist upon her right to choose between her husband and an earlier lover, which lead Nora Helmer to slam the front door behind her, are carried to a further pitch by Laura. She is all for the superiority, the supremacy of woman, and the play describes the terrible duel between her and her husband which ends by her deliberately driving him into hopeless insanity.

*Fröken Julie—Miss Julia—*is the shortest, but perhaps the most remarkable, of all Strindberg's plays. (p. 329)

Fröken Julie, according to her creator, is a modern character, not because the half-woman, the man-hater, has not existed at all times, but because it has now first attracted serious attention.

The species is unhealthy, the type is tragic, for it offers the spectacle of a desperate fight against nature; it is tragic as a romantic inheritance which will now be destroyed by naturalism, which wills only happiness, and to happiness belong only strong and healthy species. But she is also a remnant of the old warlike nobility that now sinks before the nobility of the nerves and of the brain. She is a victim of the discord a mother's fault brings into a family, a victim to the errors of the age, a victim to her own weakly constitution, all of which signifies as much as the destiny of earlier times or the universal law. (p. 332)

*Kamraterna—The Comrades—*is yet another study of the eternal duel of sex. A young painter and his wife have agreed together that marriage is an association of interest, but the comrade idea does not work. . . . Pessimism is the lesson of the piece. Pessimism is the lesson of all Strindberg's later pieces, a pessimism bitterer than Schopenhauer's, . . . the pessimism of that Frederick Nietszche whom Strindberg has taken as his master in life, a pessimism the keynote of which is a merciless misogyny. (pp. 332-33)

Pessimism does not make the whole, or anything like the whole of the interest of the plays. If one could imagine them preaching a wholly different lesson of life they would still remain attractive on account of their realism, their dexterity. Simply regarded as plays, they are exceedingly well constructed. . . . (p. 333)

Justin Huntly McCarthy, "August Strindberg," in The Fortnightly Review *(reprinted by permission of* Contemporary Review Company Limited*), n.s., Vol. CCCIX, September 1, 1892, pp. 326-34.*

H. L. MENCKEN   (essay date 1913)

When August Strindberg died in his native Stockholm, little more than a year ago, but a scant half-dozen of his plays had been done into English, and his novels and other writings were practically unknown to us, but since then our translators have been working in eight-hour shifts, like coal miners, and the result is already a formidable shelf of books. (p. 64)

No less than four non-dramatic works of the terrible Swede are in the current crop—*The Confession of a Fool, The Inferno, Married,* and *Zones of the Spirit.* All save *Married* are autobiographical, and even there the flavor of personal reminiscence is often very marked. The most coherent and interesting of the four is *The Confession of a Fool,* an extremely frank account of Strindberg's first marriage, to the Baroness Siri von Essen. (pp. 64-5)

His account of this first marriage is one long record of quarrels and suspicions. No doubt there was often a substantial basis for them. . . . But toward the end he piles up accusations with such prodigality, and they grow so wild and preposterous, that his wife's counter-accusation of insanity begins to take on a considerable plausibility. It is further borne out by *The Inferno* and *Zones of the Spirit,* which followed *The Confession of a Fool* at intervals of ten and twenty years. The first is obviously the daybook of one who has got more than halfway to lunacy. It tells of the author's chemical experiments in Paris, of his efforts to turn the baser metals into gold, of mysterious plots against him by unnamed and incredible enemies. . . . Finally he turns to religion as a solace, plowing through the incomprehensible balderdash of his countryman, Emmanuel Swedenborg. In *Zones of the Spirit,* ten years later, we find him steeped in pious credulity to the gills. He is ready to believe anything. . . . One carries away a picture of a man passing slowly into senile dementia, of the final break-up of a mind always a bit unsound, of the pathetic last act of a mental tragedy.

The twenty short stories in *Married* go back to the years 1884-88, before the accumulating bile of the author had quite dethroned his reason, and so they show him at his best. The first of them, **"Asra"** by name, is the story of two brothers, the one given to the sins of the flesh and the other chemically pure. Mark Twain treated the theme humorously in his twin stories of the good and the bad little boy; here it is treated with all of Strindberg's bitter and magnificent irony. You will go a long way, indeed, before you will find a more cruel fable: it is a devastating counterblast to all the Sunday school books. The same hot acids are to be found in some of the other stories—**"Unnatural Selection," "A Natural Obstacle," "Corinna"** and **"Compulsory Marriage"** among them. Not a touch of human kindness relieves the brutal pessimism of these tales. The author hasn't the slightest affection for his characters; he hasn't even any pity for them. His one aim seems to be to strip them to the bone; to make them dance naked to point his sardonic morals. But in certain other of the stories, for all their ruthlessness, a note of sentiment still creeps in. For example, in **"Autumn,"** a study of the transformation which the years work in love, purging it of passion and making it a thing of mutual help and mellow contentment. And again in **"A Doll's House,"** a sort of *reductio ad absurdum* of the bumptious feminism which Strindberg saw, perhaps falsely, in Ibsen's play of the same name. But these are exceptions. The general tone of the collection is that of furious misogyny. The author fancied that he had suffered much from women, and here he sought to get his revenge. Good reading for ribald and defiant old bachelors—and even better reading, I suppose, for young lovers.

But not, when all is said and done, a work of genius, nor even, perhaps, the work of a genius. I begin to fear, indeed, that some of the early estimates of Strindberg will have to be revised before long, and radically at that. I myself had the honor of being one of his first whoopers-up in this fair land; I wrote about him at great length so long ago as the year 1901, quoting Ibsen's saying that "here is one who will go further than I." But was this discreet and pondered praise, or merely a sort of emotional taking fire? I incline more and more to the fire theory. Very little of Strindberg was then to be had in English— and perceived through the muddy German veil, he took on colors that really didn't belong to him. The defects of his style were concealed; his gross and frequent blunders in construction were overlooked; ignorance conveniently took no account of his vapid essay in spiritism and theology, the general looseness and absurdity of his more serious thinking. A re-examination of him strips off most of his gauds. He left us one dramatic masterpiece—*The Father*—and half a dozen extremely clever plays—*Lady Julie, The Stronger, The Link, The Dream Play*, and the two parts of *The Dance of Death*. But he also left a lot of very shallow and silly stuff—for example, *Lucky Pehr* and *Easter*—and in his non-dramatic writings he left us far more of it. *The Inferno* and *Zones of the Spirit* (properly, *The Blue Book*) are one-fifth sense and four-fifths nonsense, and such books as *The Confession of a Fool* are interesting only when they are insane. There remain his short stories, of which some of the best are in *Married*. Are they short stories of the first rank? Are they comparable to **"Youth"** and **"Heart of Darkness,"** to **"The Attack on the Mill"** and **"The Blue Ho-**

tel"? To be sure they are not. The best thing in them is the courage of their cynicism; the author must be remembered for the hearty way in which he roared his objurgations. But there is no profundity of thinking in them; they do not impress us with any sense of their eternal verity; they are not great human documents.

The trouble with Strindberg, in brief, was that he was a second-rate artist. Over and over again he spoiled a good idea by treating it clumsily and superficially. Half of the stories in *Married* do not belong to literature at all, but merely to journalism. They suggest a busy man writing against space, with no time for that careful weighing and polishing of materials which is two-thirds of art. And many of the plays leave the same impression. They are written buoyantly, but they are not written very skillfully. There, indeed, is Strindberg in a nutshell. He was a man of striking originality and unbounded courage, and always magnificently in earnest, most of all in his lunacies. But he was without the critical faculty. He lacked a feeling for form. He was not an artist of the first caliber. (pp. 65-8)

> *H. L. Mencken, "The Drama and Some Dramatists: Strindberg—A Final Estimate" (originally published as "Strindberg—A Final Estimate," in* The Smart Set, *Vol. XL, No. 4, August, 1913), in his "Smart Set" Criticism, edited by William H. Nolte (copyright © 1968 by Cornell University; used by permission of the publisher, Cornell University Press), Cornell University Press, 1968, pp. 64-8.*

DESMOND MacCARTHY (essay date 1927)

[There] is an analogy between the sensations of fever and the aesthetic feelings inspired by a Strindberg play; . . . these feelings cannot be better described than in terms of such an analogy. (p. 89)

Everyone has experienced . . . feverish sensations. The peculiarity about them, which makes them distressful, is not so much that they are in themselves unpleasant as acutely tantalizing; they are cravings closely associated with deep satisfactions which never follow. One's whole sensuous being is continually concentrated in expectation, and continually cheated. There is no better analogy for the effect on the mind produced by works of genius which are not works of art. Strindberg's plays rouse emotional expectations and leave one thirsty, restless, and either too hot or too cold. The very fact that he possesses what is roughly conveyed by the word 'genius' makes their difference from satisfying work more obvious. They are products of the unfortunate 'cathartic' type of creation, which purges no one but the creator. The keenest form of attention they rouse is curiosity; and that curiosity, when it finds its proper direction, is concentrated upon the author, not on the work. I could see nothing in *Miss Julie* but Strindberg's 'servant' complex (see *The Son of a Servant* passim), his morbid desire to be kicked himself when loved, and the revolt of his masculine pride against that 'complex', taking the form of detestation of the object which satisfies it.

One midsummer night—thus the outline of the story runs— Julie, the only daughter of a Swedish count, bullies her father's footman into taking her to his bedroom; afterwards he has the opportunity of bullying her. They are both thoroughly frightened, and the solution which recommends itself is to lend her the razor, with which he was about to make himself respectable before carrying up his master's boots and coffee, in order that she may cut her throat. Strindberg's temperament has here stepped in and excluded all possibility of our feeling pity for the girl (he would never allow that) consequently the mood in which the fall of the curtain leaves one is: 'Well, well, she cut her throat and her father rang for his breakfast.'

This is hardly a 'catharsis'. It may have relieved Strindberg to send a high-born minx to an ugly death, but in me it inspired what is best described as a state of depressed equanimity. The dramatist's attitude towards the footman . . . is rather more difficult to determine. He is certainly innocent in all that preceded their embraces. He behaved like a natural straightforward fellow and told her she was a fool not 'to keep her place', though her tumble from it in a way rejoiced him. But when he took her canary to the kitchen dresser and chopped off its head, I am afraid, remembering the pug, or chow, or whatever it was, in *The Confessions of a Fool,* that the incident was not intended to alienate our sympathies but to illustrate 'the way of a *man* with a maid'. Julie's love of the bird, which she brought down in a cage as her sole luggage when they intended to elope together (I never quite grasped why this solution of their predicament was finally dropped) was, I fear, intended to exemplify the unfathomable falseness of feminine emotion.

There were, of course, vital and remarkable passages in the dialogue. The fact that when Julie falls, she falls, not to her servant's level but below it, was admirably brought out. The naturalness and integrity of his relations to the cook, Christine, who is his mistress, were made an excellent foil to the ugly muddle of his relations with his mistress in the other sense of the term. Of course, 'genius' was there, but—and this is my point—the very vehemence of the author's imagination served to throw into relief the disappointing emptiness and confusion of his conception behind the detail and the dialogue. (pp. 90-1)

The Pariah is a dialogue between two men admirably adapted to performance in these circumstances. They are seated at a bare table with an inkpot on it, in a bare room; the looking-glass over the mantelpiece is at the back of the younger of the two. . . .

[The elder] is studying the other with a detached curiosity which begins to get on [the younger] friend's nerves. The thunder also fidgets him. [The elder] (every pucker of his face, every pause in his slow deliberate tones tells) begins by saying that The Other One has puzzled him. 'For instance, you seem to be made up of two men. Looking at your face, you seem a man who braves life, while your back, which I see in that glass, is that of a man cringing under a burden. It is the back of a slave.'

Well, to condense—and necessarily, therefore, to spoil—the dialogue, after slowly piecing together, in a meditative and disconcerting manner, scraps of half-forgotten observation and deductions from The Other One's non-committal replies, the truth emerges: firstly, that this young man has served a term of imprisonment for forgery; secondly, for he has not the air of one who has paid for his misdeeds, that he has also done something else for which he fears, but has not yet received, punishment. [The elder] tries first to put a little self-respect into him by telling him that he himself killed a man. At this turn of the dialogue I thought that we were in for a robust Nietzschean moral, but the confession turned out to be the most innocent manslaughter. Cringing gratitude in The Other is presently replaced by the snarl of the blackmailer, the malice of the trapped jackal. Conclusion: Out you go, you cur. Thus they parted.

Now, what was the point of this little scene? I was interested because I felt I was in the room with these two men, eaves-dropping. But what was the point? There was no point. Strindberg was just working off contempt for a type, very probably identified in his mind with somebody with whom he had been in contact. Again, as always happens when insight is merely hate-directed, the dramatist did not remember that cold and half-amused probing of another's shame does not rouse in the subject the best human response. This revelation of the hopelessness of the Pariah's case was no proof of it. Again: amazingly clever, quite empty. (pp. 91-3)

Desmond MacCarthy, "Strindberg: 'Miss Julie and the Pariah'" (originally published as "Strindberg Again," in The New Statesmen, Vol. XXX, No. 756, October 22, 1927), in his Theatre (reprinted by permission of the Literary Estate of Desmond MacCarthy; in Canada by Granada Publishing Limited), MacGibbon & Kee, 1954, pp. 88-93.

BRITA M.E. MORTENSEN and BRIAN W. DOWNS (essay date 1949)

Just as the appearance of the prose version of *Master Olof* marked the beginning of a new epoch in the Swedish theatre, so the publication of *The Red Room (Röda Rummet)* in 1879 started an entirely new phase in the development of the Swedish novel. The significance of *Master Olof* was only retrospectively recognised by the Swedes; *The Red Room,* however, immediately attracted a great deal of attention and provoked much discussion, in fact, it provided Strindberg with his first taste of literary success. (p. 146)

Strindberg had no experience of novel-writing before *The Red Room.* The collected sketches printed under the title *Town and Gown (Fråan Fjärdingen och Svartbäcken)* . . . should, technically speaking, be considered . . . [with his] short stories; but it is, on other grounds, more useful to deal with them here, in that they, in a fragmentary and rudimentary form, contain something of the technique Strindberg was to employ in *The Red Room.* They are sketches of life in Uppsala, as Strindberg had observed and loathed it, during his own periods of sojourn there. In Sweden, as in most other Continental countries at this time, and especially in those under German influence, the student was a popular and glamourised figure, in both life and letters. (p. 151)

After his own struggles to exist in [Uppsala], Strindberg retained no illusions as to the romantic charm of life there, and his sketches, or stories, whilst good-humoured in tone, were designed to 'debunk' the cherished ideals of academic life. For instance, *The Victim (Offret)* describes the wretched young man who is too poor to take part in student life, because he has refused to accept any financial support from his father, who was willing to give such support only on the unacceptable condition that the son should become ordained. In the end the young man gives way, and becomes a clergyman without vocation, spiritually 'dead'. . . . In the last sketch of the series, *The Old and the New (Det Gamla och det Nya),* the most significant of them all, Strindberg shows up the lazy, sentimental attitude to life of the superannuated idealist, follower of [Christopher] Boström's philosophy, and contrasts with this the realistic young man of his own generation, in fact himself. . . . Through these sketches of real persons, whom Strindberg had himself known, Uppsala with its narrow streets and stuffy lecture-rooms is conjured up, vividly, but not nearly so vividly as Stockholm in *The Red Room.*

The Red Room takes its title from the name of the room at Bern's café in Stockholm, meeting-place of the journalists, artists, and poor intellectuals who made up Strindberg's own coterie, especially in the years 1872-4, but also later. Many of the portraits in the book are modelled on actual members of the circle, though naturally modified, for reasons of discretion; others are composite creations; but the book, as a whole, draws its strength and impetus from the fact that Strindberg was writing from his own experiences, as free-lance journalist, temporary civil servant, unsuccessful author, and member of this penurious Bohemian clique, who, sitting on the red plush sofas of Bern's, dissected life and politics over glasses of punch, and found them both *Bosch* (rubbish). (pp. 152-53)

Life in Bohemian circles as represented in fiction before Strindberg's day had often been endowed with a false glamour. The curious assembly of artists and intellectuals who doss down in Lill-Jans or Vita Bergen and drink in the Red Room, when one or other of them can raise some cash, are not intended to be romantic figures. Strindberg had begun his debunking of the contemporary scene in *Town and Gown,* in a mild way; in *The Red Room* he already manifests much greater confidence and writes with much more verve, when unmasking the financial and political hypocrisies of Swedish life. Driven by the desire to reveal the truth as he sees it, he describes with realistic detail, realistic yet impressionistic, the existence of Sellén, the artist, Olle Montanus, the self-taught philosopher and sculptor, Rehnhjelm, the actor, and the practical Lundell, who paints altar-pieces, because they pay well. Strindberg does not, like Zola, analyse his scenes as if he were making a business inventory of the furniture, the costumes, the individuals. Rather, he seizes on the significant detail, the patch of colour, just as he does in his plays, and works them up, obtaining his effect by exaggeration. Read for example the very amusing account of Sellén's and Montanus's shift to keep cold and hunger at bay, when they go to bed in the abandoned photographic studio. . . . Their struggle to survive is contrasted with the behaviour and attitude of the men who are on top of society, that is, those who have the money with which to make themselves obeyed, and even enforce a lip-service respect from their hangers-on, through the blackmailing power of money. (pp. 155-56)

Strindberg, then, as might have been expected, takes the part of the under-dog—the *déclassé* and unprivileged—but not of the working class as such. [Arvid] Falk, in his descent of the social ladder, engages himself to write for the Socialist paper *The Worker's Banner (Arbetarefanan),* and discovers that its editor is a compound of illiteracy, obsequiousness, and aggressiveness, a servile bully. Strindberg makes fun, too, of the meetings arranged by the workers' societies. Falk and Montanus are thrown out of one of these gatherings, after Olle has enraged the audience he is addressing by his outspoken critical comments on Sweden. . . . (p. 157)

As a result of all his disillusionments, . . . Falk reaches the stage of having a complete breakdown. He has absorbed the pessimistic philosophy of his friends at Bern's, to the point of nihilism, but his sensitive and high-minded nature cannot take it. (p. 158)

At this point Arvid is rescued by Borg, [a] medical student. . . . Borg is hard, cynical, and yet flexible, prepared to use the tricks his enemies employ, but maintaining his independence, in his own view, by saying what he likes when he likes. In the novel he represents the new scientific approach to life, stripped of all sentimentality. . . . Borg (while based

on a living model, Emil Kléen) also represents one side of Strindberg, an exaggeration of the tough, detached creature which Strindberg strove to be, just as Arvid Falk embodies the naïve and idealistic aspects of his creator, again in an exaggerated form. . . . Borg in some ways strikes one as a more convincingly drawn character than Arvid, probably because Strindberg generally showed greater skill in portraying the unpleasant than the attractive. (pp. 158-59)

From this analysis of *The Red Room* it must be clear how loose is the composition of the novel. The tendency to ramble stands out as one of the book's most obvious faults; in fact one may say that it is a proof of Strindberg's verve and vitality that the work does not weary a reader, this fault notwithstanding. Strindberg's prose style carries it along; it is nervous, flexible, and expressive, often picturesque, but not precious, in its selection of images and in its personifications of inanimate matter. The Dickens influence, in characterisation, subject-matter, and style must be acknowledged. Strindberg borrows Dickens's tricks of grotesque portraiture, but not so much directly as *via* Dickens's American imitators, Mark Twain and others, whom he admired indeed too much. From Dickens came the inspiration to write social satire, yet Strindberg remains more personal and even, paradoxically enough, lyrical, in his attacks. . . . Flaubert's *Madame Bovary* he knew and admired, and it certainly influenced him. Yet, though *The Red Room* led to Naturalism in Sweden, it was not a Naturalist work; hence, one may say, its lasting charm. For, in spite of the dating of the subject-matter, Strindberg has succeeded in conjuring up, fresh and yet eternal, the atmosphere of Stockholm as it was in the 'sixties. . . . (pp. 160-61)

The People of Hemsö (Hemsöborna) was composed at Lindau in Bavaria, between *The Father* and *Le Plaidoyer d'un Fou,* that is, during one of the worst phases of his first marriage. Distance and the suppressed longing for the Stockholm skerries seem to have endowed his memories of them with a quite remarkable clarity, so vivid is his presentation of Kymmendö, or Hemsö, as he christens this haunt of his in the novel. . . . Acquaintance with Gotthelf's novels, while he was living in Switzerland, decided the shape eventually given to the material, a novel about peasant life, Gotthelf's *Uli der Knecht,* being apparently the most immediate model for *The People of Hemsö.* Yet the development and moral issues of the two stories differ: Uli makes good in an aura of respectable virtue; Carlsson, the hero of Strindberg's novel, . . . meets with a more complicated lot. And the great achievement of Strindberg's work lies really in its essential Swedishness, which does not mean that chauvinistic patriotism has sentimentalized or falsified the telling: rather one may say that Strindberg's intimate knowledge and real understanding of the people and scenery which he is describing have crystallized into a story with both regional and national significance, which for this reason has a more universal appeal. (pp. 161-62)

There is no schematic ideology in the book, and its strength springs from this fact. So often Strindberg was tempted to project his own ideas by creating characters to illustrate them. Here he appears content to draw the people as he knew them, and to let them speak and act really 'in character'. Only occasionally does an exaggerated gesture or word jar, in the otherwise well-balanced whole. From the technical point of view the fact that Carlsson is a landlubber, a foreigner in the little [island] community, provides Strindberg with an excellent means of contrasting the quick, talkative, Värmland opportunist with the dourer and more taciturn people of the islands, and provides, too, convincing motivation through character for the development of the action. Note that it is the slow-witted, patient Gusten who wins in the end. Strindberg exercises unusual objectivity in his handling of Carlsson in defeat. There is a kind of lazy, 'Irish' easy-goingness about him, which rounds him off artistically. He manifests his nonchalance, for instance, at [his] wedding, when, after a Gargantuan drinking-bout, the pastor is found asleep in the marriage-bed. By dint of considerable ingenuity the pastor is manoeuvred out of the bed and into the muddy sea, after which Carlsson pretends to rescue him. . . . (pp. 164-65)

The wedding scene ranks as one of Strindberg's masterpieces of satiric, realistic description of incident and character. . . . (p. 165)

Yet even into this coarse and grotesque scene Strindberg has brought in as relief the beauty of the Swedish summer, the coolness of the dewy grass, and the scent of hay. For, whether in its garb of ice and snow, or in its adornment of young birch leaves and lilac, nature remains the ever-changing but ever-present factor in this narrative of the Hemsö people, on land and on sea. (p. 166)

In the Outer Skerries bears strong resemblances, so far as setting and personalities are concerned, to *The People of Hemsö*, but the author's attitude to his material has undergone a very marked change: he now evinces a sharp hostility to the population of the islands. As in the earlier novel the arrival of the 'foreigner' Carlsson, *der Bote von der Aussenwelt*, precipitates the action, so here it is the coming of Borg, the *fiskeri intendent* (inspector of fisheries) and his clash with his surroundings, which form the plot. Borg (who has no connection with his namesake of *The Red Room*) is depicted as an intellectual, a scientist, who, like his creator, has failed to achieve recognition by the Academies, but none the less is superior to them, and *a fortiori* to the stupid and humble people who surround him. In effect, he personifies the conception Strindberg held at this time of the 'Superman', an idea formed first independently and then under the influence of Nietzsche. (pp. 166-67)

Strindberg paints a terrifying picture of [the rejected] Borg in his misery and degradation, when the children stone him, and he totters round, dirty, exhausted from hunger, a wreck of a man. Such details of degeneration occur frequently in the Zola novels; and clearly Zola's influence has here left its mark, not only in this respect, but in Strindberg's approach to nature. Not always, but all too often, his fresh appreciation of form and colour and sound gives way to a would-be scientific analysis of the component parts of the scene he describes, as for instance in the following passage: 'When he had climbed up between the sharp stones, and reached the top, it was as if he had accomplished an Alpine ascent in ten minutes. The belt of deciduous trees lay beneath him, and on the mountain plateau the Alpine flora showed itself . . . beside the genuinely Northern cloud-berry in the damp crevices of the peat-moss, and in amongst them the little cornus, perhaps the only Swedish and the only skerry plant' . . . and so on. Even though marred by this pseudo-scientific approach—and later critics have indicated the inaccurate nature of some of Strindberg's marine biology, a criticism which cannot be levelled at his technical accounts of sailing—Strindberg's flexible prose remains a saving grace.

Borg in a state of physical and mental decay contrasts poignantly with the elegant and cool-headed savant who first makes his appearance in the opening scene. . . . Strindberg's hero,

indeed, is depicted as a dandy, an aesthete, scientist though he is, and displays certain similarities with the Parisian dandy of Baudelaire and Huysmans. Curiously enough (and this provides a further link with French aestheticism), he champions the cause of Roman Catholicism, though he himself is an atheist, on the grounds of the cultural value of the Catholic faith.

These conflicting strains make Borg interesting, but not convincing, and withal slightly comic—that most fatal characteristic for the hero of a novel. Strindberg's intellectual Superman—deliberately represented as a physical weakling—is ruined by the stupidity of his fellow-creatures; only at the end, in his madness, does he attain to the stature of a tragic hero, recalling the fate of Nietzsche, which may well have inspired Strindberg's conclusion. Obviously Strindberg's own discords, his monomaniac hatred of woman, inspired by his dependence on her, are all reflected in the development of the book. Unfortunately *In the Outer Skerries,* whilst offering much fascinating material on Strindberg's state of mind in 1890, and some interesting evidence concerning his transition from his particular brand of Naturalism, does not succeed in its objective of making the character of a genius take life before our eyes. (pp. 168-70)

The title of *The Gothic Rooms* [*Götiska Rummen*] refers back to *The Red Room;* the former meeting-place of the circle had been altered and redecorated, and twenty-five years later the members meet again, together with additions such as Dr Borg's nephew, the architect. A party in these rooms serves as introduction, just as another party forms the conclusion. Otherwise Strindberg bothers little about the claims of composition, and launches into a general attack on the decadence of Swedish society at the *fin de siècle,* a parallel to his onslaught in *The Red Room,* but lacking the earlier book's force and piquancy. Much of what he has to say is given in the form of rather tedious diatribes, or arguments. In *The Red Room* Strindberg had made his social and intellectual criticism vivid by his illustrations of the abuses prevailing; here he tends to be boring. He had changed many of his views since 1879; he was now a Christian mystic and no longer a positivist; but he still distrusted and hated emancipated women, indeed, was now openly at war with them, and *The Gothic Rooms* is full of incidents of broken marriages, ascribed to the dangerous influence of feminist doctrines. (pp. 170-71)

The pessimism and misanthropy exuded by Strindberg in *The Gothic Rooms* found a far more virulent expression in *Black Banners* [*Svarta Fanor*], which is truly a masterpiece of invective. It is a pity that much of the satire, being aimed at a definite set and time, should thus be necessarily restricted in scope, and the book dated accordingly. . . . In *Black Banners* he arbitrarily put together two works planned separately; [a] novel concerning Zachris, Jenny, and Falkenström, and their circle, and the dialogues on occult phenomena intended as a continuation of the conversations between Max and Ester in *The Gothic Rooms.* The conception of an undenominational monastery (as in *To Damascus III*), to which Max and later Falkenström retire, furnishes the pretext for these high-faluting conversations, in which Strindberg is very much in earnest. Nothing, however, could strike a more discordant note in these spiritual harmonies than the satirical exposure, in the author's most grotesque manner, of the life led in a certain section of contemporary Stockholm society. His chief victim, Zachris, was a portrait of the novelist Gustaf af Geijerstam, as Strindberg saw him. Geijerstam had used his own marriage with a consumptive as material, in romanticized form, for novels;

Strindberg takes a devilish delight in exposing this romantic fiction as a distortion of the truth; in Zachris and his wife Jenny, dissipated, futile, dishonest, and perpetually battening on other people, their ideas, their money, their friends, Strindberg has drawn two successful caricatures of unsurpassed malice. Strindberg's description of Jenny's death-bed (Geijerstam's wife had died at the turn of the century) is in extremely bad taste, even if Geijerstam, by his rather maudlin sentimental revelations of his own family life, had laid himself open to attack. Hanna Paj, with her red nose and insidious intrigues, represents Ellen Key, that active apostle of female emancipation, who was one of Strindberg's bugbears. Like horrid phantoms the whole set is assembled and exposed in the first chapter at the dinner party in Professor Stenkåhl's house, a *spökdiné*, prototype of the scene in *The Ghost Sonata.*

Over and above the immediate literary caricatures, Strindberg attacked the futility of an author's life as such, the incessant need to produce 'copy' out of his own life and emotions, a criticism levelled at himself too in the person of Falkenström, and this links the book up with his ideas in *The Red Room* and other works of the 'eighties. Strindberg also seized on the general trend of Swedish life as he saw it, its increasing materialism; it was, after all, this materialism which had helped to bring about the decadence of the literary circles. He exposes, too, the hold of materialism on society in general. Through this, Strindberg's novel, in spite of the ephemeral nature of the literary squabbles it denounces, has maintained a certain permanent value as a *description de moeurs.*

As a novelist, Strindberg never achieved all that *The Red Room* had promised. One might say that his tendency to loose composition, sketchy characterization, exaggerated grotesqueness, gained the upper hand: moreover, tormented by persecution and lack of appreciation, he used the novel more and more as an instrument for literary 'execution', to employ his own term. Only *The People of Hemsö* can be excepted from these strictures. It is worth noting that *The People of Hemsö* is usually considered to be one of Strindberg's least characteristic works in any *genre*. (pp. 171-73)

> *Brita M. E. Mortensen and Brian W. Downs, in their*
> Strindberg: An Introduction to His Life and Work,
> *Cambridge at the University Press, 1949, 233 p.*

COLIN WILSON   (essay date 1959)

For a long time now, I have had in mind a number of observations concerning Shaw's relation to his great contemporary, Strindberg, and the publication of *The People of Hemsö* offers an opportunity to state them. (p. 22)

[The novel] is by far the finest of Strindberg's long fictions. Published in 1887, the year after the self-lacerating autobiography, *The Son of a Servant,* and the savagely bitter stories of *Marriage* (part 2), it reveals a new Strindberg—a man of the open air, with a Rabelaisian sense of humour. It is the story of an amiable rascal who 'takes life as it comes', and some of its comic scenes must surely be among the finest in Swedish literature.

But the most cheering thing, for a Strindberg addict like myself, is that *The People of Hemsö* should gain him a host of admirers who might otherwise never trouble to read his works. For in some ways he is one of the most unapproachable men of genius of the nineteenth century. In Strindberg, everything is personal. It is hardly surprising if readers who are acquainted only with

The Father or *The Road to Damascus* should dismiss him as a bore and a paranoiac.

There is *some* justice in this view. And a comparison with Shaw underlines it. Strindberg wrote four astounding volumes of autobiography, one of which, *The Inferno,* is the most remarkable study in a half-insane mind ever penned. Shaw never wrote an autobiography, and could barely be persuaded to scratch together the few scraps that make up *Sixteen Self Sketches.* Strindberg was self-obsessed; Shaw had a Goethean detachment. Shaw could write: 'I was steeped in romantic opera from my childhood. I knew all the pictures and antique Greek statues in the National Gallery of Ireland. I read Byron and everything of romantic fiction I could lay my hands on. . . . I was overfed on honey dew . . .'.

And here, I think, is the really interesting point about Strindberg. He was a man of the twentieth century in his childhood and youth, in the mental cast they helped to form. *Too much* so. Strindberg's autobiographies belong on the same shelf with James Joyce's *Portrait,* John Osborne's *Look Back in Anger,* and most of the novels of the 'Angries' and the 'Beat Generation'. They are anything but Olympian. Shaw's belongs with Goethe's *Poetry and Truth* and Anatole France's autobiographical writings; the air he breathed was clear and serene. Today, literature has become totally 'personal'; a writer who attempted to brush aside his personal neuroses and tragedies would be regarded as insincere. And yet the fact that Strindberg is so little read today is evidence that the 'personal' becomes stale after two generations.

What precisely is Strindberg's value for our own age? Strindberg the iconoclast—the Strindberg Shaw admired—is certainly hopelessly out of date.

I would suggest that the importance of Strindberg—and of all 'personal' writers who possess a spark of his genius—lies in the inspiration that is inherent in his life and work. Shaw was lucky; circumstances favoured the full development of his idealism; no childhood torments left a permanent mark on him. Strindberg spent a life in torment; and at least fifty per cent of it was his own fault. . . . [He] developed the persecution mania that is detailed in *Inferno.* And the saga of insanity, betrayal and self-contempt is completed in the final volume of autobiography, **Legends,** in which Strindberg expounds at length his newly-discovered religious faith. (pp. 23-4)

Strindberg is the necessary antithesis of Shaw. Shaw stands outside his works; he very seldom descends from his mountaintops. Strindberg and his works are synonymous. There is no mountain air; he lived and wrote in an atmosphere of a thunderstorm. But a storm can be superbly exhilarating. And the calm periods between storms can possess a remarkable beauty. This is the beauty of *The People of Hemsö.* (p. 24)

> *Colin Wilson, "Shaw and Strindberg," in* The Shavian, *Vol. 1, No. 15, June, 1959, pp. 22-4.**

RAYMOND WILLIAMS   (essay date 1969)

Mention of Strindberg, to the theatregoer, usually brings as narrowly defined a response as does mention of Ibsen. With Ibsen the association is feminism, heredity, and the fully-furnished family play—usually *A Doll's House* or *Ghosts.* With Strindberg it is anti-feminism, hysteria, and the play of violent action or declaration—*The Father,* say, or **Lady Julie,** or *The Dance of Death.*

These responses, like the public projections of most artists, contain an element of truth. But Strindberg, like Ibsen, cannot be easily typed; a study of his development shows a variety of dramatic method and purpose, and an immense range of technical experiment, which ought to be appreciated if we are to form anything like a just estimate of his status as a dramatist.

Strindberg was writing plays in his late teens and early twenties, and indeed from this period can be dated the very remarkable history play—*Master Olof,* which he went on revising and rewriting until he was twenty-eight, when it was at last produced in the form in which we now have it. (pp. 75-6)

Master Olof shows in a remarkable degree that quality for which all Strindberg's historical plays may be valued: a freedom from abstraction and from what we may call historicism. Strindberg, like the maturing Shakespeare, took a series of historical events, not so much for their own sake, as for their potency to recreate the texture of [an] experience which the author might also have communicated directly. I mean that Strindberg took such stories as those of Olof, and in later years Gustav Vasa and Eric XIV, partly because they were the facts of his own history, but mainly because when communicated with his unique vigour and immediacy they became an embodiment of tangible contemporary qualities; fidelity, power, intrigue, ambition, and loyalty. The historical events provided an objective dramatic discipline.

His next important play is one of a group of three written in his early thirties: the fairy play *Lucky Peter's Travels.* . . . This play invites comparison with Ibsen's *Peer Gynt,* which had been written some fifteen years earlier. *Lucky Peter's Travels* is inferior, verbally, to *Peer Gynt;* but it shows that remarkable power of dramatic visualization which was to be so important in the later, more experimental, work of *The Road to Damascus, Dreamplay* and *Ghost Sonata.* Realism of scene is firmly set aside; the travels of Peter, the boy who achieves his manhood through a magical insight into the nature of power, are rendered with a virtuosity of scene that was quite beyond the theatre of Strindberg's own day. More clearly even than Ibsen, Strindberg was creating a kind of dramatic action—a sequence of images in language and visual composition—which became technically possible only in film. What was then only imagined is now familiar and—the stress is exact—conventional. Here is one characteristic scene movement:

> Transformation. The landscape changes from winter to summer; the ice on the brook disappears and the water runs between the stones; the sun shines over all.

It is obvious that Strindberg was using the form of a play with little thought of immediate dramatic production. Like Ibsen, after an early attempt to come to terms with the ways of the contemporary theatre, and finding them at length only shackles on his genius. Strindberg drew strength from a more general dramatic imagination, and let the theatre, for a while, take care of itself. But the "demands of the new time" soon began to exert their pressure.

> In the '80s the new time began to extend its demands for reform to the stage also. Zola declared war against the French comedy, with its Brussels carpets, its patent-leather shoes and patent-leather themes, and its dialogue reminding one of the questions and answers of the Catechism.

> (pp. 76-7)

Now Strindberg was, perhaps, in revolt against the same things as was Zola, against the "patent-leather themes" of the intrigue drama. But his own ideas for reform were different, and the experiments into which his ideas led him represent a unique and quite separate dramatic form. (p. 77)

[*The Father* and *Lady Julie*] are attempts at such a new form. By this time, of course, Ibsen's prose plays were widely known. Although Strindberg was in many ways openly contemptuous of Ibsen—he called him "that famous Norwegian blue-stocking"—Ibsen's established practice was a definite part of Strindberg's new dramatic consciousness.

The substance of *The Father* is the conflict of man and woman in the specific instance of a battle for control of their child. The woman, Laura, drives her husband, the Captain, even to insanity, in order to gain absolute control of their daughter. Her main weapon, allied to interference with his work and talebearing of his growing madness, is an induced doubt as to whether the child is really his. . . . (p. 78)

The experience with which the play deals is intended as a "revealed truth"; it is obviously, in this form, not an "everyday experience". The principal distinction is the articulacy of the exposition. And this is not merely an articulation of the imperfect conversation of everyday people. The articulacy is not that of real persons' conversation made more explicit, but rather an articulation of the author's sense of certain facts about relationship.

But one must be concerned to distinguish between this method in a play like *The Father* and in a novel, say, like *The Rainbow.* In *The Rainbow,* the characters exist within a flow of description, of their experience, their actions, their speech and their world, from which they can never really be abstracted, separated out. It is otherwise in this kind of play. Although, essentially, Laura and the Captain are simply elements of the author's statement (so that it would be secondary to ask whether a woman like Laura would reveal herself as she does in speech) the framework of the conventions remains the simulation of a separated, self-presented existence. So that, in performance, bodied forth by naturalist actors, in the fully furnished atmosphere of an everyday home, the characters inevitably aspire to a different kind of personality, and are so communicated. This is the inescapable tension of such drama. The characters lose their elemental quality in the local particularity of the presented drama. . . . Strindberg, more definitely than Ibsen in his *The Doll's House—Wild Duck* period, assumes the conventional element in his characters. He rejects the formal carpentry of the well-made play which Ibsen so often retained. *The Father* is "formless" and is played out at a single level. But while this permits more adequate expression of the central experience (compare the speeches of Laura and the Captain with those of Nora and Torvald), the very formlessness, the absence of "theatricality", only reinforces the illusion that this is a claim to be direct observation. And this illusion limits the achievement of the essentially conventional literary expression.

Strindberg realized this, and in *Lady Julie* he attempted to fashion new conventions. The "new wine had burst the old bottles"; or, more precisely, the old bottles had soured the new wine.

> In the present drama I have not tried to do anything new—for that is impossible—but merely to modernize the form in accordance with what I imagined would be required of this art from the younger generation. . . . In regard

to the character-drawing, I have made my figures rather characterless. . . . (pp. 80-1)

I do not believe in simple characters on the stage. And the summary judgements on men given by authors: this man is stupid, this one brutal, this one jealous, etc., should be challenged by naturalists, who know the richness of the soul-complex, and recognize that "vice" has a reverse side very much like virtue. . . .

. . . My souls [characters] are conglomerations from past and present stages of civilization; they are excerpts from books and newspapers, scraps of humanity, pieces torn from festive garments which have become rags—just as the soul itself is a piece of patchwork. Besides this, I have provided a little evolutionary history in making the weaker repeat phrases stolen from the stronger, and in making my souls borrow "ideas"—suggestions as they are called—from one another.

So far as this method of characterization is concerned, Strindberg's theory was at this time in advance of his practice. Julie and Jean are not "simple characters", it is true; one could define them in Strindberg's terminology as "souls", "elemental". Julie is the aristocratic girl, fixed in the conscience of inherited debt, consumed by romantic ideals of honour, and in practice a predatory "half-woman". Jean, the valet, by contrast, is "on the upgrade", "sexually, he is the aristocrat"; he is adaptable, has initiative, and hence will survive. When they meet, when they clash sexually, it is Julie who goes to pieces. (pp. 81-2)

The clash of Julie and Jean is, then, a convention to express a fact which Strindberg has perceived in relationship. And although the relationship is specific, it is hardly personal. The "drama is enacted by symbolic creatures formed out of human consciousness". But Strindberg's definition of his method of characterization hardly seems relevant to his practice in this play, although it is certainly relevant to his later, expressionist, pieces. It is true that Jean, as the stronger, imposes his ideas on Julie, the weaker, but this is rather the specific situation than an instance of the general method of the play. (p. 82)

The prose of *Lady Julie* is effective, not so much by pattern, as by force. It has a vigour wholly consonant with the dramatic speed of the action. From the first words . . . the language has the explicit, calculated violence of the whole dramatic method. But it is the rush of passionate statement rather than the patterned verbal theme which Strindberg, in the Preface, seemed to have in mind.

The whole virtue of *Lady Julie* is its speed. (pp. 83-4)

Most impressive is the "ballet" where the peasants sing a Midsummer Eve drinking song while Jean and Julie are alone in the bedroom. Kristin's mime is less successful; it has the air of simple defiance of normal theatrical practice, and serves little dramatic purpose. Strindberg, it seems, felt the need for formal devices of this kind, but felt it theoretically rather than practically. It is interesting to note that he considers the possibility of the actor working independently, being encouraged to improvise in these interludes. But in *Lady Julie,* where so much energy is concentrated for a clear single effect, it is vital that a single control should be retained. (p. 84)

After *Lady Julie* Strindberg wrote a series of naturalist plays, which gained him considerable success in the new theatres of Paris and Berlin. There is *The Stronger,* played by two people, only one of whom speaks. There are *Creditors* and *Playing with Fire*. The dramatic aim is constant: to find the crisis, the moment of struggle, and to reveal normal experience in its light. The virtue of all these plays is the intensity of the revealed experience, the unforgettable power of a savage insight into motive and situation. The limitation, as in *The Father* and *Lady Julie,* is the occasional incongruity between the bared, elemental experience of crisis and the covering apparatus of seen and spoken normality. The reduction to elements foreshadowed in the proposed conventions for *Lady Julie* is never, on the surface of the plays, achieved. It is this limitation, a limitation of convention, which led to the critical error of dismissing Strindberg as wild and abnormal, and to the further error of a search for an explanation in his autobiography. The elemental characters of Heathcliff and Catherine in *Wuthering Heights* are acceptable, to those who will read the novel as it is, because of the strict conventional form on which the novel is built. But Strindberg's interpretation of naturalism as the moment of crisis was caught up in the incongruous naturalism of the general dramatic movement, and was communicated in the apparent texture of normality. It was necessary for Strindberg to try yet again; his attempt was the wholly new dramatic form of *The Road to Damascus*. . . . (pp. 85-6)

Strindberg's genius as a dramatist was that he found, against the grain of the dramatic methods of his time, forms of expression which were adequate at least for himself. His influence, of course, has been immense: both from the conflict plays (as directly to O'Neill) and from the experiments in dramatic sequence and imagery in the later work (as notably in expressionism and in the work of many experimental directors). What has then to be said, just because of this influence, is that he worked, always, from the experience to the method; the new conventions relate, directly, to a structure of feeling, and can not be abstracted from it, as in a simple "modernism". Strindberg's view of relationships, for all its strangeness, has become characteristic, in a particular phase of society, and in some places is now even orthodox. It is a view to question, certainly, in its abstracted forms, and we have seen both the structure and the methods become mechanical. But we could never say this of Strindberg himself. There the power, the creation, the astonishing invention, are authentic and lasting: an achieved and unforgettable dramatic world. (pp. 99-100)

Raymond Williams, "A Generation of Masters," in his Drama: From Ibsen to Brecht *(copyright © 1952 and 1968 by Raymond Williams; reprinted by permission of Chatto & Windus, Ltd.), Chatto & Windus, 1968, pp. 33-114.**

BIRGITTA STEENE   (essay date 1973)

To Damascus has usually been put in the same category as *A Dreamplay* and the later chamber plays. But the fact is that when Strindberg, in his 1904 preface to *A Dreamplay,* referred to *To Damascus* as "my earlier dream-play," the statement was an afterthought. At the time of its conception, *To Damascus* was for Strindberg "a *Lucky Per's Journey* set in our own time and based on reality." Instead of emphasizing thematic unity as he was to do in *A Dreamplay,* Strindberg used the more conventional approach of unity through character. (p. 81)

Parallels certainly present themselves between *Lucky Per's Journey, Keys of Heaven,* and *To Damascus I:* all three plays employ a loose and flexible form; they deal with a man's struggle with his conscience and his gradual chastening; they suggest the Catholic church as a possibility for the seeker who, however, remains hesitant before this alternative. The basic philosophical mood is pessimistic in all three plays although the protagonist's final attitude is different in each drama, ranging from a belief in hard work (Lucky Per) to an acknowledgment of suffering as a prerequisite for salvation (the Stranger).

To Damascus I is designed as a station drama, that is, the Stranger's stops along the way are places of expiation where he is tested and forced to contemplate his situation. The play opens and closes before the entrance of a church and the protagonist's journey describes a movement forward and back, with his stay at the asylum as a turning point. The scenes unroll themselves in calculated sequence and are reversed in the latter half of the play to show life's continuous repetition, a favorite idea of Strindberg's. (pp. 81-2)

To Damascus I is not a drama of conversion so much as a drama of struggling doubt. The Stranger's nightmarish vision in the asylum does not have the immediate impact of Saul's, his biblical prototype's, terrifying revelation on his way to Damascus. Yet . . . Strindberg regarded the asylum scene as the high point of the drama, and he indicated this by casting it as a pure vision. It is a vision, however, that is realistically motivated, conditioned as it is by the protagonist's feverish state of mind. Through the Stranger's illness the spectator is forewarned of the complete shift from the real or half-real to the visionary, a crucial detail that separates *To Damascus I* from *A Dreamplay* and from later expressionist dramas.

The shift from reality to vision is also revealed in Strindberg's handling of the scenery, which is Naturalistic except in the asylum scene where a theatrical setting is used. (pp. 82-3)

The movement from an outer to an inner reality affects Strindberg's conception of the secondary characters in the drama. On one hand they are actual people whom the Stranger meets during his wanderings; on the other hand, they can be seen as projections of his wishes and fears. They offer alternatives to his present life, appear as warning examples, or loom as guilt-ridden monsters before him. Their role of imaginative dramatic images rather than independent characters stands in direct relation to the Stranger's own movement from the conscious to the subconscious level of his psyche. But whereas the Stranger, whose anonymity suggests a person who is a stand-in for all men, does not appear to be a flexible character, the other dramatis personae seem to "split and multiply," to borrow a statement from the preface to *A Dreamplay*. This has to do with their being, to some degree, either doubles or emanations of the Stranger's ego. Thus the female characters (the Lady and the Mother) often cease to be completely autonomous people; on such occasions they illustrate the two dichotomous functions of the Strindbergian woman: to save man from evil and to destroy pure, untainted love. The Lady accompanies the Stranger as a potential redeemer. The Mother ruins their relationship by tempting her daughter to read the Stranger's "evil" book. (p. 83)

To Damascus I abounds in symbolic details often suggesting madness, decadence, and death. . . . In the crucial asylum scene the setting is reminiscent of a wake, and one wall is covered by a painting representing "the archangel Michael killing the Evil One." Together with Christian references (a rosary, a chapel) and metaphorical projections of life as a repetitious dream or nightmare (e.g., an ever-grinding mill),

the visual and auditory symbolism helps build up the composite mood of frustration and restlessness that permeates the Stranger's search and points forward to the ending of the play, which is an ironic rather than emotional catharsis. The Stranger reaches neither religious peace nor a convincing reconciliation with the Lady. It is hardly surprising that Strindberg later felt compelled to write a sequel to the play.

The dramatic action of *To Damascus II* opens with a provocative argument by the Mother and the Lady whereby the Stranger's defiant attitude is rekindled. He now plunges into a disillusioning struggle of trying to win recognition and status among men; he attempts in vain to establish himself as a goldmaker. Gradually the Stranger learns that his suffering is God's just punishment of his *amour-propre,* and the Confessor leads him on a road of renunciation. (pp. 85-6)

In *To Damascus I* the Stranger suffered guilt feelings for iniquities done to his family. In the second play he moves the moral reckoning to a social plane in that he upbraids himself for his vain scientific exploits. This culminates in the most remarkable scene of the play, the gold-maker banquet, a feast that changes from a pompous gesture of homage to a derisive spurning of the Stranger's gold-making efforts: one moment he is the guest of honor among formally dressed gentlemen; the next he finds himself ridiculed by drunken derelicts in a tavern.

But apart from the expressionistic gold-making celebration and its ignominious aftermath, which foreshadows the examination scene in *A Dreamplay, To Damascus II* is little more than a tedious rumination of old marriage motifs, filled with autobiographical references that do not blend well with the main action. (p. 87)

To Damascus III indicates that the dramatic material had by now lost its visionary grip on Strindberg. The play is a desperate attempt to justify the Stranger's life, ending in a rationalized concoction of Swedenborgianism, Hegelianism, and the particular blend of misanthropy and resignation that characterizes most of Strindberg's works from 1900 on. Isolated scenes like that of the phosphorous pond have a strong visual potential, but the play as a whole lacks theatrical verve and inner dynamics. Typical is the figure of the Tempter, who accompanies the Stranger throughout the play but remains little more than an allegorical fabrication, giving the play the same intellectualized quality as some of Eugene O'Neill's dramas about split personalities (e.g. *The Great God Brown, Days Without End*). (pp. 87-8)

Strindberg's experiences during the Inferno period continued to hold a grip on him. But the trend from inner agonizing struggle to a partly intellectualized and/or moralistic view of his situation, which was noticeable in both the Inferno journals and Damascus suite, can also be observed in the two plays, *Advent* and *There are Crimes and Crimes*. . . . (p. 88)

[*Advent*], to a much larger extent than *To Damascus,* has the hysterical tone, macabre props, and ghoulish atmosphere that characterize many expressionistic *Schreidramen.* Also, the handling of the dramatis personae is basically expressionistic. The couple united in their evil represents a central consciousness, and the other characters emerge as a concretization of the thoughts and fears of the couple, something that is made clear by the wife when she asks in view of the strange phenomena that take place: "Are these shadows or ghosts or our own sick dreams?"

Strindberg once referred to *Advent* as "a Swedenborgian drama." The play has the stylized quality of a work based on a theological doctrine rather than character conflict. The judge and his wife demonstrate the Swedenborgian thesis that the devil resides in lost souls who pursue living people. (pp. 89-90)

In *There are Crimes and Crimes* Strindberg left out the stark and excessive colors from *Advent* and produced a play that is taut in structure and relatively disciplined in tone. The religious point of view is the same in both dramas, but in *There are Crimes and Crimes* Strindberg's moralistic zeal threatens to destroy the dramatic tempo of the play and fill it with frequent lectures and cants. (p. 90)

There are Crimes and Crimes is designed as a realistic drama, but its very realism proves detrimental to its success. Strindberg's rather primitive philosophical standpoint fits well into the macabre world of *Advent* but becomes almost ludicrous in a sophisticated Parisian milieu. Rather unpleasant to watch is the Swedenbogian machinery of retribution, which forms the religious core of the play and is manipulated by Strindberg in a self-defensive manner. The plot goes back to an incident during the Inferno crisis when Strindberg tried, by means of telepathy, to make his daughter Kerstin sick. Guilt feelings probably motivated him to write *There are Crimes and Crimes*. He designed it, however, as both a confession and an absolution but also justified the "happy end" to himself (and his editor) in claiming it to be a concession to the tastes of the Parisian public who demanded a light touch. (p. 91)

Guilt as a dominant motivation often becomes a central theme in Strindberg's post-Inferno production. Frequently he places the moral qualms of his characters within a Christian context. Two of his most successful dramas of this kind are [*Easter* and *The Bridal Crown*]. . . . In both of these the playwright juxtaposes individual wrongdoing and guilt with innocent or redemptive suffering. (pp. 91-2)

Easter is a morality play in which the characters embody ethical positions which are intensified by a small-town atmosphere imbued with righteous thinking. Guilt is not only a private affair but is coupled with social shame and punishment. In a sense Eleonora's isolation is only a reflection of the fate of the rest of the Heyst household. The family is a group of social failures and outcasts: the mother huddles in the house cut off from any friends; Ellis's sense of rejection leads him to believe he has lost his fiancée to another man; Benjamin, the boarder, fears ostracism after failing to pass the prestigious student examination.

The mood of social isolation and personal despair reaches its climax in act 2, on Good Friday. The dramatic action, which is rather slight, describes a movement comparable to the legendary Easter season. On Maundy Thursday there is a sense of impending disaster; on Good Friday a seeming deathblow is given to the family as Lindkvist, the creditor, appears in the neighborhood; on Easter Eve a mood of continued despair prevails as Elis is forced to review the case of his father. This is followed, however, by a happy ending in which Lindkvist, the creditor, plays a crucial role. (pp. 93-4)

Just as there was something diabolic about the offstage Lindkvist in the first half of the play, there is something divine about his final appearance. In an almost literal sense he functions as a *deus ex machina*. At first a Dickensian bogeyman, at last a celestial agent, Lindkvist belongs to the magical or supernatural sphere of the play. His clairvoyant and telepathic powers make him move closer to the world of Eleonora than

to that of the other, more realistically conceived characters. *Easter*'s happy end may easily seem like a dramatic somersault, flaunting as it does any realistic conventions of credibility. What Strindberg is trying to do is to balance off middle-class verisimilitude, as represented by the Heyst household, with a belief in a divine order and a retributive scheme on earth, visualized in the corrective figure of Lindkvist. (p. 94)

Together with his next play *Swanwhite, The Bridal Crown* is Strindberg's most stylized and lyrical drama. Its source of inspiration is to be found in Swedish folk ballads, more specifically in the antiphonal songs between a shepherd boy and a shepherd girl which Strindberg knew from Richard Dübeck's *Svenska vallvisor och hornlåtar*. (p. 95)

The Bridal Crown penetrates beyond the folk allusions of its Dalecarlian painted backdrop and conveys something of the dark lyricism and mythic anchoring of Swedish country traditions. Its rhythmic dialogue makes no attempt to reproduce a provincial idiom, but its slightly archaic tone is in keeping with the legendary material that Strindberg uses and reinforces the magical atmosphere of the play. Thematically *The Bridal Crown* dramatizes a relatively common thought in Strindberg's post-Inferno outlook: the redemptive power of certain individuals. But unlike, for instance, King Magnus in *The Saga of the Folkungs* and Eleonora in *Easter*, Kersti is a moral agent in her own right; and *The Bridal Crown* tells first and foremost of her personal destiny, of her hardened ambitions leading to the murder of the child, of her agonized conscience, materialized in her visions of specters and mythical figures, and of her final atonement for the crime.

In order for her destiny to purge society—here represented by the two rival families—Kersti's character must have stature and symbolic potential. Strindberg achieves this by casting her as a person of passion, strength, and willpower, somewhat reminiscent of the women in the old Norse sagas. But Kersti lives not only in the stark and romantic world of folk legend; the moral values of the play are Christian, with a particular reference to the Book of Job. It is Strindberg's successful fusion of legendary and Christian sources that makes *The Bridal Crown* quite unique in his dramatic production.

Swanwhite, written a few months after *The Bridal Crown*, retains much of the fatalistic quality of Kersti's drama but loses its earthy attributes. Instead the mood is ethereal, designed to sustain its main theme, the purity of self-sacrificing love. . . . (pp. 96-7)

In spite of its poetic qualities, *Swanwhite*'s tone of timid naïveté is not in keeping with Strindberg's dramatic talent. Its lyrical passages point forward, however, to *A Dreamplay*. . . . (p. 97)

In Strindberg's chamber plays [*Stormy Weather, The Burned House, The Ghost Sonata, The Pelican,* and *The Black Glove*], which proved to be very much the drama of the future, the spectator finds little of conventional character development. The emphasis is on the setting and its impact upon the dramatis personae; as [Sven] Rinman so succinctly has said: "houses, not people . . . are the central characters." These houses when viewed from the outside seem respectable enough but upon closer scrutiny they turn out to harbor hidden evils. Except in *The Pelican*, evil is not limited to a specific individual but is a state of mind permeating an entire milieu and affecting those who live on it. The drama unfolds when an outsider enters into such an environment. Then we look behind the scenes: doors open into strange rooms; self-made roles disintegrate; and voices speak up bringing back suppressed memories, revealing the guilty past, or foreshadowing an agonizing future.

The houses and buildings in the chamber plays have then the same metaphorical function as the growing castle in *A Dreamplay:* they represent life on earth in its never-ending tension between body and spirit, appearance and reality. We see its outer façade of deceit and pretension as well as its core, the human conscience experiencing shame and guilt before the inner ugliness of mankind. The dramatic action takes the form of a day of unmasking when individuals are brought to recognize their misery in being born or have to reap the result of their misdeeds. When the illusions fall, the people wake up as from an evil dream. But the telling of the truth paves the way to death; for some the end is a suicidal punishment, for others it is a liberation from agony. (pp. 106-07)

Back in 1894 Strindberg had once written: "I have passed the noonday height of my life and now when I throw a glance at my past I often see myself in the guise of a hunter." It was in this role that he cast the main character in *The Great Highway,* the work which has been called Strindberg's literary testament. (p. 118)

The Great Highway opens with the Hunter climbing the Alps, seeking his soul in the land of eternal snow. Soon, however, he is tempted to return to earth and although he wants to remain an observer, he is drawn into a series of dramatic involvements. (pp. 118-19)

The Hunter begins his circular wandering torn between a desire to settle his account on earth ("thou temptress that pulls me back") and a longing to find there a state of fulfillment ("the Land of Wishes"). His journey is designed as a *via dolorosa* between the seven stations of Golgotha; yet, his destiny is not that of a Christ-figure but as a representative of mankind. Although descending from the heights the Hunter lacks the metaphysical frame of reference of Indra's daughter in *A Dreamplay.* His next of kin, rather, is the Stranger in *To Damascus* (the similarity between the two plays extends to a conception of some of the secondary characters as projections of the protagonist's psyche). Through imagery of hindrance, aggression, and capturing, Strindberg makes the Hunter experience life on earth as a disillusioning and frustrating rat race. The Hunter has the same fighting spirit and displays the same unwillingness to accept a resigned view of life as the Stranger, but he has also absorbed some of the tired mellowness of the aging Strindberg. (p. 119)

The Hunter, having found life on earth "a lunatic asylum, a cage, a bow-net," rejects the world but not its creator. As he takes leave, he addresses a prayer to the divine power, in which he gives voice to Strindberg's lifelong and stubborn struggle with a dichotomous God whose "hard hand" conquers human beings with its "almighty goodness." (p. 120)

The Great Highway has the quality of a choral song between two voices within one person. The drama was written to be read rather than staged, but the stylized decor is also a carryover from Strindberg's experiences with the limited space of the Intimate Theatre, as well as the result of a renewed reaction against a minute, realistic stagecraft. (p. 120)

> *Birgitta Steene, in her* The Greatest Fire: A Study of August Strindberg *(copyright © 1973 by Southern Illinois University Press; reprinted by permission of Southern Illinois University Press), Southern Illinois University Press, 1973, 178 p.*

MARILYN JOHNS (essay date 1976)

[August Strindberg and Ingmar Bergman] were born and raised in strict religious homes, a fact which was to leave an indelible impression upon them throughout their lives and which was to influence the form and content of their dramaturgy. They both rejected the rigidity of this religion but could never quite rid themselves of the idea that God alone grants salvation and that man's actions cannot affect his redemption. Most of the major characters in both artists' productions are gripped by a tremendous loneliness and a despair of ever being able to achieve anything or make contact with something or someone outside themselves.

Both artists grew up subject to a hierarchical order of power in which God was the most important figure, followed by King, Father, and Family. In such an order, freedom was impossible and each artist reacted strongly against the brutality which this lack of freedom entailed. Extremely aggressive in their private as well as artistic enterprises, they rebelled not only against such authority figures, but against life itself and its harsh imperatives.

Search for a lost innocence and beauty is a common theme. Strindberg wondered if "Perhaps our illusions are ancestral memories of something better which we have once seen." Jörn Donner has noted the same quality in Bergman's work: "He seems to dream of a lost state of happiness, a lost youth."

The concept of Original Sin was one from which neither author could ever completely free himself. They learned to interpret suffering, both deserved and undeserved, as a means of appeasing guilt feelings and atoning for rebellion. One might say of Bergman's protagonists, as Einar Haugen has said of Strindberg's, that they are distinguished by their capacity for suffering.

Other similarities include attitudes toward love and sexuality. Both men perceive love as a possible redemption from the pain and agony of reality: marriage becomes an attempt to salvage meaning through human commitment, but it is an effort doomed to failure because of the incompatibility of the sexes.

Strindberg and Bergman seek a lost sense of identity and both frequently employ a journey as the structural basis of their works—a journey not from place to place, but from doubt and uncertainty to knowledge and self-confrontation. They use the journey as a revelation of truth, and the setting is often the landscape of dreams. Characters faced with an encroaching sense of meaninglessness in their lives adopt a vision of life as a dream, a state which contains possibilities for psychic regeneration.

Both Bergman and Strindberg are concerned with laying bare a deeper level of reality than that which is immediately apparent. Their theater is the inner world of the psyche and they consciously work at developing and refining a style that utilizes the full resources of their media to portray that inner world. The private nature of their searchings suggests intensely personal visions of life, but their commitment to humanity and humanistic values raises their art to the level of the universally significant.

> *Marilyn Johns, "Kindred Spirits: Strindberg and Bergman," in* Scandinavian Review *(© The American-Scandinavian Foundation 1976), Vol. 64, No. 3, September, 1976, p. 16.**

WALTER JOHNSON (essay date 1976)

Strindberg's historical dramas were composed during two periods: a handful of plays in the years before 1883, including one masterpiece, two fairly respectable plays, a few apprenticeship pieces, and, after his Inferno period, eleven masterpieces about figures from the Swedish past and four less happy ones about non-Swedish figures. (p. 174)

Easily and economically each play ties up with its predecessor and its successor: Strindberg knew well that the roots of the present lie in the past.

The never-ending struggle for power and the never-ending search for internal law and order give unity to the cycle; their treatment varies in depth and meaningfulness according to the perceptiveness of the central characters. Strindberg subtly wove into the fabric of each play the economic, political, social, artistic, religious, ethical, and intellectual elements of the evolving cultural patterns, both at home and abroad.

Such matters rarely detract from the primary core of the rich literary quality—the dynamic, complex characters, varied and individualized with as much attention to their inner beings as to their appearance and external behavior. . . . Each central character becomes a believable being of flesh and blood, a person as "characterless" (i.e., complex and dynamic) as any other human being. The secondary and minor characters are individualized to the degree their roles require. On occasion that can be very great: for example, Archbishop Gustav Trolle, "the Judas Iscariot of Sweden." In *The Last of the Knights* and *The Regent,* Trolle is as thoroughly individualized as the two men who have to cope with him. Strindberg's characters behave as people do, and they speak as people do.

Conversational language is adapted with care to the individual character, his or her mood, and the situation. The range is great: Gustav Vasa does, for example, speak as brutally and frankly as Edgar and Alice in *The Dance of Death* and as gently and tenderly as Lindquist when speaking to Eleonora. Strindberg avoids archaic language. (pp. 175-76)

Earl Birber of Bjälbo is a presentation of a strong man of action in pursuit of power to strengthen Sweden through centralizing its government and enforcing law and order. As Strindberg understood Earl Birger—and historians agree—the earl was a richly endowed human being who dared to think clearly about himself, his fellows, and their environment, who knew that he frequently had to conceal his thinking if he were to achieve his goals, and who was destined to achieve many goals but never to receive the symbolic reward, the crown. While all these matters are clearly the core of the ideational content of the folk drama, theatergoers and readers will undoubtedly find Strindberg's presentation of the earl in his many roles and the people about him in theirs even more fascinating than the attention to ideas. (p. 177)

He compressed historical events, but he insisted rightly that he "never unnecessarily violated historic truth." For many of his countrymen his interpretation of great, near-great, and minor figures has become theirs without contradicting in any major fashion interpretations by twentieth-century historians.

The Saga of the Folkungs is an even more ambitious historical drama in that it deals with the whole dynasty and a whole epoch. With King Magnus, the last of the Folkungs to occupy the Swedish throne, as the central character, Strindberg has presented an interpretation of a whole period during which crucial and civilizing changes took place in Sweden, not least because of the efforts of one Folkung after the other. (pp. 177-78)

The play has caught nicely the flavor and the atmosphere of the Middle Ages. Complementing its presentation of human beings and their dealings with each other is Strindberg's use of dreamplay elements such as the Plague Girl, the Plague Boy, the Madwoman, sleepwalking, rituals, and symbols, all of them highly appropriate in a play about an age of faith. Capitalizing on the biblical assertion that the sins of the father shall be visited on the children unto the third and fourth generations, he was able to do two things: give a realistic portrayal of the Folkungs and their environment toward the end of their generations of power and, at the same time, reveal his medieval characters' innermost feelings and thoughts through poetic techniques long used in allegory and in lyric poetry.

Strindberg knew how to provide historical atmosphere as well as salient facts about the past not only by settings and stage properties but also by folk scenes and by conversations involving analysis by deeply involved characters. The opening court-barber-shop scene in *The Saga of the Folkungs* is a superb realistic exposition of what people probably observed at the time and prepared the audience for what was likely to take place. King Magnus' analysis of the whole saga of his family's years of power in the last act is an excellent illustration of effective realistic technique. (p. 178)

[*The Last of the Knights* and *The Regent*] deal directly with Swedish struggles to be free of the union. The two are companion plays not least because they deal with the archbishop, Gustav Trolle, who was historically one of the most difficult opponents of both Sten Sture the Younger and Gustav Vasa in their struggles for independence.

In *The Last of the Knights,* Strindberg dealt with a national leader who was not only a Christian in name but a practicing one as well. . . . The presentation of a thoroughly good man is, as Strindberg well knew, likely to devolve into something embarrassingly close to cloying sentimentality and is, in fact, never accurate factually. Except for an occasional slip, Strindberg has avoided that trap by presenting Sten Sture as a good man with human frailties. (p. 179)

After his Inferno crisis was over, Strindberg wrote two sequels to *Master Olof—Gustav Vasa* and *Erik XIV*—and considered the three the Vasa trilogy. Among the links between the first two is an aging Master Olof reconciled to settling for much less than he had once dreamed, and among the links between the last two are the extremely important roles given Crown Prince Erik and his companion Göran Persson.

The structure of *Gustav Vasa* is set apart from that of the other historical plays by having everyone else keenly aware of the king whether he is on or off stage. "The wonder man of God" does not make his entrance until Act III opens, but, before that, he is constantly felt and is directly or indirectly, the center of attention: "Always this giant hand, which one never sees, only feels" and "When he's furious in the attic, people say they feel it all the way to the cellar just as when it thunders." The biblical story of Job with its accounts of the testing of one man of integrity and its revelations of his inner life serves as a parallel to Gustav's. . . . (p. 181)

Erik XIV has received more attention in the theater than *Gustav Vasa,* partly because of Erik XIV's frequently bizarre behavior rather than because of King Erik's plans and efforts on behalf of Sweden and the Swedes. . . . The play is an amazingly detailed and believable "case report" on "a characterless human being." . . .

[King Gustav Adolf, who] in Swedish opinion, had been a genius, a saint, and a martyr for the cause of Protestantism, struck Strindberg as interesting only after he had gone through his Inferno years and been converted to his own brand of Christianity. (p. 182)

Although tolerance and brotherly love are key ideas in *Gustav Adolf,* Strindberg's monumental play is much more than a plea for those virtues. It is an unbelievably effective presentation of the Thirty Years' War (1618-1648), a time when Sweden played a major role in world history. It is, moreover, a drama of character in which Strindberg made Gustav Adolf and many of the people about him live for the reader—few people have ever had a chance to see it on stage: Its length and great demands on the resources of theaters have prevented that.

The play has five acts, fifteen settings, more than fifty characters with lines to speak, many others without lines, and would take about seven hours for performance. . . .

The uncut form could serve beautifully as the basis of a scenario for a film. (p. 183)

In his historical dramas, Strindberg by no means neglected women although only in one, *Queen Christina,* did he make a woman the central character. He could, of course, have written a play about Birgitta, who helped make life miserable for King Magnus, the last of the Folkungs, and who aspired to power and canonization; he did present her in *The Saga of the Folkungs* as a gifted egotist grasping for control of her environment but not totally untrue to her nature as a woman. The women in the Strindberg plays are as human and varied as the men: Take, for example, Gustav Vasa's lovely Queen Margareta Leijonhufvud, Erik XIV's commoner queen Karin Månsdotter, Gustav Adolf's neurotic wife, the sensitive child Queen Beatrice, and the adulterous, scheming Dowager Duchess Ingeborg. (p. 184)

The four-act structure of *Queen Christina* is basically that of the well-made play, a highly artificial dramatic form remarkably well suited to the story of a crowned actress. The relevant implication is that the queen usually lived in an artificial world, a world of make-believe rather than in a world of harsh reality, that Christina was a sleepwalker. In presenting her and her story, Strindberg has combined the realism of her environment and the dreamlike quality of her sleepwalking to show not only the sleepwalking but also the awakening. Strindberg has gone far beyond a typical well-made play. (pp. 184-85)

Instead of concentrating on the sleepwalker's realistic environment and concealment of inner life as in *Queen Christina,* Strindberg, [in *Charles XII,*] deliberately placed his major emphasis on the king's innermost experiences and to represent them used the impressionistic-dreamplay techniques he had used in revealing his own inner experiences in the Damascus trilogy. Consequently, the play seemed to many early critics disjointed and loose. Later readers and theatergoers understand and appreciate the deliberate blend of reality and dream experience, the symbolism, the stress on emotions and feelings, the dark moods, and the effective use of music. (pp. 185-86)

The happy combination of realistic and dreamplay techniques gives us a synthesis and an analysis of an "arrogant egotist who believes he is the man of destiny and the center of the world . . .". *Charles XII* is the historical play that serves as counterpart to the Damascus plays: Just as the Stranger remains unknown even though the author has learned much about him, King Charles remains a stranger and an unknown even to himself. (p. 186)

[For *Gustav III,*] Strindberg chose the artificial form of the well-made play just as he had for *Queen Christina* even though King Gustav III knew very well that he was acting and Strindberg's Queen Christina had become a sleepwalker. . . . The play resembles the Scribean historical comedy with its intrigues and conspiracies, its figurative and literal fencing, its neatly arranged "scenes," and its atmosphere of superficiality.

Yet this four-act play is anything but superficial. By the time one has seen it in performance or considered it in the study one has gained insight into the king, his court, and his period. Critics and reviewers did not think the play amounted to anything as literature or theater when it first appeared in print, but, when it was produced for the first time in 1916, it was clear to the audiences throughout its long initial run that it is great theater. It is great literature as well.

In addition to the twelve great historical plays, Strindberg had written some earlier pieces that have at least historical elements in them. (p. 187)

[Three dramas]—*Moses, or From the Wilderness to the Promised Land; Socrates, or Hellas;* and *Christ, or the Lamb and the Wild Beast*—are like none of his other plays. They are essentially a series of tableaux (twenty-one for *Moses,* nineteen for *Socrates,* and fifteen for *Christ*) apparently designed to illustrate significant episodes in history and to point out the divinely designated roles of the Hebrews, the Greeks, and the Christians (the latter primarily in their struggles with Caligula, Claudius, and Nero). The plays do clarify Strindberg's view of history as controlled by the Conscious Will; they might do as imaginary conversations or dialogs to be read against backdrops of pageantry, but they lack the great Strindbergian skills in making the historic dead come alive in superbly conceived and composed dramas.

The Nightingale of Wittenberg . . . is a chronicle play, a series of episodes or tableaux divided into five acts. Its merits lie in Strindberg's interpretation of Martin Luther and his treatment of Dr. Faust.

But interesting as the trilogy and the play about Luther may be to scholars in search of minute knowledge of Strindberg and his works, they do not begin to compare with the twelve great plays about Swedish history. Those are structurally and substantially among the best plays in world literature. Taken together, they are an astonishingly effective revelation—in dramatic form—of the development of an important Western culture's ideas, values, and goals and a means of bringing into visible and audible form representations of men and women who played key roles in the development of that culture. (p. 188)

Walter Johnson, in his August Strindberg *(copyright © 1976 by Twayne Publishers, Inc.; reprinted with the permission of Twayne Publishers, a Division of G. K. Hall & Co., Boston), Twayne, 1976, 221 p.*

JOHN ERIC BELLQUIST (essay date 1981)

Insofar as Strindberg's *Sömngångarnätter på vakna dagar* comprises a sifting and weighing of possible solutions to life, it is essentially an ethical poem, whose theme is the question like its author asked so often: "What is the truth?" Like Lycko-Per or Arvid Falk, its poet confronts an array of aesthetic, intellectual, and religious alternatives, evaluates them, and finally defines his own position in their midst. But his odyssey is also psychological, for he employs the dream as a means of self-analysis. (p. 20)

Strindberg's interest in psychology, of course, is present in his works from the start—three of his earliest dramas, for example, are in part analytical studies of a Romantic, promethean type of character. Yet I think it is safe to say that ideas dominate these plays nonetheless. *Mäster Olof* is more important as an evaluation of ethical and religious perspectives upon truth than it is as a personal anatomy of Olof's nearly tragic idealism—if Strindberg had been interested primarily in the implications of Olof's individual character, he would have made the play a tragedy. So too in *Röda rummet* Arvid Falk samples thoroughly what the Oscarian society of Stockholm serves up, and in the various dramas and tales from the early 1880s, as well as in *Dikter på vers och prosa,* aesthetic and ethical viewpoints still seem to be Strindberg's chief concern. *Sömngångarnätter,* at least in retrospect, thus builds a watershed. From its conception on, Strindberg's literary interests waxed even more biographical and psychological, more subjectivistic, than they had ever been before, as he gradually evolved a psychological philosophy of human character, a new, more constant vantage that was to last him through the remainder of the decade.

It is neither my task nor my purpose to define what I call Strindberg's philosophy here at any length, but I must at least refer to it as I sketch the background for the brief continuation of *Sömngångarnätter* that he composed in 1889, a poem which so far no one has discussed in much detail. Strindberg's ideas were at first naturalistic: in *Giftas* . . . he meticulously portrays his characters as products of heredity and environment. At the same time he fuses this with his own form of Darwinism, through which he interprets man to be an animal with natural instincts and drives that propel him in the competitive struggle for survival. Even here, however, a proto-Freudian psychology is paramount: man's success in life, that which makes him able to survive most fitly, depends largely upon how well he can avoid those societal, familial, and hereditary pressures that might suppress his inherent sexuality, which in the central story "Dygdens lön" represents a kind of universal life force.

In the major works that follow *Giftas* these strains reappear variously. In *Tjänstekvinnans son* . . . man still lives within the context of naturalistic determinism. . . . In *Fröken Julie* determinism rules almost completely as a means of the analysis of character, and the heroine is a case study primarily in answer to the criticisms that Zola himself had offered Strindberg of *Fadren.* But in the rest, such as *Fadren* itself, *Fordringsägare,* the shorter one-act plays from 1888-1889 (*Paria, Samum, Den starkare*), and much of the prose from the same general period. Strindberg created what one might call, with all due respect to his professed anti-Romanticism, a mythic view of life, based on a transmutation of his Darwinism and on a reading of contemporary psychologists: what he had once seen as the struggle for survival in nature now became for him a mental act. Strindbergian man, from this point on, dwells in a mental universe, where one person's thoughts can inform another's, and where a person's thought can actually influence, control, and even shape another's physical being. Henceforth the "battle of the brains" replaces the "survival of the fittest."

No one has yet to offer an adequately encompassing designation for this segment of Strindberg's development, although traditionally all of the *plays* from the time have been called "naturalistic." Even Strindberg himself used this term to describe

his work, because he wished a clear label that would set him off from the Romantic past and present in Sweden. But, with exception made primarily for *Giftas, Fröken Julie,* and the novel *Hemsöborna,* the reference to naturalism now serves small purpose. For Strindberg's stress upon psychology, his presentation of characters in fictional contexts that seem to represent realms of mental action—manifestations, perhaps, of the author's own mind—point instead toward the definition of the typical Symbolist work as the embodiment of an *état* or a *paysage d'âme,* a suggestive landscape of consciousness. (pp. 20-2)

Because his literary work moved implicitly toward Symbolism from 1884 on, one might expect Strindberg to have frequently entertained writing poetry, but as usual the progress of his poesy and poetics was tortuously dialectical. Throughout this period his letters reveal debate over commitment to either *dikt* or *verklighet,* fiction or reality, poetry or prose, beauty or truth, literature (*skönlitteratur*) or nonfiction. *Verklighet* at this time signified for him the contents of not only purely nonfictional work, such as *Bland franska bönder* . . . but also *Tjänstekvinnans son,* with its scientific, analytical intent; *dikt* he could use in its general sense, as referring to all fictional or creative writing but also more specifically, as designating poetry. Indeed he seems to have come to view all of his creative endeavors as somehow partaking of poetry. . . . (pp. 22-3)

[When] Strindberg returned to Sweden in April 1889 after his attempt to establish an experimental theater in Copenhagen had failed, new reason for poetry naturally occurred to him; for he had now concluded his first major exile into Europe, which meant that the journeys begun in *Sömngångarnätter* had apparently reached a new end. And so he wrote the "Femte natten," as if to round the poem's circle. . . . The basic fiction of the poem is the same as in 1884: both body and spirit are returning home together, for this no longer seems to be a flight of fancy; the poet is now actually present in what was previously a dreamed landscape. At the same time, the reference to the contents of the previous "Nätternas" visions implies a restatement of emphasis, for in the first four "Nätter" Sweden was not always so much a fair oasis as a questionable context for the evaluation of standpoints that the poet found wanting. In the "Femte natten," on the other hand, the poet no longer interests himself in points of view at all.

The treatment of Paris in the "Tredje natten" allows us a fruitful means of comparison. There, the poet's experiences are certainly visionary and hence dream-like, despite the fact that they take place while he is awake, but the purpose implied in the vision is allegorical: the demonic church that the poet comes across upon his Parisian wanderings culminates a satire upon nineteenth-century urban life. Because the "Femte natten" begins with an avowed intention of putting Sweden to the test, we might expect a centrally satiric or ethical intent here too. But by now life itself had become a kind of vision for Strindberg. We can see this, first, in an epistolary response to only two days' stay in Stockholm. . . . (pp. 23-4)

His return to Stockholm meant a confrontation not only with Swedish society but also with his personal past—not just a past containing spheres of ideas, as in the first four "Nätterna," but one that called forth demons from the depths of his psyche. In the "Femte natten" the encounter reduces the poet to his barest self, as he is gradually and painfully disencumbered from the bonds of the external world, and so the poem . . . is purely psychological.

The course of the **"Femte natten"** is symmetrical: after the opening passage quoted above, the poet looks out over Stockholm, as have characters in certain of the author's previous works; he then enters the city, and the farther he goes, the deeper his quest turns inward, into himself. In the end he ascends from the city once again, leaving it behind like a sinking Atlantis. . . . The reference to waking here is important, for at the poem's beginning the return to Stockholm was defined as an awakening from the dreams that the poet had before on his travels. Now, however, even this reality of the waking state has proved a dream too, and the poet can anchor his experience only by means of his sole self. Nothing else is real. Sweden is a lost "Troja," fallen finally at the hands of barbarians . . . ; the poet is a prophet, or perhaps a superman, entering the wilderness; but he is also once again the typical Strindbergian wanderer separate from the rest of the world, which is but the stuff of his dreams.

Within this frame the poem moves gradually from the realistic to the dream-like. . . . At first his immediate impressions of the city are almost as realistic as his recollections of Europe, and indeed Stockholm seems splendid, for much construction has gone on during his absence. . . . But all this turns out to be only a "fasad". . . . On the streets, a foreign race seems to walk with creeping steps, necks bent, skin ill. Faces from his own past turn away from him too. At a café where he and his compatriots once regularly gathered he finds that they have all been broken, dispersed; and he learns from the waiter, who no longer even recognizes him, that he himself is scornfully presumed dead. In response he too becomes as the people on the streets, a victim perhaps of psychic struggle, with throat tightened, glance foggy, eyes sunken into skin's pale hue. . . . Thus the poem has moved from concrete recollection and impression to visionary dream with implications of death and annihilation. . . . The poet has sought to embrace the external world, but he cannot; and the resulting retreat into himself has led to nightmare. (pp. 24-6)

Stockholm is now a symbolic realm of the pagan and the occult, scarcely different from the Paris that Strindberg described in his subsequent "Inferno period." But as yet his own occultism was only nascent, and so the city here is doomed to sink under the waters of the flood.

The **"Femte natten"** thus serves as an indication of Strindberg's development—from the extrinsic emphasis to the psychological, from the social to the personal, from the realistic to the symbolic. It is not a Symbolist poem, because it lacks the aesthetic refinement of the work of the great French poets and because it is too much of a realistic narrative involving a poet who is the Strindberg whom we all know. . . . [Perhaps] we should speak of Strindberg at this stage as an analogue to, or a special kind of, the symbolist poet, one who in his work presents the poet moving through his own dream as he creates it and as it mutually informs and reveals his own character. For Strindberg the literary work is a mode of autoanalysis, with its end an earned purgation. As his readers we partake of this; it is why even his lesser-known poems, such as the **"Femte natten,"** may well be worth reading. (p. 27)

> *John Eric Bellquist, "Strindberg's 'Femte Natten',"*
> *in* Scandinavian Studies, *Vol. 53, No. 1, Winter,*
> *1981, pp. 20-9.*

CLIVE BARNES (essay date 1981)

What a strange but wonderful play August Strindberg wrote in *The Father*. . . . Strindberg, largely an autobiographical play-wright like O'Neill—saw life as a battle between the sexes, a battle that women are doomed to win.

Strindberg puts it explicitly enough in *The Father:* "Love between a man and a woman is a war." But of course, while Strindberg's women may be victorious, it is a pyrrhic victory, for love itself is destroyed and there are no survivors.

The Father tells of a man's descent into madness. . . .

The fault of the play—and it is a technical difficulty rather than a dramatic flaw—is that its action is too rapid. One minute we have the Captain, sane and apparently in command of his life and household, and almost the next we find him grovelling on the floor like a mock Othello in whiteface.

It is here the function of both director and actor to give the Captain some sense of impending madness, some tell-tale crack in the military facade, right from the beginning. (p. 298)

When he breaks, the Captain should erupt in a blaze of volcanic, Dionysiac madness. Years ago, I saw Michael Redgrave do just that with the role, making Strindberg's corrosively unsparing self-portrait into mother's boy gone mad.

Strindberg demands no less. It needs acting on the dangerous brink of reality, with a touch of real madness. (p. 299)

> *Clive Barnes, "Maddening 'Father' at Circle in*
> *Square," in* New York Post *(reprinted by permission*
> *of the* New York Post; © *1981, New Group Publi-*
> *cations, Inc.), April 3, 1981 (and reprinted in* New
> York Theatre Critics' Reviews, *Vol. XXXXII, No. 7,*
> *April 16, 1981, pp. 298-99).*

ADDITIONAL BIBLIOGRAPHY

Bentson, Alice N. "From Naturalism to *The Dream Play:* A Study of the Evolution of Strindberg's Unique Theatrical Form." *Modern Drama* 7, No. 4 (February 1965): 383-98.
  Traces the development of Strindberg's theatrical techniques and devices.

Björkman, Edwin. "August Strindberg: His Achievement." *The Forum* XLVII, No. 3 (March 1912): 274-88.
  Surveys the major works from Strindberg's romantic, naturalistic, and expressionistic periods.

Brandell, Gunnar. *Strindberg in Inferno.* Translated by Barry Jacobs. Cambridge: Harvard University Press, 1974, 336 p.
  Analysis of the Inferno Crisis. Brandell discusses the causes of Strindberg's breakdown, the crisis itself, and the literary style that emerged as a result.

Johannesson, Eric O. *The Novels of August Strindberg: A Study in Theme and Structure.* Berkeley, Los Angeles: University of California Press, 1968, 317 p.
  Describes Strindberg as a "psychological novelist" and demonstrates how all of his novels explore the self and the forces that condition it.

Johnson, Walter. *Strindberg and the Historical Drama.* Seattle: University of Washington Press, 1963, 326 p.
  A study of the historical dramas, particularly those written after the Inferno Crisis.

Lamm, Martin. *August Strindberg.* Edited and translated by Henry G. Carlson. New York: Benjamin Blom, 1971, 561 p.
  Definitive biographical and critical study. This volume treats the entire range of Strindberg's literature from a biographical perspective.

Lucas, F. L. "Strindberg." In his *The Drama of Ibsen and Strindberg,* pp. 303-463. New York: The Macmillan Co., 1962.
>   Vitriolic criticism of Strindberg and his plays. Lucas views the playwright as a "pathetic eccentric" whose "gifts of style and imagination . . . are cheated of real excellence by his warped and poisoned personality."

Madsen, Børge Gedsø. *Strindberg's Naturalistic Theatre: Its Relation to French Naturalism.* Seattle: University of Washington Press, 1962, 192 p.
>   Scholarly assessment of the influence of French naturalism and contemporary psychological theory on Strindberg's plays of the 1880s and 1890s.

McGill, V. J. *August Strindberg: The Bedeviled Viking.* 1930. Reprint. New York: Russell & Russell, 1965, 459 p.
>   Biography focusing on the first half of Strindberg's life. McGill quotes extensively from the author's autobiographical novels, particularly *The Confession of a Fool.*

Modern Drama 5, No. 3 (December 1962): 256-379.
>   Special issue devoted to Strindberg containing reminiscences, criticism, and a bibliography.

O'Neill, Eugene. "Strindberg and Our Theatre." In *O'Neill and His Plays: Four Decades of Criticism,* edited by Oscar Cargill, N. Bryllion Fagin, and William J. Fisher, pp. 108-09. New York: New York University Press, 1961.
>   Assesses Strindberg's importance as a world dramatist, finding that he "remains among the most modern of moderns, the greatest interpreter in the theater of the characteristic spiritual conflicts which constitute the drama—our blood—today."

Algernon Charles Swinburne

1837-1909

(Also wrote under pseudonym of Mrs. Horace Manners) English poet, dramatist, critic, essayist, and novelist.

Swinburne was renowned during his lifetime for his skill and technical mastery as a lyric poet, and he is remembered today as a preeminent symbol of rebellion against the Victorian age. The explicitly handled sensual themes in his *Poems and Ballads* delighted some, shocked many, and led Robert Buchanan to mention Swinburne in his 1866 condemnation of Charles Baudelaire and "the fleshly school of poetry." To focus on what is sensational in Swinburne, however, is to miss the assertion, implicit in his poetry and explicit in his critical writings, that in a time when poets were expected to reflect and uphold contemporary morality, Swinburne's only vocation was to express beauty.

Born into an old and wealthy Northumbrian family, Swinburne was educated at Eton and at Balliol College, Oxford, but took no degree. While at Oxford, he became friends with William Michael and Dante Gabriel Rossetti, as well as others of the pre-Raphaelite circle, later attempting a communal household arrangement with some of them. During his most productive years as a writer, Swinburne kept erratic hours and was generally believed to be an habitual patron of London's flagellation brothels. He frequently drank to excess, until physical collapse necessitated his removal to his parents' home. By 1879 his health was dangerously poor. At this point, his friend and literary agent, Theodore Watts-Dunton, isolated him at a suburban estate at Putney and gradually weaned him away from alcohol—and from his former companions and habits as well. Swinburne lived another thirty years with Watts-Dunton, whose role remains a controversial one. He did deny Swinburne's friends access to him, controlled the poet's money, and rigidly restricted his behavior. On the other hand, Swinburne, possibly suffering from premature senility, would undoubtedly have died within a few years without Watts-Dunton's intervention. French critic Georges Lafourcade is the first of Swinburne's biographers to defend Watts-Dunton, pointing out that he both encouraged the poet to continue writing and provided him "ample time and opportunities for revising, explaining and supplementing what he had written."

Throughout his career, Swinburne produced works of varied types but of a consistently high technical quality. Critics, even when taking violent exception to his subject matter, note his intricately extended and evocative imagery, his metrical virtuosity, rich use of assonance and alliteration, and his bold, complex rhythms. After publishing two verse dramas, *The Queen-Mother and Rosamond,* which were largely ignored, Swinburne had his first success with *Atalanta in Calydon,* presenting his own tragic vision in the form of classic Greek tragedy. Swinburne's lyrical gift is especially evident in the original use he makes of the chorus, which in *Atalanta in Calydon* does not supply narration as it does in the plays of Aeschylus, but provides "a vast lyric cry" to supplement the action. A second drama in the Greek mold, *Erechtheus,* received almost exclusively favorable reviews, though it was not as popular with readers as *Atalanta.* Swinburne's lifelong love of Elizabethan and Jacobean drama prompted him to write critical essays on

Shakespeare, Marlowe, and Jonson, as well as a trilogy of verse dramas—*Chastelard, Bothwell,* and *Mary Stuart*—on the life of Mary Queen of Scots.

The pre-Raphaelites stimulated in Swinburne an interest in medievalism, evident in *Poems and Ballads*. Critics have also suggested that Swinburne's lubricious verses echo in words the lush sensuousness of Dante Gabriel Rossetti's paintings. *Poems and Ballads* was at first condemned by most critics, who chose to focus on "Anactoria," "Dolores," "Laus Veneris," and "The Leper," poems which glorify the senses or treat explicitly Swinburne's fascination with violent or perverse forms of sex. Swinburne's admirers were attracted to the same poems, pointing up the "curious fact" noted by Alfred Noyes, that "the most ardent appreciation of Swinburne has usually come from the decadent, or from those who mistook his faults for his merits." Once critics turn from the content to the form of the *Poems and Ballads,* there is greater accord. They acknowledge Swinburne's technical artistry, yet admit his faults. The strong rhythms of his poems often lead the reader into a singsong chant devoid of meaning, and the poet sometimes carried his almost trademark use of alliteration to extremes. His usually effective imagery could at times become vague and imprecise, and his rhymes are, for the most part, facile but uninspired. Like many nineteenth-century poets, Swinburne became involved in political ventures. He greatly admired Giuseppe Mazzini, a leader of the Risorgimento, the movement for Italian political unity. Swinburne dedicated *A Song of Italy* to Mazzini, who urged him to write the militantly republican *Songs Before Sunrise.*

In addition to his poetry and dramas, Swinburne also published one novel, *Love's Cross-Currents,* and left another, *Lesbia Brandon,* unfinished at his death. The first, written in epistolary form, has been compared in style to the novels of William Thackeray. *Lesbia Brandon* contains themes found in the *Poems and Ballads,* and also reveals Swinburne's predilection for flagellation. Some critics have theorized that *Lesbia Brandon* was intended to be thinly disguised autobiography; however, its fragmentary form resists any sure interpretation.

Swinburne's work is limited in scope; his themes are few, and his skills did not develop noticeably throughout his career. His literary output suggested to John D. Rosenberg "a single note . . . struck early and held obsessively long." Yet within his limitations, Swinburne's achievements as a lyric poet are great.

PRINCIPAL WORKS

The Queen-Mother and Rosamond (dramas) 1860
Atalanta in Calydon (drama) 1865
Chastelard (drama) 1865
Notes on Poems and Reviews (criticism) 1866
Poems and Ballads (poetry) 1866; also published as *Laus Veneris, and Other Poems and Ballads,* 1866
A Song of Italy (poetry) 1867
Songs Before Sunrise (poetry) 1871
Under the Microscope (essay) 1872
Bothwell (drama) 1874
Essays and Studies (criticism) 1875
Songs of Two Nations (poetry) 1875
Erechtheus (drama) 1876
Poems and Ballads: Second Series (poetry) 1878
Mary Stuart (drama) 1881
Tristram of Lyonesse (poetry) 1882
Marino Faliero (drama) 1885
Locrine (drama) 1887
Poems and Ballads: Third Series (poetry) 1889
The Sisters (drama) 1892
Rosamond, Queen of the Lombards (drama) 1899
A Channel Passage, and Other Poems (poetry) 1904
Love's Cross-Currents (novel) 1905
The Duke of Gandia (drama) 1908
Contemporaries of Shakespeare (criticism) 1919
The Complete Works of Algernon Charles Swinburne. 20 vols. (poetry, dramas, novel, essays, criticism, letters) 1925-27
Lesbia Brandon (unfinished novel) 1952

ALFRED TENNYSON   (essay date 1858)

Accept my congratulations on the success of your Greek play [*Atalanta in Calydon*]. I had some strong objections to parts of it, but these I think have been modified by a re-perusal, and at any rate I daresay you would not care to hear them; here however is one. Is it *fair* for a Greek chorus to abuse the Deity something in the *style* of the Hebrew prophets?

Altogether it is many a long day since I have read anything so fine; for it is not only carefully written, but it has both strength and splendour, and shows moreover that you have a fine metrical invention which I envy you. (p. 112)

> *Alfred Tennyson, " 'Orbiter Dicta' by Contemporary Men of Letters: Alfred Tennyson'' (1858; originally published under a different title in* Alfred Lord Tennyson: A Memoir by His Son *by Hallam Tennyson, Macmillan & Co., Ltd., 1897), in* Swinburne: The Critical Heritage, *edited by Clyde K. Hyder, Barnes & Noble, Inc., 1970, pp. 112-14.*

THE SPECTATOR   (essay date 1861)

We cannot say so much of the two dramas entitled, **The Queen Mother and Rosamond.** We have with some difficulty read through them. Mr. Swinburne has chosen two painful subjects, the Massacre of St. Bartholomew and the Murder of Rosamond Clifford by Queen Eleanor. He has some literary talent, but it is decidedly not of a poetical kind. His 'thoughts are combinations of disjointed things'—and the language in which these thoughts are expressed is painfully distorted, vague, elliptical, and bristling with harsh words. Honey and rosewater verses are, we imagine, what Mr. Swinburne holds to be quite wrong in poetry; but he has mistaken reverse of wrong for right. In feeling and in thought, the daring, the disagreeable, and the violent, are in these dramas, substituted for boldness, beauty, and strength. We do not believe any criticism will help to improve Mr. Swinburne. He writes, as we believe, upon a strongly rooted bad principle. He will not, by such dramas, convince the world that it has always been wrong about poetical beauty, and that he has come to set us right. Mr. Swinburne is a man of education,—at least, we infer this from some indications in his dramas. They are fashioned on no conventional model.

> *"Unsigned Notice in 'Spectator' 1861'' (originally published under a different title in* The Spectator, *Vol. XXXIV, No. 42, January 12, 1861), in* Swinburne: The Critical Heritage, *edited by Clyde K. Hyder, Barnes & Noble, Inc., 1970, p. 1.*

ROBERT BUCHANAN   (essay date 1866)

Mr. Swinburne commenced his literary career with considerable brilliance. His **Atalanta in Calydon** evinced noticeable gifts of word-painting and of music; and his **Chastelard,** though written in monotone, contained several passages of dramatic force and power. In the latter work, however, there was too open a proclivity to that garish land beyond the region of pure thinking, whither so many inferior writers have been lured for their destruction. . . . The genuineness of the work as Art, we would suggest, can be the only absolute test of immorality in a story or poem. Truly sincere writing, no matter how forcible, seldom really offends us. When, however, we find a writer like the author of these **Poems and Ballads,** who is deliberately and impertinently insincere as an artist,—who has no splendid individual emotions to reveal and is unclean for the mere sake of uncleanness,—we may safely affirm, in the face of many pages of brilliant writing, that such a man is either no poet at all, or a poet degraded from his high estate, and utterly and miserably lost to the Muses. How old is this young gentleman, whose bosom, it appears, is a flaming fire, whose face is as the fiery foam of flowers, and whose words are as the honeyed kisses of the Shunamite? He is quite the Absalom of modern bards,—long-ringleted, flippant-lipped, down-cheeked, amorous-lidded. He seems, moreover, to have prematurely attained to the fate of his old prototype; for we now find him fixed very fast indeed up a tree, and it will be a miracle if one breath of poetic life remain in him when he is cut down. . . . Yet ere we go further, let us at once disappoint Mr. Swinburne, who would doubtless be charmed if we averred that his poems were capable of having an absolutely immoral influence. They are too juvenile and unreal for that. The strong pulse of true passion beats in no one of them. They are unclean, with little power; and mere uncleanness repulses. (pp. 30-1)

[All] the images are false and distracted,—mere dabs of colour distributed carelessly and without art. . . .

It would be idle to quote such prurient trash . . .—save for the purpose of observing that Mr. Swinburne's thought is on a fair level with his style of expression:—both are untrue, insincere, and therefore unpoetical. Absolute passion there is none; elaborate attempts at thick colouring supply the place of passion. Now, it may be fairly assumed that a writer so hopelessly blind to the simplest decencies of style, so regardless of the first principles of Art, can scarcely fail to offend if he attempt to discuss topics of importance to his fellow creatures, or deal with themes which demand the slightest exercise of thought properly so called. When, therefore, Mr. Swinburne touches on religious questions, he writes such verses as the subjoined which, though put into the mouth of a Roman, are purely personal, implying precisely the same conditions of thought as we find expressed in the lyrical poems elsewhere:—

> Wilt thou yet take all, Galilean? but these thou shalt not take,
> The laurel, the palms and the paean, the breasts of the nymphs in the brake;. . .
>
> (p. 32)

Here, as in the other poems, we find no token of sincerity. It is quite obvious that Mr. Swinburne has never thought at all on religious questions, but imagines that rank blasphemy will be esteemed very clever. He describes the Almighty as *throwing dice* with the Devil for the soul of Faustine. . . . (p. 33)

Gross insincerity in dealing with simple subjects, and rank raving on serious themes, make one suspicious of a writer's quality in all things; and a very little examination enables us to perceive that these poems are essentially imitative. Indeed, Mr. Swinburne's knack of parody is very remarkable, though it weighs heavily against his literary quality. Nothing could be cleverer than his imitation, here printed, of an old miracle-play; or than his numerous copies of the French lyric writers; or than his ingenious parrotings of the way of Mr. Browning. In no single instance does he free himself from the style of the copyist. His skill in transferring an old or modern master would be an enviable gift for any writer but one who hoped to prove himself a poet. Then again, though clever and whimsical to the last degree, he is satisfied with most simple effects. After a little while we find out there is a trick in his very versification, that it owes its music to the most extraordinary style of alliteration. . . . This kind of writing, abounding in adjectives chosen merely because they alliterate, soon cloys and sickens; directly we find out the trick our pleasure departs. We soon perceive also that Mr. Swinburne's pictures are bright and worthless. We detect no real taste for colour; the skies are all Prussian blue, the flesh-tints all vermilion, the sunlights all gamboge. The writer, who has no meditative faculty, evinces total ignorance of nature; his eye rolls like that of a drunkard, whose vision is clouded with fumes. (pp. 33-4)

Robert Buchanan, "Robert Buchanan in 'Athenaeum' 1866" (originally published under a different title in *The Athenaeum, No. 2023, August 4, 1866*), in *Swinburne: The Critical Heritage*, edited by Clyde K. Hyder, Barnes & Noble, Inc., 1970, pp. 30-5.

ALGERNON CHARLES SWINBURNE (essay date 1866)

Certain poems of mine, it appears, have been impugned by judges, with or without a name, as indecent or as blasphemous. To me, as I have intimated, their verdict is a matter of infinite indifference: it is of equally small moment to me whether in such eyes as theirs I appear moral or immoral, Christian or pagan. But, remembering that science must not scorn to investigate animalcules and infusoria, I am ready for once to play the anatomist.

With regard to any opinion implied or expressed throughout [*Poems and Ballads*], I desire that one thing should be remembered: the book is dramatic, many-faced, multifarious; and no utterance of enjoyment or despair, belief or unbelief, can properly be assumed as the assertion of its author's personal feeling or faith. Were each poem to be accepted as the deliberate outcome and result of the writer's conviction, not mine alone but most other men's verses would leave nothing behind them but a sense of cloudy chaos and suicidal contradiction. Byron and Shelley, speaking in their own persons, and with what sublime effect we know, openly and insultingly mocked and reviled what the English of their day held most sacred. I have not done this. I do not say that, if I chose, I would not do so to the best of my power; I do say that hitherto I have seen fit to do nothing of the kind.

It remains then to inquire what in that book can be reasonably offensive to the English reader. (p. 326)

I am informed, and have not cared to verify the assertion, that [*Anactoria*] has excited, among the chaste and candid critics of the day or hour or minute, a more vehement reprobation, a more virtuous horror, a more passionate appeal, than any other of my writing. Proud and glad as I must be of this distinction, I must yet, however reluctantly, inquire what merit or demerit has incurred such unexpected honour. I was not ambitious of it; I am not ashamed of it; but I am overcome by it. . . .

What my poem means, if any reader should want that explained, I am ready to explain, though perplexed by the hint that explanation may be required. What certain reviewers have imagined it to imply, I am incompetent to explain, and unwilling to imagine. I am evidently not virtuous enough to understand them. I thank Heaven that I am not. *Ma corruption rougirait de leur pudeur*. ['My depravity would blush at their modesty.'] (p. 327)

In this poem I have simply expressed, or tried to express, that violence of affection between one and another which hardens into rage and deepens into despair. The keynote which I have here touched was struck long since by Sappho. (p. 328)

[But] the descent is immeasurable from Sappho's verse to mine, or to any man's. I have striven to cast my spirit into the mould of hers, to express and represent not the poem but the poet. I did not think it requisite to disfigure the page with a footnote wherever I had fallen back upon the original text. Here and there, I need not say, I have rendered into English the very words of Sappho. I have tried also to work into words of my own some expression of their effect: to bear witness how, more than any other's, her verses strike and sting the memory in lonely places, or at sea, among all loftier sights and sounds—how they seem akin to fire and air, being themselves 'all air and fire'; other element there is none in them. As to the angry appeal against the supreme mystery of oppressive heaven, which I have ventured to put into her mouth at that point only where pleasure culminates in pain, affection in anger, and desire in despair—as to the 'blasphemies' against God or Gods of which here and elsewhere I stand accused—they are to be taken as the first outcome or outburst of foiled and fruitless passion recoiling on itself. After this, the spirit finds time to breathe and repose above all vexed senses of the weary body, all bitter labours of the revolted soul; the poet's pride of place is resumed, the lofty conscience of invincible immortality in the memories and the mouths of men. (pp. 329-30)

Next on the list of accusation stands the poem of *Dolores*. The gist and bearing of this I should have thought evident enough, viewed by the light of others which precede and follow it. I have striven here to express that transient state of spirit through which a man may be supposed to pass, foiled in love and weary of loving, but not yet in sight of rest; seeking refuge in those 'violent delights' which 'have violent ends,' in fierce and frank sensualities which at least profess to be no more than they are. This poem, like *Faustine,* is so distinctly symbolic and fanciful that it cannot justly be amenable to judgment as a study in the school of realism. (pp. 330-31)

The insight into evil of chaste and critical pressmen, their sharp scent for possible or impossible impurities, their delicate ear for a sound or a whisper of wrong—all this knowledge 'is too wonderful and excellent for me; I cannot attain unto it.'. . . I have overlooked the evidence which every day makes clearer, that our time has room only for such as are content to write for children and girls. But this oversight is the sum of my offence.

It would seem indeed as though to publish a book were equivalent to thrusting it with violence into the hands of every mother and nurse in the kingdom as fit and necessary food for female infancy. Happily there is no fear that the supply of milk for babes will fall short of the demand for some time yet. There are moral milkmen enough, in all conscience, crying their ware about the streets and byways, fresh or stale, sour or sweet, the requisite fluid runs from a sufficiently copious issue. In due time, perhaps, the critical doctors may prescribe a stronger diet for their hypochondriac patient, the reading world; or the gigantic *malade imaginaire* called the public may rebel against the weekly draught or the daily drug of MM. Purgon and Diafoirus [in Molière's *Le malade imaginaire*]. We, meanwhile, who profess to deal neither in poison nor in pap, may not unwillingly stand aside. Let those read who will, and let those who will abstain from reading. *Caveat emptor.* No one wishes to force men's food down the throats of babes and sucklings. The verses last analysed were assuredly written with no moral or immoral design; but the upshot seems to me moral rather than immoral, if it must needs be one or the other, and if (which I cannot be sure of) I construe aright those somewhat misty and changeable terms. (pp. 332-33)

To all this, however, there is a grave side. The question at issue is wider than any between a single writer and his critics, or it might well be allowed to drop. It is this: whether or not the first and last requisite of art is to give no offence; whether or not all that cannot be lisped in the nursery or fingered in the schoolroom is therefore to be cast out of the library; whether or not the domestic circle is to be for all men and writers the outer limit and extreme horizon of their world of work. For to

this we have come; and all students of art must face the matter as it stands. (p. 338)

Algernon Charles Swinburne, "Notes on Poems and Reviews" (1866), in his The Poems of Algernon Charles Swinburne, Chatto & Windus, 1904 (and reprinted in Poems and Ballads [and] Atalanta in Calydon, *edited by Morse Peckham, The Bobbs-Merrill Company, Inc., 1970, pp. 325-41).*

JAMES RUSSELL LOWELL   (essay date 1871)

Over **"Chastelard, a Tragedy,"** we need not spend much time. It is at best but the school exercise of a young poet learning to write, and who reproduces in his copy-book, more or less travestied, the copy that has been set for him at the page's head by the authors he most admires. Grace and even force of expression are not wanting, but there is the obscurity which springs from want of definite intention; the characters are vaguely outlined from memory, not drawn firmly from the living and the nude in actual experience of life; the working of passion is an *a priori* abstraction from a scheme in the author's mind; and there is no thought, but only a vehement grasping after thought. The hand is the hand of Swinburne, but the voice is the voice of Browning. With here and there a pure strain of sentiment, a genuine touch of nature, the effect of the whole is unpleasant with the faults of the worst school of modern poetry,—the physically intense school, as we should be inclined to call it. . . . (pp. 211-12)

"Atalanta in Calydon" is in every respect better than its forerunner. It is a true poem, and seldom breaks from the maidenly reserve which should characterize the higher forms of poetry, even in the keenest energy of expression. If the blank verse be a little mannered and stiff, reminding one of [Walter Savage] Landor in his attempts to reproduce the antique, the lyrical parts are lyrical in the highest sense, graceful, flowing, and generally simple in sentiment and phrase. There are some touches of nature in the mother's memories of Althea, so sweetly pathetic that they go as right to the heart as they came from it, and are neither Greek nor English, but broadly human. And yet, when we had read the book through, we felt as if we were leaving a world of shadows, inhabited by less substantial things than that nether realm of Homer where the very eidolon of Achilles is still real to us in its longings and regrets. These are not characters, but outlines after the Elgin marbles in the thinnest manner of [John Flaxman, illustrator of the *Iliad* and the *Odyssey*]. There is not so much blood in the whole of them as would warm the little finger of one of Shakespeare's living and breathing conceptions. (pp. 212-13)

The actors in the drama are unreal and shadowy, the motives which actuate them alien to our modern modes of thought and conceptions of character. (p. 213)

"Atalanta in Calydon" shows that poverty of thought and profusion of imagery which are at once the defect and the compensation of all youthful poetry, even of Shakespeare's. It seems a paradox to say that there can be too much poetry in a poem, and yet this is a fault with which all poets begin, and which some never get over. But **"Atalanta"** is hopefully distinguished, in a rather remarkable way, from most early attempts, by a sense of form and proportion, which, if seconded by a seasonable ripening of other faculties, as we may fairly expect, gives promise of rare achievement hereafter. Mr. Swinburne's power of assimilating style, which is, perhaps, not so auspicious a symptom, strikes us as something marvellous.

The argument of his poem, in its quaint archaism, would not need the change of a word or in the order of a period to have been foisted on Sir Thomas Malory as his own composition. The choosing a theme which Æschylus had handled in one of his lost tragedies is justified by a certain Æschylean flavor in the treatment. The opening, without deserving to be called a mere imitation, recalls that of the "Agamemnon," and the chorus has often an imaginative lift in it, an ethereal charm of phrase, of which it is the highest praise to say that it reminds us of him who soars over the other Greek tragedians like an eagle.

But in spite of many merits, we cannot help asking ourselves, as we close the book, whether **"Atalanta"** can be called a success, and if so, whether it be a success in the right direction. (pp. 215-16)

> *James Russell Lowell, "Swinburne's Tragedies," in his* My Study Windows, *James R. Osgood and Company, 1871, pp. 210-26.*

JOHN ADDINGTON SYMONDS   (essay date 1876)

[In his version of the lost tragedy of *Erechteus* by Euripides, Mr. Swinburne has interwoven] all the fabulous material which gives variety and colour to the legend of Erechtheus. The skill with which he has disengaged the splendid human heroism of Praxithea and Chthonia from this background of intricate and sombre mythology, and has concentrated all the interest of his drama on their two personalities, reserving the other elements of the fable for lyrical treatment in the choruses, for descriptions which produce a sense of relief, and for allusions which deepen the tragic pathos, proves the most consummate mastery of dramatic art. His *Erechtheus* is not a bare imitation of a lost tragedy by Euripides. It *is* a Greek play written in the English tongue, in the creation of which the poet has not merely adopted the forms of the Attic drama, but has thought and felt, selected his chief subject and distributed his subordinate incidents, precisely as a Greek playwright would have done. The harmony of all the parts is perfect. The tone is maintained with unerring tact. Not one word is spoken, not one note is struck, and not one sentiment is suggested which could jar upon the sympathies or tax the intelligence of an ancient Greek. And yet our *Erechtheus* is as living to us now as it would have been to an Athenian. The humanity of the two heroines, in their self-sacrifice and piety and measureless love, is so perfect that no archaisms of scholarship, mythology, and alien superstition can divide them from our affection. (p. 164)

Perhaps the greatest evidence of Mr. Swinburne's genius in this drama is this, that having chosen an essentially classic subject, and having treated it in a rigorously classic style, he has at the same time vitalised it with emotion which, though more antique than modern, still compels our own particular sympathy. In hearing the speech of Athena at the termination of the action, even the modern audience will feel that consolation of the noblest and most spiritual kind is offered, not only to the citizens of Erechtheus and the widowed queen, but also to themselves, because the poet has convinced them that the drama of Athens was the drama of liberty, and that on the fate of Athens hung the fate of civilized humanity. It is for the spiritual citadel of all mankind, the city glorious of thought and freedom, that Chthonia dies; and the promise of Athena is for us the voice of history anticipated. Such is the high and noble theme of Mr. Swinburne's youngest poem. To such al-

titudes, rarely scaled by the feet of poets in the modern age, has he ascended.

It is conceivable that some other poet might have seen the grandeur of the subject of *Erechtheus,* and, in attempting it, might have failed fully to enlist our human sympathies. In the heroines of Euripidean tragedy, for example, there is an element of frigid stoicism which repels our love as much as their self-sacrifice attracts it. This peril Mr. Swinburne, by his vivid realisation of the maternal and filial relations between Praxithea and Chthonia, has not so much avoided as annihilated. The sublimity of self-devotion to the public good can never be called cold or stern, when the patients of this exalted enthusiasm love each other as these do. . . . (pp. 165-66)

Whether general readers will find as much in the lyrical passages of *Erechtheus* to admire, separated from the drama, as they found in *Atalanta,* may perhaps be questioned. The scholar, on the contrary, will recognise in them a still greater fidelity to Greek thought and feeling, a more intimate and organic connexion between their themes and the motives of the drama. There is no competent reader who, after sufficient study of the play, will not agree with us in recognising the sublime beauty of the subject, the faith and purity and reverence which mark its large and deep humanity, and the exquisiteness of its artistic workmanship. *Erechtheus* is, in truth, a masterpiece, considered not merely as a reproduction of classical art, but also as a poem which appeals to men of all nations and of all times. (p. 169)

> *John Addington Symonds, "John Addington Symonds in Academy 1876" (originally published under a different title in* The Academy, *No. 192, January 8, 1876), in* Swinburne: The Critical Heritage, *edited by Clyde K. Hyder, Barnes & Noble, Inc., 1970, pp. 163-70.*

THEODORE WATTS   (essay date 1878)

[*Poems and Ballads: Second Series*] will not disappoint the admirers of Mr. Swinburne's poetry. At least, it will not disappoint those who had the insight to perceive what a vast advance upon *Poems and Ballads* was the *Songs before Sunrise.* In this volume, as in that, there is the same passion for anapaestic and dactyllic rhythms, and the same mastery over them; there is the same lofty aspiration and belief in the high destiny of man, and there is the same equal balance of those forces which we call 'intellectual' against those forces which we ascribe to genius. For, never was there a greater mistake than the common one of supposing that, because Mr. Swinburne is not a concise writer, therefore his intellect lags behind his genius. **'Hertha'**, the **'Hymn of Man'**, and the more daring portions of *Atalanta* showed, to any truly critical mind, that intellectually Mr. Swinburne is second to almost none of his contemporaries. (p. 177)

Mr. Swinburne is the first purely lyrical genius—judging from his work—in the English language. . . . (p. 178)

So dominant with Mr. Swinburne is the delight of lyrical movement, that even in iambics the anapaestic dance *will* come up, as we see in such lines as this, in **'In the Bay'**,—

> For surely, brother and master and lord and king,—

(where, note in passing, that, at once, he passes into the anapaestic liquefaction), and, as is still more obvious in the prologue to [**'Tristram and Iseult'**, and in the **'Sailing of the Swallow'**] . . . , where the anapaestic undulations impart a billowy movement to the lines, which sometimes suggests Homeric hexameters, and sometimes suggests the leap of M. Hugo's verse in the second series of *La Légende des Siècles*. And, again, the blank verse of *Bothwell* is far more lyrical than Fletcher's own.

In testing the amount of intellectual vigour behind the work of any artist, the first thing to ask is, What are the conditions under which an artist works? Having done this in regard to Mr. Swinburne's verse, we, for our part, have come to a conclusion which no amount of popular criticism would drive us from—that, in intellectual agility, and even in intellectual strength, Mr. Swinburne has, among contemporary English poets, no superior, unless it be Mr. Browning.

What we have said upon the relation between the 'dancing movements' and diffuseness is illustrated very forcibly by the opening poem of this volume, **'The Last Oracle'**, where the poet's intellectual strength—while wasting, so to speak, in its struggle with form, as Laocoön's strength wasted in his struggle with the serpent—is as unmistakably apparent as though it were not being wasted at all; perhaps more so.

In iambic movement the finest poem in the volume is the one on [Christopher] Marlowe, called **'In the Bay'**. . . . This is sure to be more admired than **'The Last Oracle'**, but it is not so rare and noticeable a work. The conclusion is especially fine. . . . (pp. 178-79)

That Mr. Swinburne could, before he surrendered himself entirely up to the witchery of anapaests, be concise enough, is rendered apparent by his earliest iambic writing, and especially by the early translations of [François] Villon, which form an interesting feature of this volume. (p. 179)

There is also a translation of one of Victor Hugo's beautiful poems upon children. To translate anything of Victor Hugo's must be a labour of love with Mr. Swinburne, but to render a poem upon children must be a specially grateful task. If a critic should wish to say the gracious thing to Mr. Swinburne, it would be to compare him to Victor Hugo. Such splendid praise has never, perhaps, been lavished by one living poet upon another as the fiery English lyrist has lavished upon the great Frenchman, who is at once fiery lyrist, fiery dramatist, and fiery novelist. . . .

Mr. Swinburne's language,—which, since the chastening labour that produced *Bothwell* is, though undoubtedly needing compression, nearer, at its best, to the great style than any other contemporary Englishman's—is never so lofty and never so Titanic as when he is addressing the Gallic Titan. (p. 180)

[Surely] to a superficial inquiry, nothing can be more paradoxical and anomalous than such a duo of 'mutual admiration' between men, one of whom is the English exponent of the doctrine of *l'art pour l'art*, the other the most notable example of rebellion against that doctrine. . . . (p. 181)

Yet, the moment the inquiry is pursued beyond the surface the anomaly vanishes. It is perceived that the kinship between these two lies much deeper than those superficial similarities, which are obvious to all. It is perceived that, over and above such familiar and obvious points of similarity between them as power of the 'long stroke'—an artless belief in the simplest and most familiar rhythmical effects quite inconceivable in men with such a mastery over those highest effects which, being above 'self-conscious' art, can only come to the inspired singer—such again as a lawless, reckless 'unpacking of the heart', which is mostly poetry, but sometimes rhetoric—it is perceived

that, besides these and many other points of superficial similarity, there is this, that the apostle of the doctrine of *l'art pour l'art* is no true apostle at all, but is just as ethical and just as teleological as M. Hugo himself. They are both 'God-intoxicated men' as much as ever Spinoza was.

That this should not have been seen on the publication of the first series of *Poems and Ballads* is another proof of the condition into which English criticism has sunk—another evidence of that separation between philosophy and *belles lettres* which, since the dominance of the Baconian experimental philosophy in this country, has been widening every year.

This is the truth then; as inevitably as the needle sets to the pole so do all Mr. Swinburne's imaginings and cogitations set towards teleology and the 'painful riddle of the earth'. It obtrudes itself everywhere. Even Sappho, in the very height of her unholy passion, forgets, in Mr. Swinburne's hands, all about Anactoria, and begins to challenge the inscrutable ways of God. In the **'Sailing of the Swallow'** Tristram stops in his love-passages to discourse of pantheism and evolution. And **'Dolores'**—what is that but a wail from the bed of vice?—a Jeremiad on the misery of pleasure? In Mr. Swinburne's poetry teleology and ethical preaching are positively in the way. They are almost more in the way than in M. Hugo's. The latter does grant his readers some respite. Mr. Swinburne, like Shelley, grants almost none. (pp. 181-82)

What, then, is the difference between these two—between M. Hugo and Mr. Swinburne? Simply this, that—while both are in revolt against 'the things that be'—M. Hugo's revolt is against society—against the conventions of man; whereas Mr. Swinburne's revolt—springing as it does from a more subtle, though perhaps less brilliant, intelligence—is against God as a concept of man's. (p. 182)

Mr. Swinburne, with much finer philosophical acuteness than M. Hugo, did need [moral growth], and such a growth is so apparent in him that we consider the second series of *Poems and Ballads* the most striking book—apart from its pricelessness as a body of poetry—that has appeared in England for some years. . . .

Erechtheus lifted him from the rank of fine poets to the rank of great poets. And, notwithstanding the violence of some of the political sonnets, this volume is in no way unworthy of the position he has taken. Moreover, it displays a love of nature such as was not seen in his previous books. (p. 184)

> *Theodore Watts, "Theodore Watts in Athenaeum 1878" (originally published under a different title in* The Athenaeum, *No. 2645, July 6, 1878), in* Swinburne: The Critical Heritage, *edited by Clyde K. Hyder, Barnes & Noble, Inc., 1970, pp. 177-84.*

OSCAR WILDE (essay date 1889)

Mr. Swinburne once set his age on fire by a volume of very perfect and very poisonous poetry. Then he became revolutionary, and pantheistic, and cried out against those who sit in high places both in heaven and on earth. Then he invented Marie Stuart, and laid upon us the heavy burden of "Bothwell." Then he retired to the nursery, and wrote poems about children of a somewhat over-subtle character. He is now extremely patriotic, and manages to combine with his patriotism a strong affection for the Tory party. He has always been a great poet. But he has his limitations, the chief of which is, curiously enough, an entire lack of any sense of limit. His song is nearly always too loud for his subject. His magnificent rhetoric, nowhere more significant than in the volume that now lies before us, conceals rather than reveals. It has been said of him, and with truth, that he is a master of language, but with still greater truth it may be said that Language is his master. Words seem to dominate him. Alliteration tyrannizes over him. Mere sound often becomes his lord. He is so eloquent that whatever he touches becomes unreal. (p. 146)

Verse of this kind may be justly praised for the sustained strength and vigour of its metrical scheme. Its purely technical excellence is extraordinary. But is it more than an oratorical *tour-de-force*? Does it really convey much? Does it charm? Could we return to it again and again with renewed pleasure? We think not. It seems to us empty.

Of course, we must not look to these poems for any revelation of human life. To be at one with the elements seems to be Mr. Swinburne's aim. He seeks to speak with the breath of wind and wave. The roar of the fire is ever in his ears. He puts his clarion to the lips of Spring and bids her blow, and the Earth wakes from her dreams and tells him her secret. He is the first lyric poet who has tried to make an absolute surrender of his own personality, and he has succeeded. We hear the song, but we never know the singer. We never even get near to him. Out of the thunder and splendour of words he himself says nothing. We have often had man's interpretation of Nature; now we have Nature's interpretation of man, and she has curiously little to say. Force and Freedom form her vague message. She deafens us with her clangours.

But Mr. Swinburne is not always riding the whirlwind, and calling out of the depths of the sea. Romantic ballads in Border dialect have not lost their fascination for him, and this last volume contains some very splendid examples of this curious artificial kind of poetry. The amount of pleasure one gets out of dialect is a matter entirely of temperament. To say "mither" instead of "mother" seems to many the acme of romance. There are others who are not quite as ready to believe in the pathos of provincialisms. There is, however, no doubt of Mr. Swinburne's mastery over the form, whether the form be quite legitimate or not. **"The Weary Wedding"** [in *Poems and Ballads: Third Series*] has the concentration and colour of a great drama, and the quaintness of its style lends it something of the power of a grotesque. The ballad of **"The Witch-Mother,"** a medieval Medea who slays her children because her lord is faithless, is worth reading on account of its horrible simplicity. . . . **"The Tyneside Widow,"** and **"A Reiver's Neck-verse,"** are all poems of fine imaginative power, and some of them are terrible in their fierce intensity of passion. There is no danger of English poetry narrowing itself to a form so limited as the romantic ballad in dialect. It is too vital a growth for that. So we may welcome Mr. Swinburne's masterly experiments with the hope that things which are inimitable will not be imitated. . . . Certainly "for song's sake" we should love Mr. Swinburne's work, cannot indeed help loving it, so marvellous a music-maker is he. But what of the soul? For the soul we must go elsewhere. (pp. 147-49)

> Oscar Wilde, "Mr. Swinburne's Last Volume" (originally published as an unsigned essay in Pall Mall Gazette, Vol. XLIX, No. 7574, June 27, 1889), in his The Artist As Critic: Critical Writings of Oscar Wilde, edited by Richard Ellmann (copyright © 1968, 1969 by Richard Ellmann), Random House, 1969 (and reprinted by W. H. Allen, 1970), pp. 146-49.

FRANCIS THOMPSON   (essay date 1904)

A new volume from the one living poet who survives to us out of the great Victorian choir which began with Browning and Tennyson; the one survivor, too, of the poetic movement which centred in Rossetti, and (with Rossetti himself) its greatest figure: this must always be an event of more than common interest. For the sake of the sumptuous music he has long since given us we must needs listen with hushed attention when Mr. Swinburne again breaks silence. [*A Channel Passage, and Other Poems*] is of very respectable size, and contains very various lyrics in many of Mr. Swinburne's well-known modes. There are sea rhapsodies and Nature rhapsodies, political poems and child poems, rondels and sonnets and prologues; there is a dedication, characteristically, at the end instead of the beginning. One prominent feature of the younger and typical Swinburne is absent: we hear no more the voice of passion: the roses and raptures of love are with the snows of yester-year. Nor yet do classical themes engage him now as once they did: he confines himself almost exclusively, indeed, to themes which are the direct suggestion of actuality. Even his sea rhapsodies are labelled with a place. The poems, one might say, are more purely personal and less motived by the sheer desire of artistic beauty.

It is in the rhapsodies already mentioned, especially those on sea or lake, that we find most of the Swinburne we knew of old. Here we meet again the pulse, the rush, the abandonment, the long, leaping line, the lavish profusion of cunning vocabulary. Here, too, there is much of the old ardour, something of the old beauty. **"A Channel Passage,"** for instance, is amazing work, with Mr. Swinburne's stamp throughout. But yet we seem to feel a difference. He has given us such lyrics of oceanic storm before; one remembers **"Les Casquettes."** And we prefer that older work. "Rhapsodies" we have called these poems: and it is the only word. In Mr. Swinburne's handling of such themes there has always been something rhapsodic— an unrestraint, a vehement overflowing of all bounds, an unleashed fury of words, a piling-up of phrase and epithet, an endeavour to get by accumulation of sound, diction, and imagery an effect wild, wasteful, and multitudinous as Nature's own. But in this poem the effect seems overpiled, the excess excessive, the redundance strained till impressiveness is lost through incessant threshing on the wearied nerves. There is, indeed, more than a suggestion of effort, of the poet lashing himself into the desired tempest of emotion. The imagery, too, is no longer always so fresh or various as it used to be: sometimes the splendour is somewhat factitious, while there is no little repetition of what grows to seem stock-imagery. Nevertheless, this and its brethren are the most satisfying poems in the book, despite a tendency to rhetoric; and the metre has all the music and accomplishment of old.

That metric faculty and variety are what never desert Mr. Swinburne throughout the book. He keeps it in the political poems, where, to our mind, rhetoric and invective, reinless and redundant, quite usurp the place of poetry. . . . The patriotic poems, again, are rhetoric—not, we think, of Mr. Swinburne's best. Nor, save in some poems on children, touched with his lighter grace, do the miscellaneous pieces appear to us to reach his true quality. On the whole, despite those still striking echoes of the old impetuous lyric music, this is a volume which will send the reader back to the splendid poetry which Mr. Swinburne has written. We can find in it nothing, for instance, equal to the beautiful **"Nympholept"** of his last miscellaneous volume. (pp. 221-23)

Francis Thompson, "A.C.S.," in The Academy, *Vol. LXVII, No. 1689, September 17, 1904 (and reprinted in his* Literary Criticisms, *edited by Rev. Terrence L. Connolly, S.J., E. P. Dutton and Company Inc., 1948, pp. 221-23).*

EZRA POUND   (essay date 1918)

Swinburne's art is out of fashion. The best imitations of him are by the Germans. The nineties refined upon him, and Kipling has set his 'cello-tunes to the pilly-wink of one banjo.

Swinburne recognized poetry as an art, and as an art of verbal music. Keats had got so far as to see that it need not be the pack-mule of philosophy. Swinburne's actual writing is very often rather distressing, but a deal of his verse is no worse written than Shelley's *Ode to the West Wind*. He habitually makes a fine stanzaic form, writes one or two fine strophes in it, and then continues to pour into the mould strophes of diminishing quality.

His biography is perfectly well written in his work. He is never better than in the *Ballad of Life,* the *Ballad of Death,* and the *Triumph of Time.* To the careful reader this last shows quite clearly that Swinburne was actually broken by a real and not by a feigned emotional catastrophe early in life; of this his later slow decline is a witness. There is a lack of intellect in his work. After the poems in the *Laus Veneris* volume (not particularly the title poem) and the poems of the time when he made his magnificent adaptations from Villon, he had few rallies of force, one of them in *Sienna.*

He neglected the value of words as words, and was intent on their value as sound. His habit of choice grew mechanical, and he himself perceived it and parodied his own systemization.

Moderns more awake to the value of language will read him with increasing annoyance, but I think few men who read him before their faculty for literary criticism is awakened—the faculty for purely literary discrimination as contrasted with melopoeic discrimination—will escape the enthusiasm of his emotions, some of which were indubitably real. At any rate we can, whatever our verbal fastidiousness, be thankful for any man who kept alive some spirit of paganism and of revolt in a papier-maché era, in a time swarming with Longfellows, Mables, Gosses, Harrisons.

After all, the whole of his defects can be summed up in one—that is, inaccurate writing; and this by no means ubiquitous. To quote his magnificent passages is but to point out familiar things in our landsacpe. *Hertha* is fit for professors and young ladies in boarding-school. The two ballads and the *Triumph of Life* are full of sheer imagism, of passages faultless.

No one else has made such music in English, I mean has made his kind of music; and it is a music which will compare with Chaucer's *Hide Absalon thi gilte tresses clere* or with any other maker you like. (pp. 292-93)

He and Browning are the best of the Victorian era; and Browning wrote to a theory of the universe, thereby cutting off a fair half of the moods for expression.

No man who cares for his art can be deaf to the rhythms of Swinburne, deaf to their splendor, deaf also to their bathos. The sound of *Dolores* is in places like that of horses' hoofs being pulled out of mud. The sound in a poem of sleep is so heavy that one can hardly read it aloud, the voice is drawn into a slumber. (I am not sure that this effect is not excessive, and that it does not show the author overshooting his mark; but for all that it shows ability in his craft, and has, whatever one's final opinion, an indisputable value as experiment.) Swinburne's surging and leaping dactyllics had no comparable forerunners in English.

His virtues might be largely dug from the Greeks, and his faults mostly traceable to Victor Hugo. But a perception of the beauties of Greek melopoeia does not constitute a mastery in the creation of similar melopocia. The rhythm-building faculty was in Swinburne, and was perhaps the chief part of his genius. The word-selecting, word-castigating faculty was nearly absent. Unusual and gorgeous words attracted him. His dispraisers say that his vocabulary is one of the smallest at any poet's command, and that he uses the same adjectives to depict either a woman or a sunset. There are times when this last is not, or need not be, *ipso facto* a fault. There is an emotional fusion of the perceptions, and a certain kind of verbal confusion has an emotive value in writing; but this is of all sorts of writing the most dangerous to an author, and the unconscious collapse into this sort of writing has wrecked more poets in our time than perhaps all other faults put together. (pp. 293-94)

It is the literary fashion to write exclusively of Swinburne's defects; and the fashion is perhaps not a bad one, for the public is still, and will presumably remain, indiscriminate. Defects are in Swinburne by the bushelful: the discriminating reader will not be able to overlook them, and need not condone them; neither will he be swept off his feet by detractors. There are in Swinburne fine passages, like fragments of fine marble statues; there are fine transcripts from the Greek:

> A little soul for a little bears up this corpse
> which is man.

And there is, underneath all the writing, a magnificent passion for liberty—a passion dead as mutton in most of his contemporaries, and immeasurably deader than mutton in a people who allow their literature to be blanketed by a Comstock and his successors; for liberty is not merely a catchword of politics, nor a right to shove little slips of paper through a hole. The passion not merely for political, but also for personal, liberty is the bedrock of Swinburne's writing. The sense of tragedy, and of the unreasoning cruelty of the gods, hangs over it. He fell into facile writing, and he accepted a facile compromise for life; but no facile solution for his universe. His unbelief did not desert him. . . . (p. 294)

Ezra Pound, "Swinburne versus his Biographers" (originally published as "Swinburne versus Biographers," in Poetry, *Vol. XI, No. VI, March, 1918), in his* Literary Essays of Ezra Pound, *edited by T.S. Eliot (copyright 1918, 1920, 1935 by Ezra Pound; reprinted by permission of New Directions Publishing Corporation), New Directions, 1954, Faber and Faber, 1954, pp. 290-94.*

T. S. ELIOT   (essay date 1920)

Three conclusions at least issue from the perusal of Swinburne's critical essays: Swinburne had mastered his material, was more inward with the Tudor-Stuart dramatists than any man of pure letters before or since; he is a more reliable guide to them than Hazlitt, Coleridge, or Lamb; and his perception of relative values is almost always correct. Against these merits we may oppose two objections: the style is the prose style of Swinburne, and the content is not, in an exact sense, criticism. The faults of style are, of course, personal; the tumultuous outcry of adjectives, the headstrong rush of undisciplined sentences, are the index to the impatience and perhaps laziness of a disorderly mind. But the style has one positive merit: it allows us to know that Swinburne was writing not to establish a critical reputation, not to instruct a docile public, but as a poet his notes upon poets whom he admired. And whatever our opinion of Swinburne's verse, the notes upon poets by a poet of Swinburne's dimensions must be read with attention and respect.

In saying that Swinburne's essays have the value of notes of an important poet upon important poets, we must place a check upon our expectancy. He read everything, and he read with the single interest in finding literature. (pp. 17-18)

With all his justness of judgment, however, Swinburne is an appreciator and not a critic. In the whole range of literature covered, Swinburne makes hardly more than two judgments which can be reversed or even questioned: one, that [John] Lyly is insignificant as a dramatist, and the other, that [James] Shirley was probably unaffected by [John] Webster. . . . Swinburne's judgment is generally sound, his taste sensitive and discriminating. And we cannot say that his thinking is faulty or perverse—up to the point at which it is thinking. But Swinburne stops thinking just at the moment when we are most zealous to go on. And this arrest, while it does not vitiate his work, makes it an introduction rather than a statement.

We are aware, after the *Contemporaries of Shakespeare* and the *Age of Shakespeare* and the books on Shakespeare and Jonson, that there is something unsatisfactory in the way in which Swinburne was interested in these people; we suspect that his interest was never articulately formulated in his mind or consciously directed to any purpose. As it is, there are to be no conclusions, except that Elizabethan literature is very great, and that you can have pleasure and even ecstasy from it, because a sensitive poetic talent has had the experience. (pp. 19-21)

When it is a matter of pronouncing judgment between two poets, Swinburne is almost unerring. He is certainly right in putting Webster above [Cyril] Tourneur, Tourneur above [John] Ford, and Ford above Shirley. He weighs accurately the good and evil in [John] Fletcher: he perceives the essential theatricality, but his comparison of the *Faithful Shepherdess* with *Comus* is a judgment no word of which can be improved upon. . . . (pp. 21-2)

In the longest and most important essay in the *Contemporaries of Shakespeare,* the essay on [George] Chapman, there are many such sentences of sound judgment forcibly expressed. The essay is the best we have on that great poet. It communicates the sense of dignity and mass which we receive from Chapman. But it also illustrates Swinburne's infirmities. Swinburne was not tormented by the restless desire to penetrate to the heart and marrow of a poet, any more than he was tormented by the desire to render the finest shades of difference and resemblance between several poets. . . . Swinburne's essay would have been all the better if he had applied himself to the solution of problems like this. (pp. 22-3)

He did not apply himself to this sort of problem because this was not the sort of problem that interested him. The author of Swinburne's critical essays is also the author of Swinburne's verse: if you hold the opinion that Swinburne was a very great poet, you can hardly deny him the title of a great critic. There is the same curious mixture of qualities to produce Swinburne's own effect, resulting in the same blur, which only the vigour of the colours fixes. His great merit as a critic is really one

which, like many signal virtues, can be stated so simply as to appear flat. It is that he was sufficiently interested in his subject-matter and knew quite enough about it; and this is a rare combination in English criticism. Our critics are often interested in extracting something from their subject which is not fairly in it. And it is because this elementary virtue is so rare that Swinburne must take a very respectable place as a critic. Critics are often interested—but not quite in the nominal subject, often in something a little beside the point; they are often learned—but not quite to the point either. (Swinburne knew some of the plays almost by heart.) (p. 24)

It is a question of some nicety to decide how much must be read of any particular poet. And it is not a question merely of the size of the poet. There are some poets whose every line has unique value. There are others who can be taken by a few poems universally agreed upon. There are others who need be read only in selections, but what selections are read will not very much matter. Of Swinburne, we should like to have the *Atalanta* entire, and a volume of selections which should certainly contain *The Leper, Laus Veneris* and *The Triumph of Time.* It ought to contain many more, but there is perhaps no other single poem which it would be an error to omit. A student of Swinburne will want to read one of the Stuart plays and dip into *Tristram of Lyonesse.* But almost no one, to-day, will wish to read the whole of Swinburne. It is not because Swinburne is voluminous; certain poets, equally voluminous, must be read entire. The necessity and the difficulty of a selection are due to the peculiar nature of Swinburne's contribution, which, it is hardly too much to say, is of a very different kind from that of any other poet of equal reputation. (p. 144)

We may take it as undisputed that Swinburne did make a contribution; that he did something that had not been done before, and that what he did will not turn out to be a fraud. And from that we may proceed to inquire what Swinburne's contribution was, and why, whatever critical solvents we employ to break down the structure of his verse, this contribution remains. The test is this: agreed that we do not (and I think that the present generation does not) greatly enjoy Swinburne, and agreed that (a more serious condemnation) at one period of our lives we did enjoy him and now no longer enjoy him; nevertheless, the words which we use to state our grounds of dislike or indifference cannot be applied to Swinburne as they can to bad poetry. The words of condemnation are words which express his qualities. You may say "diffuse." But the diffuseness is essential; had Swinburne practised greater concentration his verse would be, not better in the same kind, but a different thing. His diffuseness is one of his glories. That so little material as appears to be employed in *The Triumph of Time* should release such an amazing number of words, requires what there is no reason to call anything but genius. You could not condense *The Triumph of Time.* You could only leave out. And this would destroy the poem; though no one stanza seems essential. Similarly, a considerable quantity—a volume of selections—is necessary to give the quality of Swinburne although there is perhaps no one poem essential in this selection. (p. 145)

If, then, we must be very careful in applying terms of censure, like "diffuse," we must be equally careful of praise. "The beauty of Swinburne's verse is the sound," people say, explaining, "he had little visual imagination." I am inclined to think that the word "beauty" is hardly to be used in connection with Swinburne's verse at all; but in any case the beauty or effect of sound is neither that of music nor that of poetry which can be set to music. There is no reason why verse intended to be sung should not present a sharp visual image or convey an important intellectual meaning, for it supplements the music by another means of affecting the feelings. What we get in Swinburne is an expression by sound, which could not possibly associate itself with music. For what he gives is not images and ideas and music, it is one thing with a curious mixture of suggestions of all three. . . . Now, in Swinburne the meaning and the sound are one thing. He is concerned with the meaning of the word in a peculiar way; he employs, or rather "works," the word's meaning. And this is connected with an interesting fact about his vocabulary: he uses the most general word, because his emotion is never particular, never in direct line of vision, never focused; it is emotion reinforced, not by intensification, but by expansion.

> There lived a singer in France of old
> By the tideless dolorous midland sea.
> In a land of sand and ruin and gold
> There shone one woman, and none but she.

You see that Provence is the merest point of diffusion here. Swinburne defines the place by the most general word, which has for him its own value. "Gold," "ruin," "dolorous": it is not merely the sound that he wants, but the vague associations of idea that the words give him. He has not his eye on a particular place. . . . It is, in fact, the word that gives him the thrill, not the object. When you take to pieces any verse of Swinburne, you find always that the object was not there— only the word. (pp. 146-48)

The world of Swinburne does not depend upon some other world which it simulates; it has the necessary completeness and self-sufficiency for justification and permanence. It is impersonal, and no one else could have made it. The deductions are true to the postulates. It is indestructible. None of the obvious complaints that were or might have been brought to bear upon the first *Poems and Ballads* holds good. The poetry is not morbid, it is not erotic, it is not destructive. These are adjectives which can be applied to the material, the human feelings, which in Swinburne's case do not exist. The morbidity is not of human feeling but of language. Language in a healthy state presents the object, is so close to the object that the two are identified.

They are identified in the verse of Swinburne solely because the object has ceased to exist, because the meaning is merely the hallucination of meaning, because language, uprooted, has adapted itself to an independent life of atmospheric nourishment. In Swinburne, for example, we see the word "weary" flourishing in this way independent of the particular and actual weariness of flesh or spirit. The bad poet dwells partly in a world of objects and partly in a world of words, and he never can get them to fit. Only a man of genius could dwell so exclusively and consistently among words as Swinburne. His language is not, like the language of bad poetry, dead. It is very much alive, with this singular life of its own. (pp. 149-50)

> *T. S. Eliot, "Imperfect Critics" and "Swinburne As Poet," in his* The Sacred Wood: Essays on Poetry and Criticism, *Methuen & Co. Ltd., 1920 (and reprinted by Methuen & Co. Ltd., 1950, pp. 17-24, pp. 144-50).*

ALFRED NOYES (essay date 1924)

All subjects are legitimate to the artist. It is legitimate to paint an Iago; but it is not legitimate to bow down in worship before the infamy, whose every blot and stain the great poet may expose to the candour of the sun. Swinburne did not intend to make Mary Stuart "infamous": he intended to fight for her in song as his fathers fought for her in the field. We have had quite enough of the sham aestheticism which has been attempting to play the amateur Borgia in the English literature of recent years, an aestheticism which has made one of our greatest poets its special pandar, and has no more right to do so than a man would have to issue an edition of *Othello* with a scrofulous frontispiece. There never was a healthier, keener, harder, brighter, more English and open-air muse than this of Swinburne's tragedies. (p. 262)

The consensus of recent opinion seems to be that Swinburne's dramas are hardly worthy of serious consideration; but, on the whole, it is quite as mistaken as the opinion that Tennyson held in his boyhood with regard to Shakespeare. The beauty of a lyric like "O mistress mine, where are you roaming?" makes a more instant appeal to the casual reader than the larger beauty of *Macbeth;* and similarly it is possible that the five hundred closely printed pages of *Bothwell* may, in the eye of indolent readers, have weighty disadvantages as compared with the *Laus Veneris.* But those five hundred pages are written in the same lyrical blank verse as *Phoedra* in *Poems and Ballads;* in the same flawless blank verse as *Atalanta;* and, quite apart from their dramatic value, those tragedies often rise to a lyrical sublimity that is quite their own. Their songs, in French and English, have a dramatic undercurrent of meaning in the moment of their outbreak, in addition to their lyrical beauty. When Mary Stuart, for instance, walks beneath the window of Darnley on the eve of his murder, and sings the exquisite French song that Rizzio had sung to her in an earlier scene, immediately before his assassination by Darnley and his friends, the setting gives it an extraordinary dramatic force. But apart even from considerations like these, the blank verse alone, as in the passage quoted above, has often a lyrical value which places it with the best work of Swinburne. The curiously external and superficial nature of most of the criticisms which take the opposite view leads one to suppose that the chief objection to the five hundred pages of *Bothwell* is the laziness of readers who would probably be unable to lay their hands on their hearts and affirm that they can read or have read *Paradise Lost* itself in more than a very perfunctory fashion. It is an age of selections and little books; but it may safely be said that Swinburne's tragedies are not of an age or twain. They will last as long as the language, though the audience may be few.

Another accusation brought against them, and against *Bothwell* in particular, is that of "verbiage" in the uncomplimentary sense. Now it is true that John Knox sometimes makes a speech of many pages, and Mary Stuart is hardly less eloquent. But it is also true that the thunder-fraught climax and close of *Chastelard,* the crowning tragic utterance, is compressed into the last two lines of the play; two lines that would hardly appeal perhaps to a public nursed on blood and sensational pageants and carpenters' dramas; but nevertheless two of the most truly tragic lines in literature. When the execution of Chastelard is over—it takes place off the stage—the play is closed by the entry of an usher, crying:

> Make way there for the Lord of Bothwell, room,—
> Place for my Lord of Bothwell next the queen.

Similarly in *Bothwell,* amidst many speeches of all lengths, there are some, of very great importance, which consist of a single syllable. When Queen Mary speaks to George Douglas, for instance, on the eve of her flight from Scotland:

Douglas, I have not won a word of you;
What would you do to have me tarry?
George Douglas.   Die.

That is all; and it is quite as typical of Swinburne's method as
his longer speeches are. He is often very much longer than
other poets. He is often very much more concise than other
poets. The fact that the former characteristic is necessarily the
more obvious must not prevent recognition of the latter. Nor
is it true to say—as it is so often said with parrot-like insistence—that he is carried away on the wings of his music. There
never was a poet who was so consciously the master of an art
as Swinburne. His metrical gift is not essentially the gift of
music in words. The two things are quite distinct. (pp. 263-
65)

Swinburne is *not* the musician he is so often accused of
being. . . . His lines are often full of sibilants and hiss like
snakes: they are curiously monosyllabic, and sometimes they
suggest a sort of elemental language. They are welded inextricably into a perfect and artistic unity; but they are *welded.*
That is the only word to describe them. Of all their thousands,
there is not one line in which any flaw could be discovered,
not one line which errs from the laws of his art; but they are
the work of a master of metre rather than the work of a master
of music. In this he is almost exactly the opposite of Shelley,
whose lines are often "careless ordered," yet always, or almost
always, music incarnate. Swinburne, in his dramas especially,
gives one the idea of a man who grips his subject so hard as
to break it up into its component parts. The intensity of his
passion melts and resolves the world into its elements, and this
is what the critics have mistaken for "verbiage." (pp. 265-
66)

In considering these poems as dramas, *Chastelard,* the first of
the Scottish trilogy, must be regarded as the most successful.
It is flawless both as a poem and as a play. The concentrated
dramatic suggestiveness of almost every sentence is extraordinary. (pp. 266-67)

The play ends, as I noted above, with the dramatic crying of
the herald, "Place for my Lord of Bothwell," and the first
two acts of the second part of the trilogy [*Bothwell*] are occupied
with the growth of Bothwell's mastery over the Queen. Perhaps
the most marvellous feature of these two acts is the character-
study of Darnley, his vanity, his cowardice, his boyishly boast-
ful simplicity. The scene in which he "talks down to" the
subtle-souled Queen, after the success of his plot to murder
her friend Rizzio, is a masterpiece of art; and the way in which
he is gradually snared in her toils till even he feels the approaching shadow of death is second to nothing in our literature
since the Elizabethans. (p. 268)

[In] passing, it may be noted that this great master never strives
after the "mighty line," though he has written some of the
mightiest. There is here no din of gong and cymbal, no libretto-
like opportunity for pageant. His lines are not independent of
one another. All is continuity, "the long, slow slope and vast
curves of the gradual violin." In short, his work is organic
literature. (pp. 269-70)

I spoke of Swinburne's consistent exaltation of thought. Paradoxical as it may seem to his following of amateur Borgias,
and whatever his detractors may say, that is his chief characteristic, an extraordinary moral elevation. His lines appear
sometimes to have been passed through white-hot purgatorial
furnaces. Their passion has the chastity of a burning fire. All
that is of the earth earthy has been burnt out like dross. (p. 270)

> *Alfred Noyes, "Swinburne's Tragedies," in his* Some
> Aspects of Modern Poetry *(copyright, 1924, by Fred-
> erick A. Stokes Company; copyright renewed © 1952
> by Alfred Noyes; reprinted by permission of the Lit-
> erary Estate of Alfred Noyes), Stokes, 1924, pp. 261-
> 74.*

T. EARLE WELBY (essay date 1926)

As a dramatist, Swinburne "wrote for antiquity." With his
very uncertain feeling for the public, he would have come no
nearer to satisfying it if he had striven to write for the contemporary stage, in which he took no interest. . . . For one type
of mind, the dramatic pretensions of Swinburne are at once
and completely discounted by the fact that his are not acting
plays. To me, if I may venture to say so, the description of
his tragedies as closet-drama is not finally decisive of his claims.
The poetical drama that cannot be produced on the modern
stage is not necessarily an illegitimate thing. The question is
whether the form is justified by the results, whether something
of emotional and imaginative worth has been produced which
could not have been brought into existence by the adoption of
any other form.

There are dramatic poets who can compromise with stage requirements, with more or less of gain in some respects, more
or less of loss in others: there are others with whom compromise
must mean total loss. Swinburne had but little of the power,
proper to the pure novelist, the pure dramatist, of solving a
human problem in action. He had, within certain limits, a real
feeling for character, and he had an extraordinary sense of
historical and emotional atmosphere, with a rare eloquence in
the expression of erotic and of patriotic passion. To complain
of him that he did not, in quest of a merit to which he could
not have attained, sacrifice all the opportunities he secured by
ignoring the conditions of the contemporary stage is surely
foolish. *The Queen Mother, Chastelard, Bothwell, Marino Faliero,* and, apart from these, the singularly charming *Locrine,*
are works of art in which we have presented to us certain vivid
characters in an appropriate atmosphere. It is reasonable, it is
necessary, to say that in no one of these do we feel that curiosity
about the progress of events, that suspense, that profound final
satisfaction which the complete dramatist gives us. But each
offers us character, atmosphere, the expression of passion, and
in no form other than that which he has used could the poet
have given us these. We may not be at the centre of that world
in which the complete dramatist works, but assuredly we are
not merely in the province of the writer of dramatic soliloquy.
In each of the plays there are effects of contrast and co-operation; the persons influence each other powerfully; the picture
unrolled before us is not one in which we may be content to
note one figure at a time without heed to the significant grouping. *Bothwell,* indeed, owes much of its effect to the host of
personages who contribute to the tragedy, not knowing what
the remote consequences of their words and gestures will be.
The conclusion of *Mary Stuart* throws back, in the finest of
Swinburne's dramatic inventions, to the sin against love in
Chastelard, and the Queen dies in expiation. There is construction in these plays, which, in truth, though this is forgotten in
the now general contempt heaped on all quasi-Elizabethan drama,
are protests against the lax exercises in what was then supposed
to be the Elizabethan form or an improvement on it. . . . Exuberant, as much as Swinburne's own dramatic work may be,

it is ordered, and the vastness of *Bothwell* comes not of digression but of an extreme, possibly excessive, anxiety to do justice to every part of an enormous subject.

In the tragedies, and that is one of the reasons why they should receive more attention from the student of Swinburne, there is visible a development which continued to the end of his life. As a lyrist he wrote very little after 1875, and scarcely anything after 1881, which express new interests or a modification of technical ambitions; as a dramatic poet he was still evolving when he died. I do not profess that his progress as a writer of tragedy was of any startling kind, that it involved any sudden and violent break with his past, or that it has extraordinary intrinsic importance. But, having regard to the general stiffening and setting of his mind in early middle age, it does concern us to note that in this one department of his imaginative activity there was progress. (pp. 192-94)

[His first play,] *Rosamund,* with a substratum of Elizabethan drama, is superficially Pre-Raphaelite, echoing Rossetti, touched here and there by the influence of Browning. There are charming verses in it, and already there is a feeling for atmosphere, but its persons are exhibited, with some delicate distortion, as on a tapestry or canvas, in graceful languor, decoratively, without appreciation of the angularities of character, and without energy. *The Queen Mother* . . . is quite another affair. With still more feeling for atmosphere, it has a real hold on character; the speeches of Catherine are personal; pungency has come into the writing, with vigour; and the verse, which in *Rosamund* wandered down every tempting garden-path, is resolutely shaped, with a constriction it was seldom to have afterwards. No doubt the writer is still, in some ways, a disciple. There is the general Elizabethan temper, there are the careful reminiscences of Shakespeare and of George Chapman, with some recollections of his newly discovered hero, Wells. But this is the work of a man with an imagination of his own and an independent ambition.

In *Chastelard,* the product of immense labour, but in its final form so swift and song-like, there is achievement. No tragedy of Swinburne's is easier to read or more definite in effect. One thing only, but effectually, prevents it from being generally enjoyed as no other of his tragedies ever could be: the nature of its emotional content. Expressing so ardently a passion for passion which but few can share, reviving with such subtle sympathy the fantastic and fanatical devotion characteristic of the persons and the period with which it deals, it is too far removed at once from the modern mind and the usual English conception of love to find general favour. Yet to us, some few of us, to the present writer, at any rate, it is a peculiar treasure. We may, and in our seriously critical moods we must, admit that it is the masterpiece not of a broadly human poet but of a specialist in a particular, doubtless both exceptional and perilous, kind of emotion; but the union in it of luxury and energy, the swiftness with which it moves for all its exuberance, the art with which, for all the variablity of mood, its beautiful monotony is preserved, delight us long after we have lost instinctive sympathy with such cries of the youthful as ''happy days or else to die'' and of the connoisseur of life as *qualis artifex pereo*. And it is not only a lovely, exciting poem; it is, in its way, truly a dramatic poem. One aspect at least of Mary Queen of Scots has been seized with complete success; Chastelard, that exquisite and disastrous idolator of love, has been understood, in every nerve of his being; and the poet has been seen and used to the full the opportunities for contrast given by the introduction of Mary and Chastelard and other sophisticated

figures into the Scotland of that time. . . . And there is at least one scene, the last between Mary of Scots and Chastelard, which is in the full sense drama, with its great stroke of irony as she has forboding that she will somehow die sadly and he bids her think how the axe's edge would soften to such a neck.

It is in Chastelard that we become aware of the scholarship which Swinburne brought to his historical tragedies. His knowledge of Mary herself was then incomplete, but the period he already knew to perfection; and, correcting the impression of Swinburne as at that time an irresponsible romantic, it is to be noted that he had studied minutely not only the court whence Mary came, the extravagant culture which Chastelard represented, but also all that was embodied by Knox and hostile to his hero and heroine. Swinburne's recapture of the spirit of the lesser writers about Ronsard in the French lyrics of his own composition which he introduced into the play is not more remarkable, more eloquent in testimony to his power of entering into past modes of feeling, than his recapture of the spirit of the Scotland of that epoch.

With *Bothwell,* probably the most arduous task that any English dramatic poet has ever undertaken, there was at once a great broadening of interest, the assumption of enormously heavier obligations towards a complicated and in part obscure body of historical facts, and the adoption of greater sobriety of style. It is, of course, his chief work as a dramatic poet, stupendous in ambition, unflagging in energy, and it has his greatest scenes. We cannot say of it as a whole that it works steadily upon our curiosity about what is to come, but think of those pages in which apprehension deepens in the doomed Darnley! There is nothing in English drama, except the supreme scene in Marlowe's *Edward II,* which arouses such terror as that portion of the second act of *Bothwell* in which Darnley recognizes the song the Queen is singing, the song which Rizzio sang immediately before his murder. Every circumstance heightens the horror, every line tells, and at last, when Darnley has asked the dreadful, revealing question, ''How do men die?'' and cries out—

> Mary, by Christ whose mother's was your name,
> Slay me not! God, turn off from me that heart!
> Out of her hands, God, God, deliver me!—

the reader comes out of a terrible, convincing nightmare infinitely relieved that the act is at an end. And this vast and magnificent play, unlike most work on a great scale by its author, has things to set in relief against its finest ardours, its most tumultuous passages. There is modulation; there are moments when some deeply involved actor in the tragedy is visited by a doubt of the urgency, even the reality, of the cause to which he is irrevocably pledged. (pp. 194-98)

After *Bothwell, Mary Stuart* may seem somewhat flat. Swinburne himself decidedly over-valued it. . . . That which Swinburne had to do in *Mary Stuart* was extremely difficult; he did it extremely well; and I doubt whether it would be possible to point to any dramatic composition in our literature in which, having much prose matter to handle, the author has so consistently succeeded in transforming it into poetry. But however delightful the sense of difficulties overcome may be to the author, his readers can only say that *Mary Stuart,* on the whole, inspires respect rather than enthusiasm. It is only at its conclusion, in the fine invention whereby Mary is sent to her doom because she fails to recognize Chastelard's song, that the poet gets free from the merciless pressure of history.

Yet in its sobriety *Mary Stuart* is something of a development from its predecessors. *Marino Faliero,* too declamatory, perhaps, though with a really noble rhetoric, has, in its very different way, something of that continuous onward lyrical sweep which *Chastelard* possessed. But more to my purpose, as illustrating the modification of Swinburne's aims in tragedy, are the two late plays, *Rosamund, Queen of the Lombards* and *The Duke of Gandia*. In this *Rosamund,* published when Swinburne was sixty-two, for the first time the bones of the play are allowed to emerge through the poetry. Much is sacrificed that it is difficult not to mourn. The old exuberance has been replaced by a taut, for Swinburne almost naked, way of writing; but the gain in sheer dramatic quality will not be disputed. The curt speeches have in certain instances a beauty that would be perceived even in quotation, but more than the speeches in the earlier plays they tell in their context as they cannot when excerpted. (pp. 198-99)

[In *The Duke of Gandia*] this brevity, with the old art in making blank verse out of monosyllabic words, is carried much farther. It is not merely that there is severe, and even excessive, restraint put on the lyrical and rhetorical impulses of the writer: for the first time, he has learned to make unsaid things terribly eloquent to his readers. It is a very slight piece of work, and it is not, any more than its predecessors were, drama in the full sense, but there is now a strange, baleful power in suggesting the secret heat of hatred, the deadly unuttered thoughts, of the dreadful creatures that front each other, wary and venomous as snakes. (p. 200)

I do not say *The Duke of Gandia* is a great thing, but it is a very extraordinary thing, and that Swinburne should have come to write like this is astonishing. . . .

Locrine and *The Sisters* lie apart from the rest of his tragedies, experiments of very unequal value, the one a most happy, the other an entirely unfortunate exercise of virtuosity. As a piece of literature *The Sisters* is falsely based, showing us Swinburne, of all improbable experiments, striving for realism. (p. 201)

All the same, *The Sisters* is not to be wholly thrust aside. Little as the critic must think of this *tour de force,* in which early nineteenth-century persons talk a conversational, and occasionally slangy, blank verse, it has some value for the biographer, giving us as it does Swinburne's own view of his boyhood. He made, as he pleasantly boasted in private, rather a nice young fellow of the boy he had been, but he did more than that, and there must have been irony in his profession that he was simply reproducing the lineaments of a well-bred, high-spirited young Englishman. For hidden away in *The Sisters,* to be discerned only by those who have been set on the alert by passages in the correspondence and unpublishable writings of Swinburne, are strange things, evidence that, looking back on his boyhood, he saw there a boy destined never to come to full normal manhood. There are traces of a restrained self-pity, traces of a self-knowledge with which Swinburne is seldom credited. He looked back and saw himself in the bloom and brilliance of a wonderful and enchanted youth, but without failing to see what was perverse in himself.

Of *Locrine,* under reproof, I decline to speak critically. Granted that it is not what, from the moment its form, on a hint, it may be supposed, from *Selimus,* was decided upon, it never could have been made, it remains an ingenious and delightful work of art. No doubt, it might be asked whether there is in the substance at this stage or that any absolutely convincing reason why this or that metrical form should be adopted; but how can we wrangle in that spirit over a play in which the most complicated rhymed forms can yield such natural and

happy effects as this, where a child chatters so freely in intricate easy verses:

> That song is hardly even as wise as I—
> Nay, very foolishness it is. To die,
> In March before its life were well on wing,
> Before its time and kindly season—why
> Should spring be sad—before the swallows fly—
> Enough to dream of such a wintry thing?
> Such foolish words were more unmeet for spring,
> Than snow for summer when his heart is high,
> And why should words be foolish when they sing?

Skill and grace and charm are everywhere in this dramatic poem. It is without edge, without profound significance, but for my humble part I should as soon think of assailing [John] Day's happy and lovely *Parliament of Bees* because it does not compete with Marlowe or Webster or Ford as of attacking *Locrine* for not being what it could not have been, a competitor with *Chastelard* or *Bothwell.* (pp. 202-03)

> *T. Earle Welby, in his* A Study of Swinburne *(copyright 1926 by George H. Doran Company; reprinted by permission of Doubleday & Company, Inc.), George H. Doran Company, 1926 (and reprinted by Kennikat Press, Inc., 1968), 289 p.*

F. L. LUCAS (essay date 1940)

In some degree we may apply to all of [Swinburne's poetry] his own words on *Poems and Ballads I.* ''The youngest were born of boy's pastime, The eldest are young.'' His work has indeed the typical defects of youth—want of experience and judgment, of proportion and restraint. It strives and cries; at times it screeches. Having few ideas, it grows monotonous; having little knowledge of the heart, it lacks compassion. Brilliant and hard, it reflects the light of life with a glare like polished brass; with all its music, it is often brass to the ear; it is sometimes, in its taste, brass also to the tongue. There is about Swinburne a touch of the musical infant-prodigy. This immaturity did not escape his elder contemporaries. Tennyson spoke contemptuously of ''Master Swinburne'', Matthew Arnold dubbed him ''a pseudo-Shelley''; Browning described his work as ''a fuzz of words'' and Carlyle (it is said) as ''the miaulings of a delirious cat''. But they were blind if they saw no more in it than that; for the splendour of youth is also there— its fire, its generosity, its passionate high spirits, its racing pulses, its headlong speed. . . . (pp. 171-72)

Still, as time passes, the defects of youthfulness in his poetry seem to me to grow at the expense of the virtues; he wrote best, I feel, when he was really young. The heart of him is in *Atalanta* and *Poems and Ballads;* after thirty, his bloom begins to fade. (p. 172)

In *Poems and Ballads I,* the poet turns his rebellious anger less against the laws of God than against the laws of men, as the outraged Victorians were quick to realize; towards death and destiny his mood is more resigned. Yet it is still the resignation not of middle-age which learns to ignore death, but of youth which half falls in love with it, as at moments Keats had done. So Swinburne too grows dreamily fascinated by the dreamless slumber of the dead. . . . (pp. 174-75)

This passion indeed linked itself in him with that deep-rooted instinct which made him crave to suffer at the hands of what he loved. He had written in *Atalanta* of a devoted son who dies at his own mother's hand, in *Chastelard* of a Queen's lover who forces her to send him to the block; now the Goddess of Death herself became for him, as it were, a mysterious mistress whose cold caress brings peace. (p. 175)

Swinburne stands beside Byron as the poet of eloquence, and of Liberty. There is indeed a distance between them—the distance between Putney and Missolonghi. Byron acted; Swinburne did not. And accordingly Byron's poetry grew better with age; Swinburne's worse. But youthful as Swinburne's poetry essentially is, I believe that a little of the best of it, generations hence, will remain, still, full of youth. (p. 179)

F. L. Lucas, "Swinburne," in his Ten Victorian Poets, *Cambridge at the University Press, 1940 (and reprinted by Archon Books, Hamden, Connecticut, 1966), pp. 161-80.*

C. M. BOWRA (essay date 1949)

Swinburne did not adhere to the form of Greek tragedy with any servile pedantry. *Atalanta in Calydon* is half as long again as the longest Greek play. Swinburne's exuberance needed a wider scope than an ancient tragedian was allowed, and he rightly took it. Though in some ways, notably in the stichomythia or conversations in single complete lines and in his Messengers' speeches, he adheres to the old form, in other ways he breaks away from it. His choral songs have not the formality of their Greek prototypes, and are not usually composed in regular strophes and antistrophes. (p. 224)

Though the form of *Atalanta* is not always or strictly Greek, its subject and spirit are. Swinburne had so absorbed the Greek outlook that he was able to create a tragedy which in almost all essential points would be acceptable to Aeschylus and Sophocles. The tragic outlook which he displays is profoundly and inescapably Greek. Swinburne owes nothing even to Shakespeare in his approach to his subject and his handling of it. His plot is tragic in the most exacting, the most Sophoclean, sense. The harmonious order of life has been disturbed. Artemis, insulted by Oeneus' neglect of her, sends the Calydonian boar to ravage his lands; and to hunt the boar comes Atalanta, with whom Meleager falls in love. So the tragic situation rises with its elements of conflict and infatuation. Meleager kills his uncles when they affront Atalanta, and from this comes the tragic choice. Meleager's mother, Althaea, has to choose between her love for her son and her love for her brothers. In such a choice any decision brings disaster: if she forgives her son, she dishonours her brothers; if she honours her brothers, she must kill her son whom she admires and loves. She decides to kill her son, and this means not only his death but her own, since after his death she cannot endure to live. Swinburne has chosen a plot which contains the most fundamental and most essential elements of Greek tragedy. (pp. 225-26)

In making Althaea come to her decision, Swinburne shows how well he understood the deeper currents of the Greek soul. She is torn between intolerable alternatives, and she decides that loyalty to her brothers is more important than love for her son. In presenting her anguish and her decision, Swinburne makes use of a famous and disputed passage in Sophocles' *Antigone,* where Antigone says that she would not have broken the law for anyone but a brother, not for a son or a husband. Behind this apparently inhuman and sophistical argument lies a deep Greek conviction that identity of blood through common parents is a closer and more binding tie than marriage or motherhood. . . . Swinburne, with his imaginative insight into the

ways of Greek thought and his own profound sense of family ties, was entirely justified in using it. (p. 226)

Though Swinburne follows his Greek models in building his tragedy on a theological or ethical scheme, this does not in any way interfere with the free play of his poetry any more than it would in Aeschylus or Sophocles. The gods may act as they do, but that places no obligation on the poet to make less attractive those characters who fight against the divine will. Just as Sophocles throws his full imaginative power into the creation of Ajax who defies Athene, so Swinburne does his best to make his characters enjoy all the poetry which he can give them. (p. 229)

Greek tragedy demands more than a situation and a crisis. Sooner or later it raises questions about man's relations with the gods and gives to the gods, directly or indirectly, some part in its action. Swinburne was not likely to shirk this obligation. Indeed, it held dangerous attractions for him. His hatred of priests and of organized religion had been strengthened by his recent association with Landor and was one of the most abiding elements in his system of beliefs. The *Atalanta* presented him with a difficult choice. He could either present the Olympian gods and goddesses as creatures of light and beauty as he had presented them in his **"Hymn to Proserpine"** to the detriment of their Christian successors, or he could use them as targets for his own anti-religious ideas. Each alternative must have had its attractions and its disadvantages for him, but on the whole the second prevailed. There are, it is true, moments in *Atalanta* when the vision of Olympian gods infuses the poetry with light and happiness, but they are rare. Individually the gods may appear in attractive guise, but collectively they are harsh and sinister, and we cannot but feel that at times Swinburne's feelings towards them are determined by a theology later than that of Olympus. Vague, anonymous divinities cast their shadows on the action, and their presence is never quite withdrawn. (pp. 229-30)

There are moments in Greek tragedy, even in the devout Sophocles, when in the stress of anguish or despair characters break into denunciations of divine indifference or cruelty. So when Swinburne's characters do the same, he may claim august precedent. . . . This is certainly no more than some characters of Euripides say, and not much more than Sophocles' Jocasta and Philoctetes say in the agony of fear or doubt. But more difficult to justify is the way in which Swinburne uses the Chorus to state views which are beyond dispute his own and not justified by Greek example. It is not surprising that the third song of the Chorus shocked many of Swinburne's contemporaries, and that both Christina Rossetti as a Christian and Bishop Thirlwall as a scholar took exception to the Chorus which denounces

> The supreme evil, God,

and proclaims

> All we are against thee, against thee, O God
> most high.

Greek poetry provides no justification for such outbursts. Perhaps Euripides would have liked to say something of the kind, but he would hardly have been allowed to give such words to a chorus in the theatre of Dionysus. Though Sophocles may say that all the sufferings of Heracles and Deianira come from Zeus, that is not denunciation but acceptance. Swinburne goes much further than a Greek dramatist would have dared, when he extends the license allowed to a single character to the impersonal Chorus which speaks almost with his own lips. His emotions ran away with him, and it is not surprising that he has been criticized.

None the less, these outbursts occur only in one place, and the Chorus itself denies them before the end of the song. Nor have they any real relation to the plan of the poem. (pp. 230-31)

The skill with which Swinburne reproduces Greek ideas would not in itself be enough to create a poem. Indeed, the more faithful a modern poet is to an ancient outlook when he copies its form, the greater is the danger that his work will be no more than a *pastiche*. But *Atalanta* is no *pastiche*. It is poetry which catches even those who know no Greek and are not much interested in Greek ideas. And much of this success comes from the fact that Swinburne was able to put into it some things which he enjoyed in his own experience and not through his admiration for other poets. Most characteristic is the delight which he takes in sky and sea, in wide landscapes and natural forces like sun and wind and rain. In the presence of these Swinburne felt his blood tingle and his senses awaken. It was therefore right that he should introduce them into his poem. When the Chorus sings its first song, it praises the coming of spring and gives voice to the most delightful and most powerful emotions of which Swinburne was capable, his delight in the renewal of life and in the enlarged consciousness which comes with it:

> And time remembered is grief forgotten,
> And frosts are slain and flowers begotten,
> And in green underwood and cover
>   Blossom by blossom the spring begins. . . .

This is the essential voice of Swinburne, lover of wild places, the wind, and the cold.

No less characteristic are those passages where Swinburne writes from the heart about human, especially domestic, affections. His range is not very wide, but within his limits he has a special charm and tenderness. Though in later life he became sentimental when he wrote about children, in *Atalanta* he more than once touches with truth and insight on what childhood means between mother and son or between sister and brother. This is of course necessary to his plot, which turns on the conflict between Althaea's love for her son and love for her brothers, but Swinburne rises to it with noble ease. . . . There is no imitation, nothing second-hand, in this, but a real force of experience and personal feeling. Swinburne gives life to his old story by making it the vehicle for emotions which mean a great deal to him and are entirely authentic.

The great qualities of *Atalanta* are characteristic of Swinburne at his best, in his love of brave actions and his tender attachment to the sanctities of home. These inspire his best poetry and provide the core of his drama. . . . The poetry of *Atalanta* is as good as it is because the story appealed to something deeper in Swinburne than his admiration for the Greek tragedians. That is why *Atalanta* is not an imitation but stands in its own right as a true work of art. (pp. 232-35)

> *C. M. Bowra, "'Atalanta in Calydon,'" in his* The Romantic Imagination *(copyright © 1949 by the President and Fellows of Harvard College; copyright renewed © 1977 by The Estates Bursar as Executors of the Estate of C. M. Bowra; excerpted by permission), Cambridge, Mass.: Harvard University Press, 1949, pp. 221-44.*

HUMPHREY HARE (essay date 1949)

Judged as a whole, in so far as any comparison can be made, *Poems and Ballads* must take second place to *Atalanta* as a work of art. The inspiration is uneven and the order apparently haphazard. But to Swinburne himself, to his critics and, indeed, to his admirers it had a peculiar importance. Here, for those who could see, were laid bare the mechanics that had produced the philosophy of *Atalanta,* the passion of *Chastelard.* It was the revelation of the growth of a talent, of the process of the integration of a synthesis. All that had been obscure was here made clear and the vision, whatever the reaction, overwhelming. (pp. 122-23)

It is easy in these early poems to distinguish the first bloom of an undirected talent, the pristine inspirations passing across his mind like clouds across the sun, the early undergraduate enthusiasms without system and without consequence. At this stage he was a dilettante of the emotions but with an innate and unregulated desire to revolt, while his retentive mind was stored with a wide historical reading and his imagination was fired by the influence of the Pre-Raphaelites into a sumptuous, flaming magnificence. In these early poems he evokes the Queens of Antiquity: Aholibah whose

> . . . mouth's heat was the heat of flame
> For lust towards the kings that came. . . .

Hesione with all summer in her hair, Ahola whose "words were soft like dulcimers", Atarah anointed with myrrh and spikenard, Semiramis greater than "the strength of love in the blood's beat", and Chrysothemis whose face was as a rose. He describes the martyrdom of St. Dorothy, and the conversion of Theophilus; from Boccaccio he takes the story of Girolamo's dream and Andrevola's despair in the garden of love. With Villon he writes rondels. The Border ballads echo in his memory from the nurseries of Capheaton and find expression in *The Bloody Son* or *The Sea-Swallows;* the medieval chronicles inspire *A Christmas Carol.* His delight in scholarly mystification is evident in *The Leper,* where the historical note is pure *pastiche.* Sappho, Landor, and Gautier mingle their influences with Morris, while incipient revolt, thus far limited to political expression, is evident in *A Song in Time of Order.* . . . (pp. 123-24)

Indeed, here, in these early poems is the bright panoply of forming genius; under the Pre-Raphaelite cloak, covering a multiplicity of inspirations, there is a charged and personal emotion. Taken in conjunction with the early dramatic fragments, with *Rosamond* and *The Queen Mother,* there is a difference, felt as yet but obscurely, between his aspirations and those of the literature of the period. His sensitivity is unquestioned: but what form was its expression to take? . . .

Sappho and Faustine, "the sterile growths of sexless root", the cruel infecundities of the love to which he was condemned formed the intolerable basis of his fantasies. Their expression necessitated the theory of Art for Art's sake. How could desires so innate be wrong? The perfection of their expression, the beauty of their form was, indeed *must* be, a substitute for morality, was, surely, morality itself? In *A Ballad of Life* and *A Ballad of Death,* written in 1862, he pursued this theory to its farthest limits. With them he opened *Poems and Ballads.* It was an explanation of the contents of the volume, the propounding of its pervasive attitude. (p. 124)

It is in the denial of this sane and normal love, in his rejection by the one being that had the power to deliver him from the clutches of Dolores, that lie both the tragedy of his life and the tragic core of *Poems and Ballads.* Half-consciously he knew now that it was for ever beyond his grasp, that he was condemned to be "a barren stock", that his last chance had gone. . . .

The reaction was exactly what might have been expected. Having expressed his anger, his despair and his suffering in *The Triumph of Time,* he turned back "to the violent delights which have violent ends". *Anactoria* is the fierce symbol of that reaction. . . . (p. 125)

Side by side with the note of personal tragedy, though reinforced by it, the synthesis that culminated in *Atalanta* was in process of development. Throughout *Poems and Ballads* the idea of beauty is never pure: with it both pleasure and pain are inextricably confounded:

> Ah, ah, thy beauty! like a beast it bites,
> Stings like an adder, like an arrow smites.

He set himself to analyse and develop this esoteric fusion. Cruelty becomes an essential attribute of the loved one. The desire to inflict it must be there, and the craving to lie passive beneath its onslaught is ever present:

>   —O Sweet,
> Had you felt, lying under the palms of your feet,
> The heart of my heart, beating harder with pleasure
> To feel you tread it to dust and death.

But this passivity is capable of a delicate transition. If the desire to suffer at the hands of the loved one is a manifestation of love, it must be common to all lovers. Necessarily, therefore, the infliction of pain must also be one of love's attributes:

> Cruel?   But love makes all that loves him well
> As wise as heaven and crueller than hell.
>
>   (pp. 125-26)

This active sadism is expressed over and over again throughout *Poems and Ballads*. (p. 126)

But this strange paradox was not limited for Swinburne to a mere theory of love. The anguished sensibility with which he responded to the beautiful, of which the passions were only one manifestation, and the sympathetic study of Sade drove him on to discover a universal law of suffering applicable to all nature. Ruin and destruction are the great principles upon which the universe is founded: to create is to destroy, to live is to suffer. (p. 127)

Beside the Sadian rejection of Virtue and exaltation of Vice— "Come down and redeem us from virtue Our Lady of Pain"— and the cry for yet rarer and still more delicate sins—"Shall no new sin be born for men's trouble, no dream of impossible pangs?"—there is discernible the beginnings of a stoicism in face of the surrounding chaos. Anarchy is no solution; complaint, if there is no God, useless.

> Can ye beat off one wave with prayer,
> Can ye move mountains?

Here and there he sounds a note of resignation and death is "The end of all, the poppied sleep".

Nevertheless there are compensations, the contemplation of nature, the majesty of the elements, to which, as we have seen, he responded so sensitively in childhood, were not to be denied. They at least are enduring. Insensibly he passes from antitheism to pantheism. (pp. 128-29)

He identified himself with the great forces of nature. The pantheistic ecstasy, which was to find its intellectual expression in *Hertha,* is present in *Poems and Ballads,* as it is, indeed, in the more or less contemporary *Lesbia Brandon*. . . . (p. 129)

And by a natural extension he recognizes that there is in man an aspect of the divine. His human pride, his courage, his latent need for action impels him to revolt. Man, being divine, is worthy of freedom. In the love of liberty, in the battle for political emancipation he will find a new inspiration for his art. Indeed, in *Poems and Ballads,* in some of the last poems composed for it, may be found the foreshadowing of the next phase of his life. In *Félise* he proclaims the power to freedom that is latent in man:

> Why should ye bear with hopes and fears
>   Till all these things be drawn in one,
> The sound of iron-footed years,
>   And all the oppression that is done
>   Under the sun?

And with, perhaps, a more political accent in *To Victor Hugo:*

> One thing we can; to be
> Awhile, as men may, free. . . .

Thus, chronologically speaking, the forgotten fury of *A Song in Time of Order* and *A Song in Time of Revolution* was reawakened after an arduous and perilous excursion into the eccentric philosophy of Dolmancé. The synthesis was shattered, the structure had collapsed. The reverberations, unremarkable as yet, were to be extensive in their effect. (pp. 129-30)

In estimating the poems contained in *Songs before Sunrise* it is necessary to make a distinction between those that were inspired by the literal facts—or personalities—of political revolution and those, more philosophical, which belong to the *Hertha* group. Of these the most important in any attempted analysis are *Genesis* and the *Hymn of Man*. The purely political group suffer from the fact that the events of 1867-1870 were not susceptible to an afflatus which might indeed have been all very well in 1848, and that Swinburne himself had no direct experience of the events involved. A further disqualification, which was not altogether Swinburne's fault, was that, when eventually published, in 1871, the sun had very definitely set upon Mazzini's hopes with the entry into Rome of the Royal troops in September of the previous year. The clarion of revolution sounded but mutely in a Savoyard desert. Swinburne's verses, for all his assurance, were hardly "art and part" of the revolution. But these considerations, fortunately, do not apply to the central core of the book. Here the pantheism which had already been disclosed in *Poems and Ballads,* and which had led to the conception of the divinity of man and to his right to liberty, is carried a stage further. It is notable that from the first impassioned but unintegrated revolutionary ardours of 1867 it took him three years to develop the full significance of his thought which was to culminate in 1870 in the composition of *Hertha*.

Swinburne starts from the typically nineteenth-century Mazzinian doctrine "Humanity is not an aggregation of individuals but a collective Being". Mankind has a collective soul and its indestructible prerogative is Liberty. (pp. 145-46)

Swinburne saw in the conception of God as a supreme being one of the main barriers to the development of the freedom of the soul. In *Christmas Antiphones* and *Before a Crucifix* he attacks the God of the Churches:

> It was for this, that men should make
>   Thy name a fetter on men's necks,
> Poor men's made poorer for thy sake,
>   And women's withered out of sex?

It was for this, that slaves should be,
Thy word was passed to set men free?

And in *Genesis* he endeavours to show the origin of this "human figment", that God was created from human fear of the pervasive reality, the necessity even, of the co-existence of good and evil. (p. 147)

Against the background of his wide reading and the new Darwinian theories of evolution he evolved the idea of Hertha, representing the principle of growth. "Of all I have done," he wrote, "I rate *Hertha* highest as a single piece, finding in it the most of lyric force and music combined with the most of condensed and clarified thought." Indeed, here the Collective Soul of Man is coextensive with God and Liberty. (p. 148)

It is impossible on reading *Hertha* to acquit Swinburne of "the (to me) most hateful charge of optimism". It is clear that he viewed the "false God" as being in a state of decline and that the liberation of man from these figments would place him in a true relation to "the vital principle of matter", and that this process in his opinion was already taking place. How could it be otherwise when men were holding anti-Catholic Councils in Naples and dying for the cause of freedom? It was natural to suppose—and Mazzini's failure was not yet apparent—that these very proper sentiments would spread. Indeed, was it not possible that man was almost on the point of manumission? The belief has always been dear to revolutionaries that their particular success is the spark that will send a mighty flame of freedom flaring across the world. Indeed if the synthesis implicit in *Atalanta* and the central poems of *Poems and Ballads* is one founded upon a profound pessimism, that of the central poems of *Songs before Sunrise* is founded upon an optimism only proportionately more qualified. *Hertha* is necessarily, as a result, more philosophically constructive. But what promise did it hold of further poetic development? At first sight it would appear that a considerable advance had been made both in intellectual power and the control of emotion; a new and rare perfection of form had been attained; but the synthesis was exclusive. In it there was no room for the esoteric passion which until now had been the mainspring of his inspiration. And it was too violent an emotion, too important an ingredient of his sensibility, to admit of neglect in the long run if his inspiration were to maintain the quality of white heat—"pies with the devil's fingers in them"—which was so essential an element of his genius. The love of liberty and freedom was all very well, but as the inspiration of great poetry in Swinburne it seems that it required certain particular conditions. Without these conditions it was all too apt to degenerate at best into invective, at worst into irritability. And the circumstances in which *Songs before Sunrise* was composed were never to recur: the participation—Swinburne felt it to be that—in the actuality of revolution; the close communion with, and hero-worship for, that revolution's leader; and, perhaps psychologically most important of all, the temporary stilling of his erotic fantasies in the first overwhelming release provided by the "fair friend who keeps a maison de supplices à la Rodin" in the Euston Road and which there is reason to believe Swinburne only began to frequent at this time. It is possible that "Mrs. A." was as much responsible for the form of *Songs before Sunrise* as was Mazzini himself. But the fact remains that when Swinburne followed Ruskin's precept to devote himself "to the behalf of humanity, . . . 'to overthrowing its idols'," and Mazzini's command to abandon Art for Art's sake, he was, in his own way, compromising with society, attacking its tenets, not for art's sake but for its own good. And compromise was

to be fatal to his art. That his conception of Liberty as a goddess who, unrestrained and cruel in the exaction of human sacrifices, was merely a sublimation of the *femme fatale,* is irrelevant. He was not aware of it. Whereas in *Prelude* he made it quite clear that he was abandoning one basis of inspiration for another. It is therefore no paradox incapable of resolution to say that Swinburne ceased to be a revolutionary upon committing himself to a volume of revolutionary poems. It is in this sense that *Songs before Sunrise* was prophetic of a decline in his genius. (pp. 150-51)

> *Humphrey Hare, in his* Swinburne: A Biographical Approach *(reprinted by permission of H. F. & G. Witherby Ltd.), Witherby, 1949, 216 p.*

JOHN A. CASSIDY   (essay date 1964)

The accolade that greeted *Atalanta* filled [Swinburne] with confidence that the time was ripe for a frontal assault on the ramparts of British Philistinism, or Utilitarianism—such an assault as had been made in France by Gautier and Baudelaire. Swinburne saw the Philistines as more than enemies of art; they also were his personal foes. They represented the forces of political Toryism and religious orthodoxy against which he had rebelled since his days at Eton. (p. 93)

Although Swinburne never walked down Bond Street with a red rose in hand to show his contempt for the Philistines, as Oscar Wilde did at a later date, he wrote one complete novel and an extensive fragment of another for the same purpose. Even today the complete novel, first published in 1877 as *A Year's Letters* but later changed to *Love's Cross-Currents,* would be considered short, for it runs to about fifty-five thousand words. By the Victorians, so short a piece of fiction as this would not be considered a novel at all, but a tale. *Lesbia Brandon,* the fragmentary novel Swinburne wrote in spurts from 1864 into the early 1870's, runs to about seventy-five thousand words, substantially longer than *Love's Cross-Currents,* but still far short of what was considered the proper length of the novel.

I believe the significance of this matter of length is that Swinburne did not take his novels seriously, but tossed them off in the spirit of burlesque and with the idea of "poking up" the Philistines. . . . Of course, the advent of such great Victorian novelists as Dickens, Thackeray, George Eliot, and Thomas Hardy did much to overcome traditional prejudice against the novel and to raise it to such a level of respectability that even a serious poet could turn out an occasional novel without serious loss of prestige. But this turning point was not reached till the 1880's and 1890's when Swinburne had lost interest in the novel.

In the early part of his career Swinburne used the novel exclusively for such burlesques as *La Fille du Policeman, La Soeur de la Reine,* and the fiction of flagellation which he did with Lord Houghton. In something of this same spirit he wrote *Love's Cross-Currents* and *Lesbia Brandon,* or at least he began them in this spirit, though as they developed, he, like Fielding in *Joseph Andrews,* abandoned the burlesque and took them more seriously. (pp. 106-07)

The satire on Philistine morality is carried out beautifully in [*Love's Cross-Currents*], a completely cynical tale of philandering and intrigue in an English aristocratic family like the Swinburnes and Ashburnhams. The leading character and prime mover of most of the action is old Lady Midhurst, born in

1800 and now in her early sixties; completely pagan and completely frank, she has a profound contempt for Victorian hypocrisy and prudery. Superbly intelligent and realistic, she manipulates the lives and fortunes of the other members of the family with consummate finesse and resourcefulness. Her antagonist is her niece Mrs. Clara Radworth, who, born in 1836, is a complete Victorian Philistine and a whited sepulcher. Beneath a mask of piety and altruism, she attempts to conceal a character both ruthless and devious. (p. 108)

Lady Midhurst is of course the great creation of the story and one of the great characters of fiction; she is worthy of standing beside Becky Sharp, Lady Castlewood, and Elizabeth Bennet. The English novel has nobody quite like her, though Miss Crawley in [Thackeray's] *Vanity Fair* is cut from the same stout oak. Her character does not change during the story, but it is of such complexity and depth that it would be an achievement for any novel. For a work as short as *Love's Cross-Currents* and for one so restricted by the limitations of the epistolary style, her portrait is truly a work of great art. She is not only Swinburne's spokesman for "art for art's sake" in her frequent gibes at the affectations of moral and religious hypocrites, but is Swinburne himself in her paganism and religious nihilism. And yet she is still more: fierce old virago though she is, she epitomizes the indomitable British courage which conquered Napoleon's battalions and shot Hitler's Luftwaffe out of the skies. (pp. 109-10)

Lesbia Brandon shows the effects of being written during Swinburne's dark period after the unfortunate love affair with Mary Gordon. In the mood and spirit of the worst poems of *Poems and Ballads*—to which it has many similarities—and of the most frenetic scenes of *Chastelard,* this novel is a prose *Flowers of Evil.* Swinburne's purpose in it also was to roil the Philistine, but in a much more coarse and brutal fashion than in *Love's Cross-Currents.* In January, 1867, while he was still smarting from the debacle of *Poems and Ballads,* he wrote Richard Burton: "I have in hand a scheme of mixed verse and prose—a sort of étude à la Balzac *plus* the poetry—which I flatter myself will be more offensive and objectionable to Britannia than anything I have yet done. You see I have now a character to keep up, and by the grace of Cotytto I will endeavour not to come short of it—at least in my writings."

Although longer than *Love's Cross-Currents, Lesbia* is so fragmentary that the reader is hard put to make a coherent story of it. (p. 110)

In *Lesbia Brandon,* as in *Chastelard* and in *Poems and Ballads,* Swinburne was doing more than baiting the Philistines; he was expressing and exhibiting the abnormal side of his nature, the side to which, as he had threatened in *Poems and Ballads,* he would give free rein as a retaliatory measure for his defeat in love. (pp. 111-12)

In *Love's Cross-Currents* and in *Lesbia Brandon* Swinburne proved that he could have been a very good or perhaps a very great novelist. He would have had to work at the craft, for he obviously had much to learn. The cumbersome "Prologue" to *Love's Cross-Currents* is so obscure that the reader needs a character chart to straighten out the interrelationships of the characters, while the ill-advised use of the epistolary framework precludes necessary comments and interpretations by the author. Still, both novels have an immediacy, a skillful handling of scene and dialogue, depth of understanding of life, and an ability to portray character that indicate talents of a high order. (p. 112)

John A. Cassidy, in his Algernon C. Swinburne *(copyright © 1964 by Twayne Publishers, Inc.; reprinted with the permission of Twayne Publishers, a Division of G. K. Hall & Co., Boston), Twayne, 1964, 186 p.*

CECIL Y. LANG   (essay date 1964)

Swinburne has lain so long in limbo already that I would scruple to repel anyone by excessive enthusiasm, but I am bound to say, nonetheless, that **"Duriesdyke," "Roundel," "The Ballad of Villon and Fat Madge," "Father Garasse," "Les Amours Etiques. Par Félicien Cossu,"** and **"Les Abîmes. Par Ernest Clouët"** [in *New Writings by Swinburne*] all seem to me, in their several ways, little masterpieces of balladry, lyric, translation, obloquy, and satiric burlesque, that **"La Fille du policeman,"** if only Swinburne could have taken his comedy seriously, *ought* to have been an achievement comparable, in kind and quality, to [Pierre Choderlos de Laclos's] *Les Liaisons dangereuses,* to [Richard Strauss's] *Der Rosenkavalier,* to Byron's *Don Juan* or even (one ventures to hint) the great opera centering on the same superb antihero. But, though a robust comic gift was stifled, his imitative and assimilative powers were so astonishing that they win the admiration even of those hordes immune to his other charms and achievements. The ballad **"Duriesdyke"** is a triumph in its own right, but inevitably, in this fallen world, part of the "virtue" of a literary ballad consists in its very imperfections, part of our pleasure arises from being able to isolate what is too modern or too obviously contrived. A mastersinger like Swinburne, latter-day Northumbrian minstrel without peer, plays the game with such finesse and sophistication that it is almost refined out of existence. . . . (p. x)

Swinburne shares with Dryden, Coleridge, Poe, Arnold, and T. S. Eliot the distinction of being a great poet who was also a practicing critic, a galaxy in which he is neither least nor the least versatile, and despite the limitations of subject matter, tone, mood of the pieces printed [in *New Writings by Swinburne*], I believe the volume will both enlarge and deepen critical appreciation of his whole achievement. I think it might alter fundamentally the general view of his whole personality. . . . [All the works included in *New Writings by Swinburne*] tell us much about Swinburne's conception of the poet's role and of the nature of poetry, they extend our knowledge of the creative process, his working habits, critical opinions, critical assumptions, and of their evolution, they unmask more effectively than anything else I know the provinciality of English literature, the insularity of English criticism, the priggish humbuggery of the journalism, the vulgarity of popular morality, the often infirmities of received reputations. And they are one and all, whatever else they may or may not be, readable.

I am not, however, so blinded by partisanship that I consider every single piece here a masterwork, and I believe the book has a value that is not strictly literary. Whatever future study of Swinburne is not to be exclusively or primarily esthetic will have to be (I am persuaded) psychological, even psychoanalytical, before it can properly be biographical—that one shudders to imagine what will be perpetrated in the name of all this cannot fairly alter one's conviction—and it is surely significant that every piece in this volume, late as well as early, will contribute to such an investigation. This claim may be of course either a truism or a fallacy, for any piece of writing, given a key or sufficient authority or a short supply of tact, can be used as some kind of index to its creator's mind, and in the process negative evidence or no evidence at all may seem as valuable as "fact." Nevertheless, hardly anyone would deny that Swinburne's preoccupation (as revealed in this volume alone) with Sade and Villon, Webster and Marlowe, "spasmodic" poetry, Garasse, "The Maiden Tribute of Modern Babylon" and the hypocrisy of the Parisian press in dealing with it, with the actual creation of such alter egos as "Félicien Cossu" and "Ernest Clouët" and of such fantasies (I use the word in its modern psychological sense) as **"La Soeur de la reine"** and **"La Fille du policeman"** sprang from a single taproot.

And there are other considerations. Why, for instance, did he collect none of these works for publication in any of his several dozen volumes? For all the prose it is easy to turn up reasons, and for most of the verse also (though not for **"Duriesdyke"** and **"Roundel,"** the earliest and latest in date). Second, soberer thoughts doubtless led him to withhold most of the critical pieces, and the nimble-witted despair of the human condition seen in the hoaxes and burlesques is glimpsed only fleetingly in his published works.

But something more must be said. It has been suggested that in **"La Fllle du policeman"** Swinburne was motivated by a dissatisfaction with the "Victorianism" of his society. This observation, I suspect, though not inaccurate as far as it goes, finally begs the question. That certain critical stances can be assumed only with certain kinds of masks is no doubt a basic principle of satire—certainly, current fashion would have it so—and all of the hoaxes and burlesques here are, in some degree, satirical. But I think it is true that the satire and burlesque (the satire of English society, for instance, the burlesque of French writers dealing with English settings) are merely vehicles for deeper, more intimate compulsions. What satire, what burlesque can be found in the poems **"Messaline au cirque"** and **"Charenton en 1810,"** both attributed to "Félicien Cossu"? A thin edge of self-mockery, a hardly visible barrier of ironic distance. Nothing more. The undergraduate who invented Ernest Wheldrake in order to demolish him, the poet who composed his own epigraphs, the critic who, writing his essay **"Matthew Arnold's New Poems,"** created a French observer in order to controvert his elder, the novelist who issued *A Year's Letters* under the name "Mrs. Horace Manners," the mimic whose surgically incisive parodies, in *The Heptalogia,* of Tennyson, the Brownings, Rossetti, Patmore, and Owen Meredith, all anonymous, were so far superior to his parody of himself, also anonymous, was the same strange, brilliant creature whom Lady Trevelyan sketched as "the typical miss anglaise émancipée" to be passed off on George Sand or who, even earlier, had taken the role of "Mrs. Skewton in her Bath chair" in a tableau from *Dombey and Son,* who, as Herbert Seyton in an obvious self-portrait in *Lesbia Brandon,* successfully carries off a masquerade as a young girl, who, as a rising young poet, nearly became the anonymous editor of a new literary review, who had (or thought he had) an agreement with his publisher by which he could send in, as he put it, "without my name and without in any way committing myself to their authorship, MSS which I should wish you to print as though they were avowedly or probably mine." . . . Neither Stendhal, with his hundred-odd pseudonyms, nor Defoe, perpetually surrendering to the first person singular, nor such voluptuous votaries of their own egos as Rousseau and Gide, nor Emily Dickinson, with her unposted letter to the world, is a stranger case in point. The biographer and critic of Swinburne will have to recognize the pattern in all this and deal with its relation to the recurrent themes, in both the poetry and prose, of barren-

ness and sterility, Lesbianism, incest, the death of love, spiritual withdrawal and isolation ("I will keep my soul in a place out of sight," "I hid my heart in a nest of roses"), all counterpointed in a peculiarly Swinburnian way, with those of growth, fertility, liberty, freedom, and the progress of mind. (pp. x-xiii)

Cecil Y. Lang, in his preface to New Writings by Swinburne or Miscellanea Nova et Curiosa: Being a Medley of Poems, Critical Essays, Hoaxes and Burlesques, *edited by Cecil Y. Lang (copyright © 1964 by Syracuse University Press), Syracuse University Press, 1964, pp. ix-xv.*

MORSE PECKHAM   (essay date 1970)

[Before] the special problems in Swinburne's most important poetry can be explored, something needs to be said of the general problem of all of his work. There is an enormous advantage in getting interested in Swinburne at the present time. The whole literary world "knows" that Swinburne's poetry is bad; something, indeed, of a joke; something that no sensible man could possibly read for pleasure or instruction. Everyone knows that the faint signs of a Swinburne revival are but the consequences of the fact that scholars must publish, and that it does not make much difference what they publish about; that since little has been written of late about Swinburne, he makes an admirable subject for scholarship. In such a situation the man of independent and catholic taste is in a happy position; there is no official canon of what is good Swinburne and what is bad—it is all bad. Consequently it is not necessary for him to find out if the canonical judgments are to be relied upon; that trouble he can save himself. All he has to do is to read Swinburne's poetry, explore it, find out what is going in this work, find out for himself why for sixty years or so people of intelligence, learning, and exquisite taste thought Swinburne a great poet, and why a few people think so today.

But if such a reader undertakes to discover Swinburne for himself, he is immediately faced with an enormous difficulty, one which more than anything else has been responsible for the downfall of Swinburne's once great reputation. Swinburne is at once an extraordinarily seductive poet and an extraordinarily difficult one. Because of this his charm has been dismissed over and over again, an untold number of times, as simply a matter of "word-music": in Swinburne, it is alleged, there is nothing but a leaping rhythm that hurls you along and a completely irresponsible use of the various devices of euphony (or more precisely, phonic over-determination), particularly alliteration. He is recognized to be the greatest virtuoso of sound in English poetry, but that prodigious technique, it is asserted, is entirely without foundation or justification, for Swinburne *says* nothing.

It is not always recognized that the major Victorian poets are in fact difficult poets. To be sure, everyone knows that Gerard Manley Hopkins' work is difficult; so difficult that many think of him still as a "modern poet," though what of his technique he did not learn from Browning he learned from Swinburne. Arnold is admittedly quite transparent; Tennyson seems to be transparent to the point of simple-mindedness, but in fact is an exceedingly subtle, devious, and baffling writer. It is obvious that much of Browning is very difficult indeed, but the most difficult works of Browning are, for the most part, unread even by Victorian specialists, and are generally, though quite unjustifiably, dismissed. But the advantage of Browning over Tennyson is that he looks difficult, and over Swinburne that it is obvious that he is saying something. Swinburne, by contrast, seems to be almost contentless. Yet he is not. Quite the contrary. The difficulty of Browning, like the difficulty of Hopkins, is a difficulty of syntactic compression and distortion. Swinburne also offers a syntactic difficulty, but one of quite a different order. The effect of monotony comes not primarily from the unflagging splendor of the rhythm or the obviously beautiful sound, but rather from the fact that Swinburne constructs his sentences by building them up of long syntactic sub-units; the first sentence of *Atalanta,* for example, is sixteen lines long. What he exploits are the possibilities of parallel syntactic structure. The effect is that the unpracticed reader loses control over the syntax. In Hopkins and Browning the extreme use of elision and syntactic distortion confuses the reader. There is not, so to speak, enough syntactic redundance to keep the reader oriented. But in Swinburne there is too much syntactic redundance. In this he resembles to a certain extent Milton; but the difficulty of reading Milton comes from trying to follow a syntactic style of dependent syntactic units, while Swinburne exploits the possibilities of disorienting the reader by presenting him with parallel structures so far apart that it is difficult to remember and grasp their syntactical relationship. The consequence with all four of these poets is that the reader untrained in their syntactic styles loses semantic control. Yet he knows, at least, that Hopkins, Browning, and Milton are saying something; but Swinburne further confuses him by offering a continuum of beautiful sound which seems to have no relationship to anything at all. The result is that for the first three, the unpracticed reader, though baffled, is at least aware that he is not understanding what is before him, but with Swinburne he rapidly comes to the conclusion that there is nothing to understand.

To learn to read Swinburne it is necessary, therefore, to resist with all one's power both the seductiveness of the rhythm and the seductiveness of the phonic character. One must read him slowly, very slowly. The mind must always remain focused intensively on the task of comprehending the syntax, of grasping how the parallel syntactic sub-units fit into the larger sentence construction; and it must do this as they come along, in the order in which the poem offers them. It may be said that there is at every cultural level an upward limit to both the complexity and the length of the syntactic structure that may be comprehended. Obviously, the higher the cultural level, the greater the complexity and the length of the syntactical structure that can be grasped. But the fact is that today the general simplification and deterioration of the cultural milieu have meant that most people are not exposed even in prose to much opportunity for extending the range of their syntactic grasp. The power to extemporize extremely long and complex syntactic structures with an extensive use of parallelisms is rapidly disappearing, and has been for some time; and at the higher cultural levels the sentence fragment, which presents precisely the opposite difficulty from Swinburne's, has long been a standard device in both verse and prose. The first task, then, of the reader of Swinburne is to train himself by extending very far indeed the upward limit of his range of syntactic comprehension. (pp. xv-xvii)

> *Morse Peckham, in his introduction to* Poems and Ballads [and] Atalanta in Calydon *by Algernon Charles Swinburne, edited by Morse Peckham (copyright © 1970 by The Bobbs-Merrill Company, Inc.), Bobbs-Merrill, 1970, pp. xi-xxxv.*

PHILIP HENDERSON (essay date 1974)

For some time now, Swinburne has been among the most neglected of our poets. The enormous bulk of his work is partly to blame, and also the habit of judging him by his worst poems. The chief reason, however, is that our whole approach to poetry has changed, though for long he was regarded as one of the finest lyrists in the language. 'None of the more important Victorian poets is more difficult to read, with any pleasure, today, than Swinburne,' wrote John Heath-Stubbs in 1950. 'His rhythms are mechanical, his heavily stressed anapaestic and dactylic metres vulgar, his use of pause often lacking in subtlety; though a certain facility in the melodic arrangement of vowel sounds must be granted him.' Such has been the view for some time now, and one suspects that it is based on a reading of **'Dolores'** and **'The Hymn to Proserpine'**, and little else. It is usually coupled with the charge of imprecise writing, and leaves out of account the infinite variety and rhythmic subtlety of so much of his work. Swinburne is often extremely precise in his observation of nature, to take only such poems as **'The Sundew'**, **'Relics'** or **'At a Month's End'**, and the later descriptive verse is often Wordsworthian or Turnerean in feeling. There are, too, the superb elegy on the death of Baudelaire and the magnificent Villon translations. Again, few novels have more clarity and concision than *Love's Cross-Currents*. As for his letters, though they may suffer by contemporary standards from longwindedness, they are the letters of a man of immense learning and wit. Many of them bear witness, also, to a delicious sense of the absurd, as does his parody of French novels about English society, *La Fille du policeman,* which so amused his friends, and the spoof reviews of imaginary French poets with which he pulled the leg of the editor of the *Spectator*, with their masterly parodies of Hugo and Baudelaire. There is, too, his almost forgotten pioneer work on William Blake, his review of *Les Fleurs du Mal* which he said was written in a Turkish bath in Paris, his fine essays on Chapman and Ford and on the work of his elder contemporaries, Arnold, Rossetti and Morris, which caused such excitement when they first appeared in the *Fortnightly Review* in the 1860s, not to mention the excellence of much of his *Study of Shakespeare.* Nor is it recognized any longer how much Walter Pater was indebted to Swinburne's **'Notes on the Designs of the Old Masters in Florence'** of 1864, for both the style and the method of his *Renaissance*—an indebtedness acknowledged by Pater himself. These **'Notes'** are evidence of an intense sensitiveness to drawing and painting which was never developed, just as his feeling for character and drama, shown in his early novel and the fragments of *Lesbia Brandon,* went into the composition of more or less unreadable (and certainly unactable) plays on the Elizabethan model. Thanks largely to his family, who were very musical, and to his Welsh friend, George Powell, Swinburne discovered Wagner when his music was little known in England. Evidence of this is to be seen in *Tristram of Lyonesse,* which he intended to be his masterwork. In the same way, he was well before his time in England in his knowledge and appreciation of French poets and novelists, of Laclos, Stendhal, Hugo, Balzac, Baudelaire, Flaubert, Gautier, Latouche and Léon Cladel. He was also widely read in the medieval French romances, in Brantôme and all that had to do with Mary Stuart, to whom he had a romantic attachment. The scholarship that went into the writing of his enormous drama *Bothwell* was immense. Above all, he was a Greek scholar, as is shown by *Atalanta in Calydon* and *Erechtheus* and many of the shorter poems. He even assisted Jowett in his translation of Plato. In short, Swinburne is one of the most learned and richly endowed poets in the language. And since the *goût de l'horrible* is once more in fashion, then why not such poems as **'The Leper'**, **'Les Noyades'**, **'Anactoria'** and **'Faustine'**? For there, in the mid-nineteenth century, will be found all the elements that were to be taken up and developed by the symbolist and *fin de siècle* writers and painters all over Europe.

At the height of the clamour provoked by **Poems and Ballads, First Series,** the ever-perceptive Ruskin wrote to J. M. Ludlow, the social reformer, who had asked him to add his voice to the general protest: 'He is infinitely above me in all knowledge and power and I should no more think of advising him than of venturing to do it to Turner if he were alive again. As for Swinburne not being my superior, he is simply only one of the mightiest scholars of the age in Europe. . . . And in power of imagination and understanding simply sweeps me away as a torrent does a pebble.' In a letter to Swinburne himself, Ruskin compares him to 'a deadly nightshade blossom' and 'a thunder-cloud'.

The comparison with Turner has been developed by Professor John D. Rosenberg of Columbia University . . . [in his essay "Swinburne"—published in *Victorian Studies*—] which is perhaps the best contemporary analysis of Swinburne's poetry yet written: 'Swinburne's love of mixed effects gives to his descriptive verse much of its Turnerian quality. His poetry is charged with the tension of delicately poised opposites: shadows thinned to light, lights broken by shade, sunset passing into moonrise, sea merging with sky. He is obsessed with the moment when one thing shades off into its opposite, or when contraries fuse, as in **"Hermaphroditus"**. . . . Yet apart from his profound aesthetic affinity with Turner, there is the unique idiosyncrasy of Swinburne himself, who was equipped with superb senses, each of which must have transmitted a peculiar counterpoint. This basic, polarizing rhythm runs through his being and manifests itself in his compulsive use of alliterating antitheses in prose and verse. Much in Swinburne that has been criticized as mere mannerism—paradox, alliteration, elaborate antithesis—strikes me as deriving from his deepest impulses, although the question of "sincerity" is always vexing in his verse. In a sense, Swinburne *perceived* in paradoxes, and his recurrent synthetic images express perfectly that passing of pain into pleasure, bitter into sweet, loathing into desire, which lay at the root of his profoundest experiences.'

The reputation of Swinburne reached its nadir in the 1920s and 1930s after the revolution in poetry brought about by Ezra Pound and T. S. Eliot—a revolution which has now, perhaps, spent its force by making poetry often almost indistinguishable from prose. There is now evidence of the beginning of a new and more discerning interest in Swinburne in the second half of this century in the United States. . . . It is to be hoped that this new interest may not be confined to the better known, somewhat brassy Dionysian side of this extravagantly gifted being, who was once felt to be the liberator of a whole generation in revolt against Victorian pieties and repressions, but, now that we no longer need liberating, may lead to a deeper knowledge of the man who, in his less febrile moments, wrote some of the most exquisite poetry and the finest criticism of his time. (pp. 2-4)

> *Philip Henderson, in his* Swinburne: Portrait of a Poet *(reprinted with permission of Macmillan Publishing Co., Inc.; in Canada by permission of the Estate of the late Philip Henderson; copyright ©* 1974 by Philip Henderson), *Macmillan, 1974, 305 p.*

A.O.J. COCKSHUT   (essay date 1977)

[In Swinburne] the love of brother and sister is unavoidable and insistent; and it is unequivocally sexual. (p. 111)

The first and less interesting of Swinburne's two novels, **Love's Cross-Currents** was published anonymously in 1877, and acknowledged in 1905. It is a neatly-plotted epistolary story, owing more to the French tradition than to [Samuel Richardson's] *Clarissa*. The dominant personality, who appears again in the more powerful, unfinished **Lesbia Brandon,** is Lady Midhurst. She is a mask of what Swinburne in certain moods chose to fancy himself, but with his persistent, passionate weakness and naïvety, never was. She is old, bored, weary, cynical, and takes a delight in shocking the moralistic young. . . .

In **Lesbia Brandon,** this cynical note is secondary; dominant is a medley of confused torments and ecstacies, incestuous, masochistic and lesbian. A tone of lyrical joy runs through it all, even the most sombre passages, as if the normal and the conventional, who make terms with the world and even enjoy it, were infinitely pitiable to these proud, tortured spirits.

The most tiresome part of the book, of course, is that devoted to flogging fantasies. But one must concede that these were so perpetually present to the author's mind, that they would never be excluded from a lengthy piece, except when the author was on his best behaviour before the public. And, tedious and perverted as they undoubtedly are, it is perhaps not sophistical to find in them some shadowy positive value. The really disturbing feature of Swinburne's work, and what distinguished this novel from pornography, is his ability to convey sensuality as something affecting the whole personality; and this despite some languorous romantic pessimism. Pain cannot but be felt; for Swinburne, dreamy and full of illusions and megalomaniac fantasies, it was at times an anchor to reality.

Herbert, the hero, placed as the young Swinburne was, in an aristocratic milieu, and a wild Northumbrian landscape dominated by the sea, is passionately devoted to his much older married sister, Lady Wariston. His tutor, Denham, is in love with her, resents his love, and tries to exorcize it by flogging the boy. Herbert hardly needs the flogging to encourage him in a higher, more romantic, incestuous masochism. . . . Swinburne, imagining his own masochistic temperament transposed to a woman enjoying an incestuous orgasm, is a formidable conception; and formidable too is the prose he produces for the occasion. . . .

But it is characteristic of Swinburne, as of so many immoralists and antinomians, to make his moral disapprovals all the more intense for having limited their scope, and rejected so many agreed moral positions. Here his satire is reserved for Linley, Lady Wariston's uncle by marriage. At first, this is a little surprising, since his cynicism seems similar to that of Lady Midhurst, who is almost regarded as an oracle. But there is a difference. Instead of Lady Midhurst's weariness, there is a definite cruelty behind Linley's mask. (p. 113)

But Herbert has another and stronger love than his love for his sister, his love for Lesbia, the name which Swinburne, with less than his usual tact and subtlety, chose for his lesbian heroine. The plot is so arranged that when Lesbia first sees Herbert, he is dressed as a girl for some amateur theatricals. When she is dying she refers again to this moment. . . . When she tells him of his physical likeness to his beloved sister, and thus excites him once again to a dangerous level of passion, she warns:

No, not again; when I am dead if you like.

All this is neatly emblematic of Swinburnian pessimism at its most intense. The only two moments when the girl he so much loved could have tolerated his approach were—when he was disguised, and when she was dead. We are not, however, led to suppose that Herbert is actually capable of violating a corpse. His masochism can be, and at times is, transposed into a high sacrificial key. Offering his life for hers, he says:

> I know it's not worth taking, but it might be worth giving—though it's not worth keeping either.

In a few passages like this Swinburne attains to a pure and simple eloquence, reminiscent of the finest moments of his beloved Jacobean dramatists. He was, after all, a very much better writer of prose than he was a poet.

In the earlier chapter, entitled *On the Downs* when Herbert makes his declaration of love for Lesbia, he offers to die for her, in a manly, knightly way (rather than a masochistic way) though in Herbert, as in Swinburne himself, the two impulses cannot be entirely separated. It is then that Lesbia makes a reply which is perhaps the most ironical in the whole canon of Victorian love-literature:

> I don't know if you would like it or not, but I should like to feel thoroughly that we were not less than brother and sister.

How many correct young ladies in how many thousand novels, good, bad and indifferent, made just that reply. But Lesbia, a stranger as it were in Swinburne's world (for her creator obviously finds lesbianism impossible to imagine) does not know what she is saying. She is speaking as if she were in Trollope's world, or in the ordinary world of most of us, in which the relation of brother and sister is the least carnal of all kinds of affection between people of different sex. But she is not; she is in a world where the relation of brother and sister is the most carnal, tormented and deadly of all. But Herbert is an Etonian and a perfect gentleman, and he does not draw attention to her mistake.

One thing that will certainly surprise readers who come fresh to Swinburne as a novelist, knowing him only as a poet, is the convincing social milieu in which these bizarre torments find their setting. It is a very narrow aristocratic world, contemptuous or unaware of the life of unknown compatriots. But it has a surprising solidity; Swinburne is in this like his great contemporaries, Dickens, Trollope, Mrs Gaskell, just as much as he is unlike them in his sensations and moral concepts.

But we may ask, why, if he knew little and understood less of the lesbian condition, did he choose to endow his heroine with it? Because he had a fellow-feeling for all sorts and conditions of those outside the ranks of respectability. His work combines a strong social conservatism with a bitter contempt for traditional moralities. He was fond of talking of de Sade as 'the divine Marquis' and took pleasure in the fact that the most subversive of all writers on sexual questions was an aristocrat too. And he could find a link between his social conservatism and his moral revolt. Both were equally opposed to the respectable, liberal, progressive, middle-class men of the sixties whom (from such very different points of view) Ruskin and Arnold castigated. Defeat, being halfway to death, had a lasting appeal, and he had a tenderness for his family's Jacobite traditions quite as strong as his admiration for Italian nationalists, revolutionaries and anarchists.

Puerile, perverted, disgusting and grossly inconsistent in argument—Swinburne is all these. Yet in a curious way, he demands to be taken seriously for two reasons, because his fantasies spring from his depths of his being, and are never just amusements, and because a strange beauty mingles both with the absurdity and the horror. (pp. 114-16)

> *A.O.J. Cockshut, "Swinburne," in his* Man and Woman: A Study of Love and the Novel 1740-1940 *(© 1977 by A.O.J. Cockshut; reprinted by permission of Oxford University Press, Inc.; in Canada by William Collins Sons & Co., Ltd.), Collins, 1977 (and reprinted by Oxford University Press, New York, 1978), Oxford University Press, New York, 1978, pp. 111-16.*

EDMUND WILSON   (essay date 1978)

[A] special feature of Swinburne's family which made him so exceptional in Victorian England was the French strain, which gave him what can almost be called a non-English alter ego. He wrote French with facility and elegance, though occasional incorrectitudes, and cherished France as a second fatherland, with which he always kept up close connections. It is a little surprising to see how much of this correspondence is in French—his letters to Victor Hugo, [Stéphane] Mallarmé, [Auguste] Vacquerie and others; and there is a letter from Baudelaire, whom Swinburne had discovered with excitement at a time when he was apparently not known in England and had no great reputation in France. Swinburne perpetrated also, in French, a whole series of burlesques and hoaxes, from epigraphs for his poems in imitation Old French to a Hugoesque novel of which over fifteen thousand words survive. Two of his hoaxes were extremely sly attempts to impose on the editor of the *Spectator* with reviews of imaginary French authors, the quotations from whom he concocted himself. One of these was Félicien Cossu, the author of *Les Amours Etiques*. . . . The other of the bogus reviews deals with a work called *Les Abîmes*, by an author named Ernest Clouët, a prose counterpart of *Les Amours Etiques*. What is masterly in these burlesques is the contrast between the French decadents letting themselves go and the tone of the English reviewer, with his restrained but superior sarcasm. (pp. 16-17)

Swinburne wrote also, entirely in French, two burlesques of more elaborate kind—a novel called *La Fille du Policeman* and a drama called *La Soeur de la Reine*. He idolized Victor Hugo, and when *L'Homme Qui Rit* appeared defended it against the ridicule the book had provoked by its comic mistakes about English life; but in *La Fille du Policeman* he is to some extent parodying the sensational romanticism of his favorite as well as of other French novelists who have undertaken to write about England. The point of both these *jeux d'esprit*, which are also tours de force, is the opposite of the journalistic hoaxes. Instead of subjecting the French to the complacent disapproval of the English, the imaginary French author here, who is supposed to know nothing about England save a smattering of the early history of the reign of Queen Victoria and a few English words and proper names, which he invariably misunderstands and misuses, is attempting to impose on the English the conventions of French fiction and drama. (pp. 17-18)

[Swinburne's novels do not] resemble any other Victorian novels. Compare them with the usually satirical or at least ironical treatment of the class from which Swinburne came in Dickens and Thackeray and Trollope or with the highfalutin fantasies of Meredith. Swinburne is not at all class-conscious, as these middle-class writers are. He is telling about his own family entirely without constraint—which is impossible for a Dickens or a Thackeray when he is trying to deal with his. And what Swinburne has to tell, for the reader habituated to Victorian fiction, is likely to prove rather startling, as it would have been distasteful or alien to the Victorian public itself. In these novels no one has to worry about what the middle class will think or about the opinion of people above one. The characters have their own codes and standards, but many things go on among them that would horrify this middle-class public. We are brought into a world for which we have not been prepared by even the smooth lawns of Tennyson or the great ladies of Coventry Patmore—a world in which the eager enjoyment of a glorious out-of-door life of riding and swimming and boating is combined with adultery, incest, enthusiastic flagellation and quiet homosexuality. (pp. 21-2)

"Studies of life and character in our own day"—this is what one least expects from Swinburne, yet it is what one does get in [*Lesbia Brandon* and *Love's Cross-Currents*]. The mimicry of which he was a master and which we know from his literary pastiches and parodies is applied here to social types. *Love's Cross-Currents* is told mostly in letters, and the personalities are admirably conveyed through the vocabulary, the tone and the rhythm of their various epistolary styles. In *Lesbia Brandon,* the worldly conversation of the "venomous old beauty" Lady Midhurst and Mr. Linley, the scholar, collector and wit, with his eyes of which "the gravity and mockery were alike impressive and repulsive," whose whole face sometimes "bore the seal of heavy sorrow and a fatal fatigue," has something in common with the dialogue of the characters of both George Meredith and Oscar Wilde and seems to show that the latter was exploiting a vein of epigrammatic talk that had already been brought to perfection in the social life of London by the middle nineteenth century. . . . There is nothing of this kind, of course, in Swinburne's poetry, and these novels present also an unexpected contrast to Swinburne's writings in verse in their descriptions of people and landscape. He here gets away almost completely from the monotonous vocabulary of his poetry, the rhetorical abstractions and the tiresome alliterations. It is a curious deficiency of Swinburne in his poetry—for a writer so sensitive to style—that he can never surprise or delight by a colloquial turn of phrase, a sharply observed detail, a magical touch of color. He can never, like Tennyson or even Arnold, strike off something actually seen in words at once exact and sensuous. (pp. 24-5)

[But in the novels Swinburne] was able to do something quite different. In *Love's Cross-Currents,* at the beginning of Chapter 3, you are already quite out of the pre-Raphaelite world and in the presence of a recognizable England which the poet has invested with a charm that is never obscured by the wordy blur. . . . [And] especially in *Lesbia Brandon*—you get splendid descriptions of swimming and riding that convey the thrill of real experience while at the same time giving the impression that, like Swinburne's fantastic Elizabethans, they are somehow framed and varnished as painted panels in the great ornamental country houses in which the characters lived.

I know of nothing else like this in English fiction. It is obvious that Swinburne at this time in his life was attempting to effect a mutation, and it seems tragic that the obstacles he met, the restraining and stunting influences, prevented him from doing this. He would have produced something so much more interesting than the grandiose routine of his verse! How urgent to the end of his life was the need to tell his personal story,

to return to those early impressions and emotions which he had never fully described, is shown by his writing at fifty-five a blank-verse play, *The Sisters*—dedicated to the mother of Mary Leith—which is unique among Swinburne's tragedies in taking place in nineteenth-century England. Here we find the same strange snarl of inter-related characters on the same Northumberland estate, the same Reggie, with a surname different from the one he is given in *Love's Cross-Currents,* who is always Algernon himself. But the conventional poetic form to which Swinburne has become accustomed completely destroys the reality and deflects the force of the story. Swinburne is still, to be sure, attempting to do something slightly different from his dramas in the grand manner: "The tragedy of '**The Sisters,**'" he says in his introductory survey to the collected edition of his poems, "however defective it may be in theatrical interest or progressive action, is the only modern thing I know in which realism in the reproduction of natural dialogue and accuracy in the representation of natural intercourse between men and women of gentle birth have been found or made compatible with expression in genuine if simple blank verse." But it is all too easy for Swinburne here to romanticize his relations with Mary Gordon. Reggie Clevering, like Reggie Harewood in *Love's Cross-Currents,* is in love with one of his cousins, Mabel, and, in this case, she with him, but Swinburne is evidently merging himself with his successful rival, Colonel Leith, who had been gravely wounded in India, by making Reggie a brave soldier who comes back with a wound from Waterloo. The whole play becomes most implausible and artistically most inacceptable when Swinburne confuses and falsifies the family situation by the introduction of Renaissance poisonings. He was also, in another late play, *The Duke of Gandia,* to return to a favorite subject, the Borgias, which he had earlier attacked in the prose work recovered by Randolph Hughes, *The Chronicle of Tebaldeo Tebaldei.* One of the charms of the Borgias for Swinburne was that they gave him an opportunity to deal with incestuous situations, and in *The Sisters* he mixes the two milieux. The young people act a play which has been written for them by Reggie. It is a Renaissance tragedy that takes place in Italy, and the heroine's twin sister Anne, who is also in love with Reggie, enters so into the spirit of the piece that she procures a flask of real poison from a disused laboratory in the house and, after pretending in the action of the piece to poison the character played by her sister, she proceeds, after contemplating suicide, to allow Mabel actually to drink it, apparently under the impression that it is something to cure a cold. Reggie also takes a dose, and he and Mabel die together, forgiving Anne. The situation is further complicated by another cousin, who is one of Reggie's oldest friends but who is also in love with Mabel. The point is that all these young people are so closely bound by kinship and intimacy that it is impossible for Reggie and Mabel ever to extricate themselves to the point of being able to marry one another.

One's enjoyment of the splendor and wit of these novels is, however—for an American reader, at least—likely to be somewhat disturbed by an element which seems to him bizarre and repellent, and this element appears in the correspondence in an even more unpleasant form. As a result of his experience as a boy at Eton, Swinburne had made a cult of the traditional British practice of flogging, and this had become for him inseparable from his capacity for sexual gratification, which seems to have been exclusively masochistic. The pleasure and importance of being flogged are made to figure in all three of these family fictions. In *The Sisters* it is touched upon lightly; in *Love's Cross-Currents* it is dwelt upon at greater length; in

Lesbie Brandon Swinburne pulls out all the stops, and howls of pain become cries of ecstasy. (pp. 26-9)

The cruel inexorable woman is a figure that towers above everything else in all of Swinburne's writing. She is, in fact, Swinburne's ideal—Dolores Our Lady of Pain; Mary Gordon, who unthinkingly cut him down; the catalogue of perverse and destructive queens in *The Masque of Queen Bersabe;* the Messalina-Victoria of *La Soeur de la Reine;* Mary Stuart, about whom he wrote a huge trilogy and who he insists was not the pathetic victim that her sentimental admirers made her but a woman strong in intellect, passionate, and quite ruthless with enemies and lovers alike; Lady Midhurst, the relentless old schemer, who presides over *Love's Cross-Currents* and reappears in *Lesbia Brandon*. Of this character Swinburne wrote in a letter to William Rossetti, when the former novel appeared in book form, "This book stands or falls by Lady Midhurst: If she gives satisfaction, it must be all right; if not, chaos is come again," and he insists that she is entirely his own invention. Lady Midhurst is indeed at the center of *Love's Cross-Currents,* prevailing, persuading, pushing, resorting to blackmail, if necessary—always bringing pressure to bear. Part French, extremely clever, a thorough woman of the world, she enjoys reading French novels and is aware of the irregular relationships in which the members of her family are involved, but she keeps them all under control and in the end she has not a scruple about trapping her young relatives in situations that are sure to make them unhappy but that give them at least the appearance of not violating British conventions. They have been doing what they liked at home but they must not create open scandal. One would not have expected of Swinburne either restraint or psychological subtlety; yet this novel is distinguished by both. Lady Midhurst is by far his most successful incarnation of the dominating merciless woman. . . . Not only has Lady Midhurst French blood; it is evident that the book derives from Laclos's *Les Liaisons Dangereuses*. Both stories are told in letters, and though the incidents and personalities in Swinburne are quite different from those in Laclos, one can recognize that, transposed into these different terms, Swinburne's theme is the same as Laclos's—the manipulation of simple people, regardless of their own real interests, by flexible and steely intelligence. . . . Swinburne's obsession with cruelty makes itself felt more sharply in these works than it does in his other writings, because they are made to take place not in a world of history or myth but in Swinburne's own personal world. This is something that is basic to his nature, and the closer we get to the man himself, the more uncomfortable his effect on us becomes. It is not only the nostalgia for floggings that strikes this note in *Lesbia Brandon;* the whole book is shot through with a sinister satisfaction derived from inflicting pain. . . . He can never get away from this, and it is one thing that makes him so limited, in the long run so unsatisfactory. His enthusiasms are exaggerated, seem only half real (though these, too, have their masochistic element), but this masochistic excitement *is* real, and it is hard to be entirely sympathetic with someone who—though only on one side of his nature—longs so much for self-abasement. (pp. 34-6)

Edmund Wilson, "Swinburne of Capheaton and Eton" (reprinted by permission of Farrar, Straus and Giroux, Inc.; copyright © 1962 by Edmund Wilson), in The New Yorker, Vol. XXXVIII, No. 33, October 6, 1962 (and reprinted in a somewhat different form in The Novels of A. C. Swinburne by A. C. Swinburne, Greenwood Press, Publishers, 1978, pp. 3-37).

ROSS C. MURFIN   (essay date 1978)

If Swinburne is the supreme liminal poet in the English language, it is because his life, as well as the life of his age, encountered old borderlines and new horizons on every front. There was hardly an article of faith—in class structure, in material progress, in science or the function of art—that did not have to face loud and angry encounters with some strong article of doubt which had developed sometimes outside of, but just as often within, the very temple of "the dead and doubtful gods." It is little wonder that Swinburne was unable to maintain a consistent or definitive attitude towards those two faiths most crucial to his own development, Christianity and romanticism.

As a young man at Eton, Swinburne was enchanted by Shelley; one need only peruse **"The Temple of Janus,"** the poem he composed during his first year at Oxford, to realize the depth of his early devotion. By 1865, however, adoration must have turned to skepticism, for Swinburne claims that even Shelley's great works are "spoilt" by "doctrinaire views." (p. 22)

Wordsworth, no less than Shelley, was half attractive, half repulsive, to Swinburne, who wrote democratic manifestos such as **"The Eve of Revolution"** even as he satirized Wordsworth for being *"un misérable du peuple"* and who wrote pantheistic ecstasies like **"A Nympholept"** even as he assailed Wordsworth for his "pantheism." As for Christianity, Swinburne's ambivalent attitudes towards that old faith (as well as towards romanticism, with which he associates its "doctrinaire" views) can perhaps best be found in an 1875 letter to E. C. Stedman. He tells Stedman that he is a "kind of Christian (of the church of Blake and Shelley)." He then loudly decries natural religion, proclaiming that God cannot be known "by other than apocalyptic means" but later adding, in what seems a curious turn of argument, that Blake and Shelley were *not* poets of "supernatural revelation" but, rather, were discoverers of "human perfection." He ends by exclaiming that he is "in no sense a Theist" and declares himself, instead, a exponent of "clarified nihilism."

It is hardly surprising to learn that Swinburne's art, like his life, is transitional to a degree. In *Atalanta in Calydon,* his first successful work, Swinburne compresses into seventy-five powerful lines the transitions in sensibility which connect Wordsworth's ebullient celebrations of man's unity with nature and Thomas Hardy's eventual, despairing concurrence. The Chorus begins by celebrating spring, a season which seems no less than a corollary of the citizens' "winter-long hopes" for an end to trouble and strife. And yet the lyrical longing for a new season of innocence is muted. Swinburne puns on the word "traces" so that the last residues of the winter become ominous reminders both of that season's inescapable reins and of the ever-present "tracks" of the beast. . . . [The] Chorus attempts to triumph over despair, to connect nature's moods with man's own hopes and dreams. . . . But as the Chorus continues its attempted romantic ode to spring, . . . images of natural, political, and moral harmony gradually give way to images of wild, perverse, destructive power. As "the faint fresh flame . . . flushes / From leaf to flower and flower to fruit," the poet more and more blatantly reminds his audience, through the Chorus, that in the closure of nature's sadistic system, renewed life, the promised springtime resurrection, must necessarily rape—"trammel," "crush," and "feed on" the "root" of—something weaker. . . . (pp. 23-4)

Althaea knows, even better than the Chorus, that spring is all too short and that the "fire" that bursts through the veins of man and nature can hardly be a source of hope. It is only a happier manifestation of natural process, that Phoenix-like fire that simultaneously creates and consumes not only vegetative and animal nature but also the happiness and the hopes, the dreams and the prayers, harbored by the spirits of men. . . . (p. 24)

Swinburne thus suggests, through the shifting, dialectical presentations of Althaea and the Chorus, that the nature which spring revives may be more accurately described as a monstrous conflagration than as an apocalyptic flame, let alone a baptismal font, a spiritually assuaging and renewing "ripple of rain." . . . And just as Carlyle used images of gigantic size and complete indifference to describe natural process in the crisis chapters of *Sartor Resartus* ("one huge, dead, immeasurable steam-engine"), so Swinburne similarly describes the size and malign indifference of nature and nature's forces when he has Althaea refer to nature's power as that of a "boar," "the blind bulk of the immeasurable beast." . . . The goddess Artemis is another metaphorical figure Swinburne uses to describe those immeasurable, indifferent powers of nature. (pp. 25-6)

Earth's "spring" is "Barren," the poet explodes in **"Anactoria,"** for the same powers which create life also destroy it. . . . [The] fruit of the romantic poet's faith or belief in his own powers is similarly ruined by this knowledge of the violence, division, even opposition of all natural forces. Just as Hardy would fear that poetic complaints about an indifferent, omnipotent, "Immanent Will" were fruitless, since his own act of writing was necessarily a manifestation of the Will in action, Swinburne suggests in his aptly named poem **"The Triumph of Time"** that his own tortured attempts to bring love and poetry to fruition in a cruel and barren world are "ruined at root." Poetry becomes "ruined rhyme," and love, which Swinburne calls "this fruit of my heart," "will not grow again." . . .

Times does, indeed, ruin all of life at root for Swinburne. Far from being a repressive illusion, a self-constricting dream of Urizen which the imagination can pierce and transcend, time is, in Swinburne's early poetry, an inescapable facet of nature's unholy plan. It is an integral part of that larger, natural law which is symbolized in *Atalanta* by the burning brand—the law which the dying Meleager comes to understand when he says that

> . . . this death was mixed with all my life,
> Mine end with my beginning: and this law,
> This only, slays me. . . .

(pp. 26-7)

When Swinburne wrote *Atalanta in Calydon,* he was, to a great extent, caught in a middle time between faith and skepticism, and this fact no doubt has something to do with his choice of the dramatic or monodramatic form. The poet need not commit himself either to dogma or to heresy so long as he can clone his divided self into a series of soliloquies (as in *Poems and Ballads,* first series) or into dramatically opposed characters (as in *Atalanta*).

This heart's division is evident in Swinburne's poetry in oxymorons like "Adorable, detestable" . . . , a phrase used to describe the coolly perfect Atalanta, but it also compels Swinburne to create larger oxymoronic structures, too. There is a pair of monodramas entitled **"A Ballad of Life"** and **"A Ballad of Death."** There are the unresolvable conflicts of *Atalanta in Calydon,* a work in which a writer torn between dreams and despair creates a world in which every love is balanced by a loathing, every triumph by a catastrophe. (pp. 32-3)

Atalanta opens, literally and figuratively, between the moon and the sun, since the time of day is dawn and the chief huntsman's opening speech begins as an invocation to Artemis and becomes, suddenly, an invocation to Apollo. The first choral ode describes the transition from winter to spring, but Althaea quickly counters the description with a reminder that no sooner does winter turn to spring than summer, once again, turns to autumn. As the poem develops its images, we soon realize that Calydon is a world caught between seasons, between "night" and "day," "hound" and "fawn" . . . , "pain" and "pleasure," "strength" and impotence . . . , "sow[ing]" and "reap[ing]," "desire" and "death," that it lies paralyzed in an utterly divided and divisive place and time "Between a sleep and a sleep." . . . (pp. 34-5)

[*Atalanta*] ends in explosive fireworks of utter and irreconcilable divisions that have been growing ever wider since nature's inception of the dramatic action. Most of these schisms are obvious and many have been so critically belabored that a handful of examples should suffice. The Chorus is torn between describing the world as it really is and "dreaming" or "praying" that soon the natural, romantic, and social disorder will be "assuaged." (Even the choral defintion of God vacillates from "high" good . . . to "supreme evil" . . . to a perfectly oxymoronic "resolution" of these definitions ["good with bad"]). . . . Althaea's speeches are similarly divided, even from the beginning, between honeyed lines of an obsolete scripture . . . and unbearably painful descriptions of the world as it is. . . . Besides being torn between faith and doubt in the gods, Althaea is torn between two kinds of love—one for her son, the other for those brothers who have been slain by her son—and it is this inner conflict which brings about both Meleager's death and her own spiritual death. Meleager's tragic actions are similarly controlled by diametrically opposed passions and loyalties. All these divisions, plus some others, catalyze those tragic reactions that form the terrible climax of the drama, a climax without release, a "resolution" characterized not by tragic recognitions, communications, and catharsis, but rather by deafness, inarticulateness, and departure.

The tragedy of *Atalanta* is that tragedy which cannot be resolved, that catastrophe which results when romantic and religious dreams are exploded by reality and when reality, in turn, cannot be borne, when fancy and fact explode each other in one fire, leaving the characters' "speech flicker[ing] like a blown-out flame," leaving their stammering author in the analogous position of ending his work, in action, tone, and punctuation, with only questions. Does death bring Meleager release from consciousness, or only "wail[ing] by impassable streams" . . . ? Does he, through his last speech, earn his mother's forgiveness? From Atalanta, his coldly quiet beloved, does Meleager earn "honour" and the consummative "kiss" for which he pleads? Is Atalanta good or evil, human or divine? Will the slaying of the boar usher in a better, more harmonious age for nature, for lovers, for Calydonian society? Have the gods ever really existed, or have "gods" been merely the names man has given to his own irresponsible, evil propensities? Who are the "lords" with which the Chorus, in its final speech, says man must constantly "contend"—supernatural forces or man's own destructive romantic dreams? (pp. 46-7)

Ross C. Murfin, "The Agnostic Agony: Swinburne's Poetry of Loss," in his Swinburne, Hardy, Lawrence and the Burden of Belief *(reprinted by permission of*

The University of Chicago Press; © 1978 by The University of Chicago), University of Chicago Press, 1978, pp. 22-47.

ADDITIONAL BIBLIOGRAPHY

Baird, Julian. "Swinburne, Sade, and Blake: The Pleasure-Pain Paradox." *Victorian Poetry* 9, Nos. 1, 2 (Spring-Summer 1971): 49-75.
Examination of the "exploration in the separate poems [in *Poems and Ballads*] of various aspects of love and lust, pleasure and pain, God and nature, virtue and vice," and Swinburne's engagement with these themes in his reading of Sade and Blake.

Beerbohm, Max. "No. 2. The Pines." In his *And Even Now*, pp. 55-88. New York: E. P. Dutton & Co., 1921.
Sympathetic reminiscence of the later years of Swinburne and Watts-Dunton in seclusion at Putney.

Chew, Samuel C. *Swinburne*. Boston: Little, Brown and Co., 1929, 335 p.
Lengthy critical study of Swinburne's poetic achievement.

Fletcher, Ian. *Swinburne*. London: Longman, 1973, 66 p.
Overview of Swinburne's life and work.

Fuller, Jean Overton. *Swinburne: A Critical Biography*. London: Chatto & Windus, 1968, 319 p.
Biography with extensive literary criticism.

Gosse, Edmund. *The Life of Algernon Charles Swinburne*. New York: The Macmillan Co., 1917, 363 p.
First major biography.

Grierson, H.J.C. *Swinburne*. Rev. ed. London: Longmans, Green, 1959, 32 p.
Critical survey.

Harrison, Antony H. "The Aesthetics of Androgyny in Swinburne's Early Poetry." *Tennessee Studies in Literature* Vol. XXIII (1978): 87-99.
Notes Swinburne's "preoccupation with equivocal sexuality" and cites *Atalanta in Calydon* and "Hermaphroditus" as exemplifying both "his positive and negative expressions of the androgynous ideal."

Hyder, Clyde Kenneth. *Swinburne's Literary Career and Fame*. Durham, N.C.: Duke University Press, 1933, 388 p.
Biography, quoting extensively from Swinburne's critics. Hyder includes a comprehensive bibliography of works on Swinburne.

Hyder, Clyde Kenneth. Preface and Introduction to *Swinburne Replies: Notes on Poems and Reviews, Under the Microscope, Dedicatory Epistle,* by Algernon Charles Swinburne, pp. vii-xi; 1-14. Syracuse: Syracuse University Press, 1966.
Recounts the negative critical reaction to *Poems and Ballads* that led Swinburne's friends and publisher to encourage him to respond in print.

Lafourcade, Georges. *Swinburne: A Literary Biography*. London: G. Bell and Son, 1932, 314 p.

Biography concentrating on the circumstances surrounding the writing and publication of Swinburne's important works.

McGann, Jerome J. *Swinburne: An Experiment in Criticism*. Chicago: University of Chicago Press, 1972, 321 p.
Analysis of Swinburne's major works. McGann casts his criticism in the form of dialog between several contemporaries and acquaintances of Swinburne's.

Nicolson, Harold. *Swinburne*. New York: The Macmillan Co., 1926, 207 p.
Biography of Swinburne.

Ober, William B. "Swinburne's Masochism: Neuropathology and Psychopathology." In his *Boswell's Clap and other Essays: Medical Analyses of Literary Men's Afflictions,* pp. 43-88. Carbondale: Southern Illinois University Press, 1979.
Thorough recounting of what is known about Swinburne's masochistic tendencies. The critic theorizes that Swinburne's psychopathology was due to neuropathologic anoxic brain damage at birth.

Raymond, Meredith B. *Swinburne's Poetics: Theory and Practice*. The Hague: Mouton, 1971, 202 p.
Posits an aesthetic basis which applies to both Swinburne's poetry and to his criticism. Raymond analyzes Swinburne's critical style, then attempts to extract his theory of poetry from the "quasi-autobiographical" poems "Thalassius" and "On the Cliffs."

Snodgrass, Chris. "Swinburne's Circle of Desire: A Decadent Theme." In *Decadence and the 1890s*, edited by Ian Fletcher, pp. 61-87. London: Edward Arnold, 1979.
Cites as the primary theme of *Poems and Ballads* Swinburne's search for an absolute and sacred "centre" of life.

Spivey, Gaynell Callaway. "Swinburne's Use of Elizabethan Drama." *Studies in Philology* XLI, No. 2 (April 1944): 250-63.
Traces the Elizabethan sources of Swinburne's non-Hellenic dramas. Spivey cites Swinburne's use of common Elizabethan expository devices.

Thomas, Donald. *Swinburne: The Poet in his World*. New York: Oxford University Press, 1979, 256 p.
Anecdotal biography detailing Swinburne's relationships with those people who most affected his life and work: the Rossettis, Richard Burton, Richard Monckton Milnes, George Meredith, Adah Isaacs Menken, Benjamin Jowett, Guiseppe Mazzini, Mary Gordon, and Theodore Watts-Dunton.

Waugh, Arthur. "The Swinburne Letters." In his *Tradition and Change. Studies in Contemporary Literature,* pp. 180-203. London: Chapman and Hall, 1919.
Calls Swinburne "that wayward, elusive, but thoroughly lovable genius." In a review of a volume of Swinburne's letters, Waugh maintains that a perusal of them reveals "a figure refreshingly at variance from the popular conception of the fiery celebrant of strange passions and political violence."

Wymer, Thomas L. "Swinburne's Tragic Vision in 'Atalanta in Calydon'." *Victorian Poetry* 9, Nos. 1, 2 (Spring-Summer 1971): 1-16.
Analysis of the central theme of *Atalanta in Calydon* as a portrayal of Swinburne's own tragic vision. Wymer disagrees with critics such as C. M. Bowra who interpret the poem as Swinburne's attempt to deal with purely Greek themes.

Dylan (Marlais) Thomas

1914-1953

Welsh poet, short story writer, dramatist, screenplay writer, critic, and novelist.

Thomas is remembered as much for his bohemian personality as he is for his subjective and frequently abstruse poetry. In the 1930s, when a trend toward social and political commentary dominated the arts, Thomas began pursuing more personal themes whose source was his own memory and imagination. The worlds of childhood, dream, and nature are favorite aspects of existence which he celebrated with one of the richest poetic and prose styles in modern literature. Apocalypse poets such as G. S. Fraser and Henry Treece praised this new direction in writing and joined Thomas in it, while C. Day Lewis and others found the newly-formed movement lacking intellectual vigor and suffering from emotional excess.

Thomas was born and raised in Swansea, South Wales, his father a grammar school English teacher. The youth's first poems were printed in small literary journals and he published his first volume of poetry, *18 Poems,* when he was nineteen. In 1939 Thomas moved to London to work for the BBC, writing and performing radio broadcasts. After World War II, financial need prompted him to devote more energy to his lucrative short stories and screenplays rather than to poetry. Later Thomas gained public attention as a touring bohemian poet, a captivating reader of his obscure poetry and highly sonorous prose. At the height of his popularity in the early 1950s, Thomas agreed to a series of public poetry readings in America, bringing about a revival of the oral reading of poetry. Though well-received on tour, Thomas was ill equipped to handle the constant pressure to perform. Biographers report that he drank prodigiously and behaved outrageously. In late 1953, Thomas fell unconscious after one of his poetry readings and died of a brain hemorrhage.

Thomas's early work, *18 Poems,* belongs to his Swansea period of 1930-1934, when he drew upon his childhood and adolescent experiences for his poetry. Often described as incantatory, *18 Poems* records Thomas's experimentation with vibrant imagery and with sound as "verbal music." A slightly later work, *The Map of Love,* a collection of poetry and short stories, shows signs of his dabbling in surrealistic technique.

The physical and psychic havoc of World War II deeply affected Thomas, a conscientious objector, and shaped the major work of his middle period, which began with *Deaths and Entrances.* In this volume Thomas's language and imagery become simpler, calmer, and more intelligible as he directs his vision and poetry towards the events and individuals around him. In his final volume of poems, *In Country Sleep,* Thomas comes to terms with life while confronting the reality of his own death. These poems exude beauty and confidence as the poet affirms the eternal cycle of life, death, and rebirth.

Thomas wrote mostly prose and screenplays during the last years of his life. Previous to this period, his most important prose was his semiautobiographical short stories, *Portrait of the Artist as a Young Dog,* which stylistically and thematically bear comparison to Joyce's *Dubliners* and *Portrait of the Artist as a Young Man.* Both Joyce's and Thomas's works offer neg-

ative views of their respective backgrounds—Ireland and Wales—each depicting what "for artists," as Kenneth Seib observes, "is a world of death, sterility, and spiritual debasement." The most significant prose piece to issue from Thomas's later period is the "play for voices," *Under Milk Wood.* Again critics have noted similarities between Thomas and Joyce. In *Under Milk Wood* and *Ulysses,* each author captures the life of a whole society as it is reflected in a single day; for Joyce it is the urban life in Dublin, while for Thomas it is the Welsh village community of Llaregyub. David Holbrook, one of Thomas's harshest critics, finds *Under Milk Wood* unenlightening, unhumorous, and sexually perverse, reflecting an unfeeling and diseased view of life. Other critics praise the work for the life-affirming, universal significance they observe in the community of disembodied voices.

From the outset of Thomas's career there has been much critical disagreement as to his poetic stature and importance. Many commentators cite Thomas's work as being too narrow and unvarying; he essentially confines himself to the lyric expression of what Stephen Spender calls "certain primary, dithyrambic occasions," chiefly birth, love, and death. Edith Sitwell spoke for many critics as she puzzled over the poet's distorted syntax and religious symbolism. The influence of the seventeenth-century metaphysical poets is often cited in connection with Thomas's unorthodox religious imagery; while the influence of the Romantic poets is seen in his recurrent vision of a pristine beauty in childhood and nature. Thomas's vivid imagery, involved word play, fractured syntax, and personal symbology changed the course of modern poetry. Though a poet of undetermined rank, Thomas set a new standard for many mid-twentieth-century poets.

PRINCIPAL WORKS

18 Poems   (poetry)   1934
Twenty-five Poems   (poetry)   1936
The Map of Love   (poetry and short stories)   1939
The World I Breathe   (poetry and sketches)   1939
Portrait of the Artist as a Young Dog   (short stories)   1940
New Poems   (poetry)   1943
Deaths and Entrances   (poetry)   1946
Twenty-six Poems   (poetry)   1950
Collected Poems, 1934-1952   (poetry)   1952
In Country Sleep   (poetry)   1952
The Doctor and the Devils   (drama)   1953
A Prospect of the Sea, and Other Stories and Prose   (short stories and sketches)   1954
Quite Early One Morning   (sketches and essays)   1954
Under Milk Wood   (drama)   1954
Adventures in the Skin Trade, and Other Stories (unfinished novel and short stories)   1955
Letters to Vernon Watkins   (letters)   1957
Selected Letters   (letters)   1966
Poet in the Making: The Notebooks of Dylan Thomas (poetry, short stories, and sketches)   1968
The Death of the King's Canary [with John Davenport] (novel)   1976
Collected Stories   (short stories)   1980

LOUIS MacNEICE   (essay date 1938)

[Dylan Thomas] is very obscure and incoherent, but at least more human than the official surrealists; one can sometimes get into touch with him. He is like a drunk man speaking wildly but rhythmically, pouring out a series of nonsense images, the cumulative effect of which is usually vital and sometimes even seems to have a message—this message being adolescence, the discovery of the power and horror of sex and so of all the changes in nature, *natura naturans*. The statements as statements are nonsense, but it is obvious what his mind is drunkenly running on. . . . (p. 160)

> *Louis MacNeice, "Obscurity" (1938), in his* Modern Poetry: A Personal Essay *(© copyright Oxford University Press 1968; reprinted by permission of the Literary Estate of Louis MacNeice), second edition, Oxford University Press, Oxford, 1968, pp. 154-77.**

JOHN BERRYMAN   (essay date 1940)

The unmistakable signature of Dylan Thomas's poetry, so far as we have it in his three English volumes or in the forty poems . . . selected from them [for *The World I Breathe*], is certainly its diction. Here are some of the key words: blood, sea, dry, ghost, grave, straw, worm, double, crooked, salt, cancer, tower, shape, fork, marrow; and the more usual death, light, time,

sun, night, wind, love, grief. Each of these appears many times and has regularly one or several symbolic values. The verse abounds in unusual epithets (the grave for example is called, at various points in seven poems, moon-drawn, stallion, corkscrew, running, savage, outspoken, country-handed, climbing, gallow), compounds (firewind, marrowroot, fly-lord, manstring, manseed, man-iron, manshape, manwax), old, new, obsolete, coined and colloquial words (scut, fibs, hank, boxy, morsing, brawned, cockshut, mitching, nowheres, pickthank, macadam, scrams, etna, rooking, hyleg, arc-lamped, contages, natron, herods, two-gunned, pickbrain). Colors are frequent, especially green, which occurs twenty-eight times and connotes origin, innocence (green Adam, green genesis, green of beginning); red is for experience, violence. The notions of halving, doubling, quartering, dichotomy, multiplicity of function, appear often, affecting the precise look of the diction; the concept of number and division organizes several poems. Some of the language is Biblical. But the principal sources of imagery are the sea and sex. In ten poems the dominant imagery is marine, and marine imagery occurs incidentally in twenty-four others. A host of terms show the sexual emphasis: sucking, kiss, loin, naked, rub, tickle, unsex, nippled, virgin, thigh, cuddled, sea-hymen; metaphors extend the reach and importance of this area. All these words, and stranger others, meet violently to form a texture impressive and exciting. One has the sense of words set at an angle, language seen freshly, a new language.

The themes upon which this wealth of diction is employed are simple, but not I think so unimportant as Julian Symons calls them in a very bad article published some time ago. . . . I have not time to notice any considerable part of Mr. Symons's nonsense; one quotation must serve. "What is said in Mr. Thomas's poems is that the seasons change; that we decrease in vigour as we grow older; that life has no obvious meaning; that love dies. His poems mean no more than that. They mean too little." Evidently it is necessary to point out to Mr. Symons, what is elementary, that a poem means more than the abstract, banal statement of its theme: it means its imagery, the disparate parts and relations of it, its ambiguities, by extension the techniques which produced it and the emotions it legitimately produces. A poem is an accretion of knowledge, of which only the flimsiest portion can be translated into bromide. A poem that works well demonstrates an insight, and the insight may consist, not in the theme, but in the image-relations or the structure-relations; this is a value and a meaning which cannot appear in Mr. Symons's catalogue. (pp. 282-83)

What Mr. Symons misses is the value of presentation, the dramatic truth of metaphor. A good poem is not as he says restatement, but statement. His catalogue, moreover, on a simpler level is seriously incomplete. Several of the poems are religious in substance and address; two poems deal mainly, and others deal in part, with the poet's gift of speech; other examples of exceptions could be adduced. It is worth emphasizing, however, that few poems describe what may be called a human situation, a recognizable particular scene. There is a subject matter, but it is general, as indeed the diction would lead one to expect. The treatment is concrete, in the language, but the conception is abstract.

Much of Thomas's inventive energy, then, goes into technique; he faces in a lesser degree than most poets the problems of a given subject. Alliteration, internal rhyme, refrain and repetition, puns, continuous and complicated tropes, are some of the devices. He works usually in rigid stanzas, six-line in the earlier poems, the lines of equal length; recently he has used very elaborate stanzas and varied the line lengths. The metrical development is from iambics to manipulation, spondees, anapests; in the short-line poems especially, the movement is expert. Certain technical derivations there are, despite one's impression of originality: from Blake (the *Songs of Experience* and *Thel*), Hopkins, Yeats (the middle and later poetry), Auden (the 1930 *Poems*); I think it likely also that he and Auden learnt, independently, something in tone, consonance, extra syllables and feminine rhymes, from Ransom. Possibly the verse has roots in Welsh poetry, folk or professional, with which I am not familiar. Hart Crane offers a parallel development, in part similar but not influential. This brings us to the question of obscurity.

That a good many of these poems are difficult cannot be denied. The difficulty has various causes, some of them being distortion or inadequacy of syntax (sometimes the pointing is responsible), compounding of negatives, mixing of figures, the occasionally continuous novelty of expression and relation, employment of a high-pitched rhetoric as in poem 29, and the use as subjects of nightmare, fantasy, as in poem 2. Personification is so frequent and is accomplished with so little ceremony that the reference of personal pronouns is now and then erratic; in general, the practice with pronouns and antecedents is careless. In many passages, insufficient control is exerted by the context on a given verbal ambiguity; the ambiguity, indeed, may be made the basis for a further, and absolutely puzzling, extension of metaphor. Development in the poem, when it exists, may be sidewise, will probably be interrupted, may be abandoned; in the difficult poems it is never straightforward. All this is unfortunate when it interferes with communication, and the trouble is found not only in the weakest poems . . . but also in some of the best. . . . But the whole matter can be, and by most of Thomas's critics has been, exaggerated. At least fifteen poems, more than one third of those in the book, present no substantial difficulty to a conscientious reader; some present no difficulty at all. Of the rest, perhaps eight are largely insoluble or only provisionally soluble. This is not a large number, and it is simply the price one pays for what is valuable and cannot be got elsewhere. One would have more reason to complain, were not much of the finest 20th Century work difficult; Yeats, Lorca, Eliot, Stevens are sufficient reminder. Thomas's obscurity is not greater than Crane's, and their values are comparable.

This verse cannot be called "promising," however, in the ordinary way, although its author is a young man. Poets progress usually by moving to a new substance or by extending their technique to handle a new part of an old substance. But Thomas's work is so special, and his substance so restricted, that neither of these paths, if I am correct, is really open to him. This is not to say that no development can be seen in the poems. They are arranged in order roughly chronological, and the latest poems are harsher, more closely worked; some technical changes have been noted; the subjects are more often violent. The diction has partly altered; for instance, blood or a derivative occurs twenty-four times in the first twenty poems, only nine times in the second twenty, and where the concept remains it may be transformed: "my red veins full of money." But Thomas's verse does not show the major signs, such as a powerful dramatic sense, wide interests, a flexible and appropriate diction, skill over a broad range of subjects, that are clear in the work of his American contemporary Delmore Schwartz and point confidently to the future. Any large development is probably not to be expected. This circumstance, of course, cannot affect the present achievement, which is formidable. All the poems should be read with attention by anyone who is interested in poetry. In a dozen of these pieces, some of them imperfect, all brilliant—**"A saint about to fall," "Especially when the October wind," "Then was my neophyte"** and **"Light breaks where no sun shines"** may be mentioned in their four kinds—Thomas has extended the language and to a lesser degree the methods of lyric poetry. (pp. 283-85)

> *John Berryman, "Dylan Thomas: The Loud Hill of Wales" (originally published as "The Loud Hills of Wales," in* The Kenyon Review, *Vol. II, No. 4, Autumn, 1940), in his* The Freedom of the Poet *(reprinted by permission of Farrar, Straus and Giroux, Inc.; copyright © 1940, 1968, 1976 by John Berryman), Farrar, Straus and Giroux, 1976, pp. 282-85.*

C. DAY LEWIS (essay date 1946)

At the centre of Mr. Thomas's poems there is not a single image, but 'a host of images'. . . . [The] process by which this host of images creates a poem is one of conflict—the second image will 'contradict the first', and so on. . . . By 'contradictions' I think we must understand the bringing together, in images, of objects that have no natural affinity; or perhaps it might be more accurate to say, objects which would not on the face of it seem to make for consistency of impression. (p. 123)

[In a passage from *After the Funeral* there] is a pair of images, each played contrapuntally against the other. There is the actual dead woman, Ann, a simple cottager; then there is the monumental figure which 'Ann's bard' carves out of her life and death, 'Though this for her is a monstrous image blindly magnified out of praise' as he says earlier in the poem. These two images are allowed to conflict, or to 'contradict' each other: the poem shuttles backwards and forwards between the real living Ann and the dead mythical Ann. . . . The contradiction is repeated in the contrast between 'her scrubbed and sour humble hands' and 'These cloud-sopped, marble hands'. Within this contrapuntal framework, pairs of secondary images are also playing off against each other. For example, in the first six lines there is an opposition between the natural earthy woman and the religious object she has become, an opposition never commented upon or made explicit, but realized through conflicting images—'hearth' or 'ferned and foxy woods' on the one hand, and on the other the calling of 'the seas to *service*' the '*hymning* heads': and sometimes the two concepts are made to clash directly and resolve in a phrase: 'wood-tongued virtue'; or the suggestion both of natural freedom and of Christian humility in 'Bless her bent spirit with four, crossing birds', or 'That her love sing and swing through a brown chapel', with its echo of the babbling bellbuoy merging into the sound of a chapel bell, and the *brown* chapel recalling the ferned and foxy wood. At the end of the poem these wood-symbols are merged into each other; by the dialectical method Mr. Thomas described, each has in a sense turned into its opposite; the fox has become something like a fern ('The *stuffed lung* of the fox *twitch* and cry Love'), the fern moves like a fox ('And the *strutting* fern lay seeds on the black sill').

After the Funeral seems to me a most brilliant, beautiful poem. It helps us to understand what Mr. Thomas meant by his phrase 'a constant building up and breaking down of the images that come out of the central seed'. We notice, also, a constant breaking down of the distinction between the senses, so that aural, visual, tactual qualities are perpetually interfused within the image sequences and even within separate images, as they are in the poetry of Hopkins and Edith Sitwell. Moreover, when one reads the whole poem, one realizes that it does not 'move concentrically round a central image', an impression which might have been received from the strength of the 'monumental-Ann' image in the passage just discussed. Though the image pattern is most intense and closely wrought, the images are centrifugal. And yet I am very sure that it is a *whole* poem. What is it, then, that has prevented this centrifugal strain from disintegrating the texture, as so often happens with contemporary verse of this *genre,* giving us instead of a poem a handful of whirling fragments? (pp. 124-25)

> C. Day Lewis, ''Broken Images'' (originally a lecture given at Cambridge University in 1946), in his The Poetic Image (copyright © 1975 by C. Day Lewis; reprinted by permission of Literistic, Ltd.), Oxford University Press, New York, 1947, pp. 111-34.*

DYLAN THOMAS (essay date 1946)

[A] poem by myself needs a host of images, because its centre is a host of images. I make one image—though 'make' is not the word; I let, perhaps, an image be 'made' emotionally in me and then apply to it what intellectual and critical forces I possess; let it breed another, let that image contradict the first; make of the third image, bred out of the other two together, a fourth contradictory image, and let them all, within my imposed formal limits, conflict. Each image holds within it the seed of its own destruction, and my dialectical method, as I understand it, is a constant building up and breaking down of the images that come out of the central seed, which is itself destructive and constructive at the same time. . . . The life in any poem of mine cannot move concentrically round a central image, the life must come out of the centre; an image must be born and die in another; and any sequence of my images must be a sequence of creations, recreations, destructions, contradictions. . . . Out of the inevitable conflict of images—inevitable, because of the creative, recreative, destructive and contradictory nature of the motivating centre, the womb of war—I try to make that momentary peace which is a poem.

> Dylan Thomas, in an excerpt from his letter to Henry Treece in 1946 (?), in ''Broken Images'' (reprinted by permission of David Higham Associates; originally a lecture given at Cambridge University in 1946), in The Poetic Image by C. Day Lewis, Oxford University Press, New York, 1947, p. 122.

STEPHEN SPENDER (essay date 1952)

Dylan Thomas represents a romantic revolt against [the] classicist tendency which has crystallised around the theological views of Eliot and Auden. It is a revolt against more than this, against the Oxford, Cambridge and Harvard intellectualism of much modern poetry in the English language; against the King's English of London and the South, which has become a correct idiom capable of refinements of beauty, but incapable of harsh effects, coarse texture and violent colours. The romantic tendency is to regard poetry as a self-sufficient kingdom of poetic ideas, owing no allegiance to any other system of thought, in which words become sensations and sensations words. For Keats his *Ode to Psyche* was a habitable bower in which the poet who had renounced everything except poetic experience could take up his residence.

The romantic characteristic of Dylan Thomas is that his poems contain the minimum material which can be translated into prose. He does not use words with the kind of precision to which Mr. Eliot has accustomed us—just as Keats did not use them with the precision of Pope—because they are not directed to any concept outside the poetry. They are related to one another within the poem, like the colours of a painting, by the exercise of that sensuous word-choosing faculty of his imagination which cares more for the feel of words than for their intellectual meanings. A powerful emotion—we may suppose—suggests to Dylan Thomas an image or succession of images, and it is these which he puts down, without brining forward into consciousness the ideas which are associated with such images. He suppresses the intellectual links between a chain of images, because they are non-sensuous.

The few critical comments which Dylan Thomas has made on his poetry show that he is perfectly aware of what he is up to. He is a highly intelligent man, determined to keep the intellect in its place. He is also the tough boy from Wales with the ''gift of the gab'' and a suspicion of London and all it stands for: a kind of literary Lloyd George breaking up an Asquithian conspiracy of writers from Oxford and Cambridge who ruled the roost when he came to town.

Dylan Thomas is frequently described as a ''pure poet,'' but he is nothing so sophisticated, literary and (to use the word in a purely aesthetic sense) decadent. He is a romantic revolting against a thin contemporary classical tendency, and driven by a rhetorical urge. His poetry is not so much influenced by, as soaked in, childhood experiences of the Bible, and doubtless, also, Welsh bardic poetry. In his early poems there is much obscurely subjective material. As his detractors have pointed out, his metaphors are sometimes mixed and inexact; his images sometimes will not stand up to a severely ''critical examination.''

The weaker poems (mostly of what, at his present stage of development, must be called his ''middle period'') show that his poetry, unless it is galvanised into unity by some dramatically powerful situation, tends to fall apart into its separate components. It needs to be, in a quite obvious sense, inspired by a unifying vision, moment of self-realisation, great occasion, which organises the images around this centre. When this happens—as it does in the youthful poems inspired by a sense of adolescent wonder and the later ones which tend more and more to celebrate occasions—the writing becomes wonderfully coherent, and, if there are occasional obscurities, the poem as a whole is filled with joy and light.

The discipline in Thomas's best work has the quality which Goethe called ''demonic.'' It is that of a very alive person able to relate his molten, turbulent ideas to certain primary, dithyrambic occasions. In poems like *Ceremony After a Fire Raid,* and *Vision and Prayer* Dylan Thomas has discovered not a subject-matter (that he has always had) but subjects which—after the impulse of the first juvenile poems—seemed rather lacking. This poetry is concentrated on the greater sensations of living: birth and death, vision and prayer, festive celebrations, like the two poems on his birthdays. In this poetry the reader feels very close to what Keats yearned for—a ''life of sensations'' without opinions and thoughts. (pp. 780-81)

> Stephen Spender, ''A Romantic in Revolt,'' in The Spectator (© 1952 by The Spectator; reprinted by

permission of The Spectator), *Vol. 189, No. 6493, December 5, 1952, pp. 780-81.*

DAVID HOLBROOK   (essay date 1962)

According to the standards of our literary world, such as they are, this play for voices [*Under Milk Wood*] is an achieved piece of some distinction, even something towards a new poetic drama. . . . *Under Milk Wood* is the rendering of the life of a small Welsh town by the sea from the middle of one night to the middle of the next, by voices, and using two commentators. The happenings in one spring day in Llaregyb are recounted, by a kind of 'dramatized' gossip. There is no main action, though there are episodes:

Captain Cat, a blind sea captain, dreams of his long-drowned mates, and recalls his happiness with the whore Rosie Probert whom he shared with the donkeyman.

Miss Price, dressmaker and shopkeeper, has an erotic dream of Mr. Mog Edwards, a draper who is courting her.

Jack Black the cobbler dreams of driving out sin, and makes his way abroad in the woods to seek the excitements of castigating the lewd.

Evans, undertaker, dreams of his childhood, stealing buns.

Mr. Waldo, a ne'er-do-well character, dreams of his mother, dead wife, other women he has slept with, and other sins, and in the end, is having intercourse with Polly Garter, drunk.

Mrs. Ogmore-Pritchard dreams of her two dead husbands, whom she has killed by hygiene.

The milkman dreams of emptying his milk into the river, the policeman urinates into his helmet by mistake.

Mr. Willy-Nilly, the postman, knocks on Mrs. Willy-Nilly's back in bed: 'every night of her life she has been late for school'.

Hour by hour as the town wakes up we go the rounds of the characters. Each character, or group of characters, is presented with a hardness of outline, and from the outside, like caricature—Llaregyb in this way is a kind of Toy Town.

The place itself bears no relationship to modern Wales, either in village or town—no such realistic relationship as Joyce's Dublin bears to Dublin. It is rather the toy-town of Thomas's childhood, and this is why he calls it 'a place of love'—it is the place of his mother's love. The effect of the stylization of the piece is to make the world a pretend-place, with pretend-relationships, such as children play, with no morality or reality to impinge. (pp. 194-95)

Making allowances for the difference between the function of the novelist who must be as inclusive as he can, and that of the poet, who, even if he writes prose, is bound to make his effect by the economy of selection, this is Dylan Thomas's *Ulysses*. We have a similar use of characters' dreams, and, apparently, a similar investigation beneath the surface of outward appearance into people's motives and compelling inward drives as we have in Joyce. Again, in the comedy of rural life, in the approach to love and death in the small local community, where contemporary civilization impinges on vestiges of archaic social forms and values, we have something comparable with the work of T. F. Powys. Both with Joyce and Powys the rendering of local life is done to advantage by the use of

a local idiom, and this is what Dylan Thomas too sets out to do.

But as soon as one makes a comparison with writers of such gravity as Joyce or T. F. Powys the question arises—how seriously does Dylan Thomas intend his work to be taken? It *is* taken seriously: yet if it has any success it is surely only at the level of the comic radio programme, ephemeral and caricaturing? Has it a 'serious' comment to make? (pp. 195-96)

The most successful passages in *Under Milk Wood* are those where an amoral playful vigour is in order, and where the cruelty or solemnity of the child-spirit in Thomas is not maliciously drawn out, where he is not making a special plea for himself. (p. 197)

[Considered] in the light of the deeper moral functions of art—*Under Milk Wood* is trivial. And, indeed, it is really dangerous, because it flatters and reinforces the resistance to those developments we need. We need to be able to allow our tender feelings to flow—*Under Milk Wood* reinforces untenderness. It is a cruel work, inviting our cruel laughter. We need to understand love better—*Under Milk Wood* disguises and confuses. Indeed, once again, it makes special pleas for falsifications of the realities of personal relationships, as we shall see. All it may be said to have is comedy and linguistic exuberance: but these are derived rather from Joyce, often as quite direct borrowings, rather than rooted in any Rabelaisian vitality or Jonsonian irony that seeks to 'correct manners' by the laying bare of human self-deluding pretensions. Offered to us at the level of the sometime comic radio programme *It's That Man Again, Under Milk Wood* as entertainment may be acceptable and even remarkable. As art it takes us nowhere, and merely flatters the suburban prejudices.

Sex, boozing, eccentricity, cruelty, dirty behaviour, are enhanced by the implicit background of suburban respectability, the interest lying in the daring naughtiness of their revelation. The norms, or the positives of living, expressed as the potentialities of human love are absent: all is denigrated. Sometimes the denigration is relieved by humour, but only sometimes. And on the whole the breathless verbal patter is tedious. Why did the work become popular? The answer is that *Under Milk Wood* would not have had its popular success were it not essentially cruel and untender, and full of seamy hints, obscenities. The comparison with Joyce may be usefully pursued to help establish these pronouncements.

In *Ulysses* Joyce's positives are weak. Joyce's difficulty is to offer us positive values in human love without slurring into the sentimentality that one finds in his poems, *Chamber Music*. Yet behind Joyce's examination of the moral disintegration in contemporary life there is the courage of one who at least knows moral disintegration when he sees it, and fears the consequences for the European civilization to which he gratefully belongs. (The words 'London—Zurich—Paris' at the end of *Ulysses* mean a good deal.) Joyce's positives are implied in the technique of the prose and his construction—the richness of the artist's verbal power, and the structural reference to classical antiquity. This is perhaps not enough, but Joyce certainly achieved and accepted the exacting responsibility of the artist, and his work has a large metaphorical force—it enlarges sympathy.

Dylan Thomas, and the mood of his work is one which the contemporary literary world finds congenial, was happy to 'rot on the pavement'. There is no moral strength in *Under Milk Wood,* but hence no compassion, and so no real drama. The women's magazines photographed Thomas up to the neck in ivy in a Welsh churchyard, and his use of the local rural scene is as playfully contemptuous as that suggests—essentially his is the attitude of the weekender from sophisticated London, his country people toys in a model farmyard, providing an entertainment which is flattering to those playing with it. With Leopold Bloom, Marion or Stephen in *Ulysses,* in the brothel or at the adulterous riot in the bed at No. 7 Eccles Street, one feels a disturbing sympathy so that one despises or condemns them at peril of despising oneself. 'There but for the grace of God, go I'. But we laugh cruelly at Llaregyb, the 'place of love'—because 'we' are different from 'them'. This is how the child, cruelly, because it has not yet grown to the capacity to afford compassion, looks at the world. It is this infantile detachment from human reality which this work reinforces in us.

But first, to examine the 'technique'. In its plan, as I have said—'a day in the life of a Welsh seaside town'—the play has an affinity with *Ulysses.* The technique derives with little originality, and too little understanding of Joyce's purpose, from the brothel scene in *Ulysses.* The only difference is the introduction of the first and second voices to give continuity: Joyce presents the dramatic fantasia without a *compère.* (pp. 201-03)

Joyce's words, then, are not simply chosen because of a 'relish for language' or 'music' separate from their meaning. His observation is perfect. . . . But the local observation is rendered with the 'native thew and sinew' of the language: like the language of Shakespeare's mature poetry, it develops both a local situation, a local mood, the present characters, and contributes to the wider poetic themes of the work. Dylan Thomas's 'sloeblack', 'crowblack', 'jolly rodgered', 'dab-filled' merely give a 'daft' cumulative effect of 'atmosphere': 'sloe', for instance, runs contrary, if one savours the word apart from its suggestion of colour, to the salt tang of the sea, and its infertility as against land and soil.

Again, while Dylan Thomas imitates Joyce's movement, he fails to learn from its subtlety of movement and rhythm. 'The darkest-before-dawn minutely dew-grazed stir of the black, dabfilled sea' has a breathless rhythm that conveys an excitement but it is an excitement from which there is little relief in *Under Milk Wood*—it eventually becomes tedious, until the factitiousness of the energy becomes apparent. It goes with an emotional insecurity: we miss the controlled voice of the true creative understanding.

Joyce's cockle pickers actually do wade, stoop, souse and wade out *by the carefully punctuated movement:*

> Cockle pickers. They waded a little way in the water, and, stooping, soused their bags, and, lifting them again, waded out.

Under Milk Wood is deficient in any such controlled movement: the overladen, breathless patter of word relish becomes, after a while, destructive of our ability to take things in clearly and exactly:

> The lust and lilt and lather and emerald breeze and crackle of the bird praise and body of Spring with its breasts full of rivering May milk. . .
>
> (pp. 206-07)

A great deal in *Under Milk Wood,* of course, derives directly from *Ulysses:* the names are an echo of Joyce's ironic use of them in the brothel scene. 'Sinbad Sailors' is from 'Sinbad the

Sailor and Tinbad the Tailor' etc., and the rest are like a selection from Joyce's: Nogood Boyo = Blazes Boylan: Mrs. Ogmore-Pritchard = the Honourable Mrs. Mervyn Talboys: Rosie Probert = either of the three whores of Bella Cohen, or a character from Buck Mulligan's play; the Rev. Eli Jenkins = the Reverend Mr. Haines Love or Father Malachi O'Flynn. Not that the characters are parallel, but the manner of naming representative types reflects Joyce's brothel scene. We have the children's rhymes and songs added, the 'voices' giving elaborate 'stage directions' like those in *Ulysses,* and so on. (p. 213)

We miss in *Under Milk Wood* as in Thomas's poetry the essential compassion of the true artist.

In Dylan Thomas the vibration against suburbia is commingled with a tone of revolt which seems to spring from a lack of assurance that he was as superior to the suburbians as he makes himself out to be. . . . [The] suburban world is rejected because it confined him, not because it imprisons others: the vibration of the sentence shows the writer's uncertainty as to whether he has ever really escaped. (p. 218)

In *Under Milk Wood* there is not one positive love relationship—only with Rosie Probert (dead) and Polly Garter (indifferent). How is it that Dylan Thomas can offer us Llaregyb as 'a place of love?' Significantly the phrase is associated with the word 'dust'—and we remember 'his mother's breast, which was rest—and dust':

> Each cobble, donkey, goose and gooseberry street is a thoroughfare of dust; and dusk and ceremonial dust, and night's first darkening snow, and the sleep of birds, drift under and through the live dust of this place of love. Llaregyb is the capital of dusk.

This expression is typically approached through the establishment, hypnotically, of elevation of mood, by the anaesthetic *hwyl.* A special plea is being made for Llaregyb as the place of the child-love—the seaside of Thomas's childhood where he walked with his mother in Paradise, and where he attempts to lead his child-like adulthood. The passage is followed immediately by the culmination of the child's hostile rendering of married love—as with Mr Pugh with a 'poker backed nutcracker wife'—in Mrs. Ogmore-Pritchard and her two hagridden husbands. (pp. 221-22)

The whole picture of this 'place of love' is essentially a sick one, caricature though it be, and Dylan Thomas manages to involve us in the sickness, so that the work is offered in all innocence by lady teachers in girls' grammar schools. Is this how we offer the mysteries of love, sexual vitality and marriage to our children, in the hands of a neurotic writer whose whole aim is the vindication of a failure to live? (p. 224)

One successful comic theme and some hilarity does not . . . make a poetic drama, and essentially *Under Milk Wood* is not a drama. There is only the delineation of characters and their background, sometimes with a gesture at a 'Freudian' explanation of their behaviour as with Mrs. Willy Nilly, and a little vitality of observation of human nature. But there could not be any moral development, because throughout the whole of his work Dylan Thomas is concerned with only one thing: to vindicate his own inability to accept as an adult the reality of human existence on earth. To have accepted any full character, or the moral interaction of characters, to have escaped from his areal toy-village, to have exposed his own special pleas for sensual indulgence would have been unthinkable. To have begun to enact moral choice, embodied aspects of human experience in conflict, good against evil, love against lust, maturity against immaturity, reality against appearances and self-deceptions, this would have required a vast enlargement of the true voice, the true self-knowledge such as Thomas displays in his few true poems—*Out of the Sighs, I have longed to move away, Should lanterns shine, O make me a mask.* But Llaregyb itself was spun out of the false gabble of Llareggub, the world of repro modern poetry, half-art, and language with no vital engagement on life, with the help of the half-educated audience of English suburbia. It remains a plea for sickness—the sickness of Thomas, and the sickness of the society in which it became so popular. That Llaregyb can be accepted by us as 'a place of love', in all its ugliness and half-humanity is a disturbing feature of our cultural predicament. That the Llareggubian language, concealing the true voice, the language of the 'mask' of self-deception is so widely acclaimed reveals a debility in our higher literacy. There is in *Under Milk Wood* no bad and no good—there is no moral discrimination which can help us to live. Its vitality is but a substitute for the kind of search which a poet such as Chaucer made, or which folk-song made, for potentialities in living, for the benefit of human kind, to seek personal order. It may command our pity that Dylan Thomas spent his whole life disguising his weaknesses and endeavouring to involve humanity in them, to their own restriction of powers of living: but if we wish to solve those problems of Being which press on us as much as they pressed on the English poets and the English folk we must needs reject everything that Thomas stood for, the major part of his work, and the expectations of his audience.

He does not begin, in this one substantial work, to explore by metaphor aspects of personal order in relation to social order. In fact, he reinforces the imbalance of the status quo. (pp. 233-34)

> David Holbrook, "'A Place of Love': 'Under Milk Wood'," in his Llareggub Revisited: Dylan Thomas and the State of Modern Poetry (© 1962 David Holbrook), Bowes and Bowes, 1962, pp. 194-234.

CLARK EMERY (essay date 1962)

It has been said that birth, copulation, and death are [Thomas's] constant theme. This is, at least in its aphoristic statement, a gross over-simplification. True, he goes into the physiology of birth as no poet before him had done, is not unaware of and not averse to state the causal relation between copulation and birth, recognizes that what gets born also dies. He'd be a damn' fool if he didn't. But the Eliot words are too confining. Thomas is not concerned merely with birth—but with every sort of creation. He is not concerned merely with the physical act of sex—but with every form of human relation. He is not concerned merely with mortality—but with the possibility that mortality can be transcended.

To say, as also is commonly said, that for Thomas all is womb-tomb, tomb-womb is again too aphoristic; it has the unfortunate mnemonic quality and about the same relation to truth as a singing commercial. His poems about friendship, tyranny, rebellion against the bourgeoisie, man's inhumanity, faith and reason, science and myth, dogma and free thought, the integration of the personality, tradition and the individual talent, body and soul, the poetic process, the natural scene, and—above all—love belie such a narrowing of his scope. It is true

that in these latter some elementary text gives him the physiology of birth and sex, and that Freud, harnessing birth and death, love and hate, joy and guilt, offers dramatic psychological insights. But this is only where he starts, not where he ends. With Donne, Blake, Whitman, and Lawrence he raises sex (not without difficulty, of course; he was not the most integrated of persons) to love without emasculation. He is not out of accord with Whitman and Hardy in their tenderness (it is not too strong a word) for life human and natural. He explores with the Apostles, Donne, Hopkins, Thompson a more exalted love. And in Frazer and Darwin discovers conflicting testimony relative to love in man, God, and nature. He need not have studied them and scarcely even have read them. A poet takes easily what suits him from brook or conversation, and is not required to footnote.

There can be no question that in the crafting of his poems he learned from the Metaphysical poets. **"Vision and Prayer"** is the only obviously shaped poem, but the shaping process is at work in, for example, **"Now"**; in **"Author's Prologue,"** with its tricky rhyme scheme; in the experiment in caesura, **"I Dreamed My Genesis"**; in the exercise in l-endings in **"I, in My Intricate Image."**

There are other resemblances. Like the anti-Petrarchan Donne, he avoids the sugar-sweet and introduces words, images, and figures which may contribute to a poem's truth but not to its "Beauty": "spentout cancer," "maiden's slime," "blew out the blood gauze," "red, wagged root." He is not perturbed that Love has its consummation in a conjunction of sewer pipes. Like the Donne of "Batter my heart" and "Extasie," and the Hopkins of the Terrible Sonnets, he does not shudder away from agonizing stress or physical pain. Finally, a good many of his poems have the dramatic structure and quality which mark such a poem as "The Pulley." It is an illusory, almost entirely verbal drama, for very few of the poems establish conflict between real protagonists and antagonists. But Thomas has a trick of transmuting states of being or abstractions into characters which conflict with or act upon the poem's speaker in a dramatic way. Thomas does not doze off, he fellows sleep; he does not age, time tracks him down; he does not fall in love, love's rub tickles him; dreams whack their limbs, the wind punishes with frosty fingers, grief crawls off, time's mouth sucks. And always there is action: the force drives and blasts; my hero bares and unpacks; dry worlds lever; images stalk; gods thump; hands grumble.

The influence of Joyce coincides with that of the seventeenth-century poets. His denigration of "wine-dark" into "snot-green" sea, his urine-scented kidneys, his general recognition that if man is little lower than the angels he is little higher than the beasts, could not have failed to affect Thomas. Joyce followed Aquinas in organizing hierarchically the various kinds of love that man comprising body, intellect, and soul is capable of, and he did not ignore or tiptoe round its lowest manifestation. . . . To achieve a simultaneity of spectral colors and their resolution into whiteness, Joyce uses the dynamic pun, as in the title [of *Finnegans Wake*] itself with its linkage of Irish hero and workman, romance and comic song, fish and man, birth and death and rebirth. This is not word-play: the word is made to work too hard. And Thomas has a similar seriousness of purpose and a similar end in view in his exploitation of the same device. His search for the light in darkness is no less a search for the unity in variety. (pp. 10-12)

Briefly, Thomas blends the qualities of several literary lines, each different in one way or another but all related in their essential non-conformism. There is the Blake-Wordsworth-Shelley-Yeats line with its propensity toward adulation of the child or other outsider; the Donne-Blake-Whitman-Lawrence-Joyce-Yeats line with its concept of total love; the Donne-Herbert-Joyce-Eliot-Auden line with its crafting, its wit, its functional word-play; the Keats-Hopkins line with its crowding sensuosity; the Donne-Browning-Hardy-Eliot line with its verbal ruggedness and its sense of poem as drama.

Different in the sound and tone and manner of their work, all these were alike in being at outs with a prevailing dogma—a literary fashion, a moral code, a social situation, a religious creed. And all are linked, too, in that they are seeking God: a lost Christian God, the true Christian God, or a substitute in Nature or Art or History or Man.

And so is Thomas. The body of his poetry is a record of the search, a search never satisfactorily concluded. And here another problem arises: the problem of interpreting a poet whose attitude toward Christianity is never constant but who constantly uses Christian symbols. For his insistent questions, Thomas found answers that satisified the intellect, and answers that satisfied the heart. Only rarely did the answers satisfy both simultaneously. Because he made the search, he is, as Watkins has said, a religious poet. Because he affirms a crucified Christ and is witness to the test, the fall, the judgment, the agony, and the redemption *in himself*, he may be said to be a kind of Christian. But in his sectlessness and his sexfullness, he is a Christian with a difference, one who may be said by more orthodox Christians not to be one at all. (pp. 14-15)

Thomas's great appeal is to the child of the twentieth century moved by the Christian story but not led to become, or remain, an organization-Christian; seeking a faith which does not deny but assimilates Frazer, Freud, Darwin; seeking a solidarity which does not mean conformity to the tabus of the elders or the demands of the bureaucratic state; seeking a retreat from the responsibilities of the too-early adulthood compelled by the needs of a world in revolution; seeking escape from suburban monotone to pastoral idiosyncrasy.

It is an appeal heightened because Thomas is young like them (even into middle age), awkward, rash, sloppy in manner and dress, but good-hearted and "with a sense of humor"; not a Prufrock nor a Beckett (they may appreciate Eliot's resonance and wit, but they cannot identify with him, as they cannot with the aloof Yeats, the suspect Pound, the cold Joyce, the public-school Auden, the porcelain-finished Stevens, or even the erratic Cummings and too-queer Crane).

There are color and excitement, and youthfulness and honesty in Thomas's poems. And an affirmation that neither denies nor conceals the facts of existence but accepts them. Thomas offers religion in the sense that it is "the sign of the hard-pressed creature, the heart of a heartless world, the soul of soulless circumstances." The times are such that what he offers has been gratefully received because it is (in the sense of "capable of meeting") equal to even if not True. (pp. 15-16)

> *Clark Emery, in his* The World of Dylan Thomas *(copyright 1962 by University of Miami Press), University of Miami Press, 1962, 319 p.*

DEREK STANFORD (essay date 1964)

The seven stories in *The Map of Love* exhibit a typical young man's prose: not the prose of a young poet writing about poetry, but that of a poet using prose to convey what he has generally expressed in verse. (Remove the formal device of narrative and the tales in *The Map of Love* might all have been poems from that or previous volumes.) The value of these first stories, I should say, is that of Yeats' early stories. We read them, in retrospect, because they are the work of a fine poet, rather than because they succeed in themselves. But taken as a part of the poet's imaginary world, and read for the clues they offer to Thomas' literary temperament, and the confirmation of his mode of thought in verse, these tales are interesting enough. A second element in our just concern with them is that of their prophetic property—the way in which odd passages and phrases look forward to the objective consummation of the author's later prose.

The common quality in these seven stories is in the abnormal world they present. Some of them are fantasies; and others, while observing certain obligations to the claims of 'reality', make good their escape from such ties by employing themes of dementia and madness. The setting, in each case, is in Wales, within range of "the Jarvis Hills" (a fictional topographical reference). Most of the stories have pastoral backgrounds; though in one of them an industrial town is featured. But, unlike the later tales in *Portrait of the Artist as a Young Dog,* the *genius loci* or spirit of the place is only evoked in the most general terms. Place in these early stories is not a matter of particular locality but of vague associative ideas. (pp. 156-57)

Disparate passages of 'poetical' musing or of too self-conscious prose, drift like mists through the stories, depriving them of narrative economy and shape.

Lacking a grasp of particulars as being part of a general body, these tales do, however, occasionally evince that celebration of individual traits, that closeness to things, which the later prose reveals. "Upon town pavements," Thomas writes in *The Orchards,* "he saw the woman step loose, her breasts firm under a coat on which the single hairs from old men's heads lay white on black." His perception here is as shrewd as that of Maupassant or the de Goncourts.

Anticipative, too, is the vivid use of the 'character' verb in the following sentence from *The Enemies:* "In her draughty kitchen Mrs. Owen grieved over the soup."

It is small points such as these that look forward to the pincer-like perception which we get in, say, *A Story* . . . : "The charabanc pulled up outside the Mountain Sheep, a small, unhappy public house with a thatched roof like a wig with ringworm." (pp. 160-61)

Portrait of the Artist as a Young Dog, a 'touched-up' and thinly-veiled autobiography, consisting of ten stories, is a gem of humorous juvenile frankness. Allowing for its more disruptive plan, the book possesses a vivid truth similar to that of *Huckleberry Finn.* It has poetry, humour, psychological shrewdness, and an excellent swiftness in character-depiction.

In the description of farm-life and the country (see *The Peaches* and *A Visit to Grandpa's*) there are passages that prompt us to compare this aspect of Thomas with Alain-Fournier. Both have a like prose lyricism, and a kind of youthful nostalgia; but the Frenchman is more naively idealistic and sentimental than Thomas, and has not got his anodyne of humour. (p. 165)

[In the protagonist] we have a real *enfant terrible*, a quite irrepressible junior Titan thirsting for the blood of all experience.

We see him, in *Patricia, Edith and Arnold,* playing-up the house-maid and listening to her talk; scrapping with a school-boy who becomes his best friend, and with whom he exchanges fantasies of future artistic greatness (in *The Fight*); pursuing, unsuccessfully, the caresses of school-girls (in *Extraordinary Little Cough*); getting drunk in the sailors' pubs as a 'cub' reporter (in *Old Garbo*); and just missing a love-experience with a beautiful young street-walker (in *One Warm Saturday).*

But the various phases of growth through which the youthful hero passes are counter-parted, as it were, by the diversity of the book's other characters: foxy "Uncle Jim", in the course of trading his live-stock over the counter for liquor; cousin Gwilym, training for the ministry, who writes poems to actresses, practises his sermons from a cart in the barn, and masturbates himself in the farm privy while reading pornographic books; "Grandpa" who lights his pipe beneath the blankets, and sits up in bed driving imaginary horses; the drunk man who lost most of his posterior in a pit-accident (for which mischance he was awarded "Four and three! Two and three ha'pence a cheek''); the old begger who removes his cap and sets his hair on fire for a penny ("only a trick to amuse the boys", scornfully observes the young narrator)—these, and many others, vivify the *Portrait.*

And, in this book, we have proceeded from the half-mythical landscapes of *The Map of Love* to a real particularised Welsh world; not so compact and concentrated as that of Thomas' dramatic literature, yet still singularly present before the eyes. The optic nerve, on the watch for those individual splashes in the palette of local colour, vibrates finely in these stories. . . . (pp. 166-67)

From the prose to the dramatic-work of Thomas, we pass by natural transition. . . .

With Thomas' growing interest in people, and the flagging of the lyrical subjective spirit in him, it was proper that the drama should prove his next stage. From the stories it could be seen that a larger scope for spoken speech was required by him. It was clear that, with his ear for language, Thomas could do more with dialogue if he had the broader, more appropriate framework. That framework he found in dramatic writing: the film scenario of *The Doctor and the Devils* and "A Play for Voices" *Under Milk Wood.* (p. 169)

Acceptance of life . . . and the impression that acceptance brings knowledge of what it is all about, is as good for the dramatist as it may be stultifying for the lyrical poet. One of Thomas' commentators has remarked how in the early poem *Especially when the October wind,* "the poet first fully assumed his Orphic role, celebrating a particular day, a particular place." This role was often overlaid by Thomas' poetry of private enquiry; but in the stories, and finally in drama, it asserts itself in increasing splendour. Just as *18 Poems* is a landmark to adolescent isolation, so *Under Milk Wood* is a lasting monument to the world of adult community. And writing, as he does of parish happenings, the poet's language loses its cloudy probing. Powerfully experimental as it remains, the speech of this "Play for Voices" is common speech, a racy Anglo-Welsh utterance amplified out of dialect into a vivid mundane poetry. In embracing the vision of 'otherness', the language of Thomas has attained the public register. (pp. 170-71)

[The screen-play *The Doctor and the Devils* is] taken from a story-line by Donald Taylor, and based on the murders of Burke and Hare. (p. 171)

In the screen-play's opening scene, the implications of the man and the city, interpreted through visual counters, are conveyed together. From now on, we shall see them developed, for the most part, separately; but their joint or juxtaposed appearance at the beginning is imperative, since it is from the contact of two worlds—that of well-fed intellectual aristocracy and that of vicious besotted penury—that the tragedy is to spring.

The atmosphere that unifies these two separate spheres is one of caricature, of exaggeration. Both in the 'low-life' figures of this screen-play and in its characters from the drawing-room, a Dickensian spirit prevails. The presentation, in both cases, owes much to conventions of melodrama; but, here, it is a kind of melodrama in which the sinister is tempered by the facetious and grotesque. (p. 174)

Broom and Fallon, the murderers, who kill their victims before they sell their corpses to Dr. Rock for the purpose of dissection, are chiefly delineated, in visual terms, by their actions. Broom is described as "dog-haired". We see him leaping on to a barrow, which his slatternly woman is wheeling. . . .

This visualising of the characters, even so far as concerns their inner life, is a proof of just how far Thomas has borne his new medium in mind. When applied to such elementary and elemental types as Fallon and Broom, it seems entirely justified. Fallon, sitting drunk in a tavern, looking, terrified, at his strangler's hands, asserting that "there's devils in them" and that those he has killed were "my brothers . . . and my sisters . . . and my mother . . .'', speaks primarily through his movements, through the stillness and twitching of his hands. Indeed, there is only one passage in which the words of these 'low life' figures tells us more than their own actions or settings. (p. 176)

But the method of presenting character by its outward physical symptoms—appropriate to such animal types as the two murderers—has certain disadvantages when dealing with more evolved personalities. From Donald Taylor's appendix to the screen-play, we know that the tale of Dr. Rock "was written because [he] had been searching for some years to find a story that could pose the question of 'the ends justifying the means'." In other words, the originator of the play which Thomas wrote intended that the piece should be moral drama or tug-of-war with conscience, as well as a crime-and-detection story.

That Thomas in his screen-play failed completely to convey this—and failed because he found no way of representing inwardness of character—is obvious. Never, until the last scene, after the trial of the two murderers and his own public disgrace, is Dr. Rock shown as entertaining any qualms concerning the source of the bodies that are sold to him for purpose of autopsy. The only value he recognises is that of disinterested scientific research; and morality is confounded in his mind with all that is entailed by respectability. His attitude to ethical issues, as others see them, is one of arrogance. Outside of that which promotes research, he accepts no claims or checks upon his conduct: he is very much the Nietzschean super-man. There is none of that questioning and wrestling with conscience which we might expect the protagonist of a play treating of 'ends and means' to reveal. Right up to Dr. Rock's last monologue, we believe that the tragedy of the piece (in so far as it refers to the Doctor) is that of the great man punished for his pride, for the sin of *hubris* which the Greeks spoke of. Then we see that, after all, the struggle of the conscience was supposed to be embodied. (pp. 177-78)

Part of Thomas' failure here seems to derive from his exclusive use of the visualising process to indicate the thoughts and feelings of his characters. To express the inner life of Broom and Fallon in gestures and actions, rather than in words, was an entirely satisfactory resolve; but the higher complex nature of the Doctor's personality required more elaborate presentation: either a number of finer traits and gestures which should symbolise the workings of his will and his conscience, or words which in some way should suggest the direction of the conflict within him. Because Thomas provided neither of these, the figure of the Doctor remains something of a Byronic 'dummy' for all the energy of rhetoric which he tries to pump into him.

To find what is positive in *The Doctor and the Devils,* we must look at it not as high tragedy, but as a dramatic description of poverty and crime on a clearly lower level, artistically speaking. The whole richness of the story adheres to its treatment of the world of 'low life'. The upper level of Edinburgh—the professional academic world of Dr. Rock—is tamely depicted in comparison.

The grim humour—of paradox and contrast—is present in Thomas' painting of the sordid slum backgrounds. (pp. 178-79)

This is the environment of Charles Dickens—the Dickens inspired, as he often was, by Mayhew's world of the London poor, but described with a naked cynicism of speech foreign to the nineteenth-century author. (p. 180)

If the grotesquerie of Dickens is observable in *The Doctor and the Devils,* then a broader, more general, element of the novelist informs the "Play for Voices" *Under Milk Wood;* namely, his exuberance. In describing the surface tics of character, the visible oddities of individual difference, *Under Milk Wood* is truly Pickwickian. And, as with the *Pickwick Papers,* what we remember is not plot but portraiture, not the actions of people but the people who commit them.

In one point, though, the likeness breaks down. For all their robustious extrovert existence, the characters of Dickens have a certain reticence. Their observance of Victorian sexual proprieties is exemplary enough to point to inhibition. Whenever Mrs. Grundy might be offended, the assertive current that feeds their lives becomes tame, conventional, effete. There is, of course, no question of keeping the bridle on Thomas' creations. The denizens of *Under Milk Wood* are Dickensian figures with the blinkers off. The erotic for them is a spur, not a bit. They are not, like characters from Dickens, real figures too frequently flawed with a paste-board front or a card-board facet: one feels they are flesh and blood throughout. Thus, Gossamer Beynon, "demure and proud and schoolmarm in her crisp flower dress and sun-defying hat, with never a look or lilt or wriggle", tells herself, concerning an undeclared admirer, "I don't care if he *is* common. . . . I want to gobble him up. I don't care if he *does* drop his aitches . . . so long as he's all cucumber and hooves". And this irrepressible frankness informs the self-confession of most of the characters.

Sometimes this takes the form of dream-thoughts or day-dreams, of memories (as Captain Cat's of Rosie Propert), or of songs put into the character's mouths but meant as only audible to the inner ear (Polly Garter's song and that of Mr. Waldo).

Under Milk Wood is described as "A Play for Voices". This phrase primarily refers to the play's suitability for broadcasting; but it may be as well to consider more closely the specific nature of the work. Now if we begin by defining a drama as a form of stage narrative possessed of a *dénouement,* it will be hard to allow that *Under Milk Wood* is a drama at all. Like James Joyce's *Ulysses,* the form this work of Thomas takes is cyclic: an account of twenty-four hours of life in the little fishing-town of Llaregyb. But, unlike Joyce's novel, there is no hero—no Bloom or Stephan—and no substantial accession of self-knowledge to any of the characters, in *Under Milk Wood.* As things have been, so they go on: the 'bad' characters (No-good Boyo, Polly Garter, and Mr. Waldo) remain 'bad', and the 'good' characters (the Rev. Eli Jenkins and Miss Myfanwy Price) remain 'good'. There are no conversions and no retrogressions; for vice and virtue, in this work, are seen only as attributes of individuality, like winking, stammering, or jerking one's head.

This is not to say that the play does not contain a number of incidents and situation, a variety of limited dramas *in petto.* But the sum of these incidents cannot be expressed in a formula common to them all. They are just so many daily actions and intentions of separate people living in the same town. So Polly Garter continues to enjoy the intimate male company of all and sundry, Dai Bread the baker to share his two wives, Mog Edwards to woo Miss Myfanwy Price, Mr. Pugh to plan to poison Mrs. Pugh, and Mr. Waldo to drink and whore with the same alacrity as ever.

The actions, then, in *Under Milk Wood* are episodic rather than dramatic. They illustrate the nature of the characters, not in the changing fitful light of time but rather *sub specie aeternitatis.* In this sense, the characters of *Under Milk Wood* are static unephemeral creations. Their author has so fallen in love with the uniqueness of their individual make-ups that he has chosen to celebrate them by giving them a type of permanent existence. This permanence bears some relation to that which Keats intended in his *Ode on a Grecian Urn.* Llaregyb, the town in Thomas' play, is like Keats' "unravished bride of quietness": time cannot terminate the actions which take place there. But the actions are not, as in the poem, of an idealised nature. Instead of the happy piper, the lover and his girl, and the priest leading the heifer to the sacrificial alter, we have the acid bickerings of Mr. and Mrs. Pugh, the house-proud severities of Mrs. Ogmore-Pritchard, the crazy inanities of Lord Cut-Glass, and a dozen other brands of small-town boorishness. And yet, because of this un-ideal existence, the appearance of reality is the greater. Thomas has somehow learned to look at the mundane and the ordinary with such a fund of love, that the celebration of their most indifferent points has become a matter of great moment to him. He has desired to perpetuate their memory as the average man desires only to perpetuate the memory of exceptional things.

Perhaps with my talk of the 'ordinary' and 'mundane,' I may have given the impression that Thomas has employed a naturalistic approach—a restrained objective noting of detail in an almost scientific spirit. This is far from being the case. The style and presentation of *Under Milk Wood* belongs to the realm of heightened realism, of lyrical caricature, which Thomas had started to use in the 'lowlife' scenes of *The Doctor and the Devils.* The pervading air of lyricism is established by the descriptive passages spoken by the 'two voices', which act as commentators. Their utterances constitute a breathless condensed kind of prose-poetry with many colloquial over-tones:

> First Voice (Very softly)
>
> To begin at the beginning:
>
> It is spring, moonless night in the small town, starless and bible-black, the cobblestreets silent and the hunched, courters'-and-rabbits' wood

limping invisible down to the sloe-black, slow,
black, crowblack, fishing-boat-bobbing sea.

The strong evocative power of this passage derives from the same method as that of Whitman's poetry: its charm is the charm of accumulation—the recital of an inventory of objects. But the literal fascination of this list is strengthened by certain literary devices: by long dexterous trains of adjectives, by transferred epithets, and the use of the *mot juste*. The sea, for example, is conjured up by preceding a mention of it with five attributes ("the sloeblack, crowblack, fishing-boat-bobbing sea"); and in another passage in the play a noun has six adjectives before it ("the slow deep salt and silent black, bandaged night"). (pp. 180-84)

It is this vivid processional quality of words which provides the atmospheric background to the play. On the whole, it is an admirable device, a potent conjurative force; but there are occasions on which its use becomes a little monotonous. The syntax of the sentences in these background pieces is too often cut to a pattern; and though the choice of diction is excellent, the arrangement of the words tends to be repetitive. But it is only a minor criticism, and the fault could easily be remedied by shortening or omitting some of the commentaries spoken by the 'two voices'.

I have said that these passages of recitative, by the two commentators, provide the atmosphere to the entire play; but it would be quite wrong to think of that atmosphere as exclusively poetic in the elevated sense. Some of the passages are humorous in spirit, with the humour that belongs to the eccentricly absurd. (pp. 184-85)

With its natural speech-rhythms, the language of the characters provides a counter-point to the more literary idiom of the 'background' commentators. And humour (often unintentional from the speakers' point of view) is the chief element in what they have to say. One of Thomas' methods here is to construct a dialogue out of a string of conversational clichés, as in the little shorthand epitome of scandal concerning Mrs. Waldo and her trial of a husband.

When there comes a need to express themselves more deeply, the characters resort to songs; as Polly Garter does when she sings about her first sweetheart, "little Willy Wee who is dead, dead, dead". These songs serve to acquaint us both with the life-stories of the singers, and the reason why they are such people as they are. Polly Garter's song, then, is an apologia for her as a wanton: the death of her first lover turned her that way. . . . (p. 185)

The song-game of the children coming out of school is one of the finest pieces of the play. The ruthless cruel innocence of childhood is splendidly portrayed in the hard-and-fast rules with which they conduct their forfeit game. Whether Thomas invented this ritual for himself or whether he took it from some local or traditional children's song, it remains a brilliant realistic image of the juvenile world by an adult.

We have seen how *Under Milk Wood* lacks certain qualities properly associated with drama; how time in this play is not progressive but cyclic; and how vice and virtue, good and evil, are seen only as personal properties (adornments, one might almost say), and not as psychological or spiritual determinants.

Because of these aspects, *Under Milk Wood* is best considered as a pageant play, a parochial pageant play with dialogue, rather than as a more normal kind of a drama. Into this static time-free world, where action is not subject to ethical judgment in the form of some visiting nemesis, grief and mortality hardly enter. But, here and there, rumours of their workings intrude; and, though these cannot be said to impart a dramatic constitution to the play, they heighten its latent poetry and intensify our sense of the real. (p. 186)

[All] in all, *Under Milk Wood* is the gladdest thing that Thomas ever wrote. In the words of one of his own characters, "It is Spring in Llaregyb in the sun in my old age, and this is the Chosen Land". In this work, Thomas has found the Chosen Land which every artist looks for: release from one's own private obsessions and complete absorption in the outside world. Here, for the first time on such a scale, our most private of private poets speaks out largely, for all to hear, with a resounding intelligible voice. (p. 188)

> Derek Stanford, in his Dylan Thomas: A Literary Study (copyright 1954, © 1964 by Derek Stanford), revised edition, The Citadel Press, 1964, 212 p.

RUSHWORTH M. KIDDER (essay date 1973)

Dylan Thomas' *Collected Poems* comprises, with minor variations, his five published volumes of poetry: [*18 Poems, Twenty-five Poems, The Map of Love, Deaths and Entrances,* and *In Country Sleep*]. . . . The poems gathered into each of these volumes reflect an order that is something less than strictly chronological. A master of revision, Thomas put together a number of his published poems from earlier drafts that he had composed before he was twenty. Of the eighty-nine complete collected poems, forty-four are based on early work. (p. 113)

18 Poems is not remarkable as the work of a religious poet. The concomitant requirements of religion—belief, action, and obligation—are not met in this volume. None of the poems suggests that formulated religious thought prefaces its composition or is to be inferred from its statements, none calls attention to the activity of praise as a religious gesture, and none professes a sense of commitment. Yet there is, in this volume, a distinctly Biblical ambience. Titles betray its presence: **"Where once the waters of your face," "In the beginning," "Light breaks where no sun shines,"** and **"I dreamed my genesis"** all carry Biblical allusion. (p. 114)

In *18 Poems,* Thomas' concern was less with religion as theme than with Biblical imagery as metaphor. The boundary between these two is often indefinite, and the reader is often hard pressed to say just where Biblical religion stops being metaphor for the poet's experience and becomes, instead, the topic for which the poet's experience is a metaphor. Religion, not yet mistress of Thomas' poetry in this earliest volume, is still a handmaiden.

Religious imagery in *18 Poems* provides metaphors for Thomas' central subject: himself. . . .

Confirming both the universality and the significance of his own experiences, the poet (who appears as first person in thirteen of these poems and implicitly in at least two others) identifies himself with Biblical archetypes. Having been created, the poet creates; Adam, subject of the original Creation, also creates; so poet resembles Adam, and the story of the poet's creation rephrases Genesis. The poet, suffering, is martyred and reborn; Jesus, suffering, was crucified and resurrected; so the poet resembles Jesus, and paints his own existence in the Gospels' colors. Narrative, rather than faith, is involved here; for young Thomas, less explicit about holy praise than secular process, drew from the Gospels not the divinity of the Christ but the humanity of Jesus as his parallel. (pp. 115-16)

Selecting various poetic languages for the differing pieces in *Twenty-five Poems,* Thomas seemed concerned with separating religious and nonreligious matters. The unity of language characterizing *18 poems*—the particular fusion of sexual, religious, cosmic, literary, and genetic metaphor that Thomas fashioned into poetry—begins to resolve into component languages in this second volume. In the religious dimension, three categories are immediately distinguishable. There are those poems, such as **"I, in my intricate image"** and **"Then was my neophyte,"** written in a style very similar to that of the eighteen earlier poems. There are others, such as **"And death shall have no dominion"** and **"This break I break,"** that, talking religious matters as their primary topic, employ relatively unambiguous syntax and clearly religious imagery. A third group, essentially devoid of religious imagery, addresses secular concerns: examples are **"Hold hard, these ancient minutes in the cuckoo's month"** and **"Ears in the turrets hear."** Some of the best poems in this volume belong to this category; for, no longer finding divinity in all things equally, Thomas sharpened his apprehension of both the religious and the secular by keeping them, and their respective languages, separate.

The poems of religious intent that appear in this volume are not among Thomas' best. They are of interest either as developments from an earlier style or as prototypes of a later. (pp. 125-26)

[**"Altarwise by owl-light,"**] the ten-sonnet sequence that ends *Twenty-five Poems,* is one of Thomas' most ambitious poems. Resembling his early work in the range of its Biblical references and the ambiguity of its language, and his later work in its length and humor, this poem also had traditional roots. Like the best sonneteers of English literature—Shakespeare, for example, or Sidney—Thomas takes one particular topic and studies its sundry facets, producing in the process a kind of spiritual autobiography. For Shakespeare and Sidney the topic was the relationship between narrator and lover; for Thomas the topic is the relationship between narrator and Christianity. Like his Elizabethan models, Thomas develops a rough chronology as the sequence progresses: the sonnets at the beginning of "Altarwise by owl-light" concern birth, those in the middle concern growth and the coming of sexual awareness, later ones concern death and the possibilities of resurrection. The sources of metaphor know no limits; Thomas, finding analogies in myth, history, meteorology, geography, cinematography, and even poker, resembles Sidney's ideal poet, "freely ranging only within the zodiac of his own wit." Like his models, too, Thomas finds a major metaphor in writing and language: concerned not only with Christianity, these sonnets also discuss the art of poetry. (pp. 132-33)

"Altarwise by owl-light" exhibits Thomas' gymnastic ingenuity at its supplest. With an almost incredible concentration of virtuosity, he unpacks and displays the subtle meanings, puns, and allusive contents of his words, twisting them through a tortuous syntax that wrings out each hidden sense. But it is this very intensity of style that finally contributes to the failure of the poem; for every sense of his words often adds up to nonsense. The proliferation of possible meanings that lends magnificence is ultimately responsible for the diffusion of poetic statement into a fog of distractions and confusions. Ambiguity, in these sonnets, never frees itself from obscurity. (p. 133)

Composed of sixteen poems and seven prose pieces—all of which had been previously published in periodicals—*The Map of Love* is organized upon the central topic of love, and is dedicated to Thomas' wife Caitlin. Six of the stories, and most of the poems, address some of the different varieties of love: married and unmarried, happy and distressed, orthodox and perverse, sexual and platonic, divine and secular. . . .

Although this volume, unlike Thomas' previous ones, is unified by a central topic and is presented as a whole rather than as a collection of individual items, many of the poems are among the least successful in *Collected Poems.* (p. 140)

[*The Map of Love* introduces several poems whose religious language] Thomas develops into one of the strongest elements of his later poetry: the language of ritual and sacrament.

Ritual [may be] distinguished from sacrament on the basis of the consciousness of a "deeper reality" underlying the words. A ritual is a prescribed form, and ritualistic language in poetry will call attention to such form, whether it be a form of worship, of dance, of social decorum, or whatever. Ritual, as used to describe Thomas' poetry, may be taken to mean language that refers to some form and order of worship. Sacrament, involving ritual, goes farther and calls attention to the poem itself—to the process of poetic creation and to the very words on the page—as a symbol of a deeper religious realm. On those occasions when ritualistic poetry approaches gesture and act, and rises from words about things towards things in themselves, "sacramental" will be a useful description of the process.

The poems that illustrate this new departure are three: **"It is the sinners' dust-tongued bell,"** **"Because the pleasure-bird whistles,"** and **"After the funeral,"** The first is an example of ritualistic language. The second ends on an image that hints at the beginnings of sacramental language. And in **"After the funeral,"** a fine religious poem, the sacramental language is developed into a full-fledged poetic style. (p. 145)

[**"It is the sinners' dust-tongued bell,"**] instructive as an example of ritualistic language, does not become sacramental. . . . Evoking ceremony in almost every line, the vocabulary of this poem includes "Altar," "candle," "choir," "chant," "cathedral," "bell," and many other words depicting ritual. The result, however, is description rather than participation. Not written in imitation of a canticle to be used in a black mass, nor as a spell to be cast over the marriage bed, this poem is really a conceit. The extended analogy involves ritual; but the function of the language is not sacramental.

[**"Because the pleasure-bird whistles,"**] . . . lacking the concentration and consistency of fine poetry, has fine moments. Originally entitled **"January 1939,"** this poem is the meditation of an "enamoured man" as he looks back "at an old year." (p. 146)

Plagued by some of the same problems that **"Altarwise by owl-light"** encountered, this poem mixes so many metaphors that meaning is diffused into conjecture. (p. 147)

[**"After the funeral,"**] the finest piece in this volume, is an excellent poem by any standard. Not superficially religious, . . . its grand religious tone is conveyed by thematic imagery and by a carefully controlled use of ritual and sacrament. (p. 148)

From the beginning, Thomas is certain that his subject is both Ann Jones and poetic diction. One of the commonplaces of elegiac language, and one that Thomas uses frequently, is the idea that no words are good enough—or that the words already written into the elegy must be rejected as inadequate—to express the grief of the poet and the merit of the dead. . . . **"After the funeral"** engages this commonplace in a salient way. As important for what it rejects as for what it says, Thomas' poem tries and discards many ways of speaking before it settles on a final, acceptable language. This final language is Christian. Before it is reached, however, a number of approaches—the purely poetic, the pagan, and the pantheistic—have first to be examined. (pp. 148-49)

What **"And death shall have no dominion"** could only try to explain, **"After the funeral"** can confirm and demonstrate: the power of Christian love as a way of coming to terms with death. For this poem, more than any other, the title of Thomas' third volume is appropriate: **"After the funeral"** is a map of Love. (p. 154)

The major topic of *The Map of Love* was suggested by its title: most of the pieces contributed to a charting of love's topography. In *Deaths and Entrances,* too, title divulges subject. (p. 155)

Death is life's end, but life includes early poetry, euphoric youth, sexual prowess, and a religious interest that was less than a total commitment. *Entrances,* the results of such death, are the beginnings of a mature poetic style, a concern for the ordering and understanding of past youthful and sexual experience, and a submission to a greater religious commitment. But death is not without fear, and entrances are not without apprehension, even when the reward for such radical change is a whole new mode of religious awareness. As its basic overall subject, this body of poems takes the remaking of character by the deaths of old things and the entrances into new; individually, these poems try to come to terms with the poet's past, present, and future as these are seen in the light of this new religious awareness.

The poems in *Deaths and Entrances* that directly discuss this new religious awareness are three in number. The first poem in the volume, **"The Conversation of Prayer,"** introduces the reader to this subject; **"Vision and Prayer"** is devoted to a thorough development of it; and **"Holy Spring,"** one of the last poems, reconfirms the idea in no uncertain terms. (pp. 155-56)

A familiar theme in Thomas' work to this point has been that childhood's innocence is pure and desirable. Maturity, adulterating such pristine virtue, corrupts. [**"The Conversation of Prayer,"**] however, presents the child as one whose imperfect understanding and heedless unconcern render him incapable of the more mature prayers of the man. Incapable of such prayer, he is excluded from the divine beneficence granted to the adult. (pp. 157-58)

[This] poem is also an entrance into a whole new realm, a realm in which religion is not only an engaging adjunct but an unavoidable integrant of life. Entering this realm, **"Vision and Prayer"** . . . develops the theme. Twelve stanzas, diamond-shaped in the first (or Vision) half and hourglass-shaped in the second (or Prayer) half, present conversion as confrontation. Faced with a vision of a holy birth, the narrator describes his reaction, offers a prayer, and is overwhelmed by an unexpected result. . . . Although questions of interpretation arise, ambiguity is not a central element, for this poem depends less on the delights of conundrums than on the emotional and dramatic investment that the poet makes. (p. 158)

[**"Holy Spring"**] confirms the value of this commitment. This poem, with its three paradigmatic religious images and its concentrated religious vocabulary, is a celebration. What it celebrates is not the familiar Thomas topic of birth, sex, and death, although these are metaphors that enhance the language. The subject here is praise of a different sort: a praise of the very commitment the poet vainly resisted in **"Vision and Prayer,"** the very commitment that caused the man to succeed where the boy failed in **"The Conversation of Prayer."** (p. 162)

[The] poet of *Deaths and Entrances* studied aspects of his past and strove to assimilate them into the tenets of his religious principles. The three poems discussed above are the only ones in this volume that take conversion as an explicit topic. But the concept of rededication to religious principles—or what might better be called a greater awareness of his commitment to these principles—motivates a number of other poems. Submitting to the ineluctable force of his commitment, the poet examines things as they were and things as they should be and attempts to reconcile his old feelings about these things with the new rationale of his religious awareness. (pp. 163-64)

[**"Poem in October"**] is a poem about the making of poetry out of youth. The poet focuses on his present condition—through the initial metaphors of location—and then moves to a consciousness of the past in terms of this present. Inherent in the contrast between these two periods is an awareness that the art of poetry is the means for apprehending this past and making it meaningful. Youth, by itself, has no poetic existence. The mature poet—who has, paradoxically, lost the very youth he longs to capture—gives it that poetic existence. In this process he comes to understand the mature "caring" that, separating him from the child, makes it possible for the "mystery" to sing and also to be alive. In his youth he heard the "parables" that form the basis of his mature religion; that this upbringing was influential is evidenced by the fact that the poem about it ends with prayer. In his youth, also, he experienced the delights that his mature poetry expresses; and the form of this poem, with its carefully ordered structure supporting its seemingly casual tale, provides an example of the value of mature artistic care that is similar to the parable of **"The Conversation of Prayer."**

Having no introduction to place the poet in relation to his art, **"Fern Hill"** . . . speaks less about poetry and more about youth. The narrator, celebrant of a ceremonious boyhood, is "honoured," a "prince," and "lordly"; he decorates the trees, sings, and plays his horn. "Adam," "holy streams," and "fields of praise" set a religious tone; yet "Time," the deity here, controls the boy's life. Mingling a sense of joy and delight with a sense of regret, this poem, less resolved and more poignant than **"Poem in October,"** concentrates on the child's innocence and lack of understanding. Youth was "green and carefree" and "heedless." (pp. 183-84)

As the other side of the coin of **"Poem in October,"** [**"Fern Hill"**] is an experiment in coming to terms with youth in a nonreligious language. Whether or not **"Poem in October,"** because of its greater complexity and its firmer resolution, is the more successful poem is not really a relevant question. The important point is that Thomas, at a time when religious matters had such an apparently personal bearing on the rest of his poetry, could write both these poems. The problem of reconciling his desire for a return to youthful ignorance with his awareness of the value of mature understanding had no simple solution; and the authoritative statement on the subject made by the first poem of this volume is seriously qualified by this final one. *Deaths and Entrances* offers no final resolution. Fundamentally devoted to a study of the poet's awareness of an increased religious commitment, these poems range over a number of subjects and try many approaches in their search for an appropriate poetic language. While the poems are excellent, many are tentative explorations. Only with *In Country Sleep* does Thomas build, out of the findings of these explorations, a consistently religious language.

In Country Sleep, as originally published, comprised six poems: "Over Sir John's hill," "Poem on his birthday," "Do not go gentle into that good night," "Lament," "In the white giant's thigh," and "In country sleep." Certain similarities mark these poems. Each is about an individual confronting either the fact of or the threat of death, and each is an attempt to say something meaningful about the confrontation. "Death is all metaphors," asserted the poet. . . . [With *In Country Sleep*]—published less than two years before Thomas' death—the fact of physical death seems to present itself to the poet as something more than a distant event. No metaphor, the death that informs the language of these poems cannot be conquered by seeing it as a sign for something else. For *In Country Sleep* is not fundamentally concerned with the death of youth, or the death of an early poetic style, or the death of sexual fantasy. It concerns, quite simply, the poet's own death. These poems come to terms with death through a form of worship: not propitiatory worship of Death as deity, but worship of a higher Deity by whose power all things, including death, are controlled.

Of these six poems, two stand out as distinct in form from the rest. "Do not go gentle into that good night" and "Lament," metrical poems carefully patterned to rhyme schemes, contrast with the syllabic verse of the other four poems. Unlike their neighbors, these two have no poet-in-the-poem who is observer and reporter of an objective scene; on is a grand, controlled meditation, the other a humorous dramatic monologue. While each deals directly with death, the death is not the poet's: "Do not go gentle into that good night" is a poem about a father, and "Lament" a poem about an old man.

Although superficially very different, these two poems should be taken together as opposite poles of a single sphere of thought: the poet's thought about his father. (pp. 185-88)

["Do not go gentle into that good night"] honors a man who, in the words of one of Thomas' biographers, was "not so much an agnostic or an atheist as a man who had a violent and quite personal dislike for God." The poem, a villanelle, opens by urging the failing Mr. Thomas to "Rage, rage against the dying of the light." Four following stanzas, playing on the metaphor of light as life, offer the actions of four different sorts of men as examples: "wise men," "Good men," "Wild men," and "Grave men." In deference, perhaps, to Mr. Thomas' feelings, none of these is holy; no crosses, churches, or hymns lurk in the imagery or vocabulary of these verses. If anything, these four examples suggest pagan worship: the "Wild men who caught and sang the sun in flight" recall D. H. Lawrence's Indians, while the "Grave men, near death, who see with blinding sight" seem more nearly seers or astrologers. (p. 189)

Contrasting with the measured dignity of this villanelle is the boisterous ribaldry of "Lament." . . . Five stanzas detail the libidinous history of the narrator of this dramatic monologue, from his youth as "a windy boy and a bit" to his old age and the "black reward" of his impending death. (p. 190)

"Lament," in fact, seems to be an exaggerated and fanciful answer to "Do not go gentle into that good night" by a man

who plans to do anything but that. There, poet advised father. Hardly on a "sad height," and in no position to "bless," the old man in "Lament" shares the father's attitudes and retorts in an appropriate manner. (p. 191)

More overtly Christian in language and attitude, the other four poems of this volume—"In country sleep," "Over Sir John's hill," "Poem on his birthday," and "In the white giant's thigh"—share many similarities. Each presents the poet, either in the first person or as "he," as an observer and recorder. In each case a scene provides the impetus for the poem: a sleeping daughter, a hunting hawk, a day in Laugharne, and a walk on a hillside all are taken as subjects. Style, too, unites these poems: the syntax, very much in the patter of "Poem in October" and "Fern Hill," is fluid and easy; sentences tend to be long and graceful; and the lines of these syllabic poems, open and interconnected by similarities of sense and syntax, contrast greatly with the end-stopped lines of much of Thomas' earlier poetry.

Similarities extend to vocabulary as well. Since, from the book's title, the country has something to do with these poems, it is not surprising to discover that names of animals abound: numerous varieties of fish and mammals are mentioned, and the list of birds is truly impressive. Metaphors for the world surrounding the poet, these animals are the intimations of mortality that suggest the process of death working in life. . . . (pp. 192-93)

Describing animal actions, however, does not require the language of pantheism. These actions, making country holy, do not suggest an immanent deity flowing through and available in every natural object. They suggest instead that the country is holy because it is sanctified by worship, the worship of a Deity that transcends His creation. Naming that Deity, Thomas comes at last to a candid use of the word "God." (p. 194)

Thomas' poems, too, while full of animal stories, are directed at a serious end: the praise of God and the comprehension of death. Death, to be conceivable, must be apprehended through language. It comes as no surprise to find that this language is specifically and unequivocally religious. Facing the ultimate question of human life, Thomas sought answers in the praise of God. . . . [It] seems that as Thomas became less reticent about the open use of the word "God," he came to depend less on Biblical imagery and more on direct reference to the Deity. Perhaps this is to say that his conception of God gained a greater definition in his later poems. For it is also a noticeable phenomenon that the ambiguity so commonly associated with praise in his earlier work is absent here, replaced by a forthright acknowledgment of a Deity whose power, attributes, and worship all suggest that He is the Christian God. (pp. 194-95)

["Poem on his birthday"] marks the culmination of Thomas' religious poetry. Simple, personal, concerned with the ultimates of death and religion, this magnificent poem is a supreme exultation by one who, moving through the ambiguities and uncertainties of his earlier work, has at last evolved an honest and forthright language of praise. Like "After the funeral" and "Do not go gentle into that good night," this poem seeks to overcome death with religious understanding; yet the death faced is his own, and Thomas, always best when talking about himself, rises to the occasion. Like "Vision and Prayer," this twelve-stanza poem presents a scene followed by a prayer; but the tone, no longer one of terror, is one of joy. (pp. 197-98)

[This] poem is a novelty among Thomas' serious religious poems in one signal aspect: it does not focus on the past.

Rejecting the familiar appeals to the stability or capriciousness of youth, Thomas concentrates the language of this poem on the future. The entire poem is cast in the present tense, and its movement, never *away from* the beginning, is always *toward* the end. (pp. 198-99)

It is no accident that the narrator, beginning in the company of animals, ends in the company of men and angels. Appraising himself through metaphors of animals, he could only conceive of life as survival of the fittest and ultimate doom of all. . . . [The] poet here turns from a view of man as animal to a view of man as "a spirit in love"; and this view brings him to terms with death. Having learned to pray, he has brought his desires into accord with God's gifts; the result, no longer the terror that ends **"Vision and Prayer,"** is the simple grandeur of religious faith. (p. 203)

> *Rushworth M. Kidder, in his* Dylan Thomas: The Country of the Spirit *(copyright © 1973 by Princeton University Press; reprinted by permission of Princeton University Press), Princeton University Press, 1973, 234 p.*

GEOFFREY GRIGSON (essay date 1976)

Mr Fitzgibbon contrives to compare [coauthors Dylan Thomas and John Davenport] in this *Death of the King's Canary* with Wyndham Lewis earlier on in *The Apes of God*. The comparison is ludicrous, I'd say, if only in cause and intention. Lewis had the fiercest, strongest views of what human consciousness and culture should avoid like the Black Death. Thomas/Davenport displays about as much intellectual passion about anything as would butter a cocktail canapé. . . .

Between them, they invented a farce about the murder of a new Poet Laureate [*The Death of the King's Canary*]. Chapter One, in which the Prime Minister reads books of verse at Chequers at night over too much brandy, and picks the new Laureate, is enjoyable for poem-parodies nearly all, I am sure, by Davenport. At any rate, two of them, delightful take-offs of Edmund Blunden and Eliot ('West Abelard', by John Lowell Atkins) are quite beyond Dylan Thomas's skill or sophistication.

Then the joke, the sub-satirical squib, drags on—parties, boredom, bohemianism, scraps of Dylanesque description, which sound like him talking once more, and of Davenport's knowingness. There are semi-demi-take-offs of persons by the dozen—of poor old Jack Squire (whom Larkin and Betjeman have now upgraded as a poet) getting boozed and borrowing dough and toadying; or Blunden again, at the new canary's manor house at Dymmock, where 'upstairs a woman was chasing a man, a man was making his face up, a poet was screaming, a man was planning a crime, an anarchist was shaking petrol out of his boot,' and downstairs 'the pathics simpered, the anonymous female pickups ogled old artists and peers, a man in the library, out of sight, tore the pictures out of unpleasant books and put them in his pocket, women meditated upon disease and money, a temporary waiter was found asleep by the sloe gin.' In this Suffolk *Walpurgisnacht,* Blunden works on a sonnet he will call 'Tree Creepers in Dymmock Park'.

Characters from a superior world, treated as if they were of the same stripe, are slightly brought in—Wyndham Snowden (Wystan Auden), for instance, or Harry Bartatt (Henry Moore). Their names, with the others, such as 'Hamish Corbie' for Aleister Crowley, indicate the level of onomastic wit. An odd thing is that a character usually starts as a vaguely recognisable

somebody and is then allowed, without conviction, to turn into nobody in particular.

In this little knockabout, I found two authors tediously biting their own backsides; and I reflect that publishing it (see the jacket) as 'an extraordinary literary event' is about as low as English publishing, in its present low condition, can descend. Or is there still something to be fished, cynically or pertinaciously, out of the supplementary bottom of the barrel of Dylan Thomas?

> *Geoffrey Grigson, "Sub-satirical" (© British Broadcasting Corp. 1976; reprinted by permission of Geoffrey Grigson), in* The Listener, *Vol. 96, No. 2477, September 30, 1976, p. 409.*

KENNETH SEIB (essay date 1978)

Thomas' stories are artful contrivances, as complex as many of his better poems and worthy of careful consideration. (p. 240)

Admittedly the stories in [Thomas' *Portrait of the Artist as a Young Dog*] are not poetry—but neither are they potboilers. That they are "straight autobiographical stories" is equally questionable. For example, the details of **"A Visit to Grandpa's"**—grandpa's middle-of-the-night bedroom ride, . . . as well as his subsequent walk, in best waistcoat and old hat, to be buried—may very well have come from childhood experience. But the final image of the story, not straight autobiography, is clearly artistic shaping. . . . Grandpa becomes Everyman, and the story becomes clearly more than autobiography and potboiler.

But the stories *are* autobiography, in the same sense that those in Joyce's *Dubliners* are the shaped experiences of the author's life. Thomas admitted the influence of *Dubliners* on *Portrait of the Artist as a Young Dog,* but only to the extent that all modern stories are indebted to Joyce's tales composed in a style of scrupulous meanness. But the debt to Joyce goes further than that. Whatever Thomas' disclaimer, the title of his volume points irrefutably to Joyce's *A Portrait of the Artist as a Young Man.* . . . Surely several similarities exist. Both authors, for instance, disregard clear chronological sequence for the pointillist technique of portraiture, and their narratives abound with color. Both books concentrate on overall unity, each part designed to form a total "portrait" of a young man's growth to maturity. Thomas' title-change from "man" to "dog" suggests that the principal character of *Portrait of the Artist as a Young Dog,* like Joyce's Stephen Dedalus, is more failed than successful artist, a fact firmly established as well by Thomas' final story, **"One Warm Saturday,"** in which a youthful Dylan is lost and left in the dark. Finally, Thomas' stories employ much of the same symbolism found in Joyce's *Portrait:* sea, circle, light, dark, sermon, and dog. One even suspects "dog" of being a Joycean anagram for "God"; thus Thomas' title implies that his fictional Dylan is, all told, a young god become one more Welsh whelp fallen into dog days. His *Portrait,* like much of his poetry, recapitulates the Fall.

But it is with *Dubliners* that Thomas' *Portrait* most strongly compares. Thomas apparently wished to do for Welshmen what Joyce succeeded in doing for Dubliners—write a chapter of their moral history and allow them to have a good look at themselves in the "nicely polished looking-glass" of his art. What an Irishman could do, after all, any decent Welshman could equal, especially the Rimbaud of Cwmdonkin Drive. (pp. 240-41)

Like those in *Dubliners,* Thomas' stories reject "well-made" plot and commercial slickness, for controlling theme and rhetorical balance. Take handkerchiefs, for instance. . . . As ubiquitous as wheels in Samuel Beckett's writings or that man in the mackintosh in Joyce's *Ulysses,* Thomas' handkerchiefs link to part, providing overall unity.

Equally omnipresent are circles, cats, and dogs. . . .

In eight of the ten stories in *Portrait,* dogs are present in one way or another. Only in **"Extraordinary Little Cough"** and **"Where Tawe Flows"** are no dogs visible, though in one story the young lovers behave just like little dogs, and in the other, cats—traditional antagonists of dogs—are prominent. At almost the center of Thomas' collection is **"Just Like Little Dogs,"** a story that not only reinforces the title of the book, but which also emphasizes the animal-level of Welsh young manhood. (p. 242)

No dogs, but cats pervade **"Where Tawe Flows."** This story, Thomas' equivalent of "Ivy Day in the Committee Room," is a witty put-down of Welsh cultural pretension among a group of catty literary aspirants—including Dylan himself. (p. 243)

In sum, Thomas, through intricate image, has collected in *Portrait* not disparate autobiographical sketches, but rather cunning stories linked by repetitive theme and metaphor. If searching for maps, the reader can best gain entrance by first seeing . . . how each story points to others, and, second, by looking for general thematic patterns that encompass all ten stories. There are many general themes, few of them mentioned by critics. The stories, as Jacob Korg notes, "seem to trace the child's emergence from his domain of imagination and secret pleasures into an adult world where he observes suffering, pathos, and dignity." But Korg finds "loose unity" where I find tight. The narrator not only "observes suffering," he becomes part of that suffering. What Korg and others miss, it seems to me, is irony, like that in the title. The character Dylan is the artist as dog, a worthless youth who falls victim to the mediocrity around him—in short, no artist at all. The stories move from the partially Edenic innocence of childhood, with its pastoral open-spaces and imaginative adventures, to the corruption of adulthood, with its urban slums, pubs, and rotting tenements. That the character Dylan is no artist becomes apparent as the stories progress. In **"The Fight,"** Dylan is aspiring poet, with little to show for it other than Tennyson imitations, poems about bestial remorse, unfulfilled desire, tearing lust, and dark dead bodies. In **"Just Like Little Dogs,"** he is . . . a vagrant and inactive Welsh youth. **"Where Tawe Flows"** presents Dylan as posing dilettante. . . . (pp. 243-44)

To Thomas the artist, the artist was poet—not prose writer—and his fictional Dylan has abandoned genuine artistry for supernatural "potboilers."

By the final story, **"One Warm Saturday,"** Dylan's failure is complete. (p. 244)

Along with the movement from childhood to adulthood, the principal direction of the stories is from Edenic innocence to Adamic fall. Other movements exist in the book: from the private to the public, from the "safe centre of his own identity" to the exterior world in which identity is either confused or lost; from the narrator's objective witness of life around him to subjective participation in the mean and fallen Welsh world. Essentially, as in Joyce's *Dubliners,* the world of the work is a fallen one of frustration, thwarted ambition, and sterile companionship. For artists, it is a world of death, sterility, and spiritual debasement. (p. 245)

Modeled after *Dubliners, Portrait of the Artist as a Young Dog* is a composite picture of Welshmen fallen into physical decay (**"A Visit to Grandpa's"**), religious hypocrisy (**"The Peaches"**), loveless marriage (**"Just Like Little Dogs"**), provincial art (**"Where Tawe Flows"**), unrewarding work (**"Old Garbo"**), and spiritual torpor (**"One Warm Saturday"**). Unrequited love (**"Patricia, Edith and Arnold"**), broken friendship (**"The Peaches"**), loneliness and humiliation (**"Extraordinary Little Cough"**), escape into fantasy (**"The Fight"**); all are dominant in the lives of those who people Thomas' stories and all, presumably, were to Thomas dominant among the Welsh. The stories themselves even parallel in subject matter many of the stories in Joyce's *Dubliners.* Joyce's "An Encounter" and Thomas' **"Who Do You Wish Was With Us,"** for instance, both involve two young schoolboys walking seaward toward a jetty, encountering during their journeys significant views of self. **"Extraordinary Little Cough"** (a title that echoes Joyce's "A Little Could") is, like the Joyce story, one of isolation from society, insensitivity, and thwarted desire. **"Peaches,"** with its trees and religious hypocrisy, is reminiscent of Joyce's "The Sisters," with its simoniac priest and of "Araby," with its central apple tree. **"Where Tawe Flows"** is a gossipy Welsh version of Joyce's "Ivy Day in the Committee Room," a story in which Irish gossip flows freely. Finally, **"One Warm Saturday"** is Thomas' "The Dead," a story of failed love, life, and passion. *Portrait,* in fact, could easily have been called *Swanseans* or *Welshmen.* Why it was not can only be because Thomas, unlike Joyce, remained physically rooted to his birthplace—it was no accident that Thomas suffered his severe breakdowns in America. Wales was both solace and suffering to Thomas, and to write objectively of Welshmen was to distance himself from them. Instead, Thomas placed himself squarely among his countrymen; as once announced proudly, he was a Welshman, a drunkard, and a heterosexual—in that order. His main character in *Portrait* is Dylan—himself—as much a salty dog as any roistering and word-frenzied Welshman, and as susceptible to Welsh sin as the worst among them. But unlike most of his countrymen, Dylan the artist toiled with words toward "the ambush of his wounds," and, falling, achieved dominion over defeat. If the Dylan of *Portrait* is different from Dylan the author—well, then, why not? "I, in my intricate image stride on two levels," he wrote. . . . (pp. 245-46)

Kenneth Seib, " 'Portrait of the Artist As a Young Dog': Dylan's Dubliners," in Modern Fiction Studies *(© 1978 by Purdue Research Foundation, West Lafayette, Indiana 47907, U.S.A.), Vol. 24, No. 2, Summer, 1978, pp. 239-46.*

ADDITIONAL BIBLIOGRAPHY

Adams, Robert M. "Metaphysical Poets, Ancient and Modern: Donne and Eliot." In his *Strains of Discord,* pp. 105-45. Ithaca, N.Y.: Cornell University Press, 1958.*

    Compares Thomas's religious sonnets to the seventeenth-century metaphysical style of poetry characterized by elaborate effects of language and imagery.

Bayley, John. "Dylan Thomas." In his *The Romantic Survival: A Study in Poetic Revolution,* pp. 186-227. London: Constable and Co., 1957.

Examines the complex relationship between Thomas's style and his subjects.

Davies, Aneirin Talfan. *Dylan: Druid of the Broken Body*. Swansea, Wales: Christopher Davies, 1977, 124 p.
  Examination of Thomas as a religious poet, viewing his works as "decidedly Christian."

Kershner, R. B., Jr. *Dylan Thomas: The Poet and His Critics*. Chicago: American Library Association, 1976, 280 p.
  Designed to serve "as an introduction to major areas of investigation and as a guide to more intensive studies upon a single aspect of the poet's writings."

Maud, Ralph. *Dylan Thomas in Print: A Bibliographical History*. Pittsburgh: University of Pittsburgh Press, 1970, 261 p.
  Arranged to allow reader to trace growth of Thomas's reputation. Entries are arranged chronologically, with criticism listed according to nation of origin.

Moynihan, William T. *The Craft and Art of Dylan Thomas*. Ithaca, N.Y.: Cornell University Press, 1966, 304 p.
  Studies "Thomas's themes and images as an inner contest in the work between the rational and the emotional."

Reddington, Alphonsus M. *Dylan Thomas: A Journey from Darkeness to Light*. New York: Paulist Press, 1968, 100 p.
  Establishes a dialectical argument between philosophical, moral, and theological issues as the basis of Thomas's poetry.

Sweeney, John L. Introduction to *Selected Writings*, by Dylan Thomas, pp. ix-xxiii. New York: New Directions, 1946.
  Gives literary background to the period in which Thomas began writing and offers a general explication of his style.

Franz (V.) Werfel

1890-1945

Austro-Czech novelist, dramatist, poet, novella writer, and essayist.

Werfel was one of the most eminent and popular literary figures of his day. A prolific and versatile writer, he realized success in three genres. The poetry collections *Der Weltfreund, Wir Sind,* and *Einander* earned the praise of contemporaries Max Brod and Franz Kafka and placed Werfel in the vanguard of German expressionists. The experimental dramas *Spiegelmensch* and *Bocksgesang (Goat Song)* also furthered his reputation; and with the realistic novels *Die vierzig Tage des Musa Dagh (The Forty Days of Musa Dagh)* and *Das Leid von Bernadette (The Song of Bernadette),* Werfel achieved international fame.

Werfel was born in Prague to a successful Jewish merchant family. In spite of an obvious literary bent (while still in high school he belonged to a clique that included Kafka and Brod), the young Werfel was expected to follow in his father's footsteps. He dutifully attended the University of Prague, but abandoned his studies upon the success of *Der Weltfreund.* At the end of World War I, Werfel moved to Vienna, where he lived and worked until the Nazi occupation of Austria in 1938. He escaped to France, finding temporary refuge in Paris and Lourdes. When that country also fell to the Germans, Werfel fled to the United States. He spent his last years in California, where, in fulfillment of a vow made at Lourdes, he wrote *The Song of Bernadette.* Werfel completed his last novel, *Stern der Ungeborenen (Star of the Unborn),* just a few days prior to his death. In this work and in his last drama, *Jacobowsky und der Oberst (Jacobowsky and the Colonel),* the author attempted to define the effects of persecution and exile and to communicate his sense of cultural and ethnic alienation.

Werfel's work includes outstanding expressionist verse, theatrically effective dramas, and best-selling novels. The volumes *Der Weltfreund, Wir Sind,* and *Einander* contain lyrical, joyous, yet thoughtful reflections of God and humanity. Employing expressionist symbolism, Werfel conveyed his vision of a perfect and harmonious world and described his sense of identity with and affection for humankind. In the early 1920s, *Goat Song* and the "magical trilogy" *Spiegelmensch* established Werfel as a leading playwright. Both dramas depict the classic struggle between good and evil in the human soul. Though realistic in plot and setting, the plays utilize a number of expressionist and surrealist devices. Although early audiences and critics were confused, they found the dramas spectacular and entertaining. *Juarez und Maximilian (Juarez and Maximilian)* and *Paulus unter den Judan (Paul among the Jews)* concern historic and Biblical figures, focusing on critical periods of their lives. Though rich in philosophy, these works lack the dramatic appeal of *Spiegelmensch* and *Goat Song.* From the late 1920s until his death, Werfel concentrated on fiction. *Barbara; oder die Frömmigkeit (The Pure in Heart),* perhaps his most critically successful novel, provides a comprehensive and graphic account of Austria before and after the First World War. His most popular book, *The Song of Bernadette,* presents the story of young Marie Bernarde Soubirous (later canonized Saint Bernadette), whose vision of the

Virgin Mary at Lourdes made that city a place of religious pilgrimage. In *Star of the Unborn,* Werfel projected his twentieth-century narrator 100,000 years into the future, a vantage point that afforded the author an opportunity to comment on the spiritual development of humankind. *Star of the Unborn* is considered Werfel's grand finale, the novel in which he reflected upon and accounted for his life and times.

Though diverse in style, form, and subject matter, Werfel's work is thematically consistent. He embraced the ideals of piety and compassion and the belief in the essential goodness of the individual. His sympathy was for self-sacrificing characters who think only of the greater welfare of humanity. His later efforts, particularly his novels, reflect a number of the author's personal dilemmas: he was a Jew who empathized with the principles of Christianity, and he was a modern man who espoused medieval virtues and theological concepts, but questioned them in the light of contemporary scientific and philosophic thought.

Critics agree that Werfel's work is uneven, but away from this common ground they widely differ. Some contend that his poetry was his greatest achievement, praising the spontaneity and vigor of his early collections and noting the impact of his pioneering expressionist volumes on the development of German literature. Such critics find that Werfel's prose efforts are marred by tones of guilt and betrayal and lack the youthful charm and purity of feeling evident in his verse. Moreover, they dismiss his novels, especially *The Song of Bernadette,* as artistic failures and accuse the author of commercializing his art, of trading literary integrity for popular acclaim. Other reviewers believe that Werfel's finest accomplishments were in the drama and the novel. They state that his poetry exhibits an extravagance of style and an immature subjectivity. His novels, on the other hand, are free of such excesses and display an objective, mature contemplation of their subject matter. These critics also count his dramas, such as *Goat Song,* among the most stylistically effective and technically innovative of their day. Despite their differences in opinion, most critics recognize Werfel as a talented and inspired writer, notable for the constancy and sincerity of his moral-religious themes and for the life-affirming quality of his work.

PRINCIPAL WORKS

Der Weltfreund (poetry) 1911
Wir Sind (poetry) 1913
Einander (poetry) 1915
Die Mittagsgöttin [first publication] (drama) 1919
Nicht der Mörder, der Ermordete ist schuldig (novella) 1920
  [*Not the Murderer* published in *Twilight of a World,* 1937]
Spiegelmensch (drama) 1921
Bocksgesang (drama) 1922
  [*Goat Song,* 1926]
Schweiger (drama) 1923
Verdi (novel) 1924
  [*Verdi,* 1925]
Juarez und Maximilian (drama) 1925
  [*Juarez and Maximilian,* 1926]
Paulus unter den Juden (drama) 1926
  [*Paul among the Jews,* 1928]
Barbara; oder die Frömmigkeit (novel) 1929
  [*The Pure in Heart,* 1931; also published as *Hidden Child,* 1931]
Die Geschwister von Neapel (novel) 1931
  [*The Pascarella Family,* 1932]
Die vierzig Tage des Musa Dagh (novel) 1933
  [*The Forty Days of Musa Dagh,* 1934; also published as *The Forty Days,* 1934]
Der Weg der Verheissung (drama) 1937
  [*The Eternal Road,* 1937]
Das Leid von Bernadette (novel) 1941
  [*The Song of Bernadette,* 1942]
Between Heaven and Earth (essays and aphorisms) 1944
Jacobowsky und der Oberst (drama) 1944
  [*Jacobowsky and the Colonel,* 1944]
Poems (poetry) 1945
Gedichte aus den Jahren 1908-1945 (poetry) 1946
Stern der Ungeborenen (novel) 1946
  [*Star of the Unborn,* 1946]

FRANZ KAFKA (essay date 1922)

Yesterday Werfel came to see me . . . ; the visit, which otherwise would have given me pleasure, left me in despair. Werfel was well aware that I had read *Schweiger* and I foresaw that I would have to talk to him about it. Had I felt only an ordinary dislike for the play, I could somehow get around it. But the play means a great deal to me; it hits me hard, affects me horribly on the most horrible level. It had not remotely occurred to me that I would someday have to talk to Werfel about that. The reasons for my repugnance were not entirely clear to me because I had not had the slightest inner debate over the play, but merely the desire to shake it off. Though I may have been deaf to Hauptmann's *Anna,* I hear every nuance of this Anna and the tangle involving her with agonizing, uncanny acuteness. Ah well, these auditory phenomena are closely linked. If I now try to sum up the reasons for my repugnance, then it comes to something like this: Schweiger and Anna (and of course the immediate group around them: the terrible Strohschneider, the Professor, the Lecturer) are not people. (Only the peripheral group, the Curate, the Social Democrats, possess some semblance of life.) In order to make this bearable, they must invent a legend to transfigure their hellishness, the psychiatric history. But in view of their nature they can only invent something as inhuman as they are themselves, and so the horror is redoubled. But it is multiplied tenfold by the pretence of innocence and straightforwardness of the whole.

What was I to say to Werfel, whom I admire, whom I even admire in this play, although in this case only for his having the strength to wade through these three acts of mud? (pp. 364-65)

> *Franz Kafka, in his letter to Max Brod in December, 1922, in his* Letters to Friends, Family, and Editors, *translated by Richard Winston and Clara Winston (reprinted by permission of Schocken Books Inc.; copyright © 1958, 1977 by Schocken Books Inc.; originally published as* Briefe: 1902-1924, *edited by Max Brod, Schocken Books, 1958), Schocken Books, 1977, pp. 364-65.*

LLOYD MORRIS (essay date 1926)

A discrepancy between anticipation and performance accounts for the degree of my disappointment in Herr Werfel's **"Verdi."** The novel was received with unusual enthusiasm in Germany and Austria. For almost a year reports of its exceptional merit have been current in this country. A number of critics, familiar with the German text, have praised it highly. Its reputation was established before **"Verdi"** appeared in an English version. After reading this version, I am impressed chiefly by the inadequacy of the novel to its prestige.

In a brief foreword, the author remarks that a dozen years intervened between the conception of the novel and its composition. Aesthetic difficulties were responsible, in part, for this delay. Of these not the least, in the author's opinion, was the necessity of making the novel "move upon two separate planes, the poetic and the historical"; of making it march "simultaneously in the world of fable and the world of fact." This definition of his problem explains the effect of Herr Werfel's book, which marches simultaneously in two worlds that remain separate and conflicting. It is alternately a critical biography and an historical romance of outmoded pattern. It falls between exposition and narrative; it accomplishes neither. Had Herr Werfel achieved the coalescence of his two planes, the identification of his worlds of fable and fact, he would have established a consistent aesthetic foundation for his book. He did not; his book is something other than fact, but something less than fiction. (p. 475)

"**Verdi**" evokes the memory of another novel of which the action takes place in Venice during the same year and involves at least one of the same characters; d'Annunzio's "Il Fuoco." Whatever its demerits, and it has many, "Il Fuoco" is superior in power and intensity to "**Verdi**." One has but to recall d'Annunzio's dramatic representation of the carnival, and to compare with it Werfel's turgid description of the same event; the one is dynamic, vital—the other, static and expositive. Verdi, as protagonist of Werfel's fable, seems scarcely to live; he moves, like a marionette obedient to the author's hand through a series of episodes while the author speaks his lines from the wings. Wagner, who does not enter the fable as a character but is intended to enter as an influence, is reduced to the status of an hypothesis; he becomes, to the reader, the shrewd analysis of a psychological equation, the diagnosis of an influence. The subsidiary characters are, for the greater part, purely conventional; a voluble old patriot, his romantic son, the son's mistress and her husband, an ambitious prima-donna, a radical musician, a violent detractor of Verdi's fame. There is a certain irony in the signal artistic achievement recorded in this novel; the figure of a fantastic centenarian, a lifelong devotee of opera, whose all but imperceptible vitality scarcely distinguishes him from an automaton. In creating his intended automaton, the author has created convincingly. Unfortunately, however, he has created only automata when he intended the creation of living characters.

In its incidents the novel is similarly deficient. Every incident exists, not as a term in a narrative progression, but as a convenient means for the illustration of some particular virtue with which the author wishes to endow his protagonist. Thus Herr Werfel manufactures a series of insignificant episodes to exhibit Verdi as democratic, magnanimous, chivalrous, loyal; the reader becomes bored by the virtues and aware of the insignificance of the episodes as elements of a coherent narrative. From all of this Verdi fails to emerge as a synthesis equivalent to character. He remains a puppet, reverently tricked out in the counterfeit of heroic attributes.

As critical analysis, both musical and biographical, the novel sustains itself; as fiction it fails. Its failure, one suspects, is largely due to an inadequate re-creation of factual materials. (pp. 475-76)

> *Lloyd Morris, "Fact and Fable," in* The Saturday Review of Literature *(copyright © 1926 by Saturday Review; all rights reserved; reprinted by permission), Vol. II, No. 24, January 9, 1926, pp. 475-76.*

STARK YOUNG (essay date 1926)

The difficulties of managing the right degree of noise, tempo, visual movement, underscoring of points and isolation of the various dramatic motives in *Goat Song* make a problem as hard as Euripide's *Bacchae,* which the play is so much like and which it so obviously descends from. . . .

Goat Song is hard to talk about because it employs a language of inherited symbols that speak by combinations among themselves, exactly as we combine word-symbols, to express ideas. If you are familiar with these symbols in *Goat Song,* its language at least is easily read and not impossible to speak. (p. 17)

Werfel's story absolutely expresses his idea. In the language of its ideal and traditional symbols or themes the story speaks for itself. There is the Pan symbol, the shy creatures, half man, half beast, of the ancient forests and disordered grassy places;

and, beyond Pan, Dionysos, the rout, the enthusiasm, the bursting of barriers, the breaking down of a soul's entity in desire toward what is outside it; the frenzy, revolution, ecstasy by which man either is destroyed or is redeemed by losing his life to find it; the due balance of the two parts of man, that by which in the midst of millions like him he retains his own identity, that by which he participates in the beautiful alluring life, unchainable, not to be denied, drawing men to madness and orgiastic rage. There is the theme of the power within all forms to break them down; the theme of the desire, like the ravening ambition of a king, of each form to be supreme and undying; the theme of the virgin impregnated by the god, and the miraculous conception; there is the theme of that emanation from quivering nature, formless but visible, horrible but full of majesty, blasting all that meets it, like the vision of the Whole in one. In the language of these *Goat Song* speaks.

Euripides with his play enjoyed two advantages over Werfel with his. For one thing he found at hand a system of ideas into which his Dionysian theme of individual rapture, revolt, destruction, redemption, could easily establish itself in a just proportion. For another, he did not have to contend, as *Goat Song* does, with a Northern literalness. The origin of this theme is Mediterranean, and at its source there was no question of is it or is it not so? of fact and fiction, but only the question as to what was expressed. *Goat Song* keeps with the realm of literal fact; this monster is only a freak, though to the peasants and revolutionaries he represents a god of violence, change and onsweeping life. *Goat Song* is realistic detail that is charged with poetic meaning and fired with imaginative power. The *Bacchae* is supernatural, mythical, miraculous. *Goat Song* has nothing in it that is not possible; its miracle is no less intense but radiates from the actual. Its tone is less remote, magnificent, shining and final than the Greek but infinitely more human, more violent and more stirred with a pathetic sense of the human mind in the midst of chaotic universal elements, in the midst of a world of nature that is an eternal child at play.

In *Goat Song* the Theatre Guild had given us the most important play of the season. (p. 18)

> *Stark Young, "'Goat Song'" (reprinted with permission of Lewis M. Isaacs, Jr., Executor and Trustee under the will of William McKnight Bowan), in* The New Republic, *Vol. XLVI, No. 586, February 24, 1926, pp. 17-18.*

GRANVILLE HICKS (essay date 1931)

To the company of modern pilgrims—Thomas Mann's Hans Castorp, James Joyce's Stephen Dedalus, the Marcel of *The Remembrance of Things Past,* and the rest—Franz Werfel adds a new figure, Ferdinand R., the hero of *The Pure in Heart.* Like the others of that company, Ferdinand seeks the meaning of life and the way of salvation, but unlike the others he ends where he begins. For Ferdinand R. is the naturally religious man. It is true that, having been born in a secular age, he cannot rest content in the simple faith of his childhood. As one of his friends says, "To find God the man of to-day must lose him." Ferdinand has to expose himself to all the delusions of the day, has to experience the contemporary pride of the intellect, has to see the emptiness of all man-made schemes for universal happiness; but in the end he finds peace and strength and joy in a kind of mystic communion with God. (pp. vi-vii)

Surely this particular pilgrimage has not been traced before, and we can only be grateful to Werfel for describing it with so much insight and such warm conviction. Yet it may be doubted if Ferdinand R. can ever rouse in the contemporary mind the response roused by other pilgrims of recent fiction. Barbara is a credible figure, simply because she is so remote, quite as remote as any early martyr or medieval saint. But Ferdinand moves through the world that we know, suffers as we have suffered, is stirred, however briefly, by the hopes that have stirred us. We try to identify him with ourselves—and we cannot. He persistently stands apart.

That is Werfel's dilemma: he cannot take it for granted that his readers share Ferdinand's innate religiosity; and on the other hand he well knows that he cannot describe that spirit in the language of modern thought. The only way he can give Ferdinand's attitude any substance for us is by showing us what it is not. This he does, and does well enough so that we have a reasonably clear idea what he means. But that does not help us to see through Ferdinand's eyes. We remain, like the casual observer of the first and last chapters, on the outside. We have learned the route his pilgrimage followed, but we can scarcely be said to have participated in it. (pp. vii-viii)

Granville Hicks, "A Modern Pilgrim," in Forum and Century (copyright, 1931), Vol. LXXXVI, No. 1, July, 1931, pp. vi-viii.

LOUIS KRONENBERGER (essay date 1934)

Unlike most other important novels of our time—and at the outset it can be said that it is important—["**The Forty Days of Musa Dagh**"] is richest in story. In that respect it differs widely from such landmarks of twentieth-century fiction as "The Magic Mountain" or "Ulysses" or "Remembrance of Things Past," books which stand forth as socially or philosophically or psychologically eminent, but never as intensely dramatic narratives. They are all greater books, but they are different. "**Musa Dagh**" is also of consequence as a social novel, but it will first be read, and perhaps last, as a dramatic narrative; and since it stands foremost in that field today, it is as a dramatic narrative that it will seem most valuable.

It is a book to read once. We shall not go back to it, as we go back to Mann or Proust, whose novels are a little like anthologies and who, in separate passages, recall us again and again, indefinitely. But one reading of "**Musa Dagh**" will be enough to give us a lasting sense of participation in a stirring episode of history—an episode which Werfel has made his own, and vivified and enriched. He has quite rightly, even inevitably, built up the defense of Musa Dagh to heroic proportions, for it is a story of men accepting the fate of heroes and the task of supermen, and to have treated it on any smaller scale would have been to misunderstand and betray it. This is a story which, from the broadest standpoint at least, must rouse the emotions of all human beings; it could make a great poem. . . .

It is the story, in one sense, of a man returning as a stranger to his native country, finding himself bound by far stronger racial ties than he imagined and almost at once forced to accept for himself the fate of his nation. That is how, as an author, Werfel has chosen to give perspective to history. . . .

Werfel has re-created history with vigorous and terrifying power, and has made of the forsaken Armenians on their mountain an epic story. It would seem fantastic, it would seem incredible, were it not made so bitterly substantial, were it not projected from beginning to end with tremendous realistic vision. Writers

have taken many things outside our normal experience and made them live on in memory, but they have chosen nothing stranger than these forty days on Musa Dagh, and nowhere have they provided the reader with a more intimate sense of participation.

The action of the book resides at that level where drama and melodrama appear inextricably merged, where what is spectacular and what is deeply true acquire, spontaneously, a relationship. The life of these people on Musa Dagh is that of human beings under intense pressure, when peacetime codes and social amenities, when even moral laws, must be trampled upon overnight. But at the same time, curiously enough, trifling considerations and amenities can momentarily acquire great importance; for these people lead a life the reverse of ours. Fighting against death becomes the business, the daily fact, of life; trifles become the exception.

This is in every sense a true and thrilling novel; but it is concerned with a moment in history still so close to us, and with two races whose enmity has become such a byword, that it looms up as more than a novel; it is a social and historical document as well. We get insight into the feeling between Turks and Armenians—the obvious hatred of the persecuted toward their tormentors; the subtler hate, on the Turks' part, of strong barbarians for a race of superior culture and business acumen. (p. 1)

Thus, as a social document, "**Musa Dagh**" has not only a specific but also a universal application, and it is hard not to read between the lines what Werfel, as he wrote the book, must so often have perceived—the extremely close parallel between the plight of the Armenians under the Turks and that of the Jews under Hitler. It is not only that the Armenians, in character and fate, so much resemble the Jews; it is also that Nazis and Turks alike use the same methods of "government," follow the same policy, talk the same about "expediency."

What seems weakest to me in an otherwise deeply impressive book is Werfel's handling of individual characters and of their private relationships. Gabriel comes off well as a hero, a symbol, a man of the moment, a person between two worlds; even his final fate, regarded symbolically (though not realistically), seems legitimate. But if he is successful as a type, as a social figure, he is a failure as a human being with individual emotions and private concerns. Werfel hasn't seen the man in a double light as lucidly as he should have; one side of him has been sacrificed to the other.

As for Gabriel's wife, she not only doesn't come alive but is not always convincing; except as a symbol of the foreigner, the outsider, she has no validity. And Iskuhi, the girl of Armenian blood with whom Gabriel falls in love up on the mountain, seems much too shadowy and exaltée to be flesh and blood. The trouble with the whole triangle is that it is worked out not in terms of sex and emotion but as a game of races and bloods—a symbolism which Werfel may have supposed would strengthen the book's meaning, but which actually weakens and even sentimentalizes it. Into a narrative that treats elsewhere of real heroism it brings a touch of heroics.

"**Musa Dagh**" may rest upon history, but what stands out in it above everything else is a quality of orderly, sustained, robust imagination. Werfel has portrayed an extraordinary way of life with complete conviction. The book, to me, is too long, perhaps much too long, but rather because of an embarrassment of riches than because of padding or diffuseness. It is a book which, definitely and unmistakably, falls short of greatness;

that, in the midst of all praise, must be said. But it is a book which has a kind of grandeur, and it tells a story which it is almost one's duty as an intelligent human being to read. And one's duty here becomes one's pleasure also. (pp. 1, 33)

> Louis Kronenberger, "Franz Werfel's Heroic Novel: A Dramatic Narrative That Has Stirring Emotional Force," in The New York Times Book Review (© 1934 by The New York Times Company; reprinted by permission), December 2, 1934, pp. 1, 33.

GEORGE JEAN NATHAN   (essay date 1937)

Franz Werfel's **"The Eternal Road"** is a made-to-order job for the theatrical producing talents of Max Reinhardt, just as Tom Mix's old movie scenarios were made-to-order jobs for the acrobatic talents of Mr. Mix's pet horse. That it is of a very much more elevated stature and quality than the latter does not obscure the plain fact that it remains, nevertheless, a deliberately tailored affair and, as such, a dubious item. It is, of course, despite the conviction of the more dramatically pedantic and coincidentally less theatrically experienced critics, entirely possible, as the records attest, for a play to be written with a particular player or producer in mind and at the same time to prove itself an estimable work. But this doesn't seem to have been one of the occasions.

Werfel, it need not at this late hour be emphasized, is one of the most commendable of living poet-dramatists. But while it is within the range of critical belief that a dramatist may accept a commission to manufacture a play to order as a vehicle for some specific person's gifts and for the play in question to turn out a critically satisfactory and endorsable product, it is pretty hard in this modern day for criticism to believe that a poet can happily manage any such business. Werfel is patently one who cannot, which is doubtless to his credit. His play, for all its periodic traces of imagination and bits of moving literary music, is essentially a super-Sears-Roebuck catalogue of Old Testament goods, with an elaborate index of Reinhardt mobs, Bel Geddes scenic devices and Westinghouse Electrical Company dinguses. It represents the aloof and distinguished poet-dramatist that Werfel hitherto has been hanging around the Schloss Leopoldskron in Salzburg waiting for Host Reinhardt to finish lunch and talk over that first act moment when Max thinks it would be a smashing idea to introduce two hundred angels being lifted into the flies by elevators or that second act spot wherein he visualizes the *kolossal* punch of three hundred passionate supers rolling down the steps leading from Heaven to the accompaniment of a ten thousand dollar thunder storm and some Kurt Weill music.

Werfel is the kind of writer who cannot wait for lunch—at least not for someone else's lunch—and his play manuscript . . . shows it. Essaying to interpret the story of the plight of modern Jews by throwing against a background a series of Old Testament parallels, he clearly betrays a corrupting concern with the production suggestions and stage externals that were made to his extra-poetic and extra-dramatic ear. If he were a writer of Letters to the Editor, I have no doubt that he would say that all these producing suggestions and projected stage ideas met with his full and sympathetic approval. But whether they met with his approval or not isn't the point. The point is that a true poet like Werfel cannot be guided by other men's fancies, whether fragrant or not, and still retain his poetic honesty, integrity, and imaginative honor. His play, accordingly, is half Werfel and half Reinhardt, with Norman Bel Geddes adding up the total.

There is another point. **"The Eternal Road"** was arbitrarily designed as a stage spectacle and you cannot have poets arbitrarily planning stage spectacles, at least not Reinhardt stage spectacles. . . . [A] poet may no more deliberately think in terms of a half million dollars' worth of scenery, mobs, choirs, platinum blonde cherubim, and Russian ballet dancers and be faithful to his inner muse than he may, be he the greatest poet in all Christendom, sit down at his writing table under the starlit sky with a fat contract for Hollywood in his rear pants-pocket and not be in some way influenced out of his artistic probity. (pp. 17, 19)

> George Jean Nathan, "Art of the Night," in The Saturday Review of Literature (copyright © 1937, copyright renewed © 1964, by Saturday Review; all rights reserved; reprinted by permission), Vol. XV, No. 18, February 27, 1937, pp. 17, 19.

ROBERT PENN WARREN   (essay date 1942)

When Franz Werfel was attempting to escape from France, he spent some weeks at Lourdes. During that period he vowed, he tells us, to write the story of Bernadette Soubirous as an offering of thanks if he did make his escape. **"The Song of Bernadette"** is that story. As the story of Bernadette herself it is a biography in fictional form of the saint who, as a child out gathering faggots one raw February day in the middle of the last century, saw the vision of "the beautiful lady" in the niche of the cavern of Massabielle. . . . But from the first the world intervenes—her family, pious old women who wish to dominate her, the children at school. . . . [After] the first healing the world intervenes more and more violently, and the story of Bernadette, the simple, candid child, is absorbed into another story, the story of the impact of the vision upon the world.

Of this second, broader story "the lady" rather than Bernadette is the heroine. Her antagonists are numerous and constitute a panorama of nineteenth-century European society. (pp. 635-36)

Werfel has handled the personal story of Bernadette with grace and simplicity. Her character is tellingly rendered, not only in its effect upon others but in direct terms, and her conflict with the world is treated with great narrative skill. In fact, the suspense maintained by Werfel up to the point where Napoleon intervenes to open the cavern is a technical achievement of a high order. In his treatment of the larger story the novelist has perhaps been a shade less successful, if one applies the ordinary standards of fiction. It is only natural that the characters should tend to become somewhat schematic, too much like figures representing certain social forces. But this tendency has been held in check for the most part, and two of the most moving scenes in the book, that of old Lafite in the church and that of Peyramale at the death of Bernadette, involve such characters and suddenly vivify them. But even when this transformation of the intellectual shadows does not occur, the book is effective in presenting in terms of ideas the dramatic conflict of "the lady" and the world. (p. 636)

> Robert Penn Warren, "The Lady of Lourdes," in The Nation (copyright 1942 The Nation magazine, The Nation Associates, Inc.), Vol. 154, No. 22, May 30, 1942, pp. 635-36.

HARRY SLOCHOWER   (essay date 1945)

From its beginnings Werfel's work has been concerned with man's striving toward unification in the midst of divisiveness.

In his lyrical period Werfel dealt with the problem of individuation, which he regarded as man's defection from divine origins, and the source of his guilt sense. An abstract intellectualism and an atomic individualism have separated man from man and from God. In terms of social structures, the modern nationalistic state, with its cult of private property and self-assertion, was to him the insidious manifestation of the individualistic heresy. Here Werfel was at one with the body of expressionistic thinking and with writers such as Wassermann, Doeblin, Georg Kaiser and Waldo Frank in leaning toward some non-mechanistic, all-inclusive Whole as an antidote to isolative modernism.

In Werfel's early work this unity is located in the integrated reactions of the child and the childlike. Later it is translated into the Father-Mother motif (Barbara in *The Pure in Heart,* Teta in *Embezzled Heaven,* Domenico in *The Pascarella Family*). On the social plane it takes form in the notion of the patriarchal communality. The nearest modern equivalent of this sociality Werfel finds in the old Austrian Empire. And in an astounding prologue to his *Twilight of a World,* Werfel defends *Alt Oesterreich* as having embodied "the highest possible personal freedom within a highly responsible community." Austria appears to Werfel to have constituted the last European bulwark against nationalism, industrial capitalism, materialism and class warfare. (pp. 232-33)

Franz Werfel illustrates the phenomenon of a Jew who *wants to, but cannot* be a Catholic, of a modern who desires but knows it is impossible to return to the thirteenth century—for he himself has been conditioned and molded by the scientific attitude and the analytical procedure which he would repudiate. The result is that even as Werfel espouses primitiveness, metaphysics and Catholic permanence, he also questions them. This is especially evident in the dramatic nature of his art, where the opposition is accorded greatest justice. His primitive characters, such as Domenico Pascarella, Barbara, Teta, often appear pathetically futile, their naïve immediacy requiring the help of sophistication. The release of the animal in *The Goat Song,* which acts as a momentum liberating the peasants, is made possible by a doctor, a student and the ethical sensitiveness of a woman. (p. 233)

The desire for homecoming [in Werfel's work] is thwarted. But perhaps homelessness is no absolute tragedy, is in reality God's way of saving man's spirit from making itself at home in the wrong world. Possibly exile is the alternative to enslavement. In the prophet Jeremiah (*Hearken unto the Voice*), Werfel presents a Biblical prototype who *sought* exile. Finding himself surrounded by an exploiting and rapacious materialism, Jeremiah hears the call of God and isolates himself from the "herd." Jeremiah chooses alienation as his home in an age when status means servility and humiliation. His alienation becomes the "burden of the mysterious law of sanctification." By thus distancing himself from the people, he serves them by prophesying the downfall awaiting the expansionist mores of his time. (pp. 234-35)

In this sense Werfel has seen his exile as a "summons to renewal." *The Song of Bernadette* is Werfel's most recent homage to regeneration by "metaphysical faith." In this novel Werfel returns to his early lyrical mood when the child was held forth as the high instance of integration and faith—with this difference: here he would support his belief by the scientific data of history. The novel purports to be nothing more than a poetical restatement of the recorded visions of Bernadette and the miraculous cures which were subsequently to have taken place at Lourdes. The self-questioning note with which Werfel treated his post-lyrical characters has disappeared. The author does not simply state that Bernadette *claimed* to have seen visions. He would *justify* the claim by recreating her visions in a manner to suggest them as unquestionable matters of *fact.* Through labored verisimilitude, he would *persuade* the reader that it was all actually so. Werfel clearly identifies himself with the child, and it is as though he himself were experiencing the visions. The emphasis is on the complete normalcy of Bernadette's behavior and condition (she falls into a trance only *after* she has seen The Lady). The cures are presented as having the indubitable character of miracles, since they take place *immediately.* Werfel also regresses to the technique employed in *The Goat Song* and *Juarez and Maximilian,* where the protagonist or prime mover of the action remains invisible throughout. The Lady is "seen" only by virtue of the novelist's own imagination.

Werfel's method of countering a sophisticated, rationalistic age of disbelief is here of utmost disingenuousness. The limitation of modernism is seen in its failure to share the faith of Bernadette! It is such unqualified, simple faith by this highly conscious writer which raises questions as to its representation of his actual credo. (pp. 235-36)

The novel itself provides some clues that Werfel's return to the "song" of his beginnings is disturbed by the cacophony of his modern experiencing. Werfel himself records that the question of Bernadette's normalcy was raised because her visions transpired during the critical period of her adolescence. (Indeed, the category of disease hovers over the entire story and is organically bound up with faith.) Moreover, it is The Lady's beauty rather than her goodness which attracts Bernadette. Nor does the vision make her a better or a more socialized person. To be sure, as in the case of the Goat and of Juarez, The Lady's appearance leads to a kind of "people's" revolt. And once again the same aristocratic distance is maintained between the leader and the following. Bernadette remains alone and separated from everyone, even as she returns to the "anonymous mass from which she arose."

Seen in its total context, Werfel's work admits that the recapture of a primitive, socialized absolute is no longer possible. The new metaphysical unity can be reached only by travelling along the road of exile. But Werfel continues to have troubling doubts as to whether there is an end to the "eternal road." Where, in the Joseph myth, Thomas Mann chooses a story with a happy ending, Werfel's Jeremiah myth deals with an exile who remains embittered with the world. And while Mann's Joseph, travelling through Egypt's Realm of the Dead, attempts to establish communication with his fellow men, Jeremiah avoids "the community of men, the coarse, turbid world that had forsaken God." Hence, where estrangement in Mann's later characters is pointed toward bringing about their own and their people's socialization and humanization, in Werfel there is a kind of spiritual aristocracy in play which approaches a snobbishness toward the average and the ordinary. Werfel's spiritual characters remain essentially alone, communing either with themselves or with mystical essences. Werfel's quest for status remains unrequited. He drifts between a past social paternalism which he knows cannot be recaptured and a scientific socialism which he calls a "kind of aspirin." (pp. 236-37)

Harry Slochower, "Spiritual Judaism: The Yearning for Status" (originally published as "Franz Werfel and Sholom Asch: The Yearning for Status," in Accent, Vol. 5, No. 2, Winter, 1945), in his No Voice Is Wholly Lost . . . Writers and Thinkers in War and Peace (reprinted by permission of Farrar, Straus and

Giroux, Inc.; copyright 1945 by Harry Slochower; copyright renewed © 1972 by Harry Slochower), Creative Age Press, 1945 (and reprinted by Octagon Books, 1975), pp. 229-42.*

ERICH KAHLER   (essay date 1948)

Franz Werfel was a bad author and a great poet. This is rare enough in itself. But even rarer is the deep connection between the two.

His novels and plays show neither the spontaneous purity of a genuinely naive nature nor the achieved purity of an artistic conscience. They are full of guilt and betrayal. Certainly they do not belie the effervescent talent that he possessed, the impulse and joy of the born story-teller. Just as in his social intercourse, there are moments in Werfel's epical and dramatic works when he relaxed completely and gave himself up to his flowing gift, when he forgot and lost himself, and therefore found himself, exposing the childlike basis of his nature and its prankish exuberance. At such moments he told his story well—impulsively, wittily, colorfully, even dramatically. On the whole, however, he remained trapped between the spontaneity of the involuntary personal statement and the mental exertion of the work of art. (p. 186)

[The] whole style of Werfel's stories [evidence] a lack of that ultimate honor and honesty which are the premise of genuine artistic devotion.

I do not say all this in order to denigrate Werfel, I say it in order to do him the honor of applying that same high standard which he himself set in another part of his work, the only valid and pure part: that is, his poetry. How, in actual fact, could one ever evaluate the greatness of his poetry without seeing at the same time the inadequacy of his activity as an author? Indeed it is from this very inadequacy—and that, above all, is why I must expose it—that the greatness arises. Not only is Werfel's prose degraded by his poetry; in a certain sense the prose, in its turn, conditions his poetry: Werfel knew about his profound failures, knew about the badness with which he handled his great gifts, knew about his weaknesses, his lies, his sins. And the settling of accounts with himself, the ordeal he experienced in the painful recognition of his defections—it is this, exactly this, that is the source of his genuine creation. In many of his poems, the greatest, he pursued the experience of his personal defection to the very bottom of the human condition, to the point of a Job-like complaint and accusation lifted up on the part of the mortal creature.

The poems reveal his inner history: that lovable childlike quality, that openness to the world, that "friendship with the world" which lay in the depths of his nature, and the weaknesses, the abandonment to all temptations that are connected with these qualities; the urge toward union, towards communication, towards mutual effect, and the inevitable experience of the bounds separating person from person, of the impotence of speech, of being alone with oneself. The best pieces in [*Gedichte aus den Jahren 1908-1945*] . . . are direct personal statements, save for a few exceptions such as the masterly poem **"Der Dirigent."** And the salient motifs are all connected with the experience of the self. Childhood, with its warm, all-enveloping background of home, plays a mighty role; the poet's whole life is penetrated by it. Completely original also is Werfel's urge towards the Other, his extension of himself through the world, his dispersion and his loss of himself in the world. And then there comes abruptly the breaking off, the rejection and the withdrawal back into himself, the struggle for a human hold on waking reality, and the sweetness of self-surrender: sleep, sleeplessness with its specters of guilt, sickness—not only personal, acute sickness, but also the lifelong one, the "sickness unto death." It is only a step from the child to death. What is lacking is the man that he never became, and just this is the most affecting of all traits in this person. (pp. 187-88)

Because he is alone with himself, the poet is honest. And because he is altogether honest, his great powers of expression can develop freely. Only new content, just discovered for the first time, can create a new, completely direct language. Aside from slight reminiscences of the early Rilke—and these only in respect to melody—no foreign influences are to be detected even in Werfel's youthful poetry.

Werfel did not see and did not suspect, let alone penetrate with his thinking consciousness, the epic conflicts of our time, the problems of social life or of the interaction of individual and society, of the horizontal world, so to speak—in any case he was a bad thinker by and large. But what did preoccupy him in his innermost were the vertical problems, the depth problems of the self, the frailty, yes, the brittleness of personal existence, the encroachment of death, the transcendence of memory, the limits of speech. Problems, spiritual urgencies such as are awake today in all serious minds—these too occupied him in his innermost, and he gave them a metaphorical form that in its spectral buffoonery and in its tendency to allegory is often reminiscent of the lyric poetry of the German baroque period. Those most personal and most moving poems in which Werfel surrendered himself completely to the extremest remorse, and from this remorse won the truest poetic momentum, come very close in fact to the outpourings of sin and repentance of the baroque poets. . . . (p. 188)

By metaphysical impulse Werfel was a Jew, but in his need for salvation he was in truth a Christian, one might indeed say almost a Russian Christian: for it was only through sin, only driven along by sin, that he could attain to completely purified expression. (p. 189)

Erich Kahler, "Franz Werfel's Poetry," in Commentary *(reprinted by permission; all rights reserved), Vol. 5, No. 2, February, 1948, pp. 186-89.*

HEINZ POLITZER   (essay date 1950)

Franz Werfel's greatness lies precisely in the unbroken unity of his statement. In his last collection of poems [*Gedichte aus den Jahren 1908-1945*], on which he was working at the time of his death, he included incredibly vulgar verses from his early work; while parts of his novels, the conversation with the bathmaster in *Barbara*, Stephen's journey in *The Forty Days of Musa Dagh*, the "most important moment of his former life" in *Der Stern der Ungeborenen* (**"The Star of the Unborn"**), and nearly all his short stories, particularly *Das Trauerhaus* **"The House of Mourning"**), have a balladlike force and density that will preserve them from old age and death.

The phenomenal unevenness of quality evident in Werfel's work as a whole cannot be explained by the diversity of genres. It is more readily imputable to Werfel's nature, to an exuberant boyishness that surrendered itself wholly to every possible source of inspiration, and to his journalistic dependence on his subject matter. Werfel gave himself, half as an enthusiast does to the thing he loves, half as a reporter to the thing he must deal with professionally. This twofold passivity on the part of his overflowing talent accounts for both the high and the low points in his work. (p. 272)

[In the prose sketch **"Cabrinowitsch"**] we have the whole of Franz Werfel: the sharp realism, accompanied by the evil eye of the born epic poet; the courage, the foolhardy courage of the ageless schoolboy, with which he plunged from reality abruptly into the depths of the mystery; the immediate juxtaposition of surface and inner meaning; the love and sympathy, the pathos; and finally a stylistic bravura so great as to cast a doubt upon the authenticity of the vision. Ordinarily the seer pays with his blood for his vision. But to Werfel visions were given in superfluity, as melodies were given to such composers as Mozart and Verdi. What was not given to Werfel was the strict measure of music, he did not mold what he saw, and the grace that befell him did not re-create him. He reported only what he observed, in a melody all his own that runs equally through his lyrical and his epic work.

He was a sublime reporter and he took over certain elements from the tradition of Austrian journalism whose last great representative, the satirist and pamphleteer Karl Kraus, was first his teacher and then his embittered enemy. It was from Austrian journalism that Werfel learned the art of the headline—the titles of his novels, as of each single one of his poems, are cabinet pieces of summation—it was here that he learned the sudden eruption of the narrative without preparation or exposition; the blurred ending, behind which stands the question mark of mystery, the mystery of a man or of all creation; the *bon mot*, through which, as through a crevice, one perceives the abyss; the strange fusing of psychology and musicality. But he also took over certain weaknesses of this essentially ephemeral genre: a certain flatness of perspective accompanied by a heavy laying on of color to simulate depth; the point for the sake of the point; a tendency to heap up words; a weakness for digression, and longwindedness; the obtrusive "I." From the riches of the Austrian tradition and the abundance of his own imagination, he gathered at random; he had all he could do to keep pace with the flow of his own fancy; and so he had little time for arrangement and little energy for discipline. Even in his poems he was a reporter; but when in the course of a novel he paused and reflected, he became a great poet.

He was a reporter also in his highly developed flair for the "interesting" and his gift for presenting it. As Erich Kahler noted, the story of his solemn vow with which Werfel introduced his *Song of Bernadette* was pure fabrication and showmanship. . . . Like Baroque literature, his work made a public affair of faith, of the mystery of life and death, of ecstasy and repentance—did this by the seduction of words, the melody of language, by the modern dexterity with which he reported metaphysical problems and experience. And like the Baroque language, his, too, with all its elaborate display, is fundamentally without structure.

Often he was aware of the faultiness of his style. Then he attempted to lend significance to his own weakness by giving music the pre-eminence over language, by declaring the wordless to be the home and the salvation of his poor, weak word. (pp. 273-74)

Like all attempts at interpretation, this one has a certain apologetic quality and sidesteps the inner contradiction it set out to explain. With a style in which there is much local Prague jargon, much of the heritage of Viennese journalism, and a last gleam of the Hapsburg empire, of Maria Theresa no less than of Franz Joseph I, Franz Werfel was destined to plumb the depths of the modern soul. (p. 274)

Heinz Politzer, "Franz Werfel: Reporter of the Sublime," in Commentary *(reprinted by permission; all rights reserved), Vol. 9, No. 3, March, 1950, pp. 272-74.*

ADOLF D. KLARMANN   (essay date 1959)

[Werfel], whom the experiences of war had jolted from his ego-impregnated confidence in a world that redeemed itself into a deeper and more profound view, settles accounts with his vanities of madness and those of the world in his great mystery play *Spiegelmensch,* which unfortunately has been almost completely forgotten today. It is in this mystery play, which criticism at all levels has erroneously compared with Goethe's *Faust,* that he especially comes to terms with the vanities of reflected world boredom and self-satisfied salvationism, behind which the deceit of God attempts to hide itself. God and devil fight for the soul of man. Significantly Werfel calls his work "magic trilogy," and in his own commentary on it he labels it a "magic play." One notices a conscious avoiding of the terms drama, tragedy, play, or whatever the fitting traditional or customary title might be. (p. 50)

A suggestion of the familiar aversion of expressionism toward outworn and threadbare forms is obvious, but does not give the completely adequate explanation of Werfel's definition. From the very beginning of his dramatic activity the author is very much concerned in needling the audience even more than the reading public out of their emotional sluggishness and complacency and making them aware of the difference in nature of his work. . . . (pp. 50-1)

With Werfel it is not a matter of pathetic conflicts of personality and world—rather his drama is carried out in the protagonist. It is plainly theological drama, as in the case of the Spaniards of the Golden Century whom he loved so much, and also in the case of Grillparzer and Hofmannsthal. The searching man is placed in the world in order to pass a probationary test before the omnipresent divine eye. As the master of his will, it is up to him to make the choice between good and evil. Whatever his choice may turn out to be, he stands under the shelter of the divine grace which can pardon the penitent and perform miracles of redemption on the lost. Imbued early with the Messianic mission of a literary work of art, he ascribes to it metaphysical interests which, to be sure, have to be clothed in a form which the public cannot easily understand, or maybe never understand at all. (p. 51)

The substance of the drama is limited; on the other hand the ways to treat and develop it are of the greatest variety. Werfel knows, as did the Spaniards and also Shakespeare and on the other side Grillparzer and Raimund, that the lifeblood of the theater is entertainment and that the theatrical effect is not based on Lessing's or the French versions of Aristotelian concepts, but on the inner laws of the stage, which is neither a moral institution nor any other kind of institution, but again and again above all *Schau-Spiel,* show-play, spectacle. . . . [In the] *Spiegelmensch* dramaturgy, the author laid down the three basic laws of the stage, namely:

I.   The law of the varied and richly significant situation.

II. The law of the exciting and challenging possibilities for acting.

III. The law of the sparkling and effervescing theatrical gesture and language.

And later: "The dramatist must mysteriously flatter the house. He must make the consciousness of the people on the other side of the prompter's box more godlike than that of the puppets on this side. He should mold not only the scene, but also the audience, for Schiller and the teachers of the theater are wrong—the stage has nothing to do with ethics—it is subtle incitement and temptation—at best toward that which is good."

From this metaphysically rooted autochthony of the stage, Werfel drew conclusions which have given his dramatic creations their own distinctive touch and they have not been without influence on his time and ours. As already in the expressionistic drama, the dramatic structure of the acts breaks down generally, even where it is still retained as in *Bocksgesang*. There is instead of this rather an "absence of form" as seen from the architectonic standpoint which grows from its own musical tectonics. In spite of the devotion to realism which Werfel emphasized again and again, the reader cannot be content with any kind of traditional definition of the term—certainly not at all with that familiar to the Naturalists from Zola and Ibsen on—much less with that of the "Neue Sachlichkeit." Perhaps the realism of an epic Brecht theater is closest anticipated here—in spite of its contrary position in all other respects—but, to be sure, entirely without his paralyzing didacticism.

In the observations on the drama *Juarez und Maximilian* there is this in addition: "To be sure the epic nature of the story—if it is not to be violated—prescribes a certain sequence of events, which often enough runs counter to the inexorable law of tragedy. However, from days of yore the dramatic story has always been a conscious form which tries to reconcile the conflict between drama and epic." For example, consider the drama *Das Reich Gottes in Böhmen* with its alternating main stage and proscenium, the latter almost always representing a road (in the early version of the drama stagehands appear with roadsigns!), or again the deeply moving pantomime before the fifth scene. In the same work Werfel uses the triptych form of the simultaneous stage, not only to represent the same historical room—in this case the Council of Basle—but also toward the end to permit the widely separated figures of the Cardinal and Prokop to appear at the same time and in this way represent vividly and graphically the struggle for the brother's soul: "Two spotlight beams. On the right: high, open window. In front, Julian. On the left: a bed. On it the sick Prokop. Slow heavy ticking of an invisible pendulum." With these very characteristic stage directions we have already reached his suprarealism, i.e. a realism in which reality is crystalline so that the initiated not only can see through it, but understand it and also perceive its prismatic refraction. The foreground part of the stage action (and also that of the prose) is there to fascinate, to divert, to lead astray, to confuse and bewilder—or in a word—to become ironic; for that secret that is divulged is no longer a secret and becomes common knowledge. But neither God nor the poet make life that easy for man.

The frequent scenic exaggerations of his dramas are explained from this serious play instinct to give free rein to the theater magic of his baroque Austrian nature and feelings. This occurs in the early dramas such as *Spiegelmensch* or *Schweiger* and also in his last work for the stage, *Jacobowsky und der Oberst.* (pp. 51-3)

It is just this last dramatic work of the author, completed under mental and emotional torments, that is an outstanding example of Werfel's suprarealistic art, the most obscure allegory, the most successful mystery play of the present in which, as in [*Paulus unter den Juden*], but with quite different previous

suggestions and more conscious deception of the audience, the cosmic tragedy of the mission of the Christian and of the Jew is unrolled. The gentle symbolic hinting of the author extends to the naming of the characters. The stage directions—which in this very case have developed to a highly cunning artistic device—mysteriously hint at a great mystic event and transport the spectators in the fate-filled last minute before the Last Judgment. Magic theater!

This has always been the case with Werfel! (pp. 53-4)

This theater magic reaches new heights in the "magic trilogy" *Spiegelmensch* or in the depressing and yet hopeful, splendid *Bocksgesang*. The musical basic experience, which gives the primary form and which is familiar to those who know E.T.A. Hoffman, Kleist, Grillparzer, and others, is amazing also in the case of Werfel. The first idea for *Spiegelmensch* appears in the form of a ballet; at a Swiss performance of *Die Troerinnen* he felt the operatic qualities in the piece, and in *Der Weg der Verheißung* text, pantomime, scenery, dance (and Max Reinhardt) are combined with the music of Kurt Weill into a veritable pageant. Magic, enchantment, theater, tricks and illusions, overpowering thrills and excitement. Opera. Music! The drama of Werfel arises from these various worlds and reaches the stage—that which is opposed to reason and common sense and just because of that, the real trueness of opera! The dramatist as librettist of the stage. . . .

The fanatical interest in music in the works of Werfel is rooted deeply in his mission of the eternal warning that *God is*. Out of this and around this flows the music. It penetrates even into the innermost structure of his work, in the duets of the contrasting couples which complement each other to form a new unity, which, however, has always been theirs and was only temporarily separated, like two voices, that going their way mingle with each other in a higher harmony. (p. 54)

> *Adolf D. Klurmann, "Franz Werfel and the Stage," translated by Charles W. Bangert, in* The German Quarterly *(copyright © 1959 by the American Association of Teachers of German), Vol. XXXII, No. 2, March 1959 (and reprinted in* Franz Werfel: 1890-1945, *edited by Lore B. Foltin, University of Pittsburgh Press, 1961, pp. 50-6).*

WALTER H. SOKEL   (essay date 1959)

The antimodernist attitude of late Expressionism finds its climax in the work with which the movement closes—Werfel's *Verdi*. . . . In this "novel of the opera" Werfel attacks Wagner, to whom modernism in music, literature, and art owes an enormous debt, and espouses the popular musical style and the "simple" personality of Verdi as the ideal of art and the artist. Werfel equates experimental form with sickness of the soul and sees Wagner as a rootless and pathological adventurer, a neurotic and megalomaniac. He contrasts the twisted and thoroughly diseased character of Wagner with the humane normality and sanity of Verdi and opposes the humble "objectivity" or "*Sachlichkeit*" of Verdi's music to the pioneering subjectivism of Wagner's style. (p. 222)

Flying in the face of the whole modernist tradition, first originated in the aesthetics of Kant, which assumes the godlike and complete autonomy of genius, Werfel demands that the artist employ his gifts not for unbridled experiment but for the exhilaration of the people, a view which Werfel himself was to follow in practice until it carried him to the world-wide triumph of *The Song of Bernadette,* which was as far from modernist spirit and Expressionist form as anything could be. (p. 223)

In Werfel's "novel of the opera" the contrast between the ethical and the egocentric-romantic-modernist artist is a contrast between Latin and German civilization. Werfel recognizes very well that . . . the modernist aesthetics is closely linked to the social and existential crisis of the creative man which, at first apparent in Germany, spread in the course of the nineteenth century to the rest of Europe, especially to France. "Wagner was a German. And to be German means: 'You are allowed everything because no form, no past, no *relationship* binds you.' A charter of magnificence and peril." . . . The German artist as portrayed by Werfel is an innovator because he lives and creates in isolation. Since he does not write for a public with definite tastes and conventions, there is no need to abide by traditional forms. To prove himself worthy of attention, in a land of lonely individuals, he has to be original, break tradition, and rise above everything that existed before him. . . . [His] creativeness is like the "creativeness" of a volcano which offers a wonderful spectacle but devastates the countryside. (pp. 223-24)

The modernist artist, who strives for originality in order to compel the world to take notice of him, is forced by the same token, to restrict his appeal to an ever-smaller audience. Finally a point is reached where unconventionality becomes obscurity and communication ceases. (p. 225)

Verdi's audience is neither Society nor Bohemia but the people, the whole community. In such an artist Werfel draws the ideal for which he strives. It is typical, however, that this ideal artist is not a German but an Italian. In Verdi's Italy, the late Expressionist author sees art still functioning as a part of life, a daily necessity for vinegrowers, butchers, and notaries, at least as important to them as their taverns and card games. The disastrous split between art and people has not yet occurred or has already been overcome. Verdi, the Italian artist, feels at home in his country; the German Expressionist does not feel at home in Germany. An artist who feels at home among people has no need to think of startling theories of "absolute art" and *Zukunftsmusik*. He creates like the painters of the Renaissance or of seventeenth-century Holland, "who did not paint in order to solve problems of light or form but because the pious needed pictures. . . . In a like manner, Verdi wrote for people, not for excited intellects, for very definite people who crowded the theaters of Italy.". . . Art for Werfel's Verdi is functional within a human context; i.e., it fulfills very concrete human needs. (pp. 224-25)

Werfel's novel shows the artist's integration in the community, the dream that had motivated activist Expressionism from its beginning, not as a utopian goal attainable only through a revolutionary upheaval and the regeneration of mankind, but as a commonplace reality, the result of fortuitous geographical, historical, and psychological circumstances. These circumstances had always been lacking in Germany and were becoming ever rarer in the whole modern world; but neither a collective revolution nor a spectacular personal regeneration could produce them. One could humbly search for them, reverently discern them wherever they did exist, or patiently wait for their coming; but one could not hope to force them or manufacture them by either personal or collective means. With this realization the recoil from the activist euphoria had gone as far as it was possible to go. It had advanced beyond the point where the fundamental qualities and devices of Expressionism—the tense urgency, the extremism and violence, the need for the

outcry, for the breathless condensation, the hectic hyperbole, the metaphoric visualization—were still appropriate. For Werfel and the great majority of Expressionists, Expressionism had lost its *raison d'être*. (pp. 225-26)

Walter H. Sokel, "The Recoil," in his The Writer in Extremis: Expressionism in Twentieth-Century German Literature (reprinted with the permission of the publishers, Stanford University Press; © 1959 by the Board of Trustees of the Leland Stanford Junior University), Stanford University Press, 1959, pp. 192-226.*

FRANK LAMBASA (essay date 1961)

[*Goat Song*] had a distinction of being one of the first works which were to open a window across the Atlantic on the afterwar mind of Germany's young and promising men of literature. . . . Though some critics went as far as to call it "the most important play of the season" [see excerpt above by Stark Young], the American theater audience and the critics in general were just as puzzled by its dramatic complexities, its cryptic obscurities, its symbolism and ambiguity, as were their German colleagues. (p. 70)

[*Goat Song*] is built around a story allegedly reported in the press: "A monster was born to a rich peasant family—creature half beast, half man. The parents regarded it as a deep disgrace to the race of which they were proud and kept the monster a secret, hiding it in a hovel on the estate, until it grew to maturity. Finally, it escaped, causing a social upheaval in the village." With this as a central theme, Werfel has built up a drama in which traditional myths and folk tales, social and human passions, class war and rebellion are richly interwoven and interpenetrated with individual tragedies of love, hate, and anguish. (pp. 71-2)

The basic content, of course, is tragic action which Werfel directly presents. But this action is in its very essence ambiguous, so that each and every element of the play becomes readily transmutable into some sort of a symbol. In order that the symbolic level of the play be better understood, it is indispensable to know at least some of Werfel's metaphysical ideas.

The world into which man is born is essentially meaningless, asserts Werfel in one of his earliest pronouncements about the nature of tragedy. Impulse and Accident rule all things, while Reason (or Intelligence), that fearful distinction of man alone, is asked to stand unshaken before the brutal drama of the elements. Yet from this disjunction between Man and Nature spring tragedy, a spark which leaps from the pole Reason or Sensibility to the pole called Life or Accident. The tragic sentiment exists because an original sin in which the entire nature shares must be atoned by man alone. And it is this accusation that the understanding, sensitive soul of humanity brings against fate that makes the core of tragedy, and yet this tragic sentiment alone is capable of transforming the Nature's Chaos into a Cosmos.

Only after dissecting some of its philosophical framework with the help of these stated concepts do certain symbols of the play become clear and transparent. There is, first of all, the central, all-pervading symbol of Nature, whose gigantic shadow hovers eternally over the threatened humanity, descending upon it from time to time in order to disrupt and convulse the established, "rational" order. These apocalyptic disasters may assume not only divergent shapes, but they may often cow the terrorized mass into willing victims and worshipers. (pp. 74-5)

[There is also the implication] that these ''natural'' destructions that occur from time to time are necessary to man not only as a warning of his inchoate and transient nature, but also as a means of clearing his decks of the past that has piled up for so long that he feels stifled under it. But if the world starts in man, this basic disjunction which exists outside of him is concurrently mirrored in man himself. (''For man is a knot, man is a cramp. / Man is the animal crucified.'') Thus the monster may also simultaneously represent the symbol for the physical in man, the primitive, rendered evil by the puritanic repression accorded it by the parents. They have been ashamed of the offspring of their natural love, and by confining the goat-man and regarding him as monstrous, they have made him so. (pp. 75-6)

But besides this pivotal symbol of Pan, a half human and half beast creature that populates mythologies of many countries, there is the oft encountered myth of the virgin impregnated by the god, and the miraculous conception. Here, as in many other works of Werfel, the woman becomes the chosen mediator between the divine, omnipotent and unknown forces and man lost in the quandary of his existence. And then again there is a myth of the zodiacal nature of the summer solstice, of that rare magic midnoon hour—which, by the way, holds a special fascination for Werfel—when a thing could spring from quivering nature, horrible and full of majesty, like the vision of the Whole compressed into a second. (p. 77)

[Many] elements of the drama such as the gnawing shame of concealment, the smug rich, the mad student, the dispossessed, and the various individuals (the rope dancer, the scavenger, etc.) are all so sharply and suggestively drawn *and* symbolized that *Goat Song* may hold one or many meanings. But the meaning of the play, or, its spiritual content, should not be sought by attempting to resolve such ambiguities as these. For even when the whole metaphysical structure is left out, the drama retains its symbolic quality and its theatrical effectiveness. (pp. 77-8)

For Werfel's *Goat Song* is, above all, a real human drama in which the people hate, love, destroy one another, and in which crowds swirl in anger, murder carelessly, and give themselves over to a riot of abandoned drunkenness and lust. The individuals transcend mere types, which make the usual expressionistic drama appear so ponderous, and pulsate with a tremendous vitality on the stage of life. The tragicomic Jew, ubiquitous and philosophically resigned to his peddler role, when he, together with other dispossessed is refused a piece of land to settle down in the country where he was born, is a masterfully delineated figure, repeated with virtuosity also in Werfel's last play, *Jacobowsky and the Colonel*. (p. 79)

[There] is a great symbolic poignancy in this figure. For the Jew, it seems to be suggested, is, first of all, the stabilizer of society, standing before and after the revolution for order rather than chaos. He secondly appears as this society's conscience, which, though often suppressed, could never be entirely stamped out. . . .

Though most characters of the play represent types and symbols, their human reality is never put to question as it is often done in the case of the principal figure of the play [the half man and half beast] who, following the well-known Werfel technique of suspense, is never directly seen on the stage. (p. 80)

While this deliberate concealment must have increased the imminent mystery of the whole play, it also diminished its ultimate reality. Werfel himself was quite conscious of this fact, for in his (unpublished) diary under the date March 21, 1922, the following entry is found: ''In the meantime in Prague the Czech premiere of *Goat Song*. I am quite aware of the flaw of the play: the beast remains insufficiently real.''

The student Juvan and the girl Stanja, on the other hand, are naturalistically vivid creations, besides—in a true expressionistic sense—representing human types and abstract symbols. Juvan, the leader of the discontented, is clearly the intellectual revolutionary depicted from Werfel's own experience with the Viennese political upheaval that took place at the end of the First World War. He is a typical iconoclast who, dissatisfied with things as they are, would like to blaze the way for things that ought to be.

Werfel's greatest mastery, however, went into the creation of Stanja, the heroine of the play, another lively portrait in his remarkable gallery of women. There is, no doubt, a special aura surrounding these women who often appear to be a natural link in the order of things, supernaturally empowered or burdened with unique missions. . . . Stanja by her enigmatic feminine nature intensifies her symbolic significance. It is her irrationality (as, for example, when she willingly submits to the beast), her unpredictability that place her on the side with natural elements whose behavior cannot always be foreseen. It is from her that there will be recurrence of the past, that the old order will once more be resuscitated.

It is true that symbolism in the play *Goat Song* is not always sufficiently clear, and that much of it is vague and general rather than striking and specific. It nevertheless represents one of the highest dramatic achievements of Werfel. For, in spite of many disagreements as to the various meanings of the play, nobody dared to deny that the play possesses power, wonderful suggestiveness, and, above all, a high moral and spiritual appeal. (pp. 80-2)

Frank Lambasa, ''Franz Werfel's 'Goat Song','' in Franz Werfel: 1890-1945, *edited by Lore B. Foltin (reprinted by permission of the University of Pittsburgh Press; © 1961 by University of Pittsburgh Press), University of Pittsburgh Press, 1961, pp. 69-82.*

TEMIRA PACHMUSS (essay date 1963)

The works of Werfel reveal the strong influence of Dostoevskij; even a superficial comparison of their writings shows an unmistakable affinity of ideas. . . . Absorbed as he is in Dostoevskij's concept of love, Werfel uses the words of Father Zosima—''My fathers and teachers, what is hell? I think it is the pain of being no longer able to love''—as the motto for the second part of *Einander*. Like Dostoevskij, Werfel often speaks about love as the redeeming power of humanity, not only in the volumes of his poems such as **Der Weltfreund, Wir sind, Der Gerichstag, Einander,** but also in many of his later works. As we see from Werfel's poem **''Der Weise an seine Feinde''** *(Einander),* love can triumph over hatred, for it is based on Christ's teaching, ''Love thine enemy!'' Father Zosima also preaches, ''Brothers, have no fear of man's sins. Love a man in his sin, for that is . . . the highest love on earth.'' (pp. 445-46)

The similarity in Dostoevskij's and Werfel's treatment of various problems manifests itself also in their presentation of desires, passions, and conflicts in the human soul. We find in Werfel's poems the hatred of an offended person, a feeling growing into a real passion as we can see in the works of Dostoevskij. . . . (p. 446)

The importance of the fullness of experience in human life is another idea which is treated by Dostoevskij and Werfel. In *A Raw Youth* and *The Brothers Karamazov,* Dostoevskij makes it perfectly clear that man must not try to escape from life in his striving for spiritual and moral self-betterment. He must accept life with all its temptations and dangers and make his way through them toward his spiritual goal. The dying Father Zosima, sending Alëša into the temptations of the world, advises him that "life will bring you many misfortunes, but you will find your happiness in them, and you will bless life." A victory is not possible without the previous struggle of at least two opposing forces; the surrender of feelings and one's treasures, without awareness of their value, and the enjoyment they bring, cannot be considered a sacrifice. It is for that same reason that the Abbot advises Thamal in *Spiegelmensch* to experience life to the full and thus to become ripe for final perfection, to partake of the spiritual harmony of "the higher world." It is with this same purpose in mind that Mara, the symbol of the redemptive powers of Christian suffering and love in *Die Mittagsgöttin,* tells Laurentin that he must experience the full sense of material existence and thus awaken "from the external colors of pseudo-realities," in order to discover the true life and become ready for redemption. The greatness of suffering, in Father Zosima's eyes, "lies in the fact that it is a mystery, that in it the passing earthly show and the eternal truth are brought together." (p. 447)

Dostoevskij and Werfel hold that man must come to realize his share of guilt in the sins and suffering of others; he must understand and shoulder the responsibility for their failings. Both writers insist that man must develop this attitude toward his fellow men in order to prevent his painful isolation from them.

The artistic development of the theme of isolation and loneliness is at the center of Dostoevskij's ethical and moral speculations. Treating the various phases and aspects of this problem, he shows isolation as the logical consequence of man's striving to gratify his ambition. . . . While treating the same theme, Werfel points out emphatically through Franz Schweiger that absolute evil is loneliness. . . . Schweiger maintains that his former insanity, as well as his crime, was the result of his excruciating loneliness. Together with Dostoevskij, Werfel considers love to be the only remedy for isolation.

Werfel's ideas of God in his early works are almost identical with those of Dostoevskij. His poem **"Zwiegespräch an der Mauer des Paradieses"** *(Einander),* shows clearly that Werfel followed in the tracks of his Russian teacher. He underwent a painful struggle against God just as Dostoevskij had done: his logic refused to accept God. However, whereas Dostoevskij vacillated between belief and doubt all his life, Werfel soon gave himself up to religious mysticism. *Das Lied von Bernadette* and *Stern der Ungeborenen* portray this mystical faith which is devoid of reasoning. There are also mystical undercurrents in *Die Mittagsgöttin, Spiegelmensch,* [and] *Bocksgesang.* In *Die Mittagsgöttin,* a mythical goddess, "the symbol of fruitfulness and earthly vigor," intervenes by supernatural means to accomplish Laurentin's redemption. This play is too symbolic, much too mythlike to resemble even approximately the presentation of the meeting of the human and the divine, or the union of spirit and nature, in Dostoevskij's writings. *Spiegel-*

mensch, another symbolic drama, portrays, in Spengler's words, the world of "mysticism and reason," and is removed from Dostoevskij's realistic method. (pp. 448-49)

The most pronounced resemblance between Dostoevskij and Werfel is their common propensity for a certain moral masochism, which in the latter case Turrian considers a passionate longing for suffering and an inclination to martyrdom. Werfel appears also to experience a strong desire to make other people suffer through his own mental anguish. He seems to have profound delight in kindling the agonizing feeling of hatred in the poem **"Die Prozession"** *(Einander).* . . . God, having recovered from His wounds, mounts His throne and mocks the people who, driven by their feeling of guilt toward God, have gathered to worship Him. However, genuine willingness to suffer and genuine martyrdom would not be expressed in this fashion. Werfel could never say, as did Prince Myškin in *The Idiot,* "Pass by, and forgive us our happiness." Dostoevskij's Ippolit, by reading his confession before an audience, like Werfel's God, wants to appear a martyr to his fellows and to make them suffer in the process. Saddened by this attitude, Prince Myškin advises Ippolit that he must not envy the happiness of other people, nor should he make them suffer. His first moral obligation is to love them and to forgive them their happiness.

The theme of duality is yet another topic which links the two writers. Like Dostoevskij, Werfel often speaks about the duality of his own being. . . . In his writings, Werfel portrays a concept of duality of the world which resembles Dostoevskij's concept and which establishes a reality "of a higher order," distinct from that of physical phenomena. (pp. 449-50)

Dostoevskij's concept of man . . . has a strong resemblance to the Zoroastrian teaching of human nature, with its stress on the importance of the body and man's free will. Zoroastrianism, which claims that suffering lies in the very nature of man as a free being, as long as he remains in his present form, also influenced Werfel's views on the duality of the world as a world of metaphysical reality and a world of finite experience. Different from Dostoevskij's views, however, is Werfel's emphasis on the special mystic and symbolic significance of the world of "ultimate reality," which is disclosed to man only by vision and ecstasy. The idea of man's imaginative, magical relationship with the surrounding world is altogether alien to Dostoevskij's artistic presentation, even though his novels are also marked by an anti-rationalistic approach to the world of reality. Alien also to Dostoevskij's concept of the dual structure of the world is Werfel's belief that the ideal world, which stands outside of time and space, is the only real world and that the world of earth-bound reality is but an element of evil that has invaded the world of spirit. (p. 451)

Another pronounced feature of Werfel's duality concept is his belief in the unlimited magical qualities of the child, which occupies an important place in his writings. The child has a clairvoyance and ability to penetrate all the phenomena of the world behind which begins "the higher reality," and to transmit the will of God to man. Even a sensitive reader will find it difficult to link the child in Dostoevskij's novels directly with the author's theme of duality. It is only upon the suffering and tears of the innocent babe that Dostoevskij focuses his attention.

No careful reader can miss further differences between the two writers, differences which are significant for our understanding of Werfel's important deviations from his predecessor's attitudes and for a fuller comprehension of his work as a whole. Despite a preoccupation with God, with the duality in man's nature and the duality underlying the universe, with the problem of guilt, and with other spiritual matters, Werfel's interests and thoughts were mainly directed toward things of a physical and concrete nature. Even in the novel *Das Lied von Bernadette,* the physical substance—in spite of all claims to spirituality—takes precedence. Little Bernadette was primarily concerned with the outward appearance of her Lady. She fulfilled the spiritual demands of the Lady principally in order not to be deprived of her beloved presence. Dostoevskij, on the whole, gave his undivided attention to the world of the spirit, and even when he portrays really vicious and perverse people, he is in fact interested primarily in their mental condition. (p. 452)

The reader is often struck by certain morbid and perverse themes in Werfel's treatment of the physical and the erotic. He reverts continually to these themes, as we see, in *Barbara oder die Frömmigkeit, Spiegelmensch, Bocksgesang,* "Das Trauerhaus," "Die Hoteltreppe," *Stern der Ungeborenen,* etc. In the first of these works, Werfel's virtuous hero Ferdinand is attracted to Angelika, a girl full of physical and moral defects, who at twelve years was raped by her father. Gebhart's main interests were concentrated on the experimental analysis of the erotic, for which he maintained a harem, and Werfel allowed his virtuous Ferdinand to make the following statement about Gebhart upon his death, "Nothing which emanated from Gebhart was great, but he himself was great." Werfel displays a certain morbid fascination with the descriptions of various sexual scenes which we find in *Barbara, Die vierzig Tage des Musa Dagh,* in the Snake King's realm in *Spiegelmensch,* and in the portrayal of the wet-nurses' hill in *Stern.* . . . Werfel's recurring references to his distaste for the physical are reminiscent of Tolstoj's abhorrence of the erotic as evidenced in such works as "The Kreutzer Sonata," "Father Sergius," and "The Devil," the stories in which Tolstoj's heroes are unable to resist their sexual attraction to certain women.

Dostoevskij's attitude toward women differs in many respects from Werfel's. Dostoevskij was not primarily interested in the physical aspect of his female characters. Almost the only exception is Grušen'ka in *The Brothers Karamazov,* who appears as practically the only woman of the flesh in Dostoevskij's novels. Although it is true that we meet some kind, devoted, and self-sacrificing women in Werfel—to mention only Hekuba in *Die Troerrinen,* Ampheh in *Spiegelmensch,* . . . [and] Marianne in *Jacobowsky und der Oberst*—on the other hand we are often unpleasantly affected by many of his other women, who are old and ugly, depraved, jaded, addicted to drugs, sensually aroused, shameless in their nudity and in their dull indifference. There are Lesbians, nymphomaniacs, and prostitutes among them; they are in love with their own brothers (Gabriele in "Die Entfremdung"), or neglect their illegitimate children (Liza in *Barbara*). The frequent absence of all feminine dignity in these portrayals is painful. In *Stern,* Werfel explains that his peculiar attitude toward women is a result of his overwhelmingly acute feeling of personal guilt. However, one can follow only with difficulty Werfel's wandering in pure abstractions: his "masculine" guilt toward "the feminine," and his excursions into mysticism as in his idea of "transcendental love" brought down from Beyond for one short moment by a woman, as portrayed in *Die Mittagsgöttin.* . . . (pp. 453-54)

Despite the similarity in the understanding of the nature of love by the two writers, they differ greatly in their capacity to feel it. Love for one's neighbor and the acceptance of suffering,

two cardinal points in Dostoevskij's philosophy, are embodied in [Prince Myškin, Alëša Karamazov, and Father Zosima]. . . . Prepared to serve and eager to sacrifice, they consummate a union of all creation and creatures to prove that "humble love," as Father Zosima calls it, can be a powerful force. It is a love which does not crave for deeds and acknowledgements, which does not recoil from ugliness, from vice; a love which understands everything, sees everything, and still persists. Since this meek and humble love is an effective agent in the spiritual transformation of man in that it promotes his striving for the ultimate goal and inspires his advance toward man's ideal state, Dostoevskij calls it "active love." He had in mind this "active love" when he spoke about Russian Christianity. It is a similar love which Werfel depicts in his poem "Warum mein Gott" and "Jesus und der Äser-Weg" (both from the volume of poems *Einander*), and in his play *Jacobowsky.* These works reflect the poet's genuine wish to comprehend the intrinsic nature of Dostoevskij's "active love," but he considers himself too weak for such a feeling, as his poem "Des Wanderers Heimweh in die Welt" (*Der Weltfreund*) reveals: The Wanderer admits that love is too great a task for him, for his fellow men do not reciprocate it. Dismayed by their inability to love him, he wishes to leave their world of "external experience." . . . As his poem "Verzweiflung" (*Wir sind*) portrays, Werfel considers his incapacity to experience the all-embracing "active love" a deficiency from which he suffers deeply, and this produces a feeling of guilt, because the poet feels he is unable to reciprocate the love of God, the love out of which He created the world. Werfel depicts this realization in his poem "Balance der Welt" (*Wir sind*). . . . The gulf between individuals makes it impossible for them to overcome all human barriers by means of love. Man has forgotten his divine image; he can no longer love his fellows. Only a miracle can save him. (pp. 454-55)

A longing for "active love," and a striving to define his feelings toward religion, are in the foreground in almost all of Werfel's early works. All of them, including even his seemingly incoherent and perhaps absurd poem, "Das Opfer" (*Wir sind*), appear to have grown out of their author's strong desire to perceive all the phenomena in the sensory world, to fathom their depths, and to come to love them in the great harmony of God's creation.

A profound difference between Werfel and Dostoevskij appears in the father and son problem, despite its superficial similarity. The feeling of hatred which Ivan and Dmitrij Karamazov harbor in their souls is different from that of Werfel's heroes. The former hate their father because of his sensuality and greed, and most of all because they know that they have inherited his base instincts. They feel the same wild, passionate impulses and urges in themselves. These impede them in their no less passionate striving for self-perfection. Meanwhile old Karamazov has always regarded his sons, especially Dmitrij, as his enemies, and there is hardly any trace of the sort of psychological conflict or dissension which we find in Werfel's descriptions of the relationship between fathers and sons. (p. 456)

As we see in Werfel's works, such as *Spiegelmensch, Nicht der Mörder, der Ermordete ist schuldig,* the poem "Vater und Sohn" (*Wir sind*), and *Die Geschwister,* the hate-love of Werfel's fathers and sons consists of petty vainglory, envy, tyranny, servility, and passionate adoration. Their sense of guilt, and of tortured conscience, is genuine and well-grounded. The genuineness of these descriptions imparts the main charm to Werfel's early works.

Werfel's literary style also differs from Dostoevskij's. Although, as is often argued by scholars, Dostoevskij's language is far removed from the polished phrases of Turgenev, the frequent disorderliness of Werfel's style such as we see in some of his early plays, notably *Spiegelmensch* and *Bocksgesang,* is of a different nature. It may be true that the distorted grammar of these works is a result of Werfel's indulging in passionate feeling rather than in cold reason. . . . It appears at times, however, that the poet uses stylistic distortion for its own sake, that is, in order to be different, an intention obviously not characteristic of Dostoevskij. Werfel's frequently unpalatable jumble of words, his ''tortured sentence structure,'' ''Geschmacksentgleisungen,'' . . . and ''schlakkenhafte Sprache,'' show that he has little concern for the most elementary rules of prosody. In his **''Elegie des poetischen Ichs''** *(Einander),* he himself likens language to a whore, for whom he has no respect.

Dostoevskij's art is also symbolic, but in order to express his ''reinsten Wahrheiten,'' the Russian novelist developed different stylistic means such as the special technique of ''interior monologue,'' the individualization of his characters' language, ''the polyphony of ideas,'' ''urban intonation'' and ''anthropological landscape,'' contrasts in style, antitheses in composition.

As has been shown, the similiarity in the treatment of some ideas by Dostoevskij and by Werfel should not be overemphasized, for in most instances it is only superficial. The two writers actually differed greatly in their artistic approaches to the problems in which they were engrossed. The only really pronounced resemblance between Dostoevskij and Werfel consists in a common message to mankind, conveyed in gripping artistic form: love your neighbor regardless of his shortcomings and faults, and judge no one. (pp. 457-58)

> Temira Pachmuss, ''Dostoevskij and Franz Werfel,'' in The German Quarterly *(copyright © 1963 by the American Association of Teachers of German), Vol. XXXVI, No. 4, November, 1963, pp. 445-58.*

W. H. FOX (essay date 1964)

''He could not believe that the hairy-chested, unshaven image which stared vacantly out of the mirror was himself. Had not the day been like those he knew so well, blue-skied, with children and nursemaids walking in the town park?''—thus the opening of Werfel's poem *Der dicke Mann im Spiegel* in which he evokes not only the sights and sounds and smells but also the wonderment and fears of childhood. For the reader of the poem, as for the poet, these are vivid, but it is more than mere nostalgia which creates the effect in the six stanzas, for ultimately the continued undimmed existence of these memories and the longing they induce strike terror in the helpless unchildlike mirror image, which can only turn away. Why should such apparently harmless memories inspire terror? Can it be that their very vividness appears so incongruous, so inappropriate when the poet is brought face to face with himself now that childhood is past? Does he feel guilt when he still finds it possible to recall and record such innocence? Self-appraisal and a feeling of detachment are presented in this poem as frightening aspects of maturity. We are not dealing here with the sentimental reminiscences of an old man, for the poem was among those first published in the collection *Der Weltfreund* in 1911, when Werfel was only twenty-one, and just beginning a career as poet, dramatist and novelist.

Youthful ecstacy in living and in loving all that experience offers, determines the range of subject-matter and the style of these first poems. He shared with his generation distrust for cultivated form and the consciously ''beautiful'' word, and gave priority to the urgency and directness of language, even at the expense of euphony. The musicality of this verse seems so often marred by what, traditionally, counted as unpoetic and plebeian: everyday turns of phrase, a litter of journalese and foreign words, and a deliberate sloppiness and tastelessness at odds with the cool control of George or the sophisticated word music of Hofmannsthal. While this application of everyday language is in another tradition initiated by the Naturalist revolt of Arno Holz, Werfel's style involves the subordination of words to the poet's expressive intentions, so that he (as in varying degrees Heym in his mythical visions and Trakl in his elegaic melancholy) wrings new meaning out of unusual, incongruous or even grotesque word clusters. While the influence of Whitman and of the early Rilke can at times be discerned in this youthful rhapsodising, there is much that attracts the description ''anti-poetry''. But the attitude is not born of neglect nor simply out of a wish to shock. It flows freely from a personality supremely open to the world, marked by an all-embracing, insatiable sympathy, especially for the poor and oppressed, sensitive but not shrinking like the mimosa Rilke, exultantly exposed to life and to the whole cosmos. . . . (pp. 107-08)

The jarring elements of Werfel's revolutionary Expressionist style are analogous to the vision in the fat man's mirror, revealing a disparity between the wish and the reality. In *Der Weltfreund* many would see with W. H. Sokel in his *The Writer in Extremis* a cry ''symptomatic of a generation of authors who felt remote from humanity and desperately attempted to bridge the abyss between themselves and 'men' ''. This feeling of remoteness in Werfel is something attributable to his love for the world demonstrated in these early poems and well attested throughout his work—a love that in time feels it can never be adequate, such are the demands it makes of itself and of him who bears it.

In *Der Weltfreund* the euphoric state of childlike harmony is disturbed by the developing problem of individuation and by the closely related one of increasing self-awareness. . . . (p. 109)

[An] ethical strain, accompanying the process of disillusion, . . . characterises the volume *Wir sind* of 1913—a consciousness of personal responsibility for others in their suffering. . . .

This consciousness of guilt lies at the roots of the more reflective melancholy of *Einander* . . . , where Werfel turns to the godhead with longing for redemption—but it is only in and through man that God is realised. Man is still as always the focal point of Werfel's concern. . . . (p. 110)

Among the many forms adopted for his lyric verse—song, aria, hymn, ballad, ode and sonnet—one is struck by the occurrence of forms which allow for statement and counter-statement, question and answer, that is dialogue, including even stichomythia, as in the pair of poems which make up *Selbstgespräch,* or in the linked pair under the title *Des Turms Auferstehung,* or again in the dialogues *Die Prophezeiung an Alexander, Sarastro,* and *Zwiegesprëch (Einander).* In a radio talk in 1952 Willy Haas, a lifelong friend of Werfel and the character B. H. of *Der Stern der Ungeborenen,* attributed great importance to the influence of the form of the Italian operatic aria on the young poet, and compared the quartet from *Rigoletto* with poems like *Ein Gesang von Toten* (mit verteilten Rollen zu lesen) and

Gesang der Toten vor neuem Leben. But the duet form is not just an aspect of Werfel's musicality but the response to an inner need. It reflects the poet's lack of inner harmony, which more and more was demanding dramatic rather than lyrical expression. Thus there is close correspondence between the early dramatic sketches [*Der Besuch aus dem Elysium, Die Versuchung,* and *Die Mittagsgötten*] and the poetry as far as the publication of *Der Gerichtstag.* With the "magische Trilogie" *Spiegelmensch* . . . , for the first time in a full and original dramatic form, Werfel undertook to follow a path that led from delusion and vanity.

In poems like *Eitelkeit,* and repeatedly in his war poems as in *Gebet um Reinheit,* Werfel used the image of self-encounter and self-contemplation in the mirror to the end of accusing himself of vanity—vanity as a poet. There is indeed, as elsewhere in this early work, an element of the baroque about the argument which presents self-accusation as another, disguised, form of vanity. Can one suggest that the accomplished liar would feel no such pangs of conscience?

In *Spiegelmensch* the hero, Thamal, seeking asylum as a novice in a mysterious oriental monastery, shoots at his reflection in a magic mirror and, in shattering this, releases his alter ego, the Mirrorman of the title, who represents the lower and essentially megalomaniac self. (pp. 111-12)

Together with the story *Nicht der Mörder, der Ermordete ist schuldig* . . . to which it is closely related in its basic theme, *Spiegelmensch* appears to have served Werfel as a form of personal exorcism, which, while it by no means provided even a dramatically satisfying solution to the underlying problem of self-awareness, enabled him in future to debate its jumble of psychological and metaphysical problems in a more readily comprehended and less obsessively subjective way. The trilogy nevertheless shows those characteristics which are seen in all Werfel's writing for the stage. Spectacle, entertainment in the broadest theatrical sense, the intermingling of operatic and pantomime effects, all combine with the expected elements of plot and character and conflict to mark Werfel as a dramatist in the established Austrian tradition of Raimund and Grillparzer, whose *Der Traum, ein Leben* immediately springs to mind in its parallelism to *Spiegelmensch.* It is with *Brand* or *Peer Gynt* and not with the later work of Ibsen or with the Naturalist drama that the play may be compared. And when the Ich-dramas of Expressionism—those of Sorge, Czokor, Johst, Hasenclever, or Kornfeld—are considered, Werfel's drama is seen as one concerned with the inner conflict of the protagonist, not so much with the tragic outward clash of a society and the individual who claims to be its judge and saviour. Werfel continually presented realistically conceived plot and characters in a framework designed to reveal their metaphysical import, thus giving further evidence of the basic duality of his art.

Dramatic structure of the traditional type is abandoned for an organisation which owes much to musical form—which is not so unexpected when one recalls Werfel's early enthusiasm for opera, and his contribution to the Verdi renaissance of the twenties. Thus the musicality of Werfel's plays [*Juarez und Maximilian, Paulus unter den Juden,* and *Das Reich Gottes in Böhmen*], where, as A. D. Klarmann has described, "it permeates even into the innermost structure of his work, in the duets of the contrasting couples which complement each other to form a new unity, which, however, has always been theirs and was only temporarily separated, like two voices, that going their way mingle with each other in a higher harmony" [see

excerpt above]. Thus also in *Jacobowsky und der Oberst* . . . , the last of his plays, written after his escape from invaded France in 1940.

Unconventionality in dramatic form is matched in Werfel by frequent avoidance of the usual nomenclature, e.g. *Romantisches Drama, Ein Gespräch, Ein Zauberspiel, Magische Trilogie, "Bocksgesang"* (a deliberately meaningful mistranslation of the Greek "tragoedia"), *Dramatische Historie, Dramatische Legende. Jacobowsky und der Oberst* he described as *Komödie einer Tragödie!*

In their flight before the rapidly advancing German forces, a Polish Jew, Jacobowsky, and Stjerbinsky, an anti-Semitic Polish colonel, with the former's servant and later a French girl, Marianne, undergo adventures which, while they are plausible and in fact based on the accounts of refugees like Werfel himself, combine to appear as fantastic and fairy-tale-like as those of Thamal are nightmarish. This atmosphere is created by the comic way in which Jacobowsky and his companions repeatedly, by luck and his quick-wittedness, escape from the dangers, which more often than not are due to their own absurd behaviour. The comic element is in equal measure dependent on the incongruity of their behaviour and attitude in the tragic circumstances of the fall of France. This European tragedy itself gains in poignancy when seen as the background for actions and characters whose interplay can cause such laughter, and at the same time be seen as laughable by Jacobowsky himself, the truly tragi-comic figure of the piece. (pp. 112-14)

Here as in the many other works where the problem of Jewishness is debated, whether specifically or incidentally, Werfel reveals the inner tension which resulted from his own Jewish origins and his feeling for Austria. In the English foreword to the collection of stories in the volume *Twilight of a World* . . . he revealed a nostalgic and almost reactionary love for the old Austria which seemed to provide for the peaceful co-existence of so many nationalities and creeds. He nevertheless dealt with Jewishness not only in terms of history or topicality in works like *Paulus unter den Juden, Höret die Stimme, Der Weg der Verheissung* and the unfinished novel *Cella,* but also in terms of his own continual search for the cause and justification of the separateness of his kind. He turned again and again to the conception of Israel as the chosen people and found that metaphysically it has been allocated a special role until the end of time. A role which is subject to both divine grace and a divine curse. Through its suffering, persecution and destruction the Jewish race is seen as bearing witness to Christ, the unacknowledged Messiah. (p. 115)

[In both *Nicht der Mörder* and *Spiegelmensch*] the hero is afforded insight into "the mystery of unity and blood", the mystery of love and hate between succeeding generations and between man and God. The two motifs of father and son and of the maternal female figure of *Die Mittagsgöttin* are further developed and continue to play a basic role in the prose works. There follows a corresponding loss of extremism, violence and extravagance of style in the novels which Werfel wrote from the mid-twenties until the end of his life, and a more positive accent is put on the theme of integration.

In his first major novel, *Verdi* . . . , Werfel is basically concerned with the integration of the artist in the community. With a facile command of realistic detail and character delineation he depicts the Verdi of 1882 in his unproductive stage between the composition of his *Requiem* and that of *Otello* bitterly suffering his silence in Venice and eclipsed by the ascendant

Wagner. This "Roman der Oper" is antithetical in its structure, setting Verdi, opera and Italy against Wagner, Musikdrama and Germany, and examining their respective effects on the Senator, Verdi's friend, and his son, Italo. Here Werfel's sympathies are with the father figure and with Verdi, who retires behind his work. The Romantic Wagner is shown as dependent on the enthusiasms of his youthful supporters and on the force of the personality he projects through his work. Annemarie von Puttkamer points out the relevance of the implied social criticism in this novel to the events which accompanied its writing—the rise of Fascism in Italy, a new and terrible aspect of the Romanticism which in Werfel's view Wagner represented. As a Künstlerroman *Verdi* demonstrates the need for the artist to wait patiently and humbly, without asserting himself, for that combination of outward circumstances which will allow his recognition and the release of his creative ability once more. (p. 116)

Within the loose framework of what seems part chronicle, part "Entwicklungsroman" and part "Schlüsselroman" *Barbara, oder die Frömmigkeit* . . . has as its central experience, like so many contemporary novels, the First World War. The personal history it recounts however covers the childhood and youth of its hero, Ferdinand R., *and* the revolution which immediately followed the war. Here the implications of the conflict between the individual and the political and military and revolutionary powers he is helpless to resist go far beyond those of the many stories of the time about the blood and mire of trench warfare. It is an impersonal power which is portrayed and to which the orphaned boy is subjected as a military cadet and in the army. Similarly in the revolution he sees it exploiting and consuming without mercy, a whole population. The tools of this power are represented not by any enemy soldier but by the figures of Steidler, a fellow cadet and later a staff captain in the army, and by Elkan, the alien, cold-blooded revolutionary. Both have in common an inhuman and machine-like disregard for human life, and it is through Steidler that Ferdinand is brought to demonstrate a simple and unassuming humanity in the action which provides the axis for the whole novel. In 'Richtgang', the thirteenth chapter of the second of four parts, Ferdinand halts the execution of three alleged but innocent deserters and allows the men to escape. The hero is presented as relying always, even unconsciously, on the comfort and guidance of the old woman, Barbara, who since his childhood has been the source of that completely free and selfless love which is the pure expression of motherliness.

The piety of the title is a naive, uncalculating and almost undemonstrative relationship with God which corresponds to the feeling of safety and repose which Barbara in turn inspires in the child Ferdinand. It is to him that she bequeaths her life's savings, not to her relatives. Such is the love he feels for her that he consigns this symbol of her devotion to the sea, where it is beyond risk of losing that spiritual value it holds for him. Ten years later Werfel was to write a novel which, for all its dissimilarities, was essentially a variation on this theme in *Der veruntreute Himmel*. . . . (pp. 117-18)

In similar vein the novel *Die Geschwister von Neapel* published two years later demonstrates the working out of similar themes on more than one level. There is a further development of the parent and child relationship, in which the father, Domenico Pascarella, with sacrifice and suffering wins back the love and respect of his children. A love story, the only one of any account of Werfel's novels, takes on a deliberately conventionalised operatic form, which is set against the political developments of contemporary Italy, as had been the case indirectly in *Verdi*. On yet another plane the portrayal of the youthful poet Placido is the means whereby Werfel continued his own self-examination.

With *Die vierzig Tage des Musa Dagh* . . . and *Höret die Stimme* . . . Werfel shifted his attention, directed by personal observation and concern and by political developments, to larger social units—the persecuted religious communities of the Armenians during the First World War and the Jews in the story of Jeremiah. In both the scope of the subject matter allowed for the panoramic sweep and detailed character observation which he had begun to develop in the earlier novels, but the central problems still asserted themselves despite the mass of realistic detail demanded in the chronicles.

Der veruntreute Himmel and *Das Lied von Bernadette* continued the theme of religious devotion, and in the latter brought further comment on the scepticism and materialism of a self-satisfied scientific age as it gathered momentum in mid-nineteenth century. Werfel delights in showing how the representatives of authority and state, science and intellect were powerless to defeat the miracle of Lourdes and the unworthy vessel of divine grace, Bernadette Soubirous. Of the many symbolically charged figures in the novel in addition to Bernadette herself, the aristocratic nun Vauzous, her teacher as child and novice, and the poet Lafite, command most attention. Bernadette serves as the mirror for the "lady", the apparition. Divine and poetic inspiration are all but one here in the descriptions Werfel finds for the devotions and lonely suffering of Bernadette. Sister Vauzous must also suffer much mental and spiritual anguish for her hatred, envy and doubts. In the end Lafite too falls on his knees at the shrine after years of feeling privileged to dissociate himself from the spectacle of life and rejoice in his detachment.

Werfel's last novel *Stern der Ungeborenen* . . . finished only a short time before his death and written in the knowledge that this was at hand assumes the aspect of a grand finale. Ostensibly a Utopian venture with many of the appurtenances of a science fiction extravaganza, projected into the far distant world 100,000 years from now, the novel also recaptures much of Werfel's own story, including for example in a disguised form conversations between the author and his friend Willy Haas, which date from their boyhood together in Prague. Through the exercise of an alien will the author finds himself resurrected in this distant "astromental age" in order to judge it by our relatively prehistoric standards, and sub specie aeternitatis.

A playful fancy is indulged in the depiction of the topography of this strangely monotonous earth, on which Man has secured for himself a complete and uniform welfare state, which provides all his needs. He enjoys remarkable longevity and has all his mortal fears of suffering, violence and even death calmed. But they are only calmed—for these men, for all their hairless physical beauty and technical super-sophistication, are no wit different from Man today. What has happened here is that Werfel, like so many Utopian writers, has taken modern tendencies in technical development and in human aspiration to a point where he attains a more fundamental judgment of man and his condition.

But it is not merely a grand tour that F. W., as he calls himself, has in this "astromental" world of technical perfection, where one moves one's destination rather than oneself. Despite the security that intellect has created, there remains the threat of the "jungle". This is the term used for the surviving patches of original earthly vegetation which flourish on, cultivated and inhabited by a naïve pastoral folk. As in Hesse's *Glasperlenspiel* the duality of intellect and nature, which these parallel forms of life suggest, constitutes a danger for mankind.

The essential insecurity of the astromental culture is demonstrated as lying in its uniform and unoriginal qualities, and thus in the monotony which provokes even some of the younger generation to side with the ''jungle'' people when war comes. Simple, organic life re-asserts itself with the weapons against which the new culture has no defence—depression, melancholy and disappointment. (pp. 118-20)

In these last three works the wheel Werfel began to turn in his youth came full circle. The suffering he so longed to alleviate in those early poems found a positive significance. In the Jew, Saul Minjonman, of this future age we also find another projection of himself, unable to become a Catholic. . . . Even as he embraces a Romantic primitiveness, metaphysics and Catholic permanence, Werfel could not help questioning them at the same time, knowing full well that he had himself been conditioned and moulded by the scientific attitude he so often repudiated. Werfel's Romantic outlook differs essentially from that he criticised so vehemently in *Verdi*. It is graced by a sincere ethical strain, tempered by an awareness of the dangers of a poet's pride, and lent human warmth and sympathy in its avoidance of moralising. (pp. 120-21)

[Werfel] conceived his mission to be one of singing the glories of divine mystery and of the sanctity of man. For all the extravagance and violence of much of his earlier work this positive intention persists throughout all his work, and sets him apart from those of his time in whom pessimism and nihilism are so often seen as virtues. It is an element which cannot be ignored in judging him. (p. 121)

> *W. H. Fox, ''Franz Werfel,'' in* German Men of Letters: Twelve Literary Essays, Vol. III, *edited by Alex Natan (©1964 Oswald Wolff (Publishers) Limited), Wolff, 1964, pp. 107-25.*

HENRY A. LEA (essay date 1965)

In the work of Franz Werfel, the Parable of the Prodigal Son is found as a recurring theme, allegorically expressing the author's belief that man is destined to become estranged from God before he can return to Him. Whereas the Biblical son becomes alienated by yielding to wastefulness and carnality, Werfel's prodigal sons experience worldliness primarily as a separation from their spirituality. The rebellious son breaking away from the father and abandoning the ancestral faith is, for Werfel, the ever-present symbol of man's apostasy. (p. 41)

One form of apostasy to which Werfel's characters are susceptible is the attempt to change the existing social order by revolutionary means. In Werfel's view such an attempt is inherently profane, because behind the apparently good motives of the revolutionary lie the vanity and self-aggrandizement of the crusader who cannot conceive of any reform except under his own banner and who, under the corrupting influence of power, will merely replace one tyranny with another. Moreover, such an attempt is foredoomed to failure because Werfel's lyrically inspired, inward young idealists are destined to fail in any bid for political power. This is exemplified in the revolutionary episodes of *Nicht der Mörder, der Ermordete ist schuldig* . . . and *Barbara oder die Frömmigkeit*. . . . (pp. 41-2)

In both novels a sensitive young introvert joins a band of anarchists in protest against the world of the father who represents the autocratic power and hierarchic order of the army, with its glorification of military discipline for its own sake and its disregard for the individual. Humanly this rebellion is understandable and invites sympathy. . . . As overregimented young men, Karl and Ferdinand are irresistibly attracted by the lure of the illicit, the chaotic, the nihilistic. It is in a mood of defiance of authority and with the desire to strike a blow against tyranny that Karl Duschek and Ferdinand R. join the anarchists.

But it is clear at once that the appeal of the revolutionaries is a subtle temptation, all the more dangerous for posing as a design for world salvation. (p. 42)

Neither Karl nor Ferdinand escapes what Werfel considers the gravest heresy, the Messianic complex of wanting to remake the world in one's own image. They are most truly prodigal sons, lost to God, as long as they succumb to this conceit. The indications in *Nicht der Mörder* are, despite Karl's honorable motives for joining the anarchists, that his ego rather than mankind chiefly benefits from his new association. . . . Similar symptoms are apparent in Ferdinand's revolutionary phase. Momentarily he persuades himself that he is called upon to lead the downtrodden against established authority. In his dreams of grandeur he imagines himself receiving an oath of allegiance from the suffering multitudes.

Yielding to this temptation is also an escape from reality for Werfel's characters. It is a lapse into fantasy that distorts their relation to the world and to themselves. The anarchist episodes read like nightmares. Both Karl and Ferdinand are in a trance-like state when they enter the anarchist circle, and both awaken from it abruptly, as from an anxiety dream. Their emergence from this experience leads to an accounting with themselves through a re-examination of the past. Like the Prodigal Son they have to face themselves, as a necessary step toward self-knowledge and catharsis. For Karl Duschek this takes the form of filial compassion, inspired by the vision of his own future fatherhood. (pp. 43-4)

Whereas Karl and Ferdinand become alienated through political activism, Placido Pascarella's rift with his father Domenico, in *Die Geschwister von Neapel* . . . , is attributed to the son's intellectual independence. (The important feature in all three novels is the son's need to be ''different'' from his father.) (pp. 44-5)

It irritates [Domenico] that a son of his should test his authority. Being a father in the tradition of an Old Testament patriarch (his name suggests ''Lord'') he finds it difficult to tolerate his son's intractability. Structurally the novel supports him, for it is this patriarchal authority that holds the family—and the plot—together. The chapter headings (*Ein Tag des Zornes, Ein Abend der Gnade, Der Sündenfall, Das Blutopfer, Der neue Bund*, etc.) give emphasis to the Biblical cast of the story, though this theological framework is not fully justified by the plot.

Complete harmony of design and execution is achieved in *Die vierzig Tage des Musa Dagh* . . . in which the Prodigal Son motif is thematically and structurally closely integrated with the religious theme of the novel. For it soon becomes evident that Gabriel Bagradian's return to Armenia after long residence in France is preordained, leading him back to the land and faith of his fathers and thereby enabling him to liberate his people from bondage. (pp. 45-6)

It is evident from the very first pages of the novel that Gabriel Bagradian's return to Armenia is providential. On revisiting the Musa Dagh he falls asleep and dreams of leading an exodus into the mountains. . . . Like Karl and Ferdinand, Gabriel Bagradian sees his life in perspective for the first time. He knows intuitively that he has received a divine call and that there is no turning back from this mission.

Gabriel's status as an estranged Armenian who returns to his homeland is emphasized throughout the novel. . . . Thus it is evident in the theme, structure, and wording of the book that a man's life is being fulfilled in a cyclical form leading from a sheltered childhood in Armenia to worldly sophistication in Paris and back to Armenia where the cycle is completed in suffering, awareness and self-transcendence.

In Werfel's later works the Prodigal Son theme is increasingly formulated as the loss and recovery of religious affiliation, and as in *Barbara* and *Musa Dagh* the central figures end in religious exaltation. The realistic level gives way to vision and revelation, indicating a new level of experience reached after illumination. An early example is found in [*Pogrom,* a study for the chapter "Der Tanz des Wunderrabbi" in *Barbara*. A later, more fully developed one is found in *Höret die Stimme*]. In both works the protagonists have lost contact with Judaism through assimilation and rediscover it through persecution and inner transformation. Following a series of premonitory experiences, their Jewishness powerfully reasserts itself within them, after having been submerged and buried deep in their subconscious by circumstances of ancestry and upbringing. (pp. 48-9)

Like all of Werfel's major figures, his prodigal sons are selected for suffering and insight: their suffering is their alienation, their insight is the retrospective vision which enables them to re-orient their lives. Evidence of their selection is their solitude. Except for Karl Duschek in *Nicht der Mörder,* the least religious of these works, none of Werfel's prodigal sons has any prospect of marriage. Ferdinand and Sonnenfels avoid involvement with women, Bagradian and Jeeves are divested of their marital ties, and for Placido the question does not arise. Thus, they are singled out for a special mission that requires them to remain apart, the mission of prefiguring the path that mankind must take. (p. 53)

> Henry A. Lea, "Prodigal Sons in Werfel's Fiction," in The Germanic Review (reprinted by permission of Joseph P. Bowka), Vol. XL, No. 1, January, 1965, pp. 41-54.

LORE B. FOLTIN and JOHN M. SPALEK (essay date 1969)

Although Franz Werfel's fame rests on his poetry, his plays, and his fiction, he also produced a significant number of essays which ought to be assigned a more important place in the scope of his work. In taking these essays as a serious effort, we are following Werfel's own example. (p. 172)

In general we can say that Werfel's essayistic writings fall into three main categories: philosophy (Weltanschauung), literature, and music—though Werfel does not strictly observe these categories and frequently crosses from one subject to another. (p. 173)

The reader of Franz Werfel's essays is struck by his continuing desire to bring before the public what he considered vital. What does Werfel consider vital? First and foremost the necessity of spiritual awakening and the need for salvation, as expounded in his major addresses and in **"Theologumena."** The latter, dealing for the most part with the Christian-Jewish relationship,

discuss the mystery of the Trinity and other theological questions, not with the preciseness of a religious philosopher, such as Martin Buber, Karl Barth, or Thomas Merton, but with emphasis on his private beliefs. Like all beliefs, his is irrational. Because of his basically irrational attitude he sees the remedy for the ills of this world neither in socialism, revolution, or any other kind of reform, but in a turn toward inwardness. Hence his pessimistic outcries against psychology, intellectualism, and modern civilization as a whole. Werfel's increasing conservatism, especially in politics, complements his views.

One of Werfel's recurring terms of condemnation is "Abstraktion." While its specific content shifts with the context, its negative value judgment remains constant. Thus modern ideologies, e.g., socialism, are accused of operating with abstract concepts, such as a class, and of sacrificing the individual to its progress. The politician argues in abstract categories ("Stände, Nationen, Klassen, Menschheiten") which ultimately leads to the annihilation of the individual. His advocate and champion is the poet who proclaims: "Die Welt fängt im Menschen an." In exposing the dangers of "Abstraktion," Werfel himself is led astray by that mode of thinking when he tries to prove that "die Sozialdemokratie" failed to produce a poet because of its abstract character. Not only modern civilization and politics are chastized by Werfel with the word "Abstraktion," but also German music. By abstract music Werfel does not mean intellectual or atonal music, but rather music which relies on the instruments instead of the human voice and replaces melody with theme. (pp. 185-86)

The reader of Werfel's essays, be they philosophical, literary, or musicological, will find them similarly oriented. They may not be essays in a technical sense, but they are impassioned and eloquent human documents, some foreshadowing what Werfel more effectively expressed in his poetry, novels, and dramas, others restating what had already crystallized into poetic expression, with some shifts of emphasis, to be sure. In the final evaluation of Franz Werfel's literary art his essays certainly more than merely augment his creative works. (p. 186)

> Lore B. Foltin and John M. Spalek, "Franz Werfel's Essays: A Survey," in The German Quarterly (copyright © 1969 by the American Association of Teachers of German), Vol. XLII, No. 2, March, 1969, pp. 172-203.

JAMES L. ROLLESTON (essay date 1975)

[In *Star of the Unborn*] Werfel sought to isolate and magnify the polarities of modern man's fate, his cosmological potentiality and his obsessive self-destructiveness, propelling the reader into the vantage point of exile, from which what is usable after the explosion can be salvaged. (p. 57)

Werfel deals with the confusion of categories brought about by the exile experience by accelerating it and projecting it into the future. A travel novel of the present could only be ephemeral in its formulations: the main problem with Werfel's wartime play, *Jacobowsky and the Colonel,* is that his very closeness to events leads to total uncertainty of touch when he attempts to leave the comic surface in order to invoke some kind of "meaning," as with the embarrassing symbol of France, Marianne. But a travel-novel of the future, a future which, as must always be the case, is an eclectic extrapolation of trends perceived in the present—this kind of fiction offered Werfel an ideal opportunity for regaining the poet's public role. (pp. 58-59)

Politzer has called Werfel the "reporter of the sublime" [see excerpt above], and the formulation is wholly appropriate to *Star of the Unborn*. By casting the "I" of the novel as both himself A.D. 1943 and a traveller in a remote future, Werfel is able to establish a fluid continuum between constantly shifting facts and highly organized theoretical structures. He can wrap a whole series of fictional frames around any given remark and then break through these frames at will; the total relativity and uncertainty of the exile experience is thus provided with a symbolic equivalent through a unique kind of fictional reportage. The reporter F.W. is learning new things at such a breathtaking pace that it soon becomes clear that nothing he learns is definitive, indeed that his own contribution to events is of governing importance, despite his oft-repeated denigration of his own world. At one point he digresses on the difference between the impersonal exploration and the travel-novel, which has a dual focus, with the reactions of the traveller always at issue. Out of two voids, the collapsed present and the imagined future, Werfel has fashioned a texture that moves simultaneously towards ever more audacious fictions and away from all the limitations of the fictional state.

The importance of F.W. himself to the story he presents becomes clearer when we consider . . . [Werfel's] absorption of the Anglo-American Utopian tradition, of which the most widely read representatives at the time were H. G. Wells, Aldous Huxley, and Olaf Stapledon. Stapledon's influential novel *Last and First Men*, published in 1930, is especially relevant because the basic motif of Werfel's book is prefigured here, the conception of twentieth-century people as "first men" and the possibility of interaction between the beginning and the end of human time. . . . The cucial difference is in the narrative perspective. Stapledon presents his tale from the point of view of one of the Last Men, which amounts to nothing more than old-fashioned authorial omniscience. . . . [While] his vision of the world of the Last Men includes the kind of simultaneous experience of history also envisaged by Werfel, the interaction between past and future is trapped by a rigid causality. Past events cannot, by definition, be changed through their reenactment by the Last Men because, after all, the past is past. This is precisely the kind of assumption that Werfel cheerfully challenges, and in doing so he goes some way towards creating something that can genuinely be called a myth for our time. Whether consciously or not, his novel carries lightly in its baggage the Heisenberg principle that all matter is modified by the very process of observation; nothing is exempt from this process, whether it be time, space, personality, causality, or fiction itself. Indeed this circularity is embodied in one of the key sayings of the book: the whole has the shape of man. And conversely, observation is the sole purpose of the narrator F.W., unlike, say, Wells's Time Traveller, who always has the goal of return before him. F.W.'s innumerable references to the world of 1943 are enmeshed in a total mutual commitment between narrator and narrated world: the only stable frame here is the act of fiction-making itself. (pp. 59-61)

Two peculiarities will strike the reader early on in his journey through *Star of the Unborn:* the fragmentation of the narrative, which seems designed to deprive the earlier scenes of final coherence by leaving all the suggestive points hanging, unassimilated; and the unusual closeness and independence, even arbitrariness, of the narrator F.W. To someone coming to this book from another Utopian novel, or any novel at all, the narrative posture seems clumsy and sometimes tiresome: despite F.W.'s assurances that his only goal is to give us information about the future, the reader receives from the beginning

a rather different impression, as F.W., the 100,000-year-old ghost, organizes scene after scene around his own self-consciousness. But I want to argue that, taken together, the fragmentation and the narrator's insistent presence constitute the basis of a novelistic technique with very definite goals, goals that can be glimpsed from both inside and outside the novel. "True art is a kind of splitting of the atoms of subject matter" reads an epigram of Werfel's [in *Between Heaven and Earth*], and the analogy with contemporary physics is especially illuminating when read together with the speculation quoted earlier about the source of life residing in "exiled material." Clearly Werfel saw modern science as very much the ally rather than the enemy of the fiction maker, and it is not too farfetched to see in *Star of the Unborn* an extended image of the process of creation through exile imagined by Werfel in his *Theologumena*.

The two worlds, the Astromental world and that of 1943, come too close together through the agency of F.W.: the individual scenes are the seemingly inorganic lumps of stone and sand from which in fact there germinates a new form of life. In any case a very different kind of play with the processes of fiction is going on here from the modernism we are familiar with in the case of Joyce or Mann. With these recognized masters, an organic metaphor of creation is still in control: motifs anticipate and blend with each other in a continuous movement of growth and expansion. Werfel, on the other hand, wants to incorporate into his fiction both the rationalist tone of modern science, and its thematic of randomness, of particles eluding prescriptive laws. At a fairly late point in the book, F.W. reflects that the stations of his rushed, breathless journey through the Astromental world are like pieces of a jigsaw in which the connecting principle is missing. Instead of truth he has presented us with fragments, accumulating layers of apparent meaning while constantly shifting the bottom layer. And not only is the meaning of what the reader is shown in need of incessant revision, it gradually becomes clear that F.W.'s own personality is the only reliable link. Like the scientist and his experiment, the traveller and the strange world have become inextricably intertwined. (pp. 66-7)

Clearly the narrator F.W. is a consciously limited version of Werfel himself, not a falsification, but a slightly breathless caricature capable of generating the rhythms of fictional truth. For even as F.W. is denouncing his own time, he engages repeatedly in encomiums to the future age in which he finds himself, to the effect that the Astromental civilization has abolished injustice and suffering and so forth. This sort of speech sounds unconvincing even as it is made; not that the reader is to doubt in any way F.W.'s sincerity—such a reaction would be totally inimical to the essentially "flat" characterization of the novel. But each time F.W. utters his praise of the future, he is met with a melancholy insecurity which neither he nor the reader is able to understand. As a result he redoubles his Pollyanna-like efforts, as if to convince the Astromentals of their good fortune. But the device of repetition causes his words to sound hollow and as the book advances another kind of repetition gradually dominates F.W.'s reactions: the repetition of historical cycles. After his reincarnated friend B.H. has expounded the events that occurred between the two eras that are now in contact, the oscillations between excessive spiritualism and excessive materialism, F.W. comes to view the Astromental era as more and more in the grip of this cycle, its delicate achievements doomed by fundamental inner flaws.

It is at this point that the special character of the narrative posture reveals its true function: far from rejecting the future civilization or even modifying his praise of it, F.W. strives to save it or rather the valuable parts of it which could so illuminate the darkness of his own time. It is a usable future: even as F.W. is bringing his novel into being with a climax of destruction, he is almost tangibly projecting a world in which neither the achievements of the Astromental world nor its cyclical failure will be definitive, in which his own energy as a representative of the barbarian twentieth century will help conceive a truly "timeless" world born out of exile, where neither death nor evil are shunned but fruitfully confronted. This is why the frame set around the book in chapter one is not completed at the end: F.W.'s "return" is not to the year 1943 but to a world of hope beyond either realism or utopia, in which the very word "exile" will transcend its own negative connotations.

Just as the technique of narrative repetition slides into the reiteration of cyclical rhythms that undermine the situation's uniqueness, so also the technique of fragmentation and plot-disruption shades into a fictional modality with the opposite aesthetic effect, i.e., postponement. In a sense this is apparent with the very first and obviously grotesque fragmentation, namely the description of how F.W. came to write his travel novel. He was all set to write the tragedy of his own age, so he tells us, when he found he did not possess the right pencil. While looking for a suitable pencil, the experience befell him which has compelled him to write of the future instead of the present. Such light-hearted invocations of *Tristram Shandy* clearly clash horribly with the reality of the European catastrophe, but before the reader takes F.W. at his word he should remember the reality of Werfel's credentials as an author committed to his own age. It seems likely that he has not mentioned the tragedy of the present in order simply to write about something else. And in fact this is the first and most large-scale instance of postponement as a basic technique. Werfel will, in fact, be dealing with the meaning of the year 1943 as he sees it—but only obliquely, through the realization of the exile's perspective in an anti-realistic fiction.

The present cannot any longer be reported, because by the time the details have reached the writer in exile they are out of date, translatable only into banalities. But while the realistic confrontation with the present must thus be postponed indefinitely, the very technique of postponement lends itself to a reenactment of the disasters of our time on a more universal stage. As more and more important matters become postponed, especially during the first meal with F.W.'s Astromental hosts, when such issues as aging, death, and aesthetic sterility are left hanging in the air, the reader feels the building up of pressures both within the novel and within the future world. Problems are left unsolved precisely because they cannot be allowed out into the open, and even as F.W. presses against the intellectual limits of this new-old civilization, an atmosphere of anxiety and resignation thickens and presses in on him. Postponement becomes thematic, and finally the pressures explode.

Without pressing the point too hard, I see this as an abstract distillation of the build-up towards the First World War. . . . Werfel is telling us that the horrors of 1943 arose inevitably from 1914, which, in turn, derived from the repression of natural change after 1848. There is nothing original about such thoughts, which is precisely why he is not spelling them out, but instead giving them urgency and relevance through fiction. And in one sense he *is* maintaining the differentiation between present and future set out in his opening chapter. He is *not*

writing a tragedy: the unchanging presence of the indefatigably commonsensical F.W. is assurance of this. F.W. is a *perpetuum mobile,* never ceasing to test one experience against the next, and even as the reader grows irritated with his breezy tone, his boy-scout heartiness, the essential point is clear: any historical allegory is intended by the author only insofar as it helps construct a usable future. The twentieth century is to be neither side-stepped nor dwelt on, but transcended, viewed in the largest possible perspective as a pivotal moment at which a reconstruction of reality becomes possible. Werfel's expressionist evangelism has finally found aesthetic fulfillment through the exploitation of the isolation, indirection, and uprootedness of the exile experience. (pp. 68-70)

The question remains: has Werfel achieved his goal aesthetically? Does the novel work? Judging only by its respectful but somewhat detached reception, one would have to answer in the negative. It has been pigeonholed either as a summa of Werfel's theological interests or as an exemplar, along with Ernst Jünger's *Heliopolis,* of the Utopian novel of the forties. In general Werfel's manner, his jovial conservatism, his vulgarities, the almost indiscriminate richness of his material—these qualities did not endear him to the criticism of the fifties, when most of the basic work on him was done. . . . But with the breakup of what can now be seen as a somewhat restrictive aesthetic, it is surely time to read Werfel with a new sympathy, just as we are listening with new ears to Shostakovich, a composer whose emotional anti-modernism was similarly an embarrassment to the formal codes of the fifties. In the age of the nonfiction novel and other forms of overflow from fiction into life and vice versa, Werfel's intentions in **Star of the Unborn** can be assessed more fairly. The seemingly flippant turn from the tragedy of the present to an arbitrary future in chapter one, the breathless tiresomeness of the narrator almost throughout, the discontinuities between eloquence and banality, these fictional devices need to be read against the grain. The novel is in fact a veritable compendium of sophisticated fictional methods, but they are all out in the open, thrusting themselves at the reader. Technically we are perhaps not yet used to such an insistent flatness of characterization, such a literal exposition of Hofmannsthal's dictum that life's depth is in its surfaces. But form and content are as well matched as the New Criticism could desire. The style of the novel is an image of Werfel's attempt to make a fiction in defiance of all the modern saints and sages, from Marx and Lenin to Freud and Stefan George, a fiction that rests ultimately on a most unfamiliar analogy, between the fission and fusion of modern astrophysics and a radicalization of that uprooting of humanity known as exile. Only by drenching ourselves in the strangeness of these total disruptions of the past, Werfel implies, can we overcome the grim and increasingly meaningless cycles of modern history and begin anew. (pp. 78-9)

James L. Rolleston, "The Usable Future: Franz Werfel's 'Star of the Unborn' As Exile Literature" (originally presented at a symposium at the University of Alabama in 1975), in Protest—Form—Tradition: Essays on German Exile Literature, *edited by Joseph P. Strelka, Robert F. Bell, and Eugene Dobson (copyright © 1979 by The University of Alabama Press), University of Alabama Press, 1979, pp. 57-80.*

ADDITIONAL BIBLIOGRAPHY

Brod, Max. "The Young Werfel and the Prague Writers." In *The Era of German Expressionism,* edited by Paul Raabe, translated by J. M. Ritchie, pp. 53-9. Woodstock, N.Y.: The Overlook Press, 1974.*
> Memoir of Werfel's early career. Brod recalls the developing friendships among himself, Werfel, Kafka, and other prominent Prague artists.

Chandler, Frank W. "Expressionism at Its Best: Kaiser, Toller, Werfel." In his *Modern Continental Playwrights,* pp. 407-37. New York, London: Harper & Brothers, 1931.*
> Descriptive overview of dramas.

Foltin, Lore B. "The Czechs in the Work of Franz Werfel." In *Studies in Nineteenth Century and Early Twentieth Century German Literature: Essays in Honor of Paul K. Whitaker,* edited by Norman H. Binger and A. Wayne Wonderley, pp. 12-21. Lexington, Ky.: APRAP Press, 1974.
> Examines Werfel's Czech characters and how "they serve him, the writer, as an all-embracing metaphor of the human condition."

Foltin, Lore B., and Heinen, Hubert. "Franz Werfel's 'Als mich dein Wandeln an den Tod verzückte': An Interpretation." *Modern Austrian Literature* III, No. 2 (Summer 1970): 62-7.
> Indepth study of one sonnet, which, the critics contend, exemplifies Werfel's themes of piety and compassion.

Hudson, Lynton. "Symbolic Evangelism and the Philosophical Revue." In his *Life and the Theatre,* pp. 97-110. London: Harrap, 1949.*

Brief survey of Werfel's major dramatic themes, with particular emphasis on his belief in the existence of absolute evil.

Kohn-Bramstedt, Ernst. "Franz Werfel as a Novelist." *Contemporary Review* CXLVI (July 1934): 66-73.
> Thematic and stylistic outline of early novels.

Lea, Henry A. "Werfel's Unfinished Novel: Saga of the Marginal Jew." *The Germanic Review* XLV, No. 2 (March 1970): 105-14.
> Discussion of *Cella oder die Überwinder* and its theme of Jewish assimilation.

Merlan, Wilma Brun. "Franz Werfel, Poet." In *Franz Werfel: 1890-1945,* edited by Lore B. Foltin, pp. 26-38. Pittsburgh: University of Pittsburgh Press, 1961.
> Interpretative overview of poetry.

Neumann, Karl. "Franz Werfel's Early Lyrical Work with Four Poems Newly Translated." *The Southern Quarterly* XIII, No. 4 (July 1975): 241-51.
> Scholarly assessment of Werfel's early poetry. Neumann contends that Werfel was "a poet of major stature" and that his work possesses "an artistic integrity and strength that might stand even the test of translation."

Woollcott, Alexander. "Plays: Pleasant and Unpleasant: I—*Goat Song.*" In his *The Portable Woollcott,* edited by Joseph Hennessey, pp. 429-33. 1946. Reprint. Westport, Conn.: Greenwood Press, 1972.
> Descriptive and entertaining early review.

Oscar (Fingal O'Flahertie Wills) Wilde

1854-1900

Anglo-Irish dramatist, novelist, essayist, critic, poet, and short story writer.

Perhaps more than any other author of his time, Wilde is identified with the nineteenth-century "art for art's sake" movement, which defied the contemporary trend that subordinated art to ethical instruction. This credo of aestheticism, however, indicates only one facet of a man notorious for resisting any public institution—artistic, social, political, or moral—that attempted to subjugate individual will and imagination. In contrast to the traditional cult of nature, Wilde posed a cult of art in his critical essays and reviews; to socialism's cult of the masses, Wilde proposed a cult of the individual in "The Soul of Man under Socialism" and other works; and in opposition to middle-class facade of false respectability, Wilde encouraged a struggle to realize one's true nature.

Wilde was born and grew up in Dublin, though unlike other expatriate Irish writers, he did not draw upon his homeland as a subject for his works. He began his advanced education at Dublin's Trinity College and concluded it with an outstanding academic career at Oxford. In college Wilde discovered the writings of Walter Pater, a major figure of the aesthetic revival in English arts and letters. Pater advocated the pursuit of intense aesthetic experience, a doctrine which became widely influential. Pater's keenest student, Oscar Wilde, exaggerated this doctrine into a way of life. Wilde was often parodied in the English press as the popular stereotype of the lisping aesthete in velvet breeches. His first publication, *Poems*, did little to better his image, and the pieces in this collection are still regarded as highly polished and highly imitative exercises in form. Using his reputation as a self-declared saint of artistic beauty, Wilde promoted himself and his ideas with successful lecture tours of the United States, Canada, and Great Britain. In the late 1880s he continued to crusade for aestheticism as a book reviewer and as the editor of *Lady's World*, whose name he immediately changed to *Woman's World*. Wilde's first collection of prose, *The Happy Prince, and Other Tales*, further display his singleminded efforts toward ornamentation and stylistic grace in his writings.

The appearance of the critical essays and dialogues in *Intentions* defined Wilde's artistic philosophy. "The Critic as Artist" develops its author's deeply held belief that originality of form is the only enduring quality in a work of art, a quality transcending its age. "The Decay of Lying" insists on the superiority of art to nature, and puts forth the paradox that "nature imitates art," using this thesis to work out an ingenious line of argument revealing insights into the relationship between natural and aesthetic worlds. "Pen Pencil and Poison" examines the relationship between art and morality, concluding that in fact there exists none. This theme receives fictional treatment in Wilde's only novel, *The Picture of Dorian Gray*. While a number of critics have read the novel purely as a morality tale on the hazards of egoistical self-indulgence, others accept Wilde's viewpoint that the suffering and belated wisdom of the protagonist are incidental to the work's artistic form. Conceding what on his own terms was an artistic error,

Wilde freely admitted that the book does indeed contain a moral, which he summed up with the simple remark: "All excess, as well as all renunciation, brings its own punishment."

Wilde arrived at his greatest success through the production of four plays in the 1890s. The first three—*Lady Windermere's Fan*, *A Woman of No Importance*, and *An Ideal Husband*—are well-made comedies of manners revolving around social codes of the English upper classes. They are distinctively Wildean for the epigrams and witticisms delivered at frequent intervals (a show of rhetoric which often brings the action of the drama to a standstill). A fourth play, *The Importance of Being Earnest*, marked the height of Wilde's popularity and is considered his best and most characteristic drama. Bypassing the more realistic characters and situations of its predecessors, *The Importance of Being Earnest* forms the apogee of Victorian drawing-room farce. Its stylish characters, stylized dialogue, and elegant artificiality are for many readers and critics the ultimate revelation of Wilde's identity as both man and author.

In 1895, after a scandal involving Lord Alfred Douglas, the son of the Marquis of Queensberry, Wilde was convicted for committing homosexual acts. He was sentenced to, and served, two years hard labor at Reading Prison, and his final works found their source in this experience. In *The Ballad of Reading*

Gaol and *De Profundis* Wilde attempted to derive personal and artistic meaning from misery and humiliation. The first work is recognized as Wilde's one great poetic achievement. The second, written in the form of a long letter to Lord Alfred Douglas, is a document of self-examination. "I do not defend my conduct. I explain it," Wilde wrote to his future literary executor, Robert Ross, describing his motives for composing *De Profundis*. A number of critics have called the motives behind this lengthy epistle self-serving and insincere, essentially another artistic pose whether intended or not. Others find it a heroic composition which in the realm of emotion and psyche shares the same integrity that the author maintained in the realm of art.

Both Wilde's sincerity and integrity have long been issues in criticism of his works. His conception of artistic beauty was often considered a superficial liking for ornament, though for some time critics have acknowledged that this conception of beauty additionally demands, as Wilde's character Gilbert states, "thought and passion and spirituality." Commentators on Wilde have also come to stress the intellectual and humanist basis of his work; Jorge Luis Borges, for example, has written that "'The Soul of Man under Socialism' is not only eloquent; it is just." Traditionally, critical evaluation of Wilde has been complicated, primarily because his works have to compete for attention with his sensational life. Wilde himself regarded this complication as unnecessary, advising that "a critic should be taught to criticise a work of art without making reference to the personality of the author. This, in fact, is the beginning of criticism."

(See also *TCLC*, Vol. 1.)

PRINCIPAL WORKS

Poems (poetry) 1881
The Happy Prince, and Other Tales (short stories) 1888
A House of Pomegranates (short stories) 1891
Intentions (essays) 1891
Lord Arthur Savile's Crime, and Other Stories (short stories) 1891
The Picture of Dorian Gray (novel) 1891
Lady Windermere's Fan (drama) 1892
Salomé (drama) 1893
A Woman of No Importance (drama) 1893
An Ideal Husband (drama) 1895
The Importance of Being Earnest (drama) 1895
The Ballad of Reading Gaol, and Other Poems (poetry) 1898
De Profundis (letter) 1905
Collected Works. 14 vols. (poetry, essays, short stories, novel, dramas, and criticism) 1908
The Letters of Oscar Wilde (letters) 1962

*This work was not published in its entirety until 1949.

THE NATION (essay date 1881)

Quite as interesting as most of Mr. Wilde's verses is the perplexity that they have caused candid critics. Mr. Wilde is reported the original of Du Maurier's *Postlethwaite*, and yet his poetry is very fair poetry, as that article is produced by many versifiers of the present day. The contrast thus afforded between the contemptibility of his rôle of "æsthete" and the respectability of his numbers, has proved bewildering, and, so far as we have noticed, it has been explained to be, like so many things about poets, inexplicable. We fancy, however, the poetry has acquired a factitious respect from this contrast which, unheralded in this way, it would hardly have obtained, and that, on the other hand, the literalness of *Punch's* caricatures has been equally overestimated. Whatever absolute fidelity these may possess, it remains true that they are caricatures, and the essence of caricature is humorous exaggeration, not to say distortion. Nevertheless, we are bound to say there are many characteristics disclosed in the volume before us [*Poems*] which seem not wholly incompatible with the qualities ascribed to *Postlethwaite*. Traits may be ascribed to *Postlethwaite* by *Punch* which in their excess really belong more appropriately to *Postlethwaite's* admirers, the dignity of whose character and bearing, we are free to confess, is probably not distinguished. But it would be unreasonably narrow to say that the best of these poems are beyond the origination of a poet who wears long hair, sad garments, a melancholy expression, and a lily in his left hand. The distinctive trait of *Postlethwaite* and the interesting folk who emulate his sighs is, we take it, an ardent love of the love of the beautiful. And this is Mr. Wilde's most marked characteristic. He has an intense desire to delight in the things which poets delight in, and the poets are responsible for his singing as well as for himself. He declares . . . that

> Keats had lifted up his hymeneal curls from out the
> poppy seeded wine.
> With ambrosial mouth had kissed my forehead, clasped
> the hand of noble love in mine;

and, in a subjective sense, it is undeniable that this must have been the case. But the procedure thus described has by no means been confined to Keats. The sonnet "**On the Massacre of the Christians in Bulgaria**" and that "**To Milton**" would clearly never have been written if the poet of the Piedmontese Sonnet and the sedate Wordsworth had not done the same thing, and the number of kisses imprinted upon Mr. Wilde's forehead by the ambrosial mouths of Messrs. Swinburne, Rossetti, Morris, and even the fastidious Mr. Tennyson, would make any one shake his hymeneal curls to contemplate.

The result of this has been to transform Mr. Wilde into a lyric parrot. The inevitable defects of the best and most melodious parrot qualities, however, are an absence of direct inspiration, of genuine significance, and, to a measurable extent, of consciousness. One is never sure that the parrot perceives the precise bearings of his utterances, and the preponderance of the purely oral in them is an undeniable drawback to the permanence of one's enjoyment with them. In the way of modulation, measure, and propriety, too, disagreeable errors are made by the parrot-poet, since these, above all others, are only to be avoided by simplicity and unaffectedness. Nevertheless, it would be obviously unfair to say that Mr. Wilde's volume could have been written by any one who should set himself to reproduce the impression of certain English poets. He has, in the first place, a musical gift of manifest excellence. His metrical tact, so far as it depends upon his ear, is unusual, in spite of being very frequently both slip-shod and unscrupulous; one remarks with some surprise the absence of madrigals from his book, and concludes that *Postlethwaite* should be depicted from time to time strumming a guitar. In the next place, for the distinguishing verbal and metrical marks of the more sensuous school of his masters proper he has manifestly an aptness, born, doubtless, of the sympathetic inclination which his admiration of them argues. And, thirdly, he has unquestionably much perceptiveness and appreciation. This, however, is a different thing from having a natural voice of one's own, however plaintive and insignificant, from having anything to communicate, or, finally, from having any emotion to express. In all these respects Mr. Wilde's muse seems to us essentially commonplace—precisely of that perfunctory order and texture demanded for affecting affectation, which is what *Postlethwaite* and his kind are really represented as doing. (pp. 100-01)

> *"'Poems',"* in The Nation *(copyright 1881 The Nation* magazine, The Nation Associates, Inc.), Vol. *XXXIII, No. 840, August 4, 1881, pp. 100-01.*

ST. JAMES'S GAZETTE (essay date 1890)

Not being curious in ordure, and not wishing to offend the nostrils of decent persons, we do not propose to analyse *The Picture of Dorian Gray:* that would be to advertise the developments of an esoteric prurience. (p. 68)

The puzzle is that a young man of decent parts, who enjoyed (when he was at Oxford) the opportunity of associating with gentlemen, should put his name (such as it is) to so stupid and vulgar a piece of work. Let nobody read it in the hope of finding witty paradox or racy wickedness. The writer airs his cheap research among the garbage of the French *Décadents* like any drivelling pedant, and he bores you unmercifully with his prosy rigmaroles about the beauty of the Body and the corruption of the Soul. The grammar is better than Ouida's; the erudition equal; but in every other respect we prefer the talented lady who broke off with 'pious aposiopesis' when she touched upon 'the horrors which are described in the pages of Suetonius and Livy'—not to mention the yet worse infamies believed by many scholars to be accurately portrayed in the lost works of Plutarch, Venus, and Nicodemus, especially Nicodemus.

Let us take one peep at the young men in Mr. Oscar Wilde's story. Puppy No. I is the painter of the picture of Dorian Gray; Puppy No. 2 is the critic (a courtesy lord, skilled in all the knowledge of the Egyptians and aweary of all the sins and pleasures of London); Puppy No. 3 is the original, cultivated by Puppy No. I with a 'romantic friendship.' The Puppies fall a-talking: Puppy No. I about his Art, Puppy No. 2 about his sins and pleasures and the pleasures of sin, and Puppy No. 3 about himself—always about himself, and generally about his face, which is 'brainless and beautiful.' The Puppies appear to fill up the intervals of talk by plucking daisies and playing with them, and sometimes drinking 'something with strawberry in it. The youngest Puppy is told that he is charming; but he mustn't sit in the sun for fear of spoiling his complexion. When he is rebuked for being a naughty, wilful boy, he makes a pretty *moue* —this *man* of twenty! (p. 69)

Here's a situation for you! Théophile Gautier could have made it romantic, entrancing, beautiful. Mr. Stevenson could have made it convincing, humorous, pathetic. Mr. Anstey could have made it screamingly funny. It has been reserved for Mr. Oscar Wilde to make it dull and nasty. The promising youth plunges into every kind of mean depravity, and ends in being 'cut' by fast women and vicious men. He finishes with murder: the New Voluptuousness always leads up to blood-shedding—that is part of the cant. The gore and gashes wherein Mr. Rider Haggard takes a chaste delight are the natural diet for a cultivated palate which is tired of mere licentiousness. And every

wickedness or filthiness committed by Dorian Gray is faithfully registered upon his face in the picture; but his living features are undisturbed and unmarred by his inward vileness. This is the story which Mr. Oscar Wilde has tried to tell; a very lame story it is, and very lamely it is told.

Why has he told it? There are two explanations; and, so far as we can see, not more than two. Not to give pleasure to his readers: the thing is too clumsy, too tedious, and—alas! that we should say it—too stupid. Perhaps it was to shock his readers, in order that they might cry Fie! upon him and talk about him. . . . Are we then to suppose that Mr. Oscar Wilde has yielded to the craving for a notoriety which he once earned by talking fiddle-faddle about other men's art, and sees his only chance of recalling it by making himself obvious at the cost of being obnoxious, and by attracting the notice which the olfactory sense cannot refuse to the presence of certain self-asserting organisms? That is an uncharitable hypothesis, and we would gladly abandon it. It may be suggested (but is it more charitable?) that he derives pleasure from treating a subject merely because it is disgusting. The phenomenon is not unknown in recent literature; and it takes two forms, in appearance widely separate—in fact, two branches from the same root, a root which draws its life from malodorous putrefaction. One development is found in the Puritan prurience which produced Tolstoy's *Kreutzer Sonata* and Mr. [William Thomas] Stead's famous outbursts. That is odious enough and mischievous enough, and it is rightly execrated, because it is tainted with an hypocrisy not the less culpable because charitable persons may believe it to be unconscious. But is it more odious or more mischievous than the 'frank Paganism' (that is the word, is it not?) which delights in dirtiness and confesses its delight? Still they are both chips from the same block—*The Maiden Tribute of Modern Babylon* and *The Picture of Dorian Gray*—and both of them ought to be chucked into the fire. Not so much because they are dangerous and corrupt (they are corrupt but not dangerous) as because they are incurably silly, written by simpleton *poseurs* (whether they call themselves Puritan or Pagan) who know nothing about the life which they affect to have explored, and because they are mere catchpenny revelations of the non-existent, which, if they reveal anything at all, are revelations only of the singularly unpleasant minds from which they emerge. (pp. 70-1)

> *"'The Picture of Dorian Gray',"* in St. James's Gazette, *June 20, 1890 (and reprinted in* Oscar Wilde: The Critical Heritage, *edited by Karl Beckson, Barnes & Noble, Inc., 1970, pp. 67-71).*

OSCAR WILDE (essay date 1890)

[*The following excerpt is taken from the first of a series of letters Wilde wrote to the editor of the* St. James Gazette *in reaction to the magazine's review of* Dorian Gray.]

I feel bound to say that your article [on *The Picture of Dorian Gray*] contains the most unjustifiable attack that has been made upon any man of letters for many years. The writer of it, who is quite incapable of concealing his personal malice, and so in some measure destroys the effect he wishes to produce, seems not to have the slightest idea of the temper in which a work of art should be approached. To say that such a book as mine should be "chucked into the fire" is silly. That is what one does with newspapers.

Of the value of pseudo-ethical criticism in dealing with artistic work I have spoken already. But as your writer has ventured into the perilous grounds of literary criticism I ask you to allow me, in fairness not merely to myself but to all men to whom literature is a fine art, to say a few words about his critical method.

He begins by assailing me with much ridiculous virulence because the chief personages in my story are "puppies." They *are* puppies. Does he think that literature went to the dogs when Thackeray wrote about puppydom? I think that puppies are extremely interesting from an artistic as well as from a psychological point of view. They seem to me to be certainly far more interesting than prigs; and I am of opinion that Lord Henry Wotton is an excellent corrective of the tedious ideal shadowed forth in the semi-theological novels of our age.

He then makes vague and fearful insinuations about my grammar and my erudition. Now, as regards grammar, I hold that, in prose at any rate, correctness should always be subordinate to artistic effect and musical cadence; and any peculiarities of syntax that may occur in *Dorian Gray* are deliberately intended, and are introduced to show the value of the artistic theory in question. Your writer gives no instance of any such peculiarity. This I regret, because I do not think that any such instances occur.

As regards erudition, it is always difficult, even for the most modest of us, to remember that other people do not know quite as much as one does oneself. I myself frankly admit I cannot imagine how a casual reference to Suetonius and Petronius Arbiter can be construed into evidence of a desire to impress an unoffending and ill-educated public by an assumption of superior knowledge. I should fancy that the most ordinary of scholars is perfectly well acquainted with the *Lives of the Caesars* and with the *Satyricon*. The *Lives of the Caesars,* at any rate, forms part of the curriculum at Oxford for those who take the Honour School of *Literae Humaniores;* and as for the *Satyricon,* it is popular even among passmen, though I suppose they are obliged to read it in translations.

The writer of the article then suggests that I, in common with that great and noble artist Count Tolstoi, take pleasure in a subject because it is dangerous. About such a suggestion there is this to be said. Romantic art deals with the exception and with the individual. Good people, belonging as they do to the normal, and so, commonplace, type, are artistically uninteresting. Bad people are, from the point of view of art, fascinating studies. They represent colour, variety and strangeness. Good people exasperate one's reason; bad people stir one's imagination. Your critic, if I must give him so honourable a title, states that the people in my story have no counterpart in life; that they are, to use his vigorous if somewhat vulgar phrase, "mere catchpenny revelations of the non-existent." Quite so. If they existed they would not be worth writing about. The function of the artist is to invent, not to chronicle. There are no such people. If there were I would not write about them. Life by its realism is always spoiling the subject-matter of art. The supreme pleasure in literature is to realise the non-existent.

And finally, let me say this. You have reproduced, in a journalistic form, the comedy of *Much Ado about Nothing,* and have, of course, spoilt it in your reproduction. The poor public, hearing, from an authority so high as your own, that this is a wicked book that should be coerced and suppressed by a Tory Government, with no doubt, rush to it and read it. But, alas! they will find that it is a story with a moral. And the moral is this. All excess, as well as all renunciation, brings its own punishment. The painter, Basil Hallward, worshipping phys-

ical beauty far too much, as most painters do, dies by the hand of one in whose soul he has created a monstrous and absurd vanity. Dorian Gray, having led a life of mere sensation and pleasure, tries to kill conscience, and at that moment kills himself. Lord Henry Wotton seeks to be merely the spectator of life. He finds that those who reject the battle are more deeply wounded than those who take part in it. Yes; there is a terrible moral in *Dorian Gray*—a moral which the prurient will not be able to find in it, but which will be revealed to all whose minds are healthy. Is this an artistic error? I fear it is. It is the only error in the book. (pp. 238-41)

> *Oscar Wilde, in his letter to the Editor of* St. James's Gazette *on June 26, 1890, in* The Artist As Critic: Critical Writings of Oscar Wilde *by Oscar Wilde, edited by Richard Ellmann, Random House, 1969, pp. 238-41.*

BERNARD SHAW　(essay date 1895)

[Mr Oscar Wilde's *An Ideal Husband*] is a dangerous subject, because he has the property of making his critics dull. They laugh angrily at his epigrams, like a child who is coaxed into being amused in the very act of setting up a yell of rage and agony. They protest that the trick is obvious, and that such epigrams can be turned out by the score by any one lightminded enough to condescend to such frivolity. As far as I can ascertain, I am the only person in London who cannot sit down and write an Oscar Wilde play at will. The fact that his plays, though apparently lucrative, remain unique under these circumstances, says much for the self-denial of our scribes. In a certain sense Mr Wilde is to me our only thorough playwright. He plays with everything: with wit, with philosophy, with drama, with actors and audience, with the whole theatre. Such a feat scandalizes the Englishman, who can no more play with wit and philosophy than he can with a football or a cricket bat. He works at both, and has the consolation, if he cannot make people laugh, of being the best cricketer and footballer in the world. Now it is the mark of the artist that he will not work. Just as people with social ambitions will practise the meanest economies in order to live expensively; so the artist will starve his way through incredible toil and discouragement sooner than go and earn a week's honest wages. Mr Wilde, an arch-artist, is so colossally lazy that he trifles even with the work by which an artist escapes work. He distils very quintessence, and gets as product plays which are so unapproachably playful that they are the delight of every playgoer with twopenn'orth of brains. The English critic, always protesting that the drama should not be didactic, and yet always complaining if the dramatist does not find sermons in stones and good in everything, will be conscious of a subtle and pervading levity in *An Ideal Husband.* All the literary dignity of the play, all the imperturbable good sense and good manners with which Mr Wilde makes his wit pleasant to his comparatively stupid audience, cannot quite overcome the fact that Ireland is of all countries the most foreign to England, and that to the Irishman (and Mr Wilde is almost as acutely Irish an Irishman as the Iron Duke of Wellington) there is nothing in the world quite so exquisitely comic as an Englishman's seriousness. It becomes tragic, perhaps, when the Englishman acts on it; but that occurs too seldom to be taken into account, a fact which intensifies the humour of the situation, the total result being the Englishman utterly unconscious of his real self, Mr Wilde keenly observant of it and playing on the self-unconsciousness with irresistible humour, and finally, of course, the Englishman annoyed with himself for being amused at his own expense, and for being unable to convict Mr Wilde of what seems an obvious misunderstanding of human nature. He is shocked, too, at the danger to the foundations of society when seriousness is publicly laughed at. And to complete the oddity of the situation, Mr Wilde, touching what he himself reverences, is absolutely the most sentimental dramatist of the day.

It is useless to describe a play which has no thesis: which is, in the purest integrity, a play and nothing less. The six worst epigrams are mere alms handed with a kind smile to the average suburban playgoer; the three best remain secrets between Mr Wilde and a few choice spirits. The modern note is struck in Sir Robert Chiltern's assertion of the individuality and courage of his wrongdoing as against the mechanical idealism of his stupidly good wife, and in his bitter criticism of a love that is only the reward of merit. It is from the philosophy on which this scene is based that the most pregnant epigrams in the play have been condensed. Indeed, this is the only philosophy that ever has produced epigrams. In contriving the stage expedients by which the action of the piece is kept going, Mr Wilde has been once or twice a little too careless of stage illusion: for example, why on earth should Mrs Cheveley, hiding in Lord Goring's room, knock down a chair? That is my sole criticism. . . . (pp. 176-78)

> *Bernard Shaw, "'An Ideal Husband'" (reprinted by permission of The Society of Authors on behalf of the Bernard Shaw Estate), in* The Saturday Review, *London, Vol. 79, No. 2046, January 12, 1895 (and reprinted in* Oscar Wilde: The Critical Heritage, *edited by Karl Beckson, Barnes & Noble, 1970, pp. 176-78).*

W. B. YEATS (essay date 1895)

Mr. Pater once said that Mr. Oscar Wilde wrote like an excellent talker, and the criticism goes to the root. All of **'The Woman of No Importance,'** which might have been spoken by its author, the famous paradoxes, the rapid sketches of men and women of society, the mockery of most things under heaven, are delightful; while, on the other hand, the things which are too deliberate in their development, or too vehement and elaborate for a talker's inspiration, such as the plot, and the more tragic and emotional characters, do not rise above the general level of the stage. The witty or grotesque persons who flit about the hero and heroine, Lord Illingworth, Mrs. Allonby, Canon Daubeney, Lady Stutfield, and Mr. Kelvil, all, in fact, who can be characterised by a sentence or a paragraph, are real men and women; and the most immoral among them have enough of the morality of self-control and self-possession to be pleasant and inspiriting memories. There is something of heroism in being always master enough of oneself to be witty; and therefore the public of to-day feels with Lord Illingworth and Mrs. Allonby much as the public of yesterday felt, in a certain sense, with that traditional villain of melodrama who never laid aside his cigarette and his sardonic smile. The traditional villain had self-control. Lord Illingworth and Mrs. Allonby have self-control and intellect; and to have these things is to have wisdom, whether you obey it or not. "The soul is born old, but grows young. That is the comedy of life. And the body is born young and grows old. That is life's tragedy." Women "worship successes," and "are the laurels to hide their baldness." "Children begin by loving their parents. After a time they judge them. Rarely if ever do they forgive them." And many another epigram, too well known to quote, rings out like the voice of Lear's fool over a mad age. And yet one

puts the book down with disappointment. Despite its qualities, it is not a work of art, it has no central fire, it is not dramatic in any ancient sense of the word. The reason is that the tragic and emotional people, the people who are important to the story, Mrs. Arbuthnot, Gerald Arbuthnot, and Hester Worsley, are conventions of the stage. They win our hearts with no visible virtue, and though intended to be charming and good and natural, are really either heady and undistinguished, or morbid with what Mr. Stevenson has called "the impure passion of remorse." The truth is, that whenever Mr. Wilde gets beyond those inspirations of an excellent talker which served him so well in **'The Decay of Lying'** and in the best parts of **'Dorian Gray,'** he falls back upon the popular conventions, the spectres and shadows of the stage.

> *W. B. Yeats, "An Excellent Talker" (reprinted by permission of Michael and Anne Yeats), in* The Bookman, *London, Vol. VII, No. 42, March, 1895, p. 182.*

W. E. HENLEY (essay date 1898)

This elaborate appeal from the deeps [*The Ballad of Reading Gaol*] to a vain yet reasonable world is the oddest jumble: of truth and falsehood, of sincerity and affectation, of excellence and rubbish, of stuff that moves and stuff that bores, and worse. A descant on the emotions of C. 3.3 [Wilde's number in prison] and others on the occasion of a death by the rope in the gaol wherein they were immured, it is a piece of realism, yet it reeks with traditional phrases and effects. It states the fact with gloom, that everybody is engaged in killing the thing he loves; . . . yet it seems to approve, and it pleads passionately against the penalising of such excesses in emotion. In style it reminds you now of Mr. Kipling, now of 'Eugene Aram', now of 'The Ancient Mariner', now of the Border ballads, now of passionate Brompton and aesthetic Chelsea. In matter, it is a patchwork of what is and what is not. Here it is instinct and vigorous with veracity; there it is flushed and stertorous with sentimentalism. It is carefully written and elaborately designed; yet is it full fifty stanzas too long, and it is laced with such futilities as 'whisper *low*' and '*empty* space'. It is a thing of modern life, and at least a part of it is *vécue* [true to life]; yet you dance to 'flutes' and you dance to 'lutes' (Ha! Old Truepenny'), and in one stanza you make as free with Christ as Mr. Robert Buchanan ever did, and in another:—

> The warders stripped him of his clothes
>   And gave him to the flies;
> They marked the swollen, purple throat
>   And the stark and staring eyes,
> And with laughter loud they heaped the shroud
>   In which the convict lies.

Is the detail convincing? Who reads that can think it is? Is that 'swollen, purple throat' observed? It does not seem so—by the sequel. And what is a 'stark' eye? And how does the writer know the warders trampled down the poor devil's grave 'with laughter loud'? He wasn't at the trampling, evidently; for he and his fellows were carefully secluded till the horrid job was done:—

> But we knew the work they had been at
>   By the quicklime on their boots.

Without pretending to *expertise* in such matters, one may hazard the presumption that quicklime, being fully as destructive of leather as it is of flesh and bone, the warders, their work once done, would have carefully wiped their boots; so that, in the absence of complete information, this detail is not less *suspect* than certain others.

That, in fact, is the chief defect of the Poem: you do not always know when the Poet is 'putting it on'. . . . But nobody is all at once a realist; nobody all at once can tell the truth; and, in this respect, C. 3.3 is no better gifted than the most of men. His whole description of the night before the Guardsman's execution is a proof of it. It is sentimental slush—writing for the writing's sake; stuff done on the assumption that 'He who lives more lives than one, more deaths than one must die', is not peculiar to one exceptional convict, but is common to the herd of lags in which he is merged. None who reads it can believe in any word of it. It is a blunder in taste, in sentiment, in art; for it is a misstatement of fact. If C. 3.3 had been no Minor Poet, but an Artist—!

Yet, having dissented thus, one is pleased to note that sincerity, veracity, vision even, have their part in this mixty-maxty of differences. Suppress the Poet's first stanza, for example, with its impossible welter of blood and wine and the Widow's pink, and what could be better, simpler, more natural and effective than the two that follow at its heel? (pp. 214-16)

But the trail of the Minor Poet is over it all. And when the Minor Poet is at rest, then wakes the Pamphleteer. What C. 3.3 has to say about our prison system is—apart from his references to Christ, and red and white roses, and 'Tannhäuser', and quicklime, and the like—worth heeding. Or would be, *if it were true*. But is it? 'Tis not for us to say. But if it be, let C. 3.3 at once proceed to sink the Minor in the Pamphleteer, and make his name honoured among men. (p. 217)

W. E. Henley, "'De Profundis'," in Outlook, *March 5, 1898 (and reprinted under a different title in* Oscar Wilde: The Critical Heritage, *edited by Karl Beckson, Barnes & Noble, 1970, pp. 214-17).*

A[LFRED] D[OUGLAS]   (essay date 1908)

[The publication] of the complete works of Oscar Wilde marks, in a striking way, the complete literary rehabilitation which this author has achieved. When one considers that at the time of Oscar Wilde's downfall the whole of his copyrights could have been purchased for about £100, one cannot help entertaining grave suspicions as to the value of criticism in England. It must be remembered that the contempt with which Mr. Wilde's work was greeted by the general mass of contemporary criticism was not confined to the period after his condemnation. A reference to the files of the newspapers containing the criticisms of his plays as they came out would reveal the fact that almost without any exeption they were received with mockery, ridicule, and rudeness.

It is intensely amusing to read the comments in the daily papers at the present juncture on the same subject. Oscar Wilde is referred to, as a matter of course, as a great genius and a great wit, and takes his place, in the eyes of those who write these articles, if not with Shakespeare, at any rate with the other highest exponents of English dramatic art. This, of course, is as it should be, but we wonder what the gentlemen who write these glowing accounts of Mr. Wilde's genius were doing at the time when these works of genius were being poured out, and why it should have been necessary for him in order to obtain recognition to undergo the processes of disgrace and death. With the exception of the **"Ballad of Reading Gaol"**

and **"De Profundis"** every work of Oscar Wilde's was written before his downfall. If these works are brilliant works of genius now, they were so before, and the failure of contemporary criticism to appreciate this fact is a lasting slur upon the intelligence of the country.

If any one wishes to see a fair sample of the sort of criticism that used to be meted out to Oscar Wilde, let him turn to the dramatic criticism in *Truth* which appeared on the production of **Lady Windermere's Fan.** The article was, we believe, written by the late unlamented Clement Scott, and at this time of day, of course, Clement Scott's dramatic criticism is not taken seriously; but at the time it was taken quite seriously, and it is astounding to think that such a criticism should have passed absolutely unresented by anybody of importance, with the obvious exception of Oscar Wilde himself. Nowadays if a critic were to write such an article about a playwright of anything approaching the status of Oscar Wilde he would be refused admission to every theatre in London. . . .

The subject of the first great attack made by Henley on Oscar Wilde was **"The Picture of Dorian Gray."** Henley affected to think this was an immoral work, and denounced it as such. Now, anybody who having read **"Dorian Gray"** can honestly maintain that it is not one of the greatest moral books ever written, is an ass. It is, briefly, the story of a man who destroys his own conscience. The visible symbol of that conscience takes the form of a picture, the presentment of perfect youth and perfect beauty, which bears on its changing surface the burden of the sins of its prototype. It is one of the greatest and most terrible moral lessons that an unworthy world has had the privilege of receiving at the hands of a great writer.

It is characteristic of what we may call the "Henleyean School" of criticism to confuse the life of a man with his art. It would be idle to deny that Oscar Wilde was an immoral man (as idle as it would be to contend that Henley was a moral one); but it is a remarkable thing that while Oscar Wilde's life was immoral his art was always moral. At the time when the attack by Henley was made there was a confused idea going about London that Oscar Wilde was a wicked man, and this was quite enough for Henley and the group of second-rate intelligences which clustered round him to jump to the conclusion that anything he wrote must also necessarily be wicked. . . .

Wilde, putting aside his moral delinquencies, which have as much and as little to do with his works as the colour of his hair, was a great artist, a man who passionately loved his art. He as so great an artist that, in spite of himself, he was always on the side of the angels. We believe that the greatest art is always on the side of the angels, to doubt it would be to doubt the existence of God, and all the Henleys and all the Bernard Shaws that the world could produce would not make us change our opinion. It was all very well for Wilde to play with life, as he did exquisitely, and to preach the philosophy of pleasure, and plucking the passing hour; but the moment he sat down to write he became different. He saw things as they really were; he knew the falsity and the deadliness of his own creed; he knew that "the end of these things is Death;" and he wrote in his own inimitable way the words of Wisdom and Life. . . . Wilde has his school of young men in those who copy what was least admirable in him, but from a literary point of view he has no school. He stands alone, a phenomenon in literature. From the purely literary point of view he was unquestionably the greatest figure of the nineteenth century. We unhesitatingly say that his influence on the literature of Europe has been greater than that of any man since Byron died, and, unlike Byron's, it has been all for good. The evil that he did, inasmuch as he did a tithe of the things imputed to him, was interred with his bones, the good (how much the greater part of this great man!) lives after him and will live for ever.

A[lfred] D[ouglas], "The Genius of Oscar Wilde," in The Academy, No. 1888, July 11, 1908, p. 35.

ARTHUR RANSOME   (essay date 1912)

The most obvious quality of [the 1881 *Poems*], and that which is most easily and most often emphasized, is its richness in imitations. But there is more in it than that. It is full of variations on other men's music, but they are variations to which the personality of the virtuoso has given a certain uniformity. Wilde played the sedulous ape with sufficient self-consciousness and sufficient failure to show that he might himself be somebody. His emulative practice of his art asks for a closer consideration than that usually given to it. Let me borrow an admirable phrase from M. Remy de Gourmont, and say that a "dissociation of ideas" is necessary in thinking of imitation. To describe a young poet's work as derivative is not the same thing as to condemn it. All work is derivative more or less, and to pour indiscriminate contempt on Wilde's imitations because they are imitations, is to betray a lamentable ignorance of the history of poetry. There is no need too seriously to defend this early work. Wilde's reputation can stand without or even in spite of it. (p. 40)

Wilde's reputation as a poet does not rest on this first book, but on half a dozen poems that include 'The Harlot's House,' 'A Symphony in Yellow,' 'The Sphinx' and 'The Ballad of Reading Gaol,' and alone are worthy of a place beside his work in prose. (p. 51)

[*The Sphinx*] is work more personal to Wilde than anything in *Poems*. (p. 74)

The kinetic base, the obvious framework, of *The Sphinx* is an apostrophe addressed by a student to a Sphinx that lies in his room, perhaps a dream, perhaps a paperweight, an apostrophe that consists in the enumeration of her possible lovers, and the final selection of one of them as her supposed choice. It is a series rather than a whole, though an effect of form and cumulative weight is given to it by a carefully preserved monotony. In a firm, lava-like verse, the Sphinx's paramours are stiffened to a bas-relief. The water-horse, the griffon, the hawk-faced god, the mighty limbs of Ammon, are formed into a frieze of reverie; they do not collaborate in a picture, but are left behind as the dream goes on. It goes on, perhaps, just a little too long. So do some of the finest rituals; and *The Sphinx* is among the rare incantations in our language. It is a piece of black magic. (p. 75)

[Among the short stories, three] tales need detain no student of Wilde. 'The Canterville Ghost' is just so boisterous as to miss its balance, but, because it is about Americans, is very popular in America. 'The Sphinx without a Secret' betrays its secret in its title. 'The Model Millionaire' is an empty little thing no better than the popular tales it tries to imitate. 'Lord Arthur Savile's Crime,' however, is not only remarkable as an indication of what Wilde was to do both as a dramatist and as a storyteller, but is itself a delightful piece of buffoonery. Wilde is so serious. . . . The plot is no less moral than simple. Lord Arthur Savile learns from the palmist that at some period of his life it is decreed that he shall commit a murder. Unwilling to marry while a potential criminal, he sets about committing

the murder at once, to get it over, and be able to marry with the easy conscience of one who knows that his duty has been satisfactorily performed. . . . Like much of Wilde's work, this story is very clever talk, an elaborated anecdote, told with flickering irony, a cigarette now and again lifted to the lips. But, already, a dramatist is learning to use this irony in dialogue, and a decorative artist is restraining his buoyant cleverness, to use it for more subtle purposes. There is a delicate description of dawn in Piccadilly, with the waggons on their way to Covent Garden, white-smocked carters, and a boy with primroses in a battered hat, riding a big grey horse—a promise of the fairy stories. (pp. 84-6)

In reading them, I cannot help feeling that Wilde wrote one of them as an experiment, to show, I suppose, that he could have been Hans Andersen if he had liked, and his wife importuned him to make a book of things so charming, so good, and so true. He made the book, and there is one beautiful thing in it, 'The Happy Prince,' which was, I suspect, the first he wrote. The rest, except, perhaps, 'The Selfish Giant,' a delightful essay in Christian legend, are tales whose morals are a little too obvious even for grown-up people. . . . There is a moral in 'The Happy Prince,' but there is this difference between that story and the others, that it is quite clear that Wilde wanted to write it. It is Andersen, treated exactly as Wilde treated Milton in the volume of 1881, only with more assurance, and a greater certainty about his own contribution. We recognise Wilde by the decorative effects that are scattered throughout the book. He preferred a lyrical pattern to a prosaic perspective, and, even more than his wit, his love of decoration is the distinguishing quality of his work. (pp. 87-8)

Wilde wrote, with the pen of Flaubert, stories that might have been imagined by Andersen, and sometimes one and sometimes the other touches his hand. It is not impossible that Baudelaire was also present. But all this does not much concern us, except that by subtraction we may come to what we seek, which is the personal, elusive, but unmistakable quality contributed by Wilde himself. (pp. 90-1)

Wilde, always perfectly self-conscious, was not unaware of this difference between his own writing and that of most of his contemporaries. When *Dorian Gray* was attacked for immorality, Wilde wrote, in a letter to a paper: "My story is an essay on decorative art. It reacts against the brutality of plain realism." *The Picture of Dorian Gray* was written for publication in a magazine. Seven chapters were added to it to make it long enough for publication as a novel. . . . The preface was written to answer assailants of the morality of the story in its first form, and included only when it was printed as a book. These circumstances partly explain the lack of proportion, and of cohesion, that mars, though it does not spoil, the first French novel to be written in the English language. England has a traditional novel-form with which even the greatest students of human comedy and tragedy square their work. In France there is no such tradition, with the result that the novel is a plastic form, moulded in the most various ways by the most various minds. (pp. 94-5)

There are a few strange books that share the magic of some names, like Cornelius Agrippa, Raymond Lully, and Paracelsus, names that possibly mean more to us before than after we have investigated the works and personalities that lie behind them. These books are mysterious and kept, like mysteries, for peculiar moods. They are not books for every day, nor even for every night. We keep them for rare moments, as we keep in a lacquer cabinet some crystal-shrined thread of subtle perfume, or some curious gem, to be a solace in a mood that does not often recur, or, perhaps, to be an instrument in its evocation. *Dorian Gray,* for all its faults, is such a book. It is unbalanced; and that is a fault. It is a mosaic hurriedly made by a man who reached out in all directions and took and used in his work whatever scrap of jasper, or porphyry or broken flint was put into his hand; and that is not a virtue. But in it there is an individual essence, a private perfume, a colour whose secret has been lost. There are moods whose consciousness that essence, perfume, colour, is needed to intensity. (p. 98)

[In *The Portrait of Mr. W. H.*] Wilde read something of himself into Shakespeare's sonnets, and, in reading, became fascinated by a theory that he was unable to prove. Where another man would, perhaps, have written a short, serious essay, and whistled his theory down the wind that carries the dead leaves of Shakespeare's commentators, Wilde tosses it as a belief between three brains, and allows it to unfold itself as the background to a story. The three brains are the narrator, Cyril Graham, and Erskine. Graham discovers the Mr. W. H. of the Sonnets in a boy-actor called Will Hughes, and by diligent examination of internal evidence, almost persuades Erskine to believe him. (p. 101)

It would be impossible to build an airier castle in Spain than this of the imaginary William Hughes; impossible, too, to build one so delightfully designed. The prose and the reasoning seem things of ivory, Indian-carved, through which the rarest wind of criticism may freely blow and carry delicate scents away without disturbing the yet more delicate fabric. Wilde assumes that Shakespeare addressed the sonnets to William Hughes, and, that assumption granted (though there is no William Hughes to be found), colours his theory with an abundance of persuasive touches, to strengthen what is, at first, only a courtesy belief. Though all his argument is special pleading, Wilde contrives to make you feel that counsel knows, though he cannot prove, that his client is in the right. The evidence is only for the jury. You are inclined to interrupt him with the exclamation that you are already convinced. But it is a pleasure to listen to him, so you let him go on. After all, "brute reason is quite unbearable. There is something unfair about its use. It is like hitting below the intellect." Wilde's *Portrait of Mr. W. H.* is more than a refutable theory, a charming piece of speculation. It is an illustration of the critic as artist, a foretaste of *Intentions*. It is better than 'The Truth of Masks,' as good as 'The Decay of Lying.' (pp. 102-03)

Unfamiliar truth was, at first, the most noticeable characteristic of Wilde's *Intentions,* but, though paradox may fade to commonplace, "age cannot wither nor custom stale" the fresh and debonair personality that keeps the book alive, tossing thoughts like roses, and playing with them in happiness of heart. (p. 105)

Wilde loved speech for its own sake, and nothing could be more characteristic of his gift than his choice [in *Intentions*] of that old and inexhaustible form that Plato, Lucian, Erasmus and Landor, to name only a few, have turned to such different purposes. Dialogue is at once personal and impersonal. "By its means he (the thinker) can both reveal and conceal himself, and give form to every fancy, and reality to every mood." . . . Nothing could better describe Wilde's own essays in dialogue.

The first of these essays is 'The Decay of Lying,' in which a young gentleman called Vivian reads aloud an article on that subject to a slightly older and rather incredulous young gentleman called Cyril. . . . [He] envisages the history of art as a long warfare between the simian instinct of imitation and the God-like instinct of self-expression. (pp. 106-07)

It is important to remember that throughout this dialogue, Wilde is speaking of pure art, a thing which possibly does not exist, and, recognising it as an ideal towards which all artists should aspire, is engaged in pointing out the more obvious means of falling short of it. He achieves a triumph, of a kind in which he delighted, by making people read of such a subject. Not wishing to be laughed at by the British intellect, and wishing to be listened to, he laughs at it instead, and, near the end of the dialogue, is so daring as to present it with a picture of what is occurring, confident that the individual will disclaim the general, and smile without annoyance at the caricature. (pp. 111-12)

'Pen, Pencil, and Poison,' the essay on [the murderer, forger, and author Thomas Griffiths] Wainewright, not in dialogue, has some of the hard angular outlines of the set article on book or public character. It fills these outlines, however, with picturesque detail and half-ironic speculation. It is impossible not to notice the resemblance between the subject of this essay and its author. It is difficult not to suspect that Wilde, in setting in clear perspective Wainewright's poisoning and writing, is estimating the possible power of crime to intensify a personality, was analysing himself, and expressing through a psychological account of another man the results of that analysis. Perhaps, in that essay we have less analysis than hypothesis. (pp. 112-13)

But the most striking and beautiful thing in *Intentions* is that dialogue between the two young men [Ernest and Gilbert in 'The Critic as Artist'] in a library whose windows look over the kaleidoscopic swirl of Piccadilly to the trees and lawns of the Green Park. (p. 114)

[Their] talk is far too good really to have been heard. They set their excellence as a barrier between themselves and life. Not for a moment will they forget that they are the creatures of art: not for a moment will they leave that calm air for the dust and turmoil of human argument. Wilde was never so sure of his art as in this dialogue, where Ernest, that ethereal Sancho Panza, and Gilbert, that rather languid Don Quixote, tilt for their hearer's joy. They share the power of visualization that made Wilde's own talk like a continuous fairy tale. They turn their ideas into a coloured pageantry, and all the gods of Greece and characters of art are ready to grace by their visible presence the exposition, whether of the ideas that are to be confuted or of those that are to take their place. "In the best days of art," says Ernest, "there were no art critics." . . . (pp. 116-17)

"But no," says Gilbert, "the Greeks were a nation of art-critics." . . . And so the talk goes on. There is but one defect in this panoramic method of presenting ideas. Each time that Wilde empties, or seems to spill before us, his wonderful cornucopia of coloured imagery, he seems to build a wave that towers like the blue and silver billow of Hokusai's print. Now, surely, it will break, we say, and are tempted to echo Cyril in 'The Decay of Lying,' when, at the close of one of these miraculous paragraphs, he remarks, "I like that. I can see it. Is that the end?" Too many of Wilde's paragraphs are perorations. (pp. 117-18)

The fourth essay in the book ['The Truth of Masks'] is not on the high level of the others. It is more practical and less beautiful. . . . It is interesting, but less as a thing in itself than as an indication of the character of Wilde's knowledge of the theatre. (p. 129)

The character of Wilde's study of the theatre was shown in 'The Truth of Masks,' and in the dramatic criticism that he wrote in the years immediately following his marriage. It was a study of methods and concerned no less with stage-management than with the drama. Nearly thirty years ago he made a plea for beautiful scenery, and asked for that harmony between costumier and scene-painter that has been achieved in our day by Charles Ricketts and Cayley Robinson under the management of Mr. Herbert Trench. He remarked that painted doors were superior to real ones, and pointed out that properties which need light from more than one side destroy the illumination suggested by the scene-painter's shadings. From the first his dramatic criticism was written in the wings, not from the point of view of an audience careless of means, observant only of effects. *Vera* may have been dull, and *The Duchess of Padua* unplayable, but actors, at least, shall have no fault to find in the technique of *Lady Windermere's Fan*. That play seems to me to be no more than a conscious experiment in the use of the knowledge that Wilde had sedulously worked to obtain.

There was a continuity in Wilde's interest in the theatre wholly lacking in his passing fancies for narrative or essay-writing. . . . His most perfectly successful works, those which most exactly accomplish what they attempt, without sacrificing any part of themselves, are, perhaps, *The Importance of Being Earnest* and *Salomé*. Both these are plays. But neither of them seems to me so characteristic, so inclusive of Wilde as *Intentions, De Profundis, The Portrait of Mr. W. H.,* or even *The Picture of Dorian Gray*. His plays are wilfully limited, subordinated to an aim outside themselves, and, except in the two I have just mentioned, these limitations are not such as to justify themselves by giving freedom to the artist. Some limitations set an artist free for an achievement otherwise impossible. But the limitations of which I complain only made Wilde a little contemptuous of his work. They did not save his talent from preoccupations, but compelled it to a labour in whose success alone he could take an interest.

It is impossible not to feel that Wilde was impatient of the methods and the meanings of his first three successful plays, like a juggler, conscious of being able to toss up six balls, who is admired for tossing three. These good women, these unselfish, pseudonymous mothers, these men of wit and fashion discomfited to make a British holiday; their temptations, their sacrifices, their defeats, are not taken from any drama played in Wilde's own mind. He saw them and their adventures quite impersonally; and no good art is impersonal. Salome kissing the pale lips of Iokanaan may once have moved him when he saw her behind the ghostly footlights of that secret theatre in which each man is his own dramatist, his own stage-manager, and his own audience. But Lady Windermere did not return to her husband for Wilde's sake, and he did not feel that Sir Robert Chiltern's future mattered either way. He cared only that an audience he despised should be relieved at her return, and that to them the career of a politician should seem to be important. Not until the production of *The Importance of Being Earnest* did he share the pleasure of the pit. I know a travelling showman who makes "enjoy" an active verb, and speaks of "enjoying the poor folk" when, for coppers, he lets them ride on merry-go-rounds, and agitate themselves in swing-boats, which offer him no manner of amusement. In just this way Wilde "enjoyed" the London audiences with his early plays. He did not enjoy them himself. (pp. 132-36)

He consoled himself for his plots by taking extraordinary liberties with them, and amused himself with quips, bons-mots, epigrams and repartee that had really nothing to do with the business in hand. Most of his witty sayings would bear transplanting from one play to another, and it is necessary to consult the book if we would remember in whose mouth they were placed. This is a very different thing from the dialogue of Congreve on the one hand or of J. M. Synge on the other. The whole arrangement in conversation, as he might appropriately have called either *Lady Windermere's Fan, An Ideal Husband,* or *A Woman of No Importance,* was very much lighter than the story that served as its excuse and sometimes rudely interrupted it. It was so sparkling, good-humoured and novel that even the audience for whom he had constructed the story forgave him for putting a brake upon its speed with this quite separate verbal entertainment. (pp. 137-38)

It is not in the least surprising that *The Importance of Being Earnest,* the most trivial of the social plays, should be the only one of them that gives that peculiar exhilaration of spirit by which we recognise the beautiful. It is precisely because it is consistently trivial that it is not ugly. If only once it marred its triviality with a bruise of passion, its beauty would vanish with the blow. But it never contradicts itself, and it is worth noticing that its unity, its dovetailing of dialogue and plot, so that the one helps the other, is not achieved at the expense of the conversation, but at that of the mechanical contrivances for filling a theatre that Wilde had not at first felt sure of being able to do without. The dialogue has not been weighted to trudge with the plot; the plot has been lightened till it can fly with the wings of the dialogue. The two are become one, and the lambent laughter of this comedy is due to the radioactivity of the thing itself, and not to glow-worms incongruously stuck over its surface. (p. 139)

It is surprising to think that *Salomé* was not written with a view to production. (p. 144)

In writing *Salomé,* however, Wilde did not neglect the wonderful visual sense of the theatre that was, later, to suggest to him the appearance on the stage of Jack in mourning for his nonexistent brother. He was able to see the play from the point of view of the audience, and refused no means of intensifying its effect. . . . Control is never lost, and, when the play is done, when we return to it in our waking dreams, we return to that elevation only given by the beautiful, undisturbed by the vividness, the clearness with which we realise the motive of passion playing its part in that deeper motive of doom, that fills the room in which we read, or the theatre in which we listen, with the beating of the wings of the angel of death. (pp. 151-52)

In *De Profundis* Wilde wrote as harmoniously and freely as if his life were spent in conversation instead of in silence, in looking at books and pictures instead of in shredding oakum or in swinging the handle of a crank.

It is impossible too firmly to emphasize the division between the texture of the life in *De Profundis* and that of Wilde's life in prison, a division not only needing explanation but explicable in the light of later events. When he left prison he wrote *The Ballad of Reading Gaol*. Now that ballad would have been obscured or enriched by a silver cobweb of scarcely perceptible sensations if it had been written before or during his imprisonment. Wilde could not then have suffered some of the harsh and crude effects that are harmonious with its character and necessary to its success. The newly-learnt insensibility, that allowed him to use in the ballad emotions that once he would have carefully guarded himself from perceiving, had been taught in prison. In prison his nerves had been so jangled that they responded only to a violent agitation, so jarred that a delicate touch left them silent. But at the time of the writing of *De Profundis* these janglings and jarrings were too immediate to affect him. They disappeared like print held too close to the eye. He escaped from them as he wrote, for he wrote from memory. While the events were happening, had just happened, and might happen again, that produced the insensibility without which he could not have secured the broad and violent effects of his later work, he returned, in writing, to an earlier life. When he took up his pen, it was as if none of these things were, unless as material for the use of an aloof and conscious artist. He was outside the prison as he wrote, and only saw as if in vision the tall man, with roughened hands, who had once been "King of life," and now was writing in a cell. (pp. 175-77)

What is remarkable in *The Ballad of Reading Gaol,* apart from its strength, or its violence of emotion, is a change in the quality of Wilde's language. A distinction between decoration and realism, though it immediately suggests itself, is too blunt to enable us to state clearly a change in Wilde's writing that it is impossible to overlook. (p. 183)

He could not, without doing violence to himself, have written *The Ballad of Reading Gaol* before his imprisonment.

Such an alteration in his attitude became apparent when he was released: not before. And he then proceeded to write a poem whose potentiality was not won at the expense of directness. The difference between the work he did before and after his release is the same, though not so exaggerated, as that between Mallarmé and the eighteenth-century poets. The later work falls midway between these two extremes. It is writing that depends, far more nearly than anything he had yet done, in verse, upon its actual statements. *The Ballad of Reading Gaol* is not more powerfully suggestive than *The Sphinx,* but what it says, its translatable element, is more important to its effect than the catalogue of the Sphinx's lovers. (p. 187)

Nowhere else in Wilde's work is there such a feeling of tense muscles, of difficult, because passionate, articulation. And this was the effect that he was willing to achieve. The blemishes on the poem, its moments of bad verse, its metaphors only half conceived (like the filling of an urn that has long been broken) scarcely mar the impression. It is felt that a relaxed watchfulness is due to the effort of reticence. I know of no other poem that so intensifies our horror of mortality. Beside it Wordsworth's sonnets on Capital Punishment debate with aloof, respectable philosophy the expediency of taking blood for blood, and suggest the palliatives with which a tender heart may soothe the pain of its acquiescence. Even Villon, who, like Wilde, had been in prison, and, unlike Wilde, had been himself under sentence of death, is infinitely less actual. . . . [Wilde] lives an hundred times life's last moments, and multiplies the agony of the man who dies in the hearts of all those others who feel with him how frail is their own perilous hold. (pp. 190-91)

> *Arthur Ransome, in his* Oscar Wilde: A Critical Study *(reprinted by permission of the literary Estate of Arthur Ransome), Martin Secker, 1912, 213 p.*

ALFRED DOUGLAS (essay date 1914)

Wilde, who, although he insisted on his own eminence as a poet and a critic of poetry, never committed himself to what might be considered a serious theory on the subject. Piecing together the views he expressed from time to time in a casual and general way, I am convinced, indeed, that he had no theory which was in the least stable or cogent and which was not liable to be altered by the moment's whim or mood. It is certain that, while he hankered after poetic distinction and in his early manhood strove after it, his aim was not so much to produce great poetry as to turn out stuff which would provoke the critics to write about him and the witlings to talk about him. (pp. 197-98)

For myself, I do not admit that the poems have been well received by criticism, even recently, for the very simple reason that there is very little in them to receive. . . . It is plain that the only real test of poetry is its quality, and neither its reception nor its saleability can affect that quality. If we apply such a test to Wilde's early poetical work, which represents the bulk of what he accomplished, we shall not find that he shines with anything like the effulgence that his adherents have imagined for him. Wilde himself knew that he was not a great poet. His cry is, continually: "I am an artist—the supreme artist, in fact," and never: "I am a poet," or "I am the supreme poet." He knew perfectly well that that cock wouldn't fight. He was not even anxious to be known as a poet in the way that some of his contemporaries were anxious to be known. . . . Nobody who has read any poetry other than Wilde's can fail to perceive that, leaving out the **"Ballad of Reading Gaol"** and, up to a point, **"The Sphinx,"** Wilde's poetical work consists of clever, and occasionally, perhaps, brilliant imitations. Wherever one turns in the three hundred pages of his published poems one finds echoes—and little else but echoes. His sonnets are, for the most part, Miltonic in their effects; the metre and method of "In Memoriam" are used in the greater number of his lyrics; and he uses the metre which Tennyson sealed to himself for all time even in **"The Sphinx,"** which is his great set work; while in such pieces as **"Charmides," "Panthea," "Humanitad"** and **"The Burden of Itys"** he borrows the grave pipe of Matthew Arnold and what he himself called the silver-keyed flute of Keats. (pp. 198-200)

Wilde's verses are plainly a paraphrase—and a bad one to boot. It will be urged that he wrote these in his youth, and that all poets, more or less, echo one another when they are young. But when one comes to consider that out of the forty or so lyrical pieces which Wilde wrote no fewer than eighteen are in the metre of "In Memoriam," and not one of them is free from images, phrases or cadences which can easily be paralleled out of Tennyson, while the whole of **"The Sphinx"** is open to criticism on the same grounds, one cannot doubt that Oscar Wilde is a poet who has rather overdone the youthful imitation business; and one can scarcely be expected to break the alabaster box of critical adulation at his feet. (p. 204)

As for **"The Sphinx,"** even if we concede that the uneasy effect of its metre be dismissed from the question, we have left what is—on the face of it—a work of not always too successful virtuosity on a theme which is frankly bestial. There is an undoubted pomp and swing about some of the stanzas; there are pictures well visualised and put on the canvas with a fine eye for colour; and the element of curiousness or weirdness is well sustained; but right through the piece one is made to feel that it is not the poet but the mechanician who has come before us, and continually he creaks and whirrs, as it were, for want of oil and control. Wilde, doubtless, set out to build a jewelled palace for his dubious and, if you come to look at it closely, loathsome fancy. He has succeeded only in establishing a sort of Wardour Street receptacle for old, tarnished and too-vividly-coloured lots. His efforts to do things in the most dazzling and wizardly manner are at times ludicrous, and his endeavours to get up unthinkable passions provoke one to laughter rather than awe. (pp. 207-08)

[In] my view the **"Ballad of Reading Gaol"** is the only poem of Wilde's which is likely to endure. It is as different from his previous work as chalk is different from cheese, and to read it after perusal of **"The Sphinx"** or the sonnets, it might almost be the work of another hand. In point of fact, it was indeed written by a Wilde who had very little in common, whether intellectually or artistically, with the Wilde of the bulk of the poems. Up to the time of his imprisonment Oscar Wilde, poet, had encouraged, or pretended to encourage, certain very grave fallacies with regard to poetry. He asserted—largely, I think, because he knew himself to be incapable of sincerity—that poetry was, in its essence, a matter of pretence and artifice. He held that style was everything, and feeling nothing; that poetry should be removed as well from material actuality as from the actuality of the spirit, and that no great poet had ever in his greatest moments been other than insincere. He professed other odd views and used roundly to assert that he would rather have written Swinburne's "Poems and Ballads" than anything else in literature; and that Shakespeare was not, after all, a very great poet. . . . [Up] to the time of his going to prison, there can be no question that Wilde was peculiar and in a great measure heretical in his notions about what poetry should be. His opinions may or may not have altered while he was in prison. I never heard him renounce them, but after he came out he did arrive at a perception of the fact that a poet who wishes to be heard must make his appeal to the human heart as well as to the intellect, and that perversity is never by any chance poetry. And so he set about the **"Ballad of Reading Gaol."** . . . It is sufficient for us that in the **"Ballad of Reading Gaol"** we have a sustained poem of sublimated actuality and of a breadth and sweep and poignancy such as had never before been attained in this line. The emotional appeal is, on the whole, quite legitimate and, if we except a very few passages in which the old Adam Wilde crops out, the established tradition as to what is fitting and comely in a poem of this nature is not outraged or transgressed. Because of this and the general skill and deftness of its workmanship, the poem will last, and, though I cannot agree with those critics who desire to place Wilde among the Immortals, I am certainly of opinion that it is on the **"Ballad of Reading Gaol"** and on the **"Ballad of Reading Gaol"** alone that his reputation among posterity will stand. (pp. 209-11)

Alfred Douglas, in his Oscar Wilde and Myself *(copyright, 1914, by Duffield & Company), Duffield, 1914, 306 p.*

PHILIPPE JULLIAN   (essay date 1967)

Much was borrowed in [*The Picture of Dorian Gray*], but what is original is that it is a real romance of London, in the same way that Zola's *Nana* and Daudet's *L'Immortel* are novels of Paris. The reader is led from the Park to Whitechapel, from an artist's studio to a Duchess's drawing-room; Wilde is very much at home and opens all the doors, displays the treasures and the floral decorations, and from time to time actually allows the reader a glimpse behind the scenes. One of the reasons for the success of this book is that it is redolent of great luxury, a real luxury not that of Ouida's novels. Lord Henry and Dorian have their suits cut at Pooles, scent their baths with Floris bath salts, Fortnum and Mason deliver to their houses the rarest teas, the most exquisite jams; one knows that they belong to

exclusive clubs and invite their friends to shoot, they have hothouses, and yachts. They were the demi-gods watched by the crowds in Hyde Park as they rode their horses worth several hundred guineas each, whom the new-rich pointed out in the Duchess of Sutherland's box at the Opera. Like *Le Côté de Guermantes*, *The Picture of Dorian Gray* glorifies the aristocracy, even as far as its vices and its ridiculousness. It is also one of the last pictures of that world by a great writer because from the moment the nobility dismounted from their horses to get into motorcars, when they received at the Ritz rather than in their own houses, when they preferred night-clubs to the Opera, their aesthetic glamour vanished. The scene and the style was that of the Society in which for the last ten years Oscar had been entertained in the evenings, but he wanted to give his heroes one more luxury—his wit. It is Oscar who often speaks through Dorian, and always through Lord Henry. That life of walks and conversations is a little reminiscent of Oxford, but an Oxford where the college is a great house in Belgrave Square or Park Lane, where the gentlemen cultivate 'exquisite passions'. In this world, as at Oxford, women had very little place; they come, as it were, from the outside. It is conversation that plays the chief part, and which is idealised as the supreme art.

The Picture of Dorian Gray has been said to be a succession of parodies, almost a compilation: material borrowed from Balzac (*La Peau de Chagrin, Splendeurs et misères*), from Gautier (*Mademoiselle de Maupin*), from Stevenson (*The Strange Case of Dr. Jekyll and Mr. Hyde*). And from *William Wilson* in which Edgar Allan Poe tells the story of a young criminal haunted by a man who looks exactly like him; he finishes by killing him and he sees in a mirror 'his own image, but with features all pale and dabbled in blood', but it was his antagonist whom he saw and who said, 'You have conquered and I yield. Yet, henceforth art thou also dead—dead to the World, to Heaven and to Hope. In me didst thou exist—and, in my death, see by this image, which is thine own, how utterly thou hast murdered thyself.' There is also to be found something of the terrifying stories of Sheridan Le Fanu which had made such an impression on Oscar in his youth in Dublin; also an affinity with Conan Doyle (Sherlock Holmes and Dorian Gray might easily have met in a London fog on one of their respective searches for crime and pleasure). (pp. 215-17)

The bitter philosophy of these delightful pages is also Wildean, but this is not to be found so much in the paradoxes or in the elaborate reflections as in the melancholy which emerges from the story. A life dedicated to Beauty, so much luxury and so many works of Art, only hide deception and decomposition, and here . . . one is reminded of Charlus [in Marcel Proust's *Remembrance of Things Past*]. It seems as if Oscar had had a premonition of his own ruin, inevitable although delayed by success, in the way he shows Dorian's beauty suddenly crumbling into decay. The clash between the life he led, his material pleasures, and the life he dreamed of, could only lead to catastrophe. (p. 220)

Philippe Jullian, in his Oscar Wilde, *translated by Violet Wyndham (translation copyright © 1969 by Constable & Co. Ltd.; reprinted by permission of Viking Penguin Inc.; in Canada by Constable & Co. Ltd.; originally published as* Oscar Wilde, *(copyright © 1968 by Philippe Jullian), Librairie Académique Perrin, 1967), Viking Press, 1969, Constable, 1969, 420 p.*

RICHARD ELLMANN (essay date 1969)

Wilde was one of the first to see that the exaltation of the artist required a concomitant exaltation of the critic. If art was to have a special train, the critic must keep some seats reserved on it.

Wilde reached this conclusion by way of two others. The first is that criticism plays a vital role in the creative process. If this sounds like T. S. Eliot admonishing Matthew Arnold, Wilde had expressed it, also as an admonition to Arnold, almost thirty years before. The second is that criticism is an independent branch of literature with its own procedures. "I am always amused," says Wilde, "by the silly vanity of those writers and artists of our day who seem to imagine that the primary function of the critic is to chatter about their second-rate work." And he complains that "The poor reviewers are apparently reduced to be the reporters of the police-court of literature, the chroniclers of the doings of the habitual criminals of art." In protesting the independence of criticism, Wilde sounds like an ancestral Northrop Frye or Roland Barthes. These portentous comparisons do indeed claim virtue by association. . . . What I think can be urged for Wilde then, is that for his own reasons and in his own way he laid the basis for many critical positions which are still debated in much the same terms, and which we like to attribute to more ponderous names.

When Wilde formulated his theories the public was more hostile to criticism than it is now, and Wilde was flaunting his iconoclasm, his contempt for the unconsidered and so uncritical pieties of his age. This in fact was his mode: not to speak for the Victorians, or for the prematurely old writers who dithered that they were the end of an era, as if they must expire with the 1800s. (pp. ix-x)

Like Stendhal, Wilde thought of himself as a voice of the age to be, rather than of the one that was fading. Yet like anyone else writing criticism in the nineteenth century, he had to come to terms with the age that had been, and especially with everybody's parent, Matthew Arnold. . . .

Wilde's only book of criticism, *Intentions,* was written during the three years following Arnold's death and published in 1891, as if to take over that critical burden and express what Arnold had failed to say. Yeats thought the book "wonderful" and Walter Pater handsomely praised it for carrying on, "more perhaps than any other writer, the brilliant critical work of Matthew Arnold." (p. xi)

Wilde had been Pater's disciple, and in *Intentions* eighteen years later he tweaks Arnold's nose with the essay which in its first published form was entitled, **"The True Function and Value of Criticism: with Some Remarks on the Importance of Doing Nothing."** Here Wilde rounded on Arnold by asserting that the aim of criticism is to see the object as it really is not. This aim might seem to justify the highly personal criticism of Ruskin and Pater, and Wilde uses them as examples; his contention goes beyond their practice, however; he wishes to free critics from subordination, to grant them a larger share in the production of literature. While he does not forbid them to explain a book, they might prefer, he said, to deepen a book's mystery. (This purpose is amusing but out of date now; who could deepen the mystery of *Finnegans Wake*?) At any rate, their context would be different from that of the creative artist. For just as the artist claimed independence of received experience (Picasso tells us that art is "what nature is not"), so the critic claimed independence of received books. "The highest criticism," according to Wilde, "is the record of one's own soul." More closely he explained that the critic must have all literature in his mind and see particular works in that perspective rather than in isolation. (p. xii)

Each of the four essays that make up *Intentions* is to some degree subversive, as if to demonstrate that the intentions of the artist are not strictly honorable. The first and the last, **"The Decay of Lying"** and **"The Truth of Masks,"** celebrate art for rejecting truths, faces, and all that paraphernalia in favor of lies and masks. Wilde doesn't do this in the romantic way of extolling the imagination, for while he uses that word he is a little chary of it; the imagination is itself too natural, too involuntary, for his view of art. He prefers lying because it sounds more willful, because it is no outpouring of the self, but a conscious effort to mislead. "All fine imaginative work," Wilde affirms, "is self-conscious and deliberate. A great poet sings because he chooses to sing." On the other hand, "if one tells the truth, one is sure, sooner or later, to be found out!" "All bad poetry springs from genuine feeling." Wilde celebrates art not in the name of Ariel, as the romantics would, but in the name of Ananias.

He finds art to have two basic energies, both of them subversive. One asserts its magnificent isolation from experience, its unreality, its sterility. He would concur with Nabokov that art is a kind of trick played on nature, an *illicit* creation by man. "All art is entirely useless," Wilde declares. "Art never expresses anything but itself." "Nothing that actually occurs is of the smallest importance." Form determines content, not content form, a point which Auden also sometimes affirms and which is often assumed by symbolists. With this theory Wilde turns Taine upon his head; the age does not determine what its art should be, rather it is art which gives the age its character. So far from responding to questions posed by the epoch, art offers answers before questions have been asked. "It is the ages that are her symbols." Life, straggling after art, seizes upon forms in art to express itself, so that life imitates art rather than art life. ". . . This unfortunate aphorism about Art holding the mirror up to Nature, is," according to Wilde, "deliberately said by Hamlet in order to convince the bystanders of his absolute insanity in all art-matters." If art be a mirror, we look into it to see—a mask. But more precisely, art is no mirror; it is a "mist of words," "a veil." (pp. xx-xxi)

In his criticism and in his work generally, Wilde balanced two ideas which, we have observed, look contradictory. One is that art is disengaged from actual life, the other that it is deeply incriminated with it. The first point of view is sometimes taken by Yeats, though only to qualify it, the second without qualification by Genet. That art is sterile, and that it is infectious, are attitudes not beyond reconciliation. Wilde never formulated their union, but he implied something like this: by its creation of beauty art reproaches the world, calling attention to the world's faults through their very omission; so the sterility of art is an affront or a parable. Art may also outrage the world by flouting its laws or by picturing indulgently their violation. Or art may seduce the world by making it follow an example which seems bad but is discovered to be better than it seems. In these various ways the artist forces the world toward self-recognition, with at least a tinge of self-redemption. (pp. xxvi-xxvii)

Richard Ellmann, "Introduction: The Critic As Artist As Wilde," in The Artist As Critic: Critical Writings of Oscar Wilde *by Oscar Wilde, edited by Richard Ellmann (copyright © 1968, 1969 by Richard Ellmann; reprinted by permission of Random House, Inc.), Random House, 1969, pp. ix-xxviii.*

STUART N. HAMPSHIRE (essay date 1969)

One thousand and ninety-eight of Wilde's letters are collected in Mr. Hart-Davis's authoritative edition [*Letters of Oscar Wilde*]. The letters form a design that is almost a commanding work of art, as Wilde would himself have wished. Almost, but not quite; because in the middle, disturbing the symmetry of the plot, is lodged the finally, definitely definitive version of *De Profundis*. . . . And the tone of this letter notoriously makes it scarcely a letter at all. It stands out. Wilde seemed to be filing a work of literature with posterity, for the record; and posterity, in its restrained and judicial way, has not been pleased. Invited to a kind of moral banquet, with no expense of style spared, as if to a spiritual equivalent of ortolans and champagne at the Savoy Grill, it has looked severely in the opposite direction, back to *The Importance of Being Earnest*, disregarding this expensive lapse of taste. Yet its inclusion is evidently right. Here restored to its context, the too calculated style of this letter to Douglas is more easily understood, and is less offensive, because it no longer seems as false as it seemed in isolation.

For Wilde at that moment, in prison, it was a condition of sanity that he should assume the attitude of one who reclaims his past by grandly understanding it. This was indeed an assumed attitude, a necessary pose, and the quality of the writing often betrays it. But there is a psychological truth, fully recognized by the author, in this need for a theatrical success, for an exhibition of fine self-consciousness. He needed at that moment to hear the imaginary applause of a public temporarily silent, disloyal and departed. As Wilde remarked in another letter, the terror of prison was for him the vagary of emotion without action. *De Profundis* was action, a gesture. At no time in his life could he bear to be alone, because he must instantly translate overflowing feeling into extravagant performance, as physical energy must be expressed in movement. Posterity is a prig, and will always demand a terminal report on the measurable quality of the work done, abstracted from its conditions. But posterity may at last read the letter in its proper place, and judge, since judge it must, less harshly. As an oration at that stage of a drama which the public had chosen to recognize as public, the letter has force, aptness, and, in some passages, a quick psychological insight.

The real question, raised again by these letters, is the nature of the interest that we still take in Wilde, the ground of his claim to some kind of greatness and still rewarding originality. There is the obvious suspicion that this interest has little to do with achieved literature and its values, but is rather the romanticized prurience that attaches itself to the ruined rebel and to the vulgarly interpreted artistic personality: as to Gauguin, Dylan Thomas and others who, apart from their achievements, represent also commonplace dreams of scandal and of escape. Wilde himself knew that this part was open to him, and he later intermittently played it, summoning inept comparisons with Byron. But there is an evident interest elsewhere. He invented, without forethought, a style, a lightness and a verbal gaiety, which have passed in and out of English speech and writing ever since: it was as much an invention as Lear's nonsense had been, but less powerful, and wholly unpoetical, a gross trick with the English language, and it depends upon swift interruptions and an audience. (pp. 71-3)

The forming of the style can be watched in these letters. In Wilde it developed, and developed gradually, from enormous vitality, from the desire to please, from affectionate nonsense between friends, from the love of syntax and of the hard form of a sentence: certainly not from intellectual care or from any depth of reflection. It is not surprising to find in the early letters, among arrangements for shooting and riding with friends, that he placed *Aurora Leigh* alongside *Hamlet* and *In Memoriam*. He did not earnestly care for literature. It was only the idea of classical Greece, and of Flaubert, that engaged him, and never the less simple realities. Compared with the young Shaw, who was carefully to husband his physical energies, he begins and remains a free-spending amateur of letters, with massive, careless energy and with no stiffening of thin intellectual purpose. The opposing temperaments of these two Irish invaders, the one coarse and ample, the other thin and refined, are very exactly reflected in their style of wit, when their essays or letters or plays are placed side by side.

Wilde at his best achieved genial, liberating nonsense. He wrote proudly from Kansas City, during his American tour, that the miners, with whom he had been drinking, described him as 'a bully boy with no glass eye'. They were nearer the core, as disclosed in his letters, than the *Punch* cartoonists or Hichens in *The Green Carnation*. His aestheticism was a broad dramatization of a single idea—issuing from a huge enjoyment of the stage—and of the repeatable joke of mixing the conventions and artifices of comedy with ordinary social behaviour. He did not think about aesthetics closely, not even about the aesthetics of acting. He played variations on one theme: that of substituting the superficial for the profound, visible forms for spiritual states, as the proper objects of emotion; and this without any satirical intent. There was no moral and no meaning, and no one was ever threatened, except those who, in Yeats's phrase, were 'full of the secret spite of dullness'. (pp. 73-4)

Wilde was a talker, and not a great letter-writer. He remarked that many men had been ruined, when they arrived in London, by the habit of answering letters: by 'ruined' he meant, of course, that they lost 'the enjoyment of spontaneity'. The quality of his gifts has to be read through these letters rather than in them. The letters are not in themselves of the sustained quality of Fitzgerald's, even less of Byron's or Lawrence's. But they tell the story of the years during and following imprisonment more vividly than it has ever been told before. (pp. 74-5)

There is always posterity's temptation to sum up and to judge, to count the achievement and the waste, and this in defiance of Wilde's own principle of spontaneity. At least he invented a new pleasure, a new resource of language in dialogue, used by conscious and unconscious imitators ever since: 'the essence of good dialogue is interruption', he writes in a letter. The reckless, generous charm, and the 'half civilized' genius, can still be felt in his letters. (p. 77)

*Stuart N. Hampshire, " 'Letters of Oscar Wilde',"
in his* Modern Writers and Other Essays *(copyright
© 1969 by Stuart N. Hampshire; reprinted by permission of Alfred A. Knopf, Inc.; in Canada by Chatto
& Windus, Ltd.), Chatto & Windus, 1969 (and reprinted by Knopf, 1970, pp. 71-7).*

HAROLD BLOOM (essay date 1973)

[Poetic history is] indistinguishable from poetic influence, since strong poets make that history by misreading one another, so as to clear imaginative space for themselves. (p. 5)

Weaker talents idealize; figures of capable imagination appropriate for themselves. But nothing is got for nothing, and self-appropriation involves the immense anxieties of indebtedness, for what strong maker desires the realization that he has failed to create himself? Oscar Wilde, who knew he had failed as a poet because he lacked strength to overcome his anxiety of influence, knew also the darker truths concerning influence. *The Ballad of Reading Gaol* becomes an embarrassment to read, directly one recognizes that every lustre it exhibits is reflected from *The Rime of the Ancient Mariner;* and Wilde's lyrics anthologize the whole of English High Romanticism. Knowing this, and armed with his customary intelligence, Wilde bitterly remarks in *The Portrait of Mr. W. H.* that: "Influence is simply a transference of personality, a mode of giving away what is most precious to one's self, and its exercise produces a sense, and, it may be, a reality of loss. Every disciple takes away something from his master." This is the anxiety of influencing, yet no reversal in this area is a true reversal. Two years later, Wilde refined this bitterness in one of Lord Henry Wotton's elegant observations in *The Picture of Dorian Gray,* where he tells Dorian that all influence is immoral:

> Because to influence a person is to give him one's own soul. He does not think his natural thoughts, or burn with his natural passions. His virtues are not real to him. His sins, if there are such things as sins, are borrowed. He becomes an echo of someone else's music, an actor of a part that has not been written for him.

To apply Lord Henry's insight to Wilde, we need only read Wilde's review of Pater's *Appreciations,* with its splendidly self-deceptive closing observation that Pater "has escaped disciples." Every major aesthetic consciousness seems peculiarly more gifted at denying obligation as the hungry generations go on treading one another down. (pp. 5-6)

> Harold Bloom, "Introduction: A Meditation upon Priority, and a Synopsis," in his The Anxiety of Influence: A Theory of Poetry *(copyright © 1973 by Oxford University Press, Inc.; reprinted by permission), Oxford University Press, New York, 1973, pp. 5-16.*

GEOFFREY STONE   (essay date 1976)

[Oscar Wilde, in his earlier 90s plays,] is compelled to write in a spokesman, usually an Intelligent Bad Man, for the views and wit his chosen form must otherwise exclude. *A Woman of No Importance* shows the clash between his genre, Strong Society Drama as we may call it, and much of what he really wants to deal with and do. Indeed, Wilde's struggles with his awful plots are extremely like Dickens's in his early novels—and for the same reason. They even fall into the same stagy bombast at the points of greatest strain. (p. 29)

Besides unpleasant social realities, unpleasant psychological ones are buzzing in [*A Woman of No Importance*]; what is and will be the relationship between a bastard son and a mother who deliberately keeps him to herself in mediocrity? The plot, and Wilde's intelligence, are compelled to raise the theme, but since it has no place in the genre it is bundled away again as soon as raised. . . . We are here dealing with perfectly serious matters, but the characters Wilde has attempting it are quite incapable of it; they are trapped by their nature, their idiom, the very conditions of their existence—the Strong Society Drama. Now if this gap is accepted and exploited, these masks become (so to speak) not characters but meta-characters; they relate indirectly to life, and directly to a certain representation of life—that acceptable to the 90s theatre audience, or loose sentimentalists anywhere anytime. A play containing them then becomes a criticism of, or a set of variations upon, that particular mode of inadequacy to life and its highly complex relations to reality. Further, being a meta-play, a work of art whose subject is art (literally art for art's sake, in fact), many things cease to be a temptation and become an artistic necessity; for example, perfect phrasing and epigram, the greatest possible elegance of expression, of plot, of situation. The author can legitimately aim at a perfection of form usually found only in music or mathematics. At the same time, by having its roots deep in the rich manure of the 90s commercial drama and reality, the work is preserved from abstraction or triviality. . . . In fact, if Wilde is going to write a genuinely good play it must relate to at least some of the 90s otherwise unmanageable realities, it must allow his wit to work with not against his art, it must also be produceable in the 90s commercial theatre and consequently relate to the established form as well as the facts that form pretended to correspond with. It must therefore be inherently and essentially metalinguistic, a special and powerful sort of verbal structure; must be, in fact, the meta-play *The Importance of Being Earnest.* Hence its anti-natural yet legitimate stylization, its otherwise baffling combination of perfect seriousness in its internal structure with (ostensibly) perfect frivolity in its apparent structure ('a trivial comedy for serious people' is Wilde's own definition), and its numerous outcrops of granite-hard sense. These assertions will perhaps become plausible, indeed comprehensible, by a close examination of the play itself.

The people of the play are Mr. Worthing (Ernest in town, Jack in the country), his ward Cecily Cardew, his fiancée Gwendolen Fairfax (daughter of Lady Bracknell), and his friend Algernon Montcrieff (nephew of Lady Bracknell); the plot is that Algernon, as her guardian's fictitious younger brother Ernest, becomes engaged to Cecily, so both girls are engaged to 'Ernest' but neither to Ernest; more detail is unneeded. The play opens with a passage exhibiting, and implicitly commenting upon, the simple theme of master-servant relations and, by implication, those of the upper and lower orders. The social reality of the 90s was peculiarly one of power, of dominators and dominated, and in every passage of *The Importance* there is continuous conflict. Just as Byron boxed with his valet to reach physical grace-with-power, so Algernon spars verbally with his manservant. This is sporting of Algernon, and helps set the tone of civil decency that characterizes the play, because he loses every exchange. The opening question and answer ('Did you hear what I was playing, Lane?' 'I didn't think it polite to listen, sir') carry a number of elements; *(a)* regulative social conventions, (i) the upper order's access to art, and the lower orders' lack of it (cf. Yeats), (ii) the lower orders' 'knowing their place'; and *(b)* Lane's implied comments on the conventions and related facts. (i) Since society exacts deference, this exempts Lane from the duty of listening; indeed, since (ii) Algernon has no access to genuine art, it is personally polite not to have listened. In 'polite' sense (i), as a servant, Lane is outside the 'polis' or civilized group (in Athens he would have been a slave); in sense (ii), he is, as an independent intelligence, exquisitely within it. If this and the following exchanges were cruder in feeling, they would exhibit the covert insolence generated when an upper order character is attempting fraternity but being denied it; if they were coarsened the other way, by making Algernon's wit superior to Lane's, we would have the familiar figure of the comic but fundamentally inferior servant. The next exchange—on the champagne—deals with the expropriation of the expropriators, or—in the language of the time—the servant problem. Lane assumes and establishes his right to steal as much as he pleases, counters Algernon's probe with successive flank attacks on the upper order's taste, competence, major regulating social conventions (marriage, and a respectful attitude to it), and finally defeats Algernon's desperate but unsporting attempt at a snub by (judo-like) completely agreeing with him and consequently exposing a total complicity on Algernon's part with Lane's social subversion. Algernon's direct speech to the audience then points out (i) that they live off the lower orders, (ii) cant about them in several different ways at once, and (iii) their listening to and laughing at his speech shows they have publicly agreed to all that is entailed. The audience, like Algernon with Lane, has been trapped by entering the dialogue. (In Aristotelian terms, the one page of dialogue so far has supplied five peripeteias and two anagnorises. . . .) Finally, although it apparently abandons the exposition usually the business of a play's first moments, it is actually carrying out the very necessary business of training the audience in the kind of social and linguistic relations that will compose the play. We should not deny to Wilde, any more than to Marvell, that well-known 'tough reasonableness beneath the slight lyric grace'. (pp. 30-3)

Since *The Importance of Being Earnest* is itself so completely structured, there is an added elegance in the presence within it of smaller structures which by their formal quality or reversal of expectations or both operate as a kind of model of the play itself—that is, as yet another meta-level above the ostensible one. Very few works of literature are of such formal complexity. There are the traditional, the classic ironies of plot—foreshadowings and echoes; Lady Bracknell's 'the line is immaterial', 'try and acquire some relations as soon as possible' (she is addressing her nephew in his brother's flat); the prophecy 'Half an hour after they've met, they will be calling each other sister'—'Women only do that when they have called each other a lot of other things first'; and Algernon's masquerade as the younger brother he actually but unknowingly is. There is the very simple structure of the offstage running joke—Lady Harbury, Lord Bracknell; the more complex one of the onstage wit-combat, itself full of language-devices (inversion, category and subject-shift, and even points of pure logic—'There is no good offering a large reward now that the thing is found')—the battle of the cigarette-case, of Algernon-as-Ernest rebuked by Jack, of who has the right to be christened; and most complex of all, the circular sequence early in the play about the 'clever people' and the fools, which is funny at the simplest level ('What fools'), funnier when one realizes Jack has been defined as one of the fools whose non-existence he has been lamenting, and funniest when one realizes that the fool's cap also fits the audience and oneself—any critic of the play, in fact—since its characters are eminently 'clever people', and the whole audience has come to the theatre solely to meet and talk about them. So—for a second—the level-above-level structure has reached out and pulled, not this listener and that, or this common pretender and that, but the—any—audience, purely *qua* audience, inside the play—a very metalinguistic effect indeed. (pp. 36-7)

The Importance of Being Earnest is sufficiently related to the world as it is to touch the great standard themes of art—Love and Marriage, Death and Rebirth, and Appearance and Reality—though they indeed occur very obliquely. Love and Marriage is of course used structurally rather than emotionally, and the crucial insistence is not on the fact—lovers' earnestness—but the word—their Ernestness, so to speak. The theme arises in the play's first minute, and runs through to the tra-

ditional Triumph of Hymen in the last one, with such occasional strokes of appalling human truth as Gwendolen's 'I never change, except in my affections', or metalinguistic improvements on sentimental drama as 'though I may marry someone else, *and marry often*, nothing . . . can alter my eternal devotion to you'. Death and spiritual or nominal Rebirth are nearly as omnipresent. Quite early in Act I Jack announces 'I am going to kill my brother' (Jack is *totally* his 'brother's' keeper) . . . 'I am going to get rid of Ernest. And I strongly advise you to do the same with . . . your invalid friend', and accordingly in Act II he appears, a tall basalt column in 'the deepest mourning, with crepe hatband and black gloves' to announce that Ernest is 'Dead! . . . Quite dead'. Algernon carries out a parallel phantom homicide: 'Bunbury is dead . . . I killed Bunbury this afternoon . . . he was quite exploded'. The aggression usually underlying comedy, and peculiarly strongly in this play, is in these examples quite cheerfully open. And though it may be over-fussy, I cannot help feeling Lady Bracknell's phrase about persons whose origin is a Terminus, though directed against Jack's social misfortunes, both prefigures Beckett ('We give birth astride a grave') and plays on a reversal of the Christian view of death—that our end is our beginning. This is, spiritually speaking, what happens in the sacrament of baptism, in which the baptisant dies to the Old Man and regenerates as the New in his symbolic drowning and resurrection. It is again the underlying logical *structure* which makes Jack's diffident negotiations with Dr. Chasuble so funny ('if you have nothing better to do . . . I might trot round about five if that would suit you'), and with Algernon ('I have not been christened for years.' 'Yes, but you have been christened. That is the important thing'—as, theologically, it is. 'Quite so. So I know my constitution can stand it.'). Lady Bracknell brings society and sacrament—Mammon and God—together in an explosion of short-circuits—'grotesque and irreligious . . . I will not hear of such excesses. Lord Bracknell would be highly displeased if he learned that that was the way you wasted your time and money', while at a proper age she includes christening among 'every luxury that money could buy'. *The Importance* is closely if obliquely related to religion, or at least religion-in-society, even down to Gwendolen's determination to crush her doubts on Jack's sincerity—'this is not the moment for German scepticism'.

Lastly, the theme of that age-old and ultimate pair, Appearance and Reality, is overtly with us from the cigarette-case, through all the metalinguistic truths and object-level deceptions, rising to the highest points of concentration in such scenes as Algernon's masquerade as Jack's brother (yet he *is* Jack's brother), his logic ('it is perfectly childish to be in deep mourning for a man who is actually staying for a whole week with you in your house as your guest'), and the total disappearance of Ernest. The very basis of objective reality is subverted in the perfectly accurate account of Memory, which 'usually chronicles all the things that have never happened, and couldn't possibly have happened', and the proferred documentary alternative of the two diaries (respectively 'a very young girl's record of her own thoughts and impressions, and consequently meant for publication', and 'something sensational to read in the train'). The extreme difficulty of valid description is finally exampled explicit: 'Is this Miss Prism a female of repellent aspect, remotely connected with education?' 'She is the most cultivated of ladies, and the very picture of respectability.' 'It is obviously the same person.'

If the metalinguistic structure of the play and the characters is not grasped, then not only is the nature of the play unrealized, but the play and characters *look* too fragile to handle, and consequently its beautiful substructures—social and general human satire on food and power, religion, death and resurrection, appearance and reality—have to be overlooked and ignored and criticism creeps away in a flurry of embarrassed and misdirected compliments. What a Theatre of Black Comedy and the Absurd we might have had in England under Victoria if only some enlightened lover of literature had saved Wilde for thirty years more playwriting by firmly propelling Bosie [Lord Alfred Douglas] under a bus. (pp. 39-41)

> Geoffrey Stone, *"Serious Bunburyism: The Logic of 'The Importance of Being Earnest',"* in Essays in Criticism, *Vol. XXVI, No. 1, January, 1976, pp. 28-41.*

TED R. SPIVEY   (essay date 1980)

Whenever critics have taken Oscar Wilde's work seriously, it is usually with apology and denigration. Yet to omit his name from the history of modern British literature or even the history of modern fiction is to leave a gap in either. The growing interest in Harold Bloom's theory of poetry, developed in *The Anxiety of Influence* [see excerpt above], should help to bring about a resurgence of interest in Wilde, because few men of letters ever suffered more from the anxiety of influence than Wilde. That anxiety was not only because of Victorian moralists like Arnold that Wilde sought to replace but also because of those closer to him—Pater, Huysmans, and Baudelaire—whose work he thought he was making known to a large public. In fact, the two major symbolist tragedies that Wilde wrote—*Salomé* and *The Picture of Dorian Gray*—both spring from an anxiety toward both schools of letters. And if, as Bloom says, criticism "is the art of knowing the hidden roads that go from poem to poem," then we must study how Wilde took up Pater's dictum of a life burning as a flame burns and suffered it until he found his own and Dorian Gray's tragedy, and then we must go on to follow Wilde's tragedy into the poetry of André Gide, James Joyce, T. S. Eliot, and a throng of lesser symbolist poets and novelists. Having appropriately (for Bloom's theory) misread Pater's *Renaissance*, published in that pivotal period of the early seventies, Wilde plunged into a search for as large and strange a variety of sensations as he could find and then recorded his findings in his two tragedies.

The anxiety of enjoying more sensations than had been possible in most earlier ages led Wilde to depict in *The Picture of Dorian Gray* a literal attempt at superhuman transcendence. In short, Wilde made Dorian Gray's tragic flaw basically the same as that of Shakespeare's Macbeth. Macbeth listens to the plan of his wife, who has assumed leadership over him, and then accepts his wife's instructions to follow the guidance of agents of a world other than the human. Dorian follows the advice of a sinister aristocrat with vaguely Mephistophelian traits and uses a preternatural talisman to obtain the occult ability to hide his soul in a picture. The result of the tragedy for both Macbeth and Gray is that they lose their souls. The difference is that Macbeth simply follows the advice of an ambitious wife, whereas Gray is guided by an initiatory figure who promises to show by means of his knowledge the gateway to the good life but whose advice leads to death. . . . [He] is the Victorian who seems to know all but whose knowledge is deadly. Gray sees too late that it is a knowledge that denies the reality of the soul and man's need to develop the soul or lose it. Gray's tempter begins by enunciating the Pater doctrine of art for art's sake and the need to enjoy as many sensations as possible, and ends by deceiving Gray about the soul and its need for development. Too late the protagonist realizes that he is living out a tragic myth of the loss of the human soul. (pp. 58-9)

Max Beerbohm noted long ago that there were critics like Arnold who recommended that others do exactly as they had done and other critics like Pater who recommended that others do exactly the opposite of what they had done. I believe that what those who followed in Wilde's path most hid from themselves was the fact that modern man, to escape certain mythic knowledge he must embody if he is to remain fully human, flees into knowledge and art, covers his nakedness with systems of knowledge and objects of art in order to escape that art and that knowledge that it is his destiny to encounter on his own journey. Joyce partly and Yeats totally—both in part disciples of Wilde—admitted this in effect as they approached their final years. It was what Wilde had already confessed in his two greatest works in the symbolist style, *Salomé* and *The Picture of Dorian Gray.* (p. 60)

[In *The Picture of Dorian Gray*] Wilde presents his vision of evil in terms of a tempter and one who is tempted—that is Lord Henry Wotton and Dorian Gray. The brilliant and corrupt Wotton, in fact, plays the role of the devil. Wilde limits his use of the supernatural to the device of the picture which assumes Dorian's sins, but there are occasional hints that Lord Harry is more than mortal. He remains an urbane gentleman of the period, but his Christian name is traditionally associated with the devil; and in one important way he is like the biblical devil: he persuades Dorian to eat the fruit of the tree of knowledge. Lord Harry also resembles Goethe's Mephistopheles, who offers Faust a kind of knowledge that can come only through intense experience. Having tired of the inert lore of books, Faust is ready to try Mephistopheles' magic, which enables him to know a kind of heightened experience. When he is awakened with the desire to know, Dorian accepts the magic of perpetual youth and beauty from a source Wilde never makes known. Dorian's wish is mysteriously granted, but a connection between Lord Harry's remarks in the temptation scene and the granting of Dorian's desire is easy enough for the reader to make. With the help of magic, Dorian Gray is able to set out on a life of intense experience. (pp. 61-2)

I suggest that the root cause of Dorian's damnation, as well as the source of Harry's evil, is an insatiable curiosity, a never ending desire for knowledge that is essentially Victorian in its tendency to control the individual's life. It is curiosity above all else that is behind the ironclad egocentricity of Dorian and Harry. There are three key words whose meanings must be explored in order to understand this egocentricity. They are *experience, art,* and *curiosity,* and curiosity is the most important. The kind of knowledge that Lord Harry teaches Dorian to be curious about can be had only through the experience of intense sensations; thus, experience and also art . . . become only means to an end. (p. 62)

In chapter 2 Lord Harry has a good bit to say about experience: "The aim of life is self-development. To realise one's nature perfectly—that is what each of us is here for.". . . . Along with his injunction to yield always to temptation he makes a curious statement: "It is in the brain, and the brain only, that the great sins of the world take place." . . . This is the pattern of Lord Harry's philosophy throughout the book—no matter how much he honors the senses, it is always the brain that he comes back to. Actually Lord Harry recommends one set of pleasurable experiences for Dorian—the pleasures of sensation—and finds another for himself—the pleasures of the intellect. Dorian is told to go out and live the full life, to search for beauty, to yield to all temptations, to help bring about the new hedonism. Lord Harry himself, of course, does none of these things. His chief activity is manipulating the life of his disciple, Dorian, in order to satisfy better his curiosity concerning this rare youth. Harry is driven by an insatiable desire to know about the inner workings of human beings. He often speaks of theories and of analysis and he thinks of himself as a scientist, an analyst, and an experimenter. One of several passages that show the true analytical spirit and also suggest the motivating force of the newly damned Dorian is the following: "It was clear to him that the experimental method was the only method by which one could arrive at any scientific analysis of the passions; and certainly Dorian Gray was a subject made to his hand, and seemed to promise rich and fruitful results. His sudden mad love for Sibyl Vane was a psychological phenomenon of no small interest. There was no doubt that curiosity had much to do with it, curiosity and the desire for new experiences; yet it was not a simple but rather a very complex passion." . . . Thus Wilde drives home his point that curiosity is the one trait that above all other characterizes Lord Harry and incidentally now characterizes Dorian, who has become a Victorian scientist of the passions.

Along with curiosity and experience in Wilde's book goes another important idea: art. For Wilde, art is that which is shaped and molded. Experience itself must be molded and shaped so that it can be studied, and in Lord Harry's case it is mainly the experience of Dorian that is artfully arranged. As Lord Harry thinks, "There was nothing that one could not do with him. He could be made a Titan or a toy." . . . Obviously the magical preservation of Dorian's youth and beauty is the chief example in the book of the application of art to life. Works of art have their proper place in the life of sensation, but the esthetic movement was chiefly concerned with making one's life a work of art. It was enough for Lord Harry, however, to help shape Dorian's life and then observe and analyze it in order to satisfy his own curiosity. The connection between art and analysis is seen when he explains at the end of the book, "If a man treats life artistically, his brain is his heart." . . . Wilde's devil then is a kind of artist-intellectual, with particular emphasis on the intellectual. And he is an experimental scientist. (pp. 63-4)

The tragedy of Dorian Gray, as I have suggested, is the same as that of Macbeth, or even of Othello, two characters whose souls are gradually poisoned until their destructiveness forces them to face the fact that they have been deluded about their advisors, whose knowledge they have used to destroy life. Dorian is so deluded that he does not even know, until the end of his life, that he has been living out a tragedy. (p. 69)

If, as Harold Bloom says, criticism is "the art of knowing the hidden roads that go from poem to poem," then we must, in order to see Wilde in context, be aware of his reaction both to his immediate, modern precursors and to his Victorian precursors. Anxiety resulted from his reaction to both groups. All of Wilde's works are an attempt to throw off the anxiety all modern people feel in relationship to their Victorian precursors. The Victorian precursor, as created by the modern mind to free itself from anxiety, hid a manipulating, egocentric personality behind an empty morality and a supposed love and cultivation of art and science. Victorians, in the modern mind, based their vaunted morality on systems of knowledge that were pedantic and that denied the essence of life. (p. 70)

At heart Dorian's corrupter [Lord Harry] is a Victorian scientist of the sort we find in Hawthorne, one who placed life under

his own microscope in the name of some ideal. He is then the great Victorian deceiver, one of the most important characters in all of modern fiction, whose creation was one of modern man's attempts to free himself from the anxiety of Victorian influence. (p. 71)

Ted R. Spivey, "Oscar Wilde and the Tragedy of Symbolism," in his The Journey beyond Tragedy: A Study of Myth and Modern Fiction *(copyright © 1980 by the Board of Regents of the State of Florida), University Presses of Florida, 1980, pp. 57-71.*

ISAAC ELIMIMIAN (essay date 1980-81)

Oscar Wilde's *The Picture of Dorian Gray* has, in general, received unfavorable critical comments, compared with the little praise which has passed from a few sympathizers of it. Those who attack the work point to the deplorable manner in which certain aspects of it have been contrived or imitated, such as the title, such as the theme, no less than the cruel circumstances under which the actress, Sibl Vane, commits suicide. What [the following analysis] sets out to do, however, is to: (1) examine the divergences and correspondences apparent in the "Preface" to *Dorian Gray* in light of Wilde's literary criticism; and (2) establish what Wilde's aesthetic motives really are.

In the "Preface" to *Dorian Gray*, Wilde writes: "The highest as the lowest form of criticism is a mode of autobiography." . . . In *The Critic As Artist*, Wilde scoffs at the idea of writing biography and autobiography. In the "Preface" to *Dorian Gray* he says: "It is the spectator, and not life, that art really mirrors." . . . In *The Critic As Artist*, Wilde thinks differently, and speaks of "Literature" as "the perfect expression of life." . . .

On the functional quality of art, Wilde also makes statements, which, on the surface, seem contradictory. In *The Decay of Lying*, for example, he writes: "Art is our spirited protest, our gallant attempt to teach Nature her proper place." . . . In the "Preface" to *Dorian Gray*, he says: "All art is quite useless." . . . Wilde is here not only using paradox or a rhetorical style, but he is applying the Blakean concept that contraries do not imply a negation. . . . And when he adds in the "Preface" to *Dorian Gray* that "Vice and Virtue" form suitable "material for the artist," we, as readers, are made to think that the realm of artistic discourse is limitless. Art enables us to view life clearly, but art, by itself, is incapable of any permanent rendering. Similarly, when we interpret art, we interpret life, since life's colors are enshrined in it. Art and life complement each other.

The above inconsistencies notwithstanding, there are certain recurring aesthetic modes which made Wilde's work organic. For instance: "To reveal art and conceal the artist is art's aim" ("Preface" to *Dorian Gray* . . .) has been echoed in *The Truth of Masks* . . . where Wilde maintains that art, like metaphysics, conceals. The same idea is expressed also in *The Decay of Lying*, where Vivian tells Cyril: "Art . . . is a veil, rather than a mirror. She has flowers that no forests know of, birds that no woodland possesses." . . . Thus the idea of art as a mask is recurrent and common in Wilde's work. (pp. 625-26)

I have, so far, brought out some points of similarity and dissimilarity in Wilde's aesthetic theory as they relate to the "Preface" to *Dorian Gray* and his literary criticism. But one point needs to be added: such questions as whether Wilde's utterances both in his criticism and in the "Preface" to *Dorian Gray* are tenable and sincere, or whether Wilde was of a sound moral conviction (questions which have bothered some of his critics), are irrelevant. The artist need not necessarily be "sincere" and need not be of a sound moral character, so long as he can, by virtue of his good sense and the forcefulness of his artistic credo, make us think he is. By juxtaposing "beautiful" with "ugly," "moral" with "immoral," and "virtue" with "vice" ("Preface" to *Dorian Gray* . . .), Wilde shows his good sense. And by citing Christ and Caesar as figures we generally would like to emulate (*The Decay of Lying* . . .), he lends authority to his message. Besides, his attackers need to know the philosophy [in *De Profundis*] under which he worked to appreciate him:

> I have grown tired of the articulate utterances of men and things. The Mystical in Art, the Mystical in Life, the Mystical in Nature—this is what I am looking for.

(pp. 627-28)

Isaac Elimimian, "'Preface' to 'The Picture of Dorian Gray' in Light of Wilde's Literary Criticism," in Modern Fiction Studies (© 1981 by Purdue Research Foundation, West Lafayette, Indiana 47907, U.S.A.), Vol. 26, No. 4, Winter, 1980-81, pp. 625-28.

ADDITIONAL BIBLIOGRAPHY

Braybrooke, Patrick. "Oscar Wilde: A Consideration." In *Essays by Divers Hands, Being the Transactions of the Royal Society of Literature of the United Kingdom*, edited by Sir Henry Imbert-Terry, pp. 21-40. London: Oxford University Press, 1932.
Well-balanced overview which concludes that in view of the infamy of Wilde's life and the unquestionable value of much of his work, he may be best served by "a reasonable blending of forgetfulness and remembrance."

Chamberlin, J. E. *Ripe Was the Drowsy Hour: The Age of Oscar Wilde*. New York: The Seabury Press, 1977, 222 p.
Examines Wilde in the social and artistic contexts of his time.

Charlesworth, Barbara. "Oscar Wilde." In her *Dark Passages: The Decadent Consciousness in Victorian Literature*, pp. 53-80. Madison: The University of Wisconsin Press, 1965.
Biographical reading of *The Picture of Dorian Gray*.

Ellmann, Richard, ed. *Oscar Wilde: A Collection of Critical Essays*. Englewood Cliffs, N.J.: Prentice-Hall, 1969, 180 p.
Critical essays and poetical tributes by W. B. Yeats, André Gide, Alfred Douglas, John Betjeman, Thomas Mann, and Jorge Luis Borges, among others.

Ervine, St. John. *Oscar Wilde: A Present Time Appraisal*. London: George Allen & Unwin, 1951, 336 p.
Lengthy speculation on the origins of Wilde's psychological makeup using various theories of environment and heredity.

Harris, Frank. *Oscar Wilde: His Life and Confessions*. 2 Vols. New York: Privately printed: 1918, 612 p.
Biography commonly regarded as inaccurate and sensationalistic. An appendix includes a letter to Harris from Bernard Shaw on his memories of Wilde.

James, Henry. *The Letters of Henry James, Vol. I*. Edited by Percy Lubbock. New York: Charles Scribner's Sons, 1920, 434 p.*
Contains a letter to William James, dated 2 February 1895, in which the author comments in passing that *An Ideal Husband* seemed to him "so helpless, so crude, so bad, so clumsy, feeble and vulgar."

Mason, Stuart. *Oscar Wilde: Art and Morality: A Record of the Discussion Which Followed the Publication of "Dorian Gray."* 1907. Reprint. New York: Haskell House Publishers, 1971, 325 p.
Reprints numerous letters and reviews from English periodicals.

Orwell, George. "Review: *The Soul of Man under Socialism* by Oscar Wilde." In his *In Front of Your Nose: 1945-1950*, edited by Sonia Orwell and Ian Angus, pp. 226-28. The Collected Essays, Journalism and Letters of George Orwell, Vol. IV. London: Secker & Warburg, 1968.
Examines Wilde's optimistic prophecies for socialism in light of its subsequent failures in practice. Orwell concludes, however, that these prophecies may still be fulfilled.

Saltus, Edgar. *Oscar Wilde: An Idler's Impression*. 1917. Reprint. New York: AMS Press, 1968, 26 p.
Recollects several meetings with Wilde and comments that he was a "third rate poet" and that his prose "is rather sloppy." Saltus is the leading representative of the American decadent school in the late nineteenth century.

"Literature: 'De Profundis'." *The Times Literary Supplement*, No. 163 (24 February 1905): 64-5.
Early example of the prevalent critical opinion that Wilde's testament of his suffering in prison is artificial, affected, and "a triumph of the literary temperament over the most disadvantageous conditions."

Winwar, Frances. *Oscar Wilde and the Yellow 'Nineties*. Garden City, N.Y.: Blue Ribbon Books, 1940, 381 p.
Popular biography.

Woodcock, George. *The Paradox of Oscar Wilde*. London, New York: T. V. Boardman & Co., 1949, 239 p.
Devoted to resolving the contradictions of Wilde the man and the artist. Woodcock attempts an integrated view of Wilde as both serious thinker and superficial poseur, Christian and pagan, etc.

Stanisław Ignacy Witkiewicz

1885-1939

(Also wrote under pseudonym of Witkacy) Polish dramatist, novelist, philosopher, essayist, and critic.

Since the late 1950s, when artistic restraints were relaxed in communist Poland, the works of Witkiewicz have received increasing attention as literary documents revealing one of the most radical modernists of pre-World War II Europe. Witkiewicz's dramas, novels, and theoretical writings develop to their utmost limits a number of typically modern preoccupations: the nihilistic vision of a universe vacant of moral or religious absolutes, alienation as a routine fact of human existence, the decline of the individual in future societies, and the primacy of artistic form over general ideas in literature. Living in an era that cultivated an awareness of its own decadence and disorder, Witkiewicz viewed chaos, social antagonism, and a permanent state of strangeness as life's universal norms. In such works as *Tumor Mózgowicz (Tumor Brainiowicz)*, *Wariat i zakonnica (The Madman and the Nun)*, and *Nienasycenie (Insatiability)* the author presents a doctrine of pessimism which is opposed only by the frantic celebration of artistic creativity and a desperate sense of humor.

Witkiewicz took the pseudonym "Witkacy" to avoid confusion with his father, a prominent Polish author and artist who named his son after himself. The senior Witkiewicz wanted his son to realize his highest intellectual and creative potential, independent of public school conformism and mediocrity. The young Witkiewicz was therefore privately tutored, and demonstrated precocious ability in science, philosophy, art, and literature. He wrote his first play, *Karaluchy*, when he was eight years old, and by his teenage years was, like his father, an accomplished painter and a serious student of ideas. It was as a painter that Witkiewicz first adopted the tenets of strict formalism which he later incorporated into his dramas and critical writings.

Though Witkiewicz's devotion to a purist aesthetic suggests a preference for artistic rather than worldly encounters, his experiences were unusually wide-ranging. As a young man he underwent the relatively new procedure of psychoanalysis, which he later ridiculed in *The Madman and the Nun*. He also experimented extensively with mind-altering drugs, though in *Nikotyna, alkohol, kokaina, peyotl, morfina, eter* he repudiated their claims to enhance one's philosophic and artistic faculties. Working constantly to extend his cultural as well as intellectual background, Witkiewicz became fluent in several languages and acquired a cosmopolitan's familiarity with the capitals of Europe. With anthropologist Bronisław Malinowski he visited Australia, initiating the lifelong interest in non-Western and primitive cultures evidenced in *Tumor Brainiowicz, Insatiability,* and other works. During the time he lived in Russia he was an officer in the Czar's army, and after the revolution was elected political commissar by the victorious communists. In the final years of his life Witkiewicz suffered from serious physical ailments, and on the eve of the Nazi takeover of Poland he committed suicide rather than face the progress of his declining health.

In the opinion of many critics, Witkiewicz's works foretell a number of modern literary movements—including surrealism,

Antonin Artaud's Theater of Cruelty, and the Theater of the Absurd—which commonly traffic in violence, perversity, and confusion. A character in *Sonata Belzebuba (The Beelzebub Sonata)* describes his era, circa 1925, as "an epoch of artistic perversity" and adds that "*up to now* there was no greatness in that dimension." It was in this dimension that Witkiewicz set his dramatic works, and he declared two major reasons for his bizarre style and subjects: first, to revive in modern audiences a primitive sense of mystery and strangeness by presenting them with a world subversive and unfamiliar to the conventions of realistic theater; second, to create dramas whose artistic form would not be obscured by the playwright's attempts to recreate everyday life on stage.

Witkiewicz believed that true religious feeling had all but faded from modern civilization and that art was the only means by which it could be restored. Humankind had long suffered the anxieties of its sense of mystery, and there were few left who would "look the mystery straight in the eye" without the urgings of art. "Artistic creation," he wrote in *Nowe formy w malarstwie i wynikające stąd nieporozumienia (New Forms in Painting and the Misunderstandings Arising Therefrom)*, "is an affirmation of Existence in its metaphysical horror, and not a justification of this horror through the creation of a system of soothing concepts, as is the case with religion." For Witkiewicz, pure form in art—a creative display of the artist's aesthetic instinct—was the last truly human value remaining to a decayed humanity; it is "an act of despair against life which is becoming grayer and grayer," and he concludes that "art is the sole value of our times." In a time when critics often seek predecessors for the themes of absurdity and loss of order in the literature of the late twentieth century, Witkiewicz has been acclaimed as a major rediscovery.

PRINCIPAL WORKS

Nowe formy w malarstwie i wynikające stąd nieporozumienia   (criticism)   1919
  [*New Forms in Painting and the Misunderstandings Arising Therefrom* [partial translation] published in *Beelzebub Sonata: Plays, Essays, and Documents,* 1980]
Pragmatyści   (drama)   1921
  [*The Pragmatists* published in *Tropical Madness,* 1972]
Tumor Mózgowicz   (drama)   1921
  [*Tumor Brainiowicz* published in *Beelzebub Sonata: Plays, Essays, and Documents,* 1980]
Kurka wodna   (drama)   1922
  [*The Water Hen* published in *Tropical Madness,* 1972]
Teatr. Wstęp do teorii czystej formy w teatrze   (criticism)   1923
Mr. Price   (drama)   1926
  [*Mr. Price* published in *Tropical Madness,* 1972]
Nowe wyzwolenie   (drama)   1926
  [*The New Deliverance* published in journal *The Polish Review,* 1973]
Wariat i zakonnica   (drama)   1926
  [*The Madman and the Nun* published in *The Madman and the Nun, and Other Plays,* 1968]
Pożegnanie jesieni   (novel)   1927
Metafizyka dwugłowego dielecia   (drama)   1928
  [*Metaphysics of a Two-Headed Calf* published in *Tropical Madness,* 1972]
Nienasycenie   (novel)   1930
  [*Insatiability,* 1975]
Nikotyna, alkohol, kokaina, peyotl, morfina, eter   (essay)   1932
Mątwa   (drama)   1933
  [*The Cuttlefish* published in *A Treasury of the Theatre,* 1970]
Pojęcia i twierdzenia implikowane przez pojęcie istnienia   (philosophy)   1935
Szewcy   (drama)   1957
  [*The Shoemakers* published in *The Madman and the Nun, and Other Plays,* 1968]
Nadobnisie i koczkodany [first publication]   (drama)   1962
  [*Dainty Shapes and Hairy Apes* published in *Beelzebub Sonata: Plays, Essays, and Documents,* 1980]
Matka   (drama)   1964
  [*The Mother* published in *The Madman and the Nun, and Other Plays,* 1968]
Szalona lokomotywa   (drama)   1964
  [*The Crazy Locomotive* published in *The Madman and the Nun, and Other Plays,* 1968]
Oni   (drama)   1965
  [*They* published in *The Madman and The Nun, and Other Plays,* 1968]
Gyubal Wahazar   (drama)   1966
  [*Gyubal Wahazar* published in *Tropical Madness,* 1972]

Sonata Belzebuba   (drama)   1966
  [*The Beelzebub Sonata* published in *Beelzebub Sonata: Plays, Essays, and Documents,* 1980]
The Madman and the Nun, and Other Plays   (dramas)   1968
622 upadki Bunga   (novel)   1972
Tropical Madness   (dramas)   1972
Beelzebub Sonata: Plays, Essays, Documents   (dramas, essays, and criticism)   1980

STANISLAW IGNACY WITKIEWICZ   (essay date 1921)

I do not intend to say anything new, only to give a general outline of the so-called theory of Pure Form. People have accused me of being long-winded and obscure on this subject; so now I wish to condense myself as far as possible and simultaneously treat the matter with a maximum of informality lest there be implied that some special knowledge is needed to understand the idea presented here. (pp. 41-2)

I will state the basic problem as follows: how do we distinguish a work of art from other objects and phenomena? I introduce this last distinction because certain works of art exist in time, for example, musical works, poems, and theatrical plays; others exist in space, like sculpture and painting. The first I call phenomena; the second, objects. In real life, we have both types of essences. (p. 44)

Without having made any assumption as our point of departure, we shall be unable, theoretically, to separate art from other phenomena. The most we shall be able to say is that all phenomena have form and content, and we shall define art like any other phenomenon, as a certain content in a certain form and, when writing about art, we shall analyze the real-life content enclosed in it—which art and theater critics do mostly, less so critics of poetry, and least of all music critics, since, as I have observed, the feelings expressed in music are difficult to express in general. . . . Without a fundamental assumption, all additional assumptions—for example, that art is the expression of the human soul, that it is the desire to please, the imposition of one's own feelings and thoughts on others, even the saying that it is Beauty—turn out to be unsatisfactory. A great many other essences are the expression of human soul, but are not art. Thoughts and feelings we also impose in completely unartistic ways and likewise endeavor to please by means having nothing to do with art. Even an undifferentiated concept of Beauty does not apply, nor does the additional definition that art must be the creation of man. . . . If we adequately differentiate the concept of Beauty, it may appear suitable at first, but then it must be replaced by concepts that are more precise. (p. 49)

Since the single, undifferentiated concept of Beauty appears to be unsuitable, we must accept a primary assumption that the essence of art is form. The concept of Beauty can be broken down, then, into concepts of Practical Beauty, connected with the usefulness of an object or phenomenon, and Formal Beauty, which consists in order alone, in form, or in the structuralization of an object or phenomenon. This will be beauty in the precise artistic sense. It should be noted that there can be objects which possess both kinds of Beauty; correspondingly, we shall have practical likes and formal likes. (p. 50)

Form is that which imparts a certain unity to complex objects and phenomena.

And what I call aesthetic satisfaction, in contrast to other, purely practical pleasures, is precisely the apprehension of that unity, an apprehension that is immediate, not run through any intellectual calculations. I can put it in another way as the integration of a multiplicity of elements into one whole. Having thus defined Artistic Beauty, we can now designate . . . the places from which we can start reckoning works of art. They will be wherever form begins to predominate over content in our experiencing of the objects and phenomena in those places and wherever the unifying of the many into the one comes about, without any subordinate considerations, solely within a purely formal construct of these objects and phenomena, which directly affects us. Such a form, which acts through itself alone and evokes aesthetic satisfaction, I call Pure Form. It is not, however, a form deprived of content, because no living creature can create such a thing; but it is one in which real-life components are secondary. In the abstract, we can view every object and every phenomenon from the standpoint of its form. Here though, we are concerned not with the abstract but with direct experience; and only form that is felt, that acts directly upon us, do I call Pure Form. (pp. 50-1)

Since all that exists, and therefore, we ourselves, both psychologically and physically, along with objects and large complexes of phenomena in nature—since all things have this fundamental characteristic, that they form to a greater or lesser degree a certain whole and a unity and are made up of parts joined together in that whole—in other words, they are a unity in multiplicity, or vice versa—I consider this law the basic law of existence. For this reason, I assert that art always expresses one and the same thing: that law. And it is expressed in an immediate way, not subject to any subordinate considerations, either biological, practical, or intellectual. This feeling of unity in multiplicity is given to us directly in the form of the unity of our personality, our "I," and for this reason, I call art an expression of the unity of personality. Since this feeling is basic, I have called it a metaphysical feeling in contrast to other feelings, and due to this, many misunderstandings have arisen between myself and my opponents. . . .

Generally, then, we can define a work of art as a construct of arbitrary elements, both simple and mixed, created by an individual as the expression of the unity of his personality, that acts on us in an immediate way by reason of its very structuring. (p. 54)

> *Stanisław Ignacy Witkiewicz, "'On Pure Form',"*
> *translated by Catherine S. Leach (originally pub-*
> *lished as "O czystej formie," in* Zet, *1921), in* Aes-
> thetics in Twentieth-Century Poland: Selected Es-
> says, *edited by Jean G. Harrell and Alina Wierzbiańska*
> *(©1973 by Associated University Presses, Inc.),*
> *Bucknell University Press, 1973, pp. 41-65.*

ZBIGNIEW A. GRABOWSKI   (essay date 1967)

[S. I. Witkiewicz is] in my humble opinion one of the few authentic geniuses Polish literature has produced in our century. (p. 39)

[Witkiewicz's] plays were more or less dramatized philosophical treatises, extended dialogues on abstract subjects, with crude jokes or *jeux des mots* lavishly interspersed. He did not care for plots or conventional "action": his plots were fantastic, illogical; his characters were half-real, half-people, half-

ghosts; the plays were set in a twilight of reality and nightmare. Some of these plays, like *The Lunatic and the Nun,* read today like Ionesco *avant la lettre*. The Apocalypse of mankind lost at the great crossroads, unable to grasp the "nonsense of existence," babbling some inept lies to cover the unpalatable truth that life is "a tale told by an idiot." This Apocalypse is always at the back of Witkiewicz's mind. The voice which comes through that welter of strange phrases is one of vigour and despair mingled together. He wants to destroy all the cozy pretenses of our life. He wants to tear away all the masks which clutter up our view of the truth, and this monomaniac work is done with furious energy. But what is the truth? It is more depressing than the void of Kierkegaard or the *Angst* of Sartre's existentialism, which Witkiewicz anticipated in many of his writings, more penetrating than Heidegger's and Jaspers' restrained lamentations. Life has absolutely no sense and the only way out of it, the only rational protest against this mad galloping towards disaster, is suicide. This gospel of the basic nonsense of our existence is preached by Witkiewicz with a penetrating, daemoniacal force. (p. 43)

Yet those uncanny plays—and the same adjective applies to his portraits, essays and even to his absurd novels, somehow do not come off. They lack mental coherence and discipline; they are chaotic outpourings deprived of a sense of direction. Too often they disintegrate into verbosity, into a whirlwind of *calembours*. . . . It is as if the author had himself been caught in a *maelstroem* of forced hilarity *à tout prix,* of crude jokes, of verbal fireworks, with the result that the plays, intended as serious studies in a new drama and style of production, break down under the weight of carelessly piled up words. Witkiewicz shows himself his own undoer in his world of the arts. His plays misfire as a consequence of his disdain for construction. They are mines of wonderfully bold ideas, of new conceptions; they could have heralded a new era in the theatre only recently opened by Ionesco and Beckett. But in his mental cohesion, in his sense of direction, he is inferior to both Ionesco and Beckett. He does not know the great virtue of the *Beschränkung* Goethe once advised for achieving mastery, and by giving too much rein to fantasy and verbal lust he destroyed what might have been one of the finest attempts in modern drama to construct a new dimension in theatre.

The urge of self-destruction had proved in Witkiewicz more powerful than the instinct of creation. His plays and novels seem to confirm the truth that an artist must believe in his medium: if he pushes a joke too far, if he wants to demonstrate that the medium is not worth while, and that he is merely pulling our legs, the whole purpose of his creation turns into a pitiful parody. We are left with the depressing feeling that he has been wasting our time. The persiflage and the *badinage* must not exceed some mysteriously prescribed limits. "On ne badine pas avec l'amour" warned Alfred de Musset: but one also cannot play with art. It exacts a cruel revenge not only on the audience but first on the artist himself. There is an element which taints the whole production of Witkiewicz— this adolescent joke-making, these protracted jests. And eventually the laugh is on the writer himself, as he stands before us pathetic and frightened by the genie evoked by his own literary folly.

This impulse of self-destruction emerges in Witkiewicz's novels too, though here the tendency is more legitimate and rational, for he is out to destroy the traditional framework of the novel. . . . He starts his *récit* in a conventional way, obviously enjoying the game, inventing ridiculous names and situations in the Rabelaisian manner and emulating Henry Miller in the audacity of his sexual revelations and suddenly, by inserting footnotes which attack his own trend of thought, and make fun of his artistic efforts. He declares that the game is up and that this is all humbug. The novel is not a serious medium for recording people's thoughts and reactions. Brilliant ideas and ingenious situations are wasted in a wild profusion of words and dashing phrases and the reader is left with the feeling that he has been taken for a ride by the author and duped into the bargain. Both of Witkiewicz's novels [*Nienasycenie* (*Unsatiety*) and *Pozegnanie jesieni* (*Farewell to Autumn*)] are astonishing in their arrogance towards the accepted shape of the novel, and are in a way unfinished symphonies. He tired of his own sadistic exploits, and did not carry his joking to the bitter end. Both his novels are too diffused: they lack mental discipline. In my opinion, however, they are more powerful dynamite than his plays. (pp. 45-7)

All his life Witkiewicz lived cheek by jowl with despair: too early he decoded the message of life—of "the indifferent statute,"— and this in a way silenced the call to create. All his works, pictorial or literary, were a struggle with this corroding despair, were so many attempts to cover up the unbearable sights of Existence. He regarded himself as an initiate, but the truth he discovered was too horrible to be communicated. From his contemplations of the truth he had discovered, he brought the message of the uselessness of all human endeavor, of the suicide of philosophy and the dissolution of art. Thus he had no *point d'appui:* he could not find compensation in his work as an artist; he could not forget himself, because he did not believe in art's gospel. Philosophy was in all likelihood the only domain which gave the relief in which his restless mind could feel at ease. But philosophy was his "last station" and he came to it too late, when his mind and imagination had been eaten up by despair. He was his own worst enemy: through his lack of self-control he either dissipated his many talents or unnecessarily cheapened them. A curious streak of masochism can be traced in this tragic genius, and a fully developed sense of self-destruction. He was a maximalist, if one can be permitted to use such a description: a man who wanted the whole hog, who yearned for the Absolute and who could not be satisfied with any compromise with life, knowledge and truth. In this attitude of mind he reminds one of some of the Russian writers and philosophers, addicts to the Absolute. All that did not reach the level of his Absolute he treated with disdain: he "could not get used to life," as the great Polish poet Słowacki declared 130 years ago. And for this reason,—because life cannot be lived freely, in the way of a Nietzschean *Übermensch* we are all slaves to social conventions, because we cannot realize fully our potentialities, and because we have lost that metaphysical sense of "awe and amazement" in front of the gaping chasm of life, he hated life and all it represented. (pp. 48-9)

Zbigniew A. Grabowski, "S. I. Witkiewicz: A Polish Prophet of Doom," in The Polish Review *(© copyright 1967 by the Polish Institute of Arts and Sciences in America, Inc.), Vol. XII, No. 1, Winter, 1967, pp. 39-49.*

JAN KOTT   (essay date 1968)

As a precursor of the Theater of the Absurd, Witkacy was the most eminent playwright in Poland and one of the most interesting in Europe. But he was also—and this may be most astonishing—one of the most original precursors of what might be called the intellectual and artistic climate of the sixties, of its style of life and of thinking. And not only in Europe, but in America as well. Witkacy, who came too early, seemed to his contemporaries to be a man who came too late. It would be worth while to devote some attention to this very phenomenon of the precursor who swerves away from his time or, to be more precise, to the problem of the dialectic of anachronism and innovation. (pp. v-vi)

[Even] a very superficial analysis of Witkacy's *The Mother* and *The Water Hen* reveals that their author continues the destruction of naturalistic theater exactly from the point where Strindberg stopped. The same was true for Artaud. In both Artaud's and Witkiewicz' plays, even before the body of a character who has died has time to cool down, he stands up and walks.

There is a long theatrical history behind characters who, after their death, come back on stage in order to haunt living people or to give them moral lessons; this should become the subject of a separate book. The dead come back on stage both in Shakespeare and in Elizabethan drama, both in Romantic and in modern drama. The dead come back either as ghosts or as hallucinations. The ghost is a metaphysical premise; the hallucination is a psychological situation. But both imply, in the properly theatrical sense, that the ghost or hallucination can be seen only by some of the characters on the stage, that it behaves in a different way from the "living" characters, it speaks differently, it moves differently, it often wears the costume of a ghost or hallucination, and if it does not have a costume, then it still must have some special traits or marks. The theatrical tradition of the behavior of ghosts was probably undermined for the first time by Strindberg. . . . The metaphysical premise of these apparitions is ambiguous in Strindberg's play; maybe they are ghosts, maybe only hallucinations. From the theatrical point of view, however, they no longer have otherworldly attributes.

But it is only in the plays with "corpses" of Artaud and Witkiewicz that the dead characters come back on stage in an ordinary manner. In *The Water Hen* the heroine who is shot in the first act comes back in the second act as if nothing had happened. In the third act, she is shot once again, but this time definitively. In *The Mother,* old Mrs. Eely dies in the second act. In the third act she lies in state, but this does not hinder her from appearing simultaneously as a person thirty years younger and, moreover, pregnant, expecting the birth of the hero of the play. The "first" Mother who is lying in state turns out to be a dummy. In *The Madman and the Nun* the corpse of a murdered psychiatrist, which has been removed by hospital attendants, comes back after a while, smiling, with the murderer who had hanged himself in the previous scene. His corpse is still on stage and is, of course, a dummy. The same thing happens in Artaud's pantomime *The Philosopher's Stone,* where Harlequin, who has been cut in pieces a moment ago by the jealous Doctor, jumps up from the operating table and immediately has sexual intercourse with the Doctor's wife, Isabella. After a while a baby is shaken out from his skirt who resembles the doctor as closely as two peas in a pod. The Harlequin who was tortured on the operating table was, of course, a dummy. The resemblance between Artaud's and Witkiewicz' plays using corpses is all the more surprising since Artaud could in no way have known Witkacy's plays. This theatricalization of corpses is very important in the history of the contemporary, avant-garde theater; the centuries-old convention of portraying the return of the dead in European theater was completely broken. (pp. xi-xii)

Witkacy's Theater of Pure Form and Antonin Artaud's Theater of Cruelty were to serve as the last places where metaphysical experiences which had been banished from philosophy and had become dead in religion could be expressed. Artaud wrote: "In our present state of degeneration it is through the skin that metaphysics must be made to re-enter our minds." But Witkacy would have said: only through the perversion of form.

It may be most significant that in both Witkiewicz and Artaud we find the same infernal fusion, the same explosive combination of two notions, or rather of two visions, of the theater. One of them is the theater of ritual and liturgy, the theater of metaphysical transports, the theater in which—as Witkacy thought—the "Mystery of Existence" will shake even the unbelievers. Or, as Artaud wrote, which "will restore to all of us the natural and magic equivalent of the dogmas in which we no longer believe." The other is the theater of violent physical action, the theater in which gestures, words, movements, and objects are not only a system of signs, but have their own pure theatrical value, just like a hieroglyph or Chinese ideogram which not only has a meaning but is an image as well.

In fact, these are two entirely different notions of theater, although both in Artaud and in Witkiewicz they are tightly interlaced like two fibers in one cord. From the perspective of another twenty-five years, it becomes clear that one of these visions of theater was an illusion. The magic counterpart of dogmas does not exist once you cease to believe in them. Ritual and liturgy in theater are either provocation or profanation of ritual and liturgy. (p. xiv)

In the real theater created by Witkiewicz, there are no metaphysical transports, nor is there any mystery of existence. And perhaps that is the reason why this theater became understood so late. Witkiewicz' theater is sometimes bitter, but always scoffing. The unquestionable greatness of this theater consists in its historical perspective, in the perception of the end of contemporary civilization which was fatally threatened both by the egalitarian revolution coming from the East and by Western mechanization. This mechanization not only produces a society of automatons, but also impels the automatons to direct even those who had invented them. Witkacy's catastrophism only apparently belongs to the nineteenth century. In fact, it was the perspicacious and appalling vision of an inevitable clash between the civilization of computers and the levelers' revolution. For Witkacy the nineteenth century ended once and for all in 1917. In this perspective, all that followed was grim and grotesque. . . . Until the outbreak of the Second World War, Witkacy was understood only by a few—maybe, because we were all still *before,* while he was already *after.* (p. xv)

> *Jan Kott, "Foreword," translated by Bogdana Carpenter (copyright © 1968 by Jan Kott), in* The Madman and the Nun and Other Plays *by Stanislaw Ignacy Witkiewicz, edited and translated by Daniel C. Gerould and C. S. Durer, University of Washington Press, 1968, pp. v-xv.*

ADAM TARN   (essay date 1969)

Before Witkacy turned to the theatre, he was a painter and a theoretician of the Polish school of abstract painting called "Formism," and his theories of theatre were formulated in accord with many of the principles of this school. However, this is not to say that scenery or scene design were, for Witkacy, the salvation of the theatre. He passionately opposed the pre-

dominance of any one element in the theatre—text, music, scenery, or the craft of acting. For Witkacy the theatre must unify all these diverse elements; like any true work of art, a theatre piece should be a "unity within diversity," and this principle became the basic tenet of Witkacy's aesthetics and philosophy. "Unity within diversity" prescribes that each work of art should be structured according to its own logic and ruled by its own inherent laws—it should exhibit Pure Form. The actions, the characters and their psychology, the performances of the actors, the opinions of the protagonists, the plot situations—all these should be regarded as the formal elements of the theatre, just as the colors, the lines, and the composition of forms are the formal elements of painting. The theatre, or more specifically the drama—for we may now begin to speak of dramatic literature—has its own rights of deformation or transformation. The drama may deform "real-life" experience; the drama may freely transform the world, giving its heroes a fantastic psychology and leading them into actions which oppose the healthy common-sense of everyday life.

But Witkacy did not advocate nonsense merely for its own sake; his theatre is far removed from the experiments in automatic writing and from the excesses of the Dadaists, although superficially his technique appears similar. What happens on the stage in Witkacy's plays is often illogical, and the plays are often shockingly abstruse. In *The Water Hen* a woman is shot by her lover in the first act, seduces her son who is not her son in the second act, is killed in the third act, and would doubtless have been reincarnated several times if the play had more acts than three; in *The Madman and the Nun,* the hero walks nonchalantly with his lover, the nun, although he has just hanged himself and his body still hangs over the stage. But weirdness and absurdity are subordinated to an exact logic of form, the logic of the artistic "coming into being." Just as the colors and forms of a nonobjective painting acquire a meaning and pertinence within the closed, logical context of the work itself, so do the grotesqueries of Witkacy's plays seem logical and necessary within their individual contexts.

Today it may sound rather quaint to justify Witkacy's work by comparing it with nonobjective painting, but we must remember that he wrote most of his plays and formulated his aesthetic theories during the nineteen-twenties, before the world had yet recognized the significance of even Picasso's work. The chief novelty of Witkacy's theory for his own era was this translation of an advanced theory of abstract painting into a workable theory and practice for the stage. Witkacy realized fully the implications of this transformation of theory, and he extended the implications to extreme ends. His defense of an autonomous theatre form, dependent for its shape and content upon no outside forms, is still pertinent today. . . . (pp. 162-63)

As a theorist, Witkacy might be called a theatrical abstractionist. But in practice, as a playwright, he is more like the surrealists. Yet, even behind his theory and his practice, he has concealed a deeper conception, a specific metaphysic. The Pure Form—this closed, logical, artistic structure—must shock the audience metaphysically and thereby arouse in them the sensual and intellectual awareness of what he calls "the mystery of existence."

What is the significance of this "mystery of existence" in Witkacy's philosophy and artistic theory? As the phrase suggests, the term stands for questions to which there are no discernible answers other than wonderment. Witkacy's terminology suggests the metaphysical astonishment man feels before the simple fact of his existence. This fact has many astonishing facets: there is the wonder of man's existence in time and space, his singularity, the unique and unrepeatable phenomenon of his single existence within a larger, manifold Existence. Man's wonder at his singularity is reinforced by his wonder at his multiplicity as child, adult, and octogenarian; as son, husband, and father. Added to this is the wonder of man's diverse ''reflected'' existence in the minds and feelings of other men; and finally there is the simple astonishment man feels at the unity within the diversity of his interests, the unity within the contradictions of his emotions, and the unity within the variety of his activities. (pp. 163-64)

Witkacy's most important question for the contemporary theatre is stated thus: is it possible today, in the face of life's increasing mechanization and the corresponding decline of metaphysics, to originate, even if only for a short time, a form of theatre in which contemporary man, independent of lost myths and beliefs, could experience the same metaphysical feelings that men once experienced when these myths and beliefs were operative?

Witkacy's answer is affirmative: yes, it is possible in a theatre of Pure Form, or at least in a theatre which strives toward the Pure Form—a form which, because of its complexity, may never be attained. It is possible in a theatre which stimulates metaphysical response, provided it is based upon fantastic psychology and fantastic action—in a theatre which is structured simply and completely in accord with artistic logic. Such a theatre must, first, astonish that it exists at all; the shock and the violent, expressive emotions which it calls forth must impress upon the audience the strangeness, the peculiarity of all existence. Such theatre performances are like sinister, uncanny dreams in which ordinary everyday objects possess immeasurable scope and unfathomable meanings; one leaves such a performance permeated with the spirit of a primitive theatrical festival, a spirit which has largely been lost in modern theatre. This is the spirit of theatrical celebration in which religion, philosophy, and art form a unity.

And yet, Witkacy complains, the metaphysical instinct is so enfeebled in modern man, so buried beneath the thick, insensitive skin of modern life, that metaphysical shock can no longer be achieved with simple means of sublimity and harmony. Present-day man's sensitivities are dull and resistant; they must be overcome with force. Therefore, in these latter days, art must use drastic means: the grotesque, the absurd, and the shock tactics of dissonance. We require a theatre beyond the life-like laughing and crying of traditional comedy and tragedy. We must unchain perverse forms in order to free the theatre of cruelty and purity, a theatre devoid of the lies about the ''facts of life.'' The theatre of perverse form offers bizarre, comic, lofty, and dreadful objects in unlikely juxtapositions which disturb the spectator in his innermost being. Once more, before the final metamorphosis of mankind into a civilized, spiritless ant heap, the theatre must provoke an explosion of metaphysical emotions. Once more, before man sinks into the final lifelessness of materialism and technology, ''One must wake the slumbering beast, and watch what it can do. If it goes crazy, there will be time enough to shoot it down.''

Witkacy was a believer in catastrophe. He regarded the decline and disappearance of metaphysical consciousness as an unavoidable historical necessity. But before philosophy and art—which, according to Witkacy, are the expressions of metaphysical consciousness—are lost, they must be pushed to the extreme limits of their potential. Witkacy postulated no more

than a beautiful and logical ''endgame'': the dissolution of metaphysical consciousness is the dissolution of art. And yet, while painting and music, which operate according to their own simple means of expression, are already somewhat disengaged and approach the extreme limits of their potential, becoming more and more Pure Form, the situation in the theatre is desperate. The theatre is not a pure art: it operates with words, with actions, with characters and their psychology, with roles created by living actors, with three-dimensional space and movement, with music and scenic art. Compared with painting and music, the theatre is a complex art; it is a network of interdependent elements, and for this reason it is more difficult for the theatre to attain Pure Form. But the theatre can also, to a certain extent, become a free and disengaged art, and if it does not achieve Pure Form in the strict sense of the term, it can at least strive toward that goal. In this striving, according to Witkacy, the theatre has its last change. (pp. 164-65)

Adam Tarn, ''Witkiewicz, Artaud, and the Theatre of Cruelty,'' translated by Philip McCoy, Diane Hickey, and Sonja Huber (originally published in an altered version under a different title in Neue Zürcher Zeitung, *1966; translation © copyright 1969, by the Editors of* Comparative Drama; *reprinted with permission of Dr. Hansres Jacobi), in* Comparative Drama, *Vol. III, No. 1, Spring, 1969, pp. 162-67.**

JERZY R. KRZYZANOWSKI   (essay date 1969)

Witkiewicz's remarkable dramatic art is only partially literary; he himself insisted that ''the literary side of a performance is only a small part of the play being created on stage, where the author supplies only a *formal skeleton* for the creative work of the director and actors.'' Yet, as a creator of the ''formal skeleton[s]'' of his plays, Witkacy was inventive in the extreme. His imagination went beyond the surface of reality to sketch forth the grotesque with incredible vitality. He combines pathos with vulgarity, urbanity with colloquialism. The names of the characters in the plays are illustrative of his literary method in ways which have not always been noted by critics. (pp. 193-94)

The name of each character in the plays thus tells the audience what to expect of him. (p. 194)

Witkacy's *dramatis personae* are capable of division into three groups: those having Polish names, those with names of foreign and pseudo-foreign origin, and those with names representing pure neologisms. A quick glance at each group reveals some typical features of Witkiewicz's style and artistic method.

I. *Polish names.* **''Tumor Brainard [*Tumor Mozgowicz*],''** wrote Witkiewicz in his introduction to that play, ''was conceived, as is obvious from the very title of the drama, from a tumor on the brain.'' This is perhaps the most fundamental example of how the dramatist invented a Polish name for a character. He took a non-existent first name, then added to it a surname made up of a common noun with an attached *-owicz* ending. This technique thus illustrates the nature of the character and, at the same time, produces a good joke with all its improbability and absurdity. The morphological inventiveness results, then, in an expanded meaning. To the same category belong such names as Papron (dauber), Gegon (gagger), Splendorek (little splendor), Lektorowiczowna (Miss Lecturer), and Jan Maciej Karol Wscieklica (mad man).

Many names also achieve the comic by way of morphological changes. In particular, he utilizes non-existent names formed from common nouns—with attached endings typical of Polish given names. In these cases, the original meaning of the noun is still retained, e.g. Halucyna (hallucination, similar in form to names such as *Halina* and *Lucyna*), Jezory (tongue), Malpigiusz (monkey-man, similar to *Remigiusz*). Similarly, even pseudo-Latin names, once very common in Poland, find their way into the plays with comic effectiveness. In some cases, also, comic effect is achieved by deliberately juxtaposing first names with incompatible last names (Mikolaj Kwibuzda, Dyapanazy Nibek) or by placing them heavily and ludicrously out of balance (Jan Maciej Karol Wscieklica).

II. *Foreign and pseudo-foreign names*. In this category appear an abundance of odd names since Witkacy's plays usually are set in some absurd, cosmopolitan environment—a locale which breaks with the demand for realistic setting and where all nationalities might mingle freely. Furthermore, a majority of these characters are aristocrats, and hence the titles which accompany the names enhance the comic effect. Witkiewicz's imagination reaches into foreign sources without restrictions; there are French, English, Russian, Italian, Hungarian, Rumanian, Greek, and Jewish names as well as many of undefined origin.

Some of these names create comic effects because of their semantic qualities: here belong such inventions as Baron Hibiscus, Satanescu, Mikulini-Pechbauer, Princess Alicja of Nevermore—together with Duchess Irina Vsevolodovna Zbereznicka-Podberezka. Quite often, when pronounced, foreign words or their derivatives sound like certain Polish words. In **The Shoemakers,** for instance, there is a prosecuting attorney, Robert Scurvy, whose name sounds like the Polish expression which means "son of a bitch," a meaning that turns out to be quite appropriate for that character's function in the play. A pseudo-Hungarian name, Szakalyi, is invented on the reverse principle: its Polish spelling suggests an association with *szakal* (jackal). Still another group of these names is based on pure improbability (one can hardly expect to encounter in reality such names as Baron Oskar von den Binden Gnumben or Viscount Wojciech de Malensac de Troufières), though often, as in the case of the first example cited parenthetically here, the sound of the name nevertheless reflects the character's nature—in this case, his dullness. Finally, there are many names which cleverly imitate a foreign origin but which in fact are either pure neologism (Tetrafon Pneumakon, Fibroma de Mijoma) or mocking clichés (José Intriguez de Estrada).

III. *Neologisms*. In this group Witkiewicz's characters find themselves expressed through the phonetics of their names (Krakaton, Tetrykon, Teobald Rio Bamba) or find their exposition by way of imaginary forms (Monoflakon, Klawesyn Bykoblazon). This group, often overlapping with Polish and foreign names, is indicative of Witkacy's linguistic awareness and his artistic ingenuity.

On the whole, an examination of the names in all three categories in Witkacy's plays points toward a preoccupation with sex. In fact, Witkacy's works for theater and his fiction are generally permeated with eroticism manifested in the most sensational scenes, in sexual assaults, in violence, and in perversion. Sometimes Witkacy's names blatantly demonstrate his obsession with sexuality; at other times, he is more cautious. For examples of his method, one might turn to the six "Oriental women"—Yabawa, Wabaya, Bayawa, Wayaba, Yawaba, and Bawaya—in **The Independence of Triangles.** At first glance,

these names seem to be mere wordplay, with three syllables used interchangeably. However, for a reader familiar with a Russian "four-letter" word denoting copulation, those names reveal their true origin and meaning. (pp. 194-96)

Witkiewicz, like the child who is frightened, seeks out the absurdities in the world of supposedly mature adults; hence he is able to show himself a master of an art by which he is able to replace an unsatisfactory reality with his own expressionistic vision. . . .

By baptizing his characters with grotesquely significant names, he clearly expresses his contempt for a world which he found unacceptable. It is the natural gesture of a writer who used the most powerful medium at his disposal—his own language— to express himself as strongly as he could, and to create his own image of reality. (p. 196)

Jerzy R. Krzyzanowski, "Witkiewicz's Anthroponymy," in Comparative Drama *(© copyright 1969, by the Editors of* Comparative Drama*), Vol. III, No. 1, Spring, 1969, pp. 193-97.*

DANIEL GEROULD   (essay date 1971)

[*Gyubal Wahazar; or, On the Mountain Passes of the Absurd*] is often cited as a prime example of Witkiewicz's creation of an absurdist drama long before the fact. I wish to use this play—one of Witkiewicz's unquestioned masterpieces—to support my contention that his differences from the theatre of the absurd are much more important than the similarities and are, in fact, what make him most interesting. Witkiewicz's importance and appeal lie elsewhere. (p. 652)

"There aren't any tortures in Hell. There's only waiting. Hell is one gigantic waiting room," says one of the petitioners in Act I of **Gyubal Wahazar**. These lines are quoted, not only as evidence that Witkiewicz anticipated Sartre's *Huis Clos* and existentialism, but that he forecast [Samuel Beckett's] *Waiting for Godot* and the entire waiting motif in contemporary drama. The parallel, however, is verbal, and really serves to illustrate some fundamental distinctions between Witkiewicz's theatre and the theatre of the absurd. The crucial difference lies in the conception of dramatic action. Whereas the absurdists present an eternal human condition from which action is eliminated, Witkiewicz shows a dynamic world in which events are viewed sequentially, moving faster and faster through time. Institutions, exceptional individuals, and masses of people collide: History is being made.

The crowd of petitioners in **Gyubal Wahazar** talk of having waited for weeks, even months, but the play itself does not portray endless waiting, but sudden happenings. Unlike the non-appearing Godot, Wahazar—the "cruel god" for whom all the characters are waiting—rushes out within the first ten minutes of the action and begins to shout commands, abruptly disposing of the lives and destinies of his subjects.

Waiting in Witkiewicz is one of a handful of essential human activities (along with philosophical speculation, artistic creation, sexual attraction, and physical combat), but it is always a build-up to an explosion. The characters are waiting for something to happen, for an intolerable situation to blow up— and sooner or later it does. Without belief in himself, or in the past or present, the typical Witkacian "hero" longs to begin a "new life"—which most often turns out to be a sinister antiindividualist social order ushered in by a revolution overthrowing the existing political system. Someone or something new comes to power at the end of each play; in Witkiewicz, the *coup d'état* precedes the final curtain. (pp. 652, 654)

What is most characteristic about the world of *Gyubal Wahazar* (and that of all Witkiewicz's plays) is its social and political instability—which is reflected in the central figure whose explosive nature continually causes the action to erupt. Such a world can go in any direction—it veers to the right and to the left, it slows down and speeds up, it stops and starts. As Father Unguenty, High Priest of the perfidious sect of Perpendicularists, puts it, Gyubal himself is the "driving force" behind these events; his expansions and contractions propel the play forward. He has wild bursts of creative energy, then lapses into terrible apathy and inaction. Because of the elasticity of Gyubal's character, his size actually seems to change throughout the play; he grows bigger and smaller as we watch.

Endless flux is the only constant in the artificial sixth-dimensional superstate of the future, where mysticism, biology, politics, religion, diplomacy all exist in a surrealistic mixture. Not only is Wahazar changing all women into either masculettes or mechanical mothers, but also, as a result of his experiments with glands, Dr. Rypmann will soon be able to turn anyone, or anything—even a hyena, jackal, or bedbug—into a Wahazar. Already there is a Wahazar doll for Piggykins to play with, in Albania someone is pretending to be Wahazar, and Father Unguenty will turn into Wahazar II after receiving a transplant of his still warm glands. Before he is killed, Wahazar reaches a state of ecstatic indeterminateness in which he feels that he is everything.

Witkiewicz portrays the ceaseless transformations of the human personality and of whole societies on a grand scale. At about the same time Pirandello explored the question of individual identity in his plays; many of Witkiewicz's heroes are likewise bewildered by a multiplicity of selves. However, loss of identity in Witkiewicz does not remain on a personal, psychological plane; it exists on a mass social and even biological level. Metamorphoses spread throughout society in the form of group hysteria and chronic insanity. (p. 654)

The aim of much modern theatre has been a return to ritual—to the ritual of the Christian church, of Greek drama, of Asian theatre, of primitive tribes—in order to recapture the magic and mythic functions of drama. In the preface to *Tumor Brainard* and in *The Introduction to the Theory of Pure Form in the Theatre* Witkiewicz points out that although drama originally arose from religious rites, since these have long ago died out as living faith the same sense of mystery can now be created only formally. In fact, Witkiewicz creates a new mythic world. Instead of trying to revive dead mythology and ritual from the past, he looks to the future and imagines the social ceremonies, government agencies, and religious and scientific practices for social systems and institutions yet to come. . . .

The satirical and parodistic in Witkiewicz is not based on distortion of bourgeois realistic drama or *reductio ad absurdum* of senseless banalities from everyday life, as in Ionesco's *The Bald Soprano* or Albee's *The American Dream*. In fact, in plays like *Gyubal Wahazar* there is parody of something that does not precisely exist—but may or might. This purely invented quality of the rituals being parodied gives Witkiewicz's surrealistic nightmares of the future a prismatic allusiveness to many different times and places. Parody in Witkiewicz is left open to future fulfillment, and the subjects of his satire are still being created by society. Each country and generation makes its own contribution.

Citizen of a country that did not exist for the first thirty three years of his life and which once again plunged into non-being on the day he committed suicide, firsthand witness of the revolution in Russia as well as of Papuan tribal life in New Guinea, Witkiewicz was able to project in his plays with unusual accuracy the inner feeling of Europe's subsequent historical experiences of chaos, violence, dictatorship, and ideological insanity, precisely because he used such subjective techniques of dream-like distortion which made him appear something of a madman to most of his contemporaries. In Poland now Witkiewicz undoubtedly seems more of a realist. (p. 656)

Daniel Gerould, *"Discovery of Witkiewicz," in* Arts in Society *(copyright, 1971, by the Regents of The University of Wisconsin), Vol. 8, 1971, pp. 652-56.*

MARTIN ESSLIN (essay date 1972)

Stainslaw Ignacy Witkiewicz, whose importance is only now emerging more than thirty years after he died, was not only one of the earliest practitioners of the style and vocabulary of . . . contemporary drama, he was also one of the most clearsighted and lucid exponents of its theory. As a man who straddled several worlds in space as well as in time—the sophistication of Western Europe as well as the feudalism of Eastern Europe and the primitivism and mystery of the Far East; the archaic social life of Tsarist Russia as well as the utopian horror of Bolshevism—Witkiewicz had a unique vantage point; and as a playwright who was also a philosopher and painter he had the breadth of outlook and clarity of vision to diagnose the situation (which others merely sensed instinctively and intuitively) with the maximum of conscious understanding.

Witkiewicz realized that in a scientific age which was unable to provide mankind with a metaphysical explanation of the external world, a mythology which also worked on the practical external plane (thunderstorms explained as the wrath of the gods, for example), the sense of mystery must turn inwards: it is in experiencing the uniqueness of our own self, the problematic nature of our own identity, the hidden depths of our inner life that we are most directly in touch with the metaphysical dimension, the real emotional groundswell of our lives. Witkiewicz's theory of Pure Form derives from these considerations: for him Pure Form was the unfettered expression of the artist's existential experience from within, without the need to copy external appearances. Through Pure Form the sense of unity could be restored to human experience, which is constantly fragmented by the assault of external, objective, independent facts. In drama, where the presence of flesh and blood actors always provides an element of realism, the achievement of such a unified impact is much more difficult. For Witkiewicz the answer to this problem was the abandonment of any attempt to portray life as it *appears* in favor of a series of seemingly arbitrary happenings without benefit of realistic psychological motivations or external verisimilitude. Events should follow each other in a play like chords in a piece of music for no other reason than that they seemed right to the author in that sequence.

The banishment of realistic psychological motivation, on the other hand, does not mean that the psychological dimension itself is gone. On the contrary: an author who no longer has to worry about the motivations of his characters as objectively existing autonomous human beings outside himself will inevitably be projecting the subconscious contents of his own psyche. Witkiewicz's theories, which have much in common with those of the surrealists, result in a theatre of dream images which give a very deep insight into the author's mind as well as establishing, through the archetypes which spring from his depths, a level of communication with his audience which lies far deeper than that which result from realistic drama.

Again and again in Witkiewicz's plays—and [*The Pragmatists; Mr. Price: Or, Tropical Madness; Gyubal Wahazar;* and *Metaphysics of a Two-Headed Calf*] bear this out—the hero is a young man searching for his identity, deeply dissatisfied with life, hating his overpowering mother and yet in love with a younger image of that very same mother, in doubt about the identity of his true father, fascinated by female figures which either are, or could become, masculine (Masculette in *The Pragmatists,* the attempts at masculinization of girls in *Gyubal Wahazar*). And again and again the theme of suicide dominates. But perhaps the most persistent archetypal image is that of the corpse that returns to life: as in dreams where the dead live again those who have been killed reappear, sometimes as ghosts, sometimes as not having been really dead, and sometimes without out rational explanation.

The concentration on an inner, dreamlike reality does not, for an intellectual and thinker like Witkiewicz, exclude the realm of ideas. If these are dreams, they are dreams about highly lucid intellectual conversation; the characters are engaged in heated debate about the ideas of their author: artistic, philosophical, scientific and political. *Gyubal Wahazar,* dating as it does from 1921, is an astonishing piece of political prophecy: it forecasts the character of totalitarian dictators like Hitler, Mussolini and Stalin with deadly accuracy, right down to the curious mixture of madness, delusions of personal grandeur and scientific claptrap (purity of race, scientific Marxism) on which these psychopaths based their claim to absolute power. How can such prophetic power in a literature of dream images be explained? By the fact, I believe, that, as all our external reality ultimately originates from the subconscious motivations of human beings, it is in the world of subconscious fantasies that the springs of future reality lie. There is, of course, much of Witkiewicz himself in the superhuman energy and vitality of Gyubal Wahazar. In projecting his own subconscious fantasies of ruthless power he uncovered the motivations and actions of people who, less intelligent and controlled than he, actually got into situations where they could realize them.

Uniquely individual and original though he is, Witkiewicz also belongs to his national tradition. There has always been a trend toward the dreamlike and fatastic in Polish literature, exemplified, to cite but two great names, by Count Jan Potocki (1761-1815), author of the strange, fantastic novel *The Manuscript of Saragossa,* and by Zygmunt Krasinski (1812-1859) whose *Ungodly Comedy* contains political prophecy of a mechanized totalitarianism very much in tune with some of Witkiewicz's images. (pp. 2-4)

In the wider European and Western context Witkiewicz is now secure of an important place: he takes up and continues the vein of dream and grotesque fantasy exemplified by the late Strindberg or by Wedekind; his ideas are closely paralleled by those of the surrealists and Antonin Artaud which culminated in the masterpieces of the dramatists of the absurd—Beckett, Ionesco, Genet, Arrabal—of the late nineteen forties and the nineteen fifties.

It is high time that this major playwright should become better known in the English-speaking world. (p. 4)

Martin Esslin, "Introduction: The Search for Metaphysical Dimension in Drama" (copyright © 1972 by Winter House Ltd.; reprinted by permission of the author), in Tropical Madness: Four Plays *by Stanisław Ignacy Witkiewicz, translated by Daniel and Eleanor Gerould, Winter House, 1972, pp. 1-4.*

DANIEL GEROULD   (essay date 1974)

[Witkiewicz's childhood plays] offer an unusual instance of children's plays written by a child who later became a major playwright. As such, they provide direct insight into Witkiewicz's development both as a writer and as a personality. . . . [In] their own right, these short plays are charming, lively, and inventive, capable of being successfully staged. . . . (p. 6)

[In] an uncanny way these childhood plays foreshadow many techniques and themes in Witkacy's mature plays, where the "inclination for parody" and "non-serious relationship" of the author to his own creativity are characteristic traits. Anna Micinska who first discovered and published all but two of the extant plays in 1965 points out that the atmosphere of approaching danger and growing fear and panic in the face of an unknown threat—undoubtedly owing something to [Maurice] Maeterlinck—anticipates Witkacy's catastrophism in the 1920's and '30's, but of course without the apocalyptic denouement. Other typical Witkacian devices already discernible in the childhood plays, providing continuity throughout the playwright's entire work, are: accelerating action erupting in sudden violence; unexpected surprising ends; comic use of names, foreign languages, and stage directions; made-up words; offhand dialogue full of non sequitur, deflation, and anti-climax; and the use of himself and his own personal experiences—as well as of his reading—as the material for his dramas. In fact, *The Comedies of Family Life* show the realistic side of Witkacy's dramaturgy and his ability to capture the way people talk in everyday life (friends testify that he was always a master mimic) at the same time that he reveals its absurdity. (p. 9)

Daniel Gerould, "The Playwright As a Child: The Witkiewicz Childhood Plays," in yale/theatre *(copyright © 1974 by* Theatre, *formerly* yale/theatre*), Vol. 5, No. 3, 1974, pp. 6-9.*

BERNARD F. DUKORE   (essay date 1975)

[In the plays of Witkacy] tragic and comic elements reciprocate and interact; at various times, and in the same play, they both coexist and chemically fuse and this union of apparent opposites makes us aware of their opposition as well as their interconnection. (p. 292)

Generic references occasionally dot the Witkacian dramatic landscape. "Can't you see there's been a tragedy in this house?" asks Leon in the second act of *The Mother.* . . . To this question, Lucina Beer responds, "When I appear, tragedy disappears." This dialogue illustrates one of Witkacy's methods of combining tragic and comic. Apart from mocking the notion that the events are tragic, he employs comedy to undercut any potential tragedy that may have been latent in the preceding action. In this instance, in addition to undercutting Leon's anguish, the passage summarizes the preceding action, wherein another character's anguish has been undercut comically. The Mother, suddenly blinded, staggers and sits on the floor, then asks for liquor, and then, fearful that she may go mad, requests chloral hydrate. At this point, enter Lucina Beer, who shrieks her love for Leon, apologizes for the intrusion, resumes her cries of love, and next—without permitting anyone to get in a single word (nor has she since her entrance)—she asks, for she has apparently just noticed the old woman on the floor, "Madam, why are you sitting on the floor?" (pp. 292-93)

[In *The Madman and the Nun*] humor consistently mocks serious references and characters who take themselves seriously. When Sister Anna, unburdening herself to Walpurg, reveals she entered a convent after her fiance, an engineer, killed himself by blowing his brains out, Walpurg, with apparent sympathy, beseeches her not to feel sorry for him, but then adds, "So nowadays even engineers can have problems like that." . . . Nor is Walpurg himself exempt from deflation, since he takes his suffering more seriously than the author may wish us to. Not only does Walpurg puncture Anna's excessive seriousness, he also punctures his own, for instance: "Let's be happy even if it's only for a moment. You're the only woman in the world. Not because you simply happen to be the first woman I've seen for two years, but because you really are." . . . (p. 293)

In these examples, the comic alternates with tragic-tending anguish, loftiness, and seriousness. Elsewhere, they unite. . . . [The first act of *They*] contains a visual emblem of the tragicomic fusion. Although Balandash is beside himself with despair when They destroy his art collection, the Colonel forces him to laugh. A stage direction describes the scene: "*Balandash is laughing like a child who has been forced to laugh while he's crying.*" Such laughter and tearful suffering characterize Witkacian drama. *The New Deliverance* . . . begins with a comic scene that includes physical torture. In the final moments of the play, thugs—using tong, hammer, and blowtorch—torture the comically named Florestan Snakesnout. Though Snakesnout's initial appearance suggests a romantic comedy juvenile (he enters in black jacket, boater, violet-striped shirt and tie, and white flannel slacks, and announces he has come from a tennis game), his physical suffering, far from the stage world of comedy or romance, is very painful.

Illustrating the distinctiveness of Witkacian tragicomedy are two of his subtitles. *The Water Hen* he calls "**A Spherical Tragedy**" and *Dainty Shapes and Hairy Apes,* . . . "**A Comedy with Corpses.**" One does not usually regard tragedies as spherical—a defiance of the Aristotelian canon concerning a complete action with beginning, middle, and end; a defiance, too, of the practice of tragedians, whose works contain such actions. As for corpsed comedies, . . . it is tragedy rather than comedy that one associates with death. Although the corpses of *Dainty Shapes and Hairy Apes* remain properly corpsed, some of the Witkacian dead have lifelike characteristics (*The New Deliverance* contains corpses who snore), others seem oblivious to death-causing actions (in *The Shoemakers*, . . . Sajetan goes right on talking despite a dent in his head made by an axe plus two bullet holes, one in his head, one in his belly), and others return to life in various unusual ways; (Walpurg of *The Madman and the Nun* enters, rejuvenated, while his corpse lies on the floor; the dead body of the title character of *The Mother* is observed by herself thirty years younger). For that matter, *The Water Hen* might be designated "Comedy with Corpses" as well as "Spherical Tragedy." The title character, shot through the heart in the first act, calmly comments on her assailant's marksmanship, takes a good five minutes to die, and then returns in the next act looking as pretty as ever, perhaps more so. Not at all incompatible, Spherical Tragedies and Comedies with Corpses denote different emphases in Witkacian tragicomedy. First, let us examine Spherical Tragedies, whose emphasis is political. (pp. 293-94)

In Witkacy's Spherical Tragedies, in which the political aspect is important, revolution culminates the action, but though it overthrows the older order, it does not essentially change the nature of power, sometimes not even the persons who wield it. (p. 295)

The Anonymous Work, whose title may refer to revolution in general or to communist revolution specifically, follows . . . [this] pattern. Early in the play, Plasmonick voluntarily goes to jail for a fixed term (espionage is the reason) in order to live with a woman he loves; at the end of the play he goes to jail, presumably forever (since murder is the reason), to live with a different woman he now claims to love, but even apart from the duration of his stay, deterioration is revealed within the essential pattern, for he has abandoned his avant-garde notions of art (Pure Form) in favor of the more mundane, old-fashioned type (realism) of his new lady friend. (p. 296)

[In] *The Anonymous Work,* a fascist revolution topples a liberal-democratic-aristocratic government, and then a communist revolution topples the fascist one. Does it matter? (p. 298)

Witkacy's Spherical Tragedies, in which (anticipating Beckett's plays) the essential does not change, reveal what seems to me to be a major and distinguishing characteristic of modern tragicomedy. The traditional order of tragedy is from good fortune to bad, from happiness to unhappiness; that of comedy, the reverse, from bad fortune to good, from unhappiness to happiness. A cardinal characteristic of modern tragicomedy is not that a play end happily or unhappily, or that it end precisely as it began, but rather—apart from revealing an essential absence of change despite some change—that the ending deny the exclusiveness of the type of change associated with either the tragic or the comic ending. If the ending resembles that of tragedy ("unhappy"), there is nevertheless none of the affirmation, redemption, or catharsis (according to any definition of the term) characteristic of tragedy, no stature or heroism, and no revelation of a moral order. If it resembles that of comedy ("happy"), there is an absence of real comfort, a sardonic or grim quality that is almost a mockery of happiness, and a gain that is more ghastly than any death or loss; and as in the untragic quality of the apparently tragic ending, no moral order is revealed.

These characteristics also pertain in Witkacy's Comedies with Corpses, which are likewise tragicomic. Here too, essential qualities do not change. Here too is a denial of the exclusiveness of characteristics associated with the ending of either of the two major genres. Whereas Spherical Tragedies depict the death of a society, which still lives, for either the old scoundrels still live or else the old scoundrelism thrives, as practiced by new scoundrels, Comedies with Corpses depict the death of individuals, who may return. But not necessarily. In a world wherein morality and values break down, wherein the stability of the universe itself is questionable, nothing is absolute, not even death. Death is not necessarily irrevocable. Nor is it necessarily revocable. Contingency dominates. (pp. 298-99)

The nonexclusive or ambiguous nature of the conclusion of Witkacian tragicomedy is particularly vivid in *Dainty Shapes and Hairy Apes,* whose subtitle provides the second half of my title, "**Comedy with Corpses.**" Sex is one of the major motivating forces of this play, whose plot patterns are comic. But the culmination of each pattern is bitter, ironic, and usually involves one or more fatalities. The values associated with romantic comedy are disrupted, turned upside down, or negated. The chief plot pattern is the growth and development of a young boy into manhood. But the growth is perverted as well as normal, homosexual as well as heterosexual, and the results of the boy's experiences are disillusionment and death. (p. 300)

A play with corpses who return to life, **Metaphysics of a Two-Headed Calf** . . . also demonstrates the undercutting of an exclusively comic or tragic resolution. Metaphysics, which deals with what is beyond the physical, includes ontology, the nature of being. Going beyond physical or merely concrete reality, Witkacy's play takes as one of its subjects the nature of existence. It concerns being and the development of the being of sixteen-year old Patricianello, who resembles eighteen-year old Tarquinius in that each grows to manhood. During the course of the play, Patricianello shucks off his parents only to be reclaimed by them. His father and mother grab him, pack the protesting Patricianello in the car, and drive away. But the Hooded Figure *"throws off his brown robe and hood, revealing an incredibly beautiful, elegant young man about town, totally identical to Patricianello."* . . . The calf (that is, the adolescent boy) has, metaphorically, two heads, Patricianello's and the Hooded Figure's, each controlled in the end by a man who claims to be Patricianello's father (who the father really is, is never made clear: in the first act, Mikulini unequivocally states he is, while in the third, Sir Robert just as unequivocally states he himself is). Marking the transformation to an individualized identity, from adolescence to manhood, the Hooded Figure selects his own name, Kala-Azar. This name, an epidemic disease, is significant in that it carries associations of antagonism with the two men who might be Patricianello's father: one, we are led to believe in Act I, is killed by it; the other tries to perfect a serum to destroy it. In the case of one "head," the exclusiveness of a non-comic ending is denied, for though Patricianello is dragged off against his will, his alter ego, the Hooded Figure, remains. In the case of the Hooded Figure, the exclusiveness of a comic ending is also denied, for Sir Robert shoots the girl he loves, pours gin down his throat, and calls him not the name he selected (Kala-Azar) but Murphy. Whether or not this development is an allusion to Ireland's domination by England, the Hooded Figure is indeed dominated by Sir Robert. (p. 301)

Not only do Witkacy's Spherical Tragedies and Comedies with Corpses reveal no moral order, they also express human despair in an absurd universe dominated by contingency. In such a universe, the dead may or may not return. What, then, is existence? "I don't even know whether I actually exist," wonders Edgar (**The Water Hen** . . .), "although the fact that I suffer is certainly real." "Oh! How the very fact of existence torments me," cries Patricianello (**Metaphysics** . . .), who concludes that "life's worth no more than a glass of iced lemonade" and is absurd "in and of itself." . . . (p. 303)

In an absurd universe, in which ignoble man does not matter, his efforts are meaningless and he himself is in frequent danger of being crushed or nonentitized. (pp. 304-05)

I have urged that the crucial characteristic of modern tragicomedy is its denial of the exclusiveness of the order and end associated with either tragedy or comedy. This characteristic holds as well for the protagonists of tragicomedy. Where there is enlightenment, there is no death for the enlightened character, though life itself may be worse than death. Where there is no such enlightenment—for very often characters deceive themselves, refusing to face the truth about themselves and the world—the tragic pattern, which is usually the operative pattern in such an instance, is undercut. Witkacy's so-called tragedies

are spherical and lack of self-knowledge helps avoid the conclusion of a tragic thrust. His comedies are corpsed, for either suffering does not disappear with enlightenment or suffering is mitigated when enlightenment is avoided. (p. 314)

Bernard F. Dukore, "Spherical Tragedies and Comedies with Corpses: Witkacian Tragicomedy," in Modern Drama *(copyright © 1975, University of Toronto, Graduate Centre for Study of Drama; with the permission of* Modern Drama*), Vol. XVIII, No. 3, September, 1975, pp. 291-315.*

ANGELA EVONNE WEYHAUPT   (essay date 1977)

Few twentieth-century playwrights have been as obsessed with death as the Polish avant-garde dramatist Stanislaw Ignacy Witkiewicz . . . and none have more fully explored the theatrical possibilities of a corpse on the stage. . . . Death for Witkiewicz is an intriguing temptation, an opportunity for self-contemplation and a fantastic intellectual construct, rather than the annihilation of the self; his corpses are not horrifying disintegrations of the body, but comic theatrical extensions of his characters' fears and desires. The play of Witkiewicz which best illustrates how the playwright handles death and resurrection is **The Madman and the Nun,** in which death is the basis not only of the play's theme and imagery, but of its structure as well. (p. 45)

In **The Madman and the Nun,** Witkiewicz uses space and congestion as his theatrical metaphor, while at the same time drawing on religious traditions connected with death to develop these ideas in a surprising and unconventional way.

When the play opens, the poet Walpurg is confined on three levels. He is restrained spatially by both his clothing and his cell in the madhouse. The squeaking cell door and the repeated fastening and unfastening of the straitjacket emphasize his imprisonment by society. He is restrained temporally by the clock in his head, which by its directionless motion binds him to an eternal present, and by his guilt over the death of his lover which binds him to the past. And he is restrained creatively and sexually—in the asylum Walpurg is not permitted to write and, as he reiterates, he has not seen a woman for two years. The psychiatrist Bidello calls attention to this deliberate sexual confinement when he instructs Sister Anna to "behave quite naturally and directly" but "under no circumstances should you gratify his wishes." Walpurg himself aggravates the frustration: "Kiss me, I can't kiss you."

If constraint has made Walpurg into a "living corpse," as he describes himself to Sister Anna, freedom, even at the price of physical death, brings a transcendent life. The play opens with Walpurg having suffered a symbolic death. We discover him in a tomb-like cell, lit by a gloomy, solitary bulb. He is shrouded in a straitjacket with his arms crossed on his chest and above his head hangs an inscription. When he awakens from this death-like sleep he reacts according to conventional concepts of death as a time of spiritual reckoning—he expects a judgment and all the heavenly trappings: "Is this a hallucination? This has never happened to me before. What the devil? Answer me." Sister Anna consoles him with "I am not a phantom" and Walpurg sarcastically concludes "Devilish devices / Impinge on our senses / But the soul is concealed, / No one wants it revealed." . . . This traditional religious approach to death, amplified by later references to guilt and threatened damnation, is discarded because it does not loose the bonds. The "world without end" of conventional religion can have only an absurd sardonic ring for a man confined by time. "There is no eternal damnation," Walpurg maintains, "the only rewards and punishments are right here in this world.". . .

The answer is not retribution, but freedom. Anna's love, born of earthly lust as much as from romantic altruism, frees Walpurg, first from time and then from space. At Anna's kiss he declares "This moment is the only one.". . . The suspension of time becomes a blessing rather than a torment. From this starting point he welcomes the future, anticipating a new creative life, and abandons the past. Although occasionally he lapses into guilt, his progress toward sanity is marked by fewer references to the past. After killing Bidello he notes that "the clock has stopped ticking" . . . and in the end time gives way to the limitless expanse of eternity.

Walpurg's spatial release is brought about in even more powerful theatrical terms. Character after character is added to the scene—Sister Anna, Sister Barbara, Grün, two attendants and Walpurg himself—until the congested cell bursts with Walpurg's death. His metaphysical release through suicide is expressed physically by breaking out of the oppressive space—smashing the window pane and opening the locked door. Having used his straitjacket, the instrument of his confinement, to hang himself, his resurrected body is freed of his old restrictive costume—new, stylish clothes and a fresh flower replace the uniform of the asylum. This change is in keeping with the Christian tradition of the glorified resurrected body. . . . (pp. 45-7)

The consequences of Walpurg's passage through the constraint which is death are not limited to him, for freedom demands reciprocity. Just as Anna loosens his straitjacket and Walpurg responds by removing her wimple, so at the end his clean-shaven self brings a new dress and calls her by her given name to free her from her old existence. Nor is liberation restricted to the just, for Bidello also reaps the fruits of freedom. The entire universe is affected—representatives of the church and medical establishment scuffle with the enraged workers as the world of science and religion reverts to the "pulpy mass" that breeds "wonderful flowers of lust, power, creativeness, and cruelty" . . . , a fertile prelude to a new life.

Although ultimate freedom is found only in death, there is liberation in violence as well. Walpurg's killing of Bidello is, in keeping with the idealization of death, a clean, decisive action free of extended tortures and suffering. The brutality is not mitigated—after Walpurg drives a pencil through his adversary's temple, he kicks the corpse—but Witkiewicz does not dwell on it, and the body is removed with routine dispatch. As in Witkiewicz's other plays, such as *The Mother* and *The Water Hen,* violence is shown as a healthy release of hostility and aggression, a quick cure for emotional impotence. Witkiewicz places the emphasis on killing rather than dying.

The language of the play reinforces the thematic concerns. In addition to particularized imagery like the clock and the tomb-like cell, Witkiewicz draws on the death imagery of the Passion of Christ. Walpurg's passage from death to life takes three days and thunder and lightning accompany his suffering. Further, he is ministered to and prepared for the experience of death by a woman, just as the women in the Gospels stood by Christ's cross, prepared his body for burial and witnessed his resurrection. Walpurg uses Anna's cross to break the window, taking a cross-like position as he dies. Afterward the gates of hell swing open to release the good, while Grün and Sister Barbara are "cast into the confusion and darkness outside, where there is weeping and the gnashing of teeth." . . .

Unlike the Christian story, however, the resurrection of Walpurg is presented without recourse to a higher power. Rather the play abounds in references to the normal, natural life that freedom brings: "Please don't attempt to do anything out of the ordinary, Sister." Bidello orders . . . and Walpurg, having tasted release with Sister Anna says, "I want to live, to live a perfectly ordinary life.". . . Walpurg's sudden and unexpected return from the dead is made even more surprising and comic by Witkiewicz's casual, matter-of-fact treatment of it. The naturalness of his resurrection is underscored by its extension to others, since Bidello arises as well as Walpurg and the pair take not only Anna but also Walldorff on their new journey.

In its theme, structure, and imagery, then, the play is concerned with death, resurrection, and freedom as metaphysical issues. . . . In a world where death is an abstraction, the distinction between death and life is blurred. One of the consequences of this anomaly is the reduced seriousness of death—thus, Witkiewicz's subtitle for one of his plays as a "comedy with corpses" could well be applied to *The Madman and the Nun.* In such a world, suicide becomes inviting. A painless intellectual demise is more desirable than a realistic agony replete with the smells and feel of death or than continued life in a debased world. But this demise need not be permanent. The finality of death is refuted by the frequent depiction of resurrection, a fairly normal event judging by the reactions of the witnesses. The transcendent treatment of death extends to the returning corpses which are younger, better-looking, and more aggressive than before.

Although death intervenes early and often in Witkiewicz's plays, the emphasis is on the quality and attributes of life. The conflicts growing out of artistic creativity, repressed sexual drives, authoritarianism, guilt, and insanity are exposed and resolved through Walpurg's passage from death to life. Despite its darker tones, the play is not without ironic hope; in *The Madman and the Nun,* as well as in his other works, Witkiewicz has dramatized not death alone, but death and resurrection, (pp. 47-8)

Angela Evonne Weyhaupt, "Death and Resurrection in Witkiewicz's 'The Madman and the Nun'," in The Polish Review *(© copyright 1977 by the Polish Institute of Arts and Sciences in America, Inc.), Vol. XXII, No. 4, 1977, pp. 45-8.*

FRANK S. GALASSI (essay date 1977)

[Witkiewicz's *The Crazy Locomotive*] is a play which indicates that the playwright not only has a strong affiliation with the theatrical innovators of the early twentieth-century avant-garde like Jarry, Breton, Sorge, Artaurd, and Brecht, but that he anticipated well in advance how the slapstick marionette-form might be used not merely within his own dramaturgy but also by the monopolistic enterprises of the creators of the early "talkies." The slapstick caricatures which would dominate the comic cinema are numerous and celebrated. Considering Witkiewicz's antipathy to the cinema, perhaps he set for himself the challenge of utilizing the most mimetic, the most frantically spectacular aspect of his dramaturgy, to satirize, and in some manner to supersede, the cinema's mounting popularity. *The Crazy Locomotive* is a play where four major characters stand as formidable marionettes, perhaps from the Punch and Judy tradition, shouting at, and cudgelling each other as they drive a "locomotive" to its maximum acceleration and ultimate disaster. Certainly, in his directions for a replica of a "giant locomotive,'' and in the variety of other suggestions involving film, fire, and smoke, Witkicwicz obviously had the ''reality'' of the cinema satirically in mind. (p. 50)

If *The Crazy Locomotive* is in any manner Witkiewicz's satire on the rise and popularity of the cinema and its adjacent mechanisms, it also shows him using the slapstick possibilities of pantomime gesture and caricature that permeated the international silent cinema of the 1920s. Witkiewicz's innovations for the stage find him anticipating the works and concepts of Russian avant-gardists like [Lev Kuleshov, Vsevolod Pudovkin], and, of course, Eisenstein. . . .

Siegfried Tenser-Trefaldi is the ''crazy locomotive's'' engineer. Like several of Witkiewicz's hero types, he is a combination of the hero-villain, attempting to create an heroic essence out of an extreme action. In discussing his own heroism, Trefaldi questions Nicholas: ''If the two of us could only— and yet I'd rather do it entirely on my own—if we could construct a planet or a meteor, it would be much more comfortable than breaking our necks along these rails.'' . . . Nicholas reinforces: ''Only action, not contemplation, can make it clear to us. But we have so few opportunities to do something really extraordinary.'' . . . Nicholas continues: ''Just think of it: at the very same moment in history, Existence in all its infinity and the two of us, alone, on this galloping monster adrift from all mankind. Even if you tried for a thousand years, you couldn't think up anything like that.'' . . .

The complete dramatic impact of what Witkiewicz wished to accomplish here is understood when the dialogue is scrutinized as inseparable from the stage directions:

(1) When Tenser pushes the throttle down, the gestures he makes are exaggerated and impressive. All the while the locomotive chugs faster and faster. . . .
(2) Nicholas: He hits the firebox with his fist. . . .
(3) Tenser: Pushes the throttle down more vigorously; the engine chugs faster and faster. . . .
(4) Nicholas: Throwing down his shovel. . . .

(p. 52)

Each of these gestures contains a comic value particularly when they are linked to their counterpart and pompous dialogue. The ''exaggeration'' that Witkiewicz calls for reveals his slapstick intention because in his creation of Nicholas and Trefaldi as perpetrators of a seemingly mad act, he likewise endows them with a demonic energy which sustains that madness. It is this demonic energy which is the source of Witkiewicz's slapstick. Similar to the earlier description of Nicholas shovelling coal into the firebox, Witkiewicz's dialogue and stage directions establish a *unit* where a very contained but essentially explosive energy prevails. It is this very energy which will finally be unleashed in the explosion of the locomotive and its passengers. Nicholas' and Trefaldi's gestures are disjointed or ''desynchronized,'' set against their statements of grandiose accomplishment. Their gestures are the authentic indicators of their shared terror.

Since *The Crazy Locomotive* is necessarily a ''comedy,'' in Witkiewicz's sense of a grotesque or absurd ''comedy of corpses,'' the various slapstick gestures facilitate the physicalization of psychological, spiritual disorientation. First, Trefaldi ''pushing down on the throttle,'' followed by Nicholas' fist ''hitting the firebox,'' then Trefaldi pushing on the ''throttle'' more vigorously, and finally, Nicholas ''throwing down the shovel,'' are all actions which represent a ''build-up'' of tension and confusion. Like Jarry's life-sized marionette, Père

Ubu, or Chaplin, or Laurel and Hardy caricatures, Nicholas and Trefaldi represent a primitive irresponsibility, as they identify with violence, toy with its ramifications, and are ultimately immersed in it as the ''crazy locomotive'' goes berserk. Witkiewicz must also be affiliated with the bizarre comedy of Jarry, Chaplin, and Laurel and Hardy, because when the ''crazy locomotive'' ultimately collides with No. 50, and the various corpses are viscerally strewn about, Travaillac and Trefaldi survive in a fantastical manner, Travaillac running off with Minna, and Trefaldi, as seductive as ever, ranting humorously as he dies with his entrails exposed. What more slapstick Epilogue could Witkiewicz have offered than to present his heroic duo as comic ''survivors'' flaunting in the faces of law and society the absurdity of their dreams and very existences. Travaillac and Trefaldi proclaim for the philosophers and the pragmatists that absurdity is the true nature of this world, and that they themselves as fireman and engineer of the ''crazy locomotive'' have mimicked such absurdity. Just as their slapstick gestures and pompous statements are exaggerated expressions of reality, so too they represent inseparable aspects of Witkiewicz's dramatic mosaic of perception and human action. In *The Crazy Locomotive,* slapstick becomes equated with demonic energy, sometimes contained, intermittently explosive, in Travaillac and Trefaldi's battle with a frightening universe. (p. 53)

In *The Crazy Locomotive,* Witkiewicz has set down a choreography of slapstick action in Travaillac's shovelling of coal, Trefaldi's rhythmic hand on the shuttle, Julia's ''baby-doll'' gestures, Abracadabra's stylized violence, and Jeanne's marionette ravings. Witkiewicz continues to be one of the first major dramatists of the modern European theater to use the dynamism and tactile quality of slapstick for the dramatization of hallucinatory and psychological trauma. In *The Crazy Locomotive,* Witkiewicz discovered a slapstick medium for depicting modern man's frenzy in a world of mechanization, depersonalization, and savage competition. Witkiewicz's slapstick embodies the frustrated energy within our intellectual and spiritual existences. (p. 56)

> *Frank S. Galassi, ''Slapstick in Witkiewicz's 'The Crazy Locomotive','' in* The Polish Review *(© copyright 1977 by the Polish Institute of Arts and Sciences in America, Inc.), Vol. XXII, No. 4, 1977, pp. 49-56.*

LOUIS IRIBARNE (essay date 1977)

Insatiability may be viewed as an anthology of Witkiewiczian themes and styles. As a novel it shares in that genus of twentieth-century fiction known to Polish critics as ''catastrophism,'' which in the West sometimes goes under the rubric of *antiutopia* or *dystopia*. It is, in many ways, a classic of the genre. Inspired by events of modern Polish and European history, but set in the late twentieth or early twenty-first century, the novel prophesies the inevitable collapse of Western civilization in the form of a Chinese Communist invasion from the East. The novel traces the adventures of its main protagonist, Genezip Kapen (a French-Polish amalgam meaning, roughly, ''zipless''), whose own fate—that of sexual initiation, a series of unmotivated murders, and finally his complete mental breakdown in the lost military cause he serves so blindly—parallels the decline of a moribund race doomed to oblivion by historical necessity. (p. xxxii)

Witkiewicz's catastrophism is evident in the fact that bourgeois capitalism, art, religion, Western ideology, and individual heroism are all unable to reverse the course of history. Both the forces of the old (art and aristocracy) and the new (the all-leveling Chinese) are raised in the novel to the level of myth: the endgame depicted is global in dimension. In the end Genezip Kapen emerges as a symbol of a new psychology commensurate with the anthill society.

As defined in the novel *Insatiability,* Witkacy's futuristic vision would seem to defy a too narrow classification of it with this or that particular genre. It is simply not possible, for example, to ascribe to it a predominantly technological character since, apart from repeated digressions alluding to the disastrous effects of automation and technologism, machines scarcely exercise any *dramatic* function in the book. In fact, in contrast to the conventional futuristic fantasy—for example, [Yevgeny] Zamyatin's *We,* Huxley's *Brave New World,* or Orwell's *1984*—the landscape of the book is a strangely anachronistic one, reminding one more of the nineteenth than the twentieth or twenty-first century. (In this respect, it is perhaps more similar to Nabokov's novel *Invitation to a Beheading,* a pseudoantiutopian fable set somewhat incongruously against a pastoral, and even idyllic, backdrop.) And this is so, presumably, because Witkiewicz was more passionately concerned with the fate of the old *vis-à-vis* the new, and not vice versa. The lone futuristic detail found in the novel, for example, is the pill of Murti Bing (inspired, no doubt, by Witkiewicz's own experiments with narcotics), which performs a function analogous to the futuristic details in Witkacy's dramas—namely, showing the malleability of human nature and man's refusal to confront the ontological absurdity of existence. In other words, the lineaments of that vision would appear to emanate not as much from a world of pure fantasy as from Witkiewicz'a apperception of certain fatal processes undermining traditional civilization in the present, parabolically and hyperbolically transposed into a world of pseudofuturistic nightmare. Hence the noticeable absence of science fiction or fantasy in the novel—as if, for Witkacy living in the twenties, events of the present were sufficiently fantastic in themselves.

Nor is it possible to categorize the work as an antiutopian novel in the strict sense of the term, since the specific forms of the future state are only alluded to in the epilogue, even though they may be readily deduced. Witkiewicz likewise differs from such antiutopian novelists as Zamyatin, Huxley, and Orwell in the specifics of his teleology. Not only is his "brave new world" something that literally defies description because boredom is bound to reign supreme in it, but it is also a world preordained, and thus is beyond the remedial influence of men. Also absent by and large in Witkiewicz's catastrophic vision is the "fatal flaw," the individual imperfection (such as D-503's discovery of self in Zamyatin's *We*) that, as [Irving] Howe has observed, in the more conventional antiutopian novel invariably gives rise to conflict, justifies the action, and ensures a negative resolution. In Witkiewicz's novel, by contrast, individual freedom of choice is necessarily precluded from the outset by a cosmic process. Genezip's downfall is caused by the renunciation of his own intellect—Witkiewicz, in spite of everything, was a Renaissance man—making him entirely consistent with the age, the rule rather than the exception. Once this act is accomplished, all conflict is eliminated, resistance becomes futile, and "happiness" is assured. And that is so because for Witkiewicz, as much as for the Russian "catastrophist" [Andrey] Bely, the "fatal flaw" lay not so much in this or that system, much less in a psychological or moral defect, but in the defective nature of existence itself. True to the spirit of "catastrophism" (and in contrast to the antiuto-

pians), Witkacy projects a world that can be redeemed neither by the forces from without (by the revolutionaries beyond the Green Wall in Zamyatin; by the savages in Huxley) nor by individual sacrifice from within; it is, in short, . . . [a] more pessimistic vision, one devoid of the sort of moral correctives which the antiutopian traditionally seeks to apply in retrospect.

It is worth noting that Witkiewicz's catastrophic vision, despite its pronounced historical pessimism, stops short of being apocalyptic; for example, most of the characters in *Insatiability* survive the catastrophe and, once divested of their metaphysical consciousness, become ultimately reconciled to the future. On the other hand, Witkiewicz did not, and could not, share that optimistic, Spenglerian faith in the revival of traditional civilization. He could not because what he envisioned was, in the words of his narrator, "a monumental world revolution whose goal was the absolute standardization of mankind in forms completely unforeseeable in terms of traditional doctrine—for who could have possibly foreseen that the monster of civilization would ever assume such proportions?" The Chinese function symbolically in the novel as the reification of the forces of that "monumental revolution," the consummate perfection of all the various means that civilization has at its disposal for its own suicidal destruction: the collectivization of mankind, the functional rationalization of existence, the narcotization of the spirit. The images of catastrophe advanced in the novel are necessarily extreme because they derive from a recognition of history's extreme violation of the traditional belief in a personal self and the mystery of being; if they are violent, then it is only in relation to what has been violated. They terrify us, not so much by the vision of a "brave new world" gained, as by the recollection of that which has been irretrievably lost. (pp. xxxii-xxxiv)

Written some ten years before the appearance of Sartre's *La Nausée* (1938) and Camus's *L'Étranger* (written 1939—41; published 1942), [*Insatiability*] emerges as a striking precursor of what is now termed the philosophical or existential novel.

In part one of *Insatiability,* Sturfan Abnol, author of "metaphysical novels" and a persona of the author, offers the following comment on the condition of man in the modern world: "What's infinitely more interesting is man's *absolute*(!) inability to adapt to the function of existence, a phenomenon that's only possible during times of decadence. Only at such times are the metaphysical laws of existence visible in all their sheer horror. . . ." The problem that is at the center of the novel, then, is a philosophical one and may be roughly formulated as follows: how to effect a reconciliation of human essence and existence in a completely alien and incomprehensible world bent on the destruction of all traditional values—indeed, of *Homo sapiens* itself. The problem is further complicated by the fact that all freedom of choice is precluded by a historical process that sees the world threatened by a catastrophe of unprecedented proportions (symbolized by the all-leveling Chinese revolution). In more Witkiewiczian terms, the novel turns out to be a fictional rendering of what Witkiewicz the metaphysician perceived as the inherent ambiguity of human experience: the conflict between unity and plurality and what that implies about the mysteriousness of existence itself—here, of course, conceived in a certain historical context. In purely fictive terms, this constitutes the real meaning of Genezip Kapen's crisis of self-definition in the novel and is what lends the book both its form and its substance.

Modeled in part after the traditional *Bildungsroman,* the novel recounts the various critical stages in a young man's passage from youth and adolescence to manhood and madness. Out of this passage emerges a pattern symbolic of man's existential journey from a state of being to that of non-being: from the discovery of self, of consciousness and its first manifestation, the body (adolescence and young manhood); followed by metaphysical-psychological crisis (signaled on the level of action by Genezip's incipient schizophrenia and multiple crimes) provoked by the inability to wed the disparities of self; ending finally, and inevitably, in catatonic collapse and complicity in a collective disaster. (pp. xxxv-xxxvi)

The plot structure of the novel, lean as it is, follows Genezip's numerous unsuccessful attempts to reconcile his newly aroused metaphysical aspirations with those of a more carnal nature. (p. xxxvi)

The story of Genezip's psychic disintegration and "bestialization" is set in relief, and to a large extent paralleled, by a similar process at work in the social and political order. Thanks to his father's whim to see his son in the very center of the historical cauldron, the deranged adolescent suddenly finds himself part of a historical derangement: war and revolution, culminating in a Chinese invasion from the East. (p. xxxvii)

Witkiewicz subtly but unmistakably suggests a parallel relationship between the downfall of his chief protagonist and the collapse of civilization in general. For, in the final analysis, the Chinese emerge as the culminating symbol of the book's manifold forces of destructive non-being (defined in Witkiewiczian terms as collectivization, materialism, rationalized sexuality, technologism) as opposed to those of being (individualism, metaphysical consciousness, art); as such, theirs is a victory of the gregarious instinct of the species over the self-assertive instinct of the lonely personality—of ethics over metaphysics, existence over essence, slavery over freedom.

In conformity with Witkiewicz's concept of the novel as a "grab bag," *Insatiability* may be viewed as an anthology of various literary genres and styles. These are in turn parodied in order to make mercilessly manifest the agony of mankind during its penultimate phase. "The last means left for us . . . ," says the writer Sturfan Abnol, "is nonsense—after that it's all over." Parody and self-parody operate in *Insatiability* not only as a means of ridiculing the literary conventions of the past, especially the conventions of the realistic tradition aimed at verisimilitude—as in other less profound writers. Like his use of the grotesque, it is also a way of underscoring the monstrosity of the present; parody is the literary trope of pure and unmitigated catastrophism. "The final phase of a world-historical form is *comedy*," Marx wrote, and nowhere is this more painfully applicable than in the case of Witkiewicz.

Is *Insatiability* a *conte philosophique*, philosophical confession, or "novel of ideas" in the tradition of Voltaire, Diderot, Rousseau, Mann, Sartre, and Camus? To be sure; but it is nonetheless true that all the various philosophical arguments advanced in the course of the novel—Basil's neo-Catholicism, Benz's neopositivism, Bechmetev's Freudianism, the religion of Murti Bing, even Hardonne's catastrophism—are held up to ironic ridicule; all pale in comparison to the "brave new world" projected for the future. A novel of character or a work of satire? In a world where the united self has become a myth and moral absolutes a fiction, neither psychology nor the didactic-moralizing impulse of satire are relevant anymore. In such a world, instead of characters we find only grotesques; instead of values, only sham values. An epic novel or novel of adventures, perhaps? In a world where greatness and heroism

are no longer feasible and total catastrophe is inevitable, adventure is only possible in the solitude of the mind, which likewise turns out to be dispensable, while action has become so pointless that it can take the form of a footnote or parenthetic remark in a novel or else be reduced to endless garrulousness. An eighteenth-century novel of digressions in the tradition of LeSage or Sterne? Undoubtedly, but pushed to caricature, to *buffo*. And by ending his novel where he did, with a promise withdrawn concerning the future state, Witkiewicz may also have been striving for a parody of the antiutopian genre made famous by [Karel] Čapek, Zamyatin, and others.

Finally, a stylized novel in the manner of Joyce, Bely, or Woolf? But how, one might ask, is that possible in a work that gleefully parodies itself by adopting a hopelessly convoluted, baroque, self-conscious, self-mocking style? The style of *Insatiability* is a constantly shifting one, turning from the discursiveness of a scholarly treatise to lyricism (for example, in the *paysage* descriptions) and then back again to a straightforward naturalistic manner (for example, in the denouement). It is a style abundantly laced with multilingual phrases, double entendres, falsely attributed quotes, neologisms, puns, erratic punctuation, and non-narrative forms (for example, dialogue composed in dramatic form). In short, it is a style driven to such extremes that it is continually in danger of losing itself in an act of supreme resignation before the indescribable: "The situation deteriorated," says the narrator at the very end of the novel, "into something which the Polish language is not equipped to describe." Were it not for the fact that the novel preserves the appearance of a traditional novel (linear plot, "typical" characters, omniscient third-person narrator, and so on), one might almost be tempted to classify it as an antinovel; as it is, the novel seems to be a work of fiction bent on self-annihilation along with the world out of which its values spring.

In a world that has irrevocably spent itself, Witkacy seems to be arguing, the novel has likewise exhausted all the possible means at its disposal. Perhaps for that reason *Insatiability* seems to succeed most not as politics, art, or even philosophy, but as a metaphor of total suicide. (pp. xxxviii-xxxix)

Louis Iribarne, "Translator's Introduction" in Insatiability: A Novel in Two Parts *by Stanisław Ignacy Witkiewicz, translated by Louis Iribarne (© 1977 by the Board of Trustees of the University of Illinois; reprinted by permission of the author and the University of Illinois Press), University of Illinois Press, 1977, pp. vii-xlii.*

ADDITIONAL BIBLIOGRAPHY

Blonski, Jan. "Witkacy and the Western World." *Polish Perspectives* XVII, No. 3 (March 1974): 30-42.
    Examines Witkiewicz's pessimistic ideas of social catastrophe in light of modern technological and sociological trends, focusing not on "the rightness of the diagnoses but at the most the correctness of the assumptions."

Knapp, Bettina. "Stanisław Ignacy Witkiewicz's *Kurda Wodna:* 'Perform No Operation Till All Be Made of Water'." *Symposium* XXXIII, No. 1 (Spring 1979): 5-24.
    Explication of *The Water Hen* using terms derived from alchemy, such as dissolution and solution, as symbols of death and rebirth.

Milosz, Czeslaw. "Murti-Bing." In *The Intellectuals: A Controversial Portrait,* edited by George B. de Huszar, pp. 411-21. Glencoe, Ill.: The Free Press, 1960.

>   Compares Witkiewicz's concept in *Insatiability* of the Murti-Bing pill—which instills intellectual complacency—with the submission of communist-nation intellectuals to the doctrines of Marxism.

Milosz, Czeslaw. "Stanisław Ignacy Witkiewicz: A Polish Writer for Today." *Tri-Quarterly,* No. 9 (Spring 1967): 143-54.

>   Discussion of Witkiewicz's novels and dramas, his theory of pure form in the theater, and his nihilistic philosophy, concluding that he "is an acting force in Polish letters."

Peterkiewicz, Jerzy. "Metaphors of Doom." *The Times Literary Supplement,* No. 3981 (21 July 1978): 816.

>   Descriptive review of *Insatiability,* classifying it along with "all those missed-out modern classics which thrive on the generosity of critical hindsight, but are not necessarily read."

The Polish Review XVIII, Nos. 1-2 (1973): 157 p.

>   Issue devoted to the theater of Witkiewicz: his "place in the history of the drama, his relationship to some of his famous contemporaries, Polish and European, his ideas and theories as expressed in his plays, and the interpretation of his works on the contemporary stage by American directors."

Pomian, Krzysztof. "Witkacy: Philosophy and Art." *Polish Perspectives* XIII, No. 9 (September 1970): 22-32.

>   Study of Witkiewicz's portrait painting and the role of the artist in his philosophical writings.

Wirth, Andrzej. "Brecht and Witkiewicz: Two Concepts of Revolution in the Drama of the Twenties." *Comparative Drama* III, No. 1 (Spring 1969): 198-209.*

>   Contrasts Witkiewicz's pessimistic prophecy of the mechanized slavery that would follow the Russian revolution with the optimistic Marxist doctrines developed in the dramas of Bertolt Brecht.

Elinor (Morton Hoyt) Wylie (Benét)

1885-1928

American poet, novelist, short story writer, and essayist.

Wylie was considered one of the most distinguished American poets during the 1920s. Though her literary career lasted only eight years, she became extremely adept in her craft. Wylie's poetry is marked by her vivid imagination, subtle treatment of emotion, and by a detached sensibility which Louis Untermeyer has described as "a passion frozen at its source." The "fragile beauty and exquisite artificiality" seen in Wylie's poetry by H. Lüdeke is also realized in her novels. However, her decorative style—so effective in many of the poems—is not sustained in her prose. For this reason Wylie is regarded primarily as a poet.

Wylie was born in Somerville, New Jersey, the oldest child of parents well-known in society and public affairs. In 1905 she met and married Philip Hichborn, with whom she lived for several years before her relationship with Horace Wylie. After being ostracized by their families and friends and mistreated in the press, the new couple moved to England, where the poet published her first collection, *Incidental Numbers*. Though considered immature and undisciplined, this book offers a promise of its author's later development. The couple returned to the United States in 1916. During their absence Hichborn had committed suicide and Horace Wylie's wife agreed to a divorce. These events permitted the author's second marriage in 1917. Soon after Wylie became a member of a New York literary group that included William Rose Benét and Sinclair Lewis, who encouraged her to continue writing. Nine years after *Incidental Numbers*, Wylie published *Nets to Catch the Wind*, a poetry collection which she considered her first significant book. Unlike her previous effort, *Nets to Catch the Wind* conveys a deep knowledge of life and evidences a mature talent. It was followed in quick succession by three volumes of verse and four novels, several of which won high praise from America's most influential critics. One, William Rose Benét, became Wylie's third husband in 1923. Another, Carl Van Vechten, led a torchlight parade through New York City in honor of her first novel, *Jennifer Lorn: A Sedate Extravaganza,* a work he called "the only successfully sustained satire in English." In 1928, just after completing the drafts for her last work, *Angels and Earthly Creatures,* Wylie suffered a stroke and died a few months later.

Wylie was greatly influenced by the works of Percy Shelley, though this was by no means the only influence on her work. Some aspects of her verse, in particular her wit and subtlety of thought, were in the tradition of the seventeenth-century metaphysical poets, especially John Donne. In what most critics regard as her best works, *Nets to Catch the Wind* and *Black Armour,* Wylie dramatically portrays the disparities between the individual's aspirations and the limited satisfactions offered by life. In such poems as "The Eagle and the Mole" and "Velvet Shoes," Wylie achieves a genuine and consistent style altogether free from affectation. These poems demonstrate her exceptional skill in handling the materials of her ornamental and illusory "crystal world." In her later verse, however, Wylie's perceptions are often confused and incoherent, and her language redundant, highly conventional, even

Culver Pictures

trite in content and idiom. Though *Trivial Breath* and *Angels and Earthly Creatures* contain some of Wylie's most ambitious poems, including the sonnet sequence "One Person," they also suggest that the poet abandoned the themes and convictions of her earlier work in pursuit of the cult of the beautiful. Among Wylie's novels, *Jennifer Lorn* has been lauded for its satire, fantasy, and fine craftsmanship, though many critics consider *Mr. Hodge and Mr. Hazard* her best work. In the latter book Wylie tried to curb the excesses of her language, and the result is a sensitive allegory of the poet's tragedy in a world indifferent to the artist's needs. For Wylie, the gifted individual requires beauty, refinement, and variety, while the world offers commonness, coarseness, and vulgarity.

Interest in Wylie's work has decreased dramatically since her death, the peak of her literary reputation coming early in her career. Much of the early praise, in fact, was for Wylie herself, rather than her works; she was extremely beautiful and came to symbolize freedom and elegance for those who knew her. After Wylie's death her novels and verse were examined more critically. Some commentators, such as James G. Southworth, have questioned her commitment to her craft. Others have praised her talents as a lyricist, while at the same time criticizing her preciosity and sentimentality. Today Wylie is rarely read and she holds little interest outside academic circles.

Nonetheless, her work, in its crystalline artificiality, stands as a memorial to American culture of the 1920s.

(See also *Dictionary of Literary Biography*, Vol. 9: *American Novelists, 1910-1945*.)

PRINCIPAL WORKS

Incidental Numbers　(poetry)　1912
Nets to Catch the Wind　(poetry)　1921
Black Armour　(poetry)　1923
Jennifer Lorn: A Sedate Extravaganza　(novel)　1923
The Venetian Glass Nephew　(novel)　1925
The Orphan Angel　(novel)　1926; also published as *Mortal Image*, 1927
Angels and Earthly Creatures　(poetry)　1928
Mr. Hodge and Mr. Hazard　(novel)　1928
Trivial Breath　(poetry)　1928
Collected Poems of Elinor Wylie　(poetry)　1932
Collected Prose of Elinor Wylie　(novels, short stories, and essays)　1933

EDNA ST. VINCENT MILLAY　(essay date 1922)

The publication recently of Elinor Wylie's **"Nets to Catch the Wind"** is an event in the life of every poet and every lover of poetry. The book is an important one. It is important in itself, as containing some excellent and distinguished work; and it is important because it is the first book of its author, and thus marks the opening of yet another door by which beauty may enter to the world.

The material from which these poems is made is not the usual material. They are not about love, not about death, not about war, not about nature, not about God, not exclusively Elinor Wylie. They are not pourings forth. There is not a groan or a shout contained between the covers. They are carefully and skilfully executed works of art, done by a person to whom the creation of loveliness and not the expression of a personality through the medium of ink and paper is the major consideration.

One places this book, for some reason, alongside the poems of Ralph Hodgson. It contains no "Eve," no "Bull," no "Song of Honour." It is a small book of small poems, made, one would say, for the most part, out of moods and fancies, rather than out of emotions and convictions. Yet to say that Mrs. Wylie has not written a sustained and lofty poem seems as irrelevant as to say that she has not been to Taormina. One is convinced that she could go there, should she set her heart on it.

"Nets to Catch the Wind" begins badly. The opening poem is perhaps the worst poem in the book. It is called **"Beauty."** Of its twelve lines the first two are commonplace, the entire second stanza is awkward and dull, and the beginning of the last stanza is commonplace. Then, like a sword from ambush, into the sleepy consciousness of the strolling reader bites the sharp, cold wonder of the final phrase,

> Enshrine her and she dies, who had
> The hard heart of a child. . . .

It is with beating heart, as the old chronicles have it, that the reader, shaken by this first encounter, fares onward into the book, prepared for anything. . . .

[The second poem, **"The Eagle and the Mole,"**] must surely delight—and this whether or not they subscribe to its philosophy—all who admire the clean-lined and uncompromising in art. . . .

The third poem is called **"Madman's Song."** Which is another way of telling us that it is the Song of any Poet in his Right Mind. It is gracefully done, but even as it is being read is forgotten, in the rich memories of Yeats which it evokes. It is difficult to write nowadays of "silver horns," "golden pillows," and "the milk-white hounds of the moon" without finding one's-self outvoiced by one's overtones.

The book contains eight sonnets. Of these the four grouped under the title **"Wild Peaches"** are, except for **"Atavism,"** the most successful. The second and fourth of this group are especially fine, although the octave of the third—or rather the septave; it is a thirteen-line sonnet—is charming. The sonnet to **"Nancy"** is trivial and too palpably a stalk to upbear the blossom of its last line. **"Blood Feud"** is almost worthless. It is an attempt to retell a story which in the original was perhaps impressive, but which the present narrator has failed to make even interesting. It contains lines of purely statistical importance which have nothing to do with poetry, such as "He'd killed a score of foemen in the past," a line which might better be a marginal note. . . .

In order to get the full substance of Mrs. Wylie's poems one should learn them by heart. And the fact that they are easy to learn by heart speaks well for their weight and vigor and for the artistic integrity of their craftsman. Obviously the poems which are difficult to learn by heart are those poems which might as well have been written in some other way, which are too thin for their form, and have been fattened in the flesh but not in the spirit of them, whose authors have contented themselves with the time-tried figure and the approximate word. Such poems slip through the mind of the reader as they slipped through the fingers of the writer. And more often than not the author himself cannot quote them from memory. . . . [But a poem such as Mrs. Wylie's **"Escape"**] will not easily be erased or partially blotted even from the mind whereon they once have inscribed their peculiar quality.

There are other poems which I should like to quote if there were space here in which to do so: **"Water Sleep," "Village Mystery," "The Crooked Stick," "The Tortoise in Eternity,"** marred by the word "scornful" in the last line; **"The Fairy Goldsmith,"** pretty and unimportant, made by the word "monstrous" in the last stanza, a word which bulges and snores in its context like a sleeping giant; the gay and delightful **"Prinkin' Leddie,"** with her "ermine hood like the hat o' a miller," and her "cramoisie mantle that cam' frae Paris"; **"Fire and Sleet and Candlelight,"** with its interesting occasional internal rhyme, its ascetic paucity of figure, its impersonality as of a chorus of fates; **"Bronze Trumpets and Sea Water,"** twelve splendid lines which give the lie to their own thesis; and the delicate and exquisite **"Velvet Shoes,"** a poem seemingly not printed but sighed upon the paper like breath upon glass, the poem with which the book should have ended.

But if the little of Mrs. Wylie's work which I have been able to cite in this appreciation of it does not convey to the reader the conviction that she is a distinctive poet and that her book is necessary to him it would be useless to continue. . . .

There are poems in the book which are not excellent; such poems appear in every book. The author of "**Nets to Catch the Wind**" has the fine equipment of intelligence, skill, discrimination reserve, and the full powers of sorcery.

Edna St. Vincent Millay, "Elinor Wylie's Poems," in The Literary Review *(copyright, 1922, by N.Y. Evening Post, Inc.; reprinted from* The New York Post*), January 28, 1922, p. 379.*

ARCHIBALD MacLEISH (essay date 1923)

There is a difference, albeit a difference without present distinction, between the arts of expression and expression in the arts. At least there has come to be such a difference in poetry. Poetry which was once an art of communication by words has developed in the hands of some of its modern masters into an art of words extraordinarily uncommunicative. Not representation but form is its end; not the persuasion of the mind through the imagination, but the enchantment of the imagination out of mind. Such poetry does not so much use words as arrange them. It does not march them out in rows loaded with tremendous meanings, but sets them dancing in figures and lets who will be charmed. It argues that words are after all only the names of images and impressions, and these images and impressions, rather than their significance in thought, are the realities of the art. (p. 16)

If it were possible to use the phrase free of its seeming disparagement, the writers of this poetry should be described as artists in words rather than poets. And if they were so called it would be possible to say of Elinor Wylie what cannot otherwise be said, that she is, at her best, as perfect an artist in words as English has produced. She is, like Miss [Amy] Lowell, one of those to whom words are as tangible as stone. And, like Miss Lowell, she sees more often with her fingers than her eyes and writes in the sense of touch. Language is a metal to her mind and upon its surface she works patterns and dies which are only incidentally the impressions of speech. . . . [It] was a master jeweller who designed and set "**The Fairy Goldsmith**" in *Nets to Catch the Wind,* and, in *Black Armour,* the "**Unfinished Portrait.**" But even where she most resembles the craftsmen of marble and gold she most surpasses them, for she works from models which they never dared to use. She knows that art by which medallions may be coined from the intangible, and abstractions turned to stone. In "**Self Portrait**"—in her second volume—she makes of that vaguest of conceptions, the human mind,

> A lens of crystal—
> A texture polished on the horny palms
> Of vast equivocal creatures, beast or human,
> A flint, a substance finer-grained than snow
> Graved with the Graces in intaglio—

And in her lyrics she produces from materials ordinarily fragile with emotion the same sculptured and sensible effect. Her lyrics are fluent. They are exquisitely musical. But theirs is the fluency of water running in a bronze relief, and the music of unstruck bells.

It may very well be that Elinor Wylie's enduring fame, and enduring fame beyond the rest of her generation of young poets she seems very sure to have, will rest upon her mastery of the art of ponderable speech. But if her fame does rest there it will be because of her failure to free her mind from the perfection of her art. To revert again to those all but mythical distinctions

of sex which once explained so much, her mind is as curiously masculine as the method of her verse is feminine. She is, by complexion and humor, the natural and metaphysical son of the Dean of old St. Paul's. John Donne begot her out of falling stars and mandrake roots and whether or not she bears him affection is an irrelevant matter. She is the heir to that impossible clean beauty in the brain which drove him into the riddles and contradictions of his intricate conceits. She too loves those countries which lie outward of the sense. She too loves the dry sharp bitterness of the idea of death. . . . Cruelty which can burn away soft and too mortal flesh, savagery, sharp edges and keen points of pain, have a beauty which she understands. They are the weapons of the mind to lay clean the skeletons of things.

But the love of salt and steel was in Donne, and is no doubt in his natural children, a passion like other passions of desire. It cannot be represented in crystals. It cannot be expressed in any art which aims chiefly at the most perfect expression. It must make its own channels. And in Elinor Wylie's work it is never permitted that license of full flood. In a sense which perhaps she never intended her title of *Black Armour* for her second book is marvelously apt. Her verse is not only a metal of defence but a metal of captivity. The flesh, or as she would say, the bones, are prisoned in this damask work, etched over with design, and not even in those poems which she would have us believe, from their title of "**Beaver Up,**" display herself does the face of the adventurer appear. Occasionally, as in "**The Eagle and the Mole**" in *Nets to Catch the Wind* she has been explicit; but even there her passion is constrained to the limits of a perfect line. Only now and again does one catch a gesture, a movement of the mailed and articulated body, which conveys more than a suit of armor ever meant. For the most part there is only the art of the smith and the attitudes of steel.

This is perhaps more evident in the later than in the earlier volume because the art of the later volume is more closely wrought. There are no flaws for the escape of an unintended sense. There is no careless work. Even so awkward a line as "On a bedstead striped with bright-blue paint" is self-conscious and obviously planned. Every phrase bears the marks of the gold-smith's hammer, and the dints of artistry are only not apparent because they everywhere appear. But at the same time the later volume has poems which seem to promise a more flexible if a less perfected method. They are poems which seem to have been written all at once and left. They are not perhaps characteristic of what will be recognized as Elinor Wylie's distinctive art. They are certainly not expressions of the hungry ardor and the high intolerance of her mind. But they are much more than straws to show the wind, for they are amazingly beautiful. (pp. 16, 18)

It is quite idle to wonder what Elinor Wylie's poetry may become, for it is not in the process of becoming. It is as definitely shaped in its own image as any poetry that has ever been written. And it must be appreciated as it is or not at all. We may complain of her use of poetry for the etching of unutterable forms when she might use it for so large an utterance. We may object that the obtrusion between herself and her readers of such verse as she is capable of writing substitutes for a rarer beauty, a beauty less persuasive and less rare, and we may justify our objection with John Keats's phrase that "poetry should be great and unobtrusive." But when all such exceptions have been taken and all possible reservations saved the essential quality of Elinor Wylie's poetry remains. She has achieved in a great and difficult art a great distinction. And she has coined a tangible and enduring beauty out of air. (p. 18)

Archibald MacLeish, "'Black Armour'," in The New Republic *(reprinted by permission of* The New Republic; © *1923 The New Republic, Inc.), Vol. XXXVIII, No. 470 (Part II), December 5, 1923, pp. 16, 18.*

EDMUND WILSON   (essay date 1925)

Dear Madam,

It is now two years since you were so kind as to send me the first of your novels [*Jennifer Lorn*] which the vexation of other business and the exigencies of other studies then prevented me from reading. . . . [Now,] receiving your second novel in a moment of tranquillity and leisure, I have taken the opportunity to prove my candour by a careful perusal of both. (p. 259)

The merits of *Jennifer Lorn* must command a respect far beyond what we are accustomed to accord to light tales of this species, which, as they are written merely to amuse, do not often move us to admire. We are as much instructed by your knowledge of mankind as delighted by your felicity of invention; and amazed no less by the brilliance exhibited in the splendours of the style than by the vigour displayed in sustaining them. Of the character of Gerald, it may be said that our literature affords no more ingenious, and, at the same time, no more dreadful, illustration of the truth, that the most polished taste and the highest accomplishment may coexist with selfishness and cruelty; and the exercise of great abilities have for accompaniment the contempt of religion. Nor, though you stimulate us at first to admire, do you fail at last to provoke us to despise, when one who has commenced as an Atheist, is finally shewn as a thief.

Your second novel, *The Venetian Glass Nephew*, now remains to be examined; and it will not be surprising if you have not found it possible to repeat so remarkable a success in so short a time. I must say first that your choice of a subject seems less happy than in the case of its predecessor: your ignorance of the Italian language and your lack of acquaintance with the country to which it is native have rendered your scenes, on the whole, less natural and easy than in *Jennifer Lorn*. If you reply that a full third of the earlier tale is supposed to take place in Persia, a country of which you know even less than you do of Italy; I must answer that, as Persia, like Arcadia, is a country of which no one knows anything, we may be free, without fear of reprehension, to write anything of it we please; but that, in the case of Venice, we are certain to have among our readers many persons who have been there, and whom it will displease to find the scenes inappropriate or the manners reported inexactly. I must object further that you have mingled the fictitious with the real in a manner hardly allowable; in as much as, though introducing such actual and known personages as Count Gozzi and Cardinal de Bernis, you have juxtaposed to them an imaginary character whose name is a paraphrase of Casanova's and who, though in some cases spoken of in connexion with names that paraphrase those of the impostor's associates, in others is represented as the hero of Casanova's own exploits, such as the escape from the Leads. If you should plead that, since Casanova has left a history of his own life in which its events are recorded with some fulness, and that it would be incredible to ascribe to him an adventure which is not included in that account; I must reply that the same is true of Gozzi, who nowhere mentions in his memoirs the circumstances you relate.

As for the style, though distinguished by elegance and enlivened by wit, which no production of yours can fail of, I fear that the imagery has here become so copious as somewhat to impede the progress of the action. Where we are bewildered by the profusion of the trees, we become incapable of perceiving the forest. Your story is obscured by a luxuriance of phrases, which seems less suited to a novel than a poem, where exfoliation of this kind is more easily accepted; and we are forced to conclude, when we have reached the end, that the plot has not been very carefully contrived. Our attention is directed first to the Cardinal, but we presently discover that he is not among the chief actors; then we are entertained by a long conversation between the Cardinal, the Chevalier and the Count, which occupies a good third of the book, yet appears to lead nowhither, and to accomplish no purpose which might not have been accomplished better in briefer space. If the style would be more suited to a poem, the same may be asserted of the matter, which, involving so much that is supernatural and whimsical, would not invite in verse the same scrutiny to which it must be subjected in a novel, where we are less content to admit the vagueness of fancy or the abstraction of allegory.

> Your most affectionate humble servant,
> Sam. Johnson

(pp. 260-62)

Edmund Wilson, in his letter to Elinor Wylie on October 7, 1925, in The Shores of Light: A Literary Chronicle of the Twenties and Thirties *by Edmund Wilson (reprinted by permission of Farrar, Straus and Giroux, Inc.; copyright 1952 by Edmund Wilson; copyright renewed © 1980 by Helen Miranda Wilson), Farrar, Straus and Giroux, 1952, pp. 259-63.*

JAMES BRANCH CABELL   (essay date 1930)

In any regarding of the career of Elinor Wylie, it is most human to ask, What would she have done next? The question is profitless, alike in that it can have no answer and in that even if the answer were in some miraculous way provided it would be to us of no more benefit than are last week's radio programs. (p. 335)

With Elinor Wylie the poet—I mean, with the poet who wrote in verse—I plan no traffic. I can find in her verses nothing very remarkable, but then that has for many years been my attitude toward everyone's verses, all the long way from Hesiod's and Pindar's to Mr. Edgar Guest's and my own. The tale runs otherwise as concerns that more urbane, that more prismatic, and in brief that so much more poetic poetry which, after the fashion of reformed and civilised poets, Elinor Wylie wrote in prose form. To no other woman save only Helen of Troy and that unaccountable person who imprudently married me have I been indebted for more of fond delight and of unanswered surmise.

For I had the good luck to rank, along with Sinclair Lewis and Carl Van Vechten, as one of the "discoverers" of "**Jennifer Lorn**" . . . and to commend this story in the public prints (according to the testimony of my scrapbooks) as "compact of color and legerity and glitter." . . . Then it was later my fortune to be, I think, the only unsilent admirer of "**The Venetian Glass Nephew**," in the days when Elinor Wylie was dreeing the inevitable weird of every author who has scored an unlooked-for triumph in a more or less new vein—which is, of course, to hear that the successful book's successor is nothing like so good. To my mind all conceivable exploits in the way of fantastic romance then seemed to lie well within the compass of this woman's refined and impeccant ability.

Much changes, however, both within and about us, during the course of seven years. And since time, like an insane thief, robs all of all grief and disappointment eventually, there is now no hurt in conceding that "The Orphan Angel" . . . affected me very much as, in the cliché at least, does a bucket of cold water full in the face. "The Orphan Angel" really did appear a most inane wasting of wood pulp even for the Book of the Month Club to be inflicting upon its broken-spirited customers. I raged before "The Orphan Angel." I declared, as I still think, that the writing of "The Orphan Angel" was one of the most gloomy errors in all literary history. Yet out of an honest desire to avoid overstatement, I must humbly confess that, after six most conscientious onslaughts, I have not ever been able to read "The Orphan Angel"; and so perhaps speak upon insufficient information. (pp. 335-36)

[When "Mr. Hodge and Mr. Hazard" appeared] then before the dreadful forerunning rumor that yet again Elinor Wylie had rescued Shelley from the Mediterranean the hearts of the merely rational sank. Yet I at least read tentatively; and was thus allured into a peace without victory. These pleasant and innocuous doings at Lyonnesse and Gravelow by no means revealed the Elinor Wylie of her first two romances; but that reflection was drowned, as this pertinacious woman simply would not permit Percy Bysshe Shelley to be drowned upon any terms, in the glad relief of noting that, even so, in this pensive galamatias of raspberries and Greek grammars and cream buns was nowhere involved the planet-struck Elinor Wylie of her third romance. In fine, one found all rather more than satisfying, in a relatively unimportant fashion; and common-sense did not demand over much of an author convalescing from a seizure so alarming as had been manifested in "The Orphan Angel." It is upon her fifth story, I said, that the career of Elinor Wylie will pivot. Then came the news of her death and the knowledge that there would be no fifth story. Her progress stayed forever inconclusive. God alone, if one dare cite an authority so far out of touch with current literature, can say what Elinor Wylie would have done next. (pp. 336-37)

[Elinor Wylie showed] fatal gifts for being ineffectively humorous, and for confounding with the quaint that which to the candid seems unmistakably dull, and for reaching flat bathos where her avowed aim was seraphic beauty—and all this too in connection with an unbridled incapacity for self-criticism. Elinor Wylie honestly believed, as but too many of her friends learned at the cost of all friendship, that "The Orphan Angel" was an excellent fantasy made up of her finest endeavors.

Yet that delusion hardly matters now. . . . The dead past has swallowed tranquilly its dead, among whom I estimate to be that not ever really alive "Orphan Angel"; and Elinor Wylie has bequeathed to us at least two books concerning which there can be no dispute by the intelligent.

These two books, "Jennifer Lorn" and "The Venetian Glass Nephew," I regard, I admit, as something very like masterpieces in their own sharply limited romantic field. That field is not large nor is it especially lofty. Yet it now and then repays the thorny toil of bemused gardeners very prettily, with frail blossoms. (pp. 337-38)

[There is a] kind of romance which embellishes life because the writer has found life to be unendurably ugly. It embellishes life very much as one might cover the face of a leper. The origin of all such romance writing is thus appreciably removed from being love, in that if it be not entirely hate it is, at mildest, aversion. It demands, with Baudelaire, the inaccessible places and strange adorers: with Flaubert it seeks for new perfumes, for vaster flowers, and for pleasures not ever before attained. Its goals are not of this world. It does not hunt the improbable: it evokes in desperation that which it ever well knows to be impossible. (p. 339)

We may grant . . . that this is a branch of literature to which, through plain enough reasons, do belong "Jennifer Lorn" and "The Venetian Glass Nephew." (p. 340)

[In these, Elinor Wylie] created, in brief, a retreat wherein the rebuffed might encounter no more inglorious fiascos of the spirit and of the affections.

Into this quaint and brittle sanctuary of Elinor Wylie's creation neither the spirit nor the affections, or any other human plague, may enter, for the reason that there is in this sparkling place no human heart. For not only Rosalba and Virginio, but all the other inhabitants likewise, I take to be handsome porcelain figures animated by a pure and hurtless white magic. They have been shaped and colored with a pleasingly faded elegance. They have been given life: but there is no more blood in them than there is grossness. They enact their well-bred comedy, which includes a toy misery or so. It touches now and then the exaltedly tragic as if with a caress. A few of them may even pretend to die, with unruffled decorum. Their little porcelain tongues lend to their speaking a light stiffness whensoever these fine manikins converse. They converse too in their own idiom, for the vernacular of this point-device land is an ever-courteous blending of ironic epigram and neat periods and apt literary allusions. Yet a discerning audience will watch all with the connoisseur's calm approval. For this, we know, is but a make-believe land of animated figurines, wherein not lust nor death, not poverty nor bankrupt love, but the cool joys of virtuosity, and of finesse, and of each tiny triumph in phrase-making, are the sole serious matters.

For one, I still delight in the wistful humors and the fine prose of this little land: I commend to you, as I said at outset, the color and the legerity and the glitter of this sanctuary against the rude real. Yet I am far from declaring that oncoming ages will forever treasure these books. For tastes change: and in art also, we incline to forget our benefactors. It is on the cards that very few, and perhaps none, of our descendants may care to travel with Jennifer Lorn all the exotic long way of her journeying (even from the spring sunlight of Devonshire to the crimson pillows of the unvirtuous Banou's bed) or to advance happily with Rosalba Berni from the classical summer-house at Altachieri into the fires of the smelting furnace at Sèvres. Posterity, I admit, may forget both of these books. But I add that posterity will thus acquire a quite valid claim on our pity. (pp. 340-41)

James Branch Cabell, "Sanctuary in Porcelain: A Note to Elinor Wylie," in The Virginia Quarterly Review *(copyright, 1930, copyright renewed © 1957, by* The Virginia Quarterly Review, *The University of Virginia), Vol. 6, No. 3 (Summer, 1930), pp. 335-41.*

CARL VAN VECHTEN (essay date 1933)

A certain difficulty arises in writing about a book to which one awards an unreserved enthusiasm, an agreeable difficulty, no doubt, but none the less a difficulty. This unnatural situation was the cause of a great deal of perplexity on my part after my earliest reading of *Jennifer Lorn* in 1923. Determining, therefore, to discover some slight flaw, some rift in artistry, some hesitation in the creator's precision, I went straight through the book again—in vain, I may add, in so far as the purposes of my pursuit were concerned. A third and more recent reading banished all uncertainty. My enthusiasm has mounted in ten years rather than ebbed. I am confirmed in my belief that *Jennifer Lorn* is the only successfully sustained satire in English with which I am acquainted.

A satire of what? the reader may reasonably demand at this point and the rather vague reply I must give to the question is another proof to my mind of the authentic quality of this "sedate extravaganza," for, unlike most other satirists, Elinor Wylie did not aim her subtle shafts consistently at one target. On the contrary, apparently she cherished a delightfully perverse profusion of aims, lifting *Jennifer* thereby out of the class of pastiches into a niche in literature quite its own. That there are certain resemblances to the work of Philip Thicknesse and others of the elegant eighteenth century biographers is a recognizable part of the charm of this fine novel; that it is indebted now and again to the author's familiarity with the playfully heightened absurdities of [Max Beerbohm's] *Zuleika Dobson*, the elaborate oriental pageantry of [William Bockford's] *Vathek*, and the vivid narrative sense of the relators of *The One Thousand and One Nights* is unarguable. There is, certainly, inherent in this book, a curious fusion of diverse elements, a fusion which justifies itself by its success. The essential fact on which to lay emphasis, however, is that the mixture is pervaded with the distilled essence of Elinor Wylie's own glamorous personality.

We find ourselves completely in the eighteenth century, so completely that frequently we are obsessed by the credibility of this enchanting tale. The author, it is possible to believe after examination, achieved this effect by a meagre use of incident in the first hundred pages, which are peppered instead with a multiplication of fascinating details, staggering in their implication of the lady's knowledge of her selected period and milieu. At no time during her ironic recital, however, will the reader be too sure that the author has entirely forgotten that marriage is a farcical tradition which persists even into our own day, or that Jennifer's rather absurd relations with Gerald might be repeated, shorn, naturally, of their decorative adjuncts, in any Ritz Hotel. There is, indeed, a delicately sardonic smile in every line, a smile mystically sustained over a range of three hundred pages by Mrs. Wylie's instinctive reliance on her own capacity to entertain, by an apparently careless grace, abetted no end by the loveliness of her well-chosen backgrounds, by the beauty that hovers constantly like a reverent handmaiden over the wit, and by a style which may be described—surely this is ineluctable in relation to this narrative—as impeccable. Elinor Wlie's power, perchance, lay in her ability to regard life as simultaneously amusing and picturesque. (pp. 3-5)

There is, it may as well be proclaimed, a kind of perfection about *Jennifer Lorn,* the perfection of an artist who has completely realized her intention, the only perfection, perhaps, with which the critic should concern himself, although there is another approximate perfection which causes a book to arouse feelings in the reader of which the author was never aware. Certainly the perfection of this book is miniature, like the perfection of the red jasper bowl which Gerald loved so much he could not bring himself to bestow it on Jennifer, but this condition should be obvious, that perfect works of art are al-

ways conceived on a small scale. Moby Dick and Hamlet have their greatnesses; they also have their faults.

For its life, which I believe to be, if not immortal, at any rate as nearly immortal as any other work of art of its period which can be named, the story depends to a remarkable degree on the character of Gerald, that "fine flower of English gentlemen." . . . (p. 6)

Gerald, in fact, is incomparable, with his air of passive and polite contempt, his amiable and cold composure. . . . Gerald, indeed, is the epitome of maleness with all its vanity and self-importance transfigured by the smiling art of the writer, who succeeded in sympathetically identifying herself with him, into a comparatively irresistible decorative figure. So puissant is Gerald that any author who had created him might safely permit her future reputation to rest on that accomplishment alone. In this instance, moreover, the character is happily set in what can scarcely fail to continue to be regarded as a permanent masterpiece. (pp. 6-8)

> *Carl Van Vechten, in his preface to "Jennifer Lorn,"*
> *in* Collected Prose of Elinor Wylie *by Elinor Wylie (copyright 1933 by Alfred A. Knopf, Inc.; reprinted by permission of the publisher), Knopf, 1933, pp. 3-8.*

CARL VAN DOREN   (essay date 1933)

Gay, erudite, precise, *The Venetian Glass Nephew* reads like a joyful holiday. It was written under stress. In her second novel Elinor Wylie felt she had to prove, to her exacting self even more than to others, that *Jennifer Lorn* had not been an accident. (p. 217)

[The] strong native level of her mind cuts through the fantasy of *The Venetian Glass Nephew*. It is a fable of the marriage of Art and Nature, specifically Christian Art and Pagan Nature. . . . In the conflict between Art and Nature it is Nature which must yield. (p. 218)

Elinor Wylie was too much a poet to let her moral stand like bare bones in a vacuum. She chose Venice for a setting and spun the story as if her language were ductile glass. . . . Here are formal words fixed in a schematic pattern but glinting with the light which they catch and throw off. The whole book is built with [a] lovely, amused formality . . . and every paragraph flashes erudition. (p. 219)

[The] decoration of *The Venetian Glass Nephew* seems intrinsic in it. If Elinor Wylie had been as curt as a fabulist or as abstract as a moralist she would have told her story to the intellect, not to the eye. Her story as she did tell it is all pictures. Everything in her Venice is brightly visible, from the blue balloon of the opening paragraph to the whipped cream and wafers of the ending. She had ransacked a decade of history for images that could be wittily drawn and beautifully coloured. . . . Elinor Wylie was already full of her favourite century before she set herself to imagine Venice in its age of tinsel. Scrupulous as she might be about dates and streets and churches and costumes, her older memory was her major source. And her older memory served her less than her pictorial imagination. *The Nephew* was to be a poem as well as a moral tale. With a frolicking invention she enriched and confirmed the fairy story, giving it such a look of life as Casanova and Alvise Luna gave Virginio, glass within, almost flesh and blood without.

In one of her letters Elinor Wylie quoted something she had read: "He liked the flavour of an imperfect world and the preposterousness of peccant humanity." "That's the principle," she added, "upon which I write my own immortal works!" It was the principle which made *The Venetian Glass Nephew* both laughing and tender. It gave the novel its charming justice by which, in the strife of Art with Nature, sympathy is on the side of Nature but skill is on the side of Art. (pp. 220-21)

> *Carl Van Doren, in his preface to "The Venetian Glass Nephew," in* Collected Prose of Elinor Wylie *by Elinor Wylie (copyright 1933 by Alfred A. Knopf, Inc.; reprinted by permission of the publisher), Knopf, 1933, pp. 215-21.*

STEPHEN VINCENT BENÉT (essay date 1933)

In the eight, packed years of her writing life, Elinor Wylie wrote four novels. Of these, *The Orphan Angel* is the third, the longest, and the only one that has an American background. It was, to its author, a very personal book, for in it she drew at full length the mortal image of that one of the English poets to whom she gave an entire devotion.

I have heard people speak of that devotion as if it were a pose, a hobby, or a blind worship. It was none of these things. She was entirely sincere about it but she was also entirely mature. In *The Orphan Angel* she could and did show her hero, Shiloh, as sometimes pedantic, sometimes naïve and often difficult. She could laugh at him a little with no diminution of love and make of him no less an immortal because he was sometimes preposterous. As a result, in a work of fiction, a work entirely and necessarily outside of the real events of his life, she has probably come nearer to the essential character of Shelley than any of the critics. For that, too, is genius, that clairvoyance that sees beyond fact and circumstance into truth.

There are three strands woven together in the fabric of the book—a spirit, whose ruling passion is a passion for liberty in a world where liberty is the unpermitted thing—a knight-errant, whose fatal habit it is to rescue princesses from dragons, with no thought whatever of the necessary dangers of that pastime after the dragon is dead—and that lost America of rivers and forests, of wild turkeys and buckskin riflemen and the red shape in the wilderness which lies somewhere at the back of all our minds. (pp. 320-21)

[*The Orphan Angel*] is fine and ghostly as a tea-clipper under its cloud of white sail, but as solid and seaworthy, too. Beneath the incantation and the spell lie an admirable knowledge, an admirable craftsmanship. Elinor Wylie was a great lyric poet— she could also have been a great scholar, for she had many of the scholar's gifts, including an extraordinary patience and thoroughness in research. (p. 322)

[The] whole journey of Shiloh and David, across the continent, from Boston to San Diego, may seem to the reader, at times, like a fantastic fairy tale. But every stage of that journey could be plotted on a map of the period—and each stage would be right and probable, down to the number of days it took to traverse it and the means of locomotion used. . . .

The pilgrimage in search of Jasper Cross's sister across the America of the Eighteen-Twenties is the twisted silver plait that holds the book together. On this are strung the bright and diverse beads of adventure and incident. . . . (p. 323)

The book ends, and ends in grave beauty, but the soul's comedy is unfinished. It cannot, indeed, be finished—for its essence is the disparity between an ideal and the world. (p. 324)

[Here,] in a frame that has the hard bronze of Latin within it as well as the silver, is the picture of a lost America and, wandering through it, two strange companions, a Yankee boy called David Butternut and another who walks as swiftly as the West wind. Here are many adventures and one that is always the spirit's. And here is a prose that was unique in our time. (p. 325)

> *Stephen Vincent Benét, in his preface to "The Orphan Angel," in* Collected Prose of Elinor Wylie *by Elinor Wylie (copyright 1933 by Alfred A. Knopf, Inc.; reprinted by permission of the publisher), Knopf, 1933, pp. 319-25.*

WILLIAM ROSE BENÉT (essay date 1934)

I contend that [Elinor Wylie] was a great prose writer because she was a great poet. What then is a poet such as she? Such poets have puzzled fine minds through the ages for definition of the quality of their work. For one thing, she was born to welcome the most intensely arduous mental labour in passionate exploration of the utmost resources of the English language in order to express every finest shade of thought and feeling that she experienced. She was abnormally sensitive to the powers latent in language. She had an altogether unusual intuition for the exact word, and had assimilated a large vocabulary. She was unusually erudite, and had her life led her in another direction, might have been a great scholar. And because of these gifts of hers she was greatly humble before the English language. You may recall the "Dedication" to her next but last book of poems that bears the gently ironical title, **"Trivial Breath."** That dedication is a fervent tribute to the English language, one she read before the Phi Beta Kappa chapter of Columbia University, and one of the few occasional poems I know that has real poetic fire. It is a sequence of four sonnets. In it she bestows upon our great heritage of the English tongue what she chooses to call "the dull mortal homage of the mind." Her fidelity was ever to "early wells of English undefiled." And this is noteworthy in a day when a number of gifted people are calling the English language into question as insufficient in resource for the expression of the extreme subtlety of their thoughts and feelings. For the processes of Elinor Wylie's intuition and reason were the most subtle I have ever known; and she found the finest use of English sufficient, and more than sufficient, for her purposes.

Elinor Wylie wrote with extraordinary precision; but it was a precision that never for a moment sacrificed the incalculable turn of phrase, the spontaneously felicitous expression, that intuitive visitation of words that seems to us who have it not as a gift from the gods. Her subconsciousness was constantly preoccupied with the shape, look, colour, and sound of words; just as the rhythms of poetry were matters to her of second nature, and her sometimes intricate interior rhyming, art concealed by art, in the same kind. The rhythms of her prose, when she came to them, were distilled from the assimilation of an eclectic reading extensive even in childhood. And if, as Emily Dickinson says, "The soul selects its own society," Elinor's mind from the beginning selected its own society and instinctively chose the type of mind and manner of expression germane to her nature. Most catholic in her relish for good writing of every description, she yet was sure of her own particular province from the beginning. (pp. 12-14)

I have said that the most important thing about Elinor Wylie's prose was that she was a poet. To put it in another way, her prose exhibited the same unusual care in the use of words and had the same stylistic virtue that her poetry possessed. This is true up to a point. It is also true that there is an intensity of expression in poetry not possible to prose, and that in her prose Elinor displayed another facet of her mind, the singular gift that drew the attention of Max Beerbohm, and that caused Carl Van Vechten to remark:

> In my belief . . . **"Jennifer Lorn"** is the only successfully sustained satire in English with which I am acquainted [see excerpt above].

Elinor's poetry was often deeply ironic or delicately ironic or fantastic, but it is rarely satirical. Every one of her novels, on the other hand, contains satire either apparent or concealed. In their fantastic detail and in the elaboration of description the writing of these novels approaches nearest to poetry. But by the very nature of the medium, and by virtue of the fact that the best poetry must possess a deep emotional content—and this is still my contention, despite the intellectualization now rampant in much modern work—Elinor's novels have more distinctly prose values: particular sharpness of ratiocination, characterizations always played upon by subtly humorous observation of human nature (Ay, even in that best-beloved of her characters, Shiloh in **"The Orphan Angel,"**) sophistication, and the knowledge of the brittle world of manners that was also hers. They preserve the view ascribed to Thomas Love Peacock, which she was fond of quoting: "He likes the flavour of an imperfect world and the preposterousness of peccant humanity."

And yet, immediately, when one has tried to draw this distinction, one remembers certain moving passages in her novels, more perhaps in the latter two, **"The Orphan Angel"** and **"Mr. Hodge and Mr. Hazard,"** (though they can also be found in the earlier **"Jennifer Lorn"** and in **"The Venetian Glass Nephew,"**) passages of grave beauty and wisdom, of vibrant sensitivity, that flow like poetry, and that always and ever lift her prose above mere virtuosity or brilliant fantasy. You can find this moving beauty indeed, in the most fantastic of her novels, **"The Venetian Glass Nephew,"** in that most fantastic of love situations in which the young lovers find themselves, Virginio being the brittle youth created by Chastelneuf out of Venetian Glass. The book is really a profound concealed allegory of two natures. (pp. 15-17)

[Nor] do I forget other descriptions of those lovers, nor Peter Innocent feeling himself the fangs of the fire even as Rosalba is giving her body to be burned in the furnace, to become porcelain for Virginio.

Nor do I forget certain moments in that strange pilgrimage of the Shiloh who is Shelley, traversing our early nineteenth century west, with his companion and foil, in the person of the colloquially homespun David Butternut. Actually a person most like the poet Shelley, I know that Elinor Wylie also saw herself in the character of David, feeling in herself what she and her brother, as children, were wont to allude to as the "johnny-cake" portion of their inheritance; their rootedly American side. (pp. 17-18)

She leaves an imperishable name and the work of a dedicated artist. She leaves to those who loved her a guiding and luminous presence. She demonstrated what one woman's striving and courageous spirit and indomitable mind can accomplish in a few years in a bewildering world, where life may take strange turnings, but where one's purpose in life can finally be found and mastered. Now her work speaks for her to future gener-

ations, and speaks with the incorruptible accent that was all her own. (p. 24)

William Rose Benét, in his lecture delivered at Wheaton College, 1934, in his The Prose and Poetry of Elinor Wylie *(copyright by William Rose Benét 1934; reprinted by permission of Harold Ober Associates), Wheaton College Press, 1934 (and reprinted by The Folcroft Press, Inc., 1969), 24 p.*

W. B. YEATS   (essay date 1935)

Dear Lady Gerald,

Do you know the work of Elinor Wylie? Since I found your work I have had as sole excitement here **'Eagle and Mole',** a lovely heroic song. My wife tells me that Elinor Wylie had a tragic love affair; where she learnt the fact I do not know. I have written for all her work but I doubt if there will be anything else as good. I think that the true poetic movement of our time is towards some heroic discipline. . . . When there is despair, public or private, when settled order seems lost, people look for strength within or without. Auden, Spender, all that seem the new movement *look* for strength in Marxian socialism, or in Major Douglas; they want marching feet. The lasting expression of our time is not this obvious choice but in a sense of something steel-like and cold within the will, something passionate and cold. I went from Elinor Wylie to——and except one rather clumsy poem with a fine last line, found her all what my wife calls 'hot lobster'. (pp. 7-8)

W. B. Yeats, in his letter to Dorothy Wellesley on July 6, 1935, in his Letters on Poetry from W. B. Yeats to Dorothy Wellesley *(reprinted by permission of M. B. Yeats and Anne Yeats), Oxford University Press, London, 1940, pp. 7-9.*

H. LÜDEKE   (essay date 1938)

[Elinor Wylie's] first venture into print was a private edition of a selection of her earliest verse arranged in London through the agency of her mother. *Incidental Numbers* appeared anonymously in 1912. . . . Shortly after her return to America she had enough poems written to begin publishing in *Poetry* and the *Century* magazine, and in 1921 her first collection *Nets to Catch the Wind* came out. It is obviously an assortment of samples of her early work, variously reflecting her careful study of other poets. There are reminders, even reminiscences of Burns and Robert Frost and Emily Dickinson, and the themes vary from descriptions of the country-side to realistic impressions of modern life. Likewise the forms vary from the simple folk-song to the loose structure of modernist verse, and allegory and symbolism are not lacking. It is, on the whole, a variegated fare of many dishes that she set before the literary world of her day—not a surprising thing in a beginner. But what holds all these heterogeneous poems together is the strong personal note—again, not a surprising thing in a woman—, the pervasive first person singular that betrays itself even in the thickest coat of irony. (p. 243)

[Notes] of protective irony, this time much stronger and fuller, [are] struck in her second collection of verse, in *Black Armour*, which appeared two years later. In accordance with the title, itself an expression of the key-note of the whole collection, the poems are grouped under symbolical headings such as: Breastplate, Gauntlet, Helmet, etc. It is not a happy idea, since the poems hardly fit the conceptions associated with the headings and leave them in the air. But there is a decided advance in artistry in all other respects, a complete mastery of rhythm and verse, and the all-too frequent paddings, the loose-joint-edness that betrayed the beginner in the earlier volume has here been overcome. The poems are tightly constructed and with direct force the poet is now able to express what she wants to say. Her themes do not lead to exuberance of any kind: death and the cruelty and hatred of the world and her hiding from it form the burden of her song. Obviously she was still drawing from the most painful experience of her life and the solace she finds in her power of irony and the equanimity of her crystalline mind. Naturally, the collection abounds in personal touches and toward the end a new note is struck, a new love, but a quiet, impassionate one, for a man. . . . ["**Now That Your Eyes Are Shut**"] illustrates sufficiently well what is probably the salient characteristic of Elinor Wylie's work, the delicate preciosity of her imagery, the wealth of fanciful associations that flit lightly off at a tangent. It is a corollary to her irony, perhaps better: the finer, more sublimated form of this ironic spirit. And it is rooted in her mental experience, which is essentially bookish, and is mirrored in her vocabulary, an ec-lectic but usually just mixture of the romantic and the realistic. A comparison with Emily Dickinson would be trite if one did not realise that the younger woman with all the knowledge of the world that Emily lacked, still paced in her poetry a horizon hardly wider than the one the New England spinster and recluse had explored. Indeed, Emily's world is much closer to reality, since she grasped her natural surroundings with a firm hand. But there is still, above and beyond, the other world of dreams, of images and of fancy, nourished by desire and books, and here it is that the two women meet. The pure lyric note, the simple emotion in clarified expression, is rare in both, though more frequent in Emily than in Elinor. They are both poets of sophistication, Elinor Wylie more so than Emily Dickinson. (pp. 244-45)

Jennifer Lorn is an attempt to embody the spirit of an age in a fanciful prose narrative. "**Illuminating Episodes in the Lives of the Hon. Gerald Poynyard and his Bride**", is the subtitle, which does the story in so far an injustice, as the latter consists of more than mere episodes and has a consecutive thread, if not exactly a plot. For the reader follows the eccentric hero and his fairy-like bride from eighteenth century England, where they meet and spend a short part of their married life, to Paris and thence to India, where, in the course of strange adventures, Jennifer loves a fairy prince, elopes with him and dies just in time to escape being handed over to a rajah for his pleasure. There is no reality and no psychological consistency in this India of Jennifer's, just as there is no real England or real London in the book. It is not an atmosphere such as the living characters of a novel might breathe. It is a perfume, a dream-perfume, distilled not from reality but from literature. Eigh-teenth century London is suggested by the passing mention of such names as Gray, Goldsmith, Walpole, Hume, Reynolds, Gainsborough, etc., and India arises to the reader's mind on the same associative foundation. It is the mirrored picture of a picture, a world of phantoms in the centre of which move two figures who are as unreal as their environment. Gerald is a synthetic vision of the eighteenth century Englishman—Lov-elace and Tom Jones and Clive and Walpole viewed in a single individuality. Jennifer is his counterpart in sensibility and "fe-male virtue", with the romantic longings of the Gothic novel added. Such phantasms cannot be drawn seriously without be-coming ridiculous. In fact, they *are* ridiculous and their creator, in presenting them in the full iridescence of her irony, ac-knowledges the fact. But beneath the irony her sympathies are

warmly awake and she clothes the somewhat stark figures of her imagination in a rich robe of prose heavy with poetic im-agery. Lightness of touch, volatility of fancy and wealth of imaginative association go together in forming an epic fabric of rare poetic beauty.

The method found for her first book was followed out and perfected in the others. Jennifer and Gerald had been composite fictions. *The Venetian Glass Nephew* . . . places the fictional symbols in the middle ground and gives most of the space in the foreground to historical figures—taken from literature—who are the bearers of the atmosphere of eighteenth century Venice. They are the Cardinal de Bernis, Carlo Gozzi and Jacques Casanova, here masquerading as "Chastelneuf", while a realistically conceived though fictitious Peter Innocent Bon is the cardinal whose nephew (nepote) figures in the title. . . . The perfume is again evoked in the sonorous names of the Venetian aristocracy with its houses and canals, but the whole shows a more practised hand, a firmer grasp and greater con-sistency of effect than formerly. The outlines seem to be surer and the colours gathered in larger and more forceful surfaces. *Jennifer,* in comparison, had less body; the *Nephew* could draw on a much more suggestive source in the literature and art of the Venetian rococo. "Interior by Longhi" is the title of the final chapter.

From the over-wrought culture of the dying republic on the Adriatic to the raw barbarities of the young republic in the New World was a very far cry, but the temptation must have been great to test the method for which Venice was, after all, an all-too easy subject on the much more recalcitrant material offered by America in the twenties of the nineteenth century. To meet her new task, Elinor slightly changed her mode of attack. The somewhat nondescript structure of *Jennifer* had been clarified in the *Nephew* into a series of scenes and dia-logues, of *conversazioni* such as Venetian painting was so rich in at the time. The American theme is treated in the simple, straightforward narrative of the traveller, taking the reader from New England across the continent to St. Louis, at that time the outer edge of Anglo-Saxon settlement, and thence across the Plains and the Rockies to Southern California, where it stops. The plot is of the thinnest—the search of the hero for the original of the beautiful female portrait in his possession, who is the sister of his companion. The atmosphere admits of no fairy figures, but the hero is no other than Shelley. . . . (pp. 245-46)

[*The Orphan Angel*] has a double theme; against the panorama of the American democracy of the early years is placed the portrait of the ideal democrat of England. But the book is far from being a political tract. The contrast of Shelley's high humanity with the often very imperfect specimens he meets with in his wanderings is indeed one of the essential features of the story, but a repetition of *Modern Chivalry* was hardly in Elinor Wylie's mind. *The Orphan Angel* is her poetic tribute to the poetic spirit she placed above all others and it is a measure of her mastery of her art that the incongruousness inherent in the juxtaposition of two such heterogeneous elements as Shel-ley and the American coon-skin frontier is so smoothly covered over. Indeed, her difficulty lay in another direction, for the essentially earthly realism of the American atmosphere was really beyond her artistic sympathies; her American panorama remains more of a tapestry and carries less essential conviction than the literary perfumes of Venice and India. Perhaps the material was too close to her hand.

From *Jennifer* to the *Angel* there had gone with the growing clarity of outline and firmness of conception a steady approach to reality. In *Mr. Hodge and Mr. Hazard* . . . this process is continued. Her last novel is the least "tapestried" and the most realistic. The period is again the early nineteenth century—a decade or two later than that of the *Angel*—and the scene is England. It is the late Romantic age and the theme is naturally the antagonism of genius and the type of average citizen that later came to be called "Victorian". Mr. Hodge, who appears comparatively late in the story, represents such a Victorian bourgeoisie, while Mr. Hazard contains,—so her sister tells us—a great deal of Elinor Wylie herself. But, as she in real life had some of the personal characteristics of her poet-hero— her voice, when excited, became high and shrill, like his—so Mr. Hazard appears very much like a middle-aged Shelley in the rather shabby household of the Coleridge-Lamb-Southey ménage, here called the Hartleigh family. Opposed to their stuffy idealisms is the clear, sunshiny atmosphere in the country house of Lady Clara Hunting, with the youngest of whose romping daughters, Allegra, Mr. Hazard falls in love, only to be quietly and tactfully frozen out when Lady Clara becomes conscious of it—or rather, when she sees that other people have become conscious of it. In the end, Mr. Hodge wins out and Mr. Hazard goes on his way. The period-perfume has been pushed to the background and the psychological study of complex human relations is beginning to take its place. The book comes perilously near to being a problem novel—the problem of genius and society—and is perhaps a franker expression of Elinor's own experience than any of the others. The attempt to use the figures of her other novels as a perspective background for this one—Lady Clara is a daughter of Gerald Poynyard—is a reminder of how close Elinor's technique stands to that of Cabell. On the whole, the book seems to suggest that, had she lived, Elinor Wylie would finally have developed a light and realistic social comedy.

But she did not live; it was the last year of her life and it almost looks as if she realized it, for she finished in the same year besides the novel two more books of poetry. *Trivial Breath* . . . is an advance in two ways. Technically she has so far mastered her style that she begins to loosen up the verse and to experiment in freer rhythms and in assonances. There is no free verse yet, hardly an approximation to it. But there certainly seems to be an influence of the free verse world in which she was working in such Browningesque lines as those in [*Desolation Is a Delicate Thing*]. . . . And with the freer treatment there goes a more robust spirit that consciously turns away from the aspen sensitiveness of the earlier poems and accepts, even seeks, the world and life as it is. It seems to be the corollary to the growing realism of the novels.

Her poems so far had been the light, often perverse, sometimes brilliant embodiments of whims and fancies rather than of really poetic moods. A certain airy elusiveness, a quicksilvery quality of not being quite all in the reader's hand, was their characteristic and they seemed to evade one's grasp on purpose, studiously to avoid saying what really was in the poet's mind. The titles of the collections have a correspondingly apologetic ring, which sometimes belies their real worth and weight. In her last collection, *Angels and Earthly Creatures* . . . Elinor Wylie has overcome her former shyness and speaks out. And now she has a theme, for the dominant note is furnished by love. One portion of the collection, the nineteen sonnets introducing the volume and addressed to **"One Person"**, are, we are told, the fruit of her attachment during the summer before her death. Many of the other poems, however, express similar moods, though they may have been written much earlier and kept back from publication. Technically the collection shows

the poet marking time, so far as any advance in a modernist direction is concerned, and even a certain retrogression is noticeable in the vague reminiscences of Elizabethanism that occur—the shifting of the stress in three and more syllable words and the rhyming of unstressed syllables. There is an unmistakable flavor of Donne about many of the poems, especially the more thoughtful ones. (pp. 247-48)

The sonnets to **"One Person"** are generally accepted as the consummation of Elinor Wylie's poetry. There certainly is no other group among her poems that leaves so much satisfaction on so many counts. There is a warmth of feeling and directness of thought that is not usual in her work and the circle of experience that is touched upon has a much more general appeal than formerly. Technically the sonnets show a complete mastery of the form. Her experience in handling words in fanciful moods and in light, quick cadences stands her in good stead and she moves perfectly at her ease within the narrow limits of the sonnet structure. But she does not allow it to dissolve in the easy flow of the lines. The inevitable comparison with Elizabeth Barrett is interesting from this point of view as from others. The Portuguese sonnets are much looser in construction, the rhythms not only passing over the ends of the lines but frequently even from the octave to the sestet. The sonnet thus resolves itself into a series of loose rhythms that flow easily and beautifully enough without a break from the first to the last word of the poem, but which bear practically no relation to the peculiar structure of the sonnet as such. Elinor Wylie's sonnets observe the architecture of their kind with careful precision and the final line is fitted to the whole with a clinching emphasis. While Elizabeth Barrett was working with the disregard for form peculiar to the post-Romantics, Elinor Wylie obviously took the Renaissance as her model. But it denotes the difference in temperament between the two women as well; the American even here remains reticent and disciplined and what she has to say is, compared to the Victorian lady's confession, restrained and controlled for a woman of the Twentieth Century. . . .

The positions of the two women in their love, to be sure, are reversed. Elinor's was not a happy passion, with life and the world newly opened before her. Her tones are sombre and the shadow of death is palpably spreading over her. Physically much stronger than Elizabeth Barrett, she was temperamentally much more fragile. She had been familiar with the theme of death from the beginning; it was hardly a youthful moroseness in a woman of thirty, but rather an instinctive awareness of her own feeble hold on life. In the sonnets of her last collection it is almost a pervading theme and it is the burden of several other poems besides. It was as a presage of the approaching end. (p. 249)

Elinor Wylie has been acclaimed by her friends as a "great" poet. Measured, not by the quantity of her output, but by the depth and breadth of her poetical experience, the claim is exaggerated. Her world was limited by her own self and there was not much human sympathy to widen her artistic horizon. Beyond herself she experienced her books. She was essentially a library poet and even in her latest work she was only beginning to pass beyond these limits—at an age over forty. Adjectives of size and weight are inappropriate in her case; for if anything, she was a *rare* poet, expressing rather the secondary virtues of art than the primary ones. Refinement is her essential characteristic as an artist. She had an exquisite sense of the musical and associative value of words; she once wrote a sonnet (uncollected) on this her prime gift. She possessed, besides, an exceptional power of imagery that is more prevalent in her prose than her verse. Her faculty of creating human character, on the other hand, was only rudimentary and never fully developed: her "Shiloh" will hardly do as a portrait of the man Shelley. She was not a poet whose experience plumbed the depth of human life; indeed, she did not even touch bottom in her own generation. But of that post-war age, even now become historical, she was one of the finest spirits, in her quietly breezy detachment like a rest-room in a department store. Aloof as she was in her human relationships, her work will remain apart in the stream of American literature, a thing of fragile beauty and exquisite artificiality. (p. 250)

> H. Lüdeke, "Venetian Glass: The Poetry and Prose of Elinor Wylie," in English Studies (© 1938 by Swets & Zeitlinger B.V.) Vol. XX, No. 6, December, 1938, pp. 241-50.

ALFRED KAZIN   (essay date 1942)

[Like Joseph Hergesheimer, James Branch Cabell, and Thomas Beer, Elinor Wylie] felt the contemporary call to build baroque palaces in prose. But where in poetry her intensity had been spectacular, frozen, neat . . . in her novels it was feverish and artificial. Unlike the others, she did not have to plot and strain to write well; her feeling for style runs all through her work like a pang. But in her novels she was obsessed by the need to make ornate pictures. Everywhere in them human beings are wrought into marble and ironwork, draped luxuriously like silk dolls, sculptured into a frieze, and given a language so overwhelmingly rapturous as to become meaningless. Like Hergesheimer particularly, she inverted Hemingway's aphorism—"Prose is architecture, not interior decoration." For her prose actually was interior decoration, a pleasure dome in itself. If Hergesheimer carried his frank passion for interior decoration to the point where his world often appeared to be composed exclusively of furniture, she drowned her novels in color. Her aim as a novelist was not "poetic"; it was to give life the surface texture of poetry. To that end she overdressed her characters and their world with a breathless eagerness to find beauty everywhere, or fabricate it. Sacrificing good taste to the dream of elegance, she falsified even her fantasies for the sake of rhetoric. And in the end her novels rested on a profound sense of unreality in which everything was larger than life and totally unrelated to it.

The impulse behind Elinor Wylie's novels, of course, was anything but cynical or vulgar; it was rather desperate. Her despair was so fixed on words, the metallic surfaces and echoes of words, the endless pictures she could draw with them, that her novels were like the clamor of hollow gongs. Just as Hergesheimer was always ready to write a sentence like "Annette and Alice appeared with their wraps turned to exhibit the silk linings, bright like their dresses; and, at a favorable moment, they slipped out into the malice of the wind," so she seemed to be drunk on the pathetic fallacy. Her rhetoric flowered in *Jennifer Lorn*, a nightmare in technicolor which described the impossible adventures in India and London of an eighteenth-century hedonist. (pp. 242-43)

In *The Orphan Angel* Mrs. Wylie rescued Shelley from the Gulf of Spezzia, set him on a Yankee clipper, and allowed him to roam along the frontier. It was a boy's book, full of obvious contrasts; but how wonderfully did Shelley talk! . . . It was rhetoric in limbo between poetry and prose, the rhetoric of a writer who was not sure at the moment whether she wanted

to write poetry or prose, and had taken a subtle refuge in fantasy. It was poignant fantasy, where Cabell's was merely fake; but for all its mountainous splendor it could not hide her confusion, her dream of an elegance that was greater than the words that composed it.

Yet perhaps, as Elinor Wylie's lifelong passion for Shelley suggested and *Mr. Hodge and Mr. Hazard* proved, she was merely fighting out the last battle of the Romantic cause. In that last and most effective of her novels, she came closest to the modern scene. A weary stranger, who might have been [Edward John] Trelawny and should have been Byron, returns from Greece to find England already sinking into Victorianism. The conquering acquisitive middle class had succeeded the great Romantic generation after 1830; Mr. Hodge (Macaulay?) stuttered pontifically where Shelley and Keats had mounted on wings of song. *Vale*, then, the days of glory were over. Yet as she had exhumed Shelley in *The Orphan Angel*, so she would now play out Mr. Hazard's part and smolder on what was left of the romantic ecstasy to the end. Had she not, in a curious little novel . . . , *The Venetian Glass Nephew*, resurrected even Casanova? There, among the alchemists of eighteenth-century Venice, her "exquisite monsters" had gathered round for the last time. And the hero—so very appropriately—was made of glass. (pp. 245-46)

> Alfred Kazin, "The Exquisites," in his On Native Grounds: An Interpretation of Modern American Prose Literature (copyright 1942, 1970, by Alfred Kazin; reprinted by permission of Harcourt Brace Jovanovich, Inc.), Reynal & Hitchcock, 1942, pp. 227-46.*

JAMES G. SOUTHWORTH   (essay date 1954)

Miss Elinor Wylie has been favoured with a good "press" and she has often been spoken of as one of America's great women poets. . . . [Although] I can admire some fifteen of her poems, I do not think Time will continue to do what her late husband and his and her friends with ready access to the public's ear were so able to do for her. The poems on which her reputation will rest are early as well as late, serious, humorous, and ironic, and are confined to no one subject. Taken in order from her *Collected Poems*, they are "Velvet Shoes," "Let No Charitable Hope," "Cold-Blooded Creatures," "Love Song," "The little beauty that I was allowed," "I have believed that I prefer to live," "Little Elegy," "Pretty Words," "Viennese Waltz," "Golden Bough," and "A Tear for Cressid." Not all of these are of the same quality and I think none of them ranks with the truly great lyrics in our heritage of English literature. . . . (p. 35)

[Miss Wylie] has a tendency to over-emphasize her state. . . . Particularly is she apt to overstress her ability to make a synthesis out of refractory materials and to over-estimate the precision of her mind.

Death is important in her poetry, particularly as a release of the soul from the prison of the body, a release often intimately bound up with love. But it is her treatment of love that will most appeal to the majority of her readers. Her approach is what Mr. [John Crowe] Ransom calls the "heart's desire" approach, and it reaches its greatest intensity in the sonnet sequence from Section One of *Angels and Earthly Creatures*, known as "One Person." Although the reader will not question the intensity of the emotion, he may well question the artistry with which she expresses that emotion. At no time is the precision of her mind more open to question than in her treatment of details. Extravagance and confusion are often present. . . . Personally, I have always found it difficult to understand why lovers could not be friends, but Miss Wylie, being extremely feminine in her whole approach to life, believes that it is impossible, and is explicit on the subject on several occasions. Her love poems, in spite of their imperfections (or because of them) will appeal to the same readers as does Elizabeth Barrett Browning's "How do I love thee," for which I have never greatly cared. (pp. 35-6)

Certain weaknesses of Miss Wylie are obvious; others call for attention. Quite obvious, for example, is the fact that she is incapable of sustained flight. In **"Miranda's Supper,"** she not only fails with the poem as a whole, but the rhyme word often dictates the thought and some of the rhymes are inexcusable. Even in a shorter poem, such as **"Wild Peaches,"** the thought is often dictated by the rhyme rather than the reverse, as, quite obviously, it should be. Bad rhymes occur frequently throughout her poetry. (pp. 36-7)

At times Miss Wylie's rhythms, never anything but traditional, are too facile, as in **"Silver Filigree"** and some of her ocrosyllabics, always a dangerous measure.

My greatest quarrel is with the details of many of the poems. As pleasant as is **"Velvet Shoes,"** for example, I find "White as a white cow's milk" a little silly. I never thought the whiteness of the cow affected the colour of the milk. In **"Sequence,"** which I confess I find confusing in general, I think her statement that a man might find her skeleton and bury it to "circumvent the wolf" attributes to the wolf an interest in dry bones that he probably does not possess. Were these . . . isolated cases, I should not call attention to them, but such weaknesses flaw poem after poem. (p. 37)

It would be unfair to Miss Wylie, however, not to make some amends. . . . ["**Little Elegy**"] and **"Velvet Shoes"** will certainly be long remembered. In these two the rhythms are more distinctively her own. Elsewhere the music is strongly derivative. There are obvious echoes of Shakespeare, Shelley, and Keats, with an occasional echo of A. E. Housman and Emily Dickinson. Because her rhythms exact no effort from the reader before her music can be enjoyed—it being obvious rather than subtle and delicately modulated—she must pay the penalty of being sooner passed by. Max Friedlander, the great art critic, has remarked that a truly great work will repel before it begins to attract. . . . Miss Wylie's poetry begins by attracting. (pp. 39-40)

> James G. Southworth, "Elinor Wylie: 1885-1928,"
> in his More Modern American Poets, Basil Blackwell, 1954, pp. 35-40.

EVELYN T. HELMICK HIVELY (essay date 1968)

[Literary] criticism assumes a close relationship between a writer's life and his work. In the case of Elinor Eylie, whose most frequent theme was herself—as a great beauty, as a poet, as a lover—knowledge of the details of her life provides valuable insight into the creative process, particularly with her prose.

Even her poems, she readily admitted, often were disguised portraits of herself: **"Peregrine"** is herself and Horace Wylie, her second husband; **"Peter and Paul"** are herself and William Rose Benét. Benét, her third husband, has said that the reader can know her really only from descriptions in her poems. Her prose contains even more revelations, none of them inadvertent. But they are hidden under layers of allegory. She explained her extensive use of this device in an essay called **"Symbols in Literature"**:

> If you call a spade a diamond some people will think you are frivolous and affected, but other people will understand how much blacker things may be said about spades by the simple trick of pretending that they are diamonds.

She was even more specific in an interview granted to a newspaper critic: "Certain things," she said, "are so bitter that I don't want anyone to understand them—hence fantasy." By the time she wrote her novels—during the last five years of her life—she had accumulated much raw material for allegory, drawn from many bitter experiences. (p. 17)

No one realized that [in *Jennifer Lorn*] Elinor Wylie was analyzing and satirizing herself at the same time. Characters and events in the novel have very apparent parallels in her own life. Nancy Hoyt wrote of the physical resemblance of Gerald Poynyard to Horace Wylie; certainly it was Horace who taught the young, untutored Elinor the discipline of art and beauty as Gerald taught Jennifer. Elinor consciously identified with poor Jenny (as she did with all her leading characters). In a letter to Benét written as she worked on the novel, she said, "I lay supine—quite like Jennifer—all day, glad enough to be alone and neither read nor write." And the romantic Prince Abbas, whom Jennifer had to escape, most certainly represents Benét. Perhaps the more earthy, less rarified atmosphere of the world of Abbas-Benét and his journalist friends explains Elinor's strange need each summer to escape to England in order to write in the very towns where Horace Wylie had taught her about art. (p. 23)

But whether read as historical novel, satire, or allegory of her life, the book was successful. . . . [Sales] were surprisingly good, paving the way (with gold) for the publisher's eager acceptance of her second novel.

That was *Venetian Glass Nephew*, again with an eighteenth Century setting, this time in the Italy of art, religion, and magic. The good Cardinal Peter Innocent Bon asks of his old age only to have a nephew to alleviate his loneliness. Through the efforts of Chastleneuf (Casanova) and an evil glass blower, Luna, a glass nephew, Virginio, is created, then vivified. He needs, of course, a wife, and is married to Rosalba, the natural daughter of another Cardinal. They are fond of each other, but their marriage is certain to fail, given his rigid glass body and her warm flesh. Rosalba tries first to die in a fire, then agrees to be transmuted by means of that fire into porcelain herself. Elinor Wylie felt that she had undergone the same kind of transmutation, a kind of purification through emotional pain. . . . In other ways Elinor Wylie resembles Rosalba. Most observers described the author much as Rosalba appeared after her ordeal:

> There was about her an air of perfect calm; she was poised, composed, and quiet, yet without stiffness; her attitude had the grace of a bird arrested in flight, a flower flexible, but unmoved by wind.

The Cardinal is pleased by the change. He "knew instinctively that her spirit was unstirred by any pang that may not be suffered by an exemplary child of seven." This is among the lightest of the book's ironic observations that those who seem most innocent and pious, like Cardinal Innocent, can unintelligently cause much evil, and those who seem corrupt, like Chastleneuf, can know the meaning of the greatest good. Thus, her allegory serves not only as comparison between art and Nature, again, but also as an attack on the society she so despised.

Implicit in this theme is a criticism of her earlier attitude toward poetry. The most frequent theme of the poems in *Nets to Catch the Wind* had been the beauty of the passionless world of art, stated in the popular poems, **"Wild Peaches," "Winter Sleep,"** and **"Velvet Shoes."** Such poems earned for her a reputation as a brilliant, emotionless craftsman. The novels, however, suggest that she regretted the circumstances that made her art so calm. With the next two volumes of poetry, *Black Armour* and *Trivial Breath*, she moved quickly toward a more personal, less reserved expression.

Two further prose works helped to carry forward her exploration of herself. The *Orphan Angel* is again a novel of the eighteenth century. The narrative tells of the rescue of Shelley during the storm which sank his boat. He is brought to America, where his European elegance is tested by the hardships of life in the wilderness. Most critics recognize that this is not a story about America, but most fail to see that it is not a story about Shelley, either. Although Elinor Wylie's so-called Shelley obsession is well known, and her longstanding identification with him as a poet, as a thinker, as an authentic human being, becomes total in *The Orphan Angel*, he is only a part of the subject of this novel. The real subject is Elinor Wylie herself. Not only is she the aristocratic Shiloh, the Shelleyan figure, she is every major character in the book. Davy Butternut, the simple American who serves as Shiloh's companion, is the most important of these. She had always insisted that, in spite of her many years abroad, one part of her was rooted in her family's New England past. She talked often about her homespun side, and in **"Wild Peaches"** she wrote about the "Puritan marrow of my bones." Davy Butternut is all of these elements in her nature. In addition, she was gradually abandoning the baroque language of her earlier works. Dialogue between Shiloh and Davy demonstrates the extremes of language possible in the Wylie novels. Neither form of speech is close to anything a living person would use. (pp. 23-5)

The tastes of the two men in food, clothing, recreation, even women, are, similarly, on opposite ends of the scale, showing the polarities of Elinor Wylie's personality. The women Shiloh and Davy meet on their trek across the continent are also facets of Elinor Wylie's personality: the very young, naïve Melissa Dangerfield, whom they rescue from an unsuitable life with her father; Rosalie Lillie, a frontier bluestocking, who represents what the young Miss Hoyt of Washington society might have become, the lovely Anne, daughter of missionaries, who becomes an Indian princess; and finally Silver Cross, who is a symbol of Platonic intellectual beauty. Many critics think she is the soul sister Shelley sought and finally found through Elinor Wylie's intercession. But Shiloh rejects Silver Cross, in fact, after he has found her, as the author herself was rejecting the purely intellectual life. (p. 26)

[In *Mr. Hodge and Mr. Hazard*, Elinor Wylie] brought back to life not just one poet, but a composite of many poets of the Romantic age, in the person of Mr. Hazard, a poetic failure as the author declared herself to be. Mr. Hazard's attraction to the two daughters of Clara Hunting, Allegra and Rosa, again reveals two sides of Elinor Wylie's nature. Further, this novel, like *The Orphan Angel*, traces the progress of its creator's language:

> Mr. Hazard's hair had been changing from
> bronze into silver, the virgin gold of his heart

had been mixed with a sad alloy. If a heart is open, iron may very easily enter it, to alter the first purity of its metal.

Elinor Wylie became very fond of "poor Mr. Hazard" as she described him in her letters. There is no doubt that he is the author herself, since she made the statement in an interview for the New York *Sun* shortly before her death. (pp. 26-7)

Images of death appear frequently in this novel, as in her final book of poems, *Angels and Earthly Creatures*. But something more significant occurs in that final volume. With the nineteen sonnets called **"One Person"** her work arrives at that expression of herself which she had explored in her four novels. "This miracle," as she calls it, of falling in love unexpectedly produced these poems which have been compared with all the great sonnet sequences. Prepared for publication the night she died, they are a fitting final achievement for a poet who struggled so hard to find her individual voice. (p. 27)

> *Evelyn T. Helmick Hively, "Elinor Wylie's Novels, Allegories of Love," in* The Carrell *(copyright © 1968), Vol. 9, No. 2, December, 1968, pp. 17-28.*

THOMAS A. GRAY (essay date 1969)

[If Elinor Wylie's] second book of poems, *Nets to Catch the Wind*, which she and her publisher pretended was her first, had been published in 1912, it would have appeared as modern as the work of Pound, Lowell, or Frost; and it would have made its author a very important figure in American literary history. . . . [However], this second book could establish its author only as a gifted imitator, with a tenuous and ambiguous kinship to the major writers of the New Poetry. The verse in *Nets to Catch the Wind* shows that the author had not only read the makers of the New Poetry but that she had learned some of their techniques and had adopted some of their standards.

The result is that several of the poems have those qualities which had come to be regarded as indispensable: authentic tone and fresh, concrete, organically functional language. Free of feigned emotion, "poetic" posturing, "poetic" clichés, gratuitous ornament, these early poems suggest that Elinor Wylie, with Pound and others, believed poetry ought to be "at least as well written as prose" and that the "main thing [in literary art] is the genuine love and the faithful rendering of the received impression." Together, these requirements make up the first article of the artist's conscience. Though he must work hard to achieve a beguiling fiction, he must never *fake*: the one enables the natural and effortless surrender of the reader's natural reserve; the other only hardens his disbelief. (p. 20)

In *Nets to Catch the Wind* the tone of authenticity is very strong in two imagistic poems, **"Wild Peaches"** and **"August."** In the latter the apparent intention is to evoke as vividly as possible a simple, sensuous experience. "August" is a carefully arranged pattern in which images of intense sensuousness contrast with images of subdued, restrained sensuousness. . . . (pp. 20-1)

Like **"August,"** *Wild Peaches* (a sequence of four sonnets) dramatizes a distinct kind of sensibility by showing the diversity of its reactions to contrasting kinds of stimuli. **"August"** dramatizes a sensibility that responds positively to only the subtlest, most subdued sensations. *Wild Peaches* suggests a sensibility that craves outright austerity. (p. 22)

These two poems, and five others ("**The Eagle and the Mole**," "**Velvet Shoes**," "**Atavism**," "**Escape**," and "**The Tortoise in Eternity**") are an impressive demonstration of Elinor Wylie's talent. The vigor, precision, compression, concreteness, freshness, and completely functional quality of their language suggest that the author is reporting authentic, flesh-and-blood responses to her experience—not merely affecting poetic poses. These qualities, had they been consistently attained, would have put her poetry square in the tradition then being brought to maturity by her greater contemporaries. (p. 23)

That her successes in that first published volume are outnumbered by her failures is obvious and, by itself, not significant. The really memorable works of some of the more widely and consistently admired poets of the time—Pound, Cummings, Hilda Doolittle, Amy Lowell—can often be tallied up on one's fingers; for the failures of these poets were also numerous. What is significant, and ultimately damaging to Elinor Wylie's artistic stature, is the nature of her failures. The inferior poetry in *Nets to Catch the Wind* represents a violation of the most important principle in the code of the artist: the honest and "faithful rendering of the received impression." Elinor Wylie very often fakes. While some of her best poems give the impression that she aimed for excellence and elegance, her poorest poems suggest that she could readily forget the one in the effort to attain the other, and therefore fall into the role of poetaster.

The genuineness of "**August**" and *Wild Peaches* becomes even more apparent when they are contrasted with the patently contrived "**Winter Sleep**," where the poet tries to convey the same attitudes that she did so effectively in the former poems. In "**Winter Sleep**," however, instead of relying upon freshly concrete images, each of which makes a unique contribution to the achievement of complementary patterns of sound and, finally, to one unified effect, the poet depends to a large extent upon tritely pretty or "poetic" images and figures and upon flat, conventional direct statement. (p. 24)

In other poems Elinor Wylie shows even more clearly that she at times confused elegance with excellence in poetry—the usual result when "beauty" becomes the aim of the poet. In "**Silver Filigree**," for example, she uses images as if they were so many pieces of costume jewelry, just as the nineteenth-century poetasters had done and her own fellow magazine poets were still doing. Though this poem lacks the overwhelming cuteness and sentimentality of certain others of its type, a strain to create purely elegant, or "beautiful" pictorial effect is obvious in nearly every line: the syntax is awkward and out of harmony with the metrical pattern into which it is forced. The forced syntax, in turn makes images and figures of speech seem contrived and awkward; as if they were dictated by the meter rather than by their relevance to the other images of the poem or to its theme. (pp. 26-7)

The reader of *Nets to Catch the Wind* is confronted with a disagreeable paradox: a number of poems which suggest that their author had mastered the techniques of her craft and, more important, had achieved some understanding of the first duty of an artist; but on the other hand, a larger number of poems which suggest that their author was only a half-facile amateur with a trivial conception of her art. The same odd contradiction is posed by all her other volumes of verse: everywhere a similar disparity suggests that her concept of poetry, and of herself as a poet, was vague, inconsistent, and ambiguous, but, most of all, confused.

Her actual performances imply, and her critical pronouncements confirm, that she often confounded elegance with ex- cellence and that she was unwilling or unable to find a reliable basis for distinguishing between prettiness and effectiveness in poetry. Like her numerous contemporaries, the magazine poets, both male and female, she caught that "modern esthetic contagion called the beauty disease" which Whitman had observed in the debilitated poetasters of his time. (pp. 29-30)

What is true of her first volume of poems is also true of her others: her failures exist within the context of a number of impressive successes whose excellence can readily be demonstrated. Her technique in these poems attests to the positive implications of her emphasis on painstaking verse craftsmanship and to her ability to see words as more than "pretty" things "fed on cream and curds." The technique that she insisted on calling "small" and "clean" has enormous limitations, but within these Elinor Wylie managed to produce memorable effects, and a few poems which are masterpieces of their kind.

The first virtue of her technique is prosodic. Even within her "literally diminutive" lines and stanzas, for instance, she often achieved subtle effects of sound and rhythm, and some remarkable adaptations of sound to sense. The motives behind her choice of word or phrase were not always clouded by a desire for sheer elegance; she shows a degree of resistance to the "beauty disease."

The most cursory look confirms that she fully realized her ideal of writing literally diminutive lines and stanzas. Lines of over five feet are extremely rare; she preferred a tetrameter or an even shorter line. "**Peregrine**," for example, consists exclusively of dimeter lines, most of which include an extra, unaccented syllable to give the rollicking effect for which she aimed. (pp. 48-9)

Equally obvious is her preference for the smallest, most compact verse forms—simple quatrains, couplets, the sonnet— forms which, used skillfully, may help compress and intensify expression. She avoided entirely the more complicated Continental verse forms eagerly put to use by such versifiers as Austin Dobson, for example; and she went no farther toward free verse than she did in "**The Coast Guard's Cottage**" or "**Parting Gift**," both of which are composed of couplets and quatrains that are utterly conventional except for their irregular line lengths. She preferred to restrict herself to the simplest, smallest, most compact, and most common meters and verse forms. (p. 49)

Elinor Wylie required a poetic technique with which she could dramatize her desire, implicit in everything she wrote, to have existence a little better than it usually is and to refine everything earthly, polishing the palpable into near-impalpability, or if not this, then at least to lift the ordinary above itself to make it finer, rarer, more beautiful, more precious, more exotic, more fantastic, or more ethereal. Thus in "**Velvet Shoes**" or "**August**," which are direct attempts to dramatize this desire, images with these qualities are completely functional and not irrelevant or meretricious as they are in many other poems. Though fantastically exquisite, the secondary world created by the process of verbal sublimation is not just diminutively picturesque. The pretty words and the pretty things do not exist solely for their own sake; behind their choice is genuine artistic integrity. The verbal alchemy of "**Velvet Shoes**" and "**Now that Your Eyes are Shut**" seems as natural and as inevitable a choice of technique as dramatic contrast in her other successful poems.

The effort "to render" impressions faithfully appears unmistakable in her best poems. In them, technique never seems an affectation but a deliberately chosen medium for communicating emotion and thought. Though in her critical remarks and in much of her poetry, she seemed to regard technique in the same arbitrary way that one might regard a stylish wardrobe or expensive jewelry—something cute, or elegant to put on, to pose in, and to attract attention with; or something with a value apart from any plausible artistic function—seven of her lyrics demonstrate that she could rise above these unworthy conceptions of poetic art. **"Velvet Shoes," "August,"** *Wild Peaches*, **"Atavism," "Now that Your Eyes are Shut," "Sonnet XVIII,"** and **"Thunder Storm,"** taken all together, make up a modest achievement; they may save her name from oblivion. (pp. 58-9)

[*Nets to Catch the Wind* was followed by *Black Armour, Trivial Breath*, and *Angels and Earthly Creatures*.] So slight, however, is the degree of development which each of the last three books represents that all might well seem the productions of a single year. Not only is there no improvement in the quality of the writing, but there is a peculiar uniformity in the "matter" of the poetry. This obvious lack of development led Amy Lowell to refer to Elinor Wylie's work as "static." . . .

Elinor Wylie's subjects and preoccupations vary: but only as a single color varies from shade to shade. The five-year interval between *Nets to Catch the Wind* and *Angeles and Earthly Creatures* is, after all, too short a period to produce any remarkable development of style. But this short time does not altogether account for the limited variety of the subjects and themes of her poetry. By choosing to be a technician and by aspiring to be no more than the literary equivalent of an "enameller" of miniature objects, she excluded herself from a broad range of subjects and a deep range of themes. Though she suggests that she chose to be a mere artificer because she knew that her abilities as an interpreter of life were modest, she did not seem altogether aware of the actual extent to which her decision to be a jewel-smith of language might circumscribe her range of insights, limit her "vision," and practically insure that her work would fail to be great. (p. 60)

The assertion, made by reviewers of her last book, *Angels and Earthly Creatures* (and still echoed in anthologies), that her later poetry suggests a great change in her basic attitudes about existence, and hints at an accommodation to the world and the things of the world is wholly inaccurate. This assertion is based upon a shallow reading of her last poems, particularly of *One Person*, the sequence of sonnets that supposedly describe a love affair which began sometime after she took up residence in England in 1928, the last year of her life. These poems have been supposed by some to repudiate the vestal attitudes expressed in her earlier poems and to represent a strong commitment to human love and passion. Read singly and superficially, some of the sonnets might indeed give such an impression; together, however, neither these nor the other poems of *Angels and Earthly Creatures* suggest an unqualified surrender to love and passion, nor do they provide any other possible basis for an inference that Elinor Wylie had ceased to regard the flesh as anything else than a "fresh-embroidered shroud." (p. 79)

[Reading **"Sonnet VI"**], one becomes aware that *One Person* does not represent any real reversal of Elinor Wylie's basic attitudes. The octave is really a summary of the commonest attitudes found in her poetry: the preference for the fine and the delicate over the gross and the coarse, for form over substance, for essence over existence, for the spirit over the flesh; and, though **"Sonnet VI"** is also a love poem, it does not

reverse any of these preferences. It makes clear that the love experience described in *One Person* is not sensual and physical, nor yet "platonic" and "spiritual." . . . The "definition" of **"Sonnet VI"** puts the love described in *One Person* into a special perspective, which makes impossible the inference that it represents any new attachment to earthly existence. (p. 80)

Elinor Wylie's preference for the . . . [supernatural] is uniform throughout *One Person* and consistent in *Angels and Earthly Creatures*. Those readers who profess to find something "warm and human" in the later poems of Elinor Wylie must overlook her membership in a "peculiar schism," whose object of adulation—even adoration—was a "certain English man of letters," Percy Bysshe Shelley. And those who profess to see in *One Person* a commitment to things human and earthly must also ignore the two sonnets that are unmistakably addressed to the "subtle spirit," Shelley. . . . Indeed, Shelley became so natural a part of her whole consciousness that it is sometimes difficult to determine when she is speaking of him or some sublunary object of affection. She often writes of Shelley as if he did share palpable existence with her. Some poems, like **"Sonnet XIV"** of *One Person*, seem really addressed to Shelley, though ostensibly directed toward an ordinary lover. So, not only is the love in *One Person* "remote and exquisite," but its object is, on at least two occasions, and perhaps more, a particular "remote and exquisite" "subtle spirit."

However, if ignoring Elinor Wylie's adoration of Shelley helps produce one distorted interpretation of her poems, overemphasizing her affection can produce another. There can be no doubt that her preoccupation with Shelley led her to introduce him, as a well-masked "spiritual" presence, into a few of her poems. Indeed, without some hint about this practice a reader will find certain poems cryptic. On the other hand, while a small number of Wylie's poems echo Shelley, allude to him, or even covertly evoke his "presence," and some of these works—like her novel, *Orphan Angel*—even suggest an oddly intense admiration for the English Romantic, no poem or group of poems suggests that Elinor Wylie was obsessed with him. The hints of Shelley in her poetry are too few and too subtle to suggest anything that intense. Wherever he appears he is so well masked that neither the immediate context of a given poem nor that of all the poems allows even a guess at "his" identity. (pp. 81-2)

[The] total number of poems in which Shelley figures in any way at all makes up a very small percentage of *The Collected Poems of Elinor Wylie* . . . and *The Last Poems of Elinor Wylie*. . . . Thus there is a great disparity between the amount of attention given Shelley in the poems and the alleged intensity of her "Shelley obsession." . . . Even less do they suggest that, as one critic has claimed, in the last years of her life Elinor Wylie occasionally had the hallucination that she was a "reincarnated Shelley." In these poems she adores Shelley no more than any other rare, fine, exquisite, beautiful, ethereal, impalpable, delicate, or elegant object or sensation. For her he was both refuge from and spiritual ally against the rude, gross, and antagonistic world.

Elinor Wylie's poetry is largely a portrayal of the stratagems by which a fragile sensibility shields itself from the threats and shocks of existence in a world too rough for it. While such tricks hardly amount to high strategy, they all spring from a common conviction that the world is an inadequate and even hostile environment for the self. Because the stratagems often seem absurd, ill-considered, or desperately adopted tricks and sophistries . . . some critics have concluded that she had no genuine convictions and no real style. These critics, too eager to prove that she had merely "cobweb attitudes," apparently assume that behind artifice and stratagem there can be no conviction at all.

Though her Romantic conviction that the world is an unfit environment for the self may be easily attacked, or even refuted, it can not be wished out of existence. She may be wrong in her estimate of human existence, but she is not, finally, irresponsible. Her evaluations are demonstrably clear and consistent. Her poetry has no "great" theme; many of her poems do not even do that minimum, suggested by Robert Frost, of forming "a temporary stay against confusion." Some of them even add to the confusion that is a consistent feature of human life. A few, however, even if they do not form a "stay" against confusion, raise an articulate cry against it. (pp. 83-4)

The general critical reactions to the strange amalgams of style in Elinor Wylie's work have been roundly negative. Critics have judged her poetic physiognomy as a crazy mask patched together with fragments appropriated or imitated from the works of her favorite poets, and colored deeply by the attitudes and idioms of her rather undistinguished "Lyrist" contemporaries. From the point of view of such critics, she not only failed to achieve the peculiarity of expression which would unfailingly distinguish her from her models and her contemporaries, and which constitutes the simplest sense of *style*, but she also failed to achieve that perfect accommodation of form to content which is the largest modern sense of *style*. (pp. 115-16)

Elinor Wylie's later work, moreover, represents a reversal of the normal direction of development of a writer's art, in which his unique way of using language seems ever more the "necessary and inevitable" expression of his individual way of seeing and feeling. For instance, the "new" way of speaking in *One Person* does not suggest any new way of feeling. The language of the eighteen sonnets, with one or two exceptions, does not seem at all "necessary and inevitable," nor is there in the language any suggestion of a new self-consistent way of regarding experience. Even the author's word that the sonnets in *One Person* are addressed to a man with whom she fell in love is not enough to offset the impression of meretriciousness that the poems give.

Only rarely in her work is there a suggestion of that complete absorption with and penetrating comprehension of her subject which has been considered essential for achieving expression that seems necessary and inevitable for those subjects. Instead of being absorbed with them, she seems absorbed with herself; and, like a vain orator, she forever draws attention away from *what* she is saying by the *way* in which she insists on saying it. This characteristic explains the thinness of her themes and the fragility of her style: in place of fresh perceptions, she very often gives an artificially posed personality and, in place of style, stylishness. (pp. 116-17)

Thomas A. Gray, in his Elinor Wylie *(copyright © 1969 by Twayne Publishers, Inc.; reprinted with the permission of Twayne Publishers, a Division of G. K. Hall & Co., Boston), Twayne, 1969, 171 p.*

EDWARD DUCHARME (essay date 1970)

"**The Eagle and the Mole**" is a symbolic treatment of man's attitude towards his fellow men. Seemingly sympathetic towards extremes of life which foster isolation and seclusion, the poem ultimately embraces the life of man among men.

There is in the title an initial suggestion of things opposite, the eagle that soars high and the mole that burrows beneath the earth. The almost spontaneous response is indeed to think of these two objects from the natural world as opposites. Yet the title forces reconsideration of this process, for the two nouns are joined by the conjunction *and*, a consistent grammatical signal for parallelism. These words, so joined, indicate that while the eagle and the mole may be considered as opposites in the sense mentioned, there is also going to be something stated or implied that applies to both.

Wylie's method of presentation is, on the surface, straightforward. The first, second, and third stanzas deal with the eagle and his position high above the mob or herd. After the transitional first two lines of the fourth stanza, the remainder of the poem is concerned with the mole and his position beneath but clearly removed from the herd.

The opening stanza is a series of three imperatives urging the listener or reader to shy away from any contact with large groups, masses, or herds; in brief, to live like the eagle, removed and above all things. The herd and flock are described by two extremely derogatory adjectives: *reeking* and *polluted*. The eagle is described as *stoic*, a word suggesting inner strength and power to endure; further, he is spoken of as "the eagle of the rock," a phrase suggesting strength.

The use of imperatives in the first stanza and in later portions of the poem indicates that the poet is speaking to the reader or to people in general. The poet's urgings are stated so that one must compare the eagle and the mole with humanity, that the attributes ascribed to the two creatures are to have some applicability to man. While such an indication is obvious from even a careless reading of the text, one must point it out and, more importantly, insist on keeping it in mind throughout the poem. It is not the creatures that are being described so much as it is the human types they represent.

At this point one should again consider the title. Because of the pairing of the two nouns by the word *and*, it was pointed out earlier that, even though opposite in one sense, the two creatures were going to be paired in some way. Since they cannot be paired in terms of activity or appearance, a logical other point of comparison might be the symbolic use the poet makes of the two. The first stanza has, in the reading given thus far, strongly suggested the power and force of the eagle, two attributes that might be considered positive. The question that now arises is that of the use the poet will make of the mole, a creature that is, after all, a member of a class of animals that burrow underground, rarely seeking the light. One must conclude that the poet is setting an impossible task, holding back something unexpected, or not using the eagle in the positive sense thus far suggested.

The first stanza contains one clue supporting the third alternative. The word *stoic* need not be read as a positive modifier of the eagle; instead, the work may suggest not courage but withdrawal.

The second stanza furthers the suggestion that the eagle might not be a positive symbol. The poet again speaks of the herd, this time in a slightly less negative way. The crowd is marked by huddled warmth, even though the warmth does beget and foster hate at times. There is, it seems, an obvious implication of the poet's statement: something begat the huddled warmth of the crowds in the first place, perhaps the desire for companionship or a show of affection. It is clear that stoicism did not beget it. The eagle himself is described in less potentially positive terms in the second stanza; the word *inviolate* suggests an almost excessive purity, a wish not to be bothered or touched by contact with the mob.

The opening of the third stanza continues the less harsh description of the masses as the poet speaks of the flocks' being "folded warm" as the eagle "soars above the storm" and "stares into the sun." The eagle, perhaps seen earlier as a symbol for human individualism, is now seen as a symbol for the nonhuman. What kind of human, even in a symbolic way, stares into the sun? One who will, if he stares long enough, become blind like the mole. In addition, the previously suggested implication of *inviolate* is furthered in "He sails above the storm," a statement implying a solution of a problem by avoiding it.

In the three stanzas dealing with the eagle, the bird is offered as a representative of a way of life suitable for those who would avoid the masses. In a spirit of irony that marks much of the poem, the poet implies that some cannot go the route of the eagle, yet would still avoid the pack. These are offered the way of the mole, that of a burrowed existence beneath life. This death in life existence of the mole is further evidence of the author's ironic intent. She is urging that man seek "life" underground, surrounded by dead bones. Further, the tripping rhythm throughout gives the lie to the imperatives of the poem.

The poet's strategy in her treatment of the mole is similar to her treatment of the eagle. She first uses several derogatory adjectives to describe the mob: *lathered, steaming*. She more quickly notes the negative way of the mole, however, by phrases such as "would keep your soul / From spotted sight or sound." Here, of course, is the "inviolate" of the second stanza.

Finally, the follower of the eagle who cannot leap into the eagle's track is urged to hold intercourse with roots, river sources, and disembodied bones, a singularly unattractive way of life.

The poem presents two alternatives, each unattractive as ways of life for human beings. If neither the way of the eagle nor the way of the mole is appropriate, what is the way of life proposed by the poet? Is it the way of the reeking herd, the polluted flock, the lathered pack and the steaming sheep? The solution does not lie outside the crowds, at least not in the ways of life represented by the eagle and the mole. If the solution does not lie outside the crowds, it must lie within. Indeed, this is the direction the poem suggests. Supporting this conclusion are the previously noted progression of modifiers describing the crowds and the near-contempt for keeping one's soul from spotted sight or sound. The alternative to the avoiding and the hiding of the eagle and the mole is existence within.

There is another support for this conclusion. The masses are, in this poem, spoken of in terms of generating animals: *herd, flock, pack,* and *sheep*. Further, there is a succession of words suggesting, at a second level of reading, procreation: *begets, fosters, burrow,* and *intercourse*. An analysis of the last word cited will be used as an illustration.

As the poet is using the word *intercourse* in line 21, the word means discourse. Yet, placed in the poem with the presence of other words like *herds* and *flocks, begets* and *fosters,* the word takes on at the very least the suggestion of sexual intercourse. One then raises the question about what kind of sexual intercourse—even on a figurative level—one can have with roots of trees, with rivers at their sources and disembodied bones. The answer is that he can have the kind that reflects

his life: removed, distant, dead—the kind of existence attributed to the eagle and the mole. A consideration of the second level of such words as well as the other aspects noted above does reinforce the idea that the poet is, by irony and understatement, saying that life can be lived only by participating in it, despite its occasional reeking and polluted qualities, perhaps even because of them. Lone and withdrawn existence may suffice for eagles and moles but not for man. (pp. 109-12)

Edward Ducharme, "Again, Evasion of the Text," in English Record *(copyright New York State English Council 1970), Vol. XXI, No. 1, October, 1970, pp. 108-12.*

EMILY STIPES WATTS (essay date 1977)

Millay and Wylie were good friends, and their poetry is often considered together as "female Lyrist," apparently a new twentieth-century category of poetry which has been conceived especially for women poets such as Millay, Wylie, [Sara] Teasdale, [Lizette] Reese, and others. . . . Actually, the term *Lyrist* itself is a catchall and condescending critical term which is a development from the concept of "female poetry" of the nineteenth century. Moreover, the generalization which this term demands is wrong. Sara Teasdale is not Lizette Woodworth Reese is not Elinor Wylie is certainly not Edna St. Vincent Millay.

Actually, of all these women, Wylie does most closely resemble the "Lyrist" poet as that term is defined: she did wish to produce small, neat, meticulous poems; she did use traditional meters; and her images are often not essential to the poem. With influence from Shelley, her style is poetically between those of Teasdale and Millay. Poems such as **"Pity Me"** and **"Let No Charitable Hope"** are reminiscent of Teasdale's poetry of withdrawal; **"Where, O, Where?"** and **"Enchanter's Handmaiden"** suggest the independent and vigorous poetry of expansion of Millay and Dickinson. One of her most interesting poems is **"Letter to V—,"** addressed to Millay—a listing of their theological and hence for them essentially personal differences. In certain of her ballads and her self-conscious thrust toward a more general humanism, Wylie also resembles Guiney, who was writing her best poetry when Wylie was a teenager. (pp. 170-71)

Wylie did not understand the dynamic power of words (in the way, for example, Dickinson did), but she is sensitive to their sound and connotative qualities, as is evident in **"Pretty Words."** She mixes an emotional softness, as in **"Bread Alone,"** with types of poems which critics like to term "masculine," such as **"Peregrine."** At times, as in **"Heroics,"** she believes that the world is a wasteland, but she is also able to accept the truth of simple, optimistic morality (**"The Lion and the Lamb"**) and, in other poems, is willing to assert that the reality of the world is certain and "lovely," even though it is "a thin gold mask" (**"Sunset on the Spire"**). In poems such as **"Nancy"** and **"Francie's Fingers,"** there are traces of nursery rhymes in her verse. She asserts her individuality, her sense of self-value in **"Unfinished Portrait"** and **"False Prophet"**; offers a gift from a "sorceress" to the familiar female mythological figure in **"To Aphrodite, with a Talisman"**; and honors other women, as, for example, in **"On a Singing Girl"** and **"To Claudia Homonoea."** As she grew older, she came to love London; and, as in **"One Person,"** her poems began to resemble those of Elizabeth Barrett Browning. (p. 171)

Emily Stipes Watts, "1900-1945: A Rose Is a Rose with Thorns," in her The Poetry of American Women from 1632 to 1945 *(copyright © 1977 by University of Texas Press), University of Texas Press, 1977, pp. 149-76.**

STANLEY OLSON   (essay date 1979)

Unlike Lord Byron and Lytton Strachey, Elinor did not wake up one October morning in 1921 to find herself famous. The recognition she received for *Nets to Catch the Wind* was of a more somber variety, and very long in coming. . . . When critics opened [the book], they found a great deal to arrest them. The most captivating things were the certainty and the angular emotions of the poems. Phrases like Louis Untermeyer's "sparkle without burning," "frigid ecstasy," "passion frozen at its source," became critics and reader's leitmotifs in describing her work. She seemed capable of combining stunning craftsmanship with ethereal sentiments. She was a nimble, yet sure, technician of almost orgiastic images, which she destroyed as decisively as she built them up. Her ability to convey lushness through austerity was startling. All the confidence that was absent in her life was distilled on the page. (p. 184)

[Most of the poems that make up *Black Armour*] were published in periodicals beforehand. Like her headaches, [Elinor's] poetry offers an index to her feelings. While the letters reveal a certain degree of childlike absurdity, since she was playing up to Bill [Benét] and indulging in a degree of arrogance, her poems uncover a darker, almost fatalistic submission. There she descended into the emotions that in life she tried so hard to hide, and even then she was not direct. She abstracted her emotions, moving from reality to myth, and so giving them dignity. Her imagery reversed night and day. She turned standard symbolism around, equating daylight with fantasy and night with harsh reality. Truth unfolded in blackness, while fantasy thrived in full light. This extraordinary reversal had its root in nothing more complicated than her chronic fear of her own feelings. (p. 201)

Like her poetry, Elinor's novels stepped back into the eighteenth and early nineteenth centuries. She shared with Joseph Hergesheimer, Robert Nathan, James Branch Cabell, and Carl Van Vechten a deft talent for escapism. She felt more at home in the world she read about in William Hickey. And [in *Jennifer Lorn*] she produced a novel that Max Beerbohm claimed (in a letter dated November 1923, but never sent): "I feel I should like to have written myself."

Dedicated to her mother, written almost under the eye of Bill, the novel is unquestionably about Horace [Wylie]. . . . Horace is fashioned into Gerald Poynyard; Elinor is Jennifer; and other friends such as Louis Untermeyer, who figures as the not altogether complimentary figure of the prince, make an appearance. The whole novel hinges on the device of allegory. (p. 229)

While adhering to the literary conventions of the eighteenth century, Elinor created a novel that was very weak on interest. She overcame this obstacle, she believed, by being fascinating instead: "The thinness of incident in *Jennifer Lorn* is obscured by the lush descriptive foliage; where plot may appear deficient, characterization maintains the interest," maintains Nancy Potter, who has written a thesis on Elinor. The book evolves into an inventory of detail. It was as if Elinor was unable to assimilate and transform her sources; she had done too much research. (pp. 229-30)

The story of *Jennifer Lorn* is uneventful. It is a romance that moves from India, where Gerald Poynyard (later Lord Camphile) has earned a fortune, to England, where he marries Jennifer, and back again. To this slim outline Elinor adds Gothic melodrama in the latter portion of the novel: Gerald is killed—it is thought by robbers; Jennifer is imprisoned in a Persian court from which she escapes, is eventually recaptured, and dies. Upon this narrow plot Elinor weaves elaborate descriptions and florid details. Brilliant metaphors, feats of imagery, and lengthy depiction, stand in the place of events. Elinor saw the novel as an opportunity to expand the truncated skills she employed in her poetry. And if *Jennifer Lorn* is an allegory, it perhaps displays her favorite device. Defense proves the surest form of attack—the detail, the dense "foliage," and the over-ample lushness of the narrative replace action. (pp. 230-31)

[*The Venetian Glass Nephew*] is Elinor's most exquisite and famous prose creation, and indeed that is precisely what the *Nephew* was—a creation, spun from glass into the shape of an heir to satisfy the vanity of Cardinal Peter Innocent Bon, who actually descends into the pagan underworld to retrieve his nephew. The entire novel is a battle between opposites. It is constructed almost like a frieze of undigested research, across which dance like light and shade the permutations of the basic theme: reason struggling against emotion, and lust opposing chastity. White and black play an important part in the story. Virginio is introduced, as one might expect with glass, in a portrait drawn in white. His lover, Rosalba Berni, "better known among the Arcadians of Italy as Sappho the Younger, or . . . the Infant Sappho," enters swathed in black. . . . The victim of [the ensuing "unnatural warfare"]—the combat between the warm vulnerability of emotions and the frozen invulnerability not so much of reason as the absence of emotions—is Rosalba. She is the one who crosses over in a journey that takes her from life to porcelain. (pp. 251-52)

Elinor's *Nephew* is the most acute documentation of her affection for reversal. The lifeless, bloodless qualities of glass and silver heaved with animation in her mind. The exigencies of the flesh were ripe for distress. Life was, for her, a subtle progression of denial, a steep advance on the Purita; pleasure is born in denial and happiness is the result only of pain. Every sensation has its root in the destruction of sensation. Elinor understood standard values by turning them around; and if one viewed the entire *Venetian Glass Nephew* in a mirror, its reversed image would be an appropriate nursery fable. Such transitions gave Elinor's work their strength, and Elinor herself her endurance. It is a deceptively simple tale, complicated by the simple device she explained in her essay *Symbols in Literature*.

Once again the symphony of opposites is clad in the richest clothing from the wardrobe of eighteenth-century Venice, and, as in *Jennifer Lorn*, Elinor comes close to suffocating her story. (pp. 252-53)

Her novel *The Orphan Angel* was designed to retrieve Shelley from his premature death in the Gulf of Spezia on July 8, 1822, by having him found and resuscitated by the crew of an American clipper ship, *Witch of the West*. . . . Elinor's portrait of Shelley (renamed Shiloh, which she borrowed from Byron) is a mixture of accuracy and awe. . . . And her story makes heavy strides through well-researched scenes, episodes, and terrain. Her devotion to Shelley obliged her to pause too long and too often in the course of her narrative. She was hopelessly impeded by her passionate regard for her subject—a dependence that was lacking in her previous two novels.

The idea for the novel was inspired. In her Shelley/Shiloh character she merely, so she told herself, took over where history left off. To her the belief that Shelley might have been fished out of Leghorn Harbor was not so preposterous; she had been envisaging it for years. It was an extremely clever device by which she could mingle the real with the imagined. But the execution of the novel was not inspired, largely because she sensed potential opposition from her readers (a detail she rarely thought about while writing her other books) and retreated further than ever behind the protection of her researches into nineteenth-century America—a location and period she found herself as uncertain in dealing with as in her earlier excursions into eighteenth-century Venice, England, India, and Persia. Instead of enticing her readers by her irrepressible enthusiasm for Shelley, she would leave them dazed and impressed simply by the weight of her work. . . . It was the only one that would split the critics decisively between ardent admiration and utter loathing. (pp. 260-61)

Though [Elinor's] last novel was slow to find its way onto paper, once begun it was finished rapidly. "The novel of Mr. Hodge and Mr. Hazard is," she commented in her brief preface, "an everyday fable; its historical trappings are slight, and it must remain not a disguised biography but a brief symbolic romance of the mind." (p. 296)

Elinor had a talent, as E. F. Benson once expressed it, for smudging the truth. She blurred reality, and in *Mr. Hodge and Mr. Hazard* she ran her hand over a nineteenth-century English canvas that depicted scenes introduced from her life in the twentieth century. She reproduced in her books, and especially in this one, a somewhat more satisfactory version of actual scenes. "I say it is meringue," she added to Helen Young, "but you will see it is really meringue flavoured with strychnine rather than vanilla-bean. This is my only *metier;* to take a *memento mori* and trim it with rosebuds and *point d'es-prit.* . . ."

In four months Elinor produced her most mature, and for many of her readers, her best novel. It lacks the outright fantasy of *The Venetian Glass Nephew,* but it at once encompasses the imagination that made *Jennifer Lorn* so attractive and the cynicism that comes from frank awareness. It has a maturity that all her cramming had buried so well before. She is more comfortable with her characters and her narrative. In a device that Carl Van Vechten used to such advantage, characters from her previous novels crop up. Lady Clara Hunting is the daughter of Gerald Poynyard, who himself had met, at one time, Rosalba Berni before she turned into porcelain. Just as Elinor had grown older, so her characters receded further and more easily into the history she created for them. The narrative moves more gracefully, more gently, and yet there is as little incident as in the three earlier novels. (p. 297)

Mr. Hodge and Mr. Hazard is a simple tale, almost deceptively simple. Its thin story does not crack under the weight of the overwriting and florid imagery that detracted from her other novels. It has at once a freshness and depth that was denied Shiloh, Jennifer, and her Venetian characters. Some of the touches are arrestingly clever. When Hazard is suffering from influenza, he refuses to go to sleep, preferring to sit up reading Tennyson: "Presently he could read no longer. While the chill shook his bones asunder, like breakable dice in a black dice-box, he lay staring out of the window into the impenetrable

emptiness of the fog, wishing that the exaltation and valour of his mind had not been shrivelled up into scorched peas and rusty needles." The little that passed for plot was made up for in effect. It was her simplest and most successful prose achievement, less successful in terms of sales than *The Orphan Angel,* but a far more sustained, subtle work. It was her fourth, and final, novel. . . . Thereafter Elinor turned back to poetry. (pp. 298-99)

Trivial Breath, taken as a whole, was a tidying-up exercise. After disposing of the burden of Shelley, Elinor moved straight on to herself as the main subject matter for her poems. The material in these poems is entirely different from that encountered in her first two books: the Elinor here has grown weary of paradox, distrustful of striking imagery, and indeed, disdainful of her own excessive frigidity. Less antagonistic, less brittle, less harsh, she seems finally to have crossed over into the region of more human feelings—a journey she had been making steadily in her poetry since 1923, but had only recently achieved in her novels. She appeared to retire from the battle waged heroically with herself. The transition was swift and undramatic, but it is difficult to read the collection of poetry in any light other than autobiographical. The relationship with Bill is lightly touched upon in "Peter and John," . . . and her visit to the Powyses (where she stayed in a nearby cottage that had been owned by a man who had recently drowned) is celebrated in "The Coast Guard's Cottage." Rather than looking back, the sonnets that open the third section of the book hint at the "One Person" sonnets that signaled her farewell. Other poems, like "'As I Went Down by Havre de Grace . . .'"—which sings a *ritornello* on her entire life, looking far back to her father's grave at Forty Fort, Pennsylvania—and "A Strange Song," stand among the finest she ever wrote. The bitterness of her poetry six years before has been sweetened, not by greater strength or mere cleverness, but by resignation. The current of transition is strong in these poems. (pp. 300-01)

Elinor's "One Person" sonnets are, perhaps, her finest achievement. They are her testimony to the power of her emotions, distilled and purified. It is appropriate that she should have chosen the form of Petrarch, which was so suited to and famous for love. The love in these poems is not a private love, not a variety of confession, but an abstracted one, free of the protection of subjectivity. And although her expression is clear throughout, she does not ignore the pain that affection arouses; she does not, as she had done in her actual relationship with [Cliff] Woodhouse, misinterpret, overbalance, or spill into excess. The nineteen sonnets are paced with strength, energy and undeniable feeling, sustained as a group by shifting through the complexities and vicissitudes of love. And the confidence that had been born in doubt is impressive. (p. 322)

Stanley Olson, in his Elinor Wylie: A Life Apart, a Biography *(copyright © 1979 by Stanley Olson; reprinted by permission of The Dial Press), Dial Press, 1979, 376 p.*

ADDITIONAL BIBLIOGRAPHY

Brenner, Rica. "Elinor Wylie." In her *Poets of Our Time,* pp. 311-54. New York: Harcourt, Brace and Co., 1941.
    Biographical and critical commentary. Brenner focuses on Wylie's life, her struggles with society, and how these conflicts were resolved in her poetry.

Clark, Emily. "Elinor Wylie." In her *Innocence Abroad,* pp. 167-86. New York, London: Alfred A. Knopf, 1931.
> An account of Wylie's first visit to Virginia, where she met James Branch Cabell, and of her frequent trips to England.

Cluck, Julia. "Elinor Wylie's Shelley Obsession." *PMLA* LVI, No. 3 (September 1941): 841-60.
> Examination of Wylie's last two novels and selected poems from *Trivial Breath* and *Angels and Earthly Creatures.* Cluck focuses on Wylie's growing "obsession" with Shelley in an analysis of her later fiction and poetry.

Cowley, Malcolm. "The Owl and the Nightingale." *The Dial* LXXIV, No. 6 (June 1923): 624-26.
> Early review of Wylie's *Black Amour.* Cowley compares Wylie's surface qualities to T. S. Eliot's but questions her ability to combine intellect with emotion.

Deutsch, Babette. "The Ghostly Member." In her *Poetry in Our Time: A Critical Survey of Poetry in the English-Speaking World, 1900-1960,* rev. ed., pp. 243-68. Garden City, N.Y.: Anchor Books, 1963.*
> Discussion of Wylie's style as a poet. Deutsch concludes that Wylie shared "Blake's profound simplicity" and had "the craftsman's concern for phrasing, and for the sensuous qualities of words."

Gray, Thomas A. "Elinor Wylie. The Puritan Marrow and the Silver Filigree." *Arizona Quarterly* 19, No. 4 (Winter 1963): 343-57.
> Analysis of selected poems. Gray argues that Wylie, in her best poems, avoided the "raw emotion" and banality of the imagists by carefully selecting her figures and metaphors, though in her lesser works she often crossed the threshold of preciousness.

Hoyt, Nancy. *Elinor Wylie: The Portrait of an Unknown Lady.* Indianapolis, New York: The Bobbs-Merrill Co., 1935, 203 p.
> Biography by Wylie's sister, giving a personal account of the author's life both as a writer and as a woman misunderstood by those around her.

Kreymborg, Alfred. "Women, As Humans, As Lovers, As Artists." In his *A History of American Poetry: Our Singing Strength,* pp. 438-65. New York: Tudor Publishing Co., 1934.*
> Examination of selected poems from Wylie's four volumes of verse. Kreymborg calls Wylie a "craftsman" with "few peers" and an artist who attempted to voice the disillusionment after World War I on a private level according to her "aristocratic nature."

Sergeant, Elizabeth Shepley. "Elinor Wylie." In her *Fire Under the Andes: A Group of North American Portraits,* pp. 107-21. London, New York: Alfred A. Knopf, 1927.
> Biocritical discussion. Sergeant presents an imaginative portrait of Wylie's life and her development as a writer.

Untermeyer, Louis. "Bill and Nefertiti." In his *From Another World,* pp. 229-53. New York: Harcourt, Brace and Co., 1939.*
> Personal recollection. Untermeyer reconstructs the relationship between Elinor Wylie and William Rose Benét, discussing their first meeting and their eventual friendship and love.

Van Doren, Carl. "Elinor Wylie." In his *Carl Van Doren,* pp. 66-90. New York: The Viking Press, 1945.
> Tribute to Wylie by her friend and editor. Van Doren discusses the "legend" surrounding Elinor Wylie's life upon her reception in New York and the literary world.

Wood, Clement. "Elinor Wylie: The Jewelled Brain." In his *Poets of America,* pp. 262-74. New York: E. P. Dutton & Co., 1925.
> Analysis of Wylie's poetry. Wood considers the poet one of the best technicians of her time.

Wright, Celeste Turner. "Elinor Wylie: The Glass Chimaera and the Minotaur." *Twentieth Century Literature* 12, No. 1 (April 1966): 15-26.
> Examination of Wylie's four novels, emphasizing the style of her fiction. Wright suggests a number of writers, such as Shelley, Oscar Wilde, and Edgar Saltus, who might have influenced Wylie's work.

Yevgeny Ivanovich Zamyatin

1884-1937

(Also transliterated as Evgeny, Yevgenii, Yevgeni, and Eugene; also transliterated as Zamiatin, Zamjatin, and Zamayatin) Russian novelist, novella and short story writer, dramatist, essayist, critic, and autobiographer.

Zamyatin is considered one of the most influential Russian writers in the decade following the Bolshevik revolution. As a lecturer during this period, he urged young writers to renounce the methods of the nineteenth-century Russian classics and to create a new reality through experimentation with form and language. Zamyatin consistently employed new techniques in his art. His work is recognized for its arresting language, fantastic and grotesque imagery, and ironic viewpoint. Structurally his stories developed quite differently from those of the realists and symbolists. Rather than focus on objective reality or subjective experience, they revolve around a central image, what D. S. Mirsky termed a "mother metaphor." A good example of this central image is the iron stove in "Peščera" ("The Cave"). While Zamyatin argued for an escape from nineteenth-century Russian realism, his belief in the inherent goodness of humanity's irrational nature echoes tenets voiced by such realists as Tolstoy and Dostoevsky. And although his techniques were much different, Zamyatin dealt with a common concern: how to overcome individual alienation in a seemingly meaningless world.

Zamyatin, the son of an orthodox priest, was born in the central Russian town of Lebedyan. As a child he had few friends, and he turned to books for companionship. Among his favorite authors were Dostoevsky, Turgenev, and Gogol. Upon graduating from the Voronezh Gymnasium in 1902, Zamyatin entered the Petersburg Polytechnic Institute for Naval Architecture. His studies were deferred when he was arrested and exiled for revolutionary activities in 1905 and again in 1911. During this time Zamyatin published a few stories, but it wasn't until the publication of his satire on Russian provincial life, *Uezdnoe (A Provincial Tale)*, that he gained literary recognition. After the 1917 revolution Zamyatin, like so many Russian artists, became disenchanted with the Soviet regime. During this postrevolutionary era he wrote what many consider his most important work, the novel *My (We)*. Though it is not documented that *We* was a reaction specifically against Soviet communism, Zamyatin's attack on the communist's vision of a regimented civilization is hardly concealed. The novel stands as a tribute to humanity's primitive vitality—that essential characteristic which Zamyatin believed was the foundation of all individual freedom. *We* was banned from publication in Russia; when an unauthorized portion of the work appeared in a Russian *émigré* journal, Zamyatin was silenced as a writer. Soon afterward he went into voluntary exile in France, where he spent the remainder of his life.

Zamyatin's commentators, most notably Alex M. Shane, have divided his literary career into four periods. The first, which includes such works as *A Provincial Tale* and *Na kulichkakh*, deals with provincial settings and themes. Zamyatin's belief in the inherent tragedy of life is apparent throughout the works of this period, though this tragedy is often distanced by the author's penetrating irony. Also characteristic of these stories

Drawing from a photograph; reproduced by permission of Ardis Publishers

is Zamyatin's use of local dialects, colloquialisms, and the *skaz* manner of narration—a literary device in which a narrator relates his story in provincial speech. The second period begins with the tale "Ostrovityane" and ends with Zamyatin's only completed novel, *We*. The works of this period depart from the *skaz* narrative and are characterized by formal and stylistic innovations; the most important of these display Zamyatin's increasing use of the image as a unifying device. As illustrated by *We*, Zamyatin shifted his concerns from provincial backwardness to the automatization of human life and the alienation of humanity from nature. The transitional third stage in Zamyatin's career is marked by a search for new literary forms. The stories produced at this time are on the whole inferior to the earlier work. The most important, "Rasskaz o samom glavnom ("A Story about the Most Important Thing"), typifies Zamyatin's efforts to create a literary structure based on the theories outlined in his essays. In the final period Zamyatin returned to fiction based on stylistic simplicity, objective narration, and the absence of satire. Critics regard the best works of this period—"Ela" and *Navodnenie (The Flood)*—as the most powerful expressions of the author's tragic conception of life.

Zamyatin has been lauded as a master technician: few critics would disagree about the originality of his language, the strength of his imagery, and the power of his satire. On the other hand, many have criticized his tendency to overwork verbal effects. He is also faulted for concentrating too much on his central metaphors, often to the point where his characters lose their effect as human beings. But in general Zamyatin is praised for creating a peculiar brand of literature which stressed revolution and conflict, and which elevated the "heretic" to the status of hero. Critics have also commented on the integrity of his philosophy, especially as demonstrated in *We*. This book has been called the forerunner of the contemporary antiutopian novel as well as the predecessor of Aldous Huxley's *Brave New World* and George Orwell's *1984*.

Despite his relative obscurity in the Soviet Union after his death, Zamyatin has had a profound effect on other Russian writers who have appeared since the 1920s. In the words of Mirsky: "Zamyatin has been one of the strongest influences in shaping the 'formal,' technical attitude towards literature of the younger generation."

PRINCIPAL WORKS

Uezdnoe (novella) 1916
  [*A Provincial Tale* published in *The Dragon*, 1966]
Ogni svyatogo Dominika [first publication] (drama) 1922
  [*The Fires of Saint Dominic* published in *Five Plays by Yevgeny Zamyatin*, 1971]
Ostrovityane (novellas and short stories) 1922
Na kulichkakh (novellas and short stories) 1923
O literature, revolyutsii, èntropii i o pročem (essay) 1924
  [*On Literature, Revolution, and Entropy* published in *A Soviet Heretic*, 1970]
Bloxa (drama) 1925
  [*The Flea* published in *Five Plays by Yevgeny Zamyatin*, 1971]
Obščestvo početnyx zvonarei (drama) 1925
  [*The Society of Honorary Bell-Ringers* published in *Five Plays by Yevgeny Zamyatin*, 1971]
Necestivye rasskazy (short stories) 1927
Sobranie sočinenii. 4 vols. (autobiography, drama, short stories, and novellas) 1929
Navodnenie (short story) 1930
  [*The Flood* published in *The Dragon*, 1966]
Bič Božii (unfinished novel) 1939
My (novel) 1952
  [*We*, 1924]
Lica (essays) 1955
Povesti i rasskazy (autobiography, novellas, and short stories) 1963
The Dragon (letters, short stories, and novellas) 1966
A Soviet Heretic (essays and letters) 1970
Five Plays by Yevgeny Zamyatin (dramas) 1971

A. K. VORONSKY (essay date 1922)

The example of Zamyatin excellently confirms the truth that talent and intellect, however much a writer might be endowed with them, are insufficient if he has lost contact with his epoch, if his inner sensitivity has betrayed him, and in the midst of contemporaneity the artist or thinker feels as though he were a passenger on a ship, or a tourist, looking around with animosity and impatience.

With the appearance of *A Tale of the Provinces (Uezdnoe)* . . . Zamyatin immediately took a place among the prominent masters of the word. *A Tale of the Provinces* portrays our pre-revolutionary Tsarist provinces with their sleepy, comfortable, fertile, serious, thrifty, devout inhabitants. *A Tale of the Provinces* is well known to the reader both personally and through the peerless fictional models of the classics, beginning with Gogol and ending with Gorky. The fragrant geranium, the ficuses, the vicious watchdogs, the deadly nightshade, the shamelessness, the stinking coziness, and the crude psychology have been encountered time and again. Nevertheless, Zamyatin's *A Tale of the Provinces* is read with the most vivid attention and interest. Zamyatin had already at that time become established as an exceptional enthusiast for and master of the word. His language is fresh, original, and exact. It is partly folk *skaz*, stylized and modernized to be sure, and partly the simple colloquial provincial speech of the suburbs, the outlying districts, and the Rasteryaeva streets. In this fusion Zamyatin created something his own, something individual. The spontaneity and the epic quality of the narration are complicated by the ironic and satirical mood of the author. His *skaz* is not without reflection, and only appears to come straightforward from the author: actually everything here is written with a "trap," and contains a hidden mockery, smirk, and spite. This is why the epic quality of the *skaz* slips out and the work lives and emerges into the realm of the contemporary and the topical. The provinciality of the language is ennobled and well thought out. Above all it serves vividness, freshness, and picturesqueness, and enriches the language with words which have not become familiar or trite. It is as though there were before you just-minted coins, and not worn, dull, and long-circulated ones. Great austerity and economy. Nothing is said rashly; everything is joined together; there are no gaps. From the point of view of form the tale is like a monolith. Zamyatin had not yet lost control of his enthusiasm for words, as he was to do in some of his later works. There is no overloading, superfluous affectation, wordplay, literary foppery, or sleight-of-hand. He reads easily and effortlessly, and this does not at all hinder one's becoming absorbed in the contents. This is already a manifestation of the great ability of the artist to instill an image in the memory with one stroke, with one touch of the brush. (pp. 153-54)

A Tale of the Provinces is only in part a story of everyday life. It is more a satire—and not simply a satire, but a political satire, brightly painted and bold for the year 1913. In distinction from a number of authors who wrote about provincial matters, Zamyatin linked Russian Okurovism [provincialism] with the entire Tsarist mode of life and its political system, and herein lies his unquestionable merit. But, strange to say, Zamyatin's talent here achieves only half its goal. Something great, something sincere, something all-illuminating, which the reader finds in Gogol, in the satires of [Mikhail] Shchedrin, in [Gleb] Uspensky, in Gorky, and even in Chekhov, is missing. It is as if the tale, in spite of its purity of style and form, falls to pieces before the reader. It is masterfully narrated and delightfully done, but done just so it doesn't touch the reader deeply or penetrate inside, even though Baryba, Chebotarikha, Morgunov, Evsei, Timokha, and the district police officer stand before our eyes.

Zamyatin approached provincial matters from another side in a different tale—"Alatyr." Gogol already noted the Manilovism of our provinces. People live so-so, it would seem; it is not a heavenly life, but man is so inclined that he must without fail dream about something which does not exist and, perhaps, never will exist. Manilov has everything and still fantasizes. But if not everything is well with the Manilovs, and they are pressured, no matter by what, they fantasize all the more. Zamyatin tells about these peculiar dreamers in "**Alatyr.**" (p. 156)

Here also appear the provincial, the bestial, and the edible, but in addition to this there are phantasms, mirages, and dreams. The phantasms are pitiful and distorted, and they lead into a blind alley, but all the same they are phantasms. And so the meager and tedious life of Alatyr flows on between zoology and absurd fantasizing. The dreaming of the inhabitants of Alatyr, however, is distinguished from Manilovism by means of its dramatism; regardless of its absurdity, it eats into and mangles life, flying asunder as dust at the first contact with life. And perhaps that is why the inhabitants of thousands of Alatyrs do not believe in the feasibility of the great impulses of the human spirit: after all, they have before their eyes only these nonsensical, unnecessary dreams.

In "**Alatyr**" the basic features of Zamyatin's artistic talent are those which appear in *A Tale of the Provinces*. The tale is somewhat less vivid, but there is in it the same enthusiasm for the word, the same craftsmanship, the same oblique observation, the same smirk and ironical smile, the same anecdotal quality (more, perhaps, in "**Alatyr**" than *A Tale of the Provinces*), the same sharpness, abruptness, and prominence of device, the same careful selection of words and phrases, a great force of picturesqueness, unexpectedness of similes, the isolation of one or two traits, and restraint. (p. 157)

The tale "**At the World's End**" (*Na kulichkakh*) closely corresponds to *A Tale of the Provinces* and "**Alatyr**" in content and theme. . . . As in both *A Tale of the Provinces* and "**Alatyr**" it is deadly wearisome, sleepy, and absurd at the world's end. But not so much wearisome as *terrifying*. In the tale this terrifying quality is particularly emphasized by the author, and the principal part of attention is concentrated on it—in distinction from *A Tale of the Provinces* and "**Alatyr**." A terrifying quality exists in these works too, but there is more about bestiality and about provincial fantasizing in them; here it is the basic thing. Beneath the cover of a tedious, petty life Zamyatin saw this terrifying quality and pointed out to his readers not that imperceptible, grey, slowly-enveloping side of it, which Chekhov wrote about in his time, but the genuinely bloody, hideously brutal, tragic side of it. True, at the world's end, at the back of the beyond, they often fail to notice this side of it, but that is because it has entered into their everyday life. Tikhmen and the rectangular Shmit end their lives by suicide, Andrei Ivanovich becomes "ours," the soldiers are reduced to a bestial state, and the general basely, lispingly, and slobberingly rapes the tender and frail Marusia. "**At the World's End**," like *A Tale of the Provinces,* is a political and artistic satire. It makes much of what happened after 1914 understandable. In its own way it is a perhaps justified prophecy, but it also brings out, more so than the works written earlier, still another feature of Zamyatin's artistic gift. The tale is cast in a genuine, lofty, and touching lyricism. Zamyatin's lyricism has something all its own. It is womanly. In its details and subtleness it is always a kind of autumnal spider's web—a Virgin's thread. (pp. 158-59)

After a two-year stay in England during the war years, Zamyatin brought back "**The Islanders**" (*Ostrovitiane*) and "**A Fisher of Men**" (*Lovets chelovekov*). From *A Tale of the Provinces* to London and Jesmond. From dirt, pigs, and mire to stones, concrete, iron, steel, zeppelins, and underground roads.

From Chebotarikha, Baryba, and district police officers to the sedate English life, mechanized and scheduled in detail. (p. 159)

In "**The Islanders**" and "**A Fisher of Men**" there is satire on English bourgeois life—biting, sharp, effective, finished down to the details and to the point of scrupulousness. But the more carefully one reads both the long tale and the short story, the more strongly one gets the impression that neither the heart nor the bosom of life has been captured, but rather, that its surface has been captured. In essence the artist has produced a filigree work on slight material. Here are the trifles of British life; it is true that these trifles drive one to distraction, but this does not change matters. (p. 160)

Nevertheless, both "**The Islanders**" and "**A Fisher of Men**" remain masterful artistic lampoons, in spite of their limited significance. The writer's London works, like *A Tale of the Provinces,* "**At the World's End,**" and "**Alatyr**," will remain in our literature. (p. 163)

> *A. K. Voronsky, "Evgeny Zamyatin," translated by Paul Mitchell (originally published as an essay in* Red Virgin Soil, *No. 6, 1922), in* Russian Literature Triquarterly *(© 1972 by Ardis Publishers), No. 3, 1972, pp. 153-75.*

GREGORY ZILBOORG   (essay date 1924)

[*We*] is a novel that puts before every thoughtful reader with great poignance and earnestness the most difficult problem that exists today in the civilized world—the problem of the preservation of the independent, original, creative personality. Our civilization depends upon the energetic movement of great masses of people. Wars, revolutions, general strikes—all these phenomena involve great masses, large groups, enormous mobs. Despite the fact that there is hardly a corner in the world where the average man does not make the trite complaint, "What we need is leadership," the world seems for a time, at least, to have lost its capacity to produce real leaders. For our great successes in mechanical civilization, our exceptional efforts in efficiency, tend to bring into play large masses rather than great individuals. What, under these conditions, is the lot of the creative personality? The tragedy of the independent spirit under present conditions is pointed out in a unique way in *We*. The problem of the creative individual versus the mob is not merely a Russian problem. It is as apparent in a Ford factory as under a Bolshevik dictatorship.

Of course, the sincere, honest, and frank treatment of this problem seems offensive to anyone who prefers to be a member of a mob or to keep this or that part of humanity in the state of a mob. That is why *We* could not be published in Russia, and will probably be disliked by those whose spiritual activities are reduced to the mechanical standards of a mechanical civilization which is devoid of original creative effort.

A few words should be said about the method by which Zamiatin tries to drive home his main ideas to the reader. It is the method of "laughter through tears," to use an old expression of Gogol's. It is the form that is dictated by a profound love for humanity, mixed with pity for and hatred of those factors which are the cause of the disindividualization of man today. . . . Zamiatin laughs in order to hide his tears; hence amusing as *We* may seem and really is, it barely conceals a profound human tragedy which is universal today. (pp. xiv-xv)

Gregory Zilboorg, in his foreword to We *by Eugene Zamiatin, translated by Gregory Zilboorg (copyright, 1924, by E. P. Dutton & Co., Inc.; copyright renewal, 1952, by Gregory Zilboorg; reprinted by permission of the publisher, E. P. Dutton, Inc.), Dutton, 1924 (and reprinted by Dutton, 1959, pp. xiii-xviii).*

THE NEW YORK TIMES BOOK REVIEW (essay date 1925)

This singularly entitled, fantastic novel, **"We,"** pictures a civilization, scientifically perfected, a thousand years from now. Obviously, the stimulant to write it came from contemporary events and thought. Most apt that it should come from Russia, that scene of social experiment and theory applied to life, that molding of the human being to meet a precise pattern dominated by a super-State. Zamiatin drew on his native land for much of the source of his gigantic burlesque, which plays about so many general ideas and toys with infinity. Bolshevism is the main source, with the history of civilization furnishing detail trimmings. . . . Like Chekhov, [Zamiatin] has a broad, earthy sense of humor.

In this super-State, the United States of the World, many of the scientific pursuits and social problems of today have been perfected. The human being has been adjusted to the precision of machinery; reduced to a cog perfectly manipulated by the dictator, the Well-Doer, and the Bureau of Guardians. The human equation is almost non-existent—a whole people moved to a definite schedule with monotonous regularity en masse. . . . Zamiatin in his futuristic creation has loosened the imagination as fecund and lively as Jules Verne, supported by a vigorous and flexible intellect, that plays drolly upon the ideas of government and the social order. He has written a nightmare at which he sometimes laughs wistfully. (p. 16)

Zamiatin has written with power upon a theme of wide scope. His style is terse, impressionistic, futuristic, with a sort of prismatic sense to his vision. It is exciting and even terrible. His satire lashes the byplay of humans against theory. In his laughter that protests against the suppression of the individual there is pathos and terror that carries a sting. His individual characters stand out sharply, even though at times the panorama of the super-State blurs their pathetic interrelation. Mockery and passion go hand in hand across the pages of this recording journal. It is one more capital parody, the reduction ad absurdum, of the machine age, of which the cream of the jests, perhaps, lies in the fact that it came out of Russia. (pp. 16-17)

"The Standardized State," in The New York Times Book Review *(© 1925 by The New York Times Company; reprinted by permission), January 18, 1925, pp. 16-17.*

D. S. MIRSKY (essay date 1926)

Zamyatin's early stories, contained in **Uyezdnoe,** are the direct progeny of [Alexey M.] Remizov's *Stratilatov.* Provincial life is given in its most vulgar, most grotesque, and most provincial aspect. The stories are written in a studiously careful and expressive Russian, with a marked predilection for rare and provincial words. Uncannily inept vulgarity and lurid boredom form the atmosphere of these stories. In his later work, Zamyatin tears himself away from the provincial Russian soil and from the Remizovian vocabulary, and gradually evolves a manner of his own which is founded on the heightening of the expressive value of significant detail by an elaborate system of metaphor and simile. His style remains overloaded with verbal expressiveness and imagery. This excessive richness of expressive means tends to disrupt the story and transform it into a mere mosaic of details. The method is akin to the proceedings of Cubism in painting—his characters especially tend to become identified with the geometrical forms he gives them. Thus, squareness is the principal characteristic of the English hero of **Islanders.** The two English stories (**Islanders** and **The Man-hunter**) are distinctly satirical, as is **At the World's End,** a grotesquely refined and exaggerated caricature of the dreary and solitary life of an East Siberian garrison. . . . Both in this and in the English stories, Zamyatin, in spite of the great conscientiousness and elaboration of his artistic methods, shows a strange deficiency of information: his knowledge of English and of Russian army life is insufficient. This does not apply to his stories of Soviet life. One of the best of these, and perhaps his masterpiece, [is **The Cave**]. . . . It is characteristic of his methods: it is all one elaborate simile. The life of a bourgeois couple in an unheated room in Bolshevik Petersburg during a Northern winter is likened to the life of palaeolithic man in his cave; the iron stove that heats their room for an hour a day is the god of the cave, who is benevolent only when he is satisfied with their sacrifices—of fuel. This is Zamyatin's method of giving unity to his stories: a large family of metaphors (or similes) dominated by one mother metaphor. **We,** of which one does not know when it will appear, is a scientific romance of the future, written, according to accounts, in a new and striking manner, which is a further development of Zamyatin's Cubism. **The Fires of St. Dominic** is feeble as a play—too overloaded with that detail which Zamyatin cannot forgo, and which is so out of place in a play. It is a story of the Inquisition and a very transparent allegory for the Cheka. **Fables for Grown-up Children** is also pointedly satirical, and both this satirical intention and the great elaboration of its style make it recall the *Political Fables* [Fyodor] Sologub wrote in 1905.

Zamyatin has had a very considerable influence as a master, or rather as a teacher, of literature, and the great elaborateness of contemporary fiction, especially in Petersburg, is largely due to him. (pp. 297-99)

*D. S. Mirsky, "The New Prose," in his Contemporary Russian Literature: 1881-1925 (copyright 1926 by Alfred A. Knopf, Inc.; reprinted by permission of the publisher), Knopf, 1926, G. Routledge & Sons, 1926, pp. 281-315.**

YEVGENY ZAMYATIN (essay date 1930)

The paper is cut, the indelible pencil sharpened, cigarettes are prepared, and I sit down at my desk. I know only the conclusion or only one of the scenes or only one of the characters, and I need five or ten of them. And so, the first page usually witnesses the incarnation of the characters I need. I make sketches for their portraits, until I can see clearly how each one walks, smiles, eats, speaks. As soon as they come alive to me, they will begin to act unerringly on their own, or, to be more exact, they will begin to err, but only as each of them can and must err. I may try to reeducate them, I may try to build their lives according to plan, but if they are alive, they will inevitably overturn all the plans I may devise for them. And often I do not know until the last page how my story (their stories) will end. At times I do not know the conclusion even when I know it, when the whole work starts from the end.

This was true of the novella *The Islanders*. An Englishman of my acquaintance told me that there are people in London who live by a very peculiar profession—catching lovers in parks. I saw a scene of such a hunt as a suitable ending. The entire complicated plot of the novella grew out of this ending. And then—to my surprise—it turned out that the novella ended quite differently from the original plan. The hero—Campbell—refused to be the scoundrel I had meant him to be. It is worth noting that the first version of the ending, which was eliminated from the text of the novella, later took on independent life in the form of the story "**The Fisher of Men**." (p. 194)

And so the needed characters finally come, in one way or another. They are here, but they are still naked, they must be clothed in words.

A word has color and sound. From now on, painting and music go side by side.

From the very first page, the writer must determine the basic pattern of the entire musical weave; he must hear the rhythm of the entire work. But one seldom succeeds in hearing it at once. It is almost always necessary to rewrite the first page several times (the novella *At the World's End*, for example, had four different beginnings; *The Islanders* had two; "**Alatyr**," six). This is understandable. In the solution of the rhythmic problem, the prose writer is in a far more difficult position than the poet. The rhythmics of verse have long been analyzed; they have their own code of laws, and their own set penalties. But no one has yet been brought to trial for rhythmic crimes in prose. In analyzing prose rhythm, even Andrey Bely, the subtlest student of verbal music, made a mistake: he applied a verse foot to prose (hence his sickness—chronic anapaestitis). (pp. 196-97)

And what of painting? Has it been forgotten? No, the writer must hear and see simultaneously as he works. And if there are sound leitmotivs, there must also be visual ones. In the same novella, *The Islanders*, the basic visual image for Campbell is a tractor; for Lady Campbell, worms (lips); for Mrs. Dewly, pince-nez; for the lawyer O'Kelly, his double, a pug. In "**The North**," there is a constant juxtaposition of Kortoma and a smug, gleaming samovar, Kortomikha and a discarded glove. In "**The Flood**" Sofya is symbolized by a bird, Ganka by a cat.

Each of these visual leitmotivs is similar to a focus of rays in optics: it is the intersecting point of all the images connected with the given character. I rarely use individual, chance images; these are only sparks, which live for a brief moment, and then are extinguished, forgotten. A chance image is the result of inability to concentrate, to truly see, to believe. If I firmly believe in the image, it will inevitably give rise to an entire system of related images, it will spread its roots through paragraphs and pages. In a short story, the image may become integral and spread throughout the piece, from beginning to end. The six-story, fiery-eyed house on the dark, deserted street, echoing with shots in 1919, presented itself to me one night as a ship in the ocean. I believed in the image completely—and the integral image of the ship determined the entire system of images in the story "**Mamay**."

The same was true of "**The Cave**." A more complex instance is "**The Flood**." Here the integral image of the flood is followed through on two planes. The actual flood in Petersburg is reflected in the spiritual flood, and all the basic images of the story flow into their common channel. (p. 198)

There was a time when I acutely felt that I had lost one hand, that I needed a third hand. This was in England, when I first drove a car: I had to work the steering wheel, shift gears, manage the accelerator, and blow the horn, all at the same time. I had a similar feeling many years ago, when I began to write: it seemed utterly impossible at the same time to direct the movement of the plot, the emotions of the characters, their dialogues, the instrumentation, the images, the rhythms. Later I learned that two hands are quite sufficient for driving a car. This happened when most of the complex movements became a matter of reflex, were carried out without conscious effort. The same thing happens sooner or later at the desk.

The image of the automobile driver that I employed is, of course, incorrect, imprecise. Such an image is permissible only backstage; on stage, in a story or novel, I would surely have crossed it out. The image is incorrect because a good driver will guide his car unerringly—even in London—from the Strand to Euston Road. But I, after reaching Euston on paper, will return to the Strand and will take the same road a second time—and it is, perhaps, only on the third trip that I will bring my passengers to their destination. A work that would seem to be finished is not yet finished to me. I invariably begin to rewrite it from the beginning, from the first line, and, if I am still dissatisfied, I rewrite it once again (the short story "**The Land Surveyor**" was rewritten about five times). This is equally true of a novel, a story, a novella, or a play. And even of an article: to me, an article is the same as a story. I think that it is easiest for me to write a play. In a play, the writer is not overwhelmed by a multitude of possibilities; the language is limited to dialogue.

The slow process of rewriting is very useful: there is time to examine all the details, to change them before the work cools off and hardens, and to throw out all that is superfluous. These "superfluous" elements may be good in themselves, but when they are not essential, when the work can live without them, they are mercilessly eliminated. Would it not be absurd to allow an unnecessary lever to remain in a machine simply because it glitters? In the human organism there is nothing superfluous except the appendix, and doctors remove it at the first opportunity. Most frequently, such appendixes are descriptions, landscapes which do not serve as levers transmitting the psychic movements of the characters. The operation for their removal is as painful as any other; nevertheless, it is essential.

My manuscripts are deceptive; there are very few corrections, paste-ins, deletions, and everything seems to flow along easily. But this is only seeming. All the difficulties are dealt with behind the scenes. I try every scene ten times mentally before setting it down on paper. I never leave behind unfinished phrases, scenes, or situations. Tomorrow, I may not like what I wrote today, and I will start again from the beginning, but today it must look finished to me; otherwise I cannot go on. (pp. 199-200)

I spend a great deal of time on my work, probably more than the reader would require. But this is necessary for the critic, the most demanding and carping critic I know—myself. I can never deceive this critic, and until he says that everything possible has been done, I cannot put the final period to the work. (p. 201)

Yevgeny Zamyatin, "Backstage" (1930), in his A Soviet Heretic: Essays by Yevgeny Zamyatin, *edited and translated by Mirra Ginsburg (reprinted by permission of The University of Chicago Press; © 1970* by The University of Chicago), University of Chicago Press, 1970, pp. 190-201.

MAX EASTMAN (essay date 1934)

Zamyatin is unique among Russian writers—prophetic to my mind of something literature has still to attain. For besides being a gifted and imaginative artist, he is a trained man of science. (p. 82)

Being a man of intellect, however, and moreover a man of scientific intellect, Zamyatin's conception of literature is a large one, and not at all consonant with the view that all ultimate wisdom resides in the secretariat of a political party.

"A living literature," says Zamyatin, "lives not in the hours of yesterday nor of today, but of tomorrow. It is a sailor sent aloft on the mast where he can see shipwrecks, icebergs and maelstroms still invisible from the deck. . . . What we need now in literature is colossal look-out views, airplane philosophic views; we need the most ultimate, the most terrible, the most unterrified *whys?* and *what furthers?* . . . Were there in nature anything immoveable, were there truths, all this of course would be incorrect. But fortunately all truths are erroneous: the dialectic process consists in this, that today's truths become tomorrow's errors. . . ." (pp. 82-3)

With these ideals, and a training in constructive science, it is not surprising that Zamyatin wants to say something in his books about the larger destinies of man. He wants to say something about what is to come *after* the technique of capitalist machine-industry has been taken over by a successful proletarian revolution and developed to the full. His romance, *We,* . . . is an inverse utopia of the type subsequently exemplified in Aldous Huxley's *Brave New World.* Indeed its theme is identical with Huxley's, the unhappy situation of poetic people in that complete regimentation of life toward which science seems to lead the way. It is, however, a more recklessly imaginative book than Huxley's and its imaginations are realized with a greater depth of feeling. Zamyatin in 1924 considered *We* "at once the most jocular and the most earnest thing" he had written, and it is evidently the heart-spoken message of a man of poetry who has delved deeply in science. (pp. 83-4)

Max Eastman, "The Framing of Eugene Zamyatin," in his Artists in Uniform: A Study of Literature and Bureaucratism *(copyright 1934, copyright renewed © 1962, by Max Eastman; reprinted by permission of Yvette Sakay Eastman), Alfred A. Knopf, 1934, pp. 82-93.*

GLEB STRUVE (essay date 1935)

We is so far Zamyatin's only attempt at a great novel with an entertaining and complicated plot, more or less rooted in European traditions. His early stories go back to the Russian traditions. To Gogol and [Nikolai] Leskov rather than to Turgenev, Tolstoy or Dostoevsky. . . . From Gogol, Zamyatin gets his interest in depicting the meaner and baser sides of human nature—all his earlier stories of Russian provincial life bear an imprint of meanness and vulgarity. It is also meanness, coated with a thin veneer of hypocritical respectability, that he chose to see and satirize in English life. From Gogol and Leskov, Zamyatin has also inherited his predilection for verbal effects, for stylistic elaborateness, for ornamentalism of speech. Zamyatin's early manner may be described as Realism with a touch of the grotesque. Later on he developed a style of his

own, a peculiar blend of Realism with Symbolism and Imaginism which Prince Mirsky has aptly compared to Cubism in painting. (pp. 19-20)

Zamyatin's Neo-Realism certainly tends to Imaginism. Some of his best stories (*The Cave, Mamay*) have for their kernel a complex of metaphorical images round which they grow. It is, however, wrong to think that there is nothing in Zamyatin beyond these verbal effects, this love of ornamentalism. Both *The Cave* and *Mamay* convey to perfection the atmosphere of the terrible years of War Communism and have a genuinely tragic accent. . . . Zamyatin's images often reflect the mathematical turn of his mind. He has a peculiar liking for geometrical images—his characters are symbolized by geometrical figures. Squareness is the principal characteristic of Baryba in *Tales of Country Life.* It is also the main attribute of one of the characters in *Islanders.* In *We* the two heroines are geometrically contrasted: one is plump and round (and her letter is "O"); the other is thin and angular (and her letter is "I"). Like Gogol, Zamyatin characterizes his personages chiefly by their outward appearance, in which he grotesquely emphasizes some particular feature; his method is that of a cartoon artist. . . . There is a marked difference in the construction of Zamyatin's longer and shorter stories. If, in his shorter stories, the story itself can be compared to a concentric outgrowth of a central image, of a "mother-metaphor," his longer stories resemble Cubist pictures; they seem to consist of a number of broken pieces forming a peculiar pattern. In one of his critical articles (he is an acute and penetrating critic) Zamyatin champions the method of broken narrative conducted simultaneously on several planes, a method frequently applied in modern literature. It has been most thoroughly applied by Zamyatin in *The Story About What Matters Most,* in which the Revolution is regarded *sub specie aeternitatis* and which has been denounced by the Communist critics as fundamentally anti-revolutionary. But even in those of his stories which are written in a seemingly continuous manner one gets this impression of brokenness. An exception is *The Flood* . . . , a tragic story of love, jealousy and murder, written with more directness and simplicity and less ornamentalism than is usual with Zamyatin, and free from any satirical or political element, purely human in its interest, more intensely psychological, perhaps, than any of Zamyatin's work. (pp. 20-2)

By nature [Zamyatin] is a heretic, an eternal rebel against the established order of things, with a strong leaning to primitivism. Our time seems to him to offer a parallel to the age of Attila. He sees it as an age of great wars and social cataclysms. "To-morrow"—he says—"as then, we shall perhaps witness the downfall of a very great but too old civilization. . . ."

In the very first years of the Revolution Zamyatin expressed his opinion that Communist Russia would not produce a real literature. "Real literature," he said, "can exist only where it is produced, not by painstaking and well-intentioned officials, but by madmen, hermits, heretics, dreamers, rebels and sceptics." To this class of men Zamyatin himself belongs: it is very characteristic that he was a Bolshevik before the Russian Revolution and ceased to be one when Bolshevism became the official doctrine in power. (p. 22)

We is a novel that stands apart from anything else in Russian literature. It combines the methods of scientific romance somewhat in the manner of H. G. Wells—Zamyatin knows Wells's work thoroughly and in 1922 wrote a study of him—with some typical aspects of the Russian problem novel and with a trenchant political satire. The nearest thing to it in modern European literature is Aldous Huxley's *Brave New World,* although the two books are far apart in spirit because Zamyatin, with his rather strong leaning to primitivism, is more or less free from Huxley's eighteenth-century rationalism. Yet not only the general idea and presentation, but even some minor details, reveal a very striking resemblance between the two works (Zamyatin's novel was written nearly ten years and published in English five years before Huxley's).

In *We,* we are transported into the twenty-sixth century, into a perfect modern, standardized State which has no name, but is called simply "The Single State", and whose citizens have no names, but are known by their numbers. In this Zamyatin goes even one better than Huxley: the latter was unable, I think, to withstand the temptation of displaying his wit and ingeniousness in the choice of his names. In general there is more English *couleur locale* and topical humour in Huxley's novel and more universality in Zamyatin's. (p. 131)

From the purely literary point of view Zamyatin's satirical Utopia, as far as one can judge of it by the translation, is a good piece of writing. Its construction is perhaps somewhat loose in comparison with *Brave New World;* scientifically it is not so well thought out, not so elaborate in details; but its satire is more pointed, more directly inspired by actual experience, and there is in it that element of *political* satire which is absent from Mr. Huxley's novel. The Soviet critics who have written of *We* in spite of the fact that it has not been published in Russia admit its high literary qualities. In contemporary Russian literature it holds a unique place. (pp. 137-38)

> *Gleb Struve, "Pre-Revolutionary Writers after 1924" and "Counter-Revolutionary Tendencies in Soviet Literature," in his* Soviet Russian Literature *(reprinted by permission of Routledge & Kegan Paul Ltd.), Routledge & Kegan Paul, 1935, pp. 1-22, 127-52.**

D. J. RICHARDS (essay date 1962)

[An] apocalyptic atmosphere was reflected in Zamyatin's early works. The judgment which the critic I. Lezhnev made in 1924 on Zamyatin's post-revolutionary work is equally applicable to these early tales: "An artist has sensed the breathing of the age and has begun to transform that age into art."

The country town described in Zamyatin's first published work, *Uezdnoe (Tales of a District),* is a microcosm of the whole nation, seen through the eyes of the young radicals. Old Russia, tired and aimless, corrupt, brutal, and backward, is dying and is destined to be replaced by a new order. In the twenty-six vignettes, provided by the twenty-six slight chapters of *Uezdnoe,* Zamyatin describes the static, oppressive existence of a community which, lacking any faith in the future and any guiding moral principles, devotes itself to a ceaseless round of animal activities. When they find time on their hands, the people of *Uezdnoe* oscillate between abject boredom and bouts of senseless activity which often lead to cruelty and crime. (p. 30)

[The] positive characters in *Uezdnoe* are so few and so isolated that they further emphasise the atmosphere of decaying life. At the same time there is in this atmosphere a foreboding of impending catastrophe, strongly reminiscent of Gogol. . . .

[*Na Kulichkakh (At the Back of Beyond)*] continues and develops the main themes of *Uezdnoe,* but this time the setting in a garrison town in eastern Siberia led to the confiscation of

the tale by the censor and to Zamyatin's being accused of "a subversive depiction of the Imperial Army". . . .

In atmosphere *Na Kulichkakh* is very like *Uezdnoe,* though Zamyatin does add to the senseless cruelties, perpetrated from boredom, and the simple animal relationships, which he had portrayed in his first work, deeper emotional complications and a few touches of psychological nastiness, reminiscent of Dostoevsky. (p. 31)

Among Zamyatin's other pre-revolutionary works were a number of tales of peasant life, written in popular dialect. In these, in spite of outbursts of jealousy and violence, the atmosphere is predominantly clean and healthy. It is as though Zamyatin wanted to purify himself from the poisonous fumes of provincial town-life by a return to nature. Here can be seen the germ of an important later theme: modern, so-called civilised man has become alienated from nature; inflexible rationality and urban existence have combined to suppress instinctive, spontaneous behaviour to such a degree that man is no longer capable of any genuine self-fulfilment.

Much the most interesting of these peasant tales is *Chrevo (The Womb).* . . . A robust young peasant girl is so frustrated in her relations with her elderly husband that she is eventually driven to killing him. As in *Uezdnoe,* the action is motivated originally by biological drives, but here Zamyatin's attitude is quite different. Anfimya's desire for a child is idealised and described lyrically. Her actions are a manifestation of nature, life, and energy—or Revolution—in revolt against the forces of Entropy, represented by the husband. At the same time, the conspiracy of Anfimya and her young lover against the old man represents the rebellion of young, politically revolutionary Russia against the decaying old order. *Chrevo* provides the first example of Zamyatin's use of childbirth as a symbol of Revolution, political or cosmic. Here Anfimya's desire symbolises Russia's longing for a rebirth, and the child itself the new Russia-to-be. (pp. 32-3)

One of the literary themes of the early Soviet era was that of the individual out of place in the new epoch. In his tales *Peschera (The Cave)* and *Mamai 1917-ovo Goda (Mamai of 1917)* . . . , Zamyatin treats this theme in his own highly impressionistic manner. Both tales are set in the Petrograd of 1919, beleaguered by the White troops of General Yudenich. The heroes of both are literary descendants of Gogol's Akakii Akakievich, mild little men who cannot cope with the problems of life; at the same time they are Hegelian tragic heroes, crushed by the dialectic of History. Products of the pre-revolutionary era, they are educated, refined, gentle and highly moral—qualities which are pathetically out of place in the new world.

In *Peschera* Zamyatin illustrates the return to a state of primitive barbarity during the Civil War by the image of Petrograd as a prehistoric settlement, peopled by cavemen and mammoths and ruled by the basic needs for survival, food and heating; the insatiable god of this universe is the squat, rusty stove. Martin Martinych, the hero of *Peschera,* attempts to adapt himself to this new world, where the law of the jungle holds sway, by forcing himself to steal some wood from a neighbour, but his attempt is a failure, not because he is caught, but because his conscience torments him and drive him to confess his crime; he gives his dying wife the poison she craves to end her own suffering and staggers completely broken into the street below. (pp. 39-40)

Mamai is similarly an intellectual of the previous age, a henpecked, helpless soul who is suddenly forced to handle a revolver and stand on guard-duty with his tough neighbours. But Zamyatin treats Mamai less as a tragic figure than as a character of ludicrous incongruity, who applies all the aggressiveness, energy and ruthlessness, necessary for survival in the new world, to outwitting his wife, to the pursuit of books and the hunting of a mouse. Zamyatin emphasises the absurdity of the situation first by giving this gentle creature the heroic name of Mamai and then by hugely exaggerated and distorted metaphors. For instance, the book which Mamai is keen to possess becomes in his eyes a princess, whom he, the gallant knight, will rescue from her captor, the grey-bearded, bushy-browed Chornomor (the shop-keeper).

In *Mamai* the general atmosphere of uncertainty and isolation is evoked by the image of Petrograd as a dark ocean and each house as a lonely, storm-tossed ship, filled with frightened passengers who do not know whether the ship will survive its journey through the night. (pp. 40-1)

Very early Zamyatin was disturbed by the dogmatism of the new authorities. For him, Revolution meant the abolition of the old way of life but did not include a conscious, rational forging of a new social pattern. This attempt to impose a dogmatic pattern on to life was a manifestation of Entropy and could well lead to a new tyranny as bad as the old. For Zamyatin, Revolution implied *continual* change; thus, his chief criticism of the new government was that it was not revolutionary enough—in his own, essentially anarchic, sense of the word. In 1924 the critic A. Lezhnev dubbed Zamyatin the most left-wing man in Russia.

Zamyatin's first play, *Ogni Svyatovo Dominika (The Fires of Saint Dominic)* . . . , is a violent attack on dogma and an outspoken glorification of the heretic, here presented in his own right. Zamyatin's theme is universal but it was particularly relevant to the contemporary scene, where the Red Terror, proclaimed against all enemies of the state, had reached a climax.

The action is set in the Spain of Philip II, in Seville at the height of the Inquisition. . . . Zamyatin chooses the setting of Schiller's *Don Carlos,* of Lermontov's youthful drama *Ispantsy (The Spaniards),* and of Dostoevsky's *Legend of the Grand Inquisitor* for this play on the old theme of individual freedom. The dramatic form allows Zamyatin to show most clearly the clash between Entropy and Revolution, here represented by Church and heretic. The Church is convinced that it possesses the unique truth and from this it deduces the right to maintain uniformity of opinion by persecuting dissenters. The imposition of a dogmatic pattern on life results in the devaluation of the individual, who hands all moral and intellectual responsibility to the Church. (pp. 42-3)

Zamyatin emphasises the hypocrisy and time-serving which must exist in such a situation. There is both the conscious hypocrisy of those, like the two grandees, who conform to save their own skins, and the possibly half-unconscious hypocrisy among the leaders of the Church, whose primary allegiance is to the organisation for its own sake rather than to the truth.

A striking feature of *Ogni Svyatovo Dominika* is the apathy of the general populace, who stand by idly and uncomprehendingly, while the heretics, fighting for freedom and truth, are martyred in the public square. In this apathy of the masses dominated by Entropy, lies the greatest strength of the established dictator. (pp. 43-4)

In *Rasskaz o Samom Glavnom (The Most Important Thing),* of which Zamyatin was particularly fond, he returns to the theme of the brutalisation of man and the suffering brought about by the Revolution, but, as the title suggests, he also gives expression to his personal values.

The action takes place on four planes, each illustrating one aspect of cosmic Revolution and together showing that in life, viewed broadly, there is no single, absolute "most important thing". The most important thing is always subjective and relative and constantly changing. In a lilac bush a grub is turning into a cocoon, to be reborn as a bright butterfly. In the Russian countryside the menfolk of two formerly peaceful and friendly villages are slaughtering each other in the name of the Russian Revolution. On a distant star the last surviving inhabitants are dying for lack of air. This same star is rushing towards a collision with the earth which will bring human history to an end. The most important thing is: for the grub—its transformation; for the Bolshevik fighters—the capture of a little bridge; for the inhabitants of the star—air; for the star and the earth—their fusion.

The social revolution in Russia is but one of an infinite number of cosmic changes and, viewed against this broad background, the fighting appears to Zamyatin, as the Napoleonic Wars did to Tolstoy, determined by circumstances and ultimately meaningless. (pp. 44-5)

Zamyatin emphasises the vanity of human disputes by placing the action on Earth against the cosmic background of our planet's coming collision with the unknown star and by ending the tale on thoughts of new creatures who will come after us. (pp. 46-7)

[Zamyatin's utopian novel *My (We)*] is perhaps his most significant single work, not only because it reflects some of his deepest convictions but also because of its subsequent effect on the author's personal life and its influence on the English writers Huxley and Orwell.

The problems raised in *My* are perennial, but they have been brought into particular prominence in this century. Zamyatin is concerned with the compatibility of freedom with security, social and psychological, and their relationship with happiness; with the clash of reason and unreason; and with the fate of the would-be independent individual in a highly organised, conformist society. These are the themes treated earlier by Dostoevsky in his *The Legend of the Grand Inquisitor* and later by Huxley in *Brave New World* and Orwell in *1984*. (p. 54)

In *My,* as in earlier works, Zamyatin glorifies eruptions of the non-rational, or natural, side of man's personality in lyrical passages. In particular he extols the spontaneous expression of sexual love, contrasted throughout *My* with the regimented ticket-system of the Single State. During his association with I-330, D-503 at times experiences an expansion of his whole being beyond time and space—a mystic oneness with the entire universe. It is this intensified consciousness, achieved in positive freedom, which the severely rational personality can never attain, for reason not only holds in check impulses emanating from the subconscious, but also prevents the personality from expanding towards what might be called "superconscious" levels. Of course, Zamyatin does not reject reason as such, but only its misuse.

Secondly, Zamyatin claims that the state cannot maintain indefinitely the calm stability of rule by reason. For all his weakness, man is continually saved from his folly by the dialectical process: Entropy cannot withstand Revolution for ever. Unreason cannot be straitjacketed by reason. And in *My* reason and the conscious mind are the allies of Entropy and non-freedom, while unreason, the subconscious, and also what might be called the super-conscious, mind, are associated with Revolution. (pp. 59-60)

In the novel the irrational side of man's personality is paralleled by the wild world of nature, towards which D-503 feels so strongly drawn, situated outside the glass wall enclosing the artificial Single State. This wall, which the revolutionaries aim to breach, is an important symbol in *My*. It symbolises on the one hand the security and non-freedom of the Single State and on the other the frontier between the rational and the irrational areas of the mind. The destruction of the wall would mean not only the collapse of the tyranny of the Single State, but also the reunion of man with nature and the re-integration of the personality. (p. 61)

[The real hero of *My*, I-330] expresses Zamyatin's philosophy of continual flux, of permanent revolution. . . . As in the individual, so too in societies, in history itself, revolution is inevitable—an eternally static state is impossible. Zamyatin's point is essentially the same as [Boris] Pasternak's in *Dr. Zhivago* or Tolstoy's in *War and Peace*, that life is too vast and too elemental to be tamed and fashioned by the puny mind of man.

But, whereas both these writers, like Dostoevsky, find their final refuge in some form of Christianity, Zamyatin rejects this solution completely. . . . [In] *My* all Christianity is condemned by the rebels as a forerunner of the Single State. . . . Whereas for Dostoevsky the force most implacably opposed to the rational utopia was the true, uncorrupted spirit of Christianity, represented in *The Grand Inquisitor* by the silent figure of Christ and embodied in the Russian Orthodox Church, Zamyatin condemns all churches equally. Since in his view there can be no unique unchanging truth, no organisation can possess it and submission to the Orthodox Church is as absurd as submission to a rational utopia. (pp. 61-2)

However, in spite of this overtly Nietzschean, anti-Christian attitude, which is expressed more clearly in *My* than in any of his other works, there are potential parallels between Zamyatin's outlook and some of Christ's teachings. The categories into which Zamyatin divides mankind, "the living-living" and "the living-dead", might be considered Christian. His exaltation of a freer, more intensely conscious way of life, contrasted with the dull security of material well-being and mechanically accepted *mores*, is in harmony with Christ's attempt to direct men's attention beyond the superficial unsympathetic rationality of everyday life to the spiritual levels of their being. . . . Finally, Zamyatin's attack on humility is directed against the passive resignation of the vegetable life and not against that conscious humility, which stems from an awareness of man's dependence on destiny—for Zamyatin the dialectical process, for the Christian the will of God—and is an indispensable ingredient of true knowledge. Zamyatin has falsely identified the conservative dogmatism of the Church with the original "revolutionary" Christian message. (pp. 63-4)

The unifying theme of what might be called Zamyatin's "main-stream" works is that of the clash between the forces of Entropy and Revolution in various guises. In his earliest works this clash takes place in provincial Russia; after the Revolution the stage is the whole of Russia—or a comparable setting in the past (*Ogni Svyatovo Dominika*) or in the future (*My*); towards the end of his life Zamyatin produced a play (*Atilla*) and the first part of a novel (*Bich Bozhii*), where the eternal struggle

was manifested in the historical clash between the Western Roman Empire and the Eastern barbarians. This theme of warring Entropy and Revolution finds expression in short stories, novels and dramatic works. The mood is often satirical.

At the same time Zamyatin produced outside this "main-stream" several works in which attention is focused not on the cosmic struggle but primarily on personal relationships. To call these works "psychological" is perhaps a little misleading without a word of explanation. All Zamyatin's works are psychological, in the sense that he is interested above all in his heroes' states of mind, but his "main-stream" works, as is so often the case in Russian literature, are at least equally sociological—the individual's personal problems and attitudes of mind are closely linked with wider problems of social organisation, with the relationship between the individual and society in general. . . . [Several of Zamyatin's works are] psychological in the narrower, personal sense: the heroes are shown in their relations not with society in general and its values and patterns of behaviour, but with one or two individual fellow men. The larger community to which these individuals belong recedes far into the background. In these tales [*Aprel (April)*, *Zemlemer (The Land Surveyor)*, *Detskaya (The Nursery)*, and *Navodnenie (The Flood)*] Zamyatin also endeavours, rather like Chekhov, to create an atmosphere or to evoke a mood in the reader. (pp. 73-4)

During the eighteen months which he spent in England between March 1916 and September 1917 Zamyatin viewed English life with mixed feelings. Many of its features attracted him. The national reserve, modesty and *sang-froid* accorded with Zamyatin's own temperament. (p. 85)

On the other hand, Zamyatin was repelled by the superficiality, the active conformity and the pretentiousness of the English middle classes and against them he wrote the bitter satire *Ostrovityane (The Islanders)*. . . .

In *Ostrovityane* Entropy manifests itself in a tendency towards conformity and the mechanisation of life. Spontaneity is severely frowned upon and the inhabitants of Jesmond all strive to conform to a well-patterned routine of respectability in dress and behaviour. All strive to be "gentlemen". (p. 86)

This attack on social conformity and the mechanisation of life was then a new element in Zamyatin. Admittedly, in his early tales the boredom of routine and the uneventful pattern of life in provincial Russia had been seen as evil, but not as evidence of any conscious drive towards conformity for its own sake. In this way *Ostrovityane* forms a bridge between Zamyatin's early work and *My*, written three years later, where the mechanical ideal of the Reverend Dewly is largely realised in the Benefactor's rational utopia. (p. 87)

Like *Ostrovityane*, Zamyatin's other English story, *Lovets Chelovekov (The Fisher of Men)*, written after his return to Russia, is an attack on English middle-class life, here castigated largely for its hypocrisy. (p. 88)

In *Lovets Chelovekov* Zamyatin effectively employs his device of parallel planes of action by having the approach of the Zeppelin coincide with Craggs' stalking of the lovers and with Bailey's advances towards Mrs. Craggs.

Zamyatin was no friend of organised religion, seeing it as a manifestation of Entropy, and an aspect of English life which he satirises most bitterly in these stories is hypocritical piety. The Reverend Dewly is a priest and the members of Jesmond and Chiswick society are all assiduous church-goers. This attitude Zamyatin seems to have considered specifically English or Western, for his Russian priests (the monks in *Uezdnoe,* Deacon Indikoplev in *Iks* and the clerics in other short stories) are generally figures of fun, foolish, gullible and even irresponsible, though generally good-natured.

In the first years of the 'twenties Zamyatin's work centred almost exclusively on the Revolution in Russia and it was not until 1924 that he turned his gaze abroad again and concentrated attention on the question of Russia and the West. This theme remained with him until his death, finding its best expression in his two works about the old Hun leader, Atilla: the play *Atilla . . .* and the unfinished novel *Bich Bozhii (The Scourge of God).* Here the clash of Revolution and Entropy is elevated to the national-historical plane. (pp. 89-90)

In the play *Atilla,* set in the middle of the fifth century A.D., when Atilla was the ruler of a great empire in North and Central Europe, the main interest lies in the mighty clash between East and West and in the character and fate of the barbarian leader, who embraces within his person many of those qualities which Zamyatin ascribed to Russia. He is presented as a passionate and strong-willed, but insensitive man, who is, however, strictly honourable and motivated by a keen sense of justice. (p. 90)

Atilla's death can be seen as a punishment for his *hubris* in challenging fate or for his infringement of the moral law—in marrying Ildegonda he abandoned his faithful wife, Kerka. In any event, Atilla's death is not a judgment on his political views nor a sign that the Eastern advance was condemned to failure. The eventual defeat of the entropic Romans by the revolutionary Eastern barbarians is inevitable. . . . [In] Zamyatin's eyes, the eternal dialectical law must bring about the downfall of modern Western Europe.

At the same time it is perhaps possible to read into Atilla's fate a rebuke levelled against the Soviet authorities' confidence in their ability to bend life to their design.

Although Zamyatin saw as clearly as anyone the shortcomings of the new regime in Russia and the dangers inherent in it, *Atilla* demonstrates that he was no friend of Western capitalism, that he shared Marx's critical views on it. (pp. 95-6)

During his years of exile in the West, after he had left Russia in 1931, Zamyatin saw nothing to change the judgments implicit in *Atilla.* Indeed, in his last major work, the unfinished novel *Bich Bozhii (The Scourge of God),* his judgment of the West is if anything still harsher. (p. 97)

Like the play *Atilla, Bich Bozhii* is firmly based on Zamyatin's historical studies, and in its wide sweep it embraces pictures of both Rome and Constantinople and psychological portraits of Roman and barbarian leaders.

Zamyatin's main theme is again the contrast between the vigorous, animally healthy East and the soft, decaying West, hourly expecting its own downfall. The book opens with a description of this atmosphere of foreboding and doom. . . . By describing this atmosphere of economic instability and social unrest in modern terms Zamyatin suggests at once that his theme is modern as well as historical. This is not only fifth-century Rome but also Europe in the 1930's—or even later in this century. (pp. 97-8)

The characters of *Bich Bozhii* are described much more fully than those in Zamyatin's satirical works. These are no longer caricatures, but rounded personalities. At the same time Zamyatin still seizes on key characteristics and uses them as *leit-*

motifs: Atilla's father has a scar on his forehead which changes colour when he is angry; Placidia, the Emperor's sister, is characterised by her slightly squinting eyes; Atilla himself has twin forelocks which stick out like horns and at times of stress he always bows his head. (p. 99)

Zamyatin worked on *Bich Bozhii* from 1928, the year in which he finished *Atilla,* until 1935. His continued interest in the theme suggests that the question of the changing power relationship between Eastern and Western Europe was an important one for him.

Since his closer acquaintance with Western Europe in the 'thirties Zamyatin's attitude appears to have hardened. In *Atilla,* Aëtius and Vigila are much worthier figures than any of the Romans in *Bich Bozhii,* and Aëtius's arguments for peace and culture—even at the cost of social injustice—are given some weight. In *Bich Bozhii* no one defends Western values; there is no strong Western army and the old empire is almost resignedly awaiting defeat. Equally, however, on the barbarian side the moral indignation against Western values, so strongly expressed in the play *Atilla,* is less marked in the novel. (pp. 100-01)

In a world of growing fanaticism and hatred [Zamyatin] preached tolerance and the brotherhood of man; in a world of mounting dictatorial controls he championed human freedom; in a world of hypocrisy and sycophancy he spoke the truth. Like his own heroes, Zamyatin was persecuted for heresy but was strong enough to defend his ideals against overwhelming opposition and to go into voluntary exile for them. He would not consider his efforts vain: "The world is alive only through heretics"— he had played his part in the great struggle to keep the world alive. (pp. 107-08)

D. J. Richards, in his Zamyatin: A Soviet Heretic *(© D. J. Richards 1962; reprinted by permission of the author), Bowes & Bowes, 1962, 112 p.*

RICHARD A. GREGG   (essay date 1965)

"Prophetic" is a quality which few thoughtful readers would deny Zamiatin's *We.* For if its moral argument (the irreconcilability of "pure" communism and individual freedom) has, to a disturbing degree, been confirmed by the course of twentieth-century history, so have some of its boldest technological predictions (for example, state-enforced restrictions on human fertility, Communist-inaugurated space travel). Even its genre (an original blend of political satire and science fiction) has proven to be a prophecy of sorts, anticipating, as it does, the more celebrated satirical fantasies of Huxley and Orwell.

That these oracles have impressed the readers of *We* is as it should be. That they have distracted them from less obvious aspects of the work is not. For, objectively considered, *We* is a Janus-faced novel. It looks backward as well as forward. The philosophical problem it explores had engaged one of the greatest Russian minds of the previous century; its closest literary ancestor is a classic of Russian literature, and, as we shall see, underlying much of its plot is a famous myth of Judeo-Christian religion. Only when the traditional aspects of *We* have been properly assessed can the edge of its satire be fully felt.

The philosophical debt which the novel owes to Dostoevsky's thought in general, and to *Notes from the Underground* and *The Brothers Karamazov* in particular, will not detain us long, for it has received its due elsewhere. (p. 680)

Whatever ideas the *Notes* may have suggested to Zamiatin, the central metaphor or myth of his novel was drawn from a much older source, though it is possible that this debt, too, may have been suggested by Dostoevsky. The source in question is the Biblical story of Adam and Eve, which Zamiatin incorporated into his tale of a communist paradise, and the satirical uses of which Dostoevsky had—albeit in rudimentary form—anticipated in *The Possessed*. . . .

But to gauge the possible extent of Zamiatin's indebtedness to Dostoevsky is more difficult (and less important) than to see how the myth actually works itself out in the novel. (p. 682)

To do the Well-Doer's will on earth is, of course, the vocation of our hero [D-503]—a vocation which the crafty, beautiful I-330 seeks to subvert by inducing him to taste the delights of freedom and knowledge, that is, of Evil. In essence this is, of course, an imitation of Genesis. And just as the Biblical authors and their successors used certain traditional images to describe the fateful event—a forbidden food, a bite, a figurative fall, and sinful intercourse—so Zamiatin in relating D-503's loss of innocence uses his considerable ingenuity to ring the changes on these symbols. The seductive charms of Eve and her first fatal bite are thus telescoped into the recurrent images of I-330's sharp teeth and "bite-smile," which have such a fatal fascination for D-503; the moral fall of Adam becomes literal in *We*. "Down, down, down, as from a steep mountain," descends the hero into the site of his transgression (the Ancient House); it is there that a green and forbidden liqueur offered by I-330 replaces the forbidden fruit of Genesis, the consumption of which—here Zamiatin follows Milton rather than Genesis—on the hero's next visit leads to sinful and guilty intercourse with "Eve." When it is all over, the latter pointedly remarks: "Well, my fallen angel, you perished just now, did you know that?" . . .

Zamiatin exploits his myth in a manner that is neither mechanical nor, on the whole, obtrusive. Indeed, he drops his symbols so gently that their presence seems to have gone unnoticed. Perhaps it was to forestall such an event that on one occasion he expounds his Biblical design explicitly and in detail. His mouthpiece is the poet R-13, who in Entry 11 describes to D-503 the plight of the modern state in [terms of "the ancient legend of paradise"]. (p. 683)

But if *We* is to some significant degree Zamiatin's ironic retelling of Genesis chapters 1-4, where, one may ask, is the Archfiend without whose odious designs and serpent's shape no account of the story would be complete or even meaningful? The answer is provided by that enigmatic friend of Eve, S-4711, whose letter stands for Satan, serpent, and snake alike. . . . And if the frivolous reader would inquire how such a deformed creature could have ever enjoyed the favors of the beauteous I-330, Zamiatin has a no less frivolous answer ready. For who could be more ingratiating, more insinuatingly seductive than he who wears the world's most famous perfume for a name—4711? Subtlety, thy name is Eau de Cologne!

Zamiatin does not allow such occasional playfulness to blunt the edge of his satire, which cuts deepest when it diverges most widely from its model. For if the Biblical argument is that in order to be worthy of God, Adam should have resisted Eve's blandishments, the moral of *We* is that to be worthy of man the new Adam ought to succumb to them. Hence, if Genesis is tragic because Paradise was lost, and man's happiness forfeited, its modern analogue is tragic because in the end Adam is saved, and his "glass paradise"—putatively at least—preserved.

The use of ingenious mythical parallels can, as the record of contemporary fiction attests, become a habit-forming authorial indulgence. It should not, therefore, surprise us that midway through the novel Zamiatin is tempted to introduce a second Biblical pattern though it is doubtful whether its artistic integration into the novel as a whole is entirely successful. The earliest trace of this can be found in Entry 20, when Zamiatin makes his penitent hero (he has illegally gotten O-90 with child) ponder the equity of the death sentence awaiting him: "This [then] is that divine justice of which those stone-housed ancients dreamed, lit by the naive pink rays of the dawn of history. Their 'God' punished sacrilege as a capital crime." This rather shadowy equation of Christianity and communism evidently pleased the author (who was a friend of neither ideology), for two chapters later D-503, relishing the sensation of selfless solidarity with the community (he is going through one of his conformist phases), puts the case more clearly:

> In the ancient days the Christians understood
> this feeling; they are our only, though very
> imperfect, direct forerunners. They knew that
> resignation is a virtue, and pride a vice; that
> "We" is from God, "I" from the devil.

That a disciple of Dostoevskian ethics could depart from his master's metaphysics so far as to see Christianity as the father of communism was an irony which Zamiatin evidently understood and even exploited through parody. For as *We* draws to its tumultuous close, the hero finds himself in a situation . . . which bears a bizarre but unmistakable resemblance to that of Christ in the Legend of the Grand Inquisitor. . . . Like the Grand Inquisitor, the Well-Doer knows that the forced benefactions of the good society outweigh the freedom which Christ—and now D-503—would offer. And the hero, whose forty days of temptation in the wilderness of doubt (there are forty entries in his journal) and thirty-two years of age at his "death" are obvious allusions to his Christlike role, feels a solitude akin to that of Jesus before His crucifixion. (pp. 684-86)

D-503's ultimate decision is, of course, the opposite of Christ's. Instead of dying so that men may be free, he lives so that they will remain slaves. Yet, paradoxically, even as he submits himself to the machine which makes soulless robots of its victims, he is—if we accept his own identification of communism and Christianity—behaving like a Christian. And in the words written on the eve of his self-sacrifice—"Perhaps then [that is, after the operation] I shall be reborn. For only what is killed can be reborn"—one can hear ironical overtones of the Christian promise that only he who loses himself shall find himself, or that to live in the spirit is to die in the flesh.

To describe some of the more important symbolic patterns in *We* is not to affirm their artistic success. In particular, the compounded ironies occasioned by D-503's appearance as both the First and the Second Adam seem to blur and blunt more than they intensify. And other symbolic allusions (I have not tried to discuss them all) raise similar doubts. But if *We* is read today, it is less for its artistic merits (which are uneven) than for the boldness and ingenuity of its satirical concept (which are very great). In this concept the Biblical patterns described here play a role of the first importance. (p. 687)

Richard A. Gregg, "Two Adams and Eve in the Crystal Palace: Dostoevsky, the Bible, and 'We'," in Slavic Review *(copyright © 1965 by the American Association for the Advancement of Slavic Studies, Inc.), Vol. XXIV, No. 4, December, 1965, pp. 680-87.*

HELEN MUCHNIC   (essay date 1967)

[Zamyatin's] work is highly original. Fantastic but not fanciful, it is rooted in the banalities of life, rises out of them, and points to them, though it does not deal with them. Whatever the tone, that is, the reference is to the actual—actual settings and events, colloquial speech, the realities of human nature, and back of everything, implicit but unmistakable, a firm rationality and an equally firm faith. Zamyatin laughs at pettiness and stupidity, at greed, lust, and dishonesty. He can evoke such vile depravity as Sologub once conjured up in *The Petty Demon*, and yet there is always something to counterbalance the nastiness: a high sense of honor is seen surviving even in a spiritual morass or in extreme misery; passion transcends lust; a sense of guilt torments the undiscovered criminal. Zamyatin is never sentimental. He delights in ribaldry, in the violence of sexual play, and when he speaks of tenderness he mingles it with pity or brutality or the lovably absurd. It seems to him that some men will always manage to assert themselves and escape even from a totally mechanized society into the natural world; everywhere in his stories men's uncontrollable wills come welling up through drabness, viciousness, constraints. He believes that basic decency and love survive somehow and harbors a kind of unreligious, metaphysical, or scientific faith in resurrection and continuity: a distant star plunges into the earth to begin life again after the conflagration, just as the worm dies in its chrysalis, and men destroy one another in civil war for the sake of rebirth in a new and better state. His method is unique—a kind of inverted symbolism, in which the actualities of life assume fantastic shapes and become images of abstract meanings or general feelings and impressions. . . . (pp. 384-86)

> *Helen Muchnic, "The Literature of Nightmare" (originally published in* The New York Review of Books, *Vol. 8, No. 11, June 15, 1967), in her* Russian Writers: Notes and Essays *(copyright © 1971 by Helen Muchnic; reprinted by permission of Random House, Inc.), Random House, 1971, pp. 383-92.*

ALEX M. SHANE   (essay date 1968)

On the basis of thematic, structural, and stylistic considerations the greater portion of Zamjatin's prose fiction is divisible into several categories, and if in addition to these intrinsic criteria the dates of writing and other extrinsic criteria are taken into consideration, then his work can be divided into four periods.

The first period is 1908-1917. His first two stories ["Odin" and "Devuška"] . . . have but little intrinsic literary merit. One is struck by their excessive prolixity as well as the extensive influence of decadent touches such as the sensational but tasteless final paragraph of "Odin" in which the dead hero's broken skull and quivering brain are described in detail, and the use of numerous decadent clichés such as the furious caresses of dying flowers, the sickeningly sweet smell of corpses, rattling teeth, pounding heart, and the like. It is to Zamjatin's credit that these two stories were never reprinted and that their bad features were not repeated in his subsequent works. Central among the works of the early period were the three *povesti* [or novellas, "Uezdnoe," "Na Kuličkax," and "Alatyr"]. . . . (pp. 14-15)

The major themes of Zamjatin's early works—man's inhumanity, love, revolution—invariably are developed in a provincial Russian setting. In "Uezdnoe," the keynote work of this period, the ignorant Anfim Baryba, conditioned by his environment, symbolizes the negative aspects of provincial life. Expelled from school for excessive stupidity, he steals, cheats, pimps, rapes, bullies, bears false witness, and finally becomes the town constable. Whatever human feelings he may have had at the beginning are completely atrophied during the course of his career, and the final description of Baryba as "an old resurrected heathen idol, an absurd Russian stone idol" endows him with symbolic significance: that of a cruel, ossified, provincial Russia. The remainder of the characters resemble Baryba in their bestial, senseless existence, with perhaps the sole exception of the tailor Timoša, who, although Baryba's only friend, *is* capable of a human impulse and tries to save a thieving boy from being beaten to death by an irate tavern keeper: "Do you want to kill the kid because of a hundred rubles? Maybe you've already killed him? Look, he's not breathing. Devils, animals, isn't a man even worth a hundred rubles?" Zamjatin's answer to this question is an ironic negative, for Timoša's humanistic impulse is rewarded by ostracism, a court conviction of aiding the robbers (in which Baryba's false testimony is instrumental), and, finally, execution.

In "Na kuličkax," which is essentially a continuation of the same theme, some of the characters are endowed with human qualities that raise them above the level of the surrounding environment, yet the tragedy of human existence is made all the more poignant by their ultimate destruction. Andrej Ivanovič Polovec, ostensibly the central figure, possesses some capabilities and aspirations, but his love for Marusja remains unrealized and he is sucked into the drunken, bestial revelry of the other officers. . . . Here, as in "Uezdnoe," the finale takes on symbolic proportions, for the frenzied, hopeless revelry engulfs not only Polovec, but all of Russia. Although both works depict negative aspects of provincial life, there has been a shift in emphasis: in "Uezdnoe" Zamjatin has shown the successful rise to power of a provincial, animal-like inhabitant amidst others that are like him, while in "Na kuličkax" he has depicted the destruction of sensitive people endowed with some human feelings amidst animal-like inhabitants of a provincial garrison.

The theme of love has two aspects: the physical, consisting in the satisfaction of a biological urge, and the spiritual, consisting in an intellectual or emotional attachment. Zamjatin most frequently dwells on the physiological aspect, which he presents negatively or positively, depending upon the characters involved. For the characters of "Uezdnoe" there can be no question of a spiritual love; love is simply an everyday physical function, an animal necessity that does nothing to dispel the tedium of provincial life. In "Na kuličkax" the same automatic, instinctive, Baryba-like behavior is exemplified by Katjuška, who sleeps with any man, begets children yearly, and is the norm, rather than exception, for garrison behavior. By contrast, Polovec's love for Marusja is that of an idealistic dreamer, primarily spiritual in nature. However, his love is never realized, as is also the case with the other few instances of spiritual love in the early works, such as Kostja Edytkin's love for Glafira ("Alatyr") and Fedor Volkov's for a gentry girl ("Afrika"). The negative physiological treatment of the sexual urge in "Uezdnoe" and "Na kuličkax" re-enforced the basic theme of inhuman, bestial existence, but in some of the other works the physiological urge was depicted in a positive, at times even lyrical manner, as, for example, Glafira's need for fulfillment in the *povest'* "Alatyr" or Afim'ja's need for a child in the story "Črevo" . . . , which is, perhaps the best expression of Zamjatin's primitivism.

The third major theme, that of revolution, found but weak expression in Zamjatin's early works. The Potemkin Mutiny of 1905 was the subject of a brief sketch entitled **"Tri dnja"** . . . and served as a background for the denouement in the story **"Neputevyj."** . . . Of greater significance was the revolution, or rather the rebellion, of several characters, primarily of the dreamer-thinker type, against the existing environment. This rebellion, neither clearly defined nor comprising a conscious rejection of the existing environment, was always unsuccessful and frequently ludicrous, for most of the dreamer-thinkers were *čudaki* [eccentrics]. . . . (pp. 15-16)

Structurally, the increasing brevity of Zamjatin's works is indeed striking, particularly in the case of his stories, which diminished in average length from thirty to ten pages each. In the case of the *povesti*, increasing brevity was accompanied by a greater integration of action and a tightening of the narrative structure, which tended to de-emphasize the descriptive elements. The *povesti* were structurally distinguished from the stories by their greater length (averaging ninety pages each), the use of chapter titles to stress the central theme or event, a greater number of characters that played a significant role (eight or ten as opposed to two or three), and by a considerably greater scope of action depicting a whole series of events rather than only one or two. This genre distinction between *povest'* and story was retained by Zamjatin throughout the 1910's, but in the 1920's significant structural changes were to occur.

The most original aspect of Zamjatin's prose fiction, however, was his distinctive style, which was characterized by grotesque, conciseness, imagery, and *skaz* narration, and was determined by his firm belief in the primacy of the author's subjective impression. For Zamjatin, artistic truth was best achieved through the creation of a synthetic image, by focusing on a few well-chosen features that would best convey the artist's impression and reveal the essence of the object depicted. The use of grotesque, which is essentially an exaggeration of certain features at the expense of others, was most appropriate to Zamjatin's aims. . . . External description was minimal, there were no inner monologues, and the probing perambulations of the omniscient author were avoided. Emphasis was on demonstrating (*pokazyvanie*), not on narrating (*rasskazyvanie*); rather than describe a character by third-person narration, Zamjatin preferred to reveal it through action or by means of one of three standard devices: metaphoric comparison (usually with an animal), a peculiar physical characteristic, or an epithetic attributive. In all three instances the device used delineated both a physical and a basic character trait. (p. 17)

The predominance of provincial setting in Zamjatin's early works was motivated to a great degree by stylistic considerations. On the one hand it provided him with bright, new, concentrated images, and on the other it yielded rich linguistic material in the form of colloquial and regional expressions for the renovation of the literary language. In all of his *povesti* and in all but four of his earliest stories ("Odin," "Devuška," "Aprel'," "Tri dnja") Zamjatin makes use of *skaz*, a special mode of narrative prose in which a narrator, manipulated by the author, but usually differing from him in language, social position, and outlook, is introduced, either explicitly or implicitly, as a stylistic device. Zamjatin's narrator speaks a Russian which, grammatically, is basically correct, but which contains numerous regional words as well as colloquial expressions that normally would be encountered only in conversation and were not a part of standard literary Russian. The peculiarities of the narrator's language are not only lexical, but are reflected in the highly stylized syntactical structure characterized by numerous inversions. (p. 18)

In addition to the use of *skaz*, traces of rhythmic and musical stylization began to appear in some of Zamjatin's works as early as 1914 and were to acquire much greater significance in works of the subsequent period. . . . Such rhythmic and phonic organization indicates conscious manipulation on the part of the author and goes far beyond the scope of normal *skaz* narrative. (p. 19)

[Works written during the years 1917-1921] comprise the second or middle period in Zamjatin's prose fiction. Central among them are the novel *My,* the two *povesti* ["Ostrovitjane" and "Sever"] . . . and the well-known stories ["Lovec čelovekov," "Peščera," and "Mamaj"]. . . . The shift in setting to urban centers such as London, Petersburg, and a glass city of the future was indeed striking, but the juxtaposition of provincial Russia and Europe resulted in an amazing similarity: on the one hand there was provincial philistine absurdity and darkness; on the other, an inert philistine automation in the lifeless glitter of electric lamps. Philistinism, the negation of man and of human values, was the most important of Zamjatin's three major themes and remained the chief object of his satire and caustic irony. The treatment of the other two themes, love and revolution, underwent considerable modification. During this period love was usually depicted as a positive physiological force and for the first time was consistently equated with revolution, which now became a conscious and passionate attack aimed at the philistine environment. The love affairs of D-503 and I-330 (*My*), Didi and O'Kelly ("Ostrovitjane"), Mrs. Craggs and Bailey ("Lovec čelovekov"), and Marej and Pel'ka ("Sever") all are excellent examples of this new thematic formulation and have no counterpart in the early works, although a movement in this direction may be seen in the stories "Crevo" and "Krjaži." The positive aspects of the love-revolution theme were strengthened at times by the intrusion of an omniscient author and through the occasional use of characters as authorial mouthpieces.

New thematic formulation and a new setting were accompanied by stylistic changes. The use of grotesque was retained, while the three basic devices for conveying the author's impression—metaphoric comparison, physical characteristic, and epithetic attributive—were utilized more systematically and with much greater frequency. Often all three devices were applied to a single character. Kemble ("Ostrovitjane"), for example, is characterized by squarishness, rigidity, a furrowed brow (which represents his inability to place a new fact or idea into the proper compartment of his brain), and is compared to a tractor and truck. Comparisons, no longer restricted to the animal kingdom, were considerably richer in variety and originality, and the predominantly static images of the early period were at times replaced by actional images, that is, images whose development during the course of the story represented changes within the character. Kemble's movements, for example, which originally were compared to those of a tractor, are later compared to those of a tractor mired in mud, then to a stalled tractor, and finally to a tractor with a broken steering mechanism. The intensification and systematization of Zamjatin's imagery devices culminated in the creation of an integrating image, or mother metaphor as D. Mirsky has called it, which became the major unifying principle and relegated the plot to a position of secondary importance. The two most extreme examples in this respect are the stories "Mamaj" and "Peščera," where the integrating images of a cave and a ship, respectively, have determined an entire system of derivative images.

An extremely interesting innovation of the middle period was Zamjatin's use of color symbolism. Adjectives denoting color, used but rarely in the early works, appear frequently during the middle period, usually in combination with other attributives of a given object or person. Specific colors became associated with and invariably accompanied certain basic concepts. Flesh and human vivification were usually characterized by the colors pink or raspberry, while yellow and gold were attributes of the sun and frequently symbolized ardent passion, the life-giving force in man. Red, indicative of blood, flame, or revolution, and green, indicative of sprouting vegetation as another expression of the life-force, complete the four color complex which is basic to the positive manifestation of the themes of love and revolution. Blue and blue-gray, at least in *My,* were used to symbolize rationality and order, while black and white, although lacking recurrent symbolic values, were also used systematically, primarily as fixed attributives and vivid contrast.

Zamjatin's language of the middle period was characterized by two significant developments: the evolution of a condensed, staccato, elliptical style rich in rhythmic and phonic effects, and the absence of a *skaz* narrative style in the manner of his early period. . . . The use of *skaz* narrative with the presence of an implicit narrator had been motivated by the theme and setting of Zamjatin's early works, but the same style would hardly have been suitable for the depiction of London, Petersburg, or a great city of the future. Consequently, local, dialectical, and substandard words were abandoned and the presence of a narrator other than the author was not felt. What remained was a highly stylized literary prose with a sprinkling of words typical of the author's own speech.

Zamjatin's third or transitional period, consisting of works written during the years 1922-1927, was characterized by a marked decrease in output of prose fiction (only seven stories) and by a search for new literary forms. The stories [**"Rus'"** and **"Kuny"**] . . . affirmed passionate love in the style of **"Sever,"** but lacked satiric depiction of philistinism. Without question, **"Rasskaz o samom glavnom"** . . . was the single most important work of Zamjatin's transitional period and marked a unique attempt to create a new literary form on the basis of theoretical pronouncements expressed in his essays of that time. In **"Rasskaz o samom glavnom"** three worlds are depicted: the world of a yellowish-pink caterpillar Rhopalocera, the world of Kelbuj and Orel peasants who are fighting on opposite sides in the Russian Revolution, and the world of a distant, dying star. The spatial intersection of the three worlds (Rhopalocera falls into the heroine's lap as she talks with the leader of the Kelbuj rebellion, and the dying star finally collides with the Earth) is at best artificial, and the basic unity of the story rests in the underlying philosophic conceptions and in the symbolic parallelism of events on Earth and on the dying star. Although the fulfillment of sexual love is a very important theme, Zamjatin's message is much more comprehensive: life is truly life only when some basic function or purpose is being fulfilled. At such moments seconds become ages and one moment of fulfillment is worth years of unfulfilled existence. Another factor contributing to the unity and philosophic import of the story was the unusual, unmasked intrusion in several crucial instances of the author himself through use of the first person singular, which equated the sensations of the author with those of his characters. The effect is that of a fluid omniscient entity

which is a part of each and every living thing, and this all-encompassing authorial spirit creates a trans-structural unity of the three plot lines. (pp. 20-1)

[The remaining] works of the transitional period were essentially anecdotes cast in literary form with a strong admixture of parody and as such were a continuation and development of a tendency already manifest during the middle period. . . . The theme of philistinism, which had receded to the background since *My,* reappeared in the stories [**"Iks"** and **"Slove predostavljaetsja tovarišču Čuryginu"**] . . . , albeit in a new form: the superficial acceptance of the Russian Revolution by ignorant philistines who failed to understand its essence. *Skaz* narrative reappears, but is quite different from that of the early period. The narrative style in **"Iks"** is definitely oriented toward stylized oral speech and the narrator, ostensibly a Soviet citizen of good education with a literary bent, parodies various literary devices and frequently resorts to direct address to the reader. **"Slovo predostavljaetsja tovarišču Čuryginu"** stands out as a masterpiece of sustained *skaz* oratory, in which an uneducated peasant manages to misuse with consummate skill his recently acquired vague knowledge of Marxist theory and Soviet jargon. . . . (pp. 21-2)

Despite the differences that characterize the transitional works, there can be discerned in them a definite trend toward the anecdote, the narration of a story in which the action tends to assume a much greater importance than the accompanying complex of images. The extensive derivational systems of the middle period were a thing of the past. But perhaps most significant of all was a decided predilection for parody, most significant because parody precluded the possibility of working out a distinctive style that could be called the author's own. (p. 22)

[Zamjatin's late works, beginning with **"Ela"**] represent the final crystallization of his artistic techniques and stand in distinct contrast structurally, stylistically, and in thematic stress to the works of the early and middle periods. The tendency toward literary parody, so striking in the transitional stories was continued and, under the influence of O. Henry and perhaps other Western models, gave rise to a new form of story, which could be described as a short, ironic novella with a surprise ending. This new genre in Zamjatin's prose was represented by the six short stories [**"Desjatiminutnaja droma," "Mučeniki nauki," "Časy," "Lev," "Vstreča,"** and **"Videnic"**]. . . . Essentially anecdotal in nature, the sustained irony of these novellas was frequently based on the incongruity of old habits in a new environment and by the parody of literary devices and conventions, underscored by authorial instrusions that were addressed directly to the reader in a conversational tone. (pp. 22-3)

The excellent stories **"Ela"** and **"Navodnenie"** . . . sharply contrasted with the novellas and, along with the unfinished novel *Bič Božij* . . . , represent the major works of the late period. Thematically **"Ela"** is a continuation of Zamjatin's other two northern stories, **"Afrika"** and **"Sever,"** for in all three the dreamer-hero has rejected the present in the pursuit of future happiness only to find death, while the central theme of **"Navodnenie"** was essentially the same as that of **"Črevo,"** a woman's basic physiological need to bear a child. In view of the thematic similarity, the stylistic differences were all the more pronounced. Imagery continued to be used more systematically than in Zamjatin's early works, but never with the proliferation so typical of the middle period. The staccato and elliptical style of the middle period gave way to a smoother, simpler style of narration which more closely approximated the language of the author himself—polished, unconstrained, conversational. . . . Greater economy emphasized the individual descriptive image by isolating it amid relatively neutral prose and became a distinguishing characteristic of Zamjatin's late prose. The achievement of lexical purity and syntactical simplicity was accomplished by the exclusion of words that were dialectal, substandard, or too colloquial. While the lexicon of **"Afrika"** contained numerous dialectal expressions such as *ljasy* 'fishnets,' *kolguška* 'crock,' *ražyj* 'husky,' and substandard words such as *ixnij, inda, ètak,* the late works were free of such expressions. Regional flavor was created by the use of technical terms peculiar to the sea such as *ela, bot,* and *karbas,* all quite acceptable in standard literary Russian.

Another device that underwent considerable change and modification during Zamjatin's literary evolution was the use of symbolism. In his early works there was no symbolism in the strict sense of the word, although there was an attempt to create a symbolic synthesis of significant features in character depiction by means of grotesque and to endow the finales of his *povesti* with symbolic universality. The color symbolism which Zamjatin introduced and consistently used during the middle period, was, on the whole, superceded by a third form of symbolism which, lacking the philosophical implications of color symbolism, did not transcend the particular story and was used primarily as an artistic device to achieve greater esthetic effect by providing a fatalistic foreboding of the story's tragic denouement. The Norwegian widow with shaded eyes and cold hands was clearly a death symbol which stressed the inevitability of the hero's tragic death (**"Ela"**). Similar examples of prognostic symbolism occur in **"Navodnenie,"** where Sofija's dream became nightmarish reality, and the basic flood image indicated not only the rise and fall of the Neva River but the ebb and flow of human passion as well.

Although Zamjatin's literary evolution has been sketched in the preceding discussion of salient characteristics, a more concise formulation will bring major trends into sharper focus. Despite the thematic and stylistic variety of his early stories, which reflected the young writer's search for distinctive expression, philistinism in the form of provincial absurdity, bestiality, and ignorance became the major object of satiric depiction in Zamjatin's pre-Revolutionary *povesti.* Cast in an appropriate style that was characterized by striking imagery, grotesque, and *skaz,* the early *povesti* established Zamjatin's reputation as one of the most talented young writers in Russian literature of the 1910's. His year-and-a-half stay in England and the Russian Revolution profoundly affected both his thinking and writing. Although philistinism remained the central target of Zamjatin's satire, emphasis was shifted from provincial ignorance and bestiality to urban automatization, a shift that was dictated, in part, by a change in setting and which resulted in stylistic changes. The unrelieved gloom of the early *povesti* now was partially dispelled by Zamjatin's thematic treatment of love and revolution, both of which were presented as positive, primal forces capable of disrupting the existing philistine order. This artistic development was paralleled by the appearance of Zamjatin's first essays, in which he espoused maximal freedom, heresy, and neverending revolution. His anti-utopian novel *My,* which undoubtedly was inspired by the novels of H. G. Wells and Anatole France, represented a significant development in that most of Zamjatin's basic beliefs and philosophic conceptions were expressed explicitly through the words of his major characters for the first time in his prose fiction. This trend, with the sole exception of **"Rasskaz o samom glavnom,"** was not continued, although Zamjatin's

views did receive further refinement in several excellent essays. Instead, he wrote several minor stories that abounded in literary parody and satirized superficial accommodation to the Bolshevik Revolution. It was only in the late twenties that Zamjatin again returned to major prose fiction, writing two long stories that are readily distinguished from his previous works by their studied stylistic simplicity, the objectivity of the omniscient author, and the absence of satire. (pp. 22-5)

Alex M. Shane, "Zamjatin's Prose Fiction," in Slavic and East European Journal *(© 1968 by AATSEEL of the U.S., Inc.), Vol. XII, No. 1, Spring, 1968, pp. 14-26.*

DARKO SUVIN   (essay date 1971)

In Russia [the 1920s] was one of those epochs when new Heavens touch the old Earth, when the future actively overpowers the present, and the sluggish and disjointed flow of time is suddenly channelled into a wild waterfall, generating a rainbow on the near horizon and capable of dispensing light and warmth from scores of dynamos. (pp. 252-53)

The seemingly divergent concerns of Evgeny Zamyatin, when looked at more closely, turn out also to deal with the relationships of the new, future heavens and the old, present earth. The difference is that Zamyatin did not believe in any eschatological end of history. An ex-Bolshevik and rebel against tsarism, a scientist-specialist in ship-building who introduced into his novel *We* . . . the atmosphere of the shipyards and of the illegal movement, Zamyatin too despised Western capitalism as life-crushing. . . . It is thus disingenuous to present him as a primarily anti-Soviet author—even though the increasingly dogmatic and bureaucratic high priests of Soviet letters thought of him so, never allowed his novel to be printed in the USSR, and induced him to leave his country in 1931. Extrapolating the repressive potentials of every strong state and technocratic set-up, including the socialist ones, Zamyatin describes a United or Unique State 12 centuries hence having for its leader "the Benefactor" (a prototype for Orwell's Big Brother and the situation in *1984*), where art has become a public utilitarian service, and science a faultless guide for linear, undeviating happiness. Zamyatin's sarcasm against abstract utopian prescriptions (like those of the feebler Wells) takes on Dostoevskian overtones: the threat of the Crystal Palace echoes in the totally rationalized city. The only irrational element left is people, like the split (Marx would have said alienated) narrator, the mathematician and rocketship builder D-503, and the temptress from the underground movement who for a moment makes of him a deviant. But man has, as Dostoevsky's Grand Inquisitor explained to Christ, a built-in instinct for slavery, the rebellion fails, and all the citizen "Numbers" are subjected to brain surgery removing the possibility of harmful imagination.

However, Zamyatin's novel is not consistent. Of a bold general concept, it hesitates midway between Chernyshevsky and Dostoevsky—undecided as to what it thinks of science and reason. After the physician and philosopher [Alexander] Bogdanov and the mathematician [Konstantin E.] Tsiolkovsky, Zamyatin was the first practicing scientist and engineer among significant Russian SF writers. The scientific method provided the paradigm for his thinking, and he could not seriously blame it for the deformations of life. In that case, how is it that a certain type of rationalism, claiming to be scientific, can be harmful in certain social usages? This question, which came up in SF with [Samuel] Butler's *Erewhom* and Wells's best works, Zamyatin was unable to answer except in mythical, Dostoevskian terms: there is "only one conceivable victory—to be crucified. . . . Christ, when factually the victor, becomes the Grand Inquisitor" (in his essay **"Scythians?"**). The achievement of any lofty ideal inevitably causes it to founder in philistinism. To the extent that *We* equates Leninist Communism with institutionalized Christianity and models its fable on an inevitable Fall from Eden ending in an ironical crucifixion, it has a strong anti-utopian streak. Zamyatin's evocative style shifted the focus to systematic image-building at the expense of the plot, making thus a virtue of his inability to explicate the chosen situation and to reconcile its poles of rationalism and irrationalism, science and art (including the art of love). However, this obscures the problem of whether *any* utopia—even a dynamic one that refuses [Thomas] More's Platonic and Christian model—must of inherent necessity become repressive and dehumanizing. Zamyatin's social ideology conflicts with his own favorite experimental approach: a meaningful exploration of this theme and situation would have to be conducted in terms of the least alienating utopia imaginable—one in which there is no misuse of natural sciences by a dogmatic science of man.

Yet when all this is said, the basic values of *We* imply a stubborn revolutionary vision of a classless new moral world free from all social alienations, a vision common to Anarchism and libertarian Marxism. Zamyatin confronts an anti-utopian, absolutistic, military-type control—extrapolated both from the bourgeois and early socialist state practices—with a utopian-socialist norm. . . . Simultaneously with the poetry of Mayakovsky (whom he called "a magnificent beacon"), Zamyatin brought to Russian SF the realization that the new utopian world cannot be a static changeless paradise of a new religion, albeit a religion of steel, mathematics, and interplanetary flights. Refusing all canonization, the materialist utopia must subject itself to a constant scrutiny by the light of its own principles; its values are for Zamyatin centered in an ever-developing human personality and expressed in an irreducible, life-giving, and subversive erotic passion. For all its resolute one-sidedness, the uses of Zamyatin's bitter and paradoxical warning in a dialectical utopianism seem to be obvious.

The language of the novel is an interesting Expressionist medium vouching for at least some cognitive veracity. It is manipulated for speed and economy, which Zamyatin himself defined as "a high voltage of every word":

> In one second there has to be condensed what before fitted into a whole minute; the syntax becomes elliptical and airy, the complex pyramids of the paragraph are scattered into stone blocks of independent sentences. . . . The picture is sharply focussed, synthetic, it has one basic trait only, which could be noticed from a moving car. Provincialisms, neologisms, science, mathematics, engineering have invaded a vocabulary canonized by usage. . . .

Zamyatin is a heretic; in places vague and possibly confused, he probably fails to attain a fully consistent structure because of the one-sided assumptions which underlie his writing—but he is certainly not counterrevolutionary. On the contrary, in his own way he tried to work for a future different from that of the envisioned United State. His protagonist is defeated, but the novel as a whole remains concerned with the integrity of man's knowledge (science) and practice (love and art). Even the symbol of $\sqrt{-1}$ (which has an equivalent in the retribal-

ized, "hippie" Mephis in the Green World) is an antithesis to and appeal against a limited Rationalism (the United State) that does not simply reject the thesis—as Dostoevsky's Underground Man did—but includes it in a higher dialectical synthesis prefigured in D-503's oscillation between love and the Integral. Yet, as they are not in Wells, the guilt and possible solution are here placed squarely on man and not on mythical outsiders. Like the formal model of D-503's personalized notes, the laboratory conspectus, the structure of *We* remains open to new cognitions, restless, anti-entropic, and never finally complete. By systematically and sensitively subjecting the deformities it describes to the experimental examination and hyperbolic magnification of SF, Zamyatin's method makes it possible to identify and cope with them. In his own vocabulary, the protagonist's defeat is of the day but not necessarily of the epoch. The defeat in the novel *We* is not the defeat of the novel itself, but an exasperated shocking of the reader into thought and action. It is a document of an acute clash between the "cold" and the "warm" utopia; a judgment on Campanella or Bacon as given by Rabelais or Shelley. (pp. 255-59)

Darko Suvin, "Russian SF and Its Utopian Tradition," in The Modern Language Review *(© Modern Humanities Research Association 1971), Vol. 66, No. 1, January, 1971 (and reprinted in his* Metamorphoses of Science Fiction: On the Poetics and History of a Literary Genre, Yale University Press, 1979, pp. 243-69).**

SUSAN LAYTON   (essay date 1973)

Zamjatin's art offers strong evidence in support of the proposition that the roots of the complex phenomenon of Russian Modernism are located in nineteenth-century Russian culture. In examining the connections between Zamjatin's "new Realism" and this culture, valuable perspectives are provided by his aesthetic of distortion, his view of man as essentially irrational, and his concern for the human condition—characteristics which also link his work to tendencies in the international Modernist movement. . . .

As a typical Modernist, Zamjatin defended his aesthetic by insisting that an artist cannot approximate twentieth-century life by representing surface reality. He considered Einstein's discovery of the law of relativity the symbolic keynote of the age, remarking that even before this scientific confirmation artists and philosophers had intuited the nonexistence of objective reality and absolute truths. In the age of relativity life itself posed a challenge to the artist's imagination. . . . Was it not clear, he asked, that the art which arises from this modern reality must be "fantastic like a dream"? (p. 279)

In its typically Modern deformation of the actual, Zamjatin's imagery tended to annul direct reference to the external world. Rather than presenting careful descriptions of characters, he conveyed their appearance through the intensification of one or two features, often to the point of the grotesque: [in **"Mamaj"**] the bald Mamaj has a head like a pumpkin; the sickly, thin Maša in **"The Cave"** is flat, cut out of paper. Frequently the recurrent image is realized: Kortoma in **"The North"** becomes a copper samovar; Obertyšev in **"The Cave"** becomes a monster overgrown with teeth. As in *We,* Zamjatin sometimes carries metonymic representation to an extreme, reducing characters to pure lines and geometrical shapes as in a cubist painting. Like many modern painters he employs color abstractly (in **"The North,"** for example, Pelka is often visible only as a flash of red). Such techniques produce a radical metamorphosis of the actual in order to reveal the reality Zamjatin perceived beneath the surface.

Characterization by leitmotifs rather than by full, individualized descriptions is related to Zamjatin's retreat from Realism's traditional exhaustive psychological analysis; in this he participated in a main current of literary Modernism. Rather than depicting characters through lengthy analyses of their social relationships and motivations, he presented fundamental "contours". . . . Often this led him to represent them as persons whose typical experiences recur. In **"The North"** Marej's nature as a dreamer is revealed in his recollected response to the magical singing of the *rusalki,* just as it is in his captivation as an adult by a fascinating woman and a fantastic imaginary lantern. In **"Mamaj"** the ludicrous hero is constantly experiencing his past anew: books replace boyhood games, and he follows conventional codes just as he once submitted to parental supervision. D-503 in *We* relives experiences from his childhood, and he recognizes new meaning in them as his sense of individuality develops. Importantly, each of these characters illustrates another feature which Zamjatin's work shares with other works of modern literature (although in a caricatured form in **"Mamaj"**). This rejection of Realistic psychology depends upon replacing the idea of a stable, knowable ego, a "social being," with a notion of a deeper "individual being." Rather than being defined conclusively, Zamjatin's heroes are in the process of becoming, seeking sources of authenticity in existence. D-503 seeks to overcome a sense of alienation from himself and from others and to define his true self. **"The North"** and **"The Cave"** also have heroes who attempt to make life meaningful in the absence of support from religion or from society. Like D-503, Marej and Martin Martinyč make choices which assert the primacy of feeling over reason, and they experience love and the beauty of the world as absolute goods. As a caricature at the farthest remove from the human ideal, Mamaj also points to this concept of the man "genuinely alive" and creating himself. In realizing the essential individual being, the touchstone for Zamjatin's characters is love. In **"The North"** the peak of happiness for Marej and Pelka is their brief existence together in a forest world which seems magically exempt from the ravages of time. Similarly, in **"The Cave"** Martin Martinyč is overwhelmed by the harsh conditions of Soviet Petersburg and attempts to retrieve the quality of a past experience, identifying his authentic self with an enduring memory of love. And love for I-330 marks the high point in D-503's attempt to define his essential self. In each case love provides an epiphany and seems to negate the passage of time, decay, and death.

Zamjatin celebrated man's fundamentally irrational nature, an essence which transcends individual existence. In his view, passionate love, the impulse toward creation, and an awareness of beauty are human qualities which must always be defended; representing this universal human nature rather than recording topical events was the aim he ascribed to genuine art. Thus his characters participate in undying patterns of human experience. In blurring distinctions between past, present, and future periods of history Zamjatin expressed the idea of eternal recurrence. By depicting in **"The North"** Marej's experience of love and attempt to create something enduring, Zamjatin revealed in the present age a persistent, primitive sense of harmony with the natural cosmos. . . . **"Mamaj"** and **"The Cave"** display a similar intersection of historical planes. The battle of Kulikovo, the imperial age of St. Petersburg, the Russo-Japanese war, and the civil war in the Soviet Union all enter the world of Mamaj, along with the timeless feats of the

imaginary knight Ruslan. In **"The Cave"** the prehistoric ice age and the Biblical myth of creation provide perspectives on the life of Martin Martinyč and his wife in the Petersburg of 1919. By fusing such discontinuous elements into a timeless unity, Zamjatin sought to escape the confines of contemporary history to deal with the human condition.

What links can now be established between the Modernist tendencies in which Zamjatin participated and the nineteenth-century Russian heritage? His essay **"On Literature, Revolution, and Entropy"** was a definitive expression of the Modernists' sense that they were making a new beginning by breaking with the nineteenth century, a phenomenon observable throughout Western Europe. This cast of mind in Russian Modernism is related to the wide-spread nineteenth-century perception of a cultural void. (pp. 280-82)

In the political arena [during the nineteenth century] Russians of very different persuasions embraced the idea that their country's backwardness vis-à-vis the West conferred a unique potential upon it. . . . [Aleksandr I.] Herzen maintained that Russia, a "young" country, presented far more favorable conditions for a true socialist revolution than did Europe. Similarly, Russia appeared to Dostoevskij as being capable of rejuvenating the world by offering a new religious truth. But a more directly relevant product of the notion that a cultural void opens the way to originality can be observed in the conviction of major nineteenth-century Russian writers that they could not uncritically borrow literary forms characteristic of Western Europe. . . . Zamjatin, with a stridency fostered by the period in which he lived, expressed an innovative zeal similar to his predecessors, although he was reacting against the tradition they established.

Another correspondence between the avant-garde of the twenties and the educated class in nineteenth-century Russia was their position as outsiders in their societies. Dostoevskij's underground man was speaking with paralyzing self-consciousness when he proclaimed, "I have no foundations"; but his sense of being without roots was not aberrant in Russia. The superfluous man of the nineteenth century was the Russian prototype of the homeless intellectual, a sensitive person in opposition to society. In his dilemmas lay seeds of the fateful rift which developed later between artist and society not only in Russia but throughout Europe, where the avant-garde emerged as a special caste. As an internal emigré and eventual exile, Zamjatin shared this fate. (pp. 283-84)

Both in his theoretical statements and prose, Zamjatin sought to establish continuity between past, present, and future on the personal and historical levels by focusing on the human condition. This was in essence a quest for philosophical meaning, which linked him directly with much of nineteenth-century Russian literature. In calling for an art of distortion which could achieve a philosophical synthesis, he revealed his kinship with other Modernists. But his rejection of traditional Realism also identified him with a broad tendency in the works of many nineteenth-century Russian writers which distinguished them from the mainstream of Western European Realism. . . . Within this context, the most crucial heritage for Zamjatin was the "Romantic Realism" of Gogol' and Dostoevskij; it affected his structures and themes, character types, and stylistic techniques. The dense verbal texture of Zamjatin's works, his use of grotesque imagery, and his pronounced affinity for synecdoche and realized metaphors reveal the impact of Gogol'. But in its fundamental aesthetic strategy and intention Zamjatin's art finds a striking parallel, indeed a model, in Dostoevskij's "fantastic Realism."

When Zamjatin maintained that his new Realism best corresponded to the fantastic quality of contemporary life, he was following a line of thought which Dostoevskij had taken in his own time. By employing the symbolic and the fantastic, Zamjatin aspired like Doestoevskij to reveal a reality more authentic than historical fact. Although Zamjatin was commited to the quest for new forms of expression, he never considered art as the sum of its devices, maintaining instead that it must have affective significance. Opposed to the "dehumanization of art," he defended literature as a forum for philosophical speculation, thereby placing himself among modern writers who have believed they must undertake tasks traditionally performed by philosophers. . . . These two Russian artists held very different beliefs, of course, Dostoevskij affirming Orthodoxy and Zamjatin denying all absolutes and seeking a synthesis in the passionately alive individual. But in adopting styles which fused the realistic and the symbolic, they both aimed at achieving a philosophical synthesis transcending the particulars of life in a given time and place. They both explored the problem of human freedom, maintaining that human nature is essentially irrational. And despite the intensive analysis of motivation in Dostoevskij's novels, a conception of personality as a repository of mystery informs both artists' work. Focusing on the inner life and showing characters in tormented explorations of the self, Dostoevskij's work prefigured the modern writer's rejection of the stable, knowable ego.

Dostoevskij's art focuses the role of the national heritage in Russian Modernism as it was represented by Zamjatin. For all the distinctly modern tenor of Dostoevskij's ideas, we must also consider the sources and nature of his aesthetic discussed above in order to understand fully the notion that the "twentieth century was born in midnineteenth-century Russia." Because Zamjatin was both in the mainstream of the literature of his time and heavily influenced by Dostoevskij's ideas and aesthetic, his work helps in identifying the historical roots of Russian Modernism. (pp. 284-85)

> Susan Layton, "Zamjatin and Literary Modernism," in Slavic and East European Journal (© 1973 by AATSEEL of the U.S., Inc.), Vol. 17, No. 3, Fall, 1973, pp. 279-87.

CHRISTOPHER COLLINS   (essay date 1973)

Evgenij Zamjatin is perhaps best known to the general reader in the West as a champion of freedom, if not as a pure heretic. . . .

The concept of Zamjatin as a heretic derives, of course, partly from the courageous positions he took in his society, first in behalf of bolševism and later against it. (p. 15)

His writings also encourage the critic to regard Zamjatin as a pure heretic, particularly the arguments of the female revolutionary I-330 in the anti-utopian novel *We,* and the philosophy of eternal revolution expounded in his best known essay ['**O literature, revoljucii, entropii i pročem**' (**On Literature, Revolution and Entropy**)]. . . . But it should be emphasized that I-330 is not the hero of *We,* and both works were written in the early 1920's and therefore should not . . . be accepted as Zamjatin's most important or final words on life and art. Even Zamjatin's doctrine of eternal revolution for its own sake may—in its turn—be subject to a revolution of its own. (p. 16)

[Zamjatin's major works] go beyond the themes of freedom, heresy, and eternal revolution to deal with a more fundamental question: what does one do with freedom, what is the point of having it, or revolting to win it? The answer involves the primitive: an examination of Zamjatin's works shows that it plays the major role as enslaver or as potential or actual liberator.

In Zamjatin's two largest early works [*Uezdnoe* (**A Provincial Tale**) and *Na Kuličkax* (**In the Sticks**)] . . . the spheres of the natural and the provincial, the primitive, are depicted as the realm of slavery. Čebotarixa in *A Provincial Tale* and General Azančeev in *In the Sticks* are the female and male embodiments of pure, unthinking, beastly, sensual greed. Both bloat themselves on food to the point of obesity and nausea, and both have greedy, indiscriminate sexual appetites. They are the living dead, slaves to their bodies, and they are the most extreme examples of this slavery affecting almost all the inhabitants of their respective villages.

The protagonist of *A Provincial Tale* is a slow-witted, brutal villager named Baryba. . . . Baryba at times is presented with moral alternatives. Most of the time he is being 'drowned in the sweet and hot dough' . . . of sex, food, and idleness. One alternative would be the hunger, anxiety and freedom of the Balkašin yard—there he had hidden, starved and lived among dogs. The free but struggling life, so attractively presented in Zamjatin's later works, here attracts neither Baryba nor the reader as a palatable alternative even to the most deadening of well-stuffed lives. He chooses the well-stuffed life. Later Baryba must make a choice between honor and further success in the well-stuffed life: he is offered a bribe and a promotion to give false testimony against a friend accused of armed robbery. The alternative is to be honorable and to refuse to commit perjury, but in so doing, to pass up an opportunity for material advancement. Baryba does hesitate before making a decision but then gives the false testimony that sends his friend to the gallows, and that nets a promotion and a sum of money. He thus rejects the civilized values of honor and selflessness in favor of beastly selfishness. If the existence of a world of freedom and meaningful life anywhere is implied in the story, then it is in the civilized cultured world of honor, law, and decency, and not in the primitive world. (pp. 16-17)

The main characters in *In the Sticks* are not natives of the provinces, as in *A Provincial Tale,* but exiles from the civilized world. Far from civilization, this community of officers on the frontier succumbs to gluttony, lechery, alcoholism, apathy, and general depravity. The story chronicles the fall of the protagonist, the idealist and musician Andrej, and of Captain and Mrs. Šmit. Andrej begins the story back in the civilized world where he is interested in music and culture in general. He goes to the province in hopes of finding the peace and freedom and natural life he thinks he needs to write. But the provincial, the primitive, is seen to be inherently hostile to such activities, and Andrej is inevitably sucked down into the muck with the rest, not only away from art, but away from decency, life, freedom. Even the fog, such a redeeming feature of nature in Zamjatin's later works, is here a symbol of the slavery to the natural, of sluggishness, as it creeps in the door and wraps him up like a cobweb. . . . The sexual here is never so disgusting as in the case of Čebotarixa, yet still serves as a means and symbol of degradation. Unlike *A Provincial Tale,* however, the story *In the Sticks* presents an alternative form of heterosexual love, that of the pure love of Captain and Mrs. Šmit. Their love is an alternative to the world of blind, sexual greed.

The two seem to have an ideally happy marriage, one in which, however, like the idealized marriages in Gogol's early works or in Tolstoj's novels, the sexual is either absent or simply not deserving of any comment by the narrator. The newcomer bachelor Andrej is also in love with Marusja Šmit, but in a platonic way. The whiteness of the snow and the light-blue, tender face of Marusja are emphasized as images of purity. When Captain Šmit is provoked into threatening the corrupt General Azančeev, the latter blackmails Mrs. Šmit into bed, and the happiness of the pure Šmits, envied and hated by the corrupt community ever since the couple arrived, is blasted into bits. . . . As in *A Provincial Tale,* the protagonists are offered choices, opportunities to reject the slavery of the beastly and the provincial; they ponder the choices, but, like Čexov's unhappy heroes, prove too weak to break out.

These two early works display Zamjatin's fondness for downward-directed metaphors, especially for those reducing people to beasts and inanimate objects. General Azančeev is compared to an all-consuming stove . . . and frequently to an ugly frog. . . . Čebotarixa wraps herself around Baryba's body 'like a spider'. . . . (pp. 17-18)

The sexual also receives a generous share of downward-directed metaphors. The hot, greedy mouth of the incredibly obese Čebotarixa, . . . the promiscuous and stupid Mrs. Nečesa of *In the Sticks* are characteristic in Zamjatin's early works and also recall Gogol's attitude toward sex. (See especially Gogol's 'The Notes of a Madman' for the comparison of the sexual activity of people with that of dogs.)

Amid the general gloom and decay of Gogol's world and of the early Zamjatin's world there appear a few dreamers, who are necessarily doomed to frustration. Andrej does not become a great writer, but loses what humanity he had. Tixmen''s dreams of being a knight and rescuing a fair damsel . . . are interrupted by a brutal return to reality, where he is no handsome knight and his fair damsel does not even know whether her latest child is his or someone else's. And even the down-to-earth Afimja of *Črevo* [The Womb] has her long desired unborn child taken away from her. Small wonder that in this world of the primitive, Baryba becomes a stone idol and Andrej is beastly drunk by the end of their respective stories.

Two important differences should be noted in any comparison of Gogol and the early Zamjatin. The first is in the nature of their satire. Gogol was essentially a conservative who believed in God, tsar, and nation. His satire was directed at the failure of himself and man in general to live up to high ideals. Zamjatin's early works were (correctly) interpreted by the government as attacks on the existing political order. The authority figures in Gogol's fiction—despite their many sins—are not hateful scoundrels. . . . But the brutal Baryba reaches a position of authority at the end of *A Provincial Tale* and those higher up are equally corrupt. General Azančeev is the most corrupt, repulsive one in the entire *In the Sticks,* and the reader goes away disappointed that neither Andrej nor Captain Šmit murdered him. These works, especially the latter, are not to be read as expressions of the author's pessimism, but as calls to arms to overthrow the monsters in authority.

The second difference is in the two writers' attitudes toward the physical and the spiritual. When the celibate Gogol deals with sexual love in his fiction, he generally stresses its dangerous (and occasionally disgusting) aspects. Salvation is to be found in rejecting the material, physical, sexual world and finding an internal anchor of Christian faith. Zamjatin displays

Gogol's anti-sexual bias in his early works, but goes on later to find the lyrical and even the redeeming in the sexual. In his fiction (and in his life), Gogol rejects the physical in favor of the spiritual. Zamjatin discovers the spiritual *in* the physical. (pp. 18-20)

[Zamjatin's] stay in England resulted in three works set there: [*Ostrovitjane* (The Islanders), 'Lovec čelovekov' (The Fisher of Men), and (a dramatic adaptation of *The Islanders*), *Obščestvo početnyx zvonarej* (The Society of Honorary Bellringers)]. . . .

The Islanders and the other two works must not be read as attempts at a 'realistic' picture of twentieth-century England, or as anti-British satire. Zamjatin's stay in England was too short to make him an expert on *byt*, and—more importantly—his own literary inclinations led him away from 'realism'. Even early Soviet critics (hardly prone to protest anti-British satire) argued that Zamjatin's portraits of British society were not true to life. *The Islanders* is no more to be considered anti-British satire, than *The Fires of St. Dominik* is to be considered anti-Spanish satire. Nor, for that matter, should the many works set in tsarist or Soviet Russia be considered specifically anti-Russian or anti-Soviet satire. In his satires Zamjatin simply presents a manifestation of what he sees as the universal conflict between the forces of Energy and those of Entropy, the Entropy being social, moral, religious, or political, as the particular case might be. (p. 27)

If traces of [Aleksandr] Kuprin's *The Duel* show up in the tale *In the Sticks,* traces of Čexov and Dostoevskij appear in . . . *The Islanders*. The dull, materialistic Campbell and his freedom-loving fiancée recall a similar couple in the last story Čexov wrote, 'The Betrothed'. . . . Campbell's and the Vicar Dewley's passion for muffling themselves in clothes, for shutting themselves up indoors, and in general alienating themselves from nature plainly recalls Čexov's 'Man in a Box'. . . . But in neither case is Zamjatin placing his tale within the *context* of Čexov's story, in the way that Čexov, for instance, places some of his own stories within the context of certain literary classics. The Dostoevskij work recalled here does however give us the first example of Zamjatin's use of literary context. The reader who is not familiar with *The Brothers Karamazov* will miss some of the point of *The Islanders*. Zamjatin has taken Dostoevskij's Grand Inquisitor and his theories and reduced them to the pettiness of the Vicar Dewley and his 'Doctrine of Compulsory Salvation'. Much of the humor in the tale stems from the implied contrast between the dimensions of the Grand Inquisitor and the Vicar Dewley. When, for instance, Johnny the porcelain pug, a symbol of love and understanding, 'kisses' the Vicar Dewley, the reader must recognize that the irreverent Zamjatin is here presenting his version of Christ giving the kiss of forgiveness to the Grand Inquisitor. Despite this use of context, however, Zamjatin has not yet learned to place his work squarely in the context of literary classics in the way he does later in *We*, 'The Jola', and *The Flood*. (p. 28)

Christopher Collins, in his Evgenij Zamjatin: An Interpretive Study *(© copyright 1973 Mouton & Co. N.V., Publishers), Mouton Publishers, 1973, 117 p.*

MILTON EHRE (essay date 1975)

[A] dialectical motion of revolt against the Symbolist heritage and simultaneous acceptance of many of its aspects characterizes Zamjatin's aesthetics and much of his prose. His career can be understood as an attempt to do in prose what the Acmeists and Futurists were atempting in poetry—to establish in theory and exemplify in works the basis for an avant-garde literature. Zamjatin is most insistent in rejecting Realism and Naturalism, which are the dominant traditions of Russian fiction. The stable world that any realism presupposes, whether "bourgeois" or Socialist Realism, is an unreal "convention" and an "abstraction." The conventions of Realism are totally incompatible with the electric, Einsteinian, technological age in which we live. The prose fiction that would catch the quickened tempos of modern life Zamjatin calls alternately Neorealism and Synthesism. It was intended . . . to provide a temporary synthesis of Realism and Symbolism in the never-ending dialectical process that, in Zamjatin's view, constitutes literary and human history.

Zamjatin, along with almost everybody else, sees Belyj as the paradigmatic figure of the new prose. Through his polychromatic style and multileveled structures Belyj was able to capture the complexity of modern life. In Belyj, Zamjatin writes, mathematics, poetry, anthroposophy, and the foxtrot are rolled into one (the foxtrot, or jazz, is Zamjatin's metaphor for the disjointed and intense rhythms of the modern scene). (p. 289)

However, Zamjatin has certain reservations about Belyj's contribution. The former student of Remizov wonders whether one may properly say that Belyj's books are written in Russian. His language is so full of neologisms, his syntax is so unusual that it strikes us as a very special language—the language of Belyj. Also, for all of Belyj's sensitivity to the music of language, he nevertheless erred in attempting to apply metrical feet to prose. Belyj, he finds, suffered from a chronic illness—anapests. Prose and poetry, or at least poetry written in meter, have limits that preserve their integrity. . . . The "meter" of prose is not one of regular shifts of articulation; prose treats "changing quantities" instead of "constant" ones—now the tempo is slowed down, now it is quickened, according to the "emotional" emphases of the language. What Zamjatin objects to is not musicality of prose as such, but the regularity that Belyj's prose often exhibits. A prose rhythm that is too regular and too periodic, he fears, is in danger of losing its integrity as prose. (pp. 289-90)

Verbal echoes, repetitions, and syntactical parallelisms are the building blocks of Zamjatin's rhythmic prose. His rhythms are often . . . complex and intense. They always avoid mellifluousness by highlighting and dramatizing the individual word [and phrase]. . . .

Zamjatin conceives the image in terms analogous to his conception of prose style. The quickened tempos of modern life do not tolerate the "slow, horse-and-buggy descriptions" of nineteenth-century Realism. The age demands that syntax become "elliptical, volatile," and the image must also convey "quickness of motion." "The image is sharp, synthetic; there is only one basic feature in it, the kind you can manage to take note of from a speeding automobile". . . . A "synthetic" image is one that is inclusive, that summarizes a fleeting experience. . . . Character is expressed through reduction to a single image that is then threaded through the work until it becomes a leitmotif. (p. 291)

"Sharpness" of language and imagery—Zamjatin employs the same term for both—distinguishes Neorealism from Symbolism. . . . Zamjatin often calls his and his contemporaries' art "impressionistic," but if impressionism is the right term—and I do not think it is—it is an impressionism closer to the solidity of Cezanne than the fluidity of late Monet. It is a similar solidity that Picasso and Braque, looking back to Cezanne, were working for in the Cubist experiments, which were taking place in the same years that witnessed the Russian revolt against Symbolism.

The essential mode of Neorealism or Synthesism is ironic. Zamjatin employs the Hegelian dialectic to illustrate the new literature's relation to traditional Realism and Symbolism. Realism was the thesis, Symbolism the antithesis, Neorealism or Synthesism is the integration of both into a new art. Or, in a suggestive image he uses in the essay **"On Synthesism,"** first there was Eve who was all flesh, the Eve of Tolstoj, Zola, Rubens, Gor'kij (Realism). Then the artist rejected the Eve of flesh for the Eve of unattainable and tragic longing whose other name was Death (Symbolism, Idealism). Finally, contemporary man, the new Adam, returns to the Eve of flesh, but he is no longer the same. He has been poisoned by his knowledge of the second Eve. Beneath Eve's flesh the new Adam, Adam become wise, can see the skeleton. From her kisses he carries away a bittersweet taste of irony. Among the artists who represent the third stage, the synthesis, he includes Whitman, Gaugin, Seurat, and Picasso. The new art, then, assumes traditional Realism's power over the flesh and the earth. It seeks mastery of the concrete and the specific. Though it rejects Symbolism's idealistic yearning, it is unable to overcome the worldly skepticism of the Symbolists. A vivid sense of the real world combines with a profound doubt as to the possibilities of that world. This paradoxical situation of rootedness in reality and skepticism about the ultimate value of that reality leaves the modern artist with a pervasive irony.

Neorealism, in Zamjatin's aesthetic formulation as well as in his literary practice, bears little resemblance to the central tradition of nineteenth-century Realism. . . . Neorealism was a misleading term in that it suggested a stylistic affinity to Realism that it did not have. Actually it in many ways continued the Symbolist experiment in its concern with the musical powers of language, and its interest in metaphor and myth.

What distinguishes it from Symbolism is its preference for the sharp as against the hazy, for irony as against mystical and metaphysical longing. Historical periodization necessarily blurs the complexities of a given moment. Zamjatin is aware of the diversity of Symbolism, of its ironic as well as its metaphysical aspects, of its frequent use of "low" detail. Indeed the Belyj of *Petersburg* and the [Aleksandr] Blok of *The Twelve* are for him essentially Neorealists. Nevertheless, he argues, in its desire to connect with a transcendental order Symbolism remained a nineteenth-century phenomenon; it kept a bridge open to Romanticism. Neorealism is burning the bridges, and in doing so it becomes the truly modern, an art expressive of an age when absolutes have gone up in smoke. The abandonment of the vision of a transcendental order, despite continued skepticism about the world as it is, has changed the nature of art. Irony replaces high seriousness. A transcendental symbolism becomes impossible. The symbols of Neorealism, because they are deprived of higher correspondences, turn from hieratic signs into mere aesthetic tropes. The work does not strive upward to *das Ewige* [the eternal] but remains a self-contained artifact.

"The Fisher of Men" (**"Lovec čelovekov"** . . .) is characteristic of the kind of story Zamjatin wrote in the early years of the Soviet era, which was the most productive and perhaps the central period of his career. It can show us what Neorealism meant in practice. (pp. 291-92)

The story, like most of Zamjatin's fictions, turns on its imagery. Each character is expressed by one or several images. For Mr. Craggs, they are either metallic images or images taken from lower forms of animal life—rodents and crustaceans. The color pink is associated with the church organist Bailey, who seduces Mrs. Craggs; pink is also the color of the imaginary veil that seems to cover Mrs. Craggs' mouth; the beautiful girl Craggs pursues in Hampstead Heath is associated with apples and a raspberry-colored umbrella. The images, through repetition and their accessibility to categorization, turn into symbols: the metallic images represent frigidity, pink and raspberry, sexuality.

However the images are more than mere signatures of a character or signs of a value. **"The Fisher of Men"** presents a series of metamorphoses whereby characters become the things they are associated with. The first time we encounter Mr. Craggs he is eating crabs. . . . A few pages later and he has acquired crab claws. . . . Similarly, the beautiful lady under the raspberry umbrella, who is the prey of one of Craggs' voyeuristic hunts, is compared to an apple, only to become, through an exotic realization of the metaphor, Lady Apple. . . . In the manner of the grotesque, the boundaries separating human, animal, and vegetable have been obliterated. The beautiful lady is drenched with the amber of the sun; the association with ripening apples ready to fall to earth is made; the lady becomes Lady Apple; her Adam is the earth ready to receive her. Mr. Craggs rushes with "ratlike quickness"; the landscape becomes fuzzy . . . and overgrown with the "night's wool," thereby suggesting animal characteristics; a wooly Craggs, now to all appearances a huge rat, emerges from the night. (pp. 293-94)

Through metamorphosis Zamjatin converts Hampstead Heath into the landscapes of myth. The story opened with a juxtaposition of two Londons: a contemporary, mechanized London of iron arches, factory chimneys, and glittering neon signs, and a primitive London of druid temples, antediluvian black swans, and skull-like houses, with a great stone phallus at its center (the Trafalgar column). The juxtaposition of the mechanical and the sexual, as we have seen, evolves through the story. Here Hampstead Heath has been converted into a prehistoric Garden of Eden, furnished appropriately with an apple tree, an Adam, and a creature that intrudes upon the bliss of paradise. In Zamjatin's version of the myth it is a rat instead of a serpent.

But the uses of myth are purely ironic. The great drama of man's fall into sin has been lowered to the ordinary and its values have been reversed. Such lowerings and reversals are of course the essence of parody. While moving into the forests of myth we do not cease to be aware of the "daytime" incarnations of our characters. We remain conscious that our Adam and Eve are merely two ordinary Londoners out for some quick fun on a Sunday away from work, that our serpent is only a malignant and repressed voyeur disguising his fetishes behind a cloak of respectability. The original Adam and Eve fall from innocence to sex and knowledge. In Zamjatin's version sexual enjoyment is the condition of the garden; its enemy is the mechanized routines and puritanical religiosity of bourgeois civilization.

The story ends with another ironic touch, this time revealing the hand of the author. "Everything is finished" are Mrs. Craggs' last words, a double-entendre referring both to the end of the air raid and the consummation of her desire. "Everything is finished," the narrator reiterates to wrap up his story. Zamja-tin, in a manner characteristic of him, has placed an emphatic dot at the end of his work. Its symbols and myths do not reach to intimate another order of things, but stand as part of a self-enclosed artistic play that is meant to be humorous and instructive. (pp. 294-95)

Zamjatin conceived of literature as underoing a continual and dialectical process of change. His program for the prose fiction of his age was in a dialectical relation with Symbolism. Zamjatin continued Belyj's experiments in rhythmic prose, but sought a prose that would be intense and concentrated instead of melodious. The image was to convey an analogous intensity. Symbols were to have no higher correspondences. Zamjatin believed that the concreteness of language and imagery of contemporary literature and its ironic rootedness in the physical world (which did not preclude fantasy) made it a synthesis of Realism and Symbolism. We have argued that Neorealism continued the Symbolist experiment but that in its rejection of metaphysics and turn to irony it resulted in something qualitatively different. (p. 295)

> Milton Ehre, "Zamjatin's Aesthetics," in Slavic and East European Journal (© 1975 by AATSEEL of the U.S., Inc.), Vol. 19, No. 13, Fall, 1975, pp. 288-96.

ADDITIONAL BIBLIOGRAPHY

Alexandrova, Vera. "Yevgeny Zamyatin." In her *A History of Soviet Literature, 1917-1964: From Gorky to Solzhenitsyn*, pp. 97-111. Garden City, N.Y.: Anchor Books, 1964.
>   Biographical essay with some critical commentary on Zamyatin's major works.

Bayley, John. "Them and Us." *The New York Review of Books* XXIX, No. 6 (October 19, 1972): 18-21.
>   Review of *We* and *A Soviet Heretic*. Bayley examines Zamyatin's firm belief in revolution as articulated in his essays.

Brown, Edward J. "Zamjatin and English Literature." In *American Contributions to the Fifth International Congress of Slavists, Vol. II*, pp. 21-39. The Hague: Mouton & Co., 1963.
>   Study of Zamyatin's major works. Brown attempts to indicate the nature of Zamyatin's "thematic interest and stylistic behavior, and to trace certain key themes through his own work and that of the English writers who have an affinity with him."

Brown, Edward J. "Eugene Zamyatin As Critic." In *To Honor Roman Jacobson: Essays on the Occasion of His Seventieth Birthday*, pp. 402-11. The Hague: Mouton Publishers, 1967.
>   Survey of Zamyatin's criticism. Brown suggests that Zamyatin's importance as a critic lies in his search for new forms and in his defense "of the *modern* accent in literary art."

Collins, Christopher. "Zamjatin's *We* as Myth." *The Slavic and East European Journal* X, No. 2 (1966): 125-33.
>   Mythic interpretation of *We*. Collins suggests that a reading of *We* as myth "is crucial to an understanding of the work's structure, meaning, and impact."

Connors, James. "Zamjatin's *We* and the Genesis of *1984*." *Modern Fiction Studies* 21, No. 1 (Spring 1975): 107-24.*
>   Comparative study of *We* and Orwell's *1984*. Connors argues that "the chief concerns which shaped *1984*" were present in Orwell's thought long before he ever heard of Zamyatin.

Jackson, Robert Louis. "E. Zamyatin's *We*." In his *Dostoevsky's Underground Man in Russian Literature*, pp. 150-57. The Hague: Mouton & Co., 1958.

Analysis of the modern archetype of the "underground man" as portrayed in *We*.

"A New Soviet Novelist." *The Living Age* 343, No. 4393 (October 1932): 160-63.
Interview with Zamyatin. The author comments on life and literature in postrevolutionary Russia.

Mihajlov, Mihajlo. "Evgeny Zamyatin: The Chagall of Russian Literature." In his *Russian Themes*, pp. 288-97. New York: Farrar, Straus and Giroux, 1968.
Comparison of Zamyatin's writings with the paintings of Marc Chagall.

Orwell, George. "Review: 'We'." In his *The Collected Essays, Journalism and Letters of George Orwell; In Front of Your Nose, 1945-1950, Vol. IV*, edited by Sonia Orwell and Ian Angus, pp. 72-5. New York: Harcourt Brace Jovanovich, 1968.
Compares and contrasts *We* with Huxley's *Brave New World*, concluding that *We* shows more "political awareness" and is "more relevant" than Huxley's novel.

Proffer, Carl R. "Notes on the Imagery in Zamjatin's *We*." *The Slavic and East European Journal* VII, No. 3 (1963) : 269-78.
Suggests that the seemingly chaotic imagery in *We* follows a coherent pattern and serves an important function within the novel.

Ulph, Owen. "I-330: Reconsiderations on the Sex of Satan." *Russian Literature Triquarterly*, No. 9 (1974): 262-75.
Character analysis of I-330 from Zamyatin's *We*. Ulph suggests that I-330 is the embodiment of both the sensual and the revolutionary: "In her ignited person, the conflict between good and evil is eternally resolved. All opposites are synthesized. She becomes the incarnation of the Absolute . . . the unwavering advocate of the glory of permanent, unrelenting rebellion."

Woodcock, George. "Utopias in Negative." *The Sewanee Review* LXIV, No. 1 (Winter 1956): 81-97.*
Discussion of *We* as the first significant contemporary antiutopian novel and as the predecessor of Huxley's *A Brave New World* and Orwell's *1984*. Woodcock considers how *We* differs from other antiutopian works which proceeded it and how it set the pattern for those that followed.

Appendix

THE EXCERPTS IN TCLC, VOLUME 8, WERE REPRINTED FROM THE FOLLOWING PERIODICALS:

The Academy
Accent
American Quarterly
Amra
Arts in Society
The Athenaeum
The Atlantic Monthly
Australian Journal of French Studies
The Bibliophile
The Bookman (London)
The Bookman (New York)
Books Abroad
Bulletin of Hispanic Studies
Bulletin of Research in the Humanities
Canadian Literature
The Canadian Magazine
Canadian Poetry
Caribbean Quarterly
The Carrell
Catholic World
The Chap-Book
Commentary
Commonweal
Comparative Drama
Comparative Literature
Contemporary Review
The Dial
Dissertation Abstracts International
The Dublin Review
Encounter
English Literature in Transition
English Record
English Studies
Essays in Criticism
The Explicator
The Fortnightly Review
Forum
Forum and Century
Foundation
Four Decades of Poetry: 1890-1930
The French Review
French Studies
German Life & Letters

The German Quarterly
Germanic Notes
The Germanic Review
The Guardian
Harper's Weekly
International Organization
James Joyce Quarterly
Journal of Commonwealth Literature
The Journal of Narrative Technique
L'Esprit Créateur
The Listener
The Literary Review (New York)
The Literary World
Literature and Psychology
London Magazine
The London Mercury
MLN
Modern Drama
Modern Fiction Studies
The Modern Language Review
Monatshefte
MOSAIC: A Journal for the Comparative
    Study of Literature and Ideas
The Nation
The Nation and The Athenaeum
The New England Quarterly
The New Englander and Yale Review
The New Republic
New Statesman
New York Herald Tribune Book Review
New York Post
The New York Review of Books
New York Theatre Critics' Review
The New York Times Book Review
The New York Times Saturday Review of
    Books
The New Yorker
The Nineteenth Century and After
The North American Review
The Open Court
Outlook
Pacific Coast Philology
The Pall Mall Gazette

Parnassus: Poetry in Review
The Philistine
Poetry
The Polish Review
The Quarterly Review
Queen's Quarterly
Review of English Studies
Revista de Estudios Hispánicos
Rose Belford's Canadian Monthly and
    National Review
Russian Literature Triquarterly
St. James Gazette
The Saturday Review (London)
The Saturday Review of Literature
Scandinavia
Scandinavian Review
Seminar
The Sewanee Review
The Shavian
Slavic and East European Journal
Slavic Review
The Smart Set
Soviet Literature
The Spectator
Starlog
Studies in Short Fiction
Studies in the Novel
Theatre
The Times Literary Supplement
Tri-Quarterly
The Tulane Drama Review
Tulane Studies in English
The Twentieth Century
Twentieth Century Literature
University of Toronto Quarterly
Virginia Quarterly Review
The Westminster and Ford Quarterly
    Review
Woman's World
Yale French Studies
The Yale Review

THE EXCERPTS IN TCLC, VOLUME 8, WERE REPRINTED FROM THE FOLLOWING BOOKS:

Aiken, Conrad. Scepticisms: Notes on Contemporary Poetry. *Knopf, 1919.*

Alpers, Antony. The Life of Katherine Mansfield. *Viking Penguin, 1980.*

Alwroth, E. Paul. Will Rogers. *Twayne, 1974.*

Amis, Kingsley. New Maps of Hell: A Survey of Science Fiction. *Harcourt Brace Jovanovich, Inc., 1960, Arno Press, 1975.*

Balakian, Anna. Surrealism: The Road to the Absolute. *Rev. ed. Dutton, 1970.*

Barclay, Glen St. John. Anatomy of Horror: The Masters of Occult Fiction. *Weidenfeld and Nicholson, 1978, St. Martin's Press, 1979.*

Barrow, Leo L. Negation in Baroja: A Key to His Novelistic Creativity. *University of Arizona Press, 1971.*

Bates, H. E. The Modern Short Story: A Critical Survey. *T. Nelson and Sons Ltd, 1941.*

Beckson, Karl, ed. Oscar Wilde: The Critical Heritage. *Barnes & Noble, Inc., 1970.*

Beebe, Maurice. Ivory Towers and Sacred Founts: The Artist As Hero in Fiction from Goethe to Joyce. *New York University Press, 1964.*

Beerbohm, Max. Around Theatres. *Rev. ed. Rupert Hart-Davis, 1953.*

Belloc, Hilaire. Letters from Hilaire Belloc. *Hollis & Carter, 1958.*

Bellow, Saul, and others. Technology and the Frontiers of Knowledge. *Doubleday, 1975.*

Benét, Stephen Vincent. Preface to "The Orphan Angel" in Collected Prose of Elinor Wylie, *by Elinor Wylie. Knopf, 1933.*

Benét, William Rose. The Prose and Poetry of Elinor Wylie. *Wheaton College Press, 1934, The Folcroft Press, 1969.*

Bennett, Arnold. Books and Persons: Being Comments on a Past Epoch, 1908-1911. *Doran, 1917.*

Berger, Harold L. Science Fiction and the New Dark Age. *Bowling Green University Popular Press, 1976.*

Brandes, Georg. Eminent Authors of the Nineteenth Century. *Translated by Rasmus B. Anderson. T. Y. Crowell & Co., 1886.*

Brandes, Georg. Creative Spirits of the Nineteenth Century. *Translated by Rasmus B. Anderson. Thomas Y. Crowell Company, 1923.*

Brathwaite, Edward. Introduction to Brother Man, *by Roger Mais. Heinemann, 1974.*

Brooks, Van Wyck. New England: Indian Summer, 1865-1915. *Dutton, 1940.*

Brooks, Van Wyck. A Chilmark Miscellany. *Dutton, 1948.*

Brooks, Van Wyck. The Confident Years: 1885-1915. *E. P. Dutton, Inc., 1952.*

Brown, Edward J. To Honor Roman Jakobson: Essays on the Occasion of His Seventieth Birthday. *Mouton Publishers, 1967.*

Brustein, Robert. The Theatre of Revolt: An Approach to Modern Drama. *Atlantic-Little, Brown, 1964.*

Buckley, Jerome Hamilton. William Ernest Henley: A Study of the "Counter-Decadence" of the 'Nineties. *Princeton University Press, 1945.*

Burgess, Anthony. Re Joyce. *Norton, 1965.*

Cargill, Oscar; Fagin, N. Bryllion; and Fisher, William J., eds. O'Neill and His Plays: Four Decades of Criticism. *New York University Press, 1961.*

Carrington, C. E. The Life of Rudyard Kipling. *Doubleday & Company, Inc., 1956.*

Cassidy, John A. Algernon C. Swinburne. *Twayne, 1964.*

Chesterton, G. K. Heretics. *John Lane Company, 1905.*

Chesterton, G. K. The Common Man. *Sheed and Ward, Inc., 1950.*

Chesterton, G. K. A Handful of Authors: Essays on Books and Writers. *Edited by Dorothy Collins. Sheed and Ward, Inc., 1953.*

Church, Richard. British Authors: A Twentieth-Century Gallery with 53 Portraits. *Rev. ed. Longmans Green and Co., 1948.*

Closs, A. The Genius of the German Lyric: An Historic Survey of Its Formal and Metaphysical Values. *George Allen & Unwin Ltd, 1938.*

Clurman, Harold. Ibsen. *Macmillan, 1977.*

Cockshut, A.O.J. Man and Woman: A Study of Love and the Novel 1740-1940. *Oxford University Press, 1978.*

Colby, Frank Moore. Imaginary Obligations. *Dodd, Mead & Company, 1913.*

Collins, Christopher. Evgenij Zamjatin: An Interpretive Study. *Mouton Publishers, 1973.*

Connolly, Thomas E., ed. Joyce's "Portrait": Criticisms and Critiques. *Appleton-Century-Crofts, 1962.*

Cooke, Alistair. One Man's America. *Knopf, 1952.*

Cope, Jackson I. Joyce's Cities: Archeologies of the Soul. *The Johns Hopkins University Press, 1981.*

Creary, Jean. The Islands in Between: Essays on West Indian Literature. *Edited by Louis James. Oxford University Press, 1968.*

Crispin, Edmund. Introduction to Best SF Stories of C. M. Kornbluth, *by C. M. Kornbluth. Faber and Faber, 1968.*

D'Costa, Jean. Roger Mais: "The Hills Were Joyful Together" and "Brother Man." *Longman, 1978.*

de Camp, L. Sprague. Literary Swordsmen and Sorcerers: The Makers of Heroic Fantasy. *Arkham House, 1976.*

de Camp, L. Sprague, ed. The Spell of Conan. *Ace Books, 1980.*

de Madariaga, Salvador. The Genius of Spain and Other Essays on Spanish Contemporary Literature. *Oxford University Press, 1923.*

Deming, Robert H., ed. James Joyce: The Critical Heritage, 1902-1927. *Routledge & Kegan Paul, 1970.*

Deutsch, Babette. Poetry in Our Time: A Critical Survey of Poetry in the English-Speaking World, 1900 to 1960. *Rev. ed. Doubleday & Company, Inc., 1963.*

Deutsch, Babette, and Yarmolinsky, Avrahm. Introduction to Contemporary German Poetry: An Anthology. *Edited and translated by Babette Deutsch and Avrahm Yarmolinsky. John Lane, The Bodley Head Ltd., 1923.*

Dillon, E. J. Maxim Gorky: His Life and Writings. *Isbister and Company Limited, 1902.*

Dobrée, Bonamy. Rudyard Kipling: Realist and Fabulist. *Oxford University Press, 1967.*

Donchin, Georgette. Russian Literary Attitudes from Pushkin to Solzhenitsyn. *Macmillan, 1976.*

Dos Passos, John. Rosinante to the Road Again. *Doran, 1922.*

Douglas, Alfred. Oscar Wilde and Myself. *Duffield, 1914.*

Downs, Brian W. A Study of Six Plays by Ibsen. *Cambridge at the University Press, 1950.*

Doyle, Arthur Conan. Through the Magic Door. *Smith, Elder & Co., 1907.*

Drake, William A. Contemporary European Writers. *John Day, 1928, Harrap, 1929.*

Durant, Will, and Durant, Ariel. Interpretation of Life: A Survey of Contemporary Literature. *Simon & Schuster, 1970.*

Eagle, Solomon (pseudonym of J. C. Squire). Books in General. *Hoddard & Stoughton, Limited, 1921, Books for Libraries Press, 1971.*

Eastman, Max. Artists in Uniform: A Study of Literature and Bureaucratism. *Knopf, 1934.*

Eliot, T. S. The Sacred Wood: Essays on Poetry and Criticism. *Methuen & Co. Ltd., 1950.*

Eliot, T. S., ed. A Choice of Kipling's Verse Made by T. S. Eliot with an Essay on Rudyard Kipling, *by Rudyard Kipling. Charles Scribner's Sons, 1943.*

Ellmann, Richard. Introduction to The Artist As Critic: Critical Writings of Oscar Wilde, *by Oscar Wilde. Edited by Richard Ellman. Random House, 1969.*

Eloesser, Arthur. Modern German Literature. *Translated by Catherine Alison Phillips. Knopf, 1933.*

Emery, Clark. The World of Dylan Thomas. *University of Miami Press, 1962.*

Eoff, Sherman H. The Modern Spanish Novel: Comparative Essays Examining the Philosophical Impact of Science on Fiction. *New York University Press, 1961.*

Fairchild, Hoxie Neale. Religious Trends in English Poetry: Gods of Changing Poetry, 1880-1920, Vol. V. *Columbia University Press, 1962.*

Farson, Daniel. The Man Who Wrote "Dracula": A Biography of Bram Stoker. *Michael Joseph, 1975, St. Martin's Press, 1976.*

Feibleman, James. In Praise of Comedy: A Study of its Theory and Practice. *George Allen & Unwin Ltd, 1939.*

Feuerlicht, Ignace. Thomas Mann. *Twayne Publishers, 1968.*

Flora, Joseph M. William Ernest Henley. *Twayne, 1970.*

Foltin, Lore B., ed. Franz Werfel: 1890-1945. *University of Pittsburgh Press, 1961.*

Frank, Bruno. The Stature of Thomas Mann. *Edited by Charles Neider. Translated by E. B. Ashton. New Directions, 1947.*

Frye, Northrop. The Bush Garden: Essays on the Canadian Imagination. *House of Anansi Press, 1971.*

George, W. L. Introduction to Purple and Fine Women, *by Edgar Saltus. Pascal Covici, Publisher, 1925.*

Goldberg, S. L. James Joyce. *Grove Press, 1962.*

Gordon, Ian A. Katherine Mansfield. *Rev. ed. British Council, 1963.*

Gould, Jean. Amy: The World of Amy Lowell and the Imagist Movement. *Dodd, Mead & Company, 1975.*

Gray, Thomas A. Elinor Wylie. *Twayne, 1969.*

Green, Roger Lancelyn, ed. Kipling: The Critical Heritage. *Barnes & Noble, 1971.*

Gross, Harvey. The Contrived Corridor: History of Fatality in Modern Literature. *The University of Michigan Press, 1971.*

Gross, John. The Rise and Fall of the Man of Letters: A Study of the Idiosyncratic and the Humane in Modern Literature. *Macmillan, 1969.*

Gross, John, ed. The Age of Kipling. *Simon & Schuster, 1972.*

Grossvogel, David I. Twentieth Century French Drama. *Gordion Press, 1967.*

Hampshire, Stuart N. Modern Writers and Other Essays. *Knopf, 1970.*

Hare, Humphrey. Swinburne: A Biographical Approach. *H.F. & G. Witherby Ltd., 1949.*

Harrell, Jean G., and Wierzbianska, Alina, eds. Aesthetics in Twentieth-Century Poland: Selected Essays. *Bucknell University Press, 1973.*

Hart, Clive, ed. James Joyce's ''Dubliners'': Critical Essays. *Faber and Faber, 1969, Viking Penguin, 1969.*

Hart, Walter Morris. Kipling: The Story Writer. *University of California Press, 1918.*

Henderson, Philip. Swinburne: Portrait of a Poet. *Macmillan, 1974.*

Heymann, C. David. American Aristocracy: The Lives and Times of James Russell, Amy and Robert Lowell. *Dodd, Mead & Company, 1980.*

Hofacker, Erich P. Christian Morgenstern. *Twayne, 1978.*

Holbrook, David. Llareggub Revisited: Dylan Thomas and the State of Modern Poetry. *Bowes and Bowes, 1962.*

Hollingdale, R. J. Thomas Mann: A Critical Study. *Bucknell University Press, 1971.*

Horgan, Paul. Maurice Baring Restored. *Farrar, Straus and Giroux, 1970.*

Huneker, James. Iconoclasts, a Book of Dramatists: Ibsen, Strindberg, Becque, Hauptmann, Sudermann, Hervieu, Gorky, Duse and D'Annunzio, Maeterlinck and Bernard Shaw. *Charles Scribner's Sons, 1905.*

Hyder, Clyde K., ed. Swinburne: The Critical Heritage. *Barnes and Noble, Inc., 1970.*

Jackson, Rosemary. Fantasy: The Literature of Subversion. *Methuen, 1981.*

Janouch, Gustave. Conversations with Kafka. *Translated by Goronwy Rees. Rev. ed. New Directions, 1971.*

Jarrell, Randall. Introduction to The English in England: Short Stories, *by Rudyard Kipling. Anchor Press, 1963.*

Jarrell, Randall. The Third Book of Criticism. *Farrar, Straus & Giroux, 1969.*

Johnson, Lionel. Reviews and Critical Papers. *Edited by Robert Schafer. Elken Mathews, 1921.*

Johnson, Walter. August Strindberg. *Twayne, 1976.*

Jones, D. G. Butterfly on Rock: A Study of Themes and Images in Canadian Literature. *University of Toronto Press, 1970.*

Jullian, Philippe. Oscar Wilde. *Translated by Violet Wyndham. Librairie Academique Perrin, 1967, Viking Press, 1969.*

Kayser, Wolfgang. The Grotesque in Art and Literature. *Translated by Ulrich Weisstein. Indiana University Press, 1963.*

Kazin, Alfred. On Native Grounds: An Interpretation of Modern American Prose Literature. *Reynal & Hitchcock, 1942.*

Kazin, Alfred. The Inmost Leaf: A Selection of Essays. *Harcourt Brace Jovanovich, 1955.*

Keith, W. J. Charles G. D. Roberts. *Copp Clark, 1969.*

Kerrigan, Anthony. ''The World of Pio Baroja'' in The Restlessness of Shanti Andia and Other Writings, *by Pio Baroja. University of Michigan Press, 1959.*

Kidder, Rushworth M. Dylan Thomas: The Country of the Spirit. *Princeton University Press, 1973.*

Kipling, Rudyard. The Courting of Dinah Shadd and Other Stories. *Harper & Brothers, 1890, Books for Libraries Press, 1971.*

Knight, Damon. In Search of Wonder: Essays on Modern Science Fiction. *Advent: Publishers, 1967.*

Knight, Max. Introduction to Galgenlieder, *by Christian Morgenstern. Translated by Max Knight. University of California Press, 1963.*

Krispyn, Egbert. Style and Society in German Literary Expressionism. *University of Florida Press, 1964.*

Lang, Cecil Y. *Preface to* New Writings by Swinburne or Miscellanea Nova et Curiosa: Being a Medley of Poems, Critical Essays, Hoaxes and Burlesques, *by Charles Algernon Swinburne. Edited by Cecil Y. Lang. Syracuse University Press, 1964.*

Lavrin, Janko. An Introduction to the Russian Novel. *Methuen & Co., Ltd., 1945.*

Le Gallienne, Richard. Rudyard Kipling. *John Lane, 1900.*

Lewis, Allan. The Contemporary Theatre: The Significant Playwrights of Our Time. *Rev. ed. Crown, 1971.*

Lewis, C. Day. The Poetic Image. *Oxford University Press, 1947.*

Lewis, C. S. Literature and Life: Addresses to the English Association. *G. G. Harrap, 1948.*

Lewis, C. S. Selected Literary Essays. *Edited by Walter Hoopper. Cambridge at the University Press, 1969.*

Logan, J. D., and French, Donald G. Highways of Canadian Literature: A Synoptic Introduction to the Literary History of Canada (English) from 1760 to 1924. *McClelland and Stewart, 1924.*

Lord, Glenn, ed. The Last Celt: A Bio-bibliography of Robert Ervin Howard. *Berkley Publishing Corporation, 1976.*

Lovecraft, H. P. Dagon and Other Macabre Tales. *Edited by August Derleth. Arkham House Publishers, 1965.*

Lovecraft, H. P. Selected Letters: 1934-1937. *Edited by August Derleth and James Turner. Arkham House, 1976.*

Lowell, Amy. Sword Blades and Poppy Seed. *The Macmillan Company, 1914, Houghton Mifflin Company, 1925.*

Lowell, James Russell. My Study Windows. *James R. Osgood and Company, 1871.*

Lowes, John Livingston. Essays in Appreciation. *Houghton Mifflin Company, 1936.*

Lucas, F. L. Ten Victorian Poets. *Cambridge at the University Press, 1940, Archon Books, 1966.*

Lukacs, Georg. Studies in European Realism: A Sociological Survey of the Writings of Balzac, Stendhal, Zola, Tolstoy, Gorki and Others. *Translated by Edith Bone. Merlin Press, 1972.*

Lundwall, Sam J. Science Fiction: What It's All About. *Translated by Sam J. Lundwall. Ace Books, 1971.*

MacCarthy, Desmond. Theatre. *MacGibbon & Kee, 1954.*

MacNeice, Louis. Modern Poetry: A Personal Essay. *Oxford University Press, 1968.*

Magabner, Marvin, ed. A James Joyce Miscellany. *James Joyce Society, 1957.*

Manley, Norman Washington. *Foreward to* The Three Novels of Roger Mais, *by Roger Mais. Jonathan Cape Ltd., 1966.*

Manley, Norman Washington. Manley and the New Jamaica: Selected Speeches and Writings 1938-68. *Longman Caribbean, 1971.*

Mann, Erika, and Mann, Klaus. Escape to Life. *Houghton Mifflin, 1939.*

Mathewson, Rufus W., Jr. The Positive Hero in Russian Literature. *Stanford University Press, 1975.*

Maugham, W. Somerset. *Introduction to* A Choice of Kipling's Prose, *by Rudyard Kipling. Macmillan, 1952.*

Maurois, André. Prophets and Poets. *Harper and Brothers Publishers, 1935.*

Mencken, H. L. Prejudices: Fifth Series. *Alfred A. Knopf, 1926.*

Mencken, H. L. "Smart Set" Criticism. *Cornell University Press, 1968.*

Meynell, Viola, ed. Friends of a Lifetime: Letters to Sydney Carlyle Cockerell. *Jonathan Cape, 1940.*

Mirsky, D. S. Contemporary Russian Literature: 1881-1925. *Knopf, 1926, G. Routledge & Sons, 1926.*

Monkshood, G. F., and Gamble, George. Introduction to Wit and Wisdom from Edgar Saltus, *by Edgar Saltus. Gamble, Greening & Co. Ltd., 1903.*

Monro, Harold. Some Contemporary Poets. *Leonard Parsons, 1920.*

Monroe, Harriet. Poets and Their Art. *Rev. ed. Macmillan, 1932.*

Moore, Virginia. Distinguished Women Writers. *Dutton, 1934.*

Morse, A. Reynolds. The Works of M. P. Shiel: A Study in Bibliography. *Fantasy Publishing Co., Inc., 1948.*

Mortensen, Brita M. E., and Downs, Brian W. Strindberg: An Introduction to His Life and Work. *Cambridge at the University Press, 1949.*

Moskowitz, Sam. Explorers of the Infinite: Shapers of Science Fiction. *World Publishing Co., 1963.*

Muchnic, Helen. Russian Writers: Notes and Essays. *Random House, 1971.*

Murfin, Ross C. Swinburne, Hardy, Lawrence and the Burden of Belief. *University of Chicago Press, 1978.*

Murry, J. Middleton. Katherine Mansfield and Other Literary Studies. *Constable, 1959.*

Nabokov, Vladimir. Lectures on Literature. *Edited by Fredson Bowers. Harcourt Brace Jovanovich, 1980.*

Natan, Alex. ed. German Men of Letters: Twelve Literary Essays, Vol. II. *Wolff, 1963.*

Noyes, Alfred. Some Aspects of Modern Poetry. *Hodder and Stoughton Limited, 1924.*

Olson, Stanley. Elinor Wylie: A Life Apart, a Biography. *Dial Press, 1979.*

Pacey, Desmond. Introduction to Selected Poems of Sir Charles G. D. Roberts, *by Charles G. D. Roberts. Ryerson Press, 1955.*

Pacey, Desmond. Ten Canadian Poets: A Group of Biographical and Critical Essays. *Ryerson Press, 1958.*

Patt, Beatrice. Pío Baroja. *Twayne, 1971.*

Peckham, Morse. Introduction to Poems and Ballads [and] Atalanta in Calydon, *by Algernon Charles Swinburne. Edited by Morse Peckham. The Bobbs-Merrill Company, Inc., 1970.*

Perkins, Michael. The Secret Record: Modern Erotic Literature. *Rev. ed. Morrow, 1976.*

Phelps, William Lyon. Essays on Russian Novelists. *Macmillan, 1911.*

Phelps, William Lyon. Essays on Books. *Macmillan, 1922.*

Pierce, Lorne. Introduction to Sir Charles G. D. Roberts: A Biography *by E. M. Pomeroy. Ryerson Press, 1943.*

Pinto, Vivian de Sola. Crisis in English Poetry: 1880-1940. *2nd ed. Hutchinson's University Library, 1955.*

Pohl, Frederik. Introduction to Not This August, *by C. M. Kornbluth. Pinnacle Books, 1981.*

Pohl, Frederik. Introduction to The Wonder Effect, *by Frederik Pohl and C. M. Kornbluth. Ballantine Books, 1962.*

Pollard, Percival. Their Day in Court. *Neale Publishing, 1909, Johnson Reprint Corporation, 1969.*

Ramchand, Kenneth. The West Indian Novel and Its Background. *Barnes and Noble, 1970.*

Ransome, Arthur. Oscar Wilde: A Critical Study. *Martin Secker, 1912.*

Reid, John T. Modern Spain and Liberalism: A Study in Literary Contrasts. *Stanford University Press, 1937.*

Reilly, Joseph J. Of Books and Men. *Julian Messner, Inc., 1942.*

Richards, D. J. Zamyatin: A Soviet Heretic. *Bowes & Bowes, 1962.*

Hatfield, Henry, ed. Thomas Mann: A Collection of Critical Essays. *Translated by Henry Hatfield. Prentice-Hall, 1964.*

Ritchie, J. M., ed. Periods in German Literature. *Wolff, 1966.*

Ritchie, J. M. Introduction *to* Scenes from the Heroic Life of the Middle Classes: Five Plays, *by Carl Sternheim. Translated by M.A.L. Brown, M. A. McHaffie, J. M. Ritchie, and J. D. Stowall. Calder and Boyars, 1970.*

Rogers, Will, Jr. Foreword *to* The Best of Will Rogers, *by Will Rogers. Crown, 1979.*

Ruihley, Glenn Richard. The Thorn of a Rose: Amy Lowell Reconsidered. *Archon Books (The Shoe String Press, Inc.), 1975.*

Samuel, Richard, and Thomas, R. Hinton. Expressionism in German Life, Literature and the Theatre (1910-1924). *W. Heffer & Sons Ltd., 1939.*

Schmidt, Michael. A Reader's Guide to Fifty Modern British Poets. *Barnes & Noble, 1979.*

Schweitzer, Darrell. Conan's World and Robert E. Howard. *The Borgo Press, 1978.*

Shaw, Bernard. Our Theatres in the Nineties, Vol. I. *Constable and Company Limited, 1932.*

Shiel, M. P. Science, Life and Literature. *Williams and Norgate Ltd, 1950.*

Silz, Walter. Realism and Reality: Studies in the German Novelle of Poetic Realism. *University of North Carolina Press, 1954.*

Singh, Bhupal. A Survey of Anglo-Indian Fiction. *Oxford University Press, 1934, Rowman and Littlefield, 1974.*

Slochower, Harry. No Voice is Wholly Lost ... Writers and Thinkers in War and Peace. *Creative Age Press, 1945.*

Slonim, Marc. Modern Russian Literature: From Chekhov to the Present. *Oxford University Press, 1953.*

Sokel, Walter H. Introduction *to* Anthology of German Expressionistic Drama: A Prelude to the Absurd. *Edited by Walter H. Sokel. Anchor Press, 1963.*

Sokel, Walter H. The Writer in Extremis: Expressionism in Twentieth-Century German Literature. *Stanford University Press, 1959.*

Southworth, James G. More Modern American Poets. *Basil Blackwell, 1954.*

Spivey, Ted R. The Journey beyond Tragedy: A Study of Myth and Modern Fiction. *University Presses of Florida, 1980.*

Sprague, Clare. Edgar Saltus. *Twayne, 1968.*

Squire, J. C. Books Reviewed. *Hodder & Stoughton Limited, 1922.*

Steene, Birgitta. The Greatest Fire: A Study of August Strindberg. *Southern Illinois University Press, 1973.*

Steiner, George. The Death of Tragedy. *Knopf, 1961.*

Stanford, Derek. Dylan Thomas: A Literary Study. *The Citadel Press, 1964.*

Stevenson, Lionel. The History of the English Novel: Yesterday and After, Vol. XI. *Barnes & Noble, 1967.*

Stewart, J.I.M. Eight Modern Writers. *Oxford University Press, 1963.*

Stout, Joseph A., Jr., and Rollins, Peter C. Introduction *to* The Cowboy Philosopher on the Peace Conference, *by Will Rogers. Oklahoma State University Press, 1975.*

Strelka, Joseph; Bell, Robert F.; and Dobson, Eugene, eds. Protest—Form—Tradition: Essays on German Exile Literature. *University of Alabama Press, 1979.*

Struve, Gleb. Soviet Russian Literature. *Routledge & Kegan Paul, 1935.*

Summers, Montague. The Vampire: His Kith and Kin. *K. Paul, Trench, Trubner & Co., 1928, University Books, 1960.*

Suvin, Darko. Metamorphoses of Science Fiction: On the Poetics and History of a Literary Genre. *Yale University Press, 1979.*

Swales, Martin. Thomas Mann: A Study. *Rowman and Littlefield, 1980.*

Swinnerton, Frank. The Georgian Literary Scene, 1910-1935: A Panorama. *Hutchinson, 1950.*

Symons, Arthur. Dramatis Personae. *The Bobbs-Merrill Company, Inc., 1923.*

Tchekhov, Anton. The Life and Letters of Anton Tchekhov. *Edited and translated by S. S. Koteliansky and Philip Tomlinson. George H. Doran Company, 1925.*

Tennyson, Hallam. Alfred Lord Tennyson: A Memoir by His Son. *Macmillan & Co., Ltd., 1897.*

Treece, Henry. Dylan Thomas: Dog Among the Fairies. *Lindsay Drummond Ltd., 1949, Folcroft Library Editions, 1974.*

Thompson, Francis. Literary Criticisms. *Edited by Rev. Terrence L. Connolly. E. P. Dutton and Company, Inc., 1948.*

Trotsky, Leon. Leon Trotsky on Literature and Art. *Edited by Paul N. Siegel. Pathfinder Press, 1970.*

Tymn, Marshall B., ed. Horror Literature: A Core Collection and Reference Guide. *Bowker, 1981.*

Van Vechten, Carl. Excavations: A Book of Advocacies. *Knopf, 1926.*

Van Vechten, Carl. The Merry-Go-Round. *Alfred A. Knopf, 1918.*

Watts, Emily Stipes. The Poetry of American Women from 1632 to 1945. *University of Texas Press, 1977.*

Weigand, Hermann J. The Modern Ibsen: A Reconsideration. *Holt, Rinehart and Winston, 1925.*

Welby, T. Earle. A Study of Swinburne. *George H. Doran Company, 1926, Kennikat Press, 1968.*

Weil, Irwin. Gorky: His Literary Development and Influence on Soviet Intellectual Life. *Random House, 1966.*

Wells, H. G. The Outline of History: Being a Plain History of Life and Mankind, Vol. II. *The Macmillan Company, 1920.*

Wescott, Glenway. Images of Truth: Remembrances and Criticism. *Hamish Hamilton, 1963.*

Wilde, Oscar. The Artist as Critic: Critical Writings of Oscar Wilde. *Edited by Richard Ellmann. Random House, 1969.*

Williams-Ellis, A. An Anatomy of Poetry. *Basil Blackwell, 1922.*

Williams, Raymond. Drama: From Ibsen to Brecht. *Chatto & Windus, 1968.*

Wilson, Angus. The Strange Ride of Rudyard Kipling: His Life and Works. *Viking Penguin, 1978.*

Wilson, Edmund. The Wound and the Bow: Seven Studies in Literature. *Houghton Mifflin Company, 1941, Farrar, Straus and Giroux, 1978.*

Wilson, Edmund. The Shores of Light: A Literary Chronicle of the Twenties and Thirties. *Farrar, Straus and Giroux, 1952.*

Wilson, Edmund. The Devils and Canon Barham: Ten Essays on Poets, Novelists and Monsters. *Farrar, Straus and Giroux, 1973.*

Wolf, Leonard. A Dream of Dracula: In Search of the Living Dead. *Little, Brown, 1972, Popular Library, 1977.*

Woolf, Virginia. Granite and Rainbow. *Harcourt Brace Jovanovich, 1958.*

Yates, Norris W. The American Humorist: Conscience of the Twentieth Century. *Iowa State University Press, 1964.*

Yeats, W. B. Letters on Poetry from W. B. Yeats to Dorothy Wellesley. *Oxford University Press, 1940.*

Yeats, W. B. Autobiographies. *Macmillan & Co. Ltd, 1955.*

Zabel, Morton Dauwen, ed. Literary Opinion in America: Essays Illustrating the Status, Methods, and Problems of Criticism in the United States in the Twentieth Century. *Rev. ed. Harper & Row, 1951.*

Zamyatin, Yevgeny. A Soviet Heretic: Essays by Yevgeny Zamyatin. *Edited and translated by Mirra Ginsburg. University of Chicago Press, 1970.*

Zilboorg, Gregory. Foreword to We, *by Eugene Zamiatin. Translated by Gregory Zilboorg. E. P. Dutton, 1924, 1959.*

Cumulative Index to Authors

Ramal, Walter
  See De la Mare, Walter (John)
Rawlings, Marjorie Kinnan 4
Révélé, Le
  See Artaud, Antonin
Reymont, Władysław
  Stanisław 5
Richardson, Dorothy (Miller) 3
Richardson, Henry Handel 4
Rilke, Rainer Maria 1, 6
Roberts, (Sir) Charles G(eorge)
  D(ouglas) 8
Robertson, Ethel Florence
  Lindesay Richardson
  See Richardson, Henry Handel
Robinson, Edwin Arlington 5
Rogers, Will(iam Penn Adair) 8
Rostand, Edmond (Eugène
  Alexis) 6
Ruffian, M.
  See Hašek, Jaroslav (Matej
  Frantisek)
Russell, George William
  See A. E.
St. E. A. of M. and S.
  See Crowley, Aleister
Saint-Exupéry, Antoine (Jean
  Baptiste Marie Roger) de 2
Saki 3
Saltus, Edgar (Evertson) 8
Sarmiento, Félix Rubén García
  See Darío, Rubén
Sayers, Dorothy L(eigh) 2
Schmitz, Ettore
  See Svevo, Italo
Schnitzler, Arthur 4
Schulz, Bruno 5
Scott, Duncan Campbell 6
Shaw, George Bernard 3
Sherwood, Robert E(mmet) 3
Shiel, M(atthew) P(hipps) 8
Shimazaki, Tōson 5

Sienkiewicz, Henryk (Adam
  Aleksander Pius) 3
Siluriensis, Leolinus
  See Machen, Arthur (Llewellyn
  Jones)
Sinclair, Julian
  See Sinclair, May
Sinclair, May 3
Smith, Sosthenes
  See Wells, H(erbert) G(eorge)
Snodgrass, Thomas Jefferson
  See Twain, Mark
Snow, Frances Compton
  See Adams, Henry (Brooks)
Softly, Edgar
  See Lovecraft, H(oward)
  P(hillips)
Staunton, Schuyler
  See Baum, L(yman) Frank
Stein, Gertrude 1, 6
Stephens, James 4
Sternheim, (William Adolf)
  Carl 8
Stevens, Wallace 3
Stoker, Bram (Abraham) 8
Storni, Alfonsina 5
Strindberg, (Johan) August 1, 8
Sutro, Alfred 6
Svarev, Count Vladimir
  See Crowley, Aleister
Svevo, Italo 2
Swift, Augustus T.
  See Lovecraft, H(oward)
  P(hillips)
Swinburne, Algernon Charles 8
Synge, (Edmund) John
  Millington 6
Tagore, (Sir) Rabindranath 3
Taverel, John
  See Howard, Robert E(rvin)
Teasdale, Sara 4

Thākura, Sir Ravīndranāth
  See Tagore, (Sir) Rabindranath
Theobald, Jr., Lewis
  See Lovecraft, H(oward)
  P(hillips)
Therion, Master
  See Crowley, Aleister
Thomas, Dylan 1, 8
Thompson, A. C.
  See Meynell, Alice (Christiana
  Gertrude Thompson)
Thompson, Francis (Joseph) 4
Thorer, Konrad
  See Grove, Frederick Philip
Thorne, Edouard
  See Grove, Frederick Philip
Thurman, Wallace 6
Tolstoy, (Count) Leo (Lev
  Nikolaevich) 4
Tonson, Jacob
  See Bennett, (Enoch) Arnold
Towers, Ivar
  See Kornbluth, C(yril) M.
Trakl, Georg 5
Twain, Mark 6
Tynan (Hinkson), Katharine 3
Unamuno (y Jugo), Miguel de 2
Undset, Sigrid 3
Valéry, Paul (Ambroise Toussaint
  Jules) 4
Valle-Inclán (y Montenegro),
  Ramón (María) del 5
Valle y Peña, Ramón José Simón
  See Valle-Inclán (y
  Montenegro), Ramón (María)
  del
Vallejo, César (Abraham) 3
Van Druten, John (William) 2
Van Dyne, Edith
  See Baum, L(yman) Frank
Verey, Rev. C.
  See Crowley, Aleister

Verga, Giovanni 3
Verne, Jules (Gabriel) 6
Wallace, Dexter
  See Masters, Edgar Lee
Walpole, (Sir) Hugh
  (Seymour) 5
Walser, Sam
  See Howard, Robert E(rvin)
Ward, Robert
  See Howard, Robert E(rvin)
Wassermann, Jakob 6
Wedekind, (Benjamin)
  Frank(lin) 7
Weinstein, Nathan Wallenstein
  See West, Nathanael
Wells, H(erbert) G(eorge) 6
Werfel, Franz (V.) 8
West, Nathanael 1
Wetcheek, J. L.
  See Feuchtwanger, Lion
Wharton, Edith (Newbold
  Jones) 3
Wilde, Oscar (Fingal O'Flahertie
  Wills) 1, 8
Williams, Charles 1
Willie, Albert Frederick
  See Lovecraft, H(oward)
  P(hillips)
Witkacy
  See Witkiewicz, Stanisław
  Ignacy
Witkiewicz, Stanisław Ignacy 8
Wolfe, Thomas (Clayton) 4
Woolf, (Adeline) Virginia 1, 5
Woollcott, Alexander
  (Humphreys) 5
Wylie (Benét), Elinor (Morton
  Hoyt) 8
Yeats, William Butler 1
Zamyatin, Yevgeny Ivanovich 8
Zola, Émile 1, 6

Cumulative Index to Nationalities

NATIONALITY INDEX

Cumulative Index to Critics

CRITIC INDEX

583

CRITIC INDEX

CRITIC INDEX

CRITIC INDEX

CRITIC INDEX